THE CONCEPT-TUTOR™ AND CASE-TUTOR COURSEWARE FOR STUDENTS

Accompanying this textbook are two optional custom-designed supplements that you can utilize to tutor yourself and gain faster, easier command of the material.

- Concept-TUTOR™ consists of a two-question self-test for each of the 13 text chapter self-tests and two 50-question practice hour exams you can complete and have computer-graded to gauge your understanding of the text material. When you have completed each test, Concept-TUTOR™ automatically grades the answers, posts the test score in your personal "grade book," indicates the questions with wrong answers, and directs you to the text pages where the correct answers can be found. Questions incorrectly answered can be attempted as many times as needed to arrive at the correct answer.

    To get the most benefit from Concept-TUTOR™, it's recommended that you do the chapter self-tests promptly after reading each chapter to measure your level of understanding (without a solid grasp of the concepts and tools of analysis, you will struggle when it comes time to tackle the assigned cases). The practice exams can be taken as part of your preparation for the tests on the chapter material given by your instructor.

- Case-TUTOR™ contains study questions for each of the 27 cases in this book plus custom-designed case preparation exercises for 12 of the cases that walk you through the needed analysis, tutor you in appropriate use of the concepts and tools, and provide number-crunching assistance. The 12 cases for which a case preparation exercise is provided on Case-TUTOR™ are indicated by the Case-TUTOR™ logo in the Table of Contents.

    The study questions for each of the 27 cases serve as a guide for what to think about and what to analyze in preparing the assigned cases for class. You'll find the 12 custom-designed case preparation exercises valuable in learning how to think strategically about a company's situation, how to apply the tools and concepts covered in the 13 text chapters, and how to arrive at sound recommendations about what actions management should take to improve the company's performance.

    Both software supplements can be used with any Windows-based PC loaded with Microsoft® Excel® (either the Office 97 version or the Office 2000 version).

How to Obtain the Software. If use of the tutorial software intrigues you, click on the E-Learning Center at the Web site for the textbook—**www.mhhe.com/thompson**. You can use a credit card to purchase Concept-TUTOR™ and Case-TUTOR™ either singly or as a package and immediately download the files to a diskette or to your own PC's hard drive.

A SPECIAL NOTE TO STUDENTS

Unlike other business courses that concentrate narrowly on a particular function or piece of the business—accounting, finance, marketing, production, human resources, or information systems—strategic management is a big picture course. It cuts across the whole spectrum of business and management. The center of attention is the *total enterprise*—the industry and competitive environment in which it operates, its long-term direction and strategy, its resources and competitive capabilities, and its prospects for success.

Throughout the course, the spotlight will be trained on the foremost issue in running a business enterprise: What must managers do, and do well, to make the company a winner in the game of business? The answer that emerges and the theme of the course is that good strategy making and good strategy execution are always the most reliable signs of good management. The task of this course is to explore why good strategic management leads to good business performance, to present the basic concepts and tools of strategic analysis, and to drill you in the methods of crafting a well-conceived strategy and executing it competently.

You'll be called on to probe, question, and evaluate all aspects of a company's external and internal situation. You'll grapple with sizing up a company's standing in the marketplace and its ability to go head-to-head with rivals, learn to tell the difference between winning strategies and mediocre strategies, and become more skilled in spotting ways to improve a company's strategy or its execution.

In the midst of all this, another purpose is accomplished: to help you synthesize what you have learned in prior business courses. Dealing with the grand sweep of how to manage all the pieces of a business makes strategic management an integrative, capstone course in which you reach back to use concepts and techniques covered in previous courses. For perhaps the first time you'll see how the various pieces of the business puzzle fit together and why the different parts of a business need to be managed in strategic harmony for the organization to operate in winning fashion.

The journey ahead is exciting, fun, and immensely worthwhile. No matter what your major is, the content of this course has all the ingredients to be the best course you've taken—best in the sense of learning a great deal about business, holding your interest from beginning to end, and enhancing your powers of business judgment. As you tackle the subject matter, ponder Ralph Waldo Emerson's observation, "Commerce is a game of skill which many people play, but which few play well." What we've put between these covers is aimed squarely at helping you become a savvy player. Good luck!

Arthur A. Thompson
A. J. Strickland

Strategic | Management
Concepts and Cases

Arthur A. Thompson, Jr.
A. J. Strickland III
Both of the University of Alabama

Twelfth Edition

Boston   Burr Ridge, IL   Dubuque, IA   Madison, WI   New York   San Francisco   St. Louis
Bangkok   Bogotá   Caracas   Kuala Lumpur   Lisbon   London   Madrid   Mexico City
Milan   Montreal   New Delhi   Santiago   Seoul   Singapore   Sydney   Taipei   Toronto

McGraw-Hill Higher Education

A Division of The **McGraw-Hill** Companies

STRATEGIC MANAGEMENT: CONCEPTS AND CASES

Published by McGraw-Hill/Irwin, an imprint of The McGraw-Hill Companies, Inc. 1221 Avenue of the Americas, New York, NY, 10020. Copyright © 2001, 1999, 1998, 1996, 1995, 1993, 1992, 1990, 1987, 1984, 1981, 1978 by The McGraw-Hill Companies, Inc. All rights reserved. No part of this publication may be reproduced or distributed in any form or by any means, or stored in a data base or retrieval system, without the prior written consent of The McGraw-Hill Companies, Inc., including, but not limited to, in any network or other electronic storage or transmission, or broadcast for distance learning. Some ancillaries, including electronic and print components, may not be available to customers outside the United States.

This book is printed on acid-free paper.

2 3 4 5 6 7 8 9 0 VNH/VNH 0 9 8 7 6 5 4 3 2 1

ISBN 0-07-231499-0

Vice president/Editor-in-chief: *Robin J. Zwettler*
Publisher: *John E. Biernat*
Senior sponsoring editor: *John Weimeister*
Senior developmental editor: *Laura Hurst Spell*
Senior marketing manager: *Ellen Cleary*
Project manager: *Kelly L. Delso*
Senior production supervisor: *Lori Koetters*
Coordinator freelance design: *Mary L. Christianson*
Senior supplement coordinator: *Becky Szura*
Media technology producer: *Burke Broholm*
Freelance cover and interior designer: *Design Solutions*
Cover image: *©Guy Crittenden/SIS*
Compositor: *GAC Indianapolis*
Typeface: *10.5/12 Times Roman*
Printer: *Von Hoffmann Press, Inc.*

Library of Congress Cataloging-in-Publication Data

Thompson, Arthur A., 1940-
   Strategic management : concepts and cases / Arthur A. Thompson, Jr.,
A. J. Strickland, III.—12th ed.
   p. cm.
   Includes index.
   ISBN 0-07-231499-0
   1. Strategic planning. 2. Strategic planning—Case studies. I. Strickland,
A. J. (Alonzo J.) II. Title.

HD30.28.T53 2001
658.4'012—dc21

00-044786

www.mhhe.com

to Hasseline and Kitty

about the | authors

Arthur A. Thompson, Jr., earned his BS and PhD degrees in economics from the University of Tennessee in 1961 and 1965, respectively; spent three years on the economics faculty at Virginia Tech; and served on the faculty of the University of Alabama's College of Commerce and Business Administration for 24 years. In 1974 and again in 1982, Dr. Thompson spent semester-long sabbaticals as a visiting scholar at the Harvard Business School.

His areas of specialization are business strategy, competition and market analysis, and the economics of business enterprises. He has published over 30 articles in some 25 different professional and trade publications and has authored or co-authored five textbooks and four computer-based simulation exercises.

Dr. Thompson is a frequent speaker and consultant on the strategic issues confronting the electric utility industry, particularly as concerns the challenges posed by industry restructuring, re-regulation, competition, and customers' freedom of choice. He spends much of his off-campus time giving presentations to electric utility groups and conducting management development programs for electric utility executives all over the world.

Dr. Thompson and his wife of 39 years have two daughters, two grandchildren, and two dogs.

Dr. A. J. (Lonnie) Strickland, a native of North Georgia, attended the University of Georgia, where he received a bachelor of science degree in math and physics in 1965. Afterward he entered the Georgia Institute of Technology, where he received a master of science in industrial management. He earned a PhD in business administration from Georgia State University in 1969. He currently holds the title of Professor of Strategic Management in the Graduate School of Business at the University of Alabama.

Dr. Strickland's experience in consulting and executive development is in the strategic management area, with a concentration in industry and competitive analysis. He has developed strategic planning systems for such firms as the Southern Company, BellSouth, South Central Bell, American Telephone and Telegraph, Gulf States Paper, Carraway Methodist Medical Center, Delco Remy, Mark IV Industries, Amoco Oil Company, USA Group, General Motors, and Kimberly Clark Corporation (Medical Products). He is a very popular speaker on the subject of implementing strategic change and serves on several corporate boards.

He has served as director of marketing for BellSouth, where he had responsibility for $1 billion in revenues and $300 million in profits.

In the international arena, Dr. Strickland has done extensive work in Europe, the Middle East, Central America, Malaysia, Australia, and Africa. In France he developed a management simulation of corporate decision making that enables management to test various strategic alternatives.

In the area of research, he is the author of 15 books and texts. His management simulations, Tempomatic IV and Micromatic, were pioneering innovations that enjoyed prominent market success for two decades.

Recent awards for Dr. Strickland include the Outstanding Professor Award for the Graduate School of Business and the Outstanding Commitment to Teaching Award for the University of Alabama, in which he takes particular pride. He is a member of various honor leadership societies: Mortar Board, Order of Omega, Beta Gamma Sigma, Omicron Delta Kappa, and Jasons. He is past national president of Pi Kappa Phi social fraternity.

the | preface

The hallmark of the 12th edition of *Strategic Management: Concepts and Cases* is thorough coverage of the seismic strategy-related changes in the business landscape being driven by globalization, the Internet, and dot-com companies. The package features new chapters, new sections, new concepts, new cases, and a trail blazing Web site.

Much of significance has transpired since the last edition, demanding substantive adjustments and revisions in treatment and emphasis, in addition to normal updating. A defining highlight of the 12th edition is the addition of two important new chapters—one on strategy making in global markets and one on business models and strategies for e-commerce. You'll also find that this edition has been "globalized" and "e-commerced" from cover to cover, producing a significantly reshaped chapter content and an invigorating case lineup.

We attacked this revision with zeal, excited by the challenge of mirroring the changes in business strategies, business organization, and business practices being wrought by globalization, the strategy-altering embrace of the Internet by more and more companies, and further advances in the conceptual underpinning of strategic management. At the same time, we have tried our level best to satisfy the market's legitimate yearning for a comprehensive teaching/learning package that squarely targets what every student needs to know about crafting, implementing, and executing business strategies. To help keep our 12th-edition package fresh and on the leading edge of pedagogy, we are initiating a much more extensive Web site for the text that incorporates the latest in e-learning and e-publishing technology and that offers significant value-added enhancements for both students and instructors. The 12th-edition package consists of:

- Thirteen chapters of text material.
- An exciting and teachable collection of 27 cases.
- An e-library of 31 popular cases from the 10th and 11th editions that instructors can select for case assignments. Students can use a credit card to purchase assigned cases in the e-case collection; all e-cases are available immediately in the form of a downloadable file. Students can use the e-case file to print a copy for their personal use (or can read the case directly on the monitor). The e-case library at the Web site, coupled with the 27 cases in the text, effectively provides instructors with a bank of 58 high-caliber cases to choose from.
- A Concept-Tutor™ courseware supplement consisting of a series of self-tests which students can use to gauge their comprehension of the material in the 13 chapters.
- A Case-Tutor™ courseware supplement that provides students with study questions for all 27 cases plus 12 custom-designed case preparation guides that walk them through the appropriate analysis and help them arrive at soundly reasoned action recommendations.
- A Web site featuring a "learning resource center" for students and a "teaching resource center" for instructors.

- A much-enhanced seventh edition of *The Business Strategy Game*—the global simulation that functions as an integrative "strategy-in-action" decision-making exercise for capstone courses in strategic management. The simulation is available in both printed and digital formats and has a built-in e-mail feature for distance-learning situations.
- A paperback volume entitled *Crafting and Executing Strategy: Text and Readings,* which contains the 13 chapters of text material and 22 readings. This volume is particularly suitable for instructors who wish to put together their own case package (perhaps from the e-library of 53-plus preselected, proven cases on the Web site for our text).
- Seven video supplements for use with cases in this edition.
- A full array of instructional aids for adopters.

All in all, we think the enhancements and supplements take this 12th-edition package to a new plateau. This edition is designed to deliver content and teaching/learning options that will help make adopters' courses in strategic management a more valuable and timely part of the business curriculum than ever before.

CONTENT FEATURES OF THE 12TH EDITION

New concepts, analytical tools, and methods of managing continue to surface at rates that mandate important edition-to-edition changes in content and emphasis. Since the last revision, use of the term *business model* has come into widespread use, entrepreneurship has taken on renewed strategic importance, collaborative alliances have grown in scope and impact, companies have continued to globalize their operations, the effects of global competition have spread, the resource-based view of the firm has assumed still greater prominence, high-velocity change has affected more industries and company environments, and the Internet has triggered a virtual revolution in both strategy and internal operations. We have made a concerted attempt to incorporate and integrate all these developments in the text.

In this edition you'll find much discussion about business models and how they relate to strategy. We pay considerably more attention to how collaboration and alliances affect competition—indeed, the collaborative efforts between sellers and their suppliers and between sellers and buyers have been woven into our presentation of Harvard professor Michael E. Porter's five-forces model of competition, thus formally making the role of alliances and cooperative agreements part of competition analysis. We also have devoted more coverage to the demands of competing in high-velocity market environments where the swift pace of change forces companies to make frequent and sometimes very fundamental changes in their strategies and resource capabilities.

This edition gives balanced treatment to the thesis that a company's strategy must be matched *both* to its external market circumstances and to its internal resources and competitive capabilities. The two new chapters on global market environments and strategies in the Internet economy (Chapters 6 and 7), testify to the importance of these topics but you will find that all 13 chapters have been globalized and e-commerced because the impact of globalization and the Internet on strategy making and strategy implementing is pervasive. You'll find the resource-based view of the firm integrated into the coverage of crafting business strategy (Chapters 2 through 8) and crafting diversification strategies (Chapters 9 and 10). You'll also find that Chapters 11 and 12 have a strong resource-based perspective as concerns the role of intellectual capital, core competencies, competitive capabilities, and organizational resources in executing strategy.

Compared to previous editions, we've made much greater use of examples and Illustration Capsules to highlight the close connection between the conceptual presentation and real-world application. This edition is also considerably more visual, because of the addition of numerous charts and figures, color photographs, and a four-color design. As in previous editions, there's prominent treatment of ethical and social responsibility issues, plus margin notes in every chapter that highlight basic concepts, strategic management principles, and kernels of wisdom. Extensive rewriting to sharpen the presentations throughout the text has allowed us to include the new material and still cover everything in less than 435 pages—something that readers and adopters ought to welcome, given the jam-packed content of the course.

Specific Chapter Modifications and Content Improvements

The new material on strategies for globalizing market environments has been positioned as Chapter 6, and the new material on business models and strategies for e-commerce market environments immediately follows as Chapter 7. Both chapters were positioned as part of the multichapter series on strategy in single-business companies because the content of these chapters was focused chiefly on business-level strategy. Where the role of the Internet and globalization merited coverage in other chapters, we wove the treatment into the content. Otherwise, the overall chapter organization parallels that of the last several editions. The following rundown summarizes the noteworthy chapter features and topical emphasis in this edition:

- Chapter 1 contains fresh material (starting on page 1) on what the term *business model* means and how a company's business model relates to its strategy. To drive home the point that companies' business models sometimes differ quite substantially, we have included an Illustration Capsule that contrasts Microsoft's and Linux's business models in the computer operating system software industry. We've rewritten the sections on strategic visions and mission statements in Chapters 1 and 2 to hammer home the importance of clear direction setting and a motivating strategic vision. More emphasis has been placed on why companies have to rapidly adapt strategy to newly unfolding market conditions and why strategy life cycles are getting shorter. We continue to place strong emphasis on how and why a company's strategy emerges from (1) the deliberate and purposeful actions of management and (2) as-needed reactions to unanticipated developments and competitive pressures. There's a new section on corporate intrapreneuring to help underscore that a company's strategic plan is a collection of strategies devised by different managers at different levels in the organizational hierarchy. This chapter also contains discussions of why all managers are on a company's strategy-making, strategy-implementing team and why it is imperative for company personnel to be both "students of the business" and skilled users of the concepts and tools of strategic management.

- The five-forces model of competition presented in Chapter 3 has been recast to incorporate the role and importance of alliances and collaborative agreements. We argue that some competitors forge such effective collaborative arrangements with either their suppliers, their customers, or both that the whole pattern of competition in the industry is affected. Furthermore, we have added globalization and the Internet as examples of driving forces capable of reshaping the pattern and structure of industry competition—their role as driving forces in some markets has become obvious and undeniable and a factor that many companies must reckon with in forging winning strategies. Chapter 3 sets forth the now-familiar analytical tools and concepts of industry and competitive analysis, and demonstrates the importance of tailoring strategy to fit the circumstances of a company's industry and competitive environment.

- Chapter 4 establishes the importance of solid company situation analysis as a basis for matching strategy to organizational resources, competencies, and competitive capabilities. As in the prior edition, Chapter 4 contains a full-blown discussion of all the concepts and analytical tools required to understand why a company's strategy must be well matched to its internal resources and competitive capabilities. The roles of core competencies and organizational resources and capabilities in creating customer value and helping build competitive advantage are *center stage* in the discussions of company resource strengths and weaknesses. SWOT analysis is once again recast as a tool for assuring a company's resource strengths and resource weaknesses. As before, there are sections on determining the competitive value of specific company resources and assets and on selecting the competencies and capabilities with the greatest competitive advantage potential. The now-standard tools of value chain analysis, strategic cost analysis, benchmarking, and competitive strength assessments continue to have a prominent role in the method of evaluating a company's situation—we believe they are an essential part of understanding a company's relative cost position and competitive standing vis-à-vis rivals. One new feature of this chapter is a section (undergirded with timely examples and an Illustration Capsule) on how the value chains of dot-com companies differ from those of traditional brick-and-click companies.

- Together, the material in Chapter 3 and Chapter 4 creates the understanding of why managers must carefully match company strategy both to industry and competitive conditions and to company resources and capabilities. Chapter 3 sets forth the tools and concepts of industry and competitive analysis and demonstrates the importance of tailoring strategy to fit the circumstances of a company's industry and competitive environment. Chapter 4 establishes the equal importance of doing solid company situation analysis as a basis for matching strategy to organizational resources, competencies, and competitive capabilities.

- Chapter 5 focuses on how a company can achieve or defend competitive advantage through strategy and through value chain activities. There's continuing coverage of the five generic competitive strategies; new and more extensive treatments on using alliances and cooperative strategies to build competitive advantage; a new section on mergers and acquisitions; and new material on how astute use of the Internet and e-commerce technologies is allowing companies to reconfigure their value chains to speed the flow of information, enhance efficiency, and reduce costs.

- Chapter 6 examines the issues companies face in crafting strategies suitable for multinational and globally competitive market environments, drawing a careful distinction between competing internationally and competing globally and exploring the reasons why it often makes good strategic sense for a company to expand beyond domestic boundaries. There's a section on cross-country differences in cultural, demographic, and market conditions that lays the foundation for whether multicountry or global competition exists. The chapter is anchored by a major section describing the various strategy options for entering and competing in foreign markets—options ranging from an export strategy to licensing and franchising to multicountry strategies to global strategies to heavy reliance on strategic alliances and joint ventures. This chapter introduces the concepts of profit sanctuaries and cross-market subsidization, explores the special problems associated with entry into the markets of emerging countries, and concludes with a section discussing the strategic options that local companies in such emerging countries as India, China, Brazil, and Mexico can use to defend against the invasion of opportunity-seeking, resource-rich global giants.

- The all-new Chapter 7 examines the profound impact of the Internet and how it "changes everything." It covers the whole high-velocity character of the e-commerce environment; presents a bird's-eye view of Internet technology and the structure of what is being called the Internet economy; and explores how the growing use of the Internet by businesses and consumers tends to globalize the economic landscape, alter traditional industry boundaries, reconfigure industry and company value chains, and intensify competition. However, the central focus of this chapter is a thoroughgoing survey of the different business models and strategies that companies can employ in competing in industries where the Internet and e-commerce are ruling forces.

- A substantially revised Chapter 8 looks at the broad strategy options for companies competing in five different industry environments: (1) emerging industries; (2) turbulent, high-velocity markets; (3) mature, slow-growth industries; (4) stagnant and declining industries; and (5) fragmented industries. It also covers the strategy-making challenges that confront companies pursuing rapid growth, companies in industry-leading positions, companies in runner-up positions, and crisis-ridden companies. These nine situations merit special attention in strategy courses because they represent many companies and because they reinforce the point made in Chapters 3 and 4 that winning strategies have to be matched both to industry and competitive conditions and to company resources and capabilities.

- The analytical treatment of corporate diversification strategies in Chapters 9 and 10 abandons much of the attention once given to drawing business portfolio matrices and instead puts the spotlight on (1) assessing industry attractiveness, (2) evaluating the company's competitive strength in each of its lines of business, and (3) appraising both the *strategic fits* and the *resource fits* among a diversified company's different businesses. We present a strong resource-based view of the firm in the recommended method for evaluating the pros and cons of a company's diversification strategy. Chapter 10 continues to incorporate analytical use of the industry attractiveness/business strength portfolio matrix because of its conceptual soundness and practical relevance, but we have abandoned coverage of the flawed growth-share matrix and the little-used life-cycle matrix.

- The three-chapter module on strategy implementation (Chapters 11–13) continues to feature a solid, compelling conceptual framework structured around (1) building the resource strengths and organizational capabilities needed to execute the strategy; (2) developing budgets to steer ample resources into those value chain activities critical to strategic success; (3) establishing strategically appropriate policies and procedures; (4) instituting best practices and mechanisms for continuous improvement; (5) installing information, communication, and operating systems that enable company personnel to carry out their strategic roles successfully day in and day out; (6) tying rewards and incentives tightly to the achievement of performance objectives and good strategy execution; (7) creating a strategy-supportive work environment and corporate culture; and (8) exerting the internal leadership needed to drive implementation forward and to keep improving on how the strategy is being executed.

- The eight-task framework for understanding the managerial components of strategy implementation and execution is explained in the first section of Chapter 11. The remainder of the chapter focuses on building an organization with the competencies, capabilities, and resource strengths needed for successful strategy execution. You'll find coverage of what it takes for an organization to build and enhance its competencies and capabilities, develop the dominating depth in competence-related activities needed for competitive advantage, and forge the necessary degree of collaboration and cooperation both among internal departments and with outside resource providers. We have expanded our treatment of collaborative alliances and partnerships and have placed considerably more emphasis on intellectual capital and the needs to recruit talented employees and to develop a first-rate management team. Gone are the treatments of the various organizational structures, since most of this material is now covered in organization behavior and principles of management courses. But there's continuing coverage of the pros and cons of outsourcing noncritical activities, the strategic rationale for downsizing and de-layering hierarchical structures, the merits of employee empowerment, and the use of cross-functional and self-contained work teams. The result is a powerful treatment of building resource capabilities and structuring organizational activities that ties together the revolutionary organizational changes sweeping through today's corporations. So far, the efforts of companies across the world to organize the work effort around teams, reengineer core business processes, compete on organizational capabilities (as much as on differentiated product attributes), and install leaner, flatter organization structures are proving to be durable, fundamental additions to the conventional wisdom about how to manage strategy execution.

- Chapter 12 surveys strategy-supportive budgets, policies, reward structures, and internal support systems and explains why the benchmarking of best practices, total quality management, reengineering, and continuous improvement programs are important managerial tools for enhancing organizational competencies in executing strategy. Chapter 13 continues to deal with creating a strategy-supportive corporate culture and exercising the internal leadership needed to drive implementation forward. There's coverage of strong versus weak cultures, low-performance and unhealthy cultures, adaptive cultures, and the sustained leadership commitment it takes to change a company with a problem culture. Sections on ethics management and what managers can do to improve the caliber of strategy execution round out the chapter.

- Of the book's 58 Illustration Capsules (versus 41 in the last edition), 42 are new or revised. A substantial number of the new capsules concern global issues and the strategies of non-U.S. companies—these are designated by a special "global" logo.

Margin notes that highlight basic concepts, major conclusions, and core truths remain a visible and reader-friendly feature of this edition. They distill the subject matter into concise principles, bring the discussion into sharper focus for readers, and emphasize what is important.

Our top priority in preparing this edition was to ensure that the content is substantive and covers all the right bases. But, at the same time, we took pains to meet reader expectations of clarity and crispness. You won't find much fluff or filler. We strove to create conceptual discussions that go straight to the point yet contain enough relevant examples to make them realistic and interesting. We also aimed squarely at chapter presentations that are comfortably mainstream, dead center with respect to content, tightly written and convincing, readable, and representative of the best thinking of both academics and practitioners of strategic management.

THE CASE COLLECTION IN THE 12TH EDITION

The 27 cases in this edition include 19 new cases not appearing in any of our previous editions, 7 updated cases from the 10th and 11th editions, and 1 carryover case—the now-classic two-page Robin Hood case. According to our custom, we have grouped the cases under five chapter-related, topical headings to highlight the close links between the cases and strategic management concepts.

In the Section A grouping are four cases spotlighting the manager as chief strategy maker and chief strategy implementer; these cases—Steve Case, America Online, and Time Warner; The DaimlerChrysler Merger (A) and (B); and Giuseppe's Original Sausage Company—demonstrate why the discussions in Chapters 1 and 2 are relevant to a company's long-term market success. Section B contains 13 cases (including 6 cases on dot-com companies) whose central issues deal with analyzing industry and competitive situations and crafting business-level strategy; these cases call on students to apply the text material in Chapters 3 through 8. In Section C are cases on Campbell Soup and Black & Decker (both of which are updated from previous editions) that make nice follow-ons to the text coverage of strategy making in diversified companies in Chapters 9 and 10. The six cases in Section D all revolve around the managerial challenges of implementing strategy and give students an opportunity to apply the concepts presented in Chapters 11, 12, and 13. Section E contains two cases—one on Motorola and one on Levi Strauss—highlighting the links between strategy, ethics, and social responsibility.

The New Collection of e-Cases

As a way to make it simple and convenient for instructors to supplement the 27 cases included in the text, we've assembled an e-collection of 31 of the best and most popular cases from our 10th and 11th editions, giving you a total of nearly 58 cases from which to choose in making case assignments. Moreover, *the e-case collection will be expanded on an ongoing basis as fast as we are able to secure freshly written cases, get them satisfactorily formatted, and secure the rights to post them for classroom use.* Students can use a credit card to purchase assigned cases in the e-collection at the Web site for the text; all e-cases are available immediately in the form of a downloadable file. Students can either print a copy from the e-case file for their personal use or read the case directly on the monitor.

We believe that the cases from our continually updated e-library will prove valuable as supplements to the cases in the text and keep case assignments current. We hope that the e-case library will eventually consist of 60 to 70 cases eminently suitable for use with our text, and we are confident that you will find the caliber of cases in the e-collection equal to the caliber in the text. The e-case library, which instructors can browse in the "instructor center" at the Web site for the text (www.mhhe.com/thompson), is organized to make it easy and convenient for instructors to identify and select the cases that best meet their course needs. Teaching notes for all the e-cases are also available in downloadable or viewable form for instructor perusal and use.

The 27 cases in the 12th edition plus the initial 31 cases in the e-library all reflect our steadfast preference for cases that feature interesting products and companies and that are capable of sparking both student interest and lively classroom discussions. Over 40 of the 58 cases involve high-profile companies, products, or people that students will have heard of, know about from personal experience, or can easily identify with. The six dot-com company cases, plus several others, will provide students with insight into the special demands of competing in industry environments where technological developments are an everyday event, product life cycles are short, and competitive maneuvering among rivals comes fast and furious. At least 25 of the cases involve situations where company resources and competitive capabilities play as much a role in strategy making and strategy implementing as do industry and competitive conditions. Indeed, we made a special effort to ensure that the cases selected for the text and for the e-library vividly demonstrate the relevance of the resource-based view of the firm. Scattered throughout the lineup are over a dozen cases concerning non-U.S. companies, globally competitive industries, and/or cross-cultural situations; these cases, in conjunction with the globalized content of the text chapters, provide ample material for linking the study of management tightly to the ongoing globalization of the world economy—in proper keeping with the standards of the American Assembly of Collegiate Schools of Business (AACSB). You'll also find cases where the central figures are women and cases dealing with the strategic problems of family-owned or relatively small entrepreneurial businesses. Eighteen of the 27 printed cases in the text involve public companies about which students can do further research in the library or on the Internet, and 7 have videotape segments that are available from the publisher. Several cases in the e-case collection on the Web site have accompanying video segments.

The case researchers whose work appears in this edition and in our e-case collection have done an absolutely first-class job of preparing cases that contain valuable teaching points, that illustrate the important kinds of strategic challenges managers face, and that allow students to apply the tools of strategic analysis. We believe the cases available with this 12th edition are exceptionally appealing, eminently teachable, and very suitable for drilling students in the use of the concepts and analytical treatments in Chapters 1 through 13.

The Guide to Case Analysis and Use of the Internet

Following Chapter 13 and prior to Case 1, we have once again included a section called "A Guide to Case Analysis," which gives students positive direction in what the case method is all about and offers suggestions for approaching case analysis. As an integral part of this discussion, there's a section on how to use the Internet to (1) do further research on an industry or company, (2) obtain a company's latest financial results, and (3) get updates on what has happened since the case was written. The amount of information available on the Internet has increased at such a rapid-fire pace that the challenge now is to sort quickly through all that is available to find what is really pertinent to the topic at hand. We think students will find our list of suggested Web sites to be a time-saving and valuable assist in running down the information they need. And to further facilitate student use of the Internet, many of the cases include company Web site addresses.

THE CONCEPT-TUTOR AND CASE-TUTOR SOFTWARE SUPPLEMENTS FOR STUDENTS

Available with the 12th edition are third-generation Windows-based software options that serve as interactive study guides. Students can use a credit card to purchase and download the software at the publisher's Web site for the textbook (www.mhhe.com/thompson). The software consists of two separate elements which can be used singly or in tandem:

- *Concept-TUTOR™* —A series of 13 computerized self-tests that students can use to measure their comprehension, chapter-by-chapter, of the conceptual material presented in the text.
- *Case-TUTOR™* —Study questions for each of the 27 cases in the twelfth edition, plus a set of custom-designed case preparation guides for 12 of the cases that lead students through the needed analysis, provide number-crunching assistance, and tutor students in use of the concepts and tools presented in the chapters.

The Concept-Tutor Software Option

Concept-TUTOR contains (1) a 25-question self-test for each of the 13 text chapters, (2) a 50-question self-exam covering the material in Chapters 1–8, and (3) a 50-question self-exam covering the material in Chapters 9–13. The 13 chapter tests consist of a challenging assortment of true–false, multiple-choice, and fill-in-the-blank questions that thoroughly cover the text presentation. These tests were deliberately made demanding (given their open-book nature) so as to require careful reading and good comprehension of the material. When the student completes each test, Concept-TUTOR automatically grades the answers, provides a test score, posts the test score in the student's personal grade book, indicates the questions with wrong answers, and directs students to the text pages where the correct answers can be found. Questions incorrectly answered can be attempted as many times as needed to arrive at the right answer. In addition, we created multiple-choice tests covering Chapters 1–8 (50 questions) and Chapters 9–13 (50 questions) that students can use to prepare for in-class exams given by the instructor.

Used properly and in conjunction with each other, we think these tests will provide students with a welcome and effective way to gauge their readiness for the course instructor's own examinations on the 13 chapters. *None of the questions on Concept-TUTOR correspond directly to those on the instructor's test bank.*

The Case-Tutor Software Option

We've all experienced poor and uneven student preparation of cases for class discussion. Sometimes it's because of inadequate effort but more often it's because of inexperience in using the tools of strategic analysis to arrive at solid recommendations and/or uncertainty over exactly what analysis to do. To give students some direction in preparing a case for class, Case-Tutor provides study questions for all 27 cases in the 12th edition. To help them learn how to use the concepts and analytical tools properly, there's an interactive guide (not a solution!) for use in preparing 12 of the cases. Each of the 12 study guides has been custom-designed to fit the specific issues and analytical problems posed by that case. We scrupulously avoided creating one generic study guide because cases in strategic management cut across a broad range of issues and require diverse analytical approaches. (Strategy analysis in single-business situations is fundamentally different from strategy analysis of diversified companies; cases where the spotlight is on developing a strategy are fundamentally different from cases where the main issues revolve around strategy implementation and execution.)

The custom-designed case preparation guides on Case-Tutor provide:

- *Study questions* to trigger the process of thinking strategically and to point students toward the analysis needed to arrive at sound recommendations.

- A series of *interactive screens organized around the study questions* that coach students in the use of whatever analytical tools are appropriate—whether it be five-forces analysis, strategic group mapping, identification of key success factors, SWOT analysis, value chain analysis, competitive strength assessments, construction of business portfolio matrixes, industry attractiveness assessments, or strategic fit matchups. These screens are intended to help students arrive at substantive, reasoned, supportable answers to the study questions.

- *Assistance in performing calculations related to the analysis.* This can include statistics useful in evaluating industry data and company operating performance, measures of profitability, growth rates, and assorted financial ratios.

- *What-if exercises* (where appropriate) that allow students to readily develop projections of company financial performance (when such projections are germane to the case, and when data in the case permit such projections to be made).

- *Questions* specifically aimed at helping students create a set of analysis-based, supportable action recommendations.

- *The capability to make printouts* of the work done (to serve as notes students can use in the class discussion or as hand-in assignments to be checked or graded).

The interactive design of the case preparation guides keeps the ball squarely in the student's court to do the analysis, to decide what story the numbers tell about a company's situation and performance, and to think through the options to arrive at recommendations. The Case-Tutor software supplement is thus not a crutch or "answer file" for the cases; rather, it is a vehicle for using the personal computer to tutor students in strategic thinking and help them learn to correctly apply the tools and concepts of strategic management. We endeavored to design the case preparation guides to coach students in how to think strategically about business problems and issues, to drill them in the methods of strategic analysis, and to promote sound business judgment. Instructors can be assured that the case notes students develop with the aid of Case-TUTOR will represent their work, not ours.

THE NEW E-LEARNING CENTER AT THE WEB SITE

A new feature of this edition's Web site is the creation of an "e-learning center" that functions as an electronic bookstore where students can use a credit card to purchase and immediately obtain:

- The Concept-TUTOR courseware.
- The Case-TUTOR courseware.
- Downloadable portable document format (PDF) files of most of the cases in this 12th edition and selected cases from the 10th and 11th editions, plus files of freshly written cases that have become available since publication of this edition.
- A digitally delivered version of both the Player's Manual and software for *The Business Strategy Game* (described below).

The addition of the e-learning center products is intended to give instructors not only more flexibility and variety in selecting the package of case assignments for their courses but also the advantage of the Internet's speed and economies. Providing materials to students in electronic rather than in printed form or on disks and CDs is substantially more cost-efficient, thus reducing the prices that students have to pay utilizing traditional campus bookstore channels. Students can download the desired files directly to the hard disks of their own computers or to floppy disks if they are working in a university PC lab.

Our new e-learning center is a first step in what we suspect will eventually become a universal practice of delivering learning materials via the Internet. We would be delighted for you to share with us any ideas and suggestions for helping the e-learning center concept better meet the needs of both students and instructors.

THE BUSINESS STRATEGY GAME OPTION

There's an extensively revised and upgraded version of *The Business Strategy Game* to accompany this 12th edition of the textbook. The mostly new seventh-generation version of *The Business Strategy Game* has a raft of new features that we think users will find appealing and that take the simulation to a much-higher plateau of capability:

- *An easy-to-use e-mail feature that makes the simulation ideal for distance-learning situations.* This addition is a response to requests from numerous users. The e-mail feature allows company members to click on a built-in e-mail button that will send their decision file to the instructor/game administrator, lets instructors open e-mailed files and direct them into the processing sequence with a few clicks, and then lets instructors/game administrators readily e-mail the results back to company members for use in the next round of decision making.

- *A revised and integrated demand forecasting tool.* There's a new screen that allows each footwear company to develop sales projections for the number of pairs it is likely to sell in each market segment, given its contemplated marketing effort and given the overall competitive effort it expects to encounter from rival companies. Company members can use these projections as the basis for production and plant operations decisions, for shipping decisions to the various distribution centers, and for crafting a marketing strategy that will produce the desired sales and market share. However, the accuracy of the sales projections will depend on students' ability to anticipate both changes in market conditions and rivals' competitive efforts.

- *The addition of Latin America as a geographic region of the global market.* We've added Latin America to the list of geographic regions constituting the global footwear market. Companies can now locate plants and sell their footwear products in any or all of four regions—North America, Asia, Europe, and Latin America. The simulation begins with a $4 tariff on footwear imported into Europe, a $6 tariff on footwear imported into Latin America, and an $8 tariff on footwear imported into Asia. All companies start the simulation with a 1-million-pair plant in North America and a 3-million-pair plant in Asia. Exchange rate fluctuations are tied to the U.S. dollar, the euro, the Japanese yen, and the Brazilian real.

- *The Internet marketing and online sales feature.* Companies now compete online to sell direct to consumers based on three global factors (comparative selling prices, the number of models and styles offered at the Web site, and speed of delivery) and three region-specific factors (product quality, image rating, and advertising). As might be expected, there is some channel conflict between online sales and a company's attempt to secure sales through brick-and-mortar retail outlets; company co-managers have to address these "cannibalization" issues if they elect to pursue a "click-and-mortar" strategy (a situation with which many real-world companies have to contend).

- *The option to open a chain of company retail stores.* Companies now have the option of investing in building a chain of company-owned and operated retail megastores in major shopping centers to supplement or substitute for selling at wholesale through independent retail dealers. However, as with online sales, company-owned stores pose some distribution channel conflict because independent retailers see them as cannibalizing their own sales. Thus, company members now have to wrestle with which of three distribution channels to emphasize—independent dealers, company-owned stores, and online sales—and they have to cope with whatever channel conflicts result.

- *New production options.* Decision entries have been added that allow plants to produce branded and private-label footwear of a specified quality and product-line breadth. In former versions of the simulation, all production at a plant had to be of the same quality and involve the same number of models and styles—there was no distinction between producing private-label and branded footwear. The flexibility to produce both types of footwear and specify the quality and models of each gives companies a much richer and more realistic set of strategy options. We've also increased the number of plant upgrade options from three to six in order to provide more ways to match production strategy and production costs to fit the needs of a company's pricing and marketing strategy and its production capacity requirements. All these plant-related changes give company managers more ways to use plant assets and to deal with high-cost plants; they also serve to dampen the tendency that existed in prior editions for companies to invest in more plant capacity than was really needed and thus create excess supply conditions.

- *New analytical tools.* There are new menu options that players can use to assist them in evaluating capacity expansions, drawing strategic group maps, drawing charts and graphs, and preparing a long-range strategic plan. We think students will find that these analytical aids save time as well as provide valuable insights for improving the caliber of their decisions.

- *The use of Microsoft Excel.* This new seventh edition of *The Business Strategy Game* requires that the simulation be played on PCs loaded with Microsoft Excel—the version on Office 97 or Office 2000. Moreover, the PCs must have a Windows-based operating system (Windows 95, Windows 98, Windows NT, or Windows 2000) and preferably 64 MB of RAM and a 233-MHz or faster chip. (The program will run on lesser-equipped machines but at slow speeds.) If your class does not have access to PCs with a Windows-based operating system and a recent version of Microsoft Excel, then you will need to use the sixth edition version of *The Business Strategy Game.*

- *New screen designs and support calculations.* We used the reprogramming of the simulation as an opportunity to greatly improve screen layouts, to incorporate more instructions for use of the software and of the rules directly on the screen (so as to minimize the need for students to look up things in the Player's Manual), and to provide a far richer set of on-screen calculations to guide decision making. While the screens contain a lot more information and take a bit longer to digest, players will find most all of the information they need is either directly on the screens or is readily accessible on the menu bar guide at the top of each screen. If students forget some of the information in the Player's Manual, they can quickly access the information online by clicking on the Help button—the Help button takes them directly to screens displaying the related information in the Player's Manual, thus eliminating the need to look up rules and procedures in the manual.

- *A revamped Player's Manual.* The changes we've made in this edition necessitated a fundamental rewrite of the Player's Manual. So we took the opportunity to recast the whole presentation around demand forecasting, plant operations, warehousing and shipping, sales and marketing, and the financing of company operations—the very things that are the central focus of the decision screens and the overall strategy-making process. The discussion of the decisions in each area of the company's operations is integrated with the reports concerning each area of company operations. We think you'll find that the new presentation of the Player's Manual, coupled with the information-rich screen designs, will make playing of the simulation easier for students and dramatically reduce the number of questions about rules and procedures.

- *Software downloads at the McGraw-Hill/Irwin Web site for the text.* In past editions, users have encountered problems with defective disks and with getting the latest version of the software. Beginning with this edition, all of the key software that students need to play the simulation must be downloaded directly from the Web site, thus ensuring that the correct and latest version is always readily available and detouring many of the annoying problems of defective disks. Students who wish to do so can bypass the use of a printed version of the manual and, using a credit card, purchase an electronic version of the entire *Business Strategy Game* package at the Web site. Similarly, all the necessary software for instructors/game administrators is posted on the Web site for immediate availability; electronic files of the Player's Manual and the Instructor's Manual are available to instructors for immediate inspection and use.

There are numerous lesser changes and refinements that do their part to make this edition a truly next-generation product. But, while much is new, users of prior editions will still find much that is familiar; the effort to gear up for this new edition will be quite modest, and the overall time it takes to process and administer the game has been significantly reduced. As before, instructors have numerous ways to heighten competition and keep things lively as the game progresses. There are options to raise or lower interest rates, alter certain costs up or down, and issue special news flashes announcing new tariff levels, materials cost changes, shipping difficulties, or other new considerations to keep business conditions dynamic. And the built-in scoreboard of company performance keeps students constantly informed about where their company stands. Rapid advances in PC technology have cut the processing time to under 5 minutes—it should take no more than 20 minutes to turn the decisions around for an entire industry once several decisions have been processed.

What Sets This Simulation Apart

The Business Strategy Game has five features that make it an uncommonly effective teaching/learning aid for strategic management courses: (1) *the product and the industry*—as we noted earlier, students can readily identify with and understand the athletic footwear industry; (2) *the global environment*—students gain up-close exposure to what global competition is like and the kinds of strategic issues that managers in global industries have to address; (3) *the realistic quality of the simulation exercise*—we've designed the simulation to be as faithful as possible to real-world markets, competitive conditions, and revenue-cost-profit relationships; (4) *the wide degree of strategic freedom students have in managing their companies*—we've gone to great lengths to make the game free of bias as concerns use of one strategy versus another; and (5) *the long-range strategic planning and analysis capabilities it incorporates as an integral part of the exercise of running a company.*

These features, wrapped together as a package, provide an exciting and valuable bridge between concept and practice, the classroom and real-life management, and reading a textbook and learning by doing. Instructors will find opportunity after opportunity to use examples and happenings in *The Business Strategy Game* in lecturing on the text chapters.

The Value a Simulation Adds

Our own experiences, along with hours of discussions with users, have convinced us that simulation games are *the single best exercise available* for helping students understand how the functional pieces of a business fit together and giving them an integrated experience. First and foremost, the exercise of running a simulated company over a number of decision periods helps develop students' business judgment. Simulation games provide a live case situation where events unfold and circumstances change as the game progresses. Their special hook is an ability to get students personally involved in the subject matter. *The Business Strategy Game* is very typical in this respect. In plotting their competitive strategies each decision period, students learn about risk taking. They have to respond to changing market conditions, react to the moves of competitors, and choose among alternative courses of action. They get valuable practice in reading the signs of industry change, spotting market opportunities, evaluating threats to their company's competitive position, weighing the trade-offs between profits now and profits later, and assessing the long-term consequences of short-term decisions. They chart a long-term direction, set strategic and financial objectives, and try out different strategies in pursuit of competitive advantage. They become active strategic thinkers, planners, analysts, and decision makers. And by having to live with the decisions they make, they experience what it means to be accountable for decisions and responsible for achieving satisfactory results. All this serves to drill students in responsible decision making and to improve their business acumen and managerial judgment.

Second, students learn an enormous amount from working with the numbers, exploring options, and trying to unite production, marketing, finance, and human resource decisions into a coherent strategy. They begin to see ways to apply knowledge from prior courses and figure out what really makes a business tick. The effect is to help students integrate a lot of material, look at decisions from the standpoint of the company as a whole, and see the importance of thinking strategically about a company's competitive position and future prospects. Since a simulation game is, by its very nature, a hands-on exercise, the lessons learned are forcefully planted in students' minds—often with lasting impact. Third, students' entrepreneurial instincts blossom as they get caught up in the competitive spirit of the game. The resulting entertainment value helps maintain an unusually high level of student motivation and emotional involvement in the course throughout the term.

A Bird's-Eye View of the Simulation

We designed *The Business Strategy Game* around athletic footwear because producing and marketing athletic footwear is a business students can readily understand and because the athletic footwear market displays the characteristics of many globally competitive—fast growth, worldwide use of the product, competition among companies from several continents, production in low-wage locations, and a marketplace where a variety of competitive approaches and business strategies can coexist. The simulation allows the imaginary companies to manufacture and sell their brands in North America, Asia, Europe, and Latin America, plus the option to compete for supplying private-label footwear to North American chain retailers. Branded sales can be pursued through any or all of three distribution channels—independent footwear retailers, company-owned and operated retail stores, and direct sales made online at the company's Web site.

Competition is head-to-head—each team of students must match their strategic wits against the other company teams. Companies can focus their branded marketing efforts on one geographic market or two or three or all four. They also can compete aggressively or de-emphasize branded sales and specialize in private-label production (an attractive strategy for low-cost producers). They can establish a one-country production base, or they can manufacture in all four of the geographic markets to avoid tariffs and mitigate the risk of adverse exchange rate fluctuations. Low-cost leadership, differentiation strategies, best-cost producer strategies, and focus strategies are all viable competitive options. Companies can position their products in the low end of the market or the high end, or they can stick close to the middle on price, quality, and service; they can have a wide or narrow product line, small or big dealer networks, extensive or limited advertising. Company market shares are based on how each company's product attributes and competitive efforts stack up against those of rivals. Demand conditions, tariffs, and wage rates vary from geographic area to geographic area. Raw materials used in footwear production are purchased in a worldwide commodity market at prices that move up or down in response to supply-demand conditions. If a company's sales volume is unexpectedly low, management has the option to liquidate excess inventories at deep discount prices.

Each student-managed company has plants to operate; a workforce to compensate; distribution expenses and inventories to control; capital expenditure decisions to make; marketing and sales campaigns to wage; a Web site to operate; sales forecasts to consider; and ups and downs in exchange rates, interest rates, and the stock market to take into account. Students must weave functional decisions in production, distribution, marketing, finance, and human resources into a cohesive action plan. They have to react to changing market and competitive conditions, initiate moves to try to build competitive advantage, and decide how to defend against aggressive actions by competitors. And they must endeavor to maximize shareholder wealth via increased dividend payments and stock price appreciation. Each team of students is challenged to use their entrepreneurial and strategic skills to become the next Nike or Reebok and ride the wave of growth to the top of the worldwide athletic footwear industry. The whole exercise is representative of a real-world competitive market where companies try to outcompete and outperform rivals—things are every bit as realistic and true to actual business practice as we could make them.

There are built-in planning and analysis features that allow students to (1) craft a three-year strategic plan, (2) evaluate the economics of expanding capacity, (3) draw strategic group maps, (4) quickly prepare and print out an assortment of charts and graphs showing various performance trends, and (5) build different competitive strategy scenarios. Calculations at the bottom of each decision screen provide instantly updated projections of sales revenues, profits, return on equity, cash flow, and other key outcomes as each decision entry is made. The sensitivity of financial and operating outcomes to different decision entries is easily observed on the screen and on detailed printouts of projections. With the speed of today's personal computers, the relevant number-crunching is done in a split second. The game is designed throughout to lead students to decisions based on analysis and away from the quicksand of seat-of-the-pants decisions.

A separate Instructor's Manual for *The Business Strategy Game* describes how to integrate the simulation exercise into a course, provides pointers on how to administer the game, and contains step-by-step processing instructions. In the case of difficulties, technical personnel at Irwin/McGraw-Hill can provide instructors with quick assistance via a toll-free number. Assistance is also available directly from the co-authors and at the Web site.

The Business Strategy Game runs on any PC loaded with Microsoft Excel (either the Office 97 version or the Office 2000 version) and is suitable for both senior-level and MBA courses. The game can be installed to run on a network and has a new e-mail feature to facilitate use in distance-learning situations.

THE TEXT-READINGS OPTION

For instructors who want to incorporate samples of the strategic management literature into the course and assemble their own customized case package, we offer the companion paperback *Crafting and Executing Strategy: Text and Readings*. The text portion is the same as the 13 chapters in the hardbound text; instead of cases, though, it contains a selection of 22 readings. All 22 readings are suitable for seniors and MBA students. Most are articles reprinted from leading journals; they add in-depth treatment to important topic areas covered in the text and put readers at the cutting edge of academic thinking and research on the subject. A couple of the readings, drawn from practitioner sources, stress how particular tools and concepts relate directly to actual companies and managerial practices.

To emphasize the link between the selected readings and the 13 chapters of text, we have grouped the readings into five categories. Four articles examine the role of the manager as chief strategist and chief strategy implementer, and expand on the topics covered in Chapters 1 and 2. Twelve articles concern strategic analysis and strategy formation at the business unit level, and add more range and depth to the material presented in Chapters 3 through 8. There's one article dealing with strategy in diversified companies that is appropriate for use with Chapters 9 and 10. (To expand the reading assignments here, instructors can select other articles from the list of suggested readings at the end of these two chapters.) Five of the readings relate to various aspects of strategy implementation and execution, making them suitable complements for the material in Chapters 11, 12, and 13; two of these articles focus on strategy, values, and ethics. All in all, the companion volume contains a solid lineup of recently published articles that can easily be supplemented with journal articles that have appeared since this edition went to press.

In tandem, the material in *Crafting and Executing Strategy: Text and Readings* provides an effective, efficient vehicle for underpinning case assignments, using cases from the e-library at the Web site for the text or from other sources.

THE 12TH EDITION INSTRUCTOR'S PACKAGE

A full complement of instructional aids is available to assist adopters in using the 12th edition successfully. A two-volume Instructor's Manual contains suggestions for using the text materials, various approaches to course design and course organization, a sample syllabus, alternative course outlines, a thoroughly revised and expanded set of over 1,000 multiple-choice and essay questions, and a comprehensive teaching note for each case. There is a computerized test bank for generating examinations, a set of color transparencies depicting the figures and tables in the 13 text chapters, and PowerPoint presentation software containing a full set of color visuals for classrooms equipped with computer screen projection capability that can be downloaded directly from the instructor's section of the Web site. The PowerPoint files can also be used to make black-and-white transparencies for use with an overhead projector. The PowerPoint package includes over 400 visuals that thoroughly cover the material presented in the 13 chapters, thus providing plenty to select from in creating support for classroom lectures. (We deliberately created enough visuals for each chapter to allow an ample number of choices in putting together a presentation that fits both individual preferences and time constraints.) To help instructors enrich and vary the pace of class discussions of cases, there are video supplements for use with the America Online, DaimlerChrysler, Callaway Golf, Cannondale, Peapod, eBay, and Levi Strauss cases.

In concert, the textbook, the three companion supplements, and the comprehensive instructor's package provide a complete, integrated lineup of teaching materials. The package provides exceptional latitude in course design, allows adopters to capitalize on the latest computer-assisted instructional techniques, contains an assortment of visual aids, and offers rich pedagogical options for keeping the nature of student assignments varied and interesting. We've endeavored to equip instructors with all the text materials and complementary resources they need to create and deliver a course that is very much in keeping with contemporary strategic management issues and that wins enthusiastic student approval.

ACKNOWLEDGMENTS

We have benefited from the help of many people during the evolution of this book. Students, adopters, and reviewers have generously supplied an untold number of insightful comments and helpful suggestions. Our intellectual debt to those academics, writers, and practicing managers who have blazed new trails in the strategy field will be obvious to any reader familiar with the literature of strategic management.

We are particularly indebted to the case researchers whose efforts appear herein and to the companies whose cooperation made the cases possible. To each one goes a very special thank-you. The importance of timely, carefully researched cases cannot be overestimated in contributing to a substantive study of strategic management issues and practices. From a research standpoint, cases in strategic management are invaluable in exposing the generic kinds of strategic issues companies face, in forming hypotheses about strategic behavior, and in drawing experience-based generalizations about the practice of strategic management. Pedagogically, cases about strategic management give students essential practice in diagnosing and evaluating strategic situations, in learning to use the tools and concepts of strategy analysis, in sorting through various strategic options, in crafting strategic action plans, and in figuring out successful ways to implement and execute the chosen strategy. Without a continuing stream of fresh, well-researched, and well-conceived cases, the discipline of strategic management would quickly fall into disrepair, losing much of its energy and excitement. There's no question, therefore, that first-class case research constitutes a valuable scholarly contribution.

The following reviewers provided insightful advice regarding ways to improve the 12th edition text and package:

F. William Brown, Montana State University

Anthony F. Chelte, Western New England College

Gregory G. Dess, University of Kentucky

Alan B. Eisner, Pace University

John George, Liberty University

Carle M. Hunt, Regent University

Theresa Marron-Grodsky, University of Maryland

Sarah Marsh, Northern Illinois University

Joshua D. Martin, University of Delaware

William L. Moore, California State University

Donald Neubaum, University of Central Florida

George M. Puia, Indiana State University

Amit Shah, Frostburg State University

Lois M. Shelton, University of Illinois at Chicago

Mark Weber, University of Minnesota

We are also indebted to Steve Barndt, J. Michael Geringer, Ming-Fang Li, Richard Stackman, Stephen Tallman, Gerardo R. Ungson, James Boulgarides, Betty Diener, Daniel F. Jennings, David Kuhn, Kathryn Martell, Wilbur Mouton, Bobby Vaught, Tuck Bounds, Lee Burk, Ralph Catalanello, William Crittenden, Vince Luchsinger, Stan Mendenhall, John Moore, Will Mulvaney, Sandra Richard, Ralph Roberts, Thomas Turk, Gordon VonStroh, Fred Zimmerman, S. A. Billion, Charles Byles, Gerald L. Geisler, Rose Knotts, Joseph Rosenstein, James B. Thurman, Ivan Able, W. Harvey Hegarty, Roger Evered, Charles B. Saunders, Rhae M. Swisher, Claude I. Shell, R. Thomas Lenz, Michael C. White, Dennis Callahan, R. Duane Ireland, William E. Burr II, C. W. Millard, Richard Mann, Kurt Christensen, Neil W. Jacobs, Louis W. Fry, D. Robley Wood, George J. Gore, and William R. Soukup. These reviewers were of considerable help in directing our efforts at various stages in the evolution of the text.

Naturally, as custom properly dictates, we are responsible for any remaining errors of fact, deficiencies in coverage or presentation, or oversights. As always, we value your recommendations and thoughts about the book. Your comments regarding coverage and content will be most welcome, as will your calling our attention to specific errors. Please e-mail us at athompso@cba.ua.edu, fax us at (205) 348-6695, or write us at P.O. Box 870225, Department of Management and Marketing, The University of Alabama, Tuscaloosa, Alabama 35487-0225.

Arthur A. Thompson

A. J. Strickland

brief | contents

part | one   The Concepts and Techniques of Strategic Management   1

     1. The Strategic Management Process: An Overview   2

     2. Establishing Company Direction: Developing a Strategic Vision, Setting Objectives, and Crafting a Strategy   30

     3. Industry and Competitive Analysis   72

     4. Evaluating Company Resources and Competitive Capabilities   114

     5. Strategy and Competitive Advantage   148

     6. Strategies for Competing in Globalizing Markets   198

     7. New Business Models and Strategies for the Internet Economy   224

     8. Tailoring Strategy to Fit Specific Industry and Company Situations   248

     9. Strategy and Competitive Advantage in Diversified Companies   280

     10. Evaluating the Strategies of Diversified Companies   318

     11. Building Resource Strengths and Organizational Capabilities   344

     12. Managing the Internal Organization to Promote Better Strategy Execution   378

     13. Corporate Culture and Leadership—Keys to Effective Strategy Execution   408

part | two   Cases in Strategic Management   C-1

     A Guide to Case Analysis   C-2

     Section A: The Manager as Chief Strategy Maker and Chief Strategy Implementer

     * 1. Steve Case, America Online and Times Warner   C-17

     2. Daimler Chrysler Merger (A): Gaining Global Competitiveness   C-50

     3. Daimler Chrysler Merger (B): Shaping a Transatlantic Company   C-64

     4. Giuseppe's Original Sausage Company   C-74

     Section B: Crafting Strategy in Single-Business Companies

     5. The Chinese Fireworks Industry   C-90

     * 6. Competition in the U.S. Automobile Retailing Industry   C-102

     * 7. Dell Computer Corporation: Strategy and Challenges for the 21st Century   C-132

     * 8. Peapod, Inc., and the Online Grocery Business   C-174

*Cases for which there are case preparation exercises on Case-Tutor™.

* 9. Cannondale Corporation   C-196

*10. Competition in the Retail Brokerage Industry in 2000   C-225

*11. eBay: King of the Online Auction Industry   C-263

  12. CDnow in the Online Music Business   C-295

*13. Calloway Golf Company   C-314

  14. drkoop.com   C-349

  15. WingspanBank.com   C-369

  16. Ben & Jerry's—Japan   C-384

  17. Viña San Pedro   C-400

   Section C: Crafting Strategy in Diversified Companies

*18. Campbell Soup Company in 2000   C-423

*19. The Black & Decker Corporation in 2000   C-454

   Section D: Implementing and Executing Strategy

*20. Robin Hood   C-477

*21. Replacements, Ltd.: Replacing the Irreplaceable   C-479

  22. The Kimpton Hotel & Restaurant Group   C-518

  23. Brithinee Electric in 1999: Raising the Standards   C-534

  24. The Rococco New York Hotel   C-555

  25. Developing a Global Mind-Set at Johnson & Johnson, 1998   C-568

   Section E: Strategy, Ethics, and Social Responsibility

  26. Motorola: Ethical Challenges in a Multicultural Environment   C-580

  27. Levi Strauss & Company   C-601

indexes

   Name   I-1

   Organization   I-5

   Subject   I-11

 * Cases for which there are case preparation exercises on Case-TUTOR™.

table of | contents

part | one   The Concepts and Techniques of Strategic Management   1

1. The Strategic Management Process: An Overview   2

The Most Trustworthy Signs of Good Management   4
The Five Tasks of Strategic Management: A Bird's-Eye View of This Book   6
    Developing a Strategic Vision   6
    Setting Objectives   9
    Crafting a Strategy   10
    Implementing and Executing the Strategy   18
    Evaluating Performance, Monitoring New Developments, and
    Initiating Corrective Adjustments   19
Why Strategic Management Is an Ongoing Process, Not a Start-Stop
Event   20
    Characteristics of the Five-Task Process   20
Who Performs the Five Tasks of Strategic Management?   21
    How Strategies Get Crafted—What the Process Is Like and Who
    Participates   23
    The Role of the Board of Directors in Crafting and Executing Strategy   27
The Benefits of a Strategic Approach to Managing   28
Suggested Readings   29
illustration capsules
    1. Two Radically Different Business Models: Microsoft and Redhat Linux   5
    2. Examples of Strategic Visions and Company Mission Statements   8
    3. Examples of Strategic and Financial Objectives   11
    4. A Strategy Example: McDonald's   14
    5. Corporate Intrapreneuring at British Airways   26

2. Establishing Company Direction: Developing a Strategic Vision, Setting Objectives, and Crafting a Strategy   30

Developing a Strategic Vision: The First Direction-Setting Task   32
    The Three Elements of a Strategic Vision   32
    The Mission Statement: A Starting Point for Forming a Strategic Vision   32
    From Mission Statement to Strategic Vision   38
    Communicating the Strategic Vision   40
Establishing Objectives: The Second Direction-Setting Task   41
    What Kinds of Objectives to Set   42
    The Concept of Strategic Intent   45

The Need for Long-Range and Short-Range Objectives   46
How Much Stretch Should Objectives Entail?   46
Objectives Are Needed at All Organizational Levels   47
Crafting a Strategy: The Third Direction-Setting Task   48
The Strategy-Making Pyramid   49
Corporate Strategy   50
Business Strategy   54
Functional Strategy   56
Operating Strategy   57
Uniting the Strategy-Making Effort   57
The Factors That Shape a Company's Strategy   58
Societal, Political, Regulatory, and Citizenship
Considerations   59
Competitive Conditions and Overall Industry Attractiveness   61
The Company's Market Opportunities and External Threats   62
Company Resource Strengths, Competencies, and Competitive Capabilities   62
The Personal Ambitions, Business Philosophies, and Ethical Beliefs of
Managers   62
The Influence of Shared Values and Company Culture on Strategy   63
Linking Strategy with Ethics and Social Responsibility   64
Tests of a Winning Strategy   68
Key Points   69
Suggested Readings   70
illustration capsules
6. Deere and Company's Strategic Vision   33
7. Four Sample Mission Statements: Examples to Critique   37
8. Intel's Two Strategic Inflection Points   40
9. Corporate Objectives at Citigroup, General Electric, McDonald's,
Anheuser-Busch, Exodus Communications, Motorola, and
McCormick & Company   44
10. Bank One's New Internet Banking Strategy   50
11. How Enron's Vision and Values Shape Its Strategy   65
12. The Kroger Company's Commitments to Its Stakeholders   68

3. Industry and Competitive Analysis   72

The Methods of Industry and Competitive Analysis   76
Question 1: What Are the Industry's Dominant Economic
Features?   77
Question 2: What Is Competition Like and How Strong Are
Each of the Competitive Forces?   79
The Five Forces of Competition   79
Strategic Implications of the Five Competitive Forces   92
Question 3: What Is Causing the Industry's Competitive Structure and Business
Environment to Change?   93
The Concept of Driving Forces   93
Environmental Scanning Techniques   99

Question 4: Which Companies Are in the Strongest/Weakest Positions?   100
Using Strategic Group Maps to Assess the Competitive Positions of Rival Firms   100
What Can Be Learned from Strategic Group Maps   101
Question 5: What Strategic Moves Are Rivals Likely to Make Next?   103
Monitoring Competitors' Strategies   103
Evaluating Who the Industry's Major Players Are Going to Be   104
Predicting Competitors' Next Moves   105
Question 6: What Are the Key Factors for Competitive Success?   106
Question 7: Is the Industry Attractive and What Are Its Prospects for Above-Average Profitability?   108
Actually Doing an Industry and Competitive Analysis   109
Key Points   111
Suggested Readings   113
illustration capsules
13. How the Internet and New Internet-Related Technologies Are Changing the Business Landscape: Classic Examples of a Driving Force   95
14. Strategic Group Map of Competitors in the Video Game Industry   102

4. Evaluating Company Resources and Competitive Capabilities   114
Question 1: How Well Is the Present Strategy Working?   116
Question 2: What Are the Company's Resource Strengths and Weaknesses and Its External Opportunities and Threats?   117
Identifying Company Strengths and Resource Capabilities   117
Identifying Company Weaknesses and Resource Deficiencies   119
Identifying Company Competencies and Capabilities   120
Identifying a Company's Market Opportunities   125
Identifying the Threats to a Company's Future Profitability   127
The Real Value of SWOT Analysis   127
Question 3: Are the Company's Prices and Costs Competitive?   128
Strategic Cost Analysis and Value Chains   129
Benchmarking the Costs of Key Activities   134
Strategic Options for Achieving Cost Competitiveness   137
From Value Chain Activities to Competitive Capabilities to Competitive Advantage   139
Question 4: How Strong Is the Company's Competitive Position?   140
Competitive Strength Assessments   140
Question 5: What Strategic Issues Does the Company Face?   143
Key Points   146
Suggested Readings   147
illustration capsules
15. TCI's Retreat to a Vision and Strategy in Line with Its Resources and Its Subsequent Acquisition by AT&T   126

16. The Value Chain for the Recording and Distributing of Music CDs   135

17. Ford Motor Company's Benchmarking of Its Accounts Payable
Activity   136

18. Benchmarking and Ethical Conduct   137

5. Strategy and Competitive Advantage   148

The Five Generic Competitive Advantages   150

Low-Cost Provider Strategies   151

Differentiation Strategies   163

Best-Cost Provider Strategies   167

Focused (or Market Niche) Strategies   168

Cooperative Strategies and Competitive Advantage   172

The Increasingly Pervasive Use of Alliances   172

Why and How Strategic Alliances Are Advantageous   174

Merger and Acquisition Strategies   177

Vertical Integration Strategies: A Competitive Plus or a Minus   178

The Strategic Advantages of Vertical Integration   180

The Strategic Disadvantages of Vertical Integration   187

Weighing the Pros and Cons of Vertical Integration   182

Unbundling and Outsourcing Strategies—Narrowing the Boundaries of
the Business   182

Capability Considerations in Boundary Decisions   184

Using Offensive Strategies to Secure Competitive Advantage   185

Initiatives to Match or Exceed Competitor Strengths   186

Initiatives to Capitalize on Competitor Weaknesses   187

Simultaneous Initiatives on Many Fronts   188

End-Run Offensives to Move to Less Contested Ground   188

Guerrilla Offensives   189

Preemptive Strikes   189

Choosing Whom to Attack   190

Using Defensive Strategies to Protect Competitive Advantage   191

First-Mover Advantages and Disadvantages   193

Key Points   194

Suggested Readings   197

illustration capsules

19. Nucor Corporation's Low-Cost Provider Strategy   154

20. E-Business Technologies: Powerful Tools for Restructuring Value Chains
to Create a Low-Cost Advantage   161

21. Differentiating Features That Raise Performance   165

22. Toyota's Best-Cost Producer Strategy for Its Lexus Line   169

23. Focused Strategies in the Lodging Industry: Motel 6 and
Ritz-Carlton   170

24. Examples of Recent Alliances   176

25. How Clear Channel Communications Used Mergers and Acquisitions to Become a Global Leader in the Media Industry 179

26. Toyota's First-Mover Offensive in Custom-Built Cars 194

6. Strategies for Competing in Globalizing Markets 198

Why Companies Expand into Foreign Markets 200
  The Difference between Competing Internationally and Competing Globally 200

Cross-Country Differences in Cultural, Demographic, and Market Conditions 201
  The Potential for Locational Advantages Stemming from Country-to-Country Cost Variations 202
  Fluctuating Exchange Rates 202
  Host Government Restrictions and Requirements 203

Multicountry Competition or Global Competition? 203

Strategy Options for Entering and Competing in Foreign Markets 204
  Export Strategies 205
  Licensing Strategies 206
  Franchising Strategies 206
  A Multicountry Strategy or a Global Strategy? 206

Pursuing Competitive Advantage by Competing Multinationally 209
  Achieving Locational Advantages 210
  Transferring Competencies and Capabilities across Borders 211
  Coordinating Cross-Border Activities 212

Profit Sanctuaries, Cross-Market Subsidization, and Global Strategic Offensives 213
  Using Cross-Market Subsidization to Wage a Strategic Offensive 213

Strategic Alliances and Joint Ventures with Foreign Partners 213
  The Risks of Strategic Alliances with Foreign Partners 214
  Making the Most of Strategic Alliances with Foreign Partners 215

Competing in Emerging Foreign Markets 217

Strategies for Local Companies in Emerging Markets 219
  Defending against Global Competitors by Using Home-Field Advantages 219
  Transferring the Companies Expertise to Cross-Border Markets 220
  Dodging Global Entrants by Shifting to a New Business Model or Market Niche 220
  Contending on a Global Level 221

Key Points 221

Suggested Readings 223

illustration capsules

27. Multicountry Strategies: Microsoft in PC Software, McDonald's in Fast Food, and Nestlé in Instant Coffee 209

28. Cross-Border Strategic Alliances: The New Shape of Global Business 216

7. New Business Models and Strategies for the Internet Economy   224

Internet Technology and Market Structure   226
  The Supply Side of the Internet Economy   226
Strategy-Shaping Characteristics of the E-Commerce Environment   227
E-Commerce Business Models and Strategies   233
  Business Models and Strategies for Communications Equipment Suppliers   234
  Business Models and Strategies for Communications Services Suppliers   235
  Business Models and Strategies for Computer Hardware Suppliers   236
  Business Models and Strategies for Specialized E-Commerce Software Developers   236
  Business Models and Strategies for E-Commerce Retailers   237
  "Brick-and-Click" Strategies: An Alternative to Pure Brick-and-Mortar Strategies and Pure Dot-com Strategies   239
  Business Models and Strategies for E-Commerce Services Suppliers   239
  Business Models and Strategies for Media Companies and Content Providers   242
Internet Strategies for Traditional Businesses   243
Key Success Factors in E-Commerce   244
Key Points   245
Suggested Readings   246
illustration capsules
  29. How the Internet Can Revamp Manufacturing Economics and Industry Value Chains   231
  30. Office Depot's Brick-and-Click Strategy   240
  31. Fingerhut's Strategy to Provide Order-Fulfillment Services to E-tailers   241

8. Tailoring Strategy to Fit Specific Industry and Company Situations   248

Strategies for Competing in Emerging Industries of the Future   280
Strategies for Competing in Turbulent, High-Velocity Markets   252
Strategies for Competing in Maturing Industries   256
  Strategic Moves in Maturing Industries   257
  Strategic Pitfalls in Maturing Industries   259
Strategies for Firms in Stagnant or Declining Industries   259
Strategies for Competing in Fragmented Industries   261
Strategies for Sustaining Rapid Company Growth   263
Strategies for Industry Leaders   265
Strategies for Runner-Up Firms   267
Strategies for Weak and Crisis-Ridden Businesses   271
  Turnaround Strategies for Businesses in Crisis   271
  Liquidation—the Strategy of Last Resort   273

End-Game Strategies   273

10 Commandments for Crafting Successful Business Strategies   275

Key Points   277

Suggested Readings   279

illustration capsules

32. Yamaha's Strategy in the Stagnant Piano Industry   261
33. How Microsoft Used Its Muscle to Maintain Market Dominance   268
34. Continental Airlines' Turnaround Strategy   274

9. Strategy and Competitive Advantage in Diversified Companies   280

When to Diversify   282

Why Rushing to Diversify Isn't Necessarily a Good Strategy   283

The Risks of Concentrating on a Single Business   283

Factors That Signal When It's Time to Diversify   284

Building Shareholder Value: The Ultimate Justification for Diversifying   284

Three Tests for Judging a Diversification Move   284

Choosing the Diversification Path: Related versus Unrelated Businesses   285

The Case for Related Diversification Strategies   286

Cross-Business Strategic Fits along the Value Chain   287

Strategic Fit, Economies of Scope, and Competitive Advantage   291

Capturing Strategic-Fit Benefits   292

The Case for Unrelated Diversification Strategies   293

The Pros and Cons of Unrelated Diversification   294

Unrelated Diversification and Shareholder Value   298

Combination Related-Unrelated Diversification Strategies   299

Strategies for Entering New Businesses   299

Acquisition of an Existing Business   299

Internal Start-Up   300

Joint Ventures and Strategic Partnerships   301

Strategy Options for Companies That Are Already Diversified   302

Strategies to Broaden a Diversified Company's Business Base   302

Divestiture Strategies Aimed at Retrenching to a Narrower Diversification Base   304

Corporate Restructuring and Turnaround Strategies   306

Multinational Diversification Strategies   308

What Makes Multinational Diversification So Attractive: The Opportunities for Growth and Added Competitive Advantage   308

Key Points   315

Suggested Readings   317

illustration capsules

35. Koch Industries' Diversification Strategy   288

36. Examples of Companies with Related Business Portfolios   291

37. Diversified Companies with Unrelated Business Portfolios   295

38. The Global Scope of Five Prominent Diversified Multinational Corporations   310

39. Honda's Competitive Advantages   314

10. Evaluating the Strategies of Diversified Companies   318

Identifying the Present Corporate Strategy   320

Evaluating Industry Attractiveness: Three Tests   321

    Evaluating the Attractiveness of Each Industry the Company Has Diversified Into   322

    Each Industry's Attractiveness Relative to the Others   323

    The Attractiveness of the Mix of Industries as a Whole   324

Evaluating the Competitive Strength of Each of the Company's Business Units   324

    Using a Nine-Cell Matrix to Simultaneously Portray Industry Attractiveness and Competitive Strength   327

Strategic Fit Analysis: Checking for Cross-Business Competitive Advantage Potential   330

Resource Fit Analysis: Determining How Well the Firm's Resources Match Business Unit Requirements   332

    Cash Hog and Cash Cow Businesses   333

    Competitive and Managerial Resource Fits   334

Ranking the Business Units on the Basis of Past Performance and Future Prospects   336

Deciding on Resource Allocation Priorities and a General Strategic Direction for Each Business Unit   337

Crafting a Corporate Strategy   338

    The Performance Test   338

    Identifying Additional Diversification Opportunities   340

    Managing the Process of Crafting Corporate Strategy   340

Key Points   341

Suggested Readings   343

illustration capsules

40. General Electric's Approach to Managing a Broadly Diversified Business Portfolio   329

11. Building Resource Strengths and Organizational Capabilities   344

A Framework for Executing Strategy   346

The Principal Strategy-Implementing Tasks   347

Leading the Strategy Implementation and Execution Process   348

Building a Capable Organization   349

    Staffing the Organization   350

Building Core Competencies and Competitive Capabilities 355

Matching Organization Structure to Strategy 359

Organizational Structures of the Future 372

Key Points 374

Suggested Readings 376

illustration capsules

41. How General Electric Develops a Talented and Deep Management Team 352

42. How Cisco Systems Staffs Its Organization with Talented Employees 354

43. Reengineering Business Processes: How Companies Do It and the Results They Have Gotten 366

44. Cross-Unit Coordination on Technology at 3M Corporation 371

45. Organizational Approaches for International and Global Markets 373

12. Managing the Internal Organization to Promote Better Strategy Execution 378

Linking Budgets to Strategy 380

Creating Strategy-Supportive Policies and Procedures 381

Instituting Best Practices and a Commitment to Continuous Improvement 383

Total Quality Management: A Commitment to Continuous Improvement 385

Capturing the Benefits of Best Practice and Continuous Improvement Programs 388

Installing Support Systems 390

Installing Adequate Information Systems, Performance Tracking, and Controls 393

Designing Strategy-Supportive Reward Systems 395

Strategy-Supportive Motivational Practices 395

Linking the Reward System to Strategically Relevant Performance Outcomes 399

Key Points 404

Suggested Readings 405

illustration capsules

46. Granite Rock's "Short Pay" Policy 383

47. Where Best Practices Come From: The Accomplishments of Three Best Practice Award Winners 384

48. Motorola's Approach to Quality and Continuous Improvement 387

49. The Rush to Install E-Commerce Support Systems 392

50. Motivation and Reward Techniques of "Best Practice" Companies 398

51. The Folly of the Reward System in the Claims Division of a Large Insurance Company 401

13. Corporate Culture and Leadership—Keys to Effective Strategy Execution 408

Building a Strategy-Supportive Corporate Culture 410

Where Does Corporate Culture Come From? 410

Culture: Ally or Obstacle to Strategy Execution?   413
Strong versus Weak Cultures   414
Unhealthy Cultures   416
Adaptive Cultures   417
Creating a Strong Fit between Strategy and Culture   419
Building Ethics into the Culture   421
Building a Spirit of High Performance into the Culture   428

Exerting Strategic Leadership   430
Staying on Top of How Well Things Are Going   431
Leading the Effort to Establish a Strategy-Supportive Culture   432
Keeping the Internal Organization Responsive and Innovative   434
Exercising Ethics Leadership and Insisting on Good Corporate Citizenship   435
Leading the Process of Making Corrective Adjustments   437

Key Points   438

Suggested Readings   440

illustration capsules

52. The Culture at Nordstrom   411

53. Adaptive Cultures at Companies That Act and React at Internet Speed   418

54. The Johnson & Johnson Credo   423

55. Corporate Ethics and Values Statements at Lockheed Martin, Pfizer, and J. M. Smucker   424

56. How SmithKline Beecham Embedded Its Values in Its Culture   427

57. A Test of Your Business Ethics   429

58. Lockheed Martin's Corrective Actions after Being Fined for Violating U.S. Antibribery Laws   437

part | two Cases in Strategic Management   C-1

A Guide to Case Analysis   C-2

Section A: The Manager as Chief Strategy Maker and Chief Strategy Implementer

*1. Steve Case, America Online and Times Warner   C-17
Arthur A. Thompson, University of Alabama
John E. Gamble, University of South Alabama

2. Daimler Chrysler Merger (A): Gaining Global Competitiveness   C-50
George Rädler, International Institute for Management Development

3. Daimler Chrysler Merger (B): Shaping a Transatlantic Company   C-64
George Rädler, International Institute for Management Development

4. Giuseppe's Original Sausage Company   C-74
Micheal T. Smith, Christian Brothers University
Jana F. Kuzmicki, Mississippi University for Women

* Cases for which there are case preparation exercises on Case-TUTOR™.

Section B: Crafting Strategy in Single-Business Companies

5. The Chinese Fireworks Industry   C-90
    Ruihua Jany, University of Western Ontario

* 6. Competition in the U.S. Automobile Retailing Industry   C-102
    Janet Parish, University of Alabama
    Arthur A. Thompson, University of Alabama

* 7. Dell Computer Corporation: Strategy and Challenges for the
    21st Century   C-132
    Arthur A. Thompson, University of Alabama
    John E. Gamble, University of South Alabama

* 8. Peapod, Inc., and the Online Grocery Business   C-174
    Alan B. Eisner, Pace University
    Nicole Belomont, Pace University

* 9. Cannondale Corporation   C-196
    Romuald A. Stone, Keller Graduate School of Management
    John E. Gamble, University of South Alabama

*10. Competition in the Retail Brokerage Industry in 2000   C-225
    Arthur A. Thompson, University of Alabama
    John E. Gamble, University of South Alabama

*11. eBay: King of the Online Auction Industry   C-263
    Lou Marino, University of Alabama
    Patrick Kreiser, University of Alabama

12. CDNow in the Online Music Business   C-295
    Alan B. Eisner, Pace University
    Nicole Belmont, Pace University

*13. Calloway Golf Company   C-314
    John E. Gamble, University of South Alabama

14. drkoop.com   C-349
    Nicole Herskowitz, University of Michigan
    Michael Iverson, University of Michigan
    Fred Howard, University of Michigan
    Janet Mehlhop, University of Michigan
    Pilar Speer, University of Michigan

15. WingspanBank.com   C-369
    Laura Cooke, University of Michigan
    Hyung Kim, University of Michigan
    Liza Hovey, University of Michigan
    Paul Rakowski, University of Michigan

16. Ben & Jerry's—Japan   C-384
    James M. Hagen, Cornell University

17. Viña San Pedro   C-400
    David Wylie, Babson College

* Cases for which there are case preparation exercises on Case-TUTOR™.

Section C: Crafting Strategy in Diversified Companies

*18.   Campbell Soup Company in 2000   C-423
John E. Gamble, University of South Alabama
Arthur A. Thompson, Jr., University of Alabama

*19.   The Black & Decker Corporation in 2000   C-454
John E. Gamble, University of South Alabama
Arthur A. Thompson, University of Alabama

Section D: Implementing and Executing Strategy

*20.   Robin Hood   C-477
Joseph Lambel, New York University

21.   Replacements, Ltd.: Replacing the Irreplaceable   C-479
Lew G. Brown, University of North Carolina at Greensboro
Kevin B. Lowe, University of North Carolina at Greensboro
Tony R. Wingler, University of North Carolina at Greensboro
Don K. Sowers, University of North Carolina at Greensboro
Vidya Gargeya, University of North Carolina at Greensboro
Kristen M. Cashman, University of North Carolina at Greensboro
John H. Lundin, University of North Carolina at Greensboro
Charles A. Kivett, University of North Carolina at Greensboro

22.   The Kimpton Hotel & Restaurant Group   C-518
Armand Gilinsky, Jr., Sonoma State University
Richard L. McCline, San Francisco State University

23.   Brithinee Electric in 1999: Raising the Standards   C-534
Harold Dyck, California State University—San Bernardino
Sue Greenfield, California State University—San Bernardino

24.   The Rococco New York Hotel   C-555
Anna S. Mattila, The Pennsylvania State University

25.   Developing a Global Mind-Set at Johnson & Johnson, 1998   C-568
Vladimir Pucik, International Institute for Management Development

Section E: Strategy, Ethics, and Social Responsibility

26.   Motorola: Ethical Challenges in a Multicultural Environment   C-580
E. Brian Peach, The University of West Florida
Kenneth L. Murrell, The University of West Florida

27.   Levi Strauss & Company   C-601
John E. Gamble, University of South Alabama

indexes
Name   I-1
Organization   I-5
Subject   I-11

 * Cases for which there are case preparation exercises on Case-Tutor™.

part one

1

The Concepts
and Techniques
of Strategic
Management

chapter | one

1

The Strategic Management Process

An Overview

"Cheshire Puss," she [Alice] began . . . "would you tell me, please, which way I ought to go from here?"
"That depends a good deal on where you want to get to," said the Cat.

—Lewis Carroll

Without a strategy the organization is like a ship without a rudder.

—Joel Ross and Michael Kami

Strategic management is not a box of tricks or a bundle of techniques. It is analytical thinking and commitment of resources to action.

—Peter Drucker

The Internet Age implies Internet speed, a different pace and a greater sense of urgency. Clearly we need to invigorate things here.

—Carly Fiorina, CEO, Hewlett-Packard Co.

The tasks of crafting, implementing, and executing company strategies are the heart and soul of managing a business enterprise. A company's **strategy** is the game plan management is using to stake out a market position, conduct its operations, attract and please customers, compete successfully, and achieve organizational objectives. In crafting a strategy, management is saying, in effect, "Among all the paths and actions we could have chosen, we have decided to move in this direction, focus on these markets and customer needs, compete in this fashion, allocate our resources and energies in these ways, and rely on these particular approaches to doing business." A strategy thus entails managerial choices among alternatives and signals organizational commitment to specific markets, competitive approaches, and ways of operating.

Closely related to the concept of strategy is the concept of a company's **business model,** a term now widely applied to management's plan for making money in a particular business. More formally, a company's business model deals with the revenue-cost-profit economics of its strategy—the actual and projected revenue streams generated by the company's product offerings and competitive approaches, the associated cost structure and profit margins, and the resulting earnings stream and return on investment. The fundamental issue surrounding a company's business model is whether a given strategy makes sense from a money-making perspective. A company's business model is, consequently, more narrowly focused than the company's business strategy. Strategy *relates to a company's competitive initiatives and business approaches (irrespective of the financial and competitive outcomes it produces), while the term* business model *deals with whether the revenues and costs flowing from the strategy demonstrate business viability.* Companies that have been in business for a while and are making acceptable profits have a proven business model—there is clear evidence that their strategy is capable of profitability and that they have a viable enterprise. Companies that are losing money or are in a start-up mode (like many new dot-com companies) have a questionable business model; their strategies have yet to produce good bottom-line results, putting their viability in doubt. Illustration Capsule 1 contrasts the business models for Microsoft and Redhat Linux in operating system software for personal computers (PCs). Which business model do you think makes the most sense?

Crafting, implementing, and executing a strategy are top-priority managerial tasks for two very big reasons. First, there is a compelling need for managers to *proactively shape* how the company's business will be conducted. It is management's responsibility to exert strategic leadership and commit the enterprise to going about its business in one fashion rather than another. Without a strategy, managers have no prescription for doing business, no road map to competitive advantage, no game plan for pleasing customers or achieving good performance. Lack of a consciously shaped strategy is a surefire ticket for organizational drift, competitive mediocrity, internal wheel-spinning, and lackluster results. Second, there is an equally compelling need to mold the efforts and decisions of different divisions, departments, managers, and groups into a *coordinated, compatible whole*. All the actions being taken in different parts of the business—R&D, design and engineering, production, marketing, customer service, human resources, information technology, and finance—need to be mutually supportive. Absent a purposeful strategy for the entire enterprise, managers have no overarching business rationale for molding the actions and decisions initiated across the organization into a cohesive whole, no underlying business basis for uniting cross-department operations into a team effort, no conscious business model for generating profits.

THE MOST TRUSTWORTHY SIGNS OF GOOD MANAGEMENT

Among all the things managers do, nothing affects a company's ultimate success or failure more fundamentally than how well its management team sets the company's long-term direction, develops competitively effective strategic moves and business approaches, and implements what needs to be done internally to produce good day in, day out strategy execution. Indeed, *good strategy and good strategy execution are the most trustworthy signs of good management.* Managers don't deserve a gold star for designing a potentially brilliant strategy but failing to put the organizational means in place to carry it out in high-caliber fashion—weak implementation undermines the strategy's potential and paves the way for shortfalls in customer satisfaction and company performance. Competent execution of a mediocre strategy scarcely merits enthusiastic applause for management's efforts either. The standards for good management rest to a very great extent on how well-conceived the company's strategy is and how competently it is executed. Any claim of talented management that disregards these standards is likely to be false.

Granted, good strategy combined with good strategy execution doesn't *guarantee* that a company will avoid periods of so-so or even subpar performance. Sometimes organizations with well-conceived strategies, showcase practices, and very capable managers experience performance problems because of unexpected shifts in market conditions or uncontrollable technology delays or unanticipated costs. Sometimes it takes several years for competent strategy-making/strategy-implementing efforts to show good results. But neither the bad luck of unforeseeable events nor the "we need more time" reason excuses mediocre performance year after year. It is the responsibility of a

illustration capsule 1

Two Radically Different Business Models: Microsoft and Redhat Linux

MICROSOFT'S BUSINESS MODEL

Microsoft is one of the world's most successful and profitable companies, partly because of its dominant market position in operating system software for PCs—first DOS, then Windows 95 and Windows NT, and later Windows 98 and Windows 2000. Microsoft's business model for its operating system products is based on the following elements:

- Employ a cadre of highly skilled Microsoft programmers to develop proprietary code; compensate them with premium pay and lucrative stock options. Keep the source code hidden from users.

- Sell the resulting operating system to PC makers and to PC users at relatively attractive prices—around $75 to PC makers and around $100 at retail to consumers. Since most of the costs are fixed (having been incurred in developing the code), each sale generates substantial margins—the variable costs of producing and packaging the CDs provided to users amount to only a couple of dollars per copy.

- Provide technical support to users at no cost.

REDHAT LINUX'S BUSINESS MODEL

Redhat Linux, a start-up company formed to market the Linux operating system in competition with Microsoft's Windows, employs a sharply different business model:

- Give the Linux operating system away free of charge to those who download it (but charge as much as $79 to users who prefer to buy the CD-ROM version—complete with an instruction manual). Redhat is in a position to give Linux away for free because Linux has been created and upgraded through the collaborative efforts of interested programmers from all over the world who volunteer their time and contribute bits and pieces of code to improve and polish the system. The guiding force and visionary of the confederation of volunteer programmers is Linus Torvalds, age 30,

who started development of Linux in 1991 as a sideline hobby while a graduate student at the University of Helsinki and who has shepherded the cobbling together of the code in the intervening years. Torvalds encouraged other programmers to download his software, use it, test it, fix bugs, modify it, add new features as they saw fit, and post their work on the Internet. As the Linux code developed, more and more programmers joined in, contributing their ideas and improvements. The thousands of programmers around the world who work on Linux in their spare time do what they do because they love it, because they are fervent believers that software should be free (as in free speech), and in some cases because they are anti-Microsoft and want to have a part in undoing what they see as a Microsoft monopoly. Their crusade for the cause of free software and competition means that Redhat, unlike Microsoft, essentially has zero product development costs.

- Make the source code open and available to all users, allowing them to make whatever changes they may wish to create a customized version of Linux. Linux users like the ability to modify the source code at will.

- Employ a cadre of technical support personnel who provide technical support to users for a fee. The Linux operating system is a bit quirky and buggy and is said to be hard to install and use in multiserver, multiprocessor applications. Corporate users of Linux thus typically require quite a bit of handholding. Make money on technical support services, not the code.

WHO HAS THE BEST BUSINESS MODEL?

Microsoft's business model—sell proprietary code and give service away free—is a proven moneymaker. But can Redhat make money with a business model that gives software away free and charges users for technical support? What do you think?

Source: Based on information in *Business Week,* February 1, 1999, p. 36; *The New York Times Magazine,* February 21, 1999, pp. 34–37; *PC World,* March 1999, p. 64; and *Smart Money,* October 1999, p.100.

company's management team to adjust to unexpectedly tough conditions by undertaking strategic defenses and business approaches that can overcome adversity. Indeed, the essence of good strategy making is to build a market position strong enough and an organization capable enough to produce successful performance despite unforeseeable events, potent competition, a rash of delays, or cost surprises. The rationale for using the twin standards of good strategy making and good strategy execution to determine whether a company is well managed is therefore compelling: the better conceived a company's strategy and the more competently it is executed, the more likely it is that the company will be a standout performer and exhibit enviable business practices.

THE FIVE TASKS OF STRATEGIC MANAGEMENT: A BIRD'S-EYE VIEW OF THIS BOOK

The strategy-making/strategy-implementing process consists of five interrelated managerial tasks:

1. *Forming a strategic vision of where the organization is headed*—so as to provide long-term direction, delineate what kind of enterprise the company is trying to become, and infuse the organization with a sense of purposeful action.
2. *Setting objectives*—converting the strategic vision into specific performance outcomes for the company to achieve.
3. *Crafting a strategy to achieve the desired outcomes.*
4. *Implementing and executing the chosen strategy efficiently and effectively.*
5. *Evaluating performance and initiating corrective adjustments in vision, long-term direction, objectives, strategy, or execution in light of actual experience, changing conditions, new ideas, and new opportunities.*

Figure 1.1 displays this process. Together, these five components define what we mean by the term **strategic management.** Let's examine this five-task framework in enough detail to set the stage for the forthcoming chapters.

Developing a Strategic Vision

Very early in the strategy-making process, company managers need to pose a set of questions: "What is our vision for the company—where should the company be headed, what should its future technology-product-customer focus be, what kind of enterprise do we want to become, what industry standing do we want to achieve in five years?" Drawing a carefully reasoned conclusion about what the company's long-term direction should be pushes managers to take a hard look at the company's external and internal environment and form a clearer sense of whether and how its present business needs will change over the next five years and beyond.

Management's views and conclusions about what the organization's long-term direction should be, the technology-product-customer focus it intends to pursue, and its future business scope constitute a **strategic vision** for the company. A strategic vision thus reflects management's aspirations for the organization and its business, providing a panoramic view of "where we are going" and giving specifics about its future business plans. It spells out long-term business purpose and molds organizational identity. A strategic vision points an organization in a particular direction and charts a strategic path for it to follow.

The Difference between a Strategic Vision and a Mission Statement

Whereas the chief concern of a strategic vision is with "where we are going," the term **mission statement,** as it is commonly used, tends to deal with a company's *present* business scope—"who we are and what we do." The mission statements that most companies include in their annual reports or post on their Web sites almost always stress what the company's present products and services are, what types of customers it serves, and what technological and business capabilities it has. They typically say

---

Basic Concept
The term ***strategic management*** refers to the managerial process of forming a strategic vision, setting objectives, crafting a strategy, implementing and executing the strategy, and then over time initiating whatever corrective adjustments in the vision, objectives, strategy, and execution are deemed appropriate.

Basic Concept
A ***strategic vision*** is a roadmap of a company's future—providing specifics about technology and customer focus, the geographic and product markets to be pursued, the capabilities it plans to develop, and the kind of company that management is trying to create.

figure 1.1 **The Five Tasks of Strategic Management**

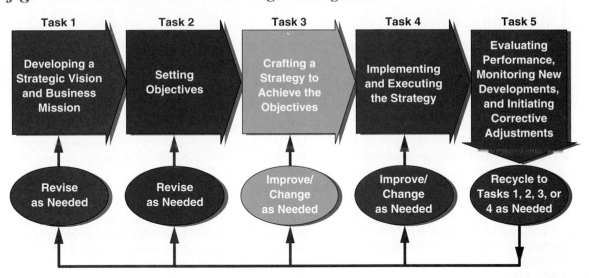

precious little about where the company is headed and its future business scope and business plans. Hence the conceptual distinction between a strategic vision and a mission statement is fairly clear-cut: A strategic vision portrays a company's future business scope ("where we are going"), whereas a company's mission statement describes its present business scope ("who we are and what we do"). Illustration Capsule 2 presents some examples of company mission and vision statements.

If a company's mission statement not only sets forth a clear definition of "who we are and what we do" but also indicates where the company is headed and what its business will become in the years ahead, then it has combined the concepts of company mission (or mission statement) and strategic vision into a single statement describing both where it is now and where it is going. In other words, a strategic vision and a future-oriented mission statement cover essentially the same ground. In practice, however, because the big majority of company mission statements say more about "what our business is now" than "what our business will be later," the distinction between company mission and strategic vision has pragmatic relevance.

> **Basic Concept**
> A company's ***mission statement*** is typically focused on its present business scope—"who we are and what we do"; mission statements broadly describe an organization's present capabilities, customer focus, activities, and business makeup.

Why a Strategic Vision Is Important   While there's a role for a mission statement that speaks to what a company is doing today, a strategic vision generally has much greater direction-setting and strategy-making value. There's an ever-present managerial imperative to look beyond today and think strategically about the impact of new technologies on the horizon, how customer needs and expectations are changing, what it will take to overtake or outrun competitors, which promising market opportunities ought to be aggressively pursued, and all the other external and internal factors that drive what the company needs to be doing to prepare for the future. Managers cannot succeed as organization leaders or strategy makers without first drawing soundly reasoned conclusions about the winds of change and then making some fundamental choices about which of several strategic paths to take. *There's no escaping the need for a strategic vision.* Armed with a clear, well-conceived business course for the organization to follow, managers have a beacon to guide resource allocation and a basis for crafting a strategy to get the company where it needs to go. Companies whose managers neglect the task of thinking strategically about the company's future business path or who are indecisive in committing the company to one direction instead of another are prone to drift aimlessly and lose any claim to being an industry leader.

illustration capsule 2
Examples of Strategic Visions and Company Mission Statements

MICROSOFT CORPORATION

For years, one vision drove what Microsoft did: "A computer on every desk and in every home using great software as an empowering tool." But the emergence of the Internet and non-PC devices like handheld computers and TV-set-top boxes as increasingly integral parts of everyday life prompted Microsoft in 1999 to broaden its vision to "Empower people through great software anytime, anyplace, and on any device." Bill Gates observed: "We see a world where people can use any computing device to do whatever they want to do anytime, anywhere. The PC will continue to have a central role . . . but it will be joined by an incredibly rich variety of digital devices accessing the power of the Internet."

INTEL

"Our vision: Getting to a billion connected computers worldwide, millions of servers, and trillions of dollars of e-commerce. Intel's core mission is being the building-block supplier to the Internet economy and spurring efforts to make the Internet more useful. Being connected is now at the center of people's computing experience. We are helping to expand the capabilities of the PC platform and the Internet."

OTIS ELEVATOR

"Our mission is to provide any customer a means of moving people and things up, down, and sideways over short distances with higher reliability than any similar enterprise in the world."

AVIS RENT-A-CAR

"Our business is renting cars. Our mission is total customer satisfaction."

TRADER JOE'S (a unique grocery store chain)

"The mission of Trader Joe's is to give our customers the best food and beverage values that they can find anywhere and to provide them with the information required for informed buying decisions. We provide these with a dedication to the highest quality of customer satisfaction delivered with a sense of warmth, friendliness, fun, individual pride, and company spirit."

AMERICAN RED CROSS

"The mission of the American Red Cross is to improve the quality of human life; to enhance self-reliance and concern for others; and to help people avoid, prepare for, and cope with emergencies."

3COM

"3Com's mission is to connect more people and organizations to information in more innovative, simple, and reliable ways than any other networking company in the world. Our vision of pervasive networking is of a world where connections are simpler, more powerful, more affordable, more global, and more available to all."

EASTMAN KODAK

"We are in the picture business."

RITZ-CARLTON HOTELS

"The Ritz-Carlton Hotel is a place where the genuine care and comfort of our guests is our highest mission.

"We pledge to provide the finest personal service and facilities for our guests who will always enjoy a warm, relaxed yet refined ambience.

"The Ritz-Carlton experience enlivens the senses, instills well-being, and fulfills even the unexpressed wishes and needs of our guests."

LONG JOHN SILVER'S

"To be America's best quick-service restaurant chain. We will provide each guest great-tasting, healthful, reasonably priced fish, seafood, and chicken in a fast, friendly manner on every visit."

BRISTOL-MYERS SQUIBB

"The mission of Bristol-Myers Squibb is to extend and enhance human life by providing the highest quality health and personal care products. We intend to be the preeminent global diversified health and personal care company."

WIT CAPITAL (an Internet start-up company)

"Our mission is to be the premier Internet investment banking firm focused on the offering and selling of securities to a community of online individual investors."

Source: Company documents and Web sites.

Setting Objectives

The purpose of setting **objectives** is to convert managerial statements of strategic vision and business mission into specific performance targets—results and outcomes the organization wants to achieve. Setting objectives and then measuring whether they are achieved or not help managers track an organization's progress. Managers of the best-performing companies tend to set objectives that require stretch and disciplined effort. The challenge of trying to achieve bold, aggressive performance targets pushes an organization to be more inventive, to exhibit some urgency in improving both its financial performance and its business position, and to be more intentional and focused in its actions. Setting objectives that require real organizational stretch helps build a firewall against complacent coasting and low-grade improvements in organizational performance. As Mitchell Leibovitz, CEO of automotive parts retailer The Pep Boys—Manny, Moe, & Jack, puts it, "If you want to have ho-hum results, have ho-hum objectives."

Objective setting is required of *all* managers. Every unit in a company needs concrete, measurable performance targets that contribute meaningfully toward achieving company objectives. When companywide objectives are broken down into specific targets for each organizational unit and lower-level managers are held accountable for achieving them, a results-oriented climate builds throughout the enterprise. There's little if any internal confusion over what to accomplish. The ideal situation is a team effort where each organizational unit strives to produce results in its area of responsibility that contribute to the achievement of the company's performance targets and strategic vision.

From a companywide perspective, two very distinct types of performance yardsticks are required: those relating to *financial performance* and those relating to *strategic performance*. Achieving acceptable financial results is crucial. Without adequate profitability, a company's pursuit of its vision, as well as its long-term health and ultimate survival, is jeopardized. Neither shareowners nor lenders will continue to sink additional funds into an enterprise that can't deliver satisfactory financial results. Even so, the achievement of satisfactory financial performance, by itself, is not enough. Managers must also pay attention to the company's strategic well-being—its competitiveness and overall long-term business position. Unless a company's performance reflects improving competitive strength and a stronger long-term market position, its progress is less than inspiring and its ability to continue delivering good financial performance is suspect.

The need for both good financial performance and good strategic performance calls for management to set financial objectives and strategic objectives. **Financial objectives** concern the financial results and outcomes that management wants the organization to achieve. They signal commitment to such outcomes as earnings growth, an acceptable return on investment (or economic value added—EVA),[1] dividend growth, stock price

> **Basic Concept**
> *Objectives* are an organization's performance targets—the results and outcomes it wants to achieve. They function as yardsticks for tracking an organization's performance and progress.

---

[1]*Economic value added (EVA)* is profit over and above the company's cost of debt and equity capital. More specifically, it is defined as operating profit less income taxes less the cost of debt less an allowance for the cost of equity capital. For example, if a company has operating profits of $200 million, pays taxes of $75 million, pays interest expenses of $25 million, has shareholders' equity of $400 million with an estimated equity cost of 15 percent (which translates into an equity cost of capital of $60 million), then the company's EVA is $200 million minus $75 million minus $25 million minus $60 million, or $40 million. The EVA of $40 million can be interpreted to mean that the company's management has generated profits well in excess of the benchmark 15 percent equity cost needed to justify or support the shareholder investment of $400 million—all of which represents wealth created for the owners *above* what they could expect from making an investment of comparable risk elsewhere. Such companies as Coca-Cola, AT&T, and Briggs & Stratton use EVA as a measure of their profit performance.

appreciation (or market value added—MVA),[2] good cash flow, and creditworthiness. In contrast, **strategic objectives** aim at results that reflect increased competitiveness and a stronger business position—outcomes such as winning additional market share, overtaking key competitors on product quality or customer service or product innovation, achieving lower overall costs than rivals, boosting the company's reputation with customers, winning a stronger foothold in international markets, exercising technological leadership, gaining a sustainable competitive advantage, and capturing attractive growth opportunities. Strategic objectives serve notice that management intends not only to deliver good financial performance but also to improve the organization's competitive vitality, business position, and long-range business prospects.

Both financial and strategic objectives ought to involve both near-term and longer-term performance targets. Short-range objectives focus organizational attention on the need for immediate performance improvements and outcomes. Long-range objectives serve the valuable purpose of prompting managers to consider what to do *now* to put the company in position to perform well over the longer term. As a rule, when trade-offs have to be made between achieving long-run objectives and achieving short-run objectives, long-run objectives should take precedence. A company rarely prospers from repeated management actions that put better short-term performance ahead of better long-run performance.

Illustration Capsule 3 shows examples of the kinds of strategic and financial objectives companies set.

Crafting a Strategy

A company's strategy represents management's answers to such fundamental business questions as whether to concentrate on a single business or build a diversified group of businesses, whether to cater to a broad range of customers or focus on a particular market niche, whether to develop a wide or narrow product line, whether to pursue a competitive advantage based on low cost or product superiority or unique organizational capabilities, how to respond to changing buyer preferences, how big a geographic market to try to cover, how to react to newly emerging market and competitive conditions, and how to grow the enterprise over the long term. A strategy thus reflects managerial choices among alternatives and signals organizational commitment to particular products, markets, competitive approaches, and ways of operating the enterprise.

Strategy making brings into play the critical managerial issue of *how* to achieve the targeted results in light of the organization's situation and prospects. Objectives are the "ends," and strategy is the "means" of achieving them. The hows of a company's strategy are typically a blend of (1) deliberate and purposeful actions, (2) as-needed reactions to unanticipated developments and fresh market conditions and competitive pressures,

---

[2]*Market value added (MVA)* is defined as the amount by which the total value of the company has appreciated above the dollar amount actually invested in the company by shareholders. MVA is equal to a company's current stock price times the number of shares outstanding less shareholders' equity investment; it represents the value that management has added to shareholders' wealth in running the business. For example, if a company's stock price is $50, there are 1 million shares outstanding, and shareholders' equity investment is $40 million, then MVA is $10 million ($50 million in market value of existing shares minus $40 million in equity investment); in other words, management has taken the shareholders' investment of $40 million in the company and leveraged it into a current company value of $50 million, creating an additional $10 million in shareholder value. If shareholder value is to be maximized, management must select a strategy and long-term direction that maximizes the market value of the company's common stock. In recent years, MVA and EVA have gained widespread acceptance as valid measures of a company's financial performance.

illustration capsule 3
Examples of Strategic and Financial Objectives

BANC ONE CORPORATION

(Strategic Objective)

"To be one of the top three banking companies in terms of market share in all significant markets we serve."

DOMINO'S PIZZA

(Strategic Objective)

"To safely deliver a hot, quality pizza in 30 minutes or less at a fair price and a reasonable profit."

FORD MOTOR COMPANY

(Strategic Objectives)

"To satisfy our customers by providing quality cars and trucks, developing new products, reducing the time it takes to bring new vehicles to market, improving the efficiency of all our plants and processes, and building on our teamwork with employees, unions, dealers, and suppliers."

ALCAN ALUMINUM

(Strategic and Financial Objectives)

"To be the lowest-cost producer of aluminum and to outperform the average return on equity of the Standard & Poor's industrial stock index."

BRISTOL-MYERS SQUIBB

(Strategic Objective)

"To focus globally on those businesses in health and personal care where we can be number one or number two through delivering superior value to the customer."

ATLAS CORPORATION

(Strategic Objectives)

"To become a low-cost, medium-size gold producer, producing in excess of 125,000 ounces of gold a year and building gold reserves of 1.5 million ounces."

3M CORPORATION

(Financial and Strategic Objectives)

"To achieve annual growth in earnings per share of 10 percent or better, on average; a return on stockholders' equity of 20–25 percent; a return on capital employed of 27 percent or better; and have at least 30 percent of sales come from products introduced in the past four years."

---

and (3) the collective learning of the organization over time—not just the insights gained from its experiences but, more important, the internal activities it has learned to perform quite well and the competitive capabilities it has developed.[3] As illustrated in Figure 1.2, strategy is typically more than what managers carefully plot out in advance and deliberately pursue as part of a visionary strategic plan. It is normal for management's planned strategy to take on a different face as new strategy features are added and others are subtracted in response to shifting market conditions, altered customer needs and preferences, the strategic maneuvering of rival firms, the experience of what is working and what isn't, newly emerging opportunities and threats, unforeseen events, and fresh thinking about how to improve the strategy. Future business conditions are sufficiently uncertain and unpredictable to prevent managers from planning every strategic action in advance without experiencing any learning or seeing any possibilities for improvement. Furthermore, common sense instructs that a company's actions, both planned and reactive, ought to bear close relationship to its competencies and competitive capabilities.

---

[3]See Henry Mintzberg and J. A. Waters, "Of Strategies, Deliberate and Emergent," *Strategic Management Journal* 6 (1985), pp. 257–72; Henry Mintzberg, Bruce Ahlstrand, and Joseph Lampel, *Strategy Safari: A Guided Tour through the Wilds of Strategic Management* (New York: Free Press, 1998), chapters 2, 5, and 7: and C. K. Prahalad and Gary Hamel, "The Core Competence of the Corporation," *Harvard Business Review* 70, no. 3 (May–June 1990), pp. 79–93.

figure 1.2   A Company's Actual Strategy Is Partly Planned and Partly Reactive

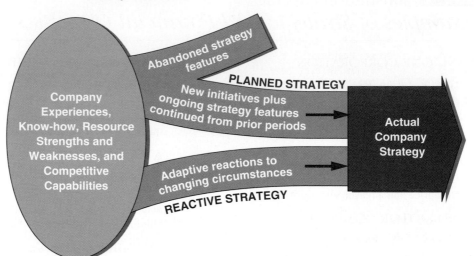

The strategy-making task thus involves developing an *intended strategy;* adapting it as events unfold *(adaptive/reactive strategy);* and linking the firm's business approaches, actions, and competitive initiatives closely to its competencies and capabilities. In short, a company's actual strategy is something managers shape and reshape as events transpire outside the company and as the company's competitive assets and liabilities evolve in ways that enhance or diminish its competitiveness.

What Does a Company's Strategy Consist Of?   Company strategies concern *how:* how to grow the business, how to satisfy customers, how to outcompete rivals, how to respond to changing market conditions, how to manage each functional piece of the business and develop needed organizational capabilities, how to achieve strategic and financial objectives. The hows of strategy tend to be company-specific, customized to a company's own situation and performance objectives. In the business world, companies have a wide degree of strategic freedom. They can diversify broadly or narrowly, into related or unrelated industries, via acquisition, joint venture, strategic alliances, or internal start-up. Insofar as a single business is concerned, prevailing market conditions usually offer enough strategy-making latitude that close competitors can easily avoid carbon-copy strategies—some pursue low-cost leadership, others stress particular differentiating attributes of their product or service, and still others concentrate on serving narrow market segments and developing unique capabilities to meet the special needs and preferences of buyers comprising these segments. Some compete only locally or regionally, others compete nationally, and still others compete globally. Because there are numerous ways for a company to conduct its business internally and position itself in the markets where it elects to compete, descriptions of the content of company strategy necessarily have to be fairly detailed in order to portray the defining characteristics of its strategy.

Figure 1.3 depicts the kinds of actions and approaches that reflect a company's overall strategy. A company's present strategy is typically a blend of holdover approaches and fresh actions and reactions, with perhaps some about-to-be-launched moves and changes that remain under wraps and in the planning stage. Because the holdover approaches and freshly initiated actions are usually visible and have been publicly discussed by company managers or explained in press releases, outside observers can deduce many key

figure 1.3   **Understanding a Company's Strategy—What to Look For**

elements of a company's strategy. Still, there's an unrevealed portion of strategy that outsiders can only speculate about—the-as-yet-unrevealed strategic actions company managers are intending to launch. Managers often, for good reason, choose not to reveal certain elements of their strategy until the company's actions become public.

To get a better understanding of the content of company strategies, see the overview of McDonald's strategy in Illustration Capsule 4.

Strategy and Entrepreneurship   Crafting strategy is partly an exercise in astute entrepreneurship—actively searching for opportunities to do new things or to do existing things in new ways.[4] The faster a company's business environment is changing, the more critical it becomes for its managers to be good entrepreneurs in making both predictions and timely strategic adjustments. Imagine, for instance, the implications for companies that downplay the potential impact of e-commerce or for retailers who ignore the exploding interest of consumers in shopping on the Internet. Managers are always under the gun to pick up on happenings in the external environment that

> Strategy making is fundamentally a market-driven and customer-driven entrepreneurial activity—the essential qualities are a talent for capitalizing on emerging market opportunities and evolving customer needs, a bias for innovation and creativity, an appetite for prudent risk taking, and a strong sense of what needs to be done to grow and strengthen the business.

---

[4]For a fuller discussion of strategy as an entrepreneurial process, see Mintzberg, Ahlstrand, and Lampel, *Strategy Safari,* chapter 5. Also see Bruce Barringer and Allen C. Bluedorn, "The Relationship between Corporate Entrepreneurship and Strategic Management," *Strategic Management Journal* 20 (1999), pp. 421–44; and Jeffrey G. Covin and Morgan P. Miles, "Corporate Entrepreneurship and the Pursuit of Competitive Advantage," *Entrepreneurship: Theory and Practice* 23, no. 3 (Spring 1999), pp. 47–63.

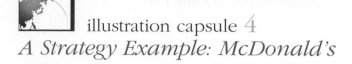

illustration capsule 4
A Strategy Example: McDonald's

In 1999 McDonald's was the leading food-service retailer in the global consumer marketplace, with a strong brand name and systemwide restaurant sales approaching $35 billion. Eighty percent of its 25,000-plus restaurants were franchised to approximately 5,000 owner/operators around the world. Over the past 10 years, the company's systemwide sales had grown an average of 8 percent annually and its stock had provided a 20 percent annual return to investors.

McDonald's food-quality specifications, equipment technology, marketing and training programs, operating systems, site selection techniques, and supply systems were considered industry standards throughout the world. Its vision was to be the world's best quick-service restaurant—*being the best* was defined as consistently satisfying customers better than rivals through outstanding quality, service, cleanliness, and value.

The company's strategic priorities were ensuring continued growth, providing exceptional customer care, remaining an efficient and quality producer, developing people at every level of the organization, sharing best practices among all units worldwide, and reinventing the fast-food concept by fostering innovation in the company's menu, facilities, marketing, operation, and technology.

GROWTH STRATEGY

● Penetrate the market not currently served by adding 1,750 restaurants annually (an average of one every five hours), some company-owned and some franchised, with about 90 percent outside the United States. Establish a leading market position in foreign countries ahead of competitors.

● Promote more frequent customer visits via the addition of attractive menu items, low-price specials, Extra Value Meals, and children's play areas.

● Explore opportunities to exploit the company's global supplier infrastructure and its core competencies in multiunit restaurant management, site location and unit construction, and product marketing.

FRANCHISING STRATEGY

● Grant franchises only to highly motivated, talented entrepreneurs with integrity and business experience, and train them to become active, on-premise owners of McDonald's. (No franchises were granted to corporations, partnerships, or passive investors.)

STORE LOCATION AND CONSTRUCTION STRATEGY

● Locate restaurants on sites offering convenience to customers and profitable growth potential. The company's research indicated that 70 percent of all decisions to eat at McDonald's were made on the spur of the moment, so its goal was to pick locations that were as convenient as possible for customers to visit. In the United States, the company supplemented its traditional suburban and urban locations with satellite outlets in food courts, airports, hospitals, universities, large shopping establishments (Wal-Mart, The Home Depot), and service stations; outside the United States, the strategy was to establish an initial presence in center cities, then open freestanding units with drive-thrus outside center cities.

● Reduce site costs and building costs by using standardized, cost-efficient store designs and by consolidating purchases of equipment and materials via a global sourcing system.

● Make sure restaurants are attractive and pleasing inside and out, and provide drive-thru service and play areas for children, where feasible.

PRODUCT LINE STRATEGY

● Offer a limited menu.

● Improve the taste appeal of the items offered (especially sandwich selections).

● Expand product offerings into new categories of fast food (chicken, Mexican, pizza, adult-oriented sandwiches, and so on) and include more items for health-conscious customers.

(continued)

signal either new opportunities for the enterprise or threats to its present way of doing business. For a company to be successful, its strategy and business model have to be well matched to the company's present and future environment. That won't happen unless managers exhibit first-rate entrepreneurship in steering company activities in whatever new directions are dictated by market conditions and customer preferences. This entails studying market trends, listening to customers and anticipating their changing needs and expectations, scrutinizing the business possibilities that spring

illustration capsule 4

(concluded)

- Roll out new, potentially appealing and exciting items in speedy fashion, but quickly drop those that fail to catch on, learning from whatever mistakes were made and moving promptly on to the next idea. (This strategy element was recently instituted and was a sharp departure from the company's long-standing practice of doing extensive testing to ensure consistent high quality and ample customer appeal before rolling out new menu items systemwide—Chicken McNuggets, for example, took seven years to develop.)

STORE OPERATIONS

- Enforce stringent standards regarding food quality; store and equipment cleanliness; restaurant operating procedures; and friendly, courteous counter service.
- Expand the "Made for You" concept to include a much larger percentage of outlets. The company's Made for You program involved the installation of advanced equipment, sophisticated computer technology, and new preparation methods to allow items to be prepared to customer order.

SALES PROMOTION, MARKETING, AND MERCHANDISING

- Enhance the McDonald's image of quality, service, cleanliness, and value globally via heavy media advertising and in-store merchandise promotions funded with fees tied to a percentage of sales revenues at each restaurant.
- Use Ronald McDonald to create greater brand awareness among children and the *Mc* prefix to reinforce the connection of menu items and McDonald's.
- Project an attitude of happiness and interest in children.

HUMAN RESOURCES AND TRAINING

- Offer wage rates that are equitable and nondiscriminatory in every location; teach job skills; reward both individual and team performance; create career opportunities; have flexible work hours for student employees.
- Hire restaurant crews with good work habits and courteous attitudes and train them to act in ways that will impress customers; promote promising employees quickly.
- Provide proper training on delivering customer satisfaction and running a fast-food business to franchisees, restaurant managers, and assistant managers. (Instructors at Hamburger University campuses in Illinois, Germany, England, Australia, and Japan annually train over 5,000 students in 22 languages.)
- Promote a global mindset by aggressively transferring best practices and new ideas developed in outlets in one part of the world to outlets in other parts of the world.

SOCIAL RESPONSIBILITY AND COMMUNITY CITIZENSHIP

- Take an active community role—support local charities and community projects; help create a neighborhood spirit; promote educational excellence.
- Sponsor Ronald McDonald Houses. (At year-end 1995, there were 168 houses in 12 countries providing a home away from home for families of seriously ill children receiving treatment at nearby hospitals.)
- Promote workforce diversity, voluntary affirmative action, and minority-owned franchises. (Over 34 percent of McDonald's franchisees and 70 percent of the franchisee applicants in training were females and minorities.)
- Support education through student scholarships, teacher awards, and free instructional resources.
- Adopt and encourage environmentally friendly practices.
- Provide nutritional information on McDonald's products to customers.

Source: Company annual reports.

from technological developments, building the firm's market position via acquisitions or new-product introductions, and pursuing ways to strengthen the firm's competitive capabilities. Good strategy making is therefore inseparable from good business entrepreneurship. One cannot exist without the other.

How fast company managers adapt to changing market conditions, how boldly they pursue new business opportunities, how much they emphasize out-innovating the competition, and how often they champion actions to improve organizational performance are good barometers of a company's entrepreneurial spirit. Entrepreneurial strategy makers are inclined to be either first-movers or rapid followers, responding quickly and opportunistically to new avenues for building the enterprise and fortifying its market position and capabilities. They are willing to take prudent risks and initiate trailblazing strategies. Today's dot-com companies are examples of entrepreneurship in action. In contrast, entrepreneurially deficient companies are risk-averse, displaying a wariness of deviating very far from the company's tried-and-true business approaches unless absolutely forced to. They either dismiss impending developments as unimportant ("we don't think it will really affect us") or move so slowly that the company is habitually late in responding and adapting to shifting conditions in the marketplace. Entrepreneurially deficient companies often minimize the disadvantages of being late-movers, pointing instead to the cost-saving benefits of avoiding whatever "mistakes" they believe first-movers have made or might make. They prefer gradual strategic change to dramatic or sweeping strategic realignment. Companies still taking a wait-and-see approach to embracing use of the Internet and e-commerce is a classic example of entrepreneurial deficiency.

Why Company Strategies Evolve   Plainly, every company encounters occasions in which it needs to adapt its strategy to shifting industry and competitive conditions, newly emerging buyer preferences and requirements, the initiatives of rival firms to grab increased market share, the appearance of fresh opportunities and threats, advancing technology, and other significant events that affect its business. On occasion, quantum changes in strategy are called for—when an opening appears to shift to a radically new strategy and drive market change, when a competitor makes a revolutionary move that demands a dramatic response, when technological breakthroughs occur, or when crisis strikes and major strategy adjustments are needed very quickly. The America Online–Time Warner merger represented a quantum strategy change for both companies. Just as plainly, ways open up to fine-tune a company's strategy, first in one department or functional area and then in another.

Because the march of external and internal events make it commonplace to initiate fresh strategic moves and business approaches of one kind or another in one part of the organization or another, *an organization's strategy re-forms over time as the number of changes and adaptations begin to mount.* It is thus normal, indeed necessary, for a company's strategy to change, sometimes gradually and sometimes rapidly, sometimes reactively (when new developments dictate a response) and sometimes proactively (when attractive new opportunities are spotted or new capabilities are acquired). Consequently, *strategy making is an ongoing process, not a one-time event.* Managers are obliged to reevaluate strategy regularly, refining and recasting it as often and as much as needed to match the organization's changing external and internal circumstances.

Another important facet of strategic change is *the need for actions to improve on how the company is competing today and the need for actions to prepare for tomorrow's markets and competitive conditions.* Whether a company takes a proactive or reactive posture in preparing for future market conditions shapes the character and speed of the adjustments it makes in its strategy over time.

Figure 1.4 illustrates the strategic postures a company can adopt in preparing for future market conditions and coping with the waves of change in the marketplace.[5] In most industries, there are pioneering entrepreneurial companies that seek to be proactive leaders in reshaping their strategies and there are cautious, conservatively managed

Basic Concept

The march of external and internal developments dictate that a company's strategy change and evolve over time—a condition that makes strategy making an ongoing process, not a one-time event.

---

[5]For a discussion of the need for strategic actions aimed at competing today coupled with strategic actions to prepare for competing tomorrow, see Derek F. Abell, "Competing Today While Preparing for Tomorrow," *Sloan Management Review* 40, no. 3 (Spring 1999), pp. 73–81.

figure 1.4   **Strategic Approaches to Preparing for Future Market Conditions**

COMPANY APPROACHES

	Reactive/Follower	Proactive/Leader
Rapid Revolutionary Change	Rushing to catch up to keep from being swamped by the waves	Aggressively altering strategy to make waves and drive change
Gradual Evolutionary Change	Revising strategy (hopefully in time) to catch the waves	Anticipating change and initiating strategic actions to ride the crest of the waves

FUTURE MARKET CONDITIONS

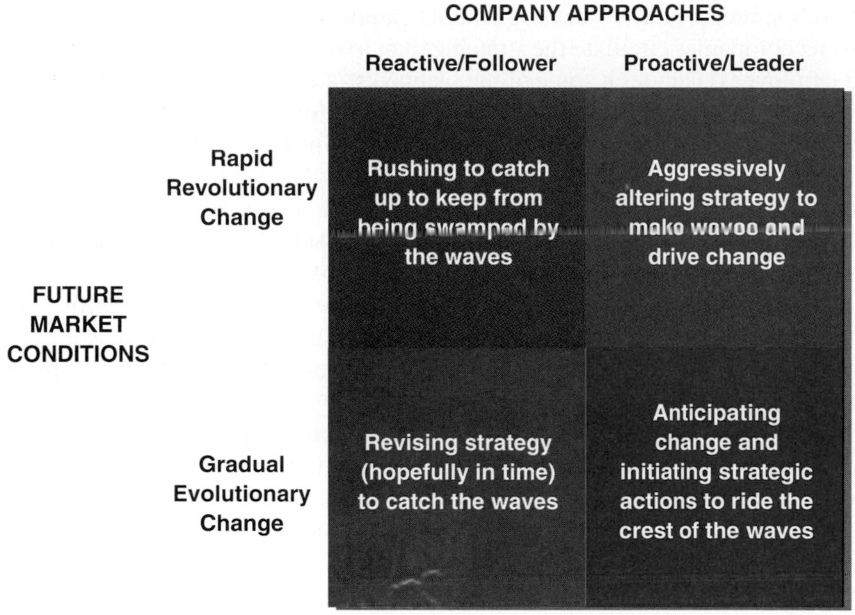

Source: Adapted from Derek F. Abell, "Competing Today While Preparing for Tomorrow," *Sloan Management Review* 40, no. 3 (Spring 1999), p. 75.

companies that end up as reactive followers. Indeed, it is typical for companies to adjust their strategies and prepare for future market conditions at varying speeds and in varying ways—the path each company takes is unique.

However, if managers decide to change strategy so fast and so fundamentally that their business model undergoes major overhaul every year, questions have to be asked. Is rapid strategy change being legitimately driven by rapid-fire technological change, swiftly changing market conditions, volatile buyer behavior, or other hard-to-foresee developments? Or is it the product of poor entrepreneurship, faulty situation analysis, and inept strategizing? As a general rule, frequent and fundamental strategy changes cannot be made repeatedly year after year without creating a zigzag market wake, generating undue confusion among customers and employees, and posing real profitability problems. In most situations, the core elements of well-crafted strategies ought to have a life of several years, even though they may have to undergo modest revision to keep them in tune with changing circumstances.

Strategy and Strategic Plans   Developing a strategic vision and mission, establishing objectives, and deciding on a strategy are basic direction-setting tasks. They map out where the organization is headed, its short-range and long-range performance targets, and the competitive moves and internal action approaches to be used in achieving the targeted business results. Together, they constitute a **strategic plan** for coping with industry and competitive conditions, the expected actions of the industry's key players, and the challenges and issues that stand as obstacles to the company's success.[6]

Basic Concept
A *strategic plan* consists of an organization's mission and future direction, near-term and long-term performance targets, and strategy.

---

[6]For an excellent discussion of why a strategic plan needs to be more than a list of bulleted points and should, in fact, tell an engaging, insightful, stage-setting story that lays out the industry and competitive situation as well as the vision, objectives, and strategy, see Gordon Shaw, Robert Brown, and Philip Bromiley, "Strategic Stories: How 3M Is Rewriting Business Planning," *Harvard Business Review* 76, no. 3 (May–June 1998), pp. 41–50.

In companies committed to regular strategy reviews and the development of explicit strategic plans, the strategic plan may take the form of a written document describing the industry's economics, key success factors, and drivers of change along with the company's strategic plan for dealing with its external and internal environment.

Some companies circulate the strategic plan to most all managers (and perhaps selected employees), although some of the planned strategic initiatives may be expressed in general terms or omitted if they are too sensitive to reveal before they are actually undertaken. In other companies, the strategic plan is not put in writing for widespread distribution but exists only in the form of oral understandings and commitments among managers about where to head, what to accomplish, and how to proceed. Organizational objectives are the part of the strategic plan most often spelled out explicitly and communicated to managers and employees. A number of companies present key elements of their strategic plans in the company's annual report to shareholders or in statements provided to the business media, while others, perhaps for reasons of competitive sensitivity, make only vague general statements about their strategic plans that could apply to most any company.

> The faster a company's external and internal environment changes, the more frequently that its short-run and long-run strategic plans have to be revised and updated—annual changes may not be adequate. In today's world strategy life cycles are growing shorter, not longer.

However, as we noted earlier, formal, written strategic plans seldom anticipate all the strategically relevant events that will transpire in upcoming months and years. Unforeseen events, unexpected opportunities or threats, and the constant bubbling up of new proposals encourage managers to modify planned actions and forge "unplanned" reactions. Postponing the recrafting of strategy until it's time to work on next year's strategic plan is both foolish and unnecessary. Once-a-year strategizing under "have-to" conditions is not a prescription for managerial or business success. *Strategy is something that ought to be modified whenever it is propitious to do so and certainly whenever unfolding events dictate.* In the "Internet economy," developments have been occurring so rapidly that quarterly, monthly, or even weekly reviews of strategy have become essential and common—the notion of annual strategic plans has been abandoned almost entirely. Internet companies have found it essential to revise demand forecasts, update financial projections, and adjust key elements of their strategies at least quarterly and often more frequently.

At Ingram-Micro, a contract manufacturer and distributor of PCs, "rolling forecasts" of financial projections are devised for five quarters out and then updated every 60 days. Bluefly.com, a clothing e-tailer, makes budget revisions weekly to keep up with strategy changes and react to daily sales patterns. To help speed company reactions to fast-changing market conditions, a number of companies have resorted to developing strategic plans for each of several different market and competitive scenarios, enabling them to react more swiftly as one or another of the scenarios turns out to best approximate unfolding events. Because of the speed of change in many of today's industries, *strategy life cycles are increasingly measured in months and single years, not decades or even five-year intervals.*[7]

Implementing and Executing the Strategy

The managerial task of implementing and executing the chosen strategy entails assessing what it will take to develop the needed organizational capabilities and to reach the targeted objectives on schedule. The managerial skill here is figuring out what must be done to put the strategy in place, carry it out proficiently, and produce good results.

---

[7]Gary Hamel, "Bringing Silicon Valley Inside," *Harvard Business Review* 77, no. 5 (September–October 1999), p. 72.

Managing the strategy execution process is primarily a hands-on, close-to-the-scene administrative task that includes the following principal aspects:

- Building an organization capable of carrying out the strategy successfully.
- Allocating company resources so that organizational units charged with performing strategy-critical activities and implementing new strategic initiatives have sufficient people and funds to do their work successfully.
- Establishing strategy-supportive policies and operating procedures.
- Putting a freshly chosen strategy into place.
- Motivating people in ways that induce them to pursue the target objectives energetically and, if need be, modifying their duties and job behavior to better fit the strategy requirements of successful execution.
- Tying the reward structure to the achievement of targeted results.
- Creating a company culture and work climate conducive to successful strategy implementation and execution.
- Installing information, communication, and operating systems that enable company personnel to carry out their strategic roles effectively day in, day out.
- Instituting best practices and programs for continuous improvement.
- Exerting the internal leadership needed to drive implementation forward and to keep improving on how the strategy is being executed.

Basic Concept
Strategy implementation concerns the managerial exercise of putting a freshly chosen strategy into place. *Strategy execution* deals with the managerial exercise of supervising the ongoing pursuit of strategy, making it work, improving the competence with which it is executed, and showing measurable progress in achieving the targeted results.

Good strategy execution involves creating a strong "fit" between the way things are done internally and what it will take for the strategy to succeed. The stronger the methods of implementation fit the strategy's requirements, the better the odds that performance targets will be achieved. The most important fits are between strategy and organizational capabilities, between strategy and the reward structure, between strategy and internal support systems, and between strategy and the organization's culture. Fitting the organization's internal practices to what is needed for strategic success helps unite the organization behind the accomplishment of strategy.

The strategy-implementing/strategy-executing task is easily the most complicated and time-consuming part of strategic management. It cuts across virtually all facets of managing and must be initiated from many points inside the organization. The action agenda for executing strategy emerges from careful assessment of what the organization needs to do differently or better. Each manager has to answer the question "What has to be done in my area to execute my piece of the strategic plan, and how can I best get it done?" How much internal change is needed depends on how much of the strategy is new, how far internal practices and competencies deviate from what the strategy requires, and how well strategy and organizational culture already match. Depending on the amount of internal change involved, full implementation and proficient execution can take several months to several years.

Strategy execution is fundamentally an action-oriented, make-it-happen process—the key tasks are developing competencies and capabilities, budgeting, policy making, motivating, culture-building, and leadership.

Evaluating Performance, Monitoring New Developments, and Initiating Corrective Adjustments

It is always incumbent on management to evaluate the organization's performance and progress. It is management's duty to stay on top of the company's situation, deciding whether things are going well internally, and monitoring outside developments closely. Subpar performance or too little progress, as well as important new external circumstances, will require corrective actions and adjustments in a company's long-term direction, objectives, business model, and/or strategy.

Likewise, one or more aspects of executing the strategy may not be going as well as intended. Revising budgets, changing policies, reorganizing, making personnel changes, building new competencies and capabilities, revamping activities and work processes, making efforts to change the culture, and revising compensation practices are typical managerial actions that may have to be taken to hasten implementation or improve strategy execution. Proficient strategy execution is always the product of much organizational learning. It is achieved unevenly—coming quickly in some areas and proving nettlesome in others. Progress reviews, ongoing searches for ways to continuously improve, and corrective adjustments are thus normal.

WHY STRATEGIC MANAGEMENT IS AN ONGOING PROCESS, NOT A START-STOP EVENT

A company's vision, objectives, strategy, and approach to implementation are never final; evaluating performance, reviewing changes in the surrounding environment, and making adjustments are normal and necessary parts of the strategic management process.

The choice of whether to continue or change the company's vision, objectives, strategy, and implementation approaches always presents itself. Strategic management is an ongoing, neverending process, not a start-stop event that, once done, can be safely put aside for a while. Managers have an ever-present responsibility for detecting when new developments require a strategic response and when they don't. Their job is to track progress, spot problems and issues early, monitor the winds of market and customer change, and initiate adjustments as needed. This is why the task of evaluating performance and initiating corrective adjustments is both the end and the beginning of the strategic management cycle.

Characteristics of the Five-Task Process

Although forming a strategic vision, setting objectives, crafting a strategy, implementing and executing the strategic plan, and evaluating performance portray what strategic management involves, actually performing these five tasks is not so cleanly divided into separate, neatly sequenced compartments. First, there is much interplay and recycling among the five tasks, as was shown in Figure 1.1. For example, deciding on a company mission and vision shades into setting objectives (both involve directional priorities). Objective-setting entails considering current performance, the strategy options available to improve performance, and whether the organization has the resources and capabilities to achieve stretch objectives when pushed and challenged. Clearly, the direction-setting tasks of developing a mission, setting objectives, and crafting strategy need to be integrated and done as a package, not individually. Deciding on a strategy is entangled with whether the organization has what it takes to execute the strategy with sufficient proficiency—it is generally foolhardy to pursue a strategic course ill-suited to the company's competencies, capabilities, and resources.

Strategic management is a tightly-knit process; the boundaries between the five tasks are conceptual, not fences that prevent some or all of them being done together.

Second, the five strategic management tasks have to be done alongside a manager's other duties and responsibilities—administering day-to-day operations, dealing with crises, going to meetings, reviewing information, handling people problems, and taking on special assignments and civic duties. Thus, while the job of managing strategy is the most important managerial function insofar as organizational success or failure is concerned, it certainly isn't all managers must do or be concerned about.

Third, crafting and implementing strategy make erratic demands on a manager's time. Change does not happen in an orderly or predictable way. Events can build quickly or gradually; they can emerge singly or in rapid-fire succession; and their implications for strategic change can be easy or hard to diagnose. Hence the task of reviewing and adjusting the strategic game plan can take up big chunks of management time in some months and little time in other months. As a practical matter, there is as much skill in knowing *when* to institute strategic changes as there is in knowing what to do.

Last, the most time-consuming aspect of strategic management involves a daily effort to get the best strategy-supportive performance out of every individual in the organization and trying to perfect the current strategy by refining its content and execution. Managers usually spend most of their efforts improving bits and pieces of the current strategy rather than developing and instituting radical or sweeping changes. Excessive changes in strategy can be disruptive to employees and confusing to customers, and they are usually unnecessary. Most of the time, there's more to be gained from improving execution of the present strategy. Persistence in making a basically sound strategy work better is often the key to successful strategy management.

WHO PERFORMS THE FIVE TASKS OF STRATEGIC MANAGEMENT?

An organization's chief executive officer, as captain of the ship, is the most visible and important strategy manager. The title of CEO carries with it the mantles of chief direction setter, chief objective setter, chief strategy maker, and chief strategy implementer for the total enterprise. Ultimate responsibility for *leading* the tasks of forming, implementing, and executing a strategic plan for the whole organization rests with the CEO, even though other senior managers normally have significant leadership roles also. What the CEO views as strategically important usually is reflected in the company's strategy, and the CEO customarily puts a personal stamp of approval on big strategic decisions and actions.

Vice presidents for production, marketing, finance, human resources, and other functional departments have important strategy-making and strategy-implementing responsibilities as well. Normally, the production VP has a lead role in developing and executing the company's production strategy, the marketing VP oversees the marketing strategy effort, the financial VP is in charge of devising and implementing an appropriate financial strategy, and so on. Usually, senior executives below the CEO are involved in proposing key elements of the overall company strategy and developing major new strategic initiatives, working closely with the CEO to hammer out a consensus strategy and coordinate various aspects of executing the strategy. Only in comparatively small companies is the strategy-making/strategy-implementing task orchestrated by a single executive.

But managerial positions with strategy-making and strategy-implementing responsibility are by no means restricted to CEOs, other senior executives, and owner-entrepreneurs. Every major organizational unit in a company—business unit, division, staff support group, plant, or district office—normally has a leading or supporting role in the company's strategic game plan. And the manager in charge of that organizational unit, with guidance from superiors, usually ends up doing some or most of the strategy making for the unit and deciding how to execute whatever strategic choices are made. While managers farther down in the managerial hierarchy obviously have a narrower, more specific strategy-making/strategy-implementing role than managers closer to the top, *every manager is a strategy maker and strategy implementer for the area he or she supervises.*

> Every company manager has a strategy-making/strategy-implementing role—it is flawed thinking to view strategic management as solely the province of senior executives.

Toshiba is a $45 billion corporation with 300 subsidiaries, thousands of products, and operations extending across the world. The notion that a few senior executives in Toshiba headquarters can orchestrate the crafting, implementing, and executing of all the thousands of pieces of Toshiba's strategy is absurd—it takes Toshiba's whole management team to pull off the strategy-making/strategy-executing process competently.

One of the primary reasons why middle- and lower-echelon managers are part of the strategy-making/strategy-implementing team is that the more geographically scattered and diversified an organization's operations are, the more unwieldy it becomes for headquarters executives to personally craft and lead the implementation of all the necessary initiatives. Managers in the corporate office seldom know enough about the situation in every geographic area and operating unit to direct every strategic move made in the field. It is common practice for top-level managers to delegate strategy-making authority to subordinates who head the organizational subunits where specific strategic results must be achieved. Such delegation fixes accountability for strategic success or failure. When the managers who implement the strategy are also its architects, it is hard for them to shift blame or make excuses if they don't achieve the target results. And, having participated in developing the strategy they are trying to execute, they are likely to support it strongly, an essential condition for effective strategy execution.

In diversified companies where the strategies of several different businesses have to be managed, there are usually four distinct levels of strategy managers:

- The chief executive officer and other senior corporate-level executives who have primary responsibility and personal authority for big strategic decisions affecting the total enterprise and the collection of individual businesses into which the enterprise has diversified.

- Managers who have profit-and-loss responsibility for one specific business unit and who are delegated a major leadership role in crafting and executing a strategy for that business.

- Functional area managers within a given business unit who have direct authority over a major piece of the business (manufacturing, marketing and sales, finance, R&D, personnel) and whose role it is to support the business unit's overall strategy with strategic actions in their own areas.

- Managers of major operating units (plants, sales districts, local offices) who have on-the-scene responsibility for developing the details of strategic efforts in their areas and for executing their piece of the overall strategic plan at the grassroots level.

Single-business enterprises need no more than three of these levels (a business-level strategy manager, functional area strategy managers, and operating-level strategy managers). Proprietorships, partnerships, and owner-managed enterprises typically have only one or two strategy managers since in small-scale enterprises the whole strategy-making/strategy-implementing function can be handled by just a few key people.

Managerial jobs involving crafting and executing strategy abound in not-for-profit organizations as well. In federal and state government, heads of local, district, and regional offices function as strategy managers in the areas they serve (a district manager in Portland may need a slightly different strategy than a district manager in Orlando). In municipal government, the heads of various departments (fire, police, water and sewer, parks and recreation, health, and so on) are strategy managers because they have line authority for the operations of their departments and thus can influence departmental objectives, the formation of a departmental strategy to achieve these objectives, and day-to-day execution of the strategy.

Managerial jobs with strategy-making/strategy-executing roles are thus the norm rather than the exception.[8] The job of crafting and executing strategy touches virtually every managerial job in one way or another, at one time or another. Strategic management is basic to the task of managing; it is not something just top-level managers deal with.

How Strategies Get Crafted—What the Process Is Like and Who Participates

Companies and managers approach the task of crafting a strategy in a variety of ways. At one extreme, strategy emerges as chiefly the product of one person—the CEO, a visionary founder of the business, or an enterprise's current owner. At the other extreme, strategy making is a group or team exercise involving managers and perhaps select other key personnel throughout the whole organization. The process of crafting strategy at most companies tends to take one of the following four forms.[9]

The Chief Architect Approach   In some enterprises, a single person—the owner or CEO—assumes the role of chief strategist and chief entrepreneur, singlehandedly shaping most or all of the major pieces of strategy. This does not mean that one person is the originator of all the ideas underlying the resulting strategy or does all the background data gathering and analysis; there may be much brainstorming with subordinates and considerable analysis by specific departments. But it does mean that one person functions as strategic visionary and chief architect of strategy, personally orchestrating the process and putting his or her imprint on what strategy to pursue. The chief architect approach to strategy formation is characteristic of companies that have been founded by the company's present CEO—Michael Dell at Dell Computer, Steve Case at America Online, Bill Gates at Microsoft, and Howard Schultz at Starbucks are prominent examples of corporate CEOs who exert a heavy hand in shaping their company's strategy. The strategies of small entrepreneurial companies, partnerships, and family-owned businesses almost always are primarily the product of the experiences, personal observations and assessments, strategic visions, and business judgments of the owner(s), with perhaps modest contributions from a few key employees or outside advisers.

The Delegation Approach   Here the manager in charge delegates big chunks of the strategy-making task to trusted subordinates, down-the-line managers in charge of key business units and departments, a high-level task force of knowledgeable and talented people from many parts of the company, self-directed work teams with authority over a particular process or function, or, more rarely, a team of consultants brought in specifically to help develop new strategic initiatives. Delegating the brainstorming, analysis, and crafting of major strategy components and certainly most of the detailed pieces of an enterprise's strategy allows for broad participation from many managers and personnel with specialized expertise and on-the-scene knowledge of market and competitive conditions—a big advantage (if not a necessity) in multiproduct, multibusiness enterprises whose operations are far-flung or fast-moving. The more that a

> Broad participation in a company's strategy-creating exercises is usually a strong plus.

---

[8]The strategy-making, strategy-implementing roles of middle managers are thoroughly discussed and documented in Steven W. Floyd and Bill Wooldridge, *The Strategic Middle Manager* (San Francisco: Jossey-Bass, 1996), chapters 2 and 3.

[9]This classification scheme is based on David R. Brodwin and L. J. Bourgeois, "Five Steps to Strategic Action," in *Strategy and Organization: A West Coast Perspective,* ed. Glenn Carroll and David Vogel (Marshfield, MA: Pitman Publishing, 1984), pp. 168–78.

company's operations cut across different products, industries, and geographical areas, the more that headquarters executives are prone to delegate considerable strategy-making authority to personnel who have firsthand knowledge of customer requirements, can better evaluate market opportunities, and are better able to keep the strategy responsive to changing market and competitive conditions. The swifter the pace of market change, the more imperative it is to delegate strategy-making responsibility to down-the-line managers who can act quickly.

While strategy delegators have less of their own imprint on individual elements of strategy, they still typically play an influential role in shaping the major components of the strategy and in turning thumbs up or down on strategy particulars proposed by subordinates. The weakness of the delegation approach is that its success hinges on the business judgments and strategy-making skills of lower-echelon personnel. For instance, the strategizing efforts of subordinates may deal more with how to address today's problems than with positioning the enterprise and adapting its resources to capture tomorrow's opportunities. Subordinates may not have either the clout or the inclination to tackle changing major components of the present strategy.[10] A second weakness is that delegation sends the wrong signal: that strategy development isn't important enough to warrant a big claim on the boss's personal time and attention. Finally, it is a mistake for executives to be too detached from the strategy-making process in case the group's deliberations bog down in disagreement or go in ill-conceived directions.

The Collaborative or Team Approach   This is a middle approach whereby a manager with strategy-making responsibility enlists the assistance and advice of key peers and subordinates in hammering out a consensus strategy. Strategy teams often include line and staff managers from different disciplines and departmental units, a few handpicked junior staffers known for their ability to think creatively, and near-retirement veterans noted for being keen observers, telling it like it is, and giving sage advice.

Electronic Data Systems conducted a year-long strategy review involving 2,500 of its 55,000 employees and coordinated by a core of 150 managers and staffers from all over the world.[11] J. M. Smucker, a maker of jams and jellies, formed a team of 140 employees (7 percent of its 2,000-person workforce) who spent 25 percent of their time over a six-month period looking for ways to rejuvenate the company's growth; the team, which solicited input from all employees, came up with 12 initiatives to double the company's revenues over the next five years. Nokia Group, a Finland-based global leader in wireless telecommunications, involved 250 employees in a strategy review of how different communications technologies were converging, how this would affect the company's business, and what strategic responses were needed. It is increasingly common for strategy teams to involve customers and suppliers in assessing the future market situation and deliberating the various strategy options.

Collaborative efforts are usually led by the manager in charge, but the result is the joint product of all concerned. Such an approach is well suited to situations where strategic issues cut across departments, product lines, and businesses and there's a need to tap the strategic thinking of people with different expertise, experiences, and perspectives. Collaborative strategy making helps win participants' wholehearted commitment to implementation of the strategy that emerges. Involving teams of people to dissect complex situations and find market-driven, customer-driven solutions is becoming increasingly necessary in many businesses. Not only are many strategic issues too far-reaching or too

> Collaborative strategy making helps win participants' wholehearted commitment to implementation.

---

[10]For a case in point of where the needed strategy changes were too big for a chartered group of subordinates to address, see Thomas M. Hout and John C. Carter, "Getting It Done: New Roles for Senior Executives," *Harvard Business Review* 73, no. 6 (November–December 1995), pp. 140–44.

[11]"Strategic Planning," *Business Week,* August 26, 1996, pp. 51–52.

involved for a single manager to handle but they often are cross-functional and cross-departmental, thus requiring the contributions of many disciplinary experts and the collaboration of managers from different parts of the organization. Giving people an influential stake in crafting the strategy they must later help implement not only builds motivation and commitment but it also means they can be held accountable for putting the strategy into place and making it work—the excuse "It wasn't my idea to do this" won't fly.

The Corporate Intrapreneur Approach   In the corporate intrapreneur approach, top management encourages individuals and teams to develop and champion proposals for new product lines and new business ventures. The idea is to unleash the talents and energies of promising corporate intrapreneurs, letting them try out business ideas and pursue new strategic initiatives. Executives serve as judges of which proposals merit support, give company intrapreneurs the needed organizational and budgetary support, and let them run with the ball. Thus, important pieces of company strategy originate with those intrapreneuring individuals and teams who succeed in championing a proposal through the approval stage and then end up being charged with the lead role in launching new products, overseeing the company's entry into new geographic markets, or heading up new business ventures.

> Corporate intrapreneuring relies upon middle and lower-level managers and teams to spot new business opportunities, develop strategic plans to pursue them, and create new businesses.

Utilizing the corporate intrapreneur approach successfully requires having an organization populated with ambitious, entrepreneurial people who want the chance to take on strategic and managerial responsibility for a new product or business. With this approach, the total strategy of a company is the collective sum of all the championed initiatives. This approach works well in enterprises where technological advances are coming at a fast and furious pace and/or compelling new opportunities are opening up in a variety of areas.

W. L. Gore & Associates, a privately owned company famous for its Gore-Tex waterproofing film, is an avid and highly successful practitioner of the corporate intrapreneur approach to strategy making. Gore expects all employees to initiate improvements and to display innovativeness. Each employee's intrapreneuring contributions are prime considerations in determining raises, stock option bonuses, and promotions. W. L. Gore's commitment to intrapreneuring has produced a stream of product innovations that has kept the company vibrant and growing for well over a decade. Illustration Capsule 5 describes an example of the corporate intrapreneur approach at British Airways.

Comparing the Approaches   These four basic managerial approaches to forming a strategy illuminate several aspects of how strategies come into being. Highly centralized strategy making works fine when the strategy commander-in-chief has a powerful, insightful vision of where to head and how to get there. The primary weakness of the chief architect approach is that the caliber of the strategy depends so heavily on one person's entrepreneurial acumen and strategic judgments. It also breaks down in enterprises with diverse businesses and product lines where there are so many particulars to the strategy that one person cannot orchestrate the strategy-making process.

On the other hand, delegating strategic decisions to others and collaborating to build a consensus strategy have their risks too. The big weakness of delegating much of strategy making to down-the-line-managers is the potential lack of sufficient top-down direction and strategic leadership on the part of senior executives. Down-the-line managers don't always have the breadth of vision or experience to make strategic decisions that later could prove to have far-reaching impact on the enterprise. Furthermore, there may be occasions when lower-level managers elect to play it safe with conservative, middle-of-the-road strategies rather than bold, creative strategies. Delegation also runs the risk that the outcome will be shaped by influential subordinates, by powerful

> Each of the four basic strategy-making approaches has strengths and weaknesses, and each is workable in the "right" situation.

illustration capsule 5
Corporate Intrapreneuring at British Airways

In 1997 Robert J. Ayling, CEO of British Airways, told Barbara Cassini, age 37, that if she came up with a business plan for a low-cost, no-frills airline showing realistic promise of profitability then the company would fund the venture and she could run it.

Cassini, an American who had an undergraduate degree from Mount Holyoke College in Massachusetts and a master's degree in public affairs from Princeton, had joined British Airways in 1987 after a stint as a consultant in the International division of Coopers & Lybrand. She worked her way up through the ranks at British Airways, playing a lead role in helping turn around Dan-Air, a small European airline that British Airways had acquired in 1992 and that was operating in the red. In 1993, Cassini moved to New York and took on the assignment of general manager for BA's U.S. operations. Then she got the offer from Ayling to look into starting a new airline subsidiary. Cassini, who considered herself a maverick, had never had an entrepreneurial role before but was intrigued by Ayling's offer and the chance to run a new company for BA.

Cassini's business plan was accepted and the new airline, Go Fly, Ltd., was created with a $40 million investment from British Airways. Cassini became the first female chief executive of any airline in the world and began the task of fleshing out the details of a strategy for Go Fly. Go Fly began operations in May 1998 with two routes. By fall 1999 it was operating flights to 15 locations from Stansted Airport and had 500 employees. A typical round-trip fare from London's Stansted Airport to Rome was $187, compared to a fare of $540 on British Airways. Like Southwest Airlines, whose operations Cassini studied carefully, Go Fly offered few frills—sandwiches and coffee were available to passengers at extra cost.

While Go Fly's low fares were probably attracting passengers away from British Airways, Cassini was unconcerned, stating that if Go Fly wasn't cutting into BA's business with its low-fare approach, some other no-frills competitor would be. Cassini expected that Go Fly would become profitable in 2001.

Source: Based on information in "Nurturing a Low-Frills Airline," *The New York Times,* September 19, 1999, Money & Business section, p. 2.

functional departments, or by majority coalitions that have a common interest in promoting their particular version of what the strategy ought to be. The collaborative approach is conducive to political strategic choices as well, since powerful departments and individuals have ample opportunity to try to build a consensus for their favored strategic approach. Politics and the exercise of power are most likely to come into play in situations where there is no consensus on what strategy to adopt. Collaborative strategy making can also suffer from slower reaction and response times, as group members meet to debate the merits of what to do.

The strength of the corporate intrapreneur approach is also its weakness. The value of corporate intrapreneuring is that it encourages people at lower organizational levels to be alert for profitable market opportunities, to propose innovative strategies to capture them, and to take on responsibility for new business ventures. Individuals with attractive strategic proposals are given the latitude and resources to try them out, thus helping renew an organization's capacity for innovation and growth. However, because they spring from many places in the organization and can fly off in many directions, the various championed actions are not likely to form a coherent pattern or result in a clear strategic direction for the company as a whole without some strong top-down leadership. With intrapreneuring, top-level executives have to work at nurturing proposals that add power to the overall organization strategy; otherwise, strategic initiatives may be launched in directions that have little or no integrating links or fits with the overall business. Another weakness of the corporate intrapreneuring approach is that top executives may be more prone to protect their reputations for prudence and risk avoidance than to support revolutionary strategies, in which case innovative ideas can be doused by corporate orthodoxy.[12] It is not easy for a low-ranking employee to champion an out-of-the-ordinary proposal up the chain of command.

Thus, all four approaches to developing a strategy have strengths and weaknesses. All four can succeed or fail depending on the company's size and business makeup, on how well the approach is managed, and on the business judgments of the individuals involved.

The Role of the Board of Directors in Crafting and Executing Strategy

Since lead responsibility for crafting and executing strategy falls to key managers, the chief strategic role of an organization's board of directors is to exercise oversight and see that the five tasks of strategic management are done in a manner that benefits shareholders (in the case of investor-owned enterprises) or stakeholders (in the case of not-for-profit organizations). The specter of stockholder lawsuits and the escalating costs of liability insurance for directors underscore the responsibility that corporate board members have for overseeing a company's strategic actions. Moreover, holders of large blocks of shares (mutual funds and pension funds), regulatory authorities, and the financial press consistently urge that board members, especially outside directors, be active in their oversight of company strategy and the actions and capabilities of executives.

It is standard procedure for executives to brief board members on important strategic moves and to submit the company's strategic plans to the board for official approval. But directors rarely can or should play a direct, hands-on role in formulating or implementing strategy. Most outside directors lack industry-specific experience; their company-specific knowledge is limited (especially if they are relatively new board members). Boards of directors typically meet once a month (or less) for six to eight hours. Board members can scarcely be expected to have detailed command of all the strategic issues or know the ins and outs of the various strategic options. It is unreasonable to expect them to come up with compelling strategy proposals of their own to debate against those put forward by management. Such a hands-on role is unnecessary for good oversight. The immediate task of directors is to be *supportive critics,* exercising their own independent judgment about whether proposals have been adequately analyzed and whether proposed strategic actions appear to have greater promise than available alternatives.[13] If executive management is bringing well-supported strategy proposals to the board, there's little reason for board members to aggressively challenge everything put before them. Asking perceptive and incisive questions is usually sufficient to test whether the case for the proposals is compelling and to exercise vigilant oversight. However, if the company is experiencing gradual erosion of profits and market share, and certainly when there is a precipitous collapse in profitability, board members have a duty to be proactive, expressing their concerns about the validity of the strategy, initiating debate about the company's strategic path, having one-on-one discussions with key executives and other board members, and perhaps directly intervening as a group to alter both the strategy and the company's executive leadership.

> **Strategic Management Principle**
> The central role of the board of directors in the strategic management process is (1) to critically appraise and ultimately approve strategic action plans and (2) to evaluate the strategic leadership skills of the CEO and others in line to succeed the incumbent CEO.

---

[12]See Gary Hamel, "Strategy as Revolution," *Harvard Business Review* 74, no. 4 (July–August 1996), pp. 80–81.

[13]For a good discussion of the role of the board of directors in overseeing the strategy-making, strategy-executing process, see Gordon Donaldson, "A New Tool for Boards: The Strategic Audit," *Harvard Business Review* 77 no. 4 (July–August 1995), pp. 99–107.

The real hands-on role of directors is to evaluate the caliber of senior executives' strategy-making and strategy-implementing skills. The board is always responsible for determining whether the current CEO is doing a good job of strategic management (as a basis for awarding salary increases and bonuses and deciding on retention or removal).[14] Recently, at AT&T, Pacific Corp., Kmart, RiteAid, and Compaq Computer, company directors concluded that top executives were not adapting their company's strategy fast enough and fully enough to the changes sweeping their markets. They pressured the CEOs to resign and installed new leadership to provide the impetus for strategic renewal. Boards must also exercise due diligence in evaluating the strategic leadership skills of other senior executives in line to succeed the CEO. When the incumbent CEO retires, the board must elect a successor, either going with an insider (frequently nominated by the retiring CEO) or deciding that an outsider is needed to perhaps radically change the company's strategic course. Board oversight and vigilance is therefore very much in play in the strategy arena.

THE BENEFITS OF A STRATEGIC APPROACH TO MANAGING

The message of this book is that doing a good job of managing inherently requires good strategic thinking. Today's managers have to think strategically about their company's position and about the impact of changing conditions. They have to monitor the company's external environment and internal capabilities closely enough to know when to institute strategy changes. They have to know the business well enough to determine what kinds of strategic changes to initiate. Simply said, the fundamentals of strategic management need to drive the whole approach to managing organizations. The chief executive officer of one successful company put it well when he said:

> In the main, our competitors are acquainted with the same fundamental concepts and techniques and approaches that we follow, and they are as free to pursue them as we are. More often than not, the difference between their level of success and ours lies in the relative thoroughness and self-discipline with which we and they develop and execute our strategies for the future.

The advantages of first-rate strategic thinking and conscious strategy management (as opposed to freewheeling improvisation, gut feel, and hoping for good luck) include (1) providing better guidance to the entire organization on the crucial point of "what it is we are trying to do," (2) making managers and organizational members more alert to new opportunities and threatening developments, (3) helping to unify the organization, (4) creating a more proactive management posture, (5) promoting the development of a constantly evolving business model that will produce sustained bottom-line success for the enterprise, and (6) providing managers with a rationale for evaluating competing budget requests—a rationale that argues strongly for steering resources into strategy-supportive, results-producing areas.

Trailblazing strategies can be the key to better long-term performance. Business history shows that high-performing enterprises often initiate and lead, not just react and defend. They launch strategic offensives to out-innovate and out-maneuver rivals

---

[14]For an excellent discussion of the board of directors' role in CEO evaluation and succession, see Jay W. Lorsch and Rakesh Khurana, "Changing Leaders: The Board's Role in CEO Succession," *Harvard Business Review* 77 no. 3 (May–June 1999), pp. 96–105.

and secure sustainable competitive advantage, then use their market edge to achieve superior financial performance. Aggressive pursuit of a creative, opportunistic strategy can propel a firm into a leadership position, paving the way for its products and services to become the industry standard. High-achieving enterprises are nearly always the product of astute, proactive management, rather than the result of lucky breaks or a long run of good fortune.

In the chapters to come, we will probe the strategy-related tasks of managers and the methods of strategic analysis much more intensively. When you get to the end of the book, we think you will see that *two factors separate the best-managed organizations from the rest: (1) superior strategy making and entrepreneurship, and (2) competent implementation and execution of the chosen strategy.* There's no escaping the fact that the quality of managerial strategy making and strategy implementing has a significant impact on organization performance. A company that lacks clear-cut direction, has vague or undemanding objectives, has a muddled or flawed strategy, or can't seem to execute its strategy competently is a company whose performance is probably suffering, whose business is at long-term risk, and whose management is lacking. In short, the better conceived a company's strategy and the more proficient its execution, the greater the chances the company will be a leading performer in its markets and truly deserve a reputation for talented management.

suggested | readings

Abell, Derek F. "Competing Today While Preparing for Tomorrow." *Sloan Management Review* 40, no. 3 (Spring 1999), pp. 73–81.

Burgelman, Robert A. *Strategy Is Destiny.* New York: The Free Press, 2000.

Collins, James C., and Jerry I. Porras. "Building Your Company's Vision." *Harvard Business Review* 74, no. 5 (September–October 1996), pp. 65–77.

Farkas, Charles M., and Suzy Wetlaufer. "The Ways Chief Executive Officers Lead." *Harvard Business Review* 74, no. 3 (May–June 1996), pp. 110–122.

Hamel, Gary. "Strategy as Revolution." *Harvard Business Review* 74, no. 4 (July–August 1996), pp. 69–82.

Lipton, Mark. "Demystifying the Development of an Organizational Vision." *Sloan Management Review,* Summer 1996, pp. 83–92.

Markides, Constantinos C. "A Dynamic View of Strategy." *Sloan Management Review* 40, no. 3 (Spring 1999), pp. 55–63.

Mintzberg, Henry. "Crafting Strategy." *Harvard Business Review* 65, no. 4 (July–August 1987), pp. 66–75.

Mintzberg, Henry. Bruce Ahlstrand; and Joseph Lampel. *Strategy Safari: A Guided Tour through the Wilds of Strategic Management.* New York: Free Press, 1998.

Moncrieff, James. "Is Strategy Making a Difference?" *Long Range Planning* 32, no. 2 (April 1999), pp. 273–76.

Porter, Michael E. "What Is Strategy?" *Harvard Business Review* 74, no. 6 (November–December 1996), pp. 61–78.

Shaw, Gordon; Robert Brown; and Philip Bromiley. "Strategic Stories: How 3M Is Rewriting Business Planning." *Harvard Business Review* 76, no. 3 (May–June 1998), pp. 41–50.

chapter | two

Establishing Company Direction

Developing a Strategic Vision, Setting Objectives, and Crafting a Strategy

The last thing IBM needs right now is a vision. (July 1993)
What IBM needs most right now is a vision. (March 1996)

—Louis V. Gerstner Jr., CEO, IBM Corporation

How can you lead if you don't know where you are going?

—George Newman, The Conference Board

Management's job is not to see the company as it is . . . but as it can become.

—John W. Teets, CEO, Greyhound Corporation

A strategy is a commitment to undertake one set of actions rather than another.

—Sharon M. Oster, Professor, Yale University

In this chapter, we present a more in-depth look at the first three of the five strategic management tasks discussed in Chapter 1: developing a strategic vision and business mission, setting performance objectives, and crafting a strategy to produce the desired results. We will also examine which kinds of strategic decisions are made at which levels of management and the major factors that shape a company's strategy. The final two sections of the chapter discuss links between strategy making and ethics, and present some tests for determining whether a proposed strategy is a winner.

DEVELOPING A STRATEGIC VISION: THE FIRST DIRECTION-SETTING TASK

Strategic Management Principle

Effective strategy making begins with a vision of where the organization needs to head.

A clear and entrepreneurially astute strategic vision is a prerequisite to effective strategic leadership. Managers cannot function effectively as either leaders or strategy-makers without a future-oriented concept of the business—what customer needs to work toward satisfying, what business activities to pursue, what kind of long-term market position to build vis-à-vis competitors, what kind of company to try to create. Charting a company's course begins with senior management looking at the road ahead and addressing the following questions: "Where do we go from here?" "What changes lie ahead in the business landscape?" and "What difference will these changes make to the company's present business?"

Forming a strategic vision is thus not merely a wordsmithing exercise designed to create a catchy company slogan; rather it is an exercise in thinking carefully about where a company needs to head to be successful. It involves selecting the market arenas in which to participate, putting the company on a strategic path, and making a commitment to follow that path.

See Illustration Capsule 6 for an example of a strategic vision describing what course a company intends to follow.

The Three Elements of a Strategic Vision

Managers have three discernible tasks in forming a strategic vision and making it a useful direction-setting tool:

- Coming up with a *mission statement* that defines what business the company is *presently* in and conveys the essence of "who we are, what we do, and where we are now."

- Using the mission statement as a basis for deciding on a *long-term* course, making choices about "where we are going," and charting a strategic path for the company to pursue.

- Communicating the strategic vision in clear, exciting terms that arouse organizationwide commitment.

The Mission Statement: A Starting Point for Forming a Strategic Vision

Coming up with a mission statement is not as simple as it might seem. Is America Online in the Internet connection business, the online content business, the information business, or the entertainment business? Is Coca-Cola in the soft-drink business (in which case management's strategic attention can be concentrated on outselling and outcompeting Pepsi, 7UP, Dr Pepper, Canada Dry, and Schweppes), or is it in the beverage business (in which case management also needs to think strategically about positioning Coca-Cola products to compete against fruit juices, ready-to-drink teas, bottled water, sports drinks, milk, and coffee)? Whether to take a soft-drink perspective or a beverage perspective is not a trivial question for Coca-Cola management—only partly because Coca-Cola is also the parent of Minute Maid and Hi-C, which make juice products. With a beverage industry vision as opposed to a soft-drink focus, Coca-Cola management can better zero in on, say, how to convince young adults to get their morning caffeine fix by drinking Coca-Cola instead of coffee.

illustration capsule 6
Deere & Company's Strategic Vision

With revenues of more than $14 billion, John Deere has been a truly international company for decades. Use of the company's agricultural equipment in many parts of the world has given the company a respected global brand name. The company has set forth in clear terms who it is, where it is going, and how it plans to get there. The following paragraphs, from Deere's Web site, spell out the company's strategic vision.

WHO ARE WE?

John Deere has grown and prospered through a long-standing partnership with the world's most productive farmers. Today, John Deere is a global company with several equipment operations and complementary service businesses. These businesses are closely interrelated, providing the company with significant growth opportunities and other synergistic benefits.

WHERE ARE WE GOING?

Deere is committed to providing genuine value to the company's stakeholders, including our customers, dealers, shareholders, employees, and communities. In support of that commitment, Deere aspires to:

- Grow and pursue leadership positions in each of our businesses.
- Extend our preeminent leadership position in the agricultural equipment market worldwide.
- Create new opportunities to leverage the John Deere brand globally.

HOW WILL WE GET THERE?

By pursuing the broader corporate goals of profitable growth and continuous improvement, each of the company's businesses is expected to:

- Achieve world-class performance by attaining a strong competitive position in target markets.
- Exceed customer expectations for quality and value.
- Earn in excess of the cost of capital over a business cycle.

By growing profitably and continuously improving, each of the company's businesses will benefit from and contribute to John Deere's unique intangible assets:

- Our distinguished brand.
- Our heritage of integrity and teamwork.
- Our advanced skills.
- The special relationships that have long existed between the company and our employees, customers, dealers, and other business partners around the world.

HOW WILL WE MEASURE OUR PERFORMANCE?

Each business will make a positive contribution to the corporation's objectives in the pursuit of creating genuine value for our stakeholders. Our "scorecard" includes:

- Human Resources—Employee Satisfaction, Training
- Customer Focus—Loyalty, Market Leadership
- Business Processes—Productivity, Quality, Cost, Environment
- Business Results—Return on Assets, Sales Growth

Source: Deere & Company Web site (www.deere.com).

The Mission Is Not to Make a Profit   Sometimes companies couch their business mission in terms of making a profit. This is misguided—profit is more correctly an *objective* and a *result* of what the company does. The desire to make a profit says nothing about the business arena in which profits are to be sought. Missions based on making a profit do not allow us to distinguish one type of profit-seeking enterprise from another—the business of Amazon.com is plainly different from the business of Toyota, even though both endeavor to earn a profit. A company that says its mission is to make a profit begs the question "What will we do to make a profit?" To understand a company's business purpose, we must know management's real answer to that question.

> One of the roles of a mission statement is to give the organization its own special identity, business emphasis, and path for development—one that typically sets it apart from other similarly situated companies.

Incorporating What, Who, and How into the Mission Statement

A strategically revealing mission statement incorporates three elements:[1]

1. Customer needs, or *what* is being satisfied.
2. Customer groups, or *who* is being satisfied.
3. The company's activities, technologies, and competencies, or *how* the enterprise goes about creating and delivering value to customers and satisfying their needs.

> A company's business is defined by what needs it is trying to satisfy, by which customer groups it is targeting, and by the technologies and competencies it uses and the activities it performs.

Defining a business in terms of what to satisfy, whom to satisfy, and how to produce the satisfaction identifies the substance of what a company does to create value for its customers. Defining a business solely in terms of the products or services it provides is incomplete. A product or service becomes a business only when it satisfies a need or want; without demand for the product there is no business. Customer groups are relevant because they pinpoint the market to be served—the geographic domain to be covered and the types of buyers the firm hopes to attract.

> Technology, competencies, and activities are important to defining a company's business because they indicate the boundaries on its operations.

Technology, competencies, and activities are important because they indicate how much of the industry's total production-distribution chain its operations will span. For instance, the business of a *fully integrated firm* extends across the entire range of industry activities that must be performed to get a product or service into the hands of end users. The business of major international oil companies like Exxon, Mobil, BP Amoco, and Royal Dutch/Shell covers all stages of the oil industry's production-distribution chain—these companies lease drilling sites, drill wells, pump oil, transport crude oil in their own ships and pipelines to their own refineries, and sell gasoline and other refined products through their own networks of branded distributors and service station outlets. A *partially integrated firm* participates in some but not all of the industry's stages—raw materials supply, components production, manufacturing and assembly, distribution, or retailing. General Motors is a partially integrated company that makes between 30 and 50 percent of the parts and components used in assembling GM vehicles; the remainder of the needed parts and systems components come from independent suppliers, and GM relies on a network of independent, franchised dealers to handle retail sales and customer service functions. A *specialized firm* concentrates on just one stage of an industry's total production-distribution chain. Wal-Mart, The Home Depot, Toys"R"Us, Lands' End, and The Limited are essentially one-stage firms that focus on the retail end of the production-distribution chain; they don't manufacture the items they sell. Southwest Airlines is a one-stage enterprise that limits its business activities to moving travelers from one location to another via commercial jet aircraft. It doesn't manufacture the airplanes it flies or operate the airports where those planes land.

An example of a company that does a pretty good job of covering the three bases of what, who, and how in its business definition is Cardinal Health, a Fortune 100 company based in Dublin, Ohio:

> Cardinal Health is a leading provider of services supporting health care worldwide. The company offers a broad array of services for health-care providers and manufacturers to help them improve the efficiency and quality of health care. These services include phar-

---

[1]Derek F. Abell, *Defining the Business: The Starting Point of Strategic Planning* (Englewood Cliffs, NJ: Prentice Hall, 1980), p. 169.

maceutical distribution, health-care product manufacturing and distribution, drug delivery systems development, pharmaceutical packaging and repackaging, automated dispensing systems manufacturing, hospital pharmacy management, retail pharmacy franchising, and health-care information systems development.

JDS Uniphase, a Canada-based high-tech telecommunications components company, also has an explicit and comprehensive business definition:

JDS Uniphase is the leading provider of advanced fiber optic components and modules. These products are sold to the world's leading telecommunications and cable television system providers, which are commonly referred to as OEMs and include Alcatel, Ciena, General Instruments, Lucent, Nortel, Pirelli, Scientific Atlanta, Siemens, and Tyco. Our products perform both optical-only (commonly referred to as "passive") functions and op-toelectronic (commonly referred to as "active") functions within fiber optic networks. Our products include semiconductor lasers, high-speed external modulators, transmitters, amplifiers, couplers, multiplexers, circulators, tunable filters, optical switches, and isolators for fiber optic applications. We also supply our OEM customers with test instruments for both system production applications and network installation. In addition, we design, manufacture, and market laser subsystems for a broad range of OEM applications, which include biotechnology, industrial process control and measurement, graphics and printing, and semiconductor equipment.

Russell Corporation, the largest U.S. manufacturer of athletic apparel and uniforms, is another company with a business definition that covers all the bases:

Russell Corporation is a vertically integrated international designer, manufacturer, and marketer of athletic uniforms, activewear, better knit shirts, leisure apparel, licensed sports apparel, sports and casual socks, and a comprehensive line of lightweight, yarn-dyed woven fabrics. The Company's manufacturing operations include the entire process of converting raw fibers into finished apparel and fabrics. Products are marketed to sporting goods dealers, department and specialty stores, mass merchandisers, golf pro shops, college bookstores, screen printers, distributors, mail-order houses, and other apparel manufacturers.

A Broad or Narrow Business Definition and Mission?

Merck, one of the world's foremost pharmaceutical companies, states that its business mission is "to provide society with superior products and services—innovations and solutions that satisfy customer needs and improve the quality of life." There's nothing specific in this statement that would allow anyone to actually identify Merck's true business; the broad, all-inclusive language Merck uses could just as easily apply to an enterprise engaged in developing innovative computer software, producing and marketing uniquely satisfying snack foods, manufacturing very appealing sports utility vehicles, or providing tax preparation services.

It is perfectly normal for companies in the same industry to have different missions and business definitions. For example, the current mission of a globally active New York bank like Citicorp (a Citigroup subsidiary) has little in common with that of a locally owned hometown bank, even though both are in the banking industry. To truly convey "who we are, what we do, and where we are now," a mission statement must be specific enough to pin down a company's real business arena. Broad-narrow definitions are relative to a company's business focus and intent, however. Consider the following business definitions:

Good mission statements are highly personalized—unique to the organization for which they are developed.

Broad Definition	Narrow Definition
● Furniture business	● Wrought-iron lawn furniture business
● Telecommunications business	● Long-distance telephone service business
● Beverage business	● Soft-drink business
● Global mail delivery business	● Overnight package delivery business
● Travel and tourism business	● Caribbean cruise ship business

"We're in the furniture business" is probably too broad a definition for a company focused on being the largest manufacturer of wrought-iron lawn furniture in North America. In contrast, "We're a provider of long-distance telephone service" has proved too narrow a definition for AT&T, which, with its desire to capitalize on the convergence of computers and communications, has ventured into cable TV (acquiring TCI and MediaOne) and is launching efforts to become the telecommunications company of the future by bundling long-distance service, local telephone service, cable TV, and Internet access into package offerings to residential and business customers. The U.S. Postal Service successfully operates with a broad definition, providing global mail-delivery services to all types of senders. Federal Express, however, operates with a narrow business definition based on handling overnight package delivery for customers who have emergencies or tight deadlines. The risks of making an overly broad mission statement are lack of business focus and dilution of effort. *Few businesses fail because they are focused on a sharply targeted market opportunity, but many fail or do badly because management's attention is divided and resources are scattered across too many areas.*

Diversified companies have broader missions and business definitions than single-business enterprises.

Diversified firms, understandably, employ more sweeping business definitions than single-business enterprises. For example, the McGraw-Hill Companies describes itself broadly as a global publishing, financial, information, and media services company (which covers a lot of ground) but then goes on to pin down its business arenas in fairly explicit terms:

> The McGraw-Hill Companies is a global publishing, financial, information and media services company with such renowned brands as Standard & Poor's, Business Week, and McGraw-Hill educational and professional materials. The Company provides information via various media platforms: through books, magazines and newsletters; online over the Internet and electronic networks; via television, satellite and FM sideband broadcast; and through software, videotape, facsimile and CD-ROM products. The McGraw-Hill Companies now creates more than 90 percent of its information on digital platforms and its business units are represented on more than 75 Web sites.

Federal Express (known formally as FDX Corporation)—also diversified—does a more precise job of laying out its targets of what, who, and how:

> FDX is composed of a powerful family of companies: FedEx®, RPS®, Viking Freight, FDX Global Logistics, and Roberts Express®. These companies offer logistics and distribution solutions on a regional, national and global scale: fast, reliable, time-definite express delivery; expedited surface and air charter delivery of time-critical freight shipments; business-to-business ground small-package delivery; expedited same-day delivery; less-than-truckload (LTL) freight service in the Western U.S.; and integrated information and logistics solutions.
>
> With all of this expertise under one umbrella, the FDX companies can provide businesses with the competitive advantage they need by providing streamlined solutions that are on the cutting edge of technology.

illustration capsule 7
Four Sample Mission Statements: Examples to Critique

Incorporating what, who, and how into a brief, revealing sentence or paragraph is not something many companies have done very well. A perusal of company Web sites, annual reports, and 10-K filings quickly reveals a surprising number of business definitions/mission statements that are deficient. Critique how well each of the following four mission statements cut to the chase in describing what the enterprise is really about and the strategic position it is trying to stake out. Which one is most revealing? Least revealing?

PFIZER INC.

Pfizer is a research-based, global pharmaceutical company. We discover and develop innovative, value-added products that improve the quality of life of people around the world and help them enjoy longer, healthier, and more productive lives.

The company has three business segments: health care, animal health and consumer health care. Our products are available in more than 150 countries.

RITZ-CARLTON HOTELS

The Ritz-Carlton Hotel is a place where the genuine care and comfort of our guests is our highest mission.

We pledge to provide the finest personal service and facilities for our guests, who will always enjoy a warm, relaxed yet refined ambience.

The Ritz-Carlton experience enlivens the senses, instills well-being, and fulfills even the unexpressed wishes and needs of our guests

APPLE COMPUTER

Apple Computer, Inc., ignited the personal computer revolution in the 1970s with the Apple II, and reinvented the personal computer in the 1980s with the Macintosh. Apple is now committed to its original mission—to bring the best personal computing products and support to students, educators, designers, scientists, engineers, business persons and consumers in over 140 countries around the world.

THE GILLETTE COMPANY

The Gillette Company is a globally focused consumer products company that seeks competitive advantage in quality, value-added personal care and personal use products. We compete in four large, worldwide businesses: personal grooming products, consumer portable power products, stationery products and small electrical appliances.

As a Company, we share skills and resources among business units to optimize performance. We are committed to a plan of sustained sales and profit growth that recognizes and balances both short- and long-term objectives.

Mission

Our mission is to achieve or enhance clear leadership, worldwide, in the existing or new core consumer product categories in which we choose to compete.

Current core categories are:

- Male grooming products, including blades and razors, electric shavers, shaving preparations and deodorants and antiperspirants.

- Female grooming products, including wet shaving products, hair removal and hair care appliances and deodorants and antiperspirants.

- Alkaline and specialty batteries and cells.

(continued)

Critically evaluate the caliber of the four mission statements in Illustration Capsule 7.

Mission Statements for Functional Departments   There's also a place for mission statements for key functions and departments within a business—R&D, marketing, finance, human resources, customer service, information systems. Every department can help focus the efforts of its personnel by developing a mission statement that sets forth its principal role and activities, the direction it is headed, and its contribution to the overall company mission. Functional and departmental managers who think through and debate with subordinates and higher-ups what their unit needs to focus on and do have a clearer view of how to lead the unit. Three examples from

illustration capsule 7

(concluded)

- Writing instruments and correction products.
- Certain areas of the oral care market, including tooth-brushes, interdental products and oral care appliances.
- Selected areas of the high-quality small household appliance business, including coffeemakers and food preparation products.

To achieve this mission, we will also compete in supporting product areas that enhance the Company's ability to achieve or hold the leadership position in core categories.

Values

In pursuing our mission, we will live by the following values:

- **People.** We will attract, motivate, and retain high-performing people in all areas of our business. We are committed to competitive, performance-based compensation, benefits, training and personal growth based on equal career opportunity and merit. We expect integrity, civility, openness, support for others and commitment to the highest standards of achievement. We value innovation, employee involvement, change, organizational flexibility and personal mobility. We recognize,

value, and are committed to the benefits in the diversity of people, ideas, and cultures.

- **Customer Focus.** We will invest in and master the key technologies vital to category success. We will offer consumers products of the highest levels of performance for value. We will provide quality service to our customers, both internal and external, by treating them as partners, by listening, understanding their needs, responding fairly and living up to our commitments. We will be a valued customer to our suppliers, treating them fairly and with respect. We will provide these quality values consistent with improving our productivity.

- **Good Citizenship.** We will comply with applicable laws and regulations at all government levels wherever we do business. We will contribute to the communities in which we operate and address social issues responsibly. Our products will be safe to make and to use. We will conserve natural resources, and we will continue to invest in a better environment.

We believe that commitment to this mission and to these values will enable the Company to provide a superior return to our shareholders.

Sources: Company annual reports and Web sites.

---

actual companies indicate how a functional mission statement puts the spotlight on a unit's organizational *role* and *scope:*

- The mission of the human resources department is to contribute to organizational success by developing effective leaders, creating high-performance teams, and maximizing the potential of individuals.
- The mission of the corporate claims department is to minimize the overall cost of liability, workers compensation, and property damage claims through competitive cost containment techniques and loss prevention and control programs.
- The mission of corporate security is to provide services for the protection of corporate personnel and assets through preventive measures and investigations.

From Mission Statement to Strategic Vision

A mission statement highlighting the boundaries of the company's current business is a logical vantage point from which to look down the road, decide what the enterprise's business makeup and customer focus need to be, and chart a strategic path for the company to take. As a rule, strategic visions should have a time horizon of five years or more unless the industry is very new or market conditions are so volatile and uncertain that it is difficult to see that far down the road with any degree of confidence. However, choosing a company's path is a daunting task that requires reasoned answers to the following questions:

1. What changes are occurring in the market arenas where we operate, and what implications do these changes have for the direction in which we need to move?
2. What new or different customer needs should we be moving to satisfy?
3. What new or different buyer segments should we be concentrating on?
4. What new geographic or product markets should we be pursuing?
5. What should the company's business makeup look like in five years?
6. What kind of company should we be trying to become?

> The entrepreneurial challenge in developing a strategic vision is to think creatively about how to prepare a company for the future.

The Crucial Role of Entrepreneurship in Forming a Strategic Vision   There's no substitute for good entrepreneurship in addressing the above six questions and making choices about which forks in the road to take.[2] Charting a promising strategic course forces managers to think both creatively and realistically about changing market, competitive, technological, economic, regulatory, and societal conditions and about the company's resources and capabilities. Sometimes, the best clues about where to head come from alertness to users' problems and complaints and listening intently when a customer says, "If only . . ." Such information, if used creatively, points to valuable customer-market-technology opportunities. Moving early and quickly to pursue emerging opportunities can result in competitive advantage.[3] *A well-chosen strategic vision prepares a company for the future.*

> Forming a strategic vision is an exercise in astute entrepreneurship, not a time for pipedreams or fantasies about the company's future.

Recognizing Strategic Inflection Points   Sometimes there's an order of magnitude change in a company's environment that dramatically alters its prospects and mandates radical revision of its strategic course. Intel's chairman Andrew Grove calls such occasions *strategic inflection points*—Illustration Capsule 8 relates Intel's two encounters with strategic inflection points and the resulting alterations in its strategic vision. As the Intel example forcefully demonstrates, when a company reaches a strategic inflection point, management has some tough decisions to make about the company's course. Often, it is a question of what to do to sustain company success, not just how to avoid possible disaster. Responding to the winds of change in timely fashion lessens a company's chances of becoming trapped in a stagnant or declining business or letting attractive new growth opportunities slip away because of inaction.

> Many successful organizations need to change direction not in order to survive but in order to maintain their success.

---

[2] For a discussion of the challenges of developing a well-conceived vision, as well as some in-depth examples, see James C. Collins and Jerry I. Porras, "Building Your Company's Vision," *Harvard Business Review* 74, no. 5 (September–October 1996), pp. 65–77; Robert A. Burgelman and Andrew S. Grove, "Strategic Dissonance," *California Management Review* 38, no. 2 (Winter 1996), pp. 8–25; and Ron McTavish, "One More Time: What Business Are You In?" *Long Range Planning* 28, no. 2 (April 1995), pp. 49–60. For a discussion of some of the alternative ways a company can position itself in the marketplace, see Michael E. Porter, "What Is Strategy?" *Harvard Business Review* 74, no. 6 (November–December 1996), pp. 65–67. Porter argues that the three basic strategic positions are based on (*a*) the range of customer needs to be served, (*b*) the variety of products to be offered (anywhere along the spectrum of one to many), and (*c*) the means by which customers are accessed—the terms Porter uses are *needs-based positioning, variety-based positioning,* and *access-based positioning.* For an empirical study of executive success in formulating and implementing a company vision, and the difficulties encountered, see Laurie Larwood, Cecilia M. Falbe, Mark Kriger, and Paul Miesing, "Structure and Meaning of Organizational Vision," *Academy of Management Journal* 38, no. 3 (June 1995), pp. 740–69.

[3] For a discussion of the role of corporate entrepreneurship in helping build competitive advantage, see Jeffrey G. Colvin and Morgan P. Miles, "Corporate Entrepreneurship and the Pursuit of Competitive Advantage," *Entrepreneurship: Theory and Practice* 23, no. 3 (Spring 1999), pp. 47–63.

illustration capsule 8
Intel's Two Strategic Inflection Points

Intel Corporation has encountered two strategic inflection points within the past 15 years. The first came in the mid-1980s, when memory chips were Intel's principal business and Japanese manufacturers, intent on dominating the memory chip business, began cutting their prices 10 percent below the prices charged by Intel and other U.S. memory chip manufacturers. Each time U.S. companies matched the Japanese price cuts, the Japanese manufacturers responded with another 10 percent price cut. Intel's management explored a number of strategic options to cope with the aggressive pricing of its Japanese rivals—building a giant memory chip factory to overcome the cost advantage of Japanese producers, investing in R&D to come up with a more advanced memory chip, and retreating to niche markets for memory chips that were not of interest to the Japanese.

At the time, Gordon Moore, Intel's chairman and co-founder, and Andrew Grove, Intel's well-known CEO, jointly concluded that none of these options offered much promise and that the best long-term solution was to abandon the memory chip business even though it accounted for 70 percent of Intel's revenue. Grove, with the concurrence of both Moore and the board of directors, then proceeded to commit Intel's full energies to the business of developing ever more powerful microprocessors for personal computers. (Intel had invented microprocessors in the early 1970s but had recently been concentrating on memory chips because of strong competition and excess capacity in the market for microprocessors.)

Grove's bold decision to withdraw from memory chips, absorb a $173 million writeoff in 1986, and go all out in microprocessors produced a new strategic vision for Intel—becoming the preeminent supplier of microprocessors to the personal computing industry, making the PC the central appliance in the workplace and the home, and being the undisputed leader in driving PC technology forward. Grove's new vision for Intel and the strategic course he charted in 1985 produced spectacular results. Going into 2001, over 80 percent of the world's PCs had "Intel inside" and Intel was one of the 10 most profitable U.S. companies in 2000, earning after-tax profits of $7.3 billion on revenues of $29.4 billion.

The company encountered a second inflection point in 1998, opting to refocus on becoming the preeminent building-block supplier to the Internet economy and spurring efforts to make the Internet more useful. Starting in early 1998 and responding to the mushrooming importance of the Internet, Intel's senior management launched major new initiatives to direct attention and resources to expanding the capabilities of the PC platform and the Internet. Management saw Intel as having a major role in getting a billion computers connected to the Internet worldwide, installing millions of servers (containing ever more powerful Intel microprocessors), and building an Internet infrastructure that would support trillions of dollars of e-commerce and serve as a worldwide communications medium.

Communicating the Strategic Vision

Communicating the strategic vision down the line to lower-level managers and employees is almost as important as setting the organization's long-term direction. People need to believe that the company's management knows where it's trying to take the company and what changes lie ahead both externally and internally. Ideally, executives should present their vision for the company in language that reaches out and grabs people, that creates a vivid image in their heads, and that provokes emotion and excitement. Expressing the strategic vision in engaging language has enormous motivational value—"building a cathedral," for example, is more inspiring than "laying stones."

Most organization members will rise to the challenge of pursuing a worthy organizational purpose and trying to be the world's best at something competitively significant and beneficial to customers. Presenting the vision as an endeavor that will please customers and perhaps benefit society is far more motivating than stressing the payoff for

> Strategic visions ought to convey a larger sense of purpose—so that employees see themselves as "building a cathedral" rather than "laying stones."

shareholders—it goes without saying that the company intends to profit shareholders.[4] When management can paint an inspiring picture of the company's strategic vision it can arouse a committed organizational effort in which people live the business instead of just coming to work. The simple, clear mission statement of the International Red Cross is a good example: "to serve the most vulnerable." Bland language, platitudes, and dull motherhood-and-apple-pie-style verbiage must be scrupulously avoided—they can be a turn-off rather than a turn-on.

> A well-articulated strategic vision creates enthusiasm for the course management has charted and engages members of the organization.

Breaking Down Resistance to a New Strategic Vision   It is particularly important for executives to provide a compelling rationale for a new strategic vision. Failure to understand or accept the need for redirecting organizational efforts often produces resistance to change among employees and makes it harder to move the organization down a newly chosen path. Hence, inducing employee buy-in, lifting spirits, and calming fears are necessary steps in getting an organization ready to move along a new course. Just stating the case for a new direction once is not enough; the vision has to be repeated often and reinforced at every opportunity, until it gains organizationwide acceptance.

Putting the Vision Statement in Writing   Many companies put the strategic visions of senior executives into written vision statements, using them as vehicles to communicate with employees, shareholders, and other constituencies. Usually it is best to keep such vision statements simple and clear, using no more words than it takes to convey unmistakable meaning. A slogan that helps generate enthusiasm for the firm's future course and inspires dedicated effort can be a strong plus. A crisp, clear, often-repeated, inspiring strategic vision has the power to turn heads in the intended direction and create a unified organizational march.

> The best-worded vision statements clearly and crisply illuminate the direction in which an organization is headed.

The Real Payoffs of a Well-Conceived, Well-Worded Vision Statement   A well-conceived, well-stated strategic vision pays off in several respects: (1) it crystallizes senior executives' own views about the firm's long-term direction; (2) it reduces the risk of rudderless decision making; (3) it conveys organizational purpose in ways that motivate organization members to go all out; (4) it provides a beacon that lower-level managers can use to form departmental missions, set departmental objectives, and craft functional and departmental strategies that are in sync with the company's overall strategy; and (5) it helps an organization prepare for the future. When these five benefits have been realized, the first step in organizational direction setting has been successfully completed.

ESTABLISHING OBJECTIVES: THE SECOND DIRECTION-SETTING TASK

Setting objectives converts the strategic vision into specific performance targets. Objectives represent a managerial commitment to achieving specific outcomes and results. Unless an organization's long-term direction is translated into specific performance targets

---

[4]Unless most managers and employees have a significant ownership stake in the enterprise, they will scarcely be motivated and energized by a vision that emphasizes making shareholders richer. Why should they go all out to enhance the pocketbooks of the owners? So, except for companies with employee stock ownership plans that empower and reward employees as owners, there is far more motivational value in a mission/vision that stresses the payoff for customers and/or the general well-being of society, not the payoff for stockholders.

and managers are pressured to show progress in reaching these targets, vision and mission statements are likely to end up as nice words, window dressing, and unrealized dreams. The experiences of countless companies and managers teach that *companies whose managers set objectives for each key result area and then press forward with actions aimed directly at achieving these performance outcomes typically outperform companies whose managers exhibit good intentions, try hard, and hope for the best.*

Basic Concept
Objectives represent a managerial commitment to achieving specific performance targets within a specific time frame—they are a call for results that connect directly to the company's strategic vision and core values.

For objectives to function as yardsticks of organizational performance and progress, they must be stated in *quantifiable,* or measurable, *terms* and they must contain a *deadline for achievement.* They have to spell out how *much* of *what kind* of performance *by when.* This means avoiding generalities like "maximize profits," "reduce costs," "become more efficient," or "increase sales," which specify neither how much or when. As Bill Hewlett, co-founder of Hewlett-Packard, once observed, "You cannot manage what you cannot measure . . . And what gets measured gets done."[5] Spelling out organization objectives in measurable terms and then holding managers accountable for reaching their assigned targets within a specified time frame (1) substitutes purposeful strategic decision making for aimless actions and confusion over what to accomplish and (2) provides a set of benchmarks for judging the organization's performance and progress.

What Kinds of Objectives to Set

Objectives are needed for each key result managers deem important to success.[6] Two types of key result areas stand out: those relating to *financial performance* and those relating to *strategic performance.* [7] Achieving acceptable financial performance is a must; otherwise the organization's financial standing can alarm creditors and shareholders, impair its ability to fund needed initiatives, and perhaps even put its very survival at risk. Achieving acceptable strategic performance is essential to sustaining and improving the company's long-term market position and competitiveness. Representative kinds of financial and strategic performance objectives are listed below:

Strategic Management Principle
Every company needs both strategic objectives and financial objectives.

---

[5]As quoted in Charles H. House and Raymond L. Price, "The Return Map: Tracking Product Teams," *Harvard Business Review* 60, no. 1 (January–February 1991), p. 93.

[6]The literature of management is filled with references to *goals* and *objectives.* These terms are used in a variety of ways, many of them conflicting. Some writers use the term *goals* to refer to the long-run outcomes an organization seeks to achieve and the term *objectives* to refer to immediate, short-run performance targets. Some writers reverse the usage, referring to *objectives* as the desired long-run results and *goals* as the desired short-run results. Others use the terms interchangeably. And still others use the term *goals* to refer to broad organizationwide performance targets and the term *objectives* to designate specific targets set by operating divisions and functional departments to support achievement of overall company performance targets. In our view, little is gained from semantic distinctions between *goals* and *objectives.* The important thing is to recognize that the results an enterprise seeks to attain vary as to both organizational scope and time frame. Nearly always, organizations need to have companywide performance targets and division/department performance targets for both the near term and the long term. It is inconsequential which targets are called goals and which objectives. To avoid a semantic jungle, we use the single term *objectives* to refer to the performance targets and results an organization seeks to attain. We use the adjectives *long-range* (or *long-run*) and *short-range* (or *short-run*) to identify the relevant time frame, and we try to describe objectives in words that indicate their intended scope and level in the organization.

[7]For another view calling for four different types of performance measures, see Robert S. Kaplan, and David P. Norton, "The Balanced Scorecard—Measures That Drive Performance," *Harvard Business Review* 70, no. 1 (January–February 1992), pp. 71–79.

Financial Objectives	Strategic Objectives
• Growth in revenues • Growth in earnings • Higher dividends • Bigger profit margins • Higher returns on invested capital • Attractive economic value added (EVA) performance* • Strong bond and credit ratings • Bigger cash flows • A rising stock price • Attractive and sustainable increases in market value added (MVA)† • Recognition as a "blue-chip" company • A more diversified revenue base • Stable earnings during periods of recession	• A bigger market share • Quicker design-to-market times than rivals (an ability to get newly developed products to market quicker) • Higher product quality than rivals • Lower costs relative to key competitors • Broader or more attractive product line than rivals • Better e-commerce and Internet sales capabilities than rivals • Superior on-time delivery • A stronger brand name than rivals • Superior customer service compared to rivals • Stronger global distribution and sales capabilities than rivals • Recognition as a leader in technology and/or product innovation • Wider geographic coverage than rivals • Higher levels of customer satisfaction than rivals

*Economic value added (EVA) is profit over and above the company's weighted average after-tax cost of capital; specifically, it is defined as operating profit less income taxes less the weighted average cost of capital. Such companies as Coca-Cola, AT&T, Briggs & Stratton, and Eli Lilly use EVA as a measure of the profit performance. For more details on EVA, consult footnote 1 in Chapter 1.

†Market value added (MVA) is defined as the amount by which the total value of the company has appreciated above the dollar amount actually invested in the company by shareholders. MVA is equal to a company's current stock price times the number of shares outstanding less shareholders' equity investment; it represents the value that management has added to shareholders' wealth in running the business. If shareholder value is to be maximized, management must select a strategy and long-term direction that maximize the market value of the company's common stock. See footnote 2 in Chapter 1.

Illustration Capsule 9 presents the strategic and financial objectives for seven different companies.

Strategic Objectives versus Financial Objectives: Which Take Precedence? Even though an enterprise places high priority on achieving both financial and strategic objectives, situations arise where a trade-off has to be made. Should a company under pressure to pay down its debt elect to kill or postpone investments in strategic moves that hold promise for strengthening the enterprise's future business and competitive position? Should a company under pressure to boost near-term profits cut back R&D programs that could help it achieve a competitive advantage over key rivals in the years ahead? The pressures on managers to opt for better near-term financial performance and to sacrifice or cut back on strategic initiatives aimed at building a stronger competitive position become especially pronounced when (1) an enterprise is struggling financially, (2) the resource commitments for strategically beneficial moves will materially detract from the bottom line for several years, and (3) the proposed strategic moves are risky and have an uncertain competitive or bottom-line payoff.

Yet there are dangers in management's succumbing time and again to the lure of immediate gains in profitability when it means forgoing strategic moves that would build a stronger business position. A company that consistently passes up opportunities to

> Strategic objectives need to be competitor-focused, often aiming at unseating a competitor considered to be the industry's best in a particular category.

illustration capsule 9

Corporate Objectives at Citigroup, General Electric, McDonald's, Anheuser-Busch, Exodus Communications, Motorola, and McCormick & Company

CITIGROUP

(Strategic Objective)

- To attain 1 billion customers worldwide.

GENERAL ELECTRIC

(Strategic Objectives)

- Become the most competitive enterprise in the world.
- Be number one or number two in each business we are in.
- Globalize every activity in the company.
- Embrace the Internet and become a global e-business.

MCDONALD'S

(Strategic Objective)

- To achieve 100 percent total customer satisfaction . . . every day . . . in every restaurant . . . for every customer.

ANHEUSER-BUSCH

(Strategic and Financial Objectives)

- To make all of our companies leaders in their industries in quality while exceeding customer expectations.
- To achieve a 50 percent share of the U.S. beer market.
- To establish and maintain a dominant leadership position in the international beer market.
- To provide all our employees with challenging and rewarding work, satisfying working conditions, and opportunities for personal development, advancement, and competitive compensation.
- To provide our shareholders with superior returns by achieving double-digit annual earnings per share growth, increasing dividends consistent with earnings growth, repurchasing shares when the opportunity is right, pursuing profitable international beer expansions, and generating quality earnings and cash flow returns.

EXODUS COMMUNICATIONS

(Exodus Communications is a leading provider of network management and Internet hosting solutions for companies with mission-critical Internet operations.)

(Strategic Objectives)

- Extend our market leadership and position Exodus as the leading brand name in the category.
- Enhance our systems and network management and Internet technology services.
- Accelerate our domestic and international growth.
- Leverage our technical expertise to address new market opportunities in e-commerce.

MOTOROLA

(Financial Objectives)

- Self-funding revenue growth of 15 percent annually.
- An average return on assets of 13 to 15 percent.
- An average return on shareholders' equity investment of 16 to 18 percent.
- A strong balance sheet.

McCORMICK & COMPANY

(Financial Objectives)

- To achieve a 20 percent return on equity.
- To achieve a net sales growth rate of 10 percent per year.
- To maintain an average earnings per share growth rate of 15 percent per year.
- To maintain total debt-to-total capital at 40 percent or less.
- To pay out 25 percent to 35 percent of net income in dividends.
- To make selective acquisitions which complement our current businesses and can enhance our overall returns.
- To dispose of those parts of our business which do not or cannot generate adequate returns or do not fit our business strategy.

Source: Company annual reports and Web sites.

strengthen its long-term competitive position in order to realize better near-term financial gains risks diluting its competitiveness, losing momentum in its markets, and impairing its ability to stave off market challenges from ambitious rivals. The danger of trading off long-term gains in market position for near-term gains in bottom-line performance is greatest when (1) there are lasting first-mover advantages in being a market pioneer (many Internet start-ups, for example, are incurring big short-term losses in their rush to stake out leadership positions in fast-emerging "industries of the future") and (2) a profit-conscious market leader has competitors who invest relentlessly in gaining market share, striving to become big and strong enough to outcompete the leader in a head-to-head market battle. The surest path to sustained future profitability quarter after quarter and year after year is to pursue strategic actions that strengthen a company's *competitiveness* and *business position*. Absent a strong position from which to compete, a company's profitability is at risk.

> **Strategic Management Principle**
> Building a stronger long-term competitive position benefits shareholders more lastingly than improving short-term profitability.

The Concept of Strategic Intent

A company's strategic objectives are important for another reason—they indicate **strategic intent** to stake out a particular business position.[8] Strategic intent can be thought of as a "big, hairy, audacious goal," or BHAG (pronounced *bee-hag*), that generally takes a long time to achieve (maybe even as long as 20 or 30 years).[9] The strategic intent of a large company may be industry leadership on a national or global scale. The strategic intent of a small company may be to dominate a market niche. The strategic intent of an up-and-coming enterprise may be to overtake the market leaders. The strategic intent of a technologically innovative company may be to pioneer a promising discovery and create a whole new array of products that change the way people work and live—as many entrepreneurial companies are now trying to do via the Internet.

> **Basic Concept**
> A company exhibits *strategic intent* when it relentlessly pursues an ambitious strategic objective and concentrates its competitive actions and energies on achieving that objective.

The time horizon underlying a company's strategic intent is *long term*. Ambitious companies almost invariably begin with strategic intents that are out of proportion to their immediate capabilities and market positions. But they set aggressive long-term strategic objectives and pursue them relentlessly, sometimes even obsessively. In the 1960s, Komatsu, Japan's leading earth-moving equipment company, was less than one-third the size of Caterpillar, had little market presence outside Japan, and depended on its small bulldozers for most of its revenue. But Komatsu's strategic intent was to eventually "encircle Caterpillar" with a broader product line and then compete globally against Caterpillar. By the late 1980s, Komatsu was the industry's second-ranking company, with a strong sales presence in North America, Europe, and Asia plus a product line that included industrial robots and semiconductors as well as a broad selection of earth-moving equipment.

The strategic intent of the U.S. government's Apollo space program was to land a person on the moon ahead of the Soviet Union. Throughout the 1980s, Wal-Mart's

---

[8]The concept of strategic intent is described in more detail in Gary Hamel and C. K. Pralahad, "Strategic Intent," *Harvard Business Review* 89, no. 3 (May–June 1989), pp. 63–76; this section draws on their pioneering discussion. See also, Michael A. Hitt, Beverly B. Tyler, Camilla Hardee, and Daewoo Park, "Understanding Strategic Intent in the Global Marketplace," *Academy of Management Executive* 9, no. 2 (May 1995), pp. 12–19. For a discussion of the different ways that companies can position themselves in the marketplace, see Michael E. Porter, "What Is Strategy?" pp. 65–67.

[9]For a discussion of BHAGs, see James C. Collins and Jerry Porras, *Built to Last: Successful Habits of Visionary Companies* (New York: HarperBusiness, 1994); James C. Collins and Jerry I. Porras, "Building Your Company's Vision," *Harvard Business Review* 74, no. 5 (September–October 1996), pp. 65–77; and Jim Collins. "Turning Goals into Results: The Power of Catalytic Mechanisms," *Harvard Business Review* 77, no. 4 (July–August 1999), p. 72.

strategic intent was to "overtake Sears" as the largest U.S. retailer (a feat accomplished in 1991). America Online's strategic intent is to build the strongest, most recognized brand name on the Internet. Internet start-up companies like E-loan, Doubleclick, eBay, etoys, Mortgage.com, and E*Trade are exhibiting strategic intent in rushing to build what they hope will prove to be dominant positions in their target e-commerce niches.

Strategic intent signals a deep-seated commitment to winning—becoming the recognized industry leader, unseating the existing industry leader, remaining the industry leader (and becoming more dominant in the process)—sometimes against long odds. Small, capably managed enterprises determined to achieve ambitious strategic objectives exceeding their present reach and resources often prove to be more formidable competitors than larger, cash-rich companies with modest strategic intents.

Sometimes a company's strategic intent takes on a heroic character, serving as a rallying cry for managers and employees alike to go all out and do their very best. Canon's strategic intent in copying equipment was to "beat Xerox." Nike's strategic intent during the 1960s was to overtake Adidas (which connected nicely with its core purpose "to experience the emotion of competition, winning, and crushing competitors"). Komatsu's motivating battle cry was "Beat Caterpillar." When Yamaha overtook Honda in the motorcycle market, Honda responded with *"Yamaha wo tsubusu"* ("We will crush, squash, slaughter Yamaha"). It is plain that America Online, Amazon.com, and Yahoo! are going all out to build globally dominant market positions in their parts of the mushrooming Internet economy.

The Need for Long-Range and Short-Range Objectives

Organizations need to establish both long-range and short-range objectives. A strong commitment to achieving long-range objectives forces managers to begin taking actions *now* to reach desired performance levels *later.* A company that has an objective of doubling its sales within five years can't wait until the third or fourth year of its five-year strategic plan to begin growing its sales and customer base. By spelling out the near-term results to be achieved, short-range objectives indicate the *speed* at which management wants the organization to progress as well as the *level of performance* being aimed for over the next two or three periods. Short-range objectives can be identical to long-range objectives if an organization is already performing at the targeted long-term level. For instance, if a company has an ongoing objective of 15 percent profit growth every year and is currently achieving this objective, then the company's long-range and short-range objectives for increasing profits coincide. The most important situation where short-range objectives differ from long-range objectives occurs when managers are trying to elevate organizational performance and cannot reach the long-range target in just one year. Short-range objectives then serve as stairsteps or milestones.

How Much Stretch Should Objectives Entail?

Company performance targets should require *organizational stretch.*

As a starter, objectives should be set high enough to produce outcomes at least incrementally better than current performance. But incremental improvements are not necessarily sufficient, especially if current performance levels are subpar. At a minimum, a company's financial objectives must aim high enough to generate the resources to execute the chosen strategy proficiently. But an "enough-to-get-by" mentality is not appropriate in objective setting. Objectives need to be set high enough to generate period-to-period results that will not only please shareholders and Wall Street but also compare favorably with competitors' performance. Ideally, objectives ought to serve as a managerial tool for truly stretching an organization to reach its full potential; this means setting them high enough to be *challenging*—to energize the organization and its strategy.

One school of thought holds that objectives should be set boldly and aggressively high—above levels that many organizational members would consider realistic. The idea here is that more organizational creativity and energy is unleashed when stretch objectives call for achieving performance levels well beyond the reach of the enterprise's immediate resources and capabilities. One of the most avid practitioners of setting stretch objectives and challenging the organization to go all out to achieve them is General Electric, arguably the world's best-managed corporation. Jack Welch, GE's CEO from 1980 to 2001, believed in setting stretch targets that seemed "impossible" and then challenging the organization to go after them. Throughout the 1960s, 1970s, and 1980s, GE's operating margins hovered around 10 percent and its sales-to-inventory ratio averaged about 5 turns per year. In 1991, Welch set stretch targets for 1995 of at least a 16 percent operating margin and 10 inventory turns. Welch's letter to the shareholders in the company's 1995 annual report said:

> 1995 has come and gone, and despite a heroic effort by our 220,000 employees, we fell short on both measures, achieving a 14.4% operating margin and almost seven turns. But in stretching for these "impossible" targets, we learned to do things faster than we would have going after "doable" goals, and we have enough confidence now to set new stretch targets of at least 16% operating margin and more than 10 turns by 1998.

GE's philosophy is that setting very aggressive stretch targets pushes the organization to move beyond being only as good as what is deemed doable to being as good as it possibly can be. GE's management believes challenging the company to achieve the impossible improves the quality of the organization's effort, promotes a can-do spirit, and builds self-confidence. Hence, a case can be made that objectives ought to be set at levels *above* what is doable with a little extra effort; there's merit in setting stretch targets that require something approaching a heroic degree of organizational effort.

Objectives Are Needed at All Organizational Levels

Objective setting does not stop when company performance targets are agreed on. Company objectives must be broken down into performance targets for each of the organization's separate businesses, product lines, functional areas, and departments. Company objectives are unlikely to be reached without each area of the organization doing its part to contribute to the desired companywide outcomes and results. This means setting strategic and financial objectives for each organization unit that support—rather than conflict with—the achievement of companywide strategic and financial objectives. Consistency between company objectives and the objectives of organizational subunits signals that each part of the organization knows its strategic role and is on board in helping the company move down the chosen strategic path and produce the desired results.

The Need for Top-Down Objective Setting. To appreciate why a company's objective-setting process needs to be more top-down than bottom-up, consider the following example. Suppose the senior executives of a diversified corporation establish a corporate profit objective of $500 million for next year. Suppose further that,

Strategic Management Principle
Objective setting needs to be more of a top-down than a bottom-up process in order to guide lower-level managers and organizational units toward outcomes that support the achievement of overall business and company objectives.

after discussion between corporate management and the general managers of the firm's five different businesses, each business is given a stretch profit objective of $100 million by year-end (i.e., if the five business divisions contribute $100 million each in profit, the corporation can reach its $500 million profit objective). A concrete result has thus been agreed on and translated into measurable action commitments at two levels in the managerial hierarchy. Next, suppose the general manager of business unit X, after some analysis and discussion with functional area managers, concludes that reaching the $100 million profit objective will require selling 1 million units at an average price of $500 and producing them at an average cost of $400 (a $100 profit margin times 1 million units equals $100 million profit). Consequently, the general manager and the manufacturing manager settle on a production objective of 1 million units at a unit cost of $400; and the general manager and the marketing manager agree on a sales objective of 1 million units and a target selling price of $500. In turn, the marketing manager breaks the sales objective of 1 million units into unit sales targets for each sales territory, each item in the product line, and each salesperson. It is logical for organizationwide objectives and strategy to be established first so they can guide objective setting and strategy making at lower levels.

A top-down process of setting companywide performance targets first and then insisting that the financial and strategic performance targets established for business units, divisions, functional departments, and operating units be directly connected to the achievement of company objectives has two powerful advantages: One, it helps produce *cohesion* among the objectives and strategies of different parts of the organization. Two, it helps *unify internal efforts* to move the company along the chosen strategic course. If top management, in the interest of involving a broad spectrum of organizational members, allows objective setting to start at the bottom levels of an organization without the benefit of companywide performance targets as a guide, then lower-level organizational units have no basis for connecting their performance targets to the company's. Bottom-up objective setting, with little or no guidance from above, nearly always signals an absence of strategic leadership on the part of senior executives.

CRAFTING A STRATEGY: THE THIRD DIRECTION-SETTING TASK

Strategies represent management's answers to *how* to achieve objectives and *how* to pursue the organization's business mission and strategic vision. Strategy making is all about *how*—how to achieve performance targets, how to outcompete rivals, how to achieve sustainable competitive advantage, how to strengthen the enterprise's long-term business position, how to make management's strategic vision for the company a reality. A strategy is needed for the company as a whole, for each business the company is in, and for each functional piece of each business.

Strategy making thus entails managerial choices. The hows that comprise the strategy represent organizational commitment to specific competitive approaches and ways of operating—in effect, strategy constitutes management's *business model* for producing good profitability and good business results. Furthermore, strategy is inherently action-oriented; it concerns what to do and when to do it. Unless there is action, unless something happens, unless somebody does something, strategic thinking and planning simply go to waste.

An organization's strategy evolves over time, emerging from the pattern of actions already initiated, the plans managers have for fresh moves, and the ongoing need to react to new or unforeseen developments. The future is too unknowable for management

Basic Concept
An organization's strategy deals with *how* to make management's strategic vision for the company a reality—it represents the game plan for moving the company into an attractive business position and building a sustainable competitive advantage.

to plan a company's strategy in advance and encounter no reason for changing one piece or another of its intended strategy as time passes. In many of today's industries—especially those where technology is advancing rapidly and those involving the Internet—the pace of industry change is intense and sometimes more than a bit chaotic. Industry environments characterized by high-velocity change require rapid strategy adaption.[10] Illustration Capsule 10 describes Bank One's attempt to adapt to high-velocity change and become a leader in online banking.

Reacting to fresh developments in the surrounding environment is thus a normal and necessary part of the strategy-making process. There is always some new strategic window opening up—whether from advancing technology, new competitive developments, budding trends in buyer needs and expectations, unexpected increases or decreases in costs, mergers and acquisitions among major industry players, new regulations, the raising or lowering of trade barriers, or countless other events that make it desirable to alter first one and then another aspect of the present strategy.[11] This is why the task of crafting strategy is neverending. And it is why a company's actual strategy turns out to be a blend of prior actions, managerial plans and intentions, and as-needed reactions to fresh developments.

While most of the time a company's strategy evolves incrementally, there are occasions when a company can function as an industry revolutionary by creating a *rule-breaking* strategy that redefines the industry or how it operates. A strategy can challenge fundamental conventions by reconceiving a product or service (like creating a single-use, disposable cameras or digital cameras), redefining the marketplace, or redrawing industry boundaries. Internet retailers are trying to become *rule-makers* by marketing their products anywhere at any time rather than being restricted to making their products available at particular locations during normal shopping times. Consumers can now get their credit cards from Shell Oil or General Motors or AOL, or have their checking account at Charles Schwab, or get a home mortgage from Merrill Lynch or Mortgage.com, or shop on the Internet instead of going to the mall.[12]

> A company's *actual strategy* usually turns out to be both more and less than the *planned strategy* as new strategy features are added and others are deleted in response to newly emerging conditions.

The Strategy-Making Pyramid

As we emphasized in Chapter 1, strategy making is not just a task for senior executives. In large enterprises, decisions about what business approaches to take and what new moves to initiate involve senior executives in the corporate office, heads of business units and product divisions, the heads of major functional areas within a business or division (manufacturing, marketing and sales, finance, human resources, and the like), plant managers, product managers, district and regional sales managers, and lower-level supervisors. In diversified enterprises, strategies are initiated at four distinct organization levels. There's a strategy for the company and all of its businesses as a whole (*corporate strategy*). There's a strategy for each separate business the company has diversified into (*business strategy*). Then there is a strategy for each specific functional unit within a business (*functional strategy*). Each business usually has a production strategy, a marketing strategy, a finance strategy, and so on. And, finally, there

---

[10]For an excellent treatment of the strategic challenges posed by high-velocity changes, see Shona L. Brown and Kathleen M. Eisenhardt, *Competing on the Edge: Strategy as Structured Chaos* (Boston, MA: Harvard Business School Press, 1998), chapter 1.

[11]Henry Mintzberg and J. A. Waters, "Of Strategies, Deliberate and Emergent," *Strategic Management Journal* 6 (1985), pp. 257–72.

[12]For an in-depth discussion of revolutionary strategies, see Gary Hamel, "Strategy as Revolution," *Harvard Business Review* 74, no. 4 (July–August 1996), pp. 69–82.

illustration capsule 10
Bank One's New Internet Banking Strategy

In 1999, after having acquired over 100 banks during the past 15 years and built an interstate banking franchise spanning 14 states with 1,900 branch offices, Chicago-based Bank One created an independent Internet bank named WingspanBank.com. The new bank operated entirely separately from Bank One and was accessible only on the Internet.

Whereas a number of other banks, such as Wells Fargo and Bank of America, had already created "Internet branches" that allow customers to pay bills and perform certain other banking functions online, Bank One opted for a strategy of creating an altogether independent Internet bank that could distance itself from Bank One and even compete against Bank One in certain areas.

John McCoy, Bank One's CEO, believed that just having a cyberbranch outpost of Bank One was not the optimal strategy for exploiting the opportunities afforded by the Internet because the financial services market was evolving too fast and because outside software and Web site developers build a full-service Internet branch for any bank in about three months for a modest $50,000 fee. McCoy believed that online mutual fund supermarkets, brokerage firms, and mortgage lenders all posed a threat to enter the online banking business and take business away from traditional banking institutions that relied on brick-and-mortar branches, ATMs, and on-site people to deliver

their services. Furthermore, in 1999 Wal-Mart was in the process of seeking approval to acquire a small savings and loan institution that would allow it to offer services ranging from car loans to credit cards in all of its stores.

Bank One's initial strategy for Wingspan included the following elements:

- Creating the capability to approve or reject customer applications for loans in less than a minute.

- Providing credit cards offering a 5 percent discount on purchases from selected Internet retailers, such as Amazon.com.

- Providing free access to Bank One's ATMs and reimbursing customers up to $5 per month for ATM fees incurred at the ATMs of other banks (so that Wingspan customers could get cash out of their accounts). To make deposits, customers had to mail the checks and slips to Wingspan's post office box in Philadelphia. Mailing deposits was considered one of the three biggest impediments to Internet banking—the other two were the difficulty of making cash withdrawals and not being able to talk to banking personnel face-to-face.

- Offering a menu of investments, mortgages, and insurance from companies not affiliated with Bank One. Whereas Bank One customers had online access to 49 mutual funds, Wingspan customers could choose from

(continued)

---

are still narrower strategies for basic operating units—plants, sales districts and regions, and departments within functional areas (*operating strategy*). In single-business enterprises, there are only three levels of strategy making (business strategy, functional strategy, and operating strategy) unless diversification into other businesses becomes an active consideration. Figure 2.1 on page 52 shows the strategy-making pyramids for diversified and single-business companies.

Basic Concept
Corporate strategy concerns how a diversified company intends to establish business positions in different industries and the actions and approaches employed to improve the performance of the group of businesses the company has diversified into.

Corporate Strategy

Corporate strategy is the overall managerial game plan for a diversified company; it extends companywide—an umbrella over all a diversified company's businesses. Corporate strategy consists of the moves made to establish business positions in different industries and the approaches used to manage the company's group of businesses. Figure 2.2 depicts the core elements that identify a diversified company's corporate strategy. Crafting corporate strategy for a diversified company involves four kinds of initiatives:

1. *Making the moves to establish positions in different businesses and achieve diversification*—In a diversified company, a key piece of corporate strategy is how many

illustration capsule 10

(concluded)

7,000 mutual funds. A special search function allowed Wingspan customers to scan the Internet for the lowest available mortgage rate and get an e-mail telling them the location of the best deal. Wingspan customers could also shop the Internet for five different kinds of insurance.

- Spending close to $100 million to promote Wingspan coast-to-coast, including pop-up ads on a wide variety of Internet sites, so as to both attract new customers and establish strong brand-name awareness. Keeping the Wingspan brand separate from the Bank One brand meant that customers would be unaffected by whatever feelings, pro or con, that they had for Bank One. Bank One executives also believed that quickly establishing dominance in Internet banking would give Wingspan/Bank One an important first-mover advantage that would allow it to out-compete later entrants. McCoy believed that there might eventually be as many as 100 Internet banks, that there would be a free-for-all battle for market leadership, and that only the biggest and strongest would capture more than a minuscule market share and end up attractively profitable.

- Creating an advisory board for Wingspan that included a student, a software programmer, and a stay-at-home mother. The iBoard, as it is called, met online as well as in person.

- Using a high-speed transaction-processing system operated by Pennsylvania-based Sanchez Computer Associates to process and account for transactions in real time, as opposed to the catch-up time that Bank One's computers often required. Outsourcing the transaction system also meant that Wingspan did not have to spend months figuring out how to link into Bank One's far-flung and complex data processing system.

- Using the feedback from customers to improve its Web site and alter its product offerings.

In its first two months of operation, Wingspan attracted 75,000 customers, nearly one-third of all customers then claimed by all the existing independent Internet banks—compared to some 9.5 million customers engaged in online banking at the Internet branches of their traditional bank. Wingspan was expected to have 500,000 customers by mid-2000. Although Bank One expects to lose money on Wingspan for the first few years, McCoy stated, "I believe this is a new way to do business, and you'd better get involved in it."

Source: The Wall Street Journal, August 25, 1999, pp. A1, A8.

and what kinds of businesses the company should be in—specifically, what industries to enter and whether to enter the industries by starting a new business or acquiring another company (an established leader, an up-and-coming company, or a troubled company with turnaround potential). This piece of corporate strategy establishes whether diversification is based narrowly in a few industries or broadly in many industries and whether the different businesses will be related or unrelated.

2. *Initiating actions to boost the combined performance of the businesses the firm has diversified into*—As positions are created in the chosen industries, corporate strategy making concentrates on ways to strengthen the long-term competitive positions and profitabilities of the businesses the firm has invested in. Corporate parents can help their business subsidiaries be more successful by financing additional capacity and efficiency improvements, by supplying missing skills and managerial know-how, by acquiring another company in the same industry and merging the two operations into a stronger business, or by acquiring new businesses that strongly complement existing businesses. Management's overall strategy for improving companywide performance usually involves pursuing rapid-growth strategies in the most promising businesses, keeping the other core businesses healthy, initiating turnaround efforts in weak-performing businesses with potential, and divesting businesses that are no longer attractive or that don't fit into the organization's long-range plans.

figure 2.1   **The Strategy-Making Pyramid**

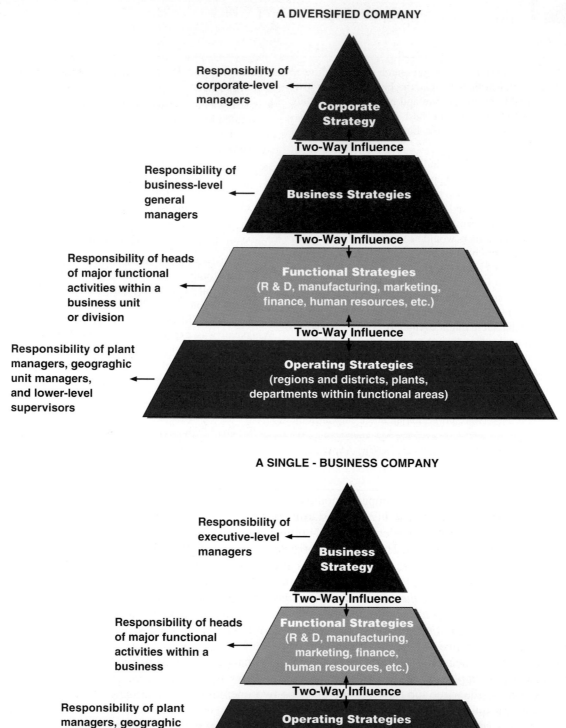

figure 2.2   **Identifying the Overall Corporate Strategy of a Diversified Company**

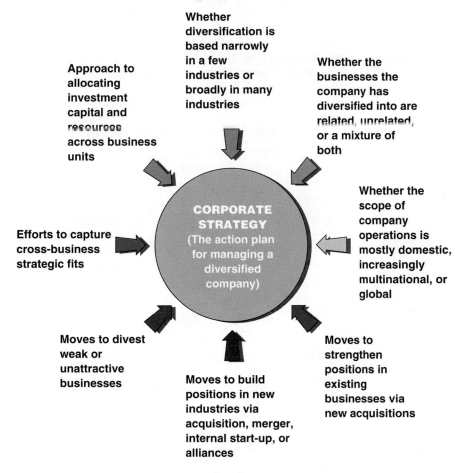

Whether diversification is based narrowly in a few industries or broadly in many industries

Whether the businesses the company has diversified into are related, unrelated, or a mixture of both

Approach to allocating investment capital and resources across business units

Whether the scope of company operations is mostly domestic, increasingly multinational, or global

CORPORATE STRATEGY (The action plan for managing a diversified company)

Efforts to capture cross-business strategic fits

Moves to divest weak or unattractive businesses

Moves to build positions in new industries via acquisition, merger, internal start-up, or alliances

Moves to strengthen positions in existing businesses via new acquisitions

3. *Pursuing ways to capture valuable cross-business strategic fits and turn them into competitive advantage*—When a company diversifies into businesses with related technologies, similar operating characteristics, common distribution channels or customers, or some other synergistic factor, it gains competitive advantage potential not open to a company that diversifies into totally unrelated businesses. When Amazon.com diversified into selling CDs and conducting online auctions, the moves presented opportunities to (*a*) transfer Amazon's skills and expertise in online book sales to online music sales, (*b*) use the same distribution facilities and order fulfillment technology to ship both books and CDs (use of shared facilities and resources meant lower joint costs), (*c*) leverage Amazon's brand name, and (*d*) lay the foundation for Amazon.com to later extend its reach into other product lines and become a one-stop shopping site for online buyers. Such cross-business "strategic fits" strengthen a company's competitiveness and provide a basis for greater profitability.

4. *Establishing investment priorities and steering corporate resources into the most attractive business units*—A diversified company's different businesses are usually not equally attractive from the standpoint of investing additional funds. This facet of corporate strategy making involves channeling resources into areas where earnings potentials

figure 2.3   **Identifying Strategy for a Single Business**

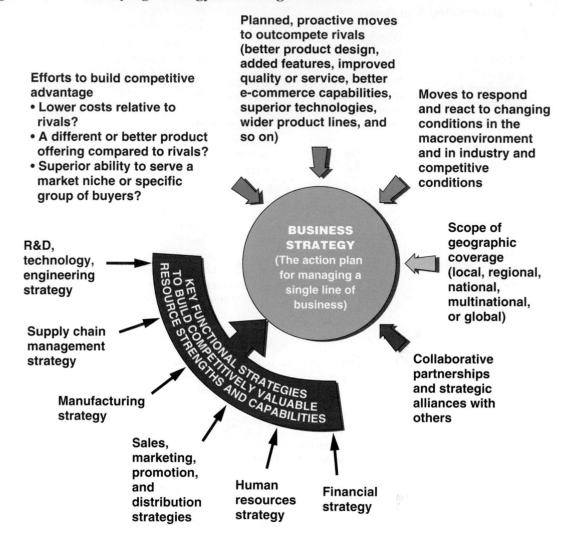

are higher and away from areas where they are lower. Corporate strategy may include divesting business units that are chronically poor performers or those in an increasingly unattractive industry. Divestiture frees up unproductive investments for redeployment to promising business units or for financing attractive new acquisitions.

Corporate strategy is crafted at the highest levels of management. Senior corporate executives normally have lead responsibility for devising corporate strategy and for choosing among whatever recommended actions bubble up from lower-level managers. Key business-unit heads may also be influential, especially in strategic decisions affecting the businesses they head. Major strategic decisions are usually reviewed and approved by the company's board of directors.

Business Strategy

The term **business strategy** (or business-level strategy) refers to the managerial game plan for a single business. It is mirrored in the pattern of approaches and moves crafted by management to produce successful performance in one specific line of business.

Basic Concept
Business strategy concerns the actions and the approaches crafted by management to produce successful performance in one specific line of business; the central business strategy issue is *how* to build a stronger long-term competitive position.

The core elements of business strategy are illustrated in Figure 2.3. For a single-business company, corporate strategy and business strategy are one and the same.

The central thrust of business strategy is *how* to build and strengthen the company's long-term competitive position in the marketplace. Toward this end, business strategy is concerned principally with (1) forming responses to changes under way in the industry, the economy at large, the regulatory and political arena, and other relevant areas; (2) crafting competitive moves and market approaches that can lead to sustainable competitive advantage; (3) building competitively valuable competencies and capabilities; (4) uniting the strategic initiatives of functional departments; and (5) addressing specific strategic issues facing the company's business.

Clearly, business strategy involves initiating whatever actions and responses managers deem prudent in light of competitive forces, economic trends, technological developments, buyer needs and demographics, new legislation and regulatory requirements, and other such broad external factors. *A good strategy is well-matched to a company's external and internal situation;* as the company's situation changes in significant ways, then adjustments in strategy typically are needed. Whether a company's response to changing conditions is quick or slow tends to be a function of how long events must unfold before managers can assess their implications and how much longer it then takes to form a strategic response. Some changes in a company's external and internal environment, of course, require little or no response, while others call for significant strategy alterations. On occasion, situational factors change in ways that pose a formidable strategic hurdle—for example, cigarette and firearms manufacturers face a tough challenge holding their own against the mounting campaigns against smoking and for stricter gun control. Conventional retailers are rushing to establish their own Internet sales capabilities to defend against competition from thousands of enterprising Internet retailers.

What separates a powerful business strategy from a weak one is the strategist's ability to forge a series of moves, both in the marketpace and internally, that are capable of producing *sustainable competitive advantage.* With a competitive advantage, a company has good prospects for above-average profitability and success in the industry. Without competitive advantage, a company risks being locked into mediocre performance. Crafting a business strategy that yields sustainable competitive advantage has three facets: (1) deciding what product/service attributes (lower costs and prices, a better product, a wider product line, superior customer service, emphasis on a particular market niche) offer the best chance to win a competitive edge; (2) developing expertise, resource strengths, and competitive capabilities that set the company apart from rivals; and (3) trying to insulate the business as much as possible from the actions of rivals and other threatening competitive developments.

> A business strategy is powerful if it produces a sizable and sustainable competitive advantage; it is weak if it results in competitive disadvantage.

A company's strategy for competing is typically both offensive and defensive—some actions are aggressive and amount to direct challenges to competitors' market positions; others aim at countering competitive pressures and the actions of rivals. Three of the most frequently used competitive approaches are (1) striving to be the industry's low-cost provider; (2) pursuing such differentiating features as higher quality, added performance, better service, more attractive styling, technological superiority, or unusually good value; and (3) focusing on a narrow market niche and doing a better job than rivals of serving the special needs and tastes of its buyers.

The most successful business strategies typically aim at building *uniquely strong or distinctive competencies* in one or more areas crucial to strategic success and then using them as a basis for winning a competitive edge over rivals. Distinctive competencies can relate to leading-edge product innovation, better mastery of a technological process, expertise in defect-free manufacturing, specialized marketing and merchandising know-how, potent global sales and distribution capability, superior e-commerce capabilities, better customer service, or anything else that constitutes a competitively valuable

> Having superior internal resource strengths and competitive capabilities is an important way to outcompete rivals.

strength in creating, producing, distributing, or marketing the company's product or service.

On a broader internal front, business strategy must also aim at uniting strategic initiatives in the various functional areas of business. Strategic actions are needed in each functional area to *support* the company's competitive approach and overall business strategy. Strategic unity and coordination across the various functional areas add power to the business strategy.

Business strategy also extends to *action plans* for addressing any special strategy-related issues unique to the company's competitive position and internal situation (such as whether to add new capacity, replace an obsolete plant, increase R&D funding for a promising technology, reduce burdensome interest expenses, form strategic alliances and collaborative partnerships, or build competitively valuable competencies and capabilities via the Internet). Such custom tailoring of strategy to fit a company's specific situation is one of the reasons why companies in the same industry employ different business strategies.

Lead responsibility for business strategy falls in the lap of whoever is in charge of the business. Even if the business head does not personally wield a heavy hand in business strategy making, preferring to delegate many strategy particulars to subordinates, he or she is still accountable for the strategy and the results it produces. The business head, as chief strategist for the business, has at least two other responsibilities. The first is seeing that supporting strategies in each of the major functional areas of the business are well conceived and consistent with each other. The second is getting major strategic moves approved by higher authority (the board of directors and/or corporate-level officers) and keeping them informed of important new developments, deviations from plan, and potential strategy revisions. In diversified companies, business-unit heads may have the additional obligation of making sure business-level objectives and strategy conform to corporate-level objectives and strategy themes.

Functional Strategy

Basic Concept
Functional strategy concerns the managerial game plan for running a major functional activity or process within a business—R&D, production, marketing, customer service, distribution, finance, human resources, and so on; a business needs as many functional strategies as it has major activities.

The term **functional strategy** refers to the managerial game plan for a particular functional activity, business process, or key department within a business. A company's marketing strategy, for example, represents the managerial game plan for running the marketing part of the business. A company's new product development strategy represents the managerial game plan for keeping the company's product lineup fresh and in tune with what buyers are looking for. A company needs a functional strategy for every major business activity and organizational unit. Functional strategy, while narrower in scope than business strategy, adds relevant detail to the overall business game plan. It aims at establishing or strengthening specific competencies calculated to enhance the company's market position. Like business strategy, functional strategy must *support* the company's overall business strategy and competitive approach. A related role is to create a managerial road map for achieving the functional area's objectives and mission. Thus, functional strategy in the production/manufacturing area represents the game plan for how manufacturing activities will be managed to support business strategy and achieve the manufacturing department's objectives and mission. Functional strategy in the finance area consists of how financial activities will be managed in supporting business strategy and achieving the finance department's objectives and mission.

Lead responsibility for conceiving strategies for each of the various important business functions and processes is normally delegated to the respective functional department heads and process managers unless the business-unit head decides to exert a strong influence. In crafting strategy, the manager of a particular business function or process ideally works closely with key subordinates and touches base often with the managers of other functions/processes and the business head. If functional or process managers plot strategy independent of each other or the business head, they open the door for uncoordinated or conflicting strategies. Compatible, collaborative, mutually reinforcing functional strategies are essential for the overall business strategy to have maximum impact. Plainly, a business's marketing strategy, production strategy, finance strategy, customer service strategy, new product development strategy, and human resources strategy should be in sync rather than serving their own narrower purposes. Coordination and consistency among the various functional and process strategies are best accomplished during the deliberation stage. If inconsistent functional strategies are sent up the line for final approval, it is up to the business head to spot the conflicts and get them resolved.

Operating Strategy

Operating strategy concerns the even narrower strategic initiatives and approaches for managing key operating units (plants, sales districts, distribution centers) and for handling daily operating tasks with strategic significance (advertising campaigns, materials purchasing, inventory control, maintenance, shipping). A plant manager needs a strategy for accomplishing the plant's objectives, carrying out the plant's part of the company's overall manufacturing game plan, and dealing with any strategy-related problems that exist at the plant. A district sales manager needs a sales strategy customized to the district's particular situation and sales objectives. A company's advertising manager needs a strategy for getting maximum audience exposure and sales impact from the ad budget.

> **Basic Concept**
> *Operating strategy* concerns how to manage front-line organizational units within a business (plants, sales districts, distribution centers) and how to perform strategically significant operating tasks (materials purchasing, inventory control, maintenance, shipping, advertising campaigns).

Operating strategies, while of limited scope, add further detail and completeness to functional strategies and to the overall business plan. Lead responsibility for operating strategies is usually delegated to front-line managers, subject to review and approval by higher-ranking managers.

Even though operating strategy is at the bottom of the strategy-making pyramid, its importance should not be downplayed. Operating-level strategies provide valuable support to higher-level strategies. Consider the case of a distributor of plumbing equipment whose business strategy emphasizes fast delivery and accurate order filling in an effort to deliver better customer service than rivals. In support of this strategy, the firm's warehouse manager (1) develops an inventory stocking strategy that allows 99.9 percent of all orders to be completely filled without back-ordering any item and (2) institutes a warehouse staffing strategy that allows any order to be shipped within 24 hours. Without such operating strategies in place, the plumbing distributor's strategy would fail.

> Front-line managers are an important part of an organization's strategy-making team because many operating units have strategy-critical performance targets and need to have strategic action plans in place to achieve them.

Another instance of the importance of operating strategy occurs in manufacturing companies. A major plant that fails in its strategy to achieve production volume, unit cost, and quality targets can undercut the achievement of company sales and profit objectives and wreak havoc with the whole company's strategic efforts to build a quality image with customers. One cannot reliably judge the strategic importance of a given action by the organizational or managerial level where it is initiated.

Uniting the Strategy-Making Effort

The previous discussion underscores that *a company's strategic plan is a collection of strategies* devised by different managers at different levels in the organizational

A company's strategy is at full power only when its many pieces are united.

Objectives and strategies that are unified from top-to-bottom of the organizational hierarchy do not come from an undirected process where managers at each level have objective-setting and strategy-making autonomy. Cross-unit and top-down coordination is essential.

hierarchy. The larger the enterprise, the more points of strategic initiative it has. Management's direction-setting effort is not complete until the separate layers and pieces of strategy are unified into a coherent, supportive pattern. Ideally the pieces and layers of strategy should fit together like a jigsaw puzzle.

To achieve this unity, the strategizing process has to proceed more from the top down than from the bottom up. Direction and guidance have to flow from the corporate level to the business level and from the business level to the functional and operating levels. *Lower-level managers cannot do good strategy making without understanding the company's long-term direction and higher-level strategies.* The strategic disarray that occurs in an organization when senior managers don't exercise strong top-down direction setting and strategic leadership is akin to what would happen to a football team's offensive performance if the quarterback decided not to call a play for the team but instead let each player pick whatever play he thought would work best at his respective position. In business, as in sports, all the strategy makers in a company are on the same team. They are obligated to perform their strategy-making tasks in a manner that benefits the whole company, not in a manner that suits personal or departmental interests. Indeed, functional and operating-level managers have a duty to set performance targets and invent strategic actions that will help achieve *business* objectives and make *business* strategy more effective.

The larger the company and the more geographically scattered its units and subsidiaries, the more tedious and frustrating the task of harmonizing objectives and strategies piece by piece and level by level. Functional managers are sometimes more interested in doing what is best for their own areas, building their own empires, and consolidating their personal power and organizational influence than they are in cooperating with other functional managers to unify behind the overall business strategy. As a result, it's easy for functional area support strategies to conflict, thereby forcing the business-level general manager to spend time and energy refereeing functional strategy conflicts and building support for a more unified approach. Broad consensus is particularly difficult when there is ample room for opposing views and disagreement.

Figure 2.4 portrays the networking of objectives and strategies through the managerial hierarchy. The two-way arrows indicate that there are simultaneous bottom-up and top-down influences on missions, objectives, and strategies at each level. Furthermore, there are two-way influences across related businesses and across related processes, functions, and operating activities within a business. The tighter that coordination is enforced, the tighter the safeguards against organizational units straying from the company's charted strategic course.

THE FACTORS THAT SHAPE A COMPANY'S STRATEGY

Many situational considerations enter into crafting strategy. Figure 2.5 on page 60 depicts the primary factors that shape a company's strategic approaches. The interplay of these factors and the influence that each has on the strategy-making process vary from situation to situation. Very few strategic choices are made in the same context. Even in the same industry, situational factors differ enough from company to company that the strategies of rivals turn out to be quite distinguishable from one another rather than imitative. This is why carefully sizing up all the various situational factors, both external and internal, is the starting point in crafting strategy.

figure 2.4 **The Networking of Strategic Visions, Missions, Objectives, and Strategies in the Strategy-Making Pyramid**

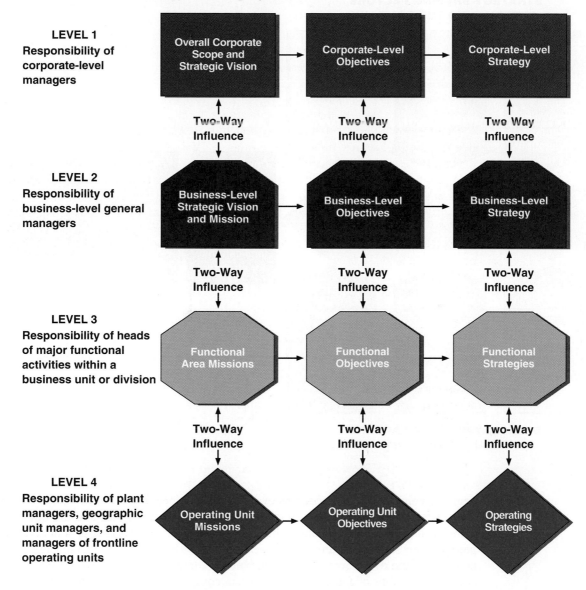

Societal, Political, Regulatory, and Citizenship Considerations

All organizations operate within the broader community of society. What an enterprise can and cannot do strategywise is always constrained by what is legal, by what complies with government policies and regulatory requirements, by what is considered ethical, and by what is in accord with societal expectations and the standards of good community citizenship. Outside pressures also come from other sources—special-interest groups, the glare of investigative reporting, a fear of unwanted political action, and the stigma of

figure 2.5   Factors Shaping the Choice of Company Strategy

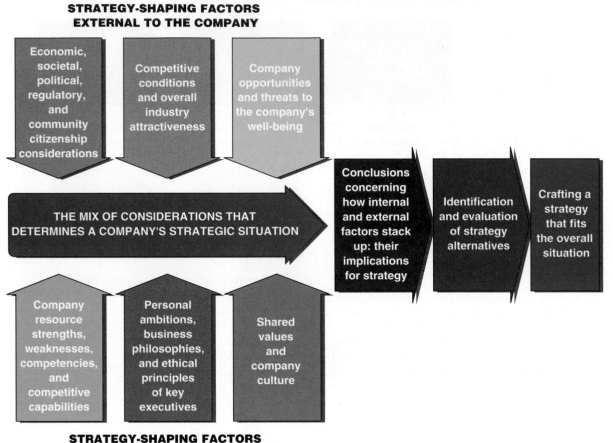

STRATEGY-SHAPING FACTORS
EXTERNAL TO THE COMPANY

Economic, societal, political, regulatory, and community citizenship considerations

Competitive conditions and overall industry attractiveness

Company opportunities and threats to the company's well-being

THE MIX OF CONSIDERATIONS THAT DETERMINES A COMPANY'S STRATEGIC SITUATION

Conclusions concerning how internal and external factors stack up: their implications for strategy

Identification and evaluation of strategy alternatives

Crafting a strategy that fits the overall situation

Company resource strengths, weaknesses, competencies, and competitive capabilities

Personal ambitions, business philosophies, and ethical principles of key executives

Shared values and company culture

STRATEGY-SHAPING FACTORS
INTERNAL TO THE COMPANY

Economic, societal, political, regulatory, and citizenship factors limit the strategic actions a company can or should take.

negative opinion. Societal concerns over gun control, health and nutrition, alcohol and drug abuse, smoking, environmental pollution, sexual harassment, and the impact of plant closings on local communities have caused many companies to temper or revise aspects of their strategies. American concerns over jobs lost to foreign manufacturers and political debate over how to cure the chronic U.S. trade deficit are driving forces in the strategic decisions of Japanese and European companies to locate plants in the United States. Heightened consumer awareness about the hazards of saturated fat and cholesterol have driven most food products companies to phase out high-fat ingredients and substitute low-fat ingredients, despite the extra costs.

Factoring in societal values and priorities, business ethics, community concerns, and the potential for onerous legislation and regulatory requirements is a regular part of external situation analysis at more and more companies. Intense public pressure and adverse media coverage make such a practice prudent. The task of making an organization's strategy socially responsible means (1) conducting organizational activities within the bounds of what is considered ethical and in the general public interest, (2) responding positively to emerging societal priorities and expectations, (3) demonstrating a willingness to take action ahead of regulatory confrontation, (4) balancing stockholder interests against the larger interests of society as a whole, and (5) being a good citizen in the community.

Corporate social responsibility is showing up in company mission statements. John Hancock, for example, concludes its mission statement with the following sentence:

> In all that we do, we exemplify the highest standards of business ethics and personal integrity, and recognize our corporate obligation to the social and economic well-being of our community.

John Hancock goes on to state its commitment to ethical behavior:

> In order to exemplify the highest standards of business ethics, we conduct the Company's affairs in strict compliance with both the letter and the spirit of the law, and will at all times treat policyholders, customers, suppliers, and all others with whom the Company does business fairly and honorably. Recognizing that our reputation of unquestioned integrity and honesty is our most valued asset, under no circumstances will what we achieve be allowed to take precedence over how we achieve it.[13]

At Sempra Energy, a San Diego–based electricity and natural gas company, management has expressed a strong commitment to enhancing the quality of life in the communities where it does business and stated it is not only good business for the company and its employees to be deeply involved in community activities but also "the right thing to do":

> We have a vested interest in ensuring that businesses thrive, community needs are met, the environment is protected, and our diverse human resources are engaged to their fullest potential.
>
> Our main focus is building and maintaining valuable relationships with communities and community leaders in markets where we do business. We also regularly encourage employee leadership and involvement in civic and community affairs, and make charitable contributions to community and civic organizations through both Sempra Energy and its key affiliates.[14]

Competitive Conditions and Overall Industry Attractiveness

An industry's competitive conditions and overall attractiveness are big strategy-determining factors. A company's strategy has to be tailored to the nature and mix of competitive factors in play—price, product quality, performance features, service, warranties, and so on. When competitive conditions intensify significantly, a company must respond with strategic actions to protect its position. Competitive weakness on the part of one or more rivals presents opportunities for a strategic offensive. Furthermore, fresh moves on the part of rival companies, changes in the industry's price-cost-profit economics, shifting buyer needs and expectations, and new technological developments often alter the requirements for competitive success and mandate reconsideration of strategy. The industry environment, as it exists now and is expected to exist later, thus has a direct bearing on a company's best competitive strategy option and where it should concentrate its efforts. *A company's strategy can't produce real market success unless it fits the industry and competitive situation.* When a firm concludes its industry environment has grown unattractive and it is better off investing company resources elsewhere, it may begin a strategy of disinvestment and eventual abandonment. A strategist, therefore, has to be a student of industry and competitive conditions.

Strategic Management Principle
A company's strategy should be tailored to fit industry and competitive conditions.

---

[13]Information posted on the company's Web site (www.johnhancock.com) as of September 1999.

[14]Information posted on the company's Web site (www.sempra.com) as of September 1999.

The Company's Market Opportunities and External Threats

The particular business opportunities open to a company and the threatening external developments that it faces are key influences on strategy. Both point to the need for strategic action. A company's strategy needs to be deliberately aimed at capturing its best growth opportunities, especially the ones that hold the most promise for building sustainable competitive advantage and enhancing profitability. Likewise, strategy should provide a defense against external threats to the company's well-being and future performance. This usually means crafting *offensive* moves to capitalize on the company's most promising market opportunities and crafting *defensive* moves to protect the company's competitive position and long-term profitability. Managers have to scrutinize the kinds of opportunities and threats presented by changes in the marketplace and be prompt and astute in making needed strategic adjustments.

Company Resource Strengths, Competencies, and Competitive Capabilities

One of the most pivotal strategy-shaping internal considerations is whether a company has or can acquire the resources, competencies, and capabilities needed to execute a strategy proficiently. These are the factors that can enable an enterprise to capitalize on a particular opportunity, give the firm a competitive edge in the marketplace, and become a cornerstone of the enterprise's strategy. The best path to competitive advantage is found where a firm has competitively valuable resources and competencies, where rivals do not have matching or offsetting resources and competencies, and where rivals can't develop comparable capabilities except at high cost or over an extended period of time. Intel's long-standing global leadership in microprocessors for PCs, servers, and workstations has much to do with its deep technological expertise, its multibillion-dollar R&D program, its state-of-the-art chip-making plants, and its ability to spend $3–$5 billion annually on new chip-making plants and the latest chip-making equipment. None of its competitors have such depth of resources and capabilities. As a rule, a company's strategy ought to be grounded in its resource strengths and in what it is good at doing (its competencies and competitive capabilities).

Even if a firm lacks competitively superior competencies and capabilities (as, in fact, many do), its managers still must tailor a strategy that fits the enterprise's particular resource strengths and weaknesses. It is foolish to craft a strategy that cannot be executed with the resources and capabilities a firm is able to assemble. And it is foolish to craft a strategy whose success depends on activities which a company performs poorly or has no experience in performing at all.

The Personal Ambitions, Business Philosophies, and Ethical Beliefs of Managers

Managers do not dispassionately assess what strategic course to steer. Their choices are typically influenced by their own vision of how to compete and how to position the enterprise and by what image and standing they want the company to have. Both casual observation and formal studies indicate that managers' ambitions, values, business philosophies, attitudes toward risk, and ethical beliefs have important influences on strategy.[15] Sometimes the influence of a manager's personal values, experiences, and emotions is conscious and deliberate; at other times it may be unconscious. As one expert noted in explaining the relevance of personal factors to strategy, "People have to have their hearts in it."[16]

Several examples of how business philosophies and personal values enter into strategy-making are particularly noteworthy. Ben Cohen and Jerry Greenfield, co-founders and major stockholders in Ben & Jerry's Homemade, Inc., have consistently insisted that the company's strategy incorporate a strong social mission and be supportive of social causes of their choosing. The strategy crafted by Starbucks' CEO, Howard Schultz, mirrors Schultz's insistence on customers having a very positive experience when patronizing a Starbucks store and his desire to "build a company with soul" and make Starbucks a great place to work. Japanese managers are strong proponents of strategies that take a long-term view and that aim at building market share and competitive position.

Attitudes toward risk also have a big influence on strategy. Risk-avoiders are inclined toward "conservative" strategies that minimize downside risk, have a quick payback, and produce sure short-term profits. Risk-takers lean more toward opportunistic strategies where visionary moves can produce a big payoff over the long term. Risk-takers prefer innovation to imitation and bold strategic offensives to defensive moves aimed at protecting the status quo.

Managerial values also shape the ethical quality of a firm's strategy. Managers with strong ethical convictions take pains to see that their companies observe a strict code of ethics in all aspects of the business. They expressly forbid such practices as accepting or giving kickbacks, badmouthing rivals' products, and buying political influence with political contributions. Instances where a company's strategic actions run afoul of high ethical standards include charging excessive interest rates on credit card balances, employing bait-and-switch sales tactics, continuing to market products suspected of having safety problems, and using ingredients that are known health hazards.

> The personal ambitions, business philosophies, and ethical beliefs of managers are usually stamped on the strategies they craft.

The Influence of Shared Values and Company Culture on Strategy

An organization's policies, practices, traditions, philosophical beliefs, and ways of doing things combine to create a distinctive culture. Typically, the stronger a company's culture, the more that culture is likely to shape the company's strategic actions, sometimes even dominating the choice of strategic moves. This is because culture-related values and beliefs are so embedded in management's strategic thinking and actions that they condition how the enterprise does business and responds to external events. Such firms have a culture-driven bias about how to handle strategic issues and what kinds of strategic moves it will consider or reject. Strong cultural influences partly account for why companies gain reputations for such strategic traits as leadership in technology

> A company's values, policies, practices, and culture can dominate the kinds of strategic moves it considers or rejects.

---

[15]The role of personal values, individual ambitions, and managerial philosophies in strategy-making has long been recognized and documented. The classic sources are William D. Guth and Renato Tagiuri, "Personal Values and Corporate Strategy," *Harvard Business Review* 43, no. 5 (September–October 1965), pp. 123–32; Kenneth R. Andrews, *The Concept of Corporate Strategy,* 3rd ed. (Homewood, IL: Richard D. Irwin, 1987), chapter 4; and Richard F. Vancil, "Strategy Formulation in Complex Organizations," *Sloan Management Review* 17, no. 2 (Winter 1986), pp. 4–5.

[16]Andrews, *The Concept of Corporate Strategy,* p. 63.

and product innovation, dedication to superior craftsmanship, a proclivity for financial wheeling and dealing, a desire to grow rapidly by acquiring other companies, having a strong people orientation and being an especially good company to work for, or unusual emphasis on customer service and total customer satisfaction.

In recent years, many companies have articulated the core beliefs, principles, and values underlying their business approaches. One company expressed its values as follows:

> We are market-driven. We believe that functional excellence, combined with teamwork across functions and profit centers, is essential to achieving superb execution. We believe that people are central to everything we will accomplish. We believe that honesty, integrity, and fairness should be the cornerstone of our relationships with consumers, customers, suppliers, stockholders, and employees.

The commitment of Ritz-Carlton Hotels to providing its guests with the finest personal service and facilities—combined with its principles of trust, respect, honesty, integrity—drive its strategy and operating practices. The company's cultural motto is "We are ladies and gentlemen serving ladies and gentlemen." Wal-Mart's founder, Sam Walton, was a fervent believer in frugality, hard work, constant improvement, dedication to customers, and genuine care for employees. The company's commitment to these values is deeply ingrained in its strategy of low prices, good values, friendly service, productivity through the intelligent use of technology, and hard-nosed bargaining with suppliers.[17] At Hewlett-Packard, the company's basic values, known internally as "the HP Way," include sharing the company's success with employees, showing trust and respect for employees, providing customers with products and services of the greatest value, being genuinely interested in providing customers with effective solutions to their problems, making profit a high stockholder priority, avoiding the use of long-term debt to finance growth, individual initiative and creativity, teamwork, and being a good corporate citizen.[18] At both Wal-Mart and Hewlett-Packard, the value systems are deeply ingrained and widely shared by managers and employees. Whenever this happens, values and beliefs are more than an expression of nice platitudes; they become a way of life within the company.[19] Illustration Capsule 11 provides yet another example of the links between vision, values, and strategy.

LINKING STRATEGY WITH ETHICS AND SOCIAL RESPONSIBILITY

Every strategic action a company takes should be ethical.

Strategy ought to be ethical. It should involve rightful actions, not wrongful ones; otherwise it won't pass the test of moral scrutiny. This means more than conforming to what is legal. Ethical and moral standards go beyond the law and the language of "thou shalt not." They address the issues of *duty* and the language of "should do and should not do." Ethics concern human *duty* and the principles on which this duty rests.[20]

---

[17]Sam Walton with John Huey, *Sam Walton: Made in America* (New York: Doubleday, 1992); and John P. Kotter and James L. Heskett, *Corporate Culture and Performance* (New York: Free Press, 1992), pp. 17, 36.

[18]Kotter and Heskett, *Corporate Culture and Performance*, pp. 60–61.

[19]For another example of the impact of values and beliefs, see Richard T. Pascale, "Perspectives on Strategy: The Real Story behind Honda's Success," in Glenn Carroll and David Vogel, *Strategy and Organization: A West Coast Perspective* (Marshfield, MA: Pitman, 1984), p. 60.

[20]Harry Downs, "Business Ethics: The Stewardship of Power," working paper provided to the authors.

illustration capsule 11
How Enron's Vision and Values Shape Its Strategy

Enron is one of the world's largest energy companies with the strategic intent of becoming *the* "blue-chip" electricity and natural gas company of the 21st century. Enron management believes it has the people and the skills in place to widen an already strong competitive advantage, and thinks it would be very difficult, if not impossible, for any other company to replicate its global energy franchise and overall capabilities in the foreseeable future. Management has stated that Enron's core natural gas and electricity businesses are positioned for significant expansion and earnings growth. The following statement of Enron's vision and values illustrates how a company's values, beliefs, and philosophy connect closely to its strategy.

WHAT WE BELIEVE

We begin with a fundamental belief in the inherent wisdom of OPEN MARKETS. Economic activities are better sorted out by markets than they are by governments. We think customers ought to be free to make a choice about buying power and natural gas. We are convinced that consumer choice and competition lead to lower prices and innovation.

Enron is a laboratory for INNOVATION. That's why we employ the best and the brightest people. And we believe that every employee can make a difference here.

We encourage people to make a difference by creating an environment where everyone is allowed to achieve their full potential and where everyone has a stake in the outcome. We think this entrepreneurial approach stimulates CREATIVITY. It calls for new insights, new ways of looking at problems and opportunities, and a strong sense of urgency. This company is all about energy; we want leaders here who create our own brand of energy.

Here we value DIVERSITY. We are committed to removing all barriers to employment and advancement based on sex, sexual orientation, race, religion, age, ethnic background, national origin, or physical limitation. It's only by being able to recruit from a diverse pool of talent that we'll be able to maintain a truly outstanding workforce.

Our success is measured by the success of our CUSTOMERS. We are committed to meeting their energy needs with solutions that offer them a competitive advantage. And we work with them in ways that reinforce the benefits of a long-term partnership with Enron.

In everything we do, we operate safely and with concern for the ENVIRONMENT. The way we do a job will affect how our children and our neighbors' children will live in the future. This is a responsibility we take seriously in all the different places around the world where we do business.

What we do here can CHANGE people's lives in significant ways. We're changing the way energy is delivered, as well as the market for it. We're reinventing the fundamentals of this business by providing energy at lower costs and in more usable forms than it has been provided before. We're even changing the way people think about energy.

Everything we do is about change. So every time you read this, try something different. Change a goal. Change a habit. Change a mind. TOGETHER we're creating the leading energy company in the world. Together, we are defining the energy company of the future.

HOW WE BEHAVE

Respect: We treat others as we would like to be treated ourselves. We do not tolerate abusive or disrespectful treatment. Ruthlessness, callousness, and arrogance don't belong here.

Integrity: We work with customers and prospects openly, honestly, and sincerely. When we say we will do something, we will do it; when we say we cannot or will not do something, then we won't do it.

Communication: We have an obligation to communicate. Here, we take the time to talk with one another . . . and to listen. We believe that information is meant to move and that information moves people.

Excellence: We are satisfied with nothing less than the very best in everything we do. We will continue to raise the bar for everyone. The great fun here will be for all of us to discover just how good we can really be.

Source: Company Web site (www.enron.com) and 1998 company annual report.

Every business has an ethical duty to each of five constituencies: owners/shareholders, employees, customers, suppliers, and the community at large. Each of these constituencies affects the organization and is affected by it. Each is a stakeholder in the enterprise, with certain expectations as to what the enterprise should do and how it should do it.[21] A company has a *duty to owners/shareholders,* for instance, who

---

[21]Ibid.

A company has ethical duties to owners, employees, customers, suppliers, the communities where it operates, and the public at large.

rightly expect a return on their investment. Even though investors may individually differ in their preferences for profits now versus profits later, their tolerances for greater risk, and their enthusiasm for exercising social responsibility, business executives have a moral duty to pursue profitable management of the owners' investment.

A company's *duty to employees* arises out of respect for the worth and dignity of individuals who devote their energies to the business and who depend on the business for their economic well-being. Principled strategy making requires that employee-related decisions be made equitably and compassionately, with concern for due process and for the impact that strategic change has on employees' lives. At best, the chosen strategy should promote employee interests as concerns compensation, career opportunities, job security, and overall working conditions. At worst, the chosen strategy should not disadvantage employees. Even in crisis situations, businesses have an ethical duty to minimize whatever hardships have to be imposed in the form of workforce reductions, plant closings, job transfers, relocations, retraining, and loss of income.

The *duty to the customer* arises out of expectations that attend the purchase of a good or service. Inadequate appreciation of this duty led to product liability laws and a host of regulatory agencies to protect consumers. All kinds of strategy-related ethical issues still abound, however. Should a seller voluntarily inform consumers that its product contains ingredients that, though officially approved for use, are suspected of having potentially harmful effects? Is it ethical for the makers of alcoholic beverages to sponsor college events, given that many college students are under 21? Is it ethical for cigarette manufacturers to advertise at all (even though it is legal)? Is it ethical to short-circuit product testing in order to rush new products to market? Is it ethical for manufacturers to stonewall efforts to recall products they suspect have faulty parts or defective designs? Is it ethical for supermarkets and department store retailers to lure customers with highly advertised "loss-leader" prices on a few select items, but then put high markups on popular or essential items?

Recently, a certain company's chief technology officer helped choose an Internet start-up company's products over that of rivals; the Internet company showed its gratitude by granting the officer rights to purchase 250 shares when the Internet company subsequently went public. The officer bought the shares at the initial offering price of $23; the stock closed at $84 at the end of the first day's trading, kept rising, then split—ultimately giving the officer a profit of about $58,000 when the officer sold the shares several months later. Is it ethical for a company to give gifts to individuals in customer companies when those individuals have had an influential role in selecting the company's products over those of its rivals? Is it ethical for the makers of athletic apparel and equipment to make substantial payments to college coaches in return for having the school's athletic teams wear their apparel or use their equipment?

A company's ethical *duty to suppliers* arises out of the market relationship that exists between them. They are both partners and adversaries. They are partners in the sense that the quality of suppliers' parts affects the quality of a firm's own product and in the sense that their businesses are connected. They are adversaries in the sense that the supplier wants the highest price and profit it can get while the buyer wants a cheaper price, better quality, and speedier service. A company confronts several ethical issues in its supplier relationships. Is it ethical to purchase goods from foreign suppliers who employ child labor, pay substandard wages, or have sweatshop working conditions in their facilities? Is it ethical for supermarket chains to demand "slotting fees" from food suppliers in return for placing their items in favorable shelf locations? Is it ethical to threaten to cease doing business with a supplier unless the supplier agrees not to do business with key competitors? Is it ethical to reveal one supplier's price quote to a rival supplier? Is it ethical to accept an offer to vacation at a supplier's beach house? Is it ethical to pay a supplier in cash? Is it ethical *not* to give present suppliers advance warning of the intent to discontinue using what they have supplied and to switch to components supplied by other enterprises?

A company's ethical *duty to the community at large* stems from its status as a member of the community and as an institution of society. Communities and society are reasonable in expecting businesses to be good citizens—to pay their fair share of taxes for fire and police protection, waste removal, streets and highways, and so on, and to exercise care in the impact their activities have on the environment, on society, and on the communities in which they operate. For example, is it ethical for a brewer of beer to advertise its products on TV at times when these ads are likely to be seen by underage viewers? (Anheuser-Busch responded to such concerns in late 1996, announcing it would no longer run its beer commercials on MTV.) Is it ethical for the manufacturers of firearms to encourage retired policemen and police departments to trade in or return automatic weapons whose manufacture has since been banned by Congress so they can gain access to a supply of resaleable weapons (a loophole in the laws allow them to traffic in such weapons that were manufactured prior to the bans)? Is it ethical for firearms makers to make just enough changes in the designs of their automatic weapons to escape the bans and prohibitions on automatic firearms instituted by Congress? Some years ago, an oil company was found to have spent $2 million on environmental conservation and $4 million advertising its virtue and good deeds—actions that seem deliberately manipulative and calculated to mislead.

A company's community citizenship is ultimately demonstrated by whether it refrains from acting in a manner contrary to the well-being of society and by the degree to which it supports community activities, encourages employees to participate in community activities, handles the health and safety aspects of its operations, accepts responsibility for overcoming environmental pollution, relates to regulatory bodies and employee unions, and exhibits high ethical standards. European consumer goods company Diageo PLC—the maker of Guinness beers and over 50 brands of liquors and wines sold across Europe and the United States—states that it has "a particular responsibility to encourage responsible use of alcohol as part of a healthy lifestyle. [We] are proud of the unique part that alcohol plays in the social lives and celebrations of many cultures. We also recognize that alcohol can be misused, and Diageo will be at the forefront of campaigns to promote moderate and sensible consumption."[22]

Living Up to Ethical Responsibilities A management that truly cares about business ethics and corporate social responsibility is proactive rather than reactive in linking strategic action and ethics.[23] It steers away from ethically or morally questionable business opportunities and business practices. And it goes to considerable lengths to ensure that its actions reflect integrity and high ethical standards. If any of a company's constituencies conclude that management is not measuring up to ethical standards, they have recourse. Concerned investors can protest at the annual shareholders' meeting, appeal to the board of directors, or sell their stock. Concerned employees can unionize and bargain collectively, or they can seek employment elsewhere. Customers can switch to competitors. Suppliers can find other buyers. The community and society

---

[22]Quoted from information appearing on the company's Web site (www.diageo.com) as of August 1999.

[23]Joseph L. Badaracco, "The Discipline of Building Character," *Harvard Business Review* 76, no. 2 (March–April 1998), pp. 115–24.

illustration capsule 12

The Kroger Company's Commitments to Its Stakeholders

Kroger, one of the leading supermarket chains in the United States, has committed itself to pursuing its mission in a manner that satisfies its responsibilities to shareowners, employees, customers, suppliers, and the communities it serves. Company documents state:

> Our mission is to be a leader in the distribution and merchandising of food, health, personal care, and related consumable products and services. In achieving this objective, we will satisfy our responsibilities to shareowners, employees, customers, suppliers, and the communities we serve.
>
> We will conduct our business to produce financial returns that reward investment by shareowners and allow the Company to grow. Investments in retailing, distribution and food processing will be continually evaluated for their contribution to our corporate return objectives.
>
> We will constantly strive to satisfy consumer needs better than the best of our competitors. Operating

procedures will reflect our belief that the organizational levels closest to the consumer are best positioned to respond to changing consumer needs.

> We will treat our employees fairly and with respect, openness and honesty. We will solicit and respond to their ideas and reward meaningful contributions to our success.
>
> We value America's diversity and will strive to reflect that diversity in our workforce, the companies with whom we do business, and customers we serve. As a company, we will convey respect and dignity to each individual.
>
> We will encourage our employees to be active, responsible citizens and will allocate researchers for activities that enhance the quality of life for our customers, our employees, and the communities we serve.

Source: Company Web site (www.kroger.com).

can do anything from staging protest marches and urging boycotts to stimulating political and governmental action.[24]

Illustration Capsule 12 indicates how the Kroger Company intends to satisfy its responsibilities to shareowners, employees, customers, suppliers, and the communities it serves.

TESTS OF A WINNING STRATEGY

What are the criteria for weeding out candidate strategies? How can a manager judge which strategic option is best for the company? What are the standards for determining whether a strategy is successful or not? Three tests can be used to evaluate the merits of one strategy over another:

1. *The Goodness of Fit Test*—A good strategy has to be well matched to industry and competitive conditions, market opportunities and threats, and other aspects of the enterprise's external environment. At the same time, it has to be tailored to the company's resource strengths and weaknesses, competencies, and competitive capabilities. Unless a strategy exhibits tight fit with a company's external situation

---

[24]Downs, "Business Ethics: The Stewardship of Power."

and internal circumstances, it is suspect and likely to produce less than the best possible business results.

2. *The Competitive Advantage Test*—A good strategy leads to sustainable competitive advantage. The bigger the competitive edge that a strategy helps build, the more powerful and effective it is.

3. *The Performance Test*—A good strategy boosts company performance. Two kinds of performance improvements are the most telling of a strategy's caliber: gains in profitability and gains in the company's competitive strength and long-term market position.

Strategic options that clearly come up short on one or more of these tests should be dropped from further consideration. The strategic option that best meets all three tests can be regarded as the best or most attractive strategic alternative. Once a strategic commitment is made and enough time elapses to see results, these same tests can be used to determine whether the chosen strategy qualifies as a winning strategy.

There are, of course, some additional criteria for judging the merits of a particular strategy: completeness and coverage of all the bases, internal consistency among all the pieces of strategy, clarity, the degree of risk involved, and flexibility. These criteria are useful supplements and certainly ought to be looked at, but they can in no way replace the three tests posed above.

> **Strategic Management Principle**
> The more a strategy fits the enterprise's external and internal situation, builds sustainable competitive advantage, and improves company performance, the more it qualifies as a winner.

key|points

Management's direction-setting tasks involve (1) charting a company's future strategic path, (2) setting objectives, and (3) crafting a strategy. Early on in the direction-setting process, managers need to address the question "What is our business and what will it be?" Management's views and conclusions about the organization's future course, the market position it should try to occupy, and the business activities to be pursued constitute a *strategic vision* for the company. A strategic vision indicates management's aspirations for the organization, providing a panoramic view of "what businesses we want to be in, where we are headed, and the kind of company we are trying to create." It spells out a direction and describes the destination. Effective visions are clear, challenging, and inspiring; they prepare a firm for the future, and they make sense in the marketplace. A well-conceived, well-worded mission/vision statement helps managers manage—serving as a beacon of the enterprise's long-term direction, helping channel organizational efforts and strategic initiatives along the path management has committed to following, building a strong sense of organizational identity and purpose, and creating employee buy-in.

The second direction-setting task is to establish *strategic* and *financial objectives* for the organization to achieve. Objectives convert the mission statement and strategic vision into specific performance targets. The agreed-on objectives need to spell out precisely how much by when, and they need to require a significant amount of organizational stretch. Objectives are needed at all organizational levels.

The third direction-setting step entails *crafting a strategy* to achieve the objectives set in each area of the organization. A corporate strategy is needed to achieve corporate-level objectives; business strategies are needed to achieve business-unit performance objectives; functional strategies are needed to achieve the performance targets set for each functional department; and operating-level strategies are needed to achieve the objectives set in each operating and geographic unit. In effect, an organization's strategic plan is a collection of unified and interlocking strategies. Typically, the strategy-making task is more top-down than bottom-up. Lower-level strategies should contribute to the achievement of higher-level, companywide objectives.

Strategy is shaped by both external and internal considerations. The major external considerations are societal, political, regulatory, and community factors; competitive conditions and overall industry attractiveness; and the company's market opportunities and threats. The primary internal considerations are company strengths, weaknesses, and competitive capabilities; managers' personal ambitions, philosophies, and ethics; and the company's culture and shared values. A good strategy must be well matched to all these situational considerations. In addition, a good strategy must lead to sustainable competitive advantage and improved company performance.

suggested|readings

Badaracco, Joseph L. "The Discipline of Building Character," *Harvard Business Review* 76, no. 2 (March–April 1998), pp. 115–24.

Brown, Shona L., and Kathleen M. Eisenhardt. *Competing on the Edge: Strategy as Structured Chaos.* Boston, MA: Harvard Business School Press, 1998.

Campbell, Andrew, and Laura Nash. *A Sense of Mission: Defining Direction for the Large Corporation.* Reading, MA: Addison-Wesley, 1993.

Collins, James C., and Jerry I. Porras. "Building Your Company's Vision." *Harvard Business Review* 74, no. 5 (September–October 1996), pp. 65–77.

Collins, Jim. "Turning Goals into Results: The Power of Catalytic Mechanisms." *Harvard Business Review* 77, no. 4 (July–August 1999), pp. 70–82.

Drucker, Peter. "The Theory of the Business." *Harvard Business Review* 72, no. 5 (September–October 1994), pp. 95–104.

Hamel, Gary. "Strategy as Revolution." *Harvard Business Review* 74 no. 4 (July–August 1996), pp. 69–82.

Hamel, Gary, and C. K. Prahalad. "Strategic Intent." *Harvard Business Review* 67, no. 3 (May–June 1989), pp. 63–76.

———. "Strategy as Stretch and Leverage." *Harvard Business Review* 71, no. 2 (March–April 1993), pp. 75–84.

Hammer, Michael, and James Champy. *Reengineering the Corporation.* New York: Harper Business, 1993, chapter 9.

Ireland, R. Duane, and Michael A. Hitt. "Mission Statements: Importance, Challenge, and Recommendations for Development." *Business Horizons* (May–June 1992), pp. 34–42.

Kahaner, Larry. "What You Can Learn from Your Competitors' Mission Statements." *Competitive Intelligence Review* 6, no. 4 (Winter 1995), pp. 35–40.

Kaplan, Robert S., and David P. Norton. "The Balanced Scorecard—Measures That Drive Performance." *Harvard Business Review* 70, no. 1 (January–February 1992), pp. 71–79.

Lipton, Mark. "Demystifying the Development of an Organizational Vision." *Sloan Management Review,* Summer 1996, pp. 83–92.

McTavish, Ron. "One More Time: What Business Are You In?" *Long Range Planning* 28, no. 2 (April 1995), pp. 49–60.

Mintzberg, Henry. "Crafting Strategy." *Harvard Business Review* 65, no. 4 (July–August 1987), pp. 66–77.

Mintzberg, Henry; Bruce Ahlstrand; and Joseph Lampel. *Strategy Safari: A Guided Tour through the Wilds of Strategic Management.* New York: Free Press, 1998.

Porter, Michael E. "Clusters and the New Economics of Competition," *Harvard Business Review* 76, no. 6 (November–December 1998), pp. 77–90.

———. "What Is Strategy?" *Harvard Business Review* 74, no. 6 (November–December 1996), pp. 65–67.

Shaw, Gordon; Robert Brown; and Philip Bromiley."Strategic Stories: How 3M Is Rewriting Business Planning." *Harvard Business Review* 76, no. 3 (May–June 1998), pp. 41–50.

Tichy, N. M.; A. R. McGill; and L. St. Clair. *Corporate Global Citizenship.* San Francisco: New Lexington Press, 1997.

Wilson, Ian "Realizing the Power of Strategic Vision." *Long Range Planning* 25, no. 5 (1992), pp. 18–28.

chapter | three 3   Industry and Competitive Analysis

Analysis is the critical starting point of strategic thinking.
—Kenichi Ohmae

Things are always different—the art is figuring out which differences matter.
—Laszlo Birinyi

Awareness of the environment is not a special project to be undertaken only when warning of change becomes deafening.
—Kenneth R. Andrews

It is not the strongest of the species that survive, nor the most intelligent, but the one most responsive to change.
—Charles Darwin

C rafting strategy is not a task in which managers can get by with opinions, good instincts, and creative thinking. Judgments about what strategy to pursue need to flow directly from *solid analysis* of a company's external environment and internal situation. The two most important situational considerations are (1) industry and competitive conditions and (2) a company's own competitive capabilities, resources, internal strengths and weaknesses, and market position.

All organizations operate in a *macroenvironment* consisting broadly of the economy at large, population demographics, societal values and lifestyles, governmental legislation and regulation, technological factors, and the company's immediate industry and competitive environment—as depicted in Figure 3.1. The

macroenvironment includes *all relevant forces* outside a company's boundaries—relevant in the sense that they are important enough to have a bearing on the decisions a company ultimately makes about its business model and strategy. While many forces in the macroenvironment are beyond a company's sphere of influence, company managements are nonetheless obliged to monitor them and adapt the company's strategy as may be needed. The forces in a company's macroenvironment having the biggest impact on a company's strategy, however, typically revolve around the company's immediate industry and competitive environment.

Figure 3.2 illustrates what is involved in sizing up a company's overall situation and deciding on a strategy. The analytical sequence is from strategic appraisal of the company's external and internal situation, to evaluation of alternatives, to choice of strategy. Accurate diagnosis of the company's situation is necessary managerial preparation for deciding on a sound long-term direction, setting appropriate objectives, and crafting a winning strategy. Without perceptive understanding of the strategic aspects of a company's external and internal environments, the chances are greatly increased

Managers are not prepared to decide on a long-term direction or a strategy until they have a keen understanding of the company's strategic situation— the exact nature of the industry and competitive conditions it faces and how these conditions match up with its resources and capabilities.

that managers will concoct a strategic game plan that doesn't fit the situation well, that holds little prospect for building competitive advantage, and that is unlikely to boost company performance.

This chapter examines the techniques of *industry and competitive analysis,* the term commonly used to refer to assessing the most strategically relevant aspects of a single-business company's macroenvironment. In Chapter 4, we'll cover the methods of *company situation analysis* and explore how to appraise the strategy-shaping aspects of a firm's internal environment and current market position.

---

figure 3.1   **A Company's Macroenvironment**

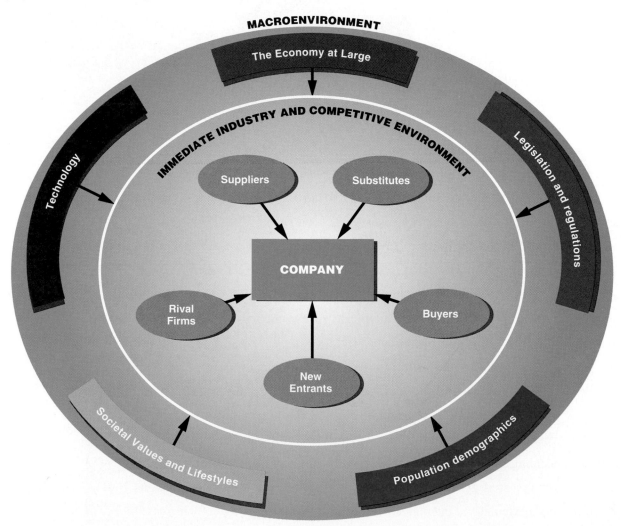

figure 3.2 **How Strategic Thinking and Strategic Analysis Lead to Good Strategic Choices**

THINKING STRATEGICALLY ABOUT INDUSTRY AND COMPETITIVE CONDITIONS

The Key Questions

1. What are the industry's dominant economic features?
2. What is competition like and how strong are each of the competitive forces?
3. What is causing the industry's competitive structure and business environment to change?
4. Which companies are in the strongest/weakest positions?
5. What strategic moves are rivals likely to make next?
6. What are the key factors for competitive success?
7. Is the industry attractive and what are the prospects for above-average profitability?

THINKING STRATEGICALLY ABOUT A COMPANY'S OWN SITUATION

The Key Questions

1. How well is the company's present strategy working?
2. What are the company's strengths, weaknesses, opportunities, and threats?
3. Are the company's prices and costs competitive?
4. How strong is the company's competitive position?
5. What strategic issues does the company face?

WHAT STRATEGIC OPTIONS DOES THE COMPANY REALISTICALLY HAVE?

- Is it locked in to improving the present strategy or is there room to make major strategy changes?

WHAT IS THE BEST STRATEGY?

The Key Criteria

- Does it have good fit with the company's situation?
- Will it help build a competitive advantage?
- Will it help improve company performance?

THE METHODS OF INDUSTRY AND COMPETITIVE ANALYSIS

Industries differ widely in their economic characteristics, competitive situations, and future profit prospects. The economic and competitive character of the trucking industry bears little resemblance to that of discount retailing. The economic and competitive traits of the fast-food business have little in common with those of Internet service providers. The cable TV business is shaped by industry and competitive considerations radically different from those that dominate the soft-drink business.

The economic character of industries varies according to such factors as overall size and market growth rate, the pace of technological change, the geographic boundaries of the market (which can extend from local to worldwide), the number and size of buyers and sellers, whether sellers' products are virtually identical or highly differentiated, the extent to which costs are affected by economies of scale, and the types of distribution channels used to access buyers. Competitive forces can be moderate in one industry and fierce, even cutthroat, in another. Moreover, in some industries competition focuses on who has the best price, while in others competition is centered on quality and reliability (as in monitors for PCs and laptops) or product features and performance (as in digital cameras) or quick service and convenience (as in online shopping and fast foods) or brand reputation (as in laundry detergents, soft drinks, and beer). In other industries, the challenge is for companies to work cooperatively with suppliers, customers, and maybe even select competitors to create the next round of product innovations and open up whole new vistas of market opportunities (as we are witnessing in wireless telecommunications and personal computers).

An industry's economic traits and competitive conditions, and how they are expected to change, determine whether its profit prospects are poor, average, or excellent. Industry and competitive conditions differ so much that leading companies in unattractive industries can find it hard to earn respectable profits, while even weak companies in attractive industries can turn in good performances.

Industry and competitive analysis uses a tool kit of concepts and techniques to get a clear fix on key industry traits, the intensity of competition, the drivers of industry change, the market positions and strategies of rival companies, the keys to competitive success, and the industry's profit outlook. This tool kit provides a way of thinking strategically about any industry's overall situation and drawing conclusions about whether the industry represents an attractive investment for company funds. The analysis entails examining a company's business in the context of a much wider environment. Industry and competitive analysis aims at developing insightful answers to seven questions:

1. What are the industry's dominant economic features?
2. What is competition like and how strong are each of the competitive forces?
3. What is causing the industry's competitive structure and business environment to change?
4. Which companies are in the strongest/weakest positions?
5. What strategic moves are rivals likely to make next?
6. What are the key factors for competitive success?
7. Is the industry attractive and what are the prospects for above-average profitability?

The answers to these questions build understanding of a firm's surrounding environment and, collectively, form the basis for matching its strategy to changing industry conditions and competitive realities.

QUESTION 1: WHAT ARE THE INDUSTRY'S DOMINANT ECONOMIC FEATURES?

Because industries differ significantly in their basic character and structure, industry and competitive analysis begins with an overview of the industry's dominant economic features. Our working definition of the word *industry* is "a group of firms whose products have so many of the same attributes that they compete for the same buyers." The factors to consider in profiling an industry's economic features are fairly standard:

- Market size.
- Scope of competitive rivalry (local, regional, national, international, or global).
- Market growth rate and position in the business life (early development, rapid growth and takeoff, early maturity, maturity, saturation and stagnation, decline).
- Number of rivals and their relative sizes—is the industry fragmented into many small companies or concentrated and dominated by a few large companies?
- The number of buyers and their relative sizes.
- Whether and to what extent industry rivals have integrated backward and/or forward.
- The types of distribution channels used to access consumers.
- The pace of technological change in both production process innovation and new product introductions.
- Whether the products and services of rival firms are highly differentiated, weakly differentiated, or essentially identical.
- Whether companies can realize economies of scale in purchasing, manufacturing, transportation, marketing, or advertising.
- Whether key industry participants are clustered in a particular location—the world's best-known cluster locations include Silicon Valley, Hollywood, Italy (for the leather fashion industry), the wineproducing regions of California and France, and New York City (for financial services).[1]
- Whether certain industry activities are characterized by strong learning and experience effects ("learning by doing") such that unit costs decline as *cumulative* output grows.
- Whether high rates of capacity utilization are crucial to achieving low-cost production efficiency.
- Capital requirements and the ease of entry and exit.
- Whether industry profitability is above/below par.

Table 3.1 provides a sample profile of the economic character of the sulfuric acid industry, using the factors (or variations of them) listed above.

An industry's economic features are important because of the implications they have for strategy. For example, in capital-intensive industries where investment in a single plant can run several hundred million dollars, a firm can spread the burden of high fixed costs by pursuing a strategy that promotes high utilization of fixed assets to generate more revenue per dollar of fixed-asset investment. Thus, commercial airlines

> An industry's economic features help frame the window of strategic approaches a company can pursue.

---

[1]For more details on the competitive relevance of clustering, see Michael E. Porter, "Clusters and the New Economics of Competition," *Harvard Business Review* 76, no. 6 (November–December 1998), pp. 77–90.

table 3.1 A Sample Profile of the Dominant Economic Characteristics of the Sulfuric Acid Industry

Market size: $400-$500 million annual revenues; 4 million tons total volume.

Scope of competitive rivalry: Primarily regional; producers rarely sell outside a 250-mile radius of plant due to high cost of shipping long distances.

Market growth rate: 2–3 percent annually.

Stage in life cycle: Mature.

Number of companies in industry: About 30 companies with 110 plant locations and capacity of 4.5 million tons. Market shares of rivals range from a low of 3 percent to a high of 21 percent.

Customers: About 2,000 buyers; most are industrial chemical firms.

Degree of vertical integration: Mixed; 5 of the 10 largest companies are integrated backward into mining operations and also forward in that sister industrial chemical divisions buy over 50 percent of the output of their plants; all other companies are engaged solely in the production of sulfuric acid.

Ease of entry/exit: Moderate entry barriers exist in the form of capital requirements to construct a new plant of minimum efficient size (cost equals $10 million) and ability to build a customer base inside a 250-mile radius of plant.

Technology/innovation: Production technology is standard and changes have been slow; biggest changes are occurring in products using sulfuric acid—1–2 newly formulated specialty chemicals products with sulfuric acid as one of the ingredients are being introduced annually, accounting for nearly all of industry growth.

Product characteristics: Highly standardized; the products of different producers are essentially identical (buyers perceive little real difference from seller to seller except as may relate to time of delivery).

Scale economies: Moderate; all companies have virtually equal manufacturing costs but scale economics exist in shipping in multiple carloads to the same customer and in purchasing large quantities of raw materials.

Learning and experience effects: Not a factor in this industry.

Capacity utilization: Manufacturing efficiency is highest between 90 and 100 percent of rated capacity; below 90 percent utilization, unit costs run significantly higher.

Industry profitability: Subpar to average; the commodity nature of the industry's product results in intense price-cutting when demand slackens, but prices strengthen during periods of strong demand. Profits track the strength of demand for the industry's products.

Basic Concept
When strong economies of learning and experience result in declining unit costs as cumulative production volume builds, a strategy to become the largest-volume manufacturer can yield the competitive advantage of being the industry's lowest-cost producer.

employ strategies to boost the revenue productivity of their multimillion-dollar jets by cutting ground time at airport gates (to get in more flights per day with the same plane) and by using multitiered price discounts to fill up otherwise empty seats on each flight. In industries characterized by one product advance after another, companies must spend enough time and money on R&D to match their technical prowess and innovative capability with that of competitors. A strategy of continuous product innovation becomes a condition of survival.

In industries like semiconductors, strong *learning/experience* effects in manufacturing cause unit costs to decline about 20 percent each time *cumulative* production volume doubles. In other words, if the first 1 million chips may cost $100 each to produce, but by the time the company reaches a production volume of 2 million the chips would cost $80 each to produce (80 percent of $100), by a production volume of 4 million each chip would cost $64 to produce (80 percent of $80), and so on. When an industry is characterized by sizable economies of experience in its manufacturing operations, a company that initiates production of a new-style product and develops a

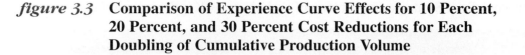

figure 3.3   **Comparison of Experience Curve Effects for 10 Percent, 20 Percent, and 30 Percent Cost Reductions for Each Doubling of Cumulative Production Volume**

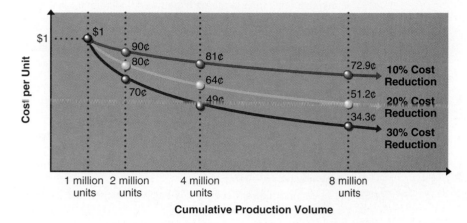

successful strategy to capture the largest market share gains sustainable competitive advantage as the low-cost producer.[2] The bigger the experience curve effect, the bigger the cost advantage of the company with the largest cumulative production volume, as shown in Figure 3.3.

Table 3.2 presents some additional examples of how an industry's economic traits are relevant to managerial strategy making.

QUESTION 2: WHAT IS COMPETITION LIKE AND HOW STRONG ARE EACH OF THE COMPETITIVE FORCES?

One important component of industry and competitive analysis involves delving into the industry's competitive process to discover what the main sources of competitive pressure are and how strong each competitive force is. This analytical step is essential because managers cannot devise a successful strategy without in-depth understanding of the industry's competitive character.

The Five Forces of Competition

Even though competitive pressures in various industries are never precisely the same, the competitive process works similarly enough to use a common analytical framework in gauging the nature and intensity of competitive forces. As Professor Michael

---

[2]There are a large number of studies of the size of the cost reductions associated with experience; the median cost reduction associated with a doubling of cumulative production volume is approximately 15 percent, but there is a wide variation from industry to industry. For a good discussion of the economies of experience and learning, see Pankaj Ghemawat, "Building Strategy on the Experience Curve," *Harvard Business Review* 64, no. 2 (March–April 1985), pp. 143–49.

table 3.2   Examples of the Strategic Importance of an Industry's Key Economic Features

Economic Feature	Strategic Importance
• Market size	• Small markets don't tend to attract big/new competitors; large markets often draw the interest of companies looking to acquire competitors with established positions in attractive industries.
• Market growth rate	• Fast growth breeds new entry; growth slowdowns spawn increased rivalry and a shake-out of weak competitors.
• Capacity surpluses or shortages	• Surpluses push prices and profit margins down; shortages pull them up.
• Industry profitability	• High-profit industries attract new entrants; depressed conditions encourage exit.
• Entry/exit barriers	• High barriers protect positions and profits of existing firms; low barriers make existing firms vulnerable to entry.
• Cost and importance of product	• More buyers will shop for lowest price on big-ticket items than on less important or expensive items.
• Standardized products	• Buyers have more power because it is easier to switch from seller to seller.
• Rapid technological change	• Raises risk factor; equipment and facilities may become obsolete before they wear out.
• Capital requirements	• Big requirements make investment decisions critical and create a barrier to entry and exit; timing becomes important.
• Vertical integration	• Raises capital requirements; often creates competitive differences and cost differences among fully versus partially versus nonintegrated firms.
• Economies of scale	• Increases volume and market share needed to be cost competitive.
• Rapid product innovation	• Shortens product life cycle; increases risk because of opportunities for rivals to bring out next-generation products quicker and leapfrog current market leader.

Porter of the Harvard Business School has convincingly demonstrated, the state of competition in an industry is a composite of *five competitive forces:*[3]

1. The rivalry among competing sellers in the industry.
2. The potential entry of new competitors.
3. The market attempts of companies in other industries to win customers over to their own *substitute* products.
4. The competitive pressures stemming from supplier–seller collaboration and bargaining.
5. The competitive pressures stemming from seller–buyer collaboration and bargaining.

Porter's *five-forces model,* depicted in Figure 3.4, is a powerful tool for systematically diagnosing the principal competitive pressures in a market and assessing how strong and important each one is. Not only is it the most widely used technique of competition analysis, but it is also relatively easy to understand and apply.

---

[3]For a thorough treatment of the five-forces model by its originator, see Michael E. Porter, *Competitive Strategy: Techniques for Analyzing Industries and Competitors* (New York: Free Press, 1980), chapter 1.

figure 3.4 **The Five-Forces Model of Competition: A Key Analytical Tool for Diagnosing the Competitive Environment**

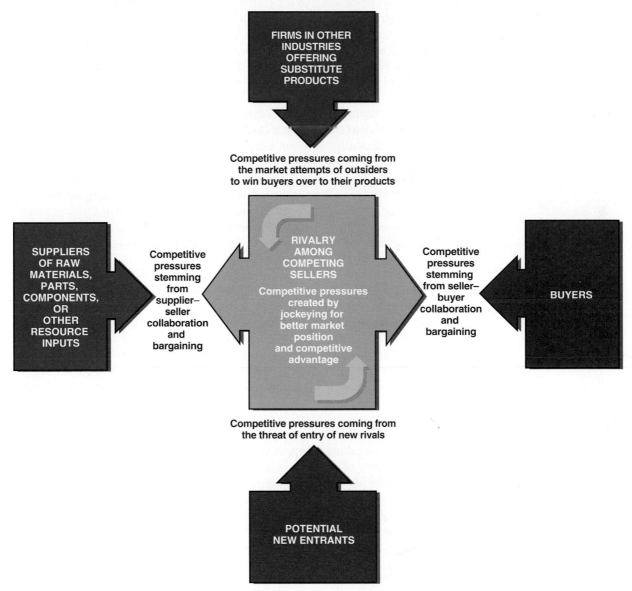

Source: Adapted from Michael E. Porter, "How Competitive Forces Shape Strategy," *Harvard Business Review* 57, no. 2 (March–April 1979), pp. 137–45.

The Rivalry among Competing Sellers   The strongest of the five competitive forces is *usually* the jockeying for position and buyer favor that goes on among rival sellers of a product or service. In some industries, cross-company rivalry is centered on price competition—competing to offer buyers the best (lowest) price is typical among Internet retailers and the sellers of such standard commodities as nails, plywood, sugar, printer paper, and gasoline. Occasionally, price competition can be so lively that market prices temporarily fall below unit costs, forcing losses on some or most rivals. In other industries, price competition is minimal to moderate and rivalry is focused on one or more of the following: offering buyers the most attractive combination of performance features (as occurs in digital cameras), being first to market with innovative products, outcompeting rivals with higher-quality or more durable products, offering buyers longer warranties (as in motor vehicles and replacement tires), providing superior after-the-sale service, or creating a stronger brand image (as in beer, cigarettes, bottled water, electronic brokerage, and quick-service restaurants).

Competitive jockeying among cross-company rivals can heat up when a competitor sees an opportunity to better please customers or is under pressure to improve its market share or profitability. *The intensity of rivalry among competing sellers is a function of how vigorously they employ such tactics as lower prices, snazzier features, expanded customer services, longer warranties, special promotions, and new product introductions.* Rivalry can range from friendly to cutthroat, depending on how frequently and how aggressively companies undertake fresh moves that threaten rivals' profitability. Ordinarily, industry rivals are clever at adding new wrinkles to their product offerings that enhance buyer appeal, and they persist in trying to exploit weaknesses in each other's market approaches.

Irrespective of whether rivalry is lukewarm or heated, every company is challenged to craft a successful strategy for competing—ideally, one that *produces a competitive edge over rivals* and strengthens its position with buyers. The big complication in most industries is that *the success of any one firm's strategy hinges on what strategies its rivals employ and the resources rivals are willing and able to put behind their strategic efforts.* The "best" strategy for one firm depends, in other words, on the competitive capabilities and strategies of rival companies. Such interdependence means that whenever one firm makes a strategic move, its rivals often retaliate with offensive or defensive countermoves.

This pattern of action and reaction makes competitive rivalry a "war-games" type of contest conducted in a market setting according to the rules of fair competition. Indeed, from a strategy-making perspective, *competitive markets are economic battlefields,* with the intensity of cross-company rivalry ebbing and flowing as competitors initiate fresh offensive and defensive maneuvers and as they endeavor to catch buyers' attention with first one mix of weapons (price, performance features, customer service, and other appealing attributes) and then another. Cross-company rivalry is thus dynamic. The current competitive scene is ever-changing as companies act and react, sometimes in rapid-fire order and sometimes methodically, to outcompete one another and build customer loyalty.

Regardless of the industry, several common factors seem to influence the tempo of cross-company rivalry:[4]

1. *Rivalry intensifies as the number of competitors increases and as competitors become more equal in size and capability.* Competition is not as strong in PC operating systems, where Linux is one of the few challengers to Microsoft, as it is in fast foods and restaurants, where buyers have many choices. Up to a point, the greater the number of competitors, the greater the probability of fresh, creative strategic initiatives. In addition, when rivals are nearly equal in size and capability, they can usually

Principle of Competitive Markets

Competitive jockeying among rival firms is a dynamic, ever-changing process as new offensive and defensive moves are initiated and emphasis swings from one blend of competitive weapons and tactics to another.

---

[4]These indicators of what to look for in evaluating the intensity of intercompany rivalry are based on Porter, *Competitive Strategy,* pp. 17–21.

compete on a fairly even footing, making it harder for one or two firms to win the competitive battle and dominate the market.

2. *Rivalry is usually stronger when demand for the product is growing slowly.* In a rapidly expanding market, there tends to be enough business for everybody to grow. Indeed, it may take all of a firm's financial and managerial resources just to keep abreast of the growth in buyer demand, let alone steal rivals' customers. But when growth slows or when market demand drops unexpectedly, expansion-minded firms and/or firms with excess capacity often cut prices and deploy other sales-increasing tactics, thereby igniting a battle for market share that can result in a shake-out of the weak and less efficient firms. The industry then consolidates into a smaller, but individually stronger, number of sellers.

3. *Rivalry is more intense when industry conditions tempt competitors to use price cuts or other competitive weapons to boost unit volume.* When a product is perishable, seasonal, or costly to hold in inventory, or when demand slacks off, competitive pressures build quickly anytime one or more firms decide to cut prices and dump excess supplies on the market. Likewise, whenever fixed costs account for a large fraction of total cost such that unit costs tend to be lowest at or near full capacity, then firms come under significant pressure to cut prices or otherwise try to boost sales. Unused capacity imposes a significant cost-increasing penalty because there are fewer units carrying the fixed-cost burden. In such cases, if market demand weakens or capacity utilization for some reason falls off, the pressure of rising unit costs can push rival firms into secret price concessions, special discounts, rebates, and other sales-increasing tactics, thus heightening competition.

4. *Rivalry is stronger when customers' costs to switch brands are low.* The lower the costs of switching, the easier it is for a rival seller to raid another seller's customers. High buyer switching costs, however, give sellers a more protected customer base and work against the efforts of rivals to promote brand switching among buyers.

5. *Rivalry is stronger when one or more competitors are dissatisfied with their market position and launch moves to bolster their standing at the expense of rivals.* Firms that are losing ground or in financial trouble often react aggressively by acquiring smaller rivals, introducing new products, boosting advertising, discounting prices, and so on. Such actions heighten cross-company rivalry and can trigger a hotly contested battle for market share.

6. *Rivalry increases in proportion to the size of the payoff from a successful strategic move.* The greater the benefits of going after a new opportunity, the more likely that one or more rivals will initiate moves to capture it. Competitive pressures nearly always intensify when several rivals start pursuing the same opportunity. For example, competition in online music sales is heating up with the entry of Amazon.com, barnesandnoble.com, Buy.com. Furthermore, the size of the strategic payoff can vary with the speed of retaliation. When competitors respond slowly (or not at all), the initiator of a fresh competitive strategy can reap benefits in the intervening period and perhaps gain a first-mover advantage that is not easily surmounted. The greater the benefits of moving first, the more likely some competitor will accept the risk and try it.

7. *Rivalry tends to be more vigorous when it costs more to get out of a business than to stay in and compete.* The higher the exit barriers (and thus the more costly it is to abandon a market), the stronger the incentive for existing rivals to remain and compete as best they can, even though they may be earning low profits or even incurring losses.

8. *Rivalry becomes more volatile and unpredictable the more diverse competitors are in terms of their visions, strategic intents, objectives, strategies, resources, and* *countries of origin.* A diverse group of sellers often contains one or more mavericks willing to rock the boat with unconventional moves and "rule-breaking" market approaches, thus generating a livelier and less predictable competitive environment. Globally competitive markets often contain rivals with different views about where the industry is headed and a willingness to employ perhaps radically different competitive approaches. Attempts by cross-border rivals to gain stronger footholds in each other's domestic markets usually boost the intensity of rivalry, especially when the aggressors have lower costs or products with more attractive features. For instance, Motorola has recently faced vigorous competition in cell phones from Europe-based Nokia and Ericcson, largely because these two companies bet on different cell phone technologies than Motorola and because, unlike Motorola, they moved aggressively to make their cell phones work on both analog and digital wireless systems.

9. *Rivalry increases when strong companies outside the industry acquire weak firms in the industry and launch aggressive, well-funded moves to transform their newly acquired competitors into major market contenders.* A concerted effort to turn a weak rival into a market leader nearly always entails launching well-financed strategic initiatives to dramatically improve the competitor's product offering, excite buyer interest, and win a much bigger market share—actions that, if successful, put added pressure on rivals to counter with fresh strategic moves of their own.

Two facets of rivalry need to be underscored. First, a powerful, successful competitive strategy employed by one rival greatly intensifies the competitive pressures on other rivals. Second, the frequency and vigor with which rivals use any and all competitive weapons at their disposal are major determinants of whether the competitive pressures associated with rivalry are cutthroat, fierce, strong, moderate, or weak. Rivalry can be characterized as *cutthroat* or *brutal* when competitors engage in protracted price wars or habitually employ other aggressive tactics that are mutually destructive to profitability. Rivalry can be considered *fierce* to *strong* when competitors are initiating frequent moves and countermoves in a battle for market share so vigorous that profit margins are being squeezed. Rivalry can be characterized as *moderate* when sellers are active in using the various weapons of competition at their command yet are still usually able to earn acceptable profits. Rivalry is *weak* when most companies in the industry are relatively well satisfied with their sales growth and market shares, rarely make concerted attempts to steal customers away from one another, and have comparatively attractive earnings and returns on investment.

The Potential Entry of New Competitors   New entrants to a market bring new production capacity, the desire to establish a secure place in the market, and sometimes substantial resources with which to compete.[5] Just how serious the competitive threat of entry is in a particular market depends on two classes of factors: *barriers to entry* and *the expected reaction of incumbent firms to new entry.* A barrier to entry exists whenever it is hard for a newcomer to break into the market or economic factors put a potential entrant at a disadvantage relative to its competitors. There are several types of entry barriers:[6]

- *Economies of scale*—Scale economies deter entry because they force potential competitors either to enter on a large scale (a costly and perhaps risky move) or to

---

[5]Michael E. Porter, "How Competitive Forces Shape Strategy," *Harvard Business Review* 57, no. 2 (March–April 1979), p. 138.

[6]Porter, *Competitive Strategy,* pp. 7–17.

accept a cost disadvantage and consequently lower profitability. Trying to overcome the disadvantages of small size by entering on a large scale at the outset can result in long-term overcapacity problems for the new entrant (until sales volume builds up), and it can so threaten the market shares of existing firms that they retaliate aggressively (with price cuts, increased advertising and sales promotion, and similar blocking actions) to maintain their positions. Either way, a potential entrant is discouraged by the prospect of lower profits. Entrants may encounter scale-related barriers not just in production but in advertising, marketing and distribution, financing, after-sale customer service, raw materials purchasing, and R&D as well.

- *Cost and resource disadvantages independent of size*—Existing firms may have cost and resource advantages not available to potential entrants. These advantages can include partnerships with the best and cheapest suppliers of raw materials and components, possession of patents and proprietary technology, existing plants built and equipped years earlier at lower costs, favorable locations, and lower borrowing costs.

- *Learning and experience curve effects*—When lower unit costs are partly or mostly a result of experience in producing the product and other learning curve benefits, new entrants face a potentially significant cost disadvantage competing against existing firms with more accumulated know-how.

- *Inability to match the technology and specialized know-how of firms already in the industry*—Successful entry may require technological capability not readily available to a newcomer or skills and know-how not easily learned by a newcomer. Key patents can effectively bar entry, as can lack of technically skilled personnel and an inability to execute complicated manufacturing techniques. Existing firms often carefully guard the know-how that gives them an edge in technology and manufacturing capability. Unless new entrants can gain access to such proprietary knowledge, they cannot compete on a level playing field.

- *Brand preferences and customer loyalty*—Buyers are often attached to established brands. Japanese consumers, for example, are fiercely loyal to Japanese brands of motor vehicles, electronics products, cameras, and film. European consumers have traditionally been loyal to European brands of major household appliances. High brand loyalty means that a potential entrant must commit to building a network of distributors and dealers, and then be prepared to spend enough money on advertising and sales promotion to overcome customer loyalties and build its own clientele. Establishing brand recognition and building customer loyalty can be a slow and costly process. In addition, if it is difficult or costly for a customer to switch to a new brand, a new entrant must persuade buyers that its brand is worth the switching costs. To overcome the switching-cost barrier, new entrants may have to offer buyers a discounted price or an extra margin of quality or service. All this can mean lower expected profit margins for new entrants—something that increases the risk to start-up companies dependent on sizable, early profits to support their new investments.

- *Capital requirements*—The larger the total dollar investment needed to enter the market successfully, the more limited the pool of potential entrants. The most obvious capital requirements are associated with manufacturing plants and equipment, working capital to finance inventories and customer credit, introductory advertising and sales promotion to establish a clientele, and cash reserves to cover start-up losses.

- *Access to distribution channels*—In the case of consumer goods, a potential entrant may face the barrier of gaining adequate access to consumers. Wholesale distributors may be reluctant to take on a product that lacks buyer recognition. A network of retail dealers may have to be set up from scratch. Retailers have to be convinced to give a new brand ample display space and an adequate trial period. The more existing producers tie up present distribution channels, the tougher entry will be. To overcome this barrier, potential entrants may have to "buy" distribution access by offering better margins to dealers and distributors or by giving advertising allowances and other promotional incentives. As a consequence, a potential entrant's profits may be squeezed unless and until its product gains enough acceptance that distributors and retailers want to carry it.

- *Regulatory policies*—Government agencies can limit or even bar entry by requiring licenses and permits. Regulated industries like cable TV, telecommunications, electric and gas utilities, radio and television broadcasting, liquor retailing, and railroads entail government-controlled entry. In international markets, host governments commonly limit foreign entry and must approve all foreign investment applications. Stringent government-mandated safety regulations and environmental pollution standards are entry barriers because they raise entry costs.

- *Tariffs and international trade restrictions*—National governments commonly use tariffs and trade restrictions (antidumping rules, local content requirements, and quotas) to raise entry barriers for foreign firms and protect domestic producers from competition. In 1996, due to tariffs imposed by the South Korean government, a Ford Taurus cost South Korean car buyers over $40,000. The government of India has required that 90 percent of the parts and components used in Indian truck assembly plants be made in India. And to protect European chip makers from low-cost Asian competition, European governments instituted a rigid formula for calculating floor prices for computer memory chips.

Whether an industry's entry barriers ought to be considered high or low depends on the resources and competencies possessed by the pool of potential entrants. Entry barriers can be formidable for start-up enterprises trying to compete against well-established companies. But interested outsiders may, given their resources, competencies, and brand-name recognition, see the industry's entry barriers as relatively easy to hurdle. Likewise, entry barriers may be low for current industry participants that are looking to enter areas of the overall market where they do not yet have a presence. A company already well-established in one market segment or geographic area may possess the resources, competencies, and competitive capabilities to hurdle the barriers of entering a different market segment or new geographic area. In evaluating the potential threat of entry, management must look at (1) how formidable the entry barriers are for each type of potential entrant—start-up enterprises, candidate companies in other industries, and current industry participants looking to expand their market reach—and (2) how attractive the profit prospects are for new entrants. *High profits act as a magnet to firms outside the industry, motivating potential entrants to commit the resources needed to hurdle entry barriers.*[7]

---

[7]When profits are sufficiently attractive, entry barriers are unlikely to be an effective entry deterrent. At most, they limit the pool of candidate entrants to enterprises with the requisite competencies and resources and with the creativity to fashion a strategy for competing with incumbent firms. For a good discussion of this point, see George S. Yip, "Gateways to Entry," *Harvard Business Review* 60, no. 5 (September–October 1982), pp. 85–93.

Even if a potential entrant has or can acquire the needed competencies and resources to attempt entry, it still faces the issue of how existing firms will react.[8] Will incumbent firms offer only passive resistance, or will they aggressively defend their market positions using price cuts, increased advertising, product improvements, and whatever else they can to give a new entrant (as well as other rivals) a hard time? A potential entrant can have second thoughts when financially strong incumbent firms send clear signals that they will stoutly defend their market positions against newcomers. A potential entrant may also turn away when incumbent firms can leverage distributors and customers to retain their business.

The best test of whether potential entry is a strong or weak competitive force in the marketplace is to ask if the industry's growth and profit prospects are attractive enough to induce additional entry. When the answer is no, potential entry is a weak competitive force. When the answer is yes and there are entry candidates with sufficient expertise and resources, then potential entry adds significantly to competitive pressures in the marketplace. The stronger the threat of entry, the more that incumbent firms are driven to fortify their positions against newcomers, endeavoring not only to protect their market shares but also to make entry more costly or difficult.

One additional point: *the threat of entry changes as the industry's prospects grow brighter or dimmer and as entry barriers rise or fall.* For example, the expiration of a key patent can greatly increase the threat of entry. A technological discovery can create an economy-of-scale advantage where none existed before or, alternatively, make it easier for newcomers to gain a market foothold—the Internet, for example, is making it much easier for new e-commerce retailers to compete against some of the strongest and best-known retail chains. New actions by incumbent firms to greatly bolster their e-commerce capabilities, increase advertising, strengthen distributor–dealer relations, step up R&D, or improve product quality can raise the roadblocks to entry. In international markets, entry barriers for foreign-based firms fall as tariffs are lowered, as host governments open up their domestic markets to outsiders, as domestic wholesalers and dealers seek out lower-cost foreign-made goods, and as domestic buyers become more willing to purchase foreign brands.

> **Principle of Competitive Markets**
> The threat of entry is stronger when entry barriers are low, when there's a sizable pool of entry candidates, when incumbent firms are unable or unwilling to vigorously contest a newcomer's efforts to gain a market foothold, and when a newcomer can expect to earn attractive profits.

Competitive Pressures from Substitute Products   Firms in one industry are quite often in close competition with firms in another industry because their respective products are good substitutes. The producers of eyeglasses compete with the makers of contact lenses and with eye specialists who perform laser surgery to correct vision problems. The sugar industry competes with companies that produce artificial sweeteners and high-fructose corn syrup. Cotton and wool producers are in head-on competition with the makers of polyester fabrics. Companies providing electric power are in competition with companies providing natural gas for such purposes as cooking, space heating, and water heating. Aspirin manufacturers compete against the makers of acetaminophen, ibuprofen, and other pain relievers. Newspapers are in competition with television in providing late-breaking news and with Internet sources in providing sports results, stock quotes, and job opportunities. E-mail is a substitute for the overnight document delivery services of FedEx, Airborne Express, and the U.S. Postal Service. Just how strong the competitive pressures are from substitute products depends on three factors: (1) whether attractively priced substitutes are available; (2) whether buyers view the substitutes as being satisfactory in terms of quality, performance, and other relevant attributes; and (3) whether buyers can switch to substitutes easily.

---

[8]Porter, "How Competitive Forces Shape Strategy," p. 140, and Porter, *Competitive Strategy,* pp. 14–15.

The presence of readily available and attractively priced substitutes creates competitive pressure by placing a ceiling on the prices an industry can charge for its product without giving customers an incentive to switch to substitutes and risking sales erosion.[9] This price ceiling, at the same time, puts a lid on the profits that industry members can earn unless they find ways to cut costs. When substitutes are cheaper than an industry's product, industry members come under heavy competitive pressure to reduce their prices and find ways to absorb the price cuts with cost reductions.

The availability of substitutes inevitably invites customers to compare quality, features, performance, ease of use, and other attributes as well as price. For example, ski boat manufacturers are experiencing strong competition from personal water-ski craft because water sports enthusiasts are finding that personal water-skis have exciting performance features that make them satisfying substitutes. The users of glass bottles and jars constantly weigh the performance trade-offs with plastic containers, paper cartons, and metal cans. Competition from substitute products pushes industry participants to heighten efforts to convince customers their product has attributes that are superior to those of substitutes.

Another determinant of the strength of competition from substitutes is how difficult or costly it is for the industry's customers to switch to a substitute.[10] Typical switching costs include extra price premiums, the costs of additional equipment, the time and cost in testing the quality and reliability of the substitute, the psychic costs of severing old supplier relationships and establishing new ones, payments for technical help in making the changeover, and employee retraining costs. If switching costs are high, sellers of substitutes must offer a major cost or performance benefit in order to entice the industry's customers away. When switching costs are low, it's much easier for sellers of substitutes to convince buyers to change over to their products.

As a rule, then, the lower the price of substitutes, the higher their quality and performance, and the lower the user's switching costs, the more intense the competitive pressures posed by substitute products. Good indicators of the competitive strength of substitute products are the rate at which their sales and profits are growing, the market inroads they are making, and their plans for expanding production capacity.

Competitive Pressures Stemming from Supplier Bargaining Power and Supplier-Seller Collaboration
Whether supplier–seller relationships represent a weak or strong competitive force depends on (1) whether suppliers can exercise sufficient bargaining power to influence the terms and conditions of supply in their favor, and (2) the extent of supplier–seller collaboration in the industry.

How Supplier Bargaining Power Can Create Competitive Pressures
Suppliers have little or no bargaining power or leverage over rivals whenever the items they provide are commodities available on the open market from numerous suppliers with ample capability to fill orders.[11] In such cases, it is relatively simple for rivals to obtain whatever is needed from any of several capable suppliers, perhaps dividing their purchases among two or more suppliers to promote lively competition for orders. Commodity product suppliers have market power only when supplies become quite tight and users are so anxious to secure what they need that they agree to terms more favorable to suppliers.

Principle of Competitive Markets
The competitive threat posed by substitute products is strong when substitutes are readily available and attractively priced, buyers believe substitutes have comparable or better features, and buyers' switching costs are low.

---

[9]Porter, "How Competitive Forces Shape Strategy," p. 142; and Porter, *Competitive Strategy,* pp. 23–24.

[10]Porter, *Competitive Strategy,* p. 10.

[11]Ibid., pp. 27–28.

Suppliers are likewise relegated to a weak bargaining position whenever there are good substitutes for the item they provide and buyers find it neither costly nor difficult to switch their purchases to the suppliers of alternative items. For example, soft-drink bottlers can counter the bargaining power of aluminum can suppliers on price or delivery by promoting greater use of plastic containers and introducing more attractive plastic container designs.

Suppliers also tend to have less leverage to bargain over price and other terms of sale when the company they are supplying is a *major customer.* In such cases, the well-being of suppliers is closely tied to the well-being of their major customers. Suppliers then have a big incentive to protect and enhance their customers' competitiveness via reasonable prices, exceptional quality, and ongoing advances in the technology of the items supplied.

In contrast, companies may have little bargaining power with *major suppliers.* Consider Intel's position as the world's dominant supplier of microprocessors for PCs. The microprocessor is not only an essential component but also a big part of the cost of a PC, as much as 20 percent in the case of chips for high-performance PCs. It thus matters a great deal to PC makers (and to PC buyers) whether Intel's price for its latest microprocessor chip is $600 or $300 and whether a chip of comparable quality and performance is available from Advanced Micro Devices (AMD), Intel's leading rival. When suppliers provide an item that accounts for a sizable fraction of the costs of an industry's product, is crucial to the industry's production process, or significantly affects the quality of the industry's product, suppliers have considerable influence on the competitive process. This is particularly true when a few large companies control most of the available supplies and have pricing leverage (as in microprocessors for PCs). Likewise, a supplier (or group of suppliers) possesses more bargaining leverage the more difficult or costly it is for users to switch to alternate suppliers. Big suppliers with good reputations and growing demand for their output are harder to wring concessions from than struggling suppliers striving to broaden their customer base or more fully utilize their production capacity.

Suppliers are also more powerful when they can supply a component more cheaply than industry members can make it themselves. For instance, most producers of outdoor power equipment (lawn mowers, rotary tillers, snowblowers, and so on) find it cheaper to source the small engines they need from outside manufacturers rather than make their own because the quantity they need is too little to justify the investment, master the process, and capture scale economies. Specialists in small-engine manufacture, by supplying many kinds of engines to the whole power equipment industry, obtain a big enough sales volume to fully realize scale economies, become proficient in all the manufacturing techniques, and keep costs well below what power equipment firms could realize making the items in-house. Small-engine suppliers, then, are in a position to price the item below what it would cost the user to self-manufacture but far enough above their own costs to generate an attractive profit margin. In such situations, the bargaining position of suppliers is strong *until* the volume of parts a user needs becomes large enough for the user to justify backward integration into self-manufacture of the component. Then the balance of power shifts from suppliers to users. The more credible the threat of such backward integration into the suppliers' business becomes, the more leverage users have in negotiating favorable terms with suppliers.

Another instance in which the relationship between industry members and suppliers is a notable competitive force is when suppliers, for one reason or another, do not have the capability or the incentive to provide items of high or consistent quality. For

Principle of Competitive Markets

The suppliers to a group of rival firms are a strong competitive force whenever they have sufficient bargaining power to put certain rivals at a competitive disadvantage based on the prices they can command, the quality and performance of the items they supply, or the reliability of their deliveries.

example, if a manufacturer's suppliers provide components that have a relatively high defect rate or that fail prematurely, they can so increase the warranty and defective goods costs of the manufacturer that its profits, reputation, and competitive position are seriously impaired.

How Collaborative Partnerships between Sellers and Suppliers Can Create Competitive Pressures   In more and more industries, rival sellers are electing to form long-term strategic partnerships and close working relationships with select suppliers in order to (1) promote just-in-time deliveries and reduced inventory and logistics costs, (2) speed the availability of next-generation components, (3) enhance the quality of the parts and components being supplied and reduce defect rates, and (4) reduce the supplier's costs and pave the way for lower prices on the items supplied. Such benefits can translate into competitive advantage for industry members who do the best job of managing supply chain relationships and form effective collaborative partnerships with suppliers.

Dell Computer has used strategic partnering with key suppliers as a major element in its strategy to be the world's low-cost supplier of branded PCs, servers, and workstations. Because Dell has managed its supply chain relationships in ways that contribute to a low-cost/high-quality competitive edge over rivals in components supply, Dell has put enormous competitive pressure on its PC rivals to try to imitate its supply chain management practices or else run the risk of being at a serious competitive disadvantage. Effective supply chain partnerships on the part of one or more industry rivals can thus become a major source of competitive pressure for other rivals.

Competitive Pressures Stemming from Buyer Bargaining Power and Seller–Buyer Collaboration
Whether seller–buyer relationships represent a weak or strong competitive force depends on (1) whether buyers have sufficient bargaining power to influence the terms and conditions of sale in their favor and (2) the extent and competitive importance of seller–buyer strategic partnerships in the industry.

How Buyer Bargaining Power Can Create Competitive Pressures   Just as with suppliers, the leverage that buyers have in negotiating favorable terms can range from strong to weak. Buyers have substantial bargaining leverage in a number of situations.[12] The most obvious is when buyers are large and purchase a sizable percentage of the industry's output. Typically, purchasing in large quantities gives a buyer enough leverage to obtain price concessions and other favorable terms.

Large retail chains like Wal-Mart, Circuit City, and The Home Depot typically have considerable negotiating leverage in purchasing products from manufacturers because of manufacturers' need for broad retail exposure and favorable shelf space for their products. Retailers may stock one or even several brands but rarely all available brands, so competition among rival manufacturers for the business of popular or high-volume retailers gives such retailers significant bargaining leverage. In the United States and Britain, supermarket chains have sufficient leverage to require food products manufacturers to make lump-sum payments to gain shelf space for new products. Motor vehicle manufacturers have significant bargaining power in negotiating to buy original equipment tires not only because they buy in large quantities but also because tire makers believe they gain an advantage in supplying replacement tires to vehicle owners if their tire brand is original equipment on the vehicle. "Prestige" buyers have

---

[12]Ibid., pp. 24–27.

a degree of clout in negotiating with sellers because a seller's reputation is enhanced by having prestige buyers on its customer list.

Even if buyers do not purchase in large quantities or offer a seller important market exposure or prestige, they may still have some degree of bargaining leverage in the following circumstances:

- *If buyers' costs of switching to competing brands or substitutes are relatively low*—Buyers who have the flexibility to fill their needs by switching brands or sourcing from several sellers often have negotiating room with sellers. When the products of rival sellers are virtually identical, it is relatively easy for buyers to switch from seller to seller at little or no cost and anxious sellers may be willing to make concessions to win a buyer's business. However, if the products of rival sellers are strongly differentiated, buyers may be less able to switch without incurring sizable changeover costs; an alert seller may conclude, often correctly, that the customer is locked in to using its product and therefore may not be inclined to make any substantive concessions.

  > High switching costs create buyer lock-in and weaken a buyer's bargaining power.

- *If the number of buyers is small or if a customer is particularly important to a seller*—The smaller the number of buyers, the less easy it is for sellers to find alternatives when a customer is lost. The prospect of losing a customer not easily replaced often makes a seller more willing to grant concessions of one kind or another.

- *If buyers are well-informed about sellers' products, prices, and costs*—The more information buyers have, the better bargaining position they are in. The mushrooming availability of information on the Internet is giving added bargaining power to individuals. It is relatively easy for buyers to use the Internet to compare prices and features of motor vehicles, obtain mortgages and loans, and purchase big-ticket items such as digital cameras. Bargain-hunting individuals can shop around for the best deal on the Internet and use that information to negotiate with sellers.

- *If buyers pose a credible threat of integrating backward into the business of sellers*—Companies like Anheuser-Busch, Coors, and Heinz have integrated backward into metal can manufacturing to gain bargaining power in obtaining the balance of their can requirements from otherwise powerful metal can manufacturers. Retailers gain bargaining power by stocking and promoting their own private-label brands alongside manufacturers' name brands. Wal-Mart, for example, has elected to compete against Procter & Gamble, its biggest supplier, by introducing its own brand of laundry detergent called Sam's American Choice, which is priced about 25 to 30 percent lower than P&G's Tide.

- *If buyers have discretion in whether and when they purchase the product*—If consumers are unhappy with the sticker prices of new motor vehicles, they can delay purchase or buy a used vehicle instead. If business customers are not happy with the prices or security features of electronic bill payment software systems, they can either delay purchase until next-generation products become available or attempt to develop their own software in-house. If college students believe that the prices of new textbooks are too high, they can purchase used copies.

Buyers typically have weak bargaining power when they buy infrequently or in small quantities and when they face high costs to switch brands. High switching costs can keep a buyer locked in to the present brand. For example, companies that have bought Compaq or Hewlett-Packard engineering and graphics workstations that use

Microsoft's Windows operating systems are not strong candidates to switch to Sun Microsystems' workstation models that run on a UNIX operating system. Switching from Windows to UNIX entails considerable time and relearning on the part of users and can also entail having to abandon all the Windows-based engineering and graphics application software that the user has accumulated over the years and replace it with software applications written for a UNIX-based operating system.

A final point to keep in mind is that *not all buyers of an industry's product have equal degrees of bargaining power with sellers*, and some may be less sensitive than others to price, quality, or service differences among competing sellers. For example, independent tire retailers have less bargaining power in purchasing tires than do Honda, Ford, and DaimlerChrysler (which buy in much larger quantities), and they are also less quality sensitive. Motor vehicle manufacturers are very particular about tire quality and tire performance because of the effects on vehicle performance, and they drive a hard bargain with tire manufacturers on both price and quality. Apparel manufacturers confront significant bargaining power when selling to retail chains like Kmart or Sears or Macy's, but they can command much better prices selling to small owner-managed apparel boutiques.

How Collaborative Partnerships between Sellers and Buyers Can Create Competitive Pressures   Partnerships between sellers and buyers are an increasingly important element of the competitive picture in *business-to-business relationships* as opposed to business-to-consumer relationships. Many sellers that provide items to business customers have found it in their mutual interest to collaborate closely on such matters as just-in-time deliveries, order processing, electronic invoice payments, and online sharing of sales at the cash register. Wal-Mart, for example, provides the manufacturers with whom it does business (like Procter & Gamble) with daily sales data from each of its stores so that they can replenish inventory stocks on time. Dell Computer has partnered with its largest customers to create online systems for over 50,000 corporate customers, providing their employees with information on approved product configurations, global pricing, paperless purchase orders, real-time order tracking, invoicing, purchasing history, and other efficiency tools. Dell also loads a customer's software at the factory and installs asset tags so that customer setup time on the PCs it orders is minimal and helps customers migrate their PC systems to next-generation hardware and software. Dell's partnerships with its customers have put significant competitive pressure on other PC makers to develop packages of offerings to corporate customers that will compare favorably with what Dell offers.

Strategic Implications of the Five Competitive Forces

The special contribution of the five-forces model is the thoroughness with which it exposes what competition is like in a given market—the strength of each of the five competitive forces, the nature of the competitive pressures comprising each force, and the overall structure of competition. *As a rule, the stronger the collective impact of competitive forces, the lower the combined profitability of participant firms.* The most brutally competitive situation occurs when the five forces create market conditions tough enough to impose prolonged subpar profitability or even losses on most or all firms. The competitive structure of an industry is clearly "unattractive" from a profit-making standpoint if rivalry among sellers is very strong, low entry barriers are allowing new rivals to gain a market foothold, competition from substitutes is strong, and both suppliers and customers are able to exercise considerable bargaining leverage. These conditions are approximated in tire manufacturing and apparel, where profit margins have historically been thin.

In contrast, when competitive forces are not collectively strong, the competitive structure of the industry is "favorable" or "attractive" from the standpoint of earning superior profits. The "ideal" competitive environment is one in which both suppliers and customers are in weak bargaining positions, there are no good substitutes, entry barriers are relatively high, and rivalry among present sellers is only moderate. However, even when some of the five competitive forces are strong, an industry can be competitively attractive to those firms whose market position and strategy provide a good enough defense against competitive pressures to preserve their ability to earn above-average profits.

To contend successfully, managers must craft strategies that shield the firm as much as possible from the five competitive forces and that help make the rules, put added pressure on rivals, and perhaps even define the business model for the industry. Managers cannot expect to develop winning competitive strategies without first identifying what competitive pressures exist, gauging the relative strength of each, and gaining a deep understanding of the industry's whole competitive structure. The five-forces model is a powerful tool for giving strategy makers the competitive insights they need to build a successful enterprise—ideally one that enjoys a sustainable competitive advantage.

> A company's competitive strategy is increasingly effective the more it provides good defenses against the five competitive forces, shifts competitive pressures in ways that favor the company, and helps create sustainable competitive advantage.

QUESTION 3: WHAT IS CAUSING THE INDUSTRY'S COMPETITIVE STRUCTURE AND BUSINESS ENVIRONMENT TO CHANGE?

An industry's economic features and competitive structure say a lot about its fundamental character but very little about the ways in which its environment may be changing. All industries are characterized by trends and new developments that gradually or speedily produce changes important enough to require a strategic response from participating firms. The popular hypothesis about industries going through a life cycle helps explain industry change but is still incomplete.[13] The life-cycle stages are strongly keyed to changes in the overall industry growth rate (which is why such terms as *rapid growth, early maturity, saturation,* and *decline* are used to describe the stages). Yet there are more causes of industry change than an industry's position in the life cycle.

The Concept of Driving Forces

While it is important to judge what growth stage an industry is in, there's more analytical value in identifying the specific factors causing fundamental industry and competitive adjustments. Industry and competitive conditions change because forces are in motion that create incentives or pressures for change.[14] The most dominant forces are called **driving forces** because they have the biggest influence on what kinds of changes will take place in the industry's structure and competitive environment. "Driving

> **Basic Concept**
> Industry conditions change because important forces are driving industry participants (competitors, customers, or suppliers) to alter their actions; the *driving forces* in an industry are the *major underlying causes* of changing industry and competitive conditions.

---

[13]For a more extended discussion of the problems with the life-cycle hypothesis, see Porter, *Competitive Strategy,* pp. 157–62.

[14]Porter, *Competitive Strategy,* p. 162.

forces" analysis has two steps: identifying what the driving forces are and assessing the impact they will have on the industry.

The Most Common Driving Forces   Many events can affect an industry powerfully enough to qualify as driving forces. Some are unique and specific to a particular industry situation, but most drivers of change fall into one of the following categories:[15]

- *The Internet and the new e-commerce opportunities and threats it breeds in the industry*—The Internet is unquestionably spawning a sweeping business revolution that alters industry boundaries, opens up all kinds of new business-to-business and business-to-consumer market opportunities and threats, sparks competition from new and entirely different breeds of enterprises, and mandates fundamental changes in business practices. Scarcely any industry or company is unaffected. But the transformation that the Internet is producing varies from industry to industry and company to company, and the industry and competitive implications are continuously evolving as new Internet-related technologies emerge and new Internet-related products hit the market. The challenge here is to assess how growing use of the Internet will alter the industry and competitive landscape. In many industries, the role and impact of the Internet is a critical, if not *the* critical, driver that must be factored into the strategy-making equation. Illustration Capsule 13 explains the power of the Internet and Internet technologies to reshape an industry's environment.

- *Increasing globalization of the industry*—Industries move toward globalization for any of several reasons. One or more nationally prominent firms may launch aggressive long-term strategies to win a globally dominant market position and precipitate a race for world leadership among the industry's major rivals. Demand for the industry's product may start to blossom in more and more countries. Countries may decide to reduce trade barriers or open up once-closed markets to foreign competitors—as is occurring in many parts of Europe, Latin America, and Asia; tariff reductions, deregulation, and privatization of government-owned enterprises bring local competitors eyeball-to-eyeball with ambitious global companies. The spread of technological know-how may pave the way for lesser-known companies in developing countries to enter the industry arena on an international or global scale. Significant differences in labor costs among countries may create a strong reason to locate global-scale plants for labor-intensive products in low-wage countries and use these plants to supply market demand across the whole world. Wages in China, Taiwan, Singapore, Mexico, and Brazil, for example, are about one-fourth those in the United States, Germany, and Japan.

  Significant cost economies may accrue to firms with world-scale volumes as opposed to national-scale volumes. Multinational companies with the ability to transfer their production, marketing, and management know-how from country to country at very low cost can sometimes gain a significant competitive advantage over domestic-only competitors. As a consequence, global competition usually shifts the pattern of competition among an industry's key players, favoring some and disadvantaging others.

  Globalization is most likely to be a driving force in industries (1) where scale economies are so large that rival companies need to market their product in many country markets to gain enough volume to drive unit costs down; (2) where low-cost

15Much of what follows draws on the discussion in Porter, *Competitive Strategy*, pp. 164–83.

illustration capsule 13

How the Internet and New Internet-Related Technologies Are Changing the Business Landscape: Classic Examples of a Driving Force

Here are three examples of how the Internet is opening up new market opportunities, affecting competition, creating a fundamentally different business environment, and prompting companies to incorporate the capabilities of online technology to transform the way they do business.

SCRAP STEEL ON THE WEB

For years, small steel companies that processed and recycled scrap steel bought their supplies by picking up the phone and calling steelmakers, brokers, and warehouse distributors to find out who might have scrap to sell and at what price. Many telephone calls had to be placed—and the game of telephone tag had to be endured—to find supplies at a decent price and with acceptable delivery dates. But now small processors can go to their PCs, click on Web sites such as Metalsite.com and e-Steel.com and check availability, prices, and delivery dates from 6 to 10 producers and locate the best deal in a matter of minutes. Moreover, companies with scrap to sell can clear their warehouses of unwanted inventory quickly by listing their surplus on the Web.

The Web sites allow a variety of companies to buy, sell, or trade metal speedily and efficiently. Metalsite and e-Steel business model is to make money by charging users a 1 to 2 percent transaction fee and collecting fees from companies wanting to advertise products and services on their Web sites. Buyers must get credit approval before bidding or negotiating.

WEYERHAEUSER'S DOORBUILDER

Some years ago, Weyerhaeuser Company's door factory in Wisconsin was besieged with high costs, slack sales, and poor employee morale. The plant—which cuts, glues, drills, and shapes customized doors according to each buyer's order—was plagued with hammering out the details of customer orders over a period of weeks and months since there were over 2 million different door configurations given the options for sizes, styles, veneer color, and hardware. Pricing was a calculation nightmare. Orders, once finalized, were stapled to each door on the production floor, and many order forms would get torn off or lost at various times during production.

Shrewd use of the Internet and creation of a company intranet turned things around. Weyerhaeuser managers installed a state-of-the-art in-house system called DoorBuilder

that uses the Internet to compare materials prices and availability from different suppliers, allows customers to design and customize doors online and obtain instant pricing, lets customers submit orders at the plant's Web site, and checks the order for possible errors (such as whether the desired door hinge conforms with building codes in a particular location). Internally, DoorBuilder has the capability to check plant inventories for all the needed components, determine the cost-price-profit margin on each custom-built door, flag less profitable or unprofitable orders, screen customers' creditworthiness, calculate the volumes a customer has ordered over a period of time to determine how profitable each customer is, track orders as they move through the plant, and completely fill 97 percent of all customer orders on time (up from 40 percent before DoorBuilder).

Since the use of DoorBuilder began, the plant's share of the U.S. commercial door market has gone from 12 to 26 percent and its return on net assets has increased from 2 to 27 percent, which compares very favorably with the companywide objective of 17 percent.

XML FORMAT FOR WEB PAGE CREATION

The Newspaper Association of America is using the new extensible markup language (XML) format for creating Web pages. XML, which is rapidly displacing hypertext markup language (HTML), allows people to find classified jobs or real estate listings from multiple newspapers with a single search. Use of XML enables the exchange of data between otherwise incompatible software systems of different enterprises. Thus, different newspapers can link their classified ads into a single searchable database.

Likewise, XML enables component suppliers, manufacturers, distributors, and end users to exchange data and link their databases, opening up a wealth of new possibilities. A Web site company could gather a fee schedule and list of routes and timetables from UPS, FedEx, and dozens of other transportation providers and offer business customers point-to-point global delivery services without owning a single truck, airplane, cargo vessel, or railcar. XML enables cyberfirms to offer such services as payment processing in multiple currencies, electronic tax processing for a variety of jurisdictions, and sophisticated searches and analyses of the Securities and Exchange Commission's huge Edgar database of corporate financial filings.

Sources: Business Week E.BIZ, July 26, 1999, pp. EB 32–EB 38; and *The Wall Street Journal,* September 16, 1999, pp. B1, B4, and B6.

production is a critical consideration (making it imperative to locate manufacturing facilities in countries where the lowest costs can be achieved); (3) where one or more globally ambitious companies are pushing hard to gain a significant competitive position in as many attractive country markets as they can; (4) where local governments are privatizing government-owned monopolies (e.g., in telecommunications and energy) and opening up their once-closed local markets to competition; and (5) where critical natural resources and raw material supplies (e.g., crude oil, copper, and cotton) are scattered all over the globe.

Globalization has triggered a frantic, fast-paced race for global market leadership in credit cards, PCs, motor vehicles, telecommunications (long-distance telephone service, Internet access, electronic communications), refined petroleum products, and energy.

- *Changes in the long-term industry growth rate*—Shifts in industry growth up or down are a driving force for industry change, affecting the balance between industry supply and buyer demand, entry and exit, and the character and strength of competition. An upsurge in long-term demand triggers a race for growth among established firms and newcomers attracted by the prospects for higher growth. Competition becomes a contest of who can capture the growth opportunities and win a place among the market leaders. A shrinking market heightens competitive pressures, producing an often intense battle for market share and inducing mergers and acquisitions that result in industry consolidation to a smaller number of participants. Some companies may exit the industry and those remaining may be forced to close less efficient plants and retrench to a smaller production base.

- *Changes in who buys the product and how they use it*—Shifts in buyer demographics and new ways of using the product can alter the state of competition by forcing adjustments in customer service offerings (credit, technical assistance, maintenance and repair); opening the way to market the industry's product through a different mix of dealers and retail outlets; and prompting producers to broaden or narrow their product lines, bringing different sales and promotion approaches into play. The mushrooming popularity of the Internet at home and at work is creating new opportunities for electronic shopping, online brokerage services, e-mail services, bulletin board services, data services, and Internet-provider services. The changing demographics generated by longer life expectancies are creating growth markets for residential golf resorts, retirement planning services, mutual funds, and health care.

- *Product innovation*—Product innovation can shake up the structure of competition by broadening an industry's customer base, rejuvenating industry growth, and widening the degree of product differentiation among rival sellers. Successful new product introductions strengthen the market position of the innovating companies, usually at the expense of companies that stick with their old products or are slow to follow with their own versions of the new product. Product innovation has been a key driving force for makers of personal computers, PC software, digital cameras, golf clubs, video games, toys, prescription drugs, frozen foods, and mobile phones.

- *Technological change*—Advances in technology can dramatically alter an industry's landscape, making it possible to produce new and better products at lower cost and opening up whole new industry frontiers. Technological developments can also produce competitively significant changes in capital requirements, minimum efficient plant sizes, distribution channels and distribution logistics, and learning or experience curve effects.

- *Marketing innovation*—When firms are successful in introducing new ways to market their products, they can spark a burst of buyer interest, widen industry demand, increase product differentiation, and lower unit costs—any or all of which can alter the competitive positions of rival firms and force strategy revisions. In today's world, the Internet is the vehicle for all kinds of marketing innovations.

- *Entry or exit of major firms*—The entry of one or more foreign companies into a market once dominated by domestic firms nearly always shakes up competitive conditions. Likewise, when an established domestic firm from another industry attempts entry either by acquisition or by launching its own start-up venture, it usually applies its skills and resources in some innovative fashion that pushes competition in new directions. Entry by a major firm often produces a new ballgame, not only with new key players but also with new rules for competing. Similarly, exit of a major firm changes the competitive structure by reducing the number of market leaders (perhaps increasing the dominance of the leaders who remain) and causing a rush to capture the exiting firm's customers.

- *Diffusion of technical know-how across more companies and more countries*—As knowledge about how to perform a particular activity or execute a particular manufacturing technology spreads, any technically based competitive advantage held by firms originally possessing this know-how erodes. The diffusion of such knowledge can occur through scientific journals, trade publications, on-site plant tours, word-of-mouth among suppliers and customers, and the hiring away of knowledgeable employees. It can also occur when those possessing technological know-how license others to use it for a royalty fee or team up with a company interested in turning the technology into a new business venture. Quite often, technological know-how can be acquired by simply buying a company that has the wanted skills, patents, or manufacturing capabilities.

  In recent years technology transfer across national boundaries has emerged as one of the most important driving forces in globalizing markets and competition. As companies worldwide gain access to technical know-how, they upgrade their manufacturing capabilities in a long-term effort to compete head-on against established companies. Examples of where technology transfer has turned a largely domestic industry into an increasingly global one include automobiles, tires, consumer electronics, telecommunications, and computers.

- *Changes in cost and efficiency*—Widening or shrinking differences in the costs and efficiency among key competitors tends to dramatically alter the state of competition. The low cost of e-mail and fax transmission has put mounting competitive pressure on the relatively inefficient and high-cost operations of the U.S. Postal Service—sending a one-page fax is cheaper and far quicker than sending a first-class letter; sending e-mail is faster and cheaper still. In the electric power industry, sharply lower costs to generate electricity at newly constructed combined-cycle generating plants has put older coal-fired and gas-fired plants under the gun to lower their production costs to remain competitive. E-tailing can have lower-cost economics than brick-and-mortar retailing. In fact, use of wired networks (the Internet and company intranets) is radically transforming the cost structure of doing business in industry after industry.

- *Growing buyer preferences for differentiated products instead of a commodity product (or for a more standardized product instead of strongly differentiated products)*—A shift to differentiated products is signaled when sellers are able to win a bigger and more loyal buyer following by offering made-to-order products, introducing new features, making style changes, offering options and accessories, and creating image differences via advertising and packaging. We have seen growing numbers of buyers decide that a customized "made-to-order" PC suits them better than standardized off-the-shelf models; a similar shift may be happening in car buying where several car manufacturers and online sellers are offering made-to-order vehicles. When a shift from standardized to differentiated products occurs, the driver of change is the contest among rivals to cleverly outdifferentiate one another.

On the other hand, buyers sometimes decide that a budget-priced, mostly look-alike product suits their requirements as well as or better than a premium-priced product with lots of snappy features and personalized services. Online brokers, for example, have used the lure of cheap commissions to attract many investors willing to place their own buy–sell orders via the Internet; growing acceptance of online trading has put significant competitive pressures on full-service brokers whose business model has always revolved around convincing clients of the value of asking for personalized advice from professional brokers and paying their sharply higher high commission fees to make trades. Pronounced shifts toward greater product standardization usually spawn lively price competition and force rival sellers to drive down their costs to maintain profitability. The lesson here is that competition is driven partly by whether the market forces in motion are acting to increase or decrease product differentiation.

- *Regulatory influences and government policy changes*—Government regulatory actions can often force significant changes in industry practices and strategic approaches. Deregulation has proved to be a potent procompetitive force in the airline, banking, natural gas, telecommunications, and electric utility industries. Government efforts to reform Medicare and health insurance have become potent driving forces in the health care industry. In international markets, host governments can drive competitive changes by opening up their domestic markets to foreign participation or closing them off to protect domestic companies.

- *Changing societal concerns, attitudes, and lifestyles*—Emerging social issues and changing attitudes and lifestyles can be powerful instigators of industry change. Growing antismoking sentiment has emerged as the major driver of change in the tobacco industry; initiatives for stricter gun control are having a big impact on gun makers. Consumer concerns about salt, sugar, chemical additives, saturated fat, cholesterol, and nutritional value have forced food producers to revamp food-processing techniques, redirect R&D efforts into the use of healthier ingredients, and compete in coming up with nutritional, good-tasting products. Safety concerns have transformed safety features into a competitive asset in the automobile, toy, and outdoor power equipment industries, to mention a few. Increased interest in physical fitness has spawned whole new industries in exercise equipment, mountain biking, outdoor apparel, sports gyms and recreation centers, vitamin and nutrition supplements, and medically supervised diet programs. Social concerns about air and water pollution have forced industries to incorporate expenditures for controlling environmental pollution into their cost structures. Shifting societal concerns, attitudes, and lifestyles alter the pattern of competition, usually favoring those players that respond quickly and creatively with products targeted to the new trends and conditions.

- *Reductions in uncertainty and business risk*—A young, emerging industry is typically characterized by unproven cost structure, much uncertainty over potential market size, how much time and money will be needed to surmount technological problems, and what distribution channels and buyer segments to emphasize.

Emerging industries tend to attract only risk-taking entrepreneurial companies. Over time, however, if the business model of industry pioneers proves profitable and market demand for the product appears durable, more conservative firms are usually enticed to enter the market. Often, these later entrants are large, financially strong firms looking to invest in attractive growth industries.

Lower business risks and less industry uncertainty also affect competition in international markets. In the early stages of a company's entry into foreign markets, conservatism prevails and firms limit their downside exposure by using less risky strategies like exporting, licensing, joint marketing agreements, and collaborative partnerships and joint ventures with local companies to accomplish entry. Then, as experience accumulates and perceived risk levels decline, companies move more boldly and more independently, making acquisitions, constructing their own plants, putting in their own sales and marketing capabilities to build strong competitive positions in each country market, and beginning to link the strategies in each country to create a more globalized strategy.

The many different *potential driving forces* explain why it is too simplistic to view industry change only in terms of the life-cycle model and why a full understanding of the *causes* underlying the emergence of new competitive conditions is a fundamental part of industry analysis.

However, while many forces of change may be at work in a given industry, no more than three or four are likely to qualify as driving forces in the sense that they will act as *the major determinants* of why and how the industry is changing. Thus, strategic analysts must resist the temptation to label everything they see changing as a driving force; the analytical task is to evaluate the forces of industry and competitive change carefully enough to separate major factors from minor ones.

> The task of driving-forces analysis is to separate the major causes of industry change from the minor ones; usually no more than three or four factors qualify as driving forces.

The Link between Driving Forces and Strategy   Sound analysis of an industry's driving forces is a prerequisite to sound strategy making. Without keen awareness of what external factors will produce the biggest potential changes in the company's business over the next one to three years, managers are ill prepared to craft a strategy tightly matched to emerging conditions. Similarly, if managers are uncertain about the implications of each driving force or if their views are incomplete or off-base, it's difficult for them to craft a strategy that is responsive to the driving forces and their consequences for the industry. So driving-forces analysis is not something to take lightly; it has practical strategy-making value and is basic to the task of thinking strategically about where the industry is headed and how to prepare for the changes.

Environmental Scanning Techniques

One way to try to detect future driving forces early on is to systematically scan the environment for new straws in the wind. **Environmental scanning** involves studying and interpreting the sweep of social, political, economic, ecological, and technological events in an effort to spot budding trends and conditions that could become driving forces. Environmental scanning involves time frames well beyond the next one to three years—for example, it could involve judgments about the demand for electric power in the year 2010, what kinds of appliances and computerized electronic controls will be in the "house of the future," how people will be communicating over long distances 10 years from now, or what will happen to the income levels and purchasing habits of retired people in the 21st century if average life expectancies continue to increase. Environmental scanning thus attempts to spot first-of-a-kind happenings and approaches that are catching on, and to extrapolate their possible implications 5 to 20 years into the

> Managers can use *environmental scanning* to spot budding trends and clues of change that could develop into new driving forces.

future. *The purpose of environmental scanning is to raise the consciousness of managers about potential developments that could have an important impact on industry conditions and pose new opportunities or threats.*

Environmental scanning can be accomplished by systematically monitoring and studying current events, constructing scenarios, and employing the Delphi method (a technique for finding consensus among a group of knowledgeable experts). Environmental scanning methods are highly qualitative and subjective. The appeal of environmental scanning, notwithstanding its speculative nature, is that it helps managers lengthen their planning horizon, translate vague inklings of future opportunities or threats into clearer strategic issues (for which they can begin to develop strategic answers), and think strategically about developments in the surrounding environment.[16] Companies that undertake formal environmental scanning on a fairly continuous and comprehensive level include General Electric, AT&T, Coca-Cola, Ford, General Motors, Du Pont, and Shell Oil.

QUESTION 4: WHICH COMPANIES ARE IN THE STRONGEST/WEAKEST POSITIONS?

The next step in examining the industry's competitive structure is to study the market positions of rival companies. One technique for revealing the competitive positions of industry participants is **strategic group mapping.**[17] This analytical tool is useful for comparing the market positions of each firm separately or for grouping them into like positions when an industry has so many competitors that it is not practical to examine each one in depth.

> **Basic Concept**
> *Strategic group mapping* is a technique for displaying the different competitive positions that rival firms occupy in the industry.

Using Strategic Group Maps to Assess the Competitive Positions of Rival Firms

A **strategic group** consists of those rival firms with similar competitive approaches and positions in the market.[18] Companies in the same strategic group can resemble one another in any of several ways: they may have comparable product-line breadth, sell in the same price/quality range, emphasize the same distribution channels, use essentially the same product attributes to appeal to similar types of buyers, depend on identical technological approaches, or offer buyers similar services and technical assistance.[19] An industry contains only one strategic group when all sellers pursue essentially identical strategies and have comparable market positions. At the other extreme, there are as many strategic groups as there are competitors when each rival pursues a distinctively

> Dividing industry members into *strategic groups* allows industry analysts to better understand the pattern of competition in complex industries and to pinpoint a firm's closest competitors.

[16]For further discussion of the nature and use of environmental scanning, see Roy Amara and Andrew J. Lipinski, *Business Planning for an Uncertain Future: Scenarios and Strategies* (New York: Pergamon Press, 1983); Harold E. Klein and Robert U. Linneman, "Environmental Assessment: An International Study of Corporate Practice," *Journal of Business Strategy* 5, no. 1 (Summer 1984), pp. 55–75; and Arnoldo C. Hax and Nicolas S. Majluf, *The Strategy Concept and Process* (Englewood Cliffs, NJ: Prentice Hall, 1991), chapters 5 and 8.

[17]Porter, *Competitive Strategy,* chapter 7.

[18]Ibid., pp. 129–30.

[19]For an excellent discussion of how to identify the factors that define strategic groups, see Mary Ellen Gordon and George R. Milne, "Selecting the Dimensions that Define Strategic Groups: A Novel Market-Driven Approach," *Journal of Managerial Issues* 11, no. 2 (Summer 1999), pp. 213–33.

different competitive approach and occupies a substantially different competitive position in the marketplace.

The procedure for constructing a *strategic group map* and deciding which firms belong in which strategic group is straightforward:

- Identify the competitive characteristics that differentiate firms in the industry—typical variables are price/quality range (high, medium, low); geographic coverage (local, regional, national, global); degree of vertical integration (none, partial, full); product-line breadth (wide, narrow); use of distribution channels (one, some, all); and degree of service offered (no-frills, limited, full).

- Plot the firms on a two-variable map using pairs of these differentiating characteristics.

- Assign firms that fall in about the same strategy space to the same strategic group.

- Draw circles around each strategic group, making the circles proportional to the size of the group's respective share of total industry sales revenues.

This produces a two-dimensional diagram like the one for the video game industry in Illustration Capsule 14.

Several guidelines need to be observed in mapping the positions of strategic groups in the industry's overall strategy space.[20] First, the two variables selected as axes for the map should *not* be highly correlated; if they are, the circles on the map will fall along a diagonal and strategy makers will learn nothing more about the relative positions of competitors than they would by considering just one of the variables. For instance, if companies with broad product lines use multiple distribution channels while companies with narrow lines use a single distribution channel, then looking at broad versus narrow product lines reveals just as much about who is positioned where as looking at single versus multiple distribution channels; one of the variables is redundant. Second, the variables chosen as axes for the map should expose big differences in how rivals position themselves to compete in the marketplace. This, of course, means analysts must identify the characteristics that differentiate rival firms and use these differences as variables for the axes and as the basis for deciding which firm belongs in which strategic group. Third, the variables used as axes don't have to be either quantitative or continuous; rather, they can be discrete variables or defined in terms of distinct classes and combinations. Fourth, drawing the sizes of the circles on the map proportional to the combined sales of the firms in each strategic group allows the map to reflect the relative sizes of each strategic group. Fifth, if more than two good competitive variables can be used as axes for the map, several maps can be drawn to give different exposures to the competitive positioning relationships present in the industry's structure. Because there is not necessarily one best map for portraying how competing firms are positioned in the market, it is advisable to experiment with different pairs of competitive variables.

What Can Be Learned from Strategic Group Maps

One thing to look for is whether *industry driving forces and competitive pressures favor some strategic groups and hurt others.*[21] Firms in adversely affected strategic groups may try to shift to a more favorably situated group; how hard such a move

---

[20]Ibid., pp. 152–54.
[21]Ibid., pp. 130, 132–38, and 154–55.

illustration capsule 14

Strategic Group Map of Competitors in the Video Game Industry

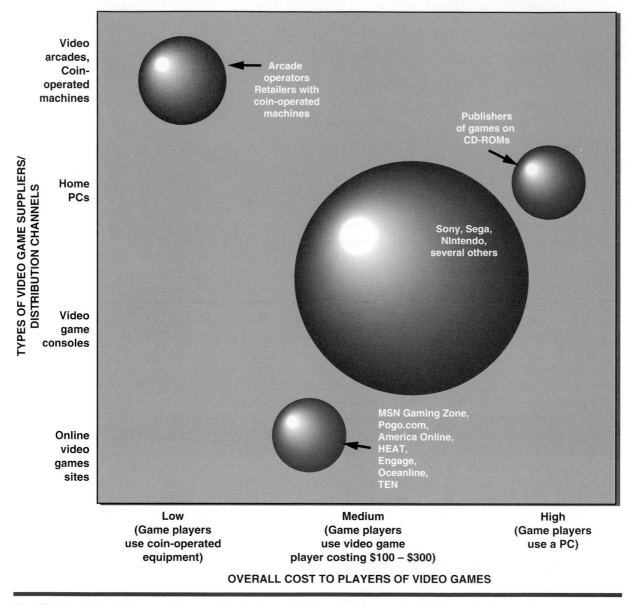

Note: The sizes of the circles are roughly proportional to the market shares of each group of competitors.

proves to be depends on whether entry barriers for the target strategic group are high or low. Attempts by rival firms to enter a new strategic group nearly always increase competitive pressures. If certain firms are known to be trying to change their competitive positions on the map, then attaching arrows to the circles showing the targeted direction helps clarify the picture of competitive jockeying among rivals.

Another consideration is whether *the profit potential of different strategic groups varies due to the strengths and weaknesses in each group's market position.* Differences in profitability can occur because of differing degrees of bargaining leverage or collaboration with suppliers and/or customers, differing degrees of exposure to competition from substitute products outside the industry, differing degrees of competitive rivalry within strategic groups, and differing growth rates for the principal buyer segments served by each group.

Generally speaking, *the closer strategic groups are to each other on the map, the stronger competitive rivalry among member firms tends to be.* Although firms in the same strategic group are the closest rivals, the next closest rivals are in the immediately adjacent groups.[22] Often, firms in strategic groups that are far apart on the map hardly compete at all. For instance, Tiffany & Co. and Wal-Mart both sell gold and silver jewelry, but their clientele and the prices and quality of their products are much too different to justify calling them competitors. For the same reason, Timex is not a meaningful competitive rival of Rolex, and Subaru is not a close competitor of Lincoln or Mercedes-Benz.

> Some strategic groups are usually more favorably positioned than other strategic groups because driving forces and competitive pressures do not affect each group evenly and because profit prospects vary among groups based on the relative attractiveness of their market positions.

QUESTION 5: WHAT STRATEGIC MOVES ARE RIVALS LIKELY TO MAKE NEXT?

Unless a company pays attention to what competitors are doing, it ends up flying blind into competitive battle. A company can't expect to outmaneuver its rivals without monitoring their actions, understanding their strategies, and anticipating what moves they are likely to make next. As in sports, scouting the opposition is essential. **Competitive intelligence** about the strategies rivals are deploying, their latest moves, their resource strengths and weaknesses, and the plans they have announced is essential to anticipating the actions they are likely to take next and what bearing their moves might have on a company's own best strategic moves. Competitive intelligence can help a company determine whether it needs to defend against specific moves taken by rivals or whether those moves provide an opening for a new offensive thrust.

> Successful strategists take great pains in gathering *competitive intelligence* about competitors' strategies, monitoring their actions, sizing up their strengths and weaknesses, and using what they have learned to anticipate what moves rivals are likely to make next.

Monitoring Competitors' Strategies

The best source of information about a competitor's strategy comes from examining what it is doing in the marketplace and from what its management is saying about the company's plans. (Figure 2.3 in Chapter 2 indicates what to look for in identifying a

---

[22]Strategic groups act as good reference points for predicting the evolution of an industry's competitive structure. See Avi Fiegenbaum and Howard Thomas, "Strategic Groups as Reference Groups: Theory, Modeling and Empirical Examination of Industry and Competitive Strategy," *Strategic Management Journal* 16 (1995), pp. 461–76. For a study of how strategic group analysis helps identify the variables that lead to sustainable competitive advantage, see S. Ade Olusoga, Michael P. Mokwa, and Charles H. Noble, "Strategic Groups, Mobility Barriers, and Competitive Advantage," *Journal of Business Research* 33 (1995), pp. 153–64.

company's business strategy.) Additional insights into what a competitor is up to and its future strategy can be gotten by considering the competitor's geographic market arena, strategic intent, market share objective, position on the industry's strategic group map, and willingness to take risks; further, it is important to know whether the competitor's recent moves are mostly offensive or defensive.[23] Good sources for such information include the company's annual report and 10-K filings, recent speeches by its managers, the reports of securities analysts, articles in the business media, company press releases, information on the company's Web site and other Web sites, its exhibits at international trade shows, and conversations with a rival's customers, suppliers, and former employees. Many companies have a competitive intelligence unit that regularly gathers information on rivals and makes it available on the company's intranet.

> It is advantageous to know more about your competitors than they know about you.

Gathering competitive intelligence on rivals, however, can sometimes tread the fine line between honest inquiry and unethical or even illegal behavior. For example, calling rivals to get information about prices, the dates of new product introductions, or wage and salary levels is legal, but misrepresenting one's company affiliation during such calls is unethical. Pumping rivals' representatives at trade shows is ethical only if one wears an accurate name tag like everyone else. In 1991, Avon Products secured information about its biggest rival, Mary Kay Cosmetics (MKC), by having its personnel search through the garbage dumpsters outside MKC's headquarters.[24] When MKC officials learned of the action and sued, Avon claimed it did nothing illegal—a 1988 Supreme Court case had ruled that trash left on public property (in this case, a sidewalk) was anyone's for the taking. Avon even produced a videotape of its removal of the trash at the MKC site. Avon won the lawsuit—but the legality of Avon's action does not mean that what the company did was ethical.

Table 3.3 provides an easy-to-apply classification scheme for profiling the objectives and strategies of rival companies. Such profiles, along with a strategic group map, provide a working diagnosis of the strategies and recent moves of rivals and are readily supplemented by whatever additional information is available about each competitor.

Evaluating Who the Industry's Major Players Are Going to Be

It's usually obvious who the *current* major contenders are, but these same firms are not necessarily positioned most strongly for the future. Some may be ill-equipped to compete on the industry's future battleground and may already be losing strength. Smaller companies may be poising for an offensive against larger but vulnerable rivals. Long-standing contenders for market leadership sometimes slide quickly down the industry's ranks; others end up being acquired. Today's market leaders don't automatically become tomorrow's.

> The company that consistently has more and better information about its competitors is better positioned to prevail, other things being equal.

In deciding which competitors are favorably or unfavorably positioned to gain market ground, company strategists need to focus on why there is potential for some rivals to do better or worse than other rivals. Usually, how securely a company holds its present market share is a function of its vulnerability to driving forces and competitive pressures, whether it has a competitive advantage or disadvantage, and whether it is the

---

[23]For a discussion of legal ways of gathering competitive intelligence on rival companies, see Larry Kahaner, *Competitive Intelligence* (New York: Simon & Schuster, 1996).

[24]Kahaner, *Competitive Intelligence*, pp. 84–85.

table 3.3 Profiling the Objectives and Strategies of Competitors

Competitive Scope	Strategic Intent	Market Share Objective	Competitive Position/ Situation	Strategic Posture	Competitive Strategy
• Local • Regional • National • Multicountry • Global	• Be the dominant leader • Overtake the present industry leader • Be among the top 5 industry leaders • Move into the top 10 • Move up a notch or two in the industry rankings • Overtake a particular rival (not necessarily the leader) • Maintain position • Just survive	• Aggressive expansion via both acquisition and internal growth • Expansion via internal growth (boost market share at the expense of rival firms) • Expansion via acquisition • Hold on to present share (by growing at a rate equal to the industry average) • Give up share if necessary to achieve short-term profit objectives (stress profitability, not volume)	• Getting stronger; on the move • Well-entrenched; able to maintain its present position • Stuck in the middle of the pack • Going after a different market position (trying to move from a weaker to a stronger position) • Struggling; losing ground • Retrenching to a position that can be defended	• Mostly offensive • Mostly defensive • A combination of offense and defense • Aggressive risk-taker • Conservative follower	• Striving for low-cost leadership • Mostly focusing on a market niche: —High end —Low end —Geographic —Buyers with special needs —Other • Pursuing differentiation based on: —Quality —Service —Technological superiority —Breadth of product line —Image and reputation —More value for the money —Other attributes

Note: Since a focus strategy can be aimed at any of several market niches and a differentiation strategy can be keyed to any of several attributes, it is best to be explicit about what kind of focus strategy or differentiation strategy a given firm is pursuing. All focusers do not pursue the same market niche, and all differentiators do not pursue the same differentiating attributes.

likely target of offensive attack from other industry participants. Pinpointing which rivals are poised to gain market position and which rivals seem destined to lose market share helps a strategist anticipate what kinds of moves they are likely to make next.

Predicting Competitors' Next Moves

Predicting competitors' next moves is the hardest yet most useful part of competitor analysis. Good clues about what moves a specific company may make next come from studying its strategic intent, monitoring how well it is faring in the marketplace, and determining how much pressure it is under to improve its financial performance. Whether a company will continue its present strategy usually depends on how well it is doing and how satisfied it is with its current performance. Content rivals are likely to continue their present strategy with only minor fine-tuning. Ailing rivals can be performing so poorly that fresh strategic moves, either offensive or defensive, are virtually certain. Aggressive rivals with ambitious strategic intent are strong candidates for pursuing emerging market opportunities and exploiting the vulnerabilities of weaker rivals.

Since managers generally operate from assumptions about the industry's future and beliefs about their own firm's situation, insights into the strategic thinking of rival managements can be gleaned from their public pronouncements about where the industry is headed and what it will take to be successful, what they are saying about their firm's situation, information from the grapevine about what they are doing, and their past actions and leadership styles. Another thing to consider is whether a rival has the flexibility to make major strategic changes or whether it is locked in to pursuing its same basic strategy with minor adjustments.

> Managers who fail to study competitors closely risk being blindsided by surprise actions on the part of rivals.

To succeed in predicting a competitor's next moves, company strategists need to have a good feel for the rival's situation, how its managers think, and what its options are. Doing the necessary detective work can be tedious and time-consuming since the information comes in bits and pieces from many sources. But scouting competitors well enough to anticipate their next moves allows managers to prepare effective countermoves (perhaps even beat a rival to the punch) and to take rivals' probable actions into account in designing the best course of action.

QUESTION 6: WHAT ARE THE KEY FACTORS FOR COMPETITIVE SUCCESS?

An industry's **key success factors (KSFs)** are those things that most affect industry members' ability to prosper in the marketplace—the particular strategy elements, product attributes, resources, competencies, competitive capabilities, and business outcomes that spell the difference between profit and loss and, ultimately, between competitive success or failure. KSFs by their very nature are so important that *all firms* in the industry must pay close attention to them—they are the prerequisites for industry success or, to put it another way, KSFs are the rules that shape whether a company will be financially and competitively successful. The answers to three questions help identify an industry's key success factors:

> **Basic Concept**
> *Key success factors* concern the product attributes, competencies, competitive capabilities, and market achievements with the greatest direct bearing on company profitability.

- On what basis do customers choose between the competing brands of sellers? What product attributes are crucial?
- What resources and competitive capabilities does a seller need to have to be competitively successful?
- What does it take for sellers to achieve a sustainable competitive advantage?

In the beer industry, the KSFs are full utilization of brewing capacity (to keep manufacturing costs low), a strong network of wholesale distributors (to gain access to as many retail outlets as possible), and clever advertising (to induce beer drinkers to buy a particular brand and thereby pull beer sales through the established wholesale/retail channels). In apparel manufacturing, the KSFs are appealing designs and color combinations (to create buyer interest) and low-cost manufacturing efficiency (to permit attractive retail pricing and ample profit margins). In tin and aluminum cans, because the cost of shipping empty cans is substantial, one of the keys is having plants located close to end-use customers so that the plant's output can be marketed within economical shipping distances (regional market share is far more crucial than national share). Table 3.4 provides a shopping list of the most common types of key success factors.

Determining the industry's key success factors, given prevailing and anticipated industry and competitive conditions, is a top-priority analytical consideration. At the

table 3.4 Common Types of Key Success Factors

Technology-related KSFs
- Scientific research expertise (important in such fields as pharmaceuticals, high-speed Internet access, mobile communications, space exploration, and other high-tech industries)
- Technical capability to make innovative improvements in production processes
- Product innovation capability
- Expertise in a given technology
- Capability to use the Internet for all kinds of e-commerce activities

Manufacturing-related KSFs
- Low-cost production efficiency (achieve scale economies, capture experience curve effects)
- Quality of manufacture (fewer defects, less need for repairs)
- High utilization of fixed assets (important in capital-intensive/high-fixed-cost industries)
- Low-cost plant locations
- Access to adequate supplies of skilled labor
- High labor productivity (important for items with high labor content)
- Low-cost product design and engineering (reduces manufacturing costs)
- Ability to manufacture or assemble products that are customized to buyer specifications

Distribution-related KSFs
- A strong network of wholesale distributors/dealers (or electronic distribution capability via the Internet)
- Gaining ample space on retailer shelves
- Having company-owned retail outlets
- Low distribution costs
- Accurate filling of customer orders
- Short delivery times

Marketing-related KSFs
- Fast, accurate technical assistance
- Courteous customer service
- Accurate filling of buyer orders (few back orders or mistakes)
- Breadth of product line and product selection
- Merchandising skills
- Attractive styling or packaging
- Customer guarantees and warranties (important in mail-order and online retailing, big-ticket purchases, new product introductions)
- Clever advertising

Skills-related KSFs
- Superior workforce talent (important in professional services like accounting and investment banking)
- Quality control know-how
- Design expertise (important in fashion and apparel industries and often one of the keys to low-cost manufacture)
- Expertise in a particular technology
- An ability to develop innovative products and product improvements
- An ability to get newly conceived products past the R&D phase and out into the market very quickly

Organizational capability
- Superior information systems (important in airline travel, car rental, credit card, and lodging industries)
- Ability to respond quickly to shifting market conditions (streamlined decision making, short lead times to bring new products to market)
- Superior ability to employ the Internet and other aspects of electronic commerce to conduct business
- Managerial experience

Other types of KSFs
- Favorable image or reputation with buyers
- Overall low cost (not just in manufacturing)
- Convenient locations (important in many retailing businesses)
- Pleasant, courteous employees in all customer contact positions
- Access to financial capital (important in newly emerging industries with high degrees of business risk and in capital-intensive industries)
- Patent protection

very least, managers need to understand the industry situation well enough to know what is more important to competitive success and what is less important. They need to know what kinds of resources are competitively valuable. Misdiagnosing the industry factors critical to long-term competitive success greatly raises the risk of a misdirected strategy. In contrast, a company with perceptive understanding of industry KSFs can gain sustainable competitive advantage by training its strategy on industry KSFs and devoting its energies to being *distinctively better* than rivals on one or more of these factors. Indeed, companies that stand out on a particular KSF enjoy a stronger market position for their efforts—*being distinctively better than rivals on one or more key success factors presents a golden opportunity for gaining competitive advantage.* Hence, using the industry's KSFs as *cornerstones* for the company's strategy and trying to gain sustainable competitive advantage by excelling at one particular KSF is a fruitful competitive strategy approach.[25]

> **Strategic Management Principle**
>
> A sound strategy incorporates efforts to be competent on all industry key success factors and to excel on at least one factor.

Key success factors vary from industry to industry and even from time to time within the same industry as driving forces and competitive conditions change. Only rarely does an industry have more than three or four key success factors at any one time. And even among these three or four, one or two usually outrank the others in importance. Managers, therefore, have to resist the temptation to include factors that have only minor importance on their list of key success factors—the purpose of identifying KSFs is to make judgments about what things are more important to competitive success and what things are less important. To compile a list of every factor that matters even a little bit defeats the purpose of concentrating management attention on the factors truly critical to long-term competitive success.

QUESTION 7: IS THE INDUSTRY ATTRACTIVE AND WHAT ARE ITS PROSPECTS FOR ABOVE-AVERAGE PROFITABILITY?

The final step of industry and competitive analysis is to use the answers to the previous six questions to draw conclusions about the relative attractiveness or unattractiveness of the industry, both near-term and long-term. Company strategists are obligated to assess the industry outlook carefully, deciding whether industry and competitive conditions present an attractive business opportunity for the company or whether the company's growth and profit prospects are gloomy. The important factors on which to base such conclusions include:

● The industry's growth potential.

● Whether competition currently permits adequate profitability and whether competitive forces will become stronger or weaker.

● Whether industry profitability will be favorably or unfavorably affected by the prevailing driving forces.

● The company's competitive position in the industry and whether its position is likely to grow stronger or weaker. (Being a well-entrenched leader or strongly positioned contender in an otherwise lackluster industry can still produce good profitability;

---

[25]Some experts dispute the strategy-making value of key success factors. Professor Ghemawat claims that the "whole idea of identifying a success factor and then chasing it seems to have something in common with the ill-considered medieval hunt for the *philosopher's stone*, a substance which would transmute everything it touched into gold." Pankaj Ghemawat, *Commitment: The Dynamic of Strategy* (New York: Free Press, 1991), p. 11.

however, having to fight an uphill battle against much stronger rivals can make an otherwise attractive industry unattractive.)

- The company's potential to capitalize on the vulnerabilities of weaker rivals (perhaps converting an unattractive *industry* situation into a potentially rewarding *company* opportunity).
- Whether the company is able to defend against or counteract the factors that make the industry unattractive.
- The degrees of risk and uncertainty in the industry's future.
- The severity of problems confronting the industry as a whole.
- Whether continued participation in this industry adds importantly to the firm's ability to be successful in other industries in which it may have business interests.

As a general proposition, *if an industry's overall profit prospects are above average, the industry can be considered attractive; if its profit prospects are below average, it is unattractive.* However, it is a mistake to think of industries as being attractive or unattractive to all industry participants and all potential entrants. Attractiveness is relative, not absolute, and conclusions one way or the other are in the eye of the beholder—industry attractiveness always has to be appraised from the standpoint of a particular company. Industry environments unattractive to weak competitors may be attractive to strong competitors. Despite the obvious problems of the cigarette industry, for example, Philip Morris has managed to grow market share and maintain reasonable profitability. Industries attractive to insiders, like soft drinks, may be unattractive to outsiders (because of high entry barriers and the global competitive capabilities of Coca-Cola and PepsiCo). Companies on the outside may look at an industry's environment and conclude that it is an unattractive business for them to get into, given the prevailing entry barriers, their particular resources and competencies, the difficulty of challenging current market leaders, and the more profitable opportunities they seem to have elsewhere. But a favorably positioned company already in the industry may survey the very same business environment and conclude that the industry is attractive because it has the resources and competitive capabilities to take sales and market share away from weaker rivals, build a strong leadership position, and earn good profits.

> A company that is uniquely well-situated in an otherwise unattractive industry can, under certain circumstances, still earn unusually good profits.

An assessment that the industry is fundamentally attractive typically suggests that current industry participants employ strategies calculated to strengthen their long-term competitive positions in the business, expanding sales efforts and investing in additional facilities and equipment as needed. If the industry and competitive situation is judged relatively unattractive, more successful industry participants may choose to invest cautiously, look for ways to protect their long-term competitiveness and profitability, and perhaps acquire smaller firms if the price is right; over the longer term, strong companies may consider diversification into more attractive businesses. Weak companies in unattractive industries may consider merging with a rival to bolster market share and profitability or, alternatively, begin looking outside the industry for attractive diversification opportunities.

ACTUALLY DOING AN INDUSTRY AND COMPETITIVE ANALYSIS

Table 3.5 provides a format for presenting the pertinent findings and conclusions of industry and competitive analysis. It embraces all seven questions discussed above and leads would-be analysts to do the strategic thinking and evaluation needed to draw perceptive conclusions about the state of the industry and competitive environment.

table 3.5   Sample Form for an Industry and Competitive Analysis Summary

1. **Dominant Economic Characteristics of the Industry Environment** (market size and growth rate, geographic scope, number and sizes of buyers and sellers, pace of technological change and innovation, scale economies, experience curve effects, capital requirements, and so on)

2. **Competition Analysis**
   - Rivalry among competing sellers (a strong, moderate, or weak force; weapons that rivals are relying upon in their efforts to outcompete one another)

   - Threat of potential entry (a strong, moderate, or weak force; assessment of entry barriers)

   - Competition from substitutes (a strong, moderate, or weak force, and why)

   - Power of suppliers (a strong, moderate, or weak force, and why)

   - Power of customers (a strong, moderate, or weak force, and why)

3. **Driving Forces**

4. **Competitive Position of Major Companies/Strategic Groups**
   - Those that are favorably positioned, and why

   - Those that are unfavorably positioned, and why

5. **Competitor Analysis**
   - Strategic approaches/predicted moves of key competitors

   - Whom to watch, and why

6. **Industry Key Success Factors**

7. **Industry Prospects and Overall Attractiveness**
   - Factors making the industry attractive

   - Factors making the industry unattractive

   - Special industry issues/problems

   - Profit outlook (favorable/unfavorable)

Two things should be kept in mind in doing industry and competitive analysis. First, the task of analyzing a company's external situation cannot be reduced to a mechanical exercise in which facts and data are plugged in and definitive conclusions come pouring out. Strategic analysis always leaves room for differences of opinion about how all the factors add up and what future industry and competitive conditions will be. There can be several appealing scenarios about how an industry will evolve, whether it will be an attractive or unattractive business to be in, and how good the profit outlook is. However, while no strategy analysis methodology can guarantee a single conclusive diagnosis, it doesn't make sense to shortcut strategic analysis and rely on opinion and casual observation. Managers become better strategists when they know what analytical questions to pose, have the skills to read clues about industry and competitive changes, and can use situation analysis techniques to find answers and identify strategic issues. This is why we concentrated on suggesting the right questions to ask, explaining concepts and analytical approaches, and indicating the kinds of things to look for.

Second, sweeping industry and competitive analyses need to be done every one to three years; in the interim, managers are obliged to continually update and reexamine their thinking as events unfold. There's no substitute for being a good student of industry and competitive conditions and staying on the cutting edge of what's happening in the industry. Anything else leaves a manager unprepared to initiate shrewd and timely strategic adjustments.

key|points

Thinking strategically about a company's external situation involves probing for answers to the following seven questions:

1. *What are the industry's dominant economic features?* Industries differ significantly on such factors as market size and growth rate, the geographic scope of competitive rivalry, the number and relative sizes of both buyers and sellers, ease of entry and exit, whether sellers are vertically integrated, how fast basic technology is changing, the extent of scale economies and experience curve effects, whether the products of rival sellers are standardized or differentiated, and overall profitability. An industry's economic characteristics are important because of the implications they have for crafting strategy.

2. *What is competition like and how strong are each of the five competitive forces?* The strength of competition is a composite of five forces: the rivalry among competing sellers, the presence of attractive substitutes, the potential for new entry, the competitive pressures stemming from supplier–seller collaboration and bargaining, and the competitive pressures stemming from seller–buyer collaboration and bargaining. The task of competition analysis is to understand the competitive pressures associated with each force; determine whether these pressures add up to a strong or weak competitive force in the marketplace, and then think strategically about what sort of competitive strategy, given the rules of competition in the industry, the company will need to employ to (*a*) insulate the firm as much as possible from the five competitive forces, (*b*) influence the industry's competitive rules in the company's favor, and (*c*) gain a competitive edge.

3. *What is causing the industry's competitive structure and business environment to change?* Industry and competitive conditions change because forces are in motion that create incentives or pressures for change. The most common driving forces are the industry changes being wrought by the Internet and mushrooming e-commerce transactions, globalization of competition in the industry, changes in the long-term industry growth rate, changes in buyer composition, product innovation, entry or exit of major firms, changes in cost and efficiency, changing buyer preferences for standardized versus differentiated products or services, regulatory influences and

government policy changes, changing societal and lifestyle factors, and reductions in uncertainty and business risk. Sound analysis of driving forces and their implications for the industry is a prerequisite to sound strategy making.

4. *Which companies are in the strongest/weakest positions?* Strategic group mapping is a valuable, if not necessary, tool for understanding the similarities, differences, strengths, and weaknesses inherent in the market positions of rival companies. Rivals in the same or nearby strategic groups are close competitors, whereas companies in distant strategic groups usually pose little or no immediate threat.

5. *What strategic moves are rivals likely to make next?* This analytical step involves identifying competitors' strategies, deciding which rivals are likely to be strong contenders and which weak contenders, evaluating their competitive options, and predicting what moves they are likely to make next. Scouting competitors well enough to anticipate their actions can help a company prepare effective countermoves (perhaps even beat a rival to the punch) and allows managers to take rivals' probable actions into account in designing their own company's best course of action. Managers who fail to study competitors closely risk being blindsided by surprise actions on the part of rivals. A company can't expect to outmaneuver its rivals without monitoring their actions and anticipating their next moves.

6. *What are the key factors for competitive success?* An industry's key success factors (KSFs) are the particular strategy elements, product attributes, competitive capabilities, and business outcomes that spell the difference between profit and loss and, ultimately, between competitive success or failure. KSFs by their very nature are so important that *all firms* in the industry must pay close attention to them—they are the *prerequisites* for industry success or, to put it another way, KSFs are *the rules* that shape whether a company will be financially and competitively successful. Frequently, a company can gain sustainable competitive advantage by training its strategy on industry KSFs and devoting its energies to being distinctively better than rivals at succeeding on these factors. Companies that only dimly or incompletely perceive what factors are truly crucial to long-term competitive success are less likely to have winning strategies.

7. *Is the industry attractive and what are its prospects for above-average profitability?* The answer to this question is a major driver of company strategy. An assessment that the industry and competitive environment is fundamentally attractive typically suggests employing a strategy calculated to build a stronger competitive position in the business, expanding sales efforts and investing in additional facilities and equipment as needed. If the industry is relatively unattractive, outsiders considering entry may decide against it and look elsewhere for opportunities, weak companies in the industry may merge with or be acquired by a rival, and strong companies may restrict further investments and employ cost-reduction strategies or product innovation strategies to boost long-term competitiveness and protect their profitability. On occasion, an industry that is unattractive overall is still very attractive to a favorably situated company with the skills and resources to take business away from weaker rivals.

Good industry and competitive analysis is a prerequisite to good strategy making. A competently done industry and competitive analysis tells a clear, easily understood story about the company's external environment. It provides the understanding of a company's macroenvironment needed for shrewdly matching strategy to the company's external situation.

suggested | readings

D'Aveni, Richard A. *Hypercompetition.* New York: Free Press, 1994, chapters 5 and 6.

Ghemawat, Pankaj. "Building Strategy on the Experience Curve." *Harvard Business Review* 64, no. 2 (March–April 1985), pp. 143–49.

Kahaner, Larry. "What You Can Learn from Your Competitors' Mission Statements." *Competitive Intelligence Review* 6 no. 4 (Winter 1995), pp. 35–40.

Langley, Ann. "Between 'Paralysis by Analysis' and 'Extinction by Instinct.'" *Sloan Management Review* (Spring 1995), pp. 63–75.

Linneman, Robert E., and Harold E. Klein. "Using Scenarios in Strategic Decision Making." *Business Horizons* 28, no. 1 (January–February 1985), pp. 64–74.

Porter, Michael E. *Competitive Strategy: Techniques for Analyzing Industries and Competitors.* New York: Free Press, 1980, chapter 1.

———. *Competitive Advantage.* New York: Free Press, 1985, Chapter 2.

———. "Clusters and the New Economics of Competition." *Harvard Business Review* 76, no. 6 (November–December 1998), pp. 77–90.

Thomas, Howard; Timothy Pollock; and Philip Gorman. "Global Strategic Analyses: Frameworks and Approaches." *Academy of Management Executive* 13, no.1 (February 1999), pp. 70–82.

Zahra, Shaker A., and Sherry S. Chaples. "Blind Spots in Competitive Analysis." *Academy of Management Executive* 7, no. 2 (May 1993), pp. 7–28.

chapter | four

Evaluating Company Resources and Competitive Capabilities

The real question isn't how well you're doing today against your own history, but how you're doing against your competitors.

—Donald Kress

Organizations succeed in a competitive marketplace over the long run because they can do certain things their customers value better than can their competitors.

—Robert Hayes, Gary Pisano, and David Upton

The greatest mistake managers make when evaluating their resources is failing to assess them relative to competitors'.

—David J. Collis and Cynthia A. Montgomery

If a company is not "best in world" at a critical activity, it is sacrificing competitive advantage by performing that activity with its existing technique.

—James Brian Quinn

Only firms who are able to continually build new strategic assets faster and cheaper than their competitors will earn superior returns over the long term.

—C. C. Markides and P. J. Williamson

In Chapter 3 we described how to use the tools of industry and competitive analysis to strategically assess a company's external environment. In this chapter we discuss the techniques of evaluating a company's resource capabilities, relative cost position, and competitive strength versus rivals. Company situation analysis prepares the groundwork for matching the company's strategy both to its external market circumstances and to its internal resources and competitive capabilities. The spotlight of company situation analysis is trained on five questions:

1. How well is the company's present strategy working?
2. What are the company's resource strengths and weaknesses and its external opportunities and threats?
3. Are the company's prices and costs competitive?
4. How strong is the company's competitive position relative to its rivals?
5. What strategic issues does the company face?

To explore these questions, we'll be using four analytical techniques: SWOT analysis, value chain analysis, strategic cost analysis, and competitive strength assessment. These techniques are basic strategic management tools that serve to illuminate a company's resource strengths and deficiencies, its best market opportunities, the outside threats to its future profitability, and its competitive standing relative to rivals. Insightful company situation analysis is a precondition for identifying the strategic issues that management needs to address and for tailoring strategy to company resources and competitive capabilities as well as to industry and competitive conditions.

QUESTION 1: HOW WELL IS THE PRESENT STRATEGY WORKING?

In evaluating how well a company's present strategy is working, a manager has to start with what the strategy is. (See Figure 2.3 in Chapter 2 to review the key components of business strategy.) The first thing to pin down is the company's competitive approach. Is the company striving to be a low-cost leader *or* stressing ways to differentiate its product offering from rivals? Is it concentrating its efforts on serving a broad spectrum of customers *or* a narrow market niche? Another strategy-defining consideration is the firm's competitive scope within the industry—how many stages of the industry's production-distribution chain it operates in (one, several, or all), what its geographic market coverage is, and the size and makeup of its customer base. The company's functional strategies in production, marketing, finance, human resources, information technology, new product innovation, and so on further characterize company strategy. In addition, the company may have initiated some recent strategic moves (for instance, price cuts, design improvements, stepped-up advertising, entry into a new geographic area, or merger with a competitor) that are integral to its strategy and that aim at securing an improved competitive position and, optimally, a competitive advantage. The strategy being pursued can be further nailed down by probing the logic behind each competitive move and functional approach.

While there's merit in evaluating the strategy from a *qualitative* standpoint (its completeness, internal consistency, rationale, and suitability to the situation), the best *quantitative* evidence of how well a company's strategy is working comes from studying the company's recent strategic and financial performance and seeing what story the numbers tell about the results the strategy is producing. The two best empirical indicators are (1) whether the company is achieving its stated financial and strategic objectives, and (2) whether the company is an above-average industry performer.[1] Persistent shortfalls in meeting company performance targets and weak performance relative to rivals are reliable warning signs that the company suffers from poor strategy making, less-than-competent strategy execution, or both. Sometimes company objectives are not explicit enough (especially to company outsiders) to benchmark actual performance against, but it is nearly always feasible to evaluate the performance of a company's strategy by looking at:

- Whether the firm's sales are growing faster, slower, or about the same pace as the market as a whole, thus resulting in a rising, eroding, or stable market share.
- Whether the company is acquiring new customers at an attractive rate as well as retaining existing customers.
- Whether the firm's profit margins are increasing or decreasing and how well its margins compare to rival firms' margins.
- Trends in the firm's net profits, return on investment, and economic value added, and how these compare to the same trends for other companies in the industry.
- Whether the company's overall financial strength and credit rating are improving or on the decline.

---

[1]For an excellent discussion of performance measures that reveal how well a company's strategy is working, see Robert S. Kaplan and David P. Norton, "The Balanced Scorecard—Measures That Drive Performance," *Harvard Business Review* 70, no. 1 (January–February 1992), pp. 71–79.

- Whether the company can demonstrate continuous improvement in such internal performance measures as unit cost, defect rate, scrap rate, employee motivation and morale, number of stockouts and customer back orders, fewer days of inventory, and so on.
- How shareholders view the company based on trends in the company's stock price and shareholder value (relative to the market value added of other companies in the industry).
- The firm's image and reputation with its customers.
- Whether the company is regarded as a leader in technology, product innovation, e-commerce, product quality, short times from order to delivery, having the best prices, getting newly developed products to market quickly, or other relevant factors on which buyers base their choice of brands.

> The stronger a company's financial performance and market position, the more likely it has a well-conceived, well-executed strategy.

The stronger a company's current overall performance, the less likely the need for radical changes in strategy. The weaker a company's financial performance and market standing, the more its current strategy must be questioned. Weak performance is almost always a sign of weak strategy, weak execution, or both.

QUESTION 2: WHAT ARE THE COMPANY'S RESOURCE STRENGTHS AND WEAKNESSES AND ITS EXTERNAL OPPORTUNITIES AND THREATS?

Sizing up a firm's resource strengths and weaknesses and its external opportunities and threats, commonly known as *SWOT analysis*, provides a good overview of whether a firm's business position is fundamentally healthy or unhealthy. SWOT analysis is grounded in the basic principle that *strategy-making efforts must aim at producing a good fit between a company's resource capability* (as reflected by its balance of resource strengths and weaknesses) *and its external situation* (as reflected by industry and competitive conditions, the company's own market opportunities, and specific external threats to the company's profitability and market standing). Perceptive understanding of a company's resource capabilities and deficiencies, its market opportunities, and the external threats to its future well-being is essential to good strategy-making. Otherwise, the task of conceiving a strategy that capitalizes on the company's resources, aims squarely at capturing the company's best opportunities, and neutralizes the threats to its well-being becomes a chancy proposition indeed.

Identifying Company Strengths and Resource Capabilities

A *strength* is something a company is good at doing or a characteristic that gives it enhanced competitiveness. A strength can take any of several forms:

- *A skill or important expertise*—low-cost manufacturing capabilities, strong e-commerce expertise, technological know-how, a proven track record in defect-free manufacture, expertise in providing consistently good customer service, excellent mass merchandising skills, or unique advertising and promotional talents.
- *Valuable physical assets*—state-of-the-art plants and equipment, attractive real estate locations, worldwide distribution facilities, ownership of valuable natural

resource deposits, cutting-edge computer networks and information systems, or sizable amounts of cash and marketable securities.

- *Valuable human assets*—an experienced and capable workforce, talented employees in key areas, motivated and energetic employees, cutting-edge knowledge and intellectual capital, astute entrepreneurship and managerial know-how, or the collective learning embedded in the organization and built up over time.[2]

- *Valuable organizational assets*—proven quality control systems, proprietary technology, key patents, mineral rights, a base of loyal customers, a strong balance sheet and credit rating, cutting-edge supply chain management systems, a well-functioning company intranet, and e-commerce systems for accessing and exchanging information with suppliers and key customers, computer-assisted design and manufacturing systems, systems for conducting business on the Internet, or a comprehensive list of customers' e-mail addresses.

- *Valuable intangible assets*—brand-name image, company reputation, buyer goodwill, or a motivated and energized workforce.

- *Competitive capabilities*—short development times in bringing new products to market, a strong dealer network, strong partnerships with key suppliers, an R&D organization with the ability to keep the company's pipeline full of innovative new products, a high degree of organizational agility in responding to shifting market conditions and emerging opportunities, a cadre of highly trained customer service representatives, or state-of-the-art systems for doing business via the Internet.

- *An achievement or attribute that puts the company in a position of market advantage*—low overall costs, market share leadership, a superior product, a wide product selection, strong name recognition, state-of-the-art e-commerce technologies and practices, or exceptional customer service.

- *Alliances or cooperative ventures*—fruitful collaborative partnerships with suppliers and marketing allies that enhance the company's own competitiveness.

Company strengths thus have diverse origins. Sometimes they relate to fairly specific skills and expertise (like know-how in researching consumer tastes and buying habits or training customer contact employees to be cordial and helpful) and sometimes they flow from different resources teaming together to create a competitive capability (like continuous product innovation—which tends to result from a combination of knowledge of consumer needs, technological know-how, R&D, product design and engineering, cost-effective manufacturing, market testing, and other types of intellectual capital).[3] The regularity with which employees from different parts of the organization pool their knowledge and expertise, their skills in exploiting and building on the organization's physical and intangible assets, and the effectiveness with which they collaborate can

---

[2]Many business organizations are coming to view cutting-edge knowledge and intellectual resources as a valuable competitive asset and have concluded that explicitly managing these assets is an essential part of their strategy. See Michael H. Zack, "Developing a Knowledge Strategy," *California Management Review* 41, no. 3 (Spring 1999), pp. 125–45 and Shaker A. Zahra, Anders P. Nielsen, and William C. Bogner, "Corporate Entrepreneurship, Knowledge, and Competence Development," *Entrepreneurship Theory and Practice,* Spring 1999, pp. 169–89.

[3]For a discussion of how to measure the competitive power of a company's resource base, see Nick Bontis, Nicola C. Dragonetti, Kristine Jacobsen, and Goran Roos, "The Knowledge Toolbox: A Review of the Tools Available to Measure and Manage Intangible Resources," *European Management Journal* 17, no. 4 (August 1999), pp. 391–401.

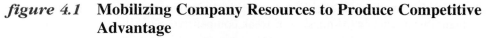

figure 4.1   **Mobilizing Company Resources to Produce Competitive Advantage**

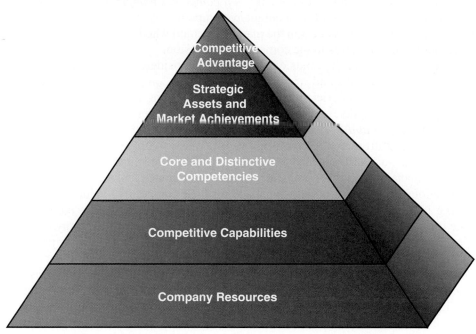

create competitive capabilities not otherwise achievable by a single department or organizational unit within the enterprise.

Taken together, a company's skills and expertise, its intellectual capital, its competitive capabilities, its uniquely strong competencies, its collection of strategically valuable assets, and its market achievements determine the complement of *resources* with which it competes. The caliber of its resources and its ability to mobilize them in a manner calculated to result in competitive advantage are the biggest determinants of how well the company will be able to perform in light of the prevailing industry and competitive conditions—see Figure 4.1.[4]

> **Basic Concept**
> A company is positioned to succeed if it has a competitively valuable complement of resources at its command.

Identifying Company Weaknesses and Resource Deficiencies

A *weakness* is something a company lacks or does poorly (in comparison to others) or a condition that puts it at a disadvantage. A company's internal weaknesses can relate to (1) deficiencies in competitively important skills or expertise or intellectual capital

[4]In the past decade, there's been considerable research into the role a company's resources and competitive capabilities play in crafting strategy and in determining company profitability. The findings and conclusions have coalesced into what is called the resource-based view of the firm. Among the most insightful articles are Birger Wernerfelt, "A Resource-Based View of the Firm," *Strategic Management Journal,* September–October 1984, pp. 171–80; Jay Barney, "Firm Resources and Sustained Competitive Advantage," *Journal of Management* 17, no. 1 (1991), pp. 99–120; Margaret A. Peteraf, "The Cornerstones of Competitive Advantage: A Resource-Based View," *Strategic Management Journal,* March 1993, pp. 179–91; Birger Wernerfelt, "The Resource-Based View of the Firm: Ten Years After," *Strategic Management Journal* 16 (1995), pp. 171–74; and Jay B. Barney, "Looking Inside for Competitive Advantage," *Academy of Management Executive* 9, no. 4 (November 1995), pp. 49–61.

of one kind or another; (2) a lack of competitively important physical, organizational, or intangible assets; or (3) missing or weak competitive capabilities in key areas. *Internal weaknesses are thus shortcomings in a company's complement of resources.* A weakness may or may not make a company competitively vulnerable, depending on how much the weakness matters in the marketplace and whether it can be overcome by the resources and strengths in the company's possession.

Table 4.1 indicates the kinds of factors to be considered in determining a company's resource strengths and weaknesses. Sizing up a company's complement of resource capabilities and deficiencies is akin to constructing a *strategic balance sheet* where resource strengths represent *competitive assets* and resource weaknesses represent *competitive liabilities*. Obviously, the ideal condition is for the company's strengths/competitive assets to outweigh its weaknesses/competitive liabilities by an ample margin—a 50-50 balance is definitely not the desired condition!

> **Basic Concept**
> A company's resource strengths represent competitive assets; its resource weaknesses represent competitive liabilities.

Once managers identify a company's resource strengths and weaknesses, the two compilations need to be carefully evaluated for their competitive value and strategy-making implications. Some resource strengths and competencies are *competitively* more important than others because they add greater power to the company's strategy or are bigger factors in contributing to a strong market position and higher profitability. Likewise, some weaknesses can prove fatal if not remedied, while others are inconsequential, easily corrected, or offset by company strengths. A company's resource weaknesses suggest a need to review its resource base: What existing resource deficiencies need to be remedied? Does the company have important resource gaps that need to be filled? What needs to be done to augment the company's future resource base?

Identifying Company Competencies and Capabilities

The Related Concepts of Company Competence and Competitive Capability   Identifying and evaluating what a company is really good at doing and what capabilities it has for competing is a critical component of assessing a company's situation. A **company competence** is nearly always the product of experience, representing an accumulation of learning over time and the buildup over time of *real proficiency*. Competencies have to be consciously built and developed—they don't just happen. A company competence originates with deliberate efforts to develop the organizational ability to do something, however imperfectly or inefficiently. Such efforts entail selecting people with the requisite knowledge and skills, upgrading or expanding individual abilities as needed, and then molding the efforts and work products of individuals into a cooperative group effort to create organizational ability. Then as experience builds, such that the company reaches a level of ability to perform the activity consistently well and at an acceptable cost, the ability begins to translate into a true competence.

> **Basic Concept**
> A *company competence* is the product of learning and experience and represents real proficiency in performing an internal activity.

Examples of competencies include skills in merchandising and product display, the ability to create attractive and easy-to-use Web sites, expertise in a specific technology, proven ability to select good locations for retail outlets, skills in working with customers on new applications and uses of the product, and expertise in just-in-time inventory management practices. Company competencies are normally bundles of skills, know-how, resources, and technologies—as opposed to a single discrete skill or resource or technology.

table 4.1   SWOT Analysis—What to Look For in Sizing Up a Company's Strengths, Weaknesses, Opportunities, and Threats

Potential Resource Strengths and Competitive Capabilities	**Potential Resource Weaknesses and Competitive Deficiencies**
• A powerful strategy supported by competitively valuable skills and expertise in key areas • A strong financial condition; ample financial resources to grow the business • Strong brand name image/company reputation • A widely recognized market leader and an attractive customer base • Ability to take advantage of economies of scale and/or learning and experience curve effects • Proprietary technology/superior technological skills/important patents • Superior intellectual capital relative to key rivals • Cost advantages • Strong advertising and promotion • Product innovation skills • Proven skills in improving production processes • Sophisticated use of e-commerce technologies and processes • Superior skills in supply chain management • A reputation for good customer service • Better product quality relative to rivals • Wide geographic coverage and/or strong global distribution capability • Alliances/joint ventures with other firms that provide access to valuable technology, competencies, and/or attractive geographic markets	• No clear strategic direction • Obsolete facilities • A weak balance sheet; burdened with too much debt • Higher overall unit costs relative to key competitors • Missing some key skills or competencies/lack of management depth/a deficiency of intellectual capital relative to leading rivals • Subpar profitability because . . . • Plagued with internal operating problems • Falling behind rivals in putting e-commerce capabilities and strategies in place • Too narrow a product line relative to rivals • Weak brand image or reputation • Weaker dealer network than key rivals and/or lack of adequate global distribution capability • Subpar e-commerce systems and capabilities relative to rivals • Short on financial resources to fund promising strategic initiatives • Lots of underutilized plant capacity • Behind on product quality and/or R&D and/or technological know-how • Not attracting new customers as rapidly as rivals due to ho-hum product attributes
Potential Company Opportunities	**Potential External Threats to Company's Well-Being**
• Serving additional customer groups or expanding into new geographic markets or product segments • Expanding the company's product line to meet a broader range of customer needs • Utilizing existing company skills or technological know-how to enter new product lines or new businesses • Using the Internet and e-commerce technologies to dramatically cut costs and/or to pursue new sales growth opportunities • Integrating forward or backward • Falling trade barriers in attractive foreign markets • Openings to take market share away from rivals • Ability to grow rapidly because of sharply rising demand in one or more market segments • Acquisition of rival firms or companies with attractive technological expertise • Alliances or joint ventures that expand the firm's market coverage or boost its competitive capability • Openings to exploit emerging new technologies • Market openings to extend the company's brand name or reputation to new geographic areas	• Likely entry of potent new competitors • Loss of sales to substitute products • Mounting competition from new Internet start-up companies pursuing e-commerce strategies • Increasing intensity of competition among industry rivals—may cause squeeze on profit margins • Technological changes or product innovations that undermine demand for the firm's product • Slowdowns in market growth • Adverse shifts in foreign exchange rates and trade policies of foreign governments • Costly new regulatory requirements • Growing bargaining power of customers or suppliers • A shift in buyer needs and tastes away from the industry's product • Adverse demographic changes that threaten to curtail demand for the firm's product • Vulnerability to industry driving forces

Companies consist of a collection of competencies and competitive capabilities.

A company competence becomes a meaningful **competitive capability** when customers deem the competence valuable and beneficial, when it helps differentiate a company from its competitors, and when it enhances its competitiveness. However, it is important to understand that competitive capabilities are not all equal—*some merely enable survival* because they are common to most all rivals while *others hold potential for changing the basis of competition* because they are unique, proprietary, and deliver considerable customer value. But *it is useful to think of a company as consisting of a collection of capabilities,* some difficult to disentangle from one another and some stronger and more competitively valuable than others.

Core Competencies: A Valuable Company Resource

One of the most valuable resources a company has is the ability to perform a competitively relevant activity very well. A competitively important internal activity that a company performs better than other competitively important internal activities is termed a **core competence.** While a core competence is something a company does well internally, what makes it a *core* competence as opposed to just a competence is that it is central to a company's competitiveness and profitability rather than peripheral. A company's core competence can relate to any of several aspects of its business: expertise in building networks and systems that enable e-commerce, speeding new or next-generation products to market, good after-sale service, skills in manufacturing a high-quality product, innovativeness in developing popular product features, speed and agility in responding to new market trends and changing competitive conditions, know-how in creating and operating a system for filling customer orders accurately and swiftly, and expertise in integrating multiple technologies to create families of new products.

A company may have more than one core competence in its resource portfolio but rare is the company that can legitimately claim more than two or three core competencies. Plainly, *a core competence gives a company competitive capability* and thus qualifies as a genuine company strength and resource.[5]

Most often, *a company's core competence resides in its people and in its intellectual capital, not in its assets on the balance sheet.* Core competencies tend to be grounded in cross-department and cross-functional combinations of skills, resources, and technologies. Knowledge and intellectual capital, more than physical assets and tangible organizational resources, are the key ingredients of a core competence and a firm's competitive capability.

Basic Concept
A *core competence* is something that a company does well relative to other internal activities; a *distinctive competence* is something a company does well relative to competitors.

Distinctive Competencies: A Competitively Superior Company Resource

Whether a company's core competence represents a **distinctive competence** depends on how good the competence is relative to what competitors are capable of—is it a competitively superior competence or just a standout internal company competence? A distinctive competence is something a company does well in comparison to its competitors.[6] Most every company does one competitively important activity enough better than the other things it does internally that it can claim that activity as a core competence. But what a company does best internally doesn't translate into a

---

[5]For a more extensive discussion of how to identify and evaluate the competitive power of a company's capabilities, see David W. Birchall and George Tovstiga, "The Strategic Potential of a Firm's Knowledge Portfolio," *Journal of General Management* 25, no. 1 (Autumn 1999), pp. 1–16; also see David Teece, "Capturing Value from Knowledge Assets: The New Economy, Markets for Know-How, and Intangible Assets," *California Management Review* 40, no. 3 (Spring 1998), pp. 55–79.

[6]For a fuller discussion of the core competence concept, see C. K. Prahalad and Gary Hamel, "The Core Competence of the Corporation," *Harvard Business Review* 68, no. 3 (May–June 1990), pp. 79–93.

distinctive competence unless the company performs that activity better than rivals and thus enjoys *competitive superiority*. For instance, most all retailers believe they have core competencies in product selection and in-store merchandising, but many retailers who build strategies on these competencies run into trouble in the marketplace because they encounter rivals whose competencies in these areas are better than theirs. Consequently, *a core competence becomes a basis for competitive advantage only when it is a distinctive competence.*

Sharp Corporation's distinctive competence in flat-panel display technology has enabled it to dominate the worldwide market for liquid crystal displays (LCDs). The distinctive competencies of Toyota and Honda in low-cost, high-quality manufacturing and in short design-to-market cycles for new models have proved to be considerable competitive advantages in the global market for motor vehicles. Intel's distinctive competence in rapidly developing new generations of ever more powerful semiconductor chips for personal computers has helped give the company a dominating presence in the personal computer industry. Starbucks' distinctive competence in store ambience and innovative coffee drinks has propelled it to the forefront among coffee retailers. Motorola's distinctive competence in virtually defect-free manufacture (six-sigma quality—an error rate of about 3.4 per million) has contributed significantly to the company's world leadership in cellular telephone equipment. Rubbermaid's distinctive competence in developing innovative rubber and plastics products for household and commercial use has made it the clear leader in its industry.

The importance of a distinctive competence to strategy-making rests with (1) the competitively valuable capability it gives a company, (2) its potential for being a cornerstone of strategy, and (3) the competitive edge it can produce in the marketplace. It is always easier to build competitive advantage when a firm has a distinctive competence in performing activities important to market success, when rival companies do not have offsetting competencies, and when it is costly and time-consuming for rivals to imitate the competence. A distinctive competence is thus potentially the mainspring of a company's success—unless it is trumped by more powerful resources of rivals.

Strategic Management Principle
A distinctive competence empowers a company to build competitive advantage.

Determining the Competitive Value of a Company Resource

No two companies are alike in their resources. They don't have the same skill sets; assets (physical, human, organizational, and intangible); competitive capabilities; or market achievements—a condition that results in different companies having different strengths and weaknesses. *Differences in company resources account for why some companies are more profitable and more competitively successful than others.* A company's success is more certain when it has appropriate and ample resources with which to compete, and especially when it has a valuable strength, asset, capability, or achievement with the potential to produce competitive advantage.

For a particular company resource to qualify as the basis for sustainable competitive advantage, it must pass four tests of competitive value:[7]

- *Is the resource hard to copy?* The more difficult and more expensive it is to imitate a resource, the greater its potential competitive value. Hard-to-copy resources limit competition, making any profit stream they are able to generate more sustainable. Resources can be difficult to copy because of their uniqueness (a fantastic real estate location, patent protection), because they must be built over time in ways

---

[7]See David J. Collis and Cynthia A. Montgomery, "Competing on Resources: Strategy in the 1990s," *Harvard Business Review* 73, no. 4 (July–August 1995), pp. 120–23.

that are difficult to imitate (a brand name, mastery of a technology), and because they carry big capital requirements (a new cost-effective plant to manufacture semiconductor chips can cost $1 to $2 billion).

- *How long does the resource last?* The longer a resource lasts, the greater its value. Some resources lose their value quickly because of the rapid speeds with which technologies or industry conditions are moving. The value of Eastman Kodak's resources in film and film processing is rapidly being undercut by the growing popularity of digital cameras. The value of 3Com's expertise in PC modem technology is fast being eroded by the onslaught of cable modems and by the efforts of chip manufacturers to incorporate modem functions directly into the microprocessor instruction set. The investments that commercial banks have made in branch offices is a rapidly depreciating asset because of growing use of direct deposits, ATMs, and telephone and Internet banking options.

- *Is the resource really competitively superior?* Companies have to guard against pridefully believing that their core competences are distinctive competences or that their brand name is more powerful than the brand names of rivals. Who can really say whether Coca-Cola's consumer marketing skills are better than Pepsi-Cola's or whether Mercedes-Benz's brand name is more powerful than BMW's or Lexus's?

- *Can the resource be trumped by the different resources/capabilities of rivals?* Many commercial airlines (American Airlines, Delta Airlines, United Airlines, Singapore Airlines) have succeeded because of their resources and capabilities in offering safe, convenient, reliable air transportation services and in providing an array of amenities to passengers. However, Southwest Airlines has been a more consistently profitable air carrier by building the capabilities to provide safe, reliable, basic services at radically lower fares. The prestigious brand names of Cadillac and Lincoln have faded as dominating factors in choosing what luxury cars to buy—Mercedes, BMW, and Lexus have introduced the most appealing luxury vehicles in recent years. Amazon.com is putting a big dent in the business prospects of brick-and-mortar bookstore chains like Barnes & Noble and Borders; likewise, eToys (with its Internet retailing capabilities) and Wal-Mart (with its lower prices) are putting major competitive pressure on Toys "R" Us, at one time the leading toy retailer.

Strategic Management Principle
Successful strategists seek to capitalize on what a company does best—its expertise, resource strengths, and strongest competitive capabilities.

The vast majority of companies are not well endowed with competitively valuable resources, much less with competitively superior resources capable of passing the above four tests with flying colors. Most businesses have a mixed bag of resources—one or two quite valuable, some good, many satisfactory to mediocre. Only a few companies, usually the strongest industry leaders or up-and-coming challengers, possess a competitively superior resource. Furthermore, nearly all companies have competitive liabilities, whether they be labeled internal weaknesses, a lack of assets, missing expertise or capabilities, or resource deficiencies.

Even if a company doesn't possess a competitively superior resource, the potential for competitive advantage is not lost. Sometimes a company derives significant competitive vitality, even competitive advantage, from a collection of good to adequate resources which, in combination, have competitive power in the marketplace. Toshiba's laptop computers were the market share leader throughout most of the 1990s—an indicator that Toshiba was good at something. Yet Toshiba's laptops were not demonstrably faster than rivals' laptops, nor did they have superior performance features (bigger screens, more memory, longer battery power, a better pointing device, and so on), nor did Toshiba provide clearly superior technical support services to buyers of its laptops. And Toshiba laptops were definitely not cheaper, model for model, than the comparable models of its rivals. Toshiba laptops seldom ranked first in the overall performance ratings done by various organizations. Rather, Toshiba's market share leadership stemmed from a *combination* of good resource strengths and capabilities—its strategic partnerships with suppliers of laptop components, its efficient assembly capability, its design expertise, its skills in choosing quality components, its creation of a wide selection of models, the attractive mix of built-in performance features found in each model when balanced against price, the much-better-than-average reliability of its laptops (based on buyer ratings), and its very good technical support services (based on buyer ratings). The verdict from the marketplace was that PC buyers considered Toshiba laptops as better, all things considered, than competing brands.

Matching Strategy to the Company's Resource Strengths and Weaknesses From a strategy-making perspective, a company's resource strengths are significant because they can form the cornerstones of strategy and the basis for creating competitive advantage. If a company doesn't have the resources and competitive capabilities around which to craft an attractive strategy, managers need to take decisive remedial action to upgrade existing organizational resources and capabilities and add others as needed. At the same time, managers have to look toward correcting competitive weaknesses that make the company vulnerable, hold down profitability, or disqualify it from pursuing an attractive opportunity. The strategy-making principle here is simple: *a company's strategy should be tailored to fit its resources—taking both strengths and weaknesses into account.* As a rule, managers should build their strategies around exploiting and leveraging company capabilities—its most valuable resources—and avoid strategies that place heavy demands on areas where the company is weakest or has unproven ability. Companies fortunate enough to have a distinctive competence or other competitively superior resource must be wise in realizing that its value will be eroded by time and competition.[8] So attention to building a strong resource base for the future and to maintaining the competitive superiority of an existing distinctive competence are ever-present needs.

Selecting the Competencies and Capabilities to Concentrate On Enterprises succeed in a competitive marketplace over time because they can do certain things that their customers value better than their rivals. The essence of astute strategy making is selecting the competencies and capabilities to concentrate on and use to underpin the strategy. Sometimes the company already has competitively valuable competencies and capabilities in place and sometimes it has be proactive in developing and building new competencies and capabilities to complement and strengthen its existing resource base. Sometimes the desired competencies and capabilities need to be developed internally and sometimes it is best to acquire them through partnerships or strategic alliances with firms possessing the needed expertise.

Identifying a Company's Market Opportunities

Market opportunity is a big factor in shaping a company's strategy. Indeed, managers can't properly tailor strategy to the company's situation without first identifying each company opportunity and appraising the growth and profit potential each one holds. Depending on the prevailing circumstances, a company's opportunities can be plentiful or

---

[8]Collis and Montgomery, "Competing on Resources: Strategy in the 1990s," p. 124.

illustration capsule 15

TCI's Retreat to a Vision and Strategy in Line with Its Resources and Its Subsequent Acquisition by AT&T

In early 1997, Tele-Communications Inc. (TCI), then the biggest cable TV provider in the United States, with 14 million subscribers, announced that its much heralded vision of transforming itself into an information superhighway and multimedia powerhouse providing cable television, telephone, Internet access, and an array of futuristic data and telecommunications services to all customers in its cable franchise territories was too sweeping, overhyped, and infeasible for the company to pursue profitably within the announced time frame. John Malone, the company's CEO, widely regarded as one of the most astute and influential visionaries of how new information superhighway technologies could transform the world of media and communications, said:

> We were just chasing too many rabbits at the same time. The company got overly ambitious about the things it could do simultaneously.
>
> If you read our annual report last year, you'd think we're one-third data, one-third telephone and one-third video entertainment, instead of 100% video entertainment and two experiments. Right now, we've got zero revenue from residential telephone service, diminishing revenue from high-speed Internet, and $6 billion in revenue from video entertainment.
>
> My job is to prick the bubble. Let's get real.

For years, Malone and TCI had been touting the potential of deploying newly discovered telecommunications technologies over the company's existing cable connections to deliver a dazzling array of information and telecommunications products and services in head-on competition against the telephone companies. TCI's aggressive investment in new technological infrastructure ($1.6 billion in 1996) to deliver the expanded array of products/ services put a strain on its cash flow and prompted bond-rating agencies to put the company on their watch lists for possible credit rating downgrade. TCI's stock price went nowhere in a strong stock market. Plus the new telecommunications bill enacted into law in 1996 created a swirl of strategic maneuvers by local and long-distance telephone companies to position themselves to compete nationwide in both the telephone business and in information superhighway products and services, a development that meant cable operators suddenly confronted a whole new set of larger, resource-rich competitors.

TCI's new, narrower vision was to focus more on the cable TV business (under attack from alternative providers using satellite dish technology as well as from the fiber-optic capability being installed by telephone companies) and to push the vision of information superhighway and multimedia provider farther out into the future, conditional on clearer technological opportunities to profit from investments to modify the existing cable system and provide a wider array of products and services to businesses and households.

But this strategy turned out to be short-lived because AT&T, seeing the same opportunities for bundling local and long distance phone service, wireless communications, cable TV, and high-speed Internet access as TCI, approached John Malone in 1998 with an offer to acquire TCI, combine resources, and pursue much the same opportunity together as Malone and TCI were pursuing independently.

Source: Based on information in "Malone Says TCI Push into Phones, Internet Isn't Working for Now," *The Wall Street Journal*, January 2, 1997, pp. A1, A3; and AT&T annual reports and press releases.

Strategic Management Principle

A company is well-advised to pass on a particular market opportunity unless it has or can build the resource capabilities to capture it.

scarce and can range from wildly attractive (an absolute "must" to pursue) to marginally interesting (low on the company's list of strategic priorities). Table 4.1 presents a checklist of things to be alert for in identifying a company's market opportunities.

In evaluating a company's market opportunities and ranking their attractiveness, managers have to guard against viewing every *industry* opportunity as a *company* opportunity. Not every company in an industry is equipped with the resources to successfully pursue each opportunity that exists in the industry. Some companies are more capable of going after particular opportunities than others, and a few companies may be hopelessly outclassed in trying to contend for a piece of the action. Deliberately adapting a company's resource base to put it in position to contend for attractive growth opportunities is something strategists must pay keen attention to. *The market opportunities most relevant to a company are those that offer important avenues for profitable growth, those where a company has the most potential for competitive advantage, and those that match up well with the company's financial and organizational resource capabilities.*

Identifying the Threats to a Company's Future Profitability

Often, certain factors in a company's external environment pose *threats* to its profitability and competitive well being. Threats can stem from the emergence of cheaper or better technologies, rivals' introduction of new or improved products, the entry of lower-cost foreign competitors into a company's market stronghold, new regulations that are more burdensome to a company than to its competitors, vulnerability to a rise in interest rates, the potential of a hostile takeover, unfavorable demographic shifts, adverse changes in foreign exchange rates, political upheaval in a foreign country where the company has facilities, and the like. External threats may pose no more than a moderate degree of adversity (all companies confront some threatening elements in the course of doing business) or they may be so imposing as to make a company's situation and outlook quite tenuous. It is management's job to identify the threats to the company's future well-being and to evaluate what strategic actions can be taken to neutralize or lessen their impact.

> **Strategic Management Principle**
> Successful strategists aim at capturing a company's best growth opportunities and creating defenses against external threats to its competitive position and future performance.

Table 4.1 presents a list of potential threats to a company's future profitability and market position. Opportunities and threats not only affect the attractiveness of a company's situation but, more important, they point to the need for strategic action. Tailoring strategy to a company's situation entails (1) pursuing market opportunities well suited to the company's resource capabilities and (2) taking actions to defend against external threats to the company's business.

The Real Value of SWOT Analysis

SWOT analysis is more than an exercise in making four lists. The really valuable part of SWOT analysis is determining what story the four lists tell about the company's situation and thinking about what actions are needed. Understanding the story involves evaluating the strengths, weaknesses, opportunities, and threats and drawing conclusions about (1) how the company's strategy can be matched to both its resource capabilities and its market opportunities, and (2) how urgent it is for the company to correct which particular resource weaknesses and guard against which particular external threats.[9] To have managerial and strategy-making value, SWOT analysis must be a basis for action. It also needs to provoke thinking and answers to several questions about what *future* resource strengths and capabilities the company will need to respond to emerging industry and competitive conditions and to produce successful bottom-line results. Will the current strengths matter as much in the future? Are there resource gaps that need to be filled? Do new types of competitive capabilities need to be put in place? Which resources and capabilities need to be given greater emphasis and which merit lesser emphasis? SWOT analysis has not served its purpose until the lessons about the company's situation have been distilled from the four lists.

> Simply listing a company's strengths, weaknesses, opportunities, and threats is not enough; the payoff of SWOT analysis comes from the evaluations and conclusions that flow from the four lists.

[9]See Jack W. Duncan, Peter Ginter, and Linda E. Swayne, "Competitive Advantage and Internal Organizational Assessment," *Academy of Management Executive* 12, no. 3 (August 1998), pp. 6–16.

QUESTION 3: ARE THE COMPANY'S PRICES AND COSTS COMPETITIVE?

Company managers are often stunned when a competitor cuts price to "unbelievably low" levels or when a new market entrant comes on strong with a very low price. The competitor may not, however, be "dumping" (an economic term for selling large amounts of goods below market price), buying market share, or waging a desperate move to gain sales; it may simply have substantially lower costs. One of the most telling signs of whether a company's business position is strong or precarious is whether its prices and costs are competitive with industry rivals. Price-cost comparisons are especially critical in a commodity-product industry where the value provided to buyers is the same from seller to seller, price competition is typically the ruling market force, and lower-cost companies have the upper hand. But even in industries where products are differentiated and competition centers on the different attributes of competing brands as much as on price, rival companies have to keep their costs *in line* and make sure that any added costs they incur and price premiums they charge create ample buyer value.

Competitors usually don't incur the same costs in supplying their products to end users. The cost disparities can range from tiny to competitively significant and can stem from any of several factors:

- Differences in the prices paid for raw materials, components parts, energy, and other items purchased from suppliers.

- Differences in basic technology and the age of plants and equipment. Because rival companies usually invest in plants and key pieces of equipment at different times, their facilities have somewhat different technological efficiencies and different fixed costs (depreciation, maintenance, property taxes, and insurance). Older facilities are typically less efficient, but if they were less expensive to construct or were acquired at bargain prices, they *may* still be reasonably cost-competitive with modern facilities.

- Differences in production costs from rival to rival due to different plant efficiencies, different learning and experience curve effects, different wage rates, different productivity levels, and the like.

- Differences in marketing costs, sales and promotion expenditures, advertising expenses, warehouse distribution costs, and administrative costs.

- Differences in inbound transportation's costs on purchased items and outbound shipping costs on goods sold.

- Differences in forward channel distribution costs (the costs and markups of distributors, wholesalers, and retailers associated with getting the product from the point of manufacture into the hands of end users).

- Differences in rival firms' exposure to the effects of inflation, changes in foreign exchange rates, and tax rates (a frequent occurrence in global industries where competitors have operations in different nations with different economic conditions and governmental taxation policies).

For a company to be competitively successful, its costs must be in line with those of close rivals. While some cost disparity is justified so long as the products or services of closely competing companies are sufficiently differentiated, a high-cost firm's market position becomes increasingly vulnerable the more its costs exceed those of close rivals.

Strategic Cost Analysis and Value Chains

Competitors must be ever alert to how their costs compare with rivals'. While every firm engages in internal cost analysis to stay on top of what its own costs are and how they might be changing, **strategic cost analysis** goes a step further to explore how costs compare against rivals. Strategic cost analysis focuses on a firm's cost position relative to its rivals'.

Every company's business consists of a collection of activities undertaken in the course of designing, producing, marketing, delivering, and supporting its product or service. Each of these activities give rise to costs. The combined costs of all these various activities define the company's internal cost structure. Further, the cost of each activity contributes to whether the company's overall cost position relative to rivals is favorable or unfavorable. The task of strategic cost analysis is to compare a company's costs activity by activity against the costs of key rivals and to learn which internal activities are a source of cost advantage or disadvantage. A company's relative cost position is a function of how the overall costs of the activities it performs in conducting business compare to the overall costs of the activities performed by rivals.

The Concept of a Company Value Chain   The primary analytical tool of strategic cost analysis is a **value chain** identifying the separate activities, functions, and business processes that are performed in designing, producing, marketing, delivering, and supporting a product or service.[10] The chain of value-creating activities it takes to provide a product or service starts with raw materials supply and continues on through parts and components production, manufacturing and assembly, wholesale distribution, and retailing to the end user of the product or service.

A company's value chain shows the linked set of activities and functions it performs internally (see Figure 4.2). The value chain includes a profit margin because a markup over the cost of performing the firm's value-creating activities is customarily part of the price (or total cost) borne by buyers—creating value that exceeds the cost of doing so is a fundamental objective of business. Disaggregating a company's operations into strategically relevant activities and business processes exposes the major elements of the company's cost structure. Each activity in the value chain incurs costs and ties up assets; assigning the company's operating costs and assets to each individual activity in the chain provides cost estimates for each activity. Quite often, there are links between activities such that the manner in which one activity is done can affect the costs of performing other activities. For instance, Japanese producers of videocassette recorders were able to reduce VCR prices from around $1,300 in 1977 to under $300 in 1984 by spotting the impact of an early step in the value chain (product design) on a later step (production) and deciding to change the product design to drastically reduce the number of parts.[11]

Why the Value Chains of Rival Companies Often Differ   A company's value chain and the manner in which it performs each activity reflect the evolution of its own particular business and internal operations, its strategy, the approaches it is

> **Basic Concept**
> *Strategic cost analysis* involves comparing how a company's unit costs stack up against the unit costs of key competitors *activity by activity,* thereby pinpointing which internal activities are a source of cost advantage or disadvantage.

> **Basic Concept**
> A company's *value chain* identifies the primary activities that create value for customers and the related support activities.

---

[10]Value chains and strategic cost analysis are described at greater length in Michael E. Porter, *Competitive Advantage* (New York: Free Press, 1985), chapters 2 and 3; Robin Cooper and Robert S. Kaplan, "Measure Costs Right: Make the Right Decisions," *Harvard Business Review* 66, no. 5 (September–October, 1988), pp. 96–103; and John K. Shank and Vijay Govindarajan, *Strategic Cost Management* (New York: Free Press, 1993), especially chapters 2–6 and 10.

[11]M. Hegert and D. Morris, "Accounting Data for Value Chain Analysis," *Strategic Management Journal* 10 (1989), p. 183.

figure 4.2 **Representative Company Value Chain**

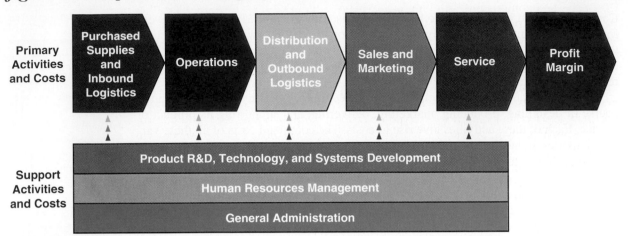

Primary Activities

- **Purchased Supplies and Inbound Logistics**—Activities, costs, and assets associated with purchasing fuel, energy, raw materials, parts components, merchandise, and consumable items from vendors; receiving, storing, and disseminating inputs from suppliers; inspection; and inventory management.

- **Operations**—Activities, costs, and assets associated with converting inputs into final product form (production, assembly, packaging, equipment maintenance, facilities, operations, quality assurance, environmental protection).

- **Distribution and Outbound Logistics**—Activities, costs, and assets dealing with physically distributing the product to buyers (finished goods warehousing, order processing, order picking and packing, shipping, delivery vehicle operations, establishing and maintaining a network of dealers and distributors).

- **Sales and Marketing**—Activities, costs, and assets related to sales force efforts, advertising and promotion, market research and planning, and dealer/distributor support.

- **Service**—Activities, costs, and assets associated with providing assistance to buyers, such as installation, spare parts delivery, maintenance and repair, technical assistance, buyer inquiries, and complaints.

Support Activities

- **Research, Technology, and Systems Development**—Activities, costs, and assets relating to product R&D, process R&D, process design improvement, equipment design, computer software development, telecommunications systems, computer-assisted design and engineering, new database capabilities, and development of computerized support systems.

- **Human Resources Management**—Activities,costs, and assets associated with the recruitment, hiring, training, development, and compensation of all types of personnel; labor relations activities; development of knowledge-based skills and core competencies.

- **General Administration**—Activities, costs, and assets relating to general management, accounting and finance, legal and regulatory affairs, safety and security, management information systems, forming strategic alliances and collaborating with strategic partners, and other "overhead" functions.

Source: Adapted from Michael E. Porter, *Competitive Advantage* (New York: The Free Press, 1985), pp. 37–43.

using to execute its strategy, and the underlying economics of the activities themselves.[12] Because these factors differ from company to company, the value chains of rival companies sometimes differ substantially—a condition that complicates the task of assessing rivals' relative cost positions. For instance, competing companies may differ in their degrees of vertical integration. Comparing the value chain for a fully integrated rival against a partially integrated rival requires adjusting for differences in scope of

---

[12]Porter, *Competitive Advantage*, p. 36.

activities performed. Clearly the internal costs for a manufacturer that *makes* all of its own parts and components will be greater than the internal costs of a producer that *buys* the needed parts and components from outside suppliers and only performs assembly operations.

Likewise, there is legitimate reason to expect value chain and cost differences between a company that is pursuing a low-cost/low-price strategy and a rival that is positioned on the high end of the market with a product that has prestige quality and a wealth of features. In the case of the low-cost firm, the costs of certain activities along the company's value chain should indeed be relatively low, whereas the high-end firm may understandably be spending relatively more to perform those activities that create the added quality and extra features.

Moreover, cost and price differences among rival companies can have their origins in activities performed by suppliers or by forward channel allies involved in getting the product to end users. Suppliers or forward channel allies may have excessively high cost structures or profit margins that jeopardize a company's cost competitiveness even though its costs for internally performed activities are competitive. For example, when determining Michelin's cost competitiveness vis-à-vis Goodyear and Bridgestone in supplying replacement tires to vehicle owners, we have to look at more than whether Michelin's tire manufacturing costs are above or below Goodyear's and Bridgestone's. Let's say that a buyer has to pay $400 for a set of Michelin tires and only $350 for a comparable set of Goodyear or Bridgestone tires; Michelin's $50 price disadvantage in the replacement tire marketplace can stem not only from higher manufacturing costs (reflecting, perhaps, the added costs of Michelin's strategic efforts to build a better-quality tire with more performance features) but also from (1) differences in what the three tire makers pay their suppliers for materials and tire-making components and (2) differences in the operating efficiencies, costs, and markups of Michelin's wholesale–retail dealer outlets versus those of Goodyear and Bridgestone. Thus, determining whether a company's prices and costs are competitive from an end user's standpoint requires looking at the activities and costs of competitively relevant suppliers and forward allies, as well as the costs of internally performed activities.

The Value Chain System for an Entire Industry   As the tire industry example makes clear, a company's value chain is embedded in a larger system of activities that includes the value chains of its upstream suppliers and downstream customers or allies engaged in getting its product or service to end users.[13] *Accurately assessing a company's competitiveness in end-use markets requires that company managers understand the entire value chain system for delivering a product or service to end users, not just the company's own value chain.* At the very least, this means considering the value chains of suppliers and forward channel allies (if any)— as shown in Figure 4.3.

Suppliers' value chains are relevant because suppliers perform activities and incur costs in creating and delivering the purchased inputs used in a company's own value chain; the cost and quality of these inputs influence a company's own cost and/or differentiation capabilities. Anything a company can do to reduce its suppliers' costs or improve suppliers' effectiveness can enhance its own competitiveness—a powerful reason for working collaboratively with suppliers.

Forward channel value chains are relevant because (1) the costs and margins of downstream companies are part of the price the end user pays and (2) the activities

> A company's cost competitiveness depends not only on the costs of internally performed activities (its own value chain) but also on costs in the value chains of suppliers and forward channel allies.

[13]Porter, *Competitive Advantage*, p. 34.

figure 4.3   **Representative Value Chain for an Entire Industry**

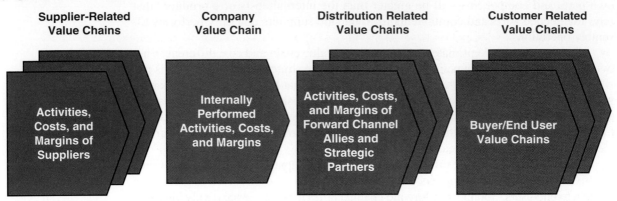

Source: Adapted from Michael E. Porter, *Competitive Advantage* (New York: Free Press, 1985), p. 35.

forward channel allies perform affect the end user's satisfaction. Thus, a company should work closely with its forward channel allies to revise or reinvent their value chains in ways that enhance their mutual competitiveness. Furthermore, a company may be able to improve its competitiveness by undertaking activities that beneficially impact both its own value chain and its customers' value chains.

For instance, some aluminum can producers constructed plants next to beer breweries and delivered cans on overhead conveyors directly to brewers' can-filling lines. This resulted in significant savings in production scheduling, shipping, and inventory costs for both container producers and breweries.[14] Many automotive parts suppliers have built plants near the auto assembly plants they supply to facilitate just-in-time deliveries, reduce warehousing and shipping costs, and promote close collaboration on parts design and production scheduling. In the California wine country, grape growers, irrigation equipment companies, suppliers of grape-harvesting and wine-making equipment, and firms making barrels, wine bottles, caps and corks, and labels are clustered together to be close to the nearly 700 wine makers they supply.[15] The lesson here is that a company's relative cost position and overall competitiveness are linked to the entire industry value chain and to customers' value chains as well.

Although the value chains in Figures 4.2 and 4.3 are representative, actual value chains vary by industry and by company. Value chains for products differ from value chains for services. The major value chain elements for the pulp and paper industry (timber farming, logging, pulp mills, papermaking, printing, and publishing) differ from the major chain elements for the home appliance industry (parts and components manufacture, assembly, wholesale distribution, retail sales). The value chain for the soft-drink industry (processing of basic ingredients, syrup manufacture, bottling and can filling, wholesale distribution, retailing) differs from that for the computer software industry (programming, disk loading, marketing, distribution). A producer of bathroom and kitchen faucets depends heavily on the activities of wholesale distributors and building supply retailers in winning sales to homebuilders and do-it-yourselfers; a producer of

---

[14]Hegert and Morris, "Accounting Data for Value Chain Analysis," p. 180.

[15]For more on how and why the clustering of suppliers and other support organizations matter to a company's costs and competitiveness, see Michael E. Porter, "Clusters and the New Economics of Competition," *Harvard Business Review* 76, no. 6 (November–December 1998), pp. 77–90.

small gasoline engines controls its own market share destiny by selling directly to the makers of lawn and garden equipment. A wholesaler's most important activities and costs deal with purchased goods, inbound logistics, and outbound logistics. A hotel's most important activities and costs are in operations—check-in and check-out, maintenance and housekeeping, dining and room service, conventions and meetings, and accounting. A global public accounting firm's most important activities and costs revolve around customer service and human resources management (recruiting and training a highly competent professional staff). Outbound logistics is a crucial activity at Domino's Pizza but comparatively insignificant at Blockbuster. Sales and marketing are dominant activities at Coca-Cola but only minor activities at interstate gas pipeline companies. Consequently, generic value chains like those in Figures 4.2 and 4.3 are illustrative, not absolute, and may require adaptation to fit a particular company's circumstances.

Developing the Data for Strategic Cost Analysis   Once the major elements of the value chain are identified, the next step in strategic cost analysis involves breaking down a firm's departmental cost accounting data into the costs of performing specific activities.[16] The appropriate degree of disaggregation depends on the economics of the activities and how valuable it is to develop cross-company cost comparisons for narrowly defined activities as opposed to broadly defined activities. A good guideline is to develop separate cost estimates for activities having different economics and for activities representing a significant or growing proportion of cost.[17]

Traditional accounting identifies costs according to broad categories of expenses—wages and salaries, employee benefits, supplies, travel, depreciation, R&D, and other fixed charges. *Activity-based costing* entails defining expense categories based on the specific activities being performed and then assigning costs to the appropriate activity responsible for creating the cost. An illustrative example is shown in Table 4.2.[18] Perhaps 25 percent of the companies that have explored the feasibility of activity-based costing have adopted this accounting approach. To fully understand the costs of activities all along the industry value chain, cost estimates for activities performed in the competitively relevant portions of suppliers' and customers' value chains also have to be developed.

To benchmark the firm's cost position against rivals, costs for the same activities for each rival must be estimated—an advanced art in competitive intelligence. But despite the tediousness of developing cost estimates activity by activity and the imprecision of some of the estimates for rivals, the payoff in exposing the costs of particular internal tasks and functions and the cost competitiveness of a company's position vis-à-vis rivals makes activity-based costing a valuable strategic analysis tool.[19] Illustration Capsule 16 shows a representative value chain for the music CD industry.

The most important application of value chain analysis is to expose how a particular firm's cost position compares with the cost positions of its rivals. What is needed

---

[16]For discussions of the accounting challenges in calculating the costs of value chain activities, see Shank and Govindarajan, *Strategic Cost Management*, pp. 62–72 and Chapter 5; and Hegert and Morris, "Accounting Data for Value Chain Analysis," pp. 175–88.

[17]Porter, *Competitive Advantage*, p. 45.

[18]For a discussion of activity-based cost accounting, see Cooper and Kaplan, "Measure Costs Right: Make the Right Decisions," pp. 96–103; Shank and Govindarajan, *Strategic Cost Management*, chapter 11; and Joseph A. Ness and Thomas G. Cucuzza, "Tapping the Full Potential of ABC," *Harvard Business Review* 73 no. 4 (July–August 1995), pp. 130–38.

[19]Shank and Govindarajan, *Strategic Cost Management,* p. 62.

table 4.2 The Difference between Traditional Cost Accounting and
Activity-Based Cost Accounting: The Case of Purchasing

Traditional Cost Accounting Categories in Purchasing Department Budget		Cost of Performing Specific Purchasing Department Activities Using Activity-Based Cost Accounting	
Wages and salaries	$340,000	Evaluate supplier capabilities	$100,300
Employee benefits	95,000	Process purchase orders	82,100
Supplies	21,500	Collaboration with suppliers on just-in-time deliveries	140,200
Travel	12,400	Data-sharing activities with suppliers	59,550
Depreciation	19,000	Check quality of items purchased	94,100
Other fixed charges (office space, utilities)	112,000	Check incoming deliveries against purchase orders	48,450
Miscellaneous operating expenses	40,250	Dispute resolution	15,250
		Internal administration	100,200
	$640,150		$640,150

Source: Adapted from information in Terence P. Paré, "A New Tool for Managing Costs," *Fortune*, June 14, 1993, pp. 124–29.

are competitor-versus-competitor cost estimates for supplying a product or service to a well-defined customer group or market segment. The size of a company's cost advantage or disadvantage can vary from item to item in the product line, from customer group to customer group (if different distribution channels are used), and from geographic market to geographic market (if cost factors vary across geographic regions).

Benchmarking the Costs of Key Activities

Benchmarking the costs of company activities against rivals provides hard evidence of a company's cost competitiveness.

Many companies today are *benchmarking* their costs of performing a given activity against competitors' costs (and/or against the costs of a noncompetitor in another industry that efficiently and effectively performs much the same activity or business process). Benchmarking is a tool that allows a company to determine whether the manner in which it performs particular functions and activities represents industry "best practices" when both cost and effectiveness are taken into account.

Benchmarking entails doing cross-company comparisons of how basic functions and processes in the value chain are performed—how materials are purchased, how suppliers are paid, how inventories are managed, how products are assembled, how fast the company can get new products to market, how the quality control function is performed, how customer orders are filled and shipped, how employees are trained, how payrolls are processed, and how maintenance is performed—and comparing the costs of these activities.[20] The objectives of benchmarking are to identify the best practices in

---

[20]For more details, see Gregory H. Watson, *Strategic Benchmarking: How to Rate Your Company's Performance Against the World's Best* (New York: John Wiley, 1993); and Robert C. Camp, *Benchmarking: The Search for Industry Best Practices That Lead to Superior Performance* (Milwaukee: ASQC Quality Press, 1989). See also Alexandra Biesada, "Strategic Benchmarking," *Financial World*, September 29, 1992, pp. 30–38.

illustration capsule 16
The Value Chain for the Recording and Distributing of Music CDs

The table below presents the representative costs and markups associated with producing and distributing a music CD that retails for $15.

1. Record company direct production costs:		$ 2.40
Artists and repertoire	$0.75	
Pressing of CD and packaging	1.65	
2. Royalties		0.99
3. Record company marketing expenses		1.50
4. Record company overhead		1.50
5. Total record company costs		6.39
6. Record company's operating profit		1.86
7. Record company's selling price to distributor/wholesaler		8.25
8. Average wholesale distributor markup to cover distribution activities and profit margins		1.50
9. Average wholesale price charged to retailer		9.75
10. Average retail markup over wholesale cost		5.25
11. Average price to consumer at retail		$15.00

Source: Developed from information in "Fight the Power," a case study prepared by Adrian Aleyne, Babson College, 1999.

performing an activity, to learn how other companies have actually achieved lower costs or better results in performing benchmarked activities, and to take action to improve a company's competitiveness whenever benchmarking reveals that its costs and results of performing an activity do not match those of other companies (either competitors or noncompetitors).

In 1979, Xerox became an early pioneer in the use of benchmarking when Japanese manufacturers began selling midsize copiers in the United States for $9,600 each—less than Xerox's production costs.[21] Although Xerox management suspected its Japanese competitors were dumping, it sent a team of line managers to Japan, including the head of manufacturing, to study competitors' business processes and costs. Fortunately, Xerox's joint venture partner in Japan, Fuji-Xerox, knew the competitors well. The team found that Xerox's costs were excessive due to gross inefficiencies in its manufacturing processes and business practices; the study proved instrumental in Xerox's efforts to become cost-competitive and prompted Xerox to embark on a long-term program to benchmark 67 of its key work processes against companies identified as having the "best practices" in performing these processes. Xerox quickly decided not to restrict its benchmarking efforts to its office equipment rivals but to extend them to any company regarded as "world class" in performing *any activity* relevant to Xerox's business.

[21]Jeremy Main, "How to Steal the Best Ideas Around," *Fortune*, October 19, 1992, pp. 102–3.

illustration capsule 17

Ford Motor Company's Benchmarking of Its Accounts Payable Activity

In the 1980s Ford Motor Company's North American accounts payable department employed more than 500 people. Clerks spent the majority of their time straightening out the relatively few situations where three documents—the purchase order issued by the purchasing department, the receiving document prepared by clerks at the receiving dock, and the invoice sent by the vendor/supplier to accounts payable—did not match. Sometimes resolving the discrepancies took weeks of time and the efforts of many people. Ford managers believed that by using computers to automate some functions performed manually, head count could be reduced to 400. Before proceeding, Ford managers decided to visit Mazda, a company in which Ford had recently acquired a 25 percent ownership interest. To their astonishment, Mazda handled its accounts payable function with only five people. Following Mazda's lead, Ford benchmarkers created an invoiceless system where payments to suppliers were triggered automatically when the goods were received. The reengineered system allowed Ford to reduce its accounts payable staff to under 200, a lot more than Mazda but much better than would have resulted without benchmarking the accounts payable activity.

Sources: Michael Hammer and James Champy, *Reengineering the Corporation* (New York: HarperBusiness, 1993), pp. 39–43, and Jeremy Main, "How to Steal the Best Ideas Around," *Fortune*, October 19, 1992, p. 106.

Basic Concept

Benchmarking
has proven to be a potent tool for learning which companies are best at performing particular activities and then utilizing their techniques (or "best practices") to improve the cost and effectiveness of a company's own internal activities.

Thus, benchmarking has quickly come to be a tool not only for comparing a company against rivals on cost but also for comparing itself to others on most any relevant activity or competitively important measure. Toyota managers got their idea for just-in-time inventory deliveries by studying how U.S. supermarkets replenished their shelves. Southwest Airlines reduced the turnaround time of its aircraft at each scheduled stop by studying pit crews on the auto racing circuit. Illustration Capsule 17 describes one of Ford Motor Company's benchmarking experiences in accounts payable. Over 80 percent of *Fortune 500* companies reportedly engage in some form of benchmarking.

The tough part of benchmarking is not whether or how to do it but rather gaining access to information about other companies' practices and costs. Sometimes benchmarking can be accomplished by collecting information from published reports, trade groups, and industry research firms and by talking to knowledgeable industry analysts, customers, and suppliers. On occasion, customers, suppliers, and joint-venture partners often make willing benchmarking allies. Usually, though, benchmarking requires field trips to the facilities of competing or noncompeting companies to observe how things are done, ask questions, compare practices and processes, and perhaps exchange data on productivity, staffing levels, time requirements, and other cost components. The problem is that benchmarking involves competitively sensitive cost information and close rivals can't be expected to be completely open, even if they agree to host facilities tours and answer questions. Making reliable cost comparisons is complicated by the fact that participants often use different cost accounting systems.

However, the explosive interest of companies in benchmarking costs and identifying best practices has prompted consulting organizations (e.g., Andersen Consulting, A. T. Kearney, Best Practices Benchmarking & Consulting, and Towers Perrin) and several newly formed councils and associations (the International Benchmarking Clearinghouse and the Strategic Planning Institute's Council on Benchmarking) to gather benchmarking data, do benchmarking studies, and distribute information about best practices and the costs of performing activities to clients or members without

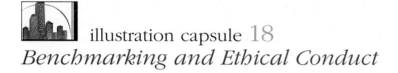

illustration capsule 18
Benchmarking and Ethical Conduct

Because discussions between benchmarking partners can involve competitively sensitive data, conceivably raising questions about possible restraint of trade or improper business conduct, the Strategic Planning Institute's Council on Benchmarking and the International Benchmarking Clearinghouse urge all individuals and organizations involved in benchmarking to abide by a code of conduct grounded in ethical business behavior. The code is based on the following principles and guidelines:

- In benchmarking with competitors, establish specific ground rules up front, such as, "We don't want to talk about those things that will give either of us a competitive advantage; rather, we want to see where we both can mutually improve or gain benefit." Do not discuss costs with competitors if costs are an element of pricing.

- Do not ask competitors for sensitive data or cause the benchmarking partner to feel that sensitive data must be provided to keep the process going. Be prepared to provide the same level of information that you request. Do not share proprietary information without prior approval from the proper authorities of both parties.

- Use an ethical third party to assemble and blind competitive data, with inputs from legal counsel, for direct competitor comparisons.

- Consult with legal counsel if any information gathering procedure is in doubt (e.g., before contacting a direct competitor).

- Treat any information obtained from a benchmarking partner as internal, privileged information. Any external use must have the partner's permission.

- Do not:
  —Disparage a competitor's business or operations to a third party.
  —Attempt to limit competition or gain business through the benchmarking relationship.
  —Misrepresent yourself as working for another employer.

- Demonstrate commitment to the efficiency and effectiveness of the process by being adequately prepared at each step, particularly at initial contact. Be professional, honest, and courteous. Adhere to the agenda and maintain focus on benchmarking issues.

Sources: The Strategic Planning Institute's Council on Benchmarking; the International Benchmarking Clearinghouse; and conference presentation of AT&T Benchmarking Group, Des Moines, Iowa, October 1993.

identifying the sources. Having an independent group gather the information and report it in a manner that disguises the names of individual companies permits companies to avoid having to disclose competitively sensitive data to rivals and reduces the risk of ethical problems. The ethical dimension of benchmarking is discussed in Illustration Capsule 18.

Strategic Options for Achieving Cost Competitiveness

Value chain analysis and benchmarking can reveal a great deal about a firm's cost competitiveness. One of the fundamental insights of strategic cost analysis is that a company's competitiveness depends on how well it manages its value chain relative to how well competitors manage theirs.[22] Examining the makeup of a company's own value chain and comparing it to rivals' indicates who has how much of a cost advantage or disadvantage and which cost components are responsible. Such information is vital in crafting strategies to eliminate a cost disadvantage or create a cost advantage.

> Strategic actions to eliminate a cost disadvantage need to be linked to the location in the value chain where the cost differences originate.

Looking again at Figure 4.2, observe that there are three main areas in a company's overall value chain where important differences in the costs of competing firms

[22]Shank and Govindarajan, *Strategic Cost Management*, p. 50.

can occur: in the suppliers' part of the industry value chain, in a company's own activity segments, or in the forward channel portion of the industry chain. If a firm's lack of cost competitiveness lies either in the backward (upstream) or forward (downstream) sections of the value chain, then reestablishing cost competitiveness may have to extend beyond the firm's own in-house operations.

Attacking the High Costs of Items Purchased from Suppliers   When a firm's cost disadvantage is principally associated with the costs of items purchased from suppliers (the upstream end of the industry chain), company managers can pursue any of several strategic actions to correct the problem:[23]

- Negotiate more favorable prices with suppliers.
- Work with suppliers on the design and specifications for what is being supplied to identify cost savings that will allow them to lower their prices.
- Switch to lower-priced substitute inputs.
- Collaborate closely with suppliers to identify mutual cost-saving opportunities. For example, finding ways to expedite just-in-time deliveries can lower a company's inventory and internal logistics costs and may also allow its suppliers to economize on their warehousing, shipping, and production scheduling costs—a win–win outcome for both (instead of a zero-sum game where the company's gains match supplier concessions).[24]
- Integrate backward to gain control over the costs of purchased items—seldom an attractive option.
- Try to make up the difference by cutting costs elsewhere in the chain—usually a last resort.

Attacking Cost Disadvantages in the Forward Portion of the Industry Value Chain   A company's strategic options for eliminating cost disadvantages in the forward end of the value chain system include:[25]

- Pushing distributors and other forward channel allies to reduce their markups.
- Working closely with forward channel allies to identify win–win opportunities to reduce costs. A chocolate manufacturer learned that by shipping its bulk chocolate in liquid form in tank cars instead of 10-pound molded bars, it could not only save its candy-bar manufacturing customers the costs associated with unpacking and melting but also eliminate its own costs of molding bars and packing them.
- Changing to a more economical distribution strategy, including switching to cheaper distribution channels (perhaps direct sales via the Internet) or perhaps integrating forward into downstream businesses.
- Trying to make up the difference by cutting costs earlier in the cost chain—usually a last resort.

---

[23]Porter, *Competitive Advantage*, chapter 3.

[24]In recent years, most companies have moved aggressively to collaborate with key suppliers to implement better supply chain management, often achieving cost savings of 5 to 25 percent. For a discussion of how to develop a cost-saving supply chain strategy, see Shashank Kulkarni, "Purchasing: A Supply-Side Strategy," *Journal of Business Strategy* 17, no. 5 (September–October 1996), pp. 17–20.

[25]Porter, *Competitive Advantage*, chapter 3.

Attacking the High Costs of Internally Performed Activities   When the source of a firm's cost disadvantage is internal, managers can use any of the following eight strategic approaches to restore cost parity:[26]

1. Implement the use of best practices throughout the company, particularly for high-cost activities.

2. Try to eliminate some cost-producing activities altogether by revamping the value chain. Examples include cutting out low-value-added activities, shifting to a different business model, bypassing the value chains and associated costs of distribution allies and marketing directly to end users (the approach used by Gateway and Dell in PCs), or using e-commerce retailing. A brokerage firm, for example, could switch to online stock trading systems rather than maintaining an elaborate network of local offices staffed by professional brokers; when investors must call or visit brokers in person to handle their trades, the commissions are sharply higher than for online trading. In retailing, Amazon.com, eToys, mortgage.com, and others have sliced brick-and-mortar activities out of the value chain.

3. Relocate high-cost activities (such as R&D or manufacturing) to geographic areas where they can be performed more cheaply.

4. Search out activities that can be outsourced from vendors or performed by contractors more cheaply than they can be done internally.

5. Invest in productivity-enhancing, cost-saving technological improvements (robotics, flexible manufacturing techniques, and state-of-the-art electronic networking).

6. Innovate around the troublesome cost components—computer chip makers regularly design around the patents held by others to avoid paying royalties; automakers have substituted lower-cost plastic and rubber for metal at many exterior body locations.

7. Simplify the product design so that it can be manufactured or assembled quickly and more economically.

8. Try to make up the internal cost disadvantage by achieving savings in the backward and forward portions of the value chain system—usually a last resort.

From Value Chain Activities to Competitive Capabilities to Competitive Advantage

How well a company manages its value chain activities relative to competitors can allow it to build valuable competencies and capabilities and leverage them into sustainable competitive advantage. With rare exceptions, a firm's products or services are not a dependable basis for sustained competitive advantage; it is too easy for resourceful competitors to clone, improve on, or find an effective substitute for them.[27] Rather, sustaining a company's competitive edge is best grounded in competencies and capabilities critical to market success and to pleasing customers—competencies and capabilities that rivals don't have or can't quite match.

Merck and Glaxo, two of the world's most competitively capable pharmaceutical companies, built their business positions around expert performance of a few competitively crucial activities: extensive R&D to achieve first discovery of new drugs, a

> **Strategic Management Principle**
> Performing value chain activities in ways that give a company the capabilities to outmatch rivals is a source of competitive advantage.

---

[26]Ibid.

[27]James Brian Quinn, *Intelligent Enterprise* (New York: Free Press, 1993), p. 54.

carefully constructed approach to patenting, skill in gaining rapid and thorough clinical clearance through regulatory bodies, and unusually strong distribution and sales force capabilities.[28] FedEx has linked and integrated the performance of its aircraft fleet, truck fleet, support systems, and personnel so tightly and smoothly across the company's different value chain activities that it has created the capability to provide customers with guaranteed overnight delivery services. McDonald's can turn out identical-quality fast-food items at some 25,000-plus outlets around the world—an impressive demonstration of its capability to replicate its operating systems at many locations via an omnibus manual of detailed rules and procedures for each activity and intensive training of franchise operators and outlet managers.

QUESTION 4: HOW STRONG IS THE COMPANY'S COMPETITIVE POSITION?

Systematic assessment of whether a company's overall competitive position is strong or weak relative to close rivals is an essential step in company situation analysis.

Using the tools of value chains, strategic cost analysis, and benchmarking to determine a company's cost competitiveness is necessary but not sufficient. A more broad-ranging assessment needs to be made of a company's competitive position and competitive strength. Particular issues that merit examination include (1) whether the firm's market position can be expected to improve or deteriorate if the present strategy is continued (allowing for fine-tuning); (2) how the firm ranks relative to rivals on each key success factor and each relevant measure of competitive strength and resource capability; (3) whether the firm enjoys a competitive advantage over rivals or is currently at a disadvantage; and (4) the firm's ability to protect and improve its market position in light of industry driving forces, competitive pressures, and the anticipated moves of rivals.

Table 4.3 lists some indicators of whether a firm's competitive position is strong or weak compared to rivals. But company managers need to do more than just identify the areas of competitive strength and weakness. They have to *judge how all the signs of strength and weakness add up*. The answers to two questions are of particular interest: Does the company have a net competitive advantage or disadvantage vis-à-vis major competitors? Can the company's market position and performance be expected to improve or deteriorate under the current strategy?

Competitive Strength Assessments

The most telling way to determine how strongly a company holds its competitive position is to *quantitatively* assess whether the company is stronger or weaker than close rivals on each industry key success factor and each competitively essential resource and capability. Much of the information for competitive position assessment comes from previous analyses. Industry and competitive analysis reveals the key success factors and competitive capabilities that separate industry winners from losers. Competitor analysis and benchmarking data provide a basis for judging the strengths and capabilities of rivals on such competitively important factors as cost, product quality, customer service, image and reputation, financial strength, technological skills, speed to market, distribution capability, and the possession of competitively important resources and capabilities.

---

[28]Quinn, *Intelligent Enterprise*, p. 34.

table 4.3 The Signs of Strength and Weakness in a Company's Competitive Position

Signs of Competitive Strength	Signs of Competitive Weakness
• Important resource strengths, core competencies, and competitive capabilities	• Confronted with competitive disadvantages
• A distinctive competence in a competitively important value chain activity	• Losing ground to rival firms with stronger positions in global and/or e-commerce markets
• Strong market share (or a leading market share)	• Eroding market share and below-average growth in revenues
• A pacesetting or distinctive strategy that is hard for rivals to copy or match	• Short on financial resources to pursue new opportunities
• Ahead of rivals in expanding into global markets and/or in building an e-commerce presence	• Weaker brand-name recognition than rivals and/or a slipping reputation with customers
• A better-known brand-name and reputation than rivals	• Trailing in product development and product innovation capability
• Growing customer base and customer loyalty	• In a strategic group destined to lose ground
• In a favorably situated strategic group	• Weak in areas where there is the most market potential—foreign markets, e-commerce
• Well-positioned in attractive market segments	• A higher-cost producer
• Strongly differentiated products	• Too small to be a major factor in the marketplace
• Cost advantages	• Not in good position to deal with emerging threats
• Above-average profit margins	• Subpar product quality
• Above-average technological and innovational capability	• Lacking skills, resources, and competitive capabilities in key areas
• A creative, entrepreneurially alert management	• Weaker distribution capability than rivals
• Ample financial resources	

Step 1 is to make a list of the industry's key success factors and most telling measures of competitive strength or weakness (6 to 10 measures usually suffice). Step 2 is to rate the firm and its rivals on each factor. Numerical rating scales (e.g., from 1 to 10) are best to use, although ratings of stronger ($+$), weaker ($-$), and about equal ($=$) may be appropriate when information is scanty and assigning numerical scores conveys false precision. Step 3 is to sum the individual strength ratings to get an overall measure of competitive strength for each competitor. Step 4 is to draw conclusions about the size and extent of the company's net competitive advantage or disadvantage based on the strength assessments and to take specific note of areas where the company's competitive position is strongest and weakest.

High competitive strength ratings signal a strong competitive position and possession of competitive advantage; low ratings signal a weak position and competitive disadvantage.

Table 4.4 provides two examples of competitive strength assessment. The first one employs an *unweighted rating scale*. With unweighted ratings each key success factor/competitive strength measure is assumed to be equally important (a rather dubious assumption). Whichever company has the highest strength rating on a given measure has an implied competitive edge on that factor; the size of its edge is mirrored in the margin of difference between its rating and the ratings assigned to rivals. Summing a company's ratings on all the measures produces an overall strength rating. The higher a company's overall strength rating, the stronger its competitive position. The bigger the difference between a company's overall rating and the scores of lower-rated rivals, the greater its implied net competitive advantage. Thus, ABC's total score of 61 (see the top half of Table 4.4) signals a greater net competitive advantage over Rival 4 (with a score of 32) than over Rival 1 (with a score of 58).

However, it is better methodology to use a weighted rating system because the different measures of competitive strength are unlikely to be equally important. In a

table 4.4   Illustrations of Unweighted and Weighted Competitive Strength Assessments

A. Sample of an Unweighted Competitive Strength Assessment
Rating scale: 1 = Very weak; 10 = Very strong

Key Success Factor/Strength Measure	ABC Co.	Rival 1	Rival 2	Rival 3	Rival 4
Quality/product performance	8	5	10	1	6
Reputation/image	8	7	10	1	6
Manufacturing capability	2	10	4	5	1
Technological skills	10	1	7	3	8
Dealer network/distribution capability	9	4	10	5	1
New product innovation capability	9	4	10	5	1
Financial resources	5	10	7	3	1
Relative cost position	5	10	3	1	4
Customer service capabilities	5	7	10	1	4
Unweighted overall strength rating	61	58	71	25	32

B. Sample of a Weighted Competitive Strength Assessment
Rating scale: 1 = Very weak; 10 = Very strong

Key Success Factor/Strength Measure	Weight	ABC Co.	Rival 1	Rival 2	Rival 3	Rival 4
Quality/product performance	0.10	8/0.80	5/0.50	10/1.00	1/0.10	6/0.60
Reputation/image	0.10	8/0.80	7/0.70	10/1.00	1/0.10	6/0.60
Manufacturing capability	0.10	2/0.20	10/1.00	4/0.40	5/0.50	1/0.10
Technological skills	0.05	10/0.50	1/0.05	7/0.35	3/0.15	8/0.40
Dealer network/distribution capability	0.05	9/0.45	4/0.20	10/0.50	5/0.25	1/0.05
New product innovation capability	0.05	9/0.45	4/0.20	10/0.50	5/0.25	1/0.05
Financial resources	0.10	5/0.50	10/1.00	7/0.70	3/0.30	1/0.10
Relative cost position	0.30	5/1.50	10/3.00	3/0.95	1/0.30	4/1.20
Customer service capabilities	0.15	5/0.75	7/1.05	10/1.50	1/0.15	4/0.60
Sum of weights	1.00					
Weighted overall strength rating		5.95	7.70	6.85	2.10	3.70

A weighted competitive strength analysis is conceptually stronger than an unweighted analysis because of the inherent weakness in assuming that all the strength measures are equally important.

commodity-product industry, for instance, having low unit costs relative to rivals is nearly always the most important determinant of competitive strength. In an industry with strong product differentiation the most significant measures of competitive strength may be brand awareness, amount of advertising, reputation for quality, and distribution capability. In a *weighted rating system* each measure of competitive strength is assigned a weight based on its perceived importance in shaping competitive success. The largest weight could be as high as 0.75 (maybe even higher) in situations where one particular competitive variable is overwhelmingly decisive or as low as 0.20 when two or three strength measures are more important than the rest. Lesser competitive strength indicators can carry weights of 0.05 or 0.10. No matter whether the differences between the weights are big or little, *the sum of the weights must add up to 1.0.*

Weighted strength ratings are calculated by deciding how a company stacks up on each strength measure (using the 1 to 10 rating scale) and multiplying the assigned rating by the assigned weight (a rating score of 4 times a weight of 0.20 gives a weighted rating of 0.80). Again, the company with the highest rating on a given measure has an implied competitive edge on that measure, with the size of its edge reflected in the difference between its rating and rivals' ratings. The weight attached to the measure indicates how important the edge is. Summing a company's weighted strength ratings for all the measures yields an overall strength rating. Comparisons of the weighted overall strength scores indicate which competitors are in the strongest and weakest competitive positions and who has how big a net competitive advantage over whom.

The bottom half of Table 4.4 shows a sample competitive strength assessment for ABC Company using a weighted rating system. Note that the unweighted and weighted rating schemes produce a different ordering of the companies. In the weighted system, ABC Company dropped from second to third in strength, and Rival 1 jumped from third into first because of its high strength ratings on the two most important factors. Weighting the importance of the strength measures can thus make a significant difference in the outcome of the assessment.

Competitive strength assessments provide useful conclusions about a company's competitive situation. The ratings show how a company compares against rivals, factor by factor or capability by capability, thus revealing where it is strongest and weakest, and against whom. Moreover, the overall competitive strength scores indicate how all the different factors add up—whether the company is at a net competitive advantage or disadvantage against each rival. The firm with the largest overall competitive strength rating enjoys the strongest competitive position, with the size of its net competitive advantage reflected by how much its score exceeds the scores of rivals.

Knowing where a company is competitively strong and where it is weak in comparison to specific rivals is valuable in deciding on specific actions to strengthen its long-term competitive position. As a general rule, a company should try to leverage its competitive strengths (areas where it scores higher than rivals) into sustainable competitive advantage and take strategic actions to protect against its competitive weaknesses (areas where it scores are below those of rivals). At the same time, the competitive strength ratings point to which rival companies may be vulnerable to competitive attack and the areas where they are weakest. When a company has important competitive strengths in areas where one or more rivals are weak, it makes sense to consider offensive moves to exploit rivals' competitive weaknesses.

> High competitive strength ratings vis-à-vis competitors signal opportunity for a company to improve its long-term market position.

> Good strategy entails looking for opportunities to leverage company strengths into competitive advantage, often by using company strengths to attack the competitive weaknesses of rivals.

QUESTION 5: WHAT STRATEGIC ISSUES DOES THE COMPANY FACE?

The final analytical task is to zero in on the strategic challenges that stand as obstacles to the company's future success. This involves using the results of both company situation analysis and industry and competitive analysis to identify as sharply and as clearly as possible the strategic issues and problems confronting the company. Pinpointing the things that management needs to worry about most sets the agenda for putting together an effective strategic action plan. The "worry list" of obstacles and issues that have to be wrestled with can include such things as *how* to meet the challenges posed by global competition, *how* to combat the product innovations of rivals, *how* to reduce the company's high costs, *how* to sustain the company's present rate of growth or grow the business at a faster rate, *how* to gain better market visibility for the company's products, or *how* to capture the e-commerce opportunities. Other issues

Identifying the strategic issues a company faces is a prerequisite to effective strategy making. It involves developing a "worry list" of strategic challenges concerning "how to . . .", whether to . . .", and "what to do about . . ."

might be *whether* to expand the company's product offerings, put more emphasis on new product R&D, add more production capacity, cut prices in response to the actions of competitors, add new features that will boost the performance of the company's products, or go forward with investments in foreign markets. Finally, managers may ask *what to do about* proposed new regulations that will significantly raise costs, lagging buyer interest in the company's latest new products, or the aging demographics of the company's customer base.

In determining the issues that merit strategic attention, managers need to draw on all the prior analysis, put the company's overall situation into perspective, and lock in on what challenges have to be overcome and what issues have to be resolved in order for the company to be financially and competitively successful in the years ahead. This step should not be taken lightly. Without a precise fix on the challenges and issues, managers are not prepared to start crafting a strategy. Questions that can help pinpoint the right strategic issues to address include the following:

- Is the present strategy adequate for protecting and improving the company's market position in light of the five competitive forces—particularly those that are expected to intensify in strength?
- Is the company vulnerable to the competitive efforts of one or more rivals?
- Should the present strategy be adjusted to better respond to the *driving forces* at work in the industry?
- Is the present strategy closely matched to the industry's *future* key success factors?
- Does the present strategy adequately capitalize on the company's resource strengths and capabilities?
- Which of the company's opportunities merit top priority? Which should be given low priority? Which are best suited to the company's resource strengths and capabilities?
- How important is it for the company need to correct its resource weaknesses? Are there things the company can do to lessen the impact of external threats?
- Does the company have competitive advantage, or must it work to offset competitive disadvantage?
- Where are the strong spots and weak spots in the present strategy?

Strategic Management Principle
A good strategy must contain ways to deal with all the strategic issues that stand in the way of the company's financial and competitive success in the years ahead.

The answers to these questions and the worries management has about "how to . . . ," "whether to . . . ," and "what to do about . . ." signal whether the company can continue the same basic strategy with minor adjustments or whether major overhaul is called for. If a company's current strategy is well matched to its external environment and to its resource strengths and capabilities, there is little need to contemplate big shifts in strategy. If, however, the present strategy is not well suited for the road ahead, the task of crafting a better strategy has got to go to the top of management's action agenda.

Table 4.5 provides a format for doing company situation analysis. It incorporates the concepts and analytical techniques discussed in this chapter and provides a way of reporting the results of company situation analysis in a systematic, concise manner.

table 4.5 Company Situation Analysis

1. Strategic performance indicators

	1997	1998	1999	2000	2001
Market share	____	____	____	____	____
Sales growth	____	____	____	____	____
Net profit margin	____	____	____	____	____
Return on equity investment	____	____	____	____	____
Other (specify): _____	____	____	____	____	____

2. Internal resource strengths and competitive capabilities:

Internal weaknesses and resource deficiencies:

External opportunities:

External threats to the company's well-being:

3. Competitive strength assessment
  Rating scale: 1 = Very weak; 10 = Very strong.

Key Success Factor/ Competitive Strength Measure	Weight	Firm A	Firm B	Firm C	Firm D	Firm E
Quality/product performance	____	____	____	____	____	____
Reputation/image	____	____	____	____	____	____
Manufacturing capability	____	____	____	____	____	____
Technological skills	____	____	____	____	____	____
Dealer network/ distribution capability	____	____	____	____	____	____
New product innovation capability	____	____	____	____	____	____
Financial resources	____	____	____	____	____	____
Relative cost position	____	____	____	____	____	____
Customer service capability	____	____	____	____	____	____
Sum of weights	1.0					
Overall strength rating		____	____	____	____	____

4. Conclusions concerning competitive position:
  (Improving/slipping? Competitive advantages/disadvantages?)

5. Major strategic issues the company must address:

key|points

There are five key questions to consider in performing company situation analysis:

1. *How well is the present strategy working?* This involves evaluating the strategy from a qualitative standpoint (completeness, internal consistency, rationale, and suitability to the situation) and also from a quantitative standpoint (the strategic and financial results the strategy is producing). The stronger a company's current overall performance, the less likely the need for radical strategy changes. The weaker a company's performance and/or the faster the changes in its external situation (which can be gleaned from industry and competitive analysis), the more its current strategy must be questioned.

2. *What are the company's resource strengths and weaknesses and its external opportunities and threats?* A SWOT analysis provides an overview of a firm's situation and is an essential component of crafting a strategy tightly matched to the company's situation. A company's resource strengths, competencies, and competitive capabilities are important because they are the most logical and appealing building blocks for strategy; resource weaknesses are important because they may represent vulnerabilities that need correction. External opportunities and threats come into play because a good strategy necessarily aims at capturing a company's most attractive opportunities and at defending against threats to its well-being.

3. *Are the company's prices and costs competitive?* One telling sign of whether a company's situation is strong or precarious is whether its prices and costs are competitive with industry rivals. Strategic cost analysis and value chain analysis are essential tools in benchmarking a company's prices and costs against rivals, determining whether the company is performing particular functions and activities cost effectively, learning whether its costs are in line with competitors, and deciding which internal activities and business processes need to be scrutinized for improvement. Value chain analysis teaches that how competently a company manages its value chain activities relative to rivals is a key to building valuable competencies and competitive capabilities and then leveraging them into sustainable competitive advantage.

4. *How strong is the company's competitive position?* The key appraisals here involve whether the company's position is likely to improve or deteriorate if the present strategy is continued, how the company matches up against key rivals on industry key success factors and other chief determinants of competitive success, and whether and why the company has a competitive advantage or disadvantage. Quantitative competitive strength assessments, using the methodology presented in Table 4.4, indicate where a company is competitively strong and weak and provide insight into the company's ability to defend or enhance its market position. As a rule a company's competitive strategy should be built around its competitive strengths and should aim at shoring up areas where it is competitively vulnerable. Also, the areas where company strengths match up against competitor weaknesses represent the best potential for new offensive initiatives.

5. *What strategic issues does the company face?* The purpose of this analytical step is to zero in on the strategic challenges that stand as obstacles to the company's future success. It involves using the results of both company situation analysis and industry and competitive analysis to identify the issues and problems that management needs to address. The objective is to pinpoint the things that management needs to worry about most. Identifying what challenges have to be overcome and

what issues have to be resolved in order for the company to be financially and competitively successful in the years ahead frames the strategic agenda that management needs to act on.

Good company situation analysis, like good industry and competitive analysis, is a crucial prerequisite to good strategy-making. A competently done evaluation of a company's resources and competencies exposes strong and weak points in the present strategy, company capabilities and vulnerabilities, and the company's ability to protect or improve its competitive position in light of driving forces, competitive pressures, and the competitive strength of rivals. Managers need such understanding to craft a strategy that fits the company's situation well.

suggested | readings

Birchall, David W., and George Tovstiga. "The Strategic Potential of a Firm's Knowledge Portfolio." *Journal of General Management* 25, no. 1 (Autumn 1999), pp. 1–16.

Bontis, Nick; Nicola C. Dragonetti; Kristine Jacobsen; and Goran Roos. "The Knowledge Toolbox: A Review of the Tools Available to Measure and Manage Intangible Resources." *European Management Journal* 17, no. 4 (August 1999), pp. 391–401.

Collis, David J., and Cynthia A. Montgomery. "Competing on Resources: Strategy in the 1990s." *Harvard Business Review* 73 no. 4 (July–August 1995), pp. 118–28.

Duncan, W. Jack; Peter M. Ginter; and Linda E. Swayne. "Competitive Advantage and Internal Organizational Assessment." *Academy of Management Executive* 12, no. 3 (August 1998), pp. 6–16.

Fahey, Liam, and H. Kurt Christensen. "Building Distinctive Competencies into Competitive Advantages." In *The Strategic Planning Management Reader*, ed. Liam Fahey. Englewood Cliffs, NJ: Prentice Hall, 1989, pp. 113–18.

Fisher, Marshall L. "What Is the Right Supply Chain for Your Product?" *Harvard Business Review* 75, no. 3 (March–April 1997), pp. 105–16.

Gadiesh, Orit, and James L. Gilbert. "Profit Pools: A Fresh Look at Strategy." *Harvard Business Review* 76, no. 3 (May–June 1998), pp. 139–47.

Kaplan, Robert S., and David P. Norton. "The Balanced Scorecard—Measures That Drive Performance." *Harvard Business Review* 70, no. 1 (January–February 1992), pp. 71–79.

Prahalad, C. K., and Gary Hamel. "The Core Competence of the Corporation." *Harvard Business Review* 70, no. 3 (May–June 1990), pp. 79–93.

Shank, John K., and Vijay Govindarajan. *Strategic Cost Management: The New Tool for Competitive Advantage.* New York: Free Press, 1993.

Stalk, George; Philip Evans; and Lawrence E. Shulman. "Competing on Capabilities: The New Rules of Corporate Strategy." *Harvard Business Review* 70, no. 2 (March–April 1992), pp. 57–69.

Teece, David. "Capturing Value from Knowledge Assets: The New Economy, Markets for Know-How, and Intangible Assets." *California Management Review* 40, no. 3 (Spring 1998), pp. 55–79.

Watson, Gregory H. *Strategic Benchmarking: How to Rate Your Company's Performance Against the World's Best.* New York: John Wiley & Sons, 1993.

Zack, Michael H. "Developing a Knowledge Strategy." *California Management Review* 41, no. 3 (Spring 1999), pp. 125–45.

chapter|five

Strategy and Competitive Advantage

Successful business strategy is about actively shaping the game you play, not just playing the game you find.
—Adam M. Brandenburger and Barry J. Nalebuff

The essence of strategy lies in creating tomorrow's competitive advantages faster than competitors mimic the ones you possess today.
—Gary Hamel and C. K. Prahalad

Competitive strategy is about being different. It means deliberately choosing to perform activities differently or to perform different activities than rivals to deliver a unique mix of value.
—Michael E. Porter

Strategies for taking the hill won't necessarily hold it.
—Amar Bhide

Nothing focuses the mind better than the constant sight of a competitor who wants to wipe you off the map.
—Wayne Calloway, Former CEO, PepsiCo

[S]trategic partnerships have become central to competitive success in fast changing global markets.
—Yves L. Doz and Gary Hamel

W inning business strategies are grounded in sustainable competitive advantage. A company has *competitive advantage* whenever it has an edge over rivals in attracting customers and defending against competitive forces. There are many routes to competitive advantage, but the most basic is to provide buyers with what they perceive as superior value—a good product at a low price,

a superior product that is worth paying more for, or a best-value offering that represents an attractive combination of price, features, quality, service, and other attributes buyers find attractive. Delivering superior value—whatever form it takes—nearly always requires performing value chain activities differently than rivals and building competencies and resource capabilities that are not readily matched.

This chapter focuses on how a company can achieve or defend competitive advantage through the strategy it employs and its management of the value chain.[1] We begin by describing the basic types of competitive strategies in some depth. Next are sections examining the merits of cooperative strategies (strategic alliances and collaborative partnerships), merger and acquisition strategies, and vertical integration versus outsourcing. There are also sections surveying the use of offensive moves to build competitive advantage and the use of defensive moves to protect competitive advantage. In the concluding section we look at the competitive importance of timing strategic moves—when it is advantageous to be a first-mover and when it is better to be a fast-follower or late-mover.

Investing aggressively in creating sustainable competitive advantage is a company's single most dependable contributor to above-average profitability.

---

[1]The definitive work on building and defending competitive advantage is Michael E. Porter, *Competitive Advantage* (New York: Free Press, 1985). A substantial portion of this chapter draws on Porter's pioneering contribution.

THE FIVE GENERIC COMPETITIVE STRATEGIES

A company's competitive strategy consists of the business approaches and initiatives it undertakes to attract customers and fulfill their expectations, to withstand competitive pressures, and to strengthen its market position. *Competitive strategy* has a narrower scope than *business strategy*. Competitive strategy deals exclusively with management's action plan for competing successfully and providing superior value to customers. Business strategy concerns not only how to compete but also how management intends to address all of the other strategic issues confronting the business.

> The objective of competitive strategy is to knock the socks off rival companies by doing a significantly better job of providing what buyers are looking for.

The competitive aim, quite simply, is to do a significantly better job of providing what buyers are looking for, thereby enabling the company to earn a competitive advantage and outcompete rivals in the marketplace. The core of a company's competitive strategy consists of its internal initiatives to deliver superior value to customers. But it also includes offensive and defensive moves to counter the maneuvering of rivals, actions to shift resources around to improve the firm's long-term competitive capabilities and market position, and tactical efforts to respond to whatever market conditions prevail at the moment.

Companies the world over are imaginative in conceiving strategies to win customer favor, outcompete rivals, and secure a market edge. Because a company's strategic initiatives and market manuevers are usually tailor-made to fit its specific situation and industry environment, there are countless variations in the competitive strategies that companies employ—strictly speaking, there are as many competitive strategies as there are competitors. However, when one strips aways the details to get at the real substance, the biggest and most important differences among competitive strategies boil down to (1) whether a company's market target is broad or narrow and (2) whether it is pursuing a competitive advantage linked to low costs or product differentiation. Five distinct competitive strategy approaches stand out:[2]

1. *A low-cost provider strategy*—appealing to a broad spectrum of customers based on being the overall low-cost provider of a product or service.

2. *A broad differentiation strategy*—seeking to differentiate the company's product offering from rivals' in ways that will appeal to a broad spectrum of buyers.

3. *A best-cost provider strategy*—giving customers more value for the money by incorporating good-to-excellent product attributes at a lower cost than rivals; the target is to have the lowest (best) costs and prices compared to rivals offering products with comparable upscale attributes.

4. *A focused (or market niche) strategy based on lower cost*—concentrating on a narrow buyer segment and outcompeting rivals by serving niche members at a lower cost than rivals.

5. *A focused (or market niche) strategy based on differentiation*—concentrating on a narrow buyer segment and outcompeting rivals by offering niche members customized attributes that meet their tastes and requirements better than rivals' products.

Each of these five generic competitive approaches stakes out a different market position—as shown in Figure 5.1. Each involves distinctively different approaches to

---

[2]The classification scheme is an adaptation of one presented in Michael E. Porter, *Competitive Strategy: Techniques for Analyzing Industries and Competitors* (New York: Free Press, 1980), chapter 2, especially pp. 35–39 and 44–46.

figure 5.1   **The Five Generic Competitive Strategies**

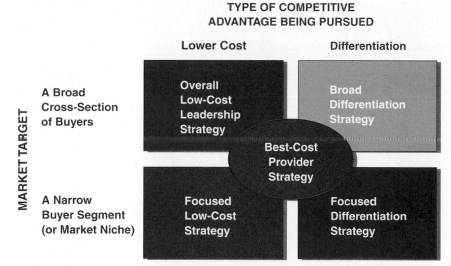

Source: Adapted from Michael E. Porter, *Competitive Strategy* (New York: Free Press, 1980), pp. 35–40.

competing and operating the business. The listing in Table 5.1 highlights the contrasting features of these five competitive strategies; for simplicity, the two strains of focused strategies are combined under one heading since they differ fundamentally on only one feature—the basis of competitive advantage.

Low-Cost Provider Strategies

Striving to be the industry's overall low-cost provider is a powerful competitive approach in markets with many price-sensitive buyers. The aim is to operate the business in a highly cost-effective manner and open up a sustainable cost advantage over competitors. A low-cost provider's strategic target is low cost relative to competitors, not the absolutely lowest possible cost—a company achieves low-cost leadership when it becomes the industry's lowest-cost provider rather than just being one of perhaps several competitors with comparatively low costs.

In trying to keep costs below those of rivals, managers must take care to include features and services that buyers consider essential—a product offering that is too spartan weakens rather than strengthens a firm's competitiveness. *Pursuing cost reduction in a manner that sabotages the attractiveness of the company's product offering turns buyers off.* Furthermore, it matters greatly whether the company achieves its cost advantage in ways difficult for rivals to copy or match. The value of a cost advantage depends on its sustainability. If rivals find it relatively easy or inexpensive to imitate the leader's low-cost methods, then the leader's advantage will be too short-lived to yield a valuable edge in the marketplace.

A low-cost provider has two options for achieving superior profit performance. Option 1 is to use the lower-cost edge to underprice competitors and attract price-sensitive buyers in great enough numbers to increase total profits. The trick to profitably underpricing rivals is either to keep the size of the price cut smaller than the size of the firm's cost advantage (thus reaping the benefits of both a bigger profit margin per unit sold and the added profits on incremental sales) or to generate enough added volume

> A low-cost leader's basis for competitive advantage is lower overall costs than competitors. Successful low-cost leaders are exceptionally good at finding ways to drive costs out of their businesses.

table 5.1   Distinctive Features of the Generic Competitive Strategies

Type of Feature	Low-Cost Provider	Broad Differentiation	Best-Cost Provider	Focused Low-Cost and Focused Differentiation
• Strategic target	• A broad cross-section of the market	• A broad cross-section of the market	• Value-conscious buyers	• A narrow market niche where buyer needs and preferences are distinctively different from the rest of the market
• Basis of competitive advantage	• Lower costs than competitors	• An ability to offer buyers something different from competitors	• More value for the money	• Lower cost in serving the niche (focused low cost) or special attributes that appeal to the tastes or requirements of niche members (focused differentiation)
• Product line	• A good basic product with few frills (acceptable quality and limited selection)	• Many product variations, wide selection, strong emphasis on differentiating features	• Good-to-excellent attributes, several-to-many upscale features	• Features and attributes that appeal to the tastes and/or special needs of the target segment
• Production emphasis	• A continuous search for cost reduction without sacrificing acceptable quality and essential features	• Creation of value for buyers; strive for product superiority	• Incorporation of upscale features and attributes at low cost	• Tailor-made for the tastes and requirements of niche members
• Marketing emphasis	• Try to make a virtue out of product features that lead to low cost	• Build in whatever features buyers are willing to pay for • Charge a premium price to cover the extra costs of differentiating features	• Either underprice rival brands with comparable features or match the price of rivals and provide better features—to build a reputation for delivering the best value	• Communicate how the focuser's product attributes and capabilities aim at catering to niche member tastes and/or specialized requirements
• Sustaining the strategy	• Offer economical prices/good value • Aim at contributing to a sustainable cost advantage—the key is to manage costs down, year after year, in every area of the business	• Communicate the points of difference in credible ways • Stress constant improvement and use innovation to stay ahead of imitative competitors • Concentrate on a few key differentiating features; tout them to create a reputation and brand image	• Develop unique expertise in simultaneously managing costs down and upscaling features and attributes	• Remain totally dedicated to serving the niche better than other competitors; don't blunt the firm's image and efforts by entering other segments or adding other product categories to widen market appeal

to increase total profits despite thinner profit margins (larger volume can make up for smaller margins provided the price reductions bring in enough extra sales). Option 2 is to refrain from price cutting altogether, be content with the present market share, and use the lower-cost edge to earn a higher profit margin on each unit sold, thereby raising the firm's total profits and overall return on investment.

Illustration Capsule 19 describes Nucor Corporation's strategy for gaining low-cost leadership in manufacturing a variety of steel products.

Ways to Achieve a Cost Advantage   To achieve a cost advantage, a firm's cumulative costs across its value chain must be lower than competitors' cumulative costs. There are two ways to accomplish this:[3]

- Do a better job than rivals of performing internal value chain activities efficiently and of managing the factors that can drive down the costs of value chain activities.

- Revamp the firm's value chain to bypass some cost-producing activities altogether.

Let's look at each of the two avenues for gaining a cost advantage.

Controlling the Cost Drivers   There are nine major cost drivers that come into play in determining a company's costs in each activity segment of the chain:[4]

1.   *Economies or diseconomies of scale*—The costs of a particular value chain activity are often subject to economies or diseconomies of scale. Economies of scale arise whenever activities can be performed more cheaply at larger volumes than smaller volumes and from the ability to spread out certain costs like R&D and advertising over a greater sales volume. Astute management of activities subject to scale economies or diseconomies can be a major source of cost savings. For example, manufacturing economies can usually be achieved by simplifying the product line, scheduling longer production runs for fewer models, and using common parts and components in different models. In global industries, making separate products for each country market instead of selling a mostly standard product worldwide tends to boost unit costs because of lost time in model changeover, shorter production runs, and inability to reach the most economic scale of production for each country model. Scale economies or diseconomies also arise in how a company manages its sales and marketing activities. A geographically organized sales force can realize economies as regional sales volume grows because a salesperson can write larger orders at each sales call or reduce travel time between calls; in contrast, a sales force organized by product line can encounter travel-related diseconomies if salespersons have to spend disproportionately more travel time calling on distantly spaced customers. Boosting local or regional market share can lower sales and marketing costs per unit, whereas opting for a bigger national share by entering new regions can create scale diseconomies unless and until market penetration in the newly entered regions reaches efficient proportions.

2.   *Learning and experience curve effects*—The cost of performing an activity can decline over time due to economies of experience and learning. Experience-based cost savings can come from much more than just personnel learning how to perform their tasks more efficiently and the debugging of new technologies. Other valuable sources of learning/experience economies include seeing ways to improve plant layout and

---

[3] Porter, *Competitive Advantage*, p. 97.

[4] The list and explanations are condensed from Porter, *Competitive Advantage*, pp. 70–107.

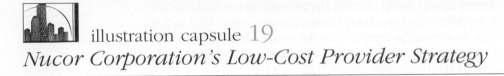

illustration capsule 19
Nucor Corporation's Low-Cost Provider Strategy

Nucor Corporation is the leading minimill producer of such steel products as rolled steel, finished steel, steel joists, joist girders, steel decks, and grinding balls. It has over $4 billion in sales annually and produces over 10 million tons of steel annually. The company has pursued a strategy that has made it among the lowest-cost producers of steel in the world and has allowed the company to consistently outperform its rivals in terms of financial and market performance.

Nucor's low-cost strategy aims to give it a cost and pricing advantage in the commodity like steel industry and leaves no part of the company's value chain neglected. The key elements of the strategy include:

• Using electric arc furnaces where scrap steel and directly reduced iron ore are melted and then sent to a continuous caster and rolling mill to be shaped into steel products, thereby eliminating an assortment of production processes from the value chain used by traditional integrated steel mills. Nucor's "minimill" value chain makes the use of coal, coke, and iron ore unnecessary; cuts investment in facilities and equipment (eliminating coke ovens, blast furnaces, basic oxygen furnaces, and ingot casters); and requires fewer employees than integrated mills.

• Nucor strives hard for continuous improvement in the efficiency of its plants, frequently investing in state-of-the-art equipment to reduce unit costs. Nucor is known for its technological leadership and its aggressive pursuit of innovation.

• The company selects its plant sites carefully to minimize inbound and outbound shipping costs and to take advantage of low rates for electricity (electric arc furnaces are heavy users of electricity). It also avoids geographic areas where labor unions are a strong influence.

• Nucor prefers a nonunion work force because it uses team-based incentive compensation systems (often opposed by unions). Operating and maintenance employees and supervisors are paid weekly bonuses based on the productivity of their work group. The size of the bonus is based on the capabilities of the equipment employed and ranges from 80 to 150 percent of an employee's base pay; no bonus is paid if the equipment is not operating. Nucor's compensation program has boosted the company's labor productivity to levels nearly double the industry average while rewarding productive employees with annual compensation packages that exceed what their union counterparts earn by as much as 20 percent. Nucor has been able to attract and retain highly talented, productive, and dedicated employees. In addition, the company's healthy culture and results-oriented self-managed work teams allow the company to employ fewer supervisors than what would be needed with an hourly union workforce. Nucor is proud of the more than 7,000 employees that make up the total Nucor team.

• Nucor puts heavy emphasis on consistent product quality and has rigorous quality systems.

• Nucor minimizes general and administrative expenses by maintaining a lean staff at its corporate headquarters (fewer than 125 employees) and allowing only four levels of management between the CEO and production workers. Headquarters offices are modestly furnished and located in an inexpensive building. The company minimizes reports, paperwork, and meetings to keep managers focused on value-adding activities. Nucor is noted not only for its streamlined organizational structure but also its frugality in travel and entertainment expenses—the company's top managers set the example by flying coach class, avoiding pricey hotels, and refraining from taking customers out for expensive dinners.

Nucor management's outstanding execution of its low-cost strategy and its commitment to drive out non-value-adding costs throughout its value chain has allowed it to grow at a considerably faster rate than its integrated steel mill rivals and maintain high industry-relative profit margins while aggressively competing on price.

Source: Company annual reports, news releases, and Web site.

work flows, to make product design modifications that enhance manufacturing efficiency, to redesign machinery and equipment to gain increased operating speed, and to tailor parts and components in ways that streamline the assembly process. Learning can also reduce the cost of constructing and operating Web sites, new retail outlets, new plants, or new distribution facilities. There are also learning benefits associated with getting samples of a rival's products and having design engineers study how they are made, benchmarking company activities against the performance of similar activities in other companies, and interviewing suppliers, consultants, and ex-employees of rival firms to tap into their wisdom. Learning tends to vary with the amount of management attention devoted to capturing the benefits of experience of both the firm and outsiders. Astute managers make a conscious effort not only to capture learning benefits but also to keep the benefits proprietary by building or modifying production equipment in-house, endeavoring to retain knowledgable employees (to reduce the risk of them going to work for rivals firms), limiting the dissemination of cost-saving information through employee publications that can fall into rivals' hands, and enforcing strict nondisclosure provisions in employment contracts.

3. *The cost of key resource inputs*—The cost of performing value chain activities depends in part on what a firm has to pay for key resource inputs. Competitors do not all incur the same costs for items purchased from suppliers or for resources used in performing value chain activities. How well a company manages the costs of acquiring key resource inputs is often a big driver of costs. Input costs are a function of three factors:

- *Union versus nonunion labor*—Avoiding the use of union labor is often a key to low-cost manufacturing, not just to escape paying high wages but rather to escape union work rules that stifle productivity. Such prominent low-cost manufacturers as Nucor and Cooper Tire are noted for their incentive compensation systems that allow nonunion workers to earn more than their unionized counterparts at rival companies.

- *Bargaining power vis-à-vis suppliers*—Many large enterprises (Wal-Mart, The Home Depot, the world's major motor vehicle producers) have used their bargaining clout in purchasing large volumes to wrangle good prices on their purchases from suppliers. Differences in buying power among industry rivals can be an important source of cost advantage or disadvantage.

- *Locational variables*—Locations differ in their prevailing wage levels, tax rates, energy costs, inbound and outbound shipping and freight costs, and so on. Opportunities may exist for reducing costs by relocating plants, field offices, warehousing, or headquarters operations.

4. *Link with other activities in the company or industry value chain*—When the cost of one activity is affected by how other activities are performed, costs can be managed downward by making sure that linked activities are performed in cooperative and coodinated fashion. For example, when a company's quality control costs or materials inventory costs are linked to the activities of suppliers, cost savings can be achieved by working cooperatively with key suppliers on the design of parts and components, quality-assurance procedures, just-in-time delivery, integrated materials supply, and online order processing. The costs of new product development can often be managed downward by having cross-functional task forces (perhaps including representatives of suppliers and key customers) jointly work on R&D, product design, manufacturing plans, and market launch. Links with forward channels tend to center on location of warehouses, materials handling, outbound shipping, and packaging. Nail manufacturers, for example, learned that nails delivered in prepackaged 1-lb., 5-lb., and 10-lb. assortments instead of 100-lb. bulk cartons could reduce a hardware dealer's labor costs in filling individual customer orders. The lesson here is that effective coordination of linked activities anywhere in the value chain system holds potential for cost reduction.

5. *Sharing opportunities with other organizational or business units within the enterprise*—Different product lines or business units within an enterprise can often share the same order processing and customer billing systems, utilize a common sales force to call on customers, share the same warehouse and distribution facilities, or rely on a common customer service and technical support team. Such combining of like activities and the sharing of resources across sister units can create significant cost savings. Cost sharing can help achieve scale economies, shorten the learning curve in mastering a new technology, and/or promote fuller capacity utilization. Furthermore, there are times when the know-how gained in one division or geographic unit can be used to help lower costs in another; sharing know-how across organizational lines has significant cost-saving potential when the activities are similar and know-how is readily transferred from one unit to another.

6. *The benefits of vertical integration versus outsourcing*—Partially or fully integrating into the activities of either suppliers or forward channel allies can allow an enterprise to detour suppliers or buyers with considerable bargaining power. Vertical integration forward or backward also has potential if there are significant cost-savings from having a single firm perform adjacent activities in the industry value chain. But, more often, it is cheaper to outsource certain functions and activities to outside specialists, who by virtue of their expertise and volume can perform the activity/function more cheaply.

7. *Timing considerations associated with first-mover advantages and disadvantages*—Sometimes the first major brand in the market is able to establish and maintain its brand name at a lower cost than later brand arrivals. This is proving true in new Internet businesses where being first and biggest creates potent brand-name recognition. Cases in point include eBay, Yahoo!, and Amazon.com. On other occasions, such as when technology is developing fast, late-purchasers can benefit from waiting to install second- or third-generation equipment that is both cheaper and more efficient; first-generation users often incur added costs associated with debugging and learning how to use an immature and unperfected technology. Likewise, companies that follow rather than lead new product development efforts sometimes avoid many of the costs that pioneers incur in performing pathbreaking R&D and opening up new markets.

8. *The percentage of capacity utilization*—Capacity utilization is a big cost driver for those value chain activities that have substantial fixed costs associated with them. Higher rates of capacity utilization allow depreciation and other fixed costs to be spread over a larger unit volume, thereby lowering fixed costs per unit. The more capital-intensive the business, or the higher the percentage of fixed costs as a percentage of total costs, the more important this cost driver becomes because there's such a stiff unit-cost penalty for underutilizing existing capacity. In such cases, finding ways to operate close to full capacity year-round can be an important source of cost advantage.

A firm can improve its capacity utilization by (*a*) serving a mix of accounts with peak volumes spread throughout the year, (*b*) finding off-season uses for its products, (*c*) serving private-label customers that can intermittently use the excess capacity, (*d*) selecting buyers with stable demands or demands that are counter to the normal peak/valley cycle, (*e*) letting competitors serve the buyer segments whose demands fluctuate the most, and (*f*) sharing capacity with sister units having a different seasonal production pattern (e.g., producing snowmobiles for the winter season and personal water-ski craft for summer water sports).

9. *Strategic choices and operating decisions*—A company's costs can be driven up or down by a fairly wide assortment of managerial decisions:

- Adding/cutting the services provided to buyers.
- Incorporating more/fewer performance and quality features into the product.

- Paying higher/lower wages and fringes to employees relative to rivals and firms in other industries.
- Increasing/decreasing the number of different channels utilized in distributing the firm's product.
- Lengthening/shortening delivery times to customers.
- Putting more/less emphasis than rivals on the use of incentive compensation to motivate employees and boost worker productivity.
- Raising/lowering the specifications for purchased materials.

Managers intent on achieving low-cost leader status have to possess a sophisticated understanding of how the above nine factors drive the costs of each activity in the value chain. Then they have to not only use their knowledge about the cost drivers to reduce costs for every activity where cost savings can be identified but do so with enough ingenuity and unswerving commitment that the company ends up with a sustainable cost advantage over rivals.

> Outperforming rivals in controlling the factors that drive costs is a very demanding managerial exercise.

Revamping the Value Chain Dramatic cost advantages can emerge from finding innovative ways to restructure processes and tasks, cut out low-value activities, eliminate frills, and provide the basics more economically. The primary ways companies can achieve a cost advantage by reconfiguring their value chains include:

- *Shifting to e-business technologies*—Use of the Internet can enable online shopping and purchases (thus reducing or eliminating the need for human order takers and brick-and-mortar stores), online order processing and bill payment, online data sharing with suppliers, fast e-mail communication and teleconferencing, and other such techniques can streamline the value chain and greatly reduce the costs of doing business. Ford Motor Company has aggressively adopted videoconferencing and computer-assisted design and manufacturing technologies—its new cars and trucks are being developed by teams of designers stationed at Ford locations around the world who use an online computer network to share ideas, create the actual designs, integrate the designs for the various parts and components (the chassis, engine, transmission, body, and instrumentation), and build and test prototypes via computer simulations.

- *Using direct-to-end-user sales and marketing approaches*—Costs in the wholesale-retail portions of the value chain frequently represent 35–50 percent of the price final consumers pay. Software developers are increasingly using the Internet to market and deliver their products directly to buyers; downloading software direct from the Internet eliminates the costs of producing and packaging CDs and cuts out the host of activities, costs, and markups associated with shipping and distributing their products through wholesale and retail channels—see Figure 5.2. By cutting all these costs and activities out of the value chain, software developers have the pricing room to boost their profit margins and still sell their products below levels that retailers would have to charge.

- *Simplifying product design*—Utilizing computer-assisted design techniques, reducing the number of parts, standardizing parts and components across models and styles, shifting to an easy-to-manufacture product design all can simplify the value chain.

- *Stripping away the extras*—Offering only basics products or services can help a company cut costs associated with multiple features and options—a favorite technique of the no-frills airlines like Southwest Airlines.

figure 5.2 **Reconfiguring Value Chain Systems to Lower Costs: The Case of the Software Industry**

A. Value Chain System of Software Developers Using Traditional Wholesale-Retail Channels

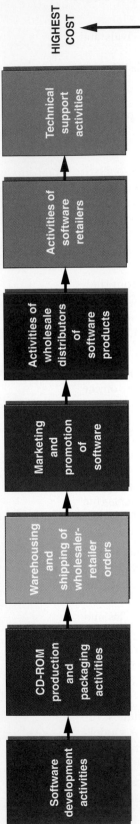

B. Value Chain System of Software Developers Using Direct Sales and Physical Delivery of CDs

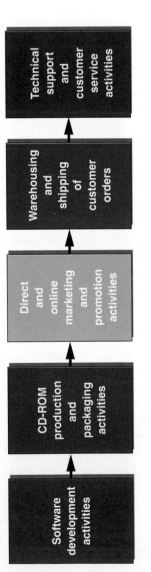

C. Value Chain System of Software Developers Using Online Sales and Internet Delivery

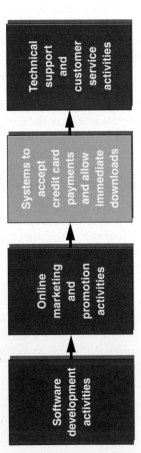

- *Shifting to a simpler, less capital-intensive, or more streamlined or flexible technological process*—Computer-assisted design and manufacture, or other flexible manufacturing systems, can accommodate both low-cost efficiency and product customization.

- *Bypassing the use of high-cost raw materials or component parts*—High-cost raw materials and parts can be designed out of the product.

- *Relocating facilities*—Moving plants closer to suppliers, customers, or both can help curtail inbound and outbound logistics costs.

- *Dropping the "something for everyone" approach*—Focusing on a limited product or service to meet a special, but important, need of the target buyer can eliminate activities and costs associated with numerous product versions.

- *Reengineering core business processes to consolidate work steps and cut out low-value-added activities*—Some companies have been able to reduce the costs of reengineered activities by 30 to 70 percent, compared to the 5 to 10 percent possible with creative tinkering and adjusting.

An example of significant cost advantages from creating altogether new value chain systems can be found in the beef-packing industry. The traditional cost chain involved raising cattle on scattered farms and ranches, shipping them live to labor-intensive, unionized slaughtering plants, and then transporting whole sides of beef to grocery retailers whose butcher departments cut them into smaller pieces and packaged them for sale to grocery shoppers. Iowa Beef Packers revamped the traditional chain with a radically different strategy—large automated plants employing nonunion workers were built near economically transportable supplies of cattle, and the meat was partially butchered at the processing plant into small, high-yield cuts (sometimes sealed in plastic casing ready for purchase) before being boxed and shipped to retailers. Iowa Beef's inbound cattle transportation expenses, traditionally a major cost item, were cut significantly by avoiding the weight losses that occurred when live animals were shipped long distances; major outbound shipping cost savings were achieved by not having to ship whole sides of beef with their high waste factor. Iowa Beef's strategy was so successful that it became the largest U.S. meatpacker, surpassing the former industry leaders, Swift, Wilson, and Armour.[5]

Federal Express innovatively redefined the value chain for rapid delivery of small parcels. Traditional firms like Emery Worldwide and Airborne Express operated by collecting freight packages of varying sizes, shipping them to their destination points via air freight and commercial airlines, and then delivering them via truck to the addressee. FedEx opted to focus only on the market for overnight delivery of small packages and documents. These were collected at local drop points during the late-afternoon hours and flown on company-owned planes during early-evening hours to a central hub in Memphis. From 11 PM to 3 AM each night all parcels were sorted, then reloaded on company planes, and flown during the early-morning hours to their destination points, where they were delivered the next morning by company personnel using company trucks.[6] FedEx's hub-and-spoke system produced a cost structure low enough to guarantee next-day delivery of a small parcel anywhere in the United States for as little as $13.

Southwest Airlines has reconfigured the traditional value chain of commercial airlines to lower costs and thereby offer dramatically lower fares to passengers. It has

---

[5]Porter, *Competitive Advantage,* p. 109.

[6]Ibid., p. 109.

mastered fast turnarounds at the gates (about 15 minutes versus 45 minutes for rivals); because the short turnarounds allow the planes to fly more hours per day, Southwest can schedule more flights per day with fewer aircraft. Southwest does not offer in-flight meals, assigned seating, baggage transfer to connecting airlines, or first-class seating and service, thereby eliminating all the cost-producing activities associated with these features. The company's online system for making reservations and purchasing an electronic ticket along with automated ticketing at its airport check-in counters encourages customers to bypass travel agents (thereby escaping payment of commisions and the costs associated with helping maintain the centralized computerized reservation systems accessed by travel agents) and also reduces the need for so many agents at check-in counters. Southwest's full-service rivals have higher costs because they must perform all the activities associated with providing meal service, assigned seating, premium classes of service, interline baggage checking, and computerized reservation systems.

Dell Computer has proved a pioneer in revamping the value chain in assembling and marketing PCs. Whereas Compaq Computer, Toshiba, Hewlett-Packard, Sony, and several other PC makers produce their models in volume and sell them through independent resellers and retailers, Dell has elected to market directly to customers, building its PCs as customers order them and shipping them to customers within a few days of receiving the order. Dell's value chain approach has proved cost-effective in coping with the PC industry's blink-of-an-eye product life cycle (new models equipped with faster chips and new features appear every few months)—the build-to-order strategy enables the company to avoid misjudging buyer demand for its various models and being saddled with fast-obsoleting excess components and finished goods inventories. Also, its sell-direct strategy slices reseller/retailer costs and margins out of the value chain (although some of these savings are offset by the cost of Dell's direct marketing and customer support activities—functions that would otherwise be performed by resellers and retailers). Partnerships with suppliers that facilitate just-in-time deliveries of components and minimize Dell's inventory costs, coupled with Dell's extensive use of e-commerce technologies (online sales of PCs exceed $30 million per day), further reduce Dell's costs. Dell's value chain approach is widely considered to have made it the global low-cost leader in the PC industry.

See Illustration Capsule 20 for how e-business technologies are fast becoming pervasive in value chain restructuring and creation of a low-cost advantage.

The Keys to Success in Achieving Low-Cost Leadership   To succeed with a low-cost-provider strategy, company managers have to scrutinize each cost-creating activity and determine what drives its cost. Then they have to use this knowledge about the cost drivers to manage the costs of each activity downward, exhaustively pursuing cost savings throughout the value chain. They have to be proactive in restructuring the value chain to eliminate nonessential work steps. Normally, low-cost producers work diligently to create cost-conscious corporate cultures that feature broad employee participation in continuous cost improvement efforts and limited perks and frills for executives. They strive to operate with exceptionally small corporate staffs to keep administrative costs to a minimum. Many successful low-cost leaders also benchmark costs against best-in-class performers of an activity to keep close tabs on how well they are doing at cost control.

But while low-cost providers are champions of frugality, they are usually aggressive in investing in resources and capabilities that promise to drive costs out of the business. Wal-Mart, for example, employs state-of-the-art technology throughout its operations—its distribution facilities are an automated showcase, it uses online systems

> Success in achieving cost advantages over rivals comes from exploring all avenues for reducing costs and pressing for continuous cost reductions across all aspects of the company's operations year after year after year.

illustration capsule 20

E-Business Technologies: Powerful Tools for Restructuring Value Chains to Create a Low-Cost Advantage

The creation of low-cost "electronic value chains" is fast becoming the norm in industry after industry. Electronic brokerages, for example, using e-business technologies and the Internet to offer online trading and deliver a growing assortment of investment information and research, are revolutionizing the business model of the stock brokerage industry. The sharply lower costs of the electronic value chains employed by online brokerages allow them to profitably execute trades for a small fraction of what traditional brokerages charge.

A number of enterprising firms have created electronic value chains that enable them to function as "Internet middlemen" and use the instant communications capability of the Internet to match buyers and sellers. Chemdex provides one-stop shopping for scientists and researchers at its Web site containing the catalogs of scores of pharmaceutical and biotech suppliers from around the world. Chemdex makes money by charging vendors a transactions fee below the percentage markup of traditional distributors; it then passes the savings on to buyers. Similarly, Wells Fargo and Chase Manhattan both operate Web sites where corporate purchasing agents can pool their purchases to get better deals or special treatment from suppliers; they too make money by charging a fee for transactions. Singapore-based Advanced Manufacturing Online provides an Internet-based system that enables Asian suppliers and customers to send orders and solicit price quotations—users include Motorola,

Matsushita, and Taiwan Semiconductor Manufacturing. These new e-markets where buyers and sellers gather electronically not only allow buyers to conveniently shop for better terms but also give sellers quick access to buyers, allowing them to save on selling and marketing costs. The whole market process becomes more efficient, compared to the traditional methods where salespeople contact customers in person or where buyers survey the offerings of various suppliers via telephone or fax.

Company Web sites can easily function as retail showrooms, thereby creating an alternative distribution channel that allows many kinds of business-to-consumer transactions in cyberspace to be handled faster, more conveniently, and less expensively than in the physical world of the marketplace—an outcome that is forcing traditional wholesalers and retailers to revamp their value chain structures to protect their sales and market shares. Internet companies (such as Carorder.com) have developed software capability that allows prospective motor vehicle buyers to place orders online for custom-equipped cars and trucks and pick up their vehicles at designated delivery points, thus bypassing the car dealership part of the automotive value chain. Other innovative Internet companies are creating electronic value chain systems to provide buyers with mortgages, loans, insurance, new and used textbooks, groceries, flowers—the list goes on and on.

---

to order goods from suppliers and manage inventories, it equips its stores with cutting-edge sales-tracking and check-out systems, and it operates a private satellite communications system that daily sends point-of-sale data to 4,000 vendors. Its information and communications systems and capabilities are more sophisticated than those of virtually any other retail chain in the world.

Companies that employ low-cost provider strategies include Lincoln Electric in arc welding equipment, Briggs & Stratton in small gasoline engines, Bic in ballpoint pens, Black & Decker in power tools, Stride Rite in footwear, Beaird-Poulan in chain saws, Nucor in steelmaking, General Electric and Whirlpool in major home appliances, and Ameritrade in electronic brokerage.

When a Low-Cost Provider Strategy Works Best　　A competitive strategy predicated on low-cost leadership is particularly powerful when:

1. *Price competition among rival sellers is especially vigorous*—Low-cost providers are in the best position to compete offensively on the basis of price, to use the appeal of lower price to grab sales (and market share) from rivals, to remain profitable in the face of strong price competition, and to survive price wars.

> In markets where rivals compete mainly on price, low cost relative to competitors is the only competitive advantage that matters.

2. *The industry's product is essentially standardized or a commodity readily available from a host of sellers*—Commoditylike conditions set the stage for lively price competition; in such markets, it is less efficient, higher-cost rivals whose profits get squeezed the most.

3. *There are few ways to achieve product differentiation that have value to buyers*— When the differences between brands do not matter much to buyers, buyers are nearly always very sensitive to price differences and shop the market for the best price.

4. *Most buyers utilize the product in the same ways*—with common user requirements, a standardized product can satisfy the needs of buyers, in which case low selling price, not features or quality, becomes the dominant factor in causing buyers to choose one seller's product over another's.

5. *Buyers incur low switching costs in changing from one seller to another*—Low switching costs give buyers the flexibility to shift purchases to lower-priced sellers having equally good products or to attractively priced substitute products. A low-cost leader is better positioned to use low price to induce its customers not to switch to rival brands or substitutes.

6. *Buyers are large and have significant power to bargain down prices*—Low-cost providers have partial profit-margin protection in bargaining with high-volume buyers, since powerful buyers are rarely able to bargain price down past the survival level of the next most cost-efficient seller.

7. *Industry newcomers use introductory low prices to attract buyers and build a customer base*—The low-cost leader can use price cuts of its own to make it harder for a new rival to win customers; the pricing power of the low-cost provider acts as a barrier for new entrants.

> A low-cost leader is in the strongest position to win the business of price-sensitive buyers, set the floor on market price, and still earn a profit.

As a rule, the more price-sensitive buyers are and the more inclined they are to base their purchasing decisions on which seller offers the best price, the more appealing a low-cost strategy becomes. A low-cost company's ability to set the industry's price floor and still earn a profit erects protective barriers around its market position.

The Pitfalls of a Low-Cost Provider Strategy   Perhaps the biggest pitfall of a low-cost provider strategy is getting carried away with overly aggressivly price cutting and ending up with lower, rather than higher, profitability. A low-cost/low-price advantage results in superior profitability only if (1) prices are cut by less than the size of the cost advantage or (2) the added gains in unit sales are large enough to bring in a bigger total profit despite lower margins per unit sold. A company with a 5 percent cost advantage cannot cut prices 20 percent, end up with a volume gain of only 10 percent, and still expect to earn higher profits!

A second big pitfall is not emphasizing avenues of cost advantage that can be kept proprietary or that relegate rivals to playing catch-up. The value of a cost advantage depends on its sustainability. Sustainability, in turn, hinges on whether the company achieves its cost advantage in ways difficult for rivals to copy or match.

> A low-cost provider's product offering must always contain enough attributes to be attractive to prospective buyers—low price, by itself, is not always appealing to buyers.

A third pitfall is becoming too fixated on cost reduction. Low cost cannot be pursued so zealously that a firm's offering ends up being too features-poor to generate buyer appeal. Furthermore, a company driving zealously to push its costs down has to guard against misreading or ignoring subtle but significant market swings—like growing buyer interest in added features or service, declining buyer sensitivity to price, or new developments that start to alter how buyers use the product. A low-cost zealot risks getting left behind if buyers begin to opt for enhanced quality, innovative performance features, faster service, and other differentiating features.

Even if these mistakes are avoided, a low-cost competitive approach still carries risk. Cost-saving technological breakthroughs or the emergence of still-lower-cost value chain models can nullify a low-cost leader's hard-won position. The current leader may have difficulty in shifting quickly to the new technologies or value chain approaches because heavy investments lock it in (at least temporarily) to its present value chain approach.

Differentiation Strategies

Differentiation strategies are an attractive competitive approach whenever buyers' needs and preferences are too diverse to be fully satisfied by a standardized product or by sellers with identical capabilities. To be successful with a differentiation strategy, a company has to study buyers' needs and behavior carefully to learn what buyers consider important, what they think has value, and what they are willing to pay for. Then the company has to incorporate buyer-desired attributes into its product or service offering that will set it visibly and distinctively apart from rivals. Competitive advantage results once a sufficient number of buyers become strongly attached to the differentiated attributes. The more that a company's differentiated offering appeals to buyers, the more customers *bond* with the company and the stronger the resulting competitive advantage.

> The essence of a differentiation strategy is to be unique in ways that are valuable to customers and that can be sustained.

Successful differentiation allows a firm to

- Command a premium price for its product, and/or
- Increase unit sales (because additional buyers are won over by the differentiating features), and/or
- Gain buyer loyalty to its brand (because some buyers are strongly attracted to the differentiating features and bond with the company and its products).

Differentiation enhances profitability whenever the extra price the product commands outweighs the added costs of achieving the differentiation. Company differentiation strategies fail when buyers don't value the brand's uniqueness enough to buy it instead of rivals' brands and/or when a company's approach to differentiation is easily copied or matched by its rivals, thus eliminating the basis of differentiation.

Types of Differentiation Themes   Companies can pursue differentiation from many angles: a unique taste (Dr Pepper, Listerine); multiple features (Microsoft Windows, Microsoft Office); wide selection and one-stop shopping (The Home Depot, Amazon.com), superior service (FedEx in next-day delivery); spare parts availability (Caterpillar guarantees 48-hour spare parts delivery to any customer anywhere in the world or else the part is furnished free); more for the money (McDonald's, Wal-Mart); engineering design and performance (Mercedes, BMW); prestige and distinctiveness (Rolex in watches); product reliability (Johnson & Johnson in baby products); quality manufacture (Karastan in carpets, Michelin in tires, Honda in automobiles); technological leadership (3M Corporation in bonding and coating products); a full range of services (Charles Schwab in stock brokerage); a complete line of products (Campbell's soups); and top-of-the-line image and reputation (Ralph Lauren in menswear, Chanel in women's fashions and accessories, Ritz-Carlton in hotels, Cross in writing instruments).

> Easy-to-copy differentiating features cannot produce sustainable competitive advantage.

The most appealing approaches to differentiation are those that are hard or expensive for rivals to duplicate. Indeed, resourceful competitors can, in time, clone almost any product or feature or attribute. If American Airlines creates a program for frequent fliers, so can Delta; if Ford offers a 50,000-mile bumper-to-bumper warranty on its new vehicles, so can Volkswagen and Nissan. This is why *sustainable* differentiation usually has to be linked to core competencies, unique competitive capabilities, and superior management of value chain activities. When a company has competencies and capabilities that competitors cannot readily match and/or manages its value chain activities in ways that promote unique differentiation, then its basis for differentiation is more sustainable. As a rule, differentiation yields a longer-lasting and more profitable competitive edge when it is based on new product innovation, technical superiority, product quality and reliability, comprehensive customer service, and unique competitive capabilities. Buyers widely perceive such differentiating attributes as having value, and they tend to be tougher for rivals to copy or offset profitably.

Where Along the Value Chain to Create the Differentiating Attributes   Differentiation is not something hatched in marketing and advertising departments, nor is it limited to the catchalls of quality and service. Differentiation opportunities can exist in activities all along an industry's value chain; possibilities include:

1. *Purchasing and procurement activities* that ultimately spill over to affect the performance or quality of the company's end product. McDonald's gets high ratings on its french fries partly because it has very strict specifications on the potatoes purchased from suppliers.

2. *Product R&D activities* that aim at improved product designs and performance features, expanded end uses and applications, more frequent first-on-the-market victories, wider product variety and selection, added user safety, greater recycling capability, or enhanced environmental protection.

3. *Production R&D and technology-related activities* that permit custom-order manufacture at an efficient cost; make production methods safer for the environment; or improve product quality, reliability, and appearance. Many manufacturers have developed flexible manufacturing systems that allow different models to be made or different options to be added on the same assembly line. Being able to provide buyers with made-to-order products can be a potent differentiating capability.

4. *Manufacturing activities* that reduce product defects, prevent premature product failure, extend product life, allow better warranty coverages, improve economy of use, result in more end-user convenience, or enhance product appearance. The quality edge enjoyed by Japanese automakers stems partly from their distinctive competence in performing assembly-line activities.

5. *Outbound logistics and distribution activities* that allow for faster delivery, more accurate order filling, and fewer warehouse and on-the-shelf stockouts.

6. *Marketing, sales, and customer service activities* that result in superior technical assistance to buyers, faster maintenance and repair services, more and better product information provided to customers, more and better training materials for end users, better credit terms, quicker order processing, or greater customer convenience.

Managers need keen understanding of the sources of differentiation and the activities that drive uniqueness to devise a sound differentiation strategy and evaluate various differentiation approaches.[7]

---

[7]Ibid., p. 124.

illustration capsule 21
Differentiating Features That Raise Performance

To enhance the performance a buyer gets from using its product or service, a company can incorporate features and attributes that:

- Provide buyers greater reliability, durability, convenience, or ease of use.

- Make the company's product or service cleaner, safer, quieter, or more maintenance-free than rival brands.

- Exceed environmental or regulatory standards.

- Meet the buyer's needs and requirements more completely, compared to competitors' offerings.

- Give buyers the option to add on or to upgrade later as new product versions come on the market.

- Give buyers more flexibility to tailor their own products to the needs of their customers.

- Do a better job of meeting the buyer's future growth and expansion requirements.

Source: Adapted from Michael E. Porter, *Competitive Advantage* (New York: Free Press, 1985), pp. 135–38.

Achieving a Differentiation-Based Competitive Advantage While it is easy enough to grasp that a successful differentiation strategy must entail creating buyer value in ways unmatched by rivals, the hard thing is to figure out *how* to create unique attributes that buyers will consider valuable. Any of four basic approaches can be used. First is to *incorporate product attributes and user features that lower the buyer's overall costs of using the company's product.* Making a company's product more economical for a buyer to use can be done by reducing the buyer's raw materials waste (providing cut-to-size components), reducing a buyer's inventory requirements (providing just-in-time deliveries), increasing maintenance intervals and product reliability so as to lower a buyer's repair and maintenance costs, using online systems to reduce a buyer's procurement and order processing costs, and providing free technical support and assistance.

> A differentiator's basis for competitive advantage is either a product/service offering whose attributes differ significantly from the offerings of rivals or a set of capabilities for delivering customer value that rivals don't have or can't quite match.

A second approach is to *incorporate features that raise the performance a buyer gets out of the product.* Illustration Capsule 21 contains differentiation avenues that enhance product performance and buyer value. A third approach is to *incorporate features that enhance buyer satisfaction in noneconomic or intangible ways.* Goodyear's new Aquatread tire design appeals to safety-conscious motorists wary of slick roads in rainy weather. Rolls-Royce, Tiffany, and Gucci have differentiation-based competitive advantages linked to buyer desires for status, image, prestige, upscale fashion, superior craftsmanship, and the finer things in life. L. L. Bean makes its mail-order customers feel secure in their purchases by providing an unconditional guarantee with no time limit: "All of our products are guaranteed to give 100 percent satisfaction in every way. Return anything purchased from us at any time if it proves otherwise. We will replace it, refund your purchase price, or credit your credit card, as you wish."

A fourth approach is to compete on the basis of capabilities—*to deliver value to customers via competitive capabilities that rivals don't have or can't afford to match.*[8] A capability has differentiating competitive value when it allows a firm to perform an activity that delivers value to customers in ways rivals cannot. The strategy-making challenge is selecting which differentiating capabilities to develop. Successful capabilities-driven

---

[8]For a more detailed discussion, see George Stalk, Philip Evans, and Lawrence E. Schulman, "Competing on Capabilities: The New Rules of Corporate Strategy," *Harvard Business Review* 70, no. 2 (March–April 1992), pp. 57–69.

differentiation begins with a deep understanding of what customers need and ends with building organizational capabilities to satisfy these needs better than rivals. The Japanese auto manufacturers have the capability to bring new models to market faster than American and European automakers, thereby allowing them to satisfy changing consumer preferences for one vehicle style versus another. CNN has the capability to cover breaking news stories faster and more completely than the major networks. Microsoft, with its Windows operating systems and assorted application software, its ability to assemble large project teams composed of highly talented and antibureaucratic programmers who thrive on developing complex products and systems, and its marketing savvy and know-how, has stronger capabilities to design, create, distribute, advertise, and sell an array of software products for PC applications than any of its rivals.

The Importance of Perceived Value and Signaling Value   Buyers seldom pay for value they don't perceive, no matter how real the unique extras may be.[9] Thus, the price premium commanded by a differentiation strategy reflects *the value actually delivered* to the buyer and *the value perceived* by the buyer (even if not actually delivered). Actual and perceived value can differ whenever buyers have trouble assessing what their experience with the product will be. Incomplete knowledge on the part of buyers often causes them to judge value based on such signals as price (where price connotes quality), attractive packaging, extensive ad campaigns (i.e., how well-known the product is), ad content and image, the quality of brochures and sales presentations, the seller's facilities, the seller's list of customers, the firm's market share, the length of time the firm has been in business, and the professionalism, appearance, and personality of the seller's employees. Such signals of value may be as important as actual value (1) when the nature of differentiation is subjective or hard to quantify, (2) when buyers are making a first-time purchase, (3) when repurchase is infrequent, and (4) when buyers are unsophisticated.

> A firm whose differentiation strategy delivers only modest extra value but clearly signals that extra value may command a higher price than a firm that actually delivers higher value but signals it poorly.

Keeping the Cost of Differentiation in Line   Company efforts to achieve differentiation usually raise costs. The trick to profitable differentiation is either to keep the costs of achieving differentiation below the price premium the differentiating attributes can command in the marketplace (thus increasing the profit margin per unit sold) or to offset thinner profit margins with enough added volume to increase total profits. It usually makes sense to incorporate extra differentiating features that are not costly but add to buyer satisfaction. Federal Express installed systems that allowed customers to track packages in transit by connecting to FedEx's Web site and entering the airbill number; some hotels and motels provide in-room coffee-making amenities or free continental breakfasts in their lobbies; many McDonald's outlets have play areas for small children.

When a Differentiation Strategy Works Best   Differentiation strategies tend to work best in market circumstances where:

- *There are many ways to differentiate the product or service and many buyers perceive these differences as having value*—Without this condition, profitable differentiation opportunities are very restricted.
- *Buyer needs and uses are diverse*—Some buyers prefer one combination of features and other buyers another. The more diverse buyer preferences are, the more

---

[9]This discussion draws from Porter, *Competitive Advantage,* pp. 138–42. Porter's insights here are particularly important to formulating differentiating strategies because they highlight the relevance of "intangibles" and "signals."

room firms have to pursue different approaches to differentiation and thereby avoid trying to outdifferentiate one another on much the same attributes.

- *Few rival firms are following a similar differentiation approach*—There is less head-to-head rivalry when differentiating rivals go separate ways in pursuing uniqueness and try to appeal to buyers on different combinations of attributes.
- *Technological change and product innovation are fast-paced and competition re-volves around rapidly evolving product features*—Rapid product innovation and frequent introductions of next-version products help maintain buyer interest in the product and provide space for companies to pursue separate differentiating paths.

The Pitfalls of a Differentiation Strategy There are, of course, no guaran tees that differentiation will produce a meaningful competitive advantage. If buyers see little value in the unique attributes or capabilities a company stresses, then its differentiation strategy will get a ho-hum market reception. In addition, attempts at differentiation are doomed to fail if competitors can quickly copy most or all of the appealing product attributes a company comes up with. Rapid imitation means that no rival achieves differentiation, since whenever one firm introduces some aspect of uniqueness that strikes the fancy of buyers, fast-following copycats quickly reestablish similarity. Thus, to build competitive advantage through differentiation a firm must search out sources of uniqueness that are time-consuming or burdensome for rivals to match. Other common pitfalls and mistakes in pursuing differentiation include:[10]

> Any differentiating element that works well tends to draw imitators.

- Trying to differentiate on the basis of something that does not lower a buyer's cost or enhance a buyer's well-being, as perceived by the buyer.
- Overdifferentiating so that price is too high relative to competitors or that product quality or service levels exceed buyers' needs.
- Trying to charge too high a price premium (the bigger the price differential the harder it is to keep buyers from switching to lower-priced competitors).
- Ignoring the need to signal value and depending only on intrinsic product attributes to achieve differentiation.
- Not understanding or identifying what buyers consider as value.

A low-cost provider strategy can defeat a differentiation strategy when buyers are satisfied with a basic product and don't think "extra" attributes are worth a higher price.

Best-Cost Provider Strategies

Best-cost provider strategies aim at giving customers *more value for the money*. The objective is to deliver superior value to buyers by satisfying their expectations on key quality-service-features-performance attributes and beating their expectations on price (given what rivals are charging for much the same attributes). A company achieves best-cost status from an ability to incorporate attractive attributes at a lower cost than rivals. To become a best-cost provider, a company must have the resources and capabilities to achieve good-to-excellent quality at a lower cost than rivals, incorporate appealing features at a lower cost than rivals, match product performance at a lower cost than rivals, provide good-to-excellent customer service at a lower cost than rivals, and so on. The term *best-cost provider* is used because this strategy entails striving to have the best (*lowest*) cost relative to rivals offering products/services with comparable attributes.

> The most successful best-cost producers have competencies and capabilities to simultaneously manage unit costs down and product caliber up.

---

[10]Porter, *Competitive Advantage*, pp. 160–62.

As Figure 5.1 indicates, best-cost provider strategies stake out a middle ground between pursuing a low-cost advantage and a differentiation advantage and between appealing to the broad market as a whole and a narrow market niche. From a competitive positioning standpoint, best-cost strategies are a *hybrid,* balancing a strategic emphasis on low cost against a strategic emphasis on differentiation (superior value). *The market target is value-conscious buyers,* perhaps a very sizable part of the market. *The competitve advantage of a best-cost provider is lower costs than rivals* in incorporating good-to-excellent attributes, putting it in a position to underprice rival brands with similar appealing attributes.

A best-cost provider strategy is very appealing in certain market situations. In markets where buyer diversity makes product differentiation the norm *and* where many buyers are also sensitive to price and value, a best-cost producer strategy can be more advantageous than either a pure low-cost producer strategy or a pure differentiation strategy keyed to product superiority. This is because a best-cost provider can position itself near the middle of the market with either a medium-quality product at a below-average price or with a very good product at a medium price. Often, substantial numbers of buyers prefer midrange products rather than the cheap, basic products of low-cost producers or the expensive products of top-of-the-line differentiators. But unless a company has the resources, know-how, and capabilities to incorporate upscale product or service attributes at a lower cost than rivals, this strategy is ill-advised.

Illustration Capsule 22 describes how Toyota has used a best-cost approach with its Lexus models.

> The most powerful competitive strategy of all is relentlessly striving to become a lower-and-lower-cost provider of a higher-and-higher-caliber product. The closer a firm can get to the ultimate of being the industry's absolute lowest-cost provider and, simultaneously, the provider of the industry's overall best product, the less vulnerable it becomes to rivals' actions.

The Big Risk of a Best-Cost Provider Strategy   The danger of a best-cost provider strategy is that a user will get squeezed between the strategies of firms using low-cost and differentiation strategies. Low-cost cost leaders may be able to siphon customers away with the appeal of a lower price. High-end differentiators may be able to steal customers away with the appeal of better product attributes. Thus, to be successful, a best-cost provider must offer buyers *significantly* better product attributes in order to justify a price above what low-cost leaders are charging. Likewise it has to achieve significantly lower costs than a high-end differentiator in providing upscale features so that it can outcompete high-end differentiators on the basis of a significantly lower price.

Focused (or Market Niche) Strategies

What sets focused strategies apart from low-cost or differentiation strategies is concentrated attention on a narrow piece of the total market. The target segment or niche can be defined by geographic uniqueness, by specialized requirements in using the product, or by special product attributes that appeal only to niche members. The aim of a focused strategy is to do a better job of serving buyers in the target market niche than rival competitors. *A focuser's basis for competitive advantage is either (1) lower costs than competitors in serving the market niche or (2) an ability to offer niche members something they perceive is better suited to their own unique tastes and preferences.* A focused strategy based on low cost depends on there being a buyer segment whose requirements are less costly to satisfy compared to the rest of the market. A focused strategy based on differentiation depends on there being a buyer segment that is looking for special product attributes or seller capabilities.

Examples of firms employing some version of a focused strategy include eBay (in online auctions); Porsche (in sports cars); Cannondale (in top-of-the-line mountain

illustration capsule 22
Toyota's Best-Cost Producer Strategy for Its Lexus Line

Toyota Motor Co. is widely regarded as a low-cost producer among the world's motor vehicle manufacturers. Despite its emphasis on product quality, Toyota has achieved absolute low-cost leadership because of its considerable skills in efficient manufacturing techniques and because its models are positioned in the low-to-medium end of the price spectrum, where high production volumes are conducive to low unit costs. But when Toyota decided to introduce its new Lexus models to compete in the luxury-car market, it employed a classic best-cost provider strategy. Toyota's Lexus strategy had three features:

- Transferring its expertise in making high-quality Toyota models at low cost to making premium-quality luxury cars at costs below other luxury-car makers, especially Mercedes and BMW. Toyota executives reasoned that Toyota's manufacturing skills should allow it to incorporate high-tech performance features and upscale quality into Lexus models at less cost than other luxury-car manufacturers.

- Using its relatively lower manufacturing costs to underprice Mercedes and BMW, both of which had models selling in the $40,000 to $75,000 range (and some even higher). Toyota believed that with its cost advantage it could price attractively equipped Lexus cars low enough to draw price-conscious buyers away from Mercedes and BMW and perhaps induce dissatified Lincoln and Cadillac owners to switch to a Lexus.

- Establishing a new network of Lexus dealers, separate from Toyota dealers, dedicated to providing a level of personalized, attentive customer service unmatched in the industry.

The Lexus 400 series models, priced in the $48,000 to $55,000 range, compete against Mercedes's 300/400E series, BMW's 540/740 series, Nissan's Infiniti Q45, Cadillac Seville, Jaguar, and Lincoln Continental. The lower-priced Lexus 300 series, priced in the $30,000 to $40,000 range, competes against Cadillac deVille, Acura Legend, Infiniti J30, Buick Park Avenue, Mercedes's C-Class series, BMW's 315 series, and Oldsmobile's Aurora line. More recently, Lexus has introduced sport-utility vehicles to compete against those from Mercedes, Lincoln, Cadillac, BMW, Infiniti, and Jeep.

Lexus's best-cost producer strategy was so successful that Mercedes introduced a new, lower-priced C-Class series, to become more competitive. The Lexus LS 400 models and the Lexus SC 300/400 models have consistently ranked among the top 10 models in the widely watched J. D. Power & Associates quality survey. In the 1999 model year, Lexus was the second best-selling luxury brand in the United States.

---

bikes); commuter airlines like Horizon, Comair, and Atlantic Southeast (specializing in low-traffic, short-haul flights linking major airports with small cities 100 to 250 miles away); Jiffy Lube International (a specialist in quick oil changes, lubrication, and simple maintenance for motor vehicles); Enterprise Rent-a-Car (specializing in providing rental cars to repair garage customers); and Bandag (a specialist in truck tire recapping that promotes its recaps aggressively at over 1,000 truck stops). Microbreweries, local bakeries, bed-and-breakfast inns, and local owner-managed retail boutiques are all good examples of enterprises that have scaled their operations to serve narrow or local customer segments. Illustration Capsule 23 describes Motel 6's focused low-cost strategy and Ritz-Carlton's focused differentiation strategy.

Focused low-cost strategies are fairly common. Producers of private-label goods are able to achieve low product development, marketing, distribution, and advertising costs by concentrating on making generic items imitative of name-brand merchandise and selling directly to retail chains wanting a basic house brand to sell at a discount to price-sensitive shoppers. Discount stock brokerage houses have lowered costs by focusing on customers who are willing to forgo the investment research, advice, and financial services offered by full-service firms like Merrill Lynch in return for 30 percent or more commission savings on their buy-sell transactions. Pursuing a cost advantage

illustration capsule 23

Focused Strategies in the Lodging Industry: Motel 6 and Ritz-Carlton

Motel 6 and Ritz-Carlton compete at opposite ends of the lodging industry. Motel 6 employs a focused strategy keyed to low cost; Ritz-Carlton employs a focused strategy based on differentiation.

Motel 6 caters to price-conscious travelers who want a clean, no-frills place to spend the night. To be a low-cost provider of overnight lodging, Motel 6 (1) selects relatively inexpensive sites on which to construct its units (usually near interstate exits and high traffic locations but far enough away to avoid paying prime site prices); (2) builds only basic facilities (no restaurant or bar and only rarely a swimming pool); (3) relies on standard architectural designs that incorporate inexpensive materials and low-cost construction techniques; and (4) has simple room furnishings and decorations. These approaches lower both investment costs and operating costs. Without restaurants, bars, and all kinds of guest services, a Motel 6 unit can be operated with just front desk personnel, room cleanup crews, and skeleton building-and-grounds maintenance. To promote the Motel 6 concept with travelers who have simple overnight requirements, the chain uses unique, recognizable radio ads done by nationally syndicated radio personality Tom Bodett; the ads describe Motel 6's clean rooms, no-frills facilities, friendly atmosphere, and dependably low rates (usually under $40 per night).

In contrast, Ritz-Carlton caters to discriminating travelers and vacationers willing and able to pay for top-of-the-line accommodations and world-class personal service. Ritz-Carlton hotels feature (1) prime locations and scenic views from many rooms; (2) custom architectural designs; (3) fine restaurants with gourmet menus prepared by accomplished chefs; (4) elegantly appointed lobbies and bar lounges; (5) swimming pools, exercise facilities, and leisure-time options; (6) upscale room accommodations; (7) an array of guest services and recreation opportunities appropriate to the location; and (8) large, well-trained professional staffs who do their utmost to make each guest's stay an enjoyable experience.

Both companies concentrate their attention on a narrow piece of the total market. Motel 6's basis for competitive advantage is lower costs than competitors in providing basic, economical overnight accommodations to price-constrained travelers. Ritz-Carlton's advantage is its capability to provide superior accommodations and unmatched personal service for a well-to-do clientele. Each is able to succeed, despite polar opposite strategies, because the market for lodging consists of diverse buyer segments with diverse preferences and abilities to pay.

---

via focusing works well when a firm can lower costs significantly by limiting its customer base to a well-defined buyer segment.

At the other end of the market spectrum, focusers like Godiva Chocolates, Chanel, Rolls-Royce, Häagen-Dazs, and W. L. Gore (the maker of Gore-Tex) employ successful differentiation-based focused strategies targeted at upscale buyers wanting products and services with world-class attributes. Indeed, most markets contain a buyer segment willing to pay a big price premium for the very finest items available, thus opening the strategic window for some competitors to pursue differentiation-based focused strategies aimed at the very top of the market pyramid. Another successful focused differentiator is a "fashion food retailer" called Trader Joe's, a 150-store East and West Coast chain that is a combination gourmet deli and food warehouse.[11] Customers shop Trader Joe's as much for entertainment as for conventional grocery items—the store stocks all

---

[11]Gary Hamel, "Strategy as Revolution," *Harvard Business Review* 74, no. 4 (July–August 1996), p. 72. For an interesting and entertaining presentation of Trader Joe's mission, strategy, and operating practices, see the information the company has posted at www.traderjoes.com.

kinds of out-of-the-ordinary culinary treats like raspberry salsa, salmon burgers, and jasmine fried rice, as well as the standard goods normally found in supermarkets. What sets Trader Joe's apart is not just its unique combination of food novelties and competitively priced grocery items but the opportunity it provides to turn an otherwise mundane shopping excursion to the grocery into a whimsical treasure hunt that is just plain fun. Blue Mountain Arts, a focused differentiator in greeting cards, stands apart from Hallmark and American Greetings not only regarding the distinctive look, feel, and content of its cards but also with respect to its focus on electronic greeting cards.

When Focusing Is Attractive   A focused strategy based either on low cost or differentiation becomes increasingly attractive as more of the following conditions are met:

- The target market niche is big enough to be profitable and offers good growth potential.
- Industry leaders do not see that having a presence in the niche is crucial to their own success—a condition that reduces rivalry from major competitiors.
- It is costly or difficult for multisegment competitors to put capabilities in place to meet the specialized needs of the target market niche and, at the same time, satisfy the expectations of their mainstream customers.
- The industry has many different niches and segments, thereby allowing a focuser to pick a competitively attractive niche suited to its resource strengths and capabilities.
- Few, if any, other rivals are attempting to specialize in the same target segment—a condition that reduces the risk of segment overcrowding.
- The focuser can compete effectively against challengers based on the capabilities and resources it has to serve the targeted niche and the customer goodwill it may have built up.

When an industry has many different niches and segments, the strength of competition varies across and within segments, a condition that makes it important for a focuser to pick a niche that is both competitively attractive and well suited to its resource strengths and capabilities. A focuser's specialized competencies and capabilities in serving the target market niche provide the strongest and most dependable basis for contending successfully with competitive forces. Rivalry in the target niche is weaker when there are comparatively few players in the niche and when multisegment rivals have trouble truly meeting the expectations of the focused firm's target clientele along with the expectations of the other types of customers they cater to. A focuser's unique capabilities in serving the market niche also act as an entry barrier—difficulties in matching a focuser's capabilities can dissuade potential newcomers from attempting entry. They also present a hurdle that makers of substitute products must overcome. Even if some niche buyers have substantial bargaining leverage, their power is blunted somewhat by the downside of shifting their business to rival companies less capable of meeting their expectations.

> Even though a focuser may be small, it still may have substantial competitve strength because of the attractiveness of its product offering and its strong expertise and capabilities in meeting the needs and expectations of niche members.

The Risks of a Focused Strategy   Focusing carries several risks. One is the chance that competitors will find effective ways to match the focused firm in serving the target niche—perhaps by coming up with more appealing product offerings or by developing expertise and capabilities that offset the focuser's strengths. A second is the potential for the preferences and needs of niche members to shift over time toward the product attributes desired by the majority of buyers. An erosion of the differences across buyer segments lowers entry barriers into a focuser's market niche and provides an open invitation for rivals in adjacent segments to begin competing for the focuser's customers. A third risk is that the segment becomes so attractive it is soon inundated with competitors, intensifying rivalry and splintering segment profits.

COOPERATIVE STRATEGIES AND COMPETITIVE ADVANTAGE

In the past 10 years, companies in all types of industries and in all parts of the world have formed strategic alliances and partnerships to complement their own strategic initiatives and strengthen their competitiveness in domestic and international markets. This is an about-face from times past, when the vast majority of companies were content to go it alone, confident that they already had or could independently develop whatever resources and know-how were needed to be successful in their markets. But globalization of the world economy, revolutionary advances in technology across a broad front, and untapped opportunities in national markets in Asia, Latin America, and Europe that are opening up, deregulation, and/or undergoing privatization have made strategic partnerships of one kind or another integral to a firm's competitiveness.

> Alliances and partnerships are a necessity in racing against rivals to build a strong global presence and/or to stake out a position in the industries of the future.

Many companies now find themselves thrust in the midst of two very demanding competitive races: (1) *the global race to build a market presence in many different national markets* and to establish an attractive position among the global market leaders and (2) *the technology race to capitalize on today's technological and information age revolution* and build the resource strengths and business capabilities to compete successfully in the industries and product markets of the future.[12] Even the largest and most financially strong companies have concluded that simultaneously running the races for global market leadership and for a stake in the industries of the future requires more diverse and expansive skills, resources, technological expertise, and competitive capabilities than they can assemble and manage alone.

Indeed, the gaps in resources and competitive capabilities between industry rivals have become painfully apparent to disadvantaged enterprises. Allowing such gaps to go unaddressed can put a company in a precarious competitve position or even prove fatal. When rivals can develop new products faster or achieve better quality at lower cost or have more resources and know-how to exploit opportunities in attractive new market arenas, a company has little option but to try to close the resource and competency gaps quickly; the fastest way to do this is often with the capabilities and strengths of new strategic allies. In today's rapidly changing world, a company that cannot position itself quickly misses important opportunities, whether they be in cyberspace or foreign countries. More and more enterprises are concluding that well-chosen alliances can allow them to bypass the comparatively slower and more costly process of building one's own capabilities internally to access new opportunities.

The Increasingly Pervasive Use of Alliances

Strategic alliances and collaborative partnerships have thus emerged as an attractive and timely means of breaching the technology and resource gaps that firms now commonly encounter. *Alliances have, in fact, become so essential to the competitiveness of*

---

[12]Yves L. Doz and Gary Hamel, *Alliance Advantage: The Art of Creating Value through Partnering* (Boston: Harvard Business School Press, 1998), pp. xiii and xiv.

companies in many industries that they are a core element of today's business strategies. They are especially prevalent in industries where change is rapid. General Electric has formed over 100 cooperative partnerships in a wide range of areas; IBM has joined in over 400 strategic alliances.[13] Oracle is said to have over 15,000 alliances. Alliances are so central to Corning's strategy that the company describes itself as a "network of organizations." Toyota has forged a network of long-term strategic partnerships with its suppliers of automotive parts and components. Microsoft collaborates very closely with independent software developers that create new programs to run on the next-generation versions of Windows. A recent study indicates that the average large corporation is involved in around 30 alliances today, versus fewer than 3 a decade ago.

> Alliances and cooperative arrangements, whether they bring together companies from different parts of the industry value chain or different parts of the world, are a fact of life in business today.

In the PC industry cooperative alliances are pervasive because the different components of PCs and the software to run them are supplied by so many different companies—one set of companies provides the microprocessors, another group makes the motherboards, another the monitors, another the disk drives, another the memory chips, and so on. Moreover, their facilities are scattered across the United States, Japan, Taiwan, Singapore, Malaysia, and parts of Europe. Close collaboration is required on product development, logistics, production, and the timing of new product releases. Consequently, Intel has formed collaborative partnerships with numerous makers of PC components and software developers to jointly pursue new technologies and to bring new products to market in parallel so that consumers can get the maximum benefits from new PCs running on Intel's next-generation microprocessors. Without extensive cooperation and collaboration between Intel, the makers of other key PC components, PC makers, and software developers in both new technology and new product development, there would be all kinds of bottlenecks, delays, and incompatibility problems in bringing new computer hardware and software products into the marketplace—obstacles that would dramatically slow the pace of advance in PC capabilities and applications.

The convergence of cable TV, telecommunications, and computer technologies is spawning entirely new kinds of services and new means of content delivery and creating a need for all kinds of alliances. Companies such as AT&T, MCI WorldCom, America Online, the regional Bell companies, Qwest Communications, Deutsche Telecom, Motorola, Nokia, Ericcson, and many others have put together webs of different alliances and partnerships, some collaborative and some competing, to pursue the races for global market leadership and for a major participating role in the telecommunication industry of the future. America Online, which from the outset formed partnerships with a host of companies to deliver content to its subscribers, has entered into alliances with Hughes Satellite, several of the regional Bell companies, and others to develop high-speed Internet access alternatives; AOL's objective is to assemble competitive alternatives to what AT&T (which has acquired two large cable companies that now make it the largest provider of cable TV service in the United States) is endeavoring to deliver via its cable TV connections. Moreover, there are assorted alliances among enterprises promoting wireless telecommunications systems going head-to-head against assorted alliances of telecommunications companies promoting fiber-optic, digital signal line (DSL), and cable types of connections. Collaborative alliances are essential in creating the capabilities for digital banking and credit card transactions on the Internet because "seamless" networks have to be built and made compatible across the operations of many different enterprises using different brands and types of hardware and software.

> Growing use of alliances is shifting the basis of competition to groups of companies against groups of companies.

---

[13]Michael A. Hitt, Beverly B. Tyler, Camilla Hardee, and Daewoo Park, "Understanding Strategic Intent in the Global Marketplace," *Academy of Management Executive* 9, no. 2 (May 1995), p. 13.

Why and How Strategic Alliances Are Advantageous

Strategic alliances are cooperative agreements between firms that go beyond normal company-to-company dealings but fall short of merger or full joint venture partnership with formal ownership ties. (Some strategic alliances do involve arrangements whereby one or more allies have minority ownership in certain of the other alliance members, however.) But the value of an alliance stems not from the agreement or deal itself but rather from the capacity of the partners to defuse organizational frictions, collaborate effectively over time, and work their way through the maze of changes that lie in front of them—technological and competitive surprises, new market developments (that may come at a rapid-fire pace), and changes in their own priorities and competitive circumstances. Collaborative alliances nearly always entail an *evolving* relationship, with the benefits and competitive value ultimately depending on mutual learning, effective cooperation over time, and successfully adapting to change. Competitive advantage emerges when a company acquires valuable resources and capabilities through alliances that it could not otherwise obtain on its own and that give it an edge over rivals—this requires real in-the-trenches collaboration between the partners to create new value together, not merely an arm's-length exchange of ideas and information. Unless partners value the skills, resources, and contributions each brings to the alliance and the cooperative arrangement results in win-win outcomes, it will amount to little or fail.

The most common reasons why companies enter into strategic alliances are to collaborate on technology or the development of promising new products, to overcome deficits in their technical and manufacturing expertise, to acquire altogether new competencies, to improve supply chain efficiency, to gain economies of scale in production and/or marketing, and to acquire or improve market access through joint marketing agreements.[14] A company that is racing for global market leadership needs alliances to help it do what it cannot easily do alone:

- Get into critical country markets quickly and accelerate the process of building a potent global market presence.
- Gain inside knowledge about unfamiliar markets and cultures through alliances with local partners.
- Access valuable skills and competencies that are concentrated in particular geographic locations (such as software design competencies in the United States, fashion design skills in Italy, and efficient manufacturing skills in Japan).

A company that is racing to stake out a strong position in an industry of the future needs alliances to:

- Establish a beachhead for participating in the target industry.
- Master new technologies and build new expertise and competencies faster than would be possible through internal efforts.
- Open up expanded opportunities in the target industry by melding the firm's own capabilities with the expertise and resources of partners.

Allies can learn much from one another in performing joint research, sharing technological know-how, and collaborating on complementary new technologies and products—sometimes enough to enable them to pursue other new opportunities on their own.

> The competitive attraction of alliances is to bundle competences and resources that are more valuable in a joint effort than when kept separate.

> Alliances are highly beneficial in racing against rivals for global market leadership.

> Alliances are also highly beneficial in racing against rivals to build the expertise and market position needed to win a strong position in the industries of the future.

---

[14]Porter, *The Competitive Advantage of Nations* (New York: Free Press, 1990), p. 66.

Manufacturers typically pursue alliances with parts and components suppliers to gain the efficiencies of better supply chain management and to speed new products to market. By joining forces in components production and/or final assembly, companies may be able to realize cost savings not achievable with their own small volumes—Volvo, Renault, and Peugeot formed an alliance to make engines together for their large car models precisely because no one of them needed enough such engines to operate their own engine plant economically. Manufacturing allies can also learn much about how to improve their quality control and production procedures by studying one another's manufacturing methods. Often alliances are formed to utilize common dealer networks or for joint promotion of complementary products, thereby mutually strengthening their access to buyers and economizing on forward channel distribution costs. Diageo (parent of Häagen-Dazs, Burger King, Pillsbury, and other name-brand foods and beverages) and Swiss-based Nestlé (the world's largest consumer foods company) recently allied in a joint venture to distribute Häagen-Dazs ice cream and Nestlé frozen dessert treats through the same U.S. distribution pipeline and to use common display cases; the allies expected to both expand the market access for their products and economize on distribution costs.

Not only can alliances offset competitive disadvantages or create competitive advantages but they also can result in the allied companies' directing their competitive energies more toward mutual rivals and less toward one another. Potential rivals can sometimes be effectively neutralized by engaging them in a collaborative alliance. Who partners with whom affects the pattern of industry rivalry. Many runner-up companies, wanting to preserve their independence, resort to alliances rather than mergers to try to close the competitive gap on leading companies—*they rely on collaboration with others to enhance their organizational capabilities, develop valuable new strategic resources, and compete effectively.* Industry leaders pursue cooperative alliances in order to better fend off ambitious rivals as well as to open up new opportunities.

Strategic cooperation is a much-favored, indeed necessary, approach in industries where new technological developments are occurring at a furious pace along many different paths and where advances in one technology spill over to affect others (often blurring industry boundaries). Whenever industries are experiencing high-velocity technological change in many areas simultaneously, firms find it virtually essential to have cooperative relationships with other enterprises to stay on the leading edge of technology and product performance even in their own area of specialization. They cooperate in technology development, in sharing R&D information, in developing new products that complement each other in the marketplace, and in building networks of dealers and distributors to handle their respective products.

Illustration Capsule 24 contains examples of recent high-profile alliances.

While a few firms can pursue their strategies alone, it is becoming increasingly common for companies to pursue their strategies in collaboration with suppliers, distributors, makers of complementary products, and sometimes even select competitors.

Alliances and Partnerships with Foreign Companies   Cooperative strategies and alliances to penetrate international markets are also common between domestic and foreign firms. Such partnerships are useful in putting together the resources and capabilities to do business over a wider number of country markets. For example, U.S., European, and Japanese companies wanting to build market footholds in the fast-growing Chinese market have all pursued partnership arrangements with Chinese companies to help in dealing with government regulations, to supply knowledge of local markets, to provide guidance on adapting their products to better match the buying preferences of Chinese consumers, to set up local manufacturing capabilities, and to assist in distribution, marketing, and promotional activities. The policy of the Chinese government has long been one of giving privileged market access to a few select outsiders while excluding others and requiring the favored outsiders to partner in one way or another with local enterprises.

illustration capsule 24
Examples of Recent Alliances

- *Pfizer and Warner-Lambert*—formed an alliance to market cholesterol-reducing drug Lipitor. Warner-Lambert contributed the product; Pfizer's contribution was the skills of its sales force in marketing the product to physicians.

- *America Online with Gateway, Motorola, Palm, Direct TV, and Hughes Electronics*—AOL has partnered with Gateway to develop and co-market Internet appliances and home networking devices; it has partnered with Motorola to make its Instant Messenger service available on Motorola wireless phones and pagers; it has teamed with Palm to put AOL's e-mail service on Palm's handheld PCs; and it has allied with satellite broadcaster Direct TV and Hughes Electronics to bring AOL to TV screens via set-top boxes.

- *Hewlett-Packard and Qwest Communications*—entered into an alliance to create a business called CyberCenters that offers end-to-end Internet solutions, with customer service available 24 hours a day, seven days a week. Hewlett-Packard contributed server hardware, software, and services; Qwest provided Internet access, a base of customers, and a lead role in delivering services to customers..

- *IBM and Dell Computer*—formed an alliance whereby Dell agreed to purchase $16 billion in parts and components from IBM for use in Dell's PCs, servers, and workstations over a three-year period. Dell determined that IBM's growing expertise and capabilities in PC components justified using IBM as a major supplier even though Dell and IBM competed vigorously in supplying laptop computers to corporate customers.

- *Johnson & Johnson and Merck*—entered into an alliance to market Pepcid AC. Merck developed the stomach distress remedy and J&J has functioned as marketer. The alliance has made Pepcid AC the best-selling such remedy.

- *General Electric's Aircraft Engines Division and Pratt & Whitney*—formed an alliance to develop and sell a new engine for Airbus Industries' super jumbo airplane, the A3XX. Both GE Aircraft and Pratt & Whitney make aircraft engines and are fierce competitiors in the market for jet engines for commercial aircraft. The partnership was formed to compete with Rolls-Royce for the Airbus contract.

- *Microsoft, Lycos, Excite, Ticketmaster, and Dell*—formed an alliance to develop an online auction network called Fairmarket, Inc., that is intended to compete against eBay.

- *Hewlett-Packard and Intel*—formed an alliance to develop a next-generation 64-bit microprocessor (code-named Merced) for powering Internet servers, engineering and graphics workstations, and high-performance PCs. In 2000, Intel began producing and marketing the first generation of chips using 64-bit architecture under the name Itanium.

- *United Parcel Service, AT&T, and Microsoft*—UPS joined with its suppliers AT&T and Microsoft to provide free Internet access for UPS's 1.7 million customers using its online shipping and digital document delivery services.

Source: Company press releases and *Business Week,* October 25, 1999, pp. 112–30.

Why Many Alliances Are Unstable or Break Apart Whether an alliance will stand the test of time or break apart hinges on how well the partners work together, their success in responding and adapting to changing internal and external conditions, and their willingness to renegotiate the bargain if circumstances so warrant. Unless partners value the skills, resources, and contributions each brings to the alliance and the cooperative arrangement results in win–win outcomes, it is doomed. A recent study by Andersen Consulting revealed that 61 percent of alliances were either outright failures or "limping along."[15]

[15]Cited in *Business Week,* October 25, 1999, p. 110.

More alliances come apart than stay together. Many reasons account for the high "divorce rate," diverging objectives and priorities, an inability to work well together, the emergence of more attractive technological paths, and marketplace rivalry between one or more allies.[16] An example of the complications caused by the unpredictability of emerging technologies comes from the efforts of Merck in the early 1990s to assemble a large group of research institutes, universities, entrepreneurial biotech companies, and other organizations to pursue the development of AIDS cures and vaccines; the market need was clear and urgent, but the uncertainities of the evolving AIDS virus and the often unsystematic manner in which miracle drugs are discovered and wind their way to market meant there was no way for Merck and its allies to judge which, if any, of the R&D alliances might prove fruitful.[17] Ongoing commitment, mutual learning, and continued close collaboration are essential to keeping alliances like Merck's functioning productively.

> Many alliances fail and break apart, never reaching their intended potential, because of frictions and conflicts among the allies.

The Strategic Dangers of Relying Heavily on Alliances and Cooperative Partnerships   The Achilles heel of alliances and cooperative strategies is the danger of becoming dependent on other companies for *essential* expertise and capabilities over the long term. To be a market leader (and perhaps even a serious market contender), a company must ultimately develop its own capabilities in areas where internal strategic control is pivotal to protecting its competitiveness and building competitive advantage. Moreover, some alliances hold only limited potential because the partner guards its most valuable skills and expertise; in such instances, acquiring or merging with a company possessing the desired resources is a better solution.

MERGER AND ACQUISITION STRATEGIES

Mergers and acquisitions are a much-used strategic option.[18] They are especially suited for situations where alliances and partnerships do not go far enough in providing a company with access to the needed resources and capabilities. Ownership ties are more permanent than partnership ties, allowing the operations of the merger/acquisition participants to be tightly integrated and creating more in-house control and autonomy.

Merging with or acquiring another company, often a competitor, can dramatically strengthen a company's market position and open new opportunities for competitive advantage. Combining operations with a rival can fill resource gaps, allowing the new company to do things which the prior companies could not do alone. Together, the companies may have stronger technological skills, more or better competitive capabilities, a more attractive lineup of products and services, wider geographic coverage, and/or greater financial resources with which to invest in R&D, add capacity, or expand into new areas. Moreover, combining operations may offer considerable cost-saving opportunities, transforming otherwise high-cost companies into a competitor with average or below-average costs.

> No company can afford to ignore the strategic and competitive benefits of acquiring or merging with another company to strenghten its market position and open up avenues of new opportunity.

---

[16]Doz and Hamel, *Alliance Advantage,* pp. 16–18.

[17]Ibid., p. 17.

[18]A *merger* is a combination and pooling of equals, with the newly created company often taking on a new name. An *acquisition* is when one company, the acquirer, purchases and absorbs the operations of another, the acquired. The difference between a merger and an acquisition relates more to the details of ownership, management control, and financial arrangements than to strategy and competitive advantage. The resources, competencies, and competitive capabilities of the newly created enterprise end up much the same whether the combination is the result of acquisition or merger.

The race for global market leadership is prompting numerous companies to make acquisitions to build a market presence in countries where they currently do not compete. Similarly, the race to establish attractive positions in the industries of the future is prompting companies to merge or make acquisitions to fill in resource or technological gaps, build important technological capabilities, and move into position to launch next-wave products and services. These benefits can be quite substantial and explain why companies resort to mergers and acquisitions.

WorldCom's bold acquisitions of MCI and Sprint has created a powerhouse company capable of challenging AT&T head-on, competing strongly in the European market, and establishing itself as a leader in the Internet-driven telecommunications industry of the future (as opposed to simply being a provider of long-distance telephone service in the United States). Nestlé, Kraft (a subsidiary of Philip Morris Companies), Unilever, Procter & Gamble, and several other prominent food and consumer products companies have all made numerous acquisitions in racing to establish a stronger global presence. Daimler-Benz merged with Chrysler to create a broader product line and a stronger global presence in the world's motor vehicle industry, enhancing the combined companies' ability to compete with Toyota, Ford, and General Motors. America Online acquired CompuServe to give it stronger appeal to customers wanting Internet access. Intel has made over 300 acquisitions in the past five or so years to broaden its technological base and put it in a stronger position to be a major supplier of Internet technology and less dependent on supplying microprocessors for PCs. Likewise, Cisco Systems has been an active acquirer, purchasing over 40 technology companies to buttress its standing as the world's biggest supplier of systems for building the infrastructure of the Internet. Illustration Capsule 25 describes how Clear Channel Communications has used mergers and acquisitions to build a leading global position in outdoor advertising and radio and TV broadcasting.

However, mergers and acquisitions do not always produce the hoped-for outcomes, sometimes because of exaggerated expectations and sometimes because capturing the benefits proves much harder than anticipated. Combining the operations of two companies, especially large and complex ones, often entails formidable resistance from rank-and-file organization members, hard-to-resolve conflicts in management styles and corporate cultures, and tough problems of integration. The expected cost savings, expertise sharing, and enhanced competitive capabilities may take substantially longer than expected to realize or, worse, may never materialize at all. A number of previously applauded acquisitions have yet to live up to expectations—AT&T's acquisition of AtHome/Excite, Ford's acquisition of Jaguar, Walt Disney's acquisition of Capital Cities/ABC, and Deutsche Bank's acquisition of Banker's Trust are prime examples. Ford paid a handsome price to acquire Jaguar but has yet to make the Jaguar brand a major factor in the luxury car segment in competition against Mercedes, BMW, and Lexus. Novell acquired WordPerfect for $1.7 billion in stock in 1994, but the combination never generated enough punch to compete against Microsoft Word and Microsoft Office; Novell sold WordPerfect to Corel for $124 million in cash and stock less than two years later. Other deals that proved disastrous are Viacom's acquisition of Blockbuster and USA Waste's acquisition of Waste Management.

VERTICAL INTEGRATION STRATEGIES: A COMPETITIVE PLUS OR A MINUS

Vertical integration extends a firm's competitive scope within the same industry. It involves expanding the firm's range of activities backward into sources of supply and/or forward toward end users of the final product. Thus, if a manufacturer invests in

illustration capsule 25

How Clear Channel Communications Used Mergers and Acquisitions to Become a Global Leader in the Media Industry

In 2000, Clear Channel Communications was the fourth largest media company in the world behind Disney, Time Warner, and Viacom/CBS. The company, founded in 1972 by Lowry Mays and Billy Joe McCombs, got its start by acquiring an unprofitable country-music radio station in San Antonio, Texas. Over the next 10 years, Mays learned the radio business and slowly bought other radio stations in a variety of states. The company went public in 1984, helping it raise the equity capital needed to fuel its strategy of expanding by acquiring radio stations in additional geographic markets.

In the late 1980s, following the decision of the Federal Communications Commission to loosen the rules regarding the ability of one company to own both radio and TV stations, Clear Channel broadened its strategy and began acquiring small, struggling TV stations. Soon thereafter, Clear Channel became affiliated with the Fox network, which was starting to build a national presence and challenge ABC, CBS, and NBC. Meanwhile, the company began selling programming services to other stations, and in some markets where it already had stations it took on the function of selling advertising for cross-town stations it did not own.

By 1998, Clear Channel had used acquisitions to build a leading position in radio and television stations. It owned, programmed, or sold airtime for 69 AM radio stations, 135 FM stations, and 18 TV stations in 48 local markets in 24 states. The TV stations included affiliates with FOX, UPN, ABC, NBC, and CBS. It had purchased a 29 percent ownership interest in Heftel Broadcasting Co., a domestic Spanish-language radio broadcaster. Clear Channel also owned two radio stations and a cable audio channel in Denmark and had acquired ownership interests in radio stations in Australia, Mexico, New Zealand, and the Czech Republic.

In 1997, Clear Channel acquired Phoenix-based Eller Media Company, an outdoor advertising company with over 100,000 billboard facings. Additional acquisitions of outdoor advertising companies quickly followed, the most important of which were:

- ABC Outdoor in Milwaukee, Wisconsin.

- Paxton Communications, with operations in Tampa and Orlando, Florida.

- Universal Outdoor.

- The More Group, with outdoor operations and 90,000 displays in 24 countries.

Then in October 1999, Clear Channel made another major strategic move, merging with AMFM, Inc., to form the world's largest out-of-home media enterprise. After divesting some 125 properties needed to gain the anticipated regulatory approval, Clear Channel Communications (the name adopted by the merged companies) had operations in 32 countries and included 830 radio stations, 19 TV stations, more than 425,000 outdoor displays, and significant ownership interests in other leading radio broadcasting and outdoor advertising properties.

The company's strategy was to buy radio, TV, and outdoor advertising properties with operations in many of the same local markets, share facilities and staffs to cut costs, improve programming, and sell advertising to customers in packages for all three media simultaneously. Packaging ads for two or three media allowed the company to combine its sales activities and have a common sales force for all three media, achieving significant cost savings and boosting profit margins.

Sources: Company documents and *Business Week,* October 19, 1999, p. 56.

---

facilities to produce certain component parts that it formerly purchased from outside suppliers, it remains in essentially the same industry as before. The only change is that it has business units in two production stages in the industry's value chain. Similarly, if a paint manufacturer, Sherwin-Williams for example, elects to integrate forward by opening 100 retail stores to market its paint products directly to consumers, it remains in the paint business even though its competitive scope extends further forward in the industry chain.

Vertical integration strategies can aim at *full integration* (participating in all stages of the industry value chain) or *partial integration* (building positions in selected stages of the industry's total value chain). A firm can accomplish vertical integration by starting its own operations in other stages in the industry's activity chain or by acquiring a company already performing the activities it wants to bring in-house.

The Strategic Advantages of Vertical Integration

The only good reason for investing company resources in vertical integration is to strengthen the firm's competitive position.[19] Unless vertical integration produces sufficient cost savings to justify the extra investment or adds materially to a company's technological and competitive strengths or truly helps differentiate its product offering, it has no real payoff profitwise or strategywise.

> A vertical integration strategy has appeal *only* if it significantly strengthens a firm's competitive position.

Integrating Backward to Achieve Greater Competitiveness   Integrating backward generates cost savings only when the volume needed is big enough to capture the same scale economies suppliers have and when suppliers' production efficiency can be matched or exceeded with no dropoff in quality. The best potential for being able to reduce costs via backward integration exists in situations where suppliers have sizable profit margins, where the item being supplied is a major cost component, and where the needed technological skills are easily mastered or can be gained by acquiring a supplier with the desired technological know-how. Integrating backward can sometimes significantly enhance a company's technological capabilities and give it expertise needed to stake out positions in the industries and products of the future. Intel, Cisco, and many other Silicon Valley companies have been active in acquiring companies that will help them speed the advance of Internet technology and pave the way for next-generation families of products and services.

Backward vertical integration can produce a differentiation-based competitive advantage when a company, by performing in-house activities that were previously outsourced, ends up with a better-quality product/service offering, improves the caliber of its customer service, or in other ways enhances the performance of its final product. On occasion, integrating into more stages along the industry value chain can add to a company's differentiation capabilities by allowing it to build or strengthen its core competencies, better master key skills or strategy-critical technologies, or add features that deliver greater customer value.

Backward integration can also spare a company the uncertainty of being dependent on suppliers of crucial components or support services, and it can lessen a company's vulnerability to powerful suppliers that raise prices at every opportunity. Stockpiling, fixed-price contracts, multiple-sourcing, long-term cooperative partnerships, or the use of substitute inputs are not always attractive ways for dealing with uncertain supply conditions or with economically powerful suppliers. Companies that are low on a key supplier's customer priority list can find themselves waiting on shipments every time supplies get tight. If this occurs often and wreaks havoc in a company's own production and customer relations activities, backward integration can be an advantageous strategic solution.

Integrating Forward to Enhance Competitiveness   The strategic impetus for forward integration is much the same as that for backward integration. In many industries, independent sales agents, wholesalers, and retailers handle competing

---

[19]See Kathryn R. Harrigan, "Matching Vertical Integration Strategies to Competitive Conditions," *Strategic Management Journal* 7, no. 6 (November–December 1986), pp. 535–56; for a discussion of the advantages and disadvantages of vertical integration, see John Stuckey and David White, "When and When *Not* to Vertically Integrate," *Sloan Management Review* (Spring 1993), pp. 71–83.

brands of the same product; they have no allegiance to any one company's brand and tend to push "what sells" and earns them the biggest profits. Halfhearted commitments by distributors and retailers can frustrate a company's attempt to boost sales and market share, give rise to costly inventory pileups and frequent underutilization of capacity, and disrupt the economies of steady, near-capacity production. In such cases, it can be advantageous for a manufacturer to integrate forward into wholesaling or retailing via company-owned distributorships, franchised dealer networks, or a chain of retail stores. But often a company's product line is not broad enough to justify stand-alone distributorships or retail outlets. This leaves the option of integrating forward into the activity of selling directly to end users—perhaps via the Internet. Bypassing regular wholesale-retail channels in favor of direct sales and Internet retailing may lower distribution costs, produce a relative cost advantage over certain rivals, and result in lower selling prices to end users.

The Strategic Disadvantages of Vertical Integration

Vertical integration has some substantial drawbacks, however. It boosts a firm's capital investment in the industry, increasing business risk (what if industry growth and profitability goes sour?) and perhaps denying financial resources to more worthwhile pursuits. A vertically integrated firm has vested interests in protecting its present investments in technology and production facilities. Because of the high costs of abandoning such investments before they are worn out, fully integrated firms tend to adopt new technologies slower than partially integrated or nonintegrated firms. Second, integrating forward or backward locks a firm into relying on its own in-house activities and sources of supply (that later may prove more costly than outsourcing) and potentially results in less flexibility in accommodating buyer demand for greater product variety.

Third, vertical integration can pose problems of balancing capacity at each stage in the value chain. In motor vehicle manufacturing, for example, the most efficient scale of operation for making axles is different from the most economic volume for radiators and different yet again for both engines and transmissions. Producing just the right number of axles, radiators, engines, and transmissions—and doing so at the lowest unit costs for each—is the exception, not the rule. If internal capacity for making transmissions is deficient, the difference has to be bought externally. Where internal capacity for radiators proves excessive, customers need to be found for the surplus. And if by-products are generated—as occurs in the processing of many chemical products—they require arrangements for disposal.

Fourth, integration forward or backward often calls for radically different skills and business capabilities. Parts and components manufacturing, assembly operations, wholesale distribution and retailing, and direct sales via the Internet are different businesses with different key success factors. Managers of a manufacturing company should consider carefully whether it makes good business sense to invest time and money in developing the expertise and merchandising skills to integrate forward into wholesaling and retailing. Many manufacturers learn the hard way that company-owned wholesale-retail networks present many headaches, fit poorly with what they do best, and don't always add the kind of value to their core business they thought they would. Selling to customers via the Internet poses still another set of problems—it is usually easier to put systems in place to use the Internet to sell to business customers than to consumers.

Integrating backward into parts and components manufacture isn't as simple or profitable as it sometimes sounds either. Personal computer makers, for example, frequently

> The big disadvantage of vertical integration is that it locks a firm deeper into the industry; unless operating across more stages in the industry's value chain builds competitive advantage, it is a questionable strategic move.

have trouble getting timely deliveries of the latest semiconductor chips at favorable prices, but most don't come close to having the resources or capabilities to integrate backward into chip manufacture; the semiconductor business is technologically sophisticated and entails heavy capital requirements and ongoing R&D effort, and mastering the manufacturing process takes a long time.

Fifth, backward vertical integration into the production of parts and components can reduce a company's manufacturing flexibility, lengthening the time it takes to make design and model changes and to bring new products to market. Companies that alter designs and models frequently in response to shifting buyer preferences often find vertical integration into parts and components burdensome because of constant retooling and redesign costs and the time it takes to implement coordinated changes throughout the value chain. Outsourcing parts and components is often cheaper and less complicated than making them in-house, allowing a company to be more flexible and more nimble in adapting its product offering to fast-changing buyer preferences. Most of the world's automakers, despite their expertise in automotive technology and manufacturing, have concluded that purchasing many of their key parts and components from manufacturing specialists results in higher quality, lower costs, and greater design flexibility as compared to the vertical integration option of supplying their own needs via in-house manufacture.

Weighing the Pros and Cons of Vertical Integration

All in all, therefore, a strategy of vertical integration can have both important strengths and weaknesses. Which direction the scales tip on vertical integration depends on (1) whether it can enhance the performance of strategy-critical activities in ways that lower cost, build expertise, or increase differentiation, (2) its impact on investment costs, flexibility and response times, and administrative overhead associated with coordinating operations across more stages, and (3) whether it creates competitive advantage. The merits of vertical integration strategies hinge on which capabilities and value-chain activities truly need to be performed in-house and which can be better performed by outsiders. Absent solid benefits, integrating forward or backward is not likely to be an attractive competitive strategy option. In a growing number of instances, companies are proving that deintegrating and focusing on a narrower portion of the industry value chain is a cheaper and more flexible competitive strategy.

UNBUNDLING AND OUTSOURCING STRATEGIES— NARROWING THE BOUNDARIES OF THE BUSINESS

Over the past decade, some companies have found vertical integration to be so competitively burdensome that they have adopted *vertical deintegration,* or *unbundling, strategies.* Moreover, a number of single-business enterprises have found it useful to focus more narrowly on certain value chain activities and rely on outsiders to perform the remaining value chain activities; they have begun *outsourcing* activities formerly performed in-house and concentrating their energies on a narrower portion of the value chain. Thus, executives at many companies are asking, "Which value chain activities should be brought within the boundary of the firm and which value chain activities should be outsourced?"

Deintegration and outsourcing involves withdrawing from certain stages/activities in the value chain system and relying on outside vendors to supply the needed products, support services, or functional activities. Outsourcing pieces of the value chain formerly performed in-house to narrow the boundaries of a firm's business makes strategic sense whenever:

● An activity can be performed better or more cheaply by outside specialists. Many PC makers, for example, have shifted from in-house assembly to utilizing contract assemblers to make their PCs because of sizable scale economies in purchasing PC components in larges volumes and in the assembly process itself. Cisco outsources most all production and assembly of its routers and switching equipment to contract manufacturers that operate 37 factories, all linked via the Internet.

● The activity is not crucial to the firm's ability to achieve sustainable competitive advantage and won't hollow out its core competencies, capabilities, or technical know-how. Outsourcing of maintenance services, data processing, accounting, and other administrative support activities to companies specializing in these services has become commonplace.

● It reduces the company's risk exposure to changing technology and/or changing buyer preferences.

● It streamlines company operations in ways that improve organizational flexibility, cut cycle time, speed decision-making, and reduce coordination costs.

● It allows a company to concentrate on its core business and do what it does best.

> Outsourcing makes good strategic sense in a number of instances.

Often, many of the advantages of bringing or keeping value chain activities in-house can be captured and many of the disadvantages avoided by forging close, long-term cooperative partnerships with key suppliers and tapping into the important competitive capabilities that able suppliers have painstakingly developed. In years past, many companies maintained arm's-length relationships with suppliers, granting them short-term contracts to supply items to precise specifications.[20] Although a company might engage the same supplier repeatedly, there was no expectation that this would be the case; price was usually the determining factor for which a supplier got a contract, and companies maneuvered for leverage over suppliers to get the lowest possible prices. The threat of switching suppliers was the company's primary weapon. To make this threat credible, short-term contracts with multiple suppliers were preferred to long-term ones with single suppliers in order to promote lively competition among suppliers. Today, most companies are abandoning such approaches in favor of alliances and strategic partnerships with fewer, highly capable suppliers. Cooperative relationships are replacing contractual, purely price-oriented relationships.

Dell Computer's partnerships with the suppliers of PC components have allowed it to operate with fewer than seven days of inventory, to realize substantial savings in inventory costs, and to get PCs equipped with next-generation components into the marketplace in less than a week after the newly upgraded components start shipping. Cisco's contract suppliers work so closely with Cisco that they can ship Cisco products to Cisco customers without a Cisco employee ever touching the gear, generating savings to Cisco of $500 to $800 million annually compared to what it would cost Cisco to own and operate the plants itself.[21] Hewlett-Packard, IBM, Silicon Graphics (now SGI), and others have sold plants to suppliers and then contracted to purchase the output. Starbucks finds purchasing coffee beans from independent growers far more advantageous than trying to integrate backward into the business.

---

[20]Robert H. Hayes, Gary P. Pisano, and David M. Upton, *Strategic Operations: Competing Through Capabilities* (New York: Free Press, 1996), pp. 419–22.
[21]"The Internet Age," *Business Week,* October 4, 1999, p. 104.

Capability Considerations in Boundary Decisions

There are numerous reasons why it is burdensome or costly for a company to create and maintain certain capabilities in-house as opposed to outsourcing them from firms that specialize in the capabilities it needs.[22] Sometimes creating or sustaining a capability involves a long, difficult learning process that is impossible to short-circuit at an acceptable cost. Sometimes it is unclear what actions a company needs to take to create or sustain a needed capability—there may be multiple competing hypotheses about how to create the capabilities and no easy way to test which hypothesis is best. Occasionally, there are hidden assets or socially complex organizational considerations involved in creating the needed capabilities, such as having the right culture, having a committed and energetic workforce, enjoying the trust of customers and suppliers—these are generally beyond the ability of managers to change in the short-term and must be put in place gradually.

While acquiring a company with the needed capabilities is an obvious option for acquiring missing capabilities, such an acquisition may pose legal problems, come with unwanted baggage, or be costly to reverse if it does not work as well as anticipated. Rarely are the desired capabilities of an acquired firm conveniently located within a single division or group; most usually they are spread across the enterprise and entangled with other of its resources and capabilities. An alliance or collaborative partnership may therefore be a much more attractive option than an acquisition. In an uncertain, fast-changing market environment, acquiring another firm to gain access to its capabilities is often a less flexible strategic option than a strategic alliance which can be terminated if conditions unexpectedly change.

The Advantages of Outsourcing

Relying on outside specialists to perform certain value chain activities offers a number of strategic advantages:[23]

- Obtaining higher quality and/or cheaper components or services than internal sources can provide.
- Improving the company's ability to innovate by interacting and allying with "best-in-world" suppliers who have considerable intellectual depth and innovative capabilities of their own.
- Enhancing the firm's strategic flexibility should customer needs and market conditions suddenly shift—seeking out new suppliers with the needed capabilities already in place is frequently quicker, easier, less risky, and cheaper than hurriedly retooling internal operations to disband obsolete capabilities and put new ones in place.
- Increasing the firm's ability to assemble diverse kinds of expertise speedily and efficiently.
- Allowing the firm to concentrate its resources on performing those activities internally that it can perform better than outsiders and/or that it needs to have directly under its own strategic control.

Using outsourcing to narrow a company's business boundaries offers significant advantages.

---

[22]Jay B. Barney, "How a Firm's Capabilities Affect Boundary Decisions," *Sloan Management Review* 40, no. 3 (Spring 1999), pp. 140–42.

[23]For more details, see James Brian Quinn, "Strategic Outsourcing: Leveraging Knowledge Capabilities," *Sloan Management Review* 40, no. 4 (Summer 1999), pp. 9–21.

The Pitfalls of Outsourcing

The biggest danger of outsourcing is that a company will farm out too many or the wrong types of activities and hollow out its own capabilities. In such cases, a company loses touch with the very activities and expertise that over the long run contribute to and determine its success. Cisco guards against loss of control and protects its manufacturing expertise by designing the production methods that its contract manufacturers must use. Cisco is thus the source of all improvements and innovations and keeps the source code for its design proprietary. Further, Cisco uses the Internet to monitor the factory operations of contract manufacturers around the clock, enabling it to know of problems immediately and to get involved when needed

USING OFFENSIVE STRATEGIES TO SECURE COMPETITIVE ADVANTAGE

Competitive advantage is nearly always achieved by successful *offensive* strategic moves—initiatives calculated to yield a cost advantage, a differentiation advantage, or a resource advantage. Defensive strategies, in contrast, can protect competitive advantage but rarely are the basis for creating the advantage. How long it takes for a successful offensive to create an edge varies with the competitive circumstances.[24] The *buildup period,* shown in Figure 5.3, can be short, if the requisite resources and capabilities are already in place awaiting deployment or if the offensive produces immediate buyer response (as can occur with a dramatic price cut, an imaginative ad campaign, or a new product that proves to be a smash hit). Or the buildup can take much longer, if winning consumer acceptance of an innovative product will take some time or if the firm may need several years to debug a new technology or put new network systems or production capacity in place. Ideally, an offensive move builds competitive advantage quickly; the longer it takes, the more likely rivals will spot the move, see its potential, and begin a counterresponse. The size of the advantage, indicated on the vertical scale in Figure 5.3, can be large (as in pharmaceuticals, where patents on an important new drug produce a substantial advantage) or small (as in apparel, where popular new designs can be imitated quickly).

> Competitive advantage is usually acquired by employing a creative offensive strategy that isn't easily thwarted by rivals.

Following a successful competitive offensive is a *benefit period* during which the fruits of competitive advantage can be enjoyed. The length of the benefit period depends on how much time it takes rivals to launch counteroffensives and begin closing the competitive gap. A lengthy benefit period gives a firm valuable time to earn above-average profits and recoup the investment made in creating the advantage. The best strategic offensives produce big competitive advantages and long benefit periods.

As rivals respond with counteroffensives to close the competitive gap, the *erosion period* begins. Competent, resourceful competitors can be counted on to counterattack with initiatives to overcome any market disadvantage they face—they are not going to stand idly by and passively accept being outcompeted without a fight.[25] Thus, to sustain

> Competent, resourceful rivals will exert strong efforts to overcome any competitive disadvantage they face—they won't be outcompeted without a fight.

---

[24]Ian C. MacMillan, "How Long Can You Sustain a Competitive Advantage?" *The Strategic Planning Management Reader,* ed. Liam Fahey (Englewood Cliffs, NJ: Prentice Hall, 1989), pp. 23–24.

[25]Ian C. MacMillan, "Controlling Competitive Dynamics by Taking Strategic Initiative," *The Academy of Management Executive* 2, no. 2 (May 1988), p. 111.

figure 5.3   The Building and Eroding of Competitive Advantage

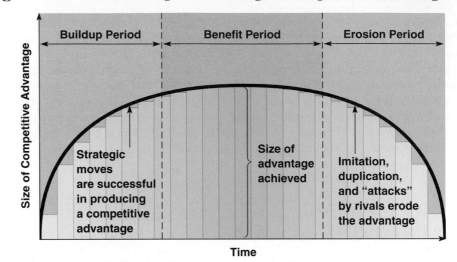

an initially won competitive advantage, a firm must come up with follow-on offensive and defensive moves. Unless the firm stays a step ahead of rivals by initiating one series of offensive and defensive moves after another to protect its market position and retain customer favor, its market advantage will erode.

There are six basic types of strategic offensives:[26]

- Initiatives to match or exceed competitor strengths.
- Initiatives to capitalize on competitor weaknesses.
- Simultaneous initiatives on many fronts.
- End-run offensives to move to less contested ground.
- Guerrilla offensives.
- Preemptive strikes.

Initiatives to Match or Exceed Competitor Strengths

One of the most powerful offensive strategies is to challenge rivals with an equally good or better product at a lower price.

There are two instances in which it makes sense to mount offensives aimed at neutralizing or overcoming the strengths and capabilities of rival companies. The first is when a company has no choice but to try to whittle away at a strong rival's competitive advantage. The second is when it is possible to gain profitable market share at the expense of rivals despite whatever resource strengths and capabilities they have. Attacking a powerful rival's strengths may be necessary when the rival has either a *superior* product offering or *superior* organizational resources and capabilities. Advanced Micro Devices (AMD), wanting to grow its sales of microprocessors for PCs, recently elected to attack Intel head-on, offering a faster alternative to Intel's Pentium chips at a lower price. AMD recognized that its survival depended on eliminating the performance gap

---

[26]Philip Kotler and Ravi Singh, "Marketing Warfare in the 1980s," *The Journal of Business Strategy* 1, no. 3 (Winter 1981), pp. 30–41; Philip Kotler, *Marketing Management,* 5th ed. (Englewood Cliffs, NJ: Prentice Hall, 1984), pp. 401–6; and Ian MacMillan, "Preemptive Strategies," *Journal of Business Strategy* 14, no. 2 (Fall 1983), pp. 16–26.

and was willing to risk that its offensive might prompt Intel to counter with lower prices of its own and accelerated development of faster Pentium chips.

The classic avenue for attacking a strong rival is to offer an equally good product at a lower price.[27] This can produce market share gains if the targeted competitor has strong reasons for not resorting to price cuts of its own and if the challenger convinces buyers that its product is just as good. However, such a strategy increases total profits only if the gains in additional unit sales are enough to offset the impact of lower prices and thinner margins per unit sold. A more potent and sustainable basis for mounting a price-aggressive challenge is to *first achieve a cost advantage* and then hit competitors with a lower price.[28] Price cutting supported by a cost advantage can be continued indefinitely. Without a cost advantage, price cutting works only if the aggressor has more financial resources and can outlast its rivals in a war of attrition.

Other strategic options for attacking a competitor's strengths include leapfrogging into next-generation technologies to make the rival's products obsolete, adding new features that appeal to the rival's customers, running comparison ads, constructing major new plant capacity in the rival's backyard, expanding the product line to match the rival model for model, and developing customer service capabilities that the targeted rival doesn't have.

As a rule, challenging a rival on competitive grounds where it is strong is an uphill struggle. Success can be long in coming and usually hinges on developing a cost advantage, a service advantage, a product with attractive differentiating features, or unique competitive capabilities (fast design-to-market times, greater technical knowhow, or agility in responding to shifting customer requirements). Absent good prospects for added profitability and a more solid competitive position, such an offensive is ill-advised.

> Challenging larger, entrenched competitors with aggressive price cutting is foolhardy unless the aggressor has either a cost advantage or greater financial strength.

Initiatives to Capitalize on Competitor Weaknesses

A company can take the initiative to gain market inroads by directing its competitive attention to the *weaknesses* of rivals. There are a number of ways to achieve competitive gains at the expense of rivals' weaknesses:

- Go after the customers of those rivals whose products lag on quality, features, or product performance; in such cases, a challenger with a better product can often convince the most performance-conscious customers to switch to its brand.

- Make special sales pitches to the customers of those rivals who provide subpar customer service. It may be relatively easy for a service-oriented challenger to win a rival's disenchanted customers.

- Try to move in on rivals that have weak brand recognition. A challenger with strong marketing skills and a recognized brand name can often win customers away from lesser-known rivals.

- Concentrate on geographic regions where a rival has a weak market share or is exerting less competitive effort.

- Pay special attention to buyer segments that a rival is neglecting or is weakly equipped to serve.

---

[27]Kotler, *Marketing Management,* p. 402.
[28]Ibid., p. 403.

As a rule, initiatives that exploit competitor weaknesses stand a better chance of succeeding than do those that challenge competitor strengths, especially if the weaknesses represent important vulnerabilities and the rival is caught by surprise with no ready defense.[29]

Simultaneous Initiatives on Many Fronts

On occasion a company may see merit in launching a grand competitive offensive involving multiple initiatives (price cuts, increased advertising, new product introductions, free samples, coupons, in-store promotions, rebates) across a wide geographic front. Such all-out campaigns can throw a rival off balance, diverting its attention in many directions and forcing it to protect many pieces of its customer base simultaneously. Microsoft employed a grand offensive to establish a prominent Internet presence that goes well beyond just being a developer for PC software. It rapidly introduced upgraded versions of Internet Explorer (to try to overtake Netscape's Navigator Web browser), incorporated Explorer in its Windows operating system, allowed Internet users to download Explorer free, negotiated deals with Internet service providers to feature Internet Explorer, put several thousand programmers to work on a variety of Internet-related projects and to reprogram Microsoft products to incorporate a host of features for creating Web pages and better interfacing with the evolving capabilities of the Internet, created a new cable channel called MSNBC in a joint venture with NBC, formed alliances with a host of companies to provide content for Microsoft Network and MSNBC, and developed software for use in cable modems and portable wireless devices that can connect to the Internet.

Multifaceted offensives have their best chance of success when a challenger not only comes up with an especially attractive product or service but also has a brand name and reputation to secure broad distribution and retail exposure. Then it can blitz the market with innovative new products and advertising, perhaps enticing large numbers of buyers to switch their brand allegiance.

End-Run Offensives to Move to Less Contested Ground

End-run offensives seek to avoid head-on challenges tied to aggressive price cutting, escalated advertising, or costly efforts to outdifferentiate rivals. Instead the idea is to maneuver *around* competitors, capture unoccupied or less contested market territory, and change the rules of the competitive game in the aggressor's favor. Examples of end-run offensives include:[30]

> A successful end-run offensive allows a company to gain a significant first-mover advantage in a new arena and force competitors to play catch-up.

- *Introducing new products that redefine the market and the terms of competition*— Netscape's Navigator, first marketed in 1994, catapulted the company to the top in Web browsers (heretofore an ignored market) and thrust Microsoft and others into a catch-up mode.
- *Launching initiatives to build strong positions in geographic areas where close rivals have little or no market presence*—The race for global market leadership in

[29]For a discussion of the use of surprise, see William E. Rothschild, "Surprise and the Competitive Advantage," *Journal of Business Strategy* 4, no. 3 (Winter 1984), pp. 10–18.

[30]For an interesting discussion of the Netscape-Microsoft battle and the use of end-run offensive strategy, see David B. Yoffie and Michael A. Cusumano, "Judo Strategy: The Competitive Dynamics of Internet Time," *Harvard Business Review* 77, no. 1 (January–February 1999), pp. 70–81.

PCs, servers, and Internet infrastructure products is prompting some contenders to launch early end-run offensives to build positions in less contested markets in Latin America and Asia.

- *Trying to create new segments by introducing products with different attributes and performance features to better meet the needs of selected buyers*—Witness the success that Lexus and BMW have had with carlike sport-utility vehicles. The introduction of PCs below $1,000 proved a smash hit. This initiative works well when new product versions satisfy certain buyer needs that heretofore have been ignored or neglected.

- *Leapfrogging into next-generation technologies to supplant existing technologies, products and/or services*—A number of telecommunications firms are trying to use new-style cable modems to displace the role of local telephone firms in providing Internet access. The makers of thin, trim flat-panel monitors are moving aggressively to improve the cost effectiveness of their technology and production processes to leapfrog the technology of heavier, more bulky CRT monitors.

Guerrilla Offensives

Guerrilla offensives are particularly well suited to small challengers who have neither the resources nor the market visibility to mount a full-fledged attack on industry leaders.[31] A guerrilla offensive uses the hit-and-run principle, selectively trying to grab sales and market share wherever and whenever an underdog catches rivals napping or spots an opening through which to lure their customers away. Guerrilla offensives can involve making scattered, random raids on the leaders' customers with such tactics as occasional lowballing on price (to win a big order or steal a key account); surprising key rivals with sporadic but intense bursts of promotional activity (offering a 20 percent discount for one week to draw customers away from rival brands); or undertaking special campaigns to attract buyers away from rivals plagued with a strike or problems in meeting delivery schedules.[32] Guerrillas can promote the quality of their products when rivals have quality control problems or announce guaranteed delivery times when competitors' deliveries are running behind or significantly boost their commitment to prompt technical support when buyers are frustrated by the caliber of the support offered by industry leaders. If rivals employ unfair or unethical competitive tactics and the situation merits it, a guerrilla can file legal actions charging antitrust violations, patent infringement, or unfair advertising.

> Guerrillas are a thorn in the side of larger competitors, quick to take advantage of whatever opportunities come their way yet careful not to provoke concerted competitive retaliation.

Preemptive Strikes

Preemptive strategies involve moving first to secure an advantageous position that rivals are foreclosed or discouraged from duplicating. What makes a move "preemptive" is its one-of-a-kind nature—whoever strikes first stands to acquire competitive assets

---

[31]For an interesting study of how small firms can successfully employ guerrilla-style tactics, see Ming-Jer Chen and Donald C. Hambrick, "Speed, Stealth, and Selective Attack: How Small Firms Differ from Large Firms in Competitive Behavior," *Academy of Management Journal* 38, no. 2 (April 1995), pp. 453-82.

[32]For more details, see Ian MacMillan, "How Business Strategists Can Use Guerrilla Warfare Tactics," *Journal of Business Strategy* 1, no. 2 (Fall 1980), pp. 63–65; Kathryn R. Harrigan, *Strategic Flexibility* (Lexington, MA: Lexington Books, 1985), pp. 30–45; and Liam Fahey, "Guerrilla Strategy: The Hit-and-Run Attack," in *The Strategic Management Planning Reader*, ed. Liam Fahey (Englewood Cliffs, NJ: Prentice Hall, 1989), pp. 194–97.

that rivals can't readily match. There are several ways a firm can bolster its competitive capabilities with preemptive moves:[33]

- Acquire a company that has exclusive control of or commanding expertise in a valuable technology, thereby giving the firm a hard-to-match technological advantage.

- Secure exclusive or dominant access to the best distributors in a particular geographic region or country.

- Tie up the best (or the most) raw material sources or the most reliable, high-quality suppliers via exclusive partnership, long-term contracts, or acquisition. DeBeers became the dominant world distributor of diamonds by buying up the production of most of the important diamond mines.

- Secure the best geographic locations. An attractive first-mover advantage can often be locked up by moving to obtain the most favorable site along a heavily traveled thoroughfare, at a new interchange or intersection, in a new shopping mall, in a natural beauty spot, close to cheap transportation or raw material supplies or market outlets, and so on.

- Obtain the business of prestigious customers, thereby boosting the company's reputation and winning the confidence of otherwise hesitant buyers.

- Expand capacity well ahead of market demand in hopes of discouraging rivals from following with expansions of their own. When rivals are "bluffed" out of adding capacity for fear of creating long-term excess supply and having to struggle with the bad profit economics of underutilized assets, the preemptor stands to win a bigger market share as market demand grows and it has the production capacity to take on new orders.

- Build an image that is unique, hard to copy, and establishes a compelling psychological appeal. Examples include Nike's "Just do it" tag line and its endorsement contract with Tiger Woods, Avis's well-known "We try harder" theme, Yahoo's image as an Internet portal, and Prudential's "piece of the rock" image of safety and permanence.

> Successful preemptive strikes relegate rivals to competing for second-best positions.

To be successful, a preemptive move doesn't have to totally block rivals from following or copying; it merely needs to give a firm a prime position that is not easily circumvented. Fox's stunning four-year, $6.2 billion contract to televise NFL football in the mid-1990s represented a bold and (successful) strategic move to transform Fox into a major TV network alongside ABC, CBS, and NBC. Du Pont's aggressive capacity expansions in titanium dioxide, while not blocking all competitors from expanding, did discourage enough to give it a leadership position in the titanium dioxide industry.

Choosing Whom to Attack

Aggressor firms need to analyze which of their rivals to challenge as well as how to outcompete them. Any of four types of firms can make good targets:[34]

1. *Market leaders*—Offensive attacks on a market leader make the best sense when the leader in terms of size and market share is not a "true leader" in terms of serving the

---

[33]The use of preemptive moves is treated comprehensively in Ian MacMillan, "Preemptive Strategies," pp. 16–26. What follows in this section is based on MacMillan's article.

[34]Kotler, *Marketing Management,* p. 400.

market well. Signs of leader vulnerability include unhappy buyers, an inferior product line, a weak competitive strategy in terms of low-cost leadership or differentiation, strong emotional commitment to an aging technology the leader has pioneered, outdated plants and equipment, a preoccupation with diversification into other industries, and mediocre or declining profitability. Offensives to erode the positions of market leaders have real promise when the challenger is able to revamp its value chain or innovate to gain a fresh cost-based or differentiation-based competitive advantage.[35] Attacks on leaders don't have to result in making the aggressor the new leader to be judged successful; a challenger may "win" by simply wresting enough sales from the leader to make the aggressor a stronger runner-up. Caution is well advised in challenging strong market leaders—there's a significant risk of squandering valuable resources in a futile effort or precipitating a fierce and profitless industrywide battle for market share.

2. *Runner-up firms*—Runner-up firms are an especially attractive target when a challenger's resource strengths and competitive capabilities are well suited to exploiting their weaknesses.

3. *Struggling enterprises that are on the verge of going under*—Challenging a hard-pressed rival in ways that further sap its financial strength and competitive position can weaken its resolve and hasten its exit from the market.

4. *Small local and regional firms*—Because these firms typically have limited expertise and resources, a challenger with broader capabilities is well-positioned to raid their biggest and best customers—particularly those who are growing rapidly, have increasingly sophisticated requirements, and may already be thinking about switching to a supplier with more full-service capability.

Choosing the Basis for Attack   A firm's strategic offensive should, at a minimum, be tied to what it does best—its core competencies, resource strengths, and competitive capabilities. Otherwise the prospects for success are indeed dim. The centerpiece of the offensive can be an important core competence, a unique competitive capability, an innovative new product, technological superiority, a cost advantage in manufacturing or distribution, or some kind of differentiation advantage. If the challenger's resources and competitive strengths amount to a competitive advantage over the targeted rivals, so much the better.

> At the very least, an offensive must be tied to a firm's resource strengths; more optimally, it is grounded in competitive advantage.

USING DEFENSIVE STRATEGIES TO PROTECT COMPETITIVE ADVANTAGE

In a competitive market, all firms are subject to challenges from rivals. Market offensives can come both from new entrants in the industry and from established firms seeking to improve their market positions. The purpose of defensive strategy is to lower the risk of being attacked, weaken the impact of any attack that occurs, and influence challengers to aim their efforts at other rivals. While defensive strategy usually doesn't enhance a firm's competitive advantage, it helps fortify a firm's competitive position, protect its most valuable resources and capabilities from imitation, and sustain whatever competitive advantage it does have. There are two basic approaches to defensive strategy: moving to block challengers and signaling the likelihood of strong retaliation.

> The foremost purpose of defensive strategy is to protect competitive advantage and fortify the firm's competitive position.

---

[35]Porter, *Competitive Advantage*, p. 518.

Blocking the Avenues Open to Challengers

The most frequently employed approach to defending a company's present position involves actions that foreclose a challenger's options for initiating competitive attack. There are any number of obstacles that can be put in the path of would-be challengers.[36] A defender can participate in alternative technologies to reduce the threat that rivals will attack with a better technology. A defender can introduce new features, add new models, or broaden its product line to close off gaps and vacant niches to would-be challengers. It can thwart the efforts of rivals to attack with a lower price by maintaining economy-priced options of its own. Shortly after America Online acquired CompuServe, it cut the price of CompuServe's service and positioned it as a lower-priced alternative to AOL, thereby countering the efforts of rivals to draw AOL users away on the basis of a cheaper price. A defender also can hire talented employees to broaden or deepen the company's base of core competencies or capabilities in key areas (so as to be able to overpower rivals that attempt to imitate its skills and resources). It can try to discourage buyers from trying competitors' brands by lengthening warranty coverages, offering free training and support services, developing the capability to deliver spare parts to users faster than rivals can, providing coupons and sample giveaways to buyers most prone to experiment, and making early announcements about impending new products or price changes to induce potential buyers to postpone switching, It can challenge the quality or safety of rivals' products in regulatory proceedings—a favorite tactic of the pharmaceutical firms in trying to delay the introduction of generic prescription drugs. It can grant dealers and distributors volume discounts or better financing terms to discourage them from experimenting with other suppliers, or it can convince them to handle its product line *exclusively* and force competitors to use other distribution outlets.

Moves such as these not only buttress a firm's present position but also present competitors with a moving target. Protecting the status quo isn't enough. A good defense entails adjusting quickly to changing industry conditions and, on occasion, being a first-mover to block or preempt moves by would-be aggressors. A mobile defense is preferable to a stationary defense.

Signaling Challengers That Retaliation Is Likely

A second approach to defensive strategy entails signaling challengers that strong retaliation is likely in the event of an attack. The goal is either to dissuade challengers from attacking at all by raising their expectations that the resulting battle will be more costly than it is worth or at least to divert them to less threatening options. Would-be challengers can be signaled by:[37]

- Publicly announcing management's commitment to maintain the firm's present market share.
- Publicly announcing plans to put adequate capacity in place to meet and possibly surpass the forecasted growth in industry volume.
- Giving out advance information about a new product, technology breakthrough, or the planned introduction of important new brands or models in hopes that challengers will be induced to delay moves of their own until they see if the announced actions actually are forthcoming.

---

[36]Ibid., pp. 489–94.

[37]Ibid., pp. 495–97. The list here is selective; Porter offers a greater number of options.

- Publicly committing the company to a policy of matching competitors' terms or prices.
- Maintaining a war chest of cash and marketable securities.
- Making an occasional strong counterresponse to the moves of weak competitors to enhance the firm's image as a tough defender.

Another way to dissuade rivals is to try to lower the profit inducement for challengers to launch an offensive. When a firm's or industry's profitability is enticingly high, challengers are more willing to tackle high defensive barriers and combat strong retaliation. A defender can deflect attacks, especially from new entrants, by deliberately forgoing some short-run profits and using accounting methods that obscure profitability.

FIRST-MOVER ADVANTAGES AND DISADVANTAGES

When to make a strategic move is often as crucial as *what* move to make. Timing is especially important when *first-mover advantages* or *disadvantages* exist.[38] Being first to initiate a strategic move can have a high payoff when (1) pioneering helps build a firm's image and reputation with buyers; (2) early commitments to new technologies, new-style components, distribution channels, and so on can produce an absolute cost advantage over rivals; (3) first-time customers remain strongly loyal to pioneering firms in making repeat purchases; and (4) moving first constitutes a preemptive strike, making imitation extra hard or unlikely. The bigger the first-mover advantages, the more attractive that making the first move becomes.[39] In e-commerce, for example, whoever is first with a new technology or a new network solution often enjoys lasting first-mover advantages in gaining the visibility and reputation needed to emerge as the dominant market leader. America Online, Amazon.com, Yahoo!, eBay, Broadcast.com, DoubleClick, Priceline.com, Inktomi, and several others have demonstrated the power of moving first and forcing rivals into a desperate race to catch up. Illustration Capsule 26 discusses Toyota's first-mover offensive in custom-built cars.

> Because of first-mover advantages and disadvantages, competitive advantage is often attached to *when* a move is made as well as to *what* move is made.

However, being a rapid follower or even a wait-and-see late-mover doesn't always carry a significant or lasting competitive penalty. There are times when a first-mover's skills, know-how, and actions are easily copied or even surpassed by late-movers, allowing them to catch or overtake the first-mover in a relatively short period. And there are times when there are actually advantages to being an adept follower rather than a first-mover. Late-mover advantages (or first-mover disadvantages) arise when (1) pioneering leadership is more costly than imitating followership and only negligible experience curve benefits accrue to the leader—a condition that allows a follower to end up with lower costs than the first-mover; (2) the products of an innovator are somewhat primitive and do not live up to buyer expectations, thus allowing a clever follower to win disenchanted buyers away from the leader with better performing products; and (3) technology is advancing rapidly, giving fast followers the opening to leapfrog a first-mover's products with more attractive and full-featured second- and third-generation products.

---

[38]Porter, *Competitive Strategy,* pp. 232–33.

[39]For research evidence on the effects of pioneering versus following, see Jeffrey G. Covin, Dennis P. Slevin, and Michael B. Heeley, "Pioneers and Followers: Competitive Tactics, Environment, and Growth," *Journal of Business Venturing* 15, no. 2 (March 1999), pp.175–210.

illustration capsule 26

Toyota's First-Mover Offensive in Custom-Built Cars

In fall 1999 Toyota Motor Company announced that it would begin a program to allow U.S. car shoppers to order custom-equipped vehicles for delivery within five days. The move was seen as an attempt to shift from a "build-for-dealer-inventory" business model in North America to a "build-to-order" business model, which was already relatively common in Japan and Europe. But the move was further interpreted as a shrewd strategic initiative by Toyota to gain competitive advantage by being the first North American manufacturer to make this transition.

Surveys of car buyers indicated that close to 50 percent were unable to find the model, color, or equipment configuration they preferred when shopping dealer lots. Traditionally, dealers made educated guesses as to what model, color, and equipment options buyers would prefer, placed their orders with manufacturers, and hoped that car buyers would find what they wanted from the array of vehicles they had in stock. To induce customers to compromise if what they wanted was not in stock, manufacturers offered rebates and dealers would make price concessions. Custom-ordered vehicles could be obtained, but delivery times often ranged from 30 to 60 days.

Toyota's competitive move to five-day delivery on custom orders was intended not only to better satisfy car buyers and encourage brand loyalty but also to gain the benefits of tighter supply chain management and reduce reliance on costly promotions to push sales of slow-selling models. A build-to-order business model (similar to that used by Dell, Gateway, and other PC makers) permitted tighter just-in-time delivery of parts and components to Toyota assembly plants, plus a reduced need for profit-eroding rebates and discounts on unpopular models and configurations. It also paved the way for dealers to drastically cut the number of vehicles kept in stock (thus driving down their inventory-financing costs). If the build-to-order approach caught on with car buyers, a dealer would only have to stock a minimal number of showroom models for inspection and test drives, a limited number of vehicles for immediate delivery, and function mainly as a pickup point for custom orders. Investing in acres of real estate at visible, high-traffic locations would be less necessary.

A build-to-order model would also work to the advantage of Internet car-buying services, since it would be easy for car shoppers to do their research online, make price comparisons, and place their orders.

From Toyota's perspective, the issue was whether its first-mover offensive would provide a lasting competitive advantage. Would buyers respond in attractive numbers? Would Toyota realize significant cost-savings and gain a valuable cost advantage over rivals? How long would it take for rival manufacturers to develop the capability to match Toyota's five-day delivery, build-to-order option?

Source: Jeffrey Bodenstab, "An Automaker Tries the Dell Way," *The Wall Street Journal,* August 30, 1999, p. 26.

While being an adept fast follower has its advantages, rarely does a company gain from being a slow follower and concentrating on avoiding the "mistakes" of early movers. Habitual late-movers, while able to survive, are usually fighting to retain their customers and struggling to keep pace with more progressive and innovative rivals.

key|points

The challenge of competitive strategy—whether it be overall low-cost, broad differentiation, best-cost, focused low-cost, or focused differentiation—is to create a competitive advantage for the firm. Competitive advantage comes from positioning a firm in the marketplace so it has an edge in coping with competitive forces and in attracting buyers.

A strategy of trying to be the low-cost provider works well in situations where:

- The industry's product is essentially the same from seller to seller (brand differences are minor).
- Many buyers are price-sensitive and shop for the lowest price.

- There are only a few ways to achieve product differentiation that have much value to buyers.
- Most buyers use the product in the same ways and thus have common user requirements.
- Buyers' costs in switching from one seller or brand to another are low or even zero.
- Buyers are large and have significant power to negotiate pricing terms.

To achieve a low-cost advantage, a company must become more skilled than rivals in controlling structural and executional cost drivers and/or it must find innovative cost-saving ways to revamp its value chain. Successful low-cost providers usually achieve their cost advantages by imaginatively and persistently ferreting out cost savings throughout the value chain. They are good at finding ways to drive costs out of their businesses.

Differentiation strategies seek to produce a competitive edge by incorporating attributes and features into a company's product/service offering that rivals don't have. Anything a firm can do to create buyer value represents a potential basis for differentiation. Successful differentiation is usually keyed to lowering the buyer's cost of using the item, raising the performance the buyer gets, or boosting a buyer's psychological satisfaction. To be sustainable, differentiation usually has to be linked to unique internal expertise, core competencies, and resources that give a company capabilities its rivals can't easily match. Differentiation tied just to unique physical features seldom is lasting because resourceful competitors are adept at cloning, improving on, or finding substitutes for almost any feature that appeals to buyers.

Best-cost provider strategies combine a strategic emphasis on low cost with a strategic emphasis on more than minimal quality, service, features, or performance. The aim is to create competitive advantage by giving buyers more value for the money; this is done by matching close rivals on key quality-service-features-performance attributes and beating them on the costs of incorporating such attributes into the product or service. To be successful with a best-cost provider strategy, a company must have unique expertise in incorporating upscale product or service attributes at a lower cost than rivals; it must have the capability to manage unit costs down and product/service caliber up simultaneously.

The competitive advantage of focusing is earned either by achieving lower costs in serving the target market niche or by developing an ability to offer niche buyers something different from rival competitors—in other words, it is either cost-based or differentiation-based. A focused strategy based either on low cost or differentiation becomes increasingly attractive as more of the following conditions are met:

- The target market niche is big enough to be profitable and offers good growth potential.
- Industry leaders do not see that having a presence in the niche is crucial to their own success—a condition that reduces rivalry from major competitiors.
- It is costly or difficult for multisegment competitors to put capabilities in place to meet the specialized needs of the target market niche and, at the same time, satisfy the expectations of their mainstream customers.
- The industry has many different niches and segments, thereby allowing a focuser to pick a competitively attractive niche suited to its resource strengths and capabilities.

- Few, if any, other rivals are attempting to specialize in the same target segment— a condition that reduces the risk of segment overcrowding.
- The focuser can compete effectively against challengers based on the capabilities and resources it has to serve the targeted niche and the customer goodwill it may have built up.

Many companies are turning to strategic alliances and collaborative partnerships as ways to help them in the global race to build a market presence in many different national markets and in the technology race to capitalize on today's technological and information age revolution. Even large and financially strong companies have concluded that simultaneously running both races requires more diverse and expansive skills, resources, technological expertise, and competitive capabilities than they can assemble and manage alone. Strategic alliances are an attractive, flexible, and often cost-effective means for companies to gain access to missing technology, expertise, and business capabilities. The competitive attraction of alliances is to bundle competences and resources that are more valuable in a joint effort than when kept separate. Competitive advantage emerges when a company acquires valuable resources and capabilities through alliances that it could not otherwise obtain on its own and that give it an edge over rivals.

Mergers and acquisitions are another attractive strategy for strengthening a firm's competitiveness. Companies racing for global market leadership frequently make acquisitions to build a market presence in countries where they currently do not compete. Similarly, companies racing to establish attractive positions in the industries of the future merge or make acquisitions to fill in resource or technological gaps, build important technological capabilities, and move into position to launch next-wave products and services. Mergers and acquisitions allow a company to fill resource gaps or correct competitive deficiencies; combining operations can result in lower costs, stronger technological skills, more or better competitive capabilities, a more attractive lineup of products and services, wider geographic coverage, and/or greater financial resources with which to invest in R&D, add capacity, or expand into new areas.

Vertically integrating forward or backward makes strategic sense only if it strengthens a company's position via either cost reduction or creation of a differentiation-based advantage. Otherwise, the drawbacks of vertical integration (increased investment, greater business risk, increased vulnerability to technological changes, and less flexibility in making product changes) outweigh the advantages (better coordination of production flows and technological know-how from stage to stage, more specialized use of technology, greater internal control over operations, greater scale economies, and matching production with sales and marketing). There are ways to achieve the advantages of vertical integration without encountering the drawbacks.

Outsourcing pieces of the value chain formerly performed in-house makes strategic sense whenever (1) an activity can be performed better or more cheaply by outside specialists; (2) the activity is not crucial to the firm's ability to achieve sustainable competitive advantage and won't hollow out its core competencies, capabilities, or technical know-how; (3) it reduces the company's risk exposure to changing technology and/or changing buyer preferences; (4) it streamlines company operations in ways that improve organizational flexibility, cut cycle time, speed decision-making, and reduce coordination costs; and/or (5) it allows a company to concentrate on its core business and do what it does best. In many situations outsourcing is a superior strategic alternative to vertical integration.

A variety of offensive strategic moves can be used to secure a competitive advantage. Strategic offensives can be aimed either at competitors' strengths or at their weaknesses; they can involve end runs or grand offensives on many fronts; they can be designed as guerrilla actions or as preemptive strikes; and the target of the offensive can be a market leader, a runner-up firm, or the smallest and/or weakest firms in the industry.

Defensive strategies to protect a company's position usually take the form of making moves that put obstacles in the path of would-be challengers and fortify the company's present position while undertaking actions to dissuade rivals from even trying to attack (by signaling that the resulting battle will be more costly to the challenger than it is worth)

The timing of strategic moves is important. First-movers sometimes gain strategic advantage; at other times, it can be cheaper and easier to be a fast follower than a pioneering leader.

suggested | readings

Barney, Jay B. *Gaining and Sustaining Competitive Advantage.* Reading, MA: Addison-Wesley, 1997, especially chapters 6, 7, 9, 10, and 14.

D'Aveni, Richard A. *Hypercompetition: The Dynamics of Strategic Maneuvering* (New York: Free Press, 1994), chapters 1, 2, 3, and 4.

Dess, Gregory G., and Joseph C. Picken. "Creating Competitive (Dis)advantage: Learning from Food Lion's Freefall." *Academy of Management Executive* 13, no. 3 (August 1999), pp. 97–111.

Hamel, Gary. "Strategy as Revolution." *Harvard Business Review* 74, no. 4 (July–August 1996), pp. 69–82.

Hayes, Robert H.; Gary P. Pisano; and David M. Upton. *Strategic Operations: Competing Through Capabilities* (New York: Free Press, 1996).

Porter, Michael E. *Competitive Advantage* (New York: Free Press, 1985), chapters 3, 4, 5, 7, 14, and 15.

———. "What Is Strategy?" *Harvard Business Review* 74, no. 6 (November–December 1996), pp. 61–78.

Schnarrs, Steven P. *Managing Imitation Strategies: How Later Entrants Seize Markets from Pioneers.* New York: Free Press, 1994.

Stuckey, John, and David White. "When and When *Not* to Vertically Integrate." *Sloan Management Review* (Spring 1993), pp. 71–83.

Venkatesan, Ravi. "Strategic Outsourcing: To Make or Not to Make." *Harvard Business Review* 70, no. 6 (November–December 1992), pp. 98–107.

Yoffie, David B., and Michael A. Cusumano. "Judo Strategy: The Competitive Dynamics of Internet Time." *Harvard Business Review* 77, no. 1 (January–February 1999), pp. 71–81.

chapter | six

Strategies for Competing in Globalizing Markets

You have no choice but to operate in a world shaped by globalization and the information revolution. There are two options: Adapt or die.

—Andrew S. Grove, Chairman, Intel Corporation

You do not choose to become global. The market chooses for you; it forces your hand.

—Alain Gomez, CEO, Thomson, S.A.

[T]here's no purely domestic industry anymore.

—Robert Pelosky and Morgan Stanley

[I]ndustries actually vary a great deal in the pressures they put on a company to sell internationally.

—Niraj Dawar and Tony Frost, Professors, Richard Ivey School of Business

Any company that aspires to industry leadership in the 21st century must think in terms of global market leadership, not domestic market leadership. The world economy is globalizing at an accelerating pace as countries heretofore closed to foreign companies open up their markets, as the Internet shrinks the importance of geographic distance, and as ambitious, growth-minded companies race to stake out competitive positions in the markets of more and more countries. Globalization of the world economy is a market condition that demands bold offensive strategies to carve out new market positions and potent defensive strategies to protect positions previously won.

This chapter examines the issues companies face in crafting strategies suitable for multinational and globally competitive industry environments. We will be introducing a number of new concepts, such as profit sanctuaries, cross-market subsidization, and the distinction between multicountry competition and global competition. There are sections on the special features of doing business in foreign markets, the different strategies for entering and competing in the foreign arena, the growing role of alliances with foreign partners, the importance of locating operations in the most advantageous countries, and the special circumstances of competing in such emerging country markets as China, India, and Brazil.

WHY COMPANIES EXPAND INTO FOREIGN MARKETS

Companies opt to expand outside their domestic market for any of four major reasons:

- *To gain access to new customers*—Expanding into the markets of foreign countries offers potential for increased revenues, profits, and long-term growth and becomes an especially attractive option when a company's home markets are mature. Firms like Cisco Systems, Intel, Sony, Nokia, and Toyota, which are racing for global leadership in their respective industries, must move rapidly and aggressively to extend their market reach into all corners of the world.

- *To achieve lower costs and enhance the firm's competitiveness*—Many companies are driven to sell in more than one country because the sales volume achieved in their own domestic markets is not large enough to fully capture manufacturing economies of scale and experience curve effects and thereby substantially improve a firm's cost competitiveness. The relatively small size of country markets in Europe explains why companies like Michelin and Nestlé long ago began selling their products all across Europe and then moved into markets in North America and Latin America.

- *To capitalize on its core competencies*—A company with competitively valuable competencies and capabilities may be able to leverage them into a position of competitive advantage in foreign markets as well as just domestic markets. Nokia's competencies and capabilities in mobile phones have propelled it to global market leadership in the wireless telecommunications business.

- *To spread its business risk across a wider market base*—A company spreads business risk by operating in a number of different foreign countries rather than depending entirely on operations in its own domestic market. Thus, if the economies of certain Asian countries turn down for a period of time, the company may be sustained by buoyant sales in Latin America or Europe.

In a few cases, companies in natural resource–based industries (like oil and gas, minerals, rubber, and lumber) often find it necessary to operate in the international arena because attractive raw material supplies are located in foreign countries.

Basic Concept
A company is an *international* (or *multinational*) *competitor* when it competes in a select few foreign markets. It is a *global competitor* when it has or is pursuing a market presence on most continents and in virtually all of the world's major countries.

The Difference between Competing Internationally and Competing Globally

Typically, a company will *start* to compete internationally by entering just one or maybe a select few foreign markets. Competing on a truly global scale comes later, after the company has established operations on several continents and is racing against rivals for global market leadership. Thus, there is a meaningful distinction between the competitive scope of a company that operates in a select few foreign countries (with perhaps modest ambitions to expand further) and a company that markets its products in 50 to 100 countries and is expanding its operations into additional country markets annually. The former is most accurately termed an **international** (or **multinational**) **competitor,** while the latter qualifies as a **global competitor.** In the discussion that follows, we'll continue to make a distinction between strategies for competing internationally and strategies for competing globally.

CROSS-COUNTRY DIFFERENCES IN CULTURAL, DEMOGRAPHIC, AND MARKET CONDITIONS

Regardless of a company's motivation for expanding outside its domestic markets, the strategies it uses to compete in foreign markets have to be *situation-driven*; cultural, demographic, and market conditions vary significantly among the countries of the world. Cultures and lifestyles are the most obvious country-to-country differences. Market demographics are close behind. Consumers in Spain do not have the same tastes, preferences, and buying habits as consumers in Norway; buyers differ yet again in Greece, in Chile, in New Zealand, and in Taiwan. Less than 10 percent of the populations of Brazil, India, and China have annual purchasing power equivalent to $20,000. Middle-class consumers represent a much smaller portion of the population in these and other emerging countries than in North America, Japan, and much of Europe.[1] Sometimes, product designs suitable for one country are inappropriate in another—for example, in the United States electrical devices run on 110-volt electrical systems, but in some European countries the standard is a 240-volt electric system, necessitating the use of different electrical designs and components. In France consumers prefer top-loading washing machines, while in most other European countries consumers prefer front-loading machines. Northern Europeans want large refrigerators because they tend to shop once a week in supermarkets; southern Europeans can get by on small refrigerators because they shop daily. In parts of Asia refrigerators are a status symbol and may be placed in the living room, leading to preferences for stylish designs and colors—in India bright blue and red are popular colors. In other Asian countries, household space is constrained and many refrigerators are only four feet high so the top can be used for something else. In Hong Kong the preference is for compact, European-style appliances, but in Taiwan large American-style appliances are more popular.

> Competing in foreign markets where there are significant cross-country variations in cultural, demographic, and market conditions poses a much bigger strategy-making challenge than just competing at home.

The potential for rapid market growth varies significantly from country to country. In emerging markets like India, China, Brazil, and Malaysia, market growth potential is far higher than in the more mature economies of Britain, France, Canada, and Japan. In India there are efficient, well-developed national channels for distributing trucks, scooters, farm equipment, groceries, personal care items, and other packaged products to the country's 3 million retailers, whereas in China distribution is primarily local and provincial and there is no national network for distributing most products. The marketplace is intensely competitive in some countries and only moderately contested in others. Industry driving forces may be one thing in Italy and quite another in Canada or Israel or Argentina or South Korea.

> Being responsive to cross-country differences in cultural, demographic, and market conditions complicates the task of competing in the world market arena. The challenge is to balance pressures to be responsive to local situations in each country against pressures for lower costs and prices.

One of the biggest concerns of companies competing in foreign markets is whether to customize their offerings in each different country market to match the tastes and preferences of local buyers or whether to offer a mostly standardized product worldwide. While being responsive to local tastes makes a company's products more appealing to local buyers, customizing a company's products country by country *may* have the effect of raising production and distribution costs due to the greater variety of designs and components, shorter production runs, and the complications of

---

[1] For an insightful discussion of how much significance these kinds of demographic and market differences have, see C. K. Prahalad and Kenneth Lieberthal, "The End of Corporate Imperialism," *Harvard Business Review* 76, no. 4 (July–August 1999), pp. 68–79.

added inventory handling and distribution logistics. Greater standardization of the company's product offering, on the other hand, can lead to scale economies and experience curve effects, thus contributing to the achievement of a low-cost advantage. The tension between the market pressures to customize and the competitive pressures to lower costs is one of the big strategic issues that participants in foreign markets have to resolve.

Aside from the basic cultural and market differences from country to country, a company also has to pay special attention to locational advantages that stem from country-to-country variations in manufacturing and distribution costs, the problems of fluctuating exchange rates, and the economic and political demands of host governments.

The Potential for Locational Advantages Stemming from Country-to-Country Cost Variations

> A company's potential for gaining competitive advantage based on where it locates its foreign activities or being at a disadvantage because rivals have lower-cost locations is a matter of considerable strategic concern.

Differences in wage rates, worker productivity, inflation rates, energy costs, tax rates, government regulations, and the like create sizable variations in manufacturing costs from country to country. Plants in some countries have major manufacturing cost advantages because of lower input costs (especially labor), relaxed government regulations, or unique natural resources. In such cases, the low-cost countries become principal production sites, with most of the output being exported to markets in other parts of the world. Companies with production facilities in low-cost countries (or that source their products from contract manufacturers in these countries) have a competitive advantage over rivals with plants in countries where costs are higher. The competitive role of low manufacturing costs is most evident in low-wage countries like Taiwan, South Korea, China, Singapore, Malaysia, Vietnam, Mexico, and Brazil, which have become production havens for goods with high labor content. Likewise, concerns about short delivery times and low shipping costs make some countries better locations than others for establishing distribution center facilities.

The quality of a country's business environment also offers locational advantages—the governments of some countries are anxious to attract foreign investments and go all out to create a business climate that outsiders will view as favorable. A good example is Ireland, which has one of the world's most pro-business environments, offering very low corporate tax rates, a government that is responsive to the needs of industry, and a policy of aggressively recruiting high-tech manufacturing facilities and multinational companies. The single biggest foreign investment in Ireland's history is Intel's largest non-U.S. chip manufacturing plant, a $2.5 billion facility employing over 4,000 people. Ireland's pro-industry policies were a significant force in making it the most dynamic, fastest-growing nation in Europe during the 1990s. Another locational advantage is the clustering of suppliers of components and capital equipment, infrastructure suppliers (universities, vocational training providers, research enterprises), trade associations, and makers of complementary products in a geographic area (the benefits of which were discussed in Chapter 4).

Fluctuating Exchange Rates

The volatility of exchange rates greatly complicates the issue of geographic cost advantages. Currency exchange rates often fluctuate as much as 20 to 40 percent annually. Changes of this magnitude can totally wipe out a country's low-cost advantage or transform a former high-cost location into a competitive-cost location. A strong U.S.

dollar makes it more attractive for U.S. companies to manufacture in foreign countries. Declines in the value of the dollar against foreign currencies can eliminate much of the cost advantage that foreign manufacturers have over U.S. manufacturers and can even prompt foreign companies to establish production plants in the United States.

Host Government Restrictions and Requirements

National governments enact all kinds of measures affecting business conditions and the operation of foreign companies in their markets. Host governments may set local content requirements on goods made inside their borders by foreign-based companies, impose tariffs or quotas on imports, put restrictions on exports to ensure adequate local supplies, and regulate the prices of imported and locally produced goods. In addition, outsiders may face a web of regulations regarding technical standards, product certification, prior approval of capital spending projects, withdrawal of funds from the country, and minority (sometimes majority) ownership by local citizens. Some governments also provide subsidies and low-interest loans to domestic companies to help them compete against foreign-based companies. Other governments, anxious to obtain new plants and jobs, offer foreign companies a helping hand in the form of subsidies, privileged market access, and technical assistance. In China, the government is hostile to the Internet and imposes severe restrictions; as a consequence fewer than 3 million Chinese were estimated to have Internet access in 1999 in a country of 1.2 billion people, and the total was not expected to reach 25 million until 2004. In contrast, it has been predicted that the percentage of the population with Internet access in 2004 would exceed 50 percent of the households in the United States, Japan, and several Western European countries.

MULTICOUNTRY COMPETITION OR GLOBAL COMPETITION?

There are important differences in the patterns of international competition from industry to industry.[2] At one extreme is **multicountry** or **multidomestic competition,** where each country market is self-contained—buyers have different expectations and like different styling and features, competition in each national market is essentially independent of competition in other national markets, and the set of rivals comprising the selling side of the market differ from country to country. For example, there is a banking industry in France, one in Brazil, and one in Japan, but market conditions and buyer expectations in banking differ markedly among the three countries, the lead banking competitors in France differ from those in Brazil or in Japan, and the competitive battle going on among the leading banks in France is unrelated to the rivalry taking place in Brazil or Japan. Because each country market is separate in multicountry competition, a company's reputation, customer base, and competitive position in one nation have little or no bearing on its ability to compete successfully in another. As a consequence, the power of a company's strategy in any one nation and any competitive advantage it yields are largely confined to that nation and do not spill over to other countries where it operates. *With multicountry competition there is no international or global market, just a collection of self-contained country markets.* Industries characterized by

> **Basic Concept**
> *Multicountry* (or *multidomestic*) *competition* exists when competition in one national market is independent of competition in another national market—there is no "international market," just a collection of self-contained country markets.

---

[2]Michael E. Porter, *The Competitive Advantage of Nations* (New York: Free Press, 1990), pp. 53–54.

multicountry competition include beer, life insurance, apparel, metals fabrication, many types of food products (coffee, cereals, canned goods, frozen foods), and many types of retailing.

At the other extreme is **global competition,** where prices and competitive conditions across country markets are strongly linked together and the term international or *global market* has true meaning. In a globally competitive industry, a company's competitive position in one country both affects and is affected by its position in other countries. Rival companies compete against each other in many different countries, but especially so in countries where sales volumes are large and where having a competitive presence is strategically important to building a strong global position in the industry. In global competition, a firm's overall competitive advantage grows out of its entire worldwide operations; the competitive advantage it creates at its home base is supplemented by advantages growing out of its operations in other countries (having plants in low-wage countries, being able to transfer expertise from country to country, having the capability to serve customers who also have multinational operations, and maintaining a brand reputation that is transferable from country to country). *A global competitor's market strength is directly proportional to its portfolio of country-based competitive advantages.* Global competition exists in automobiles, television sets, tires, telecommunications equipment, copiers, watches, and commercial aircraft.

An industry can have segments that are globally competitive and segments where competition is country by country.[3] In the hotel-motel industry, for example, the low- and medium-priced segments are characterized by multicountry competition because competitors mainly serve travelers within the same country. In the business and luxury segments, however, competition is more globalized. Companies like Nikki, Marriott, Sheraton, and Hilton have hotels at many international locations and use worldwide reservation systems and common quality and service standards to gain marketing advantages in serving businesspeople and other travelers who make frequent international trips.

In lubricants, the marine engine segment is globally competitive because ships move from port to port and require the same oil everywhere they stop. Brand reputations in marine lubricants have a global scope, and successful marine engine lubricant producers (Exxon Mobil, BP Amoco, and Shell) operate globally. In automotive motor oil, however, multicountry competition dominates. Countries have different weather conditions and driving patterns, production is subject to limited scale economies and shipping costs are high, and retail distribution channels differ markedly from country to country. Thus, domestic firms—like Quaker State and Pennzoil in the United States and Castrol in Great Britain—can be leaders in their home markets without competing globally.

All these situational considerations affecting the business and competitive environment, along with the obvious cultural and political differences between countries, shape a company's strategic approach to competing in foreign markets.

STRATEGY OPTIONS FOR ENTERING AND COMPETING IN FOREIGN MARKETS

There are a host of generic strategic options for a company that decides to expand outside its domestic market and compete internationally or globally.

---

[3]Ibid., p. 61.

1. *Maintain a national (one-country) production base and export goods to foreign markets* utilizing either company-owned or foreign-controlled forward distribution channels.

2. *License foreign firms to use the company's technology or produce and distribute the company's products.*

3. *Employ a franchising strategy.*

4. *Follow a multicountry strategy,* varying the company's strategic approach (perhaps a little, perhaps a lot) from country to country in accordance with local conditions and differing buyer tastes and preferences. The company's hoped-for competitive edge over local rivals might be lower cost in some countries, differentiated product attributes in other countries, or better value for the money in still others. The target customer base may vary from *broad* in some countries to *narrowly focused* in others. Furthermore, strategic moves in one country are made independent of initiatives taken in another country; cross-country strategy coordination is a lower priority than matching company strategy to host-country market and competitive conditions.

5. *Follow a global strategy,* using essentially the same competitive strategy approach in all country markets where the company has a presence. Any of the generic strategy options can be used. A company can employ *a global low-cost strategy* and strive for low-cost leadership over both global rivals and local rivals. Alternatively, it can opt for a *global differentiation strategy,* endeavoring to set itself apart from rivals on the same products attributes in all countries to create a globally consistent image and a consistent market position. It can follow *a global best-cost strategy* and strive to provide buyers with the overall best value in most or all of the world's major markets. Or, it can adopt *a global focus strategy,* serving the same identifiable niche in each of many strategically important country markets and striving for competitive advantage based on either low-cost or differentiation. Whichever generic theme is chosen, a global strategy entails only minimal country-to-country variation to accommodate local tastes and local market conditions. Furthermore, strategic actions are coordinated globally to achieve consistency worldwide.

6. *Use strategic alliances or joint ventures with foreign companies as the primary vehicle for entering foreign markets* and perhaps also using them as an ongoing strategic arrangement aimed at maintaining or strengthening its competitiveness.

Export Strategies

Using domestic plants as a production base for exporting goods to foreign markets is an excellent *initial strategy* for pursuing international sales. It minimizes both risk and capital requirements, and it is a conservative way to test the international waters. With an export strategy, a manufacturer can limit its involvement in foreign markets by contracting with foreign wholesalers experienced in importing to handle the entire distribution and marketing function in their countries or regions of the world. If it is more advantageous to maintain control over these functions, a manufacturer can establish its own distribution and sales organizations in some or all of the target foreign markets. Either way, a firm minimizes its direct investments in foreign countries because of its home-based production and export strategy. Such strategies are commonly favored by Chinese, Korean, and Italian companies—products are designed and manufactured at home and then distributed through local channels; the primary functions performed abroad relate chiefly to establishing a network of distributors and dealers and perhaps selected sales promotion and brand awareness activities.

Whether an export strategy can be pursued successfully over the long run hinges on the relative cost competitiveness of a home-country production base. In some industries, firms gain additional scale economies and experience curve benefits from centralizing production in one or several giant plants whose output capability exceeds demand in any one country market; obviously, to capture such economies a company must export to markets in other countries. However, an export strategy is vulnerable when manufacturing costs in the home country are substantially higher than in foreign countries where rivals have plants or when it has relatively high shipping costs. Unless an exporter can keep its production and shipping costs competitive with rivals having low-cost plants in locations close to end-user markets, its success will be limited.

Licensing Strategies

Licensing makes sense when a firm with valuable technical know-how or a unique patented product has neither the internal organizational capability nor the resources to enter foreign markets. Licensing also has the advantage of avoiding the risks of committing resources to country markets that are unfamiliar, present considerable economic uncertainty, or are politically volatile. By licensing the technology or the production rights to foreign-based firms, the firm does not have to bear the costs and risks of entering foreign markets on its own, yet it is able to generate income from royalties. The big disadvantage of licensing is the risk of providing valuable technological know-how to foreign companies and thereby losing some degree of control over its use; monitoring licensees and safeguarding the company's proprietary know-how can prove quite difficult in some circumstances.

Franchising Strategies

While licensing works well for manufacturers, franchising is often better suited to the global expansion efforts of service and retailing enterprises. McDonald's, Tricon Global Restaurants (the parent of Pizza Hut, Kentucky Fried Chicken, and Taco Bell), and Hilton Hotels have all used franchising to build a presence in foreign markets. Franchising has much the same advantages as licensing. The franchisee bears most of the costs and risks of establishing foreign locations; a franchiser has to expend only the resources to recruit, train, and support franchisees. The big problem a franchiser faces is maintaining quality control; foreign franchisees do not always exhibit strong commitment to consistency and standardization, perhaps because the local culture does not stress or put much value on the same kinds of quality concerns.

A Multicountry Strategy or a Global Strategy?

The need for a multicountry strategy derives from the sometimes vast differences in cultural, economic, political, and competitive conditions in different countries. The more diverse national market conditions are, the stronger the case for a *multicountry strategy* where the company tailors its strategic approach to fit each host country's market situation. Usually, but not always, companies employing a multicountry strategy use the same basic competitive theme (low-cost, differentiation, or best-cost) in each country, making whatever country-specific variations are needed to best satisfy customers and to position themselves against local rivals. They may aim at broad market targets in some countries and focus more narrowly on a particular niche in others.

The bigger the country-to-country variations, the more a company's overall international strategy becomes a collection of its individual country strategies. But country to country variations still allow room to connect the strategies in different countries by making an effort to transfer ideas, technologies, competencies, and capabilities that work successfully in one country market to other country markets. Toward this end, it is useful to view operations in each country as "experiments" that result in learning and in capabilities that merit transfer to other country markets.[4]

While multicountry strategies are best suited for industries where multicountry competition dominates and a fairly high degree of local responsiveness is competitively imperative, global strategies are best suited for globally competitive industries. A *global strategy* is one where the company's approach is *mostly the same* in all countries. Although *minor* country-to-country differences in strategy do exist to accommodate specific competitive conditions in host countries, the company's fundamental competitive theme (low-cost, differentiation, best-cost, or focused) remains the same worldwide. Moreover, a global strategy involves (1) integrating and coordinating the company's strategic moves worldwide and (2) selling in many if not all nations where there is significant buyer demand. Table 6.1 provides a point-by-point comparison of multicountry versus global strategies. The question of which of these two strategies to pursue is the foremost strategic issue firms face when they compete in international markets.

> A multicountry strategy is appropriate for industries where multicountry competition dominates and local responsiveness is essential. A global strategy works best in markets that are globally competitive or beginning to globalize.

The strength of a multicountry strategy is that it matches the company's competitive approach to host-country circumstances. A multicountry strategy is essential when there are significant country-to-country differences in customers' needs and buying habits (see Illustration Capsule 27), when buyers in a country insist on special-order or highly customized products, when host governments enact regulations requiring that products sold locally meet strict manufacturing specifications or performance standards, and when the trade restrictions of host governments are so diverse and complicated they preclude a uniform, coordinated worldwide market approach. However, a multicountry strategy has two big drawbacks: it is very difficult to transfer a company's competencies and resources across country boundaries, and it does not promote building a single, unified competitive advantage—especially one based on low cost. The primary orientation of a multicountry strategy is responsiveness to local country conditions, not building well-defined cross-country competencies and competitive capabilities that can ultimately produce a competitive advantage over other international or global competitors and the domestic companies of host countries. Companies employing a multicountry strategy face big hurdles in achieving low-cost leadership unless they find ways to customize their products and still be in position to capture scale economies and experience curve effects—the capability to implement mass customization assembly at relatively low cost (as Dell, Gateway, and Toyota have demonstrated) greatly facilitates effective use of a multicountry approach.

A global strategy, because it is more uniform from country to country, can concentrate on building the resource strengths to secure a sustainable low-cost or differentiation-based competitive advantage over both domestic rivals and global rivals racing for world market leadership. Whenever country-to-country differences are small enough to be accommodated within the framework of a global strategy, a global strategy is preferable to a multicountry strategy because of the value of uniting a company's efforts worldwide to create strong, competitively valuable competencies and capabilities not readily matched by rivals.

---

[4]For more details on the usefulness of such "transnational" strategy opportunities, see C. A. Bartlett and S. Ghoshal, *Managing Across Borders: The Transnational Solution*, 2nd ed. (Boston: Harvard Business School Press, 1998), pp. 79–80 and chapter 9.

table 6.1   Differences between Multicountry and Global Strategies

	Multicountry Strategy	Global Strategy
Strategic arena	● Selected target countries and trading areas	● Most countries where there is high demand for the product; most global companies will have operations in North America, the Asian Pacific, and Latin America
Business strategy	● Custom strategies to fit the circumstances of each host country situation; little or no strategy coordination across countries	● Same basic strategy worldwide; minor country-to-country variations where essential
Product-line strategy	● Adapted to local culture and the particular needs and expectations of local buyers	● Mostly standardized products sold worldwide; moderate customization where and when necessary
Production strategy	● Plants scattered across many host countries, each producing versions suitable for the surrounding locale	● Plants located on the basis of maximum competitive advantage (in low-cost countries, close to major markets, geographically scattered to minimize shipping costs, or use of a few world-scale plants to maximize economies of scale and experience curve effects—as most appropriate)
Source of supply for raw materials and components	● Suppliers in host country preferred (local facilities meeting local buyer needs; some local sourcing may be required by host government)	● Attractive suppliers from anywhere in the world
Marketing and distribution	● Adapted to practices and culture of each host country	● Much more worldwide coordination; minor adaptation to host-country situations if required
Cross-country strategy connections	● Efforts made to transfer ideas, technologies, competencies, and capabilities that work successfully in one country to another country whenever such a transfer appears advantageous	● Efforts made to use much the same technologies, competencies, and capabilities in all country markets (to promote use of a mostly standard strategy), but new strategic initiatives and competitive capabilities that prove successful in one country are transferred to other country markets
Company organization	● Form subsidiary companies to handle operations in each host country; each subsidiary operates more or less autonomously to fit host country conditions	● All major strategic decisions closely coordinated at global headquarters; a global organizational structure is used to unify the operations in each country

illustration capsule 27
Multicountry Strategies: Microsoft in PC Software, McDonald's in Fast Food, and Nestlé in Instant Coffee

MICROSOFT

In order to best serve the needs of users in foreign countries, Microsoft localizes many of its software products to reflect local languages. In France, for example, all user messages and documentation are in French and all monetary references are in French francs. In the United Kingdom, monetary references are in British pounds and user messages and documentation reflect certain British conventions. Various Microsoft products have been localized into more than 30 languages.

MCDONALD'S

McDonald's has been highly successful in markets outside the United States, partly because it has been adept in altering its menu offerings to cater to local tastes. In Taiwan and Singapore, McDonald's outlets offer a bone-in fried chicken dish called Chicken McCrispy. In Great Britain, there's McChicken Tikka Naan to appeal to British cravings for Indian food. In India, McDonald's features the Maharajah Mac sandwich (an Indian version of the Big Mac); in Japan, there's the Chicken Tatsuta sandwich and a Teriyaki Burger sandwich; in Australia, there's a McOz Burger. However, the infrastructure and operating systems that are employed in the outlets are largely the same, enabling McDonald's to achieve low-cost leadership status once it builds volume up at its outlets (sometimes a 5-year process) and once it has enough outlets operating in a country to achieve full economies of scale (sometimes a 5- to 10-year process in the largest foreign markets).

NESTLÉ

Nestlé is the world's largest food company, with over $50 billion in revenues, market penetration on all major continents, and plants in over 70 countries. A star performer in Nestlé's food products lineup is coffee, accounting for sales of over $5 billion and operating profits of $600 million. Nestlé is the world's largest producer of coffee. Nestlé produces 200 types of instant coffee, from lighter blends for the U.S. market to dark espressos for Latin America. To keep its instant coffees matched to consumer tastes in different countries (and areas within some countries), Nestlé operates four coffee research labs, to experiment with new blends in aroma, flavor, and color. The strategy is to match the blends marketed in each country to the tastes and preferences of coffee drinkers in that country, introducing new blends to develop new segments when opportunities appear and altering blends as needed to respond to changing tastes and buyer habits.

In Britain, Nescafé was promoted extensively to build a wider base of instant coffee drinkers. In Japan, where Nescafé was considered a luxury item, the company made its Japanese blends available in fancy containers suitable for gift-giving. In 1993 Nestlé began introducing Nescafé instant coffee and Coffee-Mate creamer in several large cities in China. As of 1998 the company's Nescafé brand was the leader in the instant coffee segment in virtually every national market but the United States, where it ranked number two behind Maxwell House.

Sources: Company annual reports; Shawn Tully, "Nestlé Shows How to Gobble Markets," *Fortune,* January 16, 1989, pp. 74–78; and "Nestlé: A Giant in a Hurry," *Business Week,* March 22, 1993, pp. 50–54.

PURSUING COMPETITIVE ADVANTAGE BY COMPETING MULTINATIONALLY

There are three ways in which a firm can gain competitive advantage (or offset domestic disadvantages) by expanding outside its domestic market.[5] One way exploits a multinational or global competitor's ability to deploy R&D, parts manufacture, assembly, distribution centers, sales and marketing, customer service centers and other activities among various countries in a manner that lowers costs or achieves greater product differentiation. A second way involves efficient and effective transfer of competitively

[5]Porter, *The Competitive Advantage of Nations*, p. 54.

valuable competencies and capabilities from its domestic markets to foreign markets. A third way draws on a multinational or global competitor's ability to deepen or broaden its resource strengths and capabilities and to coordinate its dispersed activities in ways that a domestic-only competitor cannot.

Achieving Locational Advantages

To use location to build competitive advantage, a company must consider two issues: (1) whether to concentrate each activity it performs in a few select countries or to disperse performance of the activity to many nations, and (2) in which countries to locate particular activities. Companies tend to concentrate their activities in a limited number of locations:

> Companies can pursue competitive advantage in world markets by locating activities in the most advantageous nations; a domestic-only competitor has no such opportunities.

- *When the costs of manufacturing or other activities are significantly lower in particular geographic locations than in others*—For example, much of the world's athletic footwear is manufactured in Asia (China and Korea) because of low labor costs; much of the production of motherboards for PCs is located in Taiwan because of both low costs and the high-caliber technical skills of the Taiwanese labor force.

- *When there are significant scale economies in performing the activity*—The presence of significant economies of scale in components production or final assembly means that a company can gain major cost savings from operating a few superefficient plants as opposed to a host of small plants scattered across the world. Important marketing and distribution economies associated with multinational operations can also yield low-cost leadership. In situations where some competitors are intent on global dominance, being the worldwide low-cost provider is a powerful competitive advantage. Achieving low-cost producer status often requires a company to have the largest worldwide *manufacturing share,* with production centralized in one or a few world-scale plants in low-cost locations. Manufacturing share (as distinct from brand share or market share) is significant because it provides more certain access to production-related scale economies. Several Japanese companies have used their large manufacturing share to establish a low-cost advantage over rivals. For example, although less than 40 percent of all the videocassette recorders sold in the United States carry a Japanese brand name, Japanese companies do 100 percent of the manufacturing—all sellers source their videocassette recorders from Japanese manufacturers.[6] In microwave ovens, Japanese brands have less than a 50 percent share of the U.S. market, but the manufacturing share of Japanese companies is over 85 percent.

- *When there is a steep learning or experience curve associated with performing an activity in a single location*—In some industries experience curve effects in parts manufacture or assembly are so great that a company establishes one or two large plants from which it serves the world market. The key to riding down the experience curve and achieving lower costs is to concentrate production in a few locations to increase the accumulated volume at a plant (and thus the experience of the plant's workforce) as rapidly as possible.

- *When certain locations have superior resources, allow better coordination of related activities, or offer other valuable advantages*—A research unit or a sophisticated production facility may be situated in a particular nation because of its pool

---

[6]C. K. Prahalad and Yves L. Doz, *The Multinational Mission* (New York: Free Press, 1987), p. 60.

of technically trained personnel. Samsung became a leader in memory chip technology by establishing a major R&D facility in Silicon Valley and transferring the know-how gained back to headquarters and its plants in South Korea. Where just-in-time inventory practices yield big cost savings and/or where the assembly firm has long-term partnering arrangements with its key suppliers, parts manufacturing plants may be clustered around final assembly plants. An assembly plant may be located in a country in return for the host government's allowing freer import of components from large-scale, centralized parts plants located elsewhere. A customer service center or sales office may be opened in a particular country to help develop strong relationships with pivotal customers.

However, in several instances, *dispersing activities is more advantageous than concentrating them.* Buyer-related activities—such as distribution to dealers, sales and advertising, and after-sale service—usually must take place close to buyers. This means physically locating the capability to perform such activities in every country market where a global firm has major customers (unless buyers in several adjoining countries can be served quickly from a nearby central location). For example, firms that make mining and oil-drilling equipment maintain operations in many international locations to support customers' needs for speedy equipment repair and technical assistance. Large public accounting firms have numerous international offices to service the foreign operations of their multinational corporate clients. A global competitor that effectively disperses its buyer-related activities can gain a service-based competitive edge in world markets over rivals whose buyer-related activities are more concentrated—this is one reason the Big Five public accounting firms have been so successful relative to second-tier firms. Dispersing activities to many locations is also competitively advantageous when high transportation costs, diseconomies of large size, and trade barriers make it too expensive to operate from a central location. Many companies distribute their products from multiple locations to shorten delivery times to customers. In addition, it is strategically advantageous to disperse activities to hedge against the risks of fluctuating exchange rates, supply interruptions (due to strikes, mechanical failures, and transportation delays), and adverse political developments. Such risks are greater when activities are concentrated in a single location.

The classic reason for locating an activity in a particular country is low cost.[7] Even though multinational and global firms have strong reason to disperse buyer-related activities to many international locations, such activities as materials procurement, parts manufacture, finished goods assembly, technology research, and new product development can frequently be decoupled from buyer locations and performed wherever advantage lies. Components can be made in Mexico, technology research done in Frankfurt, new products developed and tested in Phoenix, and assembly plants located in Spain, Brazil, Taiwan, or South Carolina. Capital can be raised in whatever country it is available on the best terms.

Transferring Competencies and Capabilities across Borders

Expanding outside the domestic market is a way for companies to leverage their core competencies and resource strengths, using them as a basis for competing successfully in additional country markets and growing sales and profits in the process.

---

[7]Porter, *The Competitive Advantage of Nations*, p. 57.

Transferring competencies, capabilities, and resource strengths from country to country contributes to the development of broader or deeper competencies and capabilities—ideally helping a company achieve *dominating depth* in some competitively valuable area. Dominating depth in a competitively valuable capability or resource or value chain activity is a strong basis for sustainable competitive advantage over other multinational or global competitors and especially so over small domestic competitors in host countries. Domestic companies are usually not able to achieve dominating depth because a one-country customer base is too small to support such a resource buildup or because their market is just emerging and sophisticated resources have not been required.

Wal-Mart is rapidly expanding its operations into other parts of the world with a strategy that involves transferring its considerable domestic expertise in distribution and discount retailing to other countries. Its status as the largest, most resource-deep, and most sophisticated user of distribution-retailing know-how has served it well in rapidly building its foreign sales and profitability.

Coordinating Cross-Border Activities

Aligning and coordinating company activities located in different countries contributes to sustainable competitive advantage in several different ways. Companies that compete in multiple locations across the world can choose where and how to challenge rivals. A multinational or global competitor may decide to retaliate against an aggressive rival in the country market where the rival has its biggest sales volume or its best profit margins in order to reduce the rival's financial resources for competing in other country markets. It may decide to wage a price-cutting offensive against weak rivals in their home markets, capturing greater market share and subsidizing any short-term losses with profits earned in other country markets.

If a firm learns how to assemble its product more efficiently at its Brazilian plant, the accumulated expertise can be easily transferred via the Internet to assembly plants in other world locations. Knowledge gained in marketing a company's product in Great Britain can readily be exchanged with company personnel in New Zealand or Australia. A company can shift production from one country to another to take advantage of exchange rate fluctuations, to enhance its leverage with host country governments, and to respond to changing wage rates, components shortages, energy costs, or changes in tariffs and quotas. Production schedules can be coordinated worldwide; shipments can be diverted from one distribution center to another if sales rise unexpectedly in one place and fall in another.

Using the Internet, companies can collect ideas for new and improved products from customers and sales and marketing personnel from all over the world, permitting informed decisions about what can be standardized and what should be customized. Likewise, the Internet can be used to involve the company's best design and engineering personnel (wherever they are located) in coming up with next-generation products. If workloads are heavy in one location, they can be shifted to locations where personnel are underutilized.

A company can enhance its brand reputation by consistently incorporating the same differentiating attributes in its products in the various worldwide markets where it competes. The reputation for quality that Honda established worldwide first in motorcycles and then in automobiles gave it competitive advantage in positioning Honda lawn mowers at the upper end of the U.S. outdoor power equipment market—the Honda name gave the company instant credibility with U.S. buyers.

PROFIT SANCTUARIES, CROSS-MARKET SUBSIDIZATION, AND GLOBAL STRATEGIC OFFENSIVES

Profit sanctuaries *are country markets in which a company derives substantial profits because of its strong or protected market position.* Japan, for example, is a profit sanctuary for most Japanese companies because trade barriers erected around Japanese industries by the Japanese government effectively block foreign companies from competing for a large share of Japanese sales. Protected from the threat of foreign competition in their home market, Japanese companies can safely charge somewhat higher prices to their Japanese customers and thus earn attractively large profits on sales made in Japan. In most cases, a company's biggest and most strategically crucial profit sanctuary is its home market, but multicountry and global companies may also enjoy profit sanctuary status in other nations where they have a strong competitive position, big sales volume, and attractive profit margins.

> **Basic Concept**
> Companies with large, protected **profit sanctuaries** have competitive advantage over companies that don't have a protected sanctuary. Companies with multiple profit sanctuaries have a competitive advantage over companies with a single sanctuary.

Using Cross-Market Subsidization to Wage a Strategic Offensive

Profit sanctuaries are valuable competitive assets, providing the financial strength to support strategic offensives in selected country markets and aid a company's race for global market leadership. The added financial capability afforded by multiple profit sanctuaries gives a global or multicountry competitor the financial strength to wage a market offensive against a domestic competitor whose only profit sanctuary is its home market. Consider the case of a purely domestic company in competition with a company that has multiple profit sanctuaries and that is racing for global market leadership. The global company has the flexibility of lowballing its prices in the domestic company's home market and grabbing market share at the domestic company's expense, subsidizing razor-thin margins or losses with the healthy profits earned in its sanctuaries—a practice called **cross-market subsidization.** The global company can adjust the depth of its price-cutting to move in and capture market share quickly, or it can shave prices slightly to make gradual market inroads over a decade or more, so as not to threaten domestic firms precipitously and perhaps trigger protectionist government actions. If the domestic company retaliates with matching price cuts, it exposes its entire revenue and profit base to erosion; its profits can be squeezed substantially and its competitive strength sapped, even if it is the domestic market leader.

> **Basic Concept**
> **Cross-market subsidization**— supporting competitive offensives in one market with resources and profits diverted from operations in other markets—is a powerful competitive weapon.

There are numerous instances across the world where domestic companies, rightly or wrongly, have accused foreign competitors of "dumping" goods at unreasonably low prices and deliberately attempting to put them in dire financial straits and perhaps drive them out of business. Many governments have antidumping laws aimed at protecting domestic firms from "unfair" pricing by foreign rivals. In the United States in 1999, for example, the federal government imposed antidumping sanctions against Japanese steel companies for selling steel products at ultralow prices.

STRATEGIC ALLIANCES AND JOINT VENTURES WITH FOREIGN PARTNERS

Strategic alliances and cooperative agreements of one kind or another with foreign companies are a favorite and potentially fruitful means for entering a foreign market or

Strategic alliances can help companies in globally competitive industries strengthen their competitive positions while still preserving their independence.

strengthening a firm's competitiveness in world markets. Historically, export-minded firms in industrialized nations sought alliances with firms in less-developed countries to import and market their products locally—such arrangements were often necessary to win approval from the host country's government to enter its market. More recently, companies from different parts of the world have formed strategic alliances and partnership arrangements to strengthen their mutual ability to serve whole continents and move toward more global market participation. Both Japanese and American companies are actively forming alliances with European companies to strengthen their ability to compete in the 12-nation European Union and to capitalize on the opening up of Eastern European markets. Many U.S. and European companies are allying with Asian companies in their efforts to enter markets in China, India, and other Asian countries.

Of late, the number of alliances, joint ventures, and other collaborative efforts has exploded, involving joint research efforts, technology sharing, joint use of production facilities, marketing one another's products, and joining forces to manufacture components or assemble finished products. Cooperative arrangements between domestic and foreign companies have strategic appeal for reasons besides gaining wider access to attractive country markets.[8] One is to capture economies of scale in production and/or marketing—the cost-reductions can be the difference that allows a company to be cost competitive. By joining forces in producing components, assembling models, and marketing their products, companies can realize cost savings not achievable with their own small volumes. A second reason is to fill gaps in technical expertise and/or knowledge of local markets (buying habits and product preferences of consumers, local customs, and so on). Allies learn much from one another in performing joint research, sharing technological know-how, studying one another's manufacturing methods, and understanding how to tailor sales and marketing approaches to fit local cultures and traditions. A third reason is to share distribution facilities and dealer networks, thus mutually strengthening their access to buyers. Fourth, allied companies can direct their competitive energies more toward mutual rivals and less toward one another; teaming up may help them close the gap on leading companies. And finally, alliances can be a particularly useful way to gain agreement on important technical standards—they have been used to arrive at standards for VCRs, assorted PC devices, Internet-related technologies, and mobile phones and other wireless communications devices.

The Risks of Strategic Alliances with Foreign Partners

Alliances and joint ventures have their pitfalls, however. Achieving effective collaboration between independent companies, each with different motives and perhaps conflicting objectives, is not easy.[9] It requires many meetings of many people working in good faith over a period of time to iron out what is to be shared, what is to remain proprietary, and how the cooperative arrangements will work. Cross-border allies typically have to overcome language and cultural barriers; the communication, trust-building, and coordination costs are high in terms of management time. Often, once the bloom is off the

---

[8]Porter, *The Competitive Advantage of Nations,* p. 66; see also Yves L. Doz and Gary Hamel, *Alliance Advantage* (Boston, MA: Harvard Business School Press, 1998), especially chapters 2–4.

[9]For an excellent discussion of company experiences with alliances and partnerships, see Doz and Hamel, *Alliance Advantage,* chapters 2–7 and Rosabeth Moss Kanter, "Collaborative Advantage: The Art of the Alliance," *Harvard Business Review* 72, no. 4 (July–August 1994), pp. 96–108.

rose, partners discover they have deep differences of opinion about how to proceed and conflicting objectives and strategies. Tensions build up, working relationships cool, and the hoped-for benefits never materialize.[10]

Another major problem is getting alliance partners to make decisions fast enough to respond to rapidly advancing technological developments. The large telecommunications companies' strategy to achieve "global connectivity" has involved extensive use of alliances and joint ventures with foreign counterparts, but they are encountering serious difficulty in reaching agreements on which of several technological approaches to employ and how to adapt to the swift pace at which all of the alternatives are advancing. AT&T and British Telecom, who formed a $10 billion joint venture to build an Internet-based global network linking 100 major cities, took eight months to find a CEO to head the project and even longer to come up with a name.

Many times allies find it difficult to collaborate effectively in competitively sensitive areas, thus raising questions about mutual trust and forthright exchanges of information and expertise. There can also be clashes of egos and company cultures. The key people on whom success or failure depends may have little personal chemistry, be unable to work closely together or form a partnership, or be unable to come to consensus. For example, an alliance between Northwest Airlines and KLM Royal Dutch Airlines linking their hubs in Detroit and Amsterdam resulted in a bitter feud among the top officials of both companies (who, according to some reports, refused to speak to each other) and precipitated a battle for control of Northwest Airlines engineered by KLM. The dispute was rooted in a clash of business philosophies (the American way versus the European way), basic cultural differences, and an executive power struggle.[11]

Another danger of collaborative partnerships is that of becoming overly dependent on another company for essential expertise and capabilities over the long term. To be a serious market contender, a company must ultimately develop internal capabilities in all areas important to strengthening its competitive position and building a sustainable competitive advantage. When learning from allies holds only limited potential (because those allies guard their most valuable skills and expertise), acquiring or merging with a company possessing the desired know-how and resources is a better solution. If a company is aiming for global market leadership, then cross-border merger or acquisition may be a better alternative than cross-border alliances or joint ventures. Illustration Capsule 28 relates the experiences of various companies with cross-border strategic alliances.

> Strategic alliances are more effective in helping establish a beachhead of new opportunity in world markets than in achieving and sustaining global leadership.

Making the Most of Strategic Alliances with Foreign Partners

Whether a company realizes the potential of alliances and collaborative partnerships with foreign enterprises seems to be a function of six factors:[12]

1. *Picking a good partner*—A good partner shares the company's vision about the purpose of the alliance and has the desired expertise and capabilities. Experience indicates that it is generally wise to avoid partnering with foreign companies

---

[10]Jeremy Main, "Making Global Alliances Work," p. 125.

[11]Details of the disagreements are reported in Shawn Tully, "The Alliance from Hell," *Fortune,* June 24, 1996, pp. 64–72.

[12]Doz and Hamel, *Alliance Advantage,* chapters 4–8.

illustration capsule 28
Cross-Border Strategic Alliances: The New Shape of Global Business

As the chairman of British Aerospace recently observed, a strategic alliance with a foreign company is "one of the quickest and cheapest ways to develop a global strategy." Cross-border strategic alliances are fast reshaping competition in world markets, pitting one group of allied global companies against other groups of allied global companies. High-profile global alliances include the following:

- Airbus Industrie, one of the world's two leading makers of commercial aircraft, was formed by an alliance of aerospace companies from Britain, Spain, Germany, and France that included British Aerospace, Daimler-Benz Aerospace, and Aerospatiale. Airbus and Boeing vie for world leadership in large commercial aircraft (over 100 passengers).

- General Electric and SNECMA, a French maker of jet engines, have had a longstanding 50-50 partnership to make jet engines to power aircraft made by Boeing and Airbus Industrie. Their partnership company is called CFM International. The GE/SNECMA alliance is regarded as a model because it has enjoyed great success since the 1970s, winning market shares for aircraft with 100+ passengers of about 35 percent through the 1980s and market shares approaching 50 percent since 1995. CFM International had over 200 customers worldwide using its engines as of 2000.

- Renault of France has recently entered into an alliance with struggling Nissan of Japan to create a global partnership capable of being more competitive with DaimlerChrysler, General Motors, Ford, and Toyota,

all of which were engaged in numerous alliances of their own. During the past decade, hundreds of strategic alliances have been formed in the motor vehicle industry as car and truck manufacturers and automotive parts suppliers moved aggressively to compete globally. Not only have there been joint marketing alliances between automakers strong in one region of the world and automakers strong in another region but there have also been strategic alliances between vehicle makers and parts suppliers.

- Vodaphone AirTouch PLC and Bell Atlantic Corporation in 1999 agreed to a collaborative partnership to create a wireless business with a single brand and common digital technology covering the entire U.S. market and to work together on global business synergies in handset and equipment purchases, global corporate account programs, global roaming agreements, and the development of new products and technologies. At the time, Vodaphone AirTouch, based in Great Britain, was the world's largest mobile communications company, and Bell Atlantic was completing a merger with GTE to make it one of the premier telecommunications service providers in the United States and a participant in the global telecommunications market, with operations and investments in 25 countries.

- American Express entered into an alliance with Tata Finance of India to provide money-changing and foreign exchange services in India.

Source: Company Web sites and press releases; Yves L. Doz and Gary Hamel, *Alliance Advantage: The Art of Creating Value through Partnering* (Boston, MA: Harvard Business School Press, 1998).

where there is strong potential of direct competition because of overlapping product lines or other conflicting interests—agreements to jointly market each other's products hold much potential for conflict unless the products are complements rather than substitutes.

2. *Being sensitive to cultural differences*—Unless the outsider exhibits respect for the local culture and local business practices and unless there is good chemistry among key personnel, productive working relationships are unlikely to emerge.

3. *Recognizing that the alliance must benefit both sides*—Information must be shared as well as gained, and the relationship must remain forthright and trustful. Many alliances fail because one or both partners grow unhappy with what they are learning. Also, if either partner plays games with information or tries to take advantage of the other, the resulting friction can quickly erode the value of further collaboration.

4. *Ensuring that both parties live up to their commitments*—Both parties have to deliver on their commitments for the alliance to produce the intended benefits. The division of work has to be perceived as fairly apportioned and the caliber of the benefits received on both sides has to be perceived as adequate.

5. *Structuring the decision-making process so that actions can be taken swiftly when needed*—In many instances, technology and competitive changes occur at such a fast pace that decisions need to be made fast. If the parties get bogged down in discussions among themselves or in gaining internal approval from higher-ups, the alliance can turn into an anchor of delay and inaction.

6. *Managing the learning process and then adjusting the alliance agreement over time to fit new circumstances*—In today's fast-moving markets, few alliances can succeed by holding only to initial plans. One of the keys to longevity and success is learning to adapt to change and adjusting the terms and objectives of the alliance as may be needed.

Most alliances with foreign companies that aim at technology-sharing or providing market access turn out to be temporary, serving their purpose after a few years because the benefits of mutual learning have occurred and because the businesses of both partners have developed to the point where they are ready to go their own ways. In such cases, it is important for the company to learn thoroughly and rapidly about a partner's technology, business practices, and organizational capabilities and then transfer valuable ideas and practices into its own operations promptly. Although long-term alliances sometimes prove mutually beneficial, most partners don't hesitate to terminate the alliance and go it alone when the payoffs run out.

Alliances are more likely to be long-lasting when (1) they involve collaboration with suppliers or distribution allies and each party's contribution involves activities in different portions of the industry value chain or (2) both parties conclude that continued collaboration is in their mutual interest, perhaps because new opportunities for learning are emerging or perhaps because further collaboration will allow each partner to extend its market reach beyond what it could accomplish on its own.

COMPETING IN EMERGING FOREIGN MARKETS

Companies racing for global leadership have to consider competing in big and *emerging-country markets* like China, India, Brazil, Indonesia, and Mexico—countries where the business risks are considerable but where the opportunities for growth are huge as their economies develop and living standards increase toward levels in the modern world.[13] With the world now comprising more than 6 billion people—fully one-third of whom are in India and China, and hundreds of millions more in other emerging countries of Asia and Latin America—a company that aspires to world market leadership (or to sustained rapid growth) cannot ignore the market opportunities or the base of technical and managerial talent such countries offer. This is especially true given that once-high protectionist barriers in most of these countries are in the process of crumbling. Coca-Cola, for example, has predicted that its $2 billion investment in China, India, and Indonesia—which together hold 40 percent of the world's population—can produce sales in those

---

[13]Much of this section is based on Prahalad and Lieberthal, "The End of Corporate Imperialism," pp. 68–79; and David J. Arnold and John A. Quelch, "New Strategies in Emerging Markets," *Sloan Management Review* 40, no. 1 (Fall 1998), pp. 7–20.

countries that double every three years for the foreseeable future (compared to a modest 4 percent growth rate that Coca-Cola averaged in the United States during the 1990s).[14]

Tailoring products for these big emerging markets often involves more than making minor product changes and becoming more familiar with their local cultures.[15] Ford's attempt to sell a Ford Escort in India at a price of $21,000—a luxury car price, given that India's best-selling Maruti-Suzuki model sold at the time for $10,000 or less, and that fewer than 10 percent of Indian households have annual purchasing power greater than $20,000—met with less than enthusiastic market response. McDonald's has had to offer vegetable burgers in parts of Asia and to rethink its prices, which are often high by local standards and affordable only by the well-to-do. Kellogg has struggled to introduce its cereals successfully because consumers in many emerging countries do not eat cereal for breakfast—changing habits is difficult and expensive. Coca-Cola has found that advertising its world image does not strike a chord with the local populace in several emerging countries. Single-serving packages of detergents, shampoos, pickles, cough syrup, and cooking oils are very popular in India because they allow buyers to conserve cash by purchasing only what they need immediately. Because telephones are not widely available in China, people use pagers to send entire messages, which prompted Motorola to redesign its pagers to display more lines and then to expand capacity to keep up with climbing demand for its product.

Strategy Implications   Consumers are highly focused on price in emerging markets, in many cases giving local low-cost competitors the edge. Companies wishing to succeed in these markets have to attract buyers with bargain prices as well as better products—an approach that can entail a radical departure from the strategy used in other parts of the world. If building a market for the company's products is likely to be a long-term process and involve reeducation of consumers, a company must not only be patient with regard to sizable revenues and profits but also prepared in the interim to invest sizable sums to alter buying habits and tastes. Also, specially designed or packaged products may be needed to accommodate local market circumstances. For example, when Unilever entered the market for laundry detergents in India, it realized that 80 percent of the population could not afford the brands it was selling to affluent consumers in India (as well as in wealthier countries). To compete against a very low-priced detergent made by a local company, Unilever came up with a low-cost formula that was not harsh to the skin, constructed new low-cost production facilities, packaged the detergent (named Wheel) in single-use amounts so that it could be sold very cheaply, utilized distribution by hand carts to local merchants, and crafted an economical marketing campaign that included painted signs on buildings and demonstrations near stores—the new brand captured $100 million in sales in a relatively short period of time. Unilever later replicated the strategy in South America with a brand named Ala.

Because managing a new venture in an emerging market requires a blend of global knowledge and local sensitivity to the culture and business practices, the management team must usually consist of a mix of expatriate and local managers. Expatriate managers are needed to transfer technology, business practices, and the corporate culture and serve as conduits for the flow of information between the corporate office and local operations; local managers bring needed understanding of the area's nuances and deep commitment to its market.

> Profitability in emerging country markets rarely comes quickly or easily—new entrants have to be very sensitive to local conditions, be willing to invest in developing the market for their products over the long term, and be patient in earning a profit.

---

[14]Arnold and Quelch, "New Strategies in Emerging Markets," p. 7.
[15]Prahalad and Lieberthal, "The End of Corporate Imperialism," pp. 72–73.

figure 6.1 **Strategy Options for Local Companies in Competing against Global Challengers**

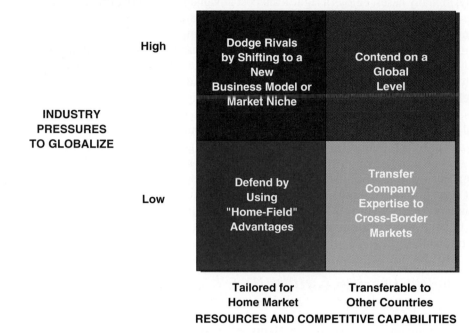

Source: Adapted from Niraj Dawar and Tony Frost, "Competing with Giants: Survival Strategies for Local Companies in Emerging Markets," *Harvard Business Review* 77, no. 1 (March–April, 1999), p. 122.

STRATEGIES FOR LOCAL COMPANIES IN EMERGING MARKETS

If large, opportunity-seeking, resource-rich companies are looking to enter the markets of emerging countries, what are the strategy options for local companies in these same markets wishing to survive against the entry of global giants? As it turns out, the prospects for local companies are by no means grim. Their optimal strategic approach hinges on (1) whether a firm's competitive assets are suitable only for the home market or can be transferred abroad and (2) whether industry pressures to move toward global competition are strong or weak. The four generic options are shown in Figure 6.1.

Defending against Global Competitors by Using Home-Field Advantages

When the pressures for global competition are weak and a local firm has competitive strengths well suited to the local market, a good strategy option is to concentrate on the advantages enjoyed in the home market, cater to customers who prefer a local touch, and accept the loss of customers attracted to global brands.[16] A local company may be

---

[16]Niraj Dawar and Tony Frost, "Competing with Giants: Survival Strategies for Local Companies in Emerging Markets," *Harvard Business Review* 77 no. 2 (March–April, 1999), pp. 122–23. See also Guliz Ger, "Localizing in the Global Village: Local Firms Competing in Global Markets," *California Management Review* 41, no. 4 (Summer 1999), pp. 64–84.

able to astutely exploit its local orientation—its familiarity with local preferences, its expertise in traditional products, its long-standing customer relationships. A local company, in many cases, enjoys a significant cost advantage over global rivals (perhaps because of simpler product design, lower operating and overhead costs), allowing it to compete on the basis of a lower price. Its global competitors often aim their products at upper- and middle-income urban buyers, who tend to be more fashion-conscious, willing to experiment with new products, and view global brands as attractive. Bajaj Auto, India's largest producer of scooters, has defended its turf against Honda (which entered the Indian market with a local joint venture partner to sell scooters, motorcycles, and other vehicles on the basis of its superior technology, quality, and brand appeal) by focusing on buyers who wanted low-cost, durable scooters and easy access to maintenance in the countryside. Bajaj designed a rugged, cheap-to-build scooter for India's rough roads, invested more in R&D to improve reliability and quality, and created an extensive network of distributors and roadside-mechanic stalls, a strategic approach that served it well—while Honda captured about an 11 percent market share, Bajaj maintained a share above 70 percent, close to its 77 percent share prior to Honda's entry. In fall 1998, Honda announced it was pulling out of its scooter manufacturing joint venture with its Indian partner.

Transferring the Company's Expertise to Cross-Border Markets

When a company has resource strengths and capabilities suitable for competing in other country markets, launching initiatives to transfer its expertise to cross-border markets becomes a viable strategic option.[17] Televisa, Mexico's largest media company, used its expertise in Spanish culture and linguistics to become the world's most prolific producer of Spanish-language soap operas. Jollibee Foods, a family-owned company with 56 percent of the fast-food business in the Philippines, combated McDonald's entry by upgrading service and delivery standards, then used its expertise in seasoning hamburgers with garlic and soy sauce and in noodle and rice meals made with fish to open outlets catering to Asian residents in Hong Kong, the Middle East, and California.

Dodging Global Entrants by Shifting to a New Business Model or Market Niche

When industry pressures to globalize are strong, any of three options make the most sense: (1) shift the business to a piece of the industry value chain where the firm's expertise and resources provide competitive advantage, (2) enter into a joint venture with a globally competitive partner, or (3) sell out to (be acquired by) a global entrant into the home market who concludes the company would be a good entry vehicle.[18] When Microsoft entered China, local software developers shifted from cloning Windows products to developing Windows application software customized to the Chinese market. When the Russian PC market opened to IBM, Compaq, and Hewlett-Packard, local Russian PC maker Vist focused on assembling very low-cost models, marketing

---

[17]Dawar and Frost, "Competing with Giants," p. 124.
[18]Ibid., p. 125.

them through exclusive distribution agreements with selected local retailers, and opening company-owned full-service centers in dozens of Russian cities. Vist focused on providing low-cost PCs, giving lengthy warranties, and catering to buyers who felt the need for local service and support. Vist's strategy allowed it to remain the market leader, with a 20 percent share.

Contending on a Global Level

If a local company in an emerging market has transferable resources and capabilities, it can sometimes launch successful initiatives to meet the pressures for globalization head-on and start to compete on a global level itself.[19] When General Motors decided to outsource the production of radiator caps for all of its North American vehicles, Sundaram Fasteners of India pursued the opportunity; it purchased one of GM's radiator cap production lines, moved it to India, and became GM's sole supplier of radiator caps in North America—at 5 million units a year. As a participant in GM's supplier network, it learned about emerging technical standards, built its capabilities, and became one of the first Indian companies to achieve QS 9000 certification, a quality standard that GM now requires for all suppliers. Sundaram's acquired expertise in quality standards enabled it then to pursue opportunities to supply automotive parts in Japan and Europe.

key|points

Companies opt to expand outside their domestic market for any of four major reasons: to gain access to new customers for their products or services, to achieve lower costs and become more competitive on price, to leverage its core competencies, and to spread its business risk across a wider market base. A company is an *international* or *multinational competitor* when it competes in several foreign markets; it is a *global competitor* when it has or is pursuing a market presence in virtually all of the world's major countries.

The strategies a company uses to compete in foreign markets have to be *situation-driven*—cultural, demographic, and market conditions vary significantly among the countries of the world. One of the biggest concerns of competing in foreign markets is whether to customize the company's offerings to cater to the tastes and preferences of local buyers in each different country market or whether to offer a mostly standardized product worldwide. While being responsive to local tastes makes a company's products more appealing to local buyers, customizing a company's products country-by-country may have the effect of raising production and distribution costs due to the greater variety of designs and components, shorter production runs, and the complications of added inventory handling and distribution logistics. Greater standardization of the company's product offering, on the other hand, enhances the capture of scale economies and experience curve effects, contributing to the achievement of a low-cost advantage. The tension between the market pressures to customize and the competitive pressures to lower costs is one of the big strategic issues that participants in foreign markets have to resolve.

Multicountry (or *multidomestic*) *competition* exists when competition in one national market is independent of competition in another national market—there is no

---

[19]Ibid., p. 126.

"international market," just a collection of self-contained country markets. *Global competition* exists when competitive conditions across national markets are linked strongly enough to form a true international market and when leading competitors compete head-to-head in many different countries. A multicountry strategy is appropriate for industries where multicountry competition dominates, but a global strategy works best in markets that are globally competitive or beginning to globalize. Other strategy options for competing in world markets include maintaining a national (one-country) production base and exporting goods to foreign markets, licensing foreign firms to use the company's technology or produce and distribute the company's products, employing a franchising strategy, and using strategic alliances and collaborative partnerships to enter a foreign market or strengthen a firm's competitiveness in world markets.

The number of global strategic alliances, joint ventures, and collaborative arrangements has exploded in recent years. Cooperative arrangements with foreign partners have strategic appeal from several angles: gaining wider access to attractive country markets, allowing capture of economies of scale in production and/or marketing, filling gaps in technical expertise and/or knowledge of local markets, saving on costs by sharing distribution facilities and dealer networks, helping gain agreement on important technical standards, and helping combat the impact of alliances that rivals have formed. Cross-border strategic alliances are fast reshaping competition in world markets, pitting one group of allied global companies against other groups of allied global companies.

There are three ways in which a firm can gain competitive advantage (or offset domestic disadvantages) in global markets. One way involves locating various value chain activities among nations in a manner that lowers costs or achieves greater product differentiation. A second way involves efficient and effective transfer of competitively valuable competencies and capabilities from its domestic markets to foreign markets. A third way draws on a multinational or global competitor's ability to deepen or broaden its resource strengths and capabilities and to coordinate its dispersed activities in ways that a domestic-only competitor cannot.

Profit sanctuaries are country markets in which a company derives substantial profits because of its strong or protected market position. They are valuable competitive assets, providing the financial strength to support competitive offensives in one market with resources and profits diverted from operations in other markets, and aid a company's race for global market leadership. The cross-subsidization capabilities provided by multiple profit sanctuaries gives a global or multinational competitor a powerful offensive weapon. Companies with large, protected profit sanctuaries have competitive advantage over companies that don't have a protected sanctuary. Companies with multiple profit sanctuaries have a competitive advantage over companies with a single sanctuary.

Companies racing for global leadership have to consider competing in *emerging-country markets* like China, India, Brazil, Indonesia, and Mexico—countries where the business risks are considerable but the opportunities for growth are huge. To succeed in these markets, it is usually necessary to attract buyers with bargain prices as well as better products—an approach that can entail a radical departure from the strategy used in other parts of the world. Moreover, building a market for the company's products in these markets is likely to be a long-term process, involving the investment of sizable sums to alter buying habits and tastes and reeducate consumers. Profitability is unlikely to come quickly or easily.

The outlook for local companies in emerging-country markets wishing to survive against the entry of global giants is by no means grim. The optimal strategic approach hinges on whether a firm's competitive assets are suitable only for the home market or can be transferred abroad and whether industry pressures to move toward global competition are strong or weak. Local companies can compete against global newcomers by (1) defending on the basis of home-field advantages, (2) transferring their expertise to cross-border markets, (3) dodging large rivals by shifting to a new business model or market niche, or (4) launching initiatives to compete on a global level themselves.

suggested | readings

Arnold, David J., and John A. Quelch. "New Strategies in Emerging Markets." *Sloan Management Review* 40, no. 1 (Fall 1998), pp. 7–20.

Bolt, James F. "Global Competitors: Some Criteria for Success." *Business Horizons* 31, no. 1 (January–February 1988), pp. 34–41.

Das, T. K., and Bing-Sheng Teng. "Managing Risks in Strategic Alliances." *Academy of Management Executive* 13, no. 4 (November 1999), pp. 50–62.

Dawar, Niraj, and Tony Frost. "Competing with Giants: Survival Strategies for Local Companies in Emerging Markets." *Harvard Business Review* 77, no. 2 (March–April 1999), pp. 119–29.

Doz, Yves L., and Gary Hamel. *Alliance Advantage: The Art of Creating Value through Partnering.* Boston, MA: Harvard Business School Press, 1998.

Ger, Guliz. "Localizing in the Global Village: Local Firms Competing in Global Markets." *California Management Review* 41, no. 4 (Summer 1999), pp. 64–84.

Inkpen, Andrew C. "Learning and Knowledge Acquisition through International Strategic Alliances." *Academy of Management Executive* 12, no. 4 (November 1998), pp. 69–81.

Kanter, Rosabeth Moss, and Thomas D. Dretler. " 'Global Strategy' and Its Impact on Local Operations: Lessons from Gillette Singapore." *Academy of Management Executive* 12, no. 4 (November 1998), pp. 60–68.

Lei, David. "Strategies for Global Competition." *Long Range Planning* 22, no. 1 (February 1989), pp. 102–9.

Ohmae, Kenichi. "The Global Logic of Strategic Alliances." *Harvard Business Review* 67, no. 2 (March–April 1989), pp. 143–54.

Parkhe, Arvind. "Building Trust in International Alliances." *Journal of World Business* 33, no. 4 (Winter 1998), pp. 417–37.

Rackham, Neil; Lawrence Friedman; and Richard Ruff. *Getting Partnering Right: How Market Leaders Are Creating Long-Term Competitive Advantage.* New York: McGraw-Hill, 1996.

Sugiura, Hideo. "How Honda Localizes Its Global Strategy." *Sloan Management Review* 33 (Fall 1990), pp. 77–82.

Thomas, Howard; Timothy Pollock; and Philip Gorman. "Global Strategic Analyses: Frameworks and Approaches." *Academy of Management Executive* 13, no. 1 (February 1999), pp. 70–82.

Zahra, Shaker A., and Hugh M. O'Neill. "Charting the Landscape of Global Competition." *Academy of Management Executive* 12, no. 4 (November 1998), pp. 36–42.

chapter | seven

New Business Models and Strategies for the Internet Economy

We have plainly arrived at one of those moments when everyone can see that things are about to change, but nobody can say for sure how that change will actually play out. The companies that mean to dominate the future must make a bet on where the world is headed—and hope they get there first.

—Joseph Nocera, Business Journalist

If you are going to be in e-commerce, you have to build a business that destroys the old brick-and-mortar model.

—John B. McCoy, CEO, Bank One Corp.

There will be thousands of winners on the Internet. But there will be only a very few really big winners.

—Mary G. Meeker, Morgan Stanley Dean Witter

If we want to stay competitive, we need to be in e-commerce.

—Jessica Chu, Marketing Manager, Aaeon Technology, Taiwan

Our strategy is to integrate the Internet into all of our core businesses.

—Thomas Middelhoff, CEO, Bertelsmann AG, Germany

The impact of the Internet and the rapidly emerging e-commerce environment is profound. As many have concluded, the advent of the Internet and online networks "changes everything." There can be no doubt that the Internet is a driving force of historical and revolutionary proportions. The coming of e-commerce has changed the character of the market, created new driving forces and key success factors, and bred the formation of new strategic groups. From an internal perspective, a company's e-commerce capabilities or lack thereof tilts the scales toward competitively valuable resource strengths or competitively threatening weaknesses. The creativeness with which a company incorporates e-commerce practices holds enormous potential for reconfiguring its value chain and affecting its company's competitiveness. With every passing day, it becomes clearer that the Internet economy presents opportunities and threats that demand strategic response and that require managers to craft bold new strategies.

This chapter examines the issues companies face in crafting strategies for competing in industries where the Internet and e-commerce are ruling forces. It covers the high-velocity character of the whole e-commerce environment, the special competitive features of e-commerce that a company must take into account, the new types of business models and strategies that dot-com companies are employing, and the offensive and defensive strategies that traditional businesses are employing to make e-commerce practices a central part of their operations.

INTERNET TECHNOLOGY AND MARKET STRUCTURE

The Internet is an integrated network of banks of servers and high-speed computers, digital switches and routers, telecommunications equipment and lines, and individual users' computers. The backbone of the Internet consists of telecommunications lines (fiber optic lines, high-capacity telephone lines) criss-crossing countries, continents, and the world that allow computers to transfer data in digital form at very high speed. The bandwidth of the line determines the capacity or speed of the data transfer. These lines are connected to computerlike digital switches that move traffic along the backbone lines; many of these switches act as routers, deciding which way to direct the traffic and how to handle the requests of users' computers to send or obtain data based on the destinations and line congestion. Users gain access to the network via a local area network (LAN) server or an Internet service provider's computerized switch that has the capability to route traffic to and from end users directly connected to it. Many different types of specialized software are required to make the Internet function and infuse it with attractive e-commerce capabilities.

The Supply Side of the Internet Economy

Projections called for an estimated 325 million people worldwide to be using the Internet regularly by year-end 2000—about 150 million in North America, close to 100 million in Europe, 58 million in the Asia-Pacific region, 11 million in Latin America, and over 7 million in the rest of the world.[1] Associated with each of the technological components and activities comprising the Internet infrastructure and value chain are a diverse and growing number of firms and industries. The major groups of firms that comprise the supply side of the Internet economy include:

> The supply side of the Internet economy consists of diverse kinds of enterprises.

- *The makers of specialized communications components and equipment*—Cisco Systems is the world's leading provider of switches and routers; other prominent companies in this group include Lucent Technologies, Motorola, Broadcom, Texas Instruments, PMC Sierra, and 3Com.

- *The providers of communications services*—These companies develop and install the communications networks that enable connectivity and traffic flow. They include backbone providers, so-called last-mile providers, and Internet service providers. Last-mile companies, which install and maintain the *physical assets* needed to connect users to the Internet, include local telephone companies, cable companies, and wireless communications providers. Leading backbone providers include WorldCom, AT&T, Qwest Communications, Deutsche Telekom, British Telecom, Vodaphone AirTouch, Bell Atlantic, SBC Communications, and Global Crossing.

- *The suppliers of computer components and computer hardware*—These companies make PCs, workstations, servers, and peripheral equipment as well as the internal devices that drive them. Examples of companies in this category include Intel, Sun Microsystems, Seagate Technology, IBM, Iomega, Fujitsu, NEC, Matsushita/Panasonic, Acer, Philips Electronics, Toshiba, Gateway, and Hewlett-Packard.

- *The developers of specialized software*—These companies write the programs that enable commercial transactions; these programs include encryption software, order/payment processing software, shopping cart software that tracks purchases, browser software, software to enable banner ads and Web page design, and software

---

[1]Reported in *Business Week*, October 7, 1999, p. 77.

that governs the functioning of cable modems, wireless devices, PCs, workstations, and LANs. DoubleClick is a developer of specialized software that collects bits of demographic information residing on the PCs of Web surfers and, then, using criteria provided by advertisers, delivers targeted ads to the Web pages popping up on Web surfers' screens; DoubleClick's software also provides its advertising clients with reports on the frequency with which surfers click particular ads and their profiles. 1ClickCharge, part of CMGI, develops payment software that allows online retailers to charge consumers a few cents per click for product reviews, music, or articles online. An entrepreneurial start-up named Blaxxun develops software for building three-dimensional Web sites, an attractive feature for some retailers. Engage Technologies, also a start-up, specializes in software that tracks Web traffic from site to site, enabling the creation of anonymous user profiles of Web surfers—information that guides users in targeting their online marketing strategies. Critical Path, another start-up, develops and markets software that allows Web sites to offer e-mail service. Other important developers of software and e-commerce systems include Microsoft, IBM, SAP, Commerce One, Seibel Systems, Ariba, Oracle, Inktomi, Baan, Sun Microsystems, Macromedia, and Novell.

- *E-commerce enterprises*—This category of businesses includes (1) business-to-business merchants (Cisco, Intel, and Dell Computer conduct most of their business with corporate customers online; General Electric does all of its business with its suppliers online); (2) business-to-consumer merchants like Emusic.com, eBay, CarParts.com, Furniture.com, MotherNature.com, Priceline.com, Buy.com, and Charles Schwab; (3) media companies such as Disney, Nintendo, Electronic Arts, and Sony that provide online entertainment; and (4) content providers like America Online, Yahoo!, Briefing.com, The Motley Fool, and iVillage.

Not surprisingly, some companies have staked out business positions in more than one of the above categories. CMGI, part holding company and part venture capitalist, consists of a portfolio of 52 Internet enterprises; among others, it owns or has equity interests in 9 content companies, 12 companies that provide software and other tools for facilitating e-commerce, and 12 e-commerce retailers. Softbank Corporation, a Japanese conglomerate headed by Masayoshi Son, is a venture capital enterprise with stakes in 100-plus high-tech enterprises whose offerings include e-commerce software, Web publishing, e-retailing, online brokerage, Web portals, assorted e-commerce services, and media and content providers. Softbank has ownership interests in Yahoo!, E*Trade, E-Loan, Critical Path, TheStreet.com, and several other U.S.-based enterprises, but the company is focusing most of its energies on commercializing the Internet in Japan, other parts of Asia, and Europe.

> Estimates are that the volume of business done via the Internet will grow to $1.3 trillion by 2003. In 1999, three companies—Dell Computer, Intel, and Cisco Systems—were doing about $100 million of business daily on the Internet.

STRATEGY-SHAPING CHARACTERISTICS OF THE E-COMMERCE ENVIRONMENT

To understand the strategies and business models that work in the new age of e-commerce, we first need to understand how growing use of the Internet by businesses and consumers reshapes the economic landscape and alters traditional industry boundaries. The following features stand out:

- *The Internet makes it feasible for companies everywhere to compete in global markets.* This is true especially for companies whose products are of good caliber and can be shipped economically. In retailing, the Internet opens up a much bigger geographic market than a traditional brick-and-mortar retailer could otherwise reach. In the brick-and-mortar world, a consumer electronics store in Tuscaloosa, Alabama, does not compete intensively with similar stores in Birmingham 60 miles away; in the virtual world of the Internet, however, it competes with electronics retailers hundreds of miles away (whose actual locations are unknown and irrelevant). Thus, *e-commerce escalates rivalry among sellers in different geographic areas to a whole new level.* National boundaries mean much less in an e-commerce world—for example, someone putting an item up for bid on eBay's auction site can connect with a buyer in Europe or Latin America, and eBay provides detailed instructions for shipping auctioned goods internationally. Growing numbers of transportation providers can handle shipments to any part of the world. However, one of the barriers to using the Internet to sell globally is the need for multilingual Web sites (although this is somewhat less necessary for selling to business enterprises since English tends to be the business language of the world). Furthermore, buyers in different countries seem to have differences preferences for the look, feel, and functioning of Web sites—some people like lots of bells and whistles while others prefer simplicity. To meet the challenges of language barriers and respond to varying Web site preferences, many companies operate multiple Web sites, sometimes one for each country or region of the world.

> Growing use of the Internet by businesses and consumers intensifies rivalry among competing sellers.

- *Competition in an industry is greatly intensified by the new e-commerce strategic initiatives of existing rivals and by the entry of new, enterprising e-commerce rivals.* Not only is the Internet an important new distribution channel that allows sellers to reach vast numbers of buyers relatively inexpensively but the use of online systems afforded by the Internet also holds considerable potential for improving business efficiency and lowering operating costs. Hence, innovative use of the Internet adds a valuable weapon to the competitive arsenal of rival sellers, giving them yet another way to jockey for market position and maneuver for competitive advantage. Many existing companies are launching Web site initiatives, sometimes for offensive reasons and sometimes for defensive reasons. At the same time, new companies are being formed by the thousands to enter the Internet economy and compete in market arenas heretofore difficult to enter. The outcome in most industries is a market environment with heightened rivalry among competing sellers.

- *Entry barriers into the e-commerce world are relatively low.* Many of the activities comprising the value chains of e-commerce businesses can be outsourced. The software necessary for establishing a Web site is readily available (if entrepreneurs do not wish to develop their own), and the costs of using a Web hosting company to manage the servers and maintain the site are relatively modest—for example, a bank can establish a new Internet banking site for under $50,000. There are now companies specializing in providing all sorts of services for dot-com companies—from Web page design and maintenance to answering e-mail inquiries to handling warehousing and shipping. Companies operating "server farms" now provide a round-the-clock server access and Web site maintenance at economical rates to enterprises who want to do business online but do not want to operate the site themselves. Manufacturing and assembly can be contracted out to others as well. Perhaps the biggest entry barriers are the sometimes significant outlays required to create brand awareness and to draw traffic to a company's Web site. Even so, there are a number of e-commerce businesses that entrepreneurs can start and operate out of their homes. *Relatively low entry barriers explain why there are already hundreds of thousands of newly formed e-commerce firms*, with perhaps millions more to spring up around the world in years to come.[2] In many markets and industries, entry barriers are low enough to make additional entry both credible and likely.

- *Online buyers gain bargaining power because they confront far fewer obstacles to comparing the products, prices, and shipping times of rival vendors.* Vendor Web sites are only a few clicks apart and are open for business 24 hours a day, every day of the year, giving buyers unprecedented ability to compare offerings and find the best value. Using online networks, a multinational manufacturer's geographically scattered purchasing groups can easily pool their orders with parts and components suppliers and bargain for volume discounts. Likewise, it is feasible for wholesalers to use online systems to research the products, prices, and features of competing manufacturers and for retailers to shop around and bargain for the best deals from manufacturers and distributors who supply them. Individual consumers can readily get reviews of products, compare the features and prices of rival brands, and put up bids for how much they are willing to pay for items. The Internet eliminates the geographic protection of distance that has traditionally given small-town businesses the advantage of being the only source within reasonable driving distance. Using the Internet, buyers can readily negotiate car purchases with dealers hundreds of miles away, order from Furniture.com, purchase music CDs at EMusic.com, or borrow money at E-Loan or Mortgage.com. Buyers of all types—manufacturers, wholesalers, retailers, and individuals—can join a buying group to pool their purchasing power and approach vendors for better terms than could be gotten individually. Purchasing agents are banding together at Web sites operated by Wells Fargo and Chase Manhattan to pool corporate purchases to get better deals or special treatment. PurchasingCenter.com operates a buying pool for industrial goods such as drill bits and motors. (Sellers are not entirely disadvantaged by buying pools, however, because they gain quick access to large, well-defined pools of buyers, allowing them to save on selling and marketing costs.)

> Growing use of the Internet and e-commerce technology can produce important shifts in one or more of an industry's five competitive forces.

- *The Internet makes it feasible for companies to reach beyond their borders to find the best suppliers and, further, to collaborate closely with them to achieve efficiency gains and cost savings.* While a number of companies have relied on foreign suppliers for low-cost components and assembly for some years, in an e-commerce environment companies can use the Internet to integrate foreign suppliers into their supply chain networks more tightly, boosting savings and speeding new products to market. All companies can extend their geographic search for suppliers and can collaborate electronically with chosen suppliers to streamline ordering and shipping of parts and components, improve just-in-time deliveries, work in parallel on the designs for new products, and communicate speedily and efficiently. But the chief point here is that new competitive pressures can spring from the e-commerce relationships between companies and their suppliers—companies not only gain added bargaining power over their suppliers but efficient online collaboration with chosen suppliers can also be a basis for gaining an edge over rivals.

- *Internet and PC technologies are advancing rapidly, often in uncertain and unexpected directions.* For example, a few years ago, both Intel and Microsoft were

---

[2]For a discussion of how e-commerce is attracting entrepreneurs and capital, see Gary Hamel, "Bringing Silicon Valley Inside," *Harvard Business Review* 77, no. 5 (September–October 1998), pp. 70–84.

focusing all their energies on expanding the role of the personal computer as a multifunctional appliance in both businesses and households. Both companies misjudged the technological and business significance of the Internet and had to initiate crash programs to redirect their efforts. Also, a few years ago, investors considered Iomega one of hottest growth stocks because of the potential for Iomega's Zip drives and high-capacity Zip disks to displace the standard 3.5-inch floppy disk. Iomega signed up numerous PC makers to include its Zip drive as an option on PCs. Its business model called for keeping prices attractively low on Zip drives to gain greater market penetration while making money on the sale of Zip disks, which retailed for about $10 each. Just as the Zip drive was gaining a solid foothold in the market, the makers of computer hard drives unexpectedly hit upon ways to greatly increase hard drive capacity (to unheard of levels—10 to 25 gigabytes) and, at the same time, lower hard drive production costs dramatically. PC makers and PC users quickly shifted to PCs with bigger hard drives and bypassed significant use of Iomega's Zip drives and Zip disks. Iomega's stock price declined steadily, and the company has fallen on hard times.

- *The Internet results in much faster diffusion of new technology and new ideas across the world.* Companies in emerging countries and elsewhere can use the Internet to monitor the latest technological developments and to stay abreast of what is transpiring in the markets of Europe, Japan, and North America and what the leading companies in these areas are doing. Distance and location matter less in a connected world; indeed, the Internet is a globalizing force that promotes the formation of a world community and, from a business perspective, reduces the importance of national boundaries.

- *The e-commerce environment demands that companies move swiftly—"in Internet time" or "at Internet speed."* Just a few years ago, companies that were nimble and operated with short response times could expect to have a competitive advantage over slower-moving rivals. In the exploding e-commerce world, speed is a condition of survival. New developments on first one front and then another occur daily. Market and competitive conditions change very quickly. Late-movers are doomed.

> The e-commerce world is characterized by high-velocity, rapid-fire change.

- *E-commerce technology opens up a host of opportunities for reconfiguring industry and company value chains.* For instance, using the Internet to link the orders of customers with the suppliers of components enables just-in-time delivery to manufacturers, slicing inventory costs and allowing production to match demand—for both components and finished goods. It also allows more accurate demand forecasting. Tight supply chain management starting with customer orders and going all the way back to components production, coupled with the use of enterprise resource planning (ERP) software and manufacturing execution system (MES) software, can make custom manufacturing just as cheap as mass production, and sometimes cheaper. It can also greatly reduce production times and labor costs. J. D. Edwards, a specialist in ERP software, teamed with Camstar Systems, a specialist in MES software, to cut Lexmark's production time for computer printers from four hours to 24 minutes. Many of the world's leading motor vehicle producers are moving rapidly to incorporate e-procurement technologies into their supply chain systems in preparation for customized mass production. Another example of how the use of e-commerce systems alters manufacturing and industry value chains to increase efficiency, reduce costs, and streamline the production process is provided in Illustration Capsule 29.

illustration capsule 29
How the Internet Can Revamp Manufacturing Economics and Industry Value Chains

In years past, companies like Compaq Computer and Hewlett Packard made PCs for their corporate and business customers by "guesstimating" which models and options customers would prefer, making variously equipped models in quantity, and shipping them to resellers. Resellers maintained inventories of a wide selection of PC models, as well as parts to reconfigure the models in stock to buyer specifications, and also handled marketing and servicing. However, pressured by the lower-cost economics of Dell Computer's build-to-order and sell-direct business model, many PC makers have been forced to revamp their value chain approach.

Recently, Compaq and Hewlett-Packard entered into arrangements with Ingram Micro, the largest PC distributor and reseller and also an assembler of PCs, and Solectron Corp., a contract manufacturer of PCs, to supply custom PCs to their corporate customers. The new value chain model the partners worked out is depicted below:

This new value chain model was expected to cut production costs substantially and reduce the amount of time a PC sat in inventory from as much as several months to a matter of hours.

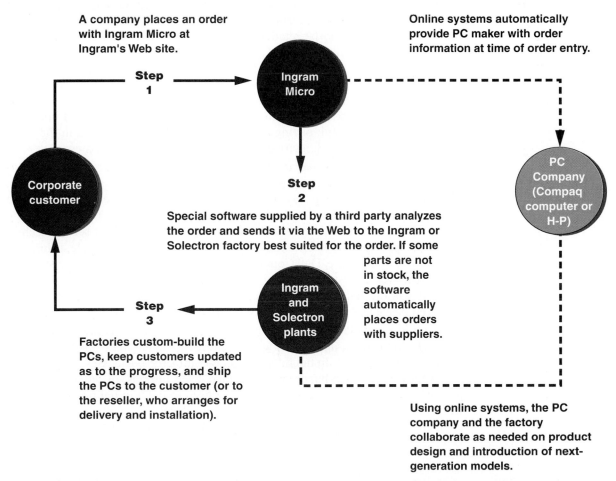

A company places an order with Ingram Micro at Ingram's Web site.

Online systems automatically provide PC maker with order information at time of order entry.

Step 1

Ingram Micro

Corporate customer

PC Company (Compaq computer or H-P)

Step 2

Special software supplied by a third party analyzes the order and sends it via the Web to the Ingram or Solectron factory best suited for the order. If some parts are not in stock, the software automatically places orders with suppliers.

Ingram and Solectron plants

Step 3

Factories custom-build the PCs, keep customers updated as to the progress, and ship the PCs to the customer (or to the reseller, who arranges for delivery and installation).

Using online systems, the PC company and the factory collaborate as needed on product design and introduction of next-generation models.

Source: Business Week, March 22, 1999, pp. EB-15 and EB-18; and information supplied by Ingram Micro, Inc., and Solectron Corp.

All of the different value chain activities associated with procuring items from suppliers and collaborating with them can be streamlined and tightened. With software from Commerce One, Oracle, SAP, Ariba, and others, company procurement personnel can—with only a few mouse clicks—check materials inventories against incoming customer orders, check suppliers' stocks, check the latest prices for parts and components at auction Web sites, and check FedEx delivery schedules, all within one seamless system. Electronic data interchange software permits the relevant details of incoming customer orders to be instantly shared with the suppliers of needed parts and components and arrangements made for just-in-time deliveries.

The instant communications features of the Internet, combined with all the real-time data-sharing and information availability, have the further effect of breaking down the need for corporate bureaucracies and reducing overhead costs. The whole "back-office" data management process (order processing, invoicing, customer accounting, and so on) can be handled fast, accurately, and with less paperwork and fewer personnel.

> The Internet paves the way for innovative reconfiguration of company and industry value chains.

Radical impacts are also occurring in the distribution portion of industry value chains. In Chapter 5, Figure 5.2 showed how software developers can use the Internet to create a low-cost value chain system for marketing and delivering their software online, thus bypassing the costs and markups of traditional software distributors and retailers. Online retailers also have other cost-saving advantages over traditional brick-and-mortar retailers. For instance, as of 1999 Amazon.com had invested about $56 million in fixed assets to achieve sales of $1.2 billion (equal to the sales of about 235 Barnes & Noble bookstores), whereas Barnes & Noble had invested about $462 million in 1,000-plus stores and was paying additional sums in rent and leasing fees.[3]

All told, the impact of e-commerce technology on industry and company value chains is profound, paving the way for fundamental changes in the ways business is conducted both internally and with suppliers and customers.

- *The Internet can be an economical means of delivering customer service.* The Internet provides innovative opportunities for handling customer service activities. Companies are discovering ways to deliver service online, thus curtailing the need to keep company personnel at the facilities of major customers, reducing staffing levels at telephone call centers, and cutting the time required for service technicians to respond to customer faxes and e-mail messages. For example, using specially designed software, Dell Computer can take a digital reading of a customer's troubled computer system, pinpoint the problem, and send repairs over the Internet—all without human intervention.[4] Direct online customer support systems may well prove less expensive and just as effective in a number of industries.

- *The capital for funding potentially profitable e-commerce businesses is readily available.* In the brick-and-mortar world, getting the capital for a new business can sometimes be difficult. In the Internet age, e-commerce businesses have found it relatively easy to raise hundreds of millions, even billions, of dollars to fund a promising new venture.[5] More capital was raised through initial public offerings (IPOs) of stock in the 1990s than in all previous decades combined.[6] Investor excitement about the business potential of the Internet has created a climate where

---

[3]As reported in *Business Week*, October 4, 1999, p. 90.

[4]As reported in *Business Week*, March 22, 1999, p. EB-31.

[5]See Hamel, "Bringing Silicon Valley Inside," pp. 77–83.

[6]According to a study cited on CNBC, January 6, 2000.

venture capitalists are quite willing to fund start-up enterprises *provided they have a promising technology or idea, an attractive business model, and a well thought-out strategic plan.* Furthermore, Internet IPOs are commonplace and their stock prices have been quickly bid up in many instances, putting such companies in a strong position to raise additional equity capital or to make acquisitions. But beginning in 2000, investors in start-up enterprises began pressuring dot-com executives to prove their business models were capable of producing near-term profitability; the stock prices of companies with sizable losses and little prospect of near-term profitability were sliding and start-up companies looking for capital infusions were experiencing much tougher scrutiny from potential investors.

> If an e-commerce venture has merit, it will attract both money and capital immediately. Capital requirements have not proved a significant barrier to entering the e-commerce arena.

- *The needed e-commerce resource in short supply is human talent—in the form of both technological expertise and managerial know-how.* While some e-commerce companies have their competitive advantage lodged in patented technology or unique physical assets or brand-name awareness, many are pursuing competitive advantage based on the expertise and intellectual capital of their personnel and on their organizational competencies and capabilities. Two of the most valuable competitive assets a company can have are dominating depth in a particular technology and a workforce with exceptional know-how and experience that gives a firm uniquely strong skills and competitive capabilities. E-commerce firms are thus competing aggressively for talent and intellectual capital; individuals with attractive qualifications and know-how can command premium compensation, including equity ownership or lucrative stock options in start-up enterprises.

This listing should make clear that growing use of e-commerce technology can produce important shifts in an industry's competitive forces—intensified rivalry, greater entry threats, a blurring of traditional industry and geographic boundaries, shifts in the balance of bargaining power both between sellers and their suppliers and between sellers and their customers, and incentives for all kinds of seller–supplier and seller–customer collaboration. Internet technology and newly emerging products and services that enable e-commerce further have the effects of altering industry value chains, spawning substantial opportunities for increasing efficiency and reducing costs, and affecting a company's resource strengths and weaknesses. Moreover, the pace of technological change is rapid and its direction is often uncertain. Market developments occur swiftly, compelling companies to make decisions at Internet speed or risk getting left behind in the dust.

E-COMMERCE BUSINESS MODELS AND STRATEGIES

Advances in Internet and e-commerce technology are creating industries of the future and giving birth to a host of new business opportunities. There are new opportunities to put a globally connected Internet infrastructure in place—building out the telecommunications system, installing millions of servers, providing high-speed Internet connections to literally billions of businesses and households, and developing the software and networks to create a wired global economy. Others relate to exploiting the business opportunities associated with day-to-day transactions in a globally wired e-commerce environment—business-to-business sales and e-procurement, business-to-consumer sales, e-retailing (or "e-tailing"), providing content, and providing services to users.

The rush of new and existing enterprises to exploit the opportunities presented by the Internet economy is giving rise to innovative business models and radically different approaches to competitive strategy and market positioning. It is also causing companies whose present businesses are threatened in one way or another by e-commerce business approaches to adapt their business models and strategies to the new environment. It is worth looking at the specific strategy elements comprising the newly emerging business models.

Business Models and Strategies for Communications Equipment Suppliers

Most all of the companies making Internet-related communications equipment use a traditional business model—selling their manufactured products to customers at prices that are attractively above costs and produce a good return on investment. Perhaps the biggest strategic problem a number of these equipment makers face is that there are competing technologies for building various components of the Internet infrastructure and creating a globally wired economy. Other things being equal, the low-cost technological solution typically wins out. But other things are seldom equal. Often, competing technologies have materially different performance pluses and minuses, with the trade-offs sufficiently unclear that industry participants disagree about which of the competing technologies represent the best option. In other cases, the competing technologies are incompatible, preventing users of one from interfacing with users of the other. If installing and maintaining parallel technological systems is prohibitively expensive, progress is slowed (and business risks are increased) until consensus emerges around one as the industry standard. There's a natural tendency for those with vested interests in a particular technological approach to maneuver to make their favored technological solution the industry standard. Technology rivals have several strategy options for trying to win the battle for technological dominance:

- *Invest aggressively in R&D to win the technological race against rivals*; spending can be aimed at improving performance features, curing performance weaknesses, and reducing the costs of installing and maintaining the company's technological approach.
- *Form strategic alliances* with suppliers, potential customers, and those with complementary technologies to build consensus for favored technological approaches and industry standards.
- *Acquire other companies with complementary technological expertise* to broaden and deepen the company's technological base and thereby drive advances in the company's technology faster than rivals are able to advance theirs.
- *Hedge the company's bets* by investing sufficient resources in mastering one or more of the competing technologies; the company can then shift to the technological approach that wins out.

A fierce competitive battle involving many of these same strategic issues is presently under way among rivals in wireless communications technologies. In the United States, there are two different technological approaches to mobile telecommunications, with some companies racing ahead with one approach and their rivals racing for market dominance with the other. The lack of a uniform technology standard is resulting in slower growth of mobile telephone communications in the United States relative to Europe and Japan. The standard used in Europe is different from the two competing U.S. technologies, and Japanese standard technology is different yet again. The four different wireless technologies in play around the world pose formidable technological and competitive challenges for all the various market participants in establishing mobile systems capable of connecting all users irrespective of location.

Cisco Systems, the world's largest provider of Internet hardware and technology, is providing start-up phone companies in Europe with the latest Internet technology at subsidized prices in a strategic offensive aimed at developing high-quality voice transmission over the Internet. If Cisco's Internet telephony effort proves successful, Europe's largest local telephone companies would be induced to purchase significantly larger amounts of Cisco equipment. And Cisco would be able to siphon revenues and market share away from the European suppliers of traditional telephone equipment—Alcatel, Siemens, and Ericcson.

Another recent technological development allows telephone calls to be routed over the Internet rather than through existing telephone lines; "gateways" can be installed that link phone systems to the Internet. The result is much cheaper rates for international phone calls and significant new competition for the world's telephone monopolies that have charged very hefty fees for handling cross-border calls.

Business Models and Strategies for Communications Services Suppliers

The companies in the communications services section of the Internet value chain have business models based on profitably selling their services for a fee—where the fee can be based on either a flat rate per month or volume of use. Since their role is to provide connectivity, Internet service providers are obliged to invest heavily in extending lines and installing equipment so as to have the capacity to provide the desired point-to-point service and handle the traffic load along their lines and systems. Investment requirements are particularly heavy for backbone providers, creating sizable up-front expenditures and heavy fixed costs. Profits come later, after the backbone has been installed and the volume of use reaches breakeven and beyond. Here, companies are racing to establish their networks ahead of rivals and to get in a position to sign up customers for their services.

Recently, fierce competition has emerged among last-mile providers—the companies that want to sell high-speed Internet access to households, small businesses, and large commercial enterprises. While local telephone companies like Bell Atlantic, Bell South, SBC Communications, and U.S. West (now part of Qwest Communications) have monopolized the market for last-mile services, their strategy to provide high-speed (broadband) Internet connections using new digital signal line (DSL) technology is meeting head-on competition from the providers of wireless broadband services and cable TV providers touting cable Internet service. AT&T is launching a three-pronged attack to enter the last-mile competition. One thrust involves a wireless strategy—giving away broadband mobile phones with Internet connection capability, selling monthly subscriptions for wireless access, eliminating roaming charges and long-distance charges, and promoting flat-rate per minute charges. A second thrust is to get the permission of regulators to compete with local telephone companies in providing local telephone service via cable connections. The third thrust involves acquiring cable TV companies (TCI and MediaOne) and promoting high-speed Internet access via cable modems that deliver data over 100 times faster than standard 56-kilobit modems. AT&T's strategy is to bundle local telephone service, long distance service, cable TV service, and Internet access into a single package, available for a single monthly fee for all four services. Other cable companies like Time Warner are also moving to develop last-mile products and services. The last-mile market is attracting attention primarily because it is viewed as such a potentially lucrative market—monthly subscriptions and fees for all four last-mile services could easily exceed $100 per month per household and several hundred dollars more for small business customers.

Name recognition and advertising have recently emerged as important elements of strategy in the just-starting battle for market share among last-mile providers. To gain attention in the race to provide high-speed Internet access, Covad—a small Silicon Valley company in the business of providing high-speed Internet access using DSL technology—launched a $40 million year-long coast-to-coast advertising campaign in late 1999 to win a place in the ranks of the leading last-mile providers; at the time, Covad had annual sales of only $20 million. Within weeks, other rivals launched advertising initiatives of their own.

Business Models and Strategies for Computer Hardware Suppliers

Like the makers of Internet-related communications equipment, the suppliers of PC components and PC hardware use a traditional business model—make money by selling the company's products at prices above costs. Again, technology is advancing at such a rapid pace in PC components that companies in this industry must stay on the cutting edge of technology, investing in R&D and being quick to imitate the technological advances and product innovations that rivals are able to come up with. Competitive success hinges on staying abreast or ahead of rivals in introducing next-generation products. A company can expect to command a premium price for its product only if it can demonstrate product superiority. Otherwise, it has to be prepared to compete on the basis of price, striving to outperform rivals by means of lower costs. More and more PC components are becoming commodities, with minimal differentiation among rivals. The same is true in PC hardware. Hence, strategies keyed to low cost are the most reliable for achieving competitive advantage, although best-cost provider strategies can work well when some buyers are willing to pay for upscale features and above-average levels of customer service and technical support.

Business Models and Strategies for Specialized E-Commerce Software Developers

The developers of e-commerce software create programming applications that enable all kinds of e-commerce activities. Their business model involves making money by investing resources (principally, the efforts of talented programmers) in designing and developing specialized software, then marketing and selling the software to other companies (e-commerce retailers, Internet service providers, content providers, and others) at what they hope will prove to be profitable prices. Since most software costs are incurred up front in the programming phase and thus are largely fixed, profitability hinges on volume—once sales reach the break-even volume, a big fraction of the additional revenue goes to the bottom line. To combat the falloff in revenues that occurs with approaching market saturation, developers upgrade the program and offer next-generation versions.

However, some software developers that market transaction-based software have adopted a business model whereby they collect a small fee for every transaction their software performs rather than sell their software outright at a set price per copy. Such a pricing approach provides them with a continuing revenue stream. The fee-per-transaction model is particularly appealing when there's a potential for the software to perform millions of transactions and the number of Web sites requiring such software is relatively small (thus limiting the potential number of copies that can be sold). The size of the transactions fee that a developer can charge is a function of competition—whether competing software is available and whether the software developer's own product is decidedly superior to alternative products. Buyers may not object strongly to a fee-per-transaction arrangement because it lowers their front-end costs for the software and they end up paying only for services rendered. Inktomi is the world's leading search-technology provider, supplying software for conducting searches, compiling directories of subject categories, doing comparison shopping, and delivering Web pages faster. Inktomi sells its search engine software to companies and Web portals, collecting a fee of about half-a-cent per Web page retrieved from each query.

Recently, software providers have launched strategies to convince PC users to rent the software they want by logging on to a Web site, connecting to a server with the desired programs, and paying a user fee, thus avoiding having to buy software, install it on their computers, and run applications from hard disks. The idea of software rental or leasing has appeal to some business users because it allows them to outsource information technology (IT) and pay IT providers a fixed fee per PC for software use and support; this can prove cheaper than having their own IT departments perform all the necessary functions in-house at costs that often overrun budgeted amounts. It can also appeal to home users who want to try out a new application or use certain applications only occasionally; pay-per-use can also make good economic sense for game and entertainment programs and educational programs for children. For about $3, customers can log on to Arepa.com's PlayNow site and run a program as often and as long as they like for a 48-hour period.

MP3.com has shaken up the music industry with its software technology that allows Web users to compress a song in digital form, download it to their computer drive, and then copy it to a recordable disk; its business model involves signing up artists to record songs and albums, then selling downloadable single songs for 99 cents and albums for $8. MP3 also distributes the songs of aspiring bands for free. MP3's technology has the potential to cut into the market shares of the five largest studios (which account for 80 percent of the music on radio and in stores) and to redefine how music is produced and distributed.

Business Models and Strategies for E-Commerce Retailers

Two categories of Web merchants stand out—those that sell primarily to businesses (referred to as business-to-business merchants) and those that sell to consumers (business-to-consumer merchants). Several business models are in play here. The simplest, and perhaps most revolutionary, is to sell products at cost (or below) and make money by selling advertising to other merchandisers who value the audience attracted to the Web site. Buy.com, for example, sells a wide variety of items at very low prices to attract a big audience, hoping to make money by selling ads on its Web site; the bigger the audience that Buy.com is able to attract, the bigger the fees it can charge advertisers. A few online merchants are willing to sell items at break-even prices or less but collect information on buyers that can be sold to other merchandisers. Car-shopping services make money not only from advertising but also by referring customers to car dealers and, further, by selling related items such as car insurance and auto accessories.

Other merchants use the mostly traditional model of purchasing goods from manufacturers and distributors, marketing them to buyers at their Web store, and filling orders from stocks held in inventory in their warehouse—their innovation is one of simply using the Internet as the sales site instead of brick-and-mortar retail outlets. Still other e-tailers operate only a Web site for marketing and selling, using contract manufacturers to make the products, and outsourcing the distribution and delivery functions to warehousing and shipping specialists. Buy.com obtains the products it sells from name-brand manufacturers and uses outsiders to stock and ship what it sells; all it does is operate an online superstore consisting of some 30,000 items.

Once an e-tailer settles on a basic business model, it can use any of the following strategy elements to undergird its competitive success:

- *Spend heavily on advertising to build widespread brand awareness, draw traffic, and start the process of developing customer loyalty.* Extravagant advertising campaigns incorporating TV, print media, radio, and online banners have become standard in launching retailing Web sites. A number of enterprises have spent amounts for advertising that were substantially in excess of current revenues, believing that it was worth incurring substantial short-term losses in order to establish name recognition, draw traffic to their Web site, and develop loyalty.

- *Add new product lines to help generate high and growing levels of traffic at the company's Web site.* Expanding a company's product lines, acquiring other Internet retailers with complementary offerings, or entering into alliances and joint marketing agreements with other enterprises desirous of boosting Internet sales all can help draw new visitors and boost traffic at the company's Web site. Amazon.com has diversified its product offerings beyond books to include music, online auctions, electronics products, toys, video games, and home improvement products. It has also allowed small specialty-item e-tailers to market their products on its Web site. In late 1999, Amazon offered approximately 18 million items at its site.

- *Be a first-mover or at worst an early-mover.* There's a strong belief among Internet entrepreneurs that being a first-mover or fast-follower significantly enhances a company's chances of being the biggest and best known online retailer for a particular category of goods, thus improving a firm's prospects for dominating its market niche and warding off challenges from newcomers.

- *Pay considerable attention to creating an attractive Web site and generating "buzz."* Web pages need to be interesting and easy-to-read, with lots of eye appeal. Moreover, the site has to be cleverly marketed. Unless Web surfers hear about the site, like what they see on their first visit, and are intrigued enough to return again and again, a company's Web site will likely not generate the desired traffic and revenues.

- *Keep the Web site innovative, fresh, and entertaining.* This means constantly adding new features and capabilities, enhancing the look and feel of the site, heightening viewer interest with audio and live video, and expanding selection and product offerings. Engaging, entertaining features add value to the experience of spending time at the site and are therefore strong competitive assets. Creating a strong sense of community among users and visitors—as eBay has done with its online auctions—can also.

On the Internet, shelf space is unlimited. The "one-stop shopping" strategy (like that of Amazon.com, described above) has the appealing economics of helping spread many one-time costs over a wide number of items and a larger customer base; it can also help an online retailer establish itself as a household name and facilitate marketing an ever-greater selection of goods to frequent visitors to the site. In contrast, some e-tailers such as eToys have adopted classic focus strategies—building a Web site aimed at a sharply defined target audience shopping for a particular product or product category. Focusers seek to build customer loyalty based on attractively low prices, better value, wide selection, convenient service, nifty options, or some other differentiating attribute. They pay special attention to the details that will please their target audience; eToys, for example, gives customers the option of having each selection gift-wrapped separately and affixed with an appropriate "To/From" tag; it also has removed its name from the outside of shipping cartons to lessen the clamor from children to open arriving boxes immediately.

"Brick-and-Click" Strategies: An Alternative to Pure Brick-and-Mortar and Pure Dot-com Strategies.

Many traditional retailers, threatened by Internet retailing, have rushed to open their own online shopping sites. Toys "R" Us, for example, has launched a Web site to combat eToys and several other online toy merchants. Merrill Lynch and Paine Webber have begun offering customers the option of trading online to prevent commission-sensitive customers from moving their accounts to cheaper online brokerages such as Charles Schwab, E*Trade, and Waterhouse. Wal-Mart has launched a Web site. Such "brick-and-click" strategies give customers the option of either shopping in stores or online and can be an effective way of combating competition from pure online retailers, especially when customer ability to see and touch a product is an important condition for going forward with the decision to purchase. Illustration Capsule 30 explains why a brick-and-click strategy can be highly attractive and competitively powerful.

Business Models and Strategies for E-Commerce Services Suppliers

The Internet economy is giving birth to a host of opportunities to provide services to e-commerce enterprises. For example, one of the key strategic issues that e-commerce retailers must resolve is how best to handle warehousing and delivery activities. A number of companies are springing up that specialize in warehousing and order shipment for e-commerce retailers. Bechtel Group is investing $1 billion to develop logistics systems, warehousing, and delivery capabilities to support online grocery retailer Webvan Group; Webvan's strategy is to create a Web site where consumers can shop for supermarket items and obtain next-day delivery—within a 30-minute time window selected by customers. Illustration Capsule 31 reports how Fingerhut is reinventing its business by exploiting the opportunities to provide warehousing, packaging, and shipping services to e-commerce retailers.

   While the Internet allows companies to connect directly with their suppliers, many companies are finding it valuable to use the services of "Internet middlemen" to efficiently sort through all the various supplier choices. The middlemen—variously referred to as "infomediaries" or "e-markets"—use the instant communications capability of the Internet to match buyers and sellers. Altra Energy Technologies allows buyers of natural gas to shop for sellers online instead of trying to contact prospective sellers to check on prices and availability via fax or telephone.[7] Using Altra's online e-market,

---

[7]*Business Week*, October 4, 1999, p. 98.

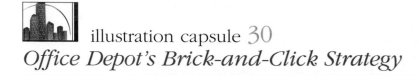

illustration capsule 30
Office Depot's Brick-and-Click Strategy

Office Depot was in the first wave of retailers to adopt an e-commerce strategy. In 1996 it began allowing business customers to use the Internet to place orders, thus avoiding having to make a call, generate a purchase order, and pay an invoice while still getting same-day or next-day delivery.

Office Depot built its Internet business around its existing network of 750 retail stores, 30 warehouses, 2,000 delivery trucks, $1.3 billion in inventories, and phone-order sales department, which handled large business customers. It already had a solid brand name and enough purchasing power with its suppliers to counter discount-minded e-commerce rivals trying to attract buyers on the basis of super-low prices. Office Depot's incremental investment to enter the e-commerce arena was almost zero since all it needed to add was a Web site where customers could see pictures and descriptions of the items it carried, their prices, and in-stock availability; marketing costs have been less than $10 million.

Office Depot set up customized Web pages for 37,000 corporate and educational customers. Sites were designed that allowed the customer's employees varying degrees of freedom to buy supplies—a clerk might be able to order only copying paper, toner cartridges, computer disks, and paper clips up to a preset dollar limit per order, while a vice president might have carte blanche to order any item Office Depot sold. Office Depot's online prices were the same as its store prices; the company's strategy was to promote

Web sales on the basis of service, convenience, and lower customer costs for order processing and inventories. Customers reported that using the Web site cut their costs of issuing purchase orders and paying invoices by up to 80 percent, plus Office Depot's same-day or next-day delivery capability gave them the ability to reduce the amount of office supplies they kept in inventory. Starting in 1998, Office Depot launched Web sales to small businesses and individuals at OfficeDepot.com.

Web site sales cost Office Depot less than $1 per $100 of goods ordered, compared to about $2 for phone orders. And since Web sales eliminate the need for Office Depot customer service representatives having to key in transactions, order-entry errors are now virtually zero and returns have been cut by 50 percent. Billing is handled electronically.

In 1999, Office Depot's Web sales accounted for about $300 million in sales and an estimated $30 million in profits. Corporate Web sales were 20 percent of the company's sales to corporations and were expected to rise to over 30 percent of total corporate sales in 2000.

Office Depot's Web rivals—Officesupplies.com and Atyouroffice.com—had not captured as much as 5 percent of the office supply sales on the Web. The leaders in Web sales of office supplies were Office Depot, Staples, and OfficeMax—the same companies whose brick-and-mortar superstores were dominating the traditional retail market for office supplies.

Source: "Why Office Depot Loves the Net," *Business Week*, September 27, 1999, pp. EB-66, EB-68; and *Fortune*, November 8, 1999, p. 17.

buyers can shop anonymously with thousands of sellers, comparing prices and avoiding the potential of price gouging from sellers when they learn of a buyer's perhaps urgent need for supplies. The convenience and efficiency of online buying and selling of natural gas has proved so popular that Altra's e-market site has emerged as the leading place to trade natural gas liquids, handling about $12 billion in trades, equal to a 40 percent market share. Altra makes its money by charging a small commission on each trade.

Priceline.com creates an e-market for the buyers and sellers of airline tickets, hotel rooms, cars, mortgages, and other items. Airline ticket buyers submit a "guaranteed offer" (typically the lowest price they think they can get away with) to Priceline. Priceline compares the bids to confidential discounted fares on unsold seats supplied to it by participating airlines. If Priceline can buy a ticket from an airline and resell it to the buyer, it executes the transaction.

Springstreet, a San Francisco–based company, provides a free listing of some 6 million apartment rentals available in the United States, along with quotes on furniture,

illustration capsule 31

Fingerhut's Strategy to Provide Order-Fulfillment Services to E-tailers

While it is a fairly simple matter for Internet entrepreneurs to build a Web site and open a cyberstore, delivering the goods to buyers in a cost-efficient manner is a more complicated task. Traditional brick-and-mortar retailers that have set up Web sites have found it difficult to pack and ship the ordered goods efficiently and promptly (to meet the holiday gift deadlines of online shoppers, for instance). A number of delivery companies are vying for the shipping business of customers—FedEx, UPS, Airborne Express, and start-ups iShip and Tandata—but others are focusing on handling the warehousing, order-picking, and packaging activities needed to get the goods in the hands of shippers.

Fingerhut is a longtime catalog company that stumbled into the opportunity to serve the warehousing and packaging needs of e-commerce retailers. In the early 1990s, Fingerhut, anticipating a surge in sales from growing popularity of home-shopping TV channels, built a new distribution center in Tennessee. When much of the center's capacity went unused because of lower-than-expected TV sales, Fingerhut began offering its services to e-commerce retailers. A manager at the center observed that employees who picked orders from the shelves would be more efficient if they didn't have to travel all over the warehouse to fill each order separately. A computer program was written to group customer orders for particular items so that employees could obtain all the needed items while they were on a particular aisle of the warehouse. Equipment was put in place to sort the collected items into individual orders.

Since then, Fingerhut has further refined its logistics and packing systems. As orders come in via fax, telephone, and the Internet, Fingerhut's mainframe computers in Minnesota group the orders into similar goods and forward the results to warehouse personnel. The goods are retrieved from warehouse shelves, at which point a computer scans the dimensions of every item to determine the smallest possible box that can be used for shipping—since eliminating air space in packages increases the number of packages that a truck can carry. Packers put the items in the boxes, affix preprinted labels, put the boxes on conveyors that route them to the appropriate bay at the shipping dock for loading onto trucks. Red lasers scan each package on the conveyor to determine if the weight of the box matches the specifications on the label; if not, the box is automatically diverted to an inspection station, where personnel check whether an item was incorrectly omitted or added. Fingerhut uses a dedicated fleet of trucks to haul packages to local post offices, saving on postage costs.

Impressed by Fingerhut's capabilities and the manner in which it was reinventing its business strategy, Federated Department Stores acquired Fingerhut for $1.7 billion in early 1999. Fingerhut immediately took on responsibilities for shipping the online orders for all of Federated's department store chains—Macy's, Bloomingdale's, Rich's, and several others.

Going into 2000, Fingerhut was shipping all the online orders for over a dozen retailers other than Federated, including eToys, Pier 1, Levi Strauss, and Wal-Mart, plus handling its own catalog orders and the online orders of several dot-com affiliates in which it had ownership interests. It operated 4.5 million square feet of warehouse space. In late 1999, Fingerhut's CEO stated, "Our business is now the Internet. Fast-forward two years, and we'll be one of the big five players doing retailing there."

Source: The Wall Street Journal, September 3, 1999, pp. B1, B3; and *Fortune,* November 8, 1999, p. 117.

moving-truck rentals, and loan possibilities. It makes money by selling ads on its site, and collecting transaction fees and commissions from about 35 partners linked to its Web site, including truck rental companies, car insurance companies, and credit card companies.

Visa, American Express, and MasterCard provide credit card services to e-commerce firms—the Internet represents a potentially huge money-making opportunity for credit card companies because credit cards are the standard mode of payment for online business-to-consumer transactions. Exodus Communications, Dell Computer, and Micron Technology offer Web hosting services to business customers. Dow-Jones (the owner of *The Wall Street Journal*), McGraw-Hill (the parent of *Business*

Week and Standard & Poors), Quote.com, Briefing.com, Bloomberg, The Motley Fool, and numerous other enterprises are providers of financial and business news to electronic brokerage firms, America Online, the Microsoft Network (MSN), and various Web portals. Some information providers charge a fee for their service, while others do not in hopes of building awareness and goodwill among users and attracting subscribers for their more complete print versions. Greenfield Online is an Internet marketing research firm that gathers data on the behavior of a proprietary panel of over 1 million Internet users across the world; using its database, it can perform surveys of either prospective or actual users of particular products for clients, help them identify which of several ad alternatives communicates best, and guide clients in enhancing their Web sites. Greenfield's competitive advantage is being able to provide clients with timely and inexpensive empirical information compared to traditional marketing research firms that rely on telephone and mail surveys.

These examples are indicative of how companies are employing focus strategies and zeroing in on particular market niches, pursuing competitive advantage based on first-mover mastery of a particular technology, product superiority, unique product attributes, convenience and ease of use, speed, or more value for the money. As with other e-commerce businesses, *there is competitive value in being first to market with an innovative product or service* and trying to become the dominant market leader in a particular niche.

Business Models and Strategies for Media Companies and Content Providers

Media companies use intellectual capital to develop music, games, video, and text. Some companies charge subscription fees, like the Interactive Edition of *The Wall Street Journal;* others rely on a pay-per-use business model to generate revenues and profits. It is relatively inexpensive to produce digital content, so it is possible to realize a profit at a fairly modest volume of sales. Because a big fraction of Internet users are unwilling to pay for such content, the primary customers of media companies tend to be what are now called *content providers.*

Content providers like Yahoo! are mainly information aggregators and portals. Their business model is built around creating content that attracts users and then selling advertising to companies wanting to get a message to users of the content—the same model used by newspapers and the major TV networks. The bigger the number of viewers/readers/users (often referred to as "eyeballs"), the easier it is to sell advertising and the higher the rate that can be charged. Companies like Charles Schwab and America Online buy information from media companies, provide the information free, and then use the attraction of the information provided to sell subscriptions (AOL) or services (Charles Schwab and other online stock brokerages). However, content providers are increasingly offering site visitors an assortment of purchasing opportunities in an effort to boost revenues and profits through collecting transactions fees. Two key success factors for content providers are to create a sense of community and to deliver convenience and entertainment value as well as information. The strategy of Web portals like Yahoo!, Excite, and AltaVista to increase audience size involves going beyond search engine capability to include news, weather, stock quotes, stock portfolio tracking, e-mail, online calendars and address books, chat rooms, personalized Web pages, and shopping opportunities.

Excite@Home paid $780 million to acquire Bluemountain.com, the dominant leader in electronic greeting cards; at the Bluemountain.com Web site visitors can select a greeting card online, add a personal message, and e-mail the greeting directly to the recipient at no charge; cards are available in eight languages. The free e-greeting service attracted an average of 9 million unique users per month in 1999, giving Bluemountain.com a 65 percent share of the electronic-greeting-card market and an audience of loyal users that ranked third in size behind Amazon.com and eBay. Hallmark and American Greetings also offer free e-greeting services. Excite@Home's strategy in acquiring Bluemountain.com included:

- Selling advertising at the Bluemountain.com site.
- Offering users of the Bluemountain.com site a range of new services—e-mail, online calendars and address books, and purchasing opportunities.
- Using the site to promote and cross-sell both its @Home broadband Internet access service and the products marketed at its Excite Web portal and search engine site.

Cross-selling products available through Internet or traditional distribution channels is a strategy that is being used with increasing frequency by e-commerce enterprises seeking to grow Web site revenues and profits.

INTERNET STRATEGIES FOR TRADITIONAL BUSINESSES

With each passing day, it becomes clearer that the Internet has forever altered the way that companies and customers learn about each other, communicate, and transact business. Few businesses, if any, can escape the need to integrate use of the Internet into their operations. The only strategic issues are: how and to what extent Internet technology will be made a core part of a "traditional" company's business. While it is too early to be definitive about what strategies will and will not work for traditional businesses, the following e-commerce initiatives are becoming common:

> In the years to come, companies now on the fringes of the Internet economy will make the use of Internet technology such a core part of their business that the distinction between e-businesses and traditional businesses will become nonexistent.

- *Using Internet technology to communicate and collaborate closely with suppliers and distribution channel allies*—Such efforts entail installing information systems to gather real-time data from wholesale and retail customers sales and using the information to create a tight supply chain network all the way back to suppliers of parts and components. The benefits include streamlined communications and significant reductions in inventories and other operating costs.
- *Revamping company and industry value chains*—Companies will change how some activities are performed and will eliminate or bypass others.
- *Making greater use of build-to-order manufacturing and assembly*—The motor vehicle industry offers a prime opportunity for this.
- *Building systems to pick and pack products that are shipped individually*—Such systems are important for business-to-consumer companies that launch Web sites for online shopping.
- *Using the Internet to give both existing and potential customers another choice of how to interact with the company*—Traditional companies can benefit from allowing customers to choose how to communicate with the company, shop for product information, make purchases, or resolve customer service problems.

- *Adopting the Internet as an integral distribution channel for accessing new buyers and geographic markets*—However, the struggle that many traditional companies are having with a combination click-and-mortar strategy is the nettlesome issue of undermining their existing dealer networks if they initiate a big push for online sales. The partnerships that many manufacturers have forged with wholesale and retail dealers are central to their marketing and sales strategies; a manufacturer that aggressively pursues online sales to consumers is signaling weaker strategic commitment to its dealers and a willingness to cannibalize their sales and growth potential in order to protect its own flanks. Needless to say, taking advantage of online sales opportunities without making traditional dealers angry can be a very tricky road to negotiate.

- *Gathering real-time data on customer tastes and buying habits, doing real-time market research, and using the results to respond more precisely to customer needs and wants*—The behavior of Web surfers is a veritable gold mine of information.

KEY SUCCESS FACTORS IN E-COMMERCE

The preceding discussion indicates that fundamentally new business models and strategies are emerging to create value for customers and build shareholder wealth. E-commerce enterprises are building elaborate networks of suppliers, distributors, service providers, and customers who communicate, exchange data, and transact business via the Internet and other electronic media in ways that produce value for customers and for one another. The networks they are constructing are both integrated (to create tight value chain links) and fluid (to respond to fast-changing conditions). At this early stage in the evolution of the Internet economy, competing successfully seems to revolve around several key factors:

> A crucial key to e-commerce success is business model innovation.

- *An innovative business model*—One of the factors that sets e-commerce enterprises apart from traditional businesses is their use of new and different business models. This newness is only partly attributable to the creative nature of Internet entrepreneurs. The fact is that Internet technology is conducive to doing business in radically different and innovative ways—the rules of business in an Internet world are different from traditional business rules.

> The market has transitioned from a state where large businesses beat small businesses to a state where fast businesses beat slow businesses.

- *The capability to adjust the company's business model and strategy quickly in response to changing conditions and emerging opportunities*—Operating at Internet speed is essential because the pace of technological and market change is so fast. Rapidly evolving business models and strategies are thus the norm, not the exception.

- *Focusing on a limited number of competencies and performing a relatively specialized number of value chain activities*—The remaining value chain activities can be delegated to outside specialists. Outsourcing enhances organizational speed and flexibility, and it allows an enterprise to concentrate on what it can do best. Hence, there is merit in outsourcing many activities from specialists—designing and managing Web sites, manufacturing, warehousing, and shipping are prime examples.

- *Staying on the cutting edge of technology*—At this stage in the development of e-commerce, technological change is a dominant and pervasive driving force. No e-commerce enterprise can hope to succeed for long without moving first or early to incorporate state-of-the-art technology. Technological expertise has to be developed and maintained internally, provided by suppliers, or accessed via new acquisitions or strategic partnerships.

- *Using innovative marketing techniques that are efficient in reaching the targeted audience and effective in stimulating purchases or whatever other actions are needed to produce a profitable revenue stream*—Competition for "eyeballs" is already fierce and will grow even more so as the number of e-commerce enterprises rises—a 1999 study conducted by the University of Texas found that 2,000 e-commerce sites were being added every month. Marketing campaigns that just result in page views alone are seldom sufficient; the best marketing test is the ratio at which page views are converted into revenues and profits (the "look-to-buy" ratio). For example, in mid-1999 the traffic at Charles Schwab's Web site averaged 6 million page views per day and generated an estimated $4.7 million in revenues; in contrast, Yahoo!'s site traffic averaged 385 million page views daily but generated only about $1.7 million in revenues.

- *Engineering an electronic value chain that enables differentiation or lower costs or better value for the money*—Striving for sustainable competitive advantage is just as essential in e-commerce as in traditional markets. This means employing strategies and value chain approaches that hold potential for low-cost leadership, competitively valuable differentiating attributes, or a best-cost provider advantage. If a firm is positioning itself as a low-cost provider, then it must possess cost advantages in those activities it performs, and it must outsource the remaining activities to low-cost specialists. If an e-commerce company is going to differentiate itself on the basis of superior customer service, then it needs to concentrate on having an easy-to-use Web site, an array of functions and conveniences for customers to use at the Web site, adequate "Web reps," and logistical capabilities to deliver products in the time frame promised. If it is going to deliver more value for the money, then it must manage value chain activities in a manner calculated to yield a cost advantage in providing customers with upscale product attributes.

key|points

The Internet is an integrated network of banks of servers and high-speed computers, digital switches and routers, telecommunications equipment and lines, and individual users' computers. The major groups of e-commerce firms that comprise the supply side of the Internet economy include the makers of specialized communications components and equipment, providers of communications services, suppliers of computer components and computer hardware, developers of specialized software, and an assortment of e-commerce enterprises—business-to-business merchants, business-to-consumer-merchants, media companies, and content providers.

Growing use of e-commerce technology produces important shifts in an industry's competitive forces—intensifying rivalry, posing greater entry threats, shifting the balance of bargaining power both between sellers and their suppliers and between sellers and their customers, and providing a new basis for all kinds of seller–supplier and seller–customer collaboration. The Internet and e-commerce further have the effects of altering industry value chains and affecting a company's resource strengths and weaknesses. Technology, market conditions, and competitive pressures change rapidly, often in unexpected directions. The e-commerce world is a high-velocity environment in which companies are compelled to move quickly and late-movers are left in the dust.

The rush to capture the opportunities presented by the Internet economy is prompting entrepreneurial companies to employ innovative new business models for making money and radically different approaches to competitive strategy. A crucial key to e-commerce success is business model innovation. The business models and strategies of various types of participants in the Internet economy vary rather significantly. The manufacturers of Internet-related communications equipment, PC hardware, and PC components use a fairly traditional business model: selling their manufactured products to customers at prices that are attractively above costs. Suppliers of communications services have business models based on profitably selling their services for a fee—where the fee can be based on a flat rate per month or on volume of use. The business model of many developers of e-commerce software involves making money by investing resources (principally, the efforts of talented programmers) in designing and developing specialized software, then marketing and selling the software to other companies (e-commerce retailers, Internet service providers, content providers, and others) at what they hope will prove to be a profitable price per copy. However, some software developers that market transaction-based software have adopted a business model whereby they sell their software based on a small fee for every transaction rather than a set price per copy.

E-commerce retailers are utilizing perhaps the most revolutionary and unorthodox business model. A number of "e-tailers" sell products at cost (or below) and make money by selling advertising on the merchant's Web site. Other merchants apply the traditional model of purchasing goods from manufacturers and distributors, marketing them to buyers at their Web store, and filling orders from stocks held in inventory in their warehouse. Still others operate only a Web site for marketing and selling, outsourcing the distribution and delivery functions to warehousing and shipping specialists. There's also a variety of business models in play among the different providers of e-commerce services.

There are several important factors underlying the competitive success of e-commerce enterprises: (1) use of an innovative business model, (2) the capability to adjust the company's business model and strategy quickly in response to changing conditions and emerging opportunities, (3) focusing on a limited number of competencies and performing a relatively specialized number of value chain activities, (4) staying on the cutting edge of technology, (5) using innovative marketing techniques that are efficient in reaching the targeted audience and effective in stimulating purchases or whatever other actions are needed to produce a profitable revenue stream, and (6) engineering an electronic value chain that enables differentiation or lower costs or better value for the money.

suggested | readings

Evans, Philip and Thomas S. Wurster. "Getting Real about Virtual Commerce." *Harvard Business Review* 77, no. 6 (November–December 1999), pp. 84–94.

Ghosh, Shikhar. "Making Business Sense of the Internet." *Harvard Business Review* 76, no. 2 (March–April 1998), pp. 126–35.

Griffith, David A., and Jonathan W. Palmer. "Leveraging the Web for Corporate Success." *Business Horizons* 42, no. 1 (January–February 1999), pp. 3–10.

Gulati, Ranjay, and Jason Garino. "Get the Right Mix of Bricks and Clicks." *Harvard Business Review* 78, no. 3 (May–June 2000), pp. 107–14.

Hamel, Gary. "Bringing Silicon Valley Inside." *Harvard Business Review* 77, no. 5 (September–October 1999), pp. 70–84.

Kaplan, Steven, and Mohanbir Sawhney. "E-Hubs: The New B2B Marketplaces." *Harvard Business Review* 78, no. 3 (May–June, 2000), pp. 97–103.

Rosenoer, Johnathan; Douglas Armstrong; and J. Russell Gates. *The Clickable Corporation: Successful Strategies for Capturing the Internet Advantage.* New York: Free Press, 1999.

Tapscott, Don; David Ticoll; and Alex Lowy. *Digital Capital: Harnessing the Power of Business Webs.* Boston, MA: Harvard Business School Press, 2000.

Timmers, Paul. "Business Models for Electronic Markets," *Electronic Markets* (www.electronicmarkets.org/netacademy/publications.nsf/all_pk949) 8, no. 2 (July 1998).

chapter|eight

Tailoring Strategy to Fit Specific Industry and Company Situations

The best strategy for a given firm is ultimately a unique
construction reflecting its particular circumstances.

—Michael E. Porter

Competing in the marketplace is like war. You have injuries
and casualties, and the best strategy wins.

—John Collins

It is much better to make your own products obsolete than
allow a competitor to do it.

—Michael A. Cusamano and Richard W. Selby

I n Chapters 6 and 7 we examined strategies for competing in global and e-commerce environments. This chapter looks at the strategy-making task in nine other commonly encountered situations:

1. Companies competing in emerging industries of the future.
2. Companies competing in turbulent, high-velocity markets.
3. Companies competing in mature, slow-growth industries.
4. Companies competing in stagnant or declining industries.
5. Companies competing in fragmented industries.
6. Companies pursuing rapid growth.
7. Companies in industry leadership positions.
8. Companies in runner-up positions.
9. Companies in competitively weak positions or plagued by crisis conditions.

We selected these situations to shed still more light on the whys and hows of matching strategy (1) to industry and competitive conditions and (2) to a company's own resource strengths and weaknesses, competitive capabilities, opportunities and threats, and market position. When you finish this chapter, you will have a strong appreciation for why it is so important for managers to customize a company's strategy and you'll have a better idea of how to weigh the various external and internal considerations and balance the pros and cons of the various strategic options that are open to a company.

STRATEGIES FOR COMPETING IN EMERGING INDUSTRIES OF THE FUTURE

An *emerging industry* is one in the early, formative stage. Examples include wireless Internet communications, high-definition TV, assisted living for the elderly, online education, and electronic banking. Most companies racing against rivals to establish a strong foothold in an emerging industry of the future are in a start-up mode; they are perfecting technology, adding people, acquiring or constructing facilities, gearing up operations, and trying to broaden distribution and gain buyer acceptance. The business models and strategies of companies in an emerging industry are unproven—what appears to be a promising business concept and strategy may stall out, never passing the test of generating attractive bottom-line profitability. Often, there are important product design problems and technological problems that remain to be worked out.

Competing in emerging industries thus presents managers with some unique strategy-making challenges:[1]

- Because the market is new and unproven, there may be much speculation and many opinions about how it will function, how fast it will grow, and how big it will get. The little historical data available is virtually useless in making sales and profit projections. There's lots of guesswork about how rapidly buyers will be attracted to use the product and how much they will be willing to pay for it. For example, digital video disc (DVD) players were much slower to catch on than expected. Currently, there is great uncertainty about how quickly the demand for high-definition TV sets will grow once the law requiring all U.S. TV stations to broadcast digital programs goes into effect in 2003.

- In many cases, much of the technological know-how underlying the products of emerging industries is proprietary and closely guarded, having been developed in-house by pioneering firms; patents and unique technical expertise are key factors in securing competitive advantage. In other cases, the technology is multifaceted, entailing parallel or collaborative efforts on the part of several enterprises and perhaps competing technological approaches.

- Often, there is no consensus regarding which of several competing technologies will win out or which product attributes will prove decisive in winning buyer favor. Until market forces sort these things out, wide differences in product quality and performance are typical. Rivalry therefore centers on each firm's efforts to get the market to ratify its own strategic approach to technology, product design, marketing, and distribution.

- Entry barriers tend to be relatively low, even for entrepreneurial start-up companies. Large, well-known, opportunity-seeking companies with ample resources and competitive capabilities are likely to enter if the industry has promise for explosive growth or if its emergence threatens their present business. For instance, many traditional local telephone companies, seeing the potent threat of wireless communications technology, have opted to enter the mobile communications business in one way or another.

- Strong experience curve effects may be present, allowing significant cost and price reductions as volume builds.

- Since in an emerging industry all buyers are first-time users, the marketing task is to induce initial purchase and to overcome customer concerns about product features, performance reliability, and conflicting claims of rival firms.

---

[1]Michael E. Porter, *Competitive Strategy* (New York: Free Press, 1980), pp. 216–23.

- Many potential buyers expect first-generation products to be rapidly improved, so they delay purchase until technology and product design mature.

- Sometimes, firms have trouble securing ample supplies of raw materials and components (until suppliers gear up to meet the industry's needs).

- Undercapitalized companies, finding themselves short of funds to support needed R&D and get through several lean years until the product catches on, end up merging with competitors or being acquired by financially strong outsiders looking to invest in a growth market.

The two critical strategic issues confronting firms in an emerging industry are (1) how to finance initial operations until sales and revenues take off, and (2) what market segments and competitive advantages to go after in trying to secure a front-runner position.[2] Competitive strategies keyed either to low cost or differentiation are usually viable. Focusing makes good sense when resources and capabilities are limited and the industry has too many technological frontiers or too many buyer segments to pursue at once. The lack of established "rules of the game" gives industry participants considerable freedom to experiment with a variety of different strategic approaches. Nonetheless, a firm with solid resource capabilities, an appealing business model, and a good strategy has a golden opportunity to shape the rules and establish itself as the recognized industry front-runner.

Dealing with all the risks and opportunities of an emerging industry is one of the most challenging business strategy problems. To be successful in an emerging industry, companies usually have to pursue one or more of the following strategic avenues:[3]

1. Try to win the early race for industry leadership with risk-taking entrepreneurship and a bold, creative strategy. Broad or focused differentiation strategies keyed to technological or product superiority typically offer the best chance for early competitive advantage.

2. Push to perfect the technology, to improve product quality, and to develop additional attractive performance features.

3. As technological uncertainty clears and a dominant technology emerges, adopt it quickly. (However, while there's merit in trying to be the industry standard bearer on technology and to pioneer the dominant product design, firms have to beware of betting too heavily on their own preferred technological approach or product design—especially when there are many competing technologies, R&D is costly, and technological developments can quickly move in surprising new directions.)

4. Form strategic alliances with key suppliers to gain access to specialized skills, technological capabilities, and critical materials or components.

5. Acquire or form alliances with companies that have related or complementary technological expertise so as to outcompete rivals on the basis of technological superiority.

6. Try to capture any first-mover advantages associated with early commitments to promising technologies, allying with the most capable suppliers, expanding product selection, improving styling, capturing experience curve effects, and getting well positioned in new distribution channels.

> Strategic success in an emerging industry calls for bold entrepreneurship, a willingness to pioneer and take risks, an intuitive feel for what buyers will like, quick response to new developments, and opportunistic strategy making.

---

[2]Charles W. Hofer and Dan Schendel, *Strategy Formulation: Analytical Concepts* (St. Paul, MN: West Publishing, 1978), pp. 164–65.

[3]Phillip Kotler, *Marketing Management,* 5th ed. (Englewood Cliffs, NJ: Prentice Hall, 1984), p. 366, and Porter, *Competitive Strategy,* chapter 10.

7. Pursue new customer groups, new user applications, and entry into new geographical areas (perhaps utilizing strategic partnerships or joint ventures if financial resources are constrained).

8. Make it easy and cheap for first-time buyers to try the industry's first-generation product. Then as the product becomes familiar to a wide portion of the market, begin to shift the advertising emphasis from creating product awareness to increasing frequency of use and building brand loyalty.

9. Use price cuts to attract the next layer of price-sensitive buyers into the market.

The short-term value of winning the early race for growth and market share leadership has to be balanced against the longer-range need to build a durable competitive edge and a defendable market position.[4] Well-financed outsiders are certain to move in with aggressive strategies as industry sales start to take off and the perceived risk of investing in the industry lessens. A rush of new entrants, attracted by the growth and profit potential, may crowd the market and force industry consolidation to a smaller number of players. Resource-rich latecomers, aspiring to industry leadership, may be able to become major players by acquiring and merging the operations of weaker competitors and then launching strategic offensives to build market share and gain quick brand-name recognition. Strategies must be aimed at competing for the long haul; often, this means sacrificing some degree of short-term profitability in order to invest in the resources, capabilities, and market recognition needed to sustain early successes.

> The early leaders in an emerging industry cannot afford to relax and rest on their laurels; they must drive forward to strengthen their resource capabilities and build a position strong enough to ward off newcomers and compete successfully for the long haul.

Young companies in fast-growing markets face three strategic hurdles: (1) managing their own rapid expansion, (2) defending against competitors trying to horn in on their success, and (3) building a competitive position extending beyond their initial product or market. Up-and-coming companies can help their cause by selecting knowledgeable members for their boards of directors, by hiring entrepreneurial managers with experience in guiding young businesses through the start-up and takeoff stages, by concentrating on out-innovating the competition, and perhaps by merging with or acquiring another firm to gain added expertise and a stronger resource base.

STRATEGIES FOR COMPETING IN TURBULENT, HIGH-VELOCITY MARKETS

More and more companies are finding themselves in industry situations characterized by rapid-fire technological change, short product life cycles (because of the pace with which next-generation products are being introduced), entry of important new rivals into the marketplace, frequent launches of new competitive moves by rivals (including mergers and acquisitions to build a stronger, if not dominant, market position), and rapidly evolving customer requirements and expectations—all occurring at once. Since news of this or that important competitive development is a daily happening, it is an imposing task just to monitor and assess developing events. High-velocity change is plainly the prevailing condition in personal computer hardware and software, video games, networking, wireless telecommunications, medical equipment, biotechnology, prescription drugs, and in the growing number of industries being swept along by the torrential changes in the whole arena of cyberspace.

> High-velocity change is the striking feature of contemporary business.

---

[4]Hofer and Schendel, *Strategy Formulation*, pp. 164–65.

The central strategy-making challenge in a turbulent market environment is managing change.[5] As illustrated in Figure 8.1, a company can assume any of three strategic postures in dealing with high-velocity change:[6]

- *It can react to change.* For instance, it can respond to a rival's new product with a better product. It can counter an unexpected shift in buyer tastes and buyer demand by redesigning or repackaging its product, or shifting its advertising emphasis to different product attributes. Reacting is a defensive strategy and is therefore unlikely to create fresh opportunity, but it is nonetheless a necessary component in a company's arsenal of options.

- *It can anticipate change.* Anticipation entails looking ahead to analyze what is likely to occur and then preparing and positioning for that future. It entails studying buyer behavior, buyer needs, and buyer expectations to get insight into how the market will evolve, then lining up ahead of time the necessary production and distribution capabilities. Like reacting to change, anticipating change is still fundamentally defensive in that forces outside the enterprise are in the driver's seat. Anticipation, however, can open up new opportunities and thus is a better way to manage change than just pure reaction.

- *It can lead change.* Leading change entails initiating the market and competitive forces that others must react and respond to—*it is an offensive strategy aimed at putting a company in the driver's seat.* Leading change means being first to market with an important new product or service. It means being the technological leader, rushing next generation products to market ahead of rivals, and having products whose features and attributes shape customer preferences and expectations. It means proactively seeking to shape the rules of the game.

> Reacting to change and anticipating change are basically defensive postures; leading change is an offensive posture.

As a practical matter, a company's approach to managing change should, ideally, incorporate all three postures (though not in the same proportion). The best-performing companies in high-velocity markets consistently seek to lead change with proactive strategies. Even so, an environment of relentless change makes it incumbent on any company to anticipate and prepare for the future and react in timely manner to unpredictable or uncontrollable new developments.

Competitive success in fast-changing markets tends to hinge on a company's ability to improvise, experiment, adapt, reinvent, and regenerate as market and competitive conditions shift rapidly and sometimes unpredictably.[7] It has to constantly reshape its strategy and its basis for competitive advantage. While the process of altering offensive and defensive moves every few months or weeks to keep the overall strategy closely matched to changing conditions is inefficient, the alternative—a fast-obsolescing strategy—is worse. The following strategic moves seem to offer the best payoffs:

> Industry leaders are proactive agents of change, not reactive followers and analyzers. Moreover, they improvise, experiment, and adapt rapidly.

---

[5]The strategic issues companies must address in fast-changing market environments are thoroughly explored in Richard A. D'Aveni, *Hyper-Competition: Managing the Dynamics of Strategic Maneuvering* (New York: Free Press, 1994). See also Richard A. D'Aveni, "Coping with Hypercompetition: Utilizing the New 7S's Framework," *Academy of Management Executive* 9, no. 3 (August 1995), pp. 45–56; and Bala Chakravarthy, "A New Strategy Framework for Coping with Turbulence," *Sloan Management Review* (Winter 1997), pp. 69–82.

[6]Shona L. Brown and Kathleen M. Eisenhardt, *Competing on the Edge: Strategy as Structured Chaos* (Boston: Harvard Business School Press, 1998), pp. 4–5.

[7]Ibid., p. 4.

figure 8.1   **Meeting the Challenge of High-Velocity Change**

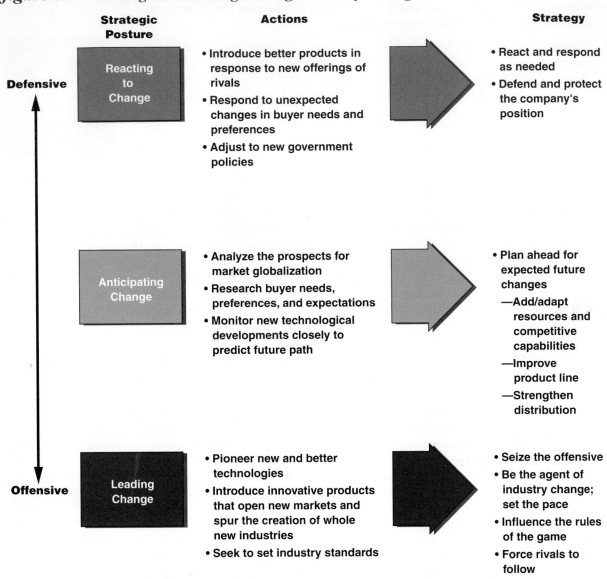

Source: Adapted from Shona L. Brown and Kathleen M. Eisenhardt, *Competing on the Edge: Strategy as Structured Chaos* (Boston: Harvard Business School Press, 1998) p. 5.

1. *Invest aggressively in R&D to stay on the leading edge of technological know-how.* Translating technological advances into innovative new products (and remaining close on the heels of whatever advances and features are pioneered by rivals) is a necessity in industries where technology is the primary driver of change. But it is often desirable to focus the R&D effort in a few critical areas not only to avoid stretching the company's resources too thin but also to deepen the firm's expertise, master the technology, fully capture learning-curve effects, and become the dominant leader in a particular technology or product category.[8] When a fast-evolving market environment

---

[8]For insight into building competitive advantage through R&D and technological innovation, see Shaker A. Zahra, Sarah Nash, and Deborah J. Bickford, "Transforming Technological Pioneering into Competitive Advantage," *Academy of Management Executive* 9, no. 1 (February 1995), pp. 32–41.

entails many technological areas and product categories, competitors have little choice but to employ some type of focus strategy and concentrate on being the leader in a particular product/technology category.

2. *Develop and maintain the organizational capability to respond quickly to the moves of rivals and surprising new developments.* Because no company can predict or foresee all of the changes that will occur, it is crucial to have the organizational capability to react, respond, and improvise quickly. This means shifting resources internally, adapting existing competencies and capabilities, creating new competencies and capabilities, and not falling far behind rivals. Companies that are habitual late-movers are destined to be industry also-rans.

3. *Rely on strategic partnerships with outside suppliers and with companies making tie-in products.* In many high-velocity industries, technology is branching off to create so many new technological paths and product categories that no company has the resources and competencies to pursue them all. Specialization (to promote the necessary technical depth) and focus strategies (to preserve organizational agility and leverage the firm's expertise) are desirable strategies. Companies build their competitive position not just by strengthening their own internal resource base but also by partnering with those suppliers making state-of-the-art parts and components and by collaborating closely with both the developers of related technologies and the makers of tie-in products. For example, personal computer companies like Gateway, Dell, Compaq, and Acer rely heavily on the makers of faster chips, the makers of monitors and screens, the makers of built-in faxes and modems, and software developers for innovative advances in PCs. None of the PC makers have done much in the way of integrating backward into parts and components because they have learned that the most effective way to provide PC users with a state-of-the-art product is to outsource the latest, most advanced components from technologically sophisticated suppliers who make it their business to stay on the cutting edge of their specialization and who can achieve economies of scale by mass-producing components for many PC assemblers. An outsourcing strategy also allows a company the flexibility to replace suppliers that fall behind on technology or product features or that cease to be competitive on price. The managerial challenge here is to strike a good balance between building a rich internal resource base that, on the one hand, keeps the firm from being at the mercy of its suppliers and allies and, on the other hand, maintains organizational agility by relying on the resources and expertise of capable (and perhaps "best-in-world") outsiders.

4. *Initiate fresh actions every few months, not just when a competitive response is needed.* In some sense, change is partly triggered by the passage of time rather than solely by the occurrence of events. A company can be proactive by making *time-paced moves*—introducing a new or improved product every four months, rather than when the market tapers off or a rival introduces a next-generation model.[9] Similarly, a company can expand into a new geographic market every six months rather than waiting for a new market opportunity to present itself; it can also refresh existing brands every two years rather than waiting until their popularity wanes. The keys to successfully using time-pacing as a strategic weapon are choosing intervals that make sense internally and externally, establishing an internal organizational rhythm for change, and choreographing the transitions. 3M Corporation has long pursued an objective of having 25 percent of its revenues come from products less than four years old, a force that established the rhythm of change and created a relentless push for new products. Recently, the firm's

---

[9]Brown and Eisenhardt, *Competing on the Edge,* pp. 14–15. See, also, Kathleen M. Eisenhardt and Shona L. Brown, "Time Pacing: Competing in Markets That Won't Stand Still," *Harvard Business Review* 76, no. 2 (March–April 1998), pp. 59–69.

CEO upped the tempo of change at 3M by increasing the percentage from 25 percent to 30 percent.

5. *Keep the company's products and services fresh and exciting enough to stand out in the midst of all the change that is taking place.* One of the risks of rapid change is that products and even companies can get lost in the shuffle of events. The marketing challenge here is to keep the firm's products and services in the limelight and, further, to keep them innovative and well matched to the changes that are occurring in the marketplace.

> In fast-paced markets, in-depth expertise, speed, agility, innovativeness, opportunism, and resource flexibility are critical organizational capabilities.

Cutting-edge know-how and first-to-market capabilities are very valuable competitive assets in fast-evolving markets. Moreover, the action-packed competition demands that a company have quick reaction times and flexible, adaptable resources—organizational agility is a huge competitive asset. Even so, companies will make mistakes and some things a company does are going to work better than others. When a company's strategy doesn't seem to be working well, it has to quickly regroup—probing, experimenting, improvising, and trying again and again until it finds something that strikes the right chord with buyers and that puts it in sync with market and competitive realities.

STRATEGIES FOR COMPETING IN MATURING INDUSTRIES

A maturing industry is one that is moving from rapid growth to significantly slower growth. An industry is said to be mature when nearly all potential buyers are already users of the industry's products; market demand thus consists mainly of replacement sales to existing users, with growth hinging on the industry's ability to attract new buyers and convince existing buyers to up their usage. Consumer goods industries that are mature typically have a growth rate under 5 percent—roughly equal to the growth of the customer base or economy as a whole.

An industry's transition to maturity does not begin on an easily predicted schedule. Industry maturity can be forestalled by the emergence of new technological advances, product innovations, or other driving forces that keep rejuvenating market demand. Nonetheless, when growth rates do slacken, the onset of market maturity usually produces fundamental changes in the industry's competitive environment:[10]

1. *Slowing growth in buyer demand generates more head-to-head competition for market share.* Firms that want to continue on a rapid-growth track start looking for ways to take customers away from competitors. Outbreaks of price cutting, increased advertising, and other aggressive tactics to gain market share are common.

2. *Buyers become more sophisticated, often driving a harder bargain on repeat purchases.* Since buyers have experience with the product and are familiar with competing brands, they are better able to evaluate different brands and can use their knowledge to negotiate a better deal with sellers.

3. *Competition often produces a greater emphasis on cost and service.* As sellers all begin to offer the product attributes buyers prefer, buyer choices increasingly depend on which seller offers the best combination of price and service.

---

[10]Porter, *Competitive Strategy,* pp. 238–40.

4. *Firms have a "topping-out" problem in adding new facilities.* Reduced rates of industry growth mean slowdowns in capacity expansion for manufacturers and slowdowns in new store growth for retail chains. With slower industry growth, adding too much capacity too soon can create oversupply conditions that adversely affect company profits well into the future.

5. *Product innovation and new end-use applications are harder to come by.* Producers find it increasingly difficult to create new product features, find further uses for the product, and sustain buyer excitement.

6. *International competition increases.* Growth-minded domestic firms start to seek out sales opportunities in foreign markets. Some companies, looking for ways to cut costs, relocate plants to countries with lower wage rates. Greater product standardization and diffusion of technological know-how reduce entry barriers and make it possible for enterprising foreign companies to become serious market contenders in more countries. Industry leadership passes to companies that succeed in building strong competitive positions in most of the world's major geographic markets and in winning the biggest global market shares.

7. *Industry profitability falls temporarily or permanently.* Slower growth, increased competition, more sophisticated buyers, and occasional periods of overcapacity put pressure on industry profit margins. Weaker, less-efficient firms are usually the hardest hit.

8. *Stiffening competition induces a number of mergers and acquisitions among former competitors, drives the weakest firms out of the industry, and produces industry consolidation in general.* Inefficient firms and firms with weak competitive strategies can achieve respectable results in a fast-growing industry with booming sales. But the intensifying competition that accompanies industry maturity exposes competitive weakness and throws second- and third-tier competitors into a survival-of-the-fittest contest.

Strategic Moves in Maturing Industries

As the new competitive character of industry maturity begins to hit full force, any of several strategic moves can strengthen a firm's competitive position: pruning the product line, improving value chain efficiency, trimming costs, accelerating sales promotion efforts, expanding internationally, and acquiring struggling competitors.[11]

Pruning Marginal Products and Models   A wide selection of models, features, and product options sometimes has competitive value during the growth stage, when buyers' needs are still evolving. But such variety can become too costly as price competition stiffens and profit margins are squeezed. Maintaining many product versions works against achieving design, parts inventory, and production economies at the manufacturing levels and can increase inventory stocking costs for distributors and retailers. In addition, the prices of slow-selling versions may not cover their true costs. Pruning marginal products from the line opens the door for cost savings and permits more concentration on items whose margins are highest and/or where a firm has a competitive advantage.

More Emphasis on Value Chain Innovation   Efforts to "reinvent" the industry value chain can have a fourfold payoff: lower costs, better product or service

---

[11]The following discussion draws on Porter, *Competitive Strategy,* pp. 241–46.

quality, greater capability to turn out multiple or customized product versions, and shorter design-to-market cycles. Manufacturers can mechanize high-cost activities, redesign production lines to improve labor efficiency, build flexibility into the assembly process so that customized product versions can be easily produced, and increase use of advanced technology (robotics, computerized controls, and automatic guided vehicles). Suppliers of parts and components, manufacturers, and distributors can collaborate on the use of Internet technology and e-commerce techniques to streamline various value chain activities and implement cost-saving innovations.

A Stronger Focus on Cost Reduction   Stiffening price competition gives firms extra incentive to drive down unit costs. Company cost-reduction initiatives can cover a broad front. Some of the most frequently pursued options are pushing suppliers for better prices, implementing tighter supply chain management practices, cutting low-value activities out of the value chain, developing more economical product designs, reengineering internal processes using e-commerce technology, and shifting to more economical distribution arrangements.

Increasing Sales to Present Customers   In a mature market, growing by taking customers away from rivals may not be as appealing as expanding sales to existing customers. Strategies to increase purchases by existing customers can involve providing complementary items and ancillary services, and finding more ways for customers to use the product. Convenience stores, for example, have boosted average sales per customer by adding video rentals, automated teller machines, gasoline pumps, and deli counters.

Purchasing Rival Firms at Bargain Prices   Sometimes a firm can acquire the facilities and assets of struggling rivals quite cheaply. Bargain-priced acquisitions can help create a low-cost position if they also present opportunities for greater operating efficiency. In addition, an acquired firm's customer base can provide expanded market coverage and opportunities for greater scale economies. The most desirable acquisitions are those that will significantly enhance the acquiring firm's competitive strength.

Expanding Internationally   As its domestic market matures, a firm may seek to enter foreign markets where attractive growth potential still exists and competitive pressures are not so strong. Many multinational companies are expanding into such emerging-country markets as China, India, Brazil, Argentina, and Malaysia, where the long-term growth prospects are quite attractive. Strategies to expand internationally also make sense when a domestic firm's skills, reputation, and product are readily transferable to foreign markets. For example, even though the U.S. market for soft drinks is mature, Coca-Cola has remained a growth company by upping its efforts to penetrate foreign markets where soft-drink sales are expanding rapidly.

Building New or More Flexible Capabilities   The stiffening pressures of competition in a maturing or already mature market can often be combated by strengthening the company's resource base and competitive capabilities. This can mean adding new competencies or capabilities, deepening existing competencies to make them harder to imitate, or striving to make core competencies more adaptable to changing customer requirements and expectations. Microsoft has responded to competitors' challenges by expanding its already large cadre of talented programmers. Chevron has developed a best-practices discovery team and a best-practices resource map to enhance the speed and effectiveness with which it is able to transfer efficiency improvements from one oil refinery to another.

Strategic Pitfalls in Maturing Industries

Perhaps the biggest strategic mistake a company can make as an industry matures is steering a middle course between low cost, differentiation, and focusing—blending efforts to achieve low cost with efforts to incorporate differentiating features and efforts to focus on a limited target market. Such strategic compromises typically result in a firm ending up stuck in the middle, with a fuzzy strategy, too little commitment to winning a competitive advantage, an average image with buyers, and little chance of springing into the ranks of the industry leaders.

Other strategic pitfalls include being slow to adapt existing competencies and capabilities to defend against stiffening competitive pressures, concentrating more on protecting short-term profitability than on building or maintaining long-term competitive position, waiting too long to respond to price cutting by rivals, overexpanding in the face of slowing growth, overspending on advertising and sales promotion efforts in a losing effort to combat the growth slowdown, and failing to pursue cost reduction soon enough or aggressively enough.

> One of the greatest strategic mistakes a firm can make in a maturing industry is pursuing a compromise between low-cost, differentiation, and focusing such that it ends up "stuck in the middle," with a fuzzy strategy, an average image, an ill-defined market identity, no competitive advantage, and little prospect of becoming an industry leader.

STRATEGIES FOR FIRMS IN STAGNANT OR DECLINING INDUSTRIES

Many firms operate in industries where demand is growing more slowly than the economywide average or is even declining. Although harvesting the business to obtain the greatest cash flow, selling out, or preparing for closedown are obvious end-game strategies for uncommitted competitors with dim long-term prospects, strong competitors may be able to achieve good performance in a stagnant market environment.[12] Stagnant demand by itself is not enough to make an industry unattractive. Selling out may or may not be practical, and closing operations is always a last resort.

Businesses competing in stagnant or declining industries must resign themselves to performance targets consistent with available market opportunities. Cash flow and return-on-investment criteria are more appropriate than growth-oriented performance measures, but sales and market-share growth are by no means ruled out. Strong competitors may be able to take sales from weaker rivals, and the acquisition or exit of weaker firms creates opportunities for the remaining companies to capture greater market share.

In general, companies that succeed in stagnant industries employ one of three strategic themes:[13]

1. *Pursue a focused strategy aimed at the fastest-growing market segments within the industry.* Stagnant or declining markets, like other markets, are composed of numerous segments or niches. Frequently, one or more of these segments is growing rapidly, despite stagnation in the industry as a whole. An astute competitor who

> Achieving competitive advantage in stagnant or declining industries usually requires pursuing one of three competitive approaches: focusing on growing market segments within the industry, differentiating on the basis of better quality and frequent product innovation, or becoming a lower cost producer.

[12]R. G. Hamermesh and S. B. Silk, "How to Compete in Stagnant Industries," *Harvard Business Review* 57, no. 5 (September–October 1979), p. 161.
[13]Ibid., p. 162.

zeroes in on fast-growing segments and does a first-rate job of meeting the needs of buyers comprising these segments can often escape stagnating sales and profits and even gain decided competitive advantage. For instance, both Ben & Jerry's and Häagen-Dazs have been successful focusing on the growing luxury or super-premium segment of the otherwise stagnant market for ice cream; revenue growth and profit margins are substantially higher for high-end ice creams sold in super-markets and in scoop shops than is the case in the other market segments.

2. *Stress differentiation based on quality improvement and product innovation.* Either enhanced quality or innovation can rejuvenate demand by creating important new growth segments or inducing buyers to trade up. Successful product innovation opens up an avenue for competing besides meeting or beating rivals' prices. Differentiation based on successful innovation has the additional advantage of being difficult and expensive for rival firms to imitate. Sony has built a solid business selling high-quality TVs, an industry where market demand has been relatively flat in the world's industrialized nations for some years.

3. *Strive to drive costs down and become the industry's low-cost leader.* Companies in stagnant industries can improve profit margins and return on investment by pursuing innovative cost reduction year after year. Potential cost-saving actions include (*a*) cutting marginally beneficial activities out of the value chain, (*b*) outsourcing functions and activities that can be performed more cheaply by outsiders, (*c*) redesigning internal business processes to exploit cost-reducing e-commerce technologies, (*d*) consolidating underutilized production facilities, (*e*) adding more distribution channels to ensure the unit volume needed for low-cost production, (*f*) closing low-volume, high-cost retail outlets, and (*g*) pruning marginal products from the firm's offerings. Nucor Steel has been one of the most successful steel producers in the United States for the past decade because of its innovative production methods and low-cost operating culture; Nucor is widely considered to be one of the most efficient producers of steel products in the world and the low-cost leader in the North American market.

These three strategic themes are not mutually exclusive.[14] Introducing innovative versions of a product can *create* a fast-growing market segment. Similarly, relentless pursuit of greater operating efficiencies permits price reductions that create price-conscious growth segments. Note that all three themes are spinoffs of the generic competitive strategies, adjusted to fit the circumstances of a tough industry environment. The most attractive declining industries are those in which sales are eroding only slowly, there is large built-in demand, and some profitable niches remain.

The most common strategic mistakes companies make in stagnating or declining markets are (1) getting trapped in a profitless war of attrition, (2) diverting too much cash out of the business too quickly (thus further eroding performance), and (3) being overly optimistic about the industry's future and spending too much on improvements in anticipation that things will get better.

Illustration Capsule 32 describes the creative approach taken by Yamaha to reverse the declining market demand for pianos.

---

[14]Ibid., p. 165.

illustration capsule 32
Yamaha's Strategy in the Stagnant Piano Industry

For some years now, worldwide demand for pianos has been declining—in the mid-1980s the decline was 10 percent annually. Modern-day parents have not put the same stress on music lessons for their children as prior generations of parents did. In an effort to see if it could revitalize its piano business, Yamaha conducted a market research survey to learn what use was being made of pianos in households that owned one. The survey revealed that the overwhelming majority of the 40 million pianos in American, European, and Japanese households were seldom used. In most cases, the reasons the piano had been purchased no longer applied. Children had either stopped taking piano lessons or were grown and had left the household; adult household members played their pianos sparingly, if at all—only a small percentage were accomplished piano players. Most pianos were serving as a piece of fine furniture and were in good condition despite not being tuned regularly. The survey also confirmed that the income levels of piano owners were well above average.

Beginning in the late 1980s, Yamaha's piano strategists saw the idle pianos in these upscale households as a potential market opportunity. The strategy that emerged entailed marketing an attachment that would convert the piano into an old-fashioned automatic player piano capable of playing a wide number of selections recorded on disks. Concurrently, Yamaha introduced Disklavier, an upright acoustic player piano model that could record and play back performances up to 90 minutes long, making it simple to monitor student progress.

Over the past 15 years, Yamaha has introduced a host of Disklavier pianos—grand pianos, minigrand, upright, and console designs in a variety of styles and finishes. It has partnered with recording artists and music studios to make thousands of digital disks available for Yamaha piano owners, allowing them to enjoy concert-caliber performances in their home. And it has created a global music education program for both teachers and students. Together, these efforts have helped rejuvenate and sustain Yamaha's piano business.

STRATEGIES FOR COMPETING IN FRAGMENTED INDUSTRIES

A number of industries are populated by hundreds, even thousands, of small and medium-sized companies, many privately held and none with a substantial share of total industry sales.[15] The standout competitive feature of a fragmented industry is the absence of market leaders with king-sized market shares or widespread buyer recognition. Examples of fragmented industries include book publishing, landscaping and plant nurseries, real estate development, convenience stores, banking, health and medical care, mail order catalog sales, computer software development, custom printing, kitchen cabinets, trucking, auto repair, restaurants and fast food, public accounting, apparel manufacture and apparel retailing, paperboard boxes, hotels and motels, and furniture.

Any of several reasons can account for why the supply side of an industry is fragmented:

● Market demand is so extensive and so diverse that very large numbers of firms can easily coexist trying to accommodate the range and variety of buyer preferences and requirements and to cover all the needed geographic locations. This is true in

---

[15]This section is summarized from Porter, *Competitive Strategy,* Chapter 9.

the hotel and restaurant industry in New York City, London, or Tokyo, and the market for apparel. Likewise, there is ample room in the marketplace for numerous auto repair outlets, gasoline and convenience store retailers, and real estate firms.

● Low entry barriers allow small firms to enter quickly and cheaply.

● An absence of scale economies permits small companies to compete on an equal cost footing with larger firms.

● Buyers require relatively small quantities of customized products (as in business forms, interior design, kitchen cabinets, and advertising). Because demand for any particular product version is small, sales volumes are not adequate to support producing, distributing, or marketing on a scale that yields advantages to a large firm.

● The market for the industry's product or service is becoming more global, putting companies in more and more countries in the same competitive market arena (as in apparel manufacture).

● The technologies embodied in the industry's value chain are exploding into so many new areas and along so many different paths that specialization is essential just to keep abreast in any one area of expertise.

● The industry is young and crowded with aspiring contenders, with no firm having yet developed the resource base, competitive capabilities, and market recognition to command a significant market share (as in online business-to-consumer retailing via the Internet).

Some fragmented industries consolidate over time as growth slows and the market matures. The stiffer competition that accompanies slower growth produces a shake-out of weak, inefficient firms and a greater concentration of larger, more visible sellers. Others remain atomistic because it is inherent in the nature of their businesses. And still others remain stuck in a fragmented state because existing firms lack the resources or ingenuity to employ a strategy powerful enough to drive industry consolidation.

Competitive rivalry in fragmented industries can vary from moderately strong to fierce. Low barriers tend to make entry of new competitors an ongoing threat. Competition from substitutes may or may not be a major factor. The relatively small size of companies in fragmented industries puts them in a relatively weak position to bargain with powerful suppliers and buyers, although sometimes they can become members of a cooperative formed for the purpose of using their combined leverage to negotiate better sales and purchase terms. In such an environment, the best a firm can expect is to cultivate a loyal customer base and grow a bit faster than the industry average. Competitive strategies based either on low cost or product differentiation are viable unless the industry's product is highly standardized or a commodity (like sand, concrete blocks, paperboard boxes). Focusing on a well-defined market niche or buyer segment usually offers more competitive advantage potential than striving for broad market appeal. Suitable competitive strategy options in a fragmented industry include

> In fragmented industries competitors usually have wide enough strategic latitude (1) to either compete broadly or focus and (2) to pursue a low-cost, differentiation-based, or best-cost competitive advantage.

● *Constructing and operating "formula" facilities*—This strategic approach is frequently employed in restaurant and retailing businesses operating at multiple locations. It involves constructing standardized outlets in favorable locations at minimum cost and then operating them superefficiently. Tricon Global Restaurants (with its Pizza Hut, Taco Bell, and Kentucky Fried Chicken restaurants), The Home Depot, and 7-Eleven pursue this strategy.

● *Becoming a low-cost operator*—When price competition is intense and profit margins are under constant pressure, companies can stress no-frills operations featuring low overhead, high-productivity/low-cost labor, lean capital budgets, and dedicated pursuit of total operating efficiency. Successful low-cost producers in a fragmented industry can play the price-discounting game and still earn profits above the industry average. Many e-retailers compete on the basis of superlow prices; so do local tire retailers and supermarkets and gasoline stations.

- *Specializing by product type*—When a fragmented industry's products include a range of styles or services, a strategy to focus on one product or service category can be very effective. Some firms in the furniture industry specialize in only one furniture type such as brass beds, rattan and wicker, lawn and garden, or early American. In auto repair, companies specialize in transmission repair, body work, or speedy oil changes.

- *Specialization by customer type*—A firm can stake out a market niche in a fragmented industry by catering to those customers who are interested in low prices, unique product attributes, customized features, carefree service, or other extras. A number of restaurants cater to take-out customers; others specialize in fine dining experiences, and still others cater to the sports bar crowd.

- *Focusing on a limited geographic area*—Even though a firm in a fragmented industry can't win a big share of total industrywide sales, it can still try to dominate a local or regional geographic area. Concentrating company efforts on a limited territory can produce greater operating efficiency, speed delivery and customer services, promote strong brand awareness, and permit saturation advertising, while avoiding the diseconomies of stretching operations out over a much wider area. Supermarkets, banks, convenience stores, and sporting goods retailers successfully operate multiple locations within a limited geographic area.

In fragmented industries, firms generally have the strategic freedom to pursue broad or narrow market targets and low-cost or differentiation-based competitive advantages. Many different strategic approaches can exist side by side.

STRATEGIES FOR SUSTAINING RAPID COMPANY GROWTH

Companies that are focused on growing their revenues and earnings at a rapid or above-average pace year after year generally have to craft a portfolio of strategic initiatives covering three horizons:[16]

Horizon 1: Strategic initiatives to fortify and extend their position in existing businesses—Horizon 1 initiatives typically include adding new items to the company's present product line, expanding into new geographic areas where the company does not yet have a market presence, and launching offensives to take market share away from rivals. The objective is capitalize fully on whatever growth potential exists in the company's present business arenas.

Horizon 2: Strategic initiatives to leverage existing resources and capabilities by entering new businesses with promising growth potential—Growth companies have to be alert for opportunities to jump into new businesses where there is promise of rapid growth and where their experience, intellectual capital, technological

---

[16]Eric D. Beinhocker, "Robust Adaptive Strategies," *Sloan Management Review* 40, no. 3 (Spring 1999), p. 101.

know-how, and capabilities will prove valuable in gaining rapid market penetration. While Horizon 2 initiatives may take a back seat to Horizon 1 initiatives as long as there is plenty of untapped growth in the company's present businesses, they move to the front as the onset of market maturity dims the company's growth prospects in its present business(es).

Horizon 3: Strategic initiatives to plant the seeds for ventures in businesses that do not yet exist—Such initiatives can entail pumping funds into long-range R&D projects, setting up an internal venture capital fund to invest in promising start-up companies attempting to create the industries of the future, or acquiring a number of small start-up companies experimenting with technologies and product ideas that complement the company's present businesses. Intel, for example, has set up a multibillion-dollar fund to invest in over 100 different projects and start-up companies, the intent being to plant seeds for Intel's future, broadening its base as a global leader in supplying building blocks for PCs and the worldwide Internet economy. Royal Dutch/Shell, with over $140 billion in revenues and over 100,000 employees, put over $20 million into rule-breaking, game-changing ideas put forth by free-thinking employees; the objective was to inject a new spirit of entrepreneurship into the company and sow the seeds of faster growth.[17]

The three strategy horizons are illustrated in Figure 8.2. Managing such a portfolio of strategic initiatives is not easy, however. The tendency of most companies is to focus on Horizon 1 strategies and devote only sporadic and uneven attention to Horizon 2 and 3 strategies. But a recent McKinsey & Company study of 30 of the world's leading growth companies revealed a relatively balanced portfolio of strategic initiatives covering all three horizons. The lesson of successful growth companies is that keeping a company's record of rapid growth intact over the long term entails crafting a diverse population of strategies, ranging from short-jump incremental strategies to grow present businesses to long-jump initiatives with a 5- to 10-year growth payoff horizon.[18] Having a mixture of short-jump, medium-jump, and long-jump initiatives not only increases the odds of hitting a few home runs but also provides some protection against unexpected adversity in present or newly entered businesses.

The Risks of Pursuing Multiple Strategy Horizons   There are, of course, risks to pursuing a diverse strategy portfolio aimed at sustained growth. A company cannot, of course, place bets on every opportunity that appears on its radar screen, lest it stretch itself too thin. And medium-jump and long-jump initiatives can cause a company to stray far from its core competencies and end up trying to compete in businesses for which it is ill suited. Moreover, it can be difficult to achieve competitive advantage in medium- and long-jump product families and businesses that prove not to mesh well with a company's present businesses and resource strengths. The payoffs of long-jump initiatives often prove elusive; not all of the seeds a company sows will bear fruit, and only a few may evolve into truly significant contributors to the company's revenue and profit growth. The losses from those long-jump ventures that do not take root may

[17]Gary Hamel, "Bringing Silicon Valley Inside," *Harvard Business Review* 77, no. 5 (September–October 1999), p. 73.

[18]Beinhocker, "Robust Adaptive Strategies," p. 101.

figure 8.2   **The Three Strategy Horizons for Sustaining Rapid Growth**

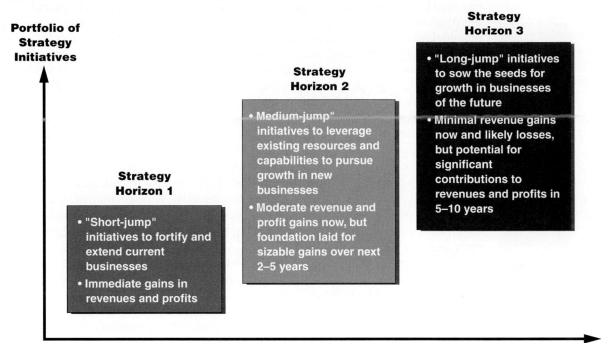

Source: Adapted from Eric D. Beinhocker, "Robust Adaptive Strategies," *Sloan Management Review* 40, no. 3 (Spring 1999), p. 101.

erode significantly the gains from those that do, resulting in disappointingly modest gains in overall profits.

STRATEGIES FOR INDUSTRY LEADERS

The competitive positions of industry leaders normally range from "stronger than average" to "powerful." Leaders typically are well known, and strongly entrenched leaders have proven strategies (keyed either to low-cost leadership or to differentiation). Some of the best-known industry leaders are Anheuser-Busch (beer), Starbucks (coffee drinks), Microsoft (computer software), McDonald's (fast food), Gillette (razor blades), Campbell's Soup (canned soups), Gerber (baby food), AT&T (long-distance telephone service), Eastman Kodak (camera film), Wal-Mart (discount retailing), Amazon.com (online shopping), eBay (online auctions), and Levi Strauss (jeans).

The main strategic concern for a leader revolves around how to defend and strengthen its leadership position, perhaps becoming the *dominant* leader as opposed to just *a* leader. However, the pursuit of industry leadership and large market share per se is primarily important because of the competitive advantage and profitability that accrue to being the industry's biggest company. Three contrasting strategic postures are open to industry leaders and dominant firms:[19]

---

[19]Kotler, *Marketing Management,* chapter 23; Michael E. Porter, *Competitive Advantage* (New York: Free Press, 1985), chapter 14; and Ian C. MacMillan, "Seizing Competitive Initiative," *Journal of Business Strategy* 2, no. 4 (Spring 1982), pp. 43–57.

1. *Stay-on-the-offensive strategy*—The central goal of a stay-on-the-offensive strategy is to be a first-mover.[20] It rests on the principle that staying a step ahead and forcing rivals into a reactive, catch-up mode is the surest path to industry prominence and potential market dominance—as the saying goes, the best defense is a good offense. Being the industry standard setter entails relentless pursuit of continuous improvement and innovation—being out front with technological improvements, new or better products, more attractive performance features, quality enhancements, improved customer service, ways to cut operating costs, and ways to make it easier and less costly for potential customers to switch their purchases from runner-up firms to its own products. A low-cost leader must set the pace for cost reduction, and a differentiator must constantly initiate new ways to keep its product set apart from the brands of imitative rivals in order to be the standard against which rivals' products are judged. The array of options for a potent stay-on-the-offensive strategy can also include initiatives to expand overall industry demand—spurring the creation of new families of products, making the product more suitable for consumers in emerging-country markets, discovering new uses for the product, attracting new users of the product, and promoting more frequent use.

Furthermore, unless a leader's market share is already so dominant that it presents a threat of antitrust action (a market share under 60 percent is usually safe), a potent stay-on-the-offensive strategy entails actions aimed at growing faster than the industry as a whole and wresting market share from rivals. A leader whose growth does not equal or outpace the industry average is losing ground to competitors.

2. *Fortify-and-defend strategy*—The essence of "fortify and defend" is to make it harder for challengers to gain ground and for new firms to enter. The goals of a strong defense are to hold on to the present market share, strengthen current market position, and protect whatever competitive advantage the firm has. Specific defensive actions can include:

> The two best tests of success of a stay-on-the-offensive strategy are (1) the extent to which it keeps rivals in a reactive mode, scrambling to keep up, and (2) whether the leader is growing faster than the industry as a whole and wresting market share from rivals

- Attempting to raise the competitive ante for challengers and new entrants via increased spending for advertising, higher levels of customer service, and bigger R&D outlays.
- Introducing more product versions or brands to match the product attributes that challenger brands have or to fill vacant niches that competitors could slip into.
- Adding personalized services and other "extras" that boost customer loyalty and make it harder or more costly for customers to switch to rival products.
- Keeping prices reasonable and quality attractive.
- Building new capacity ahead of market demand to discourage smaller competitors from adding capacity of their own.
- Investing enough to remain cost-competitive and technologically progressive.
- Patenting the feasible alternative technologies.
- Signing exclusive contracts with the best suppliers and dealer distributors.

A fortify-and-defend strategy best suits firms that have already achieved industry dominance and don't wish to risk antitrust action. It is also well suited to situations where a firm wishes to milk its present position for profits and cash flow because the indus-

---

[20]The value of being a frequent first-mover and leading change is documented in Walter J. Ferrier, Ken G. Smith, and Curtis M. Grimm, "The Role of Competitive Action in Market Share Erosion and Industry Dethronement: A Study of Industry Leaders and Challengers," *Academy of Management Journal* 42, no. 4 (August 1999), pp. 372–88.

try's prospects for growth are low or because further gains in market share do not appear profitable enough to go after. But a fortify-and-defend strategy always entails trying to grow as fast as the market as a whole (to stave off market-share slippage) and requires reinvesting enough capital in the business to protect the leader's ability to compete.

3. *Muscle-flexing strategy*—Here a dominant leader plays competitive hardball (presumably in an ethical and competitively legal manner) when smaller rivals rock the boat with price cuts or mount new market offensives that directly threaten its position. Specific responses can include quickly matching and perhaps exceeding challengers' price cuts, using large promotional campaigns to counter challengers' moves to gain market share, and offering better deals to their major customers. Dominant leaders may also court distributors assiduously to dissuade them from carrying rivals' products, provide salespersons with documented information about the weaknesses of competing products, or try to fill any vacant positions in their own firms by making attractive offers to the better executives of rivals that get out of line.

> Industry leaders can strengthen their long-term competitive positions with strategies keyed to aggressive offense, aggressive defense, or muscling smaller rivals and customers into behaviors that bolster its own market standing.

The leader may also use various arm-twisting tactics to pressure present customers not to use the products of rivals. This can range from simply forcefully communicating its displeasure should customers opt to use the products of rivals to pushing them to agree to exclusive arrangements in return for better prices to charging them a higher price if they use any competitors' products. As a final resort, a leader may grant certain customers special discounts or preferred treatment if they do not use any products of rivals.

The obvious risks of a muscle-flexing strategy are running afoul of the antitrust laws (as did Microsoft—see Illustration Capsule 33), alienating customers with bullying tactics, and arousing adverse public opinion. A company that tries to throw its weight around to protect and enhance its market dominance has got to be judicious, lest it cross the line from allowable tactics to what buyers, rivals, and antitrust officials consider unfair and unethical competitive practices.

STRATEGIES FOR RUNNER-UP FIRMS

Runner-up or "second-tier" firms have smaller market shares than "first-tier" industry leaders. Some runner-up firms are up-and-coming *market challengers,* employing offensive strategies to gain market share and build a stronger market position. Other runner-up competitors are *focusers*, seeking to improve their lot by concentrating their attention on serving a limited portion of the market. There are, of course, always a number of firms in any industry that are destined to be *perennial runners-up*, lacking the resources and competitive strengths to do more than continue in trailing positions and/or content to follow the trendsetting moves of the market leaders.

In industries where big size is definitely a key success factor, firms with small market shares have some obstacles to overcome: (1) less access to economies of scale in manufacturing, distribution, or marketing and sales promotion; (2) difficulty in gaining customer recognition; (3) weaker ability to use mass media advertising; and (4) difficulty in funding capital requirements.[21] When significant scale economies give large-volume competitors a *dominating* cost advantage, small-share firms have only two viable strategic options: initiate offensive moves to gain sales and market share (so as to build the volume of business needed to approach the scale economies enjoyed by

---

[21]Hamermesh, Anderson, and Harris, "Strategies for Low Market Share Businesses," p. 102.

illustration capsule *33*

How Microsoft Used Its Muscle to Maintain Market Dominance

In 1999 in *U.S.* v. *Microsoft*, U.S. District Judge Thomas Penfield Jackson concluded that Microsoft repeatedly had used heavy-handed tactics to routinely pressure customers, crush competitors, and throttle competition. Judge Jackson painted Microsoft as a domineering company that rewarded its friends and punished its enemies, pointing to the following examples:

- Gateway and IBM, both of which resisted Microsoft's efforts to dissuade them from using or promoting competitors' products on their PCs, were forced to pay higher prices for installing Microsoft's Windows operating system on their PCs than Dell Computer, Hewlett-Packard, and Compaq Computer, which had less contentious relationships with Microsoft. Microsoft's beef with IBM stemmed from IBM's efforts to market PCs loaded with IBM's own internally developed OS/2 operating system rather than Windows and, also, its own Lotus SmartSuite rather than Microsoft Office.

- Microsoft used a variety of bullying tactics to overcome Internet browser pioneer Netscape. It tried to persuade Netscape to halt its development of platform-level technologies for Windows 95, arguing that Netscape's Navigator browser should be designed to run on Windows 95 only rather than be designed in a way that could serve as an alternative operating system platform and substitute for use of Windows. Microsoft wanted Netscape to agree to a special alliance with Microsoft that would allow Microsoft to incorporate Navigator's functionality into Windows. When Netscape refused, Microsoft withheld information about its Windows 95 code until after it released Windows 95 and its own new version of Internet Explorer. Microsoft also refused to give Netscape a license to one of its scripting tools, thereby preventing Netscape from doing business with

certain Internet service providers for a time. Simultaneously, Microsoft pressured PC makers to install its Internet Explorer browser as the preferred alternative to Netscape Navigator. When Compaq removed the Internet Explorer icon from the opening screen of its computers and preinstalled the Navigator icon, Microsoft threatened to revoke Compaq's license to install Windows 95.

- Microsoft tried to convince Intel not to ship its newly developed Native Signal Processing (NSP) software (intended to help spark demand for Intel's most advanced microprocessors) because Microsoft felt that the NSP software represented an incursion into Microsoft's operating system platform territory. It also asked Intel to reduce the number of people working on software at Intel. Microsoft assured Intel that if it would stop promoting NSP that Microsoft would accelerate its own work to incorporate the functions of NSP into Windows. At the same time, Microsoft pressured PC makers not to install Intel's NSP software on their PCs.

- When Compaq Computer entered into an agreement with America Online to promote AOL above all online services and began to ship its computers with the Microsoft Network (MSN) icon removed and the AOL icon installed, Microsoft wrote Compaq a letter stating its intention to terminate Compaq's license for Windows 95 if it did not restore the MSN icon to its original position on the opening screen.

Judge Jackson documented numerous other occasions when Microsoft tried to leverage its monopoly position in operating systems to thwart competition from rivals and gain wider use of Internet Explorer, Microsoft Office, MSN, and other Microsoft products.

Source: Transcript of Judge Jackson's findings of fact in *U.S.* v. *Microsoft*, November 5, 1999.

larger rivals) or withdraw from the business (gradually or quickly). The competitive strategies most underdogs use to build market share and achieve critical scale economies are based on (1) using lower prices to win customers from weak, higher-cost rivals; (2) merging with or acquiring rival firms to achieve the size needed to capture greater scale economies; (3) investing in new cost-saving facilities and equipment, perhaps relocating operations to countries where costs are significantly lower; and

(4) pursuing technological innovations or radical value chain revamping to achieve dramatic cost savings.

But *it is erroneous to view runner-up firms as inherently less profitable or unable to hold their own against the biggest firms.* Many small and medium-sized firms earn healthy profits and enjoy good reputations with customers. Assuming that scale economies or experience curve effects are relatively small and result in no important cost advantage for big-share firms, runner-up companies have considerable strategic flexibility and can consider any of the following six approaches.

Offensive Strategies to Build Market Share   A challenger firm interested in improving its market standing needs a strategy aimed at building a competitive advantage of its own. Rarely can a runner-up firm improve its competitive position by imitating the strategies of leading firms. A cardinal rule in offensive strategy is to avoid attacking a leader head-on with an imitative strategy, regardless of the resources and staying power an underdog may have.[22] Moreover, if a challenger has a 5 percent market share and needs a 20 percent share to earn attractive returns, it needs a more creative approach to competing than just "Try harder."

> Rarely can a runner-up firm successfully challenge an industry leader with a copycat strategy.

Ambitious runner-up companies desirous of joining the ranks of first-tier industry leaders have to make some waves in the marketplace if they want to make big market share gains. The best "mover-and-shaker" offensives usually involve one of the following approaches:

- Pioneering a leapfrog technological breakthrough.
- Getting new or better products into the market consistently ahead of rivals and building a reputation for product leadership.
- Being more agile and innovative in adapting to evolving market conditions and customer expectations than slower-to-change market leaders.
- Forging attractive strategic alliances with key distributors, dealers, or marketers of complementary products.
- Finding innovative ways to dramatically drive down costs and then using the attraction of lower prices to win customers from higher-cost, higher-priced rivals. A challenger firm can pursue aggressive cost reduction by eliminating marginal activities from its value chain, streamlining supply chain relationships, improving internal operating efficiency, using various e-commerce techniques, and merging with or acquiring rival firms to achieve the size needed to capture greater scale economies.
- Crafting an attractive differentiation strategy based on premium quality, technological superiority, outstanding customer service, rapid product innovation, or convenient online shopping options.

Without a potent offensive strategy to capture added market share, runner-up companies have to patiently nibble away at the lead of first-tier firms and build sales at a more moderate pace over time.

Growth-via-Acquisition Strategy   One of the most frequently used strategies employed by ambitious runner-up companies is merging with or acquiring rivals to form an enterprise that has greater competitive strength and a larger share of the overall market. For an enterprise to succeed with this strategic approach, senior management must have the skills to assimilate the operations of the acquired companies,

---

[22]Porter, *Competitive Advantage,* p. 514.

eliminating duplication and overlap, generating efficiencies and cost savings, and structuring the combined resources in ways that create substantially stronger competitive capabilities. Many banks owe their growth during the past decade to acquisition of smaller regional and local banks. Likewise, a number of book publishers have grown by acquiring small publishers. HealthSouth, an operator of outpatient surgery centers and rehabilitation and diagnostics clinics, has grown into a $4 billion health care provider by acquiring hundreds of clinics and facilities across the United States and in several foreign countries.

Vacant-Niche Strategy   This version of a focused strategy involves concentrating on customer or end-use applications that market leaders have bypassed or neglected. An ideal vacant niche is of sufficient size and scope to be profitable, has some growth potential, is well suited to a firm's own capabilities and skills, and for one reason or another is hard for leading firms to serve. Two examples where vacant-niche strategies have worked successfully are (1) regional commuter airlines serving cities with too few passengers to fill the large jets flown by major airlines and (2) health-food producers (like Health Valley, Hain, and Tree of Life) that cater to local health-food stores—a market segment traditionally given little attention by Pillsbury, Kraft General Foods, Heinz, Nabisco, Campbell Soup, and other leading food products firms.

Specialist Strategy   A specialist firm trains its competitive effort on one technology, product or product family, end use, or market segment (often one in which buyers have special needs). The aim is to train the company's resource strengths and capabilities on building competitive advantage through leadership in a specific area. Smaller companies that successfully use a specialist focused strategy include Formby's (a specialist in stains and finishes for wood furniture, especially refinishing); Blue Diamond (a California-based grower and marketer of almonds); Canada Dry (known for its ginger ale, tonic water, and carbonated soda water); and American Tobacco (a leader in chewing tobacco and snuff). Many companies in high-tech industries concentrate their energies on being the clear leader in a particular technological area; their competitive advantage is superior technological depth, technical expertise that is highly valued by customers, and the capability to consistently beat out rivals in pioneering technological advances.

Superior Product Strategy   The approach here is to use a differentiation-based focused strategy keyed to superior product quality or unique attributes. Sales and marketing efforts are aimed directly at quality-conscious and performance-oriented buyers. Fine craftsmanship, prestige quality, frequent product innovations, and/or close contact with customers to solicit their input in developing a better product usually undergird this superior product approach. Some examples include Bombay and Tanqueray in gin, Tiffany in diamonds and jewelry, Chicago Cutlery in premium-quality kitchen knives, Baccarat in fine crystal, Cannondale in mountain bikes, Bally in shoes, and Patagonia in apparel for outdoor recreation enthusiasts.

Distinctive Image Strategy   Some runner-up companies build their strategies around ways to make themselves stand out from competitors. A variety of strategic approaches can be used: creating a reputation for charging the lowest prices, providing prestige quality at a good price, going all out to give superior customer service, designing unique product attributes, being a leader in new product introduction, or devising unusually creative advertising. Examples include Dr Pepper's strategy in calling attention to its distinctive taste, Apple Computer's making it easier and more interesting for people to use its Macintosh PCs, and Mary Kay Cosmetics' distinctive use of the color pink.

Content Follower Strategy Content followers deliberately refrain from initiating trendsetting strategic moves and from aggressive attempts to steal customers away from the leaders. Followers prefer approaches that will not provoke competitive retaliation, often opting for focus and differentiation strategies that keep them out of the leaders' paths. They react and respond rather than initiate and challenge. They prefer defense to offense. And they rarely get out of line with the leaders on price. They are content to simply maintain their market position, albeit sometimes struggling to do so. Followers have no urgent strategic questions to confront beyond "What strategic changes are the leaders initiating and what do we need to do to follow along and maintain our present position?" The marketers of private-label products tend to be followers, imitating many of the features of name-brand products and content to sell to price-conscious buyers at prices modestly below those of well-known brands.

STRATEGIES FOR WEAK AND CRISIS-RIDDEN BUSINESSES

A firm in an also-ran or declining competitive position has four basic strategic options. If it can come up with the financial resources, it can launch an *offensive turnaround strategy* keyed either to low-cost or "new" differentiation themes, pouring enough money and talent into the effort to move up a notch or two in the industry rankings and become a respectable market contender within five years or so. It can employ a *fortify-and-defend* strategy, using variations of its present strategy and fighting hard to keep sales, market share, profitability, and competitive position at current levels. It can opt for an *immediate abandonment strategy* and get out of the business, either by selling out to another firm or by closing down operations if a buyer cannot be found. Or it can employ an *end-game strategy,* keeping reinvestment to a bare-bones minimum and taking actions to maximize short-term cash flows in preparation for an orderly market exit.

> The strategic options for a competitively weak company include waging a modest offensive to improve its position, defending its present position, being acquired by another company, or employing an end-game strategy.

Turnaround Strategies for Businesses in Crisis

Turnaround strategies are needed when a business worth rescuing goes into crisis; the objective is to arrest and reverse the sources of competitive and financial weakness as quickly as possible. Management's first task in formulating a suitable turnaround strategy is to diagnose what lies at the root of poor performance. Is it an unexpected downturn in sales brought on by a weak economy? An ill-chosen competitive strategy? Poor execution of an otherwise workable strategy? High operating costs? Important resource deficiencies? An overload of debt? Can the business be saved, or is the situation hopeless? Understanding what is wrong with the business and how serious its strategic problems are is essential because different diagnoses lead to different turnaround strategies.

Some of the most common causes of business trouble are taking on too much debt, overestimating the potential for sales growth, ignoring the profit-depressing effects of an overly aggressive effort to "buy" market share with deep price cuts, being burdened with heavy fixed costs because of an inability to use plant capacity, betting on R&D efforts to boost competitive position and profitability and failing to come up with effective innovations, betting on technological long shots, being too optimistic about the ability to penetrate new markets, making frequent changes in strategy (because the previous strategy didn't work out), and being overpowered by more successful rivals.

Curing these kinds of problems and achieving a successful business turnaround can involve any of the following actions:

- Selling off assets to raise cash to save the remaining part of the business.
- Revising the existing strategy.
- Launching efforts to boost revenues.
- Pursuing cost reduction.
- Using a combination of these efforts.

Selling Off Assets   Asset-reduction strategies are essential when cash flow is a critical consideration and when the most practical ways to generate cash are (1) through sale of some of the firm's assets (plant and equipment, land, patents, inventories, or profitable subsidiaries) and (2) through retrenchment (pruning of marginal products from the product line, closing or selling older plants, reducing the workforce, withdrawing from outlying markets, cutting back customer service). Sometimes crisis-ridden companies sell off assets not so much to unload losing operations and to stem cash drains as to raise funds to save and strengthen the remaining business activities. In such cases, the choice is usually to dispose of noncore business assets to support strategy renewal in the firm's core businesses.

Strategy Revision   When weak performance is caused by bad strategy, the task of strategy overhaul can proceed along any of several paths: (1) shifting to a new competitive approach to rebuild the firm's market position; (2) overhauling internal operations and functional area strategies to better support the same overall business strategy; (3) merging with another firm in the industry and forging a new strategy keyed to the newly merged firm's strengths; and (4) retrenching into a reduced core of products and customers more closely matched to the firm's strengths. The most appealing path depends on prevailing industry conditions, the firm's particular strengths and weaknesses, its competitive capabilities vis-à-vis rival firms, and the severity of the crisis. A situation analysis of the industry, major competitors, and the firm's own competitive position and its skills and resources is a prerequisite for action. As a rule, successful strategy revision must be tied to the ailing firm's strengths and near-term competitive capabilities and directed at its best market opportunities.

Boosting Revenues   Revenue-increasing turnaround efforts aim at generating increased sales volume. There are a number of revenue-building options: price cuts, increased promotion, a bigger sales force, added customer services, and quickly achieved product improvements. Attempts to increase revenues and sales volumes are necessary (1) when there is little or no room in the operating budget to cut expenses and still break even, and (2) when the key to restoring profitability is increased utilization of existing capacity. If buyer demand is not especially price sensitive because of differentiating features, the quickest way to boost short-term revenues may be to raise prices rather than opt for volume-building price cuts.

Cutting Costs   Cost-reducing turnaround strategies work best when an ailing firm's value chain and cost structure are flexible enough to permit radical surgery, when operating inefficiencies are identifiable and readily correctable, when the firm's costs are obviously bloated and there are many places where savings can be quickly achieved, and when the firm is relatively close to its break-even point. Accompanying a general belt-tightening can be an increased emphasis on paring administrative overheads, elimination of nonessential and low-value-added activities in the firm's value chain, modernization of existing plant and equipment to gain greater productivity, delay of nonessential capital expenditures, and debt restructuring to reduce interest costs and stretch out repayments.

Combination Efforts   Combination turnaround strategies are usually essential in grim situations that require fast action on a broad front. Likewise, combination actions frequently come into play when new managers are brought in and given a free hand to make whatever changes they see fit. The tougher the problems, the more likely the solutions will involve multiple strategic initiatives—see the story of the turnaround at Continental Airlines in Illustration Capsule 34.

Turnaround efforts tend to be high-risk undertakings, and they often fail. A landmark study of 64 companies found no successful turnarounds among the most troubled companies in eight basic industries.[23] Many of the troubled businesses waited too long to begin a turnaround. Others found themselves short of both the cash and entrepreneurial talent needed to compete in a slow-growth industry characterized by a fierce battle for market share. Better-positioned rivals simply proved too strong to defeat in a long, head-to-head contest. Even when successful, turnaround may involve numerous attempts and management changes before long-term competitive viability and profitability are finally restored.

Liquidation—the Strategy of Last Resort

Sometimes a business in crisis is too far gone to be salvaged or is not worth salvaging given the resources it will take and its profit prospects. Closing a crisis-ridden business down and liquidating its assets is sometimes the best and wisest strategy. Of all the strategic alternatives, liquidation is the most unpleasant and painful because of the hardships of job eliminations and the effects of business closings on local communities. Nonetheless, in hopeless situations, an early liquidation effort usually serves owner-stockholder interests better than an inevitable bankruptcy. Prolonging the pursuit of a lost cause merely exhausts an organization's resources further and leaves less to salvage, not to mention the added stress and potential career impairment for all the people involved. The problem, of course, is differentiating between when a turnaround is achievable and when it isn't. It is easy for owners or managers to let their emotions and pride overcome sound judgment when a business gets in such deep trouble that a successful turnaround is remote.

End-Game Strategies

An *end-game strategy* steers a middle course between preserving the status quo and exiting as soon as possible. *Harvesting* is a phasing-down strategy that involves sacrificing market position in return for bigger near-term cash flows or current profitability. The overriding financial objective is to reap the greatest possible harvest of cash to deploy to other business endeavors. The operating budget is chopped to a rock-bottom level; reinvestment in the business is held to a bare minimum. Capital expenditures for

---

[23]William K. Hall, "Survival Strategies in a Hostile Environment," *Harvard Business Review* 58, no. 5 (September–October 1980), pp. 75–85. See also Frederick M. Zimmerman, *The Turnaround Experience: Real-World Lessons in Revitalizing Corporations* (New York: McGraw-Hill, 1991), and Gary J. Castrogiovanni, B. R. Baliga, and Roland E. Kidwell, "Curing Sick Businesses: Changing CEOs in Turnaround Efforts," *Academy of Management Executive* 6, no. 3 (August 1992), pp. 26–41.

illustration capsule 34
Continental Airlines' Turnaround Strategy

In the early 1990s, Continental Airlines was in disastrous condition for a $6 billion company. It was just emerging from its second bankruptcy proceeding in nine years and had a reputation for lousy service and late departures, poor maintenance practices, weak management at the top, a nonexistent strategy, and negative cash flows. The company, a product of seven mergers, had gone through 10 presidents in 10 years. It ranked 10th out of the 10 largest airlines in all customer-service areas measured by the Department of Transportation: on-time arrivals, baggage handling, customer complaints, and involuntary denied boardings. The company had not posted a profit outside of bankruptcy since 1978.

In late 1994, new owners took over Continental; Gordon Bethune became Continental's new CEO and Greg Brenneman, a former specialist in turnaround strategy at Bain & Co., became president and chief operating officer. Together, Bethune and Brenneman engineered a turnaround strategy for Continental called the Go Forward Plan, built around four key themes:

- *Fly to Win*—This meant focusing on core assets to increase revenues and deliver a profit. Key actions included eliminating flights that were losing money; reducing costs by cutting the advertising budget in half, reducing the size of the workforce by 7,000 people, and trimming the amount spent on aircraft maintenance from $777 million to $495 million; building up the company's hubs at Houston, Newark, and Cleveland; expanding the customer mix to include more business travelers; and building better relationships with travel agents, corporations, and frequent fliers.

- *Fund the Future*—This facet of the turnaround strategy involved a series of actions to strengthen the balance sheet and track cash flows carefully, reduce the number of different aircraft types in the fleet from 13 to 4 (which helped reduce maintenance costs), put

programs in place to do a much better job of matching airplane size with market size and traffic patterns, renegotiate high-cost leases on the company's aircraft, and sell nonstrategic assets (to raise needed cash).

- *Making Reliability a Reality*—Continental management launched a series of initiatives to paint the interiors and exteriors of its aircraft, reupholster the seats, add phones and first-class seating, improve aircraft cleanliness, improve food service, and get Continental in the top 50 percent of the industry on four measures: on-time arrivals, baggage handling, customer complaints, and involuntary denied boardings. The goal of these initiatives was to improve Continental's product offering and become an airline that people found pleasant to fly.

- *Working Together*—The goal here was to build a new, results-oriented corporate culture featuring consistent and reliable flight schedules, peace among the company's various work groups, and attempts to restore employee confidence in management. Fifty of Continental's 61 senior executives were asked to resign (their contracts were honored); they were replaced with 20 new individuals who were identified as smart team players, driven to get things done. Employees were offered on-time incentives of $65 per month, and a new profit-sharing plan was created. People were empowered to do their jobs without interference, employee-management communication was improved, and emphasis was put on treating one another with dignity and respect.

The plan was sold to employees with energetic zeal, and Continental's progress on 15 performance measures was tracked monthly. Three years later, Continental was profitable, passenger traffic was rising, employee morale was high, and the company compared favorably with rivals on the measures of on-time arrivals and departures, baggage handling, and customer complaints.

Source: Greg Brenneman, "Right Away and All at Once: How We Saved Continental," *Harvard Business Review* 76, no. 5 (September–October 1998), pp. 162–79.

new equipment are put on hold or given low financial priority (unless replacement needs are unusually urgent); instead, efforts are made to stretch the life of existing equipment and make do with present facilities as long as possible. Promotional expenses may be cut gradually, quality reduced in not-so-visible ways, nonessential customer services curtailed, and the like. Although such actions may result in shrinking sales and market share, if cash expenses can be cut even faster, then after-tax profits and cash flows are bigger (at least temporarily). The business gradually declines, but not before sizable amounts of cash have been harvested.

An end-game strategy is a reasonable strategic option for a weak business in the following circumstances:[24]

1. When the industry's long-term prospects are unattractive—as seems to be the case for the cigarette industry, for the manufacture and sale of VCRs and videocassettes (which are now being replaced by DVD players and both CDs and DVDs), and for the 3.5-inch floppy disk business.

2. When rejuvenating the business would be too costly or at best marginally profitable—as could be the case at Iomega, which is struggling to maintain sales of its Zip drives in the face of rapidly expanding hard disk drives on PCs, or at Polaroid, which has experienced stagnant sales for its instant-developing cameras and film.

3. When the firm's market share is becoming increasingly costly to maintain or defend—as could be the case with the makers of film for traditional cameras.

4. When reduced levels of competitive effort will not trigger an immediate or rapid falloff in sales—the makers of dot-matrix printers will not likely experience much of a decline in sales of either dot-matrix printers or ribbons if they spend all of their ad budgets on laser printers.

5. When the enterprise can redeploy the freed resources in higher-opportunity areas—the makers of dot-matrix printers are better off devoting their resources to the production and sale of low-cost, good-quality laser printers.

6. When the business is not a crucial or core component of a diversified company's overall lineup of businesses—gradually letting a sideline business decay is strategically preferable to deliberately letting a mainline or core business decline.

7. When the business does not contribute other desired features (sales stability, prestige, a well-rounded product line) to a company's overall business portfolio.

The more of these seven conditions that are present, the more ideal the business is for harvesting.

End-game strategies make the most sense for diversified companies that have sideline or noncore business units in weak competitive positions or in unattractive industries. Such companies can withdraw the cash flows from unattractive, noncore business units and reallocate them to business units with greater profit potential or spend them on the acquisition of new businesses.

10 COMMANDMENTS FOR CRAFTING SUCCESSFUL BUSINESS STRATEGIES

Business experiences over the years prove again and again that disastrous strategies can be avoided by adhering to good strategy-making principles. We've distilled the lessons learned from the strategic mistakes companies most often make into 10 commandments that serve as useful guides for developing sound strategies:

---

[24]Phillip Kotler, "Harvesting Strategies for Weak Products," *Business Horizons* 21, no. 5 (August 1978), pp. 17–18.

1. *Place top priority on crafting and executing strategic moves that enhance the company's competitive position for the long term.* An ever-stronger competitive position pays off year after year, but the glory of meeting one quarter's or one year's financial performance targets quickly fades. Shareholders are never well served by managers who let short-term financial performance considerations rule out strategic initiatives that will meaningfully bolster the company's longer-term competitive position and competitive strength. The best way to protect a company's long-term profitability is with a strategy that strengthens the company's long-term competitiveness.

2. *Be prompt in adapting to changing market conditions, unmet customer needs, buyer wishes for something better, emerging technological alternatives, and new initiatives of competitors.* Responding late or with too little often puts a company in the precarious position of having to play catch-up. While pursuit of a consistent strategy has its virtues, adapting strategy to changing circumstances is normal and necessary. Moreover, long-term strategic commitments to achieve top quality or lowest cost should be interpreted relative to competitors' products as well as customers' needs and expectations; the company should avoid singlemindedly striving to make the absolute highest quality or lowest cost product possible no matter what.

3. *Invest in creating a sustainable competitive advantage.* Having a competitive edge over rivals is the single most dependable contributor to above-average profitability. As a general rule, a company must play aggressive offense to build competitive advantage and aggressive defense to protect it.

4. *Avoid strategies capable of succeeding only in the most optimistic circumstances.* Expect competitors to employ countermeasures and expect times of unfavorable market conditions. A good strategy works reasonably well and produces tolerable results even in the worst of times.

5. *Don't underestimate the reactions and the commitment of rival firms.* Rivals are most dangerous when they are pushed into a corner and their well-being is threatened.

6. *Consider that attacking competitive weakness is usually more profitable and less risky than attacking competitive strength.* Attacking capable, resourceful rivals is likely to fail unless the attacker has deep financial pockets and a solid basis for competitive advantage.

7. *Be judicious in cutting prices without an established cost advantage.* Only a low-cost producer can win at price cutting over the long term.

8. *Strive to open up very meaningful gaps in quality or service or performance features when pursuing a differentiation strategy.* Tiny differences between rivals' product offerings may not be visible or important to buyers.

9. *Avoid "stuck in the middle" strategies that represent compromises between lower costs and greater differentiation and between broad and narrow market appeal.* Compromise strategies rarely produce sustainable competitive advantage or a distinctive competitive position—well-executed best-cost producer strategies are the only exception where a compromise between low cost and differentiation succeeds. Usually, companies with compromise strategies end up with average costs, average differentiation, an average image and reputation, a middle-of-the-pack industry ranking, and little prospect of industry leadership.

10. *Be aware that aggressive moves to wrest market share away from rivals often provoke retaliation in the form of a marketing "arms race" or price war—to the*

detriment of everyone's profits. Aggressive moves to capture a bigger market share invite cutthroat competition, particularly when the market is plagued with high inventories and excess production capacity.

key|points

It is not enough to understand a company's basic competitive strategy options, overall low-cost leadership, broad differentiation, best cost, focused low cost, and focused differentiation, and that there are a variety of offensive, defensive, first-mover, and late-mover initiatives and actions to choose from. The lessons of this chapter are that some strategic options are better suited to certain specific industry and competitive environments than others and that some strategic options are better suited to certain specific company situations than others. This chapter portrays the multifaceted task of matching strategy to a firm's external and internal circumstances in nine types of situations.

Rather than try to summarize the main points we made about choosing strategies for these nine sets of circumstances (the relevant principles are not readily capsuled in three or four sentences each), we think it more useful to conclude by outlining a broader framework for matching strategy to *any* industry and company situation. Aligning a company's strategy with its overall situation starts with a quick diagnosis of the industry environment and the firm's competitive standing in the industry:

1. What basic type of industry environment does the company operate in (emerging, rapid-growth, high-velocity, mature, global, commodity-product)? What strategic options and strategic postures are usually best suited to this generic type of environment?

2. What position does the firm have in the industry (leader, runner-up, or also-ran; strong, weak, or crisis-ridden)? How does the firm's market standing influence its strategic options given the industry and competitive environment—in particular, which courses of action have to be ruled out?

Next, strategists need to factor in the primary external and internal situational considerations (as discussed in Chapters 3 and 4—see again Figure 3.2 for a convenient overview) and decide how all the factors add up. Nearly always, weighing the various considerations makes it clear that some strategic options can be ruled out. Listing the pros and cons of the remaining options can help reach a decision as to the best overall strategy.

The final step is to custom-tailor the chosen generic strategic approach (low-cost, differentiation, best-cost, focused low-cost, focused differentiation) to fit *both* the industry environment and the firm's standing vis-à-vis competitors. Here, it is important to be sure that (1) the customized aspects of the proposed strategy are well matched to the firm's competencies and competitive capabilities and (2) the strategy addresses all issues and problems the firm confronts.

In weeding out less attractive strategic alternatives and weighing the pros and cons of the most attractive ones, the answers to the following questions often help point to the best course of action, all things considered:

● What kind of competitive edge can the company *realistically* achieve? Can the company execute the strategic moves necessary to secure this edge?

● Does the company have the organizational capabilities and financial resources to succeed in these moves and approaches? If not, can they be acquired?

table 8.1   Sample Format for a Strategic Action Plan

1. Strategic Vision and Mission	**5. Supporting Functional Strategies** • Production
2. Strategic Objectives • Short-term • Long-term	• Marketing/sales • Finance • Personnel/human resources
3. Financial Objectives • Short-term • Long-term	• Other **6. Recommended Actions to Improve Company Performance** • Immediate
4. Overall Business Strategy	• Longer-range

- Once built, how can the competitive advantage be protected? Is the company in a position to lead industry change and set the rules by which rivals must compete? What defensive strategies need to be employed? Will rivals counterattack? What will it take to blunt their efforts?
- Are any rivals particularly vulnerable? Should the firm mount an offensive to capitalize on these vulnerabilities? What offensive moves need to be employed?
- What additional strategic moves are needed to deal with driving forces in the industry, specific threats and weaknesses, and any other issues/problems unique to the firm?

As the choice of strategic initiatives is developed, there are several pitfalls to avoid:

- Designing an overly ambitious strategic plan—one that overtaxes the company's resources and capabilities.
- Selecting a strategy that represents a radical departure from or abandonment of the cornerstones of the company's prior success—a radical strategy change need not be rejected automatically, but it should be pursued only after careful risk assessment.
- Choosing a strategy that goes against the grain of the organization's culture or that conflicts with the values and philosophies of the most senior executives.
- Being unwilling to *commit wholeheartedly* to one of the five competitive strategies—picking and choosing features of the different strategies usually produces so many compromises between low cost, best cost, differentiation, and focusing that the company fails to achieve any kind of advantage and ends up stuck in the middle.

Table 8.1 provides a generic format for outlining a strategic action plan for a single-business enterprise. It contains all of the pieces of a comprehensive strategic action plan that we discussed at various places in the previous seven chapters.

suggested | readings

Afuah, Allan. "Strategies to Turn Adversity into Profits." *Sloan Management Review* 40, no. 2 (Winter 1999), pp. 99–109.

Beinhocker, Eric D. "Robust Adaptive Strategies." *Sloan Management Review* 40, no. 3 (Spring 1999), pp. 95–106.

Bleeke, Joel A. "Strategic Choices for Newly Opened Markets." *Harvard Business Review* 68, no. 5 (September–October 1990), pp. 158–65.

Brenneman, Greg. "Right Away and All at Once: How We Saved Continental." *Harvard Business Review* 76, no. 5 (September–October 1998), pp. 162–79.

Cooper, Arnold C., and Clayton G. Smith. "How Established Firms Respond to Threatening Technologies." *Academy of Management Executive* 6, no. 2 (May 1992), pp. 55–57.

D'Aveni, Richard A. *Hypercompetition: Managing the Dynamics of Strategic Maneuvering.* New York: Free Press, 1994, chapters 3 and 4.

Day, George S. "Strategies for Surviving a Shakeout." *Harvard Business Review* 75, no. 2 (March–April 1997), pp. 92–102.

Feldman, Lawrence P., and Albert L. Page. "Harvesting: The Misunderstood Market Exit Strategy." *Journal of Business Strategy* 5, no. 4 (Spring 1985), pp. 79–85.

Finkin, Eugene F. "Company Turnaround." *Journal of Business Strategy* 5, no. 4 (Spring 1985), pp. 14–25.

Gordon, Geoffrey L.; Roger J. Calantrone; and C. Anthony di Benedetto. "Mature Markets and Revitalization Strategies: An American Fable." *Business Horizons* (May–June 1991), pp. 39–50.

Mayer, Robert J. "Winning Strategies for Manufacturers in Mature Industries." *Journal of Business Strategy* 8, no. 2 (Fall 1987), pp. 23–31.

Rackham, Neil; Lawrence Friedman; and Richard Ruff. *Getting Partnering Right: How Market Leaders Are Creating Long-Term Competitive Advantage.* New York: McGraw-Hill, 1996.

Zimmerman, Frederick M. *The Turnaround Experience: Real-World Lessons in Revitalizing Corporations.* New York: McGraw-Hill, 1991.

chapter | nine 9

Strategy and Competitive Advantage in Diversified Companies

...to acquire or not to acquire: that is the question.
—Robert J. Terry

Strategy is a deliberate search for a plan of action that will develop a business's competitive advantage and compound it.
—Bruce D. Henderson

Fit between a parent and its businesses is a two-edged sword: a good fit can create value: a bad one can destroy it.
—Andrew Campbell, Michael Goold, and Marcus Alexander

In this chapter and the next, we move up one level in the strategy-making hierarchy, from strategy making in a single-business enterprise to strategy making in a diversified enterprise. Because a diversified company is a collection of individual businesses, corporate strategy making is a bigger-picture exercise than line-of-business strategy making. In a single-business enterprise, management has to contend with only one industry environment and the

question of how to compete successfully in it. But in a diversified company corporate managers must strategize for several different business divisions competing in diverse industry environments and craft a multi-industry, multi-business strategy.

The task of crafting corporate strategy for a diversified company encompasses four areas:

1. *Picking the new industries to enter and deciding on the means of entry*—The first concern in diversifying is what new industries to get into and whether to enter by starting a new business from the ground up, acquiring a company already in the target industry, or forming a joint venture or strategic alliance with another company. A company can diversify narrowly into a few industries or broadly into many industries. The choice of whether to enter an industry via a new start-up operation or a collaborative joint venture or by acquisition of an established leader, an up-and-coming company, or a troubled company with turnaround potential shapes what position the company will initially stake out for itself.

2. *Initiating actions to boost the combined performance of the businesses the firm has entered*—As positions are created in the chosen industries, corporate strategists typically focus on ways to strengthen the long-term competitive positions and profitabilities of the businesses the firm has invested in. Corporate parents can help their business subsidiaries be more successful by providing financial resources, by supplying missing skills or technological know-how or managerial expertise to better perform key value chain activities, or by providing new avenues for cost reduction. They can also acquire another company in the same industry and merge the two operations into a stronger business, or acquire new businesses that strongly complement existing businesses. Typically, a company will pursue rapid-growth strategies in its most promising businesses, initiate turnaround efforts in weak-performing businesses with potential, and divest businesses that are no longer attractive or that don't fit into management's long-range plans.

3. *Pursuing opportunities to leverage cross-business value chain relationships and strategic fits into competitive advantage*—A company that diversifies into businesses with related value chain activities (pertaining to technology, supply chain logistics, production, overlapping distribution channels, common customers), gains competitive advantage potential not open to a company that diversifies into businesses whose value chains are totally unrelated. Related diversification presents opportunities to transfer skills, share expertise, or share facilities, thereby reducing overall costs, strengthening the competitiveness of some of the company's products, or enhancing the capabilities of particular business units.

4. *Establishing investment priorities and steering corporate resources into the most attractive business units*—A diversified company's different businesses are usually not equally attractive from the standpoint of investing additional funds. It is incumbent on corporate management to (*a*) decide on the priorities for investing capital in the company's different businesses, (*b*) channel resources into areas where earnings potentials are higher and away from areas where they are lower, and (*c*) divest business units that are chronically poor performers or are in an increasingly unattractive industry. Divesting poor performers and businesses in unattractive industries frees up unproductive investments for redeployment to promising business units or for financing attractive new acquisitions.

These four tasks are sufficiently demanding and time-consuming that corporate-level decision makers generally refrain from becoming immersed in the details of crafting and implementing business-level strategies, preferring instead to delegate lead responsibility for business strategy to the heads of each business unit.

In this chapter we describe the various paths through which a company can become diversified, explain how a company can use diversification to create or compound competitive advantage for its business units, and survey the strategic options an already-diversified company has to improve its overall performance. In Chapter 10 we will examine the techniques and procedures for assessing the strategic attractiveness of a diversified company's business portfolio.

WHEN TO DIVERSIFY

So long as a company has its hands full trying to capitalize on profitable growth opportunities in its present industry, there is no urgency to pursue diversification. But when growth opportunities in the company's mainstay business begin to peter out, diversification is usually the most viable option for reviving the firm's prospects. Diversification also has to be considered when a firm possesses technological expertise, core competencies, and resource strengths that are uniquely well suited for competing successfully in other industries.

When to diversify depends partly on a company's growth opportunities in its present industry and partly on the opportunities to utilize its resources, expertise, and capabilities in other market arenas.

As part of the decision to diversify into new businesses, the company must ask itself, "What kind and how much diversification?" The strategic possibilities are wide open. A company can diversify into closely related businesses or into totally unrelated businesses. It can expand into industries whose technologies and products complement and enhance its present business. It can leverage existing competencies and capabilities by expanding into businesses where these same resource strengths are key success factors and valuable competitive assets. It can pursue opportunities to get into other product markets where its present technological know-how can be applied and possibly yield competitive advantage. It can diversify to a small extent (less than 10 percent of total revenues and profits) or to a large extent (up to 50 percent of revenues and profits). It can move into one or two large new businesses or a greater number of small ones. Joint ventures in new fields of endeavor are another possibility.

Why Rushing to Diversify Isn't Necessarily a Good Strategy

Companies that continue to concentrate on a single business can achieve enviable success over many decades without relying on diversification to sustain their growth. McDonald's, Southwest Airlines, Coca-Cola, Domino's Pizza, Apple Computer, Wal-Mart, Federal Express, Timex, Campbell Soup, Anheuser-Busch, Xerox, Gerber, and Ford Motor Company all won their reputations in a single business. In the nonprofit sector, continued emphasis on a single activity has proved successful for the Red Cross, Salvation Army, Christian Children's Fund, Girl Scouts, Phi Beta Kappa, and American Civil Liberties Union. Coca-Cola, wanting to escape market maturity for soft drinks in the United States, abandoned most of its early efforts to diversify (into wine and into entertainment) when management concluded that the opportunities to sell Coca-Cola products in foreign markets (especially in China, India, and other parts of Asia) could produce attractive sales and profit growth well into the 21st century.

> Diversification doesn't need to become a strategic priority until a company begins to run out of attractive growth opportunities in its main business.

Concentrating on a single line of business (totally or with a small dose of diversification) has important advantages. It entails less ambiguity about "who we are and what we do." The energies of the total organization are directed down one business path, creating less chance that senior management's time will be diluted or organizational resources will be stretched thin by the demands of several different businesses. The company can devote the full force of its organizational resources to expanding into geographic markets it doesn't serve and to becoming better at what it does. Important competencies and competitive skills are more likely to emerge. Entrepreneurial efforts can be trained exclusively on keeping the firm's business strategy and competitive approach responsive to industry change and evolving customer preferences and buying patterns. With management's attention focused exclusively on one business, the probability is higher that good ideas will emerge on how to improve production technology, better meet customer needs with innovative new product features, and enhance efficiencies or differentiation capabilities along the value chain. All the firm's managers, especially top executives, can have hands-on contact with the core business and in-depth knowledge of operations. Most senior officers will usually have risen through the ranks and possess firsthand experience in field operations. (In broadly diversified enterprises, corporate managers seldom have had the opportunity to work in more than one or two of the company's businesses.) The more successful a single-business enterprise is, the more able it is to parlay its accumulated experience, distinctive competence, and reputation into a sustainable position as one of the leading firms in its industry.

> There are important organizational, managerial, and strategic advantages to concentrating on just one business.

The Risks of Concentrating on a Single Business

The big risk of remaining concentrated on a single business, of course, is putting all of a firm's eggs in one industry basket. If the market becomes saturated, competitively unattractive, or is eroded by the appearance of new technologies or new products or fast-shifting buyer preferences, then a company's prospects can quickly dim. It is not unusual for changing customer needs, technological innovation, or new substitute products to undermine or wipe out a single-business firm. Consider, for example, what digital cameras are doing to the market for film and film processing, what compact disc technology is doing to the market for cassette tapes and 3.5-inch disks, and what good-tasting, low-fat food products are doing to the sales of high-fat food products.

Factors That Signal When It's Time to Diversify

There's no formula for determining when a company ought to diversify. Judgments about when to diversify have to be made on the basis of a company's own situation. Generally speaking, a company is a prime candidate for diversifying when it has: (1) diminishing growth prospects in its present business, (2) opportunities to add value for its customers or gain competitive advantage by broadening its present business to include complementary products or technologies, (3) attractive opportunities to transfer its existing competencies and capabilities to new business arenas, (4) cost-saving opportunities that can be exploited by diversifying into closely related businesses and (5) the financial and organizational resources to support a diversification effort. Indeed, because companies in the same industry occupy different market positions and have different resource strengths and weaknesses, it is entirely rational for them to choose different diversification approaches and launch them at different times.

BUILDING SHAREHOLDER VALUE: THE ULTIMATE JUSTIFICATION FOR DIVERSIFYING

Diversification is justifiable only if it builds shareholder value. To enhance shareholder value, the company must accomplish more than simply spreading its business risk across various industries. Shareholders can easily diversify risk on their own by purchasing stock in companies in different industries or investing in mutual funds. Strictly speaking, *diversification does not create shareholder value unless the chosen businesses perform better under a single corporate umbrella than they would perform operating as independent, stand-alone businesses.* For example, let's say that company A diversifies by purchasing company B. If A and B's consolidated profits in the years to come prove no greater than what each could have earned on its own, then A's diversification won't provide its shareholders with added value. Company A's shareholders could have achieved the same $1 + 1 = 2$ result by merely purchasing stock in company B. Shareholder value is not created by diversification unless it produces a $1 + 1 = 3$ effect where sister businesses perform better together as part of the same firm than they could have performed as independent companies.

> To create shareholder value, a diversifying company must get into businesses that can perform better under common management than they could perform as stand-alone enterprises.

Three Tests for Judging a Diversification Move

The problem with such a strict rule for whether diversification is justified is that it requires speculative judgments about how well a diversified company's businesses would have performed on their own. Comparisons of actual and hypothetical performances are never very satisfactory, and besides they represent after-the-fact assessments. Strategists have to base diversification decisions on *expectations.* Attempts to gauge the impact of particular diversification moves on shareholder value do not have to be abandoned, however. Corporate strategists can make before-the-fact assessments of whether a particular diversification move is capable of increasing shareholder value by using three tests:[1]

1. *The industry attractiveness test:* The industry chosen for diversification must be attractive enough to yield consistently good returns on investment. Whether an industry is attractive depends chiefly on the presence of favorable competitive conditions and a market environment conducive to long-term profitability. Such factors as rapid growth or a currently hot-selling product are unreliable as indicators of attractiveness.

2. *The cost-of-entry test:* The cost to enter the target industry must not be so high as to erode the potential for good profitability. A catch-22 can prevail here, however. The more attractive the industry, the more expensive it can be to get into. Entry barriers for start-up companies are nearly always high; were barriers low, a rush of new entrants would soon erode the potential for high profitability. And buying a company already in an industry with strong appeal often entails a high acquisition cost. Costly entry undermines the prospects of above-average profitability and enhanced shareholder value.

3. *The better-off test:* Diversifying into a new business must offer potential for the company's existing businesses and the new business to perform better together than apart. The best chance of a 1 + 1 = 3 outcome occurs when a company diversifies into businesses that have competitively important value chain matchups with its existing businesses—matchups that offer opportunities to reduce costs, to transfer skills or technology from one business to another, to create valuable new competencies and capabilities, or to leverage existing resources (such as brand name reputation). Absent such strategic fits, a firm ought to be skeptical about the potential for the businesses to perform better together than apart.

Diversification moves that satisfy all three tests have the greatest potential to build shareholder value over the long term. Diversification moves that can pass only one or two tests are suspect.

CHOOSING THE DIVERSIFICATION PATH: RELATED VERSUS UNRELATED BUSINESSES

Once the decision is made to pursue diversification, the firm must choose whether to diversify into **related** businesses, **unrelated** businesses, or some mix of both—see Figure 9.1. *Businesses are said to be related when there are competitively valuable relationships among the activities comprising their respective value chains.* The appeal of related diversification is exploiting these value chain matchups to realize a 1 + 1 = 3 performance outcome and build shareholder value. *Businesses are said to be unrelated when the activities comprising their respective value chains are so dissimilar that no real potential exists to transfer skills or technology from one business to another or to combine similar activities and reduce costs or to otherwise produce competitively valuable benefits from operating under a common corporate umbrella.*

Most companies favor related diversification strategies, attracted by the performance-enhancing potential of cross-business synergies. However, some companies

[1]Michael E. Porter, "From Competitive Advantage to Corporate Strategy," *Harvard Business Review* 45, no. 3 (May–June 1987), pp. 46–49.

figure 9.1   **Strategy Alternatives for a Company Looking to Diversify**

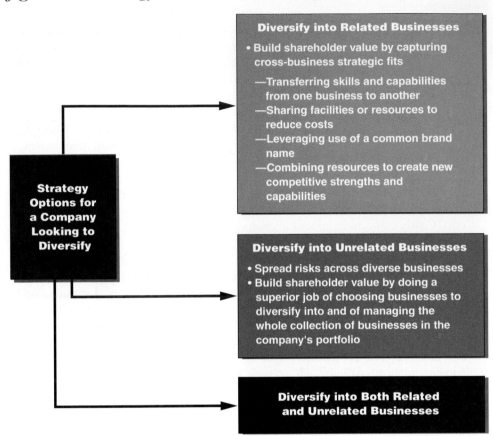

have, for one reason or another, pursued unrelated diversification. And a few have diversified into both related and unrelated businesses. The next two sections explore the ins and out of related and unrelated diversification.

THE CASE FOR RELATED DIVERSIFICATION STRATEGIES

A related diversification strategy involves adding businesses whose value chains possess competitively valuable "strategic fits" with the value chain of the company's present business, as shown in Figure 9.2. *Strategic fit* exists whenever one or more activities comprising the value chains of different businesses are sufficiently similar as to present opportunities for:[2]

---

[2]Michael E. Porter, *Competitive Advantage* (New York: Free Press, 1985), pp. 318–19 and pp. 337–53; Kenichi Ohmae, *The Mind of the Strategist* (New York: Penguin Books, 1983), pp. 121–24; and Porter, "From Competitive Advantage to Corporate Strategy," pp. 53–57. For an empirical study confirming that strategic fits are capable of enhancing performance (provided the resulting resource strengths are competitively valuable and difficult to duplicate by rivals), see Constantinos C. Markides and Peter J. Williamson, "Corporate Diversification and Organization Structure: A Resource-Based View," *Academy of Management Journal* 39, no. 2 (April 1996), pp. 340–67.

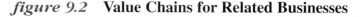

figure 9.2 Value Chains for Related Businesses

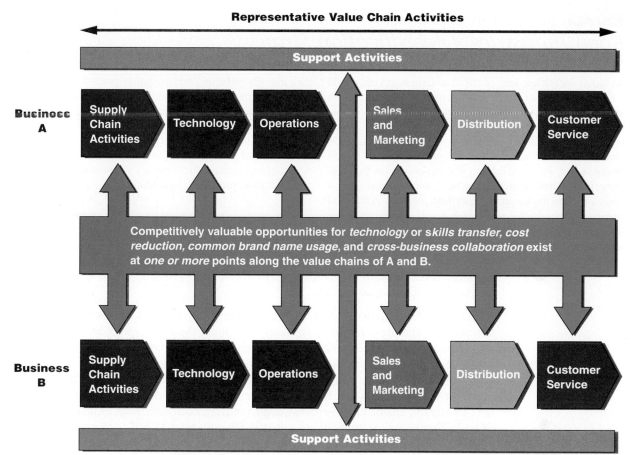

- Transferring competitively valuable expertise or technological know-how or capabilities from one business to another.
- Combining the related activities of separate businesses into a single operation to achieve lower costs.
- Exploiting common use of a well-known brand name.
- Cross-business collaboration to create competitively valuable resource strengths and capabilities (see Illustration Capsule 35).

Related diversification thus has strategic appeal from several angles. It allows a firm to reap the competitive advantage benefits of skills transfer, lower costs, common brand names, and/or stronger competitive capabilities and still spread investor risks over a broad business base. Furthermore, the relatedness among the different businesses provides sharper focus for managing diversification and a useful degree of strategic unity across the company's various business activities.

Cross-Business Strategic Fits along the Value Chain

Cross-business strategic fits can exist anywhere along the value chain—in R&D and technology activities, in supply chain activities and relationships with suppliers, in

> Strategic fits among related businesses offer the competitive advantage potential of *(a)* efficient transfer of key skills, technological expertise, or managerial know-how from one business to another, *(b)* lower costs, *(c)* ability to share a common brand name, or *(d)* creation of competitively valuable resource strengths and capabilities.

![Koch Industries logo] illustration capsule *35*
Koch Industries' Diversification Strategy

At Koch Industries, one of the five largest privately held companies in America, development of a company vision and strategy involved an analysis of the company's competencies and capabilities, and of how to match these competencies and capabilities with perceived market opportunities. One executive observed, "We thought we were in the oil business, but we found out our real expertise is in the gathering, transportation, processing, and trading business." This realization led the company to expand into gas liquids, and

then into gas gathering, transportation, processing, and trading. Involvement in gas operations led Koch into ammonia transportation and trading—operations more closely related to Koch's oil business than service station operations. More recent acquisitions have involved transferring Koch's core capabilities to grain gathering and cattle feedlots—business activities that draw on the company's expertise in gathering, transportation, processing, and trading.

Source: Tyler Cowen and Jerry Ellig, "Market-Based Management at Koch Industries: Discovery, Dissemination, and Integration of Knowledge," *Competitive Intelligence Review* 6, no. 4 (Winter 1995), p. 7.

manufacturing, in sales and marketing, in distribution activities, or in administrative support activities.[3]

R&D and Technology Activities   Diversifying into businesses where there is potential for sharing common technology, exploiting the full range of business opportunities associated with a particular technology and its derivatives, or transferring technological know-how from one business to another has considerable appeal. Businesses with technology-sharing benefits can perform better together than apart because of potential cost savings in R&D, because of potentially shorter times in getting new products to market, and/or because technological advances in one leads to increased sales of both. Technological innovations were the driver behind AT&T's diversification into cable TV (via the acquisition of TCI and MediaOne). Now that there are ways to provide local and long-distance telephone service, cable TV service, and Internet access to residential and commercial customers in a single "pipe," AT&T can offer its customers all of these services in a single package.

Supply Chain Activities   Businesses that have supply chain strategic fits can perform better together because of the potential for skills transfer in procuring materials, greater bargaining power in negotiating with common suppliers, the benefits of added collaboration with common supply chain partners, and/or added leverage with shippers in securing volume discounts on incoming parts and components. Dell Computer's strategic partnerships with leading suppliers of microprocessors, motherboards, disk drives, memory chips, monitors, modems, flat-panel displays, long-life batteries, and other desktop and laptop components have been an important component of its strategy to diversify into servers and workstations—products that include many components common to PCs and that can be sourced from the same strategic partners that provide Dell with PC components.

Manufacturing Activities   Cross-business strategic fits in production-related activities can represent an important source of competitive advantage in situations

[3]For a discussion of the strategic significance of cross-business coordination and insight into how it works, see Jeanne M. Liedtka, "Collaboration across Lines of Business for Competitive Advantage," *Academy of Management Executive* 10, no. 2 (May 1996), pp. 20–34.

where a diversifier's expertise in quality manufacture, in cost-efficient production methods, in just-in-time inventory practices, or in training and motivating workers can be transferred to another business. When Emerson Electric diversified into the chain-saw business, it transferred its expertise in low-cost manufacture to its newly acquired Beaird-Poulan business division; the transfer drove Beaird-Poulan's new strategy to be the low-cost provider of chain-saw products and fundamentally changed the way Beaird-Poulan chain saws were designed and manufactured. Another benefit of value chain matchups in production may involve cost-saving opportunities stemming from the ability to perform manufacturing or assembly activities jointly in the same facility rather than independently, thus making it feasible to consolidate production into a smaller number of plants and significantly reduce overall production costs. When snowmobile maker Bombardier diversified into motorcycles, it was able to set up assembly lines for its motorcycles in the same manufacturing facility where it was assembling its snowmobiles.

Distribution Activities   Businesses with closely related distribution activities can perform better together than apart because of potential cost savings in sharing the same distribution facilities or using many of the same wholesale distributors and retail dealers to access customers. When Sunbeam acquired Mr. Coffee, it was able to consolidate the distribution centers for its own line of small household appliances and the distribution centers for Mr. Coffee's lineup of coffeemakers; cutting back on the number of distribution centers the company had to operate generated considerable cost savings. Likewise, since Sunbeam products were sold to many of the same retailers as Mr. Coffee products (Wal-Mart, Kmart, department stores, home centers, hardware chains, supermarket chains, and drugstore chains), Sunbeam was able to convince many of the retailers carrying Sunbeam appliances to also take on the Mr. Coffee line and to convince retailers that stocked Mr. Coffee products to also begin carrying Sunbeam products.

Sales and Marketing Activities   A variety of cost-saving opportunities spring from diversifying into businesses with closely related sales and marketing activities. Sales costs can often be reduced by using a single sales force for the products of both businesses rather than having separate sales forces for each business. When the products are distributed through many of the same wholesale and retail dealers or are sold directly to the same customers, it is usually feasible to give one salesperson the responsibility for handling the sales of both products (rather than have two different salespeople call on the same customer). The products of related businesses can be promoted at the same Web site, and included in the same media ads and sales brochures. After-sale service and repair organizations for the products of closely related businesses can often be consolidated into a single operation. There may be opportunities to reduce costs by coordinating delivery and shipping, coordinating order processing and billing, and using common promotional tie-ins (cents-off couponing, free samples and trial offers, seasonal specials, and the like). When global power-tool maker Black & Decker acquired General Electric's domestic small household appliance business, it was able to use its own global sales force and global distribution facilities in power tools to sell and distribute small appliances (toasters, irons, mixers, and coffeemakers) because the types of customers that carried its power tools (discounters like Wal-Mart and Kmart, home centers, and hardware stores) also stocked small appliances. The economies of combining and then downsizing the sales forces and distribution centers for power tools and small appliances were substantial.

A second category of benefits arises when different businesses use similar sales and marketing approaches; in such cases, there may be competitively valuable opportunities to transfer selling, merchandising, advertising, and product differentiation skills from one business to another. Philip Morris, a leading cigarette manufacturer, pursued a related diversification strategy by purchasing Miller Brewing, General Foods, and Kraft Foods and transferring its competencies and capabilities in advertising, promoting, and marketing cigarettes to the marketing of beer and food products. Procter & Gamble's lineup of products includes Jif peanut butter, Duncan Hines cake mixes, Folger's coffee, Tide laundry detergent, Crisco vegetable oil, Crest toothpaste, Ivory soap, Charmin toilet tissue, and Head and Shoulders shampoo. All of these have different competitors and different supply chain and production requirements, but they all move through the same wholesale distribution systems, are sold in common retail settings to the same shoppers, are advertised and promoted in the same ways, and require the same marketing and merchandising skills.

A third set of benefits arises from related sales and marketing activities when a company's brand name and reputation in one business is transferable to other businesses. Black & Decker's strong brand name in power tools and cordless items like the Dustbuster vacuum greatly facilitated a successful transfer of the B&D brand name to the products in GE's household appliance line. Honda's name in motorcycles and automobiles gave it instant credibility and recognition in entering the lawn-mower business, allowing it to achieve a significant market share without spending large sums on advertising to establish a brand identity for its lawn mowers. Canon's reputation in photographic equipment was a competitive asset that facilitated the company's diversification into copying equipment. Panasonic's name in consumer electronics (radios, TVs) was readily transferred to microwave ovens, making it easier and cheaper for Panasonic to diversify into the microwave oven market.

Managerial and Administrative Support Activities   Often, different businesses require comparable types of skills, competencies, and managerial know-how, thereby allowing know-how in one line of business to be transferred to another. Ford transferred its automobile financing and credit management know-how to the savings and loan industry when it acquired some failing savings and loan associations during the 1989 bailout of the crisis-ridden S&L industry. At General Electric, managers who were involved in GE's geographic expansion into Russia were able to expedite entry because of information gained from GE managers involved in expansions into other emerging-country markets. The lessons GE managers learned in China were passed along to GE managers in Russia, allowing them to anticipate that the Russian government would demand that GE build production capacity in the country rather than enter the market through exporting or licensing and that GE would be required to aid in the country's national economic development efforts. In addition, GE's managers in Russia were better able to develop realistic performance expectations and make tough up-front decisions since experience in China and elsewhere warned them (1) that there would likely be increased short-term costs during the early years of start-up and (2) that if GE committed to the Russian market for the long term and aided the country's economic development it could eventually expect to be given the freedom to pursue profitable penetration of the Russian market.[4]

Likewise, different businesses sometimes entail the same types of administrative support facilities. For instance, an electric utility that diversifies into natural gas, water, cable TV, appliance sales and repair services, and home security services can use the same customer data network, the same customer call centers and local offices, the same billing and customer accounting systems, and the same customer service infrastructure to support all of its products and services.

---

[4]"Beyond Knowledge Management: How Companies Mobilize Experience," *The Financial Times*, February 8, 1999, p. 5.

illustration capsule 36
Examples of Companies with Related Business Portfolios

Presented below are the business portfolios of four companies that have pursued related diversification. See if you can identify the strategic fits and value chain relationships that exist among their businesses.

GILLETTE

- Blades and razors
- Toiletries (Right Guard, Foamy, Dry Idea, Soft & Dry, White Rain)
- Oral-B toothbrushes
- Writing instruments and stationery products (Paper Mate pens, Parker pens, Waterman pens, Liquid Paper correction fluids)
- Braun shavers, coffeemakers, alarm clocks, mixers, hair dryers, and electric toothbrushes
- Duracell batteries

DARDEN RESTAURANTS

- Olive Garden restaurant chain (Italian-themed)
- Red Lobster restaurant chain (seafood-themed)
- Bahama Breeze restaurant chain (Caribbean-themed)

JOHNSON & JOHNSON

- Baby products (powder, shampoo, oil, lotion)
- Band-Aids and other first-aid products
- Women's health and personal care products (Stayfree, Carefree, Sure & Natural)
- Neutrogena and Aveeno skin care products
- Nonprescription drugs (Tylenol, Motrin, Pepcid AC, Mylanta, Monistat)
- Prescription drugs
- Prosthetic and other medical devices
- Surgical and hospital products
- Accuvue contact lenses

PEPSICO, INC.

- Soft drinks (Pepsi, Diet Pepsi, Pepsi ONE, Mountain Dew, Mug, Slice, Storm)
- Fruit juices (Tropicana and Dole)
- New Age and other beverages (Aquafina bottled water, Lipton ready-to-drink tea, Starbucks ready-to-drink coffee, All Sport isotonic beverages)
- Snack foods (Fritos, Lays, Ruffles, Doritos, Tostitos, Santitas, Smart Food, Rold Gold pretzels, Chee-tos, Grandma's cookies, Sun Chips, Cracker Jack, salsas, sandwich crackers)

Source: Company annual reports.

Illustration Capsule 36 shows the business portfolios of four companies that have pursued a strategy of related diversification.

Strategic Fit, Economies of Scope, and Competitive Advantage

As the preceding discussion illustrates, related diversification can lead to cost savings whenever there are opportunities to consolidate one or more of the value chain activities being performed in different businesses. Such savings are termed **economies of scope**—a concept distinct from *economies of scale*. Economies of *scale* are cost savings that accrue from increases in size or number; for example, unit costs are lower in a large plant than in a small plant, lower in a large distribution center than in a small one, lower for large-volume purchases of components than for small-volume purchases. Economies of *scope* are cross-business cost-saving opportunities.

Economies of scope are pretty much a phenomenon of related diversification, arising whenever it is less costly to perform certain value chain activities for two or more

> **Basic Concept**
> *Economies of scope* arise from the ability to eliminate costs by operating two or more businesses under the same corporate umbrella; the cost-saving opportunities can stem from strategic fit relationships anywhere along the businesses' value chains.

businesses operated under centralized management than it is for these activities to be performed independently. Sharing technology, performing R&D together, sharing manufacturing or distribution facilities, using a common sales force or distributor/dealer network, sharing an established brand name, and sharing administrative support functions can all help a diversified company save money. *The greater the economies of scope associated with cross-business cost-saving opportunities, the greater the potential for creating a competitive advantage based on lower costs.*

> What makes related diversification attractive is the opportunity to turn cross-business strategic fits into competitive advantage.

What makes related diversification an attractive strategy is the opportunity to convert the strategic fit relationships between the value chains of different businesses into competitive advantage over business rivals that have not diversified or that have diversified in ways that don't give them access to such strategic-fit benefits. The greater the relatedness among the businesses of a diversified company, the greater the opportunities for skills transfer and/or combining value chain activities to achieve lower costs and/or collaborating to create new resource strengths and capabilities and the bigger the window for creating competitive advantage.

> Competitive advantage achieved through cross-business strategic fits adds to the performance potential of the firm's individual businesses; this extra source of competitive advantage allows related diversification to have a 1 + 1 = 3 effect on shareholder value.

Moreover, *a diversified firm that exploits cross-business value-chain matchups and captures the benefits of strategic fit can achieve a consolidated performance greater than the sum of what the businesses can earn pursuing independent strategies.* The competitive edge flowing from strategic fits along the value chains of related businesses provides a dependable basis for them performing better together than as stand-alone enterprises where no such competitive edge exists. The bigger the strategic-fit benefits, the more that related diversification is capable of 1 + 1 = 3 performance—thereby satisfying the better-off test for building shareholder value.

Capturing Strategic-Fit Benefits

It is one thing to diversify into industries with strategic fit and another to actually capture the benefits associated with having interrelated value chains.[5] To capture the cost-saving benefits of cross-business strategic fits, the related value chain activities must usually be merged into a single functional unit and coordinated; then the cost savings must be squeezed out. Because merging functions can entail reorganization costs, management must decide whether the benefit of some centralized strategic control is great enough to warrant sacrifice of business-unit autonomy. Likewise, where skills or technology transfer is the cornerstone of strategic fit, managers must find a way to make the transfer effective without stripping too many skilled personnel from the business that has the expertise. The more a company's diversification strategy is tied to skills or technology transfer, the more it has to develop a big enough and talented enough pool of specialized personnel not only to supply new businesses with the skill or technology but also to master the skill or technology sufficiently to create competitive advantage.

> A company that can expand its stock of strategic assets faster and at lower cost than rivals obtains sustainable competitive advantage.

There is one additional benefit that flows from becoming adept at capturing cross-business strategic fits: the competitive advantage potential for the firm to expand its pool of resources and strategic assets and to create new ones *faster and more cheaply* than rivals who are not diversified across related businesses.[6] One reason some diversified firms perform better over the long term than others is that they are more accomplished in

---

[5]For one view of how to capture strategic fit benefits, see Kathleen M. Eisenhardt and D. Charles Galunic, "Coevolving: At Last, a Way to Make Synergies Work," *Harvard Business Review* 78, no. 1 (January–February 2000), pp. 91–101.

[6]Constantinos C. Markides and Peter J. Williamson, "Related Diversification, Core Competences and Corporate Performance," *Strategic Management Journal* 15 (Summer 1994), pp. 149–65.

exploiting the links between their related businesses; such know-how translates into an ability to *accelerate* the creation of valuable new core competencies and competitive capabilities. Given the rapid pace of change in many industries in today's world, having the ability to build new resource strengths and capabilities faster than rivals is a potent and dependable way for a diversified company to earn superior returns over the long term.

THE CASE FOR UNRELATED DIVERSIFICATION STRATEGIES

Despite the strategic-fit benefits associated with related diversification, a number of companies opt for unrelated diversification strategies. These companies exhibit a willingness to diversify into *any industry* with a good profit opportunity. *In unrelated diversification there is no deliberate effort to seek out businesses having strategic fit with the firm's other businesses*—see Figure 9.3. While companies pursuing unrelated diversification may try to make certain their diversification targets meet the industry-attractiveness and cost-of-entry tests, the conditions needed for the better-off test are either disregarded or relegated to secondary status. Decisions to diversify into one industry versus another are the product of an opportunistic search for "good" companies to acquire—*the basic premise of unrelated diversification is that any company that can be acquired on good financial terms and that has satisfactory profit prospects represents a good business to diversify into.* Much time and effort goes into finding and screening acquisition candidates, using such criteria as:

> A strategy of unrelated diversification involves diversifying into whatever industries and businesses hold promise for attractive financial gain; exploiting strategic-fit relationships is secondary.

- Whether the business can meet corporate targets for profitability and return on investment.
- Whether the new business will require substantial infusions of capital to replace out-of-date plants and equipment, fund expansion, and provide working capital.
- Whether the business is in an industry with significant growth potential.
- Whether the business is big enough to contribute significantly to the parent firm's bottom line.
- Whether there is a potential for union difficulties or adverse government regulations concerning product safety or the environment.
- Whether there is industry vulnerability to recession, inflation, high interest rates, or shifts in government policy.

Sometimes, companies with unrelated diversification strategies concentrate on identifying acquisition candidates that offer quick opportunities for financial gain because of their "special situation." Two types of businesses may hold such attraction:

- *Companies whose assets are undervalued*—Opportunities may exist to acquire such companies for less than full market value and make substantial capital gains by reselling their assets and businesses for more than their acquired costs.
- *Companies that are financially distressed*—Such businesses can often be purchased at a bargain price, their operations turned around with the aid of the parent company's financial resources and managerial know-how, and then either held as long-term investments in the acquirer's business portfolio (because of their strong earnings or cash flow potential) or sold at a profit, whichever is more attractive.

Companies that pursue unrelated diversification nearly always enter new businesses by acquiring an established company rather than by forming a start-up subsidiary

figure 9.3 **Value Chains for Unrelated Businesses**

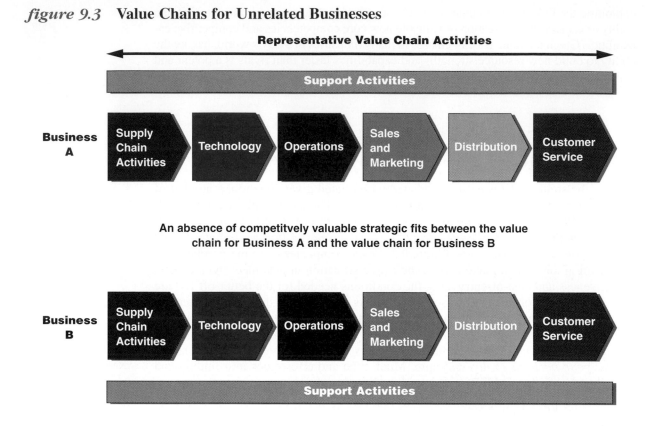

within their own corporate structures. Their premise is that growth by acquisition translates into enhanced shareholder value. Suspending application of the better-off test is seen as justifiable so long as unrelated diversification results in sustained growth in corporate revenues and earnings and so long as none of the acquired businesses end up performing badly.

Illustration Capsule 37 shows the business portfolios of several companies that have pursued unrelated diversification. Such companies are frequently labeled *conglomerates* because their business interests range broadly across diverse industries.

The Pros and Cons of Unrelated Diversification

Unrelated diversification has appeal from several financial angles:

1. Business risk is scattered over a set of *diverse* industries—a superior way to diversify financial risk as compared to related diversification because the company's investments can be spread over businesses with totally different technologies, competitive forces, market features, and customer bases.[7]

---

[7]While such arguments have logical appeal, there is research showing that related diversification is less risky from a financial perspective than is unrelated diversification; see Michael Lubatkin and Sayan Chatterjee, "Extending Modern Portfolio Theory into the Domain of Corporate Diversification: Does It Apply?" *Academy of Management Journal* 37, no. 1 (February 1994), pp. 109–36.

illustration capsule 37
Diversified Companies with Unrelated Business Portfolios

DIAGEO PLC

- Burger King fast-food restaurants
- Guinness—a leading beer brewer and maker of stout
- Häagen-Dazs ice cream products
- Pillsbury and Martha White flours and baking products
- Old El Paso Mexican food products
- Progresso soups
- Totino's pizza
- Frescarina fresh pasta
- B&M baked beans
- Green Giant, Giant Vert, and Gigante brands of canned and frozen vegetables
- Spirits and wines—Smirnoff, Popov vodka, Johnny Walker, Gordon's, Tanqueray, George Dickel, J&B, Moët, Henessey, Gilbey's, Bailey's, Cinzano, Jose Cuervo, Beaulieu Vineyards, Glen Ellen Wines, Rutherford Estates wines, Dom Perignon, and some 50 other brands of liquors, cordials, wines, and brandies

UNITED TECHNOLOGIES, INC.

- Pratt & Whitney aircraft engines
- Carrier heating and air-conditioning equipment
- Otis elevators
- Sikorsky helicopters
- Hamilton Substrand aerospace subsystems and components

THE WALT DISNEY COMPANY

- Theme parks
- Disney Cruise Line
- Resort properties
- Movie production (for both children and adults)
- Video production
- Television broadcasting (ABC, Disney Channel, Toon Disney, Classic Sports Network, ESPN, E!, Lifetime, and A&E networks)
- Radio broadcasting (Disney Radio)
- Theatrical productions
- Musical recordings
- Animation art sales
- Anaheim Mighty Ducks NHL franchise
- Anaheim Angels Major League Baseball franchise (25 percent ownership)
- Book and magazine publishing
- Interactive software and Internet sites
- The Disney Store retail shops

COOPER INDUSTRIES

- Crescent wrenches, pliers, and screwdrivers
- Nicholson files and saws
- Diamond horseshoes and farrier tools
- Lufkin measuring and layout products
- Gardner-Denver electric power tools
- Electrical construction materials
- Lighting fixtures, fuses, and circuit protection devices
- Electric utility products (transformers, relays, capacitor controls, switches)
- Emergency lighting, fire detection, and security systems

TEXTRON, INC.

- Bell helicopters
- Cessna Aircraft
- E-Z-Go golf carts
- Textron Automotive (instrument panels, plastic fuel tanks, plastic interior and exterior trim)
- Textron Fastening Systems (the global leader)
- Fluid and power systems
- Textron Financial Services
- Jacobsen turf care equipment
- Ransomes turf care and utility vehicles
- Tools and testing equipment for the wire and cable industry

(continued)

 illustration capsule 37

(concluded)

AMERICAN STANDARD

- Trane and American Standard furnaces, heat pumps, and air conditioners
- Plumbing products (American Standard, Ideal Standard, Standard, Porcher lavatories, toilets, bathtubs, faucets, whirlpool baths, and shower basins)
- Automotive products (commercial and utility vehicle braking and control systems)
- Medical systems (DiaSorin disease assessment and management products)

VEBA GROUP

VEBA is a German-based company with revenues of $43 billion and a ranking of 46 on the Fortune Global 500.

- PreussenElektra—Germany's second largest generator of electricity

- Degussa-Huls—one of the world's largest specialty chemicals companies whose products include feed additives, hydrogen peroxide, industrial carbon black, silicic acids, and phenol
- VEBA Oel—a crude oil producer and a refiner of petroleum and petrochemical products
- MEMC Electronic Materials—a Missouri-based manufacturer of silicon wafers, with production facilities in the United States, Asia, and Europe
- VEBA Telecom—a seller of wireless service to private and business customers and a participant in the telecommunications markets in Switzerland and France
- Viterra—Germany's market leader in real estate and real estate services
- VEBA Electronics and Stinnes—business interests in distribution/logistics

Source: Company annual reports.

2. The company's financial resources can be employed to maximum advantage by investing in *whatever industries* offer the best profit prospects (as opposed to considering only opportunities in related industries). Specifically, cash flows from company businesses with lower growth and profit prospects can be diverted to acquiring and expanding businesses with higher growth and profit potentials.

3. Company profitability may prove somewhat more stable because hard times in one industry may be partially offset by good times in another—ideally, cyclical downswings in some of the company's businesses are counterbalanced by cyclical upswings in other businesses the company has diversified into.

4. To the extent that corporate managers are exceptionally astute at spotting bargain-priced companies with big upside profit potential, shareholder wealth can be enhanced.

> The two biggest drawbacks to unrelated diversification are the difficulties of competently managing many different businesses and being without the added source of competitive advantage that cross-business strategic fit provides.

While entry into an unrelated business can often pass the industry attractiveness and cost-of-entry tests (but rarely the better-off test), a strategy of unrelated diversification has drawbacks. One Achilles' heel of conglomerate diversification is the big demand it places on corporate-level management to make sound decisions regarding fundamentally different businesses operating in fundamentally different industry and competitive environments. The greater the number of businesses a company is in and the more diverse they are, the harder it is for corporate managers to oversee each subsidiary and spot problems early, to have real expertise in evaluating the attractiveness of each business's industry and competitive environment, and to judge the caliber of strategic actions and plans proposed by business-level managers. As one president of a diversified firm expressed it:

We've got to make sure that our core businesses are properly managed for solid, long-term earnings. We can't just sit back and watch the numbers. We've got to know what the real issues are out there in the profit centers. Otherwise, we're not even in a position to check out our managers on the big decisions.[8]

With broad diversification, corporate managers have to be shrewd and talented enough to (1) discern a good acquisition from a bad acquisition, (2) select capable managers to run each of many different businesses, (3) discern when the major strategic proposals of business-unit managers are sound, and (4) know what to do if a business unit stumbles.[9] Because every business tends to encounter rough sledding, a good way to gauge the risk of diversifying into new unrelated areas is to ask, "If the new business got into trouble, would we know how to bail it out?" When the answer is no, unrelated diversification can pose significant financial risk and the business's profit prospects are more chancy.[10] As the former chairman of a Fortune 500 company advised, "Never acquire a business you don't know how to run." It takes only one or two big strategic mistakes (misjudging industry attractiveness, encountering unexpected problems in a newly acquired business, or being too optimistic about how hard it will be to turn a struggling subsidiary around) to cause a precipitous drop in corporate earnings and crash the parent company's stock price.

Second, without the competitive advantage potential of strategic fit, consolidated performance of an unrelated multibusiness portfolio tends to be no better than the sum of what the individual business units could achieve if they were independent, and it may be worse to the extent that corporate managers meddle unwisely in business-unit operations or hamstring them with corporate policies. Except, perhaps, for the added financial backing that a cash-rich corporate parent can provide, a strategy of unrelated diversification does nothing for the competitive strength of the individual business units. Each business is on its own in trying to build a competitive edge. Unrelated diversification offers no basis for cost reduction, skills transfer, or technology sharing. In a widely diversified firm, the value added by corporate managers depends primarily on how good they are at deciding what new businesses to add, which ones to get rid of, how best to deploy available financial resources to build a higher-performing collection of businesses, and the quality of the decision-making guidance they give to the general managers of their business subsidiaries.

Third, although in theory unrelated diversification offers the potential for greater sales-profit stability over the course of the business cycle, *in practice, attempts at countercyclical diversification fall short of the mark*. Few attractive businesses have opposite up-and-down cycles; the great majority of businesses are similarly affected by economic good times and hard times. There's no convincing evidence that the consolidated profits of broadly diversified firms are more stable or less subject to reversal in periods of recession and economic stress than the profits of less diversified firms.

---

[8]Carter F. Bales, "Strategic Control: The President's Paradox," *Business Horizons* 20, no. 4 (August 1977), p. 17.

[9]For a review of the experiences of companies that have pursued unrelated diversification successfully, see Patricia L. Anslinger and Thomas E. Copeland, "Growth through Acquisitions: A Fresh Look," *Harvard Business Review* 74, no. 1 (January–February 1996), pp. 126–35.

[10]Of course, management may be willing to assume the risk that trouble will not strike before it has had time to learn the business well enough to bail it out of almost any difficulty. But there is research that shows this is very risky from a financial perspective; see, for example, Lubatkin and Chatterjee, "Extending Modern Portfolio Theory," pp. 132–33.

Despite these drawbacks, unrelated diversification can sometimes be a desirable corporate strategy. It certainly merits consideration when a firm needs to diversify away from an endangered or unattractive industry and has no distinctive competencies or capabilities it can transfer to an adjacent industry. There's also a rationale for pure diversification to the extent that owners have a strong preference for investing in several unrelated businesses instead of a family of related ones. Otherwise, the argument for unrelated diversification hinges on the case-by-case prospects for financial gain.

A key issue in unrelated diversification is how wide a net to cast in building the business portfolio. In other words, should the corporate portfolio contain few or many unrelated businesses? How much business diversity can corporate executives successfully manage? A reasonable way to resolve the issue of how much diversification comes from answering two questions: "What is the least diversification it will take to achieve acceptable growth and profitability?" and "What is the most diversification that can be managed given the complexity it adds?"[11] The optimal amount of diversification usually lies between these two extremes.

Unrelated Diversification and Shareholder Value

Unrelated diversification is *a financial* approach to creating shareholder value; related diversification, in contrast, represents a *strategic* approach.

Unrelated diversification is fundamentally a *financial* approach to creating shareholder value, whereas related diversification is fundamentally *strategic*. Related diversification represents a strategic approach to building shareholder value because it is predicated on exploiting the links between the value chains of different businesses to lower costs, transfer skills and technological expertise across businesses, and gain other strategic-fit benefits. As we stressed earlier, the objective is to convert cross-business strategic fits into an extra measure of competitive advantage that goes beyond what business subsidiaries are able to achieve on their own. The added competitive advantage a firm achieves through related diversification is the driver for building greater shareholder value.

In contrast, unrelated diversification is predicated on astute deployment of corporate financial resources and executive skill in spotting financially attractive business opportunities. Since unrelated diversification entails no cross-business strategic-fit opportunities of consequence, corporate strategists can't build shareholder value by acquiring companies that exploit value chain matchups to perform better together than as stand-alone entities—in a conglomerate of unrelated businesses, competitive advantage doesn't go beyond what each business subsidiary can achieve independently through its own competitive strategy. Consequently, for unrelated diversification to result in enhanced shareholder value (above the $1 + 1 = 2$ effect that shareholders could obtain by purchasing ownership interests in a variety of businesses to spread investment risk on their own behalf), corporate strategists must exhibit superior skills in creating and managing a portfolio of diversified business interests. This specifically means:

For corporate strategists to build shareholder value in some way other than through strategic fits and competitive advantage, they must be smart enough to produce financial results from a group of businesses that exceed what business-level managers can produce.

- Doing a superior job of diversifying into new businesses that can produce consistently good returns on investment (satisfying the attractiveness test).
- Doing an excellent job of negotiating favorable acquisition prices (satisfying the cost-of-entry test).
- Making astute moves to sell previously acquired business subsidiaries at their peak and getting premium prices. (This requires skills in discerning when a business subsidiary is on the verge of confronting adverse industry and competitive conditions and probable declines in long-term profitability.)

---

[11]Peter Drucker, *Management: Tasks, Responsibilities, Practices* (New York: Harper & Row, 1974), pp. 692–93.

● Being shrewd in shifting corporate financial resources out of businesses where profit opportunities are dim and into businesses where rapid earnings growth and high returns on investment are occurring.

● Doing such a good job overseeing the firm's business subsidiaries and contributing to how they are managed (by providing expert problem-solving skills, creative strategy suggestions, and decision-making guidance to business-level managers) that the businesses perform at a higher level than they would otherwise be able to do (a possible way to satisfy the better-off test).

To the extent that corporate executives are able to craft and execute a strategy of unrelated diversification that produces enough of the above outcomes for an enterprise to consistently outperform other firms in generating dividends and capital gains for stockholders, a case can be made that shareholder value has truly been enhanced. Achieving such results consistently requires supertalented corporate executives, however. Without them, unrelated diversification is a very dubious and unreliable way to try to build shareholder value. There are far more who have tried it and failed than who have tried it and succeeded.

COMBINATION RELATED-UNRELATED DIVERSIFICATION STRATEGIES

There's nothing to preclude a company from diversifying into both related and unrelated businesses. Indeed, in actual practice the business makeup of diversified companies varies considerably. Some diversified companies are really *dominant-business enterprises*—one major "core" business accounts for 50 to 80 percent of total revenues and a collection of small related or unrelated businesses accounts for the remainder. Some diversified companies are *narrowly diversified* around a few (two to five) related or unrelated businesses. Some diversified companies are *broadly diversified* and have a wide-ranging collection of either related businesses or unrelated businesses or a mixture of both. And a few multibusiness enterprises have diversified into unrelated areas but have a collection of related businesses within each area—thus giving them a business portfolio consisting of *several unrelated groups of related businesses.* There's ample room for companies to customize their diversification strategies to incorporate elements of both related and unrelated diversification, as may suit their own risk preferences and strategic vision.

STRATEGIES FOR ENTERING NEW BUSINESSES

Entry into new related or unrelated businesses can take any of three forms: acquisition, internal start-up, and joint ventures/strategic partnerships.

Acquisition of an Existing Business

Acquisition is the most popular means of diversifying into another industry. Not only is it a quicker way to enter the target market than trying to launch a brand-new operation from the ground up but it offers an effective way to hurdle such entry barriers as acquiring technological experience, establishing supplier relationships, becoming big enough to match rivals' efficiency and unit costs, having to spend large sums on introductory advertising and promotions to gain market visibility and brand recognition, and securing adequate distribution.[12] In many industries, going the internal start-up route and trying to develop the knowledge, resources, scale of operation, and market reputation necessary to become an effective competitor can take years. Acquiring an already established concern allows the entrant to move directly to the task of building a strong market position in the target industry.

However, finding the right kind of company to acquire sometimes presents a challenge.[13] The big dilemma an acquisition-minded firm faces is whether to pay a premium price for a successful company or to buy a struggling company at a bargain price. If the buying firm has little knowledge of the industry but ample capital, it is often better off purchasing a capable, strongly positioned firm—unless the price of such an acquisition is prohibitive and flunks the cost-of-entry test. However, when the acquirer sees promising ways to transform a weak firm into a strong one and has the resources, the know-how, and the patience to do it, a struggling company can be the better long-term investment.

The cost-of-entry test requires that the expected profit stream of an acquired business provide an attractive return on the total acquisition cost and on any new capital investment needed to sustain or expand its operations. A high acquisition price can make meeting that test improbable or difficult. For instance, suppose that the price to purchase a company is $3 million and that the business is earning after-tax profits of $200,000 on an equity investment of $1 million (a 20 percent annual return). Simple arithmetic requires that the acquired business's profits be tripled for the purchaser to earn the same 20 percent return on the $3 million acquisition price that the previous owners were getting on their $1 million equity investment. Building the acquired firm's earnings from $200,000 to $600,000 annually could take several years—and require additional investment on which the purchaser would also have to earn a 20 percent return. Since the owners of a successful and growing company usually demand a price that reflects their business's future profit prospects, it's easy for such an acquisition to fail the cost-of-entry test. A would-be diversifier can't count on being able to acquire a desirable company in an appealing industry at a price that still permits attractive returns on investment.

Internal Start-Up

Achieving diversification through *internal start-up* involves creating a new company under the corporate umbrella to compete in the desired industry. A newly formed organization not only has to overcome entry barriers but also has to invest in new production capacity, develop sources of supply, hire and train employees, build channels of distribution, grow a customer base, and so on. Generally, forming a start-up company is more attractive when (1) there is ample time to launch the business from the ground up, (2) incumbent firms are likely to be slow or ineffective in responding to a new entrant's efforts to crack the market, (3) internal entry has lower costs than entry via acquisition, (4) the company already has in-house most or all of the skills it needs to compete effectively, (5) adding new production capacity will not adversely impact the supply-demand balance in the industry, and (6) the targeted industry is populated

> One stumbling block to entering attractive industries by acquisition is the difficulty of finding a suitable company at a price that satisfies the cost-of-entry test.

> The biggest drawbacks to entering an industry by forming a start-up company internally are the costs of overcoming entry barriers and the extra time it takes to build a strong and profitable competitive position.

---

[12]In recent years, hostile takeovers have become a hotly debated and sometimes abused approach to acquisition. The term *takeover* refers to the attempt (often sprung as a surprise) of one firm to acquire ownership or control over another firm against the wishes of the latter's management (and perhaps some of its stockholders).

[13]Michael E. Porter, *Competitive Strategy: Techniques for Analyzing Industries and Competitors* (New York: Free Press, 1980), pp. 354–55.

with many relatively small firms so the new start-up does not have to compete head-to-head against larger, more powerful rivals.[14]

Joint Ventures and Strategic Partnerships

Joint ventures typically entail forming a new corporate entity owned by the partners, whereas strategic partnerships represent a collaborative arrangement that usually can be terminated whenever any one of the partners so chooses. Most joint ventures have involved two partners and, historically, were normally formed to pursue opportunities that were somewhat peripheral to the strategic interests of the partners; very few companies have used joint ventures to diversify into new industries central to their corporate strategy. In recent years, strategic partnerships/alliances have replaced joint ventures as the favored mechanism for joining forces to pursue strategically important diversification opportunities because they can readily accommodate multiple partners and are more flexible and adaptable to rapidly changing technogological and market conditions than a formal joint venture.

A strategic partnership or joint venture can be a useful way to gain access to a new business in at least three types of situations.[15] First, a strategic alliance/joint venture is a good way to pursue an opportunity that is too complex, uneconomical, or risky for a single organization to pursue alone. Second, strategic alliances/joint ventures make sense when the opportunities in a new industry require a broader range of competencies and know-how than any one organization can marshal. Many of the opportunities in satellite-based telecommunications, biotechnology, and network-based systems that blend hardware, software, and services call for the coordinated development of complementary innovations and integrating a host of financial, technical, political, and regulatory factors. In such cases, pooling the resources and competencies of two or more independent organizations is essential to generate the capabilities needed for success.

Third, joint ventures are sometimes the only way to gain entry into a desirable foreign market when market entry is restricted by government and companies must secure a local partner to gain entry; for example, the Chinese government closed entry in the automotive industry to all but a few select automakers and in the elevator industry it originally permitted only Otis, Schindler, and Mitsubishi to establish joint ventures with local partners. (Although this number was later expanded, the three early entrants were able to retain a market advantage over later entrants.)[16] Joint ventures with local partners can also be a useful way to surmount tariff barriers and import quotas. Alliances with local partners have become a favorite mechanism for global companies to establish footholds in desirable foreign country markets. Local partners offer outside companies the benefits of local knowledge about market conditions, local customs and cultural factors, and customer buying habits; they can also be a source of managerial and marketing personnel and provide access to distribution outlets. The foreign partner's role is usually to provide specialized skills, technological know-how, and other resources needed to crack the local market and serve it efficiently.

However, such partnerships are not without their difficulties, often posing complicated questions about how to divide efforts among the partners and about who has effective control.[17] Conflicts between foreign and domestic partners can arise over

---

[14]Ibid., pp. 344–45.

[15]Yves L. Doz and Gary Hamel, *Alliance Advantage: The Art of Creating Value through Partnering* (Boston: Harvard Business School Press, 1998), chapters 1 and 2. See also Drucker, *Management: Tasks, Responsibilities, Practices,* pp. 720–24.

[16]Doz and Hamel, *Alliance Advantage*, p. 46.

[17]Porter, *Competitive Strategy*, p. 340.

whether to use local sourcing of components, how much production to export, whether operating procedures should conform to the local partner's or the foreign company's standards, and the extent to which the local partner is entitled to make use of the foreign partner's technology and intellectual property. As the foreign partner acquires experience and confidence in the local market, its need for the local partner typically diminishes, posing the strategic issue of whether the alliance/joint venture should be dissolved. This happens frequently in alliances between global manufacturers and local distributors.[18] Japanese car makers have abandoned their European distribution partners and set up their own dealer networks; BMW did the same thing in Japan. On the other hand, several ambitious local partners have used their alliances with global companies to master technologies and build key competitive skills, then capitalized on the acquired know-how to launch their own entry into the international arena. Taiwan's Acer Computer Group used its alliance with Texas Instruments as a stepping stone for entering the world market for desktop and laptop computers.

STRATEGY OPTIONS FOR COMPANIES THAT ARE ALREADY DIVERSIFIED

We can better understand the strategic issues corporate managers face in managing a diversified group of businesses by looking at four post-diversification strategy alternatives:

1. Broadening the firm's business base by diversifying into additional businesses.
2. Retrenching to a narrower diversification base by divesting some of its present businesses.
3. Corporate restructuring and turnaround strategies.
4. Multinational diversification strategies.

Figure 9.4 summarizes the central thrust of each of these diversification options.

Strategies to Broaden a Diversified Company's Business Base

Diversified companies sometimes find it desirable to build positions in new related or unrelated industries, perhaps because the company's growth is sluggish and it needs the revenue and profit boost of a newly acquired business, because it has resources and capabilities that are eminently transferable to other related or complementary businesses, or because the opportunity to acquire an attractive company unexpectedly lands at its doorstep. Making new acquisitions to broaden a company's diversification base can become close to imperative when rapidly changing conditions in one of a company's core industries are blurring the boundaries with adjoining industries. For instance, the recent passage of legislation in the United States allowing banks, insurance companies, and stock brokerages to enter each other's businesses is likely to propel a blurring between these historically distinct industries and result in the creation of enterprises that offer banking, insurance, and brokerage services to their customers. Already companies with business interests in one of the three industries are acquiring companies in the others and merging their operations so as to reposition themselves as financial services firms of the future.

---

[18]Doz and Hamel, *Alliance Advantage*, p. 48.

figure 9.4   **Strategy Options for a Company That Is Already Diversified**

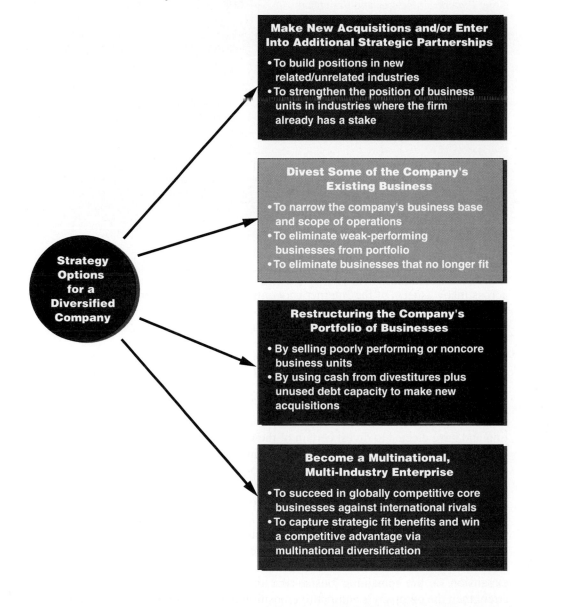

Alternatively, a diversified company may find it highly desirable to make new acquisitions to complement and strengthen the market position and competitive capabilities of one or more of its present businesses. Viacom's acquisition of CBS strengthened and extended its reach into various media businesses (shown at top of page 304).

Numerous pharmaceutical and high-tech companies have been active in acquiring new businesses to broaden their competitive reach and extend their technological expertise into new areas. The latest diversification rage has been for companies to diversify broadly into numerous types of Internet-related businesses. Companies like CMGI, Internet Capital Group, and Softbank Corporation have invested in Internet technology and hardware providers, e-commerce software developers, Web publishers, e-retailers, online brokerages, Web portals, assorted e-commerce service providers, and media and content providers to create diversified enterprises broadly positioned

Viacom's Businesses	CBS's Businesses
• Paramount Pictures and Paramount Home Video	• CBS Television Network
• Paramount Television (production); 50% ownership of UPN TV broadcasting network	• King World Productions (programs include *The Oprah Winfrey Show* and *Wheel of Fortune*); Infinity Broadcasting (radio)
• 19 local TV stations	• 15 local TV stations
• Cable TV networks (MTV, MTV2, Nickelodeon, VH1, Showtime, The Movie Channel, Comedy Central, and several others)	• CBS Cable (Country Music Television, The Nashville Network, Home Team Sports)
• Simon & Schuster (book publishing)	• TDI Outdoor Advertising
• Internet businesses (Red Rocket online educational toy retailer, SonicNet.com, vh1.com, mtv.com, nick.com)	• Internet businesses (Sportsline USA, CBS Marketwatch.com, Medscape, Rx.com, office.com, Hollywood.com)
• Blockbuster video and music	
• Famous Players and United Cinemas International movie theaters	

across many aspects of the Internet economy. A number of Internet-focused venture capital companies are building broadly diversified portfolios of Internet start-up companies, some investing in several new companies each month.

Divestiture Strategies Aimed at Retrenching to a Narrower Diversification Base

A number of highly diversified firms have had difficulty managing broad diversification and have elected to divest certain of their businesses to focus their total attention and resources on a lesser number of core businesses. Retrenching to a narrower diversification base is usually undertaken when corporate management concludes that the firm's diversification efforts have ranged too far afield and that the key to improved long-term performance lies in concentrating on building strong positions in a smaller number of businesses. Retrenchment is usually accomplished by divesting businesses (1) that have little or no strategic fit with the businesses that management wants to concentrate on, or (2) that are too small to make a sizable contribution to earnings. Divesting such businesses frees resources that can be used to reduce debt, to support expansion of the remaining businesses, or to make acquisitions that materially strengthen the company's competitive position in one or more of the remaining core businesses. Hewlett-Packard recently spun off its testing and measurement businesses into a new company called Aligent Technologies so that it could better concentrate on its PC, workstation, server, printer and peripherals, and electronics businesses. PepsiCo divested its entire restaurant group of businesses, consisting of KFC, Pizza Hut, Taco Bell, and California Pizza Kitchens, so that it could better focus its attention and resources on its soft-drink business (which had recently been losing market share to Coca-Cola) and its faster-growing and more profitable Frito-Lay snack foods business. Kmart divested itself of its OfficeMax, Sports Authority, and Borders Bookstores businesses in order to refocus its efforts on discount retailing.

Focusing corporate resources on a few core businesses is usually a superior strategy to diversifying broadly and potentially stretching resources and management attention too thin.

These and other similarly-motivated divestitures confirm the difficulties that companies encounter when trying to manage broad diversification. So few companies have demonstrated the capability to profitably manage broad diversification that investors question the wisdom of broad diversification and place a lower valuation on companies that pursue such strategies. Indeed, because conglomerates often have lower price-earnings ratios than companies with narrow diversification, some broadly diversified companies have divested a number of their businesses and retrenched to a narrower business base. Recent research indicates that pruning businesses and narrowing a firm's diversification base improves corporate performance.[19]

But there are other important reasons for divesting a portion of a company's present businesses. Sometimes diversified firms retrench because they can't make certain businesses profitable after several frustrating years of trying or because they lack funds or other resources to support the operating and investment requirements of all of their business subsidiaries. Even a shrewd corporate diversification strategy can result in the acquisition of business units that, down the road, just do not work out. Mistakes cannot be completely avoided because it is difficult to foresee how getting into a new line of business will actually work out. In addition, long-term industry attractiveness changes with the times; what was once a good diversification move into an attractive industry may later turn sour because of deteriorating market and competitive conditions. Subpar performance by some business units is bound to occur, thereby raising questions of whether to divest them or keep them and attempt a turnaround. Other business units, despite adequate financial performance, may not mesh as well with the rest of the firm as was originally thought.

> A business needs to be considered for divestiture when corporate strategists conclude it no longer fits or is an attractive investment.

Sometimes, a diversification move that seems sensible from a strategic-fit standpoint turns out to be a poor *cultural fit*.[20] Several pharmaceutical companies had just this experience. When they diversified into cosmetics and perfume, they discovered their personnel had little respect for the "frivolous" nature of such products compared to the far nobler task of developing miracle drugs to cure the ill. The absence of shared values and cultural compatibility between the medical research and chemical-compounding expertise of the pharmaceutical companies and the fashion-marketing orientation of the cosmetics business was the undoing of what otherwise was diversification into businesses with technology-sharing potential, product-development fit, and some overlap in distribution channels.

When a particular line of business loses its appeal, the most attractive solution usually is to sell it. Normally such businesses should be divested as fast as is practical. To drag things out serves no purpose unless time is needed to get it into better shape to sell. The more business units in a diversified firm's portfolio, the more likely that it will have occasion to divest poor performers and misfits. A useful guide to determine if and when to divest a business subsidiary is to ask, "If we were not in this business today, would we want to get into it now?"[21] When the answer is no or probably not, divestiture should be considered. Another useful signal that a business should become a divestiture candidate is whether it is worth more to another company than to the present parent.[22]

Options for Accomplishing Divestiture   Divestiture can take either of two forms—spinning the business off as a financially and managerially independent company or selling it outright. When a corporate parent decides to spin off one of its businesses as a separate company, there's the issue of whether to retain partial ownership

> Divestiture usually takes one of two forms—spinning a business off as an independent company or selling it to another company.

[19]See, for example, Constantinos C. Markides, "Diversification, Restructuring and Economic Performance," *Strategic Management Journal* 16 (February 1995), pp. 101–18.

[20]Drucker, *Management: Tasks, Responsibilities, Practices,* p. 709.

[21]Ibid., p. 94.

[22]See David J. Collis and Cynthia A. Montgomery, "Creating Corporate Advantage," *Harvard Business Review* 76, no. 3 (May–June 1998), pp. 72–80.

or forgo any ownership interest whatsoever in the new company. Retaining partial ownership makes sense when the business to be divested has good profit prospects. When 3Com elected to divest its Palm Pilot business, which investors saw as having very promising profit potential, it elected to retain a substantial ownership interest in the newly formed company.

When the parent decides to sell a business outright, the problem becomes finding a buyer. This can prove hard or easy, depending on the business. As a rule, a company selling a business should not ask, "Whom can we pawn this business off on, and what is the most we can get for it?"[23] Instead, it is wiser to ask, "For what sort of company would this business be a good fit, and under what conditions would it be viewed as a good deal?" Enterprises for which the business is a good fit are likely to pay the highest price. Sometimes a parent, anxious to divest itself of a particular business and not finding a buyer with ready cash, will agree to a *leveraged buyout*. A leveraged buyout typically involves selling the business to the managers who have been running it (and perhaps other outside investors brought in as partners) for a minimal equity down payment and loaning the balance of the purchase price to the new owners. Of course, if a buyer willing to pay an acceptable price cannot be found, then the decision must be made whether to keep the business until a buyer appears, whether to spin it off as a separate company, or whether, in the case of a crisis-ridden business that is losing substantial sums, to simply close it down and liquidate the remaining assets. Liquidation is obviously a last resort.

Corporate Restructuring and Turnaround Strategies

Corporate restructuring and turnaround strategies come into play when a diversified company's management has to restore an ailing business portfolio to good health. Diversified companies may find themselves struggling because of large losses in one or more business units that pull the corporation's overall financial performance down, a disproportionate number of businesses in unattractive industries, a bad economy adversely affecting many of the firm's business units, an excessive debt burden with interest costs that eat deeply into profitability, ill-chosen acquisitions that haven't lived up to expectations, or the appearance of new technologies that threaten the survival of one or more of the company's important core businesses. *Restructuring strategies* involve divesting some businesses and acquiring new businesses so as to put a whole new face on the company's business makeup; *corporate turnaround strategies,* in contrast, concentrate exclusively on restoring a diversified company's money-losing businesses to profitability.

Strategies to Restructure a Diversified Company's Business Mix

> Corporate restructuring involves making radical changes in the composition of the businesses in the company's portfolio.

Corporate restructuring efforts attack poor overall performance by performing radical surgery on the nature and mix of businesses in the portfolio. For instance, one struggling diversified company over a two-year period divested 4 business units, closed down the operations of 4 others, and added 25 new lines of business to its portfolio, 16 through acquisition and 9 through internal start-up. Other diversified companies have approached restructuring from the standpoint of splitting their businesses up into two or more independent companies. AT&T, for instance, in the mid-1990s divided into three companies—one for long-distance and other telecommunications services that retained the AT&T name, one for manufacturing telecommunications equipment (called Lucent Technologies), and one for computer systems (called NCR) that essentially represented the divestiture of AT&T's earlier acquisition of NCR. A few years after the split-up, AT&T acquired TCI Communications and MediaOne, both cable companies, and

---

[23]Ibid., p. 719.

restructured itself into a "new-age" telecommunications company offering bundled local and long-distance service, cable TV, and high-speed Internet access to its customers.

Restructuring can be prompted by any of several conditions: (1) when a strategy review reveals that the firm's long-term performance prospects have become unattractive because the portfolio contains too many slow-growth, declining, or competitively weak business units; (2) when one or more of the firm's principal businesses fall prey to hard times; (3) when a new CEO takes over and decides to redirect the company; (4) when "wave-of-the-future" technologies or products emerge and a major shake-up of the portfolio is needed to build a position in a potentially big new industry, (5) when the firm has a unique opportunity to make an acquisition so big that it has to sell several existing business units to finance the new acquisition; (6) when major businesses in the portfolio have become more and more unattractive, forcing a shake-up in the portfolio in order to produce satisfactory long-term corporate performance; or (7) when changes in markets and technologies of certain businesses proceed in such different directions that it is better to split the company into separate pieces rather than remain together under the same corporate umbrella.

Candidates for divestiture typically include not only weak or up-and-down performers or those in unattractive industries, but also those that no longer fit a company's revised diversification strategy (even though they may be profitable or in an attractive industry). Business units incompatible with the new related diversification criteria are divested, the remaining units regrouped and aligned to capture more strategic-fit benefits, and new acquisitions made to strengthen the parent company's business position in the industries it has chosen to emphasize.[24] Recently, a few broadly diversified companies have pursued restructuring by splitting into several independent companies. Notable examples include ITT, Westinghouse, and Britain's Imperial Chemical and Hanson, PLC. Before beginning to divest in 1995, Hanson owned companies with more than $20 billion in revenues in industries as diverse as beer, exercise equipment, tools, construction cranes, tobacco, cement, chemicals, coal mining, electricity, hot tubs and whirlpools, cookware, rock and gravel, bricks, and asphalt; understandably, investors and analysts had a hard time making sense of the company and its strategies. By early 1997, Hanson had restructured itself into a $3.8 billion enterprise focused more narrowly on gravel, crushed rock, cement, asphalt, bricks, and construction cranes; the remaining businesses were divided into four groups and divested.

Strategies to Turn Ailing Businesses Around   Corporate turnaround strategies focus on efforts to restore a diversified company's money-losing businesses to profitability instead of divesting them. The intent is to get the whole company back in the black by curing the problems of those businesses in the portfolio that are most responsible for pulling overall performance down. Turnaround strategies are most appropriate in situations where the reasons for poor performance are short term, the ailing businesses are in attractive industries, and divesting the money-losers does not make long-term strategic sense.

The specifics of the turnaround efforts in each poorly performing business necessarily need to vary according to the causes underlying each business's weak performance and flow from a diagnosis of prevailing industry and competitive conditions and the business's particular resource strengths, weaknesses, opportunities, and threats. The strategic options for turning a poorly performing business around in a diversified company are the same as discussed in Chapter 8 for a single-business company:

---

[24]Evidence that corporate restructuring produces improved corporate performance is contained in Markides, "Diversification, Restructuring and Economic Performance."

- Selling or closing down a portion of its operations (usually those where losses are greatest and/or future prospects are poorest).
- Shifting to a different, and hopefully better, business-level strategy.
- Launching new initiatives to boost the business's revenues.
- Pursuing cost reduction.
- Using a combination of these efforts.

However, turnaround efforts in a diversified company as compared to a single-business company have the advantage of being able to draw on the corporate parent for needed financial resources and managerial know-how and perhaps on related businesses for an infusion of competitively valuable skills and expertise.

Multinational Diversification Strategies

The distinguishing characteristics of a multinational diversification strategy are a *diversity of businesses* and a *diversity of national markets*.[25] Such diversity makes multinational diversification a particularly challenging and complex strategy to conceive and execute. Managers have to develop business strategies for each industry (with as many multinational variations as conditions in each country market dictate). Then, opportunities for cross-business and cross-country collaboration and strategic coordination have to be pursued and managed in ways calculated to result in competitive advantage and enhanced profitability.

Moreover, the geographic operating scope of individual businesses within a diversified multinational company (DMNC) can range from one country only to several countries to many countries to global. Thus, each business unit within a DMNC often competes in a somewhat different combination of geographic markets than its sister businesses—adding another element of strategic complexity—and perhaps an element of opportunity to try to grow certain lines of business by entering country markets where sister businesses already have a market presence.

What Makes Multinational Diversification So Attractive: The Opportunities for Growth and Added Competitive Advantage

Despite their complexity, multinational diversification strategies have considerable appeal. They offer two avenues for long-term growth in revenues and profitability. One is to grow by entering additional businesses and the other is to grow by extending the operations of existing businesses into additional country markets. Moreover, multinational diversification offers six ways to build competitive advantage:

1. Full capture of economies of scale and experience curve effects.
2. Opportunities to capitalize on cross-business economies of scope.
3. Opportunities to transfer competitively valuable resources from one business to another and from one country to another.
4. Ability to leverage use of a well-known and competitively powerful brand name.
5. Ability to capitalize on opportunities for cross-business and cross-country collaboration and strategic coordination.[26]

---

[25]C. K. Prahalad and Yves L. Doz, *The Multinational Mission* (New York: Free Press, 1987), p. 2.
[26]Ibid., p. 15.

6. Opportunities to use cross-business or cross country subsidization to outcompete rivals.

Each of these will be discussed in turn below.

Illustration Capsule 38 shows the scope of five prominent diversified multinational corporations.

Opportunities to Capture Full Economies of Scale and Experience Curve Effects

In some businesses, the volume of sales needed to realize full economies of scale and/or benefit from experience curve effects is rather sizable, perhaps exceeding the volume that can be achieved operating within the boundaries of a single country market, especially a small one. *The chance to drive down unit costs through expanding sales to additional country markets is one reason why a diversified multinational may seek to acquire a business and then expand its operations into additional foreign markets as fast as possible.* Expanding into additional country markets to capture scale economies makes good strategic sense when cross-country buyer preferences are homogeneous; it is then feasible to market common product versions across different country markets. Expansion also makes sense if a company has the capability to pursue customized mass production and economically produce different versions of a product for different country markets. With the greater sales volumes provided from selling to buyers in a greater number of country markets, companies can drive harder bargains with components suppliers. Plants can gain the economies of longer production runs in world-scale plants, make efficient use of high-speed equipment, and/or accelerate capture of learning-curve effects. Distribution facilities can be scaled to a size that justifies use of state-of-the-art technology and automated processes. Both plants and distribution facilities can be located in whatever country locations prove most cost effective. In short, expanding into additional country markets is advantageous whenever it helps a company achieve an efficient scale of operation in production, distribution, or marketing and spread fixed overhead costs over a greater volume of unit sales.

> Expanding into additional country markets helps a company capture full economies of scale and experience curve effects.

Opportunities to Capitalize on Cross-Business Economies of Scope

Diversifying into related businesses can help a multinational firm benefit from cost-reducing economies of scope. For example, a diversified multinational company that utilizes much the same distributors and retail dealers worldwide can diversify into new businesses using these same worldwide distribution channels at relatively little incremental expense by piggybacking distribution for the newly entered businesses on the dealer network already in place. Likewise, diversifying into new distribution-related businesses may present opportunities to draw on existing distribution capabilities in many or all of the same country markets where it already has operations and a solid base of customers. A third source of distribution-related economies of scope comes from gaining added bargaining leverage with retailers in securing attractive display space for any new products and businesses as its family of businesses grows in number and sales importance to the retailer.

> Multinational diversification can open up opportunities to achieve economies of scope, reduce costs, and build a low-cost advantage over less diversified rivals.

Sony, for example, has enjoyed competitive advantage in diversifying into the video game industry to take on giants like Nintendo and Sega because (1) it has well-established distribution capabilities in consumer electronics worldwide that can be used for video game products; (2) it has in-place capability to go after video game sales in all country markets where it presently does business in other product categories (TVs, computers, DVD players, VCRs, radios, CD players, and digital and video cameras); and (3) it has the marketing clout to persuade retailers and e-tailers to give Sony video game products prominent visibility in their merchandising efforts. The cost-savings that flow from economies of scope open up opportunities to build a low-cost advantage over less diversified rivals.

illustration capsule 38

The Global Scope of Five Prominent Diversified Multinational Corporations

Sony, Philip Morris, Nestlé, Siemens, and Samsung are among the world's most prominent diversified multinational companies. The table below provides a glimpse of their reach into different lines of business and the geographic scope of their operations across the various countries of the world.

Company	Global Scope	Businesses into Which the Company Has Diversified
Sony	Operations in more than 100 countries and sales offices in more than 200 countries	• Televisions, VCRs, DVD players, radios, CD players and home stereos, digital cameras and video equipment, PCs and Trinitron computer monitors • PlayStation game consoles and video game software • Columbia, Epic, and Sony Classical pre-recorded music • Columbia TriStar motion pictures, syndicated television programs • Insurance • Other businesses (financing, entertainment complexes, Internet-related businesses)
Philip Morris Companies	Operations in 92 countries and sales offices in more than 150 countries	• Cigarettes (Marlboro, Virginia Slims, Benson & Hedges, and numerous other brands) • Miller Brewing Company (Miller Genuine Draft, Miller Lite, Icehouse, Red Dog, Molson, Foster's, and numerous other brands) • Kraft Foods (Maxwell House, Sanka, Oscar Mayer, Kool-Aid, Jell-O, Post cereals, Miracle Whip, Bullseye barbecue sauce, Kraft cheeses, Crystal Light, Tombstone pizza)
Nestlé	Operations in 70 countries and sales offices in more than 200 countries	• Beverages (Nescafe and Taster's Choice coffees, Nestea, Perrier, Arrowhead, & Calistoga mineral and bottled waters) • Milk products (Carnation, Gloria, Neslac, Coffee Mate, Nestlé ice cream and yogurt) • Pet foods (Friskies, Alpo, Fancy Feast, Mighty Dog) • Contadina, Libby's, and Stouffer's food products and prepared dishes • Chocolate and confectionery products (Nestlé Crunch, Smarties, Baby Ruth, Butterfinger, KitKat) • Pharmaceuticals (Alcon opthalmic products, Galderma dermatological products)
Siemens	Operations in 160 countries and sales offices in more than 190 countries	• Electrical power generation, transmission, and distribution equipment and products • Manufacturing automation systems, industrial motors, industrial computers, industrial machinery, industrial tools, plant construction and maintenance • Information and communications (solutions and services needed for corporate communication networks, telephones, PCs, mainframes, computer network products, consulting services)

 illustration capsule 38

(concluded)

Company	Global Scope	Businesses into Which the Company Has Diversified
Samsung	Operations in more than 60 countries and sales in more than 200 countries	• Mass transit and light rail systems, rail cars, locomotives • Medical equipment, health care management services • Semiconductors, memory components, microcontrollers, capacitors, resistors • Lighting (bulbs, lamps, theater and television lighting systems) • Home electronics, large home appliances, vacuum cleaners • Financial services (commercial lending, pension administration, venture capital) • Procurement and logistics services, business consulting services • Electronics (computers, peripherals, displays, televisions, telecommunications equipment, semiconductors, memory chips, circuit boards, capacitors, information technology services, systems integration) • Machinery and heavy industry (shipbuilding, oil and gas storage tank construction, marine engines, aircraft and aircraft parts, gas turbines, military hardware, industrial robots, factory automation systems) • Automotive (passenger cars, commercial trucks) • Chemicals (general chemicals, petrochemicals, fertilizers) • Financial services (insurance, credit card services, securities trading, consumer credit services, trust management) • Other affiliated companies (theme parks, hotels, medical centers, apparel, professional sports teams, film, music, and television production)

Source: Company annual reports and Web sites.

Opportunities to Transfer Competitively Valuable Resources from One Business to Another and from One Country to Another

Diversification into new businesses with resource-related strategic fits at various points along the value chain offers significant competitive advantage potential. Technological expertise and know-how in one business can be transferred to other existing or newly entered businesses with opportunities to make competitively advantageous use of such expertise. Manufacturing skills, sales and marketing skills, e-commerce capabilities, and managerial expertise can likewise be transferred across businesses, allowing the receiving businesses to perform better as part of the diversified multinational company than as a stand-alone enterprise.

> Multinational diversification offers a firm the opportunity to build competitive advantage through cross-business and cross-country resource transfer.

Furthermore, competing multinationally allows a company to transfer the experience and expertise it has gained in operating in particular country markets to sister businesses that are in the process of entering these same country markets. It can also transfer its multicountry operating experiences and know-how to newly entered country markets. The understanding of local markets and buyer behavior and customs gained in one country often provides valuable clues and faster learning about markets and buyer behavior in new country markets that a multinational company is presently entering or planning to enter.

Opportunities to Leverage Use of a Competitively Powerful Brand Name

A number of diversified multinational companies have gone to great lengths to establish brand names that are well known and respected in many parts of the world. Such companies can deliberately exploit the value of that name by transferring it to newly entered businesses and benefiting from the added sales and market share they can gain simply on the strength of the trust that buyers have in their brand name. For example, Sony's well-established, global brand-name recognition gives it an important marketing and advertising advantage over rivals with lesser-known brands. When Sony diversifies into new businesses or product families and goes into the marketplace with the stamp of the Sony brand on them, it can command prominent display space with retailers. It can expect to win sales and market share simply on the confidence that buyers place in products carrying the Sony name. While it may spend money to make consumers aware of the availability of its new products, it does not have to spend as heavily to gain brand recognition and market acceptance as would a lesser known competitor looking at the marketing and advertising costs of entering the same new product/business/country markets and trying to go head-to-head against Sony. Further, if Sony moves into a new country market for the first time and does well selling Sony PlayStations and video games, it faces lower market barriers in proceeding to introduce the products of its other businesses (say, consumer electronics products) in that same country. Once it has established the Sony brand strongly in the minds of buyers in one product family or line of business, it can leverage its investment in establishing its brand name by marketing its other product families and business lines under the same brand. In short, a diversified multinational company's global brand name is more than a valuable competitive or strategic asset; it is a source of potential competitive advantage.

Ability to Coordinate Strategic Activities and Strategic Initiatives across Businesses and Countries

Multinational diversification presents a host of opportunities for cross-business and cross-country coordination of a company's strategic activities and initiatives. For instance, by channeling corporate resources directly into a combined R&D/technology effort for all related businesses, as opposed to letting each business unit fund and direct its own R&D effort however it sees fit, a diversified multinational company can merge its expertise and efforts *worldwide* to advance the core technology, pursue promising technological avenues to create altogether new businesses, generate technology-based manufacturing economies within and across product/business lines, expedite across-the-board product improvements in existing businesses, and develop new products that complement and enhance the sales of existing products—all significant contributors to competitive advantage and better corporate performance.

If, on the other hand, R&D activities are decentralized and put totally under the direction of each existing business unit, R&D/technology investments are more prone to end up narrowly aimed at each business's own product-market opportunities. A splintered R&D effort is unlikely to produce the range and depth of strategic fit benefits as a broad, coordinated companywide effort to advance and exploit the company's full

---

Diversified multinational companies with well-known and respected brand names have lower barriers to entering new businesses in those country markets where they already have a presence.

A diversified multinational company with expertise in a core technology and a family of businesses using this technology can capture competitive advantage through a collaborative and strategically coordinated R&D effort on behalf of all the related businesses as a group.

technological expertise.[27] Illustration Capsule 39 describes how Honda has exploited gasoline engine technology and its well-known name by diversifying into a variety of products powered by gasoline engines.

Aside from cross-business technological coordination, a company can gain cost savings by cross-business and cross-country coordination of purchasing and procurement from suppliers, from collaborative introduction and shared use of e-commerce technologies and online sales efforts, and from coordinated product introductions and promotional campaigns. Firms that are less diversified and less global in scope have less such cross-business and cross-country collaborative opportunities.

Opportunities to Use Cross-Business or Cross-Country Subsidization to Outcompete Rivals   A diversified multinational company can use the financial and organizational resources it has from operations in other countries or other lines of business to cross-subsidize a competitive assault on the market position of rivals. Both a one-country competitor and a one-business competitor are at a disadvantage defending their market positions against a DMNC determined to establish a solid long-term competitive position in their market and willing to accept lower short-term profits in order to do so. A one-business domestic company has only one profit sanctuary—its home market. A diversified one-country competitor may have profit sanctuaries in several businesses but all are in the same country market. A one-business multinational company may have profit sanctuaries in several country markets, though all are in the same business. All three are vulnerable to an aggressive DMNC that launches a major strategic offensive in their profit sanctuaries and lowballs its prices and/or spends extravagantly on advertising to win market share at their expense. A DMNC's ability to keep hammering away at competitors with lowball prices year after year may reflect either a cost advantage growing out of its related diversification strategy or a willingness to cross-subsidize low profits or even losses with earnings from its profit sanctuaries in other country markets and/or its earnings from other businesses. Sony, for example, by pursuing related diversification keyed to product-distribution-technology strategic fit and managing its product families on a global scale, has the ability to put strong competitive pressure on its two main video game rivals, Nintendo and Sega, neither of which are diversified. If need be, Sony can lowball its prices on its PlayStations or fund extravagant promotions for its latest video game products, using earnings from its other business lines to help wrest market share away from Nintendo and Sega in video games. At the same time, Sony can draw on its considerable resources in R&D, its ability to transfer electronics technology from one electronics product family to another, and its expertise in product innovation to introduce better video game players, perhaps players that are multifunctional and do more than just play video games. Such competitive actions not only enhance Sony's own brand image but also make it very tough for Nintendo and Sega to match its prices, advertising, and product development efforts and still earn acceptable profits. Sony can turn its attention to making its video game business more attractively profitable once the battle for market share and competitive position against Nintendo and Sega is won.[28]

The Combined Effects of These Advantages Is Potent   Companies with a strategy of (1) diversifying into *related* industries and (2) competing *globally* in each of these industries thus can draw on any of several competitive advantage opportunities to overcome a domestic-only rival or a single-business rival. There's evidence that

> A well-diversified family of businesses and a multinational market base give a DMNC the power and resource strength to subsidize a long-term market offensive against one-market or one-business competitors with earnings from profit sanctuaries in other countries or businesses.

> Although cross-subsidization is a potent competitive weapon, it can only be used sparingly because of its adverse impact on overall corporate profitability.

---

[27]Prahalad and Doz, *The Multinational Mission,* pp. 62–63.
[28]Ibid.

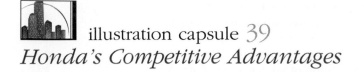

illustration capsule *39*
Honda's Competitive Advantages

At first blush anyone looking at Honda's lineup of products—cars, motorcycles, lawn mowers, power generators, outboard motors, snowmobiles, snowblowers, and garden tillers—might conclude that Honda has pursued unrelated diversification. But underlying the obvious product diversity is a common core: Honda's expertise in the technology of gasoline engines.

Honda's strategy involves transferring the company's expertise in gasoline engine technology to additional products, exploiting its capabilities in low-cost/high-quality manufacturing, using the widely known and respected Honda brand name on all the products, and promoting several

products in the same ad. One Honda ad teased consumers with the question "How do you put six Hondas in a two-car garage?" and then showed a garage containing a Honda car, a Honda motorcycle, a Honda snowmobile, a Honda lawn mower, a Honda power generator, and a Honda outboard motor.

The relatedness in the value chains for the products in Honda's business lineup produces competitive advantage for Honda in the form of economies of scope, beneficial opportunities to transfer technology and capabilities from one business to another, and economical use of a common brand name.

Honda's Competitive Advantage

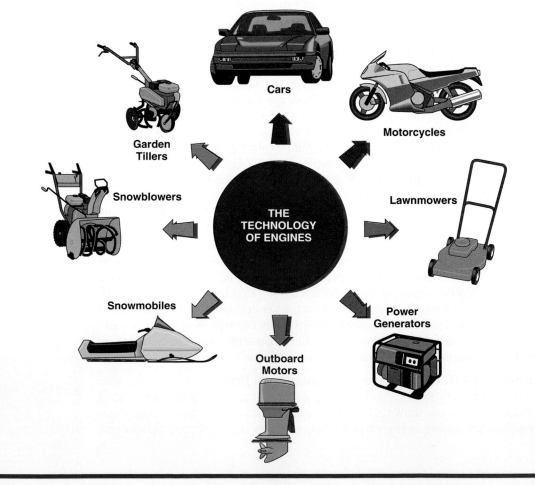

Source: Adapted from C. K. Prahalad and Yves L. Doz, *The Multinational Mission* (New York: Free Press, 1987), p. 62.

these advantages are significant enough to help a DMNC achieve above-average returns and have lower overall business risk.[29] A DMNC's biggest competitive advantage potential comes from concentrating its diversification efforts in those industries where there are resource-sharing and resource-transfer opportunities and where there are important economies of scope and brand-name benefits. The more a company's diversification strategy yields these kinds of strategic-fit benefits, the more powerful a competitor it becomes and the better its profit and growth performance is likely to be. Relying on cross-business strategic fit advantages to outcompete rivals is inherently more attractive than resorting to the profit-eroding tactics of cross-subsidization.

While a DMNC can employ cross-subsidization tactics to help muscle its way into attractive new markets or outcompete a particular rival, its ability to use cross-subsidization is limited by the need to maintain respectable levels of overall company profitability. It is one thing to occasionally use a portion of the profits and cash flows from existing businesses to cover reasonable short-term losses to gain entry to a new business or a new country market or wage a competitive offensive against certain rivals. It is quite another thing to regularly use cross-subsidization tactics to fund competitive inroads in new areas and weaken overall company performance on an ongoing basis. A DMNC is under the same pressures as any other company to demonstrate consistently acceptable profitability across its whole business portfolio. At some juncture, every business and every market entered needs to make a profit contribution or become a candidate for abandonment. So using cross-subsidization as a competitive tactic is constrained by the need to preserve acceptable levels of corporate profitability. As a general rule, *cross-subsidization is justified only if there is a good prospect that the short-term impairment to corporate profitability will be offset by stronger competitiveness and better overall profitability over the long term.*

key|points

Most companies have their business roots in a single industry. Even though they may have since diversified into other industries, a substantial part of their revenues and profits still usually comes from the original or "core" business. Diversification becomes an attractive strategy when a company runs out of profitable growth opportunities in its core business. The purpose of diversification is to build shareholder value. Diversification builds shareholder value when a diversified group of businesses can perform better under the auspices of a single corporate parent than they would as independent, stand-alone businesses and thereby realize important $1 + 1 = 3$ performance benefits. Whether a particular diversification move is capable of increasing shareholder value hinges on the attractiveness test, the cost-of-entry test, and the better-off test.

There are two fundamental approaches to diversification—into related businesses and into unrelated businesses. The rationale for *related* diversification is *strategic:* diversify into businesses with strategic fits along their respective value chains, capitalize on strategic-fit relationships to gain competitive advantage, and then use competitive advantage to achieve the desired $1 + 1 = 3$ impact on shareholder value. Businesses have strategic fit when their value chains offer potential (1) for realizing economies of scope or cost-saving efficiencies associated with sharing technology, facilities, functional activities, distribution outlets, or brand names; (2) for competitively valuable cross-business transfers of technology, skills, know-how, or other resource capabilities;

---

[29]See, for example, W. Chan Kim, Peter Hwang, and Willem P. Burgers, "Multinationals' Diversification and the Risk-Return Trade-off," *Strategic Management Journal* 14 (May 1993) pp. 275–86.

(3) for leveraging use of a well-known and trusted brand name, and (4) for competitively valuable cross-business collaboration.

The basic premise of unrelated diversification is that any business that has good profit prospects and can be acquired on good financial terms is a good business to diversify into. *Unrelated* diversification is basically a *financial* approach; strategic fit is a secondary consideration compared to the expectation of financial gain. Unrelated diversification surrenders the competitive advantage potential of strategic fit in return for such advantages as (1) spreading business risk over a variety of industries and (2) providing opportunities for quick financial gain (if candidate acquisitions have undervalued assets, are bargain-priced and have good upside potential given the right management, or need the backing of a financially strong parent to capitalize on attractive opportunities). In theory, unrelated diversification also offers greater earnings stability over the business cycle, a third advantage. However, achieving these three outcomes consistently requires corporate executives who are smart enough to avoid the considerable disadvantages of unrelated diversification. The greater the number of businesses a conglomerate is in and the more diverse these businesses are, the harder it is for corporate executives to know enough about each business to distinguish a good acquisition from a risky one, select capable managers to run each business, know when the major strategic proposals of business units are sound, or wisely decide what to do when a business unit stumbles. Unless corporate managers are exceptionally shrewd and talented, unrelated diversification is a dubious and unreliable approach to building shareholder value when compared to related diversification.

Entry into new related or unrelated businesses can take any of three forms: acquisition, internal start-up, and joint ventures/strategic partnerships. Each has its pros and cons, but acquisition is the most frequently used.

Once diversification is accomplished, corporate management's task is to manage the collection of businesses for maximum long-term performance. There are four different strategic paths for improving a diversified company's performance: (1) broadening the firm's business base by diversifying into additional businesses, (2) retrenching to a narrower diversification base by divesting some of its present businesses, (3) corporate restructuring and turnaround strategies, and (4) multinational diversification.

Broadening the diversification base is attractive when growth is sluggish and the company needs the revenue and profit boost of a newly acquired business, when it has resources and capabilities that are eminently transferable to related or complementary businesses, or when the opportunity to acquire an attractive company unexpectedly lands on its doorstep. Furthermore, there are occasions when a diversified company makes new acquisitions to complement and strengthen the market position and competitive capabilities of one or more of its present businesses.

Retrenching to a narrower diversification base is usually undertaken when corporate management concludes that the firm's diversification efforts have ranged too far afield and that the best avenue for improving long-term performance is to concentrate on building strong positions in a smaller number of businesses. Retrenchment is usually accomplished by divesting businesses (1) that have little or no strategic fit with the businesses that management wants to concentrate on and/or (2) that are too small to make a sizable contribution to earnings. Divesting such businesses frees resources that can be used to reduce debt, to support expansion of the remaining businesses, or to make acquisitions that materially strengthen the company's competitive position in one or more of the remaining core businesses. Most of the time, companies divest businesses by selling them to another company, but sometimes they spin them off as financially and managerially independent enterprises in which the parent company may or may not retain an ownership interest.

Corporate restructuring and turnaround strategies come into play when corporate management has to restore an ailing business portfolio to good health. Poor performance can be caused by large losses in one or more businesses that pull overall corporate performance down, by too many business units in unattractive industries, by an excessive debt burden, or by ill-chosen acquisitions that haven't lived up to expectations. Corporate turnaround strategies aim at restoring money-losing businesses to profitability instead of divesting them. Restructuring strategies involve radical portfolio shake-ups, divestiture of some businesses and acquisition of others to create what is perceived as a more attractive group of businesses with better long-term performance potential.

Multinational diversification strategies feature a diversity of businesses and a diversity of national markets. Despite the complexity of having to devise and manage so many strategies (at least one for each industry, with as many variations for country markets as may be needed), multinational diversification strategies have considerable appeal. They offer two avenues for long-term growth in revenues and profitability—one is to grow by entering additional businesses and the other is to grow by extending the operations of existing businesses into additional country markets. Moreover, multinational diversification offers six ways to build competitive advantage: (1) full capture of economies of scale and experience curve effects, (2) opportunities to capitalize on cross-business economies of scope, (3) opportunity to transfer competitively valuable resources from one business to another and from one country to another, (4) ability to leverage use of a well-known and competitively powerful brand name, (5) ability to capitalize on opportunities for cross-business and cross-country collaboration and strategic coordination, and (6) opportunities to use cross-business or cross-country subsidization to wrest sales and market share from rivals.

suggested | readings

Barney, Jay B. *Gaining and Sustaining Competitive Advantage.* Reading, MA: Addison-Wesley, 1997, chapters 11 and 13.

Campbell, Andrew; Michael Goold; and Marcus Alexander. "Corporate Strategy: The Quest for Parenting Advantage." *Harvard Business Review* 73, no. 2 (March–April 1995), pp. 120–32.

————. "The Value of the Parent Company." *California Management Review,* 38, no. 1 (Fall 1995), pp. 79–97.

Collis, David J., and Cynthia A. Montgomery. "Creating Corporate Advantage." *Harvard Business Review* 76, no. 3 (May–June 1998), pp. 70–83.

Doz, Yves L., and Gary Hamel. *Alliance Advantage: The Art of Creating Value through Partnering.* Boston: Harvard Business School Press, 1998.

Eisenhardt, Kathleen M., and D. Charles Galunic. "Coevolving: At Last, a Way to Make Synergies Work." *Harvard Business Review* 78, no. 1 (January–February 2000), pp. 91–101.

Goold, Michael, and Andrew Campbell. "Desperately Seeking Synergy." *Harvard Business Review* 76, no. 5 (September–October 1998), pp. 130–43.

Goold, Michael, and Kathleen Luchs. "Why Diversify? Four Decades of Management Thinking." *Academy of Management Executive* 7, no. 3 (August 1993), pp. 7–25.

Hax, Arnoldo, and Nicolas S. Majluf. *The Strategy Concept and Process.* Englewood Cliffs, NJ: Prentice Hall, 1991, chapters 9, 11, and 15.

Hoffman, Richard C. "Strategies for Corporate Turnarounds: What Do We Know about Them?" *Journal of General Management* 14, no. 3 (Spring 1989), pp. 46–66.

Liedtka, Jeanne M. "Collaboration across Lines of Business for Competitive Advantage." *Academy of Management Executive* 10, no. 2 (May 1996), pp. 20–34.

chapter|ten

Evaluating the Strategies of Diversified Companies

If we can know where we are and something about how we got there, we might see where we are trending—and if the outcomes which lie naturally in our course are unacceptable, to make timely change.

—Abraham Lincoln

The corporate strategies of most companies have dissipated instead of created shareholder value.

—Michael Porter

Achieving superior performance through diversification is largely based on relatedness.

—Philippe Very

The acid test for any corporate strategy is that the company's businesses must not be worth more to another owner.

—David G. Collis and Cynthia A. Montgomery

Make winners out of every business in your company. Don't carry losers.

—Jack Welch, CEO, General Electric

O nce a company diversifies and has operations in a number of different industries, three issues dominate the agenda of the company's top strategy makers:

1. How attractive is the group of businesses the company is in?
2. Assuming the company sticks with its present lineup of businesses, how good is its performance outlook in the years ahead?
3. If the answers to the previous two questions are not satisfactory:
   a. Should the company divest itself of low-performing or unattractive businesses?
   b. What actions should the company take to strengthen the growth and profit potential of the businesses it intends to remain in?
   c. Is further diversification into additional businesses warranted to boost the company's long-term performance prospects?

Crafting and implementing action plans to improve the overall attractiveness and competitive strength of a company's business lineup is the central strategic task of corporate-level managers.

Strategic analysis of diversified companies builds on the concepts and methods used for single-business companies. But there are also new aspects to consider and additional analytical approaches to master. The evaluation procedure involves the following steps:

1. *Identifying the present corporate strategy*—whether the company is pursuing related or unrelated diversification (or a mixture of both), the nature and purpose of any recent acquisitions and divestitures, and the kind of diversified company that corporate management is trying to create.
2. *Applying the industry attractiveness test*—evaluating the long-term attractiveness of each industry the company is in and the attractiveness of all the industries as a group.
3. *Applying the competitive strength test*—evaluating the competitive strength of the company's business units to see which ones are strong contenders in their respective industries.
4. *Applying the strategic-fit test*—determining the competitive advantage potential of cross-business value chain relationships and strategic fits among the company's various business units.

5. *Applying the resource-fit test*—determining whether the firm's resource strengths match the resource requirements of its present business lineup.

6. *Ranking the businesses*—analyzing both historical performance and future prospects.

7. *Ranking the business units in terms of priority for resource allocation*—deciding whether the strategic posture for each business unit should be aggressive expansion, fortify and defend, overhaul and reposition, or harvest/divest. (The task of initiating specific business-unit strategies to improve the business unit's competitive position is usually delegated to business-level managers, with corporate-level managers offering suggestions and having authority for final approval.)

8. *Crafting new strategic moves to improve overall corporate performance*—changing the makeup of the portfolio via acquisitions and divestitures, improving coordination among the activities of related business units to achieve greater cost-sharing and skills-transfer benefits, and steering corporate resources into the areas of greatest opportunity.

The rest of the chapter describes this eight-step process and introduces analytical techniques managers need in order to arrive at sound corporate strategy appraisals.

IDENTIFYING THE PRESENT CORPORATE STRATEGY

Analysis of a diversified company's situation and prospects needs to begin with an understanding of its present strategy and business makeup. As shown in Figure 10.1, we can get a good handle on a diversified company's corporate strategy by looking at

> Evaluating a diversified firm's business portfolio needs to begin with a clear identification of the firm's diversification strategy.

- The extent to which the firm is diversified (as measured by the proportion of total sales and operating profits contributed by each business unit and by whether the diversification base is broad or narrow).

- Whether the firm is pursuing related or unrelated diversification, or a mixture of both.

- Whether the scope of company operations is mostly domestic, increasingly multinational, or global.

- Any moves to add new businesses to the portfolio and build positions in new industries.

- Any moves to divest weak or unattractive business units.

- Recent moves to boost performance of key business units or strengthen existing business positions.

- Management efforts to capture cross-business strategic-fit benefits and leverage cross-business value chain relationships into competitive advantage.

- The percentage of total capital expenditures allocated to each business unit in prior years (a strong indicator of the company's resource allocation priorities).

Getting a clear fix on the current corporate strategy and its rationale sets the stage for probing the strengths and weaknesses in its business portfolio and, subsequently, for drawing conclusions about whatever refinements or major alterations in strategy are appropriate.

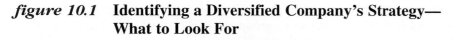

figure 10.1 **Identifying a Diversified Company's Strategy—
What to Look For**

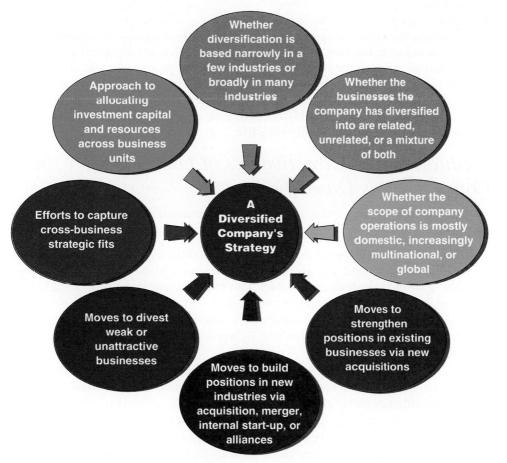

EVALUATING INDUSTRY ATTRACTIVENESS: THREE TESTS

A principal consideration in evaluating a diversified company's business makeup and the caliber of its strategy is the attractiveness of the industries into which it has diversified. The more attractive these industries, the better the company's long-term profit prospects. Industry attractiveness needs to be evaluated from three angles:

1. *The attractiveness of each industry represented in the business portfolio*—Each industry must be scrutinized from the standpoint of whether it represents a good business for the company to be in. What are the industry's prospects for long-term growth? Are competitive conditions and the overall market environment conducive to long-term profitability? Ideally, each industry in which the firm operates will pass the attractiveness test.

2. *Each industry's attractiveness relative to the others*—The question here is "Which industries in the portfolio are the most attractive and which are the least attractive?" Comparing the attractiveness of the industries and ranking them from most

> The more attractive the industries that a company has diversified into, the better its performance prospects.

attractive to least attractive is a prerequisite to drawing conclusions about the attractiveness of the industries as a group and deciding how to allocate corporate resources across the various businesses.

3. *The attractiveness of all the industries as a group*—The question here is "How appealing is the whole group of industries in which the company has invested?" The answer points to whether the company may be in too many relatively unattractive businesses, whether the portfolio of industries holds promise for attractive growth and profitability, or whether some form of portfolio restructuring needs to be considered. A company whose revenues and profits come chiefly from businesses in unattractive industries probably needs to look at building positions in additional industries that qualify as highly attractive.

Evaluating the Attractiveness of Each Industry the Company Has Diversified Into

All the industry attractiveness considerations discussed in Chapter 3 come into play here:

- *Market size and projected growth rate*—Big industries are more attractive than small industries, and fast-growing industries tend to be more attractive than slow-growing industries or industries with uncertain prospects, other things being equal.

- *The intensity of competition*—Industries where competitive pressures are relatively weak are more attractive than industries where competitive pressures are strong.

- *Emerging opportunities and threats*—Industries with promising opportunities and minimal threats on the near horizon are more attractive than industries with modest opportunities and imposing threats.

- *Seasonal and cyclical factors*—Industries where buyer demand is relatively steady year-round and not unduly vulnerable to economic ups and downs are more attractive than industries where there are wide swings in buyer demand within or across years.

- *Resource requirements*—Industries having resource requirements within the company's reach are more attractive than industries where capital and other resource requirements could strain corporate financial resources and organizational capabilities.

- *The presence of cross-industry strategic fits and resource fits*—An industry is more attractive to a particular firm if its value chain and resource requirements match up well with the value chain activities of other industries the company has diversified into and with the company's resource capabilities.

- *Industry profitability*—Industries with healthy profit margins and high rates of return on investment are generally more attractive than industries where profits have historically been low or where the business risks are high.

- *Social, political, regulatory, and environmental factors*—Industries with significant problems in such areas as consumer health, safety, or environmental pollution or that are subject to intense regulation are less attractive than industries where such problems are not burning issues.

- *Industry uncertainty and business risk*—Industries with less uncertainty on the horizon and lower overall business risk are more attractive than industries whose future prospects for one reason or another are quite uncertain, especially when the industry has formidable resource requirements.

How well each industry stacks up on these factors determines how many are able to satisfy the attractiveness test. The ideal situation is for all of the industries represented in the company's portfolio to be attractive.

Each Industry's Attractiveness Relative to the Others

It is not enough, however, that an industry be attractive. There is strong reason for corporate managements to steer resources into those industries of *greatest* long-term opportunity. Shrewd resource allocation is aided by ranking the industries in the company's business portfolio from most attractive to least attractive—an analytical procedure that calls for quantitative measures of industry attractiveness.

The first step in arriving at a formal, quantitative measure of long-term industry attractiveness is to select a set of industry attractiveness measures (such as those listed above). Next, weights are assigned to each attractiveness measure—it is weak methodology to assume that the various measures are equally important. While judgment is obviously involved in deciding how much weight to put on each attractiveness measure, it makes sense to place the most weight on those measures that are important to achieving corporate objectives and that fit the company's circumstances. The weights must add up to 1.0. Each industry is then rated on each of the chosen industry attractiveness measures, using a rating scale of 1 to 5 or 1 to 10 (where a *high* rating signifies *high* attractiveness and a *low* rating signifies *low* attractiveness or unattractiveness). Weighted attractiveness ratings are calculated by multiplying the industry's rating on each factor by the factor's weight. For example, a rating score of 8 times a weight of 0.25 gives a weighted rating of 2.00. The sum of weighted ratings for all the attractiveness factors provides a quantitative measure of the industry's long-term attractiveness. The procedure is shown below:

Industry Attractiveness Factor	Weight	Attractiveness Rating	Weighted Industry Rating
Market size and projected growth	0.10	5	0.50
Intensity of competition in the industry	0.25	8	2.00
Strategic fits and resource fits with other industries represented in the company's business portfolio	0.15	5	0.75
Resource requirements	0.15	7	1.05
Emerging industry opportunities and threats	0.05	6	0.30
Seasonal and cyclical influences	0.05	4	0.20
Social, political, regulatory, and environmental factors	0.05	2	0.10
Industry profitability	0.10	4	0.40
Industry uncertainty and business risk	0.10	5	0.50
Sum of the assigned weights	1.00		
Industry attractiveness rating			**5.80**

Rating scale: (1 = Very unattractive; 10 = Very attractive)

Once industry attractiveness ratings are calculated for each industry in the corporate portfolio, it a simple task to rank the industries from most to least attractive.

There are two difficulties with calculating industry attractiveness scores. One is deciding on appropriate weights for the industry attractiveness measures. The other is getting reliable data on which to assign accurate and objective ratings. Without good information, the ratings necessarily become subjective, and their validity hinges on whether management has probed industry conditions sufficiently to make dependable judgments. Generally, a company can come up with the statistical data needed to compare its industries on such factors as market size, growth rate, seasonal and cyclical influences, and industry profitability. The presence of important cross-industry value chain relationships and strategic fits with other industries or businesses represented in the company's business portfolio typically greatly enhances an industry's attractiveness because of the competitive advantage potential such relationships can yield. The attractiveness measure where judgment weighs most heavily is in comparing the industries on intensity of competition. It is not always easy to conclude whether competition in one industry is stronger or weaker than in another industry because of the different types of competitive influences that prevail and the differences in their relative importance. Nonetheless, industry attractiveness ratings are a reasonably reliable method for ranking a diversified company's industries from most attractive to least attractive—they tell a valuable story about just how and why some of the industries a company has diversified into are more attractive than others.

The Attractiveness of the Mix of Industries as a Whole

For a diversified company to be a strong performer, a substantial portion of its revenues and profits must come from business units judged to be in attractive industries—those with relatively high attractiveness scores. It is particularly important that the company's principal businesses be in industries with a good outlook for growth and above-average profitability. Having a big fraction of the company's revenues and profits come from industries that are growing slowly or have low returns on investment tends to drag overall company performance down. Business units in the least attractive industries are potential candidates for divestiture, unless they are positioned strongly enough to overcome the unattractive aspects of their industry environments or they are a strategically important component of the portfolio.

EVALUATING THE COMPETITIVE STRENGTH OF EACH OF THE COMPANY'S BUSINESS UNITS

The task here is to evaluate whether each business unit in the corporate portfolio is well positioned in its industry and the extent to which it already is or can become a strong market contender. Doing an appraisal of each business unit's strength and competitive position in its industry not only reveals its chances for industry success but also provides a basis for comparing the relative competitive strength of the different business units to determine which ones are strongest and which are weakest. Quantitative measures of each business unit's competitive strength and market position can be calculated using a procedure similar to that for measuring industry attractiveness.[1] Assessing the competitive strength of a diversified company's business subsidiaries should be based on such factors as:

---

[1]The procedure also parallels the method for doing competitive strength assessments presented in Chapter 4 (see Table 4.4).

- *Relative market share*—Business units with higher relative market shares normally have greater competitive strength than those with lower shares. A business unit's *relative market share* is defined as the ratio of its market share to the market share held by the largest rival firm in the industry, with market share measured in unit volume, not dollars. For instance, if business A has a 15 percent share of its industry's total volume and A's largest rival has 30 percent, A's relative market share is 0.5. If business B has a market-leading share of 40 percent and its largest rival has 30 percent, B's relative market share is 1.33.[2] Using relative market share is analytically superior to using actual or absolute market share to measure competitive strength. A 10 percent market share, for example, is not very strong if the leader's share is 50 percent, but a 10 percent share is actually quite strong if the leader's share is 12 percent.[3]

- *Costs relative to competitors*—Business units that are very cost competitive tend to be more strongly positioned in their industries than business units struggling to maintain cost parity with major rivals.

- *Ability to match or beat rivals on key product attributes*—A company's competitiveness depends in part on being able to satisfy buyer expectations with regard to features, product performance, reliability, service, and other important attributes.

- *Ability to exercise bargaining leverage with key suppliers or customers*—Having bargaining leverage signals competitive strength and can be a source of competitive advantage.

- *Caliber of alliances and collaborative partnerships with suppliers and/or buyers*—Well-functioning alliances and partnerships may signal a potential competitive advantage vis-à-vis rivals and thus add to a business's competitive strength.

- *Ability to benefit from strategic-fit relationships with sister businesses*—Strategic-fit relationships with sister businesses are a source of added competitive advantage.

- *Technology and innovation capabilities*—Business units recognized for their technological leadership and track record in product innovation are usually strong competitors in their industry.

- *How well the business unit's competitive assets and competencies match industry key success factors*—The more a business unit's resource strengths and competitive capabilities match the industry's key success factors, the stronger its competitive position tends to be.

---

[2]Given this definition, only business units that are market share leaders in their respective industries will have relative market shares greater than 1.0. Business units that trail rivals in market share will have ratios below 1.0. The further below 1.0 a business unit's relative market share, the weaker is its competitive strength and market position relative to the industry's market share leader.

[3]Equally important, relative market share is likely to reflect relative cost based on experience in producing the product and economies of large-scale production. Businesses with large relative market shares may be able to operate at lower unit costs than low-share firms because of technological and efficiency gains that attach to larger production and sales volume. As was discussed in Chapter 3, the phenomenon of lower unit costs can go beyond just the effects of scale economies; as the cumulative volume of production increases, the knowledge gained from the firm's growing production experience can lead to the discovery of additional efficiencies and ways to reduce costs even further. For more details on how the relationship between experience and cumulative production volume results in lower unit costs, see Figure 3.1 in Chapter 3. A sizable experience curve effect in an industry's value chain places a strategic premium on market share: the competitor that gains the largest market share tends to realize important cost advantages that, in turn, can be used to lower prices and gain still additional customers, sales, market share, and profit. Such conditions are an important contributor to the competitive strength that a company has in that business.

- *Brand-name recognition and reputation*—A strong brand name is a valuable competitive asset in most industries.
- *Profitability relative to competitors*—Business units that consistently earn above-average returns on investment and have bigger profit margins than their rivals usually have stronger competitive positions than business units with below-average profitability for their industry. Moreover, above-average profitability signals competitive advantage, while below-average profitability usually denotes competitive disadvantage.

Other competitive strength indicators include uniquely strong knowledge of customers and markets, unique production capabilities, skills in supply chain management, marketing skills, ample financial resources, and the caliber of management (particularly whether management has experience, knowledge, and depth in making the kinds of major business changes that may be needed).

Analysts have a choice between rating each business unit on the same generic factors or rating each business unit on those strength measures most pertinent to its industry. Either approach can be defended, although using strength measures specific to each industry is conceptually stronger because the relevant measures of competitive strength, along with their relative importance, vary from industry to industry. Where adequate information is available, it is desirable to do a SWOT analysis (see Chapter 4) of each business unit and use the results in doing the competitive strength assessments.

As was done in evaluating industry attractiveness, weights need to be assigned to each of the strength measures to indicate their relative importance. Using different weights for different business units is conceptually stronger when the importance of the strength measures differs significantly from business to business. As before, the weights must add up to 1.0. Each business unit is then rated on each of the chosen strength measures, using a rating scale of 1 to 5 or 1 to 10 (where a *high* rating signifies *high* competitive strength and a *low* rating signifies *low* strength). Weighted strength ratings are calculated by multiplying the business unit's rating on each strength measure by the assigned weight. For example, a strength score of 8 times a weight of 0.20 gives a weighted strength rating of 1.60. The sum of weighted ratings across all the strength measures provides a quantitative measure of a business unit's overall market strength and competitive standing. The procedure is shown below:

Competitive Strength Measure	Weight	Strength Rating	Weighted Strength Rating
Relative market share	0.15	5	0.75
Costs relative to competitors	0.20	8	1.60
Ability to match rivals on key product attributes	0.05	7	0.35
Bargaining leverage with suppliers/buyers; caliber of alliances	0.10	6	0.60
Strategic-fit relationships with sister businesses	0.15	7	1.05
Technology and innovation capabilities	0.05	4	0.20
How well resources are matched to industry key success factors	0.10	7	0.70
Brand-name reputation/image	0.10	4	0.40
Degree of profitability relative to competitors	0.10	5	0.50
Sum of the assigned weights	1.00		
Competitive strength rating			**6.15**

Rating scale: (1 = Low strength; 10 = High strength)

Business units with relatively high overall competitive strength ratings (above 6.7 on a rating scale of 1 to 10) are strong market contenders in their industries. Businesses with relatively low overall ratings (below 3.3 on a rating scale of 1 to 10) are in competitively weak market positions.[4] Managerial evaluations of which businesses in the portfolio are strong and weak market contenders are a valuable consideration in deciding where to steer resources.

> Shareholder interests are generally best served by concentrating corporate resources on businesses that can contend for market leadership in their industries.

Using a Nine-Cell Matrix to Simultaneously Portray Industry Attractiveness and Competitive Strength

The industry attractiveness and business strength scores can be used to portray the strategic positions of each business in a diversified company. Long-term industry attractiveness is plotted on the vertical axis and competitive strength on the horizontal axis. A nine-cell grid emerges from dividing the vertical axis into three regions (high, medium, and low attractiveness) and the horizontal axis into three regions (strong, average, and weak competitive strength). High attractiveness is associated with scores of 6.7 or greater on a rating scale of 1 to 10, medium attractiveness is assigned to scores of 3.3 to 6.7, and so on; likewise, strong competitive strength is defined as a score greater than 6.7, average strength entails scores of 3.3 to 6.7, and so on—as shown in Figure 10.2. Each business unit in the corporate portfolio is plotted on the nine-cell matrix according to its overall attractiveness score and strength score, and then shown as a "bubble." The size of each bubble is scaled to what percentage of revenues the business generates relative to total corporate revenues.

> In the attractiveness-strength matrix, each business's location is plotted using quantitative measures of long-term industry attractiveness and business strength/competitive position.

The attractiveness-strength matrix helps in assigning investment priorities to each of the company's business units. Top investment priority is normally given to businesses in the three cells at the upper left, where long-term industry attractiveness and competitive strength/competitive position are both favorable. The general strategic prescription for businesses falling in these three cells is "grow and build," with businesses in the high-strong cell having the highest claim on investment funds. Next in priority come businesses positioned in the three diagonal cells stretching from the lower left to the upper right. These businesses are usually given medium or intermediate priority. They merit *selective* reinvestment, depending on their specific circumstances—size, profitability, strategic and resource fits, role in the company's overall strategy, and so on.

Some businesses in the medium-priority diagonal cells are likely to be more attractive than others. For example, a small business in the upper right cell of the matrix, despite being in a highly attractive industry, may occupy too weak a competitive position in its industry relative to stronger rivals to justify the investment and resources needed to turn it into a strong market contender and shift its position leftward in the matrix over time. If, however, a business in the upper right cell has an unusually attractive strategic opening to win a stronger market position, it may merit a higher investment priority and be given the resources to pursue a "grow-and-build" strategy.

> A company may earn larger profits over the long term by investing in a business with a competitively strong position in a moderately attractive industry than by investing in a weak business in a glamour industry.

---

[4]If analysts lack sufficient data to do detailed strength ratings, they can rely on their knowledge of each business unit's competitive situation to classify it as being in a "strong," "average," or "weak" competitive position. If trustworthy, such subjective assessments of business-unit strength can substitute for quantitative measures.

figure 10.2 **A Representative Nine-Cell Industry Attractiveness–Competitive Strength Matrix**

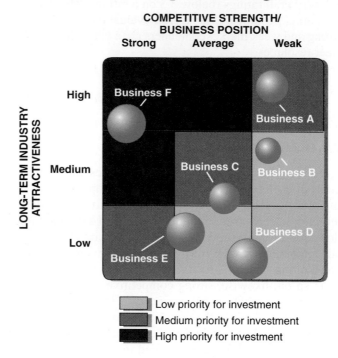

The strategy prescription for businesses in the three cells in the lower right corner of the matrix is typically "harvest or divest." In exceptional cases where good turnaround potential exists, it can be "overhaul and reposition" using some type of turnaround approach.[5]

The nine-cell attractiveness-strength grid provides strong logic for concentrating resources in those businesses that enjoy a higher degree of attractiveness and competitive strength, being very selective in making investments in businesses with intermediate positions, and withdrawing resources from businesses that are lower in attractiveness and strength unless they offer exceptional turnaround potential. This is why a diversified company needs to consider both industry attractiveness and business strength in allocating resources and investment capital to its different businesses.

More and more diversified companies are concentrating their resources on industries where they can be strong market contenders and divesting businesses that are not good candidates for becoming market leaders. At General Electric, the whole thrust of corporate strategy and corporate resource allocation over the past two decades has been to put GE's businesses into a number one or two position in both the United States and globally—see Illustration Capsule 40.

---

[5]At General Electric, each business actually ended up in one of five types of categories: (1) *high-growth-potential businesses* deserving top investment priority, (2) *stable base businesses* deserving steady reinvestment to maintain position, (3) *support businesses* deserving periodic investment funding, (4) *selective pruning or rejuvenation businesses* deserving reduced investment funding, and (5) *venture businesses* deserving heavy R&D investment.

illustration capsule 40
General Electric's Approach to Managing a Broadly Diversified Business Portfolio

Most knowledgeable observers believe General Electric has done a superlative job of profitably operating a broadly diversified portfolio of most unrelated businesses, anointing it as the world's most successful conglomerate.

GE's climb to global prominence began when Jack Welch became CEO of General Electric in 1981 and launched a series of corporate revitalization initiatives to reshape the company's diversified business portfolio. Early on, Welch issued a challenge to GE's business-unit managers to become number one or number two in their industry. Failing that, the business units either had to capture a decided technological advantage translatable into a competitive edge or face possible divestiture. By 1990, GE was a different company, having divested operations worth $9 billion, made additional acquisitions totaling $24 billion, and cut its workforce by 100,000. Twelve of GE's 14 primary business groups had attained a leading market position in the United States and/or globally. (The company's financial services and TV broadcasting businesses served markets too fragmented to rank.)

Under Welch's leadership, acquisitions, divestitures, and portfolio reshuffling continued at a fast and furious pace during the 1990s. GE acquired hundreds of new companies during the 1990s, including 108 in 1998 and 64 during a 90-day period in 1999. Most of the acquisitions were in Europe, Asia, and Latin America and aimed at transforming GE into a truly global enterprise. Weak-performing businesses were either divested or merged with stronger GE businesses.

GE'S BUSINESS PORTFOLIO IN 2000

Going into 2000, General Electric's business portfolio consisted of over 250 business divisions grouped into 10 business categories:

- *Aircraft Engines*—the world's largest producer of large and small jet engines for commercial and military aircraft. Throughout the 1990s, more than 50 percent of the world's large commercial jet engine orders were awarded to GE businesses.
- *Appliances*—one of the largest manufacturers of major appliances in the world, producing Monogram, Profile Performance, Profile, GE, and Hotpoint refrigerators and freezers, ovens, ranges and cooktops, microwave

ovens, washers and dryers, dishwashers, disposals and compactors, room air conditioners, and water purification systems.
- *Capital Services*—a diversified financial services group of 28 businesses in the areas of equipment management, consumer services, midmarket financing, specialized financing, and specialty insurance.
- *Industrial Systems*—a leading supplier of products used to distribute, protect, operate and control electrical power and equipment, as well as services for commercial and industrial applications. Major products and services include circuit breakers, switches, transformers, switchboards, switchgear, meters, relays, adjustable-speed drives, control and process automation systems, a full range of AC and DC electric motors and comprehensive technical engineering and power management solutions.
- *Lighting*—a leading supplier of lighting products for global consumer, commercial, and industrial markets. Products include incandescent, fluorescent, high-intensity discharge, halogen and holiday lamps, along with portable lighting fixtures, lamp components, and quartz products. GE also manufactures outdoor lighting fixtures, residential wiring devices, and commercial lighting controls.
- *Medical Systems*—a world leader in medical diagnostic imaging technology, services, and health care productivity. Products include computed tomography (CT) scanners, x-ray equipment, magnetic resonance imaging (MRI) systems, nuclear medicine cameras, ultrasound systems, patient monitoring devices, and mammography systems.
- *NBC*—included the NBC Television Network, 13 television stations, CNBC, MSNBC (in partnership with Microsoft), and partial ownership of such cable channels as Arts & Entertainment and the History Channel. The group also had equity stakes in CNET, Talk City, iVillage, Telescan, Hoover's, and 24/7 Media. Several of NBC's Internet assets were merged with Snap.com and XOOM.com, Inc., in 1999 to form NBCi, the seventh largest Internet site and the first publicly traded Internet company integrated with a major broadcaster.

(continued)

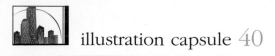

- *Plastics*—a world leader in versatile, high-performance engineered plastics used in the computer, electronics, data storage, office equipment, automotive, building, and construction industries.

- *Power Systems*—a global leader in the design, manufacture, and service of gas, steam, and hydroelectric turbines and generators for power production, pipeline and industrial applications. Power Systems also provides nuclear fuels, services, and related equipment.

- *Transportation Systems*—manufactures more than half of the diesel freight locomotives in North America. Its locomotives also operate in 75 countries worldwide. Other products include passenger locomotives, diesel engines for marine and stationary markets, electrical propulsion and control systems for rapid transit cars, motorized electric wheel systems for large mining trucks, and advanced railway signaling and control systems.

GE'S INTERNAL INITIATIVES TO PROFITABLY MANAGE BROAD DIVERSIFICATION

During the 1990s, Jack Welch orchestrated a series of internal initiatives to dramatically boost productivity in all of the company's businesses, reduce the size of the corporation's bureaucracy, and create a "boundaryless" organization where new ideas, technology, experience, and other forms of intellectual capital could be readily transferred from one GE business to another. Company programs to profitably manage a broadly diversified and global portfolio of businesses included:

- Emphasis on being a learning organization with no boundaries. Stress was placed on finding better ways to do things—borrowing ideas from other companies and relentlessly transferring ideas and best practices from one GE business to another. The operative assumption at GE was that someone, somewhere has a better idea; and the operative compulsion was to find who has that better idea, learn it, and put it into action as quickly as possible. Cross-business idea sharing was promoted by job rotations and transfers of people across businesses and geographic areas and by sending individuals or teams to visit facilities inside or outside the company that had put an innovative idea in place and achieved outstanding results. For example, when the company transferred a manager from its aircraft engine business to a GE appliance plant, that manager was expected to learn firsthand the success of the appliance division's Quick Response Plan that reduced the division's inventory by $200 million and increased its return on investment by 8.5 percent; on returning, the individual was under the gun to use that learning to help implement inventory savings in the aircraft engine business. Transfers and regular job rotations also built personal relationships between individuals across business units that aided in continued knowledge transfer after the rotation and helped block out insular thinking within each business unit.

- Instituting a six sigma quality program (led and taught by highly trained GE employees) all across GE that introduced rigorous thinking and analysis into the management process—a six sigma quality program

(continued)

STRATEGIC FIT ANALYSIS: CHECKING FOR CROSS-BUSINESS COMPETITIVE ADVANTAGE POTENTIAL

One essential part of evaluating a diversified company's strategy is to check its business portfolio for the extent to which there are competitively valuable matchups (i.e., strategic fit) among the company's existing businesses:

- Which business units have value chain matchups that offer opportunities to combine the performance of certain activities and thereby reduce costs? Potential value chain matchups typically include purchasing (where combining materials purchases could lead to greater bargaining leverage with suppliers), common use of e-commerce systems, manufacturing (where it may be possible to share manufacturing facilities),

(concluded)

generates fewer than 3.4 defects per million operations in a manufacturing or service process. GE's six sigma initiative was introduced in late 1995 (when it was running at a sigma level between 3 and 4) in a concerted effort to reduce costs, improve efficiency, and boost customer satisfaction. The gap between GE's sigma level of 3 to 4 and the target level of 6 was estimated to cost GE between $8 billion and $14 billion in inefficiencies and lost productivity. By year-end 1998, GE reported that its six sigma initiative had improved the company's operating margins to 16.7 percent (from 13.6 percent in 1995) and helped increase GE's working capital turns to 9.2 (from 5.8 in 1995).

- Strong reliance on "workout sessions" where GE managers and employees gathered in a room for as many hours or days as it took to focus on a problem or an opportunity, confront issues, share and debate their views, and develop a decisive plan of action for taking swift corrective action and moving the business or company forward. Workout, like the concept of a boundaryless company, was an integral component of GE's global culture.

- Encouraging managers and employees to fight bureaucracy and to go all out to kill bureaucratic practices and behavior at GE.

- Becoming an Internet company—the company's newest initiative. The goal was to fully incorporate use of the Internet and e-commerce practices in all of GE's 250 business divisions within 18 months and transform GE into a global e-business.

- Consciously molding a deep, talent-rich team of managers with strong leadership skills, the ability to make tough decision, and the ability to produce good business results. In a *Business Week* interview, Jack Welch said, "This place runs by its great people. The biggest accomplishment I've had is to find great people. An army of them . . . They are big hitters . . . We're in the cat-and-dog insurance business in England. I don't really want to be in that business, but the guy who brought me that idea wanted to be in it, and I trust him. He'll take it and make it work."

GE's commitments to cross-business learning, its determination to create a boundaryless organization, its use of workout sessions to confront and resolve issues quickly, and its movement of management talent around the company were widely viewed as integral to its success in managing a highly diverse portfolio of businesses and to having successfully assimilated the hundreds of acquisitions (mostly foreign) that the company made during the 1990s to build and strengthen its global business positions. Going into 2000, GE had sales of $112 billion, profits of $197 billion, and a market capitalization of over $400 billion (among the world's top five companies).

Source: Company documents; www.generalelectric.com; John A. Byrne, "How Jack Welch Runs GE," *Business Week*, June 8, 1998, pp. 88–95; and assorted other articles in the business press.

or distribution (where it may be possible to share warehousing, sales forces, distributors, dealers, or online sales channels).

- Which business units have value chain matchups that offer opportunities to transfer skills or technology or intellectual capital from one business to another?

- Which business units offer opportunities to use a common and well-respected brand name to command prominent display space with retailers and gain credibility with buyers?

- Which business units have value chain matchups that offer opportunities to create valuable new competitive capabilities or to leverage existing resources?

Figure 10.3 illustrates the process of searching for competitively valuable cross-business strategic fits and value chain matchups. Absent significant strategic fits, one has to be skeptical about the potential for a diversified company's businesses to perform better together than apart.

figure 10.3   **Comparing Value Chains to Identify Strategic Fits among a Diversified Company's Business Units**

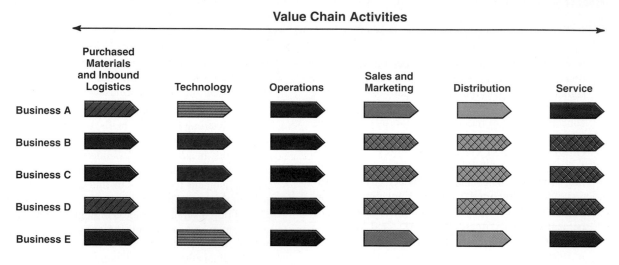

Value Chain Activities

	Purchased Materials and Inbound Logistics	Technology	Operations	Sales and Marketing	Distribution	Service
Business A						
Business B						
Business C						
Business D						
Business E						

Opportunities to combine purchasing activities and gain greater leverage with suppliers

Opportunities to share technology, transfer technical skills, combine R&D

Opportunities to combine/share sales and marketing activities, utilize common distribution channels, leverage use of a common brand name, and/or combine after-sale service activities.

No strategic fit opportunities

A second aspect of strategic fit that bears checking out is whether there are any businesses in the portfolio that do not fit in well with the company's overall long-term direction and strategic vision. Sometimes a business, despite possessing certain value chain matchups, doesn't mesh well with the strategic markets or customer groups or product categories that corporate management is concentrating on—in other words, it doesn't fit strategically into the company's future plans and performance objectives. A business may also lack long-term strategic appeal if it lacks growth potential or is marginally profitable or requires sizable annual capital investments to replace outdated plants and equipment. Such businesses probably need to be considered for divestiture despite having value chain fits with sister businesses. Businesses with little long-term strategic value often end up being treated like an unwanted stepchild and are a distraction to top management.

RESOURCE FIT ANALYSIS: DETERMINING HOW WELL THE FIRM'S RESOURCES MATCH BUSINESS UNIT REQUIREMENTS

The businesses in a diversified company's lineup need to exhibit good *resource fit* as well as good strategic fit. Resource fit exists when (1) businesses add to a company's resource strengths, either financially or strategically, and (2) a company has the resources to adequately support its businesses as a group without spreading itself too thin. One important dimension of resource fit concerns whether the company's business lineup is well matched to its financial resources.

Cash Hog and Cash Cow Businesses

Different businesses have different cash flow and investment characteristics. For example, business units in rapidly growing industries are often *cash hogs*—so labeled because the annual cash flows they are able to generate from internal operations aren't big enough to cover their annual capital requirements. To keep pace with rising demand, rapid-growth businesses frequently are looking at sizable annual capital investments for some years to come—for new facilities and equipment, for new product development or technology improvements, and for additional working capital to support inventory expansion and a larger base of operations. A business in a fast-growing industry becomes an even bigger cash hog when it has a relatively low market share and is pursuing a strategy to outgrow the market and gain enough market share to become an industry leader. When a rapid-growth business cannot generate a big enough cash flow from operations to finance its capital requirements internally, the needed financial resources must be provided by the corporate parent. Corporate management has to decide whether it is strategically and financially worthwhile to fund the perhaps considerable investment requirements of a cash hog.

A *cash hog* business is one whose internal cash flows are inadequate to fully fund its needs for working capital and new capital investment.

Business units with leadership positions in mature industries may, however, be *cash cows*—or businesses that generate substantial cash surpluses over what is needed for capital reinvestment and competitive maneuvers to sustain their present market position. Market leaders in slow-growth industries often generate sizable positive cash flows *over and above what is needed for reinvestment in operations* because their industry-leading position tends to give them the sales volumes and reputation to earn attractive profits and because the slow-growth nature of their industry often entails relatively modest annual investment requirements. Cash cows, though not always attractive from a growth standpoint, are valuable businesses from a financial resource perspective. The surplus cash flows they generate can be used to pay corporate dividends, finance acquisitions, and provide funds for investing in the company's promising cash hogs. It makes good financial and strategic sense for diversified companies to keep cash cows in healthy condition, fortifying and defending their market position so as to preserve their cash-generating capability over the long term and thereby have an ongoing source of financial resources to deploy elsewhere.

A *cash cow* business is a valuable part of a diversified company's business portfolio because it generates cash for financing new acquisitions, funding the capital requirements of cash hogs, and paying dividends.

Viewing a diversified group of businesses as a collection of cash flows and cash requirements (present and future) is a major step forward in understanding the financial aspects of corporate strategy. Determining which businesses in a diversified company's portfolio are cash hogs and which are cash cows highlights opportunities for shifting financial resources between business subsidiaries to optimize the performance of the whole corporate portfolio, explains why priorities for corporate resource allocation can differ from business to business, and provides good rationalizations for both invest-and-expand strategies and divestiture. For instance, a diversified company can use the excess cash generated by cash cows to fund the investment requirements of promising cash hogs, eventually growing the hogs into self-supporting "stars" having strong competitive positions in attractive, high-growth markets.[6] *Star businesses* are the cash cows of the future—when the markets of star businesses begin to mature and their growth

---

[6]A star business, as the name implies, is one with a leading market share, a widely respected reputation, a solid track record of profitability, and excellent future growth and profit opportunities. Star businesses vary as to their cash hog status. Some can cover their investment needs with self-generated cash flows; others require capital infusions from their corporate parents to stay abreast of rapid industry growth. Normally, strongly positioned star businesses in industries where growth is beginning to slow tend to be self-sustaining in terms of cash flow and make little claim on the corporate parent's treasury. Young stars, however, may require substantial investment capital *beyond what they can generate on their own* and still be cash hogs.

slows, their competitive strength should produce self-generated cash flows more than sufficient to cover their investment needs. The "success sequence" is thus cash hog to young star (but perhaps still a cash hog) to self-supporting star to cash cow.

If, however, a cash hog has questionable promise (either because of low industry attractiveness or a weak competitive position), then it becomes a logical candidate for divestiture. Pursuing an aggressive invest-and-expand strategy for a competitively weak cash hog seldom makes sense because it requires the corporate parent to keep pumping more capital into the business to keep abreast of fast-paced market growth *and* to build an attractively strong competitive position. Such businesses are a financial drain and lack good financial resource fit. Divesting a less attractive cash hog business is usually the best alternative unless (1) it has valuable strategic fits with other business units or (2) the capital infusions needed from the corporate parent are modest relative to the funds available and there's a decent chance of growing the business into a solid bottom-line contributor yielding a good return on invested capital.

Aside from cash flow considerations, a business has good financial fit when it contributes to the achievement of corporate performance objectives (profit growth, above-average return on investment, recognition as an industry leader, and so on) and when it materially enhances shareholder value. A business exhibits poor financial fit if it soaks up a disproportionate share of the company's financial resources, if it is a subpar or inconsistent bottom-line contributor, if it is unduly risky and failure would jeopardize the entire enterprise, or if it is too small to make a material earnings contribution even though it performs well. In addition, a diversified company's business portfolio lacks financial fit if its financial resources are stretched across too many businesses. Severe financial strain can occur if a company borrows so heavily to finance new acquisitions that it has to trim way back on new capital expenditures for existing businesses and use the big majority of its financial resources to meet interest obligations and to pay down debt. Some diversified companies have found themselves so financially overextended or overleveraged that they have had to sell off some businesses to raise the money to meet existing debt obligations and fund essential capital expenditures for the remaining businesses.

Competitive and Managerial Resource Fits

A diversified company's strategy must aim at producing a good fit between its resource capability and the competitive and managerial requirements of its businesses.[7] Diversification is more likely to enhance shareholder value when the company has or can develop the competitive and managerial capabilities to be successful in the businesses/industries it has diversified into. Businesses where resource fit is lacking is a serious enough problem to make such businesses prime divestiture candidates. Likewise, when a company's resources and capabilities match the key success factors of industries it is not presently in, it makes sense to take a hard look at acquiring companies in these industries and expanding the company's business lineup.

> Business subsidiaries that don't exhibit good strategic fit and good resource fit should be considered for divestiture unless their financial performance is outstanding.

Checking a diversified company's business portfolio for competitive and managerial resource fits involves the following:

- *Determining whether the company's resource strengths are well matched to the key success factors of the businesses it has diversified into*—A close match between

---

[7]For an excellent discussion of how to assess these fits, see Andrew Campbell, Michael Goold, and Marcus Alexander, "Corporate Strategy: The Quest for Parenting Advantage," *Harvard Business Review* 73, no. 2 (March–April 1995), pp. 120–32.

industry key success factors and company resources and capabilities is a solid sign of good resource fit.

- *Determining whether the company has ample resource depth to support all its businesses*—A diversified company has to guard against stretching its resource base too thin and trying to do too many things. The broader the diversification, the greater the concern about whether the company has sufficient managerial depth and expertise to cope with the diverse range of managerial and operating problems its wide business lineup presents (plus those it may be contemplating getting into).

- *Determining whether one or more businesses can benefit from the transfer of resources and/or competitive capabilities from sister businesses*—Capabilities that are often good candidates for transfer include short development times in bringing new products to market, strong partnerships with key suppliers, an R&D organization capable of generating technological and product opportunities in several different industry arenas simultaneously, a high degree of organizational agility in responding to shifting market conditions and emerging opportunities, or state-of-the-art systems for doing business via the Internet. The ability to transfer competitively valuable resources or capabilities from one business to another is a strong signal of resource fit.

- *Determining whether the company needs to invest in upgrading its resources or capabilities in order to stay ahead of (or at least abreast of) the efforts of rivals*—In a world of fast-paced change and competition, managers have to be alert to the need to continually invest in and upgrade the company's resources, however potent its current resources are. All resources depreciate in value as competitors mimic them or retaliate with a different (and perhaps more attractive) resource combination.[8] Upgrading resources and competencies often means going beyond just strengthening what the company already is capable of doing. It may involve adding new capabilities (like the ability to manage a group of diverse international manufacturing plants, technological expertise in related or complementary disciplines, a state-of-the-art-company intranet, or an innovative Web site that draws many visits and gives all business units greater market exposure); building competencies that allow the company to enter another attractive industry; or widening the company's range of capabilities to match certain competitively valuable capabilities of rivals.

The complement of resources and capabilities at a firm's command determines its competitive strengths. The more a company's diversification strategy is tied to leveraging its resources and capabilities in new businesses, the more it has to develop a big enough and deep enough resource pool to supply these businesses with sufficient capability to create competitive advantage. Otherwise its strengths end up being stretched too thin across too many businesses and the opportunity for competitive advantage is lost.

Some Notes of Caution   Many diversification strategies built around cross-business transfer of resource capabilities never live up to their promise because the transfer process proves problematic. Developing a resource capability in one business nearly always involves much trial and error and much organizational learning, the product of close collaboration among many people over a period of time. The first step in transferring knowledge from one business to another involves moving people with the requisite know-how to the new business. These people not only have to learn the

> Diversifying into businesses with seemingly good resource fit is, by itself, not sufficient to produce success.

[8]David J. Collis and Cynthia A. Montgomery, "Competing on Resources: Strategy in the 90s," *Harvard Business Review* 73, no. 4 (July–August 1995), p. 124.

ins and outs of the new business well enough to see how best to integrate the capability into the operations of the receiving business but they also have to be adept in implanting all the appropriate organizational learning from the donor business. As a practical matter, resource transfers require the receiving business to undergo significant organizational learning and team building on its own to get up to speed in executing the transferred capability. It takes time, money, and patience for the transferred capability to become operational. Sometimes unforeseen problems result in debilitating delays or prohibitive expenses or inability on the part of the receiving business to execute the capability proficiently. As a consequence, the business receiving the resource transfer may never perform up to expectations.

A second reason for the failure of a diversification move into a new business with seemingly good resource fit is that the causes of a firm's success in one business are sometimes quite entangled and hard to replicate.[9] It is easy to be overly optimistic about the ease with which a company that has hit a home run in one business can enter a new business with similar resource requirements and hit a second home run. Noted British retailer Marks & Spencer, despite possessing a range of impressive resource capabilities (ability to choose excellent store locations, having a supplier chain that gives it both low costs and high merchandise quality, loyal employees, an excellent reputation with consumers, and strong management expertise) that have made it one of Britain's premier retailers for 100 years, has failed repeatedly in its efforts to diversify into department store retailing in the United States.

A third reason for diversification failure, despite apparent resource fit, is misjudging the resource strengths of rivals. For example, even though Philip Morris had built powerful consumer marketing capabilities in its cigarette and beer businesses, it floundered in soft drinks and ended up divesting its acquisition of 7UP after several frustrating years because of difficulties in competing against strongly entrenched and resource-capable rivals like Coca-Cola and PepsiCo.

RANKING THE BUSINESS UNITS ON THE BASIS OF PAST PERFORMANCE AND FUTURE PROSPECTS

Once a diversified company's businesses have been rated on the basis of industry attractiveness, competitive strength, strategic fit, and resource fit, the next step is to evaluate which businesses have the best performance prospects and which ones the worst. The most important considerations in judging business-unit performance are sales growth, profit growth, contribution to company earnings, and the return on capital invested in the business. (As we noted in Chapter 1, more and more companies are evaluating business performance on the basis of economic value added—the return on invested capital over and above the firm's cost of capital.) Sometimes, cash flow generation is a big consideration, especially for cash cows and businesses with potential for harvesting.

Information on each business's past performance can be gleaned from a company's financial records.[10] While past performance is not necessarily a good predictor of future performance, it does signal which businesses have been strong performers

---

[9]Ibid., pp. 121–22.

[10]Financial performance by line of business is typically contained in a company's annual report, usually in the notes to corporate financial statements. Line-of-business performance can also be found in a publicly owned firm's 10-K report filed annually with the Securities and Exchange Commission.

and which have been weak performers. The industry attractiveness–business strength evaluations should provide a solid basis for judging future prospects. Normally, strong business units in attractive industries have significantly better prospects than weak businesses in unattractive industries.

The growth and profit outlooks for a diversified company's principal or core businesses generally determine whether its portfolio as a whole is capable of strong, mediocre, or weak performance. Noncore businesses with subpar track records and hazy or uncertain long-term prospects are logical candidates for divestiture. Business subsidiaries with the brightest profit and growth prospects and solid strategic and resource fits generally should head the list for corporate resource support.

DECIDING ON RESOURCE ALLOCATION PRIORITIES AND A GENERAL STRATEGIC DIRECTION FOR EACH BUSINESS UNIT

Using the information and results of the preceding evaluation steps, corporate strategists can allocate resources to the various business units and settle on a general strategic direction for each business unit. The task here is to draw some conclusions about which business units should have top priority for corporate resource support and new capital investment and which business units should carry the lowest priority. In doing the ranking, managers need to give special attention to whether and how corporate resources and capabilities can be used to enhance the competitiveness of particular business units.[11] Opportunities for resource transfer, activity combining, or infusions of new financial capital become especially important when improvement in some key success area could make a big difference to a particular business unit's performance.

Ranking a diversified company's businesses from highest to lowest priority should also reveal the most appropriate strategic approach for each business unit—*invest-and-grow* (aggressive expansion), *fortify-and-defend* (protect current position by strengthening and adding resource capabilities in needed areas), *overhaul-and-reposition* (make major competitive strategy changes to move the business into a different and ultimately stronger industry position), or *harvest-divest*. In deciding whether to divest a business unit, corporate managers should rely on a number of evaluating criteria: industry attractiveness, competitive strength, strategic fit with sister businesses, resource fit, performance potential (profit, return on capital employed, economic value added, contribution to cash flow), compatibility with the company's strategic vision and long-term direction, and ability to contribute to enhanced shareholder value.

To get ever-higher levels of performance out of a diversified company's business portfolio, corporate managers have to do an effective job of steering resources out of low-opportunity areas into high-opportunity areas. Divesting marginal businesses is one of the best ways of freeing unproductive assets for redeployment. Surplus funds from cash cows and businesses being harvested also add to the corporate treasury. Options for allocating a diversified company's financial resources include (1) investing in ways to strengthen or expand existing businesses, (2) making acquisitions to establish positions in new industries, (3) funding long-range R&D ventures, (4) paying off

> Improving a diversified company's long-term financial performance entails concentrating company resources on businesses with the best prospects and most solid strategic and resource fits.

---

[11]Collis and Montgomery, "Competing on Resources: Strategy in the 90s," pp. 126–28; Hofer and Schendel, *Strategy Formulation: Analytical Concepts,* p. 80; and Michael E. Porter, *Competitive Advantage* (New York: Free Press, 1985), chapter 9.

existing long-term debt, (5) increasing dividends, and (6) repurchasing the company's stock. The first three are *strategic* actions to add shareholder value; the last three are *financial* moves to enhance shareholder value. Ideally, a company will have enough funds to do what is needed, both strategically and financially. If not, strategic uses of corporate resources should usually take precedence unless there is a compelling reason to strengthen the firm's balance sheet or divert financial resources to pacify shareholders.

CRAFTING A CORPORATE STRATEGY

The preceding analytical steps set the stage for crafting strategic moves to improve a diversified company's overall performance. The basic issue of "what to do" hinges on the conclusions drawn about the strategic and financial attractiveness of the group of businesses the company has diversified into.[12] Key questions here are: Does the company have enough businesses in very attractive industries? Will the proportion of mature or declining businesses cause corporate growth to be sluggish? Are the company's businesses overly vulnerable to seasonal or recessionary influences or to threats from emerging new technologies? Are the prospects hazy or uncertain for too many of the industries or businesses the company is in? Is the firm burdened with too many businesses in average-to-weak competitive positions? Is there ample strategic fit among the company's different businesses? Does the portfolio contain businesses that the company really doesn't need to be in? Is there ample resource fit among the company's business units? Does the firm have enough cash cows to finance the cash hogs with potential to be star performers? Can the company's principal or core businesses be counted on to generate dependable profits and/or cash flow? Does the makeup of the business portfolio put the company in good position for the future? Answers to these questions indicate whether corporate strategists should consider divesting certain businesses, making new acquisitions, restructuring the makeup of the portfolio, significantly altering the pattern of corporate resource allocation, or sticking closely with the existing business lineup and pursuing the opportunities they present.

The Performance Test

A good test of the strategic and financial attractiveness of a diversified firm's business portfolio is whether the company can attain its performance objectives with its current lineup of businesses and resource capabilities. If so, no major corporate strategy changes are indicated. However, if a performance shortfall is probable, corporate strategists can take any of several actions to close the gap:[13]

1. *Alter the strategic plans for some or all of the businesses in the portfolio.* This option involves renewed corporate efforts to get better performance out of its present business units. Corporate managers can push business-level managers for strategy changes that yield better business-unit performance and perhaps provide higher-than-planned corporate resource support for these efforts. However, pursuing better short-term performance by zealously trimming resource initiatives aimed at

---

[12]Barry Hedley, "Strategy and the Business Portfolio," *Long Range Planning* 10, no. 1 (February 1977), p. 13; and Hofer and Schendel, *Strategy Formulation,* pp. 82–86.

[13]Hofer and Schendel, *Strategy Formulation,* pp. 93–100.

bolstering a business's long-term competitive position has dubious value—it merely trades off better long-term performance for better short-term financial performance. In any case there are limits on how much extra near-term performance can be squeezed out to reach established targets.

2. *Add new business units to the corporate portfolio.* Boosting overall performance by making new acquisitions or starting new businesses internally raises some new strategy issues. Expanding the corporate portfolio means taking a close look at (*a*) whether to acquire related or unrelated businesses, (*b*) what size acquisitions to make, (*c*) how the new units will fit into the present corporate structure, (*d*) what specific features to look for in an acquisition candidate, and (*e*) whether acquisitions can be financed without shortchanging present business units on their new investment requirements. Nonetheless, adding new businesses is a major strategic option, one frequently used by diversified companies to escape sluggish earnings performance.

3. *Divest weak-performing or money-losing businesses.* The most likely candidates for divestiture are businesses in a weak competitive position, in a relatively unattractive industry, or in an industry with minimal strategic fit with sister business and/or a lack of resource fit. Funds from divestitures can, of course, be used to finance new acquisitions, pay down corporate debt, or fund new strategic thrusts in the remaining businesses.

4. *Form cooperative alliances to try to alter conditions responsible for subpar performance potentials.* In some situations, cooperative alliances with domestic or foreign firms, suppliers, customers, or special interest groups may help ameliorate adverse performance prospects.[14] Instituting resource sharing agreements with suppliers, select competitors, or firms with complementary products and collaborating closely on mutually advantageous initiatives are often fruitful avenues for improving the competitiveness and performance potential of a company's businesses. Forming or supporting a political action group may be an effective way of lobbying for solutions to import-export problems, tax disincentives, and onerous regulatory requirements.

5. *Upgrade the company's resource base.* Achieving better performance may well hinge on corporate efforts to develop new resource strengths that will help select business units match the competitively valuable capabilities of their rivals or, better still, allow them to secure competitive advantage. One of the biggest ways that corporate-level managers of diversified companies can contribute to added shareholder value is to lead the development of cutting-edge capabilities and to marshal new kinds of corporate resources for deployment in a number of the company's businesses.

6. *Lower corporate performance objectives.* Adverse market circumstances or declining fortunes in one or more core business units can render companywide performance targets unreachable. So can setting overly ambitious objectives. Closing the gap between actual and desired performance may then require downward revision of corporate objectives to bring them more in line with reality. Lowering performance objectives is usually a last resort, used only after other options come up short.

---

[14]For an excellent discussion of the benefits of alliances among competitors in global industries, see Kenichi Ohmae, "The Global Logic of Strategic Alliances," *Harvard Business Review* 67, no. 2 (March–April 1989), pp. 143–54.

Identifying Additional Diversification Opportunities

One of the major corporate strategy-making concerns in a diversified company is whether to pursue further diversification and, if so, how to identify the "right" kinds of industries and businesses to get into. For firms pursuing unrelated diversification, the issue of where to diversify next is relatively wide open—the search for acquisition candidates is based more on spotting a good financial opportunity and having the financial resources to pursue it than on industry or strategic criteria. Decisions to diversify into additional unrelated businesses are usually based on such considerations as whether the firm has the financial ability to make another acquisition, whether new acquisitions are badly needed to boost overall corporate performance, whether one or more acquisition opportunities have to be acted on before they are purchased by other firms, whether the timing is right for another acquisition (corporate management may have its hands full dealing with the current portfolio of businesses), and whether corporate management believes it possesses the range and depth of expertise to take on the supervision of an additional business.

> Firms with unrelated diversification strategies hunt for businesses that offer attractive financial returns—regardless of what industry they're in.

With a related diversification strategy, however, the search for new industries to diversify into is aimed at identifying other businesses (1) whose value chains have fits with the value chains of one or more businesses represented in the company's business portfolio and (2) whose resource requirements are well matched to the firm's corporate resource capabilities.[15] Once corporate strategists identify strategic-fit and resource-fit opportunities in attractive new industries, they must determine which ones have important competitive advantage potential. The size of the competitive advantage potential depends on whether the fits are competitively significant or marginal and on the costs and difficulties of merging or coordinating the business unit interrelationships to capture the fits.[16] Often, careful analysis reveals that while there are many actual and potential business unit interrelationships, only a few have enough strategic importance to generate meaningful competitive advantage.

> Further diversification in firms with related diversification strategies involves identifying attractive industries having good strategic or resource fit with one or more existing businesses.

Managing the Process of Crafting Corporate Strategy

Although formal analysis and entrepreneurial brainstorming normally undergird the corporate strategy-making process, there is more to where corporate strategy comes from and how it evolves. Rarely is there an all-inclusive grand formulation of the total corporate strategy. Instead, corporate strategy in major enterprises emerges incrementally as many different internal and external events unfold; it is the result of probing the future, experimenting, gathering more information, sensing problems, building awareness of the various options, spotting new opportunities, developing ad hoc responses to unexpected crises, communicating consensus as it emerges, and acquiring a feel for all the strategically relevant factors, their importance, and their interrelationships.[17]

Strategic analysis is not something that the executives of diversified companies do all at once in comprehensive fashion. Such big reviews are sometimes scheduled, but research indicates that major strategic decisions emerge gradually rather than from

---

[15]Porter, *Competitive Advantage,* pp. 370–71.

[16]Ibid., pp. 371–72.

[17]Ibid., pp. 58, 196.

periodic, full-scale analysis followed by prompt decision. Typically, top executives approach major strategic decisions a step at a time, often starting from broad, intuitive conceptions and then embellishing, fine-tuning, and modifying their original thinking as more information is gathered, as formal analysis confirms or modifies their judgments about the situation, and as confidence and consensus build for what strategic moves need to be made. Often attention and resources are concentrated on a few critical strategic thrusts that illuminate and integrate corporate direction, objectives, and strategies.

key|points

Strategic analysis in diversified companies is an eight-step process:

Step 1: *Get a clear fix on the present strategy.* Determine whether the company's strategic emphasis is on related or unrelated diversification; whether the scope of company operations is mostly domestic or increasingly multinational, what moves have been made recently to add new businesses and build positions in new industries, the rationale underlying recent divestitures, the nature of any efforts to capture strategic fits and create competitive advantage based on economies of scope and/or resource transfer, and the pattern of resource allocation to the various business units. This step sets the stage for thorough evaluation of the need for strategy changes.

Step 2: *Evaluate the long-term attractiveness of the industries into which the firm has diversified.* Industry attractiveness needs to be evaluated from three angles: the attractiveness of each industry on its own, the attractiveness of each industry relative to the others, and the attractiveness of all the industries as a group. Quantitative measures of industry attractiveness tell a valuable story about just how and why some of the industries a company has diversified into are more attractive than others. The two hardest parts of calculating industry attractiveness scores are deciding on appropriate weights for the industry attractiveness measures and knowing enough about each industry to assign accurate and objective ratings.

Step 3: *Evaluate the relative competitive strength of each of the company's business units.* Again, quantitative ratings of competitive strength are preferable to subjective judgments. The purpose of rating the competitive strength of each business is to gain clear understanding of which businesses are strong contenders in their industries, which are weak contenders, and the underlying reasons for their strength or weakness. Join the conclusions about industry attractiveness with the conclusions about competitive strength by drawing an industry attractiveness/competitive strength matrix displaying the positions of each business on a nine-cell grid; use the attractiveness/strength matrix to help determine the prospects of each business and what priority they should have in allocating corporate resources and investment capital.

Step 4: *Check for cross-business value chain relationships and strategic fit.* A business is more attractive strategically when it has value chain relationships with sister business units that present opportunities to transfer skills or technology, reduce overall costs, share facilities, or share a common brand name—any of which can represent a significant avenue for producing competitive advantage beyond what any one business can achieve on its own. The more businesses with competitively valuable strategic fits, the greater a diversified company's potential for achieving economies of scope, enhancing the competitive capabilities of particular business units, and/or strengthening the competitiveness of its product and business lineup, thereby realizing a combined performance greater than the units could achieve operating independently.

Step 5: *Determine whether the firm's resource strengths fit the resource requirements of its present business lineup.* The businesses in a diversified company's lineup need to exhibit good *resource fit* as well as good strategic fit. Resource fit exists when (1) businesses add to a company's resource strengths, either financially or strategically, (2) a company has the resources to adequately support the resource requirements of its businesses as a group without spreading itself too thin, and (3) there are close matches between a company's resources and industry key success factors. One important dimension of resource fit concerns whether the company's business lineup is well matched to its financial resources. Assessing the cash requirements of different businesses in a diversified company's portfolio and determining which are cash hogs and which are cash cows highlights opportunities for shifting corporate financial resources between business subsidiaries to optimize the performance of the whole corporate portfolio, explains why priorities for corporate resource allocation can differ from business to business, and provides good rationalizations for both invest-and-expand strategies and divestiture.

Step 6: *Rank the different business units on past performance and future prospects.* The most important considerations in judging business-unit performance are sales growth, profit growth, contribution to company earnings, and the return on capital invested in the business. Sometimes, cash flow generation is a big consideration. Normally, strong business units in attractive industries have significantly better performance prospects than weak businesses or businesses in unattractive industries.

Step 7: *Decide on priorities for resource allocation and whether the general strategic direction for each business unit should be aggressive expansion, fortify and defend, overhaul and reposition, or harvest/divest.* In doing the ranking, special attention needs to be given to whether and how corporate resources and capabilities can be used to enhance the competitiveness of particular business units. Options for allocating a diversified company's financial resources include (1) investing in ways to strengthen or expand existing businesses, (2) making acquisitions to establish positions in new industries, (3) funding long-range R&D ventures, (4) paying off existing long-term debt, (5) increasing dividends, and (6) repurchasing the company's stock. Ideally, a company will have the financial strength to accomplish what is needed strategically and financially; if not, strategic uses of corporate resources should usually take precedence.

Step 8: *Use the preceding analysis to craft a series of moves to improve overall corporate performance.* Typical actions include (1) making acquisitions, starting new businesses from within, entering into new strategic alliances, and divesting marginal businesses or businesses that no longer match the company's long-term direction and strategy; (2) devising moves to strengthen the long-term competitive positions of the company's businesses; (3) capitalizing on strategic-fit and resource-fit opportunities and turning them into long-term competitive advantage; and (4) steering corporate resources out of low-opportunity areas and into high-opportunity areas.

suggested | readings

Campbell, Andrew; Michael Goold; and Marcus Alexander. "Corporate Strategy: The Quest for Parenting Advantage." *Harvard Business Review* 73, no. 2 (March–April 1995), pp. 120–32.

Collis, David J., and Cynthia A. Montgomery. "Creating Corporate Advantage." *Harvard Business Review* 76, no. 3 (May–June 1998), pp. 70–83.

Eisenhardt, Kathleen M., and Shona L. Brown. "Patching: Restitching Business Portfolios in Dynamic Markets." *Harvard Business Review* 77, no. 3 (May–June 1999), pp. 72–82.

Haspeslagh, Phillippe C., and David B. Jamison. *Managing Acquisitions: Creating Value through Corporate Renewal.* New York: Free Press, 1991.

Porter, Michael E. "From Competitive Advantage to Corporate Strategy." *Harvard Business Review* 65, no. 3 (May–June 1987), pp. 43–59.

chapter | eleven

11

Building Resource Strengths and Organizational Capabilities

The best game plan in the world never blocked or tackled anybody.
—Vince Lombardi

Strategies are intellectually simple; their execution is not.
—Lawrence A. Bossidy, Former CEO, Allied-Signal

We would be in some form of denial if we didn't see that execution is the true measure of success.
—C. Michael Armstrong, CEO, AT&T

Organizing is what you do before you do something, so that when you do it, it is not all mixed up.
—A. A. Milne

Flat organizations of empowered people are critical to gaining quick decisions in a global marketplace that moves at Net speed.
—John Byrne

Managers can't assume that strategy and capability will come together automatically.
—Thomas M. Hout and John C. Carter

Once managers have decided on a strategy, the emphasis turns to converting it into actions and good results. Putting a strategy into place and getting the organization to execute it well call for different sets of managerial skills. Whereas crafting strategy is largely a market-driven activity, implementing strategy is primarily an operations-driven activity revolving around the management of people and business processes. Whereas successful strategy making depends on business vision, shrewd industry and competitive analysis, and good resource fit, successful strategy implementation depends on doing a good job of leading, working with and through others, allocating resources, building and strengthening competitive capabilities, installing strategy-supportive policies, and shaping

how the organization performs its core business activities. Executing strategy is an action-oriented, make-things-happen task that tests a manager's ability to direct organizational change, motivate people, develop core competencies, build valuable organizational capabilities, achieve continuous improvement in business processes, create a strategy-supportive corporate culture, and meet or beat performance targets.

Experienced managers, savvy in strategy making and strategy implementing, are emphatic in declaring that it is a whole lot easier to develop a sound strategic plan than it is to execute the plan and achieve the planned outcomes. According to one executive, "It's been rather easy for us to decide where we wanted to go. The hard part is to get the organization to act on the new priorities."[1] What makes executing strategy a tougher, more time-consuming management challenge than crafting strategy is the wide array of managerial activities that have to be attended to, the many ways managers can proceed, the demanding people-management skills required, the perseverance necessary to get a variety of initiatives launched and moving, the number of bedeviling issues that must be

> The manager's task is to convert the strategic plan into action and get on with what needs to be done to achieve the vision and targeted objectives.

----

[1]As quoted in Steven W. Floyd and Bill Wooldridge, "Managing Strategic Consensus: The Foundation of Effective Implementation," *Academy of Management Executive* 6, no. 4 (November 1992), p. 27.

worked out, the resistance to change that must be overcome, and the difficulties of integrating the efforts of many different work groups into a smoothly functioning whole.

Just because managers announce a new strategy doesn't mean that subordinates will agree with it or cooperate in implementing it. Senior executives cannot will things to happen when they launch new strategic initiatives, nor can they simply communicate with a few hundred people at the top of the organization and expect change to occur. Some managers and employees may be skeptical about the merits of the strategy, seeing it as contrary to the organization's best interests, unlikely to succeed, or threatening to their own careers. Moreover, different employees may interpret the new strategy differently, be uncertain about how their departments will fare, and have different ideas about what internal changes are needed to execute the new strategy. Long-standing attitudes, vested interests, inertia, and ingrained organizational practices don't melt away when managers decide on a new strategy and start to implement it—especially when only a handful of people have been involved in crafting the strategy and when the rationale for strategic change has to be sold to enough organizational members to root out the status quo. It takes adept managerial leadership to convincingly communicate the new strategy and the reasons for it, overcome pockets of doubt and disagreement, build consensus and enthusiasm for how to proceed, secure the commitment and energetic cooperation of concerned parties, and move forward to get all the implementation pieces into place and integrated. Depending on how much consensus building, motivating, and organizational change is involved, the implementation process can take several months to several years.

> Companies don't implement and execute strategies, people do.

A FRAMEWORK FOR EXECUTING STRATEGY

Implementing and executing strategy entails converting the organization's strategic plan into action and then into results. Like crafting strategy, it's a job for the whole management team, not just a few senior managers. While an organization's chief executive officer and the heads of major units (business divisions, functional departments, and key operating units) are ultimately responsible for seeing that strategy is implemented successfully, the implementation process typically affects every part of the firm, from the biggest operating unit to the smallest frontline work group. Every manager has to think through the answer to "What has to be done in my area to implement our part of the strategic plan, and what should I do to get these things accomplished?" In this sense, *all managers become strategy-implementers in their areas of authority and responsibility, and all employees are participants.*

> Every manager has an active role in the process of executing the firm's strategic plan and all employees are participants.

One of the keys to successful implementation is for management to communicate the case for organizational change so clearly and persuasively to organizational members that there is determined commitment throughout the ranks to carry out the strategy and meet performance targets. The ideal condition is for managers to arouse enough enthusiasm for the strategy to turn the implementation process into a companywide crusade. *Management's handling of the strategy implementation process can be considered successful if and when the company achieves the targeted strategic and financial performance and shows good progress in realizing its long-range strategic vision.*

Unfortunately, there are no 10-step checklists, no proven paths, and few concrete guidelines for tackling the job. Strategy implementation is the least charted, most open-ended part of strategic management. The best dos and don'ts come from the reported experiences and "lessons learned" of managers and companies—and the wisdom they yield is inconsistent. What's worked well for some managers has been tried by others and found lacking. The reasons are understandable. Not only are some managers more effective than others in employing this or that recommended approach to organizational change but each instance of strategy implementation takes place in a different organizational context. Different business practices, competitive circumstances, work environments, cultures, policies, compensation incentives, mixes of personalities, and organizational histories all require a customized approach to strategy implementation—one based on individual company situations and circumstances, the strategy-implementer's best judgment, and the implementer's ability to use particular change techniques adeptly.

> Managing strategy implementation is more art than science.

THE PRINCIPAL STRATEGY-IMPLEMENTING TASKS

While managers should tailor their approaches to the situation, certain bases have to be covered no matter what the organization's circumstances; these include:

1. Building an organization with the competencies, capabilities, and resource strengths to carry out the strategy successfully.
2. Developing budgets to steer ample resources into those value chain activities critical to strategic success.
3. Establishing strategy-supportive policies and procedures.
4. Instituting best practices and pushing for continuous improvement in how value chain activities are performed.
5. Installing information, communication, e-commerce, and operating systems that enable company personnel to carry out their strategic roles successfully day in and day out.
6. Tying rewards and incentives to the achievement of performance objectives and good strategy execution.
7. Creating a strategy-supportive work environment and corporate culture.
8. Exerting the internal leadership needed to drive implementation forward and keep improving on how the strategy is being executed.

These managerial tasks crop up repeatedly in the strategy implementation process, no matter what the specifics of the situation, and drive the priorities on the strategy implementer's agenda—as depicted in Figure 11.1. One or two of these tasks usually end up being more crucial or time-consuming than others, depending on whether there are important resource weaknesses to correct or new competencies to develop, the strength of ingrained behavior patterns that have to be changed, any pressures for quick results and near-term financial improvements, and other such factors particular to the company's circumstances.

In devising an action agenda, *strategy implementers should begin with a probing assessment of what the organization must do differently and better to carry out the strategy successfully.* They should then consider how to make the necessary internal changes as rapidly as possible. Successful strategy implementers have a knack for diagnosing what their organizations need to do to execute the chosen strategy well, and they are creative in finding ways to perform key value chain activities effectively and efficiently.

figure 11.1   **The Eight Big Managerial Components of Implementing Strategy**

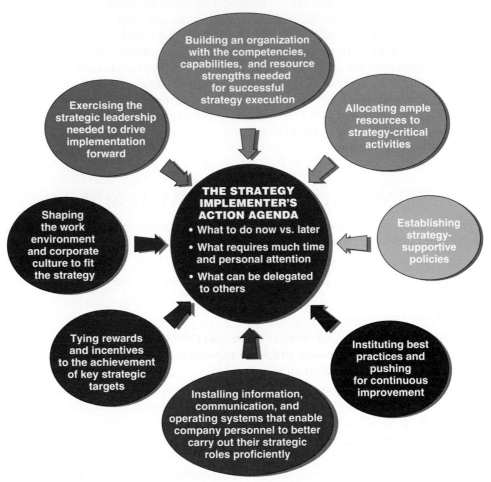

LEADING THE STRATEGY IMPLEMENTATION AND EXECUTION PROCESS

One make-or-break determinant of successful strategy implementation and execution is how well management leads the process. Managers can employ any of several leadership styles in pushing the implementation process along. They can play an active, visible, take-charge role or a quiet, low-key, behind-the-scenes one. They can make decisions authoritatively or on the basis of consensus; delegate much or little; be personally involved in the details of implementation or stand on the sidelines and coach others; proceed swiftly (launching implementation initiatives on many fronts) or deliberately (remaining content with gradual progress over a long time frame). How managers lead the strategy execution process tends to be a function of (1) their experience and knowledge of the business; (2) whether they are new to the job or veterans; (3) their network of personal relationships in the organization; (4) their own diagnostic, administrative, interpersonal, and problem-solving skills; (5) the authority they've been given; (6) the leadership style they're comfortable with; and (7) their view of the role they need to play to get things done.

Although major initiatives to implement corporate and business strategies usually have to be led by the CEO and other senior officers, top-level managers still have to rely on the active support and cooperation of middle and lower managers to push strategy changes into functional areas and operating units and to carry out the strategy effectively on a daily basis. Middle and lower-level managers not only are responsible for initiating and supervising the execution process in their areas of authority but also are instrumental in getting subordinates to continuously improve on how strategy-critical value chain activities are performed and in producing the front-line results that allow company performance targets to be met. How successful middle and lower managers are in using the resources at their command to strengthen organizational capabilities determines how proficiently the company executes its strategy on a daily basis—their role on the company's strategy execution team is by no means minimal.

> It is the job of middle and lower-level managers to push needed implementation actions on the front lines and to see that the strategy is well executed on a daily basis.

In big organizations with geographically scattered operating units, the action agenda of senior-level strategy implementers mostly involves communicating the case for change to others, building consensus for how to proceed, installing strong allies in positions where they can push implementation along in key organizational units, urging and empowering subordinates to get the process moving, establishing measures of progress and deadlines, recognizing and rewarding those who achieve implementation milestones, reallocating resources, and personally presiding over the strategic change process. Thus, the bigger the organization, the more the success of the chief strategy implementer depends on the cooperation and implementing skills of operating managers who can push needed changes at the lowest organizational levels. In small organizations, the chief strategy implementer doesn't have to work through middle managers and can deal directly with frontline managers and employees, personally orchestrating the action steps and implementation sequence, observing firsthand how implementation is progressing, and deciding how hard and how fast to push the process along. Regardless of the organization's size and whether implementation involves sweeping or minor changes, the most important leadership trait is a strong, confident sense of "what to do" to achieve the desired results. Knowing what to do comes from understanding the circumstances of both the organization and the industry as a whole.

> The real strategy-implementing skill is being good at figuring out what it will take to execute the strategy proficiently.

In the remainder of this chapter and the next two chapters, we survey the manager's role as chief strategy implementer. The discussion is framed around the eight managerial components of the strategy implementation process shown in Figure 11.1 and the most often-encountered issues associated with each. This chapter explores the management tasks of building a capable organization. Chapter 12 looks at budget allocations, policies, best practices, internal support systems, and strategically appropriate reward structures. Chapter 13 deals with creating a strategy-supportive corporate culture and exercising strategic leadership.

BUILDING A CAPABLE ORGANIZATION

Proficient strategy execution depends heavily on competent personnel, better-than-adequate competitive capabilities, and effective internal organization. Building a capable organization is thus always a top priority in strategy execution. As shown in Figure 11.2, three types of organization-building actions are paramount:

figure 11.2   **The Components of Building a Capable Organization**

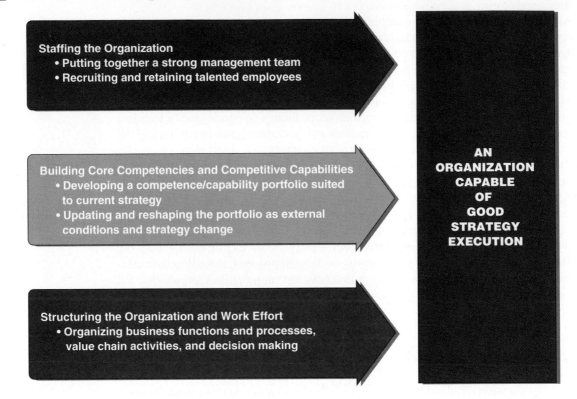

- *Staffing the organization*—includes putting together a strong management team, and recruiting and retaining employees with the needed experience, technical skills, and intellectual capital.
- *Building core competencies and competitive capabilities* that will enable good strategy execution and then keeping the competence/capability portfolio updated as strategy and external conditions change.
- *Structuring the organization and work effort*—organizing business functions and processes, value chain activities, and decision making in a manner conducive to successful strategy execution.

Staffing the Organization

No company can hope to perform the activities required for successful strategy execution without attracting capable managers and without employees that give it a suitable knowledge base and portfolio of intellectual capital.

Putting Together a Strong Management Team   Assembling a capable management team is one of the first cornerstones of the organization-building task. Strategy implementers must determine the kind of core management team they need and then find the right people to fill each slot on the team. Sometimes the existing management team is suitable; sometimes it needs to be strengthened or expanded by promoting qualified people from within or by bringing in outsiders whose experience, skills, and leadership styles suit the situation. In turnaround and rapid-growth situations, and in instances when a company doesn't have insiders with the requisite experience and management know-how, filling key management slots from the outside is a fairly standard organization-building approach. In 1998 Gateway founder Ted Waitt determined that the company, whose sales had rocketed to over $6 billion but whose profits were sagging, needed a fundamental shaking up in the top executive ranks.[2] He brought in consultants Smart & Associates to evaluate Gateway's top 100 managers, many of whom he had hired and who had good credentials. The company decided to replace 10 of the top 14 executives with outsiders and to recruit a new CEO. Following the consultants' recommendations, Waitt decided to recruit only "A players," coach the company's B and C players to become A players or move them into positions where they could become A players, or, failing that, move them out. Two years later, in early 2000, all of the major new hires were still in their jobs and the company's earnings and profit margins were much improved.

The important skill in assembling a core executive group is discerning what mix of backgrounds, experiences, know-how, values, beliefs, management styles, and personalities will contribute to successful strategy execution. The personal chemistry needs to be right, and the talent base needs to be appropriate for the chosen strategy. Picking a solid management team is an essential organization-building function—often the first strategy implementation step to take.[3] Until key managerial slots are filled with able people, it is hard for strategy implementation to proceed at full speed.

Illustration Capsule 41 describes General Electric's approach to assembling an "A" caliber management team to execute its strategy of broad diversification.

> Putting together a strong management team with the right personal chemistry and mix of skills is one of the first strategy-implementing steps.

Recruiting and Retaining Talented Employees   A good management team is not enough. Staffing the organization with talented people must go much deeper than managerial jobs in order to assemble the human resources and knowledge base needed for effective strategy execution. Companies like General Electric, Procter & Gamble, PepsiCo, Hewlett-Packard, Nike, Electronic Data Systems (EDS), Cisco, Microsoft, and McKinsey & Company (one of the world's premier management consulting companies) make a concerted effort to recruit the best and brightest talent they can find and then retain them with excellent compensation packages, opportunities for rapid advancement and professional growth, and challenging and interesting assignments. Having a cadre of people with strong skill sets and budding management potential is essential to their business. EDS requires college graduates to have at least a 3.5 grade point average (on a 4.0 scale) just to qualify for an interview. Microsoft makes a point of hiring the very brightest and most talented programmers it can find and motivating them with both good monetary incentives and the challenge of working on cutting-edge software design projects. McKinsey recruits MBAs only at the top 10 business schools. The Big Five accounting firms endeavor to screen candidates not only on the basis of their accounting expertise but also on whether they possess the people skills needed to relate well with clients and colleagues. Southwest Airlines goes to considerable lengths to hire people who can have fun and be fun on the job; it uses specially developed methods, including interviews with customers, to determine whether applicants for customer-contact jobs have outgoing personality traits that match its strategy of creating a high-spirited, fun-loving, in-flight atmosphere for passengers. The company is so selective that only about 3 percent of the candidates interviewed are offered jobs.

> Talented people in possession of superior intellectual capital are not only a resource that enables proficient strategy execution but also a prime source of competitive advantage.

For dot-com companies trying to carve out a future in the Internet economy, the resource in shortest supply is intellectual capital. Their biggest challenge is to staff their organizations with gifted, imaginative, and energetic people who can bring life to new

---

[2]Geoffrey Colvin, "The Truth Can Hurt—Get Used to It," *Fortune,* February 7, 2000, p. 52.

[3]For an analytical framework in top-management team analysis, see Donald C. Hambrick, "The Top Management Team: Key to Strategic Success," *California Management Review* 30, no. 1 (Fall 1987), pp. 88–108.

illustration capsule 41
How General Electric Develops a Talented and Deep Management Team

General Electric is widely considered to be one of the best-managed companies in the world, with capabilities that go deep into the management ranks and one of the world's best programs for developing managers into people with outstanding leadership, business, and decision-making skills. The company focuses on attracting talented people with high potential for executive leadership and then goes to great lengths to develop their leadership, business, and decision-making skills. There are several key elements of GE's strategy for assembling a talent-rich stable of managers and executives:

- GE makes a practice of transferring managers across divisional, business, or functional lines for sustained periods of time. Such transfers allow managers to develop relationships with colleagues in other parts of the company, help break down insular thinking in business "silos," and promote cross-business idea sharing and best practice sharing. There is an enormous emphasis at GE on transferring ideas and best practices from business to business and making GE a "boundaryless" company despite its strategy of broad, mostly unrelated diversification (see Illustration Capsule 40 in Chapter 10).

- In selecting executives for key positions, GE is strongly disposed to candidates who exhibit what are called the four E's—enormous personal *energy*, the ability to motivate and *energize* others, *edge* (a GE code word for instinctive competitiveness and the ability to make tough decisions in a timely fashion (saying yes or no, and not maybe), and *execution* (the ability to carry things through to fruition).

- All managers are expected to be proficient at what GE calls "workout"—a process where managers and employees come together to confront issues as soon as they come up, pinpoint the root cause of the issue, and bring about quick resolutions to the issue so the business can move forward. In 1999 and early 2000, managers and employees in all of GE's businesses were engaged in workout sessions on how to make proficient use of the Internet, "e-commerce" the whole company, and transform GE into a global e-business.

- GE operates a Leadership Development Center in Croton-on-Hudson, New York (referred to as Crotonville by GE managers), that is regarded as one of the best corporate training centers in the world. Each

---

> In the Internet economy and many other industries, there is a seismic shift under way from the importance of capital investment to the importance of investing in intellectual capital.

ideas quickly and inject into the organization what one Dell Computer executive calls "hum."[4] In a very real way, their most important investment is in intellectual capital, not in tangible assets such as facilities and equipment. The saying "People are our most important asset" may seem hollow elsewhere, but it fits Internet and high-technology companies dead on. This is why such companies as Amazon.com, DoubleClick, America Online, Cisco Systems, and Dell are breaking new ground in recruiting, hiring, cultivating, developing, and retaining talented employees—most all of whom are in their 20s and 30s. Compensation packages include not only attractive pay and benefits but also lucrative stock options. Much attention is devoted to creating exciting work environments where people work hard but have fun and are passionate about being on the cutting edge and doing incredible new things that will affect the future of the world. DoubleClick puts all new employees through a week-long orientation program called ClickerCamp, where all senior executives discuss what the company is doing and a concerted effort is made to explain the company's vision, introduce new hires to DoubleClick's culture, and begin making them a part of the DoubleClick team.[5] All Dou-

---

[4] John Byrne, "The Search for the Young and Gifted," *Business Week*, October 4, 1999, p. 108.
[5] Ibid., p. 112.

illustration capsule 41

(concluded)

year GE sends about 10,000 newly hired and long-time managers to Crotonville for a three-week course on the company's six sigma quality initiative. More than 5,000 "Master Black Belt" and "Black Belt" six sigma experts have graduated from Crotonville to drive forward thousands of quality initiatives throughout the corporation. Almost every GE professional manager holds at least a "Green Belt" in six sigma education. CEO Jack Welch's inspirational lectures on quality and performance are seen on video by nearly all of GE's employees. Six sigma training is an ironclad requirement for promotion to any professional and managerial position and any stock option award.

Welch has visited the company's training facility more than 250 times over the past 17 years to lecture, cajole, and engage 15,000-plus GE managers in discussions. Welch encourages managers attending the three-week development course to speak their minds, challenge, argue and disagree with his positions, and offer up their own thoughts.

GE's Crotonville development center also offers advanced courses for senior managers that may focus on a single management topic for a month. All classes at Crotonville involve managers from different GE businesses and different parts of the world. Some of the most valuable learning at Crotonville comes in between formal class sessions when GE managers from different businesses trade ideas about how to improve processes and better serve the customer. This knowledge sharing not only spreads best practices throughout the organization but also improves each GE manager's knowledge.

- Each of GE's 85,000 managers and professionals is graded in an annual process that divides them into five groups: the top 10 percent, the next 15 percent, the middle 50 percent, the next 15 percent, and the bottom 10 percent. Everyone in the top tier gets stock options, nobody in the fourth tier gets options, and most of those in the fifth tier become candidates for being weeded out. Business heads are pressured to wean out "C" players. Jack Welch personally reviews the performance of GE's top 3,000 managers. Senior executive compensation is heavily weighted toward six sigma commitment and producing successful business results.

According to Jack Welch, "The reality is, we simply cannot afford to field anything but teams of 'A' players."

Sources: 1998 Annual Report; www.ge.com; John A. Byrne, "How Jack Welch Runs GE," *Business Week,* June 8, 1998, p. 90; Miriam Leuchter, "Management Farm Teams," *Journal of Business Strategy,* May 1998, pp. 29–32; and "The House That Jack Built, *The Economist,* September 18, 1999.

bleClick employees rate their manager annually on 25 criteria, intended to reveal whether managers hired good people and whether employees liked working for them. Besides checking closely for functional and technical skills, Dell Computer tests applicants for their tolerance of ambiguity and change, their capacity to work in teams, and their ability to learn on the fly. Illustration Capsule 42 discusses Cisco Systems' approach to recruiting talented employees.

The best companies use a variety of practices to develop their knowledge base and build intellectual capital:

1. Spend considerable effort in screening and evaluating job applicants, selecting only those with suitable skill sets, energy, initiative, judgment, and aptitudes for learning and adaptability to the company's work environment and culture. Many companies take extraordinary pains to seek out the right people to fill job openings—in 1997, Southwest Airlines got 150,000 resumés but hired only 5,000 people.

2. Put employees through training programs that continue not just through their early years but usually throughout their careers.

3. Give them challenging, interesting, and skills-stretching assignments.

illustration capsule 42
How Cisco Systems Staffs Its Organization with Talented Employees

Cisco Systems is the world's leading producer of switches, routers, and other network components used to access the Internet. The company's revenues and earnings have increased approximately 50 percent annually since 1995. The company's rapid growth has required workforce additions of as many as 1,000 new employees per quarter, making it responsible for as much as 10 percent of Silicon Valley's job growth. In early 2000, Cisco had more than 23,000 employees worldwide, including over 10,000 in Silicon Valley and the San Francisco Bay area. Cisco focuses on hiring only the highest-caliber people; according to Cisco CEO John Chambers, "Cisco has an overall goal of getting the top 10% to 15% of people in our industry. Our philosophy is very simple—if you get the best people in the industry to fit into your culture and you motivate them properly, then you're going to be an industry leader."

Finding so many star engineers, programmers, managers, salespeople, and support personnel has been a challenge for Cisco, given the superheated job market and the competition for top talent. Because Cisco operates with few levels of management, it requires employees who not only have strong skill sets but also work well without direct supervision and can make quick, sound decisions. The innovative tactics Cisco uses to staff its organization with talented high performers include the following:

- Cisco does not advertise specific jobs in newspapers, but runs ads featuring its Web address and an invitation to apply at Cisco. The employment opportunities section of Cisco's Web site contains job listings for all Cisco locations around the world and provides a great deal of information about each job. To attract applicants, Cisco also runs ads in movie theaters and on billboards along commuter routes and sends recruiters to art fairs, microbrewery festivals, and home and garden shows in Silicon Valley and other locations where it has facilities to collect business cards and speak informally with potential prospects.

- Since many prospects visit Cisco's Web site from their jobs (peak usage of the employment Web pages occurs between 10 AM and 3 PM), it can tell where they work (with software that automatically checks the Internet address of those who visit its site) and, at times, has greeted visitors from highly regarded firms with a screen that says "Welcome to Cisco. Would you like a job?" Cisco's employment Web pages contain an escape button featuring a grimacing face with the caption "Oh no: My boss is coming." When job seekers click on the face, they are immediately taken to a page that lists "Seven habits of a successful employee," "Lists of gift ideas for my boss and workmates," and "Things to do today."

- Job prospecting visitors to Cisco's Web site can fill out an application online. Part of the online application process involves use of a tool Cisco calls Profiler that asks a series of questions tailored to the applicant's experience. The profile gives Cisco recruiters more detailed information about an applicant than what might be included in a resumé.

- Cisco recruiters target passive job seekers—people who are happy and successful where they are. According to

4. Rotate them through jobs that not only have great content but that span functional and geographic boundaries. Providing people with opportunities to gain experience in a variety of international settings is increasingly considered an essential part of career development in multinational or global companies.

5. Encourage employees to be creative and innovative, to challenge existing ways of doing things and offer better ways, and to submit ideas for new products or businesses. Progressive companies work hard at creating a work environment where ideas and suggestions bubble up from below rather than proceed from the top down. Employees are made to feel their opinions count.

6. Foster a stimulating and engaging work environment, such that employees will consider the company "a great place to work."

illustration capsule 42

(concluded)

Cisco's human resources vice president, "The top 10% are not typically found in the first round of layoffs from other companies, and they usually aren't cruising through the want ads." To learn how to find and entice talented people to move to Cisco, the company held focus groups with such recruiting targets as marketing professionals and senior engineers at other companies to discover how happily employed people could be persuaded to interview for a job. These sessions revealed that people were most likely to consider a job change if a friend told them about a job opportunity that was better than their current job. So the company launched an initiative to get Cisco personnel actively involved in making friends with prospects, telling them what it was like to work at Cisco, mentioning attractive job openings, and putting them in touch with Cisco employees in the same job or with similar interests who could give them a realistic preview of the job and attempt to remove the fear and uncertainty from a job move. At one point, a thousand Cisco employees participated in the "friends initiative," enticed by a referral fee (starting at $500) and a lottery ticket for a free trip to Hawaii for each prospect they befriended who was ultimately hired. The program was so successful that a Friends@Cisco section was added to the company's website, giving prospects a way to communicate directly with Cisco employees in job functions or departments of interest and get their views on Cisco's work environment, culture, and career opportunities.

- The company has a staff of 100 in-house professional headhunters to review applicant profiles and resumés and submit a short list of qualified applicants to line managers for interviews. Cisco management believes that it is best to hire people when they are "hot" and that any compensation premium for "hot" prospects (as well as the costs of headhunters and recruiting) is more than offset by the benefits of quickly hiring top-tier people to support Cisco's own rapid growth.

- One of Cisco's core strategies for growing its business is to acquire companies with promising products or technological capabilities that complement Cisco's present business lineup. Very often, one of the prime purposes underlying such acquisitions is gaining the acquired company's engineering and R&D talent. As a rule, Cisco endeavors to retain the employees of acquired companies.

Cisco's recruiting team is constantly coming up with new innovative ideas for finding, interviewing, and hiring top-tier talent. So rapidly are new initiatives and approaches being used that the life cycle of the human resources department's recruiting strategy is 6 to 12 months. We suggest visiting www.cisco.com and looking at the company employment pages to learn about the company's latest practices (and perhaps to check out an employment opportunity for yourself).

Sources: Cisco's Web site (www.cisco.com) and Patricia Nakache, "Cisco's Recruiting Edge," *Fortune*, September 29, 1997, pp. 275–76.

---

7. Exert efforts to retain high-potential, high performing employees with salary increases, performance bonuses, stock options and equity ownership, and other long-term incentives. Average performers are coached to do better, while underperformers and benchwarmers are weeded out.

Building Core Competencies and Competitive Capabilities

High among the organization-building concerns in the strategy implementing/executing process is the need to build competitively valuable core competencies and organizational capabilities that give the firm a competitive edge over rivals in performing one or more critical value chain activities. When it is relatively easy for rivals to copy smart strategies, making it difficult or impossible to outstrategize rivals and beat them on the

> **Strategic Management Principle**
>
> Building core competencies, resource strengths, and organizational capabilities that rivals can't match is a sound foundation for sustainable competitive advantage.

basis of a superior strategy, the other main avenue to lasting competitive advantage is to outexecute them (beat them with superior strategy execution). Superior strategy execution is essential in situations where rival firms can readily duplicate one another's successful strategic maneuvers. Building core competencies, resource strengths, and organizational capabilities that rivals can't match is one of the best ways to outexecute them. This is why one of management's most important strategy-implementing tasks is to guide the building of core competencies and organizational capabilities in competitively advantageous ways.

Developing and Strengthening Core Competencies   Core competencies can relate to any strategically relevant factor. Honda's core competence is its depth of expertise in gasoline engine technology and small engine design (see Illustration Capsule 39 in Chapter 9). Intel's is in the design of complex chips for personal computers. Procter & Gamble's core competencies reside in its superb marketing-distribution skills and its R&D capabilities in five core technologies—fats, oils, skin chemistry, surfactants, and emulsifiers.[6] Sony's core competencies are its expertise in electronic technology and its ability to translate that expertise into innovative products (cutting-edge video game hardware, miniaturized radios and video cameras, TVs and DVDs with unique features, attractively designed PCs). Most often, a company's core competencies emerge incrementally as it moves either to bolster skills that contributed to earlier successes or to respond to customer problems, new technological and market opportunities, and the competitive maneuverings of rivals.[7] Wise company managers try to foresee changes in customer-market requirements and proactively build new competencies and capabilities that offer a competitive edge over rivals.

Four traits concerning core competencies and competitive capabilities are important to organization building:[8]

- Core competencies rarely consist of narrow skills or the work efforts of a single department. More often, they are bundles of skills and know-how growing out of the combined efforts of cross-functional work groups and departments performing complementary activities at different locations in the firm's value chain.

- Because core competencies typically reside in the combined efforts of different work groups and departments, individual supervisors and department heads can't be expected to see building the overall corporation's core competencies as their responsibility. Rather, the building and nurturing of core competencies is a senior management responsibility.

- The key to leveraging a company's core competencies into competitively valuable capabilities with potential for long-term competitive advantage is concentrating more effort and more talent than rivals on deepening and strengthening these competencies.

- Because customers' needs and market conditions change in often unpredictable ways, it is difficult to fully anticipate the specific know-how and intellectual capital needed for future competitive success. A company's selected bases of competence thus need to be broad enough and flexible enough to respond to an unknown future.

---

[6]James Brian Quinn, *Intelligent Enterprise* (New York: Free Press, 1992), p. 76.
[7]Ibid.
[8]Ibid., pp. 52–53, 55, 73, and 76.

Thus, building and strengthening core competencies is an exercise in (1) managing human skills, knowledge bases, and intellect, and (2) coordinating and networking the efforts of different work groups and departments at every related place in the value chain. It's an exercise best orchestrated by senior managers who appreciate the strategy-executing significance of creating valuable competencies/capabilities and who have the clout to enforce the necessary networking and cooperation among individuals, groups, departments, and external allies. Moreover, organization builders have to concentrate enough resources and management attention on core competence–related activities to achieve the *dominating depth* needed for competitive advantage.[9] This does not necessarily mean spending more money on such activities than present or potential competitors, but it does mean consciously focusing more talent on them and making appropriate internal and external benchmarking comparisons to move toward best-in-industry, if not best-in-world, status.

> Core competencies don't come into being or reach strategic fruition without conscious management attention.

To achieve dominance on lean financial resources, companies like Cray in large computers, Lotus in software, and Honda in small engines leveraged the expertise of their talent pool by frequently re-forming high-intensity teams and reusing key people on special projects.[10] The experiences of these and other companies indicate that the usual keys to successfully building core competencies are superior employee selection, thorough training and retraining, powerful cultural influences, cooperative networking, motivation, empowerment, attractive incentives, organizational flexibility, short deadlines, and good databases—not big operating budgets.[11]

Developing and Strengthening Organizational Capabilities   Whereas the essence of astute strategy making is selecting the competencies and capabilities to underpin the strategy, the essence of good strategy execution is *building and strengthening* the company's competencies and capabilities. Sometimes the company already has the needed competencies and capabilities in place, in which case managers can concentrate on nurturing them to promote better strategy execution. More usually, however, management has to be proactive in upgrading existing capabilites to promote more proficient strategy execution and developing new competencies and capabilities to execute new strategic initiatives.

Capability-building is a time-consuming, hard-to-replicate exercise. Capabilities are difficult to purchase (except through outsiders who already have them and will agree to supply them) and difficult to acquire just by watching others. Just as one cannot become a good golfer by watching Tiger Woods play golf, a company cannot put a new capability in place by creating a new department and assigning it the task of emulating a capability rivals have. Building capability requires a series of organizational steps:

> Building capabilities takes time, conscious effort, and considerable organizing skill.

- First, the organization must develop the *ability* to do something, however imperfectly or inefficiently. This entails selecting people with the requisite skills and experience, upgrading or expanding individual abilities as needed, and then molding the efforts and work products of individuals into a cooperative group effort to create organizational ability.

---

[9]Ibid., p. 73.
[10]Ibid.
[11]Ibid., pp. 73–74.

- Then as experience builds, and the organization reaches a level of ability to accomplish the activity consistently well and at an acceptable cost, the ability begins to translate into a *competence* or a *capability*.

- Should the organization get so good (by continuing to polish and refine and deepen its skills and know-how) that it is better than rivals at the activity, the capability becomes a *distinctive competence* and carries the potential for competitive advantage.

One organization-building question is whether to develop the desired competencies and capabilities internally or to outsource them by partnering with key suppliers or forming strategic alliances. The answer depends on what can be safely delegated to outside suppliers or allies versus what internal capabilities are key to the company's long-term success. Either way, though, calls for action. Outsourcing means launching initiatives to identify the most attractive providers and to establish collaborative relationships. Developing the capabilities in-house means hiring new personnel with relevant skills and experience, linking the individual skills to form organizational capability, building the desired levels of proficiency through repetition (practice makes perfect), and establishing links with related value chain activities.[12] Strong links with related activities are important. Complex activities (like designing and manufacturing a sports utility vehicle or creating software that allows secure credit card transactions over the Internet) usually involve a number of component skills, technological disciplines, competencies, and capabilities—some performed in-house and some provided by suppliers/allies. An important part of the organization-building function is to think about which competencies and capabilities need to be linked and made mutually reinforcing and then to forge the necessary collaboration both internally and with outside resource providers.

> Organizational competencies and capabilities can emerge from collaborative efforts with allies and from acquiring a company having the desired capabilities.

Sometimes these steps can be short-circuited by acquiring the desired capability through collaborative efforts with external allies or by buying a company that has the requisite capability and integrating its competencies into the firm's value chain. Indeed, a pressing need to acquire certain capabilities quickly is one reason to acquire another company—an acquisition aimed at building greater capability can be every bit as competitively valuable as an acquisition aimed at adding new products or services to the company's business lineup. Capabilities-motivated acquisitions are essential (1) when an opportunity can disappear faster than a needed capability can be created internally, and (2) when industry conditions, technology, or competitors are moving at such a rapid clip that time is of the essence.

Updating and Reshaping Competencies and Capabilities as External Conditions and Company Strategy Change

Even after core competencies and competitive capabilities are in place and functioning, company managers can't relax. Competencies and capabilities that grow stale can impair competitiveness unless they are refreshed and modified, with some even being phased out and replaced with altogether new ones, in response to ongoing customer-market changes and to shifts in company strategy. Indeed, the buildup of knowledge and experience over time, coupled with the imperatives of keeping capabilities in step with ongoing

---

[12]Robert H. Hayes, Gary P. Pisano, and David M. Upton, *Strategic Operations: Competing through Capabilities* (New York: Free Press, 1996), pp. 503–7.

strategy and market changes, makes it appropriate to view a company as *a bundle of evolving competencies and capabilities.* Management's organization-building challenge is one of continuously adapting and adjusting the company's portfolio of competencies and capabilities, deciding when and how to tune and recalibrate existing competencies and capabilities, and when and how to develop new ones. Although the task is formidable, ideally it produces a dynamic organization with "hum" and momentum. But dedicated and ongoing management efforts to keep core competencies finely honed and in step with shifting external and internal circumstances provide a big executional advantage. Moreover, cutting-edge core competencies and organizational capabilities are not easily duplicated by rival firms; thus any competitive edge they produce is likely to be sustainable, paving the way for above-average organizational performance.

The Strategic Role of Employee Training   Training and retraining are important when a company shifts to a strategy requiring different skills, competitive capabilities, managerial approaches, and operating methods. Training is also strategically important in organizational efforts to build skills-based competencies. And it is a key activity in businesses where technical know-how is changing so rapidly that a company loses its ability to compete unless its skilled people have cutting-edge knowledge and expertise. Successful strategy implementers see to it that the training function is both adequately funded and effective. If the chosen strategy calls for new skills, deeper technological capability, or building and using new capabilities, training should be placed near the top of the action agenda.

The strategic importance of training has not gone unnoticed. Over 600 companies have established internal "universities" to manage the task of keeping employee and managerial skills and expertise up-to-date, facilitate continuous organizational learning, and aid in the task of upgrading company competencies and capabilities. Many companies conduct orientation sessions for new employees, fund an assortment of competence-building training programs, and reimburse employees for tuition and other expenses associated with obtaining additional college education, attending professional development courses, and earning professional certification of one kind or another. A number of companies offer online, just-in-time training courses to employees around the clock. Increasingly, employees at all levels are expected to take an active role in their own professional development, assuming responsibility for continuous learning.

Matching Organization Structure to Strategy

There are few hard-and-fast rules for organizing the work effort to support strategy. Every firm's organization chart is idiosyncratic, reflecting prior organizational patterns, varying internal circumstances, executive judgments about reporting relationships, and the politics of who gets which assignments. Moreover, every strategy is grounded in its own set of key success factors and value chain activities. So a customized organization structure is appropriate. But despite the need for situation-specific organization structures, some considerations are common to all companies. These are summarized in Figure 11.3 and discussed in turn below.

Identifying Strategy-Critical Activities   In any business, some activities in the value chain are always more critical to strategic success and competitive advantage than others. From a strategy perspective, a certain portion of an organization's work

> Continuously tuning and recalibrating a company's competencies and capabilities to match new strategic requirements, evolving market conditions, and customer expectations is a solid basis for sustaining both effective strategy execution and competitive advantage.

figure 11.3   **Structuring the Organization to Promote Successful Strategy Execution**

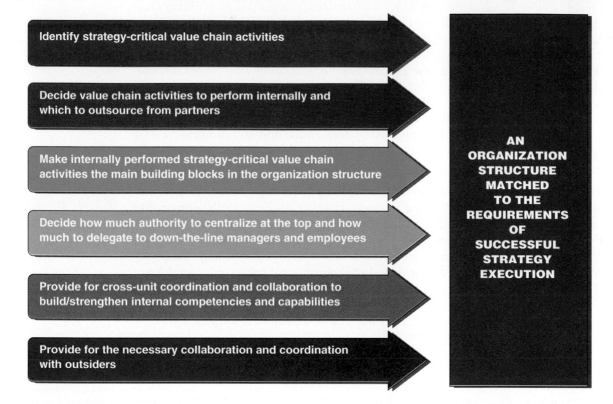

<table>
<tr><td>Identify strategy-critical value chain activities</td></tr>
<tr><td>Decide value chain activities to perform internally and which to outsource from partners</td></tr>
<tr><td>Make internally performed strategy-critical value chain activities the main building blocks in the organization structure</td></tr>
<tr><td>Decide how much authority to centralize at the top and how much to delegate to down-the-line managers and employees</td></tr>
<tr><td>Provide for cross-unit coordination and collaboration to build/strengthen internal competencies and capabilities</td></tr>
<tr><td>Provide for the necessary collaboration and coordination with outsiders</td></tr>
</table>

AN ORGANIZATION STRUCTURE MATCHED TO THE REQUIREMENTS OF SUCCESSFUL STRATEGY EXECUTION

> Strategy-critical activities and capabilities vary according to the particulars of a firm's strategy, value chain make-up, competitive requirements, and external market conditions.

involves routine administrative housekeeping (doing the payroll, administering employee benefit programs, managing cash flows, handling grievances and the usual assortment of people problems, providing corporate security, managing stockholder relations, maintaining fleet vehicles, and complying with regulations). Other activities are support functions (information technology and data processing, accounting, training, public relations, market research, legal and legislative affairs, and purchasing). Among the primary value chain activities are certain crucial business processes that have to be performed either exceedingly well or in closely coordinated fashion for the organization to deliver on the capabilities needed for strategic success. For instance, hotel/motel enterprises have to be good at fast check-in/check-out, room maintenance, food service, and creating a pleasant ambience. A manufacturer of chocolate bars must be skilled in purchasing, production, merchandising, and promotional activities; buying quality cocoa beans at low prices is vital, and reducing production costs by a fraction of a cent per bar can mean a seven-figure improvement in the bottom line. In discount stock brokerage, the strategy-critical activities are fast access to information, accurate order execution, efficient record keeping and transactions processing, and good customer service. In specialty chemicals, the critical activities are R&D, product innovation, getting new products onto the market quickly, effective marketing, and expertise in assisting customers. In consumer electronics, where advancing technology drives new product innovation, rapidly getting cutting-edge, next-generation products to market is a critical organizational capability.

Two questions help pinpoint an organization's strategy-critical activities: "What functions or business processes have to be performed extra well or in timely fashion to achieve sustainable competitive advantage?" and "In what value chain activities would poor execution seriously impair strategic success?"[13] The answers generally point to the crucial activities where attentive, strategy-supportive organization is required.

Reasons to Consider Outsourcing "Noncritical" Value Chain Activities   Managers too often spend inordinate amounts of time, psychic energy, and resources wrestling with functional support groups and other internal bureaucracies, which diverts their attention from the company's strategy-critical activities. One way to reduce such distractions is to cut the number of internal staff support activities and, instead, source more support functions and noncritical value chain activities from outside vendors.

Each supporting activity in a firm's value chain and within its traditional staff groups can be considered a "service."[14] Indeed, most of a company's overhead consists of services the company chooses to produce internally. However, many such services can be purchased from outside vendors. What makes outsourcing attractive is that an outsider, by concentrating specialists and technology in its area of expertise, can frequently perform certain services as well or better, and usually more cheaply, than a company that performs these services only for itself.

But there are strong reasons to consider outsourcing besides lower costs and less internal hassle. Approached from a strategic point of view, outsourcing noncrucial support activities can decrease internal bureaucracies, flatten the organization structure, speed decision making, heighten the company's strategic focus, improve its innovative capacity (through interaction with "best in world" suppliers), and increase competitive responsiveness.[15] The experiences of companies that obtain many support services from outside vendors indicate that such outsourcing allows a company to concentrate its own energies and resources on those value chain activities where it can create unique value, where it can be best in the industry (or, better still, best in the world), and where it needs strategic control to build core competencies, achieve competitive advantage, and manage key customer-supplier-distributor relationships.[16]

Critics contend that the danger of outsourcing is that a company can go overboard and hollow out its knowledge base and capabilities, leaving itself at the mercy of outside suppliers and short of the resource strengths to be master of its own destiny.[17] However, a number of companies have found ways to successfully rely on outside components suppliers, product designers, distribution channels, advertising agencies,

> Outsourcing noncritical value chain activities can produce many advantages—lower costs, less internal bureaucracy, speedier decision making, more flexibility, and heightened strategic focus.

---

[13]Peter F. Drucker, *Management: Tasks, Responsibilities, Practices* (New York: Harper & Row, 1974), pp. 530, 535.

[14]Quinn, *Intelligent Enterprise,* p. 32.

[15]Quinn, *Intelligent Enterprise,* pp. 33 and 89; and James Brian Quinn, "Strategic Outsourcing: Leveraging Knowledge Capabilities," *Sloan Management Review* 40, no. 3 (Summer 1999), p. 9. See also James Brian Quinn and Frederick G. Hilmer, "Strategic Outsourcing," *Sloan Management Review* (Summer 1994), pp. 43–55.

[16]Quinn, *Intelligent Enterprise,* p. 47; and Quinn, "Strategic Outsourcing: Leveraging Knowledge Capabilities," p. 9.

[17]Quinn, *Intelligent Enterprise,* pp. 39–40.

and financial services firms to perform significant value chain activities.[18] For years Polaroid Corporation bought its film from Eastman Kodak, its electronics from Texas Instruments, and its cameras from Timex and others, while it concentrated on producing its unique self-developing film packets and designing its next generation of cameras and films. Nike concentrates on design, marketing, and distribution to retailers, while outsourcing virtually all production of its shoes and sporting apparel. Likewise, a number of PC manufacturers outsource the assembly of the PCs, concentrating their energies on product design, sales and marketing, and distribution. Many mining companies outsource geological work, assaying, and drilling. Ernest and Julio Gallo Winery outsources 95 percent of its grape production, letting farmers take on the weather and other grape-growing risks while it concentrates on wine production and the marketing-sales function.[19] The major airlines outsource their in-flight meals even though food quality is important to travelers' perception of overall service quality. Eastman Kodak, Ford, Exxon, Merrill Lynch, and Chevron have outsourced their data processing activities to computer service firms, believing that outside specialists can perform the needed services at lower costs and equal or better quality. Prior to merging with Germany's Daimler-Benz, Chrysler tranformed itself from a high-cost producer into a low-cost producer by abandoning internal production of many parts and components and instead outsourcing them from more efficient parts/components suppliers; greater reliance on outsourcing enabled Chrysler to shorten its design-to-market cycle for new models. Companies like Ford, Boeing, Aerospatiale, AT&T, BMW, and Dell Computer have learned that their central R&D groups cannot begin to match the innovative capabilities of a well-managed network of suppliers.[20] Consequently, deciding what activities to perform internally and what activities to outsource is indeed of considerable strategic significance.

Reasons to Consider Partnering with Others to Gain Added Competitive Capabilities   There is another, equally important reason to look outside for resources to compete effectively aside from just the cost savings and agility that outsourcing can permit. *Partnerships can add to a company's arsenal of capabilities and contribute to better strategy execution.* By building, continually improving, and then leveraging collaborative partnerships, a company enhances its overall organizational capabilities and builds resource strengths—strengths that deliver value to customers, that rivals can't quite match, and that consequently pave the way for competitive success.

Automobile manufacturers work closely with their suppliers to advance the design and functioning of parts and components, to incorporate new technology, to better integrate individual parts and components to form engine cooling systems, transmission

---

[18]The growing tendency of companies to outsource important activities and the many reasons for building cooperative, collaborative alliances and partnerships with other companies is detailed in James F. Moore, *The Death of Competition* (New York: HarperBusiness, 1996); see especially chapter 3.

[19]Quinn, *Intelligent Enterprise,* p. 43.

[20]Quinn, "Strategic Outsourcing: Leveraging Knowledge Capabilities," p. 17.

systems, electrical systems, and so on—all of which helps shorten the cycle time for new models, improve the quality and performance of those models, and boost overall production efficiency. Soft-drink producers (Coca-Cola and PepsiCo) and beer producers (Anheuser-Busch and Miller Brewing) all cultivate their relationships with their bottlers and distributors to strengthen access to local markets and build the loyalty, support, and commitment for corporate marketing programs, without which their own sales and growth are weakened. Similarly, fast-food enterprises like McDonald's and Taco Bell find it essential to work hand-in-hand with franchisees on outlet cleanliness, consistency of product quality, in store ambience, courtesy and friendliness of store personnel, and other aspects of store operations. Unless franchisees continuously deliver sufficient customer satisfaction to attract repeat business, a fast-food chain's sales and competitive standing will suffer quickly. *Strategic partnerships, alliances, and close collaboration with suppliers, distributors, the makers of complementary products, and even competitors all make good strategic sense whenever the result is to enhance organizational resources and capabilities.*

Making Strategy-Critical Activities the Main Building Blocks The rationale for making strategy-critical activities the main building blocks in structuring a business is compelling: if activities crucial to strategic success are to have the resources, decision-making influence, and organizational impact they need, they have to be centerpieces in the organizational scheme. Plainly, implementing a new or changed strategy is likely to entail new or different key activities, competencies, or capabilities and, therefore, require new or different organizational arrangements. If workable organizational adjustments are not forthcoming, the resulting mismatch between strategy and structure can open the door to execution and performance problems.[21] Hence, attempting to carry out a new strategy with an old organizational structure is usually unwise. Just as a company's strategy evolves to stay in tune with changing external circumstances, so must an organization's structure evolve to fit shifting requirements for proficient strategy execution.

> **Strategic Management Principle**
> Matching structure to strategy requires making strategy-critical activities and strategy-critical organizational units the main building blocks in the organization structure.

---

[21]The importance of matching organization design and structure to the particular needs of strategy was first brought to the forefront in a landmark study of 70 large corporations conducted by Professor Alfred Chandler of Harvard University. Chandler's research revealed that changes in an organization's strategy bring about new administrative problems that, in turn, require a new or refashioned structure for the new strategy to be successfully implemented. He found that structure tends to follow the growth strategy of the firm—but often not until inefficiency and internal operating problems provoke a structural adjustment. The experiences of these firms followed a consistent sequential pattern: new strategy creation, emergence of new administrative problems, a decline in profitability and performance, a shift to a more appropriate organizational structure, and then recovery to more profitable levels and improved strategy execution. That managers should reassess their company's internal organization whenever strategy changes is pretty much common sense. A new or different strategy is likely to entail new or different key activities, competencies, or capabilities, and therefore to require new or different internal organizational arrangements. For more details, see Alfred Chandler, *Strategy and Structure* (Cambridge, MA: MIT Press, 1962).

Although the stress here is on designing the organization structure around the needs of effective strategy execution, it is worth noting that structure can and does influence the choice of strategy. A good strategy must be doable. When an organization's present structure is so far out of line with the requirements of a particular strategy that the organization would have to be turned upside down to implement it, the strategy may not be doable and should not be given further consideration. In such cases, structure shapes the choice of strategy. The point here, however, is that once strategy is chosen, structure must be modified to fit the strategy if, in fact, an approximate fit does not already exist. Any influences of structure on strategy should, logically, come before the point of strategy selection rather than after it.

The primary organizational building blocks within a business are usually a combination of traditional functional departments (R&D, engineering and design, production and operations, sales and marketing, information technology, finance and accounting, and human resources) and process-complete departments (supply chain management, filling customer orders, customer service, speeding new products to market, quality control, e-commerce).[22] In enterprises with operations in various countries around the world, the basic building blocks may also include geographic organizational units, each of which has profit-loss responsibility for its assigned geographic area. In vertically integrated firms, the major building blocks are divisional units performing one (or more) of the major processing steps along the value chain (raw materials production, components manufacture, assembly, wholesale distribution, retail store operations); each division in the value chain may operate as a profit center for performance measurement purposes. The typical building blocks of a diversified company are its individual businesses, with each business unit usually operating as an independent profit center and with corporate headquarters performing assorted support functions for all the businesses.

Managers need to be particularly alert to the fact that in traditional functionally organized structures, pieces of strategically relevant activities and capabilities often end up scattered across many departments. Consider, for example, how a functional structure ends up with pieces of the following strategy-critical activities and organizational capabilities being performed in different departments:

1. *Filling customer orders accurately and promptly*—a process that cuts across sales (which wins the order); finance (which may have to check credit terms or approve special financing); production (which must produce the goods and replenish warehouse inventories as needed); warehousing (which has to verify whether the items are in stock, pick the order from the warehouse, and package it for shipping); shipping (which has to choose a carrier to deliver the goods and release the goods to the carrier).[23]

2. *Speeding new products to market*—a process that is fragmented among R&D, engineering, purchasing, manufacturing, and marketing.

---

[22]There are many ways a company can organize around functions other than those just cited. A technical instruments manufacturer may be organized around research and development, engineering, production, technical services, quality control, marketing, personnel, and finance and accounting. A hotel may have a functional organization based on front-desk operations, housekeeping, building maintenance, food service, convention services and special events, guest services, personnel and training, and accounting. A discount retailer may organize around such functional units as purchasing, warehousing and distribution, store operations, advertising, merchandising and promotion, customer service, and corporate administrative services. Likewise, process organization assumes a form that matches a company's processes.

[23]Michael Hammer and James Champy, *Reengineering the Corporation* (New York: HarperBusiness, 1993), pp. 26–27.

3. *Improving product quality*—a process that often involves the collaboration of personnel in R&D, engineering and design, components purchasing from suppliers, in-house components production, manufacturing, and assembly.

4. *Supply chain management*—a collaborative process that cuts across such functional areas as purchasing, engineering and design, components purchasing, inventory management, manufacturing and assembly, and warehousing and shipping.

5. *Building the capability to conduct business via the Internet*—a process that involves personnel in information technology, supply chain management, production, sales and marketing, warehousing and shipping, customer service, finance, and accounting.

6. *Obtaining feedback from customers and making product modifications to meet their needs*—a process that involves personnel in customer service and after-sale support, R&D, engineering and design, components purchasing, manufacturing and assembly, and marketing research.

So many handoffs lengthen completion time and frequently drive up administrative costs, since coordinating the fragmented pieces can soak up hours of effort on the parts of many people.[24] This is not a fatal condemnation of functional organization—organizing around specific functions has worked to good advantage in support activities like finance and accounting, human resource management, and engineering, and in such primary activities as R&D, manufacturing, and marketing, despite the fragmentation of strategy-critical activities which accompanies such organization structures. But fragmentation is an important weakness of functional organization, accounting for why we indicated that a company's competencies and capabilities are a composite of activities and do not reside in the activities of a single functional department.

Increasingly during the last decade, companies have found that rather than continuing to scatter related pieces of a business process across several functional departments and scrambling to integrate their efforts, it is better to reengineer the work effort and create *process departments*. This is done by pulling the people who performed the pieces in functional departments into a group that works together to perform the whole process. Pulling the pieces of strategy-critical processes out of the functional silos and creating process departments or cross-functional work groups charged with performing all the steps needed to produce a strategy-critical result has been termed *business process reengineering*. Bell Atlantic used business process reengineering to streamline its bureaucratic procedures for connecting a telephone customer to its long-distance carrier.[25] In Bell Atlantic's functional structure, when a business customer requested a connection between its telephone system and a long-distance carrier for data services, the request traveled from department to department; the internal processing required two to four weeks. In reengineering that process, Bell Atlantic pulled workers from the many functional departments and put them on teams that could handle most customer requests in a matter of days or even hours. Because the work was recurring—similar customer requests had to be processed daily—the teams were permanently grouped into a process department. In the electronics industry, where product life cycles run

---

[24]Although functional organization incorporates Adam Smith's division-of-labor principle (every person/department involved has specific responsibility for performing a clearly defined task) and allows for tight management control (everyone in the process is accountable to a functional department head for efficiency and adherence to procedures), *no one oversees the whole process and its result.* Hammer and Champy, *Reengineering the Corporation,* pp. 26–27.

[25]Hammer and Champy, *Reengineering the Corporation,* pp. 66–68.

illustration capsule 43

Reengineering Business Processes: How Companies Do It and the Results They Have Gotten

Reengineering strategy-critical business processes to reduce fragmentation across traditional departmental lines and cut bureaucratic overhead has proved to be a legitimate organization design tool. It's not a passing fad or another management program-of-the-month. Process organization is every bit as valid an organizing principle as functional specialization. Strategy execution is improved when the pieces of strategy-critical activities and core business processes performed by different departments are properly integrated and coordinated.

Companies that have reengineered some of their business processes have ended up compressing formerly separate steps and tasks into jobs performed by a single person and integrating jobs into team activities. Reorganization then follows as a natural consequence of task synthesis and job redesign. Successes in this area suggest attacking process fragmentation and overhead reduction in the following fashion:

- Develop a flow chart of the total business process, including its interfaces with other value chain activities.

- Try to simplify the process first, eliminating tasks and steps where possible and streamlining the performance of what remains.

- Determine which parts of the process can be automated (usually those that are repetitive, time-consuming, and automatic); consider introducing

advanced technologies that can be upgraded to achieve next-generation capability and provide a basis for further productivity gains down the road.

- Reengineer, then reorganize.

- Evaluate each activity in the process to determine whether it is critical or not. Strategy-critical activities are candidates for benchmarking to achieve best-in-industry or best-in-world performance status.

- Weigh the pros and cons of outsourcing activities that are noncritical or that contribute little to organizational capabilities and core competencies.

- Design a structure for performing the activities that remain; reorganize the personnel and groups who perform these activities into the new structure.

When done properly, reengineering can produce dramatic gains in productivity and organizational capability. In the order-processing section of General Electric's circuit breaker division, elapsed time from order receipt to delivery was cut from three weeks to three days by consolidating six production units into one, reducing a variety of former inventory and handling steps, automating the design system to replace a human custom-design process, and cutting the organizational layers between managers and workers from three to one. Productivity rose 20 percent in one year, and unit manufacturing costs dropped 30 percent.

(continued)

three to six months due to the speed of advancing technology, companies have formed process departments charged with cutting the time it takes to bring new technologies and products to commercial fruition. Illustration Capsule 43 discusses the procedures for reengineering fragmented processes and the results that several organizations have gotten from their reengineering efforts. [26]

Determining the Degree of Authority and Independence to Give Each Unit and Each Employee   Companies must decide how much authority to give managers of each organization unit (especially the heads of business subsidiaries, functional departments, and process departments) and how much decision-making latitude to give individual employees in performing their jobs. *In a highly centralized organization structure, top executives retain authority for most strategic and operating decisions and keep a tight rein on business-unit heads and department heads; compara-*

---

[26]For a detailed review of one company's experiences with reengineering, see Donna B. Stoddard, Sirkka L. Jarvenpaa, and Michael Littlejohn, "The Reality of Business Reengineering: Pacific Bell's Centrex Provisioning Process," *California Management Review* 38, no. 3 (Spring 1996), pp. 57–76.

illustration capsule 43

(concluded)

Northwest Water, a British utility, used reengineering to eliminate 45 work depots that served as home base to crews who installed and repaired water and sewage lines and equipment. Now crews work directly from their vehicles, receiving assignments and reporting work completion from computer terminals in their trucks. Crew members are no longer employees but contractors to Northwest Water. These reengineering efforts not only eliminated the need for the work depots but also allowed Northwest Water to eliminate a big percentage of the bureaucratic personnel and supervisory organization that managed the crews.

At acute care hospitals such as Lee Memorial in Fort Myers, Florida, and St. Vincent's in Melbourne, Australia, medical care has been reengineered so that it is delivered by interdisciplinary teams of health care professionals organized around the needs of the patients and their families rather than around functional departments within the hospital. Both hospitals created focused care or treatment-specific wards within the hospital to treat most of a patient's needs, from admission to discharge. Patients are no longer wheeled from department to department for procedures and tests; instead, teams have the equipment and resources within each focused care unit to provide total care for the patient. While the hospitals had some concern about functional inefficiency in the use of some facilities, process organization has resulted in substantially lower operating cost, faster patient recovery, and greater satisfaction on the part of patients and caregivers.

There's no escaping the conclusion that reengineering, in concert with electronic communication systems, empowerment, and the use of self-directed work teams, provides company managers with the means to:

- Flatten organizational hierarchies and remove middle-management layers.

- Push responsibility and decision-making authority downward and outward to those places in the organization where customer contacts are made.

- Unify strategy-critical processes and perform them more quickly and at lower cost.

- Generate big gains in organizational creativity and employee productivity.

Sources: Based on information in James Brian Quinn, *Intelligent Enterprise* (New York: Free Press, 1992), p. 162; T. Stuart, "GE Keeps Those Ideas Coming," *Fortune,* August 12, 1991; Gene Hall, Jim Rosenthal, and Judy Wade, "How to Make Reengineering Really Work," *Harvard Business Review* 71, no. 6 (November–December 1993), pp. 119–31; Ann Majchrzak and Qianwei Wang, "Breaking the Functional Mind-Set in Process Organizations," *Harvard Business Review* 74, no. 5 (September–October 1996), pp. 93–99; and Iain Somerville and John Edward Mroz, "New Competencies for a New World," in *The Organization of the Future,* ed. Frances Hesselbein, Marshall Goldsmith, and Richard Beckard (San Francisco: Jossey-Bass, 1997), p. 71.

tively little discretionary authority is granted to subordinate managers and individual employees. The command-and-control paradigm of centralized structures is based on the underlying assumption that the people actually performing work have neither the time nor the inclination to monitor and control it, and that they lack the knowledge to make informed decisions about how best to do it—hence the need for prescribed procedures, close supervision, and tight managerial control. A serious shortcoming of hierarchical command-and-control is that it makes an organization sluggish because of the time it takes for the review-approval process to run up all the layers of the management bureaucracy. Furthermore, to work well, centralized decision making requires top-level managers to gather and process whatever knowledge is relevant to the decision. When the relevant knowledge resides at lower organizational levels or is technical, detailed, or hard to express in words, it is difficult and time-consuming to get all of the facts and nuances in front of a high-level executive located far from the scene of the action—knowledge cannot be readily copied from one mind to another. Very often, it is better (and certainly faster) to put decision-making authority in the hands of the people closest to and most familiar with the situation and train them to exercise good judgment.

> There are serious disadvantages to having a small number of top-level managers micromanage the business by personally making decisions or by requiring they approve the recommendations of lower-level subordinates before actions can be taken.

In a highly decentralized organization, managers (and, increasingly, many non-managerial employees) are empowered to act on their own in their areas of responsibility. Plant managers are empowered to order new equipment as needed and make arrangements with suppliers for parts and components; work teams are empowered to manage and improve their assigned process; and employees with customer contact are empowered to do what it takes to please customers. At Starbucks, for example, employees are empowered to exercise initiative in promoting customer satisfaction—there's the story of a store employee who, when the computerized cash register system went offline, enthusiatically offered free coffee to waiting customers.[27] In a diversified company operating on the principle of decentralized decision making, business-unit heads have broad authority to run the subsidiary with comparatively little interference from corporate headquarters; moreover, the business head gives functional and process department heads considerable decision-making latitude.

> The purpose of decentralization is not to push decisions down to lower levels but to lodge decision-making authority in those persons or teams closest to and most knowledgeable about the situation.

Delegating greater authority to subordinate managers and employees creates a more horizontal organization structure with fewer management layers. Whereas in a centralized vertical structure managers and workers have to go up the ladder of authority for an answer, in a decentralized horizontal structure they develop their own answers and action plans—making decisions and being accountable for results is part of their job. Decentralized decision making usually shortens organizational response times, plus it spurs new ideas, creative thinking, innovation, and greater involvement on the part of subordinate managers and employees.

During the past decade, there's been a growing shift from authoritarian, multilayered hierarchical structures to flatter, more decentralized structures that stress employee empowerment. The new preference for leaner management structures and empowered employees is grounded in three tenets:

1. *With the world economy moving swiftly into the Internet Age, traditional hierarchical structures built around functional specialization have to undergo radical surgery to capitalize on both the external market and internal operating potentials of e-commerce technologies.* Companies the world over are having to reinvent their organization structures and internal business approaches in order to (*a*) incorporate productivity-enhancing, cost-reducing benefits of Internet technologies; (*b*) enhance their capabilities to act and react quickly; and (*c*) create, package, and rapidly move information to the point of need.

2. *Decision-making authority should be pushed down to the lowest organizational level capable of making timely, informed, competent decisions.* In practice this means giving meaningful decision-making authority to those people (managers or nonmanagers) nearest the scene who are knowledgeable about the issues and trained to weigh all the factors. Insofar as the five tasks of strategic management are concerned, decentralization means that the managers of each organizational unit should not only lead the crafting of their unit's strategy but also lead the decision making on how to execute it. Decentralization thus requires selecting strong managers to head each organizational unit and holding them accountable for crafting and executing appropriate strategies for their units. Managers who consistently produce unsatisfactory results have to be weeded out.

3. *Employees below the management ranks should be empowered to exercise judgment on matters pertaining to their jobs.* The case for empowering employees to make decisions and holding them accountable for their performance is based on the belief

---

[27]Iain Somerville and John Edward Mroz, "New Competencies for a New World," in *The Organization of the Future,* ed. Frances Hesselbein, Marshall Goldsmith, and Richard Beckard (San Francisco: Jossey-Bass, 1997), p. 70.

that a company that draws on the combined intellectual capital of all its employees can outperform a command-and-control company. The thesis is that employee empowerment shortens organizational response times and spurs new ideas, creative thinking, innovation, and greater involvement on the part of subordinate managers and employees. With employee empowerment, jobs can be defined more broadly, several tasks can be integrated into a single job, and people can direct their own work. Fewer managers are needed because deciding how to do things becomes part of each person's or team's job. Further, given today's electronic communication systems, it is easy and relatively inexpensive for people at all organizational levels to have direct electronic access to data, other employees, managers, suppliers, and customers. They can access information quickly (via the Internet or company intranet), readily check with superiors or whomever else as needed, and take responsible action. Typically, there are genuine morale and productivity gains when well-informed people are allowed to operate in a self-directed way.

Increasing numbers of organizations all across the world are acknowledging the wisdom of these three tenets. There's strong and growing consensus that authoritarian, hierarchical organizations are not as well suited to implementing and executing strategies in an era where they use electronic technologies to operate at Internet speed and where a big fraction of the organization's most valuable assets is intellectual capital and resides in the knowledge and capabilities of its employees. Many companies have therefore begun empowering lower-level managers and employees throughout their organizations, giving them greater discretionary authority to make strategic adjustments in their areas of responsibility and decide what needs to be done to put new strategic initiatives into place and execute them proficiently. But empowerment presents its own organizing challenge: how to exercise adequate control over the actions of empowered employees so that the business is not put at risk at the same time that the benefits of empowerment are realized.[28]

> Decentralization of authority is an appropriate response to today's seismic shifts toward an Internet economy and toward the dominating role of intellectual capital.

Further, decentralizing strategy-related decisions and giving business heads full operating rein poses a problem in diversified companies with related businesses. Cross-business strategic fits are often best captured by either centralizing strategic-fit-related decision-making authority at the corporate level or else by enforcing close cooperation and shared decision making.[29] For example, if businesses with overlapping process and product technologies have their own independent R&D departments, each pursuing their own priorities, projects, and strategic agendas, it's hard for the corporate parent to prevent duplication of effort, capture either economies of scale or economies of scope, or broaden the company's R&D efforts to embrace new technological paths, product families, end-use applications, and customer groups. Likewise, centralizing control over the related activities of separate businesses makes sense when there are opportunities to share a common sales force, use common distribution channels, rely on a common field service organization to handle customer requests for technical assistance or provide maintenance and repair services, use common e-commerce systems

> In diversified companies, there's merit in retaining some strategy-implementing authority at the corporate level to enforce cross-business collaboration and achieve tight coordination of related value chain activities.

---

[28]Exercising adequate control in businesses that demand short response times, innovation, and creativity is a serious requirement. For example, a prominent Wall Street securities firm lost $350 million when a trader allegedly booked fictitious profits; Sears took a $60 million write-off after admitting that employees in its automobile service departments recommended unnecessary repairs to customers. For a discussion of the problems and possible solutions, see Robert Simons, "Control in an Age of Empowerment," *Harvard Business Review* 73 (March–April 1995), pp. 80–88.

[29]For a discussion of the importance of cross-business coordination, see Jeanne M. Liedtka, "Collaboration across Lines of Business for Competitive Advantage," *Academy of Management Executive* 10, no. 2 (May 1996), pp. 20–34.

and approaches, and so on. And for reasons previously discussed, limits also have to be placed on the independence of functional managers when pieces of strategy-critical processes are located in different organizational units and require close coordination for maximum effectiveness.

Providing for Cross-Unit Coordination The classic way to coordinate the activities of organizational units is to position them in the hierarchy so that those most closely related report to a single person (a functional department head, a process manager, a geographic area head). Managers higher up in the pecking order generally have authority over more organizational units and thus the clout to coordinate, integrate, and arrange for the cooperation of units under their supervision. In such structures, the chief executive officer, chief operating officer, and business-level managers end up as central points of coordination because of their positions of authority over the whole unit. When a firm is pursuing a related diversification strategy, coordinating the related activities of independent business units often requires the centralizing authority of a single corporate-level officer. Also, diversified companies commonly centralize such staff support functions as public relations, finance and accounting, employee benefits, and information technology at the corporate level.

But, as explained earlier, the functional organization structures employed in most businesses often result in pieces of certain strategy-critical activities being fragmented across several departments rather than being unified under the coordinating authority of a single executive. To combat fragmentation, most companies supplement their functional organization structures with coordinating teams, cross-functional task forces, dual reporting relationships, informal organizational networking, voluntary cooperation, incentive compensation tied to group performance measures, and strong executive-level insistence on teamwork and cross-department cooperation (including removal of recalcitrant managers who stonewall collaborative efforts). At ABB, a $30 billion European-based company that makes power generation and electrical equipment and offers a wide range of engineering services, a top executive promptly replaced the managers of several plants who were not fully committed to collaborating closely on eliminating duplication in product development and production efforts among plants in several different countries. Earlier, the executive, noting that negotiations among the managers had stalled on which labs and plants to close, had met with all the managers, asked them to cooperate to find a solution, discussed with them which options were unacceptable, and given them a deadline to find a solution. When the asked-for teamwork wasn't forthcoming, several managers were replaced.

See Illustration Capsule 44 for how 3M Corporation puts the necessary organizational arrangements into place to create worldwide coordination on technology matters.

The key in weaving support activities into the organization design is to establish reporting and coordinating arrangements that

- Maximize how support activities contribute to enhanced performance of the primary functional and strategy-critical capabilities in the firm's value chain.
- Contain the costs of support activities and minimize the time and energy internal units have to spend on doing business with each other.

Without such arrangements, the cost of transacting business internally becomes excessive, and the managers of individual organizational units, forever diligent in guarding their turf and protecting their prerogatives to run their areas as they see fit, can weaken the strategy execution effort and become part of the strategy-implementing problem rather than part of the solution.

illustration capsule 44
Cross-Unit Coordination on Technology at 3M Corporation

At 3M, technology experts in more than 100 laboratories around the world have come to work openly and cooperatively without resorting to turf protection tactics or not-invented-here mind-sets. 3M management has been successful in creating a collegial working environment that results in cooperation among scientists and in rapid technology transfer.

Management formed a Technical Council, composed of the heads of the major labs; the council meets monthly and has a three-day annual retreat to discuss ways to improve cross-unit transfer of technology and other issues of common interest. In addition, management created a broad-based Technical Forum, composed of scientists and technical experts chosen as representatives, to facilitate grassroots communication among employees in all the labs. One of the forum's responsibilities is to organize employees with similar technical interests from all the labs into chapters; chapter members attend regular seminars with experts from outside the company. There's also an annual three-day technology fair at which 3M scientists showcase their latest findings for colleagues and expand their network of acquaintances.

As a result of these collaborative efforts, 3M has developed a portfolio of more than 100 technologies and created the capability to routinely use these technologies in product applications in three different divisions that each serve multiple markets.

Source: Adapted from Sumantra Ghoshal and Christopher A. Bartlett, "Changing the Role of Top Management: Beyond Structure to Process," *Harvard Business Review* 73, no. 1 (January–February 1995), pp. 93–94.

Assigning Responsibility for Collaboration with Outsiders

Someone or some group must be authorized to collaborate as needed with each major outside constituency involved in strategy execution. Forming alliances and cooperative relationships presents immediate opportunities and opens the door to future possibilities, but nothing valuable is realized until the relationship grows, develops, and blossoms. Unless top management sees that constructive organizational bridge-building with strategic partners occurs and that productive working relationships emerge, the value of alliances is lost and the company's power to execute its strategy is weakened. If close working relationships with suppliers are crucial, then supply chain management must be given formal status on the company's organization chart and a significant position in the pecking order. If distributor/dealer/franchisee relationships are important, someone must be assigned the task of nurturing the relationships with forward channel allies. If working in parallel with providers of complementary products and services contributes to enhanced organizational capability, then cooperative organizational arrangements have to be put in place and managed to good effect.

> The key to cooperative alliances and partnerships is effectively managing the relationship and capturing the potential gain in resource capability, not in doing the deal.

Building organizational bridges with external allies can be accomplished by appointing "relationship" managers with responsibility for making particular strategic partnerships or alliances generate the intended benefits. Relationship managers have many roles and functions: getting the right people together, promoting good rapport, seeing that plans for specific activities are developed and carried out, helping adjust internal organizational procedures and communication systems to link the partners better and iron out operating dissimilarities, and nurturing interpersonal ties. Multiple cross-organization ties have to be established and kept open to ensure proper communication and coordination.[30] There has to be enough information sharing to make the relationship work and periodic frank discussions of conflicts, trouble spots, and changing situations.[31]

---

[30]Rosabeth Moss Kanter, "Collaborative Advantage: The Art of the Alliance," *Harvard Business Review* 72, no. 4 (July–August 1994), pp. 105–6.

[31]For an excellent review of ways to effectively manage the relationship between alliance partners, see Kanter, "Collaborative Advantage," pp. 96–108.

Perspectives on Organizing the Work Effort and Building Capabilities   All organization designs have their strategy-related strengths and weaknesses. To do a good job of matching structure to strategy, strategy implementers first have to pick a basic design and modify it as needed to fit the company's particular business makeup. They must then (*a*) supplement the design with appropriate coordinating mechanisms (cross-functional task forces, special project teams, self-contained work teams, and so on), and (*b*) institute whatever networking and communication arrangements it takes to support effective execution of the firm's strategy. While companies may not set up "ideal" organizational arrangements to avoid disturbing certain existing reporting relationships or to accommodate the personalities of certain individuals involved, internal politics, and other situational idiosyncracies, they must work toward the goal of building a competitively capable organization.

> There's no perfect or ideal organization structure.

The ways and means of developing stronger core competencies and organizational capabilities (or creating altogether new ones) tend to be idiosyncratic to each company, its culture, and its circumstances. Not only do different companies and executives tackle the capabilities-building challenge in different ways but different capabilities require different organizing techniques. Thus, generalizing about how to build capabilities has to be done cautiously. What can be said unequivocally is that building an organization with the competencies and capabilities to execute strategy proficiently entails a process of consciously knitting the efforts of individuals and groups together. Competencies and capabilities emerge from establishing and nurturing cooperative working relationships among people and groups to perform activities in a more customer-satisfying fashion, not from rearranging boxes on an organization chart. Furthermore, organization building is a task senior management must lead and be deeply involved in. Indeed, effectively managing both internal organization processes and external collaboration to create and develop competitively valuable competencies and capabilities ranks very high on the "to-do" list of senior executives in today's companies.

> Organizational capabilities emerge from a process of consciously knitting together the efforts of different work groups, departments, and external allies, not from how the boxes on the organization chart are arranged.

ORGANIZATIONAL STRUCTURES OF THE FUTURE

Many of today's companies are winding up the task of remodeling their traditional hierarchical structures once built around functional specialization and centralized authority. Much of the corporate downsizing movement in the late 1980s and early 1990s was aimed at recasting authoritarian, pyramidal organizational structures into flatter, decentralized structures. The change was driven by growing realization that command-and-control hierarchies were proving a liability in businesses where customer preferences were shifting from standardized products to custom orders and special features, product life cycles were growing shorter, custom mass production methods were replacing standardized mass production techniques, customers wanted to be treated as individuals, the pace of technological change was accelerating, and market conditions were fluid. Layered management hierarchies with lots of checks and controls that required people to look upward in the organizational structure for answers and approval were bogging down, failing to deliver responsive customer service and adapt fast enough to changing conditions. Likewise, functional silos, task-oriented work, and fragmentation of strategy-critical activities further contributed to an erosion of competitiveness in fluid or volatile business environments.

> During the past decade, new strategic priorities and rapidly shifting competitive conditions have triggered revolutionary changes in how companies are organizing the work effort.

illustration capsule 45

Organizational Approaches for International and Global Markets

A study of 43 large U.S.-based consumer products companies conducted by McKinsey & Co., a leading management consulting firm, identified internal organizational actions with the strongest and weakest links to rapidly growing sales and profits in international and global markets.

ORGANIZATIONAL ACTIONS STRONGLY LINKED TO INTERNATIONAL SUCCESS

- Centralizing international decision making in every area except new product development.

- Having a worldwide management development program and more foreigners in senior management posts.

- Requiring international experience for advancement into top management.

- Linking global managers with video conferencing and electronic mail.

- Having product managers of foreign subsidiaries report to a country general manager.

- Using local executives to head operations in foreign countries. (However, this is rapidly ceasing to distinguish successful companies because nearly everyone has implemented such a practice.)

ORGANIZATIONAL ACTIONS WEAKLY LINKED TO INTERNATIONAL SUCCESS

- Creating global divisions.

- Forming international strategic business units.

- Establishing centers of excellence where a single company facility takes global responsibility for a key product or emerging technology (too new to evaluate pro or con).

- Using cross-border task forces to resolve problems and issues.

- Creating globally integrated management information systems.

However, the lists of organizational dos and don'ts are far from decisive. In general, the study found that internal organizational structure doesn't matter as much as having products with attractive prices and features. It is wrong to expect good results just because of good organization. Moreover, certain organizational arrangements, such as centers of excellence, are too new to determine whether they positively affect sales and profit growth.

Source: Based on information reported by Joann S. Lublin, "Study Sees U.S. Businesses Stumbling on the Road to Globalization," *The Wall Street Journal,* March 22, 1993, p. B4B.

In today's fast-changing markets where many companies are racing for global leadership in their industries and/or racing to build strong positions in the industries of the future, the necessary organizational themes are lean, flat, agile, responsive, and innovative. The necessary tools of organizational design are managers and workers empowered to act on their own judgments, reengineered work processes, self-directed work teams, rapid incorporation of Internet technologies and a cutting-edge e-commerce infrastructure, and networking with outsiders to improve existing organization capabilities and create new ones. The necessary organizational imperative is building a company capable of outcompeting rivals on the basis of superior resource strengths and competitive capabilities—capabilities that are increasingly based on intellectual capital. In a growing number of companies and industries, there is no alternative but to restructure the internal organization so it can operate at Internet speed and to ingrain e-commerce business practices in day-to-day operations throughout the company.

Illustration Capsule 45 reports the results of a study of trends in organizational arrangements in multinational and global companies.

The organizations of the future will have several new characteristics:

- Fewer barriers between different vertical ranks, between functions and disciplines, between units in different geographic locations, and between the company and its suppliers, distributors/dealers, strategic allies, and customers.
- A capacity for change and rapid learning.
- Collaborative efforts among people in different functional specialities and geographic locations—essential to create organization competencies and capabilities.
- Extensive use of e-commerce technology and e-commerce business practices—real-time data and information systems, heavy reliance on e-commerce systems for transacting business with suppliers and customers, and Internet-based communication and collaboration with suppliers, customers, and strategic partners.

key|points

The job of strategy execution is to convert strategic plans into actions and good results. The test of successful strategy execution is whether actual organization performance matches or exceeds the targets spelled out in the strategic plan. Shortfalls in performance signal weak strategy, weak execution, or both.

In deciding how to implement a new or revised strategy, managers have to determine what internal conditions are needed to execute the strategic plan successfully. Then they must create these conditions as rapidly as practical. The process of implementing and executing strategy involves:

- Building an organization with the competencies, capabilities, and resource strengths to carry out the strategy successfully.
- Developing budgets to steer ample resources into those value chain activities critical to strategic success.
- Establishing strategy-supportive policies and procedures.
- Instituting best practices and pushing for continuous improvement in how value chain activities are performed.
- Installing support systems that enable company personnel to carry out their strategic roles successfully day in and day out.
- Tying rewards and incentives to the achievement of performance objectives and good strategy execution.
- Creating a strategy-supportive work environment and corporate culture.
- Exerting the internal leadership needed to drive implementation forward and to keep improving on how the strategy is being executed.

The challenge is to create a series of tight fits (1) between strategy and the organization's competencies, capabilities, and structure; (2) between strategy and budgetary allocations; (3) between strategy and policy; (4) between strategy and internal support systems; (5) between strategy and the reward structure; and (6) between strategy and the corporate culture. The tighter the fits, the more powerful strategy execution becomes and the more likely targeted performance can actually be achieved.

Implementing strategy is not just a top-management function; it is a job for the whole management team. *All managers function as strategy implementers* in their respective areas of authority and responsibility. All managers have to consider what actions to take in their areas to achieve the intended results—they each need an action agenda.

The three major organization-building actions are (1) filling key positions with able people, (2) building the core competencies and organizational capabilities needed to perform value chain activities proficiently, and (3) structuring the internal work effort and melding it with the collaborative efforts of strategic allies. Selecting able people for key positions tends to be one of the earliest strategy implementation steps because it takes a full complement of capable managers and employees to get changes in place and functioning smoothly.

Building strategy-critical core competencies and competitive capabilities not easily imitated by rivals is one of the best ways to gain a competitive advantage. Core competencies emerge from skills and activities performed at different points in the value chain that, when linked, create unique organizational capability. The key to leveraging a company's core competencies into long-term competitive advantage is to concentrate more effort and more talent than rivals do on strengthening and deepening organizational competencies and capabilities. The multiskill, multiactivity character of core competencies and capabilities makes achieving dominating depth an exercise in (1) managing human skills, knowledge bases, and intellect, and (2) coordinating and networking the efforts of different work groups, departments, and collaborative allies. It is a task that senior mangement must lead and be deeply involved in chiefly because it is senior managers who are in the best position to guide and enforce the necessary networking and cooperation among individuals, groups, departments, and external allies.

Building organizational capabilities means more than just strengthening what a company already does. There are times when management has to be proactive in developing new competencies and capabilities to complement the company's existing resource base and promote more proficient strategy execution. It is useful here to think of companies as a bundle of evolving competencies and capabilities, with the organization-building challenge being one of developing new capabilities and strengthening existing ones in a fashion calculated to achieve competitive advantage through superior strategy execution.

One capability-building issue is whether to develop the desired competencies and capabilities internally or whether it makes more sense to outsource them by partnering with key suppliers or forming strategic alliances. Decisions about whether to outsource or develop in-house capability often turn on the issues of (1) what can be safely delegated to outside suppliers versus what internal capabilities are key to the company's long-term success and (2) whether noncritical activities can be outsourced more effectively or efficiently than they can be performed internally. Either way, though, calls for action. Outsourcing means launching initiatives to identify the most attractive providers and to establish collaborative relationships. Developing the capabilities in-house means hiring new personnel withs skills and experience relevant to the deired organizational competence/capability, then linking the individual skills/know-how to form organizational capability.

Matching structure to strategy centers around making strategy-critical activities the main organizational building blocks, finding effective ways to bridge organizational lines of authority and coordinate the related efforts of separate internal units and individuals, and effectively networking the efforts of internal units and external collaborative partners. Other big considerations include what decisions to centralize and what decisions to decentralize.

All organization structures have strategic advantages and disadvantages; *there is no one best way to organize*. Functionally specialized organization structures have traditionally been the most popular way to organize single-business companies. Functional organization works well where strategy-critical activities closely match discipline-specific activities and minimal interdepartmental cooperation is needed. But it has significant drawbacks: functional myopia, empire building, interdepartmental rivalries, excessive process fragmentation, and vertically layered management hierarchies. In recent years, *business process reengineering* has been used to circumvent many of the disadvantages of functional organization.

Whatever basic structure is chosen, it usually has to be supplemented with interdisciplinary task forces, incentive compensation schemes tied to measures of joint performance, empowerment of cross-functional and/or self-directed work teams to perform and unify fragmented processes and strategy-critical activities, special project teams, relationship managers, and special top management efforts to knit the work of different individuals and groups into valuable competitive capabilities. Building core competencies and competitive capabilities emerges from establishing and nurturing collaborative working relationships between individuals and groups in different departments and between a company and its external allies, not from how the boxes are arranged on an organization chart.

New strategic priorities like short design-to-market cycles, multiversion production, personalized customer service, aggressive pursuit of e-commerce opportunities, and winning the race for positions of leadership in global markets and/or industries of the future have prompted increasing numbers of companies to create lean, flat, horizontal structures that are responsive and innovative. Such designs for matching structure to strategy involve fewer layers of management authority, managers and workers empowered to act on their own judgment, reengineered work processes to reduce cross-department fragmentation, collaborative partnerships with outsiders (suppliers, distributors/dealers, companies with complementary products/services, and even select competitors), increased outsourcing of selected value chain activities, leaner staffing of internal support functions, and rapidly growing use of e-commerce technologies and business practices.

suggested | readings

Argyris, Chris. "Empowerment: The Emperor's New Clothes." *Harvard Business Review* 76, no. 3 (May–June 1998), pp. 98–105.

Hall, Gene; Jim Rosenthal; and Judy Wade. "How to Make Reengineering Really Work." *Harvard Business Review* 71, no. 6 (November–December 1993), pp. 119–31.

Hambrick, Donald C. "The Top Management Team: Key to Strategic Success." *California Management Review* 30, no. 1 (Fall 1987), pp. 88–108.

Hammer, Michael, and James Champy. *Reengineering the Corporation.* New York: HarperBusiness, 1993, chapters 2 and 3.

Kanter, Rosabeth Moss. "Collaborative Advantage: The Art of the Alliance." *Harvard Business Review* 72, no. 4 (July–August 1994), pp. 96–108.

Katzenbach, Jon R., and Douglas K. Smith. "The Discipline of Teams." *Harvard Business Review* 71, no. 2 (March–April 1993), pp. 111–24.

Majchrzak, Ann, and Qianwei Wang. "Breaking the Functional Mind-Set in Process Organizations." *Harvard Business Review* 74, no. 5 (September–October 1996), pp. 93–99.

Markides, Constantinos C., and Peter J. Williamson. "Corporate Diversification and Organizational Structure: A Resource-Based View." *Academy of Management Journal* 39, no. 2 (April 1996), pp. 340–67.

Pfeffer, Jeffrey. *The Human Equation: Building Profits by Putting People First.* Boston, MA: Harvard Business School Press, 1999.

————. "Producing Sustainable Competitive Advantage through the Effective Management of People." *Academy of Management Executive* 9, no. 1 (February 1995), pp. 55–69.

Pfeffer, Jeffrey, and John F. Veiga. "Putting People First for Organizational Success." *Academy of Management Executive* 13, no. 2 (May 1999), pp. 37–48.

Prahalad, C. K., and Gary Hamel. "The Core Competence of the Corporation." *Harvard Business Review* 68 (May–June 1990), pp. 79–93.

Rackham, Neil; Lawrence Friedman; and Richard Ruff. *Getting Partnering Right: How Market Leaders Are Creating Long-Term Competitive Advantage.* New York: McGraw-Hill, 1996.

Stalk, George; Philip Evans; and Lawrence E. Shulman. "Competing on Capabilities: The New Rules of Corporate Strategy." *Harvard Business Review* 70, no. 2 (March–April 1992), pp. 57–69.

Wetlaufer, Suzy. "Organizing for Empowerment: An Interview with AES's Roger Sant and Dennis Bakke." *Harvard Business Review* 77, no. 1 (January–February 1999), pp. 110–23.

chapter | twelve 12 Managing the Internal Organization to Promote Better Strategy Execution

Winning companies know how to do their work better.
—Michael Hammer and James Champy

If you talk about change but don't change the reward and recognition system, nothing changes.
—Paul Allaire, former CEO, Xerox Corporation

If you want people motivated to do a good job, give them a good job to do.
—Frederick Herzberg

You ought to pay big bonuses for premier performance . . . be a top payer, not in the middle or low end of the pack.
—Lawrence Bossidy, former CEO, AlliedSignal

In Chapter 11 we emphasized the importance of building organization capabilities and structuring the work effort so as to perform strategy-critical activities in a coordinated and highly competent manner. In this chapter we discuss five additional managerial tasks common to the strategy-implementing/strategy-executing process:

1. Reallocating resources to ensure that strategy-critical units have sufficient budgets to do their work successfully.
2. Establishing strategy-supportive policies.
3. Instituting best practices and mechanisms for continuous improvement.
4. Installing support systems that enable company personnel to carry out their strategic roles proficiently day in, day out.
5. Motivating and compensating employees in ways that enhance organizationwide commitment to good strategy execution.

LINKING BUDGETS TO STRATEGY

Implementing and executing strategy forces managers to consider how the firm's resources are being allocated. Organizational units need sufficient budgets and resources to carry out their parts of the strategic plan effectively and efficiently. There has to be ample funding of efforts to strengthen existing competencies and capabilities and/or to develop new ones. Managers with budgetary responsibility must screen subordinates' requests for more people, bigger operating budgets, and more or better facilities and equipment, distinguishing between requests that would be nice and requests that hold promise for making a cost-justified contribution to strategy execution and enhanced competitive capabilities. Moreover, strategy implementers have to make a persuasive, documented case to superiors to acquire the resources they need to execute their assigned pieces of company strategy.

Strategic-Management Principle
Depriving strategy-critical groups of the resources needed to execute their pieces of the strategy can undermine the implementation process.

How well budget allocations are linked to the needs of strategy can either promote or impede the implementation process. Too little funding slows progress and impedes the ability of organizational units to execute their pieces of the strategic plan proficiently. Too much funding wastes organizational resources and reduces financial performance. Both outcomes argue for managers charged with implementing and executing strategy to be deeply involved in the budgeting process, closely reviewing programs and budget proposals and endeavoring to ensure adequate resources are allocated to strategy-critical organization units.

A change in strategy nearly always calls for budget reallocations. Units important in the prior strategy may now be oversized and overfunded. Units that now have a bigger and more critical strategic role may need more people, new equipment, additional facilities, and above-average increases in their operating budgets. Strategy implementers need to be active and forceful in shifting resources, downsizing some areas and upsizing others, to not only amply fund activities with a critical role in the new strategy but also avoid inefficiency and achieve profit projections. They have to exercise their power to put enough resources behind new strategic initiatives to make things happen and make the tough decisions to kill projects and activities that are no longer justified. The essential condition is that the funding requirements of the new strategy must drive how capital allocations are made and the size of each unit's operating budgets. Underfunding organizational units and activities pivotal to strategic success can defeat the whole implementation process.

New strategies usually call for significant budget reallocations.

Forceful actions to reallocate operating funds and move people into new organizational units signal a determined commitment to strategic change and are frequently needed to catalyze the implementation process and give it credibility. Microsoft has made a practice of regularly shifting hundreds of programmers to new high-priority programming initiatives within a matter of weeks or even days. At Harris Corporation, where the strategy was to diffuse research ideas into areas that were commercially viable, top management regularly shifted groups of engineers out of government projects and moved them as a group into new commercial venture divisions. But fast-moving developments in many markets are prompting companies to move at Internet speed in reallocating resources and updating budgets. Companies are finding it desirable, if not necessary, to abandon traditional annual or semiannual budgeting and resource allocation cycles in favor of cycles that match the strategy changes a company makes in response to newly developing events. Annual or semiannual budget and resource reallocation reviews do not work when companies make strategic shifts weekly. Bluefly.com, a discount Internet apparel retailer, revises its budgets and shifts resources weekly. Bluefly.com's CEO observed, "For us, 11 months is long-term planning."[1]

Fine-tuning the implementation of a company's existing strategy seldom requires big movements of people and money from one area to another. The desired improvements can usually be accomplished through above-average budget increases to organizational units where new initiatives are contemplated and below-average increases (or even small cuts) for the remaining organizational units. The chief exception occurs where a prime ingredient of strategy is to create altogether new capabilities or to generate fresh products and business opportunities within the existing budget. Then, as proposals and business plans worth pursuing bubble up from below, managers have to make decisions regarding where the needed capital expenditures, operating budgets, and personnel will come from. Companies like 3M, GE, and Boeing shift resources and people from area to area as needed to support the launch of new products and new business ventures. They empower "product champions" and small bands of would-be entrepreneurs by giving them financial and technical support and by setting up organizational units and programs to help new ventures blossom more quickly.

CREATING STRATEGY-SUPPORTIVE POLICIES AND PROCEDURES

Changes in strategy generally call for some changes in work practices and internal operations. Asking people to alter established procedures always upsets the internal order of things. It is normal for pockets of resistance to develop and for people to exhibit some degree of stress and anxiety about how the changes will affect them, especially when the changes may eliminate jobs. Questions are also likely to arise over what activities need to be done in rigidly prescribed fashion and where there ought to be leeway for independent action.

Prescribing policies and operating procedures aids the task of implementing strategy in several ways:

1. New or revised policies and procedures provide top-down guidance to operating managers, supervisory personnel, and employees regarding how certain things now need to be done and what behavior is expected, thus establishing some degree of regularity, stability, and dependability in how management has decided to try to execute the strategy and operate the business.

2. Policies and procedures help align actions and behavior with strategy throughout the organization, placing limits on independent action and channeling individual and group efforts along the intended path. Policies and procedures counteract tendencies for some people to resist or reject common approaches. Most people refrain from violating company policy or ignoring established practices without first gaining clearance or having strong justification.

3. Policies and standardized operating procedures help enforce needed consistency in how particular strategy-critical activities are performed in geographically scattered operating units (different plants, sales regions, customer service centers, or the individual outlets in a chain operation). Eliminating significant differences in the

---

[1]Marcia Stepanek, "How Fast Is Net Fast?" *Business Week*, November 1, 1999, pp. EB-52–EB-54.

operating practices and procedures of organizational units performing common functions is frequently desirable to avoid sending mixed messages to internal personnel and to customers who do business with the company at multiple locations.

4. Because dismantling old policies and procedures and instituting new ones invariably alter the internal work climate, strategy implementers can use the policy-changing process as a powerful lever for changing the corporate culture in ways that produce a stronger fit with the new strategy.

Company managers therefore need to be inventive in devising policies and practices that can provide vital support to effective strategy implementation and execution.

McDonald's policy manual, in an attempt to steer "crew members" into stronger quality and service behavior patterns, spells out procedures in detail; for example, "Cooks must turn, never flip, hamburgers. If they haven't been purchased, Big Macs must be discarded in 10 minutes after being cooked and french fries in 7 minutes. Cashiers must make eye contact with and smile at every customer." Caterpillar Tractor has a policy of guaranteeing its customers 24-hour parts delivery anywhere in the world; if it fails to fulfill the promise, it supplies the part for free. Hewlett-Packard requires R&D people to make regular visits to customers to learn about their problems, talk about new product applications, and in general keep the company's R&D programs customer-oriented. Mrs. Fields Cookies has a policy of establishing hourly sales quotas for each store outlet; furthermore, it is company policy that cookies not sold within two hours after being baked have to be removed from the case and given to charitable organizations. Illustration Capsule 46 describes Granite Rock's "short pay" policy for promoting high levels of customer service and customer satisfaction.

Thus, there is a definite role for new and revised policies and procedures in the strategy implementation process. Wisely constructed policies and procedures help channel actions, behavior, decisions, and practices in directions that promote good strategy execution. When policies and practices aren't strategy-supportive, they become a barrier to the kinds of attitudinal and behavioral changes strategy-implementers are trying to promote. Often, people opposed to certain elements of the strategy or certain implementation approaches will hide behind or vigorously defend long-standing policies and operating procedures in an effort to stall implementation or divert the approaches to implementation along a different route. Anytime a company alters its strategy, managers should review existing policies and operating procedures, proactively revise or discard those that are out of sync, and formulate new ones to facilitate execution of new strategic initiatives.

> Well-conceived policies and procedures aid implementation; out-of-sync policies are barriers.

None of this implies that companies need thick policy manuals to guide strategy execution and daily operations. Too much policy can be as stifling as wrong policy or as chaotic as no policy. There is wisdom in a middle approach: prescribe enough policies to give organization members clear direction in implementing strategy and to place desirable boundaries on their actions, then empower them to act within these boundaries however they think makes sense. Allowing company personnel to decide and act anywhere between the "white lines" is especially appropriate when individual creativity and initiative are more essential to good strategy execution than standardization and strict conformity. Creating a strong supportive fit between strategy and policy can therefore mean more policies, fewer policies, or different policies. It can mean policies that require things to be done a certain way or policies that give employees leeway to do activities the way they think best.

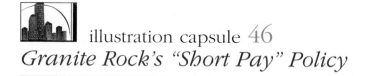

illustration capsule 46
Granite Rock's "Short Pay" Policy

The owners of Granite Rock, a 100-plus-year-old supplier of crushed gravel, sand, concrete, and asphalt in Watsonville, California, set two big, hairy, audacious goals (BHAGs) for the company: to achieve total customer satisfaction and a reputation for service that met or exceeded that of Nordstrom, the upscale department store famous for pleasing its customers. To drive the implementation effort, the owners decided to forgo all the various hoopla events it could have used to fire up its 725-plus employees. Instead it instituted a radical new policy called "short pay," to signal to both employees and customers that Granite Rock was deadly serious about its two strategic commitments. At the bottom of every Granite Rock invoice was the following statement:

> If you are not satisfied for any reason, don't pay us for it. Simply scratch out the line item, write a brief note about the problem, and return a copy of this invoice along with your check for the balance.

Customers did not have to call and complain and were not expected to return the product. They were given complete discretionary power to decide whether and how much to pay based on their satisfaction level.

The policy has worked exceptionally well, providing unmistakable feedback and spurring company managers to correct any problems quickly in order to avoid repeated short payments. Granite Rock has enjoyed market share increases, while charging a 6 percent price premium for its commodity products in competition against larger rivals. Its profit margins and overall financial performance have improved. Granite Rock won the prestigious Malcolm Baldrige National Quality Award in 1992, about five years after instituting the policy. *Fortune* rated it as one of the 100 best companies to work for in America in 1997 (ranked 23rd), 1998 (ranked 33rd), and 1999 (ranked 19th). Company employees receive an average of 43 hours of training annually. Entry-level employees, called job owners, start at $16 per hour and progress to such positions as "accomplished job owner" and "improvement champion" (base pay of $26 per hour). The company has a no-layoff policy.

Source: Based on information in Jim Collins, "Turning Goals into Results: The Power of Catalytic Mechanisms," *Harvard Business Review* 77, no. 4 (July–August 1999), pp. 72–73; and Robert Levering and Milton Moskowitz, "The 100 Best Companies to Work For," *Fortune*, January 10, 2000, p. 88.

INSTITUTING BEST PRACTICES AND A COMMITMENT TO CONTINUOUS IMPROVEMENT

If value chain activities are to be performed as effectively and efficiently as possible, each organizational unit needs to benchmark how it performs specific activities against best-in-industry or best-in-world performers. A strong commitment to searching out and adopting best practices is integral to implementing strategy and then continuously improving on how well it is executed—especially for strategy-critical and big-dollar activities where better quality or lower costs significantly impact bottom-line performance.[2]

As we noted in Chapter 4, benchmarking how well a company performs particular activities and processes against "best in industry" and "best in world" performers provides valuable yardsticks for gauging how well a company is executing pieces of its strategy and represents a solid methodology for identifying areas in which to improve. It can also be useful to look at "best in company" performers of an activity if a company has a number of different organizational units performing much the same function at different

> Identifying and implementing best practices is a journey, not a destination.

---

[2]For a discussion of the value of benchmarking in implementing strategy, see Yoshinobu Ohinata, "Benchmarking: The Japanese Experience," *Long-Range Planning* 27, no. 4 (August 1994), pp. 48–53.

illustration capsule 47

Where Best Practices Come From: The Accomplishments of Three Best Practice Award Winners

Arthur Andersen sponsors a Best Practices Awards program to help businesses learn the innovative practices of small and mid-sized companies from different parts of the world. Three of the award winners in 1998 were Cloud 9 Shuttle, the Amalgamated Sugar Company, and Great Plains Software (which has been selected four times as one of the top 100 companies to work for in America).

CLOUD 9 SHUTTLE

Cloud 9 Shuttle, San Diego's largest "share ride" airport ground transportation company, was created in 1994 out of the ashes of a predecessor company whose dispatchers used magnets on a map to track the location of company vehicles. The predecessor stored customer service information in rarely used file folders and put customers through a lengthy procedure when they called to make reservations.

The new owners had a good vision of where they wanted to take the company, recognizing that service standards had to be increased and costs lowered. But resources were limited. They opted to use technology in very pragmatic ways. One innovation was to use a cellular telephone technology called cellular triangularization that allows reservationists and dispatchers to see the location of any Cloud 9 vehicle in San Diego County on a computer screen around the clock; the system identifies each vehicle's speed and direction as well as the street and nearest cross street.

New information systems were installed that permitted the integration of reservations, dispatch, and cashiering functions, both to provide better customer service and to provide key operating data to management—passengers per hour, revenue per hour per driver, passengers per gallon of fuel, and so on. This information is used to control costs and schedule drivers—driver hours were reduced by 11 percent while their income rose 7 percent.

The new systems and practices—coupled with employee empowerment, training, and a progressive company culture—have allowed Cloud 9 to deploy a fleet of more than 100 vehicles (the precedessor company could only handle 60 vehicles with its operating practices), triple revenues, and operate profitably.

THE AMALGAMATED SUGAR COMPANY

Amalgamated's business is converting sugar beets into sugar. A key success factor is how much sugar can be extracted from the beets before it is lost to molasses. Since sugar sells for $550 per ton versus $75 per ton for molasses, the incentive to improve sugar yield is high.

Amalgamated engineers developed and patented a computer-optimized separator system based on "simulated

locations. The innovative manner in which activities or processes are performed by companies considered "best in industry" or "best in world" (or internal units considered "best in company")—commonly termed *best practices*—provides useful performance targets for organization units to achieve or compare themselves against. But it is not enough just to identify the best practices of other companies, especially companies in other industries, because copying them exactly is usually neither feasible nor desirable owing to differences from one situation and application to another. More usually, the best practices of other companies need to be modified and adapted to a company's own specific situation—and then later improved on as time passes. Hence, benchmarking nearly always involves creativity and innovative application of the best practices of outsiders.

A substantial number of companies engage in benchmarking. A recent survey of over 4,000 managers in 15 countries indicated that over 85 percent were using benchmarking to measure the efficiency and effectiveness of their internal activities. During the past decade, growing numbers of companies have instituted best practice programs as an integral part of their efforts to fine-tune strategy execution. Such programs, creatively pursued, tend to result in company personnel being innovative in developing best practices out of their own efforts as well as searching out and adapting the best

illustration capsule 47

(concluded)

moving bed chromatography" that has enabled the company to recover more than 80 percent of the sugar ordinarily lost to the molasses by-product.

Amalgamated also developed a computer technology to perform 1,500 individual analytic tests daily at each of its four plants to maximize plant performance. Company representatives also developed software that helped the company's sugar beet growers to set standards and use sophisticated agronomic practices in producing sugar beets.

Amalgamated's management believes the company's constant innovation and use of advanced technology has enabled it to become the most efficient sugar beet processor in the world.

GREAT PLAINS

Great Plains, based in Fargo, South Dakota, is a leading provider of enterprise business management software for mid-sized companies. The company has annual revenues of about $135 million and nearly 1,000 employees; it was rated 15th on the 1999 list of the 100 best companies to work for in America. It won awards for best practices in exceeding customer expectations and in motivating and retaining employees.

Great Plains' management believes superior customer service is a key success factor in the enterprise software business. In 1987, in an effort to provide immediate solutions to customers' problems, Great Plains established "guaranteed response times" to set customer expectations for prompt service and technical support. Although Great Plains' customer support teams handle more than 20,000 cases each month (most of them involving "how-to" questions and productivity issues), they have met the company's guaranteed response times more than 99 percent of the time. In 1998, the company broke its own record by serving more than 250,000 consecutive customer support calls without missing a single guarantee.

Among the key employee-oriented practices are an automated performance management process, company-wide and team-based recognition events, stock ownership opportunities for all employees, on-site services for employees such as dry cleaning, discounts for health clubs and retail stores, flexible work hours, and paid sabbaticals. There's also a no-layoff policy. Employees have strong feelings of belonging to a family; according to one employee, "Work feels a whole lot more like hanging out with your friends than going to work."

Source: Arthur Andersen and articles in *Fortune* reporting the 100 best companies to work for: January 12, 1998, and January 10, 2000.

practices of others. Illustration Capsule 47 provides examples of three small and mid-sized companies that have won best practice awards because of their own innovations.

Total Quality Management: A Commitment to Continuous Improvement

The benchmarking movement to search out, study, implement, and improve on best practices has stimulated greater management awareness of the importance of business process reengineering, *total quality management* (TQM), and other continuous improvement techniques. *TQM is a philosophy of managing a set of business practices that emphasizes continuous improvement in all phases of operations, 100 percent accuracy in performing activities, involvement and empowerment of employees at all levels, team-based work design, benchmarking, and fully satisfying customer expectations.* Management interest in quality improvement programs has historically originated in such activities as fabrication and assembly in manufacturing enterprises, teller transactions in banks, order picking and shipping at catalog firms, and customer-contact interfaces at Web sites and in service organizations. Occasionally, interest begins with executives who hear TQM presentations, read about TQM, or talk to people in other companies that have benefited from total quality programs. Usually, interested managers either have quality

table 12.1   Components of Popular TQM Approaches and 1992 Baldrige Award Criteria

DEMING'S 14 POINTS	THE JURAN TRILOGY	CROSBY'S 14 QUALITY STEPS
1. Constancy of purpose	1. *Quality planning*	1. Management commitment
2. Adopt the philosophy	• Set goals	2. Quality improvement teams
3. Don't rely on mass inspection	• Identify customers and their needs	3. Quality measurement
4. Don't award business on price	• Develop products and processes	4. Cost of quality evaluation
5. Constant improvement	2. *Quality control*	5. Quality awareness
6. Training	• Evaluate performance	6. Corrective action
7. Leadership	• Compare to goals and adapt	7. Zero-defects committee
8. Drive out fear	3. *Quality improvement*	8. Supervisor training
9. Break down barriers	• Establish infrastructure	9. Zero-defects day
10. Eliminate slogans and exhortations	• Identify projects and teams	10. Goal-setting
11. Eliminate quotas	• Provide resources and training	11. Error cause removal
12. Pride of workmanship	• Establish controls	12. Recognition
13. Education and retraining		13. Quality councils
14. Plan of action		14. Do it over again

THE 1992 BALDRIGE AWARD CRITERIA (1,000 points total)

1. *Leadership* (90 points)
   - Senior executive
   - Management for quality
   - Public responsibility
2. *Information and analysis* (80 points)
   - Scope and management of quality and performance data
   - Competitive comparisons and benchmarks
3. *Strategic quality planning* (60 points)
   - Strategic quality and planning process
   - Quality and performance plans
4. *Human resource development and management* (150 points)
   - Human resource management
   - Employee involvement
   - Employee education and training
   - Employee performance and recognition
   - Employee well-being and morale

5. *Management of process quality* (140 points)
   - Design and introduction of products and services
   - Process management—production and delivery
   - Process management—business and support
   - Supplier quality
   - Quality assessment
6. *Quality and operational results* (180 points)
   - Product and service quality
   - Company operations
   - Business process and support services
   - Supplier quality
7. *Customer focus and satisfaction* (300 points)
   - Customer relationships
   - Commitment to customers
   - Customer satisfaction determination
   - Customer satisfaction results
   - Customer satisfaction comparisons
   - Future requirements and expectations

Source: As presented in Thomas C. Powell, "Total Quality Management as Competitive Advantage," *Strategic Management Journal* 16, no. 1 (January 1995), p. 18, and based on M. Walton, *The Deming Management Method* (New York: Pedigree, 1986); J. Juran, *Juran on Quality by Design* (New York: Free Press, 1992); Philip Crosby, *Quality Is Free: The Act of Making Quality Certain* (New York: McGraw-Hill, 1979); and S. George, *The Baldrige Quality System* (New York: Wiley, 1992).

and customer-satisfaction problems they are struggling to solve or are under the gun of competition and customer expectations to dramatically improve certain quality attributes. Surveys indicate that over 95 percent of manufacturing companies and 70 percent of service companies have used some form of quality improvement program.[3] Another survey found that 55 percent of American executives and 70 percent of Japanese executives used quality improvement information at least monthly as part of their assessment of overall

---

[3]Judy D. Olian and Sara L. Rynes, "Making Total Quality Work: Aligning Organizational Processes, Performance Measures, and Stakeholders," *Human Resource Management* 30, no. 3 (Fall 1991), p. 303; and Darrell K. Rigby, "What's Today's Special at the Consultant's Café?" *Fortune*, September 7, 1998, p. 163.

table 12.2 12 Aspects Common to TQM and Continuous
Improvement Programs

1. **Committed leadership:** a near-evangelical, unwavering, long-term commitment by top managers to the philosophy, usually under a name something like Total Quality Management, Continuous Improvement (CI), or Quality Improvement (QI).
2. **Adoption and communication of TQM:** using tools like the mission statement, and themes or slogans.
3. **Closer customer relationships:** determining customers' (both inside and outside the firm) requirements, then meeting those requirements no matter what it takes.
4. **Closer supplier relationships:** working closely and cooperatively with suppliers (often sole-sourcing key components), ensuring they provide inputs that conform to customers' end-use requirements.
5. **Benchmarking:** researching and observing operating competitive practices.
6. **Increased training:** usually includes TQM principles, team skills, and problem-solving.
7. **Open organization:** lean staff, empowered work teams, open horizontal communications, and a relaxation of traditional hierarchy.
8. **Employee empowerment:** increased employee involvement in design and planning, and greater autonomy in decision-making.
9. **Zero-defects mentality:** a system in place to spot defects as they occur, rather than through inspection and rework.
10. **Flexible manufacturing:** (applicable only to manufacturers) can include just-in-time inventory, cellular manufacturing, design for manufacturability (DFM), statistical process control (SPC), and design of experiments (DOE).
11. **Process improvement:** reduced waste and cycle times in all areas through cross-departmental process analysis.
12. **Measurement:** goal-orientation and zeal for data, with constant performance measurement, often using statistical methods.

Source: Thomas C. Powell, "Total Quality Management as Competitive Advantage," *Strategic Management Journal* 16, no. 1 (January 1995), p. 19.

business performance.[4] An Arthur D. Little study reported that 93 percent of the 500 largest U.S. firms had adopted TQM in some form as of 1992, and a 1998 *Fortune* survey of over 4,000 managers in 15 countries showed that TQM usage was just under 60 percent in 1997. Analysts have credited TQM with helping propel Japanese companies to global prominence in manufacturing quality products. Table 12.1 displays the different kinds of features emphasized by the leading proponents of TQM and the criteria employed in selecting winners of the Malcolm Baldrige Award for Quality.

While TQM concentrates on the production of quality goods and the delivery of excellent customer service, it is more successful when it is extended to employee efforts in all departments—HR, billing, R&D, engineering, accounting and records, and information systems—that may lack less-pressing customer-driven incentives to improve. This is because the institution of best practices and continuous improvement programs involves re-forming the corporate culture and shifting to a total quality/continuous improvement business philosophy that permeates every facet of the organization—see Table 12.2 for the features common to most TQM programs.[5] TQM aims at instilling enthusiasm and commitment to doing things right from top to bottom of the

> Quality improvement processes have now become a globally pervasive part of the fabric of implementing strategies keyed to defect-free manufacture, superior product quality, superior customer service, and total customer satisfaction.

> TQM entails creating a total quality culture bent on continuously improving the performance of every task and value chain activity.

---

[4]Olian and Rynes, "Making Total Quality Work," p. 303.

[5]For a discussion of the shift in work environment and culture that TQM entails, see Robert T. Amsden, Thomas W. Ferratt, and Davida M. Amsden, "TQM: Core Paradigm Changes," *Business Horizons* 39, no. 6 (November–December 1996), pp. 6–14.

organization. It entails a restless search for continuing improvement, the little steps forward each day that the Japanese call *kaizen.* TQM is thus a race without a finish. The managerial objective is to kindle an innate, burning desire in people to use their ingenuity and initiative to progressively improve on how tasks and value chain activities are performed. TQM preaches that there's no such thing as "good enough" and that everyone has a responsibility to participate in continuous improvement. See Illustration Capsule 48, which describes Motorola's success in pursuing its version of TQM and continuous improvement.

> The ability to generate continuous improvements in important value chain activities is a valuable competitive asset and resource strength.

Effective use of TQM/continuous improvement techniques is a valuable asset in a company's resource portfolio—one that can produce important competitive capabilities (in product design, cycle time, cost, product quality and reliability, service, and customer satisfaction) and be a source of competitive advantage.[6] Not only do ongoing incremental improvements add up over time and strengthen organizational capabilities but TQM/continuous improvement programs have hard-to-imitate aspects. While it is relatively easy for rivals to undertake benchmarking, process improvement, and quality training, it is much more difficult for them to implant a total quality culture, do an effective job of empowering employees, and generate deep and genuine management commitment to TQM philosophy and practices throughout their organizations. Successful implementation of TQM initiatives requires a substantial investment of management time and effort; some managers and employees resist TQM, viewing it as ideological or faddish. It is expensive (in terms of training and meetings), and it seldom produces short-term results. The long-term payoff depends heavily on management's success in instilling a culture within which TQM philosophies and practices can thrive.

The Difference between TQM and Process Reengineering   Best practices, business process reengineering, and continuous improvement efforts like TQM all aim at improved efficiency and reduced costs, better product quality, and greater customer satisfaction. The essential difference between business process reengineering and TQM is that reengineering aims at quantum gains on the order of 30 to 50 percent or more whereas total quality programs stress incremental progress, striving for inch-by-inch gains again and again in a never-ending stream. The two approaches to improved performance of value chain activities are not mutually exclusive; it makes sense to use them in tandem. Reengineering can be used first to produce a good basic design that yields dramatic improvements in performing a business process. Total quality programs can then be used as a follow-on to gradually make improvements in the efficiency and effectiveness of the process over time. Such a two-pronged approach to implementing organizational change is like a marathon race where you run the first four laps as fast as you can, then gradually pick up speed the remainder of the way.

> Reengineering seeks one-time quantum improvement; TQM seeks ongoing incremental improvement.

Capturing the Benefits of Best Practice and Continuous Improvement Programs

Research indicates that some companies benefit from reengineering and TQM and some do not.[7] Usually, the biggest beneficiaries are companies that view such programs not

---

[6]Thomas C. Powell, "Total Quality Management as Competitive Advantage," *Strategic Management Journal* 16 (1995), pp. 15–37. See also, Richard M. Hodgetts, "Quality Lessons from America's Baldrige Winners," *Business Horizons* 37, no. 4 (July–August 1994), pp. 74–79; and Richard Reed, David J. Lemak, and Joseph C. Montgomery, "Beyond Process: TQM Content and Firm Performance," *Academy of Management Review* 21, no. 1 (January 1996), pp. 173–202.

[7]See, for example, Gene Hall, Jim Rosenthal, and Judy Wade, "How to Make Reengineering Really Work," *Harvard Business Review* 71, no. 6 (November–December 1993), pp. 119–31.

![illustration capsule logo] illustration capsule 48

Motorola's Approach to Quality and Continuous Improvement

Motorola is rated as one of the world's leading companies in promoting total quality practices that lead to continuous improvement. Motorola implemented a quality improvement program in 1987 and was selected in 1988 as one of the first winners of the Malcolm Baldrige Quality Award. Since then it has further refined its award-winning efforts.

At Motorola, continuous improvement is an ongoing quest and a fundamental part of the company's approach to strategy execution. Motorola was part of a 1987 consortium that conceived the six sigma quality concept—six sigma quality represents fewer than 3.4 defects per million operations. Over the past 11 years, Motorola has implemented the six sigma process with dramatic results:

- Increased productivity an average of 12.3 percent per year.

- Reduced the cost of poor quality by more than 84 percent.

- Eliminated 99.7 percent of in-process defects.

- Saved more than $11 billion in manufacturing costs.

The success of the company's six sigma quality effort led to the development of a Black Belt level of expertise. Today, throughout Motorola, an extensive infrastructure of trained experts leads increasing dedication to virtually defect-free processes. In 1999 and 2000 Motorola's initiatives to improve quality and reduce cycle time took on renewed urgency, both in terms of the manufacturing process and the cycles of creating new products and bringing them to market. The programs broadened companywide and integrated the concept of "delighting" Motorola customers.

Motorola University is a major factor in training employees in quality enhancement and continuous improvement, offering 10 courses in six sigma quality concepts and techniques plus workshops for senior managers and special projects to build application skills.

Another technique Motorola has used to ingrain a total quality culture is a year-long contest highlighting the successes of employee teams from around the world in improving internal company practices, making better products, saving money, pleasing customers, and sharing best practices with other Motorola groups. One year the contest, known as the Total Customer Satisfaction Team Competition, attracted entries from nearly 4,000 teams involving nearly 40,000 of Motorola's 107,000 employees. Preliminary judging eventually reduced the finalists to 24 teams from around the world, all of which were invited to Chicago to make a 12-minute presentation to a panel of 15 senior executives, including the CEO. Twelve teams were awarded gold medals and 12 silver medals.

Source: Based on information in Motorola's 1998 annual report; information posted on the company Web site (www.motorola.com); and Barnaby J. Feder, "At Motorola, Quality Is a Team Sport," *New York Times,* January 21, 1993, pp. C1 and C6.

as ends in themselves but as tools for implementing and executing company strategy more effectively. The skimpiest payoffs from best practices, TQM, and reengineering occur when company managers seize them as something worth trying—novel ideas that could improve things. In most such instances, they result in strategy-blind efforts to simply manage better. There's an important lesson here. Best practices, TQM, and reengineering all need to be seen and used as part of a bigger-picture effort to execute strategy proficiently. Only strategy can point to which value chain activities matter and what performance targets make the most sense. Absent a strategic framework, managers lack the context in which to fix things that really matter to business-unit performance and competitive success.

To get the most from benchmarking, best practices, reengineering, TQM, and related tools for enhancing organizational competence in executing strategy, managers have to start with a clear fix on the indicators of successful strategy execution. Examples of such performance indicators include minimal manufacturing defects, on-time delivery percentages, low overall costs relative to rivals, few customer complaints and survey data indicating high percentages of pleased customers, shorter cycle times, and a higher percentage of revenues coming from recently introduced

> When best practices, reengineering, and TQM are not part of a wider-scale effort to improve strategy execution and business performance, they deteriorate into strategy-blind efforts to manage better.

products. Benchmarking best-in-industry and best-in-world performance of most or all value chain activities provides a realistic basis for setting internal performance milestones and longer-range targets.

Then comes the managerial task of building a total quality culture and instilling the necessary commitment to achieving the targets and performance measures that the strategy requires. The action steps managers can take include:[8]

- Visible, unequivocal, and unyielding commitment to total quality and continuous improvement, including a quality vision and specific, measurable objectives for boosting quality and making continuous improvement.
- Nudging people toward TQ-supportive behaviors by initiating such organizational programs as
  - Screening job applicants rigorously and hiring only those with attitudes and aptitudes right for quality-based performance.
  - Quality training for most employees.
  - Using teams and team-building exercises to reinforce and nurture individual effort (expansion of a TQ culture is facilitated when teams become more cross-functional, multitask, and increasingly self-managed).
  - Recognizing and rewarding individual and team efforts regularly and systematically.
  - Stressing prevention (doing it right the first time), not inspection (instituting ways to correct mistakes).
- Empowering employees so that authority for delivering great service or improving products is in the hands of the doers rather than the overseers.
- Using online systems to provide all relevant parties with the latest best practices and actual experiences with them, thereby speeding the diffusion and adoption of best practices throughout the organization and also allowing them to exchange data and opinions about how to upgrade the prevailing best practices.
- Preaching that performance can, and must, be improved because competitors are not resting on past laurels and customers are always looking for something better.

If the targeted performance measures are appropriate to the strategy and if all organizational members (top executives, middle managers, professional staff, and line employees) buy into the process of continuous improvement, then the work climate will be conducive to proficient strategy execution and good bottom-line business performance.

Strategic Management Principle

Innovative, state-of-the-art support systems can be a basis for competitive advantage if they give a firm capabilities that rivals can't match.

INSTALLING SUPPORT SYSTEMS

Company strategies can't be implemented or executed well without a number of support systems for business operations. Southwest, American, United, Delta, and other major airlines cannot hope to provide world-class passenger service without a computerized reservation system, an accurate and expeditious baggage handling system, and a strong

---

[8]Olian and Rynes, "Making Total Quality Work," pp. 305–6 and 310–11; and Paul S. Goodman and Eric D. Darr, "Exchanging Best Practices Information through Computer-Aided Systems," *Academy of Management Executive* 10, no. 2 (May 1996), p. 7.

aircraft maintenance program. FedEx has internal communication systems that allow it to coordinate its 44,500 vans nationwide to handle an average of 3.2 million packages per day. Its leading-edge flight operations systems allow a single controller to direct as many as 200 FedEx aircraft simultaneously, overriding their flight plans should weather or special emergencies arise. In addition, FedEx has created a series of e-business tools for customers that allow them to ship and track packages online (either at FedEx's Web site or on their own company intranets or Web sites), create address books, review shipping history, generate custom reports, simplify customer billing, reduce internal warehousing and inventory management costs, purchase goods and services from suppliers, and respond faster to changing customer demands. All of FedEx's systems support the company's strategy of next-day package delivery when "it absolutely, positively has to be there" and boost its competitiveness against UPS, Airborne Express, and the U.S. Postal Service.

Otis Elevator has a sophisticated support system called OtisLine to coordinate its maintenance efforts nationwide.[9] Trained operators take all trouble calls, input critical information on a computer screen, and dispatch people directly via a beeper system to the local trouble spot. From the trouble-call inputs, problem patterns can be identified nationally and the information communicated to design and manufacturing personnel, allowing them to quickly alter design specifications or manufacturing procedures when needed to correct recurring problems. Also, much of the information needed for repairs is provided directly from faulty elevators through internally installed microcomputer monitors, further lowering outage time.

Arthur Andersen uses the Internet and digital technology to link more than 70,000 people in 382 offices in 81 countries. Its Knowledge Xchange system has data, voice, and video capabilities and includes an electronic bulletin board for posting customer problems, allowing personnel from all over the world to organize around a customer's problem. The system also has the capability to collect, index, and distribute files containing information on particular subjects, customers, solutions, and company resources.[10] Knowledge Xchange thus helps Andersen personnel capture the lessons learned in the company's daily work and research and makes those lessons available to all other Andersen personnel 24 hours a day. Wal-Mart's computers transmit daily sales data to Wrangler, a supplier of blue jeans; Wrangler then uses a model that interprets the data, and software applications that act on these interpretations, in order to ship specific quantities of specific sizes and colors to specific stores from specific warehouses—the system lowers logistics and inventory costs and leads to fewer stockouts.[11] Domino's Pizza has computerized systems at each outlet to facilitate ordering, inventory, payroll, cash flow, and work control functions, thereby freeing managers to spend more time on supervision, customer service, and business development activities.[12] Most telephone companies, electric utilities, and TV broadcasting systems have online monitoring systems to spot transmission problems within seconds and increase the reliability of their services. At

[9]James Brian Quinn, *Intelligent Enterprise* (New York: Free Press, 1992), p. 186.

[10]James Brian Quinn, Philip Anderson, and Sydney Finkelstein, "Leveraging Intellect," *Academy of Management Executive* 10, no. 3 (November 1996), p. 9.

[11]Stephan H. Haeckel and Richard L. Nolan, "Managing by Wire," *Harvard Business Review* 75, no. 5 (September–October 1993), p. 129.

[12]Quinn, *Intelligent Enterprise,* p. 181.

illustration capsule 49
The Rush to Install E-Commerce Support Systems

Companies everywhere are rushing to install the support systems they need to participate in one or more segments of the rapidly expanding Internet economy and enable better execution of their business strategies. Investment in Internet-related support systems is occurring in a host of different arenas:

- Building attractive, user-friendly Web sites and installing adequate and reliable server capacity.

- Creating electronic data interchange capabilities, starting with the details of sales to customers and flowing real-time information all the way back through company supply chains to the relevant suppliers.

- Developing software and systems to gather and analyze data from online sales, thus enabling "real-time market research" and rapid response to shifting customer demand.

- Installing software and systems to handle buyer credit card payments (in the case of business-to-consumer transactions) and electronic payment of invoices (in the case of business-to-business transactions).

- Installing the hardware systems and software to handle and tie together such "back-office" functions as automated order processing and invoicing for both customers and suppliers, accounts receivable and other customer/supplier-related accounting functions, management of both materials and finished goods inventories, and distribution logistics. Companies such as Computer Associates, Oracle, Ariba, Siebel Systems, i2 Technologies, and Germany's SAP (the world's largest) supply complex software allowing companies to weave together such basic internal operations as procurement, accounting, manufacturing, shipping, order processing, and all interactions with customers.

- Putting warehousing and shipping facilities and systems in place to follow through on delivering customers' online orders in a timely and economical manner.

- Installing software and systems to enable customers to track their orders online and to get online technical support and customer service.

- Connecting more employees to the Internet and company intranets so that (1) e-mail can be used as the prime means of internal and external communication, (2) employees can readily access needed databases, (3) company personnel can engage in online collaboration with external allies and partners, (4) communications with target customer groups can be optimized, and (5) internal activities can be tied together with software and coordinated easily and more quickly.

Rapidly advancing Internet and e-commerce technologies are revolutionizing the manner in which company operations are conducted internally, as well as the manner in which business is conducted externally—with suppliers and customers and alliance partners. Because this revolution is only in its early stages, it is difficult to forecast the outcome, except to say that it is generating major gains in productivity, lowering costs, and spawning an overhaul of daily operating practices that no business can afford to ignore. There can be no doubt that cutting-edge e-commerce support systems can greatly enrich a company's long-term competitiveness and strategy execution capabilities.

Mrs. Fields Cookies, computer systems monitor hourly sales and suggest product mix changes, promotional tactics, or operating adjustments to improve customer response. Many companies have installed software systems on their company intranets to catalog best practices information and promote faster best practices transfer and implementation organizationwide.[13]

Well-conceived, state-of-the-art support systems not only facilitate better strategy execution but also can strengthen organizational capabilities enough to provide a

---

[13]Such systems speed organizational learning by providing fast, efficient communication, creating an organizational memory for collecting and retaining best practice information, and permitting people all across the organization to exchange information and updated solutions. See Goodman and Darr, "Exchanging Best Practices Information through Computer-Aided Systems," pp. 7–17.

competitive edge over rivals. For example, a company with a differentiation strategy based on superior quality has added capability if it has systems for training personnel in quality techniques, tracking product quality at each production step, and ensuring that all goods shipped meet quality standards. A company striving to be a low-cost provider is competitively stronger if it has a benchmarking system that identifies opportunities to implement cost-saving best practices and drive costs out of the business. Fast-growing companies get an important assist from having the internal capabilities in place to recruit and train new employees in large numbers and from investing in high-capacity systems and infrastructure that give them the capability to handle rapid growth as it occurs. It is nearly always better to put infrastructure and support systems in place ahead of the time they are actually needed than to be caught short and have to scramble to catch up to customer demand. In businesses such as public accounting and management consulting where large numbers of professional staff need cutting-edge technical know-how, companies need well-functioning systems for training and retraining employees regularly and keeping them supplied with up-to-date information. Companies that rely on empowered customer service employees to act promptly and creatively in pleasing customers have to have state-of-the-art information systems that put essential data at employees' fingertips and give them instantaneous communications capabilities.

> In today's business environment, competitive advantage goes to those firms most able to mobilize information and create systems to use knowledge effectively.

Installing Adequate Information Systems, Performance Tracking, and Controls

Accurate information is an essential guide to action. Every organization needs systems for gathering and storing data, tracking key performance indicators, identifying and diagnosing problems, and reporting strategy-critical information. Telephone companies have elaborate information systems to measure signal quality, connection times, interrupts, wrong connections, billing errors, and other measures of reliability. To track and manage the quality of passenger service, airlines have information systems to monitor gate delays, on-time departures and arrivals, baggage handling times, lost baggage complaints, stockouts on meals and drinks, overbookings, and maintenance delays and failures. Virtually all companies now provide customer-contact personnel with instant electronic access to customer databases so that they can respond effectively to customer inquiries and personalize customer services. Companies that rely on empowered employees need measurement and feedback systems to monitor the performance of empowered workers and guide them to act within specified limits so that unwelcome surprises are avoided.[14]

> Accurate, timely information allows organizational members to monitor progress and take corrective action promptly.

The age of real-time information spawned by the Internet allows company managers to monitor implementation initiatives and daily operations, steering them to a successful conclusion in case early steps don't produce the expected progress or things seem to be drifting off course. Information systems need to cover five broad areas: (1) customer data, (2) operations data, (3) employee data, (4) supplier/partner/collaborative ally data, and (5) financial performance data. All key strategic performance indicators have to be measured as often as practical. Many retail companies generate daily sales reports for each store and maintain up-to-the-minute inventory and sales records on each

---

[14]For a discussion of the need for putting appropriate boundaries on the actions of empowered employees and possible control and monitoring systems that can be used, see Robert Simons, "Control in an Age of Empowerment," *Harvard Business Review* 73 (March–April 1995), pp. 80–88.

Effective companies gather, analyze, and communicate data and information at Internet speed.

item. Manufacturing plants typically generate daily production reports and track labor productivity on every shift. Many retailers and manufacturers have online data systems connecting them with their suppliers that monitor the status of inventories, process orders and invoices, and track shipments. Monthly profit-and-loss statements and monthly statistical summaries, long the norm, are fast being replaced by daily statistical updates and even up-to-the-minute performance monitoring that electronic technology makes possible. Such diagnostic control systems allow managers to detect problems early, intervene as appropriate, and adjust either the strategy or how it is being implemented. Early experiences are sometimes difficult to assess, but they yield the first hard data and should be closely scrutinized as a basis for corrective action. Ideally, data analysis procedures should flag big or unusual variances from preset performance standards.

Statistical information gives the strategy implementer a feel for the numbers; reports and meetings provide a feel for new developments and problems; and personal contacts add a feel for the people dimension. All are good barometers of overall performance and good indicators of which things are on and off track. Managers have to identify problem areas and deviations from plan before they can take actions either to improve implementation or fine-tune strategy.

Exercising Adequate Controls over Empowered Employees   A major problem facing today's managers is how to ensure that the actions of empowered subordinates stay within acceptable bounds and don't expose the organization to excessive risk.[15] There are dangers to leaving employees to their own devices in meeting performance standards. Media stories abound with reports of employees whose decisions or behavior went awry, sometimes costing a company huge sums or producing lawsuits aside from just generating embarrassing publicity. Managers can't spend all their time making sure that everyone's decisions and behavior are between the white lines, yet they have a clear responsibility to institute adequate checks and balances and protect against unwelcome surprises. One of the main purposes of diagnostic control systems to track performance is to relieve managers of the burden of constant monitoring and give them time for other issues. But diagnostic controls are only part of the answer. Another valuable lever of control is establishing clear boundaries on behavior without telling employees what to do. Strictly prescribed rules and procedures that leave no room for discretion can discourage employee creativity and turn work into pure drudgery. It is better to set forth what not to do, allowing freedom of action within specified limits. Another control device is face-to-face meetings to review information, assess progress and performance, reiterate expectations, and discuss the next action steps.

When a company relies on team-based organizations and self-managed work groups, one of the biggest payoffs is that teams substitute peer-based control for hierarchical control of work.[16] This is because team members feel accountable and responsible for the success and performance of the whole team and tend to be relatively intolerant of a team member's behavior or actions that weaken team performance or put team accomplishments at risk. Because peer evaluation is so powerful a control device, companies organized on the basis of teams find that they can remove some layers of the management hierarchy, avoiding the costs of having people whose job it is to

---

[15]Ibid. See also, David C. Band and Gerald Scanlan, "Strategic Control through Core Competencies," *Long Range Planning* 28, no. 2 (April 1995), pp. 102–14.

[16]Jeffrey Pfeffer and John F. Veiga, "Putting People First for Organizational Success," *Academy of Management Executive* 13, no. 2 (May 1999), pp. 41–42.

watch other people do the work. This is especially true when a company has the information systems capability to closely monitor team performance.

DESIGNING STRATEGY-SUPPORTIVE REWARD SYSTEMS

It is important for both organization subunits and individuals to be enthusiastically committed to executing strategy and achieving performance targets. Company managers typically try to enlist organizationwide commitment to carrying out the strategic plan by motivating people and rewarding them for good performance. A manager has to do more than just talk to everyone about how important new strategic practices and performance targets are to the organization's future well-being. No matter how inspiring, talk seldom commands people's best efforts for long. *To get employees' sustained, energetic commitment, management has to be resourceful in designing and using motivational incentives—both monetary and nonmonetary.* The more a manager understands what motivates subordinates and the more he or she relies on motivational incentives as a tool for implementing strategy, the greater will be employees' commitment to good day in, day out execution of the company's strategic plan.

While financial incentives (salary increases, performance bonuses, stock options, and retirement packages) are the core component of most companies' reward systems, managers normally make extensive use of such nonmonetary carrot-and-stick incentives as frequent words of praise (or constructive criticism), special recognition at company gatherings or in the company newsletter, more (or less) job security, stimulating assignments, opportunities to transfer to attractive locations, increased (or decreased) job control and decision-making autonomy, and rapid promotion (or the risk of being "sidelined" in a routine or dead-end job). Effective managers are further alert to the motivating power of giving people a chance to be part of something exciting, giving them an opportunity for greater personal satisfaction, challenging them with ambitious performance targets, creating a stimulating and engaging work environment, and the intangible bonds of group acceptance and a "family" work environment. But the motivation and reward structure has to be used *creatively* and tied directly to achieving the performance outcomes necessary for good strategy execution.

> The role of the reward system is to align the well-being of organization members with realizing the company's vision, so that organization members benefit by helping the company execute its strategy competently and fully satisfy customers.

Strategy-Supportive Motivational Practices

Successful strategy implementers inspire and challenge employees to do their best. They get employees to buy into the strategy and commit to making it work. They structure individual efforts into teams and work groups in order to facilitate an exchange of ideas and foster a climate of support. They allow employees to participate in making decisions about how to perform their jobs, and they try to make jobs interesting and satisfying and the company's whole work climate engaging and fun. They devise strategy-supportive motivational approaches and use them effectively. Consider some actual examples:

> One of the biggest strategy implementing challenges is to employ motivational techniques that build wholehearted commitment and winning attitudes among employees.

- Several Japanese automobile producers, believing that providing employment security is a valuable contributor to worker productivity and company loyalty, elect not to lay off factory workers but instead put them out in the field to sell vehicles when business slacks off for a period. Mazda, for example, during a sales downturn in Japan in the 1980s, shifted factory workers to selling its models door-to-door, a common practice in Japan. At the end of the year, when awards were given out to the best salespeople, Mazda found that its top 10 salespeople were all factory workers, partly because they were able to explain the product effectively. When business picked up and the factory workers returned to the plant, their experiences in talking to customers yielded useful ideas in improving the features and styling of Mazda's product line.[17] Southwest Airlines, FedEx, Lands' End, and Harley-Davidson (all companies that have been listed among the 100 best companies to work for in America), along with over a dozen other companies on the same list, have also instituted no-layoff policies and use employment security as both a positive motivator and a means of reinforcing good strategy execution.[18] At Southwest Airlines (ranked second on the 1999 list), for example, the company's partnership with employees is a critical component of its strategy to make flying a fun experience for passengers and to have a more productive workforce that helps it contain costs and keep its fares lower than competitors. Southwest management believes that its no-layoff policy keeps workers from fearing that by boosting their productivity they will work themselves out of their jobs.[19]

- More than 35 of the 58 publicly held companies on *Fortune*'s 1999 list of the 100 best companies to work for in America (including Cisco Systems, Procter & Gamble, Merck, Charles Schwab, General Mills, Amgen, and Tellabs) provide stock options to all employees. Tellabs gives every employee options on 200 shares every year. Having employee-owners who share in a company's success is widely viewed as a positive motivator, most especially when a company's stock is rising sharply and making employees wealthy—as has been the case at numerous dot-com companies that have gone public in the last several years. A big majority of Internet companies have found it necessary to use lucrative stock options to attract the kinds of talented, innovative, energetic, committed employees needed to run and win the race for leadership in some niche of the Internet economy.

- Nordstrom typically pays its retail salespeople an hourly wage higher than the prevailing rates paid by other department store chains, plus it pays them a commission on each sale. Spurred by a culture that encourages salespeople to go all out to satisfy customers, to exercise their own best judgment, and to seek out and promote new fashion ideas, Nordstrom salespeople often earn twice the average incomes of sales employees at competing stores.[20] Nordstrom's rules for employees are simple: "Rule #1: Use your good judgment in all situations. There will be no additional rules."

- Cisco Systems offers on-the-spot bonuses of up to $2,000 for exceptional performance.

- Microsoft, realizing that software creation is a highly individual effort, interviews hundreds of prospective programmers to find the few most suited to write code for its programs. It places new recruits onto teams of three to seven people under experienced mentors to work on the next generation of software programs. While project team members can expect to put in 60- to 80-hour workweeks to meet

---

[17]Ibid., p. 62.

[18]*Fortune*'s 1997 and 1999 lists of the 100 best companies to work for in America—see the January 12, 1998, and January 10, 2000, issues.

[19]Pfeffer and Veiga, "Putting People First for Organizational Success," p. 40.

[20]Jeffrey Pfeffer, "Producing Sustainable Competitive Advantage through the Effective Management of People," *Academy of Management Executive* 9, no. 1 (February 1995), pp. 59–60.

deadlines for getting new programs to market, the best programmers seek out and stay with Microsoft largely because they believe that Microsoft will determine where the industry moves in the future and that working for Microsoft will allow them to share in the excitement, challenge, and rewards of working on this frontier (and only partly because of Microsoft's very attractive pay scales and lucrative stock option program).[21]

- Lincoln Electric, a company deservedly famous for its piecework pay scheme and incentive bonus plan, rewards individual productivity by paying workers for each good piece produced. Workers have to correct quality problems on their own time—defects can be traced to the worker who caused them. The piecework plan motivates workers to pay attention to both quality and volume produced. In addition, the company sets aside a substantial portion of its profits above a specified base for worker bonuses. To determine bonus size, Lincoln Electric rates each worker on four equally important performance measures: dependability, quality, output, and ideas and cooperation. The higher a worker's merit rating, the higher the incentive bonus earned; the highest rated workers in good profit years receive bonuses of as much as 110 percent of their piecework compensation.[22]

- At a California automobile assembly plant run by Toyota, there's a big emphasis on symbolic egalitarianism. All employees (managers and workers alike) wear blue smocks, there are no reserved spaces in the employee parking lot, there's no executive dining room—everyone eats in the same plant cafeteria, and there are only two job classifications for skilled trades and only one job classification for all other workers.[23] Many companies are discovering that reducing the status distinctions that separate individuals and groups makes organization members feel important and raises their commitment.

- Monsanto, FedEx, AT&T, Whole Foods Markets, Advanced Micro Devices, W.L. Gore & Associates, and many other companies have tapped into the motivational power of self-managed teams and achieved very good results. Team performance is enhanced because team members put considerable peer pressure on co-workers to pull their weight and help achieve team goals and expectations. At W.L. Gore (a regular member on annual listings of the 100 best companies to work for), each team member's compensation is based on other team members' rankings of his or her contribution to the enterprise.

- GE Medical Systems uses a program called Quick Thanks! in which an employee can nominate any colleague to receive a $25 gift certificate redeemable at certain stores and restaurants in appreciation of a job well done. Employees often hand out the award personally to deserving co-workers (in a recent 12-month period over 10,000 Quick Thanks! awards were presented). Peers prove to be tougher than executives in praising colleagues; for the recipient, the approving acknowledgment of co-workers matters more than the $25.[24]

The above approaches to motivation, compensation, and people management (and those presented in Illustration Capsule 50) accentuate the positive; others blend positive

---

[21]Quinn, Anderson, and Finkelstein, "Leveraging Intellect," p. 8.

[22]Pfeffer, "Producing Sustainable Competitive Advantage through the Effective Management of People," p. 59.

[23]Ibid., p. 63.

[24]Steven Kerr, "Risky Business: The New Pay Game," *Fortune,* July 22, 1996, p. 95.

illustration capsule 50

Motivation and Reward Techniques of "Best Practice" Companies

Companies have been innovative in coming up with all kinds of novel motivational and reward practices to help create a work environment that supports strategy execution. Here's a glimpse of what some companies believe are best practices:

- *Providing attractive perks and benefits*—The various options here include on-site child care, on-site gym facilities and massage therapists, vacation and getaway opportunities at company-owned recreational facilities (beach houses, ranches, resort condos), personal concierge services, subsidized cafeterias and free lunches, casual dress every day, personnel travel services, paid sabbaticals, profit-sharing plans, maternity leaves, paid leaves to care for ill family members, telecommuting, compressed workweeks (four 10-hour days, instead of five 8-hour days), reduced summer hours, college scholarships for childen, on-the-spot bonuses for exceptional performance, and relocation services.

- *Making sure that the ideas and suggestions of employees are valued and respected*—Research indicates that the moves of many companies to push decision making down and empower employees increases employee motivation and satisfaction, as well as boosting their productivity. The use of self-managed teams has much the same effect.

- *Creating a work atmosphere where there is genuine sincerity, caring, and mutual respect among workers and between management and employees*—Companies where people are on a first-name basis and there is strong camaraderie are increasingly the rule because of the beneficial impact on the work climate.

- *Providing inspiring leadership and making employees feel they are a part of doing something very worthwhile in a larger social sense*—Jobs with noble purpose tend to turn employees on. At Medtronic, Merck,

and most other pharmaceutical companies, it is the notion of helping sick people get well and restoring patients to full life; at Whole Foods Market (a natural-foods grocery chain), it is improving human health and nutrition; at many Internet companies, it is creating a global village and revolutionizing the world landscape.

- *Sharing information with employees about financial performance, strategy, operational measures, market conditions, and competitors' actions*—This conveys to people that they are trusted and that there are no secrets. Keeping employees in the dark denies them information useful to performing their job, prevents them from being "students of the business," and usually turns employees off.

- *Having "knockout facilities"*—An impressive corporate compound for employees to work in usually has decidedly positive effects on morale and productivity.

- *Relying on promotion from within whenever possible*—This practice helps bind workers to their employer and employers to their workers, plus it is an incentive for good performance. Promotion from within also helps ensure that people in positions of responsibility actually know something about the business, technology, and operations they are managing.

- *Being flexible in how the company approaches people management (motivation, compensation, recognition, recruitment) in multinational, multicultural environments*—Managers and employees in countries whose customs, habits, values, and business practices vary from those at the "home office" often become frustrated with insistence on consistent people management practices worldwide. But the one area where consistency is essential is conveying the message that the organization values people of all races and cultural backgrounds and that discrimination on the basis of race, gender, or culture will not be tolerated.

Sources: Articles in *Fortune* on the 100 best companies to work for (1998, 1999, and 2000); Jeffrey Pfeffer and John F. Veiga, "Putting People First for Organizational Success," *Academy of Management Executive* 13, no. 2 (May 1999), pp. 37–45; and Linda K. Stroh and Paula M. Caligiuri, "Increasing Global Competitiveness through Effective People Management," *Journal of World Business* 33, no. 1 (Spring 1998), pp. 1–16.

and negative features. At companies such as McKinsey & Company and other management consulting firms, General Electric, the leading public accounting firms, and other companies that put a premium on high performance, there's an "up-or-out" policy—managers and professionals whose performance is considered marginal or not good enough to warrant promotion are denied bonuses and stock options and systematically weeded out. Some companies, despite having attractive pay packages, expect employees to put in long hours (nights and weekends), put them under the pressure of heavy workloads and tight deadlines, and push them hard to achieve ambitious stretch objectives. Business heads and other senior managers in underperforming organization units are usually under the gun to boost performance to acceptable levels or risk being replaced.

Balancing Positive and Negative Motivational Considerations   If an organization's motivational approach and reward structure induces too much stress, internal competitiveness, and job insecurity, the impact on work force morale and strategy execution can be counterproductive. Evidence shows that a manager's push for improving strategy execution should incorporate more positive than negative motivational elements because when cooperation is positively enlisted and rewarded, rather than strong-armed by orders and threats (implicit or explicit) of retribution, people tend to respond with more enthusiasm, effort, creativity, and initiative. Yet it is unwise to completely eliminate pressure for good individual and group performance and the stress and anxiety it evokes. There is no evidence that a no-pressure work environment leads to superior strategy execution or sustained high performance. As the CEO of a major bank put it, "There's a deliberate policy here to create a level of anxiety. Winners usually play like they're one touchdown behind."[25] *High-performing organizations need a cadre of ambitious people who relish the opportunity to climb the ladder of success, love a challenge, thrive in a performance-oriented environment, and find some competition and pressure useful to satisfy their own drives for personal recognition, accomplishment, and self-satisfaction.* Unless meaningful compensation, career, and job satisfaction consequences are associated with successfully implementing strategic initiatives and hitting strategic performance targets, few people will respond to top management urgings for dedicated effort to execute strategic initiatives and achieve the company's vision and objectives.

> Positive motivational approaches generally work better than negative ones, but completely eliminating pressure for good performance lacks merit.

Linking the Reward System to Strategically Relevant Performance Outcomes

The most dependable way to keep people focused on organizational objectives and to make achieving these performance targets a way of life up and down the organization is to *generously* reward and recognize individuals and groups who achieve their assigned performance targets and deny rewards and recognition to those who don't. *The use of incentives and rewards is the single most powerful tool management has to win strong employee commitment to diligent, competent strategy execution.* Failure to use these tools wisely and powerfully weakens the entire strategy implementation/execution process. Decisions on salary increases, incentive compensation, promotions, key assignments, and the ways and means of awarding praise and recognition are potent attention-getting, commitment-generating devices. Such decisions seldom escape the closest employee scrutiny, saying more about what is expected and who is considered to be doing a good job than any other factor. A company's system of incentives and rewards thus ends up being the vehicle by which its strategy is emotionally ratified in the form of real workforce commitment. Performance-based incentives make it in employees' self-interest to exert

> **Strategic Management Principle**
> A properly designed reward structure is management's most powerful tool for mobilizing organizational commitment to successful strategy execution.

[25]As quoted in John P. Kotter and James L. Heskett, *Corporate Culture and Performance* (New York: Free Press, 1992), p. 91.

their best efforts to achieve strategy-critical performance targets and to execute the strategy competently.[26]

The key to creating a reward system that promotes good strategy execution is to make strategically relevant measures of performance *the dominating basis* for designing incentives, evaluating individual and group efforts, and handing out rewards. Strategy-driven performance targets have to be established for every organization unit, every manager, every team or work group, and perhaps every employee—targets that measure whether strategy execution is progressing satisfactorily. If the company's strategy is to be a low-cost provider, the incentive system must reward actions and achievements that result in lower costs. If the company has a differentiation strategy predicated on superior quality and service, the incentive system must reward such outcomes as zero defects, infrequent need for product repair, low numbers of customer complaints, and speedy order processing and delivery. If a company's growth is predicated on a strategy of new product innovation, incentives should be tied to factors such as the percentages of revenues and profits coming from newly introduced products.

A number of prominent companies—Southwest Airlines, W. L. Gore & Associates, Bank One, Nucor Steel, Lincoln Electric, Wal-Mart, Remington Products, and Mary Kay Cosmetics—owe much of their success to a set of incentives and rewards that induce people to do the things critical to good strategy execution and competing effectively in the marketplace. At Bank One (one of the 10 largest U.S. banks and also one of the most profitable based on return on assets), operating in a manner that produces consistently high levels of customer satisfaction makes a big competitive difference in how well the company fares against rivals; customer satisfaction ranks high on Bank One's list of strategic priorities. To enhance employee commitment to the task of pleasing customers, Bank One ties the pay scales in each branch office to that branch's customer satisfaction rating—the higher the branch's ratings, the higher that branch's pay scales. By shifting from a theme of equal pay for equal work to one of equal pay for equal performance, Bank One has focused the attention of branch employees on the task of pleasing, even delighting, their customers.

Nucor's strategy is to be *the* low-cost producer of steel products. Because labor costs are a significant fraction of total cost in the steel business, successful implementation of Nucor's low-cost leadership strategy entails achieving lower labor costs per ton of steel than competitors'. Nucor management designed an incentive system to promote high worker productivity and drive labor costs per ton below rivals'. Management organized each plant's workforce into production teams (each assigned to perform particular functions) and, working with the teams, has established weekly production targets for each team. Base pay scales are set at levels comparable to wages for similar manufacturing jobs in the local areas where Nucor has plants, but workers can earn a 1 percent bonus for each 1 percent that their output exceeds target levels. If a production team exceeds its weekly production target by 10 percent, team members receive a 10 percent bonus in their next paycheck; if a team exceeds its quota by 20 percent, team members earn a 20 percent bonus. Bonuses are paid every two weeks based on the prior two weeks' actual production levels measured against the targets. Nucor's piece-rate incentive plan has resulted in labor productivity levels 10 to 20 percent above the average of the unionized workforces of large, integrated steel producers like U.S. Steel and Bethlehem Steel, given Nucor a cost advantage over most rivals, and made Nucor workers among the best-paid in the U.S. steel industry.

---

[26]For a countervailing view on the merits of incentives, see Alfie Kohn, "Why Incentive Plans Cannot Work," *Harvard Business Review* 71, no. 6 (September–October 1993), pp. 54–63.

illustration capsule 51
The Folly of the Reward System in the Claims Division of a Large Insurance Company

The past reward practices of the health care claims division of a large insurance company demonstrate the folly of hoping for one behavior but rewarding another behavior. Seeking to encourage employees to be accurate in paying surgical claims, the company tracked the number of returned checks and letters of complaint filed by policyholders. However, employees in the claims department frequently found it hard to tell from physician filings which of two surgical procedures, with different allowable benefits, was performed. Since writing to the physicians for clarification greatly reduced the number of claims paid within two days of receipt (a performance standard the company stressed), the workers' norm quickly became "When in doubt, pay it out." Thus, while it appeared that employee accuracy increased (since fewer policyholders complained about nonpayment), the company lost money to overpayment of claims.

This practice was made worse by the firm's reward system, which called for merit increases of 5 percent for "outstanding" employees, 4 percent for "above-average" employees (most employees not rated as outstanding were designated as above average), and 3 percent for all other employees. Many employees were indifferent to the potential of an extra 1 percent reward for avoiding overpayment errors and working hard enough to be rated as outstanding.

However, employees were not indifferent to a rule that stated that employees forfeited their entire merit raise at the next six-month merit review if they were absent or late for work three or more times in any six-month period. The company, while hoping for performance, was rewarding attendance. But the absent-late rule was not as stringent as it might seem because the company counted the number of "times" rather than the number of "days"—a one-week absence counted the same as a one-day absence. A worker in danger of getting a third absence within a six-month period could sometimes stay away from work during the second absence until the first absence was over six months old; the limiting factor was that after a certain number of days the worker was paid sickness benefits instead of his or her regular pay. For workers with 20 or more years of service, the company provided tax-free sickness benefits of 90 percent of normal salary.

Source: Steven Kerr, "On the Folly of Rewarding A While Hoping for B," *Academy of Management Executive* 9, no. 1 February 1995), p.11.

As the example in Illustration Capsule 51 so vividly demonstrates, compensating and rewarding organization members on criteria not directly related to successful strategy execution undermines organization performance and condones the diversion of time and energy in less strategically relevant directions.

The Importance of Basing Incentives on Achieving Results, Not on Performing Assigned Functions

To create a strategy-supportive system of rewards and incentives, a company must emphasize rewarding people for accomplishing results, not for just dutifully performing assigned functions. Focusing jobholders' attention and energy on what to *achieve* as opposed to what to *do* makes the work environment results-oriented. It is flawed management to tie incentives and rewards to satisfactory performance of duties and activities in hopes that the by-products will be the desired business outcomes and company achievements.[27] In any job, performing assigned tasks is not equivalent to achieving intended outcomes. Working hard, staying busy, and diligently attending to assigned duties do not guarantee results. (As any student knows, just because an instructor teaches and students are going to class

> It is folly to reward one outcome in hopes of getting another outcome.

---

[27]See Steven Kerr, "On the Folly of Rewarding A While Hoping for B," *Academy of Management Executive* 9, no. 1 (February 1995), pp. 7–14; Kerr, "Risky Business: The New Pay Game," pp. 93–96; and Doran Twer, "Linking Pay to Business Objectives," *Journal of Business Strategy* 15, no. 4 (July–August 1994), pp. 15–18.

doesn't mean students are learning. Teaching and going to class are activities, and learning is a result. The enterprise of education would no doubt take on a different character if teachers were rewarded for the result of what is learned instead of the activity of teaching.)

The whats to accomplish—the performance measures on which rewards and incentives are based—must be tightly connected to the requirements of successful strategy execution and good company performance.

Incentive compensation for top executives is typically tied to company profitability (earnings growth, return on equity investment, return on total assets, economic value added), the company's stock price performance, and perhaps such measures as market share, product quality, or customer satisfaction that indicate the company's market position, overall competitiveness, and future prospects have improved. However, incentives for department heads, teams, and individual workers may be tied to performance outcomes more closely related to their strategic area of responsibility. In manufacturing, incentive compensation may be tied to unit manufacturing costs, on-time production and shipping, defect rates, the number and extent of work stoppages due to labor disagreements and equipment breakdowns, and so on. In sales and marketing, there may be incentives for achieving dollar sales or unit volume targets, market share, sales penetration of each target customer group, the fate of newly introduced products, the frequency of customer complaints, the number of new accounts acquired, and customer satisfaction. Which performance measures to base incentive compensation on depends on the situation—the priority placed on various financial and strategic objectives, the requirements for strategic and competitive success, and what specific results are needed in different facets of the business to keep strategy execution on track.

Guidelines for Designing Incentive Compensation Systems   The concepts and company experiences discussed above yield the following prescriptive guidelines for creating an incentive compensation system to help drive successful strategy execution:

1. *The performance payoff must be a major, not minor, piece of the total compensation package.* Payoffs must be at least 10 to 12 percent of base salary to have much impact. Incentives that amount to 20 percent or more of total compensation are big attention-getters, likely to really drive individual or team effort; incentives amounting to less than 5 percent of total compensation have comparatively weak motivational impact. Moreover, the payoff for high-performing individuals and teams must be substantially greater than the payoff for average performers, and the payoff for average performers substantially bigger than for below-average performers.

2. *The incentive plan should extend to all managers and all workers, not just top management.* It is a gross miscalculation to expect that lower-level managers and employees will work their hardest to hit performance targets just so a few senior executives can get lucrative rewards.

3. *The reward system must be administered with scrupulous care and fairness.* If performance standards are set unrealistically high or if individual/group performance evaluations are not accurate and well documented, dissatisfaction with the system will overcome any positive benefits.

4. *The incentives must be tightly linked to achieving only those performance targets spelled out in the strategic plan.* Incentives should not include factors that get thrown in because they are thought to be nice occurrences. Performance evaluation based on factors not tightly related to the strategy signal that either the strategic

plan is incomplete (because important performance targets were left out) or management's real agenda is something other than what was stated in the strategic plan.

5. *The performance targets each individual is expected to achieve should involve outcomes that the individual can personally affect.* The role of incentives is to enhance individual commitment and channel behavior in beneficial directions. This role is not well served when the performance measures an individual is judged by are outside his or her arena of influence.

6. *Keep the time between the performance review and payment of the reward short.* A lengthy interval between review and payment breeds discontent and works against reinforcing cause and effect.

7. *Make liberal use of nonmonetary rewards; don't rely solely on monetary rewards.* When used properly, money is a great motivator, but there are potent advantages to be gained from praise, special recognition, handing out plum assignments, and so on.

8. *Absolutely avoid skirting the system to find ways to reward nonperformers.* It is debatable whether exceptions should be made for people who've tried hard, gone the extra mile, yet still come up short because of circumstances beyond their control—arguments can be made either way. The problem with making exceptions for unknowable, uncontrollable, or unforeseeable circumstances is that once good excuses start to creep into justifying rewards for nonperformers, the door is open for all kinds of reasons why actual performance failed to match targeted performance. In short, people at all levels have to be held accountable for carrying out their assigned parts of the strategic plan, and they have to know their rewards are based on the caliber of their strategic accomplishments.

Once the incentives are designed, they have to be communicated and explained. Everybody needs to understand how their incentive compensation is calculated and how individual/group performance targets contribute to organizational performance targets. Moreover, the reasons for anyone's failure or deviations from targets have to be explored fully to determine whether the causes are attributable to poor individual/group performance or to circumstances beyond the control of those responsible. The pressure to achieve the targeted strategic and financial performance and continuously improve on strategy execution should be unrelenting. A "no excuses" standard has to prevail.[28] But with the pressure to perform must come deserving and meaningful rewards. Without an ample payoff, the system breaks down, and the strategy implementer is left with the unworkable option of barking orders and pleading for compliance.

Performance-Based Incentives and Rewards in Multinational Enterprises

In some foreign countries, incentive pay runs counter to local customs and cultural norms. Professor Steven Kerr cites the time he lectured an executive education class on the need for more performance-based pay and a Japanese manager protested, "You shouldn't bribe your children to do their homework, you shouldn't bribe your wife to prepare dinner, and you shouldn't bribe your employees to work for the company."[29] Singling out individuals and commending them for unusually good

---

[28]Tom Peters and Nancy Austin, *A Passion for Excellence* (New York: Random House, 1985), p. xix.

[29]Kerr, "Risky Business: The New Pay Game," p. 96. For a more general criticism of why performance incentives are a bad idea, see Kohn, "Why Incentive Plans Cannot Work," pp. 54–63.

effort can also be a problem; Japanese culture considers public praise of an individual an affront to the harmony of the group. In some countries, employees have a preference for nonmonetary rewards—more leisure time, important titles, access to vacation villages, and nontaxable perks. Thus, multinational companies have to build some degree of flexibility into the design of incentives and rewards in order to accommodate cross-cultural traditions and preferences.

key | points

A change in strategy nearly always calls for budget reallocations. Reworking the budget to make it more strategy-supportive is a crucial part of the implementation process because every organization unit needs to have the people, equipment, facilities, and other resources to carry out its part of the strategic plan (but no more than what it really needs). Implementing a new strategy often entails shifting resources from one area to another—downsizing units that are overstaffed and overfunded, upsizing those more critical to strategic success, and killing projects and activities that are no longer justified.

Anytime a company alters its strategy, managers are well advised to review existing policies and operating procedures, deleting or revising those that are out of sync and deciding if additional ones are needed. Prescribing new or freshly revised policies and operating procedures aids the task of implementation (1) by providing top-down guidance to operating managers, supervisory personnel, and employees regarding how certain things need to be done; (2) by putting boundaries on independent actions and decisions; (3) by promoting consistency in how particular strategy-critical activities are performed in geographically scattered operating units; and (4) by helping to create a strategy-supportive work climate and corporate culture. Thick policy manuals are usually unnecessary. Indeed, when individual creativity and initiative are more essential to good execution than standardization and conformity, it is better to give people the freedom to do things however they see fit and hold them accountable for good results rather than try to control their behavior with policies and guidelines for every situation. Hence, creating a supportive fit between strategy and policy can mean many policies, few policies, or different policies.

Competent strategy execution entails visible, unyielding managerial commitment to best practices and continuous improvement. Benchmarking, the discovery and adoption of best practices, reengineering core business processes, and total quality management programs all aim at improved efficiency, lower costs, better product quality, and greater customer satisfaction. *All these techniques are important tools for learning how to execute a strategy more proficiently.* Benchmarking provides a realistic basis for setting performance targets. Instituting "best-in-industry" or "best-in-world" operating practices in most or all value chain activities provide a means for taking strategy execution to a higher plateau of competence and nurturing a high-performance work environment. Reengineering is a way to make quantum progress toward becoming a world-class organization, while TQM instills a commitment to continuous improvement. Effective use of TQM and continuous improvement techniques is a valuable competitive asset in a company's resource portfolio—one that can produce important competitive capabilities (in reducing costs, speeding new products to market, or improving product quality, service, or customer satisfaction) and be a source of competitive advantage.

Company strategies can't be implemented or executed well without a number of support systems to carry on business operations. Well-conceived, state-of-the-art support systems not only facilitate better strategy execution but can also strengthen organizational capabilities enough to provide a competitive edge over rivals. In the age of the Internet, real-time information and control systems, growing use of e-commerce technologies and business practices, company intranets, and wireless communications capabilities, companies can't hope to outexecute their competitors without cutting-edge information systems and technologically sophisticated operating capabilities that enable fast, efficient, and effective organization action.

Strategy-supportive motivational practices and reward systems are powerful management tools for gaining employee buy-in and commitment. The key to creating a reward system that promotes good strategy execution is to make strategically relevant measures of performance *the dominating basis* for designing incentives, evaluating individual and group efforts, and handing out rewards. Positive motivational practices generally work better than negative ones, but there is a place for both. There's also a place for both monetary and nonmonetary incentives.

For an incentive compensation system to work well (1) the monetary payoff should be a major percentage of the compensation package, (2) the use of incentives should extend to all managers and workers, (3) the system should be administered with care and fairness, (4) the incentives should be linked to performance targets spelled out in the strategic plan, (5) each individual's performance targets should involve outcomes the person can personally affect, (6) rewards should promptly follow the determination of good performance, (7) monetary rewards should be supplemented with liberal use of nonmonetary rewards, and (8) skirting the system to reward nonperformers should be scrupulously avoided.

suggested | readings

Denton, Keith D. "Creating a System for Continuous Improvement." *Business Horizons* 38, no. 1 (January–February 1995), pp. 16–21.

Grant, Robert M.; Rami Shani; and R. Krishnan. "TQM's Challenge to Management Theory and Practice." *Sloan Management Review* (Winter 1994), pp. 25–35.

Herzberg, Frederick. "One More Time: How Do You Motivate Employees?" *Harvard Business Review* 65, no. 4 (September–October 1987), pp. 109–20.

Katzenbach, Jon R., and Jason A Santamaria. "Firing Up the Front Line." *Harvard Business Review* 77, no. 3 (May–June 1999), pp. 107–17.

Kerr, Steven. "On the Folly of Rewarding A While Hoping for B." *Academy of Management Executive* 9, no. 1 (February 1995), pp. 7–14.

Kohn, Alfie. "Why Incentive Plans Cannot Work." *Harvard Business Review* 71, no. 5 (September–October 1993), pp. 54–63.

Luthans, Fred, and Alexander D. Stajkovic. "Reinforce for Performance: The Need to Go beyond Pay and Even Rewards." *Academy of Management Executive* 13, no. 2 (May 1999), pp. 49–57.

Ohinata, Yoshinobu. "Benchmarking: The Japanese Experience." *Long Range Planning* 27, no. 4 (August 1994), pp. 48–53.

Olian, Judy D., and Sara L. Rynes. "Making Total Quality Work: Aligning Organizational Processes, Performance Measures, and Stakeholders." *Human Resource Management* 30, no. 3 (Fall 1991), pp. 303–33.

Pfeffer, Jeffrey. "Producing Sustainable Competitive Advantage through the Effective Management of People." *Academy of Management Executive* 9, no. 1 (February 1995), pp. 55–69.

———. "Six Dangerous Myths about Pay." *Harvard Business Review* 76, no. 3 (May–June 1998), pp. 108–19.

Pfeffer, Jeffrey, and John F. Veiga. "Putting People First for Organizational Success." *Academy of Management Executive* 13, no. 2 (May 1999), pp. 37–48.

Simons, Robert. "Control in an Age of Empowerment." *Harvard Business Review* 73 (March–April 1995), pp. 80–88.

chapter | thirteen 13

Corporate Culture and Leadership— Keys to Effective Strategy Execution

Weak leadership can wreck the soundest strategy; forceful execution of even a poor plan can often bring victory.

—Sun Zi

Leadership is accomplishing something through other people that wouldn't have happened if you weren't there . . . Leadership is being able to mobilize ideas and values that energize other people . . . Leaders develop a story line that engages other people.

—Noel Tichy

[A] leader lives in the field with his troops.

—H. Ross Perot

An organization's capacity to execute its strategy depends on its "hard" infrastructure—its organizational structure and systems—and on its "soft" infrastructure—its culture and norms.

—Amar Bhide

Ethics is the moral courage to do what we know is right, and not to do what we know is wrong.

—C. J. Silas

The biggest levers you've got to change a company are strategy, structure, and culture. If I could pick two, I'd pick strategy and culture.

—Wayne Leonard, CEO, Entergy

In the previous two chapters we examined six of the strategy-implementer's tasks—building a capable organization, steering ample resources into strategy-critical activities and operating units, establishing strategy-supportive policies, instituting best practices and programs for continuous improvement, creating internal support systems to enable better execution, and employing appropriate motivational

practices and compensation incentives. In this chapter we explore the two remaining implementation tasks: creating a strategy-supportive corporate culture and exerting the internal leadership needed to drive implementation forward.

BUILDING A STRATEGY-SUPPORTIVE CORPORATE CULTURE

Every company has a unique organizational culture. Each has its own business philosophy and principles, its own ways of approaching problems and making decisions, its own work climate, its own embedded patterns of "how we do things around here," its own lore (stories told over and over to illustrate company values and what they mean to stakeholders), its own taboos and political don'ts—in other words, its own ingrained beliefs, behavior and thought patterns, business practices, and personality that define its **corporate culture.** The bedrock of Wal-Mart's culture is dedication to customer satisfaction, zealous pursuit of low costs, a strong work ethic, Sam Walton's legendary frugality, the ritualistic Saturday-morning headquarters meetings to exchange ideas and review problems, and company executives' commitment to visiting stores, talking to customers, and soliciting suggestions from employees. At McDonald's the constant message from management is the overriding importance of quality, service, cleanliness, and value; employees are drilled over and over on the need for attention to detail and perfection in every fundamental of the business. At General Electric, the culture is founded on a hard-driving, results-oriented atmosphere (where all of GE's businesses are held to a standard of being number one or two in their industries as well as achieving good business results); the concept of a boundaryless organization (where ideas, best practices, and learning flow freely from business to business); the reliance on "workout sessions" to identify, debate, and resolve burning issues; a commitment to six sigma quality; and globalization of the company. At Microsoft, there are stories of the long hours programmers put in, the emotional peaks and valleys in encountering and overcoming coding problems, the exhilaration of completing a complex program on schedule, the satisfaction of working on cutting-edge projects, the rewards of being part of a team responsible for a popular new software program, and the tradition of competing aggressively. Illustration Capsule 52 describes the culture at Nordstrom.

> **Basic Concept**
> *Corporate culture* refers to a company's values, beliefs, business principles, traditions, ways of operating, and internal work environment.

Where Does Corporate Culture Come From?

The taproot of corporate culture is the organization's beliefs and philosophy about how its affairs ought to be conducted—the reasons why it does things the way it does. A company's culture is manifested in the values and business principles that management preaches and practices, in its ethical standards and official policies, in its stakeholder relationships (especially its dealings with employees, unions, stockholders, vendors, and the communities in which it operates), in the traditions the organization maintains, in its supervisory practices, in employees' attitudes and behavior, in the legends people repeat about happenings in the organization, in the peer pressures that exist, in the organization's politics, and in the "chemistry" and the "vibrations" that permeate the work environment. All these sociological forces, some of which operate quite subtly, combine to define an organization's culture.

> An organization's culture is bred from a complex combination of sociological forces operating within its boundaries.

Beliefs and practices that become embedded in a company's culture can originate anywhere: from one influential individual, work group, department, or division, from the bottom of the organizational hierarchy or the top.[1] Very often, many components of the culture originate with a founder or certain strong leaders who articulated them as a company philosophy or as a set of principles to which the organization should rigidly

---

[1]John P. Kotter and James L. Heskett, *Corporate Culture and Performance* (New York: Free Press, 1992), p. 7.

illustration capsule 52
The Culture at Nordstrom

The culture at Nordstrom, a department store retailer noted for exceptional commitment to its customers, revolves around the company's motto: "Respond to unreasonable customer requests." Living up to the company's motto is so strongly ingrained in behavior that employees learn to relish the challenges that some customer requests pose. Usually, meeting customer demands entails little more than gracious compliance and a little extra personal attention. But occasionally it means paying a customer's parking ticket when in-store gift wrapping takes longer than normal or hand-delivering items to the airport for a customer with an emergency need.

At Nordstrom, each out-of-the-ordinary customer request is seen as an opportunity for a "heroic" act by an employee and a way to build the company's reputation for great service. Nordstrom encourages these acts by promoting employees noted for outstanding service, keeping scrapbooks of heroic acts, and basing the compensation of salespeople mainly on commission. It is not unusual for good salespeople at Nordstrom to earn double what they would at other department stores.

For go-getters who truly enjoy retail selling and pleasing customers, Nordstrom is a great company to work for. But the culture weeds out those who can't meet Nordstrom's demanding standards and rewards those who are prepared to be what Nordstrom stands for.

Nordstrom starts new employees, even those with advanced degrees, out on the sales floor. Promotion is strictly from within, and when a new store is opened, its key people are recruited from other stores around the country to help perpetuate Nordstrom's culture and values and to make sure the new store is run the Nordstrom way.

Source: Based on information in Tracy Goss, Richard Pascale, and Anthony Athos, "Risking the Present for a Powerful Future," *Harvard Business Review* 71, no. 6 (November–December 1993), pp. 101–2; and Jeffrey Pfeffer, "Producing Sustainable Competitive Advantage through the Effective Management of People," *Academy of Management Executive* 9, no. 1 (February 1995), pp. 59–60, 65.

adhere or as company policies. Over time, these cultural underpinnings take root, become embedded in how the company conducts its business, come to be shared by company managers and employees, and then persist as new employees are encouraged to adopt and follow the professed values and practices. Fast-growing companies risk creating a culture by chance rather than by design if they rush to hire employees mainly for their technical skills and credentials and neglect to screen out candidates whose values, philosophies, and personalities aren't compatible with the organizational character, vision, and strategy being articulated by the company's founder and top managers.

The Role of Stories   Frequently, a significant part of a company's culture emerges from the stories that get told over and over again to illustrate to newcomers the importance of certain values and beliefs and ways of operating. FedEx, of course, is world renowned for the reliability of its next-day package delivery guarantee. One of the folktales at FedEx is about a deliveryman who had been given the wrong key to a FedEx drop box. Rather than leave the packages in the drop box until the next day when the right key was available, the deliveryman unbolted the drop box from its base, loaded it into the truck, and took it back to the station. There, the box was pried open and the contents removed and sped on their way to their destination the next day. The story vividly communicates the kind of commitment the company wants every employee to exhibit in helping the company live up its reputation of reliable delivery.

Perpetuating the Culture   Once established, company cultures can be perpetuated by screening and selecting new group members according to how well their values and personalities fit in (as well as on the basis of talents and credentials), by systematic indoctrination of new members in the culture's fundamentals, by the efforts of senior group members to reiterate core values in daily conversations and pronouncements, by the telling and retelling of company legends, by regular ceremonies honoring members who display cultural ideals, and by visibly rewarding those who follow cultural norms and penalizing those who don't.[2] The staffing of an organization with new employees is one of the most important ways in which a company's culture is perpetuated. Company managers tend to hire people they feel comfortable with and think will fit in—which tends to mean hiring people with values and beliefs and personalities that will embrace the prevailing culture. Job seekers tend to accept jobs at companies where they expect to be comfortable and happy. Employees who don't hit it off at a company tend to leave quickly, while employees who thrive and are pleased with the work environment move into senior roles and positions of greater responsibility. The longer people stay at an organization, the more their values and beliefs tend to be molded by mentors, fellow workers, company training programs, and the reward structure and the more that they come to embrace and mirror the corporate culture. Sometimes gradually and sometimes more rapidly, the culture takes root, the agglomeration and product of all the social forces at work.

Forces That Can Cause Culture to Evolve   However, even stable cultures aren't static—just like strategy and organization structure, they evolve, if only slightly. Internal crises, revolutionary technologies (like the Internet), and new challenges breed new ways of doing things and cultural evolution. Arrival of new leaders and turnover of key members often spawn new or different values and practices that alter the culture. Diversification into new businesses, expansion into different geographical areas (especially foreign countries), rapid growth that adds new employees, and merger with or acquisition of another company can all precipitate cultural changes. Indeed, globalization and the Internet are today driving significant changes in the culture of companies all over the world.

Company Subcultures: The Problems Posed by New Acquisitions and Multinational Operations   Although it is common to speak about corporate culture in the singular, companies typically have multiple cultures (or subcultures).[3] Values, beliefs, and practices can vary significantly by department, geographic location, division, or business unit. A company's subcultures can clash, or at least not mesh well, if they have conflicting managerial styles, business philosophies, and operating approaches or if important differences between a company's culture and those of recently acquired companies have not yet been ironed out. *Global and multinational companies tend to be at least partly multicultural* because cross-country organization units have different operating histories and traditions, as well as members who have different values and beliefs and who speak different languages. The human resources manager of a global pharmaceutical company who took on an assignment in the Far East discovered, to his surprise, that one of his biggest challenges was to persuade his company's managers in China, Korea, Malaysia, and Taiwan to accept promotions—their cultural values were such that they did not believe in competing with their peers for career rewards or personal gain, nor did they relish breaking ties to their local communities to assume cross-national responsibilities.[4] Many companies that have merged with or acquired foreign companies have to deal with language- and custom-based cultural differences.

---

[2]Ibid., pp. 7–8.

[3]Ibid., p. 5.

[4]John Alexander and Meena S. Wilson, "Leading across Cultures: Five Vital Capabilities," in *The Organization of the Future,* ed. Frances Hesselbein, Marshall Goldsmith, and Richard Beckard (San Francisco: Jossey-Bass, 1997), pp. 291–92.

Nonetheless, the different subcultures that may exist within a global or multinational company's culture do not preclude there being important areas of commonality and compatibility. For example, General Electric's cultural traits of boundarylessness, workout, and six sigma quality can be implanted and practiced successfully in different countries. Multinational companies are learning how to make strategy-critical cultural traits travel across country boundaries and create a workably uniform culture worldwide. Likewise, company managements have learned to consider the importance of cultural compatibility in making acquisitions and the importance of addressing how to merge and integrate the cultures of newly acquired companies.

Culture: Ally or Obstacle to Strategy Execution?

The beliefs, vision, objectives, and business approaches and practices underpinning a company's strategy may be compatible with its culture or they may not. When they are, the culture becomes a valuable ally in strategy implementation and execution. When the culture is in conflict with some aspect of the company's direction, performance targets, or strategy, the culture becomes a stumbling block that impedes successful strategy implementation and execution.[5]

> An organization's culture is either an important contributor or an obstacle to successful strategy execution.

How Culture Can Promote Better Strategy Execution   A culture grounded in values, practices, and behavioral norms that match what is needed for good strategy execution helps energize people throughout the company to do their jobs in a strategy-supportive manner, adding significantly to the power and effectiveness of strategy execution. For example, a culture where frugality and thrift are values strongly shared by organizational members is very conducive to successful execution of a low-cost leadership strategy. A culture where creativity, embracing change, and challenging the status quo are pervasive themes is very conducive to successful execution of a product innovation and technological leadership strategy. A culture built around such business principles as listening to customers, encouraging employees to take pride in their work, and giving employees a high degree of decision-making responsibility is very conducive to successful execution of a strategy of delivering superior customer service.

> Strong cultures promote good strategy execution when there's fit and hurt execution when there's little fit.

A tight culture–strategy alignment acts in two ways to channel behavior and influence employees to do their jobs in a strategy-supportive fashion:[6]

- *A work environment where the culture matches the conditions for good strategy execution provides a system of informal rules and peer pressure regarding how to conduct business internally and how to go about doing one's job.* Strategy-supportive cultures shape the mood, temperament, and motivation of the workforce, positively affecting organizational energy, work habits and operating practices, the degree to which organizational units cooperate, and how customers are treated. Culturally approved behavior thrives, while culturally disapproved behavior gets squashed and often penalized. In a company where strategy and culture are misaligned, ingrained values and operating philosophies don't cultivate strategy-supportive ways of operating; often, the very kinds of behavior needed to execute strategy successfully run afoul of the culture and attract negative recognition rather than praise and reward.

> A deeply rooted culture well matched to strategy is a powerful lever for successful strategy execution.

- *A strong strategy-supportive culture nurtures and motivates people to do their jobs in ways conducive to effective strategy execution; it provides structure, standards,*

---

[5]Kotter and Heskett, *Corporate Culture and Performance*, p. 5.
[6]Ibid., pp. 15–16.

and a value system in which to operate; and it promotes strong employee identification with the company's vision, performance targets, and strategy. All this makes employees feel genuinely better about their jobs and work environment and the merits of what the company is trying to accomplish. Employees are stimulated to take on the challenge of realizing the company's vision, do their jobs competently and with enthusiasm, and collaborate with others as needed to bring the strategy to fruition.

This says something important about the task of leading strategy implementation: *anything so fundamental as implementing a strategic plan involves moving the organization's culture into close alignment with the requirements for proficient strategy execution.* The optimal condition is a work environment that mobilizes organizational energy in strategy-supportive fashion, promoting "can-do" attitudes and acceptance of change where needed, enlisting and encouraging people to perform strategy-critical activities in superior fashion, and breeding needed organizational competencies and capabilities.

The Perils of Strategy–Culture Conflict   Conflict between culture and strategy sends mixed signals to organization members and forces an undesirable choice. Should organization members be loyal to the culture and company traditions (as well as their own personal values and beliefs, which are likely to be compatible with the culture) and resist actions to pursue the strategy? Or should they go along with announced strategic priorities and engage in actions that will erode certain valued aspects of the culture and go against their own ingrained values and beliefs? Such conflict weakens commitment to culture or strategy or both.

   When a company's culture is out of sync with what is needed for strategic success, the culture has to be changed as rapidly as can be managed—this, of course, presumes that it is one or more aspects of the culture that are out of whack rather than the strategy. While correcting a strategy–culture conflict can occasionally mean revamping strategy to produce cultural fit, more usually it means revamping the mismatched cultural features to produce strategy fit. The more entrenched the mismatched aspects of the culture, the greater the difficulty of implementing new or different strategies until better strategy–culture alignment emerges. A sizable and prolonged strategy–culture conflict weakens and may even defeat managerial efforts to make the strategy work.

Strong versus Weak Cultures

Company cultures vary widely in the degree to which they are embedded in company practices and behavioral norms. Some are strong and go directly to a company's heart and soul; others are weak, with shallow roots that support little in the way of a definable corporate character.

In a strong-culture company, values and behavioral norms are like crabgrass: deeply rooted and difficult to weed out.

Strong-Culture Companies   A company's culture can be strong and cohesive in the sense that the company conducts its business according to a clear and explicit set of principles and values, that management devotes considerable time to communicating these principles and values to organization members and explaining how they relate to its business environment, and that the values are shared widely across the company—by senior executives and rank-and-file employees alike.[7] Strong-culture

---

[7]Terrence E. Deal and Allen A. Kennedy, *Corporate Cultures* (Reading, MA: Addison-Wesley, 1982), p. 22.

companies typically have creeds or values statements, and executives regularly stress the importance of using these values and principles as the basis for decisions and actions taken throughout the organization. In strong-culture companies, values and behavioral norms are so deeply rooted that they don't change much when a new CEO takes over—although they can erode over time if the CEO ceases to nurture them. And they may not change much as strategy evolves and the organization acts to make strategy adjustments, either because the new strategy is compatible with the present culture or because the dominant traits of the culture are strategy neutral and can be used to support any number of plausible strategies.

Three factors contribute to the development of strong cultures: (1) a founder or strong leader who establishes values, principles, and practices that are consistent and sensible in light of customer needs, competitive conditions, and strategic requirements; (2) a sincere, long-standing company commitment to operating the business according to these established traditions, thereby creating an internal environment that supports decision making and strategies based on cultural norms; and (3) a genuine concern for the well-being of the organization's three biggest constituencies—customers, employees, and shareholders. Continuity of leadership, small group size, stable group membership, geographic concentration, and considerable organizational success all contribute to the emergence and sustainability of a strong culture.[8]

During the time a strong culture is being implanted, there's nearly always a good strategy–culture fit (which partially accounts for the organization's success). Mismatches between strategy and culture in a strong-culture company tend to occur when a company's business environment undergoes significant rapid-fire change, prompting a drastic strategy revision that clashes with the entrenched culture. In such cases, a major culture-changing effort has to be launched. IBM went through wrenching culture changes to adapt to the new computer industry environment now driven by the so-called Wintel standard—Microsoft (with its Windows operating systems for PCs and its Windows-based PC software programs) and Intel (with its successive generations of faster microprocessors for PCs). IBM's bureaucracy and mainframe culture clashed with the shift to a PC-dominated world and the emergence of the Internet economy. Many electric utilities, long used to operating as slow-moving regulated monopolies with captive customers, are in the midst of a massive cultural shift, as they try to cope with the transition to a competitive marketplace and freedom of customer choice. The new circumstances of electric utilities are prompting a shift away from cultures predicated on risk avoidance, centralized control of decision making, and the politics of regulatory relationships to cultures where the new values and beliefs revolve around entrepreneurial risk taking, innovation, competitive thinking, superior customer service, and growing the business.

> A strong culture is a valuable asset when it matches strategy and a dreaded liability when it doesn't.

Weak-Culture Companies   In direct contrast to strong-culture companies, a company's culture can be weak and fragmented in the sense that many subcultures exist, few values and behavioral norms are widely shared, and there are few sacred traditions. In weak-culture companies, there's little cohesion and glue across organization units— top executives don't repeatedly espouse any business philosophy or exhibit commitment to particular values or extoll use of particular operating practices. Because of a dearth of common values and ingrained business approaches, organization members typically have no deeply felt sense of corporate identity. While they may have some bonds of identification with and loyalty toward their department, their colleagues, their

---

[8]Vijay Sathe, *Culture and Related Corporate Realities* (Homewood, IL: Richard D. Irwin, 1985).

union, or their boss, the weak company culture breeds no strong employee allegiance to what the company stands for. The lack of a definable corporate character tends to result in many employees viewing the company as a place to work and their job as a way to make a living. As a consequence, *weak cultures provide little or no strategy implementing assistance* because there are no traditions, beliefs, values, common bonds, or behavioral norms that management can use as levers to mobilize commitment to executing the chosen strategy. While a weak culture does not usually pose a strong barrier to strategy execution, it provides no assist either.

Unhealthy Cultures

There are a number of unhealthy cultural characteristics that can undermine a company's business performance.[9] One unhealthy trait is a politicized internal environment that allows influential managers to operate autonomous "fiefdoms" and resist needed change. In politically dominated cultures, many issues get resolved on the basis of turf, vocal support or opposition by powerful executives, personal lobbying by a key executive, and coalitions among individuals or departments with vested interests in a particular outcome. What's best for the company plays second fiddle to personal aggrandizement.

A second unhealthy cultural trait, one that can plague companies suddenly confronted with fast-changing business conditions, is hostility to change and to people who champion new ways of doing things. Executives who don't value managers or employees with initiative often put a damper on experimentation and on efforts to improve. Avoiding risks, not fouling up, not rocking the boat, and accepting the status quo become more important to a person's career advancement than entrepreneurial successes, innovative accomplishments, and championing better ways to do things. Hostility to change is most often found in companies with multilayered management bureaucracies that have enjoyed considerable market success in years past but whose business environments have been hit with accelerating change. General Motors, IBM, Sears, and Eastman Kodak are classic examples—all four gradually became burdened by a stifling bureaucracy that rejected innovation and are now struggling to reinvent the cultural approaches that caused them to succeed in the first place.

A third unhealthy characteristc is promoting managers who are good at staying within their budgets, exerting close supervisory control over their units, and handling administrative detail as opposed to managers who understand vision, strategies, and culture building and who are good leaders, motivators, and decision makers. While the former are adept at internal organizational maneuvering, they may lack the entrepreneurial skills a company needs among its senior executives to introduce new strategies, reallocate resources, build new competitive capabilities, and fashion a new culture—and such a lack will ultimately erode long-term performance.

A fourth characteristic of unhealthy cultures is an aversion to looking outside the company for superior practices and approaches. Sometimes a company enjoys such great market success and reigns as an industry leader for so long that its management becomes inbred and arrogant. It believes it has all the answers or can develop them on its own. Insular thinking, inward-looking solutions, and a must-be-invented-here syndrome often precede a decline in company performance. Kotter and Heskett cite Avon, BankAmerica, Citicorp, Coors, Ford, General Motors, Kmart, Kroger, Sears, Texaco,

---

[9]Kotter and Heskett, *Corporate Culture and Performance,* chapter 6.

and Xerox as examples of companies that had unhealthy cultures during the late 1970s and early 1980s.[10] Several—most notably General Motors, Kmart, and Sears—still exhibit many unhealthy culture traits.

Adaptive Cultures

In fast-changing business environments, the capacity to introduce new strategies and organizational practices is a necessity if a company is to achieve superior performance over long periods of time.[11] Strategic agility requires a culture that quickly accepts and supports company efforts to adapt to environmental change rather than a culture that has to be coaxed and cajoled to change.

> Adaptive cultures are a valuable competitive asset—sometimes a necessity—in fast-changing environments.

In adaptive cultures, members share a feeling of confidence that the organization can deal with whatever threats and opportunities come down the pike; they are receptive to risk taking, experimentation, innovation, and changing strategies and practices whenever necessary to satisfy the legitimate interests of stakeholders—customers, employees, shareowners, suppliers, and the communities where the company operates. Hence, members willingly embrace a proactive approach to identifying issues, evaluating the implications and options, and implementing workable solutions. There's a spirit of doing what's necessary to ensure long-term organizational success *provided core values and business principles are upheld in the process.*[12] Entrepreneurship is encouraged and rewarded. Managers habitually fund product development initiatives, evaluate new ideas openly, and take prudent risks to create new business positions. Strategies and traditional operating practices are modified as needed to adjust to or take advantage of changes in the business environment. The leaders of adaptive cultures are adept at changing the right things in the right ways, not changing for the sake of change and not compromising core values or business principles. Adaptive cultures are very supportive of managers and employees at all ranks who propose or help initiate useful change; indeed, executives consciously seek, train, and promote individuals who display these leadership traits.

> Today's dot-com companies are classic examples of adaptive cultures.

Today's dot-com companies are perfect illustrations of adaptive cultures. Internet-related companies thrive on change—driving it, leading it, and capitalizing on it (but sometimes also succumbing to change when they make the wrong move or are swamped by better technologies or the superior business models of rivals). From the outset, Internet companies established cultures with the capability to act and react rapidly. They are avid practitioners of entrepreneurship and innovation, with a demonstrated willingness to take bold risks to create altogether new products, new businesses, and new industries. They have carefully and deliberately staffed their organizations with people who are proactive, who rise to the challenge of change, and who have an aptitude for adapting. Because of the revolution in business strategies, business organization, and business practices spawned largely by companies comprising the Internet economy, traditional companies are overhauling their cultures to become more adaptive and are learning to move at

---

[10]Ibid., p. 68.

[11]This section draws heavily from Kotter and Heskett, *Corporate Culture and Performance,* chapter 4.

[12]There's no inherent reason why new strategic initiatives should conflict with core values and business principles. While conflict is always possible, most strategy makers lean toward choosing strategic initiatives that are compatible with the company's character and culture and that don't go against ingrained values and beliefs. After all, the company's culture is usually something that strategy makers have had a hand in building and perpetuating, so they are not often anxious to undermine core values and business principles without serious soul-searching and compelling business reasons.

illustration capsule 53

Adaptive Cultures at Companies That Act and React at Internet Speed

Fast-changing industry and competitive conditions, driven partly by the e-commerce revolution and mushrooming use of the Internet, have made it more desirable than ever for companies to establish adaptive cultures. Acting and responding at Internet speed is rapidly becoming a cultural and business necessity. Internet retailers typically monitor consumer buying preferences every few days and make changes to their product lineup whenever it appears that buying preferences have changed. Companies like software and e-services firm Portera Systems hold weekly meetings to analyze sales reports and customer requests and decide whether to institute changes in their software products or shifts in strategy. New entrants can become viable competitors before they are even noticed by most industry incumbents—for example, within 10 weeks, home furnishings start-up GoodHome.com went from an idea to a business plan to venture capital funding to a merger.

The ability to act and react at Internet speed hinges largely on having an adaptive culture. Corporate cultures that are resistant to change impede actions to quickly plot and pursue a new strategic course when customer preferences or other circumstances so dictate. Companies with adaptive organizational cultures typically create flat organizational structures that push decision making to the front lines. They staff the organization with people who thrive on change and ambiguity. And they foster a "sensing-and-responding mind-set" that comes from ongoing communications with customers, attentive monitoring of rivals' actions, and awareness of technological developments. The CEO of Accompany, an online buying club, reports that his company is "not interested in people who can only deal in black and white—they'd slow us down."

Building an adaptive culture that moves at Internet speed also entails providing employees with timely information about strategic changes. According to an IBM executive, "You can't keep people in the dark when you're moving really fast or they start thinking that change is something sinister." Accompany uses e-mail and group meetings to communicate strategy shifts to its employees within hours of management's decisions.

Solutia, a Monsanto spin-off, speeds its ability to respond to market changes by building scenarios in its strategic planning sessions. For every new strategic initiative, the company's managers plan four different short-term outcomes and establish "signposts" to indicate when it's time to change strategic direction. When signpost events begin to appear, management relies on its scenarios and discussions to alter strategy, sometimes within hours.

Sun Microsystems has weekly "whack-o-meter" sessions where the company's president and key decision makers meet to assess the company's vulnerabilities or ways that competitors might "whack" Sun. Sun's managers then try to identify responses that can be implemented at the first sign of a rival's offensive move.

Source: Based on Marcia Stepanek, "How Fast Is Net Fast?" *Business Week*, November 1, 1999, pp. EB 52–EB 54.

Internet speed. Illustration Capsule 53 describes what dot-com companies are doing to build adaptive cultures that can act and react at Internet speed.

One outstanding trait of adaptive cultures is that top management, while orchestrating responses to changing conditions, proceeds in a manner that demonstrates genuine care for the well-being of all key constituencies—customers, employees, stockholders, major suppliers, and the communities where the company operates—and tries to satisfy all their legitimate interests simultaneously. No group is ignored, and fairness to all constituencies is a decision-making principle—a commitment often described as "doing the right thing."[13] Pleasing customers and protecting, if not enhancing, the company's long-term well-being is seen as the best way of looking out for the interests of employees, stockholders, suppliers, and communities where the company operates. Management concern for the well-being of employees is a big factor in gaining employee support for

---

[13]Kotter and Heskett, *Corporate Culture and Performance,* p. 52.

change—employees understand that changes in their job assignments are part of the process of adapting to new conditions and that their employment security will not be threatened in the process of adapting to change unless the company's business unexpectedly reverses direction. In cases where workforce downsizing becomes necessary, management concern for employees dictates that separation be handled humanely, making employee departure as pleasant as possible. Management efforts to make the process of adapting to change fair for customers, employees, stockholders, suppliers, and communities where the company operates, keeping adverse impacts to a minimum insofar as possible, breeds acceptance of and support for change among all organization stakeholders.

In less-adaptive cultures where skepticism about the importance of new developments and resistance to change are the norm, managers avoid risk taking and prefer waiting until the fog of uncertainty clears before steering a new course or making fundamental adjustments to their product line or embracing a major new technology.[14] They believe in moving cautiously and conservatively, preferring to follow others rather than take decisive action to be in the forefront of change. In change-resistant cultures, there's a premium placed on not making mistakes, prompting managers to lean toward safe, "don't-rock-the-boat" options that will have only a ripple effect on the status quo, protect or advance their own careers, and guard the interests of their immediate work groups.

Creating a Strong Fit between Strategy and Culture

It is the *strategy maker's* responsibility to select a strategy compatible with the "sacred" or unchangeable parts of prevailing corporate culture. It is the *strategy implementer's* task, once strategy is chosen, to change whatever facets of the corporate culture hinder effective execution.

Changing a Problem Culture   Changing a company's culture to align it with strategy is among the toughest management tasks—easier to talk about than do. Changing problem cultures is very difficult because of the heavy anchor of deeply held values and habits—people cling emotionally to the old and familiar. It takes concerted management action over a period of time to replace an unhealthy culture with a healthy culture or to root out certain unwanted cultural obstacles and instill ones that are more strategy-supportive.

> Once a culture is established, it is difficult to change.

The first step is to diagnose which facets of the present culture are strategy-supportive and which are not. Then, managers have to talk openly and forthrightly to all concerned about those aspects of the culture that have to be changed. The talk has to be followed swiftly by visible, aggressive actions to modify the culture—actions that everyone will understand are intended to establish a new culture more in tune with the strategy. The menu of culture-changing actions includes revising policies and procedures in ways that will help drive cultural change, altering incentive compensation (to reward the desired cultural behavior), visibly praising and recognizing people who display the new cultural traits, recruiting and hiring new managers and employees who have the desired cultural values and can serve as role models for the desired cultural behavior, replacing key executives who are strongly associated with the old culture, and taking every opportunity to communicate to employees the basis for cultural change and its benefits to all concerned.

---

[14]Ibid., p. 50.

Sometimes executives succeed in changing the values and behaviors of small groups of managers and even whole departments or divisions, only to find the changes eroded over time by the actions of the rest of the organization. What is communicated, praised, supported, and penalized by an entrenched majority undermines the new emergent culture and halts its progress. Executives, despite revamping the formal organization, bringing in managers from the outside, introducing new technologies, and opening new facilities, can still fail at altering embedded cultural traits and behaviors because of skepticism about the new directions and covert resistance to altering traditional methods.

Symbolic Culture-Changing Actions   Managerial actions to tighten the culture–strategy fit need to be both symbolic and substantive. Symbolic actions are valuable for the signals they send about the kinds of behavior and performance strategy-implementers wish to encourage. The most important symbolic actions are those that top executives take to serve as role models—leading cost reduction efforts by curtailing executive perks; emphasizing the importance of responding to customers' needs by requiring all officers and executives to spend a significant portion of each week talking with customers and understanding their requirements; and initiating efforts to alter policies and practices identified as hindrances in executing the new strategy. Another category of symbolic actions includes the events organizations hold to designate and honor people whose actions and performance exemplify what is called for in the new culture. Many universities give outstanding teacher awards each year to symbolize their commitment to and esteem for instructors who display exceptional classroom talents. Numerous businesses have employee-of-the-month awards. The military has a long-standing custom of awarding ribbons and medals for exemplary actions. Mary Kay Cosmetics awards an array of prizes—from ribbons to pink automobiles—to its beauty consultants for reaching various sales plateaus.

> Awards ceremonies, role models, and symbols are a fundamental part of culture-shaping and reshaping efforts.

The best companies and the best executives expertly use symbols, role models, ceremonial occasions, and group gatherings to tighten the strategy–culture fit. Low-cost leaders like Wal-Mart and Nucor are renowned for their spartan facilities, executive frugality, intolerance of waste, and zealous control of costs. Executives sensitive to their role in promoting strategy–culture fits make a habit of appearing at ceremonial functions to praise individuals and groups that "get with the program." They honor individuals who exhibit cultural norms and reward those who achieve strategic milestones. They participate in employee training programs to stress strategic priorities, values, ethical principles, and cultural norms. Every group gathering is seen as an opportunity to repeat and ingrain values, praise good deeds, reinforce cultural norms, and promote changes that assist strategy execution. Sensitive executives make sure that current decisions and policy changes will be construed by organizational members as consistent with cultural values and supportive of the company's new strategic direction.[15]

Substantive Culture-Changing Actions   While being out front personally and symbolically leading the push for new behaviors and communicating the reasons for new approaches is crucial, strategy implementers have to convince all those concerned that the culture-changing effort is more than cosmetic. Talk and symbolism have to be complemented by substantive actions and real movement. The actions taken have to be credible, highly visible, and unmistakably indicative of the seriousness of

---

[15]Judy D. Olian and Sara L. Rynes, "Making Total Quality Work: Aligning Organizational Processes, Performance Measures, and Stakeholders," *Human Resource Management* 30, no. 3 (Fall 1991), p. 324.

management's commitment to new strategic initiatives and the associated cultural changes. There are several ways to accomplish this. One is to engineer some quick successes that highlight the benefits of strategy–culture changes, thus making enthusiasm for the changes contagious. However, instant results are usually not as important as having the will and patience to create a solid, competent team psychologically committed to pursuing the strategy in a superior fashion. The strongest signs that management is truly committed to creating a new culture include replacing old-culture traditionalist managers with "new-breed" managers, changing long-standing policies and operating practices that are dysfunctional or that impede new initiatives, undertaking major reorganizational moves that bring structure into better alignment with strategy, tying compensation incentives directly to the new measures of strategic performance, and making major budgetary reallocations that shift substantial resources from old-strategy projects and programs to new-strategy projects and programs.

Implanting the needed culture-building values and behavior depends on a sincere, sustained commitment by the chief executive coupled with extraordinary persistence in reinforcing the culture at every opportunity through both word and deed. Neither charisma nor personal magnetism is essential. However, personally talking to many departmental groups about the reasons for change *is* essential; organizational changes are seldom accomplished successfully from an office. Moreover, creating and sustaining a strategy-supportive culture is a job for the whole management team. Major cultural change requires many initiatives from many people. Senior officers, department heads, and middle managers have to reiterate values, "walk the talk," and translate the organization's philosophy into everyday practice. In addition, for the culture-building effort to be successful, strategy implementers must enlist the support of firstline supervisors and employee opinion leaders, convincing them of the merits of practicing and enforcing cultural norms at the lowest levels in the organization. Until a big majority of employees join the new culture and share an emotional commitment to its basic values and behavioral norms, there's considerably more work to be done in both instilling the culture and tightening the culture–strategy fit.

The task of making culture supportive of strategy is not a short-term exercise. It takes time for a new culture to emerge and prevail; it's unrealistic to expect an overnight transformation. The bigger the organization and the greater the cultural shift needed to produce a culture–strategy fit, the longer it takes. In large companies, changing the corporate culture in significant ways can take two to five years. In fact, it is usually tougher to reshape a deeply ingrained culture that is not strategy-supportive than it is to instill a strategy-supportive culture from scratch in a brand-new organization.

Building Ethics into the Culture

A strong corporate culture founded on ethical business principles and moral values is a vital driving force behind continued strategic success. Many executives are convinced that *a company must care about how it does business*; otherwise a company's reputation, and ultimately its performance, is put at risk. Corporate ethics and values programs are not window dressing; they are typically undertaken to create an environment of strongly held values and convictions and to make ethical conduct a way of life. Moral values and high ethical standards nurture the corporate culture in a very positive way—they connote integrity, "doing the right thing," and genuine concern for stakeholders. *Value statements serve as a cornerstone for culture building; a code of ethics*

An ethical corporate culture has a positive impact on a company's long-term strategic success; an unethical culture can undermine it.

table 13.1   Topics Frequently Covered in Value Statements and Codes of Ethics

Topics Covered in Values Statements	Topics Covered in Codes of Ethics
• Importance of customers and customer service	• Honesty and observance of the law
• Commitment to quality	• Conflicts of interest
• Commitment to innovation	• Fairness in selling and marketing practices
• Respect for the individual employee and the duty the company has to employees	• Using inside information and securities trading
• Importance of honesty, integrity, and ethical standards	• Supplier relationships and procurement practices
• Duty to stockholders	• Payments to obtain business/Foreign Corrupt Practices Act
• Duty to suppliers	• Acquiring and using information about others
• Corporate citizenship	• Political activities
• Importance of protecting the environment	• Use of company assets, resources, and property
	• Protection of proprietary information
	• Pricing, contracting, and billing

serves as a cornerstone for developing a corporate conscience.[16] Table 13.1 indicates the kinds of topics such statements cover.

Companies establish values and ethical standards in a number of different ways.[17] Tradition-steeped companies with a rich folklore rely heavily on word-of-mouth indoctrination and the power of tradition to instill values and enforce ethical conduct. But many companies today convey their values and codes of ethics to stakeholders and interested parties in their annual reports, on their Web sites, and in documents provided to all employees. They are hammered in at orientation courses for new employees and in refresher courses for managers and employees. The trend of making stakeholders aware of a company's commitment to ethical business conduct is partly attributable to greater management understanding of the role these statements play in culture building and partly attributable to a growing trend by consumers to search out "ethical" products, a greater emphasis on corporate social responsibility by large investors, and increasing political and legal pressures on companies to behave ethically.

However, there is a considerable difference between saying the right things (having a well-articulated corporate values statement or code of ethics) and truly managing a company in an ethical and socially responsible way. Companies that are truly committed to ethical conduct make ethical behavior *a fundamental component of their corporate culture.* They put a stake in the ground, explicitly stating what the company intends and expects. Values statements and codes of ethical conduct are used as benchmarks for judging both company policies and individual conduct. Illustration Capsule 54 presents the Johnson & Johnson Credo, one of the most publicized and celebrated codes of ethics among U.S. companies; J&J's CEO has called the credo "the unifying

---

[16]For a discussion of the strategic benefits of formal statements of corporate values, see John Humble, David Jackson, and Alan Thomson, "The Strategic Power of Corporate Values," *Long Range Planning* 27, no. 6 (December 1994), pp. 28–42. For a study of the status of formal codes of ethics in large U.S. corporations, see Patrick E. Murphy, "Corporate Ethics Statements: Current Status and Future Prospects," *Journal of Business Ethics* 14 (1995), pp. 727–40.

[17]The Business Roundtable, *Corporate Ethics: A Prime Asset,* February 1988, pp. 4–10.

illustration capsule 54
The Johnson & Johnson Credo

- We believe our first responsibility is to the doctors, nurses, and patients, to mothers and all others who use our products and services.

- In meeting their needs everything we do must be of high quality.

- We must constantly strive to reduce our costs in order to maintain reasonable prices.

- Customers' orders must be serviced promptly and accurately.

- Our suppliers and distributors must have an opportunity to make a fair profit.

- We are responsible to our employees, the men and women who work with us throughout the world.

- Everyone must be considered as an individual.

- We must respect their dignity and recognize their merit.

- They must have a sense of security in their jobs.

- Compensation must be fair and adequate, and working conditions clean, orderly, and safe.

- Employees must feel free to make suggestions and complaints.

- There must be equal opportunity for employment, development, and advancement for those qualified.

- We must provide competent management, and their actions must be just and ethical.

- We are responsible to the communities in which we live and work and to the world community as well.

- We must be good citizens—support good works and charities and bear our fair share of taxes.

- We must encourage civic improvements and better health and education.

- We must maintain in good order the property we are privileged to use, protecting the environment and natural resources.

- Our final responsibility is to our stockholders.

- Business must make a sound profit.

- We must experiment with new ideas.

- Research must be carried on, innovative programs developed, and mistakes paid for.

- New equipment must be purchased, new facilities provided, and new products launched.

- Reserves must be created to provide for adverse times.

- When we operate according to these principles, the stockholders should realize a fair return.

Source: 1982 Annual Report and company Web site.

force for our corporation." Illustration Capsule 55 presents the ethics and values statements for Lockheed Martin, Pfizer, and J. M. Smucker.

Once values and ethical standards have been formally set forth, they must be institutionalized and ingrained in the company's policies, practices, and actual conduct. Implementing the values and code of ethics entails several actions:

- Incorporation of the statement of values and the code of ethics into employee training and educational programs.

- Explicit attention to values and ethics in recruiting and hiring to screen out applicants who do not exhibit compatible character traits.

- Communication of the values and ethics code to all employees and explaining compliance procedures.

- Management involvement and oversight, from the CEO down to firstline supervisors.

- Strong endorsements by the CEO.

- Word-of-mouth indoctrination.

> Values and ethical standards must not only be explicitly stated but must also be ingrained into the corporate culture.

illustration capsule 55

Corporate Ethics and Values Statements at Lockheed Martin, Pfizer, and J. M. Smucker

LOCKHEED MARTIN

Our Value Statements

- *Ethics*—We will be well informed in the regulations, rules, and compliance issues that apply to our businesses around the world. We will apply this knowledge to our conduct as responsible employees of Lockheed Martin, and will adhere to the highest standards of ethical conduct in all that we do.

- *Excellence*—The pursuit of superior performance infuses every Lockheed Martin activity. We excel at meeting challenging commitments even as we achieve total customer satisfaction. We demonstrate leadership by advancing new technologies, innovative manufacturing techniques, enhanced customer service, inspired management, and the application of best practices throughout our organization. Each of us leads through our individual contributions to Lockheed Martin's core purpose.

- *"Can-Do"*—We demonstrate individual leadership through a positive approach to every task, a "can-do" spirit, and a restless determination to continually improve upon our personal bests. We aggressively pursue new business, determined to add value for our customers with ingenuity, determination and a positive attitude. We utilize our ability to combine strength with speed in responding enthusiastically to every new opportunity and every new challenge.

- *Integrity*—Each of us brings to the workplace personal values which guide us to meet our commitments to customers, suppliers, colleagues, and others with whom we interact. We embrace truthfulness and trust, and we treat everyone with dignity and respect—as we wish to be treated ourselves.

- *People*—Outstanding people make Lockheed Martin unique. Success in rapidly changing markets requires that we continuously learn and grow as individuals and as an organization. We embrace lifelong learning through individual initiative, combined with company-sponsored education and development programs, as well as challenging work and growth opportunities.

- *Teamwork*—We multiply the creativity, talents, and contributions of both individuals and businesses by focusing on team goals. Our teams assume collective accountability for their actions, share trust and leadership, embrace diversity, and accept responsibility for prudent risk-taking. Each of us succeeds individually . . . when we as a team achieve success.

Our Ethical Principles

- *Honesty*—To be truthful in all our endeavors; to be honest and forthright with one another and with our customers, communities, suppliers, and shareholders.

- *Integrity*—To say what we mean, to deliver what we promise, and to stand for what is right.

- *Respect*—To treat one another with dignity and fairness, appreciating the diversity of our workforce and the uniqueness of each employee.

- *Trust*—To build confidence through teamwork and open, candid communication.

- *Responsibility*—To speak up—without fear of retribution—and report concerns in the workplace, including violations of laws, regulations and company policies, and seek clarification and guidance whenever there is doubt.

- *Citizenship*—To obey all the laws of the United States and the other countries in which we do business and to do our part to make the communities in which we live better.

PFIZER, INC.

To fulfill our purpose and achieve our mission, we abide by the enduring values that are the foundation of our business:

- *Integrity*—We demand of ourselves and others the highest ethical standards, and our products and processes will be of the highest quality. Our conduct as a company, and as individuals within it, will always reflect the highest standards of integrity. We will demonstrate open, honest, and ethical behavior in all dealings with customers, clients, colleagues, suppliers, partners, the public, and governments. The Pfizer name is a source of pride to us and should inspire trust in all with whom we come in contact. We must do more than simply do things right—we must also do the right thing.

- *Respect for People*—We recognize that people are the cornerstone of Pfizer's success. We come from many

illustration capsule 55

different countries and cultures, and we speak many languages. We value our diversity as a source of strength. We are proud of Pfizer's history of treating employees with respect and dignity and are committed to building upon this tradition.

We listen to the ideas of our colleagues and respond appropriately. We seek a business environment that fosters personal and professional growth and achievement. We recognize that communication must be frequent and candid and that we must support others with the tools, training, and authority they need to succeed in achieving their responsibilities, goals, and objectives.

- *Teamwork*—We know that to be a successful company we must work together, frequently transcending organizational and geographic boundaries to meet the changing needs of our customers.

We want all of our colleagues to contribute to the best of their ability, individually and in teams. Teamwork improves the quality of decisions and increases the likelihood that good decisions will be acted upon. Teamwork sustains a spirit of excitement, fulfillment, pride, and passion for our business, enabling us to succeed in all of our endeavors and continually learn as individuals and as a corporation.

- *Performance*—We strive for continuous improvement in our performance. When we commit to doing something, we will do it in the best, most complete, most efficient, and most timely way possible. Then we will try to think of ways to do it better the next time. We will measure our performance carefully, ensuring that integrity and respect for people are never compromised. We will compete aggressively, establishing challenging but achievable targets and rewarding performance against those targets. We wish to attract the highest caliber employees, providing them with opportunities to develop to their full potential and to share in the success that comes from winning in the marketplace.

- *Innovation*—Innovation is the key to improving health and sustaining Pfizer growth and profitability. The quest for innovative solutions should invigorate all of our core businesses and pervade the Pfizer community worldwide.

In our drive to innovate, we support well-conceived risk-taking and understand that it will not always lead to success. We embrace creativity and consistently pursue new opportunities. We look for ways to make our research and development capabilities, our products and services more useful to our customers, and our business practices, processes, and systems more efficient and effective. We listen to and collaborate with our customers to identify and make widely available potential new products.

- *Customer Focus*—We are deeply committed to meeting the needs of our customers and constantly focus on customer satisfaction. We take genuine interest in the welfare of our customers, whether internal or external. We recognize that we can prosper only if we anticipate and meet customer needs, respond quickly to changing conditions, and fulfill customer expectations better than our competitors. We seek long-term relationships based on our comprehensive understanding of all our customers' needs and on the value we provide through superior products and services.

- *Leadership*—Leaders advance teamwork by imparting a clarity of purpose, a shared sense of goals, and a joint commitment to excellence. Leaders empower those around them by sharing knowledge and authority and by recognizing and rewarding outstanding individual effort. We are dedicated to providing opportunities for leadership at all levels in our organization.

Leaders are those who step forward to achieve difficult goals, envisioning what needs to happen and motivating others. They utilize the particular talents of every individual and resolve conflict by helping others to focus on common goals. Leaders build relationships with others throughout the company to share ideas, provide support, and help assure that the best practices prevail throughout Pfizer.

- *Community*—We play an active role in making every country and community in which we operate a better place to live and work. We know that the ongoing vitality of our host nations and localities has a direct impact on the long-term health of our business. As a company and as individuals, we give of ourselves to serve the needs of communities and people in need throughout the world.

THE J. M. SMUCKER COMPANY

Our Basic Beliefs are an expression of the values and principles that guide corporate and individual behavior at the

(*continued*)

 illustration capsule 55

(concluded)

Company. These Basic Beliefs are deeply rooted in the philosophy and heritage of the Company's founder, J. M. Smucker. Present policies are based on these time-honored principles:

- *Quality*—Quality applies to our products, our manufacturing methods, our marketing efforts, our people, and our relationships with each other. We will only produce and sell products that enhance the quality of life and well-being. These will be the highest quality products offered in our respective markets because the Company's growth and business success have been built on quality. We will continuously look for ways to achieve daily improvements which will, over time, result in consistently superior products and performance.

  At The J. M. Smucker Company, quality comes first. Sales growth and earnings will follow.

- *People*—We will be fair with our employees and maintain an environment that encourages personal responsibility within the Company and the community. In return, we expect our employees to be responsible for not only their individual jobs but for the Company as a whole.

  We will seek employees who are committed to preserving and enhancing the values and principles inherent in our Basic Beliefs through their own actions. We firmly believe that the highest quality people produce the highest quality products and services; that the highest business ethics require the highest personal ethics; and that responsible people produce exceptional results.

- *Ethics*—The same strong, ethical values on which our Company was founded provide the standards by which we conduct our business as well as ourselves. We accept nothing less regardless of the circumstances. Therefore, we will maintain the highest standards of business ethics with our customers, suppliers, employees, and shareholders and with the communities in which we work.

- *Growth*—Along with day-to-day operations, we are also concerned with the potential of our Company. Growing is reaching for that potential whether it be in the development of new products and new markets, the discovery of new manufacturing or management techniques, or the personal growth and development of our people and their ideas.

  We are committed to strong balanced growth that will protect or enhance our consumer franchise within prudent financial parameters. We want to provide a fair return for our stockholders on their investment in us.

- *Independence*—We have a strong commitment to stewardship of the Smucker name and heritage. We will remain an independent company because of our desire and motivation to control our own direction and succeed on our own. We strive to be an example of a company which is successful by operating under these Basic Beliefs within the free enterprise system.

These Basic Beliefs regarding quality, people, ethics, growth and independence have served as a strong foundation throughout our history, and will continue to be the basis for future strategy, plans, and achievements.

Sources: Company Web sites and annual reports.

Illustration Capsule 56 describes the interesting and effective way that SmithKline Beecham, one of the world's leading phamaceutical manufacturers, embedded its values into its culture and operating practices.

In the case of codes of ethics, special attention must be given to sections of the company that are particularly vulnerable—procurement, sales, and political lobbying. Employees who deal with external parties are in ethically sensitive positions and often are drawn into compromising situations. Company personnel assigned to subsidiaries in foreign countries can find themselves trapped in ethical dilemmas if bribery and corruption of public officials are common practices or if suppliers or customers are accustomed to kickbacks of one kind or another.

illustration capsule 56

How SmithKline Beecham Embedded Its Values in Its Culture

SmithKline Beecham (SB), the maker of such products as Tagamet, Tums, and Augmentin, ranks among the world's largest pharmaceutical companies with 1999 sales of more than $13 billion. The company is known for having taken its five simply stated values and integrated them into its corporate culture:

- *Customer*: To achieve full customer satisfaction.

- *Innovation*: To be one step ahead of the competition.

- *Integrity*: To be a team people trust.

- *People*: To be the best place to work for the best people.

- *Performance*: To be the benchmark for success in our industry.

SB managers have embedded these five values into its culture by demonstrating top management support for the values initiative, creating an inclusive values development process, giving values a high priority within the organization, and requiring training programs that are values specific. The company's values initiative originated in 1989 after the merger of SmithKline Beckman and the Beecham Group. The newly formed company's chairman and chief executive officer both agreed that the merger created an ideal opportunity to shape an organizational culture that embraced ethical business conduct and other behaviors that reflected principles that would help ensure the success of the new company.

Months after the merger, the chairman and CEO jointly called a meeting of the company's top 15 managers to discuss the need for a new organizational culture and values statement. The team of 17 met over six weekend retreats to agree on core values and leadership practices that

would define SmithKline Beecham as a company. The company's managers and legal department later developed a Corporate Code covering 73 specific policies related to employment, legal compliance, external relations, and internal processes. The Code is available as a printed document and on the company intranet.

Shortly after the first anniversary of the merger, the integration of SB's five agreed-on values into the company's culture began through its Simply Better Way program, which was led by top management, delivered by insiders (rather than consultants), and aligned with the company's strategic priorities. The SB Way initiates newly hired employees into the company's culture through an orientation program that provides an overview of the company's core values. In addition, all SB employees agree as part of their employment contract to observe the company's Corporate Code.

The company also requires all employees to participate in business conduct and values training programs that offer interactive sessions where employees are asked to respond to scenarios that are similar to what they might encounter when interacting with those inside and outside the company. The following scenario is taken from a session that discusses the company's guidelines on political contributions: "It is your first assignment in a new country, and it soon becomes apparent to you that competitors are making payments to the Health Minister to place and keep their drugs on the reimbursement list. Although it is against your principles, it appears this is the way business is done here." Other such scenarios deal with conflicts of interest, gifts and entertainment, product recalls, proprietary and confidential information, and employment policies.

(continued)

Structuring the Ethics Enforcement Process   Procedures for enforcing ethical standards and handling potential violations have to be developed. The compliance effort must permeate the company, extending into every organizational unit. The attitudes, character, and work history of prospective employees must be scrutinized. Every employee must receive adequate training. Line managers at all levels must give serious and continuous attention to the task of explaining how the values and ethical code apply in their areas. In addition, they must insist that company values and ethical standards become a way of life. In general, instilling values and insisting on ethical conduct must be looked on as a continuous culture-building, culture-nurturing exercise. Whether the effort succeeds or fails depends largely on how well corporate values and ethical standards are visibly integrated into company policies, managerial practices, and actions at all levels.

As a test of your ethics, take the quiz in Illustration Capsule 57 on page 429.

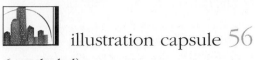

illustration capsule 56

(concluded)

Performance evaluations of SB managers include ratings on such leadership criteria as: (1) demonstrates principled and sound business ethics, (2) shows consistency among principles, (3) shares credit with others, (4) follows or applies company policies consistently and fairly, (5) admits personal mistakes, (6) communicates openly and honestly to employees and customers, and (7) builds trust with others through own authenticity and follow-through on commitments. Managers whose behavior closely matches the company's values or who show commendable improvement in values-based leadership are eligible for the company's biannual Simply the Best Awards. In addition, the SB Way requires that 50 percent of the annual performance evaluation rating for the company's top 250 managers be tied to their support of company's values and desired leadership practices.

SmithKline Beecham also administers a biannual values survey that measures employee satisfaction with their own integrity, co-workers' integrity, SB's level of business ethics, the extent to which SB managers share information with employees, open communications within the company, management's actions matching their words, and being open about failure as well as successes. SB managers believe that the company should strive for continuous improvement in values-related behaviors and use the biannual survey results to evaluate the company's culture and plan new initiatives to build a tighter values–culture link in the company.

Sources: Ian W. Jones and Michael G. Pollitt, "Putting Values into Action: Lessons from Best Practice," *Long Range Planning* 32, no. 2 (April 1999), pp. 162–65; Ian W. Jones and Michael G. Pollitt, "From Promise to Compliance: The Development of 'Integrity' at SmithKline Beecham," *Long Range Planning* 32, no. 2 (April 1999), pp. 190–98; and company annual reports.

Building a Spirit of High Performance into the Culture

A results-oriented culture that inspires people to do their best is conducive to superior strategy execution.

An ability to instill strong individual commitment to strategic success and to create an atmosphere in which there is constructive pressure to perform is one of the most valuable strategy-implementing/strategy-executing skills. When an organization performs consistently at or near peak capability, the outcome is not only improved strategic success but also an organizational culture permeated with a spirit of high performance. Such a spirit should not be confused with whether employees are happy or satisfied or whether they get along well together, although the latter are certainly desirable conditions. *An organization with a spirit of high performance emphasizes achievement and excellence. Its culture is results-oriented, and it uses people-management practices that inspire workers to do their best.*[18]

Companies with a spirit of high performance typically are intensely people-oriented, and they reinforce their concern for individual employees on every conceivable occasion in every conceivable way. They treat employees with dignity and respect, train each employee thoroughly, encourage employees to use their own initiative and creativity in performing their work, set reasonable and clear performance expectations, use the full range of rewards and punishment to enforce high-performance standards, hold managers at every level responsible for developing the people who report to them, and grant employees enough autonomy to stand out, excel, and contribute. Creating a results-oriented organizational culture generally entails making champions out of the people who turn in

---

[18] For a more in-depth discussion of what it takes to create a climate and culture that nurture success, see Benjamin Schneider, Sarah K. Gunnarson, and Kathryn Niles-Jolly, "Creating the Climate and Culture of Success," *Organizational Dynamics,* Summer 1994, pp. 17–29.

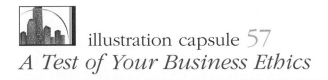

illustration capsule 57
A Test of Your Business Ethics

As a gauge of your own ethical and moral standards, take the following quiz and see how you stack up against other members of your class. How do you think your future employer would want you to answer each of these questions—in which instances would an employer be indifferent as to your answers?

1. Is it unethical to make up data to justify the introduction of a new product if, when you start to object, your boss tells you to "just do it"?
   _____ Yes   _____ No   _____ Need more information

2. Do you think that it is acceptable to give your boss a $100 gift to celebrate a birthday or holiday?
   _____ Yes   _____ No   _____ Need more information

3. Would it be wrong to accept a $100 gift from your boss (who is of the opposite sex) to celebrate your birthday?
   _____ Yes   _____ No   _____ Need more information

4. Is it unethical to accept an invitation from a supplier to spend a holiday weekend skiing at the supplier company's resort home in Colorado? (Would your answer be different if you were presently considering a proposal from that supplier to purchase $1 million worth of components?)
   _____ Yes   _____ No   _____ Need more information

5. Is it unethical to give a customer company's purchasing manager free tickets to the Super Bowl if he or she is looking for tickets and is likely to make a large purchase from your company?
   _____ Yes   _____ No   _____ Need more information

6. Is it unethical to use sick days provided in your company benefits plan as personal days so that you can go shopping or leave early for a weekend vacation?
   _____ Yes   _____ No   _____ Need more information

7. Would it be wrong to keep quiet if you, as a junior financial analyst, had just calculated that the projected return on a possible project was 18 percent and your boss (*a*) informed you that no project could be approved without the prospect of a 25 percent return and (*b*) told you to go back and redo the numbers and "get them right"?
   _____ Yes   _____ No   _____ Need more information

8. Would it be unethical to allow your supervisor to believe that you were chiefly responsible for the success of a new company initiative if it actually resulted from a team effort or major contributions by a co-worker?
   _____ Yes   _____ No   _____ Need more information

9. Is it unethical to fail to come forward to support an employee wrongfully accused of misconduct if that person is a source of aggravation for you at work?
   _____ Yes   _____ No   _____ Need more information

10. Is it wrong to use your employer's staff to prepare invitations for a party that you will give provided clients or customers are among those invited?
    _____ Yes   _____ No   _____ Need more information

11. Is it wrong to browse the Internet while at work if all your work is done and there is otherwise nothing you ought to be doing? (Would your answer be the same if the Web sites you visited were pornographic?)
    _____ Yes   _____ No   _____ Need more information

12. Is it unethical to keep quiet if you are aware that a co-worker is being sexually harassed by his or her boss?
    _____ Yes   _____ No   _____ Need more information

13. Is there an ethical problem with using your employer's copier to make a small number of copies for personal use (for example, your tax returns, your child's school project, or personal correspondence)?
    _____ Yes   _____ No   _____ Need more information

14. Is it unethical to install company-owned software on your home computer without the permission of your supervisor and the software vendor?
    _____ Yes   _____ No   _____ Need more information

15. Is it unethical to okay the shipment of products to a customer that do not meet the customer's specifications without first checking with the customer?
    _____ Yes   _____ No   _____ Need more information

ANSWERS:

We think a strong case can be made that the answers to questions 1, 3, 4, 5, 6, 7, 8, 9, 10, 11, 12, 13, 14, and 15 are yes and that the answer to question 2 is no. Most employers would consider the answers to questions 10 and 13 to be yes unless company policy allows personal use of company resources under certain specified conditions.

winning performances. Some companies symbolize the value and importance of individual employees by referring to them as Cast Members (Disney), crew members (McDonald's), co-workers (Kinko's and CDW Computer Centers), job-owners (Granite Rock), partners (Starbucks), or associates (Wal-Mart, Lenscrafters, W. L. Gore, Edward Jones, Publix Supermarkets, and Marriott International). Companies like Mary Kay Cosmetics, Tupperware, and McDonald's actively seek out reasons and opportunities to give pins, buttons, badges, and medals for good showings by average performers—the idea being to express appreciation and give a motivational boost to people who stand out in doing "ordinary" jobs. General Electric and 3M Corporation make a point of ceremoniously honoring individuals who believe so strongly in their ideas that they take it on themselves to hurdle the bureaucracy, maneuver their projects through the system, and turn them into improved services, new products, or even new businesses.

What makes a spirit of high performance come alive is a complex network of people-management practices, words, symbols, styles, values, and policies pulling together that produces extraordinary results with ordinary people. The drivers of a spirit of high performance are a belief in the worth of the individual, strong company commitment to job security and promotion from within, managerial practices that encourage employees to exercise individual initiative and creativity in doing their jobs, and pride in doing the "itty-bitty, teeny-tiny things" right.[19] A company that treats its employees well generally benefits from increased teamwork, higher morale, greater loyalty, and increased employee commitment to making a contribution.

While promoting and nurturing a spirit of high performance nearly always accentuates the positive, there are negative reinforcers too. Managers whose units consistently perform poorly have to be replaced. Low-performing workers and people who reject the cultural emphasis on dedication and high performance have to be weeded out or at least moved to out-of-the-way positions. Average performers have to be candidly counseled that they have limited career potential unless they put forth more effort and acquire better skills and work habits.

EXERTING STRATEGIC LEADERSHIP

The litany of good strategic management is simple enough: craft a sound strategic plan, implement it, execute it to the fullest, adjust as needed, win! But it's easier said than done. Exerting take-charge leadership, being a "spark plug," ramrodding things through, and getting things done by coaching others to do them are difficult tasks.[20] Moreover, a strategy manager has many different leadership roles to play: visionary, chief entrepreneur and strategist, chief administrator and strategy implementer, culture builder, resource acquirer and allocator, capabilities builder, process integrator, coach, crisis solver, taskmaster, spokesperson, negotiator, motivator, arbitrator, consensus builder, policy maker, policy enforcer, mentor, and head cheerleader.[21] Sometimes it is

---

[19]Jeffrey Pfeffer, "Producing Sustainable Competitive Advantage through the Effective Management of People," *Academy of Management Executive* 9, no.1 (February 1995), pp. 55–69.

[20]For an excellent survey of the problems and pitfalls in making the transition to a new strategy and to fundamentally new ways of doing business, see John P. Kotter, "Leading Change: Why Transformation Efforts Fail," *Harvard Business Review* 73, no. 2 (March–April 1995), pp. 59–67. See also, Thomas M. Hout and John C. Carter, "Getting It Done: New Roles for Senior Executives," *Harvard Business Review* 73, no. 6 (November–December 1995), pp. 133–45 and Sumantra Ghoshal and Christopher A. Bartlett, "Changing the Role of Top Management: Beyond Structure to Processes," *Harvard Business Review* 73, no. 1 (January–February 1995), pp. 86–96.

[21]For a very insightful and revealing report on how one CEO leads the organizational change process, see Noel Tichy and Ram Charan, "The CEO as Coach: An Interview with Allied Signal's Lawrence A. Bossidy," *Harvard Business Review* 73, no. 2 (March–April 1995), pp. 68–78.

useful to be authoritarian and hardnosed; sometimes it is best to be a perceptive listener and a compromising decision maker; sometimes a strongly participative, collegial approach works best; and sometimes being a coach and adviser is the proper role. Many occasions call for a highly visible role and extensive time commitments, while others entail a brief ceremonial performance with the details delegated to subordinates.

For the most part, major change efforts have to be top-down and vision-driven. Leading change has to start with diagnosing the situation and then deciding which of several ways to handle it. Managers have five leadership roles to play in pushing for good strategy execution:

1. Staying on top of what is happening, closely monitoring progress, ferreting out issues, and learning what obstacles lie in the path of good execution.

2. Promoting a culture and esprit de corps that mobilizes and energizes organizational members to execute strategy in a competent fashion and perform at a high level.

3. Keeping the organization responsive to changing conditions, alert for new opportunities, bubbling with innovative ideas, and ahead of rivals in developing competitively valuable competencies and capabilities.

4. Exercising ethics leadership and insisting that the company conduct its affairs like a model corporate citizen.

5. Pushing corrective actions to improve strategy execution and overall strategic performance.

Staying on Top of How Well Things Are Going

To stay on top of how well the strategy execution process is going, a manager needs to develop a broad network of contacts and sources of information, both formal and informal. The regular channels include talking with key subordinates, attending presentations and meetings, reading reviews of the latest operating results, talking to customers, watching the competitive reactions of rival firms, exchanging e-mail and holding telephone conversations with people in outlying locations, and gathering information firsthand through on-site visits and listening to rank-and-file employees. However, some information is more trustworthy than the rest, and the views and perspectives offered by different people can vary widely. Presentations and briefings by subordinates may represent the truth but not the whole truth. Bad news or problems may be minimized or in some cases not reported at all as subordinates delay conveying failures and problems in hopes that more time will give them room to turn things around. Hence, strategy managers have to make sure that they have accurate information and a feel for the existing situation. They have to confirm whether things are on track, identify problems, learn what obstacles lie in the path of good strategy execution, and develop a basis for determining what, if anything, they can personally do to move the process along.

One way strategy leaders stay on top of things is by making regular visits to the field and talking with many different people at many different levels. The technique of *managing by walking around (MBWA)* is practiced in a variety of styles. Wal-Mart executives have had a long-standing practice of spending two to three days every week visiting Wal-Mart's stores and talking with store managers and employees. Sam Walton, Wal-Mart's founder, insisted, "The key is to get out into the store and listen to what the associates have to say." Jack Welch, CEO of General Electric, not only spends several days each month personally visiting GE operations and talking with major customers but also arranges his schedule so that he can spend time talking with and listening to GE managers from all over the world who are attending classes at the

MBWA is one of the techniques effective leaders use to stay informed on how well strategy implementation and execution are proceeding.

company's leadership development center near GE's headquarters. Some companies have weekly get-togethers in each division (often on Friday afternoons), attended by both executives and employees, to create a regular opportunity for tidbits of information to flow freely between down-the-line employees and executives. In a number of offices, executives operate out of open cubicles in big spaces populated with open cubicles for other office personnel so that they can interact easily and frequently with co-workers. Some manufacturing executives make a point of strolling the factory floor talking with workers and meeting regularly with union officials.

Most managers rightly attach great importance to spending time with people at various company facilities and gathering information and opinions firsthand from diverse sources about how well various aspects of the strategy execution process are going. Such contacts give managers a feel for the progress being made, the problems being encountered, and whether additional resources or different approaches may be needed. Just as important, on-site visits and MBWA provide opportunity to talk informally to many different people at different organizational levels, speak with encouragement, lift spirits, shift attention from the old to the new priorities, and create some excitement—all of which generate positive energy and help mobilize organizational efforts behind strategy execution.

Leading the Effort to Establish a Strategy-Supportive Culture

Managers with responsibility for crafting and executing strategy have to be out front in establishing a strategy-supportive organizational climate and culture. When major strategic changes are being implemented, a manager's time is best spent personally leading the changes for whatever cultural adjustments are needed. Showing gradual incremental progress is often not enough. Conservative incrementalism seldom leads to major cultural adaptations; more usually, gradualism is defeated by the resilience of entrenched cultures and the ability of vested interests to thwart or minimize the impact of piecemeal change. Only with bold leadership and concerted action on many fronts can a company succeed in tackling so large and difficult a task as major cultural change. When only strategic fine-tuning is being implemented, it takes less time and effort to bring values and culture into alignment with strategy, but there is still a lead role for the manager to play in pushing ahead and prodding for continuous improvements.

> Successful culture changes have to be personally led by top mangement; it's a task that can't be delegated to others.

The single most visible factor that distinguishes successful culture-change efforts from failed attempts is competent leadership at the top. Effective culture-changing leadership has several attributes:[22]

- A "stakeholders-are-king" philosophy that links the need for culture change to the need to serve the long-term best interests of all key constituencies.

- Challenging the status quo with very basic questions: Are we giving customers what they really need and want? Why aren't we taking more business away from rivals? Why do our rivals have lower costs than we do? How can we drive costs out of the business and be more competitive on price? Why can't design-to-market cycle time be halved? Why aren't we moving faster to make better use of the Internet and e-commerce technologies and practices? How can we grow company revenues at 15 percent instead of 10 percent? What can we do to speed up our decision making and shorten response times?

---

[22]Kotter and Heskett, *Corporate Culture and Performance,* pp. 84, 144, and 148.

- Creating events where everyone in management is forced to listen to angry customers, dissatisfied strategic allies, alienated employees, or maybe disenchanted stockholders—a tactic that raises awareness levels and helps lay the basis for realistically assessing which traits of the culture support strategy and which do not.

- Making a compelling case for why the company's new direction and a different cultural atmosphere are in the organization's best interests and why individuals and groups should commit themselves to making it happen despite the obstacles. Skeptics have to be convinced that all is not well with the status quo. And the messages of strategic and cultural change have to be repeated at every opportunity to continue to drive the points home.

- Initiating substantive and forceful actions to flush out the undesirable cultural traits and replace them with the desired new ones.

- Recognizing and generously rewarding those who exhibit new cultural norms and who lead successful change efforts—this helps cultivate expansion of the coalition for change.

> What organizational leaders say *and do* plants the seeds of cultural change.

Great power is needed to force major cultural change—to overcome the spring-back resistance of entrenched cultures—and great power normally resides only at the top. But senior executives must not only use the power and influence that come with their position, they must also *lead by example*. For instance, if the organization's strategy involves a drive to become the industry's low-cost producer, senior managers must display frugality in their own actions and decisions: inexpensive decorations in the executive suite, conservative expense accounts and entertainment allowances, a lean staff in the corporate office, scrutiny of budget requests, and so on. The CEO of SAS Airlines, Jan Carlzon, symbolically reinforced the primacy of quality service for business customers by flying coach instead of first class and by giving up his seat to wait-listed travelers.[23] In addition, effective culture-change leaders frequently rely on stories to convey new values, create new role models, and connect the case for change to organization members.

> Only top management has the power and organizational influence to bring about major change in a company's culture.

Leading Culture Change Efforts in Multinational and Global Companies In multinational and global companies, where some cross-border diversity in the corporate culture is normal, the leadership requirements of culture-changing efforts are even more complex. Company personnel in different countries sometimes fervently insist on being treated as distinctive individuals or groups, making a one-size-fits-all rationale for cultural change and a common leadership approach potentially inappropriate. Leading cross-border culture-change initiatives requires sensitivity to prevailing cross-border cultural differences, discerning how to adapt the case for cultural change to each situation and discerning when diversity has to be accommodated and when cross-border differences can be and should be narrowed.[24] Many multinational and global companies are finding, however, that most of their core cultural values and beliefs travel well across country borders and strike a chord with managers and workers in many different areas of the world, despite the diversity of local cultures and behavioral norms. AES Corporation, which operates power plants in a growing number of culturally diverse companies across the world, has managed to institute a reasonably uniform corporate culture by relying on a set of corporate values

---

[23]Olian and Rynes, "Making Total Quality Work," p. 324.

[24]For a discussion of this dimension of leadership, see Alexander and Wilson, "Leading across Cultures: Five Vital Capabilities," pp. 287–94.

and beliefs that are well received in virtually all of the countries where it has plants.[25] At AES, the culture is built around respect for the worth and dignity of individuals, a strong sense of social responsibility and corporate citizenship, respect for the environment, decentralization of authority and decision making to local country managers (most of whom are natives to the country), and heavy reliance on employee empowerment at each of its power plants.

Keeping the Internal Organization Responsive and Innovative

Generating fresh ideas, identifying new opportunities, and developing innovative products and services are not solely managerial tasks. They are organizationwide tasks, particularly in large corporations. One of the toughest parts of exerting strategic leadership is generating a dependable supply of fresh ideas and suggestions for improvement from the rank and file, along with promoting an entrepreneurial spirit among managers and employees. A flexible, responsive, innovative internal environment is critical in fast-moving high-technology industries, in businesses where products have short life cycles and growth depends on new product innovation, in companies with widely diversified business portfolios (where opportunities are varied and scattered), in markets where successful product differentiation depends on out-innovating the competition, and in situations where low-cost leadership hinges on continuous improvement and new ways to drive costs out of the business. Managers cannot mandate such an environment by simply exhorting people to "be creative."

> The faster a company's business environment changes, the more attention managers must pay to keeping the organization innovative and responsive.

Empowering Champions   One useful leadership approach is to take special pains to foster, nourish, and support people who are willing to champion new technologies, new operating practices, better services, new products, and new product applications and are eager for a chance to try turning their ideas into better ways of operating, new product families, new businesses, and even new industries. One year after taking charge at Siemens-Nixdorf Information Systems, Gerhard Schulmeyer produced the first profit in the merged company, which had been losing hundreds of millions of dollars annually since 1991; he credited the turnaround to the creation of 5,000 "change agents," almost 15 percent of the workforce, who volunteered for active roles in the company's change agenda while continuing to perform their regular jobs. As a rule, the best champions are persistent, competitive, tenacious, committed, and fanatic about their idea and seeing it through to success.

> Identifying and empowering champions helps promote an environment of innovation and experimentation.

To promote an organizational climate where champion innovators can blossom and thrive, strategy managers need to do several things:

- Individuals and groups have to be encouraged to be creative, hold informal brainstorming sessions, let their imaginations fly in all directions, and come up with proposals. The culture has to nurture, even celebrate, experimentation and innovation. Everybody must be expected to contribute ideas, exercise initiative, and pursue continuous improvement. The trick is to keep a sense of urgency alive in the business so that people see change and innovation as necessities.

- People with maverick ideas or out-of-the-ordinary proposals have to be tolerated and given room to operate. Above all, would-be champions who advocate radical or different ideas must not be looked on as disruptive or troublesome.

---

[25]Suzy Wetlaufer, "Organizing for Empowerment: An Interview with AES's Roger Sant and Dennis Bakke," *Harvard Business Review* 77, no. 1 (January–February 1999), pp. 110–23.

- Managers have to induce and promote lots of "tries" and be willing to tolerate mistakes and failures. Most ideas don't pan out, but the organization learns from a good attempt even when it fails.

- Strategy managers should be willing to use all kinds of ad hoc organizational forms to support ideas and experimentation—venture teams, task forces, "performance shootouts" among different groups working on competing approaches, informal "bootlegged" projects composed of volunteers, and so on.

- Strategy managers have to see that the rewards for successful champions are large and visible and that people who champion an unsuccessful idea are not punished or sidelined but rather encouraged to try again.

In effect, the leadership task is to create an adaptive, innovative culture that embraces organizational responses to changing conditions rather than fearing the new conditions or seeking to minimize them. Companies with conspicuously innovative cultures include Sony, 3M, Nokia, Amazon.com, W. L. Gore, Dell Computer, and Enron.

Leading the Process of Developing New Capabilities   Often, effectively responding to changing customer preferences and competitive conditions requires top management intervention. Senior management usually has to lead the effort because core competencies and competitive capabilities typically reside in the combined efforts of different work groups, departments, and collaborative allies. The tasks of managing human skills, knowledge bases, and intellect and then integrating them to forge competitively advantageous competencies and capabilities is an exercise best orchestrated by senior managers who appreciate their strategy-implementing significance and who have the clout to enforce the necessary networking and cooperation among individuals, groups, departments, and external allies.

Effective company managers try to anticipate changes in customer-market requirements and proactively build new competencies and capabilities that offer a competitive edge over rivals. Senior managers are in the best position to see the need and potential of new capabilities and then to play a lead role in the capability-building, resource-strengthening process. Proactively building new competencies and capabilities ahead of rivals to gain a competitive edge is strategic leadership of the best kind, but strengthening the company's resource base in reaction to newly developed capabilities of pioneering rivals occurs more frequently.

Exercising Ethics Leadership and Insisting on Good Corporate Citizenship

For an organization to display consistently high ethical standards, the CEO and those around the CEO must be openly and unequivocally committed to ethical and moral conduct. It is never enough for senior executives to assume activities are being conducted ethically, nor can it be assumed that employees understand they are expected to act with integrity. Leading the enforcement of ethical behavior means iterating and re-iterating to employees that it is their duty not only to observe the company's ethical codes but also to report ethical violations. While ethically conscious companies have provisions for disciplining violators, *the main purpose of enforcement is to encourage compliance rather than administer punishment.*

There are several concrete things managers can do to exercise ethics leadership. First and foremost, they must set an excellent ethical example in their own behavior and establish a tradition of integrity. Company decisions have to be seen as ethical—actions speak louder than words. Second, managers and employees have to be educated about what is ethical and what is not; ethics training programs may have to be established and

> It's a constant organization-building challenge to broaden, deepen, or modify organization capabilities and resource strengths in response to ongoing customer-market changes.

> High ethical standards cannot be enforced without the open and unequivocal commitment of the chief executive.

Managers are an or-ganization's ethics teachers—what they do and say sends signals and what they don't do and don't say sends signals.

gray areas pointed out and discussed. Everyone must be encouraged to raise issues with ethical dimensions, and such discussions should be treated as a legitimate topic. Third, top management should regularly reiterate its unequivocal support of the company's ethical code and take a strong stand on ethical issues. Fourth, top management must be prepared to act as the final arbiter on hard calls; this means removing people from key positions or terminating them when they are guilty of a violation. It also means repri-manding those who have been lax in monitoring and enforcing ethical compliance. Fail-ure to act swiftly and decisively in punishing ethical misconduct is interpreted as a lack of real commitment.

If a company is really serious about enforcing ethical behavior, it probably needs to do two things:

- Conduct an annual audit of each manager's efforts to uphold ethical standards and formal reports on the actions taken by managers to remedy deficient conduct.
- Require all employees to sign a statement annually certifying that they have com-plied with the company's code of ethics.

See Illustration Capsule 58 for a discussion of the actions Lockheed Martin took when it was fined nearly $25 million for an ethics violation and its status as a major U.S. defense contractor was put in jeopardy.

Corporate Citizenship and Social Responsibility: Another Dimension of Model Ethical Behavior
Strong enforcement of a corporate code of ethics by itself is not sufficient to make a company a good corporate citizen. Business leaders who want their companies to be regarded as exemplary corporate citizens not only must see that their companies operate ethically but also must display a social conscience in decisions that affect stakeholders, especially employees, the communi-ties in which they operate, and society at large. Corporate citizenship and socially reponsible decision making are demonstrated in a number of ways: having family-friendly employment practices, operating a safe workplace, taking special pains to protect the environment (beyond what is required by law), taking an active role in community affairs, interacting with community officials to minimize the impact of layoffs or hiring large numbers of new employees (which could put a strain on local schools and utility services), and being a generous supporter of charitable causes and projects that benefit society. For example, Chick-fil-A, an Atlanta-based fast-food chain with 700 outlets, has a charitable foundation, supports 10 foster homes and a summer camp, funds two scholarship programs, and participates in a number of one-on-one programs with children.[26] Toys "R" Us supports initiatives addressing the is-sue of child labor and fair labor practices around the world. Community Pride Food Stores is assisting in revitalizing the inner city of Richmond, Virginia, where the com-pany is based. The owner of Malden Mills Industries in Malden, Massachusetts, kept employees on the company's payroll for months while a fire-razed plant was rebuilt and re-equipped.

What separates companies that make a sincere effort to carry their weight in be-ing good corporate citizens from companies that are content to do only what is legally required of them are strategy leaders who believe strongly in good corporate citizen-ship. Companies with socially conscious strategy leaders and with cultures where cor-porate social responsibility is a core value are the most likely to conduct their affairs in a manner befitting a good corporate citizen.

---

[26]Archie B. Carroll, "The Four Faces of Corporate Citizenship," *Business and Society Review* 100/101 (1998), p. 6.

illustration capsule 58

Lockheed Martin's Corrective Actions after Being Fined for Violating U.S. Antibribery Laws

Lockheed Martin Corporation is among the world's leading producers of aeronautics and space systems with 1999 sales of over $25 billion. Since 1914, when the company first delivered aircraft to the U.S. Army Signal Corps, Lockheed has designed and built military aircraft and spacecraft for the U.S. military and its allies, including the P-38 fighter, B-29 bomber, U-2 and SR-71 reconnaissance aircraft, C-130 cargo planes, F-104 Starfighter, F-16 Fighting Falcon, F-22 Raptor, and Titan and Trident missiles. It has been a major contractor on the Mercury, Gemini, Apollo, Skylab, and Shuttle space programs. In 1999 the company's sales to the U.S. government accounted for more than 70 percent of its annual revenues.

Lockheed Martin's status as a U.S. government contractor was jeopardized in 1995 when company officials admitted that the company had conspired to violate U.S. antibribery laws. The infraction occurred in 1990 when Lockheed Martin paid an Egyptian lawmaker $1 million to help the company secure a contract to supply Egypt with C-130 cargo planes. The U.S. government fined Lockheed Martin $24.8 million and placed it on a three-year probationary period during which further ethics violations could bar the company from bidding on government contracts.

After the conviction, Lockheed Martin's CEO and other senior executives engineered the development of a comprehensive ethics compliance program that used the company's computer systems and Internet capabilities to guard against subsequent violations. Software programs like Qwizard and Merlin allow employees to go online to complete mandatory ethics training related to the Lockheed Martin's Code of Ethics and Business Conduct. The system records when employees complete online sessions on such topics as sexual harassment, security, software-license compliance, labor charging, insider trading, and gratuities. The Internet-based training program also allows the company to conduct up-to-the-minute ethics audits to determine how many hours of training have been completed by each of Lockheed Martin's 170,000 employees.

Lockheed Martin's ethics software programs also provide company managers with a variety of statistics related to ethics violations that do occur at the company. The system compiles data and prepares reports concerning detected violations like misuse of company resources, conflicts of interest, and security breaches. In addition, the system gives an accounting of the number of Lockheed Martin employees discharged, suspended, and reprimanded for ethics violations. The information maintained by Lockheed Martin's systems has aided both managers and the U.S. government in assessing the state of business ethics at the company.

Lockheed Martin's renewed commitment to honesty, integrity, respect, trust, responsibility, and citizenship and its method for monitoring ethics compliance not only reduced the likelihood of being barred from the defense contracting business but also paved the way for the company to receive the 1998 American Business Ethics Award. Upon receiving the award, the company's chairman and CEO Vance Coffman said, "At Lockheed Martin, we have stressed that the first and most important unifying principle guiding us is ethical conduct, every day and everywhere we do business. Receiving the American Business Ethics Award is a strong signal that we are achieving our goal of putting our Corporation on a firm ethical foundation for the challenges of the 21st Century."

Sources: Lockheed Martin Web site; and *The Wall Street Journal*, October 21, 1999, p. B1.

Leading the Process of Making Corrective Adjustments

The leadership challenge here is twofold: deciding when to make adjustments and deciding what adjustments to make. Both decisions are a normal and necessary part of a strategy manager's job since no strategic plan and no scheme for implementing and executing strategy can foresee all the events and problems that will arise. There comes a time at every company when managers have to alter the company's direction, revise objectives, modify strategy, or fine-tune the approaches to strategy execution.

The *process* of making corrective adjustments varies according to the situation. In a crisis, the typical leadership approach is to have key subordinates gather information,

> Corrective adjustments in the company's approach to executing strategy are normal and have to be made as needed.

identify and evaluate options (crunching whatever numbers may be appropriate), and perhaps prepare a preliminary set of recommended actions for consideration. The strategy leader then usually meets with key subordinates and personally presides over extended discussions of the proposed responses, trying to build a quick consensus among members of the executive inner circle. If no consensus emerges and action is required immediately, the burden falls on the strategy manager to choose the response and urge its support.

When the situation allows managers to proceed more deliberately in deciding when to make changes and what changes to make, strategy managers seem to prefer a process of incrementally solidifying commitment to a particular course of action.[27] The process that managers go through in deciding on corrective adjustments is essentially the same for both proactive and reactive changes: they sense needs, gather information, broaden and deepen their understanding of the situation, develop options and explore their pros and cons, put forth action proposals, generate partial (comfort-level) solutions, build a managerial consensus, and finally formally adopt an agreed-on course of action.[28] The time frame for deciding what corrective changes in vision, objectives, strategies, capabilities, implementation/execution approaches to initiate can take a few hours, a few days, a few weeks, or even a few months if the situation is particularly complicated. Success usually hinges on thorough analysis of the situation and the exercise of good business judgment.

All this, once again, highlights the fundamental nature of strategic management: the job of crafting, implementing, and executing strategy is a five-task process with much looping and recycling to fine-tune and adjust strategic visions, objectives, strategies, capabilities, implementation approaches, and cultures to fit one another and to fit changing circumstances. The process is continuous, and the conceptually separate acts of crafting and executing strategy blur and join together in real-world situations. The best tests of good strategic leadership are whether the company has a good strategy and whether that strategy is being competently executed. If these two conditions exist, the chances are excellent that the company is improving its financial and strategic performance, is capable of adapting to multiple changes, and is a good place to work.

key | points

Building a strategy-supportive corporate culture is important to successful strategy execution because it produces a work climate and organizational esprit de corps that thrive on meeting performance targets and being part of a winning effort. An organization's culture emerges from why and how it does things the way it does, the values and beliefs that senior managers espouse, the ethical standards expected of organization members, the tone and philosophy underlying key policies, and the traditions the organization maintains. Culture thus concerns the atmosphere and feeling a company has and the style in which it gets things done.

Very often, the elements of company culture originate with a founder or other early influential leaders who articulate the values, beliefs, and principles to which the company should adhere, and that then get incorporated into company policies, a creed or values statement, strategies, and operating practices. Over time, these values and practices become shared by company employees and managers. Cultures are perpetuated as new leaders act to reinforce them, as new employees are encouraged to adopt

---

[27]James Brian Quinn, *Strategies for Change: Logical Incrementalism,* Homewood, IL: Richard D. Irwin, 1980, pp. 20–22.
[28]Ibid., p. 146.

and follow them, as stories of people and events illustrating core values and practices are told and retold, and as organization members are honored and rewarded for displaying cultural norms.

Company cultures vary widely in strength and in makeup. Some cultures are strongly embedded, while others are weak and fragmented. Some cultures are unhealthy; these are often dominated by self-serving politics, resistance to change, and inward focus. Such cultural traits are often precursors to declining company performance. In fast-changing business environments, adaptive cultures are best because people tend to accept and support company efforts to adapt to environmental change; the work climate in adaptive-culture companies is receptive to new ideas, experimentation, innovation, new strategies, and new operating practices provided such changes are compatible with core values and beliefs. One significant defining trait of adaptive cultures is that top management genuinely cares about the well-being of all key constituencies—customers, employees, stockholders, major suppliers, and the communities where it operates—and tries to satisfy all their legitimate interests simultaneously.

The philosophy, goals, and practices implicit or explicit in a new strategy may or may not be compatible with a firm's culture. A close strategy–culture alignment promotes implementation and good execution; a mismatch poses real obstacles. Changing a company's culture, especially a strong one with traits that don't fit a new strategy's requirements, is one of the toughest management challenges. Changing a culture requires competent leadership at the top. It requires symbolic actions and substantive actions that unmistakably indicate serious commitment on the part of top management. The stronger the fit between culture and strategy, the less managers have to depend on policies, rules, procedures, and supervision to enforce what people should and should not do; rather, cultural norms are so well observed that they automatically guide behavior.

Healthy corporate cultures are also grounded in ethical business principles, moral values, and socially responsible decision making. Such standards connote integrity, "doing the right thing," and genuine concern for stakeholders and for how the company does business. To be effective, corporate ethics and values programs have to become a way of life through training, strict compliance and enforcement procedures, and reiterated management endorsements. Moreover, top managers must practice what they preach, serving as role models for ethical behavior, values-driven decision making, and a social conscience.

Successful managers do a number of things to exercise strategy-executing leadership. They keep a finger on the organization's pulse by spending considerable time outside their offices, listening and talking to organization members, coaching, cheerleading, and picking up important information. They take pains to reinforce the corporate culture through the things they say and do. They encourage people to be creative and innovative in order to keep the organization responsive to changing conditions, alert to new opportunities, and anxious to pursue fresh initiatives. They support champions of new approaches or ideas who are willing to stick their necks out and try something innovative. They work hard at building consensus on how to proceed, what to change, and what not to change. They enforce high ethical standards and insist on socially responsible corporate decision making. And they actively push corrective actions to improve strategy execution and overall strategic performance.

Because each instance of executing strategy occurs under different organizational circumstances, a strategy implementer's action agenda always needs to be situation-specific—there's no neat generic procedure to follow. And, as we said at the beginning, executing strategy is an action-oriented, make-the-right-things-happen task that challenges a manager's ability to lead and direct organizational change, create or reinvent business processes, manage and motivate people, and achieve performance targets. If you now better understand the nature of the challenge, the range of available approaches, the issues that need to be considered, and why the action agenda for implementing and executing strategy sweeps across so many aspects of administrative and managerial work, then we will look on our discussion in these last three chapter as a success.

suggested|readings

Badaracco, Joseph L. *Defining Moments: When Managers Must Choose between Right and Wrong.* Boston: Harvard Business School Press, 1997.

Badaracco, Joe, and Allen P. Webb. "Business Ethics: A View from the Trenches." *California Management Review* 37, no. 2 (Winter 1995), pp. 8–28.

Carroll, Archie B. "The Four Faces of Corporate Citizenship." *Business and Society Review* 100/101 (1998), pp. 1–7.

Clement, Ronald W. "Culture, Leadership, and Power: The Keys to Organizational Change." *Business Horizons* 37, no. 1 (January–February 1994), pp. 33–39.

Driscoll, Dawn-Marie, and W. Michael Hoffman. "Gaining the Ethical Edge: Procedures for Delivering Values-Driven Management." *Long Range Planning* 32, no. 2 (April 1999), pp. 179–89.

Farkas, Charles M., and Suzy Wetlaufer. "The Ways Chief Executive Officers Lead." *Harvard Business Review* 74, no. 3 (May–June 1996), pp. 110–22.

Floyd, Steven W., and Bill Wooldridge. "Managing Strategic Consensus: The Foundation of Effective Implementation." *Academy of Management Executive* 6, no. 4 (November 1992), pp. 27–39.

Ghoshal, Sumantra, and Christopher A. Bartlett. "Changing the Role of Top Management: Beyond Structure to Processes." *Harvard Business Review* 73, no. 1 (January–February 1995), pp. 86–96.

Goffee, Robert, and Gareth Jones. *The Character of a Corporation.* New York: HarperCollins, 1998.

Goleman, Daniel. "What Makes a Leader." *Harvard Business Review* 76, no. 6 (November–December 1998), pp. 92–102.

Hamel, Gary. "Reinvent Your Company." *Fortune* 141, no. 12 (June 12, 2000), pp. 98–118.

Heifetz, Ronald A., and Donald L. Laurie. "The Work of Leadership." *Harvard Business Review* 75, no. 1 (January–February 1997), pp. 124–34.

Kirkpatrick, Shelley A., and Edwin A. Locke. "Leadership: Do Traits Matter?" *Academy of Management Executive* 5, no. 2 (May 1991), pp. 48–60.

Kotter, John P. "What Leaders Really Do." *Harvard Business Review* 68, no. 3 (May–June 1990), pp. 103–11.

———."Leading Change: Why Transformation Efforts Fail." *Harvard Business Review* 73, no. 2 (March–April 1995), pp. 59–67.

Kotter, John P., and James L. Heskett. *Corporate Culture and Performance.* New York: Free Press, 1992.

Miles, Robert H. *Corporate Comeback: The Story of Renewal and Transformation at National Semiconductor.* San Francisco: Jossey-Bass, 1997.

Murphy, Patrick E. "Corporate Ethics Statements: Current Status and Future Prospects." *Journal of Business Ethics* 14 (1995), pp. 727–40.

Paine, Lynn Sharp. "Managing for Organizational Integrity." *Harvard Business Review* 72, no. 2 (March–April 1994), pp. 106–17.

Schneider, Benjamin; Sarah K. Gunnarson; and Kathryn Niles-Jolly. "Creating the Climate and Culture of Success." *Organizational Dynamics* (Summer 1994), pp. 17–29.

Scholz, Christian. "Corporate Culture and Strategy—The Problem of Strategic Fit." *Long Range Planning* 20 (August 1987), pp. 78–87.

part|two 2

Cases in
Strategic
Management

A Guide to Case Analysis

I keep six honest serving men
(They taught me all I knew);
Their names are What and Why and When;
And How and Where and Who.
—Rudyard Kipling

In most courses in strategic management, students use cases about actual companies to practice strategic analysis and to gain some experience in the tasks of crafting and implementing strategy. A case sets forth, in a factual manner, the events and organizational circumstances surrounding a particular managerial situation. It puts readers at the scene of the action and familiarizes them with all the relevant circumstances. A case on strategic management can concern a whole industry, a single organization, or some part of an organization; the organization involved can be either profit-seeking or not-for-profit. The essence of the student's role in case analysis is to diagnose and size up the situation described in the case and then to recommend appropriate action steps.

WHY USE CASES TO PRACTICE STRATEGIC MANAGEMENT?

A student of business with tact
Absorbed many answers he lacked.
But acquiring a job,
He said with a sob,
"How does one fit answer to fact?"

The above limerick was used some years ago by Professor Charles Gragg to characterize the plight of business students who had no exposure to cases.[1] The truth is that the mere act of listening to lectures and sound advice about managing does little for anyone's management skills. Accumulated managerial wisdom cannot effectively be passed on by lectures and assigned readings alone. If anything had been learned about the practice of management, it is that a storehouse of readymade textbook answers does not exist. Each managerial situation has unique aspects, requiring its own diagnosis, judgment, and tailor-made actions. Cases provide would-be managers with a valuable way to practice wrestling with the actual problems of actual managers in actual companies.

The case approach to strategic analysis is, first and foremost, an exercise in learning by doing. Because cases provide detailed information about conditions and problems of different industries and companies, your task of analyzing company after company and situation after situation has the twin benefit of boosting your analytical skills and exposing you to the ways companies and managers actually do things. Most college students have limited managerial backgrounds and only fragmented knowledge

---

[1]Charles I. Gragg, "Because Wisdom Can't Be Told," in *The Case Method at the Harvard Business School*, ed. M. P. McNair (New York: McGraw-Hill, 1954), p. 11.

about companies and real-life strategic situations. Cases help substitute for on-the-job experience by (1) giving you broader exposure to a variety of industries, organizations, and strategic problems; (2) forcing you to assume a managerial role (as opposed to that of just an onlooker); (3) providing a test of how to apply the tools and techniques of strategic management; and (4) asking you to come up with pragmatic managerial action plans to deal with the issues at hand.

OBJECTIVES OF CASE ANALYSIS

Using cases to learn about the practice of strategic management is a powerful way for you to accomplish five things:[2]

1. Increase your understanding of what managers should and should not do in guiding a business to success.
2. Build your skills in sizing up company resource strengths and weaknesses and in conducting strategic analysis in a variety of industries and competitive situations.
3. Get valuable practice in identifying strategic issues that need to be addressed, evaluating strategic alternatives, and formulating workable plans of action.
4. Enhance your sense of business judgment, as opposed to uncritically accepting the authoritative crutch of the professor or "back-of-the-book" answers.
5. Gaining in-depth exposure to different industries and companies, thereby acquiring something close to actual business experience.

If you understand that these are the objectives of case analysis, you are less likely to be consumed with curiosity about "the answer to the case." Students who have grown comfortable with and accustomed to textbook statements of fact and definitive lecture notes are often frustrated when discussions about a case do not produce concrete answers. Usually, case discussions produce good arguments for more than one course of action. Differences of opinion nearly always exist. Thus, should a class discussion conclude without a strong, unambiguous consensus on what do to, don't grumble too much when you are *not* told what the answer is or what the company actually did. Just remember that in the business world answers don't come in conclusive black-and-white terms. There are nearly always several feasible courses of action and approaches, each of which may work out satisfactorily. Moreover, in the business world, when one elects a particular course of action, there is no peeking at the back of a book to see if you have chosen the best thing to do and no one to turn to for a provably correct answer. The only valid test of management action is *results*. If the results of an action turn out to be good, the decision to take it may be presumed right. If not, then the action chosen was wrong in the sense that it didn't work out.

   Hence, the important thing for a student to understand in case analysis is that the managerial exercise of identifying, diagnosing, and recommending builds your skills; discovering the right answer or finding out what actually happened is no more than frosting on the cake. Even if you learn what the company did, you can't conclude that it was necessarily right or best. All that can be said is "Here is what they did . . . "

---

[2]Ibid., pp. 12–14; and D. R. Schoen and Philip A. Sprague, "What Is the Case Method?" in *The Case Method at the Harvard Business School,* ed. M. P. McNair, pp. 78–79.

The point is this: *The purpose of giving you a case assignment is not to cause you to run to the library or surf the Internet to discover what the company actually did but, rather, to enhance your skills in sizing up situations and developing your managerial judgment about what needs to be done and how to do it.* The aim of case analysis is for *you* to become actively engaged in diagnosing the business issues and managerial problems posed in the case, to propose workable solutions, and to explain and defend your assessments—this is how cases provide you with meaningful practice at being a manager.

PREPARING A CASE FOR CLASS DISCUSSION

If this is your first experience with the case method, you may have to reorient your study habits. Unlike lecture courses in which you can get by without preparing intensively for each class and have latitude to work assigned readings and reviews of lecture notes into your schedule, a case assignment requires conscientious preparation before class. You will not get much out of hearing the class discuss a case you haven't read, and you certainly won't be able to contribute anything yourself to the discussion.

To get ready for class discussion of a case, you must study the case, reflect carefully on the situation presented, and develop some reasoned thoughts. Your goal should be to end up with a sound, well-supported analysis of the situation and a sound, defensible set of recommendations. The Case-TUTOR software package that accompanies this edition will assist you in preparing the cases—it contains a set of study questions for each case and step-by-step tutorials to walk you through the process of analyzing and developing reasonable recommendations.

To prepare a case for class discussion, we suggest the following approach:

1. *Skim the case rather quickly to get an overview of the situation it presents.* This quick overview should give you the general flavor of the situation and indicate the kinds of issues and problems you will need to wrestle with. If your instructor has provided you with study questions for the case, now is the time to read them carefully.

2. *Read the case thoroughly to digest the facts and circumstances.* On this reading, try to gain full command of the situation presented in the case. Begin to develop some tentative answers to the study questions from your instructor or in the Case-TUTOR software package, which you can download at the Web site for the text. If your instructor has elected not to give you assignment questions or has not recommended regular use of the Case-TUTOR, then start forming your own picture of the overall situation being described.

3. *Carefully review all the information presented in the exhibits.* Often, there is an important story in the numbers contained in the exhibits. Expect the information in the case exhibits to be crucial enough to materially affect your diagnosis of the situation.

4. *Decide what the strategic issues are.* Until you have identified the strategic issues and problems in the case, you don't know what to analyze, which tools and analytical techniques are called for, or otherwise how to proceed. At times the strategic issues are clear—they are either stated directly in the case or easily inferred from it. At other times you will have to dig out the issues from all the information

given; if so, the study questions and the case preparation exercises provided in the Case-TUTOR software will guide you.

5. *Start your analysis of the issues with some number crunching.* A big majority of strategy cases call for some kind of number crunching—calculating assorted financial ratios to check out the company's financial condition and recent performance, calculating growth rates of sales or profits or unit volume, checking out profit margins and the makeup of the cost structure, and understanding whatever revenue-cost-profit relationships are present. See Table 1 on the next page for a summary of key financial ratios, how they are calculated, and what they show. If you are using Case-TUTOR, some of the number crunching has been computerized and you'll spend most of your time interpreting the growth rates, financial ratios, and other calculations provided.

6. *Apply the concepts and techniques of strategic analysis you have been studying.* Strategic analysis is not just a collection of opinions; rather, it entails applying the concepts and analytical tools described in Chapters 1 through 13 to cut beneath the surface and produce sharp insight and understanding. Every case assigned is strategy related and presents you with an opportunity to usefully apply what you have learned. Your instructor is looking for you to demonstrate that you know *how* and *when* to use the material presented in the text chapters. The case preparation guides on Case-TUTOR will point you toward the proper analytical tools needed to analyze the case situation.

7. *Check out conflicting opinions and make some judgments about the validity of all the data and information provided.* Many times cases report views and contradictory opinions (after all, people don't always agree on things, and different people see the same things in different ways). Forcing you to evaluate the data and information presented in the case helps you develop your powers of inference and judgment. Resolving conflicting information comes with the territory because a great many managerial situations entail opposing points of view, conflicting trends, and sketchy information.

8. *Support your diagnosis and opinions with reasons and evidence.* Most important is to prepare your answers to the question "Why?" For instance, if after studying the case you are of the opinion that the company's managers are doing a poor job, then it is your answer to "Why do you think so?" that establishes just how good your analysis of the situation is. If your instructor has provided you with specific study questions for the case or if you are using the case preparation guides on Case-TUTOR, by all means prepare answers that include all the reasons and number-crunching evidence you can muster to support your diagnosis. Work through the case preparation exercises on Case-TUTOR *conscientiously,* or, if you are using study questions provided by the instructor, *generate at least two pages of notes!*

9. *Develop an appropriate action plan and set of recommendations.* Diagnosis divorced from corrective action is sterile. The test of a manager is always to convert sound analysis into sound actions—actions that will produce the desired results. Hence, the final and most telling step in preparing a case is to develop an action agenda for management that lays out a set of specific recommendations. Bear in mind that proposing realistic, workable solutions is far preferable to casually tossing out top-of-the-head suggestions. Be prepared to explain why your recommendations

table 1   Key Financial Ratios, How They Are Calculated, and What They Show

Ratio	How Calculated	What It Shows
Profitability ratios		
1. Gross profit margin	$\dfrac{\text{Sales} - \text{Cost of goods sold}}{\text{Sales}}$	An indication of the total margin available to cover operating expenses and yield a profit.
2. Operating profit margin (or return on sales)	$\dfrac{\text{Profits before taxes and before interest}}{\text{Sales}}$	An indication of the firm's profitability from current operations without regard to the interest charges accruing from the capital structure.
3. Net profit margin (or net return on sales)	$\dfrac{\text{Profits after taxes}}{\text{Sales}}$	Shows after-tax profits per dollar of sales. Subpar profit margins indicate that the firm's sales prices are relatively low or that costs are relatively high, or both.
4. Return on total assets	$\dfrac{\text{Profits after taxes}}{\text{Total assets}}$ or $\dfrac{\text{Profit after taxes} + \text{interest}}{\text{Total assets}}$	A measure of the return on total investment in the enterprise. It is sometimes desirable to add interest to the after-tax profits to form the numerator of the ratio since total assets are financed by creditors as well as by stockholders; hence, it is accurate to measure the productivity of assets by the returns provided to both classes of investors.
5. Return on stockholders' equity (or return on net worth)	$\dfrac{\text{Profits after taxes}}{\text{Total stockholders' equity}}$	A measure of the rate of return on stockholders' investment in the enterprise.
6. Return on capital employed	$\dfrac{\text{Profits after taxes} - \text{Preferred stock dividends}}{\text{Total stockholders' equity} + \text{total debt} - \text{Par value of preferred stock}}$	A measure of the rate of return on the total capital investment in the enterprise.
7. Earnings per share	$\dfrac{\text{Profits after taxes and after preferred stock dividends}}{\text{Number of shares of common stock outstanding}}$	Shows the earnings available to the owners of each share of common stock.
Liquidity ratios		
1. Current ratio	$\dfrac{\text{Current assets}}{\text{Current liabilities}}$	Indicates the extent to which the claims of short-term creditors are covered by assets that are expected to be converted to cash in a period roughly corresponding to the maturity of the liabilities.
2. Quick ratio (or acid-test ratio)	$\dfrac{\text{Current assets} - \text{Inventory}}{\text{Current liabilities}}$	A measure of the firm's ability to pay off short-term obligations without relying on the sale of its inventories.
3. Inventory to net working capital	$\dfrac{\text{Inventory}}{\text{Current assets} - \text{Current liabilities}}$	A measure of the extent to which the firm's working capital is tied up in inventory.
Leverage ratios		
1. Debt-to-assets ratio	$\dfrac{\text{Total debt}}{\text{Total assets}}$	Measures the extent to which borrowed funds have been used to finance the firm's operations. Debt includes both long-term debt and short-term debt.
2. Debt-to-equity ratio	$\dfrac{\text{Total debt}}{\text{Total stockholders' equity}}$	Provides another measure of the funds provided by creditors versus the funds provided by owners.

table 1   (*concluded*)

Ratio	How Calculated	What It Shows
Leverage ratios (*cont.*)		
3. Long-term debt-to-equity ratio	$$\frac{\text{Long-term debt}}{\text{Total stockholders' equity}}$$	A widely used measure of the balance between debt and equity in the firm's long-term capital structure.
4. Times-interest-earned (or coverage) ratio	$$\frac{\text{Profits before interest and taxes}}{\text{Total interest charges}}$$	Measures the extent to which earnings can decline without the firm becoming unable to meet its annual interest costs.
5. Fixed-charge coverage	$$\frac{\text{Profits before taxes and interest} + \text{Lease obligations}}{\text{Total interest charges} + \text{Lease obligations}}$$	A more inclusive indication of the firm's ability to meet all of its fixed-charge obligations.
Activity ratios		
1. Inventory turnover	$$\frac{\text{Sales}}{\text{Inventory of finished goods}}$$	When compared to industry averages, it provides an indication of whether a company has excessive or perhaps inadequate finished goods inventory.
2. Fixed assets turnover	$$\frac{\text{Sales}}{\text{Fixed assets}}$$	A measure of the sales productivity and utilization of plant and equipment.
3. Total assets turnover	$$\frac{\text{Sales}}{\text{Total assets}}$$	A measure of the utilization of all the firm's assets; a ratio below the industry average indicates the company is not generating a sufficient volume of business, given the size of its asset investment.
4. Accounts receivable turnover	$$\frac{\text{Annual credit sales}}{\text{Accounts receivable}}$$	A measure of the average length of time it takes the firm to collect the sales made on credit.
5. Average collection period	$$\frac{\text{Accounts receivable}}{\text{Total sales} \div 365}$$ or $$\frac{\text{Accounts receivable}}{\text{Average daily sales}}$$	Indicates the average length of time the firm must wait after making a sale before it receives payment.
Other ratios		
1. Dividend yield on common stock	$$\frac{\text{Annual dividends per share}}{\text{Current market price per share}}$$	A measure of the return to owners received in the form of dividends.
2. Price-earnings ratio	$$\frac{\text{Current market price per share}}{\text{After-tax earnings per share}}$$	Faster-growing or less-risky firms tend to have higher price-earnings ratios than slower-growing or more-risky firms.
3. Dividend payout ratio	$$\frac{\text{Annual dividends per share}}{\text{After-tax earnings per share}}$$	Indicates the percentage of profits paid out as dividends.
4. Cash flow per share	$$\frac{\text{After-tax profits} + \text{Depreciation}}{\text{Number of common shares outstanding}}$$	A measure of the discretionary funds over and above expenses that are available for use by the firm.

Note: Industry-average ratios against which a particular company's ratios may be judged are available in *Modern Industry and Dun's Reviews* published by Dun & Bradstreet (14 ratios for 125 lines of business activities), Robert Morris Associates' *Annual Statement Studies* (11 ratios for 156 lines of business), and the FTC-SEC's *Quarterly Financial Report* for manufacturing corporations.

are more attractive than other courses of action that are open. You'll find Case-Tutor's case preparation guides helpful in performing this step, too.

As long as you are conscientious in preparing your analysis and recommendations, and have ample reasons, evidence, and arguments to support your views, you shouldn't fret unduly about whether what you've prepared is "the right answer" to the case. In case analysis there is rarely just one right approach or set of recommendations. Managing a company and crafting and executing strategies are not such exact sciences that there exists a single provably correct analysis and action plan for each strategic situation. Of course, some analyses and action plans are better than others; but, in truth, there's nearly always more than one good way to analyze a situation and more than one good plan of action. So, if you have carefully prepared the case using either the Case-Tutor case preparation guides or your instructor's assignment questions, don't lose confidence in the correctness of your work and judgment.

PARTICIPATING IN CLASS DISCUSSION OF A CASE

Classroom discussions of cases are sharply different from lecture classes. In a case class students do most of the talking. The instructor's role is to solicit student participation, keep the discussion on track, ask "Why?" often, offer alternative views, play the devil's advocate (if no students jump in to offer opposing views), and otherwise lead the discussion. The students in the class carry the burden of analyzing the situation and of being prepared to present and defend their diagnoses and recommendations. Expect a classroom environment, therefore, that calls for *your* size-up of the situation, *your* analysis, what actions *you* would take, and why *you* would take them. Do not be dismayed if, as the class discussion unfolds, some insightful things are said by your fellow classmates that you did not think of. It is normal for views and analyses to differ and for the comments of others in the class to expand your own thinking about the case. As the old adage goes, "Two heads are better than one." So it is to be expected that the class as a whole will do a more penetrating and searching job of case analysis than will any one person working alone. This is the power of group effort, and its virtues are that it will help you see more analytical applications, let you test your analyses and judgments against those of your peers, and force you to wrestle with differences of opinion and approaches.

To orient you to the classroom environment on the days a case discussion is scheduled, we compiled the following list of things to expect:

1. Expect the instructor to assume the role of extensive questioner and listener.
2. Expect students to do most of the talking. The case method enlists a maximum of individual participation in class discussion. It is not enough to be present as a silent observer; if every student took this approach, there would be no discussion. (Thus, expect a portion of your grade to be based on your participation in case discussions.)
3. Be prepared for the instructor to probe for reasons and supporting analysis.
4. Expect and tolerate challenges to the views expressed. All students have to be willing to submit their conclusions for scrutiny and rebuttal. Each student needs to learn to state his or her views without fear of disapproval and to overcome the hesitation of speaking out. Learning respect for the views and approaches of others is an integral part of case analysis exercises. But there are times when it is OK to

swim against the tide of majority opinion. In the practice of management, there is always room for originality and unorthodox approaches. So while discussion of a case is a group process, there is no compulsion for you or anyone else to cave in and conform to group opinions and group consensus.

5. Don't be surprised if you change your mind about some things as the discussion unfolds. Be alert to how these changes affect your analysis and recommendations (in the event you get called on).

6. Expect to learn a lot in class as the discussion of a case progresses; furthermore, you will find that the cases build on one another—what you learn in one case helps prepare you for the next case discussion.

There are several things you can do on your own to be good and look good as a participant in class discussions:

- Although you should do your own independent work and independent thinking, don't hesitate before (and after) class to discuss the case with other students. In real life, managers often discuss the company's problems and situation with other people to refine their own thinking.

- In participating in the discussion, make a conscious effort to contribute, rather than just talk. There is a big difference between saying something that builds the discussion and offering a long-winded off-the-cuff remark that leaves the class wondering what the point was.

- Avoid the use of "I think," "I believe," and "I feel"; instead, say, "My analysis shows—" and "The company should do . . . because—" Always give supporting reasons and evidence for your views; then your instructor won't have to ask you "Why?" every time you make a comment.

- In making your points, assume that everyone has read the case and knows what it says; avoid reciting and rehashing information in the case—instead, use the data and information to explain your assessment of the situation and to support your position.

- Bring the printouts of the work you've done on Case-TUTOR or the notes you've prepared (usually two or three pages' worth) to class and rely on them extensively when you speak. There's no way you can remember everything—especially the results of your number crunching. To reel off the numbers or to present all five reasons why, instead of one, you will need good notes. When you have prepared thoughtful answers to the study questions and use them as the basis for your comments, *everybody* in the room will know you are well prepared, and your contribution to the case discussion will stand out.

PREPARING A WRITTEN CASE ANALYSIS

Preparing a written case analysis is much like preparing a case for class discussion, except that your analysis must be more complete and put in report form. Unfortunately, though, there is no ironclad procedure for doing a written case analysis. All we can offer are some general guidelines and words of wisdom—this is because company situations and management problems are so diverse that no one mechanical way to approach a written case assignment always works.

Your instructor may assign you a specific topic around which to prepare your written report. Or, alternatively, you may be asked to do a comprehensive written case analysis, where the expectation is that you will (1) *identify* all the pertinent issues that management needs to address, (2) perform whatever *analysis* or *evaluation* is appropriate, and (3) propose an *action plan* and *set of recommendations* addressing the issues you have identified. In going through the exercise of identify, evaluate, and recommend, keep the following pointers in mind.[3]

Identification

It is essential early on in your paper that you provide a sharply focused diagnosis of strategic issues and key problems and that you demonstrate a good grasp of the company's present situation. Make sure that you can identify the firm's strategy (use the concepts and tools in Chapters 1–10 as diagnostic aids) and that you can pinpoint whatever strategy implementation issues may exist (consult the material in Chapters 11–13 for diagnostic help). Consult the key points we have provided at the end of each chapter for further diagnostic suggestions. Review the study questions for the case on Case-TUTOR. Consider beginning your paper with an overview of the company's situation, its strategy, and the significant problems and issues that confront management. State problems/ issues as clearly and precisely as you can. Unless it is necessary to do so for emphasis, avoid recounting facts and history about the company (assume your professor has read the case and is familiar with the organization).

Analysis and Evaluation

This is usually the hardest part of the report. Analysis is hard work! Check out the firm's financial ratios, its profit margins and rates of return, and its capital structure, and decide how strong the firm is financially. Refer back to Table 1, which contains a summary of various financial ratios and how they are calculated. Use it to assist in your financial diagnosis. Similarly, look at marketing, production, managerial competence, and other factors underlying the organization's strategic successes and failures. Decide whether the firm has valuable resource strengths and competencies and, if so, whether it is capitalizing on them.

Check to see if the firm's strategy is producing satisfactory results and determine the reasons why or why not. Probe the nature and strength of the competitive forces confronting the company. Decide whether and why the firm's competitive position is getting stronger or weaker. Use the tools and concepts you have learned about to perform whatever analysis or evaluation is appropriate. Work through the case preparation exercise on Case-TUTOR if one is available for the case you've been assigned.

In writing your analysis and evaluation, bear in mind four things:

1. You are obliged to offer analysis and evidence to back up your conclusions. Do not rely on unsupported opinions, overgeneralizations, and platitudes as a substitute for tight, logical argument backed up with facts and figures.

---

[3]For some additional ideas and viewpoints, you may wish to consult Thomas J. Raymond, "Written Analysis of Cases," in *The Case Method at the Harvard Business School,* ed. M. P. McNair, pp. 139–63. Raymond's article includes an actual case, a sample analysis of the case, and a sample of a student's written report on the case.

2. If your analysis involves some important quantitative calculations, use tables and charts to present the calculations clearly and efficiently. Don't just tack the exhibits on at the end of your report and let the reader figure out what they mean and why they were included. Instead, in the body of your report cite some of the key numbers, highlight the conclusions to be drawn from the exhibits, and refer the reader to your charts and exhibits for more details.

3. Demonstrate that you have command of the strategic concepts and analytical tools to which you have been exposed. Use them in your report.

4. Your interpretation of the evidence should be reasonable and objective. Be wary of preparing a one-sided argument that omits all aspects not favorable to your conclusions. Likewise, try not to exaggerate or overdramatize. Endeavor to inject balance into your analysis and to avoid emotional rhetoric. Strike phrases such as "I think," "I feel," and "I believe" when you edit your first draft, and write in "My analysis shows," instead.

Recommendations

The final section of the written case analysis should consist of a set of definite recommendations and a plan of action. Your set of recommendations should address all of the problems/issues you identified and analyzed. If the recommendations come as a surprise or do not follow logically from the analysis, the effect is to weaken greatly your suggestions of what to do. Obviously, your recommendations for actions should offer a reasonable prospect of success. High-risk, bet-the-company recommendations should be made with caution. State how your recommendations will solve the problems you identified. Be sure the company is financially able to carry out what you recommend; also check to see if your recommendations are workable in terms of acceptance by the persons involved, the organization's competence to implement them, and prevailing market and environmental constraints. Try not to hedge or weasel on the actions you believe should be taken.

By all means state your recommendations in sufficient detail to be meaningful—get down to some definite nitty-gritty specifics. Avoid such unhelpful statements as "The organization should do more planning" or "The company should be more aggressive in marketing its product." For instance, do not simply say, "The firm should improve its market position" but state exactly how you think this should be done. Offer a definite agenda for action, stipulating a timetable and sequence for initiating actions, indicating priorities, and suggesting who should be responsible for doing what.

In proposing an action plan, remember there is a great deal of difference between, on the one hand, being responsible for a decision that may be costly if it proves in error and, on the other hand, casually suggesting courses of action that might be taken when you do not have to bear the responsibility for any of the consequences. A good rule to follow in making your recommendations is: *Avoid recommending anything you would not yourself be willing to do if you were in management's shoes.* The importance of learning to develop good managerial judgment is indicated by the fact that, even though the same information and operating data may be available to every manager or executive in an organization, the quality of the judgments about what the information means and which actions need to be taken does vary from person to person.[4]

---

[4]Gragg, "Because Wisdom Can't Be Told," p. 10.

It goes without saying that your report should be well organized and well written. Great ideas amount to little unless others can be convinced of their merit—this takes tight logic, the presentation of convincing evidence, and persuasively written arguments.

PREPARING AN ORAL PRESENTATION

During the course of your business career it is very likely that you will be called on to prepare and give a number of oral presentations. For this reason, it is common in courses of this nature to assign cases for oral presentation to the whole class. Such assignments give you an opportunity to hone your presentation skills.

The preparation of an oral presentation has much in common with that of a written case analysis. Both require identification of the strategic issues and problems confronting the company, analysis of industry conditions and the company's situation, and the development of a thorough, well-thought-out action plan. The substance of your analysis and quality of your recommendations in an oral presentation should be no different than in a written report. As with a written assignment, you'll need to demonstrate command of the relevant strategic concepts and tools of analysis, and your recommendations should contain sufficient detail to provide clear direction for management. The main difference between an oral presentation and a written case is in the delivery format. Oral presentations rely principally on verbalizing your diagnosis, analysis, and recommendations and visually enhancing and supporting your oral discussion with colorful, snappy slides (usually created with Microsoft's PowerPoint software).

Typically, oral presentations involve group assignments. Your instructor will provide the details of the assignment—how work should be delegated among the group members and how the presentation should be conducted. Some instructors prefer that presentations begin with issue identification, followed by analysis of the industry and company situation analysis, and conclude with a recommended action plan to improve company performance. Other instructors prefer that the presenters assume that the class has a good understanding of the external industry environment and the company's competitive position and expect the presentation to be strongly focused on the group's recommended action plan and supporting analysis and arguments. The latter approach requires cutting straight to the heart of the case and supporting each recommendation with detailed analysis and persuasive reasoning. Still other instructors may give you the latitude to structure your presentation however you and your group members see fit.

Regardless of the style preferred by your instructor, you should take great care in preparing for the presentation. A good set of slides with good content and good visual appeal is essential to a first-rate presentation. Take some care to choose a nice slide design, font size and style, and color scheme. We suggest including slides covering each of the following areas:

- An opening slide covering the "title" of the presentation and names of the presenters.
- A slide showing an outline of the presentation (perhaps with presenters' names by each topic).
- One or more slides showing the key problems and strategic issues that management needs to address.
- A series of slides covering your analysis of the company's situation.

- A series of slides containing your recommendations and the supporting arguments and reasoning for each recommendation—one slide for each recommendation and the associated reasoning has a lot of merit.

You and your team members should carefully plan and rehearse your slide show to maximize impact and minimize distractions. The slide show should include all of the pizzazz necessary to garner the attention of the audience, but not so much that it distracts from the content of what group members are saying to the class. You should remember that the role of slides is to help you communicate your points to the audience. Too many graphics, images, colors, and transitions may divert the audience's attention from what is being said or disrupt the flow of the presentation. Keep in mind that visually dazzling slides rarely hide a shallow or superficial or otherwise flawed case analysis from a perceptive audience. Most instructors will tell you that first-rate slides will definitely enhance a well-delivered presentation but that impressive visual aids accompanied by weak analysis and poor oral delivery still add up to a substandard presentation.

RESEARCHING COMPANIES AND INDUSTRIES VIA THE INTERNET AND ONLINE DATA SERVICES

Very likely, there will be occasions when you need to get additional information about some of the assigned cases, perhaps because your instructor has asked you to do further research on the industry or company or because you are simply curious about what has happened to the company since the case was written. These days it is relatively easy to run down recent industry developments and to find out whether a company's strategic and financial situation has improved, deteriorated, or changed little since the conclusion of the case. The amount of information about companies and industries available on the Internet and through online data services is formidable and expanding rapidly.

It is a fairly simple matter to go to company Web sites, click on the investor information offerings and press release files, and get quickly to useful information. Most company Web sites are linked to databases containing the company's quarterly and annual reports and 10K and 10Q filings with the Securities and Exchange Commission. Frequently, you will find mission and vision statements, values statements, codes of ethics, and strategy information, as well as charts of the company's stock price. The company's recent press releases typically contain reliable information about what of interest has been going on—new product introductions, recent alliances and partnership agreements, recent acquisitions, and other late-breaking company developments. Some company Web pages also include links to the home pages of industry trade associations where you can find information about industry size, growth, recent industry news, statistical trends, and future outlook. Thus, an early step in researching a company on the Internet is always to go to its Web site and see what's available.

Online Data Services

Lexis-Nexis, Bloomberg Financial News Services, and other online subscription services available in many university libraries provide access to a wide array of business reference material. For example, the Web-based Lexis-Nexis Academic Universe contains business news articles from general news sources, business publications, and industry trade publications. Broadcast transcripts from financial news programs are also available through Lexis-Nexis, as are full-text 10-Ks, 10-Qs, annual reports, and company profiles for more than 11,000 U.S. and international companies. Your business librarian should be able to direct you to the resources available through your library that will aid you in your research.

Public and Subscription Web sites with Good Information

In addition to company Web pages and online services provided by your university library, almost every major business publication has a subscription site available on the Internet. *The Wall Street Journal Interactive Edition* not only contains the same information that is available daily in its print version of the paper but also maintains a searchable database of all *Wall Street Journal* articles published during the past few years. The newspaper's online subscription site also has a Briefings Books section that allows you to conduct research on a specific company and track its financial and market performance in near–real time. *Fortune* and *Business Week* also make the content of the most current issue available online to subscribers as well as provide archives sections that allow you to search for articles related to a particular keyword that were published during the past few years.

The following Web sites are particularly good locations for company and industry information:

Securities and Exchange Commission EDGAR database (contains company 10-Ks, 10-Qs etc.)	www.sec.gov/cgi-bin/srch-edgar
NASDAQ	www.nasdaq.com
CNNfn: The Financial Network	www.cnnfn.com
Hoover's Online	www.hoovers.com
The Wall Street Journal Interactive Edition	www.wsj.com
Business Week	www.businessweek.com
Fortune	www.fortune.com
MSN Money Central	www.moneycentral.msn.com
Yahoo! Finance	www.quote.yahoo.com
Individual News Page	www.individual.com

Some of these Internet sources require subscriptions in order to access their entire databases.

Using a Search Engine

Alternatively, or in addition, you can quickly locate and retrieve information on companies, industries, products, individuals, or other subjects of interest using such Internet search engines as Lycos, Go, Excite, Snap, and Google. Search engines find articles and other information sources that relate to a particular industry, company name, topic, phrase, or keyword of interest. Search engine technology is becoming highly intuitive in retrieving Web pages related to your query and will likely direct you to the company Web site and other sites that contain timely and accurate information about the company. However, keep in mind that the information retrieved by a search engine is unfiltered

table 2   The 10 Commandments of Case Analysis

To be observed in written reports and oral presentations, and while participating in class discussions.

1. Go through the case twice, once for a quick overview and once to gain full command of the facts; then take care to explore the information in every one of the case exhibits.

2. Make a complete list of the problems and issues that the company's management needs to address.

3. Be thorough in your analysis of the company's situation. Either work through the case preparation exercises and/or study questions on Case-Tutor or make a minimum of one to two pages of notes detailing your diagnosis.

4. Use every opportunity to apply the concepts and analytical tools in the text chapters— all of the cases in the book have very definite ties to the concepts/tools in one or more of the text chapters and you are expected to apply them in analyzing the cases.

5. Do enough number crunching to discover the story told by the data presented in the case. (To help you comply with this commandment, consult Table 1 in this section to guide your probing of a company's financial condition and financial performance.)

6. Support any and all opinions with well-reasoned arguments and numerical evidence; don't stop until you can purge "I think" and "I feel" from your assessment and instead are able to rely completely on "My analysis shows."

7. Prioritize your recommendations and make sure they can be carried out in an acceptable time frame with the available resources.

8. Support each recommendation with persuasive argument and reasons as to why it makes sense and should result in improved company performance.

9. Review your recommended action plan to see if it addresses all of the problems and issues you identified—any set of recommendations that does not address all of the issues and problems you identified is incomplete and insufficient.

10. Avoid recommending any course of action that could have disastrous consequences if it doesn't work out as planned; therefore, be as alert to the downside risks of your recommendations as you are to their upside potential and appeal.

and may include sources that are not reliable or that contain inaccurate or misleading information. Be wary of information that is provided by authors who are unaffiliated with reputable organizations or publications or that doesn't come from the company or a credible trade association—be especially careful in relying on the accuracy of information you find posted on various bulletin boards. Articles covering a company or issue should be copyrighted or published by a reputable source. If you are turning in a paper containing information gathered from the Internet, you should cite your sources (providing the Internet address and date visited); it is also wise to print Web pages for your research file (some Web pages are updated frequently).

The Learning Curve Is Steep

With a modest investment of time, you will learn how to use Internet sources and search engines to run down information on companies and industries quickly and efficiently. And it is a skill that will serve you well into the future. Once you become familiar with the data available on the different Web sites mentioned above and with one or more search engines, you will know where to go to look for the particular information that you want. Search engines nearly always turn up too many information sources that match your request rather than too few; the trick is to learn to zero in on those most relevant to what you are looking for. As with most things, once you get a little experience under your belt on how to do company and industry research on the Internet, you will find that you can readily find the information you need.

THE 10 COMMANDMENTS OF CASE ANALYSIS

As a way of summarizing our suggestions about how to approach the task of case analysis, we have compiled what we like to call "The 10 Commandments of Case Analysis." They are shown in Table 2 on the previous page. If you observe all or even most of these commandments faithfully as you prepare a case either for class discussion or for a written report, your chances of doing a good job on the assigned cases will be much improved. Hang in there, give it your best shot, and have some fun exploring what the real world of strategic management is all about.

case 1 Steve Case, America Online, and Time Warner

Arthur A. Thompson
The University of Alabama

John E. Gamble
University of South Alabama

Every day, millions of people across the world log on to America Online to check their e-mail, track their stock portfolios, visit their favorite spots on the Internet, and send instant messages to friends on their buddy lists. In early 2000 AOL had 22 million subscribers and handled 110 million e-mails, 200 million stock quotes, and 562 million instant messages daily. Many subscribers used AOL features to create online photo albums, online calendars, and electronic jukeboxes. The company's members could also use AOL to purchase an airline ticket, reserve a car or hotel, or get a map from the airport to the hotel. They could purchase an unlimited variety of merchandise and services through Shop@AOL and pay their bills with an AOL Visa or through electronic banking provided by AOL and Intuit.

Other AOL brands brought the company millions more sets of eyeballs each day. Netscape Netcenter had 27.5 million registrants; Digital City, the number one local online network, had more than 6 million visitors each month from 60 U.S. cities; and ICQ, the number one communication community, had 53.1 million registrants and averaged 8 million daily users. Over 150 million movie tickets were purchased from AOL's MovieFone Web site each year. This combined traffic made AOL the leading interactive Internet medium, with more than $4.7 billion in 1999 revenues, nearly $400 million in net earnings, and a market capitalization of nearly $200 billion at year-end 1999. Exhibit 1 presents selected financial and operating highlights for America Online during the 1992–99 period. The performance of the company's stock price is shown in Exhibit 2.

Much of the company's success through 1999 was attributable to CEO and chairman Stephen Case's visionary leadership and his efforts to make AOL an essential and ubiquitous component of everyday life. During the last half of the 1990s, Case's entrepreneurship, his strategic vision for AOL, and AOL's undeniably significant market impact had made him one of the most prominent and influential top executives in the United States. His views on the Internet economy were paid close attention in industry

exhibit 1　Selected Financial and Operating Highlights, America Online, Inc., 1992–99

	Year Ended June 30				
	1999	1998	1997	1996	1995
Statement of operations data					
Subscription services	$3,321	$2,183	$1,478	$1,024	$ 352
Advertising, commerce, and other	1,000	543	308	111	50
Enterprise solutions	456	365	411	188	23
Total revenues	4,777	3,091	2,197	1,323	425
Income (loss) from operations	458	(120)	(485)	64	(41)
Net income (loss)	$ 762	$ (74)	$ (485)	$ 35	$ (55)
Income (loss) per common share					
Net income (loss) per share—diluted	$ 0.60	($ 0.08)	($ 0.58)	$ 0.04	($0.09)
Net income (loss) per share—basic	$ 0.73	($ 0.08)	($ 0.58)	$ 0.05	($0.09)
Weighted average shares outstanding					
Diluted	1,277	925	838	944	587
Basic	1,041	925	838	751	587
Net cash provided by operating activities	$1,099	$ 437	$ 131	$ 2	$ 18
Earnings before interest, taxes, depreciation and amortization (EBITDA)	968	302	111	138	11
Balance sheet data					
Working capital (deficiency)	$ 254	$ 108	($ 40)	$ 72	$ 18
Total assets	5,348	2,874	1,501	1,271	459
Total debt	364	372	52	25	24
Stockholders' equity	3,033	996	610	707	242

Source: America Online 1999 annual report.

circles and by the news media. Then on January 10, 2000, AOL stunned the business world with an announcement of potentially far-reaching consequences for business. Steve Case, Time Warner co-chairmen Gerald Levin and Ted Turner, and other America Online and Time Warner executives held a joint press conference describing plans to merge the two companies. The new company, to be named AOL Time Warner, would combine one of the largest "old-economy" media companies with the world's largest "new-economy" media company to create a company positioned, they said, to lead the second Internet revolution and capitalize on the convergence of entertainment, information, communications, and online services. Combined sales of the two companies would approach $33 billion.

America Online's brands included AOL, AOL.com, AOL MovieFone, ICQ, CompuServe, Netscape, Digital City, iPlanet, Spinner, Winamp, and AOL Instant Messenger. Time Warner's brands included *Time, Fortune, Sports Illustrated, People, Money, Southern Living, Parenting, Entertainment Weekly,* Book-of-the-Month Club, Warner Bros., CNN, TBS, TNT, Turner Classic Movies, World Championship Wrestling, Cartoon Network, HBO, Cinemax, Warner Music Group (five studios and over 70 artists), and Looney Tunes; in addition, Time Warner was the second largest provider of cable TV services, serving 12.4 million homes in over 34 areas of the country. Top executives at the

exhibit 2   Monthly Performance of America Online, Inc.'s Stock Price, 1992 to March 2000

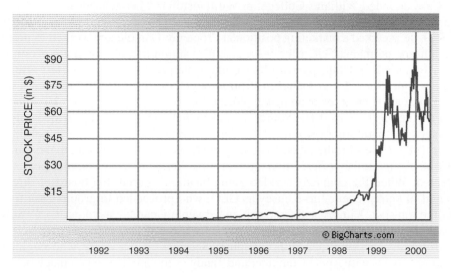

two companies believed the merger would allow Time Warner to bring its entertainment brands to consumers in a digital environment, in addition to traditional formats, while AOL could use Time Warner's broadband cable resources and satellite television capabilities to deliver online content to consumers at speeds much greater than possible over telephone lines. If approved by shareholders and regulators, the merger would convert each company's shares to AOL Time Warner shares at a fixed ratio. Each Time Warner share was to be exchanged for 1.5 shares of the new company's shares, and each AOL share was to be exchanged for 1 share of the new company's stock. The new stock would be traded under the symbol AOL on the New York Stock Exchange.

Steve Case would become chairman of AOL Time Warner, and Gerald Levin would serve as CEO. Case believed the merger was so important to securing AOL's future that he was willing for Levin to function as AOL Time Warner's CEO in order to win the support of Time Warner management for the merger. The impetus for the merger had come from Steve Case and AOL—it was Case's vision for the merged company that had prompted him to initiate merger discussions, and he was the person most responsible for sparking the excitement of Time Warner executives and leading the effort to pull the deal together.

STEPHEN M. CASE: CHAIRMAN, PRESIDENT, AND CEO OF AMERICA ONLINE

Steve Case was born and raised in Honolulu, Hawaii, where his father was a lawyer and his mother a teacher. Case's entrepreneurial spirit surfaced at an early age. When Case was six, he and his brother opened a juice stand and charged 2 cents a cup, but many of their customers gave them a nickel and let them keep the change—an experience that taught the boys the value of high margins. A few years later, the two brothers started a business selling a variety of products door-to-door and by mail. Then they began selling ad circulars and, in addition, shared a newspaper route.

Case attended Williams College, in Williamstown, Massachusetts, where he majored in political science and was the lead singer in two rock groups. After graduating in 1980, he accepted a marketing position at Procter & Gamble and worked to promote Lilt, a home permanent kit, after unsuccessfully attempting to obtain a position with Time, Inc.'s HBO. Unhappy with managing a mature business, Case left after two years to join Pizza Hut as manager of pizza development. The job involved a lot of travel, and he often spent evenings exploring his new laptop computer. He joined an early online service called The Source, and even though the service provided only text messages at a painfully slow rate, Steve Case became fascinated by the possibilities.

In 1983, Case's brother, then an investment banker, introduced him to the founders of Control Video; they offered him a job as a marketing assistant on the spot, and he accepted. When the company's video game business soured, the board of directors brought in entrepreneur Jim Kimsey as CEO, who proceeded to groom Case to take over the top spot. Kimsey and Case convinced venture capitalists to put up $5 million to back their idea of forming an online service for users of Commodore computers, and Control Video became Quantum Computer Services. It was Case who engineered Quantum's deals with Apple Computer and Tandy (although he used up much of the $5 million in capital in the process and had some of the venture capital board members calling on Kimsey to fire him). And it was Case who, when the Apple deal fell through, helped turn the basis for it into America Online.

When he was made CEO of America Online in 1992, Case quickly fashioned a growth-at-any-cost strategy and charged ahead. Despite industry observers' numerous predictions over the years that AOL would stumble or that its membership growth would soon slow to a crawl, Steve Case kept making new acquisitions, forging new alliances, adjusting the company's marketing strategies, and adapting AOL's services and content to fast-paced changes in the marketplace.

When Microsoft announced that it would bundle its new Microsoft Network software in with its Windows 95 operating system software, Steve Case was a leader in urging the Justice Department to block the move as an unfair advantage. Microsoft, however, was allowed to proceed. Later, in March 1996, Case negotiated a head-turning pact with Microsoft whereby AOL would integrate Microsoft's Internet Explorer (a Web browser) into its online software; Microsoft, in return, would include AOL software in every copy of its Windows 95 operating system. Case explained the reasons for choosing Microsoft's Internet Explorer over Netscape's Navigator, the market share leader in Web browsers:

> . . . there were a number of reasons we went with Microsoft. We think the Internet Explorer technology is evolving at a rapid rate and its modular design will enable us to plug it in to AOL quickly. Strategically, we thought it would be smart for us to make sure there were two strong providers of Web technology in the marketplace. We didn't want anyone, whether Microsoft or Netscape, to have the kind of monopoly in Web technology that Microsoft has in operating systems.[1]

Within four years as CEO, Case had led AOL in becoming the largest online service, with more than 5 million users. In 1998, Case stated that the mission of AOL was

---

[1]As quoted in "AOL CEO Steve Case," *Forbes,* October 7, 1996, p. 95.

"to build a global medium as central to people's lives as the telephone or television . . . and even more valuable."[2] In 2000, AOL's 22 million subscribers easily made it the world's largest online service.

Because of his success in transforming AOL into what many observers believed was the most potent force in cyberspace, Case was often asked to speak at PC-related conventions, usually drawing packed audiences. His views were widely sought by business reporters, industry analysts, and executives from Internet-related companies. He discussed the growth of AOL's subscriber base and the Internet revolution at one such event during the fall of 1999 as follows:

> Today, the Internet is becoming as central to everyday life as the phone and the TV. Right now, 53 percent of U.S. households own a PC—up from 39 percent in 1995. Already, 37 percent of households have online access—when just eight or nine years ago, most Americans didn't know what online access was. At AOL, it took us about a decade to get our first 1 million members. Now we add an additional million members every few months. When we started, 90 percent of AOL users were men. Today, more than half are women—about the same proportion as the overall U.S. population. The Internet is becoming a mass medium. I knew this for sure a few years ago when my parents finally understood what I did for a living.[3]

Even before AOL's success was evident, those who knew Steve Case were impressed by his vision and his ability to forge success in an emerging industry. Although Case functioned as an ardent and visible spokesman for AOL and had fashioned a hard-charging image for the company, he displayed a low-key, non-egotistical management style in his relationships with AOL executives and employees. Case was also a hands-on manager who stayed on top of how things were going. In 1996, former U.S. general Alexander Haig, an AOL board member, said that Case "borders on genius. If you look at how this young fella has positioned this company, he has ventures with every big player in the business. Instead of being beaten to death by Microsoft, as everyone predicted, they came courting him."[4] "When I met Steve," recalled another AOL board member, "he was 30 years old, and he already had a messianic vision of a connected world where the Internet was going to be part of daily life in every way imaginable. AOL is about being the leader in making this medium all that it has the potential to be."[5] Another close observer of Case and AOL said, "Every time people ask 'How is he going to survive?' he makes the right moves."[6]

Nonetheless, Case had taken a number of potshots from critics. Ned Brainard of *HotWired,* for example, labeled Case a "shameless self-promoter." Disgruntled AOL members had, from time to time, posted messages on AOL bulletin boards "flaming" Steve Case and AOL for policies and practices they disagreed with, long wait times for customer support, excessive busy signals at peak hours (which spurred such labels as America On Hold), and assorted other grievances.

---

[2]As stated in America Online's 1998 annual report.

[3]Speech given to the National School Boards Association, 13th Annual Technology and Learning Conference, Dallas, Texas, November 11, 1999.

[4]As quoted in "The Online World of Steve Case," *Business Week,* April 15, 1996, p. 80.

[5]"These Guys Want It All," *Fortune,* February 7, 2000, p. 72.

[6]Ibid.

COMPANY HISTORY AND BACKGROUND

Control Video Corporation was founded in the early 1980s with the business purpose of creating an online service that specialized in video games for users of Atari computer-game machines. At the time, two brands of home computers, the Apple II and the Commodore 64, dominated the market for playing online computer games. But because of maddeningly slow modems and modest processing power, playing video games online was not popular, and thus Control Video soon failed. The company was reorganized by James Kimsey and Steve Case as Quantum Computer Services in 1985; the new company focused its energies on developing customized online services for other companies. Quantum created a service for Commodore, then a leading computer company, called Q-Link. Commodore ended up selling millions of its home computers, and Q-Link was a hit with Commodore users. Quantum generated enough revenues to keep the company going. During the next several years, Quantum expanded to serve other computer users. Steve Case made a deal with Apple Computer in 1987 to create software packages for its Apple II and Macintosh models, and in 1988 he convinced Tandy Corporation to support a new online service, PC-Link, for purchasers of its DOS-based Radio Shack computers. Then in 1989 Apple withdrew from its deal at the last minute. Frustrated by the turn of events with Apple, Quantum decided to introduce the software service it designed for Apple under the name America Online.

Quantum's promotional strategy for its online service was to blanket home computer users with diskettes containing the America Online software. It gave the disks away at trade shows, got them included in magazine subscription mail-outs, had them attached to magazine covers at newsstands, and mailed them to selected households. By 1990, management had decided to bring all of its segmented online services together under one overall service. Quantum changed its name to America Online in 1991 and went public in 1992, raising $66 million to fund its expansion. Steve Case was named CEO shortly thereafter.

When Case took over as CEO, America Online, with only 200,000 subscribers and 250 employees, was well behind CompuServe and Prodigy, the two leading online services. In early 1993, AOL cut its monthly fee well below what CompuServe and Prodigy were charging and began mailing out massive numbers of diskettes with free trial offers. The company also made its start-up disks available to United Airlines passengers with their meals, inserted AOL CDs in boxes of cereal, and even included AOL disks with deliveries of Omaha Steaks. AOL's membership growth accelerated to the point where it had trouble handling the influx of new subscribers. Users would get abruptly disconnected, and logging on in peak periods sometimes took over an hour. Numerous complaints led Case to issue a letter of apology and to promise network improvements. Case proceeded to initiate agreements with NBC, the *New York Times,* CNN, *Time,* and others to provide AOL with content for its service. AOL made investments to handle a bigger volume of users; acquired new companies to boost its network and multimedia expertise and its software development capabilities; and continued to solicit new members with aggressive marketing.

By early 1995, America Online had 1 million subscribers but still trailed Prodigy (which had 1.5 million subscribers) and industry leader CompuServe (which had over 2 million subscribers). The company then began offering members Internet and World Wide Web access and kept flooding the market with diskettes, running arresting ads and come-ons, and offering consumers first 10 then 15 free hours to try the service, all the while improving the breadth and quality of the content of its services. AOL launched AOL Germany in 1995 through a joint venture with Bertelsmann AG, the world's third largest publisher. AOL UK, AOL Canada, and AOL France were all launched in early 1996. By mid-1996 the company's enhanced services, international expansion, and aggressive marketing built its membership to more than 6 million subscribers.

AOL's Setbacks during 1996

In July 1996 AOL, pressured by inquiries from the Federal Trade Commission and several state attorneys general, settled a class-action lawsuit concerning its billing practices by agreeing to give members free time online. The agreement cost AOL about $8 million. On August 7, AOL's system crashed during an equipment upgrade and the network went dead for 19 hours; the failure made headlines in newspapers and on TV and users complained about being deprived of e-mail and World Wide Web connections. In an apology to subscribers, Steve Case wrote, "I would like to be able to tell you this sort of thing will never happen again, but frankly, I can't make that commitment."

AOL encountered additional problems in August 1996, when the National Basketball Association sued the company in federal court, charging it with misappropriating proprietary data and violating intellectual property laws by providing real-time updates on NBA games in progress, not only giving the scores as each point was made but also providing summaries of player performance. AOL claimed that it was exercising its constitutional right to free speech and that the NBA didn't own the underlying facts about its basketball games. The three other major professional sports leagues (for baseball, football, and ice hockey) filed briefs supporting the NBA's lawsuit. AOL subsequently altered its practice of reporting on games in progress by delaying its updates.

In October 1996, the company's shares fell 10 percent the day following its 10-K filing with the Securities and Exchange Commission that noted its difficulties in retaining subscribers. AOL management attributed its problems with customer retention (referred to as "customer churn") to an increased number of lower-priced competitors and to the flat-rate monthly service pricing of many Internet service providers. In the October–December 1995 quarter, AOL signed up 1.8 million new subscribers but 950,000 members canceled, for a net gain of 850,000. Analysts estimated that in the January–March 1996 quarter AOL signed up 2.3 million new users and 1.4 million users quit. One analyst estimated that up to 45 percent of AOL's subscriber base canceled service each year; the same analyst observed that AOL spent more than $300 million in marketing in 1996 to add a net of 3.2 million subscribers to its membership base.[7] Steve Case indicated in the fall of 1996 that AOL's cost to acquire a subscriber averaged about $45 and that the company's customer churn was running under 40 percent.

Later in October, reacting to mounting criticism that the manner in which it accounted for its marketing expenses resulted in greatly overstated profits, America Online announced that it was changing its accounting practice of amortizing its marketing expenditures for acquiring new subscribers. Whereas the typical company charged marketing expenses against earnings as the expenses were incurred, it was AOL's practice

---

[7]*The Wall Street Journal,* October 2, 1996, p. B5.

to spread those costs over a 24-month period; AOL's accounting methods (agreed to by its auditors, Ernst & Young) had the effect of increasing the company's reported short-term profits—an outcome that critics said was misleading to investors. AOL's decision to switch to a practice of charging subscriber acquisition costs as a current operating expense resulted in an immediate charge against prior earnings of $350 million—an amount over 50 times greater than the company's total profits in the five preceding years combined (see again Exhibit 1).

AOL's Move to Flat-Rate Pricing

In November 1996, AOL announced that starting in December it would give members the option to switch to unlimited usage for $19.95 per month instead of paying $9.95 for basic service of five hours per month and $2.95 for each additional online hour. It also offered several other pricing plans, including advance renewal rates of $14.95 per month for customers paying two years in advance, advance renewal rates of $17.95 for customers paying one year in advance, and a light usage program of 3 hours per month for $4.95 (with additional time at $2.95 per hour). In addition to its new pricing options, America Online sought to further spur new subscriber sign-ups in November by boosting its trial offer from 15 free hours to 50 free hours.

The response to these marketing initiatives was overwhelming, greatly exceeding what AOL had expected and prepared for. Over 1.2 million new members signed on in the last quarter of 1996, and an estimated 75 percent of existing members switched to the new flat-rate, unlimited-use pricing plan. Virtually overnight, usage of AOL's service jumped dramatically (especially during the peak hours of 8 PM until midnight), straining existing capacity and causing members to get busy signals when they tried to sign on. In November 1996, the month before the unlimited use pricing plan went into effect, AOL members spent 66 million hours collectively online, more than double the 30 million hours they averaged during the summer months of 1996 and 50 percent more than the 44 million hours logged in September. In December 1996, the total soared to more than 100 million hours and rose further to about 125 million hours in January 1997. The number of daily sessions rose from 6.2 million in October to more than 10 million in January 1997 and over 11 million in February. AOL users averaged more than 32 minutes per day in January 1997, compared to 14 minutes per day in September 1996. And the number of simultaneous users increased from 185,000 in November 1996 to more than 260,000 in January 1997. Member complaints about busy signals and congested network traffic escalated, even though AOL had added about 20,000 modems to its network to accommodate increased call-ins and was adding thousands more weekly. One member's experience was typical: "It's literally impossible to get on AOL at night. I do business on the Internet and this has really hurt me."

In January 1997, five AOL members filed a class-action lawsuit in a state court in Los Angeles, alleging they were not getting the promised services due to repeated busy signals; similar suits were filed in three other states as well. State attorneys general from 36 states quickly joined in, reacting to a chorus of customer complaints. AOL responded by announcing it would spend $350 million to upgrade its network over the next five months by adding 150,000 modems, building new data centers, hiring 600 additional customer service representatives, adding 1-800 access numbers, and cutting back on the recruitment of new members. In an open letter to members, Steve Case said:

Last fall, you told us you wanted an unlimited use plan, and we delivered. Naturally, we anticipated more usage, and prepared for it, but we seriously underestimated the surge in demand that actually occurred. We know that you are having problems getting online and we are working day and night to improve the situation . . .

The events of the past few weeks have vividly reminded us of the responsibilities we have, as the service that 8 million members rely on each day. We take these responsibilities seriously, and I can assure you we will do everything in our power to meet them.

AOL'S EVOLVING STRATEGY, 1997–99

In early 1997 America Online, under mounting pressure of legal action, formally agreed to issue refunds or credit toward future service to cover network access and service problems during December 1996 and January 1997. Under terms of the agreement, customers could choose whether to receive credit for a free month of service or qualify for cash rebates up to $39.90. By March 1997, AOL had a total of 250,000 modems in place, was handling more than 11 million connections per day, and was distributing 10.5 million e-mail messages daily. On an average day, AOL members were, collectively, spending just over 4 million hours online and accounting for 225 million Web hits daily.

Steve Case saw the move to flat-rate pricing and the ensuing system overloads as hard evidence that Internet users were adopting his vision of the future and AOL's role in their lives: "What was happening, for really the first time, was that we impacted people's daily lives in a significant way. Suddenly, almost overnight, we became part of their everyday life. That's why there was this national outrage and tremendous passion and frustration, because people needed us, and many of them loved us, and we had disappointed them. It was a coming of age for the medium."[8]

AOL's Use of Alliances and Acquisitions to Enhance the Online Experience

America Online began making acquisitions to build its capabilities to deliver interesting online content in 1994. The company's acquisitions added expertise in creating multimedia experiences, improving the performance of its software, bringing new functionality to AOL's service, and improving the performance of AOL's network. Exhibit 3 presents AOL's acquisitions from August 1994 through December 1999. Through the company's acquisitions and its own internal product development efforts, it was able to offer a richer interactive experience than most of its online and Internet rivals.

In 1997 AOL launched its version 4.0 software that built on the resources gained through the company's numerous acquisitions and alliances and was faster, more responsive, and more interactive than its 3.0 predecessor. AOL 4.0 allowed members to send other members e-mail with embedded color photographs, custom backgrounds, multiple attachments, and different fonts. On the chat side, members could display a photograph, graphic image, or live video camera footage while they were chatting. Users could also click on a button and request an AOL phone conversation with the person they were chatting with. Another new feature was Driveway, an automated offline information option that could be customized by members to retrieve particular content from e-mail, newsgroups, the Web, and other places. Other new features included e-mail spelling and grammar checking, greeting card creation, address book enhancements,

---

[8]"The Internet Is Mr. Case's Neighborhood," *Fortune,* March 30, 1998, p. 72.

exhibit 3   America Online's Acquisitions, August 1994–December 1999

Date	Price in Stock	Company Acquired
August 1994	$34 million	Redgate Communications, Ted Leonis's company, which made multimedia CD-ROMs with online links
November 1994	$6 million	Navisoft, a maker of software for creating Web sites
December 1994	$41 million	BookLink Technologies, which provided AOL's first browser
February 1995	$35 million	ANS, creator of the Internet network
May 1995	$30 million	Medior, interactive media developer
May 1995	$15 million	WAS, developer of Web server software
June 1995	$11 million	Global Network Navigator, which provided the foundation for AOL's new Internet browser
September 1995	$15 million	Ubique, maker of software for 3-D worlds
February 1996	$59 million	Johnson-Grace, provider of data compression
August 1996	Not disclosed	ImagiNation Network, producer of online multiplayer games
March 1997	Not disclosed	Lightspeed Media, online program developer
January 1998	Not disclosed	PLS, developer of information indexing and search technologies
February 1998	$1.3 billion deal involving AOL's ANS, H&R Block, and WorldCom	CompuServe
June 1998	$29 million	NetChannel, a Web-enhanced television company
June 1998	$287 million	Mirabilis, producer of ICQ instant communications technology
November 1998	Not disclosed	PersonaLogic, maker of online decision tree software
March 1999	$10.2 billion	Netscape
April 1999	Not disclosed	When, Inc., an Internet calendar developer
May 1999	Not disclosed	MovieFone, Inc.
June 1999	$400 million	Winamp, Spinner.com, and SHOUTcast music brands
June 1999	$15 million	Digital Marketing Services, online marketing research and online incentive marketing

Source: America Online press releases and *Business Week,* April 15, 1996, p. 82.

16-character screen names, additional security and control, and streaming video and multimedia enhancements for the World Wide Web.

In 1997, AOL began an alliance with Tel-Save, a small long-distance company, that allowed the company to offer its customers long-distance service at 9 cents per minute. AOL furthered its global reach in 1997 with the launch of AOL Japan and AOL Australia to gain more than 1 million international subscribers by the end of the year. AOL also announced an "AOL Anywhere" initiative in December 1997 that would ultimately make the company's services available beyond PCs through alliances and investments in interactive television, handheld connected devices, and broadband technology.

In 1998 AOL expanded its paying membership to 14.5 million through its continued aggressive marketing and the acquisition of CompuServe. Steve Case saw the interactive experience not as separate online and Internet markets but as a seamless product; he therefore made acquisitions to ensure that AOL would become a notable Internet destination. The company expanded its content available to AOL.com non-subscribers and acquired both instant communication provider ICQ and Web community Digital City. AOL's combined brands were visited by tens of millions of different people in 1998.

AOL also acquired a Web-enhanced television company called NetChannel and PLS, the leading developer of information indexing and search technologies, to improve the functionality of upcoming versions of AOL's software. AOL entered into an alliance with Sun Microsystems in November 1998 to build end-to-end electronic solutions and to help other companies put their businesses on the Internet. The company created a number of other alliances in 1998 with companies such as eBay to improve the diversity of its content, and added a mixture of e-commerce sites through alliances with 1-800-FLOWERS, J. Crew, Barnes & Noble, Preview Travel, DLJ Direct, E*Trade, Intuit, and others. AOL also created an investment unit in 1998 to examine interactive investment opportunities related to the Internet. The company expanded its international presence in 1998 with the launch of AOL Austria with the help of Bertelsmann AG.

AOL's Acquisition of Netscape

During 1999 AOL acquired Netscape for $10.2 billion in AOL stock. The Netscape acquisition provided AOL with the browser technology necessary to enhance its product development resources and provided the company with a West Coast location for job candidates unwilling to move to Virginia, but more importantly it gave AOL the resources necessary to provide electronic commerce services to business customers. Even though AOL customers could buy goods and services through the company's online service, prior to the Netscape acquisition AOL's e-commerce capabilities were primarily restricted to its efforts to offer an online shopping mall to Internet retailers.

In 1996, AOL attempted to develop the computer software and services necessary for companies to put their business online, but firms were hesitant to contract with AOL for their e-commerce requirements. AOL's senior vice president of its enterprise solutions group said that the company's failure in landing commercial accounts was largely attributable to the "psychic clash" encountered by business executives considering purchasing software from a consumer online service—many companies thought that it "bordered on a joke" that AOL's technology could reliably handle their mission-critical operations.[9]

The Netscape acquisition, along with AOL's existing agreement with Sun Microsystems, allowed the company to offer e-commerce solutions under a brand that would appeal to the business customer. Furthermore, the addition of Netscape to AOL's brands brought more daytime visitors to AOL sites and added a highly talented pool of workers needed to develop newer generations of AOL's software and browser capabilities. Steve Case commented on the importance of the addition of Netscape to AOL's portfolio of brands shortly after the company had been reorganized to fully capture the strategic fit benefits of the acquisition:

---

[9]"AOL's New State: Firm Faces Challenge Selling Software, Services to Business," *Washington Post,* November 29, 1998, p. H01.

This acquisition will greatly accelerate our business momentum by advancing our multiple-brand, multiple-product strategy and helping us take e-commerce to a new level. We are especially excited about adding Netscape's talented-people—highly regarded in Silicon Valley and elsewhere—to our team. We will continue to build Netscape's successful businesses, including expanding the audience for popular Netscape NetCenter and extending both the Navigator and Communicator browsers to the emerging market of next-generation Internet devices.[10]

Some industry analysts suggested that America Online should integrate the Netscape Navigator and Communicator browsers into the upcoming versions of its online software in lieu of using Microsoft's Internet Explorer.

Other Recent Acquisitions and Alliances

In 1999 AOL acquired When.com and PersonaLogic, the developers of Web-based calendar services; online music brands Spinner.com, Winamp, and SHOUTcast; and MovieFone, the premier movie information and ticketing brand. Also in 1999, the company acquired online incentive marketing and marketing research firm Digital Marketing Services, Inc.

AOL signed an alliance with CBS to become its exclusive provider of broadcast news, formed alliances with Bell Atlantic, SBC, Ameritech, and GTE to provide high-speed digital subscriber line (DSL) access to AOL customers, forged an advertising partnership with First USA, and formed alliances with Gemstar DIRECTV, Hughes Network Systems, Philips Electronics, and Liberate Technologies to create a television-based online service. In addition, AOL and 3Com Corporation created an alliance that would allow AOL subscribers to access their e-mail with their PalmPilots; AOL and Motorola began to develop wireless applications for AOL's Instant Messenger; and the company partnered with Gateway to introduce a family of specialized Internet appliances that would automatically launch AOL when the device was switched on. The new appliances would be a low-cost alternative to PCs and would come in countertop, desktop, or wireless handheld models.

Many of America Online's alliances were accompanied by equity investments in the company's partners. AOL had made investments in more than 70 publicly and closely held companies that were valued at more than $2 billion in early 2000. In addition, America Online had invested $1.5 billion in Hughes Electronics and $800 million in Gateway. A list of AOL's content and e-commerce partners is presented in Exhibit 4.

America Online's Strategy to Finance Its Growth

The company's rapid growth had been financed largely through new issues of common stock. The company had raised nearly $1.5 billion from the issue of new shares of common and preferred stock in fiscal years 1993–99 to pay for the costs of attracting new subscribers; new product development; and investments in modems, servers, and other equipment needed to operate and expand its online network capability. America Online had also generated the more than $12 billion needed for its many acquisitions through the issuance of new shares. The company's cash flows from operations had remained

---

[10]"America Online Announces New Organization to Integrate Netscape and Extend Industry Leadership," *Business Wire,* March 24, 1999.

exhibit 4   America Online's Content and E-Commerce Partners

Auto, Travel American Airlines Norwegian Cruise Line Budget Rent-a-Car Preview Travel The Hertz Corporation AutoTrader.com **Babies, Children, and Toys** Gymboree.com eToys Healthtex BabyCenter iBaby Sesame Street Toysrus.com KBKids.com Americasbaby.com **Books, Videos, Movies, Music, Electronics and Computers** DIRECTV barnesandnoble.com Amazon.com CDNow DVD Express New Line Cinema Beyond.com 800.COM Onsale **Cards, Office Supplies, Gifts, Art, and Collectibles** americangreetings.com eBay 1-800-FLOWERS.com Godiva Chocolatier Art.com Sharper Image	Office Max Red Envelope.com **Clothing, Apparel, Fashion, and Accessories** J. Crew Fossil JCPenney bluefly.com eBags Brooks Brothers Guess Steve Madden Levi Strauss **Educational Programming** Nickelodeon MamaMedia New York Times Learning Network Cartoon Network Time for Kids **Food, Cooking, and Consumer Products** OmahaSteaks.com Procter & Gamble Cooking.com Hickory Farms Tavolo **Health, Pharmacy, Beauty, and Fitness** PlanetRx.com Drugstore.com Healthquick HealthAxis.com AmericasDoctor.com Avon	**News, Sports, Entertainment, and General Interest** CBS News CBS SportsLine The Weather Channel iVillage Oxygen Media Inc. People Online E! Online MTV Bloomberg **Insurance, Real Estate, Banking, and Financial Services** E*Trade TD Waterhouse The Motley Fool Ameritrade Century 21 Real Estate Corporation Realtor.com First USA Intuit DLJdirect iOwn.com Bank of America BankOne Citibank Scudder Investments The Kaufmann Fund Union Bank of California **Pets, Hobbies, and Outdoors** Chipshot.com PetSmart Eastman Kodak Company L. L. Bean Mammoth Golf

Source: AOL Web site.

negative until 1997, when America Online generated $131 million from its operating activities. AOL began to record investment gains from many capital investments in strategic allies after those companies had later gone public. At year-end 1999 the company had not yet paid a dividend to its shareholders. Exhibits 5, 6, and 7 show America Online's income statements, balance sheets, and cash flow statements for 1994–99.

The Costs of Marketing, Acquiring New Subscribers, and Developing New Products

Acquiring new subscribers absorbed a sizable fraction on America Online's financial resources. In 1999 AOL's current marketing expenses were $808 million, up from $77 million in 1995. The company's marketing expenditures had amounted to as much as 28

exhibit 5   Consolidated Statements of Operations, America Online, Inc., 1994–99
(In Millions, Except Per Share Data)

	Year Ended June 30					
	1999	1998	1997	1996	1995	1994
Revenues						
Subscription services	$3,321	$2,183	$1,478	$ 992	$ 334	$ 98
Advertising, commerce and other	1000	543	308	102	50	17
Enterprise solutions	456	365	411	—	—	—
Total revenues	4,777	3,091	2,197	1,094	394	116
Costs and expenses						
Cost of revenues	2,657	1,811	1,162	627	230	69
Sales and marketing	808	623	608	213	77	24
Write-off of deferred subscriber acquisition costs	—	(385)	—	—	—	—
Product development	286	239	195	54	14	5
General and administrative	408	328	220	110	43	14
Amortization of goodwill and other intangible assets	65	24	6	7	2	—
Acquired in-process research and development	—	94	9	17	50	—
Merger, restructuring and contract termination charges	95	75	73	—	—	—
Settlement charges	—	17	24	—	—	—
Total costs and expenses	4,319	3,211	2,682	1,029	416	112
Income (loss) from operations	458	(120)	(485)	65	(21)	4
Other income, net	638	30	10	(2)	3	2
Income (loss) before provision for income taxes	1,096	(90)	(475)	62	(21)	6
(Provision) benefit for income taxes	(334)	16	(10)	(33)	(15)	(4)
Net income (loss)	$ 762	($ 74)	($ 485)	$ 30	($ 36)	$ 2
Earnings (loss) per share						
Earnings (loss) per share—diluted	$ 0.60	($ 0.08)	($ 0.58)	$ 0.28	($0.51)	$0.03
Earnings (loss) per share—basic	$ 0.73	($ 0.08)	($ 0.58)	$ 0.28	($0.51)	$0.03
Weighted average shares outstanding—diluted	1,277	925	838	108	70	69
Weighted average shares outstanding—basic	1,041	925	838	108	70	69

Source: America Online annual reports.

percent of revenues in prior years but totaled less than 20 percent in 1999. Prior to 1997, these expenses did not include all that the company actually spent in soliciting new members. As noted earlier, AOL employed an accounting practice whereby it treated a large portion of the solicitation costs of new subscribers (including the costs of printing, producing, and shipping starter kits; obtaining mailing lists of qualified prospects; and creating direct response advertising) as a capital investment rather than a current expense; it then depreciated these "capital investments" over the next 12 to 18 months. In 1996, AOL spent approximately $275 million on subscriber acquisition efforts that it classified as capital investment. Moreover, company accountants opted in 1996 to increase the time frame over which AOL amortized subscriber acquisition costs from 12 and 18 months to 24 months, a change that had the effect of increasing the company's reported 1996 earnings by $48 million (actions and outcomes that were described in the

exhibit 6   Consolidated Balance Sheets, America Online, Inc., 1998–99 (In Millions)

	June 30 1999	June 30 1998
Assets		
Current assets		
Cash and cash equivalents	$ 887	$ 677
Short term investments	537	146
Trade accounts receivable, less allowances of $54 and $34, respectively	323	192
Other receivables	79	93
Prepaid expenses and other current assets	153	155
Total current assets	1,979	1,263
Property and equipment at cost, net	657	503
Other assets		
Investments including available-for-sale securities	2,151	531
Product development costs, net	100	88
Goodwill and other intangible assets, net	454	472
Other assets	7	17
Total assets	$5,348	$2,874
Liabilities and Stockholders' Equity		
Current liabilities		
Trade accounts payable	$ 74	$ 120
Other accrued expenses and liabilities	795	461
Deferred revenue	646	420
Accrued personnel costs	134	78
Deferred network services credit	76	76
Total current liabilities	1,725	1,155
Long-term liabilities		
Notes payable	348	372
Deferred revenue	30	71
Other liabilities	15	7
Deferred network services credit	197	273
Total liabilities	2,315	1,878
Stockholders' equity		
Preferred stock, $.01 par value; 5 million shares authorized, no shares issued and outstanding at June 30, 1999 and 1998, respectively	—	—
Common stock, $.01 par value, 1.8 billion shares authorized; 1,100,893,933 and 973,150,052 shares issued and outstanding at June 30, 1999 and 1998, respectively.	11	10
Additional paid-in capital	2,703	1,431
Accumulated comprehensive income—unrealized gain on available-for-sale securities, net	168	145
Retained earnings (accumulated deficit)	151	(590)
Total stockholders' equity	3,033	996
Total liabilities and stockholders' equity	$5,348	$2,874

Source: America Online annual reports.

***exhibit* 7**   Consolidated Statements of Cash Flows, America Online, Inc., 1997–99
(In Millions)

	June 30		
	1999	**1998**	**1997**
Cash flows from operating activities			
Net income (loss)	$762	($74)	($485)
Adjustments to reconcile net income (loss) to net cash provided by operating activities			
Write-off of deferred subscriber acquisition costs	—	—	385
Non-cash restructuring charges	7	32	22
Depreciation and amortization	298	191	93
Amortization of deferred network services credit	(76)	(32)	—
Charge for acquired in-process research and development	—	94	9
Compensatory stock options	20	33	2
Deferred income taxes	334	(18)	(1)
Gain on sale of investments	(564)	(28)	—
Amortization of subscriber acquisition costs	—	—	59
Changes in assets and liabilities, net of the effects of acquisitions and dispositions			
Trade accounts receivable	(123)	78	(122)
Other receivables	12	(67)	2
Prepaid expenses and other current assets	(63)	28	(50)
Deferred subscriber acquisition costs	—	—	(130)
Other assets	4	(5)	(15)
Investments including available-for-sale securities	(16)	(40)	(30)
Accrued expenses and other current liabilities	319	141	130
Deferred revenue and other liabilities	185	104	262
Total adjustments	337	511	616
Net cash provided by operating activities	1,099	437	131
Cash flows from investing activities			
Purchase of property and equipment	(301)	(384)	(230)
Product development costs	(49)	(51)	(57)
Proceeds from sale of investments	769	87	26
Purchase of investments, including available-for-sale securities	(2,289)	(166)	(208)
Maturity of investments	133	103	83
Net (payments) proceeds for acquisitions/dispositions of subsidiaries	30	(98)	30
Other investing activities	(69)	(22)	(11)
Net cash used in investing activities	(1,776)	(531)	(367)
Cash flows from financing activities			
Proceeds from issuance of common and preferred stock, net	836	141	251
Proceeds from sale and leaseback of property and equipment	8	70	20
Principal and accrued interest payments on line of credit and debt	(22)	(2)	(22)
Proceeds from line of credit and issuance of debt	65	371	1
Net cash provided by financing activities	887	580	250
Net increase in cash and cash equivalents	210	486	14
Cash and cash equivalents at beginning of year	677	191	177
Cash and cash equivalents at end of year	$887	$677	$191
Supplemental cash flow information			
Cash paid during the year for interest	$17	$10	$2

Source: America Online annual reports.

exhibit 9   (*continued*)

Composition of Time Warner's Business Units

1999 Financial Performance Summary, by Business Segment

Business Segment	Revenues	Operating Income	EBITDA
Cable networks	$ 6.1 billion	$ 1.2 billion	$ 1.4 billion
Publishing	4.7 billion	627 million	679 million
Music	3.8 billion	179 million	452 million
Filmed entertainment	8.1 billion	796 million	997 million
Broadcasting (WB Network)	384 million	(96) million	(92) million
Cable systems	5.4 billion	3.4 billion	3.9 billion

Turner Entertainment Group

TBS Superstation (most-watched cable TV network)

TNT (available in 75 percent of U.S. homes)

Cartoon Network (50 million-plus U.S. subscribers, plus 20 million foreign subscribers in 120 countries)

Turner Classic Movies (30 million U.S. subscribers)

Atlanta Braves (Major League baseball franchise)

Atlanta Hawks (NBA franchise)

Atlanta Thrashers (NHL franchise)

World Championship Wrestling

Goodwill Games

New Line Cinema

Fine Line Features

CNN News Group (more than 75 million U.S. subscribers; reaches nearly 150 million households in 212 countries; more than 1 billion people worldwide have access to a CNN service)

Home Box Office (34.6 million U.S. subscribers and 12 million foreign subscribers)

HBO

Cinemax

Publishing Business Segment

Magazines (32 publications with combined readership of 130 million)

Time

Fortune

Sports Illustrated

People

Entertainment Weekly

Life

Money

Southern Living

Southern Accents

Cooking Light

Parenting

Health

20 others

Book-of-the-Month Club   (*continued*)

exhibit 9 (*concluded*)

Warner Books
Time-Life Books
Sunset Books (a publisher)
Oxmoor House (a publisher)

Filmed Entertainment Business Group
Warner Bros. motion pictures (5,700 full-length and feature films and 13,500 animated titles)
Warner Bros. television series (32,000 episodes of various programs)
Castle Rock motion pictures
New Line Cinema
Telepictures Productions
Warner Bros. Television Animation
The WB Network
Hanna-Barbera Studios

Music Business Segment
Warner Music Group (5 studios, over 1,000 recording artists, 1 million music copyrights, 20 percent market share of U.S. album sales, world's most diversified and vertically integrated music company)
The Atlantic Group music production
Elektra Entertainment Group
Sire Records Group
Warner Bros. Records
Warner Music International
Columbia House Records (joint venture with Sony)

Cable Systems Business Segment
Time Warner Cable (this division had 100,000-plus subscribers in each of 34 areas of the United States and served 12.4 million homes)
Road Runner (a jointly owned high-speed online service with 320,000-plus customers and approximately 10,000 new customers being added weekly)
Local news channels (a total of 4)

*"AOL, Time Warner Set Plan to Link in Mammoth Merger," *The Wall Street Journal Interactive Edition,* January 11, 2000.

- **Gerald Levin, Chairman and CEO of Time Warner:**
  This strategic combination with AOL accelerates the digital transformation of Time Warner by giving our creative and content businesses the widest possible canvas. The digital revolution has already begun to create unprecedented and instantaneous access to every form of media and to unleash immense possibilities for economic growth, human understanding, and creative expression. AOL Time Warner will lead this transformation, improving the lives of consumers worldwide.

- **Bob Pittman, AOL's president:**
  The value of this merger lies not only in what it is today but in what it will be in the future. We believe that AOL Time Warner will provide companies worldwide with a convenient, one-stop way to put advertising and commerce online as well as take advantage of the best in traditional marketing. We will accelerate the development of Time Warner's cable broadband assets by bringing AOL's hallmark ease-of-use to this platform. We expect America Online to help drive the growth of cable broadband audiences, and we will use our combined infrastructure and cross-promotional strengths to enhance the growth and development of both America Online and Time Warner brands around the world.

exhibit 10 Combined AOL–Time Warner Statistics

Selected financials*	
Revenue	$32.8 billion
EBITDA	7.5 billion
Net income	2.4 billion
Cash and cash equivalents	3.7 billion
Long-term debt	19.8 billion
Employees	82,100
Customer relationships	
Online subscribers	24 million
Magazine subscribers	25.4 million
Cable TV network subscribers	73 million
ICQ, AOL Instant Messenger, and Netscape NetCenter registrants	107 million

*Based on the combined year-end 1999 financials of each company.
Source: "The Men Who Would Be King," *Fortune,* February 7, 2000.

- **Richard Parsons, Time Warner's president:**

  This is a defining event for Time Warner and America Online as well as a pivotal moment in the unfolding of the Internet age. By joining the resources and talents of these two highly creative companies, we can accelerate the development and deployment of a whole new generation of interactive services and content. The heightened competition and expanded choices this will bring about will be of great benefit to consumers. For the creative and innovative people who are the lifeblood of our companies, it means a truly exciting range of new opportunities to explore and give shape to. For our shareholders, it means we'll be able to grow in ways we couldn't have as separate companies, producing superior returns in both the short and long term.

Steve Case later further discussed the benefits of the merger and how AOL Time Warner would be positioned to lead the second Internet revolution:

One thing the last few years have made crystal clear is that in such a rapidly changing, Internet-charged economy, companies must constantly reinvent themselves to attract new customers. And today, it's not how many assets your company has, it's how you connect those assets and constantly innovate to better serve consumers.

In this new environment, it is critical to integrate the new technologies for consumers. Whether in wireless or other new markets, both individual companies and industries must build bridges between platforms, mediums, content and services—capitalizing on new synergies, creating new businesses, and taking advantage of transforming business opportunities.

That, in fact, is our game plan for AOL Time Warner. And we believe we are uniquely positioned to put it into play, for a number of reasons.

First, our combined assets are unrivaled—not only because of their range and value, but because of the way they fit together like pieces of a puzzle. From the world's most popular media, Internet and communications brands and properties, to our technological expertise and infrastructure, we are poised to lead the next wave of growth.

Second, we have strong, sticky relationships with our customers, including more than 110 million paying subscribers between the two companies. In fact, our combined brands touch consumers more than 2.5 billion times monthly, all around the world.

Third, our combined resources give us the strength to take full advantage of new opportunities. With significant revenues, critical strategic partnerships, a world-class operational team, management vision, and a deep talent pool, we will drive strong and consistent growth.

Finally, we are committed to putting the interests of both our customers and shareholders first. AOL and Time Warner have always believed that the best way to return shareholder value is to bring new value into the lives of consumers.

That's what we'll do as a combined company. Just as *Time* has been a part of people's lives for 75 years, and CNN for 20, we plan to entwine our brands into the fabric of society, improving our customers' lives . . . and becoming the most valuable company in the world.[16]

Preliminary Plans of How the Merged Companies Would Operate

As part of the merger agreement announcement, the two companies said they would begin new marketing, commerce, content, and promotional agreements that would immediately expand various relationships already in place. Subsequently, AOL's online service added Time Warner content that included *InStyle* magazine, *People, Teen People,* and *Entertainment Weekly.* Time Warner's CNN.com and Entertaindom.com programming was prominently featured on various America Online services, and AOL members were given access to a wide range of Time Warner promotional music clips from Time Warner's selection of popular artists. In addition, Time Warner and AOL MovieFone participated in online–offline cross-promotion of Time Warner movies and related content, including live events.

AOL also planned to use Time Warner's broadband capabilities and content to help launch AOL Plus, AOL's broadband service scheduled for a spring 2000 release. Time Warner began making a series of special offers exclusively to AOL members that included discounts on magazine subscriptions, premium cable subscriptions, and movie passes. Time Warner began aiding AOL in building its online membership by distributing AOL disks in its Warner Bros. retail stores and including AOL trial-offer disks in promotional mailings and product shipments. AOL services such as Instant Messenger, Digital City, AOL Search, and MovieFone were to be made available to the subscribers of Road Runner, Time Warner's broadband service.

Other specific opportunities that AOL and Time Warner executives identified as revenue- and profit-enhancing synergies between the two companies included the following:

1. Combining Time Warner's music labels with America Online's online marketing and e-commerce capacities presented opportunities for growing Time Warner's music revenues.

2. Combining America Online's AOL TV and MovieFone with Time Warner's cable networks and Warner Bros. movies and television offered valuable programming, cross-promotional, and e-commerce opportunities.

3. AOL's ability to use Time-Warner's broadband capabilities could expedite Internet access at high speeds via cable modem, DSL, wireless, or satellite.

4. AOL could enhance its online news offering with content from CNN, *Time,* and local all-news channels such as NY1 News.

5. AOL Time Warner could develop and leverage technology across all of the businesses, creating new opportunities to expand services and share infrastructure.

---

[16]Speech given at CS First Boston Global Telecom Conference, March 8, 2000.

6. AOL Time Warner could offer businesses and consumers a communications platform that combined America Online's popular instant messaging products with Time Warner's ability to offer local telephony over cable.

7. AOL could devote a large percentage of its advertising budget to Time Warner publications and broadcast media outlets.

Planned Roles of AOL Time Warner's Top Executives   Steve Case's role as AOL Time Warner's chairman of the board was to oversee the new company's technological developments and global expansion initiatives. As CEO, Gerald Levin would set the company's strategy and oversee its management. Ted Turner would have the title of vice chairman of the new company. AOL president and COO Bob Pittman and Time Warner president Richard Parsons would act as co-chief operating officers of the new company. When questioned by analysts and business reporters about whether AOL Time Warner would be top heavy, with highly-talented executives whose egos and management styles might conflict, Steve Case responded, "There's a big meal to serve."[17] He and Levin expressed the opinion that a deep, talented senior management team was a strong asset, given the ambitious objectives of the new company; the broad range of products, brands, and services to be integrated; and the fast-paced changes occurring in the marketplace.

Reaction to the Merger

Reactions to the proposed merger were quite mixed. Some analysts were unconvinced that the merger made good sense for AOL, arguing that the combined companies could not increase net income and cash flows at rates sufficient to keep AOL's stock price at its former levels, much less keep it rising. Other analysts saw the merger as beneficial, making comments like "The merger of America Online with Time Warner is one of the greatest strategic alliances in the history of the Internet."[18] Merger proponents saw very little downside risk in the merger and great potential for the new company to be a global leader in interactive communications. One communications industry analyst commented, "They don't stand to lose much. And what they stand to gain is enormous." Another characterized the merger benefit as "one plus one equals four."[19]

Skeptics predicted that AOL Time Warner would have difficulty integrating AOL's technology-oriented culture with the celebrity-based culture of Time Warner's entertainment business and the no-nonsense culture of its cable business. Negative analysis centered on the price AOL had agreed to pay for Time Warner's shares and the level of cash flows needed to justify the rising stock price to which AOL investors had become accustomed. While there were obvious synergies between the two companies (like AOL's ability to offer broadband service over Time Warner cable's cable lines, which served 20 percent of all U.S. cable subscribers), there were concerns that AOL's proposed buyout price gave Time Warner shareholders a far-too-rich 71 percent premium over its market valuation at the time of the merger agreement. The premium would

---

[17]"Investors Puzzle as AOL, Time Warner Integration Begins," The Associated Press State & Local Wire, January 12, 2000.

[18]"Fletcher and Faraday Announce Investment Opinion," PR Newswire, January 14, 2000.

[19]"AOL: You've Got Content, but Is Content Still King?" *Investors Business Daily,* January 13, 2000.

create a $150 billion goodwill charge resulting from the difference between the company's purchase price and book value that AOL would be required to write off over the next 10 years—the $15 billion per year goodwill writeoff would result in the company's reporting a loss each year for an indefinite time. This was why AOL executives and some Wall Street analysts were arguing that the profitability of the combined companies had to be viewed from the perspective of earnings before interest, taxes, depreciation, and amortization (EBITDA) rather than net earnings. But even using this measure, many analysts believed that the new AOL Time Warner would need to increase EBITDA to approximately $11 billion soon after the merger to maintain the growth of its share price.

Analysts were additionally concerned that the market would have trouble choosing earnings multiples to set a price on the new company's shares. Prior to the merger, Time Warner shares traded at a multiple of 14 times EBITDA, which was consistent with many old-economy firms, while AOL traded at 55 times EBITDA, which was consistent with the multiples of most growing new-economy firms. Some analysts were concerned that the new AOL Time Warner would become an old-economy company rather than a more competitively powerful new-economy company, since Time Warner's media properties accounted for about 80 percent of the combined company's 1999 cash flow. An analyst for J. P. Morgan Securities remarked, "That's what everyone is trying to get their arms around now: what this new entity is, and how to value it. This is going to continue to evolve. I think we need to take some time and see how things settle out."[20] Investment company Edward Jones's chief market strategist said that he no longer considered AOL a high-flying Internet company that could "grow 40 or 50 percent per year."[21]

An analyst for Merrill Lynch stated that if the new AOL could achieve $11 billion in EBITDA and a multiple of 40, the company's shares could trade as high as $90 within a year of the merger. If the market saw the company as less of an Internet company and more of a traditional media company, then an EBITDA multiple of 25 might be more realistic. The Merrill Lynch analyst stated that under the latter valuation scenario, AOL's message to shareholders would be "You've got losses."[22] AOL's shares, trading in the $90 to $95 per share range in the weeks prior to the merger, subsequently drifted downward to trade in the $55 to $65 range in March–April 2000.

In a speech given in April 2000, Steve Case reflected on AOL's growth and discussed how convergence would affect the future of the interactive medium:

> The average AOL user has gone from being online one hour a week to one hour a day. And while that's been gratifying for us and a sign of real progress, it's just scratching the surface. Having gotten a taste of interactivity, people are starting to say, "Why can't my PC be as simple and visually compelling as my TV—and why can't my TV be as powerful and flexible as my PC?" They're starting to ask, "Why can't I send instant messages from my cell phone?" And, "Why can't all these new devices work together in a way that's simple and easy to understand?"
>
> These days, we call it convergence—and it is turbo-charging a second Internet Revolution that will make the first one look almost quaint by comparison.
>
> Just think about the four devices we rely on the most in our homes: the television, the PC, the telephone, and the stereo. Already, the distinctions between these four devices are

---

[20]"Investors Puzzle as AOL, Time Warner Integration Begins.

[21]"Wall Street Doubts AOL's Staying Power after Its Merger with Time-Warner," *St. Louis Post-Dispatch,* January 15, 2000, p. B1.

[22]"Welcome to the 21st Century," *Business Week,* January 24, 2000, p. 39.

blurring—and interactivity is starting to connect all of them—giving people access to the Internet wherever they are and whenever they want.

Soon, televisions will come equipped with interactive program guides, and people will be able to bookmark their favorite programs like they bookmark their favorite Web sites. They will even be able to access interactive services like e-mail and Instant Messaging while they're watching TV—and trade comments on breaking stories or sports events.

The role of the PC will change, too. Just as the TV has evolved in many houses from a single console in the living room, people will have interactive devices all through the house. A recent AOL survey found that 52 percent of people online are already rearranging the furniture for the PC.

The fact is, the first steps of convergence already are driving consumers' expectations—and the more they get, the more they want.

The Internet has already changed the landscape of our lives. Ten years ago, the Internet was the exclusive province of researchers. Just five years ago, the World Wide Web barely existed, there was no talk about a "new economy," and, hard though it may be to believe, "e" was just the fifth letter in the alphabet.

Today, more than 200 million people are online worldwide, and if projections hold true—as I think they will—that number will more than double in the next three years. There are around 800 million Web pages, covering everything from world markets to world wrestling. And "e" has become the prefix for a massive social and economic transformation.[23]

---

[23]Speech given at ASNE Conference, April 14, 2000

case | 2 The DaimlerChrysler Merger (A)

Gaining Global Competitiveness

George Rädler
International Institute for Management Development

> In interviews, the men who run Detroit's Big 3 auto companies squinted at the horizon and offered similar descriptions of the future they see, one dominated by fewer car companies and smarter, more demanding customers. Perhaps the agreement is surprising, but it is based on the certainty that what once was a comfortable, predictable, nationalistic industry is gone forever. It's a clear sign that global reach and critical mass are needed to survive the ferocious future envisioned by the auto chiefs.
> —*USA Today*, September 29, 1998

The car industry is the world's largest manufacturing industry, and the most global. Many car companies consider the world market their home market; they have production sites around the globe and produce "global cars."

However, the surprise was big when Daimler-Benz AG and Chrysler Corporation announced on May 7, 1998, their coming together in a "merger of equals." The first true transatlantic merger, the DaimlerChrysler fusion created a company with revenues of $132 billion and approximately 440,000 employees. An international union of this size was without precedent, and it set the stage for more mergers. Previously unthinkable deals, such as Ford's acquisition of Volvo and the Renault–Nissan connection, were suddenly concluded in a matter of weeks.

How could an industry of former national champions change so fast?

Car Industry at Another Breakpoint?

Since Henry Ford's invention of the conveyor belt, the automotive industry has been shaped by breakpoints. Each signals a dramatic change in the industry. After World War II, for example, Japanese carmakers were able to provide fuel-efficient cars with good price/performance ratios during the oil crises of both 1973 and 1979. Within 15 years, Japanese car companies had secured about 30 percent of the American market and a considerable share of the European market (although protectionistic measures hindered the penetration). To a lesser extent, Korean manufacturers replicated this success.

Prepared under the supervision of Professor Ulrich Steger as a basis for class discussion rather than to illustrate either effective or ineffective handling of an administrative situation.

Copyright © 1999 by IMD—International Institute for Management Development, Lausanne, Switzerland. Used with permission.

exhibit 1   Value Chain (as a Percent of Total Price to the Consumer)

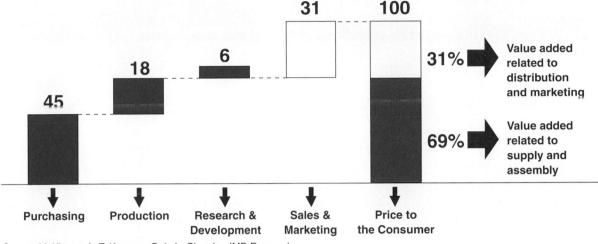

Source: McKinsey, A. T. Kearney, DaimlerChrysler, IMD Research.

Another breakpoint was the arrival of "lean manufacturing systems" around the globe. A 1990 study revealed that, in production hours per vehicle and inventory control, respectively, Japanese car plants were more than twice to more than 10 times as efficient as their European competitors. In order to survive, car companies optimized their operations within a few years. (Refer to Exhibit 1 for the value chain of a typical car company.)

The global drive for rationalization led to an estimated overcapacity of 20 to 30 percent and decreasing price levels. This overcapacity was one of the drivers of consolidation in the industry. Already, some industry experts expected only six car companies to survive this round of megamergers. They referred to this scenario as the end game.

THE WORLDWIDE MARKET FOR CARS AND COMMERCIAL VEHICLES

During the past five decades, the world population has doubled; at the same time, the number of cars on the road has increased tenfold to 500 million units (which is in addition to almost 300 million trucks and motorbikes). The global market for motor vehicles as measured by the number of registrations of both cars and commercial vehicles has grown from 46.4 million units in 1993 to 50.9 million units in 1998. (Refer to Exhibit 2 for an overview of new car registrations.)

The three main regions (North America, Western Europe, and Japan) accounted for 75 percent of all vehicles sold in 1998 and are still the most important markets. These traditional markets in the industrialized countries were saturated, and growth was expected from expansion in developing countries in Asia and Latin America. Nevertheless, economic difficulties resulted in large idle capacity in these formerly promising markets, too. Moreover, due to currency volatility, high inflation, and competitive pressure, developing markets have proven difficult.

exhibit 2   The Worldwide Market for Cars (in 000s of Units)

New registration of cars and commercial vehicles by region							Forecast	
	1993	1994	1995	1996	1997	1998	1999	2000
Cars								
Western Europe	11,451	11,934	12,021	12,790	13,408	14,341	13,800	12,700
NAFTA	9,656	10,154	9,424	9,390	9,333	9,358	8,930	8,335
South America	1,485	1,737	1,898	1,938	2,215	1,703	1,120	1,460
Japan	4,200	4,210	4,444	4,669	4,492	4,093	4,200	4,450
Asia (excluding Japan)	2,700	2,972	3,267	3,533	3,599	2,468	2,743	3,098
Eastern Europe	1,879	1,560	1,533	1,729	1.906	1,820	1,534	1,580
Other markets	988	880	1,072	1,150	1,208	1,268	1,289	1,345
Total	**32,358**	**33,447**	**33,658**	**35,199**	**36,161**	**35,051**	**33,616**	**32,968**
% change	−3.6	3.4	0.6	4.6	2.7	−3.1	−4.1	−1.9
Commercial vehicles								
Western Europe	1,328	1,421	1,528	1,647	1,766	1,958	1,854	1,750
NAFTA	6,315	7,118	7,056	7,623	8,086	8,617	8,230	8,160
South America	451	478	485	558	590	576	370	480
Japan	2,267	2,316	2,421	2,409	2,233	1,781	1,995	2,276
Asia (excluding Japan)	2,448	2,550	2,850	2,830	2,450	2,050	2,270	2,550
Eastern Europe	625	350	310	360	395	405	420	490
Other markets	634	535	618	625	632	442	450	460
Total	**14,068**	**14,767**	**15,267**	**16,052**	**16,152**	**15,829**	**15,589**	**16,166**
% change	4.5	5	3.4	5.1	0.6	−2	−1.5	3.7
Total cars and commercial vehicles	**46,426**	**48,214**	**48,925**	**51,251**	**52,313**	**50,880**	**49,205**	**49,134**
% change	−1.3	3.9	1.5	4.8	2.1	−2.7	−3.3	−0.1

Source: The Economist Intelligence Unit, April 1999.

Although Western markets were very competitive, a few profitable market niches existed; some of the highest growth rates were found in the segment for light trucks. This segment has been extremely successful in North America and to a lesser extent in Europe and Japan. (Refer to Exhibit 3 for more detailed descriptions of new segments in the U.S. auto market.) The light truck segment included:

- *Pickup trucks*—accounted for 19.1 percent of the American market, with Ford as the market leader.
- *Multipurpose vehicles (MPVs)—minivans*—invented by Chrysler; the flexibility of MPVs (spaciousness, good handling) made them extremely popular among American families (market share: 10.5 percent in 1998).
- *Sport utility vehicles (SUVs or 4 × 4s)*—represented the fastest growing segment of the U.S. market for automobiles. They reached a record market share of 18 percent of all newly sold vehicles in 1998.
- *Minicars*—mainly popular in Europe.

exhibit 3   New Segments in the U.S. Auto Market

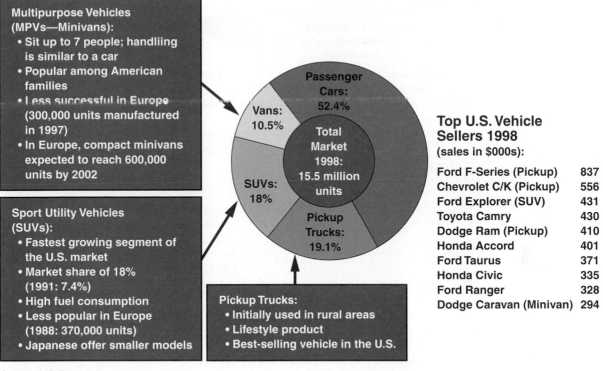

Multipurpose Vehicles (MPVs—Minivans):
- Sit up to 7 people; handliing is similar to a car
- Popular among American families
- Less successful in Europe (300,000 units manufactured in 1997)
- In Europe, compact minivans expected to reach 600,000 units by 2002

Sport Utility Vehicles (SUVs):
- Fastest growing segment of the U.S. market
- Market share of 18% (1991: 7.4%)
- High fuel consumption
- Less popular in Europe (1988: 370,000 units)
- Japanese offer smaller models

Pickup Trucks:
- Initially used in rural areas
- Lifestyle product
- Best-selling vehicle in the U.S.

Passenger Cars: 52.4%

Vans: 10.5%

Total Market 1998: 15.5 million units

SUVs: 18%

Pickup Trucks: 19.1%

Top U.S. Vehicle Sellers 1998
(sales in $000s):

Ford F-Series (Pickup)	837
Chevrolet C/K (Pickup)	556
Ford Explorer (SUV)	431
Toyota Camry	430
Dodge Ram (Pickup)	410
Honda Accord	401
Ford Taurus	371
Honda Civic	335
Ford Ranger	328
Dodge Caravan (Minivan)	294

Source: IMD Research.

The number of available models has also increased considerably over the past two decades. In 1981, 60 brands with a total of 268 models were available on the German market. By 1998, the number of brands had gradually increased to 67; however, the number of models had increased sharply to over 550. Many car manufacturers had switched to a so-called platform design, and they could produce several models on the same platform. Volkswagen optimized this system and was planning to use only four platforms for its annual production capacity of over 4.2 million units, thus combining economies of scale with model scope. (Refer to Exhibit 4 for more about Volkswagen's platform strategy.)

However, lowering production costs was not enough to satisfy customers. Increasingly, customers were demanding features at no extra cost. Features such as power windows, power locks, and air conditioning were included in the base package or were available at reduced prices.

THE AUTO INDUSTRY—SURVIVAL OF THE FITTEST

Trends in the Industry

Overcapacity   Overcapacity in this high-fixed-cost industry was not distributed equally around the globe. Already in the 1980s, America's Big Three started removing

exhibit 4   Volkswagen's Platform Strategy

Each platform consists of:
- **bottom part of the chassis**
- **various modules of:**
  - **steering**
  - **power train**

 60% of manfacturing cost

In 1996, Volkswagen started its concept of four platforms. The platforms are used for the Volkswagen, Seat, Audi, and Skoda brands. The number in parentheses () indicates the 1999 retail price range of each model sold in Switzerland (prices in 000s of Swiss francs, including value-added tax).

Platform	Volkswagen	Seat	Audi	Skoda	Capacity
Compact Class	Polo (16-26) Lupo (15-20)	Arosa (14-19) Cordoba (19-28)		Felicia (15-21)	Over 1 million
Golf Class	Golf (22-36) Jetta (26-38) Beetle (30)	Toledo (24-36)	A3 (28-38) TT (46-54)	Octavia (21-41)	Over 2 million
Middle Class	Passat (31-47)		A4 (37-72) A6 (43-67)		Over 1.2 million
Luxury			A8 (78-125)		Over 15,000

Models of the Golf Class Platform:

Seat Toledo   Audi TT   VW Golf   Skoda Octavia   VW Bora   VW Beetle   Audi A3

Note: Exchange rate: 1 U.S.$ = 1.5 Swiss francs.

Source: Volkswagen AG, HypoVereinsbank Research.

overcapacity by closing a total of 30 plants in the United States and Canada. American market research companies expected North American utilization to remain above 80 percent and Western European around 70 percent. Asian utilization was a concern as Japanese companies expanded recklessly in the late 1980s and had idle capacity. Mazda, for example, was running at a utilization rate of 60 percent during most of the 1990s.

Continuing overcapacity has decreased the number of car companies. In 1960, a total of 42 independent car manufacturers existed; by 1999, only 17 remained. (See Exhibit 5 for an overview of consolidation in the auto industry.) However, although mergers and acquisitions often made sense on paper, their implementation frequently proved to be more difficult and expensive than expected. It took Ford more than five years to see a profit from its Jaguar acquisition. For BMW's acquisition of Rover, optimistic forecasts expected a profit by 2001—seven years after the company was acquired.

Changing Role of Suppliers   Components accounted, on average, for 45 percent of the value chain. Instead of merely supplying batches of parts to order, component suppliers increasingly had to manufacture very complex modules, from complete suspension packages to ready-to-build-in driver cockpits. Suppliers were required to design, develop, and produce the modules according to strict quality standards. Moreover, they needed to be able to manage the complex system of subassemblies. In return, car manufacturers granted suppliers long-term supply contracts, in many cases as the sole supplier. In some of the most modern factories, suppliers already accounted for 80 percent of the value, leaving manufacturers the role of running "systems integrators" and marketing functions. The surviving companies were becoming systems integrators, establishing closer relationships with the manufacturers.

exhibit 5   Consolidation in the Automotive Industry

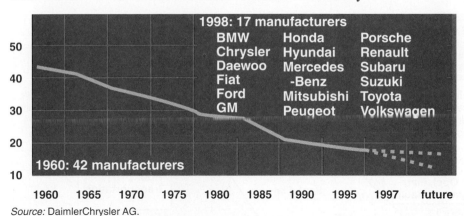

Source: DaimlerChrysler AG.

Large suppliers with the necessary capital backing had a better chance of offering their products globally. Pressure to reduce prices and to establish a global presence had forced many suppliers to merge or to exit the industry. Even heavyweight ITT, one of the five largest American component suppliers in 1995, decided in early 1998 to leave the automotive industry altogether. Overall, the effect of "lean manufacturing" and heavy concentration was changing the structure in the auto industry—only two suppliers remained for producing fuel injection systems (Lucas and Robert Bosch) and sunroofs (Rockwell and Webasto). The situation was similar for seats, clutches, and windscreens. Experts believed that the profit margins of these powerful suppliers could increase from their current 6 percent of sales.

Marketing and Brand Image Is Key   The distribution channel, including marketing expenses, accounted for up to 30 percent of a vehicle purchase price. Manufacturers had started streamlining this channel by reducing excessive stocks and the number of dealers. Dealers, already struggling because of a heavy reliance on after-sales service (40 percent of the dealer's revenue, but 90 percent of profits), were facing new competitors:

- In 1997, Auto-by-Tel, a General Electric (GE) subsidiary, sold 750,000 cars over the Internet (1995: 50,000 units). Microsoft and Dell have also entered this retail sector.

- GE had entered the financing market and financed around 850,000 vehicles in Europe.

- "Megadealer" companies such as CarMax successfully entered the market for used cars by opening large superstores. They offered a wide variety and good consultation at attractive prices.

- AutoNation, a megadealer, created a new business concept based on selling, renting, leasing and servicing. The company already owned around 200 car dealerships in North America. This consolidation strengthened the position of the surviving dealers vis-à-vis the manufacturers. In an attempt to limit the power of dealers, the manufacturers had taken legal action to prevent megadealers from buying more independent sales outlets.

On the marketing side, the traditional market segmentation became more difficult and in some cases obsolete due to overlapping segments. (See Exhibit 6 for an

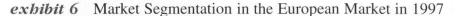

exhibit 6   Market Segmentation in the European Market in 1997

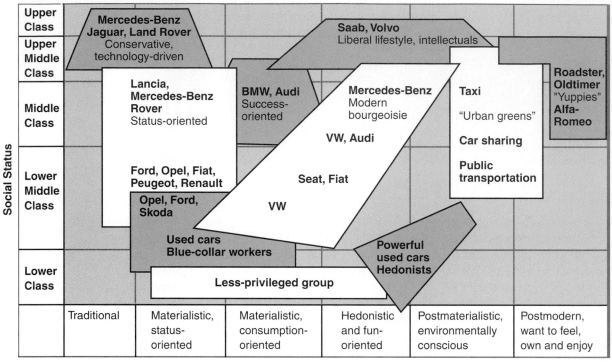

Source: *Manager Magazine,* Marketing Systems, IMD Research.

overview of the market segmentation in Europe.) Hence, car manufacturers were forced to focus more on the power of brands. The power of brands could be clearly seen in the case of the New United Motor Manufacturing, Inc. (NUMMI) plant in California. Since 1989, the plant has produced two almost-identical cars: the Toyota Corolla and the GM Geo Prizm. The Toyota car sold at $9,000 in 1989, about 10 percent higher than its American counterpart. Over five years, the Corolla depreciated more slowly; its secondhand value was 18 percent higher than GM's Geo Prism. This difference accounted for the strength of Toyota's brand name.

Impact of Technology

- On average, R&D expenses accounted for around 6 percent of sales, but Daimler-Benz spent 8 percent on R&D in 1997. Ford's Mondeo world car set records for development costs—a total of $6 billion—but Ford boasted an average profit margin of around $1,000 per vehicle sold in 1997. The auto industry had become knowledge-intensive, and R&D was a crucial aspect of differentiating cars (which have become a lot more similar due to the usage of platforms, and aerodynamic and regulatory constraints). Since the time-to-market of cars has gotten shorter (from 60 months in 1988 to 24 months in 1998), even large manufacturers have decided to cooperate to reduce R&D expenses per vehicle. Overall, about 500 co-operation agreements existed in the automotive industry.

- Traffic jams had become a reality in almost all urban areas. Authorities took various approaches for reducing overcongestion. One of the most promising was using computers to help increase the flow of traffic ("telematics"). Computers calculated the optimal speed for maintaining a flow of traffic and then adjusted the maximum posted speed limit on roadside digital screens. The European market was estimated to grow from DM 1 billion in 1998 to over DM 10 billion in 2004.

- Dealing with heavy pollution, the California Air Resources Board made a directive to increase the proportion of cars with lower emissions. Although this directive sanctioned the use of electric vehicles, their market potential was still limited due to high cost, limited reach, and safety problems. As a result, many car companies started to invest in fuel cells. Mercedes-Benz was expected to introduce a fuel cell car in 2003.

DAIMLER-BENZ: SHAKE OR BE SHAKEN

With good reason, Daimler-Benz AG (DB) was perceived as the incarnation of German engineering competence. Its luxury cars were regarded as the best-engineered cars (overengineered, some would say) with a constant stream of innovations in safety, quality, electronic features, comfort, and design. DB cars sold in more than 200 countries, and Mercedes was one of the strongest global brands.

However, in the early 1990s, Daimler-Benz took several hits: Its ambitious diversification process into a "technology concern" did not produce the anticipated synergies. The European truck division produced heavy losses. And Japanese rivals pressed DB's luxury cars with similar quality and technology, but at much lower prices.

DB staged a thunderous turnaround, especially after Jürgen Schrempp took over as CEO in early 1995. In an operation called "stop the bleeding," all unprofitable business units were restructured, closed, or sold, very much in a U.S. style never before seen in Germany. Although DB reversed the diversification process so that it remained a kind of "transportation company" (cars, trucks, buses, railway, aerospace, telecommunications, and related services), DB still covered a much broader range than its competitors (and Chrysler).

How to Survive in a Consolidating Industry

Once the restructuring got on its way, Schrempp started to think about the future of Daimler-Benz and the car industry. Schrempp saw the writing on the wall. He noticed that:

- Except for niche players (e.g., BMW, Porsche, Volvo), none of the luxury car brands was still independent. Big global players owned most brands: Ford Motors controlled Jaguar, and GM sat in the driver's seat at Saab.
- Since the mid-1980s, the number of brands competing in the luxury segment had increased from 9 to 19.
- The world economy was experiencing the longest expansion cycle in several decades. Overcapacity was estimated at 20 to 30 percent, and what would happen during the next downturn?
- Mercedes-Benz's attempts to expand outside its traditional target segment met with more obstacles than expected. The most visible experience was the "moose test," a cornering test performed by journalists, where a Mercedes A-class subcompact model tipped. As a result, the model had to be redesigned. The establishment of the "Smart" brand (initially a joint venture with Swatch) for "city cars" was also challenging. Mercedes-Benz invested over DM 2 billion, but the development took longer than expected. The market introduction had to be delayed by six months.
- Mercedes-Benz's 8 percent R&D cost-on-turnover was far above the industry average (and nearly three times the Chrysler figure). Due to the small production volume, suppliers had to be given permission to transfer innovations to competing

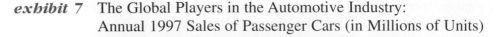

exhibit 7   The Global Players in the Automotive Industry:
Annual 1997 Sales of Passenger Cars (in Millions of Units)

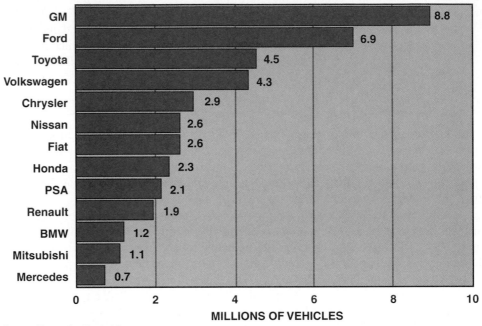

Source: Deutsche Bank AG.

car brands within six months. (Refer to Exhibit 7 for annual global sales of passenger cars.) Hence, the advantage of technological superiority was becoming difficult to communicate to customers.

- Although Mercedes-Benz was trying to become a global player (e.g., the new M-class production site in Alabama or the E-Class assembly in India and South Africa), it was basically still a German company (some would even insist, *Swabian*) with huge factories (e.g., the Sindelfingen plant outside Stuttgart still employed around 30,000 people in the late 1990s).

- The acquisition of Freightliner Trucks in the United States went smoothly. The company almost tripled its sales within a decade; however, it was run as a completely separate entity, with little interference from Stuttgart.

Schrempp and his team knew that more change was needed in order to remain in the top league of global players in the automotive industry. Otherwise they could be shaken by the industry consolidation. So in 1997, Schrempp commissioned, in addition to internal studies, a study by an investment bank identifying possible partners.

HOW TO AVOID THE THREAT OF ANOTHER BANKRUPTCY AT CHRYSLER

If DB was run by blue-ribbon engineers, Chrysler had to adopt more of a street-fighter mentality. Being the smallest and the most vulnerable of the U.S. Big Three, Chrysler had been to the edge of the cliff of bankruptcy twice in the last two decades. Moreover, it was the target of a hostile takeover battle by its largest shareholder, Kirk Kerkorian.

When Bob Eaton took over as CEO in 1994, he had a clear message: "I want to be the first CEO who does not lead the company back from bankruptcy."

exhibit 8   1997 Financial Performance of Selected Automakers
        (All Annual Data in Billions of U.S. Dollars)

	Daimler-Benz AG	Chrysler Corp.	General Motors	Ford
Domestic sales	$ 23.0	$ 57.0		
International sales	46.6	4.2		
Total Sales	**$ 69.6**	**$ 61.2**	**$ 178.0**	**153.6**
Net Earnings	$ 1.8	$ 2.8	$ 6.7	6.9
Domestic employees	225,266			
International employees	74,802			
Total Employees	**300,068**	**121,000**	**608,000**	**360,000**

Note: Chrysler's domestic sales include sales in Canada.

Exchange rate: $1 = DM 1.78 (this rate was used in the combination agreement).

Net earnings of Daimler-Benz AG does not include tax benefits (around $2.8 billion in 1997).

Source: Annual reports.

After diversification had led to a dramatic cash drain in the late 1980s, Chrysler focused only on cars and light trucks. It was praised for developing the new markets for minivans (market share of almost 50 percent in the United States), sport utility vehicles (sales of the Jeep brand more than doubled between 1990 and 1997), and pickup trucks.

But fighting for survival had turned Chrysler into a strong competitor during the 1990s. Its time-to-market design and development times (due to conventional platform models) set world standards and were still widely considered best for cost-effectiveness. Overall, Chrysler was the leanest manufacturer of the Big Three. Compared to GM, Chrysler had one-third the sales but only one-fifth of the employees. (Refer to Exhibit 8 for GM, DB, and Chrysler financial results and employee numbers.) Cost effectiveness became an obsession. As a result, the profitability per employee stood at around $23,000, more than double the value for GM.

Although Chrysler was characterized to be a "fast follower" in technology and mostly bought technology from suppliers, trendy and fashionable design has been instrumental in the market success in recent years.

Chrysler—the Smallest of the Big Three

Although Chrysler was doing very well in the late 1990s, Bob Eaton was also concerned about the future:

- Any decline in the U.S. economy could hit Chrysler harder than the larger Big Three rivals and the Japanese competitors.
- Competition was also catching up in the market segments for minivans and sport utility vehicles, where Chrysler was the leader.
- Chrysler's position in the car segment was weakening. Between 1990 and 1997, its U.S. production rate of passenger cars fell by 40 percent to 440,000 units, while GM and Ford had decreases of less than 20 percent.
- Chrysler's plans to expand the company beyond the North American Free Trade Area (NAFTA) were stagnating due to a lack of management depth and products suited to non-NAFTA markets. The company sold less than 10 percent of its cars outside NAFTA.

- The rapid dissemination of electronic systems in cars (e.g., global positioning system) raised a question about the company's strategy of buying most car technology from suppliers. Might this approach erode Chrysler's core competencies to the degree that it risked becoming more of an assembler than a manufacturer, which could result in a weakened position in the value creation chain?

- The emerging distribution systems in the U.S. car industry (megadealers, e-commerce, car management companies) with their higher retailer power could affect Chrysler more deeply than competitors because of its smaller market share.

In light of these facts, Schrempp approached Eaton in January 1998. Given the circumstances of the industry, Eaton was very responsive to Schrempp's proposal to discuss a merger. Within four months and under strict secrecy, a team of only 20 to 30 managers from both companies worked out the details of this merger. The merger of Daimler-Benz AG and Chrysler Corporation was announced on May 7.

THE MERGER FOR GROWTH AND THE MERGER OF EQUALS: RHETORIC OR REALITY?

In communicating the merger to the boards, investors, employees, customers and the public, Schrempp and Eaton constantly stressed the following themes:

- This was a merger of equals, not an acquisition. The U.S. press in particular doubted this claim, noting that the 58:42 distribution of shares represented a significant premium for Chrysler. Although Chrysler was relatively more profitable, its price-earnings ratio was much lower, in the range of 13.5; Daimler-Benz, in contrast, tracked with a price-earnings ratio of approximately 21.5.

- This was a "merger for growth"—no layoffs, no plant closures, no scrapping of brands or products. Both brands were kept separate, and financial analysts were quick to point out that this strategy limited the potential synergies that the merged companies might otherwise have reaped. Overall, the combined company expected cost savings of $1.4 billion in its first year of operation.

- The merger was going to be the "best-implemented merger." The integration phase was expected to last for three years. The "merger of equals" philosophy was also expected to lead to the "best of two worlds" state, where the strength and best practices of Daimler and Chrysler would combine to form a stronger new entity, outpacing competition. Every process was reviewed in order to pick the best solution. For more details refer to Case 3, "The DaimlerChrysler Merger (B): Shaping a Transatlantic Company."

The geographic spread and product portfolio showed very little overlap between both companies, due to the simple fact that Mercedes-Benz was only in the upper market segments, whereas the Chrysler brands were more mid-market and stronger in specialized segments like minivans, SUVs or pickups. (Refer to Exhibits 9 and 10 for the geographic spread and market segments of the two companies.) Some financial analysts were fast to point out the difficulty of achieving cost savings in purchasing due to a lack of overlapping products.

For most of Daimler-Benz's other activities (heavy trucks, aerospace, etc.), no similar Chrysler division existed. Even in financial services, Chrysler was much more focused on captive customers (e.g., dealers) than the Debis subsidiary of Daimler-Benz.

exhibit 9 Geographic Sales and Production Volume of Chrysler Corporation and Daimler-Benz AG, 1997

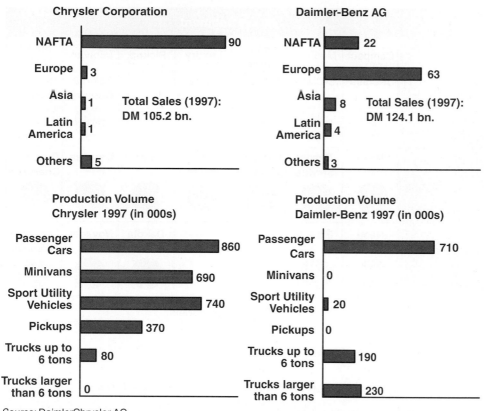

Source: DaimlerChrysler AG.

However, the complementarity of products didn't mean that there were no bumps on the road to the merger agreement. One was the price premium for Chrysler. Even more contentious were the questions of where and how to incorporate the new company, and what to name it. In order to discuss these delicate questions, the representatives from DB and Chrysler considered three options for the incorporation of the new company:

● A U.S. company.
● A German company.
● A neutrally incorporated company (e.g., in the Netherlands).

The team agreed to let the facts speak for the decision (and it was clear that the facts were mainly monetary). The exchange rate for the stocks was decided three weeks before the merger announcement. However, other issues proved to be more complex. For American managers it was difficult to imagine operating with a German two-tier board system (management board and supervisory board) with co-determination (having labor representation on the supervisory board). Nevertheless, DB's loss-carry forward and a tax-free solution for Deutsche Bank, DB's major shareholder, and other shareholders led to the establishment of DaimlerChrysler in Germany. After that, the slogan "Let the facts speak for the solution" became a model for conflict resolution in the merger process.

exhibit 10   Geographic Spread of Daimler-Benz AG and
              Chrysler Corporation

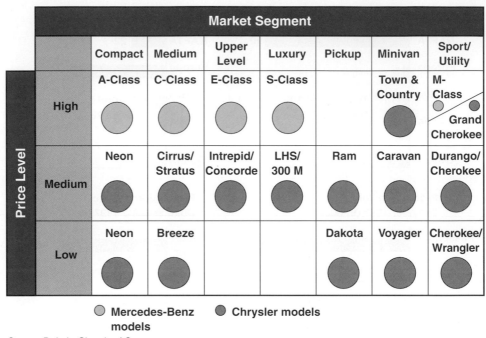

| Source: DaimlerChrysler AG. |

Triggering a New Round of Consolidation

The DaimlerChrysler merger sent shock waves through the global automobile industry, issuing in a new round of consolidation. Ford bought the Volvo car division and was forming a premium brand division called Premier Automotive, run by BMW's former number two manager, Wolfgang Reitzle. DaimlerChrysler showed a strong interest in acquiring Nissan, the second largest player in Japan. Only a few weeks after DaimlerChrysler decided not to bid for Nissan, Renault joined forces with Nissan. Within one year, the number of Korean manufacturers fell from five to two—Hyundai and Daewoo.

A Recession Just around the Corner?

The portents for an economic slowdown on the horizon were numerous:

● Although the North American market was currently not showing any indications of a slowdown, analysts had become increasingly nervous about the long expansion cycle in the United States. Moreover, Chrysler's most profitable cars (SUVs, pickups, and minivans) were being attacked by new models from Honda, Toyota, and BMW.

● Europe's business outlook was uncertain—growth was slower than expected, and a weakening Euro was a good indicator of this uncertainty.

● Growth expectations had been considerably dampened, not only in emerging countries in Asia and Latin America but also in Japan, the third largest market in the world. Japanese car and truck sales had fallen by 12 percent in 1998—the worst sales decline in two decades.

Was the DaimlerChrysler merger solid enough to stand a recession in an industry that had a global capacity of 71 million units but sold only 52 million at the peak of the cycle? What would happen in a downturn? Said Thomas Stallkamp, the president of DaimlerChrysler:

> I wouldn't want to hope for a crisis, but sometimes it brings people together even faster.

Thinking about the industry, Schrempp wanted to shake things up, rather than be shaken. But the end game in the global auto industry has more than one round. . . .

The DaimlerChrysler Merger (B)

Shaping a Transatlantic Company

George Rädler

International Institute for Management Development

> Since the announcement of the merger, we have not only kept our promises, we have exceeded them. As a result, your company shines more brightly than even we dared to imagine.
> —Bob Eaton, co-chairman of DaimlerChrysler, to shareholders

> Our merger has become a model for others throughout the entire business world. DaimlerChrysler has been named the most respected company in Europe by the Financial Times.
> —Jürgen Schrempp, co-chairman of DaimlerChrysler

In late May 1999, one year after the initial merger announcement, the two co-chairmen and other board members of DaimlerChrysler AG (DCX) met in Stuttgart to review the progress of the merger. The mood was good because the General Assembly on May 18 had gone very well. Despite some criticism of the few small dark spots (surprising losses from the new Smart "city-car"), the results for the first year of consolidated operations were better than expected: sales had risen by 12 percent to $146.5 billion, and the operating profit had grown by 38 percent to $9.6 billion. Overall, DCX was the world's most profitable car company in 1998 and, on top of that, over 19,000 new employees had been hired. Other divisions (aerospace, Debis/Chrysler Financial Services) had achieved record results. (Refer to Exhibit 1 for an overview of DCX.)

The board members were proud of their achievements so far, but there were numerous challenges for the future. Increasingly, financial analysts were questioning whether DCX had gone too far with its strict brand separation: Was the company running the risk of hindering anticipated cost savings?

The board members were well aware that in today's volatile world, neither the shareholders, the financial analysts, nor the media, who were following the merger closely, would give any credit for past successes. Some critical voices remained.

Although the integration plan was clearly working, the wear and tear on the organization was becoming visible. Indeed, some top managers complained about spend-

---

Prepared under the supervision of Professor Ulrich Steger as a basis for class discussion rather than to illustrate either effective or ineffective handling of an administrative situation.

exbibit 1 Financial Overview of DaimlerChrysler AG, Financial Year 1998

	Mercedes-Benz Passenger Cars, Smart	Chrysler, Plymouth, Jeep, Dodge	Commercial Vehicles Mercedes-Benz, Freightliner, Sterling, Setra	Chrysler Financial Services	Debis Services (Financial Services, IT, Telecom)	DaimlerChrysler Aerospace	Others
Revenue (in $ million)	38,234	66,101	27,175	3,376	11,232	10,290	4,019
Growth in % over 1997	*18.3%*	*8.5%*	*15.7%*	*19.5%*	*21.5%*	*12.1%*	*(12.1%)*
Operating profit (in $ million)	2,338	4,942	1,110	765	460	731	(171)
Growth in % over 1997	*15.7%*	*25.1%*	*176.6%*	*11.3%*	*59.3%*	*119.4%*	—
Unit sales	922,795	3,093,716	489,680	—	—	—	—
Growth in % over 1997	*29%*	*7.2%*	*17.3%*	—	—	—	—
Employees	95,158	123,180	89,711	3,513	20,221	45,858	32,581

Note: Due to double counting, the revenue figure is larger than $146.5.
Source: Annual report.

exhibit 2   Share Price of DaimlerChrysler AG, April 1997–June 1999

Source: Reuters.

ing up to 40 percent of their time on merger activities, rather than running their day-to-day operations. Notes Dr. Rüdiger Grube, senior vice president of corporate strategy:

> After the honeymoon is over, you sort out the easy things first. Then you come to the more difficult items—and here comes the real test for the merger of equals. Do you work things out and look for the best solutions, wherever you find it? Or do you go on war for your system? The pressure does not allow you to play politics but forces a constructive attitude, because you have to deliver results. There is no place to hide, and this sometimes causes stress. But the complexity makes it difficult to keep everything on a speedy track.

Although the first year of the merger was indeed successful in many respects, the board members were debating how to improve the performance of the stock and how to continue in increasingly uncertain times. (See Exhibit 2 for the development of the stock.)

Implementation Is Everything

From research, DCX executives knew that most mergers fail. (Refer to Exhibit 3 for an overview of why mergers fail.) Many unsuccessful mergers are not ill-designed from the beginning; failure occurs during implementation. That was perhaps why Schrempp

exhibit 3   Why Do Mergers Fail?

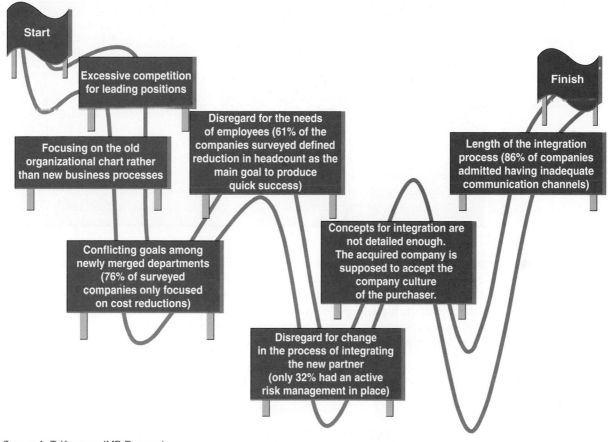

Source: A. T. Kearney, IMD Research.

had committed himself to making the DaimlerChrysler merger the best strategically, and the best-implemented and communicated. As Dr. Christoph Walther, head of communications, noted:

> We always try to raise issues before we were asked.

For Dr. Alexander Dibelius, managing partner of Goldman Sachs and one of the leading bankers behind the merger, one issue stood out above all others:

> Lack of speed is the single most important reason for failure. What you don't achieve in the beginning, you never see materialized.

Knowing this, the key players in the DCX merger had set the internal goal of concluding the merger in two years (abandoning the former official goal of three years)—the maximum time Bob Eaton would serve as co-chairman. Eaton stated publicly that he was going to retire in 2001.

But speed was not an eminent characteristic of the German model of corporate governance. Not only was the strict division of supervisory board and management

exhibit 4   Co-determination—German Model of Corporate Governance

Management board versus supervisory board
Management board: runs day-to-day operations
Supervisory board: hires and controls the management board

Supervisory board
- 20 members for companies >20,000 employees
- The members of the board are divided equally between representatives from shareholders and employees
  - Representatives from the employee side are voted in
  - At least two union members have to be on the supervisory board
  - At least one blue-collar worker has to be on the supervisory board
  - One senior manager (white collar) also has to be on the supervisory board
- Shareholders elect members of the supervisory board for the capital side
- Chairman (always from the capital side) has two votes in case of a 50/50 split

board slowing down decisions, but the necessary consensus with the workers' councils and workers' representative on the supervisory board also had to be built on all important issues of employment. (Refer to Exhibit 4 for an overview of co-determination.) Given both the high dependency on public contracts in aerospace and railways and the regulatory framework for cars and trucks, other stakeholders couldn't be ignored either. Schrempp didn't see this as a disadvantage:

> It takes more time to come to a decision, but you can implement faster, because everybody is on board. However, you have to communicate intensively—both internally and externally.

Speed, Speed, Speed—and Monitoring Results

The so-called proxy statement of the merger specified the financial targets, and included savings of $1.4 billion in the first year of combined operations, as well as annual benefits of approximately $3 billion within three to five years of the merger agreement. Soon after signing the merger agreement, co-chairmen Schrempp and Eaton clearly defined a framework for the postmerger integration phase. Speed was priority number one, followed by accountability and transparency. In the integration effort, it was important to have all of top management involved in the process.

The Chairmen's Integration Council (CIC) was founded in order to monitor the integration. The CIC was co-chaired by both Eaton and Schrempp. (Refer to Exhibit 5 for an overview of the Postmerger Integration Structure.) Further members included two executives from Chrysler and four from Daimler-Benz. The integration process was divided into 12 clusters, which were called Issue Resolution Teams (IRTs). Twelve IRTs were grouped around functional areas (e.g., purchasing) and identified and realized the synergies between the two companies. For example, one team analyzed the various e-mail systems and came up with a proposal for the board. Daimler-Benz used to have a different e-mail system for each division while Chrysler just had one e-mail system. Subsequently the team proposed to have only one e-mail system for DaimlerChrysler. Each IRT was jointly run by one management board

exhibit 5   Postmerger Integration at DaimlerChrysler AG

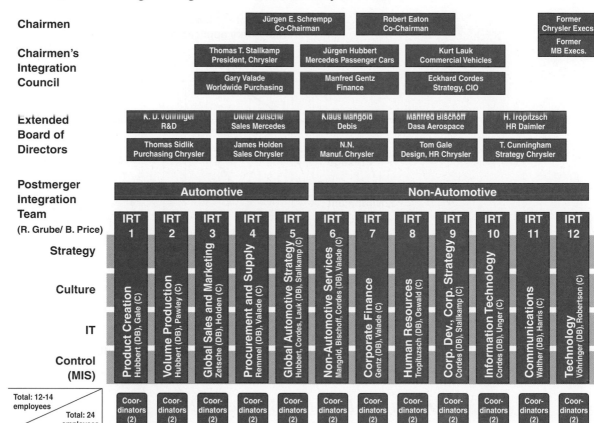

member from Chrysler and one from Daimler; they reported directly to the CIC. Due to the board members' heavy workloads, each IRT had two coordinators who stayed in close contact with their counterparts from other IRTs. In addition to a dedicated team of around 10 individuals, these coordinators formed the Postmerger Integration (PMI) Team. The PMI Team supported and helped monitor the integration process. Altogether, this PMI structure was referred to as distributed leadership and included around 50 dedicated individuals. This relatively small coordination structure, in turn, oversaw around 80 integration projects involving hundreds of managers across the organization.

The "war room" was the center for aggregating and monitoring the progress of the different PMI projects. Located in Stuttgart, the war room was equipped with the most modern information technology equipment. The project coordinators had to input their progress on a weekly basis. Each project was constantly monitored by a set of "traffic lights." A green light signaled that everything was on track; a yellow light indicated a few delays; and a red light implied serious difficulties. Top executives could access this system from any computer. In case of a red light, members of the CIC normally sent an e-mail to the team leader asking for reasons for the slow progress.

exhibit 6   Brand Profiles of Chrysler and Mercedes

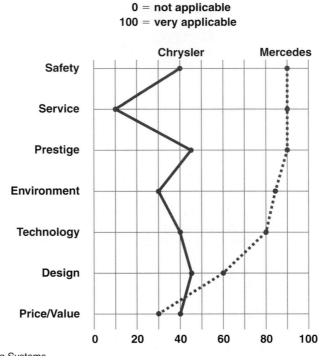

Source: Marketing Systems.

Combining a Luxury Brand with a Mass-Volume Producer

The brand value of both Mercedes-Benz and Chrysler was undisputed. Before the merger, Mercedes-Benz was ranked as one of the world's 10 most powerful brands, and Chrysler had an established position in North America. However, the perception of both brands was very different. (Refer to Exhibit 6 for brand profiles.) As the brands were often considered the most valuable asset, both brands even had their own members on the board, James Holden (former Chrysler vice president of sales and marketing) and Dr. Dieter Zetsche (former Mercedes-Benz vice president of sales and marketing). They also headed the IRT sales and marketing. This committee discussed a broad range of issues. The guidelines for both brands were listed in the "Guidelines for DaimlerChrysler Brand Management." This book (internally it was referred to as the "bible") outlined the clear separation of both brands. The bible prohibited a common platform strategy for the Mercedes-Benz/Chrysler brands as well as the establishment of combined Mercedes-Benz/ Chrysler dealers in Europe. However, financial analysts started to wonder where the financial savings would be found if there were so few common parts. In addition, critics pointed out that Chrysler was lacking appropriate products for the European market and developing countries.

Beyond the Figures and Organization Charts

The cultural issues, the "soft" feature of the merger, were discussed intensively, particularly in the media. Many American journalists didn't buy into the "merger of equals" concept at all—they referred to DaimlerChrysler as an acquisition of the Chrysler Corporation. They eagerly tried to find signs of a takeover, especially when executives from Chrysler were leaving. But as one observer stated:

> These reports are missing the point. In Detroit, there has always been a fluctuation of executives among the Big Three. In every merger, there are winners and losers. Not only that some functions double, more important: some made it to the new headquarters and others were downgraded to becoming brand managers.

Top management reminded the employees that this was a merger of equals and encouraged them to pay close attention to cultural issues. Moreover, managers were expected to first identify the changes that would have a large impact on the organization.

In Europe, the public focused on differences in compensation. Bob Eaton's salary in 1997 ($16 million) was estimated to be eight times that of Jürgen Schrempp, who was one of the best-paid executives in Germany. By American standards, even Eaton's salary looked small—Alex Trotman, ex-CEO of Ford, had received a total salary of $73.1 million in 1998. However, these high salaries did not sell well in the more egalitarian German society. Hilmar Kopper, the chairman of the supervisory board, tried to steer a middle ground for the compensation of the board:

> There won't be an Americanization of the German executive pay system.

As part of the business combination agreement, all Chrysler employees' salaries were guaranteed for two years. For the future executive salaries, Kopper proposed four elements: a base salary depending on the executive's responsibilities, an annual bonus payment, stock-option plans, and phantom share payouts linked to certain key earnings targets. Some employees saw this as a move towards the U.S. model, with higher performance-related pay for members of the management board and executives. Kopper also had to deal with salary differences in other parts of the organization. In order to retain the most capable managers, the new company would pay its 200 top managers a globally competitive salary.

Dividend payments were also Americanized. DCX adopted a dividend similar to former Chrysler payments rather than the much lower payment by Daimler-Benz. However, the U.S. media was not convinced by these moves, because DCX decided not to release a proxy statement (includes details on top executive compensation) with the 1998 annual report. DCX, incorporated in Germany, was legally not required to file the proxy statement but could have supplied it voluntarily. Being incorporated in Germany also led to DCX's removal from the Standard & Poor 500 Index (S&P 500). Because many American investment funds were limited to investing their money in the S&P 500, a major shift in shareholder structure took place. After the merger, American shareholders accounted for only 25 percent of the shareholders, compared to 44 percent at the announcement. (Refer to Exhibit 7 for the changing structure of shareholders.)

In order to convince critics and lessen internal concerns and uncertainties, DCX created a vision and mission statement. It was developed by a working group and presented for discussion at the first DCX top management meeting (executive board and vice presidents) in Seville in December 1998. Then it was rolled out in the spring of 1999 in a trickle-down process. Management had to explain the mission/vision, outlining the goals of DaimlerChrysler to their direct reports. (Refer to Exhibit 8 for the main goals.) Videos, overhead slides, and a proposed schedule for each session supported the rollout.

***exhibit* 7**   Shareholder Structure of DaimlerChrysler AG

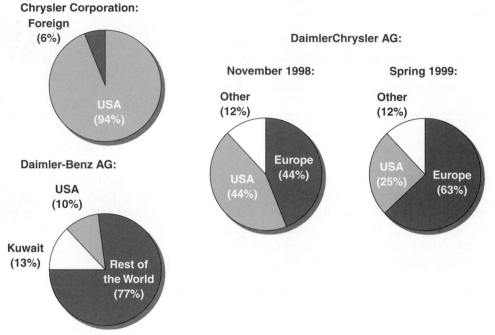

Source: DaimlerChrysler AG.

What Next?

Critics pointed out that integration of processes and brand separation might not be the right way for two companies as diverse as Daimler and Chrysler. To make their point, they referred to the example of the U.S. Freightliner and Sterling divisions, which were U.S. market leaders in heavy trucks despite not being integrated with the Mercedes truck division.

Other critics argued that because there was little overlap between Daimler and Chrysler, there were also few synergies to reap. As the Economist Intelligence Unit wrote: "Current harmony is little surprise—but complementarity reduces potential for synergies."[1] Financial analysts, ever hard to satisfy, pointed out that $1.4 billion in savings for year one of the merger, and $3 billion in years three to five, was not much for a sales volume of approximately $146 billion.

One huge synergy, the use of Mercedes' European and global distribution system, could not be leveraged, because as Tom Stallkamp, number two after Schrempp/Eaton, admitted:

Chrysler does not yet have the right product for the markets.

---

[1]EIU Motor Business Europe, 1st Quarter 1999. London: The Economist Intelligence Unit Limited, 1999, pp. 74–102.

exhibit 8   DaimlerChrysler's Mission, Goals, and Values

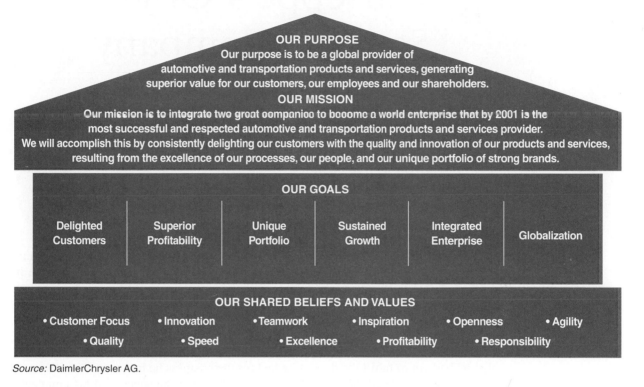

OUR PURPOSE
Our purpose is to be a global provider of
automotive and transportation products and services, generating
superior value for our customers, our employees and our shareholders.

OUR MISSION
Our mission is to integrate two great companies to become a world enterprise that by 2001 is the
most successful and respected automotive and transportation products and services provider.
We will accomplish this by consistently delighting our customers with the quality and innovation of our products and services,
resulting from the excellence of our processes, our people, and our unique portfolio of strong brands.

OUR GOALS

Delighted Customers	Superior Profitability	Unique Portfolio	Sustained Growth	Integrated Enterprise	Globalization

OUR SHARED BELIEFS AND VALUES

• Customer Focus   • Innovation   • Teamwork   • Inspiration   • Openness   • Agility
• Quality   • Speed   • Excellence   • Profitability   • Responsibility

Source: DaimlerChrysler AG.

How to move forward was therefore very much on the CIC agenda. As Schrempp stated:

> The DaimlerChrysler merger was only the necessary precondition to remaining a player in the global automobile industry.

Although the first year of integration was successful, the members of the CIC wondered whether they were still well positioned for the future challenges.

case 4 Giuseppe's Original Sausage Company

Michael T. Smith
Christian Brothers University

Jana F. Kuzmicki
Mississippi University for Women

As Joseph Cotrone, president and CEO of Giuseppe's Original Sausage Company, drove back to his office after conducting a promotion at a Seessel's grocery store in East Memphis, he wondered what the recently announced sale of Seessel's to the much larger Albertson's chain of grocery stores meant to his business. This was the second time within two years that Cotrone's first, and most important, customer was undergoing a change in ownership. Even though his seven-year-old company had finally broken even, Cotrone could not escape the feeling that he was just spinning his wheels, that he had yet to fulfill the dreams he had for the business he had started in 1991.

Cotrone pondered the issues he felt were hindering the success of his company: time involved in developing and establishing new accounts, lack of consistency in sales volume, inability to develop long-term relations with major customers, and financial instability. While sales continued to increase, the company did not have a core group of customers it could count on year in and year out. Cotrone's vision was to grow the business to a stage where he could afford to hire the necessary staff to run the day-to-day operations. Then he could spend his time in the kitchen creating new varieties of sausages—culinary works of art—which was his long-term goal.

COMPANY BACKGROUND AND HISTORY

When Joe Cotrone relocated to Memphis, Tennessee, in the late 1980s, he had a vision of operating a sausage company in which he could create a variety of different sausages using exotic meats and spices. Having moved from New Jersey, Cotrone missed the various types of high-quality sausages available in the Northeast. In the South, sausage (only links or patties) was viewed primarily as a meat to be served with breakfast. Cotrone was used to a much broader selection of sausages, typically featured as the main meat for breakfast, lunch, or dinner. In the Northeast, sausage often took center stage at meals other than breakfast, in both restaurants and homes.

The art of making sausage came naturally to Cotrone. He began by making custom sausages out of the kitchen in his home in the early 1990s. His original customers included friends, associates, and patrons at the restaurant where he worked as a bartender. In addition to serving his specialty sausages at the bar, Cotrone also sold them from a cooler he kept in his car. Customer demand soon exceeded Cotrone's production capabilities (maximum of 100 pounds per week), so he made plans to open a full-scale sausage company outside his home.

Giuseppe's Original Sausage Company began to take shape in late 1991. On November 1, 1991, Cotrone signed a six-month lease for space in a commercial building. This marked the beginning of a long journey, filled with numerous challenges, for Cotrone's gourmet sausage company. Although the space leased had once been used as a facility to manufacture sandwiches, it required additional renovations in order to meet the U.S. Department of Agriculture (USDA) regulations to produce sausage on a commercial scale. The regulations required the interior of the facility to be modified with new freezers, floors, walls, plumbing, and doors. Delays in construction and government-mandated renovations pushed back the scheduled opening (late March 1992) of Giuseppe's Original Sausage Company. Demands of the USDA, the Health Department, and various other government agencies exacted a toll on Cotrone's financial resources. As his personal capital dwindled, Cotrone had no choice but to initiate a search for external investors.

In the midst of regulation-driven renovations and the search for capital, Cotrone grabbed an opportunity, Memphis in May, to market his fledgling company. Memphis in May was an annual month-long series of cultural, social, and entertainment events that had a unifying theme of honoring a specific country. Fortunately for Cotrone, the 1991 Memphis in May festival spotlighted Italy and thus presented an ideal opportunity to introduce and market his newly formed company. Cotrone rented a booth from which to sell his specialty sausages to festival attendees. Sales were brisk, and Cotrone received a lot of very favorable comments from the festival participants.

In late 1992, Giuseppe's opened its doors to business, with sales to Seessel's (a local upscale grocery chain) and local restaurants. Sales were slow during the initial years. Sales to local restaurants quickly took priority over those to Seessel's. The sales projections that Cotrone had originally forecasted proved to be too optimistic. The outside investors Cotrone had recruited kept Giuseppe's afloat through the lean times before sales began to slowly increase by the mid-1990s. While Cotrone focused the majority of his attention on sales to local restaurants, Seessel's, and Kroger (a national retail grocery chain) during the mid-1990s, he also developed a flyer that featured his specialty sausages and could be sent or given to his ever-expanding individual customers.

By late 1997, Giuseppe's had sales of over $250,000 due to larger-order quantities from an expanding customer base, including the newly established Tunica, Mississippi, casinos. Giuseppe's staff included a plant manager, a full-time sausage maker, and a part-time salesperson. While a computer and basic business software (Microsoft Office, Small Business Edition) had been purchased, neither Cotrone nor his newly hired staff had been able to invest the necessary time to operationalize the computer system's potential contributions.

THE SPECIALTY SAUSAGE INDUSTRY

The results of an A. C. Nielsen study indicated that consumers nationwide purchased almost 462 million pounds of dinner sausage during 1997. According to a 1996 USDA study, the projected average total meat and poultry weight per capita was 208.8 pounds per year. The specialty dinner sausage market consisted of two segments: retail (supermarket) and food service (restaurants; institutions such as hospitals, schools, and nursing homes; and other establishments). In 1997, the retail segment exceeded $2 million

exhibit 1   Meals Purchased at Commercial Restaurants per Person, 1984–1996

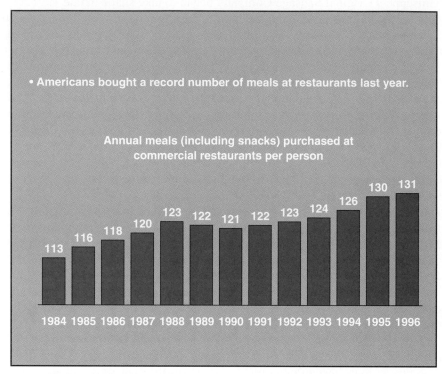

• Americans bought a record number of meals at restaurants last year.

Annual meals (including snacks) purchased at commercial restaurants per person

113	116	118	120	123	122	121	122	123	124	126	130	131
1984	1985	1986	1987	1988	1989	1990	1991	1992	1993	1994	1995	1996

Source: The NPD Group's CREST Service.

in sales, and the industry as a whole had grown at a rate of 18.3 percent from 1996. The most popular flavor was the "smoked flavor" sausage (45.7 percent). Other popular flavors included Polish flavor (21.3 percent), hot flavor (7.7 percent), and Italian flavor (4.3 percent). There was significant variation in the growth rates according to the flavor of sausage. Italian flavor sausage had experienced the most growth, at 31.2 percent from 1996 to 1997, followed by Polish flavor sausage at 24 percent, and smoked flavor sausage at 15.6 percent.

Restaurants were critical customers of the sausage industry. According to a 1996 Crest report from the NAPD Group (the seventh largest research consulting firm in the United States), the average number of meals eaten in U.S. restaurants by individuals had steadily increased since 1990 (see Exhibit 1). The study's results also indicated that 72 percent of households purchased a processed meat product every month.

There had also been an explosion of interest in ethnic specialty foods. In 1992, a survey conducted by Research Advantage to monitor dining-out habits revealed that 84 percent of the surveyed customers ate Italian foods other than pizza, 40 percent of the consumers enjoyed Cajun foods, and 32 percent had a taste for French cuisine.

One significant characteristic that was likely to affect the sausage industry in the near future was revealed in a 1998 study conducted by the NAPD Pantry Check. The study's results indicated the average time taken to prepare meals in the U.S. household was decreasing. The study stated that "70 percent of households spend no more than 45 minutes preparing a typical meal." This finding was likely to affect the amount of time people would spend preparing dinner sausages. If buyers felt sausage took too long to cook, they might bypass dinner sausages for a less time-intensive alternative.

Health and Nutrition Issues   Numerous studies had been conducted on the nutritional value of all types of food products. Government regulations specified that nutrition facts were to be included on almost every food product. This encouraged consumers to be more knowledgeable about the nutritional value of the foods they were purchasing and eating. For some food companies, the regulations tended to be damaging because they exposed the high fat content of their food items. According to a U.S. Food and Drug Administration study conducted in 1996, nutrition labels were 91 percent accurate, up 4 percent from 1994. Companies that elected to enter the low-fat segments of the sausage market had created a shift in marketing techniques by creating niche segments. While most sausages ranged from 15 to 25 grams of fat per pound, low-fat varieties ranged between 1.5 and 5 grams. Although reducing fat content had the notorious reputation of altering taste, low-fat sausages did present alternatives to regular sausage products.

Competition in the Specialty Sausage Industry

The dinner sausage industry was a competitive market. For example, approximately 25 to 30 major brands were sold in the Memphis retail market. In the retail segment, the major competitors included Bryan, Jimmy Dean, and Johnsonville. Exhibit 2 contains a profile of the major competitors and information regarding their sausage products. Many of these companies competed on a national scale. While competition among the companies often centered on price, other competitive features included special promotions, advertising, and the variety of product offerings. Shelf space and competitive interbrand pricing were keys to success in this market. Opportunities did exist for specialty sausage companies to market unique, high-quality products at premium prices. Price competition in the food-service segment was probably more severe because sausage typically lost its brand identity as it was prepared and served. Upscale restaurants might be willing to pay premium prices for high-quality, unique sausage that they could promote to their clientele, but institutions were going to be much more concerned about average taste and quality and below-average prices. Specialty sausage products had the potential to generate somewhat higher margins, but competitive copying and interbrand price comparisons served to limit the premium that could be realized on a consistent basis.

Large supermarkets (Piggly Wiggly, Kroger, Seessel's, Megamarket, and Jitney Premier) controlled over 50 percent of the available supermarkets in the Memphis area. This level of concentration was typical of most major metropolitan areas and was forcing many small grocers out of business. Thus, ever-increasing numbers of consumers were shopping at the large supermarkets. Nontraditional outlets of grocery products were also playing an increasing role in grocery sales. Companies such as Kmart with its Super Kmart, Wal-Mart with its Super Wal-Mart, and Sam's Club represented new retail grocery outlets. Large organizations with centralized buying and professional buyers made business more difficult for the small sausage producer.

exhibit 2   Major Competitors in the Sausage Industry

Manufacturer	Product	Price	Weight	Package	Fat Content	Characteristics
Johnsonville	Mild Italian sausage	$3.99	1.24 lb.	Tray	25 g	Instructions inside package; no sell-by date
	Bratwurst	3.99	1.24 lb.	Tray	25 g	
	Beer-n-bratwurst	3.99	1.24 lb.	Tray	25 g	
Dino's	Garlic Italian	N/A	3.29/lb.	Tray	N/A	Instructions on package; sell-by date
	Italian sausage	N/A	3.29/lb.	Tray	N/A	
	Cajun style charice	N/A	3.29/lb.	Tray	N/A	
King Cotton	Reduced fat smoked sausage	$1.99	1 lb.	Vacuum sealed	15 g	No instructions on package; no sell-by date
	Cajun style smoked sausage	1.99	1 lb.	Vacuum sealed	15 g	
	Smoked sausage	1.99	1 lb.	Vacuum sealed	16 g	
Jimmy Dean	Polska kielbasa	$2.59	1 lb.	Vacuum sealed	15 g	No instructions on package; no sell-by date
Bryan	Smoked bratwurst	$3.39	1 lb.	Vacuum sealed	22 g	No instructions on package; no sell-by date
	Smoked sausage	2.19	1 lb.	Vacuum sealed	16 g	
	Beef smoked sausage	3.29	1 lb.	Vacuum sealed	17 g	
	Polska kielbasa	3.29	1 lb.	Vacuum sealed	17 g	
	Cajun style smoked	3.29	1 lb.	Vacuum sealed	17 g	
John Morrell	Skinless Polish	$1.39	1 lb.	Vacuum sealed	22 g	Instructions on package; sell-by date
	Skinless Smoked	$1.39	1 lb.	Vacuum sealed	22 g	
Mr. Turkey	Turkey Polish kielbasa	$2.84	1.15 lb.	Vacuum sealed	5 g	No instructions on package; sell-by date
	Turkey smoked	2.84	1.15 lb.	Vacuum sealed	5 g	
	Italian style turkey Smoked sausage	2.84	1.15 lb.	Vacuum sealed	5 g	
Healthy Choice	Smoked	$2.94	.875 lb.	Vacuum sealed	1.5 g	Instructions on package; sell-by date
Giuseppe's	Chorizo	$3.99	1 lb.	Vacuum sealed	N/A	Instructions on package; sell-by date
	Bratwurst	3.99	1 lb.	Vacuum sealed	N/A	
	Cajun style Andouilles	2.79	.5 lb.	Vacuum sealed	N/A	
	Chaurice	2.79	.5 lb.	Vacuum sealed	N/A	
	Hot Italian	3.99	1 lb.	Vacuum sealed	15 g	
	Mild Italian	3.99	1 lb.	Vacuum sealed	15 g	
	Turkey Italian	3.99	1 lb.	Vacuum sealed	7 g	
	Hot turkey Italian	3.99	1 lb.	Vacuum sealed	7 g	

The retailers controlled shelf space, and food-service operations controlled menus as well as specific ingredients in the meals they prepared. The willingness of distributors to carry a manufacturer's product could mean the difference between ultimate market success or failure, especially for the small sausage makers. It was highly unlikely that consistent volume and profits were possible without the support of distributors. The implication was that downstream channel members had the ability to reduce profits that might be realized by sausage manufacturers.

As the market for dinner sausage continued to grow, new entrants were expected. As evidenced by Giuseppe's, it was possible for a new company to enter the industry in a relatively short time. Government regulations erected some barriers to entry, but the major barrier came from the ability of the large companies to wage significant marketing campaigns. Large meatpackers not currently in the sausage business also represented a potential threat if they decided to enter this market on a major scale.

Suppliers provided meats, spices, and packaging materials; they had relatively little ability to extract higher-than-normal profits from manufacturers. Sausage manufacturers could potentially improve their purchasing position and costs as their volume increased.

The Specialty Sausage Industry in Memphis

The retail segment of the dinner sausage industry in Memphis was a 6.1-million-pound, $12.25 million market as of 1997. The total market had grown at a rate of 15.4 percent from 1996. There were significant variations in the growth rate based on the flavor of sausage; growth rates ranged from a low of 3.9 percent for Polish-flavor sausage to a high of 45.8 percent for Italian-flavor sausage. The potential customer base for the sausage industry was growing as more people in the Mid-South gained experience with dinner sausages. Not only were new varieties of sausages being introduced on a regular basis, but the notion that sausages were cooked only for breakfast was being replaced with the idea that sausage represented an attractive alternative dinner meat. This represented a change that the Memphis area had not previously witnessed. The changing view of the role of sausage presented new opportunities and challenges for both large and small sausage manufacturers.

The larger regional and national companies, such as Bryan, Jimmy Dean, and Johnsonville, had a difficult time competing with the specialty dinner sausage products from small local producers such as Giuseppe's. Small companies could offer a wider variety of specialty sausages in smaller volumes, whereas large companies tended to concentrate on fewer varieties and a larger volume of sales per variety. Conversely, smaller companies confronted obstacles such as the much larger production volume and the marketing campaigns waged by the large companies. Specialty sausage makers were more likely to maintain their primary volume of sales in their local regions, whereas national competitors were able to generate sales over a wider geographical area.

As Memphis grew larger, so did communities and cities in the surrounding area. Over the past decade, the establishment of casinos in Tunica, Mississippi, located only 20 miles from Memphis, had had an incredible economic impact on the Mid-South. The growth of this small Mississippi town had caused significant changes in the local and surrounding economies by introducing the tourism industry on a much grander scale than in the past. According to the Memphis Community Network, an estimated 16 million people traveled to Memphis every year. The casinos were responsible for the large size of that number. The connection with sausage was that tourists, as well as Memphis citizens, wanted to enjoy the same types of food they were familiar with at home. Thus, the casinos were inclined to serve foods such as dinner sausages to the people in their establishments. For example, Giuseppe's Original Sausage generated nearly 19 percent of its total sales from just one casino, the Sheraton Casino, in 1997. There were eight other casinos in Tunica that did just as much, if not more, business. The casinos were willing to do whatever it took to attract people; serving quality dinner products was a nice extra.

GIUSEPPE'S ORIGINAL SAUSAGE COMPANY

Giuseppe's Original Sausage Company prided itself on producing high-quality premium sausages in a variety of different forms and flavors. Cotrone was committed to producing exceptional, distinctive-tasting sausages, many of which were made individually to suit his customers' preferences. His strategy involved purchasing only top-of-the-line ingredients, requiring employees to take extra precautions when producing the various types of sausage, and insisting that every aspect of the production process follow a specific set of procedures he had personally developed.

Giuseppe's product line consisted of more than 80 different sausage-related products. There were four primary markets for Giuseppe's sausage: supermarkets, restaurants, casinos, and mail-order/individual call-in. Three of these customer groups were consolidated into two categories: retailers and food services. Retail sales consisted of supermarkets, and food-service sales consisted of restaurants and casinos. Mail-order/individual call-ins did not represent a significant portion of sales. It was common for individual orders not to be picked up or paid for. Giuseppe's did not currently have the ability to handle credit card sales to individuals.

One of Cotrone's primary objectives was to generate enough sales in a given week to cover expenses and overhead. Cotrone aspired to expand his volume, thereby increasing both sales and profits. He also wanted to assure his customers that Giuseppe's sausage had the reputation of being the best in the industry. Customer satisfaction was another primary concern. Giuseppe's also took pride in keeping its work facility and sausage-making areas above the required standards stipulated by the USDA and local health department regulations.

The price of Giuseppe's sausage was pegged at the upper end of the spectrum, usually averaging a few cents above competitors' prices. While this approach established the company's position as a leader in the market, it was problematic in that no one knew how much, or even if, profits were being realized on the different varieties of sausage, let alone on individual orders. Methods for establishing prices lacked consistency. An accurate product costing system did not exist. Consequently, Cotrone was unable to determine the exact costs for the individual batches and varieties of sausage that were produced. Prices for the standard products were based on competitors' current prices. Prices for the specialty products were based on Cotrone's instinct—a general feel for what he thought his costs were for making the specialty sausage.

The Sausage-Making Process at Giuseppe's

Giuseppe's Original Sausage Company operated on the basis of a weekly production schedule due to the small size and unique nature of the company. Giuseppe's customers placed orders through either their distributor or direct contact with the company. This weekly scheduling placed unusual but manageable constraints on the company.

The meats used in the sausages were ordered weekly; the majority of the other sausage ingredients were kept in stock. This approach to ordering was required to maintain the quality standards that Cotrone had established for his sausage. Freshness was ensured with the weekly arrival of meats; however, production delays could occur if the deliveries did not arrive at the scheduled time. Dry ingredients were stored in separate containers in a moisture-controlled room to ensure freshness. Vegetables and fruits were stored in separate containers in refrigerators for freshness and taste considerations. The various types of meats used in the sausages were stored at freezing temperatures in temperature-controlled refrigeration units until needed for production. Meats for the next day's production were defrosted the previous night; this approach allowed production to begin with a thawed and pliable meat product. Exhibit 3 presents an overview of the process used in making the various sausage products.

The defrosted meats for each day's production schedule were removed from the refrigeration units in the morning and were then moved to the sausage production facility. The plant manager gathered the necessary spices and other ingredients, while the sausage maker prepared the meat for grinding. Regular (branded) sausage had the fat

exhibit 3   The Art of Sausage-Making: Process Flow Chart

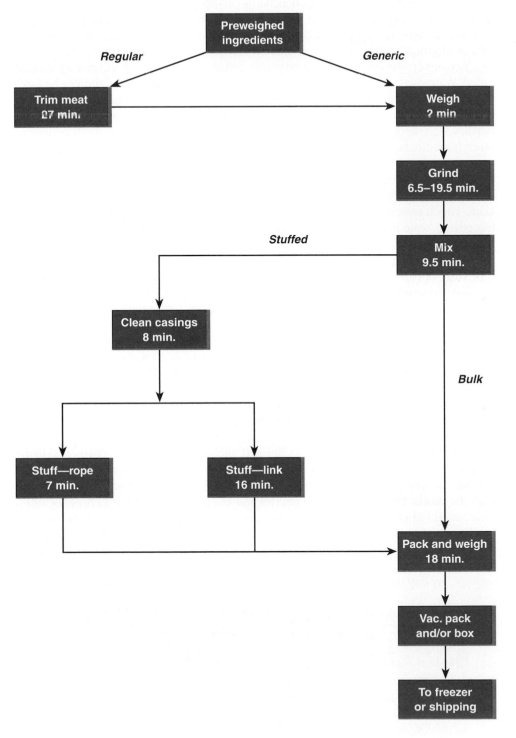

trimmed from the meat, whereas the generic (unbranded) sausage did not. The prepared meat was put in the grinder, where, depending on the type of sausage being produced, it could be ground up to three times. The various meats were ground in batches of up to 120 pounds, based on the size of the sausage order being manufactured. As soon as the meat was ground to the desired consistency, it was moved to the mixer.

The mixer was where the ground meats and other required ingredients were combined. Water was usually added to the ingredients to ensure proper and thorough blending. The thoroughness of the mix was the prime factor for the dependable taste of Giuseppe's sausages. The mixer had a capacity of 150 pounds, although the majority of batches were approximately 130 pounds (120 pounds of meat and about 10 pounds of other ingredients). During the mixing process, the plant manager and sausage maker prepared either the stuffing or the bulk packaging of the sausage. Sausages that were sold in nonbulk form were transferred to the stuffer for stuffing. The stuffer had the ability to stuff up to 50 pounds of sausage at a time into the natural casings. The natural skins, which were used for taste considerations, had to be thoroughly cleaned before the ingredients were injected into them. The stuffing process required a minimal amount of time due to the efficiency of the stuffer. The packaging process usually followed the stuffing process right away. Once the sausage was stuffed, it was either left in a straight rope stage or twisted into a link stage before being packaged. Packaging and labeling of the finished sausage product was custom-tailored to the specific customer's order.

Sausage that was either prepared for individuals or left in the bulk stage was vacuum sealed and labeled as individual packages, whereas sausage for restaurants and other institutional customers was placed in bulk plastic bags and boxed before labels were applied. Vacuum-sealed packaging ensured freshness of the sausage purchased by individual customers either at supermarkets or via UPS/FedEX shipment. The boxed rope and linked sausage was not vacuum packaged because it was either immediately shipped to the customer for prompt use or frozen for future shipment. Both freezing and immediate shipment ensured the freshness of the sausage without the added cost of vacuum packaging.

When the packaging process was finished, the sausage products were moved to the walk-in refrigeration units, where they were inventoried and stored until shipment occurred. The sausage-making process required 46 to 97 minutes per batch depending on both the product type (regular or generic) and the product form (bulk, rope, or link). There could also be up to 10 minutes of downtime between the end of one sausage batch and the beginning of the next to allow for equipment cleaning. Whenever possible, batches were sequenced to either avoid or minimize the time required for cleaning. As shown in the table below, current capacity ranged from 603 to 1,271 pounds of sausage per day depending on the type of product.

Production Capacity per Day (Excluding Cleanouts)			
Product	Minutes/Batch	Batches/Day (7.5 hours/day)	Pounds/Day (130 pounds/batch)
Generic			
Bulk	46	9.78	1,271
Rope	61	7.38	959
Regular			
Bulk	75	6.00	780
Rope	88	5.11	664
Link	97	4.64	603

exhibit 4   Meat Marketing and Distribution Channels

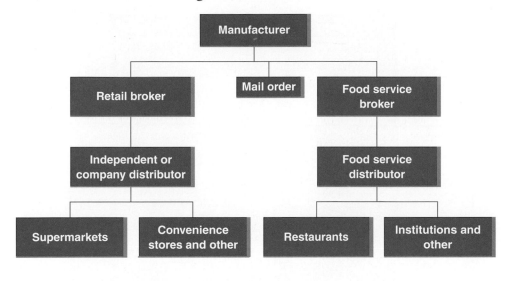

Marketing and Distribution

Food products, specifically meats, were normally marketed through a broker and distributor intermediary system to the retailer or ultimate end user. There were two distinct market segments served by different brokers and distributors: the retail market and the food-service market. Exhibit 4 portrays an overview of the distribution system.

The retail market segment consisted of retailers such as supermarkets and convenience stores. In 1997, there were 23 multistore grocery chains in the Memphis area. The notable multistore grocery store chains included Piggly Wiggly (27 stores), Kroger (25 stores), Seessel's (11 stores), Megamarket (4 stores), and Jitney Premier (4 stores). Giuseppe's had significant sales potential in the major supermarket chains, particularly in the large upscale markets located in the more affluent geographic areas of Memphis. If Giuseppe's decided to market its sausages to these supermarkets, it would have to deal with their distributors. Several supermarkets purchased their products from affiliated distributors such as Flemming, Kroger, and Albertson's. However, there were some independent distributors that provided additional products. Primary brokers, including Empire/Pyramid, Bud Mayer Company, and Sales Mark, handled sausage products in the Memphis area.

The food-service segment consisted of restaurants, education facilities, and large food-preparation companies. Potential customers were restaurants (> 300), hospitals (42), educational institutions (259), and nursing homes (29). Although there were over 300 restaurants in the Memphis metropolitan area, their significance as potential outlets for Giuseppe's sausage varied significantly depending on menu, image, and location. For example, there were about 100 Italian restaurants that could be potential customers. Other potential customers in this segment were primarily concerned with the price of the sausage, since sausage was not a featured item in their menu offerings.

The majority of food-service operators in Memphis purchased their product primarily from Alliant or Sysco. Combined, these two companies controlled over 80 percent of the Memphis food-service market. Brokers serving this market segment included Norbert, Delta Brokerage, and Sales Marketing Consultants.

exhibit 5   Major Customers of Giuseppe's Original Sausage Company

Company Name	Total Sales
Sheraton	$ 48,155
American Seafood	45,735
Nanda	8,192
Seessel's #1	5,158
Garibaldi's	4,402
Kroger	3,576
Seessel's #10	3,121
Seessel's #2	3,013
Flying Saucer	3,008
Seessel's #6	2,688
Seessel's #5	2,392
Seessel's #3	1,595
Seessel's #8	843
Seessel's #4	817
Seessel's #9	752
Methodist	730
Seessel's #7	356
Total of found invoices	$134,534
Total pounds from invoices	39,659
Total 1997 sales	$257,625

Difficulties in building volume were likely to occur if a company did not use the established distribution system. There were obviously efficiencies to be realized by supermarkets and food-service operators, as it was their common practice to consolidate purchasing and delivery with the distributors. The broker's primary role was to serve as the manufacturer's local sales force and assume responsibility for a major part of the manufacturer's local marketing efforts. A company that elected to work on a direct basis was unlikely to secure enough time with the final purchaser or a distributor's sales staff to significantly influence sales. For example, Sysco indicated it would consider a new specialty product, especially on a regional basis, only if it was offered by a broker. Due to their expertise, brokers were a valuable source of market information and marketing ideas that were not easily accessible to small manufacturers. At the present time, the majority of Giuseppe's sales did not originate from using the broker/distributor channel. Exhibit 5 contains information regarding 1997 sales to Giuseppe's major customers.

Financial Performance

Giuseppe's was a subchapter S corporation; Cotrone owned 60 percent and outside investors (primarily friends and acquaintances) owned the remaining 40 percent. While sales had continued to increase each year, profits remained elusive. In 1997, Cotrone was extremely pleased to have finally broken even, but he wondered what 1998 would bring. Much remained to be accomplished if he wanted to earn a reasonable income.

exhibit 6a Income Statement of Giuseppe's Original Sausage
Company, 1994–1997

	Year			
	1994	1995	1996	1997
Sales	$139,821	$166,655	$210,686	$257,625
Cost of goods	81,348	74,891	107,964	155,918
Gross profit	58,473	91,764	102,722	101,707
Wages and salaries	60,388	33,288	42,188	44,659
Professional services	825	1,175	1,200	1,075
Auto and truck	17,364	2,387	3,234	5,486
Insurance	2,263	1,306	5,022	3,058
Travel and entertainment	1,153	206	1,018	1,130
Office expense	2,991	2,528	2,915	3,636
Telephone	1,927	2,626	2,830	3,834
Advertising	3,137	9,939	9,378	2,801
Repair and maintenance	2,407	4,434	4,918	1,342
Rent	13,016	13,939	16,959	10,913
Taxes and licenses	4,799	5,185	5,269	939
Interest	—	119	1,128	8,400
Depreciation	6,471	4,652	4,652	4,550
Utilities	6,817	6,889	7,435	2,18
Other	2,543	2,459	2,752	5,641
Total Operating Expenses	26,101	91,132	110,898	99,648
Operating income	(67,628)	632	(8,176)	2,059
Other income	(2,282)	(2,650)	(3,478)	(2,235)
Net income	$ (69,910)	$ (2,018)	$ (11,654)	$ (176)

One of Cotrone's primary goals was to hire additional staff to handle the daily operations so he could spend more of his time in the kitchen developing new sausage varieties. Exhibits 6 and 7 present recent financial data.

Cotrone decided a useful starting place to evaluate the company's financial soundness was to review sales and costs for 1997. He looked in his files for materials invoices to review the costs of the products sold in 1997 but did not find invoices for some of the materials needed to produce the products shown in Exhibit 8. Using the financial statements, he developed an analysis of cost of goods sold (see Exhibit 9) and estimated overhead costs per pound of sausage (see Exhibit 10). Next, he pulled out his box of sales invoices and reviewed them to see what he could learn. On further examination of the financial data, Cotrone realized that the sales invoices he found in the box represented only slightly more than 50 percent of his total 1997 sales—where were the remainder of the invoices?

The Future

While Joe Cotrone was proud of what Giuseppe's had accomplished over the past seven years, he knew the company's market and financial position was tenuous.

exhibit 6b   Giuseppe's Percentage Composition of Income Statement, 1994–1997

	Year			
	1994	1995	1996	1997
Sales	100.00%	100.00%	100.00%	100.00%
Cost of goods	58.18	44.94	51.24	60.52
Gross profit	41.82	55.06	48.76	39.48
Wages and salaries	43.19	19.97	20.02	17.33
Professional services	0.59	0.71	0.57	0.42
Auto and truck	12.42	1.43	1.53	2.13
Insurance	1.62	0.78	2.38	1.19
Travel and entertainment	0.82	0.12	0.48	0.44
Office expense	2.14	1.52	1.38	1.41
Telephone	1.38	1.58	1.34	1.49
Advertising	2.24	5.96	4.45	1.09
Repair and maintenance	1.72	2.66	2.33	0.52
Rent	9.31	8.36	8.05	4.24
Taxes and licenses	3.43	3.11	2.50	0.36
Interest	0.00	0.07	0.54	3.26
Depreciation	4.63	2.79	2.21	1.77
Utilities	4.88	4.13	3.53	0.85
Other	1.82	1.48	1.31	2.19
Total Operating Expenses	90.19	54.68	52.64	38.68
Operating income	−48.37	0.38	−3.88	0.80
Other income	−1.63	−1.59	−1.65	−0.87
Net income	−50.00%	−1.21%	−5.53%	−0.07%

Intense competition, ambiguous policies and procedures surrounding product costing and product pricing, uncertain distribution of Giuseppe's sausage products, combined with investor uncertainty, presented unique challenges to Giuseppe's future. For Giuseppe's Original Sausage Company to be successful over the long term, the company would need a sound strategy, ample capital, and more formal procedures related to its operations.

exhibit 7   Balance Sheet of Giuseppe's Original Sausage Company, 1994–1997

	Year			
	1994	1995	1996	1997
Assets				
Cash	$ 3,773	$ 1,364	$ 135	$ 6,400
Accounts receivable	9,163	14,194	18,360	30,153
Inventory	4,995	7,700	11,900	17,105
Building and assets	45,615	45,615	45,615	47,985
Less depreciation	−20,952	−25,037	−29,689	−36,609
Intangibles	4,469	4,469	4,469	4,469
Less amortization	−1,936	−3,427	−4,321	−4,469
Other expenses	75	75	75	75
Loans to shareholders	22,623	25,665	27,729	0
Total assets	$ 67,825	$ 70,618	$ 74,273	$ 65,109
Liabilities and Equity				
Accounts payable	$ 10,965	$ 12,075	$ 14,988	$ 7,416
Mortgages/notes/bonds—1 year			10,153	2,194
Other current liabilities	1,382	1,589	1,614	11,040
Loans from shareholders	14,000	17,600	14,000	14,000
Long-term debt			6,252	
Capital stock	155,500	155,500	155,500	160,000
Retained earnings	−114,022	−116,146	−128,234	−129,541
Total liabilities and equity	$ 67,825	$ 70,618	$ 74,273	$ 65,109

exhibit 8   Sales by Product Line for Giuseppe's Original Sausage
Company, 1997

Product	Amount	Pounds	Cost/Pound (Ingredients only)
Original Italian	$17,630	7,567	$1.29
Chicken	12,933	2,281	2.40
Cajun Andouille	8,547	2,546	1.20
Bratwurst	8,202	3,479	1.18
Turkey	7,190	2,933	1.06
Boudin	6,609	1,256	1.24
Lamb	5,647	953	2.46
Duck & Bacon	4,648	811	2.92
Sicilian	3,937	1,691	1.18
Santa Fe	3,364	634	1.54
Chorizo	2,955	1,231	1.19
Knackwurst	2,772	781	?
Smoky Catfish & Tail	2,730	408	?
Kielbasa	2,708	863	?
Jerked Pork & Banana	2,528	384	?
Cajun Style	2,460	1,535	.55
Seafood Boudin	2,136	430	3.51
Duck	1,845	264	2.92
Bangers	1,380	355	?
Crawfish Boudin	1,337	235	2.65
Boudin Blanc	1,325	541	.83
Items with sales between $500 and $1,000: 11	8,713	3,147	
Items with sales between $100 and $500: 16	4,258	2,115	
Items with sales below $100: 28	1,126	525	
One-time items	13,445	945	
Nonsausage Items			
Potato Salad	2,408		
Kraut	1,955		

exhibit 9   Cost of Goods Sold for Giuseppe's Original Sausage
Company, 1994–1997

	Year			
	1994	1995	1996	1997
Inventory—beginning	$ 2,600	$ 4,995	$ 7,700	$ 11,900
Purchases	69,955	66,523	97,970	156,573
Labor	62,169	34,991	44,344	44,659
Depreciation			12,038	4,550
Total	136,718	108,504	164,048	219,679
Inventory—ending	4,995	7,700	11,900	17,105
Cost of goods sold	$131,723	$100,804	$152,148	$202,574

exhibit 10   Estimated Overhead per Pound of Sausage for Giuseppe's
Original Sausage Company, 1997

Overhead Item	Expenses	Cost per Pound
Wages and salaries	$44,659	$0.59
Professional services	1,075	0.01
Auto and truck expense	5,486	0.07
Insurance	3,058	0.04
Travel and entertainment	1,130	0.01
Office expense	3,636	0.05
Telephone	3,834	0.05
Advertising	2,801	0.04
Repairs and maintenance	1,342	0.02
Rent	10,913	0.14
Taxes and licenses	939	0.01
Interest	8,400	0.11
Depreciation	4,550	0.06
Utilities	2,184	0.03
Other	5,641	0.07
Total	$99,648	$1.32

Total Pounds Produced = 75,562

case 5 The Chinese Fireworks Industry

Ruihua Jiang
The University of Western Ontario

Paul Beamish
The University of Western Ontario

In February 1999, Jerry Yu was spending the Chinese New Year holidays in Liuyang (lee-ou-yang), a small city known as "the home of firecrackers and fireworks," located in Hunan Province in China. Jerry was an ABC (America-Born-Chinese). With an MBA, he was now running a small family-owned chain of gift stores in Brooklyn, New York. Liuyang was his mother's hometown. During his visit, his relatives invited him to invest in a fireworks factory that was owned by a village. Mr. Yu had been impressed by the extravagant fireworks shows he had seen during the festival; however, he wanted to assess how attractive the Chinese fireworks industry was before he even looked at the financial details of the factory.

HISTORY OF FIREWORKS AND FIRECRACKERS

Fireworks referred to any devices designed to produce visual or audible effects through combustion or explosion. The art of making fireworks was formally known as pyrotechnics. Firecrackers were a special kind of fireworks, usually in the form of a noisemaking cylinder. Firecrackers were often strung together and fused consecutively, a staple of Chinese New Year celebrations, weddings, grand openings, births, deaths and other ceremonial occasions.

The main ingredient of fireworks was the black powder: a ground-up mixture of potassium nitrate (saltpetre), sulfurs, and charcoal. The proportions of its ingredients had remained almost the same over the past thousand years: 75 parts-by-weight potassium

Ruihua Jiang prepared this case under the supervision of Professor Paul Beamish solely to provide material for class discussion. The authors do not intend to illustrate either effective or ineffective handling of a managerial situation. The authors may have disguised certain names and other identifying information to protect confidentiality.

nitrate, 15 parts charcoal, and 10 parts sulfur. It burned briskly when lighted, but did not erupt or make any noise. When it was found that a projectile could be thrust out of a barrel by keeping the powder at one end and igniting it, black powder became known as gunpowder. Today, smokeless powder has replaced black powder as the propellant in modern weaponry, but black powder remains a main ingredient in fireworks, both as a propellant and as a bursting charge.

It was generally believed that the Chinese were the first makers of fireworks. The Chinese made war rockets and explosives as early as the sixth century. One legend said that a Chinese cook, while toiling in a field kitchen, happened to mix together sulfur, charcoal, and saltpetre, and noticed that the pile burned with a combustible force when ignited. He further discovered that when these ingredients were enclosed in a length of bamboo sealed at both ends, it would explode rather than burn, producing a loud crack. This was the origin of firecrackers. In fact, the Chinese word for firecrackers—*bao-zhu*—literally means "exploded bamboo."

The loud reports and burning fires of firecrackers and fireworks were found to be perfect for frightening off evil spirits and celebrating good news at various occasions. For more than a thousand years, the Chinese had been seeing off past years and welcoming in new ones by firing firecrackers.

Fireworks made their way first to Arabia in the seventh century, then to Europe sometime in the middle of the 13th century. By the 15th century, fireworks were widely used for religious festivals and public entertainment. Most of the early pyrotechnicians in Europe were Italians. Even today, the best-known names in the European and American fireworks industry were Italian in origin. From the 16th to the 18th century, Italy and Germany were the two best known areas in the European continent for fireworks displays, representing two different styles. The Italians tended to display their fireworks with elaborate, ornamental structures—the "machines" that were often known as "temples." The Germans, on the other hand, tended to rely more on fireworks themselves. Referred to as the Northern School, most of these pyrotechnicians were from Nürnberg.

In 1777, the United States used fireworks in its first Independence Day celebration, and fireworks have became closely associated with July Fourth celebrations ever since. Today, most of the fireworks sales in the United States are made around July Fourth. Fireworks' popularity was highlighted and enhanced through memorable fireworks extravaganzas at the 400-year celebration of Columbus' landing in 1892, the Bicentennial Celebration in 1976, and Inauguration Day celebrations in 1997.

Up until the 1830s, the colors of the early fireworks were limited to the amberlike shades produced from the burning of charcoal and iron filings. After that, color advancement was swift, with blue being the last color added to the spectrum. In 1999, there were six basic colors used in fireworks: white, produced by magnesium or aluminum; yellow, by sodium salts; red, by strontium nitrate or carbonate; green, by barium nitrate or chlorate; blue, by copper salts in the presence of a volatile chlorine donoe; and orange or amber, by charcoal or iron.

LIUYANG—THE HOMETOWN OF FIRECRACKERS AND FIREWORKS

According to historical records in China, firecrackers and fireworks "emerged during the Tang dynasty (618–907 AD), flourished during the Song Dynasty (960–1279 AD), and originated in Liuyang." For more than a thousand years, Liuyang had been known

exhibit 1   Liuyang Firecrackers and Fireworks: Total Revenue
and Export Sales (In U.S. $000)

	1992	1993	1994	1995	1996
Total revenue	49,639	55,542	86,747	126,506	134,940
Tax revenue	5,099	7,010	11,829	15,422	18,434
Export sales	15,100	30,200	51,240	84,030	85,560

Source: Liuyang Firecrackers and Fireworks Exhibition, 1998.

as the "hometown of firecrackers and fireworks of China," a title that was officially conferred to Liuyang by the State Council of China in 1995.

As early as 1723, Liuyang fireworks were chosen as official tributes to the imperial family and were sold all over the country. Exports started early: by 1875, firecrackers and fireworks were being shipped to Japan, Korea, India, Iran, Russia, Australia, England, the U.S., and other countries. In China, the name Liuyang had become almost synonymous with firecrackers and fireworks. Liuyang-made firecrackers and fireworks won numerous awards over its long history of fireworks making. In 1929, Liuyang fireworks won first place in the China National Commodity Exhibition; in 1933, they won an "Award of Excellence" at the Chicago World's Fair; in 1986, they won the first prize in the 21st Monaco International Fireworks Competition; and they also won several prizes in the "International Music-Fireworks Competition" held annually in Canada.

The long history and tradition had made fireworks more than just a livelihood for the Liuyang people. Almost every native person in the area knew something about fireworks making, or had actually made firecrackers or fireworks in their lifetime. As a result, Liuyang claimed an impressive pool of skilled labor.

Firecrackers and fireworks had become the pillar industry of Liuyang, employing more than 400,000 people in peak seasons, about one-third of the total population in the Liuyang District (including Liuyang City and the surrounding counties). Liuyang had more than 500 fireworks manufacturers. Among them, only one was a state-owned enterprise (SOE) with more than 1,000 workers. The rest were owned either by villages or families. Among them, about a dozen or so were medium to large factories with employment between 100 to 500 workers. The rest were small workshops employing anywhere from 10 to 50 people, depending on market demand.

Liuyang was the top fireworks exporter in the world, accounting for 80 percent of fireworks export sales of Hunan Province and 60 percent of those of China (see Exhibit 1 for information on revenue and export sales of Liuyang fireworks). The trademarked brand "Red Lantern" had become well known to fireworks-lovers around the world.

The Product

Fireworks could be classified into two categories: display fireworks and consumer fireworks. The display fireworks, such as aerial shells, maroons, and large Roman candles, were meant for professional (usually licensed) pyrotechnicians to fire during large public display shows. They were devices that were designed to produce certain visual or audio effects at a greater height above the ground than the consumer fireworks, which the general public could purchase in convenience stores and enjoy in their own backyards. Roughly, the display fireworks were known as Explosives 1.3 (Class B prior to 1991) in the U.S. The consumer fireworks belonged to Explosives 1.4 (Class C prior to 1991). The difference lay mainly in the amount of explosive components contained in the product. Canada had a similar classification system. In the U.K., it was more carefully divided into four categories: category one was indoor fireworks; category two was garden fireworks; category three was display fireworks; and category four was display fireworks for professionals only.

There were many varieties of fireworks. Liuyang made 13 different types with more than 3,000 varieties. The major types included fountains, rockets, hand-held novelties, nail and hanging wheels, ground-spinning novelties, jumping novelties, floral shells, parachutes, and firecrackers.

Historically, firecrackers made up 90 percent of the total production and sales. Over the past 50 years or so, however, there had been a shift away from firecrackers to fireworks. In 1999, firecrackers made up only about 20 percent of the total sales. The skill levels of fireworks-making had been greatly improved. For instance, the old-time fireworks could reach no more than 20 metres into the sky, while the new ones could go as high as 400 metres.

Not much had changed in fireworks-making. Over the last few decades, numerous novelties were added to the fireworks family. However, innovation had never reached beyond product variations. The ingredients had remained more or less the same. The process technology had not changed much either, although some manual processes, such as cutting the paper, rolling the cylinders, mixing powder, and stringing the cylinders could now be done by machines.

Safety Issues

The fact that fireworks were made with gunpowder and listed under explosives brought up the issue of safety. Numerous accidents involving fireworks had resulted in tragic human injuries and considerable property damages. As a result, fireworks had become heavily regulated in most countries.

According to the manufacturers, fireworks were the most dangerous during the production process. Powder mixing and powder filling, in turn, were the two most dangerous procedures. The workers had to abide by strict safety measures. Even a tiny spark caused by the dropping of a tool on the floor or the dragging of a chair could start a major explosion. The quality of the ingredients was also of significant importance. Impure ingredients could greatly increase the possibility of accidents. In Liuyang, almost every year, there would be one or more accidents that resulted in deaths and damages.

Once the fireworks were made, they were relatively safe to transport and store. Even in firing, good quality fireworks rarely caused any problems if everything was done properly. Most of the fireworks-related accidents occurred during private parties or street displays, and quite often involved children playing with fireworks that needed to be handled by adults, or laymen firing shells that required professional expertise. It was also often the case that illegal and/or inferior fireworks were used in the accidents. Most accidents were linked to consumer backyard events rather than to public displays.

According to the United States Consumer Products Safety Commission's (CPSC) data, injuries related to fireworks had declined by 44 percent, even though their use had increased (see Exhibit 2). For 1997, there were an estimated 8,300 fireworks-related injuries, 32 percent of which were caused by firecrackers. Of all the injuries related to firecrackers, 42 percent involved illegal firecrackers.

Children from ages 5 to 14 were the most frequently involved in fireworks-related injuries. However, fireworks were not the only consumer product that might cause injuries to this age group. According to a 1997 CPSC Injury Surveillance Report, fireworks

exhibit 2   Total Fireworks Consumption and Estimated Fireworks-
Related Injuries in the U.S.: 1990 to 1998

Year	Fireworks Consumption, Millions of Pounds	Estimated Fireworks-Related Injuries	Injuries per 100,000 Pounds
1990	67.6	12,100	17.8
1991	73.7	11,000	14.9
1992	87.1	12,600	14.5
1993	101.9	12,300	12.0
1994	117.0	12,500	10.7
1995	115.0	10,900	9.4
1996	118.0	7,800	6.2
1997	132.8	8,300	6.2
1998	112.6	7,000	6.2

Source: American Pyrotechnics Association.

were actually safer than some much more benign-looking products, like baseballs, pens and pencils (see Exhibit 3).

However, fireworks-related injuries were usually the most dramatic and the most widely publicized accidents, which partly explained the fact that fireworks was the only category among the products listed in Exhibit 3 for which prohibition, instead of education and adult supervision, was often urged.

In the United States, multiple government agencies were involved in regulating fireworks. The Bureau of Alcohol Tobacco and Firearms (BATF) controlled the manufacture, storage, sales and distribution of explosives, i.e., Class B fireworks. The CPSC regulated Class C consumer fireworks, and the Department of Transportation dealt with the transportation of fireworks.

Although at the federal level, fireworks and firecrackers were allowed as long as the safety features were up to the standard, local governments had their own different regulations regarding fireworks consumption. Out of the 50 states, 10 would not allow any fireworks, 5 would allow novelty fireworks, 18 would allow "safe and sane" fireworks, while the remaining 17 would allow essentially all consumer fireworks. For display fireworks, permits would have to be obtained from federal and local authorities and fire departments.

All legal consumer fireworks offered for sale in the United States had been tested for stability by the Bureau of Explosives and approved for transportation by the U.S. Department of Transportation. Because of the limited amount of pyrotechnic composition permitted in each individual unit, consumer fireworks would not ignite spontaneously during storage, nor would they mass-explode during a fire. Therefore, no special storage was required.

In most of Europe, similar regulations were in place for safety considerations, only the requirements were regarded as less stringent. In Canada, however, regulations were extremely restrictive. The Explosives Research Department under the Ministry of Natural Resources was in charge of regulating fireworks as one type of explosives. The Canadian Explosives Research Laboratory was responsible for setting standards and testing products. On the list of fireworks companies that were allowed to sell fireworks to Canada, no Chinese companies were found.

exhibit 3   Estimated Emergency Room Treatment per 100,000 Youths (Ages 5 to 14)

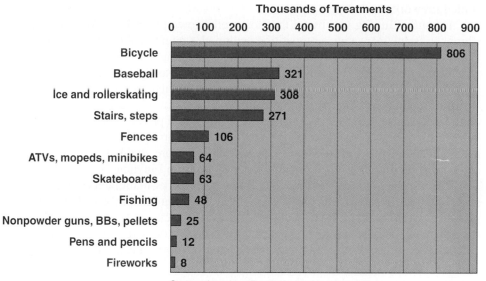

Thousands of Treatments

Bicycle	806
Baseball	321
Ice and rollerskating	308
Stairs, steps	271
Fences	106
ATVs, mopeds, minibikes	64
Skateboards	63
Fishing	48
Nonpowder guns, BBs, pellets	25
Pens and pencils	12
Fireworks	8

Source: American Pyrotechnics Association.

THE FIRECRACKERS AND FIREWORKS INDUSTRY IN CHINA

The firecrackers and fireworks industry in China was dominated by small family-owned-and-operated workshops. It was essentially a low-tech, highly labor-intensive industry. After 1949, government-run factories replaced the family-owned workshops. The increased scale and government funds made possible the automation of some processes. However, the key processes such as installing powder, mixing color ingredients, and putting in fuses were still manually done by skilled workers.

The factories themselves were made up of small workshops that stood away from each other, so that in case of an accident the whole factory would not explode. For the same safety consideration, the workshops were usually located near a water source and in sparsely populated rural areas, to reduce the noise and explosion hazard.

After the reform toward a market economy started in 1979, most of the factories were broken up and became family-run units of production again. It was hoped that this privatization might help to motivate people better, to increase their productivity, and consequently raise the output. However, this move also served to restrict further technological innovations. There were hardly any research and development (R&D) facilities nor human and capital resources allocated to R&D in most fireworks companies. The few resources that were available were all spent on product varieties. Even in Liuyang, out of the 400,000 or so people working in the industry, only four were engineers with advanced professional training and titles. The approximately 40 research facilities scattered in the Liuyang area were poorly funded and equipped.

In fact, the majority of the workers were regular farmers who had learned how to make fireworks just by watching and following their elders. They would come to work in fireworks workshops when there were jobs to be done, and return to till their fields if there were none. In Liuyang, for instance, only four to five factories were operating year-round. The rest of the 500-plus workshops would operate as orders came in. Since the fireworks-making communities were very concentrated geographically and had lasted for generations, only a few places (like Liuyang) came to claim a large pool of skilled fireworks-makers.

Although Liuyang was by far the most well-known place for making fireworks in China, it faced increasing competition within the country. Also located in Hunan Province, Liling was another major manufacturing community of fireworks. Liling fireworks might not enjoy the same reputation and variety as Liuyang products, but they were fierce in price competition. In the neighboring Jiangxi Province, Pingxiang and Wanzai fireworks had become strong competitors both in price and quality, especially on the low- and medium-priced market. In the high-end product market, especially in large display fireworks and the export market, Dongguan in Guangdong Province had taken advantage of its closeness to Hong Kong and more sophisticated management and marketing practices and snatched market share from Liuyang.

The initial capital requirement for starting a fireworks-manufacturing facility was relatively low. To set up a factory with the necessary equipment for making large display shells would require RMB 1,000,000.[1] However, setting up a small family workshop making consumer firecrackers and fireworks would require less than RMB 100,000. Consequently, the number of small manufacturers mushroomed after the government started to encourage private business ventures.

The labor cost was low in the area. Skilled workers engaged in major processes would earn an average of RMB 800 to RMB 1,000 per month. A nonskilled worker would be paid only RMB 300 to RMB 400 every month. Therefore, the labor cost took no more than 20 percent of the total cost. For the small private workshops, the percentage would be around 10 percent.

The main raw materials for fireworks were gunpowder, color ingredients, paper, fuse and clay soil. None would be difficult to procure. The prices and supply were both quite stable. The one possible problem in supply was quality. Major manufacturers would usually establish long-term relationships with their suppliers to guarantee the quality of materials. The small workshops would often go with the lowest prices, sometimes at the cost of quality, which could lead to fatal results.

The emergence of the small companies intensified competition. The private workshops were flexible and quick in responding to market demand. They did not entail much administrative cost. Compared to government-owned or some collectively owned factories, they did not have the social responsibilities of health care, retirement benefits, and housing. They usually did not do any product research or design. Oblivious to intellectual property protection, they would copy any popular product design and sell it for much less. The resulting price drop had become a serious problem for the whole industry. As the profit margin kept shrinking, some workshops would hire cheap unskilled workers, and use cheap equipment and raw materials to cut down on cost. The results could be disastrous. Low-quality-fireworks-related damages and injuries as well as factory accidents were reported every year, pushing the authorities to impose stricter regulations regarding fireworks.

THE DOMESTIC MARKET

Firecrackers and fireworks had long been an integral part of any ceremonies held in China. Firecrackers had to be fired for grand openings, weddings, funerals, festivals or

---

[1]In 1999, the exchange rate was around 8.30 yuan per U.S. $1.00.

any special occasions, both for good luck and to attract public attention. Until recently, demand had been stable, and on the rise in the past two decades because of increased economic development and living standards. Economically, market reform and unprecedented growth had given rise to the daily appearance of multitudes of new companies and new stores. As people's income level and living standards kept rising, fancier and pricier fireworks and firecrackers were desired over the cheap simple firecrackers, thereby creating more profit opportunities for fireworks manufacturers. Almost every household would spend at least a couple of hundred yuan on firecrackers and fireworks during the Spring Festival.

However, since the beginning of the 1990s, increased concerns over environmental pollution and safety of human life and property led more and more cities to regulate the consumption of fireworks and firecrackers. Every year, high profile fireworks-related accidents that led to human injuries or property damages were reported and emphasized on mass media before and after the traditional Spring Festival. Some articles even condemned firecrackers and fireworks as an old, uncivilized convention that created only noise, pollution, and accidents. In a wave of regulations, city after city passed administrative laws regarding the use of fireworks. By 1998, one-third of the cities in China had completely banned the use of firecrackers and fireworks. Another one-third had partially banned their use, allowing fireworks only in designated places. This led to a decline in domestic market demand.

In the meantime, domestic competition grew intensely. The reform toward a market economy made it possible for numerous family-run workshops to appear. They competed mainly on price. Almost every province had some fireworks-making workshops or factories, many set up and run with the help of skilled worked who had migrated from Liuyang. These small establishments usually were located in rural, underdeveloped areas where labor cost was minimal. The manufacturing was done manually, sometimes without safety measures, using cheap raw materials and simplified techniques. The products were sold locally at low prices, making it difficult for Liuyang fireworks to sell in those areas. To make things worse, these products would often copy any new or popular product designs coming out of Liuyang or other traditional fireworks communities, even using their very brand names.

Within the Liuyang area, similar small workshops bloomed in the past few years. The number of the workshops could exceed 500 in peak time and drop to half that number in a slow period. Since their cost was very low, they could be extremely flexible in price. To create sales, they would underprice each other, thereby bringing down the overall profit margin of the industry.

In the past, fireworks were sold through the government-run general merchandise companies. Eventually, private dealers took over a large part of the business. Overall, the distribution system was rather fragmented and messy. The old government-run channels were not very effective any more, especially for general merchandise. The new distribution channels were still rather chaotic. It was necessary to be close to the market to make any sense of it. Usually, wholesale dealers would get shipments directly from the manufacturers, and then resell to street peddlers and convenience stores.

In the countryside, wholesale markets would appear in focal townships, with wholesale dealers and agents of the manufacturers setting up booths promoting their products. Small peddlers in the surrounding areas would get supplies from the market and then sell them in small towns or villages. The wholesale markets in China were important outlets for distributing general merchandise like fireworks.

In the display fireworks market, the buyers were often central and local governments, who would purchase the product for public shows on national holidays or special celebrations. Obviously, a local company would have advantages in supplying to local government in its area. Large fireworks shows usually would use invited bidding to decide on suppliers. The amount of fireworks used could range from RMB 100,000 to several million yuan, depending on the scale of a fireworks show.

Another serious issue, account receivables and bad debt control, was a problem not just for fireworks manufacturers, but for all businesses operating in China. Bad debts and lack of respect for business contracts had created a credit crisis in the business world in China. The bad debt problem greatly increased transaction costs, slowed down the cash turnover, and had become a headache for fireworks manufacturers. Some had chosen to withdraw from selling in the domestic market, although the profit margin was higher than in the export market.

Legal restrictions, local protectionism, cutthroat price competition, hard-to-penetrate distribution channels, and bad debt were impacting negatively on the domestic sales of Liuyang fireworks. In 1997, seeing the decline of its fireworks sales, Liuyang Firecrackers and Fireworks Industry Department, the government agency in charge of the overall development of the pillar industry, decided to start an offensive strategy. First, it opened local offices in most of the 29 provinces, major cities, and regions to promote Liuyang fireworks. Second, it regulated the prices that Liuyang fireworks companies could quote and sell in export sales. Third, it resorted to a government-to-government relationships in order to secure contracts for large public fireworks displays in each province. One year after introducing the offensive strategy, Liuyang fireworks sales had increased.

The next two years would be big years for the fireworks industry in China. In October 1999, China would celebrate the 50th anniversary of the founding of the People's Republic; the central government, each province, and each city would hold its own celebration. Then, the turn of the millennium would certainly be celebrated with extravagant fireworks displays, both public and private.

THE EXPORT MARKET

Since the opening of the Chinese economy in 1979, exporting had become a major market for the Chinese fireworks industry. As one of the most celebrated products out of China, export sales of fireworks had risen between 1978 and 1998. According to government statistics, the recorded export sales of firecrackers and fireworks reached U.S.$143 and U.S.$172 million in 1994 and 1995, respectively. The estimate for 1998 was about U.S.$200 million.

The general belief was that China-made fireworks actually made up about 80 percent to 90 percent of the world's fireworks market. The products from China were rich in variety and low in price, but also had a lower reputation in quality control, packaging, and timing control, compared to the products made in Japan and Korea. China-made fireworks also would wholesale for much lower prices, usually 80 percent lower than similar products made in Japan or Korea.

Due to the lack of technology and management input, the Chinese fireworks industry had not made much progress in advancing the fireworks-making and packaging techniques, nor in quality control and marketing capabilities. There was little overall coordination of the export sales. As more and more companies were allowed to export directly, the competition kept intensifying and the profit margin of the export sales kept slipping. Some manufacturers would even sell at or below cost, just looking to get the tax refund that the government set aside to encourage export, which could sometimes reach 20 percent. As a result, underpricing each other became a common practice. Therefore, despite its dominant share of the world market, the Chinese fireworks export

exhibit 4 Comparison of FOB Import Prices from China and
Wholesale Prices of Chinese Fireworks in the U.S.

Name	Packing	FOB China[1] (U.S.$)	Wholesale in U.S.[2] (U.S.$)
Consumer Fireworks			
Thunderbombs	12/80/16	$12.40	$ 42.00
Tri-Rotating Wheel	24/12	15.50	48.50
Changing Color Wheel	72/1	20.70	57.60
Jumping Jack	20/48/12	16.70	60.00
Cuckoo	24/6	14.50	50.40
Ground Bloom Flower	20/12/6	16.50	62.40
Color Sparkler	24/12/8	16.40	66.74
Moon Traveller	25/12/12	9.20	40.00
Crackling Whips	72/12	16.99	50.40
Aerial Display	4/1	19.40	68.00
Evening Party	12/1	12.60	60.00
Assorted Fountain	18/4	10.30	64.20
Assorted Rockets	36/12	24.20	68.00
Display Fireworks			
4" Display Shell w/Tail	36/1	52.65	165.00
6"	10/1	41.82	160.00
8"	6/1	54.53	190.00
12"	2/1	60.95	190.00

[1]FOB major ports in South China. Cost, insurance, freight to major ports in the U.S. would be $3.00 to $4.00 more per carton.
[2]U.S. import duty rate for fireworks from China was 12.5 percent.

industry enjoyed limited profitability. Exhibit 4 provides a comparison of the free on board (FOB) prices quoted by the Chinese companies to U.S. markets versus the prices quoted by the U.S. importers and wholesalers to the retailers and end users on some consumer and display fireworks items. The importers enjoyed a high markup even after paying the 12.5 percent U.S. import duty. Of course, the importers had to absorb the cost of getting permits, shipping, storing and carrying the inventory for three to four months before making the sales.

Besides suffering from low profit margin, the Chinese fireworks makers were also risking losing their brand identities. Given the low cost and reasonably good quality of the Chinese fireworks, many large fireworks manufacturers and dealers in the West started to outsource the making of their brand-name fireworks. Failing to see the importance of brand equity, the Chinese fireworks manufacturers were sometimes reduced to mere manufacturing outfits for foreign companies, gradually losing their own brands.

There were also fireworks merchants in Korea, Japan, or Spain, who would buy the products from China, and then repackage them, or replace the fuses with better quality ones, then resell them for much higher prices.

The export market was usually divided into five blocks: Southeast Asia, North America, Europe, South America, and the rest of the world. The most popular market had been Europe, where the regulations on fireworks were less stringent, and orders were of larger quantities and better prices. The United States was considered a tough market because of complex regulations and high competition, nevertheless a necessary one if a company wanted to remain a viable world-player. The Canadian market was virtually closed to Chinese fireworks due to its regulations, although most of the fireworks consumed in Canada were imported, and had probably originated in China before being repackaged in other countries. The result of the stricter regulations in Canada was higher prices for consumers. It was estimated that a fireworks display that cost less than $3,500 in the U.S. would cost Canadians $8,000.

The foreign importers were powerful buyers for several reasons. First, they were very well informed, both through past dealings with China and the Internet. Second, they were able to hire agents who were very familiar with the industry in China. Third, they could deal directly with the factories that were willing to take lower prices. Fourth, there were basically no switching costs, so they could play the suppliers against each other.

The diversity of the cultures in the destination countries greatly reduced the seasonality of the fireworks production and sales. As a result, orders evened out throughout the year. However, the peak season was still toward the end of the year. For the U.S., it was before July 4. Usually, the importers would receive the shipment two or three months beforehand.

The Internet was gradually becoming a marketing outlet for Chinese fireworks. According to a fireworks company's office in Shenzhen, 20 percent to 30 percent of the business inquiries they got were through the Internet. However, export sales were still made mainly through foreign trade companies or agents.

In recent years, foreign investments were also funneled into the fireworks industry. In Liuyang, four of the large fireworks factories had foreign investments, made mainly by the fireworks trading companies in Hong Kong.

In 1999, out of the 5,000 or so containers of fireworks exported from China annually, about four-fifths were consumer fireworks. However, the demand for display fireworks was growing at a faster pace. It was predicted that the demand for display fireworks would increase as organized public shows grew more popular; at the same time, demand for consumer fireworks was expected to decline as regulations were getting stricter. Fireworks shows were increasingly being used in promotional campaigns, and were finding customers among amusement parks, sports teams, and retailers (for store openings, anniversaries and holiday celebrations). The massive annual Fourth of July fireworks put on by Macy's in New York City was one well-known example.

The Future of the Fireworks Industry in China

The managers of the Chinese fireworks companies that Jerry Yu talked to expressed mixed feelings toward the future outlook of their industry. One pessimistic view was that this was a sunset industry. This view held that regulations were killing the industry. Moreover, as people in general became more environmentally conscious and more distracted by the endless diversities of modern entertainment, traditional celebrations using firecrackers and fireworks would die a gradual death. As to the function of attracting public attention for promotional purposes, fireworks also faced challenges from new technologies, such as laser beams combined with sound effects.

In fact, make-believe "firecrackers" already appeared as substitutes in China. These make-believe firecrackers were made of red plastic tubes strung together like firecrackers. Electric bulbs were installed inside the tubes. When the power was turned on, the lights would emit sparks, accompanied by crackling reports that sounded like firecrackers. These were being used at weddings and grand openings in cities where firecrackers and fireworks were banned. More interesting substitutes were spotted at some weddings in Beijing, where people paved the road with little red balloons, and made the limousine carrying the bride and groom run over the balloons to make explosive cracking sounds as well as leave behind red bits and pieces of debris. On the other hand, more and more young couples were getting married in Western styles, in a church or a scenic green meadow outdoors, where serene and quiet happiness prevailed over the traditional noisy way of celebrating. Therefore, some managers believed that firecrackers and fireworks were doomed to fade off into history.

The more optimistic view, however, was that the industry would not die at all. If the right moves were made by the industry, it could even grow. Some said that tradition would not die so easily. It was in their national character for the Chinese to celebrate with an atmosphere of noisy happiness. Moreover, even in the West, the popularity of fireworks was not suffering from all the regulations. No real substitutes could replace fireworks, which combined the sensual pleasures of visual, audio, and emotional stimuli. For instance, the U.S. Congressional resolution in 1963 to use bells to replace fireworks in celebrating Independence Day never really caught on.

Fireworks were also being combined with modern technologies like laser beams, computerized firing, and musical accompaniment to make the appeal of fireworks more irresistible. The safety problem was not really as serious as people were made to believe, and would only improve with new technological innovations like smokeless fireworks.

However, both sides agreed that the Chinese fireworks industry would have to change its strategy, especially in international competition, to stay a viable and profitable player.

THE DECISION

Meanwhile, Jerry had to decide whether it was worthwhile to invest in the fireworks industry. He wondered whether he could apply the industry analysis framework he had studied in his MBA program.

The Richard Ivey School of Business gratefully acknowledges the generous support of The Richard and Jean Ivey Fund in the development of this case as part of the RICHARD AND JEAN IVEY FUND ASIAN CASE SERIES.

case | 6 Competition in the U.S. Automotive Retailing Industry

Janet Parish
University of Alabama

Arthur A. Thompson
University of Alabama

Two perhaps interrelated revolutions are under way in the business of selling cars. One is the Web. The other is the consolidation of traditional dealers into national organizations like Wayne Huizenga's AutoNation or into manufacturer-controlled retail chains.
—From an article in *Forbes,* October 25, 1999

In early 2000, the automotive retailing industry seemed on the front edge of fundamental change. For a number of years, there had been rumblings of dissatisfaction among vehicle buyers with their purchasing experiences at local franchised dealerships. Apart from all the jokes about car salesmen, many customers reportedly found price haggling and high-pressure sales tactics distasteful or intimidating. Moreover, industry analysts believed there were many inefficiencies in the sales, marketing, and distribution of automobiles through the present franchised dealer networks of the major vehicle manufacturers, owing to costs that were believed to add as much as 30 percent to the sales prices of new vehicles. Automakers were looking at ways to overhaul their franchised dealer networks to squeeze some of these distribution inefficiencies out of the industry value chain. At the same time, hometown dealers were facing unprecedented competition from megaretailers, like AutoNation, and from a host of enterprising dot-com car-buying services that threatened to reshape the role and function of franchised dealers.

Increasingly, when shoppers went to local dealers to look for a new vehicle, they were armed with information gathered from the Internet concerning the invoice prices paid by dealers, the markups and margins that dealers had on each model and each option, the trade-in value of their present model, and perhaps price quotes from the new breed of dot-com auto retailers. Over 60 percent of car buyers were said to be using the Internet for research and price comparisons. Interested shoppers could go to hundreds of Internet sites to get free, detailed information on the various brands and models, read reviews of vehicle performance, and check out prices, rebates, and financing.

There were three types of Internet firms racing to get a slice of the budding market for online vehicle sales:

- *Lead generators* like Microsoft's CarPoint, cars.com, Autoweb.com, and car-club.com. The Web sites of lead generators let customers peruse all the various manufacturers' brands and models and make side-by-side model comparisons. They also provided base sticker prices and the prices of all the various options, and allowed visitors to check the models, colors, and optional equipment they wanted. Shoppers could fill out a simple form online requesting a price quote; the lead generator forwarded the customer requests for price quotes to nearby participating dealers, who followed up with an e-mail price quote and perhaps a telephone contact if a phone number was provided on the site form.

- *Direct sellers* like CarsDirect.com, carOrder.com, DriveOff.com, and Green light.com. The Web sites of direct sellers went a step further than lead generators, providing an immediate price quote and letting shoppers place an order online, then partnering with area franchised dealers to deliver the vehicle ordered.

- *Hybrid sites,* like Autobytel.com, that provided content for research, generated leads for participating dealers, took orders online, and used their franchised dealer networks for order fulfillment. Autobytel.com and some other hybrid sites also conducted auctions and provided online classified advertising that customers could use to sell a vehicle through online channels.

Online sales accounted for approximately 2.7 percent of the 15.5 million new vehicles sold in the United States in 1999.[1]

Meanwhile, manufacturers had launched Internet sites where vehicle buyers could get information, compare models and features, and be referred to nearby dealers for price quotes; visitors to Toyota's Web site could order custom-built cars and receive delivery within a week. As of mid-2000, more than 85 percent of the franchised dealers had launched Internet sites of their own to display their inventories and prices and to allow customers to fill out financing applications and request service appointments. In addition to their own sites, more than 50 percent of the 22,400 U.S. dealerships subscribed to one or more third-party Internet shopping services such as CarPoint (a service of the Microsoft Network), car.com, Autoweb.com, and Autobytel.com, which referred shoppers to nearby dealers to get price quotes on vehicles they were interested in. At the same time, thousands of franchised dealers had joined the dealer networks of the direct sellers and were providing the vehicles sold online. These developments reflected a growing understanding among both manufacturers and franchised dealers that the Internet had changed the dynamics of automotive retailing.

THE U.S. MOTOR VEHICLE RETAILING MARKET

Since Henry Ford's first Model T, more than 670 million new vehicles had been sold in the United States as of early 2000. Automotive retailing in the United States was nearly a $700 billion market in 2000, with annual sales of new cars and trucks running close to 15.5 million units in 1998 and 1999 and annual sales of used vehicles equal to

---

[1]Based on information compiled by J. D. Power and Associates.

exhibit 1 Number of Franchised Dealerships, 1978–99 (Beginning of Year)

Year	Number of Dealerships	Year	Number of Dealerships
1978	29,000	1989	25,000
1979	28,500	1990	24,825
1980	27,900	1991	24,200
1981	26,350	1992	23,500
1982	25,700	1993	22,950
1983	24,725	1994	22,850
1984	24,725	1995	22,800
1985	24,725	1996	22,750
1986	24,825	1997	22,700
1987	25,150	1998	22,600
1988	25,025	1999	22,400

Source: NADA Industry Analysis Division.

about 40 million units. There were an estimated 205 million vehicles in operation in the United States as of 1999.

Automotive retailers in the United States consisted of some 22,400 franchised dealers, who accounted for virtually 100 percent of new-car sales ($370 billion in revenues) and about 30 percent of the used-car sales ($120 billion in revenues). In addition, there were close to 35,000 independent used-car lots accounting for annual sales of $270 billion and close to 22 million used vehicles, plus a handful of blossoming online car sellers with sales of about 500,000 vehicles in 1999. Private-party sales of used vehicles were estimated to run close to 5 million units annually. Used vehicles had gained greater acceptance over the past 15 years due to improved vehicle quality and upward creep in the prices of new vehicles.

The Plight of the Small-Town Dealers

The number of new-car dealerships had declined gradually over the last three decades of the 20th century (see Exhibit 1). Dealer mergers and acquisitions, combined with manufacturers' efforts to weed out weak dealerships and reduce the overall number of dealer locations, were responsible for much of the decline. As shown in Exhibit 2, it was small-volume dealerships that were disappearing; dealerships selling more than 400 units annually were on the increase. In 1979 there were 11,500 dealer locations with sales of less than 150 new vehicles per year; in 1999, there are only 4,256 such dealerships. In contrast, in 1999 there were over 5,800 dealerships that sold more than 750 new units per year, compared to only 4,100 in 1979. Small-town dealers, lacking the scale of operation and market base of dealers in larger cities and towns, had found it hard to remain price-competitive and were either closing their doors or being acquired. Mounting price competition among both manufacturers anxious to build market share and dealers anxious to clear out inventories had made the retailing of new vehicles a low-margin, high-volume business in the 1990s. With the prices of new vehicles rising steadily, buyers had become quite price-sensitive and were shopping harder for the best

exhibit 2   Annual New-Unit Sales

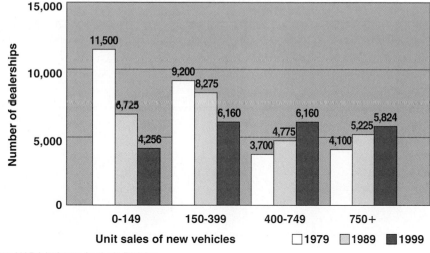

Source: NADA Industry Analysis Division.

deal, often driving 50 or 100 miles to shop at metropolitan dealers who were willing to accept bigger discounts off the sticker price. Small-volume dealers in mostly rural areas could not match the deeper discounts of high-volume dealers on new-vehicle sales and still cover their operating costs, hence the steady decline in the number of low-volume dealers. Those small-town dealers that were able to survive in the 1990s did so by taking on additional brands, both foreign and domestic, to build up their sales volume of both new and used vehicles.

By 2000, it was commonplace for dealers in most geographic locations, both rural and urban, to handle more than one manufacturer's brand. The National Automobile Dealers Association reported that its 19,500 members held nearly 40,000 separate franchises from domestic and foreign manufacturers. Exhibit 3 shows unit sales by dealership and average unit selling prices during the 1988–98 period.

The Emergence of Large-Volume, Multilocation Dealerships

Since the late 1980s and early 1990s, there had been a pronounced trend in auto retailing toward megadealerships offering not only a big selection of new models but also a wider variety of brands from multiple manufacturers. A number of aggressive, growth-minded dealers went on the acquisition trail, purchasing dealerships in several different cities and expanding their geographical reach. Then, in 1997, AutoNation, Inc., shook up the local dealer-dominated industry by acquiring hundreds of existing dealers and opening huge megalots to display and sell a variety of brands at a single metropolitan location. In less than three years, AutoNation had become the world's largest retailer of motor vehicles, boosting its revenues from $9 billion in 1997 to over $16 billion in 1998 to over $20 billion in 1999. Going into 2000, AutoNation had more than 400 automotive franchises in 23 states, representing 39 manufacturer brands. It also operated or

exhibit 3   Average Number of New Vehicles Sold per Dealership and
Average Retail Selling Prices, 1988–98

Year	New Vehicles Sold per Dealership	Average Retail Selling Price
1988	617	$14,100
1989	584	15,400
1990	567	15,900
1991	517	16,050
1992	555	17,100
1993	608	18,200
1994	661	19,200
1995	648	20,450
1996	664	21,900
1997	668	22,650
1998	691	23,600

Source: NADA Industry Analysis Division.

franchised 42 AutoNation USA used-vehicle megastores in 13 states. In 1999, Auto-Nation sold approximately 1 million vehicles, the equivalent of two vehicles per minute, 24 hours a day, seven days a week.

Dealer Marketing and Sales Strategies

Franchised dealers relied heavily on advertising to attract the attention of people who were in the market for a new vehicle and especially to draw price-sensitive customers to their showrooms and lots. Dealer ads tended to emphasize the wide selection of models and styles, discounts off sticker prices, special manufacturer rebates and promotions, low-cost financing, and low monthly payments. When shoppers drove onto the lot, they were usually quickly greeted by a salesperson who inquired about their interests and guided them to the selection of models in inventory. Salespeople normally strived to build a relationship with customers and win their confidence, touting the features of various models and offering test drives of those models that buyers found most appealing. Most dealerships worked at making the buying experience pleasant and paid considerable attention to delivering good after-the-sale service so that customers would be loyal in returning for their next purchase.

Dealer Revenue-Cost-Profit Economics

Combined revenues of the 22,400 new-car dealers in the United States in 1998 were a record $533.6 billion. Exhibit 4 shows the composition of dealer revenues. New-vehicle department sales were up 7 percent in 1998 over 1997, used-vehicle sales up 4 percent, and service and parts sales up 2 percent. Pretax profits at the typical dealership averaged $403,000. Exhibit 5 shows profit trends for new-car sales, used-car sales, and service and parts sales. Exhibit 6 shows the trends in revenues and expenses for the average U.S. dealership for the 1988–98 period. The biggest expense dealers incurred was for labor:

Payroll	$1,766,000
Advertising	234,800
Rent and equivalent	225,300
Floor-plan interest	87,700

In 1999, franchised dealers collectively spent $5.7 billion for advertising; this total included $2.9 billion for newspaper ads, $900 million for TV spots, $800 million for radio ads, and $272 million for Internet advertising. Advertising costs amounted to an average of $209 per new vehicle sold and $217 per used vehicle sold.

Dealer Pricing of New Vehicles   Dealers stocked their showrooms and lots with models they ordered directly from manufacturers. Dealers placed orders for specific models and styles based on the experience of what their customers liked and what styles, colors, and equipment options were selling best. However, as part of the bargain of filling dealer orders, manufacturers pressured dealers to take delivery of slow-selling, less-popular models and styles that they needed to move out of their own inventories of freshly produced models. The price that dealers paid manufacturers (called the dealer invoice cost) was usually 10 to 18 percent below the manufacturer's suggested retail price (MSRP)—the so-called sticker price customarily fixed to the rear window; the percentage markup over dealer invoice varied by make and model and was usually bigger for luxury makes and models than for low-end makes and models. However, it was standard practice for manufacturers to give dealers a small discount—termed a *holdback*—from the official invoice price for meeting certain sales targets. Dealers received the holdbacks at the end of the year; the size of each holdback varied from make to make and model to model, but was typically between 2 and 3 percent of the sales price. Because of the holdback, dealers anxious to make added sales often ran highly advertised "special clearance sales" at $100 (or some similarly small amount) over dealer invoice price. Many vehicle buyers did not know about the existence of holdbacks.

Dealers had discretion over the actual price at which they could sell a vehicle; some discount off the MSRP was typical. High-volume dealers generally operated on a lower margin over dealer invoice than did low-volume dealers; normally, dealers were unwilling to grant as large a discount off the MSRP on fast-selling vehicles in short supply from manufacturers. Traditionally, the size of the discount off the MSRP was the subject of back-and-forth bargaining between the dealer and the customer—a process

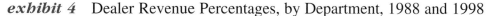

exhibit 4   Dealer Revenue Percentages, by Department, 1988 and 1998

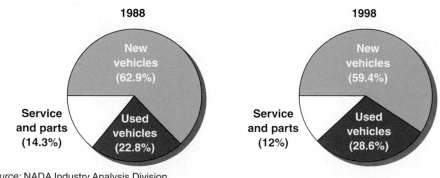

Source: NADA Industry Analysis Division.

exhibit 5   Profit Trends of Franchised Dealers, by Department, 1984–98

NEW-VEHICLE DEPARTMENT NET PROFIT
Average dealership, in thousands of dollars

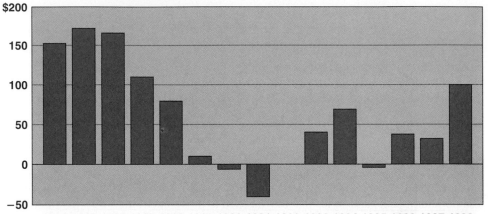

SERVICE AND PARTS DEPARTMENT NET PROFIT
Average dealership, in thousands of dollars

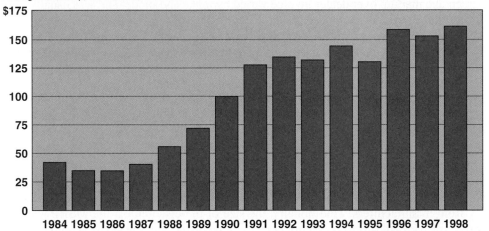

USED-VEHICLE DEPARTMENT NET PROFIT
Average dealership, in thousands of dollars

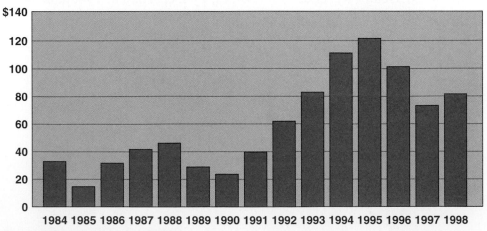

Source: NADA Industry Analysis Division.

exhibit 6 Selected Financial Statistics of Average Automotive Dealership, 1992–98

	1992	1993	1994	1995	1996	1997	1998	% Change 1997–1998
Total dealership sales	$14,372,487	$16,457,502	$18,865,279	$20,029,989	$21,562,332	$22,407,329	$23,712,667	5.8%
Total dealership gross	$ 1,983,403	$ 2,207,717	$ 2,471,352	$ 2,583,869	$ 2,788,010	$ 2,861,416	$ 3,058,934	6.9%
As % of total sales	13.8%	13.4%	13.1%	12.9%	12.9%	12.8%	12.9%	
Total dealership expense	$ 1,783,626	$ 1,944,109	$ 2,131,777	$ 2,303,449	$ 2,458,106	$ 2,554,435	$ 2,655,819	4.0%
As % of total sales	12.4%	11.8%	11.3%	11.5%	11.4%	11.4%	11.2%	
Net profit before taxes	$ 199,778	$ 263,608	$ 339,575	$ 280,420	$ 392,904	$ 306,980	$ 403,115	31.3%
As % of total sales	1.4%	1.6%	1.8%	1.4%	1.5%	1.4%	1.7%	
Net pretax profit in constant 1982 dollars	$ 137,409	$ 176,043	$ 221,113	$ 177,562	$ 198,926	$ 184,571	$ 238,508	29.2%
New-vehicle department sales	$ 8,609,119	$ 9,885,301	$11,375,763	$11,737,574	$12,527,715	$13,130,695	$14,085,324	7.3%
As % of total sales	59.9%	60.0%	60.3%	59.6%	59.1%	58.6%	59.4%	
Used-vehicle department sales	$ 3,650,612	$ 4,349,533	$ 5,074,760	$ 5,808,697	$ 6,360,888	$ 6,498,125	$ 6,781,823	4.4%
As % of total sales	25.4%	26.4%	25.9%	29.0%	29.5%	29.0%	29.6%	
Service and parts sales	$ 2,112,756	$ 2,240,668	$ 2,414,756	$ 2,483,719	$ 2,673,729	$ 2,778,509	$ 2,845,520	2.4%
As % of total sales	14.7%	13.6%	12.8%	12.4%	12.4%	12.4%	12.0%	
New-vehicle average selling price	$ 17,100	$ 18,200	$ 19,200	$ 20,450	$ 21,900	$ 22,650	$ 23,600	4.2%
Used-vehicle average selling price	$ 8,310	$ 9,130	$ 10,140	$ 11,050	$ 11,850	$ 12,100	$ 12,500	3.3%
Average net worth (as of 12/31)	$ 965,244	$ 1,022,053	$ 1,131,690	$ 1,220,597	$ 1,330,257	$ 1,389,052	$ 1,490,451	7.3%
Net profit as % of net worth	20.7%	25.8%	30.0%	23.0%	24.8%	22.1%	27.0%	

Source: NADA Industry Analysis Division.

that could consume hours and sometimes extend over several days. Most customers felt they were not getting a good deal unless they were able to negotiate what they considered a big discount off sticker price; some went from dealer to dealer in search of the best price. Many buyers were using the Internet to research dealer invoice costs and the value of the vehicle they wanted to trade in so that they could do a better job of negotiating. As part of their negotiating strategy, dealers tried to disguise the discount they were granting by presenting their offer to sell in terms of the difference between the sticker price and the trade-in allowance on the customer's used vehicle.

Used-Car Sales   Franchised new-car dealers sold 12 million used vehicles at retail in 1998 and 1999. Another 7.5 million used vehicles were wholesaled at auction or to other dealers. Franchised dealers acquired about 70 percent of their used-car inventories through trade-ins; the remaining 30 percent came from auction purchases, street purchases, and other sources. During the 1990s, the percentage of used cars obtained from auctions rose steadily from 10 percent in 1988 to 31 percent in 1998. Throughout the 1990s, the average retail price of used vehicles rose steadily from $7,400 in 1990 to $10,600 in 1995 to $12,500 in 1998.

The Service Department   Dealers considered after-the-sale service as one of the keys to building a strong relationship with the customers to whom they sold new and used vehicles. Vehicle owners who were highly satisfied with a dealer's repair and maintenance services and service department personnel were more likely to return to the dealership to purchase their next vehicles. Moreover, the service department was a dealer's biggest contributor to the bottom line (see Exhibit 5).

National Automobile Dealers Association

Approximately 19,500 of the 22,400 franchised dealers were members of the National Automobile Dealers Association (NADA), which fought vigorously to represent the best interests of its members. In recent years, NADA had spent considerable time and energy fighting both the Internet car-selling firms and the attempts of manufacturers to integrate forward into manufacturer-owned dealerships.

While NADA officials anticipated that growing buyer use of the Internet would affect motor vehicle retailing, they took comfort in the fact that the laws of most states prevented anyone other than a franchised dealer from selling directly to new-vehicle buyers—an obstacle that online car sellers were busily strategizing to get around. Moreover, NADA and most of its dealer members believed that the majority of buyers would want to personally look at the vehicle, check out the exterior and interior, and take a test drive before committing to a purchase that was typically the second-largest purchase they made (after buying a home).

In a keynote speech at the National Automobile Dealers Association 2000 Convention, James A. Willingham, NADA chairman, said:

> It's important to understand that dealers do much more than simply "sell" cars and trucks. We hire and train skilled sales and service professionals. We perform safety recalls and consumer education, such as the proper installation of child safety seats. We invest millions in technology, training, and facilities. In short, we bring tangible value to the transaction—dealer-added value.[2]

---

[2]www.nada.org.

Willingham suggested that while the Web was a great way to reach a new generation of consumers, it was not a replacement for traditional dealers. He expressed the view that there was more to motor vehicle retailing than agreeing on a price and delivering the vehicle:

> Most importantly, there's the feeling that someone—a real person—is standing behind the product. Now, combine a well-designed, dealer-based Web presence with the personal customer service of a top dealership, and you have a powerful "click-and-mortar" auto retailing strategy for the 21st century.[3]

Nonetheless, NADA felt compelled to look for ways to take advantage of the Internet on behalf of its 19,500 member dealers and to counter the emerging competition of online car-buying services. In 1999, NADA launched a Web site that fielded leads for member dealerships. The site was developed to offer shoppers the largest online new- and used-vehicle inventory of any automobile Web site. In April 2000, NADA launched its own car-shopping Web site (NADAdealers.com), providing consumers with:

- Access to the invoice prices of new vehicles. (However, the site did not reveal the incentives or holdbacks that manufacturers rebated to dealers for meeting sales targets—information that was available on some independent Internet sites.) NADA's move to disclose invoice prices was a radical departure from its long-standing opposition to disclosing dealers' costs for new cars and trucks, but observers felt it was necessary if dealers were to counter the e-challenge from dot-com companies.
- An online inventory of new and used vehicles at the 6,000 participating dealers. (Other dealers could post their inventories of new and used cars for $150 per month.)
- Links to used-car trade-in values and dealer sites.

NADA hoped that eventually all 19,500 of its dealer-members (about 90 percent of the 22,400 franchised dealers) would be accessible through its portal.[4] The NADA site provided shoppers with the names of three dealers in their geographic area that carried the brands they wanted to buy and made those referrals at no charge to the dealer, thus undercutting the referral sites that charged fees either to buyers or dealers for acting as middlemen in a transaction. NADA also began a program in which members could get software packages enabling them to set up their own Web sites or upgrade existing sites. NADA said it developed the site to reduce dealers' Internet marketing costs and to give dealers a direct relationship with online customers. NADA believed that its new initiatives would encourage dealers to affiliate with the NADA site and eventually allow consumers to search dealer inventories at all its members' locations.

AUTOMOBILE BUYER DEMOGRAPHICS

Exhibit 7 shows the demographic makeup of U.S. households in 1998, with projections to 2008. Whereas in the 1970s married couples with children under 18 accounted for close to 50 percent of all U.S. households, in 1998 this group made up only 25 percent, or about 25 million households. That number is not expected to increase in the next decade. More than 30 percent of the 102 million U.S. households were comprised of people either living alone or with nonfamily members; their numbers were expected to

---

[3]www.nada.org.
[4]"Auto Dealers to Launch a Web Site," *The Wall Street Journal,* March 16, 2000, p. A3.

exhibit 7   Selected U.S. Population Statistics, 1998, with Projections to 2008

	1998	2008	Change	1998 to 2008 Percent Change
All households	102,022,000	112,433,000	10,411,000	10.20%
Family households, total	70,938,000	77,864,000	6,926,000	9.80
Married couples without children < 18	28,977,000	34,335,000	5,458,000	18.80
Married couples with children < 18	25,166,000	25,155,000	−11,000	0.00
Female householder, no husband	12,917,000	14,061,000	1,144,000	8.90
Male householder, no wife	3,878,000	4,213,000	335,000	8.60
Nonfamily households, total	31,084,000	34,569,000	3,485,000	11.20
Living alone, total	25,637,000	28,780,000	3,089,000	12.00
Females living alone	15,154,000	17,255,000	2,101,000	13.90
Males living alone	10,537,000	11,525,000	988,000	9.40
Living with nonrelatives	5,393,000	5,789,000	396,000	7.30
Female householder	2,124,000	2,334,000	210,000	9.90
Male householder	3,269,000	3,455,000	186,000	5.70

Source: TGE Demographics.

increase 11 percent by 2008. Married couples without children at home accounted for 28 percent of all households and were expected to grow 19 percent by 2008, the strongest growth among all household types. One of the fastest-growing age groups was people over 65. During the 1998–2008 period, African American households were expected to grow to 14.3 million, a 16.6 percent growth rate. Hispanic households were expected to grow 36 percent, or to 11.6 million by 2008. The number of Asian American households will also increase to 36.5 percent by 2008. Children will be a large component of these numbers. Nearly 35.7 percent of Hispanic married couple households had children under 18 at home in 1998, followed by 32 percent of Asians, 25 percent of whites, and 18.3 percent of blacks. Market research indicated that the type of new vehicle purchased was strongly affected by whether or not children were present in a vehicle buyer's household and, if so, by their numbers and ages (see Exhibit 8).

Market research showed that used-vehicle buyers tended to be somewhat younger and less affluent than new-vehicle buyers. However, used vehicles were becoming more appealing to buyers between the ages of 35 and 49 with annual incomes ranging between $50,000 and $75,000. This was partly attributable to the widespread availability of low-mileage, nicely equipped vehicles in good condition that were coming off two-year and three-year lease programs.

Types of Vehicle Shoppers

A recent study by J. D. Power and Associates, a leading research authority on buyer experiences with motor vehicles, classified vehicle shoppers into four categories—armed unfriendlies, relationship seekers, low-involved pragmatists, and highly involved deal seekers.[5]

Armed unfriendlies (33 percent) were said to be a relatively antagonistic group of shoppers. They tended to be precise and systematic, and came equipped with

---

[5]J. D. Power and Associates, Press Release, June 24, 1999. Posted at www.jdpower.com.

exhibit 8   Share of New Vehicle Purchase by Family Type, July 1998–June 1999

	Married Couples with Children	Married Couples without Children	Multiple Adults with Children	Multiple Adults without Children	One Adult with Children	One Adult, Living Alone
Small car	11.8%	11.1%	14.8%	13.5%	17.4%	15.9%
Midsize car	18.4	21.3	19.1	21.6	21.0	22.7
Large car	1.3	4.0	1.4	2.9	0.9	2.4
Sports car	4.2	4.5	4.8	5.0	4.5	5.6
Luxury car	7.0	10.1	0.7	0.2	0.7	0.0
Minivan	14.6	7.5	10.6	5.5	11.5	4.6
Sport utility vehicle	22.0	19.4	19.9	18.8	21.2	19.5
Pickup truck	19.6	21.3	21.6	22.7	15.9	19.8
Full-size van	1.4	0.8	1.1	0.8	0.9	0.5
Total	100.0%	100.0%	100.0%	100.0%	100.0%	100.0%

Source: The Polk Company.

information in order to better negotiate with sales personnel. This group of shoppers consisted of the youngest and most educated of the four groups of buyers.

Relationship seekers (25 percent) tended to be outgoing and loyal to brands and dealerships. They enjoyed the process of shopping and negotiating for a new vehicle.

Low-involved pragmatists (24 percent) were said to be private, reserved, and convenience-minded. Approximately 45 percent were female. Members of this group believed that shopping around for the perfect vehicle was not the best use of their time and were somewhat indifferent to the kind of car they drove.

Highly involved deal seekers (18 percent) were 73 percent male, younger than the average new-vehicle shopper, and usually shopped many dealerships before making a final selection. They tended to gather a significant amount of information before shopping. These buyers were said to be strong-willed, direct, and competitive. They enjoyed shopping for a new vehicle and were generally friendly toward dealerships and salespeople.

Growing Buyer Use of the Internet to Shop for Vehicles

More and more consumers were using the Internet as a tool to gather information about various models, to compare the features of one vehicle against another in trying to decide what to buy, to learn dealer invoice prices and rebate incentives, to search out the best prices from various dealers, and to avoid the high-pressure sales tactics that salespeople sometimes employed. One newspaper reported the experience of a buyer who had used the Internet to shop for a new vehicle as follows:

> Beth Trane knew she wanted to buy a new sport utility vehicle. But after visiting car dealerships near her home in Orlando, Fla., Trane knew she didn't want to buy her new SUV there.
>
> While researching options and prices on the Internet, Trane started to feel the Orlando dealerships were not offering her a good deal. She returned to the Internet, which pointed her to Miracle Toyota in Winter Haven, Fla.
>
> A few e-mails to that dealership helped her decide what to buy and what to pay for it. That prompted Trane, 38, to call Miracle Toyota to seal the deal. The first time she set foot on the lot was to pick up her 1999 Toyota 4Runner Limited.

exhibit 9   Example of Pricing Data Available from Online
Vehicle Sellers

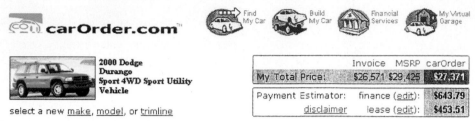

Source: www.carorder.com, April 2000.

"I was not happy with the shopping experience in Orlando," Trane said. "It's very pressured. Over the Internet, we were able to work out the numbers very easily. I just felt more comfortable."[6]

J. D. Power and Associates estimated that the share of new-car buyers using the Internet to help them with their car purchases had grown from 25 percent in 1998 to 60 percent during the last quarter of 1999, and projected that at least 65 percent would make use of the Internet by the end of 2000. The Internet sales manager of a suburban dealership in Birmingham, Alabama, said, "I'd say about 50 percent of the people who come onto our lot have gotten information off the Internet before they come here. Folks who use the Web are some of the most educated customers we have—they're sharp."[7] J. D. Power also reported that more than 60 percent of new-vehicle buyers believed they were able to find out the dealer invoice price during the shopping process.[8] Exhibit 9 illustrates the pricing information available from carOrder.com. According to Forrester Research, 8 million customers were expected to use the Internet for car buying by 2003 (up from an estimated 5 million in 1999), resulting in 500,000 vehicles sold over the Internet and sales totaling $12 billion. Some observers and executives of Internet car-buying companies, however, believed online vehicle sales would grow much more quickly.

J. D. Power's 1999 New Autoshopper.com Study predicted that the growing influence of the Internet would hit domestic manufacturers the hardest:

> The more time a person spends online, the less likely he or she is to purchase a domestic vehicle. Overall, domestic manufacturers currently have approximately 70 percent market share; however, this share drops to 58 percent among Internet shoppers. Furthermore, only half the shoppers who submit a purchase request to an online buying service purchase a domestic vehicle.[9]

MANUFACTURER EFFORTS TO ENTER THE AUTOMOTIVE RETAILING MARKET

Since 1998 Ford and General Motors had been trying to acquire franchised dealers in certain markets to begin setting up their own retail distribution network—a practice forbidden by the franchising laws in a number of states and a move vigorously opposed by

---

[6]Chris Brennan, "Will the Web Lure Buyers to Dealerships or Drive Them Away?" *The Tuscaloosa News* (a New York Times Regional Newspaper), January 23, 2000, p. D1.

[7]As quoted in "Kicking Tires in Cyberspace," *The Birmingham News,* February 6, 2000, p. D6.

[8]www.jdpower.com.

[9]1999 New Autoshopper.com Study, J. D. Power and Associates.

franchised dealers. In 1999 GM announced a controversial plan to buy up to 10 percent of its 7,000-plus dealerships; dealers complained loudly and bitterly, prompting GM to agree to consult with dealers in the future on such moves. Daewoo, a South Korean car maker that had entered the U.S. market in late 1998, had recently opened several factory-owned retail locations. Daewoo's retail distribution strategy for the U.S. market was to have a mix of 25 percent company-owned stores and 75 percent dealer-owned stores. Its plan had led to legislation in some states limiting or banning manufacturer-owned retail distribution. Ford had formed co-owned companies with local dealers in Tulsa, Oklahoma City, San Diego, Salt Lake City, and Rochester, New York, whereby participating dealers either sold their franchise rights to Ford or partnered with Ford at a newly open location. Either way, several dealership locations in the area were closed. Several manufacturers were also said to be developing or pursuing plans to begin advertising and selling used cars coming off company-leasing programs directly over the Internet.

Dealer Efforts to Combat Manufacturer-Owned Dealerships

Dealers had lobbied state lawmakers and regulators to block manufacturer-owned dealerships and also to prevent online sales of new cars by dot-com companies; they had put pressure on government officials in many states to strictly uphold existing franchise laws that made it all but impossible for anyone other than a franchised dealer to sell a new car to a customer—even the U.S. employees of Ford, GM, and other U.S.-based automakers had to buy through dealers rather than buying factory-direct. In 1999 franchised dealers in North Carolina successfully lobbied the state legislature to ban manufacturer-owned dealerships within 45 miles of a franchised dealer selling the same brand; dealers arguing in favor of the restriction expressed a fear that factory-owned franchises would get special treatment, such as a bigger supply of the best-selling models and easy credit approval for vehicle buyers.[10] Other dealers complained that entry of manufacturer-owned stores into the automotive retailing business created an unlevel playing field for dealers because it put them into direct competition with their suppliers. Opposing consumer groups argued that manufacturers wanted to get into retailing to consolidate and eliminate dealerships so they could get better control over pricing. Strong dealer opposition, coupled with restrictive legislation in certain states, was prompting car manufacturers to rethink their strategies and begin to cooperate more with dealers to ward off the dot-com car-buying services.

DEALER–MANUFACTURER ALLIANCES TO BLOCK MARKET INVASION BY THE DOT-COM COMPANIES

To combat the challenge of Internet car-buying services, dealers and manufacturers—despite their many acrimonious battles with each other over the years and the recent flap over manufacturer entry into automotive retailing—were cooperating to try to minimize buyers' use of dot-com companies in finding or buying a new or used vehicle. Dealers were lobbying state legislatures to maintain and enforce the laws that prohibited anyone other than a franchised dealer from selling a new vehicle within their borders—and so far they had been successful.

A strong manufacturer–dealer alliance put independent Web sites at a disadvantage. The strategy of Internet sites such as CarsDirect.com was to guarantee shoppers

---

[10]"Car Sellers, Automakers Haggle over Dealerships," *USA Today,* November 15, 1999, p. 10B.

a price for a vehicle, arrange to buy it from a dealer at a relatively modest markup over dealer cost, then deliver it to the buyer's home. Dot-com companies could not buy vehicles directly from the manufacturer and, so far, manufacturers had refused to do business with wholesale brokers who wanted to make a business of providing vehicles to dot-com sellers. Most observers believed that until online car sellers like CarsDirect.com and Autobytel.com had their own factory-direct source for vehicles it would be difficult for them to satisfy customers and capture more than a token share of the market for new-vehicle sales.

THE RESPONSES OF DEALERSHIPS TO BUYER USE OF THE INTERNET

Dealer-operated Web sites were growing in importance from the standpoint of providing a new source of leads and sales. While the majority of dealer sites received an average of 50 hits per month during the last quarter of 1999, 14 percent received more than 500 hits per month. And the numbers were trending upward each quarter. More than 50 percent of the dealers had partnered with lead-generating Internet sites like Microsoft's CarPoint, cars.com, and Autoweb.com by agreeing to pay monthly or per-hit fees for steering buyers to their dealerships.

Virtually all dealers had begun actively courting sales generated from Internet leads and e-mail inquiries from customers and had hired a new breed of salesperson—one who was computer and Internet savvy and could respond promptly and effectively to customer inquiries without scaring the customer away with high-pressure sales tactics. Over 95 percent of the dealers with Web sites had salespeople specifically assigned to handle Internet-generated leads. And most all dealers and their Internet salespeople were working on how to perfect their Internet sales techniques. So far, it was clear that a very quick response was critical; people wanted to know their message had been received and was being taken seriously. A good Internet rapport and knowledgeable, forthcoming answers to questions could often lead to sales, sometimes without any contact other than the Internet. Close to 50 percent of dealer Web sites allowed customers to fill out financing applications and request service appointments, as well as view inventories and prices.

Miracle Toyota in Winter Haven, Florida, was selling 35–40 cars per month through Internet contacts, most of which turned out to be comparison-shopping buyers in Tampa and Orlando. Lute Riley Honda in suburban Dallas sold nearly 100 cars a month from online contacts.[11] King Acura in Birmingham, Alabama, generated 325 leads in October 1999 from 45 different Internet sites ranging from www.acura.com (the manufacturer's site) to Yahoo! In January 2000, a slow month for vehicle sales, King Acura got 507 referrals from 62 sites.[12]

E-COMMERCE STRATEGIES OF VEHICLE MANUFACTURERS

Exhibit 10 shows the current market share trends for vehicle sales, by manufacturer. While manufacturers were developing a presence online, they were cognizant of the fact that their dealers were the ones who were in contact with the customers. They realized

---

[11]"Car Dealers Say: Follow the Mouse," *Business Week,* April 10, 2000, p. 110.
[12]"Kicking Tires in Cyberspace."

exhibit 10 New-Vehicle Sales in the United States and Market Share by Manufacturer, 1988–98

Year	Chrysler	Ford	GM	Toyota	Honda	Nissan	Volkswagen	Other Imports	Total
1988	2,208,100	3,751,900	5,511,400	936,000	769,000	642,500	197,200	1,359,000	15,374,900
	14.36%	24.40%	35.85%	6.09%	5.00%	4.18%	1.28%	8.84%	
1989	2,004,000	3,579,900	5,106,200	945,400	783,100	664,200	154,900	1,302,700	14,540,500
	13.78%	24.62%	35.12%	6.50%	5.39%	4.57%	1.07%	8.96%	
1990	1,698,100	3,317,100	4,934,300	1,058,000	854,900	621,600	157,500	1,216,300	13,857,700
	12.25%	23.94%	35.61%	7.63%	6.17%	4.49%	1.14%	8.78%	
1991	1,507,700	2,867,400	4,319,700	1,010,500	803,400	583,400	109,000	1,109,000	12,310,000
	12.25%	23.29%	35.09%	8.21%	6.53%	4.74%	0.89%	9.01%	
1992	1,713,000	3,192,500	4,397,500	1,023,600	768,800	585,500	90,500	1,089,000	12,860,600
	13.32%	24.82%	34.19%	7.96%	5.98%	4.55%	0.70%	8.47%	
1993	2,014,800	3,562,400	4,667,000	1,033,200	717,400	687,700	62,100	1,118,400	13,896,000
	14.74%	25.64%	33.59%	7.44%	5.16%	0.05%	0.45%	8.05%	
1994	2,204,000	3,818,100	5,015,900	1,088,100	788,200	774,300	109,600	1,260,400	15,058,600
	14.64%	25.35%	33.31%	7.23%	5.23%	5.14%	0.73%	8.37%	
1995	2,164,300	3,801,000	4,841,600	1,083,400	794,600	770,300	106,600	1,166,300	14,728,000
	14.70%	25.81%	32.87%	7.36%	5.40%	5.23%	0.72%	7.92%	
1996	2,450,800	3,843,400	4,743,600	1,159,700	843,900	749,800	163,200	1,142,700	15,097,200
	16.23%	25.46%	31.42%	7.68%	5.59%	4.97%	1.08%	7.57%	
1997	2,303,800	3,807,100	4,734,100	1,230,100	940,400	728,400	172,000	1,214,400	15,130,200
	15.23%	25.16%	31.29%	8.13%	0.06%	4.81%	1.14%	8.03%	
1998	2,510,000	3,860,200	4,570,100	1,361,000	1,009,600	624,600	267,200	1,342,300	15,541,900
	16.15%	24.84%	29.41%	8.76%	6.50%	4.00%	1.72%	8.64%	
Average	**2,073,782**	**3,581,909**	**4,803,764**	**1,084,455**	**824,845**	**675,391**	**144,545**	**1,210,955**	**14,399,600**
1988–98	**14.40%**	**24.88%**	**33.36%**	**7.53%**	**5.73%**	**4.69%**	**1.00%**	**8.41%**	

Source: NADA Industry Analysis Division.

the potential risk of channel conflict if the dealers felt threatened by their online presence. Until early 2000, manufacturers' Web sites served mainly to provide information for consumers and a referral service for dealerships. Virtually all of the leading manufacturers had Web sites that provided information about their various models and allowed consumers to configure the vehicles they were interested in—including optional equipment, exterior colors, and interior trim. This information was then transmitted to nearby dealers, whose salespeople would promptly be in touch with the prospect by e-mail or phone with a price quote and follow-up sales information. From there, visits to the dealer for a test drive or on-site inspection of the vehicles matching the buyer's preferences and negotiation and haggling over price proceeded in much the same fashion that it had prior to the advent of the Internet. In addition to the product information that was available on these sites, the manufacturers offered information to vehicle owners relating to service, financing, and safety issues.

However, in recent months there had been some new developments on the part of manufacturers.

Toyota Motor Corporation

In the fall of 1999, Toyota Motor Corporation announced that it would begin producing its Camry Solara coupe to customer order in only five days. Toyota planned to include other models in its five-day order-to-production-to-delivery strategy as soon as it perfected the process for the Camry. The move was seen as a possible first step in shifting from a build-for-dealer-inventory business model in North America to a build-to-order business model, which was already relatively common in Japan and Europe. Surveys of car buyers indicated that close to 50 percent were unable to find the model, color, or equipment configuration they preferred when shopping dealer lots. Traditionally, dealers made educated guesses as to what model, color, and equipment options buyers would prefer, placed their orders with manufacturers, and hoped that car buyers would find what they wanted from the array of vehicles they had in stock. To induce customers to compromise if what they wanted was not in stock, manufacturers offered rebates and dealers made price concessions. Custom-ordered vehicles could be obtained, but delivery times often ranged from 30 to 60 days.

Industry observers believed Toyota's competitive move to five-day delivery on custom orders was intended not only to better satisfy car buyers and encourage brand loyalty but also to gain the benefits of tighter supply chain management and reduce reliance on costly promotions to push sales of slow-selling models. A build-to-order business model permitted tighter just-in-time delivery of parts and components to Toyota assembly plants, plus a reduced need for profit-eroding rebates and discounts on unpopular models and configurations. It also paved the way for dealers to drastically cut the number of vehicles kept in stock (thus driving down their inventory-financing costs). If the build-to-order approach caught on with vehicle buyers, a dealership would have to stock only a minimal number of showroom models for inspection and test-drives, and a limited number of vehicles for immediate delivery; it would function mainly as a pickup point for custom orders. Dealer investments in acres of prime expensive real estate at visible, high-traffic locations would be less necessary. A build-to-order model would also work to the advantage of Internet car-buying services. It would be easy for car shoppers to do their research online, make price comparisons, and place their order.[13] According to one estimate, build-to-order assembly could reduce average vehicle costs by over $1,500.[14]

Ford Motor Company

In April 2000, Ford was in the midst of embracing the Internet and e-commerce on a number of fronts. In mid-1999, an internal team made a presentation to senior executives that envisioned (1) factories that built cars to customers' orders, (2) dealers that reported repair and maintenance problems on particular models or components via the Internet as vehicles came in for service so that assembly plants and suppliers could make corrective adjustments promptly, (3) suppliers that controlled inventories at Ford assembly plants and delivered most parts and components on a just-in-time basis, (4) links to suppliers and assembly plants such that when a customer hit the button to order a custom-equipped Ford Explorer online, all the relevant information would be instantaneously transmitted to suppliers providing the parts and components, to assembly plants building the vehicle, to the dealer who would deliver it, to the finance and insurance companies doing the underwriting, and to the Ford designers doing the brainstorming for new SUV models. Ford's CEO and other senior executives were impressed and began a series of initiatives called CustomerConnect to make the vision a reality and link buyers, parts suppliers, assembly plants, dealers, finance companies, and designers. In early 2000, Ford put in place a new online trading market for the company's 30,000 suppliers worldwide and began using the Internet to arrange for purchases and to communicate and coordinate more closely with its suppliers.

---

[13]"An Automaker Tries the Dell Way," *The Wall Street Journal,* August 30, 1999.

[14]"Detroit Goes Digital," *Fortune,* April 17, 2000, p. 172.

To pacify its dealers, Ford had pledged at the 2000 convention of the National Automobile Dealers Association to continue to partner with its franchised dealers in executing its e-commerce strategy and refrain from selling vehicles directly to buyers via the Internet. While Ford had eased back on its initiatives to acquire dealer franchises, its long-term strategic intent regarding forward integration into automotive retailing via acquiring dealerships remained unclear.

General Motors

General Motors launched an e-GM initiative in mid-1999 to link its suppliers and dealers and to forge closer ties to consumers via the Internet. Established as a separate venture within the company, e-GM had set up 150 consumer Web sites around the world to help buyers pick the vehicles they wanted to buy and to try to build relationships with prospective buyers. It had plans to integrate these sites, make them much easier to navigate (in response to complaints), and streamline the process of doing transactions online. GM's U.S. Web site, www.gmbuypower.com, had software that allowed shoppers to configure the vehicle they wanted and a locator service to determine whether any nearby dealers had that vehicle in stock. GM's TradeXchange initiative to move to online procurement with all of its suppliers was expected to cut the administrative costs of filling a purchase order from $100 to $10. During mid-1999, GM had moved to begin selling cars coming off lease programs to consumers in an Internet-based business in Houston, Texas, but Texas refused to issue a business license for GM's venture because of prevailing franchise laws; GM was forced to find a Texas dealership to function as a partner in its venture.

In the fall of 1999 GM began studying what it would have to do to take orders online, custom-produce the vehicles, and deliver them on a promised date. The internal changes were rather dramatic and far-reaching. By early 2000, a team of 100 GM executives and experts from all over the world had forged a plan to put custom-order manufacturing capabilities in place by at least 2003. The key time frames and capabilities that were needed included:[15]

- Reducing times from order to manufacture from 10 days (the minimum) in 1999 to 3 days.
- Reducing normal shipping times from the 11-day average in 1999 to 1–8 days. (Most vehicles were shipped by rail, then transferred to trucks for delivery to dealers.)
- Creating the capability to achieve shipping times of 1–4 days for "premium" orders or special delivery requests.
- Reducing the present elapsed order-to-delivery time from as much as 8 weeks to 4–11 days.

Top executives speculated that as many as 70 percent of GM's customers would take advantage of the opportunity to order custom-equipped vehicles by 2003. In addition, GM executives believed that a well-executed custom-order system could result in a 50 percent reduction in the $40 billion in inventories that dealers stocked and that GM maintained in parts inventories at its assembly plants. GM hoped that capturing information as consumers configured their cars online would help GM designers reduce the number of possible combinations, simplifying parts procurement and assembly. GM's plans included linking suppliers into its Web site so that they could track what was needed and so that the necessary components could be ordered in real time as customers

---

[15]"GM Retools to Sell Cars Online," *The Wall Street Journal,* February 22, 2000, p. B23.

submitted vehicle orders. Harold Kutner, GM's executive in charge of the new plan said, "I envision one day having a 'war room' crammed with computers and monitors where we could track any customer's order anywhere in the world."[16]

GM believed that offering customers quick delivery of custom vehicles would give it a significant competitive advantage over independent Internet sites. Internet car-buying services could not offer custom-built vehicles given the present restrictive franchising laws; their only option was to search through dealer stocks to find vehicles in nearby dealer inventories that closely matched what an individual buyer wanted. Like Ford, GM had pledged that it would stay out of the Internet retail business and would not undermine dealers with Internet-direct factory sales.

Ford-GM-DaimlerChrysler Online Purchasing Alliance

In early 2000, Ford, General Motors, and DaimlerChrysler announced the formation of an unprecedented alliance to build an online network to jointly handle the procurement of the $240 billion in materials, parts, components, and supplies that they used world-wide each year. The venture was expected to result in the creation of the world's largest business-to-business Internet company in terms of revenues and scale of operation. The purpose of the venture was to bring together all their suppliers, allowing them to transact purchases at a single Internet site and thereby streamline their entire supply chain. The three automakers had an equal ownership stake in the venture, which was expected to operate independently. Plans called for the supplier exchange site to be opened to other automakers and to offer them ownership stakes in the new company. Several analysts expected that online parts purchasing would ultimately cut the costs of the average vehicle by about $1,100.[17]

BUSINESS MODELS AND STRATEGIES OF THE DOT-COM COMPETITORS IN AUTOMOTIVE RETAILING

The first generation of automotive-related Internet sites began as pure information providers. They sought to attract site traffic by providing credible and useful information on brands and models, dealer invoice prices (always of great interest to buyers desirous of bargaining hard with dealers), the latest incentive and rebate offers from manufacturers, vehicle performance reviews, and other such topics of interest to vehicle shoppers. The business model of information providers called for covering the costs of the site by selling advertising. These early information providers quickly concluded that their strategy was too revenue-constrained and, seeing larger revenue-growth opportunities, transitioned to lead generators or direct sellers. One of the best sites for research and information was Edmunds.com, but starting in 2000 Edmunds.com expanded into lead generation and referrals, leaving no pure information providers among the major high-traffic automotive-related sites.

The Business Model of Lead Generators

A number of entrepreneurial companies saw early on that the Internet presented considerable opportunities in automotive retailing beyond just providing information. The

---

[16]Ibid.

[17]"Detroit Goes Digital," *Fortune,* April 17, 2000. p. 172.

first generation of online car services acted as content providers and dealer referral services. They developed sites with a wealth of information that car shoppers could peruse in the course of researching what to buy, and they also incorporated links to the Web sites of providers of auto-related products and services. Typically, the content at their sites consisted of both original information developed internally by their own editorial staffs and information assembled from a wide variety of outside sources. The leading outside source was Chrome Data, a company based in Portland, Oregon, that had pioneered the technology of online vehicle configuration and that collected and maintained a database of production specifications for all makes and models, descriptions of standard and optional equipment, vehicle photographs, and manufacturers' suggested retail prices (MSRPs). Chrome Data had incorporated all this information into software products that it sold commercially. Most of the online content providers used Chrome Data's software products as primary tools for giving site visitors the ability to configure custom-equipped models and check out the resulting sticker prices. Chrome Data was the only independent provider of such information, and its vehicle and pricing information precisely matched manufacturers' data, thus providing vehicle shoppers with very accurate product and pricing information.

Most sites had features that allowed shoppers to compare several different models side-by-side. When site visitors decided on a vehicle type equipped the way they wanted it, they could fill out a brief form containing an e-mail address, a zip code, and perhaps other information and click on a button requesting a price quote. The requests for price quotes were then forwarded to area dealers who had signed on with the online car-buying service to provide quotes; dealers either paid the online car-buying service a monthly fee for all such lead referrals or a fixed fee per referral. Competition was active among the growing number of lead generators to sign up dealers and gain the capability to provide quotes to shoppers nationwide.

The business model of car-buying sites that specialized in providing content and generating lead referrals was to cover costs and make a profit by (1) selling advertising and sponsorships to companies wishing to promote their own goods and services to the Web site audience, and (2) signing up dealerships as affiliates and charging them a fee for lead referrals. Such sites had shied away from trying to sell cars directly to car shoppers because of the barriers posed by state franchise laws, the costs of getting the vehicle to the buyer's home without having a number of local distribution points, and a general belief that only a very few shoppers would be willing to complete an entire transaction online without first having test-driven or seen the vehicle or talked to a salesperson.

The Business Model of Online Direct Sellers

The second generation of online car-buying services elected to go a step beyond referring leads to local franchised dealers and take on the task of brokering the entire transaction. Their strategy was to immediately quote customers a price for vehicles as shoppers configured their choices of makes, models, and optional equipment online. The price quotes typically included a total cash price for the vehicle, the monthly payment if the car was leased, and the monthly payment if the car was financed; shoppers could select from any of several leasing or monthly payment plans. Along with these quotes, shoppers were shown the dealer invoice cost and the MSRP. Once customers were ready to place an order, they could enter their credit card number authorizing a deposit of around $250 (usually refundable) to start the transaction rolling and get information as to the time and place of delivery. Online sellers filled customer orders by prearranging with area franchised dealers to supply particular makes and models and function as the actual seller (to comply with state franchise laws). Online sellers were able to provide instantaneous price quotes because they had already negotiated discounts from the vehicle's MSRP with participating area dealers; online brokers added a fee (usually in the neighborhood of $250) to the dealer's discounted price to arrive at the price quoted to online shoppers.

In effect, the business model of online direct sellers was to function as middleman or broker in making the sale. They had two primary revenue sources: (1) the fee earned from brokering the transaction, and (2) the sales of advertising and site sponsorship—especially ad sales to partners interested in providing financing or vehicle insurance or companies selling automotive-related goods and services. Their value added in the transaction was twofold—providing the area dealer with an additional sale and sparing the customer the time-consuming experience of visiting dealer showrooms and the nuisance of negotiating and haggling with dealers. However, like referral services, the strategies of direct sellers were currently constrained by the need to make the sale through franchised dealers and by an inability to source vehicles directly from manufacturers. Virtually all direct sellers were busily putting together nationwide dealer networks that would give them the capability to deliver all makes and models to customers in all geographic locations. A few direct sellers had signed on several thousand franchised dealers, giving them close to total national coverage; others had less than 100 participating dealers and were rushing to woo additional dealers and expand their geographic coverage. Direct sellers also relied on dealers to provide local support for the car-buying process not completed online, serve as a place where shoppers could test-drive vehicles, and potentially handle after-the-sale service of the automobile. The most ambitious and well-funded direct sellers were moving to expand their online buying service to shoppers in foreign countries; several had launched foreign Web sites and begun recruiting foreign dealers to function as distribution outlets for online sales in the targeted country markets.

The discounts off sticker price that direct sellers quoted to online shoppers were typically a function of a model's popularity—slow-selling makes and models carried bigger discounts, and popular makes and models carried smaller discounts. Most franchised dealers were reluctant to supply direct sellers with the best-selling models that were in short supply from the factory at much below MSRP because these could be sold right off their own lots without the added cost of paying a fee to the online broker to win an incremental sale. On the other hand, dealers were usually quite willing to supply makes and models that were readily available from the factory to direct sellers at big discounts from MSRP, allowing direct sellers, in turn, to quite lower prices to online shoppers. Shoppers in different zip codes or states were frequently quoted slightly different prices due to varying destination charges and to differences in the sizes of the discounts from MSRP that direct sellers had been able to negotiate with local dealers. It was not unusual for the prices quoted to online shoppers located in metropolitan areas to be somewhat lower than those quoted to shoppers located in outlying towns and rural areas where dealer competition was weaker and direct sellers could not negotiate as favorable terms.

All things considered, selling vehicles online was considered to cost less than using franchised dealer networks. If franchised dealers could be eliminated from the equation, some analysts estimated that about $1,050 could be trimmed off the $26,000 average price of a new vehicle.[18]

Price competition was becoming a factor among online sellers. Exhibit 11 shows the prices quoted by selected direct sellers for three representative makes and models.

---

[18]Ibid.

exhibit 11   Comparative Prices of Selected Online Vehicle Retailers, Standard Equipped
Models, April 2000

	MSRP	Dealer Invoice	carOrder.com Price	CarsDirect.com Price	Greenlight.com Price
2000 Toyota Camry 4dr Sedan LE	$20,843	$18,304	$19,216	$18,572	$18,004
Monthly payment if leased			$300.36	$308	$245.98
Monthly payment if purchased			$444.70	$371	$370.77
2000 Jeep Grand Cherokee 2x2 Laredo w/26E	$27,465	$24,937	$26,142	$25,180	$24,892
Monthly payment if leased			$442.81	$434	$356.56
Monthly payment if purchased			$613.79	$502	$513.37
2000 Mercedes-Benz ML320 Base	$35,945	$33,474	$35,816	$35,896	$35,177
Monthly payment if leased			$750.49	$566	$532.33
Monthly payment if purchased			$898.78	$715	$811.24

Source: Company Web sites.

PROFILES OF SELECTED ONLINE COMPETITORS IN AUTOMOTIVE RETAILING

Brief profiles of selected lead generators and direct sellers are presented below.

Microsoft's CarPoint

Among the automotive websites, CarPoint had drawn the most traffic as of fall 1999. CarPoint was one of the main features on the Microsoft Network portal. The site was widely praised for its ease of use and its depth of national content (said to be six times as much as some sites). It offered good side-by-side comparisons of models, rebate reports, maintenance reminders, personalized car pages with special offers, chat, and such services as financing and insurance. CarPoint had more than 50 "surround" video clips that let users take a 360-degree tour of a vehicle's exterior and interior. CarPoint had over 2,500 dealer members to whom it forwarded leads. CarPoint had transitioned its strategy from being a content provider to being a lead generator early on in its existence; starting in 2000, CarPoint seemed to be in the early stages of changing its strategy to become a direct seller.

Cars.com

The cars.com site was a comprehensive car information Web site that provided users with extensive local and national inventories of new and used vehicles. Vehicle shoppers could search the inventory listing by zip code, make, model, and year and easily submit quote requests to dealers by e-mail, fax, or telephone. Cars.com had more than 130 local newspaper affiliates that supplied classified ads for used vehicles; it displayed inventories in 26 of the top 30 U.S. metropolitan markets and was the only service that updated dealer inventories daily. It was the second most visited automotive retailing site during the September 1999–February 2000 period, according to Media Metrix.

Tom and Ray Magliozzi (the hosts of the popular "Car Talk" program on National Public Radio) and their award-winning CarTalk Web site were an integral part of the cars.com site. The site also offered rich editorial content on such topics as how to purchase a vehicle and tips for parents of young drivers, plus over 3,500 independent reviews on various makes and models going back to 1983.

Cars.com was a subsidiary of Classified Ventures, based in Chicago. Classified Ventures was formed by eight leading media companies: Gannett Co. (the published of *USA Today* and a number of local newspapers), Knight Ridder (another newspaper chain), the New York Times Co., the Washington Post Co., the Tribune Company, the Times Mirror Company (which was being acquired by the Tribune Company), and the McClatchy Company. Classified Ventures provided nationally branded online services for e-commerce opportunities relating to the market for classified advertising. In addition to the cars.com Web site, Classified Ventures operated four other national Web sites—Apartments.com, auctions.com, MovingCenter.com, and NewHomeNetwork.com; it also operated HomeHunter, a local resale real estate service.

CarsDirect.com

CarsDirect.com was a privately held company founded by Scott Painter, a former marketing vice president of 1-800-Dentist, and Internet entrepreneur Bill Gross, head of idealab!; the company had a number of corporate and institutional backers that included Goldman Sachs, Morgan Stanley Dean Witter, Michael Dell's MSD Capital, Oracle, Hambrecht & Quest (a prominent investment bank that specialized in helping finance Internet companies), Primedia Ventures (affiliated with the largest U.S. publisher of automotive publications, one of whose brands was IntelliChoice) and eight other venture capital firms. Nationally launched in May 1999, CarsDirect operated a research-rich Web site, covering more than 2,500 makes and models, and sold vehicles online. Shoppers could look at vehicle specifications, equipment options, safety features, value ratings, pricing data compiled by IntelliChoice, and IntelliChoice reports on vehicle performance. They could custom-configure a vehicle, compare CarsDirect's price against dealer invoice costs and MSRP, make side-by-side model comparisons, buy the vehicle of their choice online, and have it delivered to their home. By fall 1999, CarsDirect.com was selling about 1,000 vehicles per month and by March 2000 the company had over 2,000 participating dealers.

To arrive at the price it quoted shoppers, the company polled the more than 1,700 dealerships it did business with and created a bell-shaped curve of the dealer prices of every vehicle it offered for sale. It was the company's practice to price the vehicle in the bottom 10th percentile of the bell-shaped curve. According to Scott Painter, "We can guarantee that nine times out of ten, a car bought on our site is cheaper than if a consumer went to a dealership."[19] There was no price negotiation, and the price was consistent for all buyers. CarsDirect had teamed with Bank One, the fifth largest U.S. bank and a major automotive lender, to provide online financing for purchases and leases. They could also purchase vehicle insurance and extended warranties equal to double or triple the standard manufacturers' warranties. In March 2000, CarsDirect introduced a new "zero driveoff" leasing option whereby qualified buyers in 39 states could lease a new vehicle with no down payment.

CarsDirect had recently entered into strategic alliances with Autoweb, a major lead referral service, and cars.com. The alliance with Autoweb provided for the launch of a co-branded direct new-car-buying service on Autoweb.com, placement of exclusive links between the company's sites, and licensing of data content and tools. CarsDirect

---

[19]As quoted in "CarsDirect.com Cuts Auto-Buying Hassles," *Information Week,* November 8, 1999, p. 48.

customers were given the opportunity to list their used cars for sale on Autoweb's site. To signal long-term commitment to the alliance, the two companies each bought ownership stakes in the other. CarsDirect's alliance with cars.com provided a link on cars.com's site where shoppers who wanted to buy a vehicle direct could click directly to CarsDirect's site.

Gomez Advisors, a specialist in rating numerous types of online companies, had given CarsDirect top honors as the best overall car buying site on the Internet for three consecutive quarters (the latest being in March 2000). Gomez gave CarsDirect accolades for its customer service, up-front pricing, online leasing programs, the functionality of its new site design, and the attractive features of its financial calculator tool.

StoneAge.com

Headquartered in Detroit, StoneAge.com's mission was "to eliminate the hassle and stress of the car buying and selling experience." To try to make the whole process easier, more convenient, and worry free, StoneAge's Web site offered comprehensive information and three ways to buy a vehicle: a free service that provided a quote from an affiliated dealer along with invoice information; a $250-deposit service in which StoneAge conducted a search for the best price possible on a customer-specified vehicle; and an auction service in which shoppers sent a quote request to multiple dealers (at a cost of $1 per dealer) and dealers returned a bid via e-mail. Shoppers interested in used vehicles could search through the company's database of over 200,000 vehicles compiled from Internet and newspaper classified ads; StoneAge was putting in place the capability to list over 2 million used vehicles for sale in locations all across the United States. The service also had loan and lease payment calculators, as well as tools to apply for financing, insurance, and leasing. StoneAge had an extensive network of what it termed "top-rated" dealer affiliates; it strived to recruit dealer affiliates that had high customer satisfaction ratings in their locales. Its Web site attracted approximately 500,000 visitors per month.

CarPrices.com

CarPrices.com sought to differentiate its car buying service by *guaranteeing* customers the best purchases prices on the Internet or paying them double the difference in cash. Using its New Car PriceWar feature, customers specified their vehicle of choice (make, model, optional equipment, and colors), then sat back and waited while multiple dealers placed the bids to fill the order. The bid process typically took about 24 hours, and customers could log back on to CarPrices.com to view the bid comparison screen for their custom-equipped vehicle. CarPrices.com provided shoppers with dealer invoice cost and MSRP to help them evaluate the bids. According to CarPrices.com's promotional advertising, consumers who visited dealer showrooms to make their purchase bought cars from dealers, on average, at 8 percent above dealer invoice while the average online purchase was a 6 percent above invoice cost. Consumers who bought through CarPrices.com's PriceWar paid on average only 2 percent over invoice.

While the PriceWar feature was available only to residents of the San Diego area in the spring of 2000, CarPrices.com had recruited a sufficient number of participating dealers to roll out the feature in Los Angeles, Miami, Chicago, and Washington/Baltimore by mid-2000 and was expecting to have a national rollout sometime in 2001.

Like most of its rivals, CarPrices.com had a feature-rich site that provided a broad variety of information, news about new models, used-car prices and a search of used-car classified ads, special articles on automotive-related topics, insurance and financing options, calculators, a "lemon" check, manufacturers' rebates, and reviews of models.

DriveOff.com

DriveOff.com offered shoppers the ability to finalize all the terms and conditions of buying a vehicle online. Shoppers could research detailed specifications, standard and optional equipment, and safety features, and compare multiple vehicles side-by-side. Articles from USAutoNews.com were available for review. Once shoppers had configured the vehicle they wanted and selected which options were essential and which they would be willing to forgo, DriveOff.com provided a binding price and monthly payment (exclusive of state and local taxes and transportation charges, which varied according to the shopper's location). Shoppers still interested provided contact information, completed a credit application, and entered a credit card number to make a fully refundable $250 cash deposit on the vehicle. When DriveOff located a list of vehicles matching the shopper's preferences, the shopper was notified by e-mail to go to his or her Personal Auto Center on DriveOff's Web site to view the information. A shopper who accepted one of the matches could track every step of the transaction as it unfolded. Buyers were e-mailed a Deal Kit containing all the documents necessary to close the transaction and take delivery from a participating DriveOff dealer affiliate. All that remained was for the customer to pick up the vehicle at the dealership at the scheduled time, sign the closing documents, get a quick tutorial on how to operate the vehicle, and then drive off. If DriveOff could not find an acceptable match and the customer did not want to place a factory order for the vehicle, the credit card deposit was immediately refunded.

Greenlight.com

Greenlight.com was formed in 1999 by entrepreneurs with experience in both e-commerce and the automotive industry who saw an opportunity to improve the car-buying experience and put customers in control. The new company had received financial backing from a prominent Silicon Valley venture capital firm and from Asbury Automotive, a privately held U.S. group of 100-plus franchised automobile dealers representing virtually all makes and models. In January 2000, Amazon.com acquired 5 percent of the outstanding shares of Greenlight.com and contracted to make Greenlight its exclusive partner in the market for online car-buying. Under the agreement, Amazon provided Greenlight exclusive exposure to its 16 million-plus online shoppers; in return, Greenlight agreed to pay Amazon $82.5 million over five years and give Amazon warrants to increase its ownership stake to as much as 30 percent. In February 2000, Greenlight.com and AutoTrader.com announced a strategic partnership whereby Greenlight would become the exclusive online car-buying service offered by AutoTrader. Auto-Trader.com had one of the largest selections of used cars for sale in the United States, with more than 40,000 listings from 40,000 U.S. auto dealers and more than 250,000 private sellers. The site had 5 million unique visitors in February 2000. AutoTrader.com was a venture of Trader Publishing Company, the publisher of *AutoTrader* and *AutoMart* magazines, which were distributed in more than 136,000 retail locations and had an estimated weekly circulation of 2.5 million copies. One of the investors in AutoTrader.com was the same Silicon Valley venture capital firm that had invested in Greenlight.com.

Greenlight was a direct seller of new vehicles; its site used vehicle configuration software and had a tool for helping shoppers choose a vehicle based on price range, body type, engine, or transmission. When shoppers selected the customized vehicle they wanted, Greenlight provided a no-haggle price; the company claimed that its everyday-low-pricing approach resulted in prices that were "low (often at invoice!)." Greenlight provided the vehicle's MSRP and the dealer invoice cost as a basis for comparison. Greenlight asked for a $200 refundable deposit to guarantee its price, reserve the vehicle, and process an order. Customer service representatives were available 24 hours a day to help with a purchase. The company provided home delivery, except where it was prevented from doing so by state franchise laws or manufacturers. In April 2000, Greenlight's service was available only in seven cities but the company planned to have national coverage before Fall 2000.

CarOrder.com

Headquartered in Austin, Texas, carOrder.com was launched in January 1999 as a spin-off business of Trilogy Software, also an Austin-based company. One of Trilogy's new products was software that allowed consumers to buy cars online. CarOrder.com's strategy was to acquire approximately 100 small, rural, typically underperforming dealerships with about 200 new-car franchises and turn them into what it termed "e-dealerships"—distribution centers for its Internet car buyers. The company was particularly interested in acquiring the worst-performing dealerships with the worst customer satisfaction ratings so that it could hold dealer acquisition costs down to around $1 million each. To finance its acquisitions, carOrder.com completed arrangements for $100 million in funding from Trilogy in September 1999. Company officials indicated they expected to raise another $500 million from private investors and a public stock offering in 2000.

Management's plan was to acquire the 100 dealerships region by region across the United States and turn them into e-dealers, eventually building national distribution and direct-delivery capability for its online sales. The strategy was for the company's Web site to attract vehicle shoppers and tie down the sales of new vehicles online. Vehicles sold online would be routed through the national chain of local dealers, thus allowing carOrder.com to comply with state franchise laws. The primary function of the acquired local dealerships was to provide a place where online shoppers could test-drive vehicles and where truckloads of new vehicles arriving from manufacturer assembly plants could be unloaded onto dealer lots. Newly unloaded vehicles would be run through the service department and made ready for either buyer pickup or for loading onto carOrder.com flatbed trucks for home delivery to the buyer.

The newly acquired dealerships would still handle local walk-in traffic and perhaps stock a small new-vehicle and used-vehicle inventory for local customers, but 60–90 percent of their sales volume was expected to eventually originate from Internet-generated sales at carOrder.com's Web site. Costs of operating the dealership would be smaller because they would need a minimal sales force and would need to keep smaller numbers of vehicles in inventory. Since carOrder.com could order directly from manufacturers, the company planned to give customers the opportunity to order custom-equipped vehicles, thus promoting wider use of a build-to-order business model. CarOrder.com's management believed that a build-to-order configured value chain could eventually cut $2,000 to $4,000 out of the cost of getting a new vehicle to a consumer, producing a significant pricing advantage over traditional dealers.

When NADA learned of carOrder.com's strategy, it immediately put pressure on manufacturers to sign agreements saying that they would not transfer any franchises to dot-com companies. So far, NADA's efforts had not derailed carOrder.com's strategy. In commenting on the challenges to carOrder.com's strategy, its CEO remarked, "We may be one of the only Internet companies with more lawyers than software engineers."[20]

Exhibit 12 shows carOrder.com's home page.

---

[20] As quoted in Fara Warner, "Web Auto Retailer CarOrder.com Receives Funds to Buy Dealerships," *The Wall Street Journal,* September 29, 1999, p. B4.

exhibit 12   carOrder.com's Home Page, April 2000

Source: www.carorder.com

Autobytel.com

Autobytel.com was a hybrid site. It began as a content provider and lead-referral service but its strategy had recently evolved to include direct sales at its new AutobytelDirect.com site. The company offered shoppers three ways to buy a vehicle: (1) shoppers could search the inventories of dealers, find a car that suited them, and, for a refundable credit card deposit, submit a purchase request to bid on vehicles at the Autobytel.com Auction; (2) they could buy direct online through the "Click and Buy" on posted inventory at AutobytelDirect; or (3) if customers wished, they could use the services of a personal shopper in locating and buying a vehicle. Autobytel also had auto auction and classified ad features for car owners who wanted to sell a vehicle. Autobytel's dealer affiliates had an online searchable inventory of over 50,000 vehicles. Customers could get real-time insurance quotes from any of three sources, purchase extended warranties, get free service quotes, check out vehicle recall, and check the value of their present vehicle.

Autobytel was launched in March 1995 and had served over 4 million customers since its inception. In 1999, Autobytel reported revenues of $40.3 million and losses of $23.3 million; its year-end cash balance was $85.5 million. It generated 1.06 million purchase requests in the last half of 1999, resulting in sales averaging about 50,000 vehicles per month. Autobytel received a fee of $100 to $300 from a dealer upon the completion of a sale, depending on the gross selling price of the vehicle.

In the first quarter of 2000, Autobytel's market share of vehicle sales on the Internet was about 45 percent. Its sales volume was bigger than the next two direct sellers combined. Autobytel completed its acquisition of CarSmart.com, a leading online buying site for new and used vehicles, in March 2000, giving it a database of over 6.5 million customers, a network of over 4,800 dealer affiliates, established relationships with over 200 credit unions, and strategic marketing agreements with 10 of the top Internet portals, including AOL, AltaVista, and Snap.com. The company generated vehicle sales totaling more than $3.4 billion through participating dealers (equal to vehicle sales of $1.6 million per hour) in the first quarter of 2000 and had a record-breaking 3 million site users.

Autobytel was aggressively pursuing international expansion. In addition to the United States, Autobytel had Web sites in Sweden, Australia, the United Kingdom, Japan, and Canada. Autobytel Europe was formed in January 2000 as a platform for expanding across Europe and partnering with strong vehicle distribution firms in Europe. Autobytel's strategic objective was to become the largest Internet car dealer in the world.

AUTONATION'S BRICK-AND-CLICK STRATEGY

Going into the new millennium, AutoNation was the world's largest automotive retailer, with 406 franchises in 21 states, 41 multiacre AutoNation USA used-vehicle megastores in 13 states, 350 Web sites, 1999 revenues of $20.1 billion and 1999 earnings of $283 million. AutoNation also owned Alamo Rent-a-Car and National Car Rental. The company (formerly named Republic Industries, with business interests extending beyond the automotive business) was formed in 1995 by corporate entrepreneur and billionaire H. Wayne Huizenga, a founder of Blockbuster and owner of the Miami Dolphins National Football League franchise. Huizenga's vision was to make AutoNation the Home Depot of the car-retailing business and build the first national automotive retail brand. The company's initial strategy had been to acquire strong franchised dealerships, build them into a national retail network, and then redefine the customer's vehicle-buying experience by changing the sales and services processes to better please customers and meet their expectations. The prices of all new and used vehicles at AutoNation's dealerships were posted on the vehicles and fixed—there was no price haggling. Salespeople were trained to be courteous and helpful. The company's multiacre used-car superstores located throughout a given metropolitan area were all served by a central used-car reconditioning center.

But the strategy so far had met with only modest success, partly because the dealerships could not achieve a large enough unit volume to justify the capital investment and operating costs associated with superstores. AutoNation's strategy had gone through several revisions to try to find the right combination. One revision involved buying Alamo Rent-a-Car and National Car Rental to serve as sources for funneling late-model used cars into AutoNation's inventory and avoid having to compete with other dealers for attractive late-model car inventory. But buyers were not excited about the "plain-vanilla" models that rental car companies favored. Starting in early 1999 Huizenga took the string of dealerships in the Denver area acquired earlier and renamed them all John Elway AutoNation USA. (AutoNation had purchased six John Elway dealerships in the Denver area in 1998.) To promote the one-price concept, a major advertising campaign was launched to saturate the Denver market. Salespeople were put through 60 days of training to learn how to deal with customers and sell a vehicle without getting into price haggling. Sales commissions were based on volume, as opposed to the normal practice of tying commission size to the amount of gross profit on each sale. The strategy boosted market share from 19 percent to 28 percent, but profit margins suffered. Huizenga commented, "There are a lot of moving parts in this business. It isn't just a simple thing like renting a video or picking up the trash. It is difficult, but you just have to keep working at it."[21] In September 1999, Huizenga relinquished his position as CEO and to fill the spot, brought in Michael Jackson, a former car dealer who had been the head of Mercedes-Benz's sales and marketing operations in North America.

In February 2000, with AutoNation's stock price languishing in single digits (down from a high of $46 in 1997), Michael Jackson announced that the company was putting new acquisitions on hold and shelving plans to make the AutoNation brand a household name for car buying.[22] Instead, Jackson said the company was shifting its focus to leverage its scale of operations to be the low-cost provider and concentrating on expanding the reach of its AutoNationDirect.com e-commerce site. He indicated that greater use of the Internet to reach prospective vehicle buyers would allow the company to grow its market share without spending heavily to acquire brick-and-mortar dealerships. AutoNation's new strategy was to market its Web site nationally and use its existing franchises as distribution points for delivering vehicles to customers. To serve buyers in cities where it did not already own franchises, the strategy was to license non-AutoNation dealers to serve as distribution and service locations for buyers. In addition to its own Web site, AutoNation announced plans to sell thousands of cars through Internet companies that steered leads to dealers to meet its goal of generating $1.5 billion in online cars sales in 2000 and $3 billion in 2001; toward this end, it signed national contracts with four lead-referral dot-com car services—Autoweb.com, AutoVantage.com, StoneAge.com, and CarPoint. AutoNation also expected to cooperate with dot-com companies that sold vehicles to buyers online; several had approached AutoNation to serve as a source for new and used vehicles (AutoNation maintained online listings of some 90,000 vehicles on the lots of its dealers which could easily be searched). To boost the sales that it was getting from lead-referral companies and from hits on its own Web sites, AutoNation had begun using its newly installed software capability to track which lead generators had the highest sales closures and which car brands sold best through which referral services; its software also tracked buyer requests sent to other AutoNation dealers, helping salespeople know what other types of vehicles the buyer was considering. Management believed such information would allow AutoNation to be more effective in selling vehicles from Internet contacts.

To further drive down costs and streamline operations, Michael Jackson announced that AutoNation would shut down its megastores for used cars, cut the size of AutoNation's workforce, and curtail corporate spending. Management was implementing efforts to use the Internet to combine and streamline back-office operations in its 400-plus dealerships and to let its dealers go online to search its inventory and bid for any of the 45,000 used cars in its inventory—actions that were expected to boost profit margins. Jackson's goal was to boost profit margins at the company's dealerships from 3.3 percent in the fourth quarter of 1999 to 3.8 percent in 2000—the industry average in 1999 was 2.8 percent. He called a halt to the plan of prior management to replace local dealership brands such as John Elway AutoNation in Denver with just the AutoNation brand.

It remained to be seen whether Jackson would alter AutoNation's one-price, no-haggle strategy. Many auto industry executives believed that the one-price, no-haggle

---

[21]As quoted in Alex Taylor, "Would You Buy a Car from This Man?" *Fortune,* October 25, 1999, p. 166.
[22]"AutoNation Goes Back to Basics with an Internet Twist," *The Wall Street Journal,* February 25, 2000, p. B4.

system was fundamental to reforming the automotive retailing business. Others, however, saw a one-price strategy as flawed because it put a dealer at a disadvantage to cross-town competitors who were willing to make a sale for $50 less, especially in an industry ruled by overcapacity in manufacturing and dealers who always had the incentive to make an additional sale. When Michael Jackson was running Mercedes-Benz's sales and marketing operation for North America, he had installed a system he called credible pricing, which involved reducing the sticker price to such a small margin over dealer invoice that it was uneconomical for dealers to trim much off the sticker price in negotiating price with customers.

AutoNationDirect.com   AutoNation launched AutoNationDirect.com in June 1999. Shoppers could explore product specifications for all makes and models of new vehicles, check sticker prices, view interior and exterior photographs, and see descriptions of standard and optional equipment. The site offered the largest inventory of new and used vehicles in the United States, featuring every major manufacturer, make, and model and covering all of AutoNation's dealerships. Shoppers could conduct their own searches for vehicles using the site's "Tour the Lot" feature. All prices were fixed, with no haggling. Buyers could reserve a vehicle with a credit card. If customer wished, they could arrange financing with Giggo.com, a financing division of DaimlerChrysler, and purchase car insurance from Progressive Insurance Co. without ever leaving the site. Buyers could pick up their vehicle at an AutoNation dealership or make arrangements for home delivery. The site offered shoppers the ability to study and compare reviews and independent commentary on all vehicle makes and models, and site visitors could write and share their own reviews. Over 600 dedicated Internet sales guides were available to assist customers in the selection and purchase process. In 1999 AutoNation-Direct's "Tour the Lot" feature along with AutoNation's 200-plus individual dealership Web sites contributed to more than $1 billion in vehicle sales via the Internet.

In March 2000 AutoNationDirect.com introduced two new features on its Web site called "Build Your Dream Car" and "Let Us Find It for You." The Dream Car feature recorded a shopper's preferences—make, model, optional equipment, trim levels, and interior and exterior colors—and instantly e-mailed the profile to one of AutoNation's Internet sales guides; the sales guide searched the entire online inventory of 100,000 new and used vehicles for a match. If a match was not available, the sales guide could order the desired vehicle from the manufacturer or through a secondary source. The Let Us Find It feature offered shoppers a short form they could use to have the Internet sales guides conduct similar searches including searches of vehicles leaving manufacturers' assembly plants en route to nearby AutoNation-owned dealerships. AutoNation management believed that the positive customer reaction to the AutoNationDirect.com site and its new features made it likely the company would achieve its target of $1.5 billion in online sales in 2000.

case 7 Dell Computer Corporation: Strategy and Challenges for the 21st Century

Arthur A. Thompson
The University of Alabama

John E. Gamble
University of South Alabama

> You don't ever really know whether you've come up with the right plan until much later—when it either works or it doesn't. What is the right plan? It's the one that helps you identify what you need to do to ensure success. It's the one that rallies your employees around a few common goals—and motivates them to achieve them. It's one that involves your customers' goals and your suppliers' goals and brings them altogether in a unified focus.
> —Michael Dell

In 1984, at the age of 19, Michael Dell founded Dell Computer with a simple vision and business concept—that personal computers could be built to order and sold directly to customers. Michael Dell believed his approach to the PC business had two advantages: (1) Bypassing distributors and retail dealers eliminated the markups of resellers, and (2) building to order greatly reduced the costs and risks associated with carrying large stocks of parts, components, and finished goods. While the company sometimes struggled during its early years trying to refine its strategy, build an adequate infrastructure, and establish market credibility against better-known rivals, Dell's build-to-order, sell-direct approach proved appealing to growing numbers of customers worldwide during the 1990s as global PC sales rose to record levels. And, as Michael Dell had envisioned, the direct-to-the-customer strategy gave the company a substantial cost and profit margin advantage over rivals that manufactured various PC models in volume and kept their distributors and retailers stocked with ample inventories.

DELL COMPUTER'S MARKET POSITION IN EARLY 2000

Going into 2000, Dell Computer was the U.S. leader in PC sales, with nearly a 17 percent market share, about 1 percentage point ahead of second-place Compaq. Gateway

---

Copyright © 2000 by Arthur A. Thompson and John E. Gamble. All rights reserved.

was third with 8.9 percent, followed by Hewlett-Packard with 8.8 percent and IBM with 7.2 percent. Dell overtook Compaq as the U.S. sales leader in the third quarter of 1999, and it had moved ahead of IBM into second place during 1998 (see Exhibit 1). World-wide, Dell Computer ranked second in market share (10.5 percent) behind Compaq (14.0 percent). IBM ranked third worldwide, with an 8.2 percent share, but this share was erod-ing. Since 1996, Dell had been gaining market share quickly in all of the world's mar-kets, growing at a rate more than triple the 18 percent average annual increase in global PC sales. Even though Asia's economic woes in 1997–98 and part of 1999 dampened the market for PCs, Dell's PC sales across Asia in 1999 were up a strong 87 percent. Dell was also enjoying strong sales growth in Europe.

Dell's sales at its Web site (www.dell.com) surpassed $35 million a day in early 2000, up from $5 million daily in early 1998 and $15 million daily in early 1999. In its fiscal year ending January 31, 2000, Dell Computer posted revenues of $25.3 billion, up from $3.4 billion in the year ending January 29, 1995—a compound average growth rate of 49.4 percent. Over the same time period, profits were up from $140 million to $1.67 billion—a 64.1 percent compound average growth rate. Since its initial public of-fering of common stock in June 1988 at $8.50 per share, the company had seen its stock price split seven times and increase 45,000 percent. Dell Computer was one of the top 10 best-performing stocks on the NYSE and the NASDAQ during the 1990s. In recent years, Dell's annual return on invested capital had exceeded 175 percent.

Dell's principal products included desktop PCs, notebook computers, workstations, servers, and storage devices. It also marketed a number of products made by other man-ufacturers, including CD-ROM drives, modems, monitors, networking hardware, mem-ory cards, speakers, and printers. The company received nearly 3 million visits weekly at its Web site, where it maintained 50 country-specific sites. It was a world leader in mi-grating its business relationships with both customers and suppliers to the Internet. In 1998 the company expanded its Internet presence with the launch of www.gigabuys.com, an online source for more than 30,000 competitively priced computer-related products. Sales of desktop PCs accounted for about 65 percent of Dell's total systems revenue; sales of notebook computers generated 20–25 percent of revenues, and servers and work-stations accounted for 10–15 percent of revenues. Dell products were sold in more than 170 countries. In early 2000, the company had 33,200 employees in 34 countries, up from 16,000 at year-end 1997; approximately one-third of Dell's employees were located in countries outside the United States, and this percentage was growing.

COMPANY BACKGROUND

When Michael Dell was in the third grade, he responded to a magazine ad with the headline "Earn Your High School Diploma by Passing One Simple Test." At that age, he was both impatient and curious—always willing to try ways to get something done more quickly and easily. Early on, he became fascinated by what he saw as "commer-cial opportunities." At age 12, Michael Dell was running a mail-order stamp-trading business, complete with a national catalog, and grossing $2,000 per month. At 16, he was selling subscriptions to the *Houston Post,* and at 17 he bought his first BMW with the more than $18,000 he had earned. He enrolled at the University of Texas in 1983 as a pre-med student (his parents wanted him to become a doctor) but soon became im-mersed in the commercial opportunities he saw in computer retailing and started selling PC components out of his college dormitory room. He bought random-access memory (RAM) chips and disk drives for IBM PCs at cost from IBM dealers, who often had ex-cess supplies on hand because they were required to order large monthly quotas from

exhibit 1 Leading PC Vendors Worldwide and in the United States, Based on Factory Shipments, 1996–99

A. Worldwide Market Shares of the Leading PC Vendors*

1999 Rank	Vendor	1999 Market Shipments of PCs	1999 Market Share	1998 Market Shipments of PCs	1998 Market Share	1997 Market Shipments of PCs*	1997 Market Share	1996 Market Shipments of PCs*	1996 Market Share	Compound Growth Rate, 1996–99
1	Compaq Computer	15,732,000	14.0%	13,266,000	14.5%	10,064,000	12.6%	7,211,000	10.4%	29.7%
2	Dell Computer	11,883,000	10.5	7,770,000	8.5	4,648,000	5.8	2,996,000	4.3	58.3
3	IBM	9,287,000	8.2	7,946,000	8.7	7,239,000	9.1	6,176,000	8.9	14.6
4	Hewlett-Packard	7,577,000	6.7	5,743,000	6.3	4,468,000	5.6	2,984,000	4.3	36.4
5	Packard Bell/ NEC	5,989,000	5.3	5,976,000	6.5	4,150,000	5.2	4,230,000	6.1	12.1
6	Gateway	4,685,000	4.2	3,540,000	n.a.	n.a.	n.a.	n.a.	n.a.	n.a.
	Others	57,573,000	55.2	50,741,000	55.5	49,369,000	61.8	45,727,000	66.0	10.8
	All vendors	112,726,000	100.0%	91,442,000	100.0%	79,938,000	100.0%	69,324,000	100.0%	17.6%

B. U.S. Market Shares of the Leading PC Vendors, 1998–99

1999 Rank	Vendor	1999 Market Shipments of PCs*	1999 Market Share	1998 Market Shipments of PCs*	1998 Market Share	Percent Growth 1998–99
1	Dell Computer	7,492,000	16.6%	4,799,000	13.2%	56.1%
2	Compaq Computer	7,222,000	16.0	6,052,000	16.7	19.3
3	Gateway	4,001,000	8.9	3,039,000	8.4	31.6
4	Hewlett-Packard	3,955,000	8.8	2,832,000	7.8	39.6
5	IBM	3,274,000	7.2	2,983,000	8.2	9.8
	Others	19,248,000	42.6	16,549,000	45.6	16.3
	All vendors	45,192,000	100.0%	36,254,000	100.0%	24.7%

*Includes branded shipments only and excludes OEM sales for all manufacturers.

Source: International Data Corp.

IBM. Dell resold the components through newspaper ads (and later through ads in national computer magazines) at 10–15 percent below the regular retail price.

By April 1984 sales were running about $80,000 per month. Michael Dell at age 18 dropped out of college and formed a company, PCs Ltd., to sell both PC components and PCs under the brand PCs Limited. He obtained his PCs by buying retailers' surplus stocks at cost, then powering them up with graphics cards, hard disks, and memory before reselling them. His strategy was to sell directly to end users; by eliminating the retail markup, Dell's new company was able to sell IBM clones (machines that copied the functioning of IBM PCs using the same or similar components) at about 40 percent below the price of an IBM PC. The price-discounting strategy was successful, attracting price-conscious buyers and producing rapid growth. By 1985, with a few people working on six-foot tables, the company was assembling its own PC designs. The company had 40 employees, and Michael Dell worked 18-hour days, often sleeping on a cot in his office. By the end of fiscal 1986, sales had reached $33 million.

During the next several years, however, PCs Limited was hampered by growing pains—a lack of money, people, and resources. Michael Dell sought to refine the company's business model; add needed production capacity; and build a bigger, deeper management staff and corporate infrastructure while at the same time keeping costs low. The company was renamed Dell Computer in 1987, and the first international offices were opened that same year. In 1988 Dell added a sales force to serve large customers, began selling to government agencies, and became a public company—raising $34.2 million in its first offering of common stock. Sales to large customers quickly became the dominant part of Dell's business. By 1990 Dell Computer had sales of $388 million, a market share of 2 to 3 percent, and an R&D staff of over 150 people. Michael Dell's vision was for Dell Computer to become one of the world's top three PC companies.

Thinking its direct-sales business would not grow fast enough, in 1990–93, the company began distributing its computer products through Soft Warehouse Superstores (now CompUSA), Staples (a leading office products chain), Wal-Mart Stores, Sam's Club, and Price Club (now Price/Costco). Dell also sold PCs through Best Buy stores in 16 states and through Xerox in 19 Latin American countries. But when the company learned how thin its margins were in selling through such distribution channels, it realized it had made a mistake and withdrew from selling to retailers and other intermediaries in 1994 to refocus on direct sales. At the time, sales through retailers accounted for only about 2 percent of Dell's revenues.

Further problems emerged in 1993, when Dell reportedly lost $38 million in the second quarter from engaging in a risky foreign-currency hedging strategy; had quality difficulties with certain PC lines made by the company's contract manufacturers; and saw its profit margins decline. Also that year, buyers were turned off by the company's laptop PC models. To get laptop sales back on track, the company took a charge of $40 million to write off its laptop line and suspended sales of those products until it could get redesigned models into the marketplace. The problems resulted in losses of $36 million for the company's fiscal year ending January 30, 1994.

Because of higher costs and unacceptably low profit margins in selling to individuals and households, Dell Computer did not pursue the consumer market aggressively until sales on the company's Internet site took off in 1996 and 1997. Management noticed that while the industry's average selling price to individuals was going down, Dell's was going up—second- and third-time computer buyers who wanted powerful computers with multiple features and did not need much technical support were choosing Dell. It became clear that PC-savvy individuals liked the convenience of buying direct from Dell, ordering exactly what they wanted, and having it delivered to their door within a matter of days. In early 1997, Dell created an internal sales and marketing group dedicated to serving the individual consumer segment and introduced a product line designed especially for individual users.

By late 1997, Dell had become the global industry leader in keeping costs down and wringing efficiency out of its direct-sales, build-to-order business model. Going into 2000, Dell Computer had made further efficiency improvements and was widely regarded as having the most efficient procurement, manufacturing, and distribution process in the global PC industry. The company was a pioneer and acknowledged world leader in incorporating e-commerce technology and use of the Internet into its everyday business practices. The goal was to achieve what Michael Dell called "virtual integration"—a stitching together of Dell's business with its supply partners and customers in real time such that all three appeared to be part of the same organizational team.[1] The company's mission was "to be the most successful computer company in the world at delivering the best customer experience in the markets we serve."[2]

Exhibits 2–5 contain a five-year review of Dell Computer's financial performance and selected financial statements.

Michael Dell

Michael Dell was widely considered one of the mythic heroes of the PC industry, and was labeled "the quintessential American entrepreneur" and "the most innovative guy for marketing computers in this decade." In 1992, at the age of 27, Michael Dell became the youngest CEO ever to head a Fortune 500 company; he was a billionaire at the age of 31. Once pudgy and bespectacled, Michael Dell at the age of 35 was physically fit, considered good-looking, wore contact lenses, ate only health foods, and lived in a three-story 33,000 square-foot home on a 60-acre estate in the Austin, Texas, metropolitan area. In early 2000 Michael Dell owned about 14 percent of Dell Computer's common stock, worth about $12 billion. The company's glass-and-steel headquarters building in Round Rock, Texas (an Austin suburb), had unassuming, utilitarian furniture, abstract art, framed accolades to Michael Dell, laudatory magazine covers, industry awards plaques, bronze copies of the company's patents, and a history wall that contained the hand-soldered guts of the company's first personal computer.[3]

In the company's early days Michael spent a lot of his time with the engineers. He was said to be shy, but those who worked with him closely described him as a likable young man who was slow to warm up to people.[4] Michael described his experience in getting the company launched as follows:

> There were obviously no classes on learning how to start and run a business in my high school, so I clearly had a lot to learn. And learn I did, mostly by experimenting and making a bunch of mistakes. One of the first things I learned, though, was that there was a relationship between screwing up and learning: The more mistakes I made, the faster I learned.
>
> I tried to surround myself with smart advisors, and I tried not to make the same mistake twice. . . . Since we were growing so quickly, everything was constantly changing.

[1]Michael Dell used the term "virtual integration" in an interview published in the *Harvard Business Review.* See Joan Magretta, "The Power of Virtual Integration: An Interview with Dell Computer's Michael Dell," *Harvard Business Review,* March–April 1998, p. 75.

[2]Information posted on www.dell.com, February 1, 2000.

[3]As described in *Business Week,* March 22, 1993, p. 82.

[4]"Michael Dell: On Managing Growth," *MIS Week,* September 5, 1988, p. 1.

exhibit 2 Financial Performance Summary, Dell Computer, 1995–2000 (In Millions, Except Per Share Data)

	January 28, 2000	January 29, 1999	February 1, 1998	February 2, 1997	January 28, 1996	January 29, 1995
Results of operations data						
Net revenue	$25,265	$18,243	$12,327	$7,759	$5,296	$3,475
Gross margin	5,218	4,106	2,722	1,666	1,067	738
Operating income	2,263	2,046	1,316	714	377	249
Income before extraordinary loss	$ 1,666	1,460	944	531	272	149
Net income	$ 1,666	$ 1,460	$ 944	$ 518	$ 272	$ 149
Income before extraordinary loss per common share[a][b]						
Basic	$0.66	$0.58	$0.36	$0.19	$0.09	$0.06
Diluted	$0.61	$0.53	$0.32	$0.17	$0.08	$0.05
Number of weighted average shares outstanding[a]						
Basic	2,536	2,531	2,631	2,838	2,863	2,473
Diluted	2,728	2,772	2,952	3,126	3,158	3,000
Balance sheet data						
Working capital	—	$ 2,644	$ 1,215	$ 1,089	$1,018	$ 718
Total assets	$11,471	6,877	4,268	2,993	2,148	1,594
Long-term debt	508	512	17	18	113	113
Total stockholders' equity	5,308	2,321	1,293	806	973	652

[a]All share and per share information has been retroactively restated to reflect the two-for-one splits of common stock.

[b]Excludes extraordinary loss of $0.01 basic per common share for fiscal year 1997.

Source: Dell Computer Corporation 2000 annual report.

exhibit 3 Dell Computer's Consolidated Statements of Income, Fiscal Years 1997–2000 (In Millions, Except Per Share Data)

	Fiscal Year Ended			
	January 28, 2000	January 29, 1999	February 1, 1998	February 2, 1997
Net revenue	$25,265	$18,243	$12,327	$7,759
Cost of revenue	20,047	14,137	9,605	6,093
Gross margin	5,218	4,106	2,722	1,666
Operating expenses				
Selling, general and administrative	2,387	1,788	1,202	826
Research, development and engineering	374	272	204	126
Purchased research and development	194	—	—	—
Total operating expenses	2,955	2,060	1,406	952
Operating income	2,263	2,046	1,316	714
Financing and other	188	38	52	33
Income before income taxes and extraordinary loss	2,451	2,084	1,368	747
Provision for income taxes	785	624	424	216
Income before extraordinary loss	1,666	1,460	944	531
Extraordinary loss, net of taxes	—	—	—	(13)
Net income	$ 1,666	$ 1,460	$ 944	$ 518
Basic earnings per common share (in whole dollars)				
Income before extraordinary loss	$ 0.66	$ 0.58	$ 0.36	$ 0.19
Extraordinary loss, net of taxes	—	—	—	(0.01)
Earnings per common share	$ 0.66	$ 0.58	$ 0.36	$ 0.18
Diluted earnings per common share (in whole dollars)	$ 0.61	$ 0.53	$ 0.32	$ 0.17
Weighted average shares outstanding				
Basic	2,536	2,531	2,631	2,838
Diluted	2,728	2,772	2,952	3,126

Source: Dell Computer Corporation's annual reports.

exhibit 4   Dell Computer's Consolidated Statements of Financial Position, Fiscal Years 1999 and 2000 (In Millions of Dollars)

	January 28, 2000	January 29, 1999
Assets		
Current assets		
Cash and cash equivalents	$ 3,809	$1,726
Short term investments	323	923
Accounts receivable, net	2,608	2,094
Inventories	391	273
Other	550	791
Total current assets	7,681	5,807
Property, plant, and equipment, net	765	523
Other	3,025	547
Total assets	$11,471	$6,877
Liabilities and Stockholders' Equity		
Current liabilities		
Accounts payable	$ 3,538	$2,397
Accrued and other	1,654	1,298
Total current liabilities	5,192	3,695
Long-term debt	508	512
Other	463	349
Commitments and contingent liabilities	—	—
Total liabilities	6,163	4,556
Stockholders' equity		
Preferred stock and capital in excess of $.01 par value; shares issued and outstanding: none	—	—
Common stock and capital in excess of $.01 par value; shares issued and outstanding: 2,543 and 2,575, respectively		1,781
Retained earnings		606
Other		(66)
Total stockholders' equity	5,308	2,321
Total liabilities and stockholders' equity	$11,471	$6,877

Source: Dell Computer Corporation's 2000 annual report.

We'd say, "What's the best way to do this?" and come up with an answer. The resulting process would work for a while, then it would stop working and we'd have to adjust it and try something else. . . . The whole thing was one big experiment.

From the beginning, we tended to come at things in a very practical way. I was always asking, "What's the most efficient way to accomplish this?" Consequently, we eliminated the possibility for bureaucracy before it ever cropped up, and that provided opportunities for learning as well.

Constantly questioning conventional thinking became part of our company mentality. And our explosive growth helped to foster a great sense of camaraderie and a real "can-do" attitude among our employees.

exhibit 5 Geographic Area Information, Dell Computer, Fiscal 1998–2000 (In Millions of Dollars)

	Americas	Europe	Asia Pacific and Japan	Eliminations	Consolidated
Fiscal year 2000					
Net revenue from unaffiliated customers	$17,879	$5,590	$1,796	—	$25,265
Transfers between geographic segments	48	5	2	(55)	—
Total net revenue	$17,927	$5,595	$1,798	$ (55)	$25,265
Operating income	$ 2,173	$ 403	$ 97	$(194)	$ 2,479
Corporate expenses					(216)
Total operating income					$ 2,263
Depreciation and amortization	$ 82	$ 41	$ 14	—	$ 137
Corporate depreciation and amortization					19
Total depreciation and amortization					$ 156
Identifiable assets	$ 2,456	$1,147	$ 413	—	$ 4,016
General corporate assets					7,455
Total assets					$11,741
Fiscal year 1999					
Net revenue from unaffiliated customers	$12,420	$4,674	$1,149	—	$18,243
Transfers between geographic segments	33	5	1	−39	—
Total net revenue	$12,453	$4,679	$1,150	($39)	$18,243
Operating income	$ 1,802	$ 446	$ 78	—	$ 2,326
Corporate expenses					−(280)
Total operating income					$ 2,046
Depreciation and amortization	$ 59	$ 29	$ 8	—	$ 96
Corporate depreciation and amortization					7
Total depreciation and amortization					$ 103
Identifiable assets	$ 1,640	$1,017	$ 234	—	$ 2,891
General corporate assets					3,986
Total assets					$ 6,877
Fiscal year 1998					
Net revenue from unaffiliated customers	$ 8,531	$2,956	$ 840	—	$12,327
Transfers between geographic segments	67	17	—	−84	—
Total net revenue	$ 8,598	$2,973	$ 840	($84)	$12,327
Operating income	$ 1,152	$ 255	$ 33	—	$ 1,440
Corporate expenses					−(124)
Total operating income					$ 1,316
Depreciation and amortization	$ 42	$ 16	$ 5	—	$ 63
Corporate depreciation and amortization					4
Total depreciation and amortization					$ 67
Identifiable assets	$ 1,363	$ 605	$ 172	—	$ 2,140
General corporate assets					2,128
Total assets					$ 4,268

Source: Dell Computer Corporation's 1998 and 2000 annual reports.

> We challenged ourselves constantly, to grow more or to provide better service to our customers; and each time we set a new goal, we would make it. Then we would stop for a moment, give each other a few high fives, and get started on tackling the next goal.[5]

In 1986, to provide the company with much-needed managerial and financial experience, Michael Dell brought in Lee Walker, a 51-year-old venture capitalist, as president and chief operating officer. Walker had a fatherly image, came to know company employees by name, and proved to be a very effective internal force in implementing Michael Dell's ideas for growing the company. Walker became Michael Dell's mentor, built up his confidence and managerial skills, helped him learn how to translate his fertile entrepreneurial instincts into effective business plans and actions, and played an active role in grooming him into an able and polished executive.[6] Under Walker's tutelage, Michael Dell became intimately familiar with all parts of the business, overcame his shyness, learned the ins and outs of managing a fast-growing enterprise, and turned into a charismatic executive with an instinct for motivating people and winning their loyalty and respect. Walker also proved instrumental in helping Michael Dell recruit distinguished and able people to serve on the board of directors when the company went public in 1988. When Walker had to leave the company in 1990 because of health reasons, Dell turned for advice to Morton Meyerson, former CEO and president of Electronic Data Systems. Meyerson provided guidance on how to transform Dell Computer from a fast-growing medium-sized company into a billion-dollar enterprise.

Though sometimes given to displays of impatience, Michael Dell usually spoke in a quiet, reflective manner and came across as a person with maturity and seasoned judgment far beyond his age. His prowess was based more on having a pragmatic combination of astute entrepreneurial instincts, good technical knowledge, and marketing savvy rather than on being a pioneering techno-wizard. By the late 1990s, he was a much-sought-after speaker at industry and company conferences. (He received 100 requests to speak in 1997, 800 in 1998, and over 1,200 in 1999.) He was considered an accomplished public speaker and his views and opinions about the future of PCs, the Internet, and e-commerce practices carried considerable weight both in the PC industry and among executives worldwide. His speeches were usually full of usable information about the nuts and bolts of Dell Computer's business model and the compelling advantages of incorporating e-commerce technology and practices into a company's operations. A *USA Today* article labeled him "the guru of choice on e-commerce" because top executives across the world were so anxious to get his take on the business potential of the Internet and possible efficiency gains from integrating e-commerce into daily business operations.[7]

Michael Dell was considered a very accessible CEO and a role model for young executives because he had done what many of them were trying to do. He delegated authority to subordinates, believing that the best results came from "[turning] loose talented people who can be relied upon to do what they're supposed to do." Business associates viewed Michael Dell as an aggressive personality and an extremely competitive risk-taker who had always played close to the edge. Moreover, the people Dell hired had similar traits, which translated into an aggressive, competitive, intense corporate culture with a strong sense of mission and dedication. Inside Dell, Michael was

---

[5]Michael Dell, *Direct from Dell* (New York: HarperBusiness, 1999), pp. 17–20.
[6]"The Education of Michael Dell," *Business Week,* March 22, 1993, p. 86.
[7]"E-Commerce's Guru of Choice," *USA Today,* April 15, 1999, p. 3B.

noted for his obsessive, untiring attention to detail—a trait which employees termed "Michaelmanaging."

Michael Dell's Business Philosophy   In the 15 years since the company's founding, Michael Dell's understanding of what it took to build and operate a successful company in a fast-changing, high-velocity marketplace had matured considerably. His experience at Dell Computer and in working with both customers and suppliers had taught him a number of valuable lessons and shaped his leadership style. The following quotes provide insight into his business philosophy and practices:

> Believe in what you are doing. If you've got an idea that's really powerful, you've just got to ignore the people who tell you it won't work, and hire people who embrace your vision.

> It is as important to figure out what you're not going to do as it is to know what you are going to do.

> We instituted the practice of strong profit and loss management. By demanding a detailed P&L for each business unit, we learned the incredible value of facts and data in managing a complex business. As we have grown, Dell has become a highly data- and P&L- driven company, values that have since become core to almost everything we do.

> For us, growing up meant figuring out a way to combine our signature, informal style and "want to" attitude with the "can do" capabilities that would allow us to develop as a company. It meant incorporating into our everyday structure the valuable lessons we'd begun to learn using P&Ls. It meant focusing our employees to think in terms of shareholder value. It meant respecting the three golden rules at Dell: (1) Disdain inventory, (2) Always listen to the customer, and (3) Never sell indirect.

> I've always tried to surround myself with the best talent I could find. When you're the leader of a company, be it large or small, you can't do everything yourself. The more talented people you have to help you, the better off you and the company will be.

> A company's success should always be defined by its strategy and its ideas—and it should not be limited by the abilities of the people running it . . . When you are trying to grow a new business, you really need the experience of others who have been there and can help you anticipate and plan for things you might have never thought of.

> For any company to succeed, it's critical for top management to share power successfully. You have to be focused on achieving goals for the organization, not on accumulating power for yourself. Hoarding power does not translate into success for shareholders and customers; pursuing the goals of the company does. You also need to respect one another, and communicate so constantly that you're practically of one mind on the most important topics and issues that face the company.

> I have segmented my own job twice. Back in 1993–1994, it was becoming very clear to me that there was far too much to be done and far more opportunities than I could pursue myself . . . That was one of the reasons I asked Mort Topfer to join the company (as vice-chairman) . . . As the company continued to grow, we again segmented the job. In 1997, we promoted Kevin Rollins, who had been a key member of our executive team since 1996, to what we now call the office of the chairman. The three of us together run the company.

> Beyond winning and satisfying your customer, the objective must be to delight your customer—not just once but again and again. I spend about 40 percent of my time with customers . . . Customers know that I am not looking for insincere praise, or an affirmation of our strengths. They know by the quantity of the time that I spend and the kinds of questions that I ask that I want to hear the truth, and that I want to walk away with a list of ideas about how we can work to make a valued partnership that much more significant . . . When you delight your customers—consistently—by offering better products and better services, you create strong loyalty. When you go beyond that to build a meaningful, memorable total experience, you win customers for life. Our goal, at the end of the day, is for our customers to say, "Dell *is* the smarter way to buy a computer."

The pace of decisions moves too quickly these days to waste time noodling over a decision. And while we strive to always make the right choice, I believe it's better to be first at the risk of being wrong than it is to be 100 percent perfect two years too late. You can't possibly make the quickest or best decisions without data. Information is the key to any competitive advantage. But data doesn't just drop by your office to pay you a visit. You've got to go out and gather it. I do this by roaming around. I don't want my interactions planned; I want anecdotal feedback. I want to hear spontaneous remarks . . . I want to happen upon someone who is stumped by a customer's question—and help answer it if I can . . . I show up at the factory to talk to people unannounced, to talk to people on the shop floor and to see what's really going on. I go to brown-bag lunches two or three times a month, and meet with a cross-section of people from all across the company.[8]

Developments at Dell in Early 2000

Dell's unit shipments in the fourth quarter of 1999 were 3.36 million units, compared to 2.3 million units in the fourth quarter of 1998. In laptop PCs, Dell moved into second place in U.S. sales and fourth place worldwide in 1999. In higher-margin products like servers and workstations running on Windows NT, Windows 2000, and Linux, Dell ranked number two in market share in the United States and number three worldwide. In Europe, Dell ranked first in market share in Great Britain, third in market share in France, and second overall behind Compaq Computer. In Asia, Dell's sales were up 87 percent over 1998, despite sluggishness in the economies of several important Asian countries.

In 1999, about half of the industry's PC sales consisted of computers selling for less than $1,000. Dell's average selling price was $2,000 per unit in 1999, down from $2,500 in the first quarter of 1998. The company had recently introduced a line of WebPCs that was intended mainly for browsing the Internet. To counter the decline in the average selling prices of PCs, the company was placing increased emphasis on its line of PowerEdge servers and its Precision line of workstations, where average selling prices were $4,000 and higher, depending on the model.

MARKET CONDITIONS IN THE PC INDUSTRY IN 2000

There were an estimated 350 million PCs in use worldwide in 2000. Annual sales of PCs were approaching 130 million units annually (see Exhibit 6). About 50 million of the world's 350 million PCs were believed to have Intel 486 or older microprocessors with speeds of 75 megahertz or less. The world's population was over 6 billion people. Many industry experts foresaw a time when the installed base of PCs would exceed 1 billion units, and some believed the total would eventually reach 1.5 billion—a ratio of one PC for each four people. Forecasters also predicted that there would be a strong built-in replacement demand as microprocessor speeds continued to escalate past 1,000 megahertz. A microprocessor operating at 450 megahertz could process 600 million instructions per second (MIPS); Intel had forecast that it would be able to produce microprocessors capable of 100,000 MIPS by 2011. Such speeds were expected to spawn massive increases in computing functionality and altogether new uses and applications for PCs and computing devices of all types.

---

[8]Dell, *Direct from Dell,* pp. 29, 57, 50, 59, 60, 64, 65, 69, 139–40, 168–69, and 116.

exhibit 6   Actual and Projected Worldwide Shipments of PCs

Year	PC Volume (Millions)
1980	1
1985	11
1990	24
1995	58
1996	69
1997	80
1998	91
1999	113
2000	130 (projected)
2003	190 (projected)

Source: International Data Corp.

At the same time, forecasters expected demand for high-end servers carrying price tags of $5,000 to over $100,000 to continue to be especially strong because of the rush of companies all across the world to expand their Internet and e-commerce presence. Full global build-out of the Internet was expected to entail installing millions of high-speed servers.

Declining PC Prices and Intense Competition

Sharp drops in the prices of a number of PC components (chiefly, disk drives, memory chips, and microprocessors) starting in late 1997 had allowed PC makers to dramatically lower PC prices—sales of PCs priced under $1,500 were booming by early 1998. Compaq, IBM, Hewlett-Packard, and several other PC makers began marketing sub-$1,000 PCs in late 1997. In December 1997, the average purchase price of a desktop computer fell below $1,300 for the first time. It was estimated that about half of all PCs sold in 1998 were computers carrying price tags under $1,500; by 1999, close to half of all PCs sold were units under $1,000. Growth in unit volume was being driven largely by sub-$1,000 PCs. The low prices were attracting first-time buyers into the market and were also causing second- and third-time PC buyers looking to upgrade to more powerful PCs to forgo top-of-the-line machines priced in the traditional $2,000–$3,500 range in favor of lower-priced PCs that were almost as powerful and well-equipped. Powerful, multifeatured notebook computers that had formerly sold for $4,000 to $6,500 in November 1997 were selling for $1,500 to $3,500 in December 1999. The profits at Compaq, IBM, and several other PC makers began sliding in early 1998 and continued under pressure in 1999. Declining PC prices and mounting losses in PCs prompted IBM to withdraw from selling desktop PCs in 1999.

However, unexpected shortages of certain key components (namely, memory chips and screens for notebook computers) drove up prices for these items in late 1999 and moderated the decline in PC prices somewhat. But the shortages were expected to last only until suppliers could gear up production levels.

Continuing Economic Problems in Parts of Asia

Economic woes in a number of Asian countries (most notably, Japan, South Korea, Thailand, Indonesia, and to some extent, China) had put a damper on PC sales in Asia starting in 1997 and continuing through much of 1999. Asian sales of PCs in 1998 grew minimally (though sales were fairly robust in China); sales improved in 1999 but remained depressed in Thailand, Indonesia, and several other countries. China began experiencing some economic problems in 1999. In addition, sharp appreciation of the U.S. dollar against Asian currencies had made U.S.-produced PCs more expensive in terms of local currency to Asian buyers. In contrast, sales growth in the United States and Europe in 1999 remained strong, despite all the Y2K fears, mainly because of lower PC prices.

Disk-drive manufacturers and the makers of printed circuit boards, many of which were in Asia, were feeling the pressures of declining prices and skimpy profit margins. Industry observers were predicting that competitive conditions in the Asia-Pacific PC market favored growing market shares by the top four or five players and the likely exit of PC makers that could not compete profitably.

The Uncertain Near-Term Outlook for PC Industry Growth

While few industry observers doubted the long-term market potential for PC sales, there were several troubling signs on the near-term horizon, along with differences of opinion about just how fast the market for PCs would grow. A number of industry observers were warning of a global slowdown in the sales of PCs in 2000 and beyond, partly due to the economic difficulties in several Asian countries and partly due to approaching market maturity for PCs in the United States, Japan, and parts of Europe. Consequently, some analysts were forecasting gradual slowing of the industry growth rates from the 20–25 percent levels that characterized the 1990s down to the 10–12 percent range by 2005. However, U.S. shipments of PCs in the 1997–99 period had grown 20–25 percent annually, a much higher rate than most industry analysts had expected. Some 45 million new PCs were sold in the United States alone in 1999. Sales of servers, along with low-end PCs and workstations, were the fastest-growing segments of the PC industry in 1999 and were expected to be the segment growth leaders in 2000 and beyond.

On the positive side, some analysts expected that worldwide computer hardware sales in 2000–2003 period would grow at a compound annual rate of 15 to 20 percent, following cautious corporate buying in the second half of 1999 in preparation for meeting Y2K deadlines. Their expectations for 15–20 percent growth were based on (1) the introductions of Windows 2000 and Intel's new 64-bit Itanium microprocessors, (2) rapidly widening corporate use of the Internet and e-commerce technologies, (3) wider availability of high-speed Internet access, and (4) growing home use of PCs—as first-time purchasers succumbed to the lure of reasonably equipped sub-$1,000 PCs and as more parents purchased additional computers for use by their children. The three most influential factors in home ownership of PCs were education, income, and the presence of children in the household.

COMPETING VALUE CHAIN MODELS IN THE GLOBAL PC INDUSTRY

When the personal computer industry first began to take shape in the early 1980s, the founding companies manufactured many of the components themselves—disk drives, memory chips, graphics chips, microprocessors, motherboards, and software. Subscribing to a philosophy of "We have to develop key components in-house," they built expertise in a variety of PC-related technologies and created organizational units to produce components as well as to handle final assembly. While certain "noncritical" items were typically outsourced, if a computer maker was not at least partially vertically integrated and an assembler of some components, then it was not taken seriously as a manufacturer.

But as the industry grew, technology advanced quickly in so many directions on so many parts and components that the early personal computer manufacturers could not keep pace as experts on all fronts. There were too many technological innovations in components to pursue and too many manufacturing intricacies to master for a vertically integrated manufacturer to keep its products on the cutting edge. As a consequence, companies emerged that specialized in making particular components. Specialists could marshal enough R&D capability and resources to either lead the technological developments in their area of specialization or else quickly match the advances made by their competitors. Moreover, specialist firms could mass-produce a component and supply it to several computer manufacturers far cheaper than any one manufacturer could fund the needed component R&D and then make only whatever smaller volume of components it needed for assembling its own brand of PCs.

Thus, in recent years, computer makers had begun to abandon vertical integration in favor of a strategy of outsourcing most all components from specialists and concentrating on efficient assembly and marketing their brand of computers. Exhibit 7 shows the value chain model that such manufacturers as Compaq Computer, IBM, Hewlett-Packard, and others used in the 1990s. It featured arm's-length transactions between specialist suppliers, manufacturer/assemblers, distributors and retailers, and end users. However, Dell, Gateway, and Micron Electronics employed a shorter value chain model, selling direct to customers and eliminating the time and costs associated with distributing through independent resellers. Building to order avoided (1) having to keep many differently equipped models on retailers' shelves to fill buyer requests for one or another configuration of options and components and (2) having to clear out slow-selling models at a discount before introducing new generations of PCs. Selling direct eliminated retailer costs and markups. (Retail dealer margins were typically in the 4 to 10 percent range.) Dell Computer was far and away the world's largest direct seller to large companies and government institutions, while Gateway was the largest direct seller to individuals and small businesses. Micron Electronics was the only other PC maker that relied on the direct-sales, build-to-order approach for the big majority of its sales.

DELL COMPUTER'S STRATEGY

Dell management believed it had the industry's most efficient business model. The company's strategy was built around a number of core elements: build-to-order manufacturing, partnerships with suppliers, just-in-time components inventories, direct sales to customers, award-winning customer service and technical support, and pioneering use of the Internet and e-commerce technology. Management believed that a strong

exhibit 7   Comparative Value Chains of PC Manufacturers

Traditional PC industry value chain (utilized by Compaq Computer, IBM, Hewlett-Packard, most others)

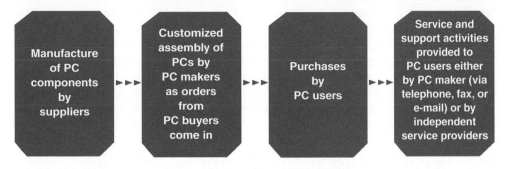

Build-to-order/direct sales value chain (employed by Dell Computer, Gateway, and Micron Electronics)

first-mover advantage accrued to the company from its lead over rivals in making e-commerce a centerpiece in its strategy.

Build-to-Order Manufacturing

Dell built its computers, workstations, and servers to order; none were produced for inventory. Dell customers could order custom-built servers and workstations based on the needs of their applications. Desktop and laptop customers ordered whatever configuration of microprocessor speed, random access memory (RAM), hard disk capacity, CD-ROM drive, fax/modem, monitor size, speakers, and other accessories they preferred. The orders were directed to the nearest factory. In 2000, Dell had PC assembly plants in Austin, Texas; Nashville/Lebanon, Tennessee; Limerick, Ireland; Xiamen, China; Penang, Malaysia; and El Dorado do Sul, Brazil. All six plants manufactured the company's entire line of products.

Until 1997, Dell operated its assembly lines in traditional fashion, with each worker performing a single operation. An order form accompanied each metal chassis across the production floor; drives, chips, and ancillary items were installed to match customer specifications. As a partly assembled PC arrived at a new workstation, the operator, standing beside a tall steel rack with drawers full of components, was instructed what to do by little red and green lights flashing beside the drawers containing the components the operator needed to install. When the operator was finished, the drawers containing the used components were automatically replenished from the other side, and the PC chassis glided down the line to the next workstation. However, Dell had reorganized its plants in 1997, shifting to "cell manufacturing" techniques whereby a team of workers operating at a group workstation (or cell) assembled an entire PC according to customer specifications. The shift to cell manufacturing reduced Dell's assembly times by 75 percent and doubled productivity per square foot of assembly space. Assembled computers were tested, then loaded with the desired software, shipped, and typically delivered within five to six business days of the order placement.

Dell's build-to-order, sell-direct strategy meant, of course, that Dell had no in-house stock of finished goods inventories and that, unlike competitors using the traditional value chain model (Exhibit 7), it did not have to wait for resellers to clear out their own inventories before it could push new models into the marketplace—resellers typically operated with 60 to 70 days' inventory. Equally important was the fact that customers who bought from Dell got the satisfaction of having their computers customized to their particular liking and pocketbook.

Quality Control Programs   All assembly plants had the capability to run testing and quality control processes on components, parts, and subassemblies obtained from suppliers, as well as for the finished products Dell assembled. Suppliers were urged to participate in a quality certification program that committed them to achieving defined quality specifications. Quality control activities were undertaken at various stages in the assembly process. In addition, Dell's quality control program included testing of completed units after assembly, ongoing production reliability audits, failure tracking for early identification of problems associated with new models shipped to customers, and information obtained from customers through its service and technical support programs. All of the company's plants had been certified as meeting ISO 9002 quality standards.

Partnerships with Suppliers and Just-in-Time Inventory Practices

Michael Dell believed it made much better sense for Dell Computer to partner with reputable suppliers of PC parts and components rather than integrate backward and get into parts and components manufacturing on its own. He explained why:

> If you've got a race with 20 players all vying to make the fastest graphics chip in the world, do you want to be the twenty-first horse, or do you want to evaluate the field of 20 and pick the best one?[9]

A central element of Dell Computer's strategy, therefore, was to evaluate the various makers of each component, pick the best one or two as suppliers, and partner with them for as long as they remained leaders in their specialty. Management believed long-term partnerships with reputable suppliers yielded several advantages. First, using name-brand processors, disk drives, modems, speakers, and multimedia components enhanced the quality and performance of Dell's PCs. Because of varying performance of different brands of components, the brand of the components was as important or more important to some end users than the brand of the overall system. Dell's strategy was to partner with as few outside vendors as possible and to stay with them as long as they maintained their leadership in technology, performance, and quality. Second, because Dell's partnership with a supplier was long term and because it committed to purchase a specified percentage of its requirements from that supplier, Dell was assured of getting the volume of

---

[9]As quoted in Magretta, "The Power of Virtual Integration," p. 74.

components it needed on a timely basis even when overall market demand for a particular component temporarily exceeded the overall market supply. Third, Dell's formal partnerships with key suppliers made it feasible to have some of their engineers assigned to Dell's product design teams and for them to be treated as part of Dell. When new products were launched, suppliers' engineers were stationed in Dell's plant, and if early buyers called with a problem related to design, further assembly and shipments were halted while the supplier's engineers and Dell personnel corrected the flaw on the spot.[10]

Fourth, Dell's long-run commitment to its suppliers laid the basis for just-in-time delivery of suppliers' products to Dell's assembly plants. Many of Dell's vendors had plants or distribution centers within a few miles of Dell assembly plants and could deliver daily or even hourly if needed. To help suppliers meet its just-in-time delivery expectations, Dell openly shared its daily production schedules, sales forecasts, and new-model introduction plans with vendors. Using online communications technology, Dell communicated inventory levels and replenishment needs to vendors on a daily or even hourly basis. Michael Dell explained what delivery capabilities the company expected of its suppliers:

> We tell our suppliers exactly what our daily production requirements are. So it's not, "Well, every two weeks deliver 5,000 to this warehouse, and we'll put them on the shelf, and then we'll take them off the shelf." It's, "Tomorrow morning we need 8,562, and deliver them to door number seven by 7 AM."[11]

Dell also did a three-year plan with each of its key suppliers and worked with suppliers to minimize the number of different stock-keeping units of parts and components in designing its products. Current initiatives included using the Internet to further improve supply chain management and achieve still greater manufacturing and assembly efficiencies.

Why Dell Was Committed to Just-in-Time Inventory Practices   Dell's just-in-time inventory emphasis yielded major cost advantages and shortened the time it took for Dell to get new generations of its computer models into the marketplace. New advances were coming so fast in certain computer parts and components (particularly microprocessors, disk drives, and modems) that any given item in inventory was obsolete in a matter of months, sometimes quicker. Having a couple of months of component inventories meant getting caught in the transition from one generation of components to the next. Moreover, it was not unusual for there to be rapid-fire reductions in the prices of components—in 1997 and early 1998, prices for some components fell as much as 50 percent (an average of 1 percent a week). Intel, for example, regularly cut the prices on its older chips when it introduced newer chips, and it introduced new chip generations about every three months. The prices of hard disk drives with greater and greater memory capacity had dropped sharply in recent years as disk drive makers incorporated new technology that allowed them to add more gigabytes of hard disk memory very inexpensively.

The economics of minimal component inventories were dramatic. Michael Dell explained:

> If I've got 11 days of inventory and my competitor has 80 and Intel comes out with a new 450-megahertz chip, that means I'm going to get to market 69 days sooner.
>
> In the computer industry, inventory can be a pretty massive risk because if the cost of materials is going down 50 percent a year and you have two or three months of inventory

---

[10]Ibid.

[11]Ibid.

versus 11 days, you've got a big cost disadvantage. And you're vulnerable to product transitions, when you can get stuck with obsolete inventory.[12]

Collaboration with suppliers was close enough to allow Dell to operate with only a few days of inventory for some components and a few hours of inventory for others. Dell supplied data on inventories and replenishment needs to its suppliers at least once a day—hourly in the case of components being delivered several times daily from nearby sources. In a couple of instances, Dell's close partnership with vendors allowed it to operate with no inventories. Dell's supplier of monitors was Sony. Because the monitors Sony supplied with the Dell name already imprinted were of dependably high quality (a defect rate of fewer than 1,000 per million), Dell didn't even open up the monitor boxes to test them.[13] Nor did it bother to have them shipped to Dell's assembly plants to be warehoused for shipment to customers. Instead, using sophisticated data exchange systems, Dell arranged for its shippers (Airborne Express and UPS) to pick up computers at its Austin plant, then pick up the accompanying monitors at the Sony plant in Mexico, match up the customer's computer order with the customer's monitor order, and deliver both to the customer simultaneously. The savings in time, energy, and cost were significant.

The company had, over the years, refined and improved its inventory tracking capabilities, its working relationships with suppliers, and its procedures for operating with smaller inventories. In fiscal year 1995, Dell averaged an inventory turn ratio of 32 days. By the end of fiscal 1997 (January 1997), the average was down to 13 days. The following year, it was 7 days, which compared very favorably with Gateway's 14-day average, Compaq's 23-day average, and the estimated industrywide average of over 50 days. In fiscal year 1999, Dell operated with an average of 6 days' supply in inventory. The company's long-term goal was to get its inventories down to a 3-day average supply.

Direct Sales

Selling direct to customers gave Dell firsthand intelligence about customer preferences and needs, as well as immediate feedback on design problems and quality glitches. With thousands of phone and fax orders daily, $35 million in daily Internet sales, and daily contacts between the field sales force and customers of all types, the company kept its finger on the market pulse, quickly detecting shifts in sales trends and getting prompt feedback on any problems with its products. If the company got more than a few of the same complaints, the information was relayed immediately to design engineers, who checked out the problem. When design flaws or components defects were found, the factory was notified and the problem corrected within a matter of days. Management believed Dell's ability to respond quickly gave it a significant advantage over rivals, particularly PC makers in Asia, that operated on the basis of large production runs of standardized products and sold them through retail channels. Dell saw its direct-sales approach as a totally customer-driven system, with the flexibility to change quickly to new generations of components and PC models.

Despite Dell's emphasis on direct sales, industry analysts noted that the company sold perhaps 10 percent of its PCs through a small, select group of resellers.[14] Most of

[12]Ibid.
[13]Ibid.
[14]"Dell Uses Channel to Move System Inventory," *Computer Reseller News,* January 12, 1998.

exhibit 8   Rapid Expansion of Dell Computer's Target Customer Segments, 1994–2000

Target Customer Segments			
1994	**1996**	**1997**	**2000**
• Large customers (both corporate and governmental buyers) • Small customers (both small businesses and individuals)	• Large companies • Midsize companies • Government agencies and educational institutions • Small customers (both small businesses and individuals)	• Global enterprise accounts • Large companies • Midsize companies • Federal agencies • State and local government agencies • Educational institutions • Small companies • Individual consumers	• Global enterprise accounts • Large and midsize companies (over 400 employees) • Health care businesses (over 400 employees) • Federal government • State and local government • Education—K–12 and higher education institutions (including special programs for personal-use purchases by faculty, staff, and students) • Small companies (under 400 employees) • Home and home office

Source: Joan Magretta, "The Power of Virtual Integration: An Interview with Dell Computer's Michael Dell," *Harvard Business Review,* March–April 1998, p. 78, and www.dell.com, February 1, 2000.

these resellers were systems integrators. It was standard for Dell not to allow returns on orders from resellers or to provide price protection in the event of subsequent declines in market prices. From time to time, Dell offered its resellers incentive promotions at up to a 20 percent discount from its advertised prices on end-of-life models. Dell was said to have no plans to expand its reseller network, which consisted of 50 to 60 dealers.

Dell's Use of Market Segmentation   To make sure that each type of computer user was well served, Dell had made a special effort to segment the buyers of its computers into relevant groups and to place managers in charge of developing sales and service programs appropriate to the needs and expectations of each market segment. Until the early 1990s, Dell had operated with sales and service programs aimed at just two market segments: (1) corporate and governmental buyers who purchased in large volumes and (2) small buyers (individuals and small businesses). But as sales took off in 1995–97, these segments were subdivided into finer, more homogeneous categories (see Exhibit 8).

In 1999, 65 percent of Dell's sales were to large corporations, government agencies, and educational institutions. Many of these large customers typically ordered thousands of units at a time and bought at least $1 million in PCs annually. Dell had hundreds of sales representatives calling on large corporate and institutional accounts. Its customer list included Shell Oil, Sony, Exxon-Mobil, MCI, Ford Motor, Toyota, Eastman Chemical, Boeing, Goldman Sachs, Oracle, Microsoft, Woolwich (a British bank with $64 billion in assets), Michelin, Unilever, Deutsche Bank, Wal-Mart, and First Union (one of the 10 largest U.S. banks). However, no one customer represented more than 2 percent of total sales.

Dell's sales to individuals and small businesses were made by telephone, fax, and the Internet. It had a call center in the United States with toll-free phone lines; customers could talk with a sales representative about specific models, get information faxed or mailed to them, place an order, and pay by credit card. Internationally, Dell had set up toll-free call centers in Europe and Asia.[15] The call centers were equipped with technology that routed calls from a particular country to a particular call center. Thus, for example, a customer calling from Lisbon, Portugal, was automatically directed to the call center in Montpelier, France, and connected to a Portuguese-speaking sales rep. Dell began Internet sales at its Web site (www.dell.com) in 1995, almost overnight achieving sales of $1 million per day. In 1997 sales reached an average of $3 million daily, hitting $6 million on some days during the Christmas shopping period. Dell's Internet sales averaged nearly $4 million daily in the first quarter of 1997, reached $14 million daily by year-end 1998, and climbed sharply to $35 million daily at the close of 1999. In early 2000, visits to Dell's Web site for information and order placement were approaching 2.5 million weekly, about 20 times more that the number of phone calls to sales representatives. In early 2000, about 43 percent of Dell's sales were Web-enabled and the percentage was increasing.

Dell in Europe   In fiscal year 1999, $6.6 billion of Dell's $18.2 billion in sales came from foreign customers. Europe, where resellers were strongly entrenched and Dell's direct sales approach was novel, was Dell's biggest foreign market, accounting for sales of $4.7 billion, up from $3.0 billion the prior year. Dell's European revenues were growing over 50 percent annually, and unit volume was increasing at nearly a 35 percent annual rate. Sales of PCs in Europe were 19.7 million units in 1997, 25.4 million units in 1998, and 29.9 million units in 1999. Expectations were for continued growth of 18 to 22 percent for the next several years. Europe's population and economy were roughly the same as those of the United States, but computer usage was only half that of the United States in 1999. Germany led Europe in sales of PCs, with 6.6 million units in 1999 (up 21.6 percent over 1998); Great Britain was second, with unit sales of 5.5 million (up 25.2 percent over 1998); and France was third, with 1999 unit sales of 4.4 million (up 26.7 percent over 1998). According to Dataquest, the top five market leaders in PCs in Europe were as follows:

Company	1999 Shipments	1999 Market Share (%)	1998 Shipments	1998 Market Share (%)	Percent Growth
Compaq	4,675,400	15.6	4,123,900	16.2	13.4
Fujitsu Siemens	3,471,600	11.5	2,615,000	10.3	32.8
Dell	2,612,200	8.7	1,943,600	7.7	34.4
IBM	2,340,300	7.8	2,107,400	8.3	11.1
Hewlett-Packard	1,897,600	6.3	1,482,900	5.8	28.0
Others	14,934,800	49.9	13,128,700	51.7	13.8
Totals	29,931,900	100.0	25,401,500	100.0	17.8

---

[15]"Michael Dell Rocks," *Fortune,* May 11, 1998, p. 66.

Fujitsu and Siemens had merged their PC operations in 1999 to move ahead of Dell in the ratings in Europe during 1999 (based on the combined market shares of the two brands); based on individual brand, however, Dell ranked second in Europe, ahead of both the Fujitsu brand and the Siemens brand.

Dell in China Dell Computer entered China in 1998 and by 2000 had achieved a market share close to 2 percent. China was the fifth largest market for PCs in the world, behind the United States, Japan, Germany, and Britain. But with unit volume expanding 30 percent annually and a population of 1.2 billion people, the Chinese market for PCs was expected to become the second largest in the world by 2005 (with annual sales of $25 billion) and to become the world's largest PC market sometime thereafter. The market leader in China was Legend, a local company; other major local PC producers were Founder (ranked fourth) and Great Wall (ranked sixth). IBM, Hewlett-Packard, and Compaq were among the top five market share leaders in China—all three relied on resellers to handle sales and service. Other companies among the top 10 in market share in China included Toshiba, NEC Japan, and Acer (a Taiwan-based company). Dell, ranked eighth in market share in 1999, was the only market contender that employed a direct-sales business model. Dell's sales in China in 1999 were up 87 percent over 1998 levels.

Dell management believed that in China, as in other countries around the world, the company could be very price-competitive by cutting out middlemen and selling direct via the Internet, telephone, and a sales force that called on large customers. Dell's primary market target in China was large corporate accounts. Management believed that many Chinese companies would find the savings from direct sales appealing, that they would like the idea of having Dell build PCs to their requirements and specifications, and that—once they became Dell customers—they would like the convenience of Internet purchases and telephone orders. Dell recognized that its direct-sales approach would temporarily put it at a disadvantage in appealing to small-business customers and individual consumers. According to an executive from rival Legend, "It takes two years of a person's savings to buy a PC in China. And when two years of savings is at stake, the whole family wants to come out to a store to touch and try the machine."[16] But Dell believed that over time, as Chinese consumers became more familiar with PCs and more comfortable with making online purchases, it would be able to attract growing numbers of small-business customers and consumers through Internet and telephone sales.

IBM was the market leader in 1999 in the entire Asia-Pacific region, with an estimated 8.4 percent share, up from 8.1 percent in 1998.[17] Compaq had a second-place 7.3 percent share but was the market leader in a number of individual countries within the region. China-based Legend had a 7.1 percent share, most all of which came from sales in China. Samsung had the fourth largest market share, followed by Hewlett-Packard.

Dell in Latin America In 2000, PC sales in Latin America were approaching 5 million units annually. Latin America had a population of 450 million people. Dell management believed that in the next few years use of PCs in Latin America would reach 1 for every 30 people (one-tenth the penetration in the United States), pushing annual sales up to 15 million units. The company's new plant in Brazil, the largest market in Latin America, was opened to produce, sell, and provide service and technical support for customers in Brazil, Argentina, Chile, Uruguay, and Paraguay.

---

[16]As quoted in Neel Chowdhury, "Dell Cracks China," *Fortune,* June 21, 1999, p. 121.

[17]According to data compiled by International Data Corporation and provided to the case researchers by IDC.

Customer Service and Technical Support

Service became a feature of Dell's strategy in 1986 when the company began providing a year's free on-site service with most of its PCs after users complained about having to ship their PCs back to Austin for repairs. Dell contracted with local service providers to handle customer requests for repairs; on-site service was provided on a next-day basis. Dell also provided its customers with technical support via a toll-free phone number, fax, or e-mail. Dell received close to 40,000 e-mail messages monthly requesting service and support and had 25 technicians to process the requests. Bundled service policies were a major selling point for winning corporate accounts. If a customer preferred to work with its own service provider, Dell supplied that provider with the training and spare parts needed to service the customer's equipment.

Value-Added Services   Selling direct allowed Dell to keep close track of the purchases of its large global customers, country by country and department by department—information that customers found valuable. And its close customer relationships resulted in Dell being quite knowledgeable about what each customer needed and how its PC network functioned. Aside from using this information to help customers plan their PC needs and configure their PC networks, Dell used it to add to the value it delivered to its customers. For example, Dell could load a customer's software at the factory, thereby eliminating the need for the customer's PC personnel to unpack the PC, deliver it to an employee's desk, hook it up, place asset tags on the PC, then load the needed software from an assortment of CD-ROMs and diskettes—a process that could take several hours and cost $200 to $300.[18] Dell's solution was to load the customer's software onto large Dell servers at the factory and, when a particular version of a customer's PC came off the assembly line, to use its high-speed server network to load whatever software the customer had specified onto the PC's hard disk in a few seconds. If the customer so desired, Dell would place the customer's asset tags on the PC at the factory. Dell charged customers only $15 or $20 for the software-loading and asset-tagging services—the savings to customers were thus considerable. One large customer reported savings of $500,000 annually from having Dell load its software and place asset tags on its PCs at the factory.[19] In 1997, about 2 million of the 7 million PCs Dell sold were shipped with customer-specific software already loaded on the PCs.

In late 1997, in another effort to add value for its customers, Dell, following Compaq's lead, created a financial services group to assist customers with financing their PC networks.

Premier Pages   Dell had developed customized, password-protected Web sites (called Premier Pages) for 40,000 corporate, governmental, and institutional customers worldwide. Premier Page sites gave customer personnel online access to information about all Dell products and configurations the company had purchased or that were currently authorized for purchase. Employees of Dell's large customers could use Premier Pages to (1) obtain customer-specific pricing for whatever machines and options they wanted to consider, (2) place an order online that would be electronically routed to higher-level managers for approval and then on to Dell for assembly and delivery, and (3) seek advanced help desk support. Customers could also search and sort all invoices and obtain purchase histories. These features eliminated paper invoices, cut ordering time, and reduced the internal labor customers needed to staff corporate purchasing and

---

[18]Magretta, "The Power of Virtual Integration," p. 79.
[19]"Michael Dell Rocks," p. 61.

accounting functions. A customer's Premier Pages also contained all of the elements of its relationship with Dell, including who the Dell sales and support contacts were in every country where the customer had operations, what software Dell loaded on each of the various types of PCs the customer purchased, and service and warranty records for each machine. So far, customer use of Premier Pages had boosted the productivity of Dell salespeople assigned to these accounts by 50 percent. Dell was providing Premier Page service to thousands of additional customers annually and adding more features to further improve functionality.

www.dell.com   At the company's Web site, which underwent a global redesign in late 1999 and had 50 country-specific sites in local languages and currencies, prospective buyers could review Dell's entire product line in detail, configure and price customized PCs, place orders, and track those orders from manufacturing through shipping. The closing rate on sales coming through www.dell.com were 20 percent higher than sales inquiries received via telephone or fax. The company was adding Web-based customer service and support tools to make a customer's online experience pleasant and satisfying. Already the company had implemented a series of online technical support tools:

- *Support.Dell.com*—This Web-based feature allowed customers to create a customized support home page; review technical specifications for Dell systems; obtain information and answers from an extensive database collected by Dell technicians, service providers, and customers; click on online links to Dell's primary suppliers; and take three online courses on PC usage at no charge. The site enabled customers to select how they received online help, based on their comfort and experience with PC technology. The information available at this part of Dell's Web site was particularly helpful to the internal help-desk groups at large companies. In late 1999, customer visits to support.Dell.com were running at a rate of 19 million per year.

- *E-Support*—Dell had developed advanced technology called "E-Support—Direct from Dell" that helped Dell systems detect, diagnose, and resolve most of their own problems without the need for users to interact with Dell's support personnel. The goal of Dell's E-Support technology was to create computing environments where a PC would be able to maintain itself, thus moving support from a reactive process to a preventive one. Michael Dell saw E-Support as "the beginning of what we call self-healing systems that we think will be the future of online support."[20] Dell expected that by the end of 2000 more than 50 percent of the customers needing technical help would use E-Support—Direct from Dell. Management believed the service would shorten the time it took to fix glitches and problems, reduce the need for service calls, cut customer downtimes, and lower Dell's tech-support costs.

- *Dell Talk*—An online discussion group with 100,000 registered users, Dell Talk brought users and information technology (IT) professionals together to discuss common IT problems and issues.

- *Ask Dudley*—The Ask Dudley tool gave customers instant answers to technical service and support questions. Customers typed in the question in their native language and clicked on "ask."

In February 2000, 40 to 45 percent of Dell's technical support activities were being conducted via the Internet. Dell was aggressively pursuing initiatives to enhance its on-

---

[20]As quoted in *Austin American-Statesman,* August 26, 1999.

line technical support tools. Its top priority was the development of tools (as described in the above list) that could tap into a user's computer, make a diagnosis, and if the problem was software related, perform an online fix. Dell expected that such tools would not only make it easier and quicker for customers to resolve technical problems but would also help it reduce the costs of technical support calls (currently running at 8 million calls a year). The company estimated that its online technical support tools had resulted in 25 percent fewer support calls from users, generating savings of between $5 and $10 per call.

Management believed that the enhancements it was making to www.dell.com made it easier and faster for customers to do business with Dell by shrinking transaction and order fulfillment times, increasing accuracy, and providing more personalized content. According to management, a positive Web site experience was a bigger driver of "e-loyalty" than traditional attributes like price and product selection.

On-Site Service   Corporate customers paid Dell fees to provide support and on-site service. Dell generally contracted with third-party providers to make the necessary on-site service calls. Customers notified Dell when they had PC problems; such notices triggered two electronic dispatches—one to ship replacement parts from Dell's factory to the customer sites and one to notify the contract service provider to prepare to make the needed repairs as soon as the parts arrived.[21] Bad parts were returned to Dell for diagnosis of what went wrong and what could be done to see that the problems wouldn't happen again. Problems relating to faulty components or flawed components design were promptly passed along to the relevant supplier, who was expected to improve quality control procedures or redesign the component. Dell's strategy was to manage the flow of information gleaned from customer service activities to improve product quality and reliability.

On-Site Dell Support   A number of Dell's corporate accounts were large enough to justify dedicated on-site teams of Dell employees. Customers usually welcomed such teams, preferring to focus their time and energy on the core business rather than being distracted by PC purchasing and servicing issues. For example, Boeing, which had 100,000 Dell PCs, was served by a staff of 30 Dell employees who resided on-site at Boeing facilities and were intimately involved in planning Boeing's PC needs and configuring Boeing's network. While Boeing had its own people working on what the company's best answers for using PCs were, there was close collaboration between Dell and Boeing personnel to understand Boeing's needs in depth and to figure out the best solutions.

Migration to New Technology   Dell had opened facilities in both Europe and North America to assist its customers and independent software providers in migrating their systems and applications to Windows 2000, Intel's new 64-bit Itanium computer chip technology, and other next-generation computing and Internet technologies. Dell was partnering with Intel, Microsoft, Computer Associates, and other prominent PC technology providers to help customers make more effective use of the Internet and the latest computing technologies. Dell, which used Intel microprocessors exclusively in its computers, had been a consistent proponent of standardized Intel-based platforms because it believed those platforms provided customers with the best total value and performance. Dell management considered both Intel and Microsoft as long-term strategic partners in mapping out its future.

---

[21]Kevin Rollins, "Using Information to Speed Execution," *Harvard Business Review,* March–April, 1998, p. 81.

Customer Forums   In addition to using its sales and support mechanisms to stay close to customers, Dell held regional forums to stimulate the flow of information back and forth with customers. The company formed "Platinum Councils," composed of its largest customers in the United States, Europe, Japan, and the Asia-Pacific area; regional meetings were held every six to nine months.[22] In the larger regions, there were two meetings—one for chief information officers and one for technical personnel. As many as 100 customers and 100 Dell executives and representatives, including Michael Dell, attended the three-day meetings. At the meetings, Dell's senior technologists shared their views on the direction of the latest technological developments, what the flow of technology really meant for customers, and Dell's plans for introducing new and upgraded products over the next two years. There were also breakout sessions on such topics as how to manage the transition to Windows NT, how to manage the use of notebooks by people out in the field, and whether leasing was better than buying. Customers were provided opportunities to share information and learn from one another (many had similar problems) as well as exchange ideas with Dell personnel. Dell found that the information gleaned from customers at these meetings assisted in forecasting demand for the company's products.

Pioneering Leadership in Use of the Internet and E-Commerce Technology

Michael Dell believed that the Internet had revolutionary business potential, and he was instrumental in making Dell Computer a pioneering first-mover in using the Internet and e-commerce technologies. In a 1999 speech to 1,200 Dell customers, he said:

> The world will be changed forever by the Internet . . . The Internet will be your business. If your business isn't enabled by providing customers and suppliers with more information, you're probably already in trouble. The Internet provides a dramatic reduction in the cost of transactions and the cost of interaction among people and businesses, and it creates dramatic new opportunities and destroys old competitive advantages. The Internet is like a weapon sitting on a table ready to be picked up by either you or your competitors.[23]

Michael Dell believed that for a company to harness the power of the Internet and succeed in revolutionizing the way business was done, it had to observe three rules:

1. Give customers a better experience online than they could get offline.
2. Execute efficiently.
3. Recognize that compressing time and distance in business relationships with suppliers and customers to enhance the velocity of business transactions is the ultimate source of competitive advantage. (Dell was convinced that transacting business with suppliers and customers in real time drove big improvements in business efficiency—requiring fewer people, less inventory, and fewer physical assets and speeding new products to market.)

Dell Computer was rapidly gaining valuable experience and know-how in applying these rules to its business. For example, the company had created valuechain.dell.com, which provided suppliers with secure personalized access to Dell's operations through a single portal. This tool facilitated real-time collaboration on the quality of the items being supplied, helped assure continuity of supply and minimal components inventories,

---

[22]Magretta, "The Power of Virtual Integration," p. 80.

[23]Keynote speech given on August 25, 1999, in Austin, Texas, at Dell's "DirectConnect Conference."

and made it possible for engineers at Dell and its suppliers to jointly develop online designs of next-generation components and products. Dell had also created an online "scorecard" for suppliers showing their performance against the quality standards that had been agreed on and how well they were doing against other suppliers in the same class. Both tools helped the company achieve its strategic objectives of product quality and reliability, rapid inventory turnover, and low costs.

Dell was using the Internet to improve its execution efficiency in several ways. By greatly improving the company's capability to provide order status information quickly and conveniently over the Internet, the company had been able to eliminate tens of thousands of order status inquiries coming in by phone. Order status inquiries handled by phone typically cost the company between $3 and $10; however, the cost could be considerably more if a customer had 100 orders and the status of each one had to checked. Close to 80 percent of Dell's order status inquiries in 2000 were being handled via the Internet at a cost close to zero, saving Dell an estimated $21 million annually and freeing personnel to do higher-value-added activities.

Although Dell was doing a very good job in solving 80 percent of customer issues over the phone (compared to an industry average of 27 percent) and saving money by not having to dispatch an on-site service provider, the company was working to greatly improve its online diagnostic technical support tools—Support.Dell.com, Dell Talk, and Ask Dudley. Management believed that Web-enabled technical support would make it easier and quicker for users to get the technical support they needed, as well as reduce the costs of handling the current total of 8 million technical support calls a year.

In 1998 the company had used technology to tackle the challenge of reducing its infrastructure cost of handling messages from customers. Michael Dell explained:

> The needs for our e-mail structure had grown beyond the support we had internally. We faced a very serious challenge. We were receiving 2.7 million messages per week within Dell's system, 4.3 million per month over the Internet, and our user base was growing at the rate of 50 percent per year. To solve this, we consolidated 200 servers into about 25 PowerEdge servers running Microsoft Exchange. There was a 10 times reduction in the number of servers and the associated management costs. We migrated to Exchange and lowered our user cost by 29 percent.[24]

Other Elements of Dell's Business Strategy

Other element of Dell's strategy, in addition to those mentioned above, are discussed below.

Demand Forecasting   Management believed that accurate sales forecasts were key to keeping costs down and minimizing inventories, given the complexity and diversity of the company's product line. Because Dell worked diligently at maintaining a close relationship with its large corporate and institutional customers and because it sold direct to small customers via telephone and the Internet, it was possible to keep a finger on the pulse of demand—what was selling and what was not. Moreover, the company's market segmentation strategy paved the way for in-depth understanding of customers' current needs, evolving requirements, and expectations. Having credible real-time information about what customers were actually buying and having firsthand knowledge of large customers' buying intentions gave Dell strong capability to forecast demand. Furthermore, Dell passed that information on to suppliers so they could

---

[24]Ibid.

plan their production accordingly. The company worked hard at managing the flow of information it got from the marketplace and quickly sending that information to both internal groups and vendors.

Forecasting was viewed as a critical sales skill. Sales-account managers were coached on how to lead large customers through a discussion of their future needs for PCs, workstations, servers, and peripheral equipment. Distinctions were made between purchases that were virtually certain and those that were contingent on some event. Salespeople made note of the contingent events so they could follow up at the appropriate time. With smaller customers, there was real-time information about sales, and direct telephone sales personnel often were able to steer customers toward configurations that were immediately available to help fine-tune the balance between demand and supply.

Research and Development   Company management believed that it was Dell's job to sort out all the new technology coming into the marketplace and help steer customers to options and solutions most relevant to their needs. The company talked to its customers frequently about "relevant technology," listening carefully to customers' needs and problems and endeavoring to identify the most cost-effective solutions. Dell had about 1,600 engineers working on product development and spent about $250 million annually to improve users' experience with its products—including incorporating the latest and best technologies, making its products easy to use, and devising ways to keep costs down. The company's R&D unit also studied and implemented ways to control quality and to streamline the assembly process. Much time went into tracking all the new developments in components and software to ascertain how they would prove useful to computer users. For instance, it was critical to track vendor progress in making longer-lasting batteries because battery life was very important to the buyers of portable computers. Dell was the first company to put lithium ion batteries with a 5.5- to 6-hour life in all of its laptop models.

Advertising   Michael Dell was a strong believer in the power of advertising and frequently espoused its importance in the company's strategy. His competitive zeal resulted in the company's being the first to use comparative ads, throwing barbs at Compaq's higher prices. Although Compaq won a lawsuit against Dell for making false comparisons, Michael Dell was unapologetic, arguing that the ads were "very effective" and that they allowed the company "to increase customer awareness about value."[25] Dell insisted that the company's ads be communicative and forceful, not soft and fuzzy.

The company regularly had prominent ads describing its products and prices in such leading computer publications as *PC Magazine* and *PC World,* as well as in *USA Today, The Wall Street Journal,* and other business publications. In the spring of 1998, the company debuted a major multiyear worldwide TV campaign to strengthen its brand image—the theme for the campaign was "Be Direct." A number of the ads featured Michael Dell talking about the importance of direct customer relationships, the company's attentive and responsive customer service, and the unique value created by the company's direct-sales and build-to-order approaches. One of Dell's tag lines was "Empower Your Business Through the Internet with Dell."

Dell's Increased Emphasis on Servers and Storage Devices   Dell entered the market for low-end PC servers (under $25,000) in the second half of 1996. Its entry strategy included adding 23,000 square feet of production capacity suitable for cell manufacturing techniques and self-contained work teams, training 1,300 telemarketers

---

[25]"The Education of Michael Dell," p. 85.

to sell servers, assigning 160 sales reps with systems know-how to big customer accounts, and recruiting a staff of systems experts to help the sales reps. It also contracted with companies such as Electronic Data Systems, which had in-depth systems and networking expertise, to help provide service to large customers with extensive server networks.

There were several drivers behind Dell's entry into servers. The use of servers by corporate customers was growing rapidly. The margins on servers were large. Moreover, purchase price was not as significant a factor in selecting which brand of server to buy because servers required far more in the way of service, support, and software. Several of Dell's rivals, most notably Compaq Computer, were using their big margins on server sales to subsidize price cuts on desktops and notebooks in an attempt to win corporate PC accounts away from Dell. According to Michael Dell,

> We had to meet the challenge of extending the Dell brand beyond our strong desktop and notebook franchises. The next logical step was servers. Entering the server business was not only a huge opportunity but clearly a competitive necessity. An explosion of networked and internetworked systems was occurring throughout corporations, which meant that our present customers—the techno-savvy, second- or third-time buyers who were our core market—would be looking to make big purchases.
>
> At the same time, the emergence of industry standards for operating systems (Windows NT) and multiprocessor servers meant that Dell could develop its own server systems based on these standards and avoid massive investments in new proprietary technologies that would ultimately become very costly for our customers. It also meant that we did not have to acquire a competitor to enter the server business.
>
> We could profit by offering lower prices through the direct model. We could, in effect, shatter the price premiums customers were paying for proprietary server technologies.
>
> The alternative wasn't pretty. Servers were a force literally big enough to change the operating environment. If we ignored them, the market would consolidate around the top three providers—Compaq, IBM, and HP. We would be seen as a bit player, and would lose our standing with technology providers. And our operating margins would start to thin.
>
> Our large competitors also were using excessively high margins in servers to subsidize the less profitable parts of their business, like desktops and notebooks. If we didn't move into servers, we would be greatly exposed to attack in the desktop and notebook market.
>
> We had the opportunity to do with servers what we had originally done with desktops and then notebooks: rapidly build market share by offering higher performance at a lower price, simultaneously forcing our competitors to lower their server prices and collapse their margins to the point where they couldn't afford to subsidize their other product lines. We couldn't afford not to take such an opportunity.[26]

As Michael Dell predicted, Dell Computer's build-to-order, sell-direct strategy gave it a significant cost and pricing advantage over rival sellers of servers. When Dell launched its new PowerEdge server line, the servers from such competitors as Compaq, IBM, and Hewlett-Packard, all of which relied on networks of resellers, were priced 15 to 20 percent higher than comparable Dell models. To communicate to Dell employees the importance of achieving success in the server market, the company sent out companywide "Message from Michael" e-mails, put up posters in high-traffic areas, and talked through the strategy at numerous brown-bag lunches and company get-togethers.[27] It also staged an event called "The Great Dell Torch Event" for 7,000 employees in a downtown Austin auditorium, opened by Michael Dell running into the auditorium carrying an

[26]Dell, *Direct from Dell,* pp. 82–83.

[27]Ibid., p. 84.

Olympic-sized torch. In meetings with customers Michael Dell and Dell salespeople told customers to ask their server vendors to meet Dell's pricing so they could at least save money on server purchases if they did not opt to buy from Dell. In the first year that Dell competed in servers, rivals cut prices about 17 percent on their competing models.

Dell's objective was to achieve a double-digit share of the server market by year-end 1998; it achieved that goal in the middle of 1997. By year-end 1997, Dell had gone from 10th to 4th in market share worldwide. By the fall of 1998, Dell had passed IBM and Hewlett-Packard in the U.S. market, moving into second place with a 19 percent share; and Dell was the only server provider growing substantially faster than the rest of the market. During the 1997–99 period, Dell expanded its lineup of server products to include more powerful models, added modular features, and boosted its service capabilities for servers. By 2000, the company had captured a sizable share of the market for low-end servers and was a significant competitive force in the server segment.

More recently, Dell had expanded its product line to include storage devices designed to handle a variety of customers' needs for high-speed data storage and retrieval. Dell's PowerVault line of storage products had data protection and recovery features that made it easy for customers to add and manage storage and simplify consolidation. Dell management saw storage devices as a growth opportunity because the computing systems of corporate and institutional customers were making increasing use of storage devices.

Dell's Introduction of a WebPC   In December 1999, Dell unveiled a new line of PCs stripped of fancy features and equipped for easy, quick Internet access by novices. The new line included three models, ranging in price from $999 to $2,349. Each came with a monitor, printer, technical support options, and one-year subscription to Dell's Internet service, DellNet. Each of the new WebPCs could be plugged in and made Internet-ready in three steps. The main unit was 6 inches wide, 11 inches high, and 10 inches deep and weighed 10 pounds. Dell believed the new line would help broaden the market for its products and give it a growing presence in the consumer and small-business segments. According to Michael Dell, "If Dell executes in the consumer and small business market alone this could add an additional $10 billion in revenue over the next several years."[28] Two competitors were planning to launch comparable products. Compaq Computer had announced it would begin selling an iPaq PC in early 2000 for $499 without a monitor. Advanced Micro Devices planned to introduce its EasyNow model in late December at prices of $500 to $1,000.

Dell's Efforts to Promote Good Strategy Execution

Michael Dell was a strong believer that good planning and good strategy amounted to little without good strategy execution. To promote effective strategy execution, the company had adopted a number of policies and operating practices. The company stressed use of facts and data in daily decision making—"Facts are your friend" was a common phase at Dell and an integral part of the corporate culture. The company had developed detailed profit and loss statements for each part of the business, and managers were expected to make fact-based decisions according to their impact on the bottom line; those who resisted were forced out.

---

[28]As quoted in Connie Mabin, "Dell Focuses on Novice Users with Simple WebPC," The Associated Press State and Local Wire, December 1, 1999.

Because much of what had contributed to Dell's success went against the grain of conventional wisdom, Dell Computer made a conscious effort to hire employees who had open, questioning minds and were always ready to learn and try something new.[29] Job applicants were screened carefully; the company looked for people who not only were results-oriented, self-reliant, and intelligent but also expected change to be the norm and liked looking at things from a different angle and coming up with unprecedented, innovative solutions. People were hired not so much for their ability to come in and fill a job opening as for their capacity to grow and develop with the company over the long term. Once hired, Dell employees were encouraged to be innovative, to look for breakthrough ideas, to challenge the status quo, and to experiment with new or better ways of doing things. Self-criticism and acceptance of periodic "course corrections" were ingrained in the Dell culture; everyone could question how things were being done and offer suggestions for improvement. Michael Dell preached against complacency and satisfaction with the status quo:

> We try to avoid being too proud of our accomplishments . . . If we start to think we've made it, we're just setting ourselves up to be eclipsed by someone else . . . It's easy to fall in love with how far you've come and how much you've done. It's definitely harder to see the cracks in the structure you've built yourself, but that's all the more reason to look hard and look often. Even if something seems to be working, it can always be improved.[30]

A substantial part of the work process at Dell was organized around teams. Teams were given objectives and were held accountable for their performance. For example, on the factory floor people worked in teams of two to receive, manufacture, and pack an order for delivery to a customer. Profit-sharing incentives encouraged members to be productive as a team. Hourly metrics for team performance were posted on monitors on the factory floor so that each team could see how it was doing relative to other teams and to performance targets. Ratings of individual performance were based on a 360-degree performance appraisal that involved input from everyone with whom an employee worked rather than just supervisors.

The vast majority of Dell's employees were also stockholders as a result of the company's employee stock purchase plans, stock option grants, and a 401(K) plan in which Dell matched employee contributions with stock rather than cash. The compensation and incentives of Dell employees were tied to the health of Dell's business, measured chiefly by the company's return on invested capital (ROIC) and growth rate. Tying compensation increases and incentive awards to ROIC began in 1995 with a companywide push to educate all employees to the benefits of boosting ROIC that included e-mail "Messages from Michael," articles in the company newsletter, posters, and talks by managers. The company explained how employees could contribute to a higher ROIC by helping reduce cycle times, eliminating scrap and waste, increasing inventory turns, forecasting accurately, boosting sales volumes, controlling operating expenses, collecting accounts receivable more efficiently, and doing things right the first time.[31] Dell executives believed that focusing attention on ROIC mobilized employees around a single company goal. And they believed that treating employees as owners helped employees understand the drivers of the business, fostered a sense of pride, and got them much more involved in the process of questioning procedures, experimenting with new ideas, and learning better ways to do things.

To spur the process of looking for innovations and new opportunities, Dell management made a practice of setting stretch objectives. In 1997, the company set a target

---

[29]Dell, *Direct from Dell,* pp. 109–11.

[30]Ibid., pp. 128–29.

[31]Ibid., pp. 134–35.

of selling 50 percent of its systems at www.dell.com within the next few years. At the time, Web site sales were averaging $1 million per day and annual revenues were $12 billion. The 50 percent target was not picked out of the air but was based on the company's growth, the market potential of the company's products, and the perceived potential of online sales.

Dell management spent a lot of time communicating to employees—explaining what was going on, what the company's strategy was, where the company stood in the market, what its future plans were, and what the organization needed to do to achieve its objectives. Michael Dell conducted "town hall" meetings at various locations annually and spent a lot of time answering questions. Company successes were celebrated at get-togethers and via e-mail communications congratulating teams on big account wins or other special achievements. Best practices in one area were shared with other areas. Much communication took place in real time via extensive use of e-mail and the company intranet.

The company made a concerted effort to avoid hierarchical structure, believing that hierarchy stymied communication and resulted in slower response times. Michael Dell explained:

> We're allergic to hierarchy. Hierarchical structure to me fundamentally implies a loss of speed. It implies that there's congestion in the flow of information. It implies the need for layers of approval and command and control, and signoffs here, there, and everywhere. That's inconsistent with the speed with which we all need to make decisions, both as leaders and as a company, in this fast-paced marketplace . . . Time is everything—the sooner you deal with an issue, the sooner it's resolved.[32]

RECENT CHANGES IN THE STRATEGIES OF PC MAKERS

Rivalry among the world's makers of PCs was quite strong in 2000. As the CEO of Gateway put it in January, "The environment in which we are operating is tough and getting tougher." Competitive pressures, which had been mounting since 1997, had prompted a number of companies to alter their strategies for competing.

The Attempts of Several Manufacturers and Retailers to Clone Dell's PC Strategy

Dell's competitors—Compaq, IBM, Packard Bell NEC, and Hewlett-Packard—were shifting their business models to build-to-order manufacturing to reduce their inventories and speed new models to market. Compaq launched its build-to-order initiative in July 1997 and hoped to cut costs 10 to 12 percent. Compaq's revamped assembly plants were able to turn out a custom-built PC in three to four hours and could load the desired software in six minutes. Packard Bell NEC's program allowed customers to place orders by phone. But all three were finding that it was hard to duplicate Dell's approach because of the time it took to develop just-in-time delivery schedules with suppliers, to coordinate their mutual production schedules, and to shift smoothly to next-generation parts and components as they appeared on the market. It took extensive collaboration to plan smooth technology transitions. Compaq and Hewlett-Packard had spent 18 months planning their build-to-order strategies and expected it would take another 18 or more months to achieve their inventory- and cost-reduction goals.

---

[32]Ibid., pp. 133, 137.

At the same time, such computer retailers as Tandy Corporation's Computer City, CompUSA, OfficeMax, and Wal-Mart Stores had gotten into the build-to-order, sell-direct business. CompUSA was offering customers two lines of desktop computers that could be ordered at any of its 134 stores, by phone, at its Web site, or through its corporate sales force; its goal was to undercut Dell's price by $200 on each configuration. Wal-Mart was offering build-to-order PCs made by a contract manufacturer at its Web site.

Dell was seen as having the right strategy to appeal to customers well versed in PC technology who knew what options and features they wanted and who were aware of the price differences among brands. According to one industry analyst, "Dell is everybody's target. No matter who you talk to in the industry, Dell is the brand to beat."[33]

The Moves of PC Makers to Broaden Their Business

Several leading players in the PC industry made moves in late 1997 and early 1998 to expand into selling more than just PCs in an effort to improve profitability. The sharp declines in the prices of PCs had crimped gross profit margins and prompted such companies as Dell, Compaq, Gateway, Hewlett-Packard, and IBM to view selling PCs as an entrée to providing a bigger lineup of products.

To move beyond simple PC manufacturing, Compaq in late 1997 acquired Digital Equipment Company (DEC), which derived $6 billion in revenues from providing a range of PC services to corporate customers. Both Hewlett-Packard and IBM had always viewed the PC business as part of a larger portfolio of products and services they offered customers. A substantial portion of Hewlett-Packard's revenues and profits came from sales of servers and printers. IBM derived a big portion of its revenues from mainframe computers, software, and technical and support services.

Dell, Gateway, and several other makers of PCs for the home market had begun offering Internet access service to purchasers of their PCs. Gateway's chairman, Ted Waitt, explained, "We're about customer relations a lot more than we are about PCs. If we get a 5 percent margin on a $1,500 PC, we make $75. But if we can make $3 a month on Internet access, that's another $100 over three years. Three years from now, I don't think just selling PC hardware will allow anyone to have a great business."[34] PC makers were also selling printers, scanners, Zip drives, assorted software packages, and other computer-related devices at their Web sites to boost revenues and overall margins. Several PC makers had begun leasing PCs to individuals and households and to finance PCs on low monthly payment plans in hopes of getting the customer to trade in the old PC for a new PC later when the lease expired or the last payment was made.

PROFILES OF SELECTED COMPETITORS IN THE PC INDUSTRY

Below are brief profiles of Dell's principal competitors in the global PC market.

Compaq Computer

In 1999 Compaq Computer Corporation was the world's largest supplier of personal computer systems and the second largest global computing company (behind IBM),

---

[33]As quoted in *Business Week,* September 29, 1997, p. 38.

[34]David Kirkpatrick, "Old PC Dogs Try New Tricks," *Fortune,* July 6, 1998, pp. 186–88.

with annual sales of $38.5 billion and profits of $569 million. Compaq became the world's largest seller of PCs in 1995, displacing IBM as the world leader. Compaq acquired Tandem Computer in 1997 and Digital Equipment Corporation in 1998 to give it capabilities, products, and service offerings that allowed it to compete in every sector of the computer industry.[35] When Compaq purchased Digital, Digital was a troubled company with high operating costs, an inability to maintain technological leadership in high-end computing, and a nine-year string of having either lost money or barely broken even.[36] The acquisitions gave Compaq a product line that included PCs, servers, workstations, mainframes, peripherals, and such services as business and e-commerce solutions, hardware and software support, systems integration, and technology consulting. Compaq management believed that additional unit volume provided by the Digital acquisition permitted greater economies of scale in production and gave it more leverage in securing favorable pricing from component suppliers.[37] Digital's extensive service and support network allowed Compaq to offer a comprehensive portfolio of professional computing services and technical support through a global network of approximately 27,000 employees as well as 30,000 service delivery partners.[38] Compaq had very strong brand recognition because of its status as the global market share leader in the PC market.

Compaq's Strategy Compaq's strategy was to sell almost exclusively through resellers—distributors and PC retailers, particularly large computer stores like CompUSA. In 1998 Compaq, responding to mounting competition in PCs, launched internal actions to emulate some of the key elements of Dell Computer's strategy. Compaq began efforts to switch from a build-to-stock to a build-to-order production model and intended to maintain Internet connections with its suppliers and customers to achieve a five-day or less cycle time between the receipt of an order and product shipment.[39] However, as of mid-1999 the company's order-to-delivery time was approximately 12 days (versus an order-to-delivery time of 3.1 days at Dell).[40] Compaq was also striving to improve inventory management and reduce transportation costs, but the results going into 2000 had been modest.[41] Because Compaq had bigger components inventories than Dell and because its resellers sometimes had sizable inventories of Compaq's models on hand, Compaq was slower than Dell in getting new generations of its PCs into the marketplace.

Compaq's extensive network of authorized reseller partners gave it strong distribution capability that covered more than 100 countries across the world. But Compaq's strategy of using reseller partners as its primary distribution channel was a weakness as well as a strength. Reliance on resellers put Compaq at a cost disadvantage relative to Dell, since Dell's direct sales approach entailed lower sales and marketing costs than

---

[35]"Can Compaq Catch Up?" *Business Week,* May 3, 1999, p. 163.

[36]Digital's competitive position is discussed in "Compaq-Digital: Let the Slimming Begin," *Business Week,* June 22, 1998.

[37]A discussion of the benefits of the Digital Equipment Corporation acquisition is presented in Compaq Computer Corporation's 1998 annual report; see www.compaq.com/corporate/1998ar/financials/MDA/purchased_nf.html.

[38]Compaq Computer Corporation 1998 10-K.

[39]Compaq Computer Corporation 1998 annual report; see www.compaq.com/corporate/1998ar/letter/english01_nf.html.

[40]"Can Compaq Catch Up?" p. 166.

[41]Compaq was said to have adopted a program that would reduce the number of destinations that the company shipped to by 70 percent by eliminating all but four distributors in North America in a May 10, 1999, *ComputerWorld* online news article; see www.computerworld.com/home/news.nsf/all/9905101compaq2.

Compaq's use of resellers. (Resellers had to mark up the factory price they paid Compaq to cover their own selling, general, and administrative costs and realize an adequate return on investment.) Compaq made a push in 1998 to promote direct sales over its Web site, an effort that irritated its 20 distributors and hundreds of reseller partners and may have prompted some resellers to push rival PC/server/workstation brands.[42] Nonetheless, there continued to be much debate among Compaq investors and Wall Street securities analysts about whether Compaq needed to put considerably more emphasis on direct sales and cut back its number of distributors in North America. Despite the pressures, Compaq management had so far refrained from further attempts to increase direct sales.

Compaq offered a full line of desktop PCs, from sub-$1,000 PCs to top-of-the-line models. It was an aggressive seller of PCs priced under $1,000. It also offered a broad line of laptop PCs. Compaq was also the market leader in PC servers priced under $25,000. Compaq's market strength was greatest among Fortune 1000 companies; it had weaker penetration in the small and medium business segments. To combat the volume discounts that Dell and other direct vendors typically used to help win the accounts of small and medium businesses, Compaq had recently begun working more closely with its resellers on special pricing to make the Compaq brand more competitive in the bidding process for these accounts. To boost its subpar 3 percent share of the Japanese market for PCs, in 1997 Compaq signed a deal that gave Canon Sales Company exclusive distribution and sales rights to Compaq's consumer-oriented Presario models.

Compaq's Acquisition of Digital Equipment Company   In early 1998, Compaq acquired the floundering Digital Equipment Company for $9.6 billion, a move intended to turn Compaq into more of a full-spectrum global supplier of computer hardware and services and put it into better position to challenge IBM as a "global enterprise computing company." Digital had 1997 revenues of $13 billion (versus $14.5 billion in 1996) and net earnings of $141 million (versus a loss of $112 million in 1996). The merged companies would have combined revenues of $37.6 billion, making Compaq the second largest computer company in the world. Following the merger, Compaq set a goal of $50 billion in revenues in 2000.

Digital considered itself a "network solutions company" with strengths in multivendor integration, Internet security, continuous computing, high-availability data, and high-performance networked platforms. Its chief products were large servers (those priced over $1 million), entry servers (those priced under $100,000), large computers and workstations, and personal computers (55 percent of revenues). Services accounted for 45 percent of revenues (about $6 billion); Digital had 25,000 engineers and support people in the field working with customers. (Compaq had 8,000 sales and support people in the field, many of whom spent much of their time servicing retailers of Compaq PCs.) Digital's gross margins on services averaged 34 percent compared to Compaq's 25 percent margins on PC sales. Compaq's corporate customers had been requesting the company to provide more service for years.

In May 1998, Compaq announced plans to cut about 15,000 jobs at Digital when the acquisition was completed; the layoffs were concentrated mainly in Digital's personal computer division, portions of its sales force, and corporate computer operations—where there were significant overlaps with Compaq's business. Digital had a total of 53,500 employees, down from a peak of 130,000 in the 1980s. But despite its recent

---

[42]"Can Compaq Catch Up?" p. 164. Many distributors and resellers carry more than one brand and can push sales of one brand over another if they are so inclined.

workforce downsizings, Digital in 1997 employed about 65 percent more people than Compaq to produce about half the volume of sales revenues. Compaq also moved aggressively to reduce Digital's high selling, general, and administrative (SG&A) costs (equal to 24 percent of total 1997 revenues) and bring them more in line with Compaq's SG&A expense ratio of 12 percent of revenues.

Compaq believed that Digital's expertise in networking and information systems integration, coupled with the combined product lines, would give it an advantage with large corporate customers over companies like Dell that offered mainly PC-related services. Compaq also believed that Digital's worldwide service and support capabilities would help it win corporate business for PCs, workstations, and servers away from IBM. (Prior to the Compaq-Digital merger, Dell had contracted with Digital's service organization to maintain its PowerEdge line of servers at a number of corporate accounts; following the merger announcement, Dell replaced Digital as a service provider.)

Problems at Compaq   Despite its status as the world's leading PC manufacturer and the new capabilities seemingly gained from the Tandem and Digital acquisitions, Compaq struggled throughout the 1997–99 period to maintain market share and profitability in the face of mounting price competition and declining PC prices. Furthermore, Compaq management got bogged down in trying to make a success of its acquisition of Digital. While Compaq was described as a company that was "consistently doing the right things and doing them well" at the time of the Digital acquisition, its efforts to get Digital's operations on track and integrated with those of Compaq were behind schedule and not going as well as had been anticipated.[43]

In April 1999, Compaq's board of directors removed CEO Eckhard Pfeiffer because of difficulty with the Digital acquisition and problems in executing the company's plans to copy Dell Computer's build-to-order, just-in-time-inventory, and direct-sales approaches.[44] After a three-month search to find a replacement for Pfeiffer from outside the company, the board chose an insider, Michael Capellas, the company's former chief information officer, to fill the vacant CEO position. Despite the leadership change and aggressive actions initiated by Capellas to return Compaq to profitable growth, Compaq's market share in PCs continued to erode in the United States, Europe, and Asia during the remainder of 1999. Compaq lost its claim to market share leadership to Dell in the U.S. market in the third quarter of 1999 and seemed in danger of losing its global market share leadership to Dell in 2000 if Capellas's turnaround efforts did not produce results. The financial performance of the company's three major business groups was as follows:

Business Group	1999 Revenues	1999 Operating Profit
Enterprise Solutions and Services	$20.1 billion	$2.3 billion
Products	13.5 billion	
Services	6.6 billion	
Commercial Personal Computing	12.2 billion	(448 million)
Consumer PCs	6.0 billion	262 million

---

[43]"Desktop and Mobile Weekly Update," *Dataquest,* February 12, 1998, p. 7.

[44]Compaq's difficulty in making a success of its Digital acquisition is discussed in "Compaq Chief Executive Pfeiffer Ousted," Associated Press Wire, April 19, 1999, and "Can Compaq Catch Up?" pp. 162–66.

Despite the weak 1999 performance, by early 2000 Compaq management believed that the aggressive actions taken in the last six months of 1999 were taking hold and laying the foundation for a comeback in 2000. Capellas said, "During the fourth quarter, we made great strides in defining a clear strategy, realigning for success, getting our cost structure in order, and re-energizing employees . . . We upped the pace in launching innovative new products, signing strategic partnership deals and alliances, and securing major customer wins."[45] Capellas went on to say that the performance of the Enterprise Solutions and Services group indicated "growing market acceptance of Compaq's high-end systems, solutions, and services, which customers are demanding to build nonstop 24 × 7 Internet computing environments." In January 2000, Compaq announced that it was spending $370 million to acquire certain assets of Inacom Corporation that would reduce inventories, speed cycle time, and enhance its capabilities to do business with customers via the Internet.

IBM

With 1999 sales of $87.5 billion and earnings of $7.7 billion, IBM was the world's largest seller of computer systems. IBM was considered a "computer solutions" company and operated in more segments of the overall computer industry than Dell. It had the broadest and deepest capabilities in customer service, technical support, and systems integration of any company in the world. The company's slow-growing computer hardware business had total 1999 revenues of over $37 billion from its internal and external sales of mainframe computers, PCs, servers, workstations, display devices, semiconductors, hard disk drives, printer systems, and storage and networking devices. IBM's global services business group, the company's fastest-growing group, was the world's largest information technology services provider, with 1999 sales of nearly $32.2 billion. The company's software business group had 1999 sales of over $12.7 billion and supported more than 29,000 independent software vendors (ISVs) to ensure that the company's software and hardware was included in ISV partner solutions.[46] In 2000, IBM had a lineup of over 40,000 hardware and software products.

IBM's Troubles in PCs   IBM's market share in PCs was in a death spiral—it had lost more market share in the 1990s than any other PC maker. Once the dominant global and U.S. market leader in the late 1980s and early 1990s, with a market share exceeding 50 percent, it was fast becoming an also-ran in PCs, with a global market share under 8 percent. Its last stronghold in PCs was in laptop computers, where its ThinkPad line was a consistent award winner on performance, features, and reliability. The vast majority of IBM's laptop and desktop sales were to corporate customers that had IBM mainframe computers and had been long-standing IBM customers.

Despite its eroding market share, IBM's position as the longtime global leader in mainframe computers and, more recently, as a broad line supplier of computer products and services gave it strong global distribution capability and potent brand-name credibility throughout the world. IBM distributed its PCs, workstations, and servers through reseller partners but relied on its own direct sales force for most corporate customers. IBM competed against its PC rivals by emphasizing confidence in the IBM brand and the company's long-standing strengths in software applications, service, and technical support. IBM had responded to the direct sales inroads Dell had made in the

[45]Compaq Press Release, January 25, 2000.
[46]IBM 1998 annual report, pp. 84–86.

corporate market by allowing some of its resellers to custom-assemble IBM PCs to buyer specifications; it was hoping this effort would cut costs up to 10 percent.

Going into 2000, IBM's personal systems (PCs and workstations) and server businesses accounted for just under 30 percent of corporate revenues, but both groups turned in weak performances in 1998 and 1999 and lost market share to rivals:

	Revenues		Pretax Profit	
	1998	1999	1998	1999
Personal Systems	$12.8 billion	$15.3 billion	($992 million)	($557 million)
Servers	$11.1 billion	$9.0 billion	$2.8 billion	$1.6 billion

IBM's PC group had higher costs than rivals, making it virtually impossible to match rivals on price and make a profit. In late 1999, IBM announced that it was discontinuing sales of its Aptiva Desktop PCs through retail channels in North America, although it would continue to sell Aptivas at its Web site. It also announced layoffs of up to 10 percent of its PC workforce and up to 6 percent of its server workforce. Like Dell, IBM was trying to cut technical support costs by getting its customers to use Internet-based support tools; for every service call handled through www.ibm.com, the company estimated it saved 70 to 90 percent of the cost of having a person take the call.[47] In 1999, IBM handled 35 million online service requests, saving an estimated $750 million in customer support costs.

To offset its declining share of PC and server sales, in 1998 and 1999 IBM moved to boost its R&D and manufacturing efforts to become a leading global supplier of computing components (hard drives and storage devices) and microelectronics products. During 1999, for example, it signed a long-term agreement with Dell to supply over $7 billion in components; it was increasing its sales of parts and components to other PC makers as well.

IBM's E-Business Strategy   Throughout the 1990s IBM had struggled to reinvent itself as the growing use of PCs continued to erode corporate dependence on mainframe computers and made mainframe sales and services a stagnating business. (Mainframe prices were falling faster than sales were rising.) While the company added new hardware and software products, revenue growth lagged and lower-cost rivals undercut many of IBM's strategic initiatives to grow. IBM's sales of computer hardware remained flat; revenue growth came chiefly from services and software. IBM's global dominance as a computer hardware systems provider faded. No cohesive new strategic theme really took root at IBM during the 1990s.

However, starting in 1998 and continuing on into 2000, the company's efforts to reinvent itself began to take on a distinct Internet and e-business theme. By early 2000 IBM was directing most of its strategic initiatives toward "e-business services" where it saw explosive growth opportunities. More than 50 percent of IBM's R&D budget was directed to Internet projects. Senior management believed that software and services were the soul of e-business and that the company had a full complement of resources to help corporate customers put integrated e-business capabilities in place. A growing majority of the company's 130,000 consultants were working to provide customers with integrated e-commerce and Internet technology solutions. The company

---

[47]Ira Sager, "Inside IBM: Internet Business Machines," *Business Week,* December 13, 1999, p. EB 34.

was opening e-business integration centers around the world where customers could meet with IBM specialists to develop next-generation e-business solutions. During the past three years, IBM had handled 18,000 Internet-related jobs for customers, ranging from Web page design to hosting entire online storefronts to hooking corporate databases into new online systems. IBM's revenues from pure e-business projects totaled $3 billion in 1999, but the company estimated that some $20 billion of its revenues was driven by customer demand for e-business solutions, an amount that was expected to grow significantly.

Most observers, as well as IBM executives, seemed to believe that IBM's future success depended far more on becoming the world's leading provider of e-business services than on strengthening its position as a provider of computer hardware. But it faced significant competition in e-business services and software from Intel (which was spending over $1 billion to set up rooms of servers to host Internet sites); Hewlett-Packard (which had a variety of initiatives aimed at do-it-yourself Internet technologies that required minimal consulting services and support); Microsoft (which was focusing increasing efforts on Internet-related software and serving e-business customers); Sun Microsystems; and numerous others.

Hewlett-Packard

Going into 2000, Hewlett-Packard (HP) was the world's leading seller of computer printers, the second-ranking seller of workstations, and a top-tier seller of PCs and servers. HP's product line also included scanners, digital cameras, storage devices, and networking software and equipment. The company recorded 1999 revenues and earnings of $42.4 billion and $3.1 billion, respectively.[48] Dell regarded Hewlett-Packard as a strong competitor because of the company's global leadership in printers (a 52 percent market share), HP's strong reputation with corporate customers in most all parts of the world, and its growing strategic emphasis on PCs, workstations, and servers. HP ranked fourth worldwide in desktop PC sales, first in worldwide sales of workstations, first in worldwide sale of handheld PCs, first in worldwide sales of both midrange and high-end servers running on UNIX operating systems, and among the top five worldwide vendors of servers running on Windows NT and Windows 2000. HP Pavillion PCs were the top-selling PC brand in U.S. retail stores. HP was a co-designer of Intel's new family of 64-bit Itanium microprocessors. HP's partnership with Intel on the Itanium was expected to put HP on the cutting edge of computer technology for the next several years and boost its brand image in PCs, workstations, and servers. The company spent $2.4 billion on R&D in 1998 and the same amount in 1999.

Hewlett-Packard marketed its PC line through resellers. HP's resellers could deliver orders to major corporate accounts within 12 to 24 hours. Hewlett-Packard had the capability to offer after-sale support to PC, workstation, and server purchasers around the world through 600 support offices, 35 response center locations in 110 countries, and a support staff of 17,500 people. The company had won numerous awards for the caliber of its services and technical support. It had 83,200 employees worldwide.

Over the past several years, HP had moved to improve operating efficiencies by outsourcing manufacturing assembly, reducing inventory and field-sales costs, and improving supply chain management. These efforts, combined with lowered component

---

[48]Hoover's, Inc., "Hoover's Company Profile Database for Hewlett-Packard," 1998, p. 1. HP's test and measurement business, which accounted for approximately 16 percent of 1998 sales, was spun off as a stand-alone company in March 1999; Hewlett-Packard Company 8-K (filed March 2, 1999), p. 1.

prices, had made HP aggressive in competing on price against its PC, workstation, and server rivals. Nonetheless, Hewlett-Packard's PC division, despite growing unit volume, was thought to be only marginally profitable. However, the company's sales of workstations and servers were major contributors to revenues and profits. In early 2000, the company reported that sales of home PCs and laptops were particularly strong.

Hewlett-Packard's board of directors chose Carly Fiorina, the head of Lucent Technology's Global Service Provider Business, as the company's new CEO in July 1999, to replace the company's retiring CEO. Fiorina had been designated by *Fortune* as the most powerful woman in business in 1998 and 1999. Believing that HP had grown sluggish and lacked entrepreneurial drive, Fiorina had immediately spearheaded initiatives to boost HP's revenue growth and profitability through increased attention to inventiveness and innovation. Fiorina's top priorities were to renew the company's energy and focus and to develop a stream of innovative products and new types of electronic services aimed at making the Internet "more warm, friendly, pervasive and personal." In late 1999, Fiorina announced a new global brand campaign and a new logo to reflect the reinvented, reenergized Hewlett-Packard.

Gateway

Gateway, formerly called Gateway 2000, was a San Diego–based company (recently relocated from South Dakota) with 1999 revenues of $8.6 billion and profits of $428 million. Founder and chairman Ted Waitt, 38, and his brother owned over 40 percent of the company. Waitt had dropped out of college in 1985 to go to work for a computer retailer in Des Moines, Iowa; after nine months, he quit to form his own company. The company, operating out of a barn on his father's cattle ranch, sold add-on parts by phone for Texas Instruments PCs. In 1987, the company, using its own PC design, started selling fully equipped PCs at a price near that of other PC makers. Sales took off, and in 1991 Gateway topped the list of *Inc.* magazine's list of the fastest-growing private companies. The company went public in 1993, achieving sales of $1.7 billion and earnings of $151 million. The company had differentiated itself from rivals with eye-catching ads; some featured cows with black-and-white spots, while others featured company employees (including one with Waitt dressed as Robin Hood). Gateway, like Dell, built to order and sold direct. It had entered the server segment in 1997. To promote the Gateway name in the retail marketplace, the company had opened 280 Gateway Country Stores—227 in the United States, 27 in Europe, and 26 in the Asia-Pacific region—that stocked Gateway PCs and peripheral products and that conducted classes for individuals and businesses on the use of PCs.

Going into 2000, Gateway was the number one seller of PCs to consumers. It was also a major contender in the small-business, educational, and government segments. Despite growing at a rate of nearly 38 percent annually in the 1994–97 period, Gateway saw its profit margins erode steadily from a high of 9.6 percent in 1992 to only 1.7 percent in 1997. Since then, however, company cost-cutting efforts and efficiency improvements had resulted in eight straight quarters of year-over-year margin improvement. Profits in 1999 were at record levels. Nonetheless, Gateway was feeling the pressures of falling PC prices and stiff price competition—although 1999 unit sales were up 32.3 percent over 1998 levels, revenues increased only 15.8 percent. The company's entry-level PC models, which started at $799, accounted for 20 percent of its sales to consumers.

To reduce its reliance on traditional PC sales, Gateway took aggressive steps in 1999 to diversify its revenue stream. In February, Gateway became the first PC maker to bundle its own Internet service with its PCs; at the same time, following Dell, Gateway launched an online software and peripheral Web store with more than 30,000 products. Meanwhile, Gateway increased its service and training offerings to consumers and small businesses at its 280 Country Store locations worldwide. In October, Gateway entered into a wide-ranging strategic alliance with America Online to accelerate distribution of each company's products and services. By the end of 1999, after adding 400,000 new subscribers in less than three months, Gateway's joint Internet service with AOL had more than 1 million subscribers. Gateway management believed its "beyond-the-box" strategy positioned the company extremely well for the future.

Gateway also took aggressive steps in 1999 to boost its sales to small businesses, government agencies, and educational institutions. It established a sales force operating out of its 280 Country Stores that called on area businesses and other organizations. An alliance with GE Capital was formed to promote technology solutions for large enterprises. In Europe, Gateway entered into a two-year partnership with ComputaCenter, Europe's leading information technology systems and services company, to sell and support Gateway PC products throughout Europe. During 1999, Gateway increased its sales over the Internet by 100 percent over 1998 levels.

To further enhance the Gateway brand with consumers, Gateway committed to sponsorship of the 2002 Winter Olympic Games in Salt Lake City, plus it entered into brand-enhancing alliances with Fidelity Investments and Nickelodeon. Gateway planned to open more than 100 new Country Store locations worldwide during 2000, including 75 in the United States. In early 2000, Gateway introduced a new line of home and small-business desktop PCs powered by Athlon microprocessors made by Advanced Micro Devices (AMD). The new Gateway Select PC line represented an effort to counter the difficulties the company was having in obtaining adequate supplies of Pentium microprocessors from Intel.

Toshiba Corporation

Toshiba was a $45 billion diversified Japanese electronics and electrical equipment manufacturer with 300 subsidiaries and affiliates worldwide; it ranked as the world's 26th largest corporation in terms of revenues and the world's seventh largest computer and electronics company. Toshiba produced and marketed portable and desktop computers, servers, voice-mail systems, digital business telephone systems, interactive voice-response systems, cable modems, networking systems, and digital, medical, and PC cameras. In the PC arena, Toshiba's biggest strength was in notebook PCs, where it had an 18 percent global share in 1999.

The company's Toshiba America Information System (TAIS) division, headquartered in Irvine, California, had annual sales of approximately $2.5 billion across the United States and Latin America. The TAIS division offered a wide array of portable PCs, selling both direct and through dealers—one of its largest U.S. dealers was Computer Discount Warehouse. In the mid-1990s, TAIS enjoyed a commanding lead over its U.S. laptop rivals in both channels, but its lead had been shrinking in recent years. During the 1996–99 period, TAIS's share of portable computer sales in the United States was in the 15 to 20 percent range. It had a negligible share of the desktop PC market.

Providers of House-Label Brands

There were about 30,000 resellers of generic, or "house-label," PCs in North America alone and countless thousands more worldwide. The generic segment constituted a $7 to $8 billion market in the United States and Canada, representing shipments of about 7 million units and 25 to 30 percent of sales through resellers. No single generic brand, however, accounted for more than 0.25 percent market share, and most had a lot smaller percentage share. Generic PCs assembled in" "screwdriver shops" had been a part of the PC business since its inception—Steve Wozniak and Steve Jobs launched Apple Computer from a garage using components they purchased. Rising technological savvy about how PCs worked and the widespread availability of individual components made it fairly easy for an enterprising operation to assemble a generic PC. Contract manufacturers of PCs, many of whom assembled name brands of PCs for several PC makers, were a major source of house-label PCs marketed by retailers. To keep costs and prices low, the makers of generic PCs typically incorporated components from low-end suppliers. Generic PCs appealed mainly to very price-conscious buyers. The quality and reliability of generic PCs varied from good to poor, depending on the caliber of their components. The makers of generic PCs generally took little responsibility for providing technical support; whatever technical support was available to users typically had to come from resellers.

MICHAEL DELL'S VIEW OF DELL COMPUTER'S BIGGEST CHALLENGES

Michael Dell believed Dell Computer's biggest challenge in the marketplace was to gain as much acceptance for the company's direct business model outside the United States as it had gained inside the United States. But an even bigger challenge, he believed, was gathering enough talented people to help the company pursue the opportunities in other countries. Dell was active in recruiting foreign nationals graduating from U.S. business schools. Those who hired on with Dell were sent to Austin, Texas, for a couple of years to learn about Dell and the Dell model and to work in various parts of the company's operations. Then they were given assignments to help in Dell's global expansion effort. Michael Dell believed the company needed the expertise of foreigners who knew Dell from the inside and who could help Dell Computer understand different cultures and respond in a sensitive manner to local customs and behaviors.

For the most part, Michael Dell was not particularly concerned about the efforts of competitors to copy many aspects of Dell's build-to-order, sell-direct strategy:

> The competition started copying us seven years ago. That's when we were a $1 billion business. Now we're $25 billion. And they haven't made much progress to be honest with you. The learning curve for them is difficult. It's like going from baseball to soccer . . . We're more challenged by new technologies on the market, some new computing model, something we haven't anticipated.[49]

Michael Dell's near-term vision was for the company to reach $50 billion in annual sales by growing more aggressively in the consumer and small-business segments in computer services, by increasing its market share in foreign countries, and by selling more powerful and more expensive servers to corporate customers.

---

[49]Comments made to students at the University of North Carolina and reported in the *Raleigh News & Observer,* November 16, 1999.

case | 8 Peapod, Inc., and the Online Grocery Business

Alan B. Eisner
Pace University

Nicole Belmont
Pace University

Peapod, Inc., cofounded by brothers Andrew B. Parkinson and Thomas L. Parkinson in 1989, was a $68 million online grocery service that used both its own central warehouses and the retail stores of supermarket partners to fill customers' grocery orders. Peapod was a pioneer of the online grocery industry, getting its start on the Internet well before the Internet became a global phenomenon and well before such competitors as HomeGrocer.com, Webvan, and NetGrocer.com were even organized. However, the company had grown more slowly than first anticipated, revising its trial-and-error strategy several times to find a formula that would attract more customers and make the company profitable. In September 1999, Andrew Parkinson relinquished the position of CEO and turned the reins over to a new president and CEO, Bill Malloy, who had been recruited from AT&T Wireless to fine-tune and execute Peapod's latest order fulfillment strategy and capitalize on what the cofounders believed was a blossoming opportunity in online grocery sales. Andrew Parkinson stayed on as chairman of Peapod's board of directors.

Malloy faced three daunting challenges at Peapod. He had to prove that the company's newly revised business model was viable; that the company could be made profitable after six years of mounting losses; and that it could withstand competition from HomeGrocer.com, which had recently allied itself with Amazon.com, and from newly formed Webvan, which raised over $350 million in its initial public offering of common stock in the second half of 1999.

COMPANY BACKGROUND

As noted above, Peapod was an early pioneer in e-commerce, inventing an online home-shopping service for grocery items years ahead of the commercial emergence of the Internet. With its tagline "Smart Shopping for Busy People," the company began

---

providing home shopping in the early 1990s, going so far as to install modems in consumers' homes to provide an online connection. Until 1998, the company's business model involved filling customer orders by forming alliances with traditional grocery retailers. The company chose a retail partner in each geographic area where it operated and used the partner's local network of retail stores to pick and pack orders for delivery to customers. Peapod personnel would cruise the aisles of a partner's stores to select the items each customer ordered, pack and load them into Peapod vehicles, and then deliver them at times chosen by customers. Peapod charged customers a fee for its service and also collected fees from its retail supply partners for using their products in its online service. In its first years, Peapod built delivery capabilities in eight market areas:

Chicago, Illinois

Columbus, Ohio

Houston, Texas

Boston, Massachusetts

San Francisco/San Jose, California

Dallas, Texas

Austin, Texas

Long Island, New York

The company steadily built a base of about 90,000 to 100,000 customers across all eight markets; it filled over 700,000 orders in 1999. Peapod's revenues rose from $8.0 million in 1994 to $73.1 million in 1999 (see Exhibit 1). Meanwhile, the company made improvements in its Web site (www.peapod.com) and invested in proprietary software technologies to facilitate efficient order fulfillment and delivery routes, accumulate data on customer buying patterns, and better integrate pricing, merchandising, and product promotion. The company went public in June 1997, offering shares at $16. During 1999 and early 2000, Peapod's stock (listed on the NASDAQ National Market under the symbol "PPOD") traded mostly in the $8 to $12 range.

In 1997, faced with mounting losses despite growing revenues, Peapod management determined that its original, partner-based business model entailed too high a cost structure for the company to achieve profitable growth. The cofounders opted to shift to a new order fulfillment business model using a local company-owned, company-operated central distribution warehouse to store, pick, and pack customer orders for delivery. By mid-1999 the company had opened new distribution centers in three of the eight markets it served (Chicago, Long Island, and Boston); a fourth distribution center was under construction in San Francisco. Peapod stocked its distribution centers with products purchased at wholesale from a variety of food and household products companies, including Kellogg's, Kraft, Colgate-Palmolive, Frito-Lay, Coca-Cola, Clorox, Kimberly-Clark, Procter & Gamble, Nabisco, Ralston Purina, Nestlé, Walgreens, and in some cases, traditional retailers. Peapod management had announced plans to use the centralized distribution model in all eight markets over time and in all new areas it entered. The company was reportedly losing money in five of the markets it served in mid-1999.

PEAPOD IN EARLY 2000

Going into the new millennium, Peapod was the largest Internet supermarket, with over 90,000 customers (based on a count of customers who had placed an order within the past 12 months). It had a 30 percent share of the estimated $235 million market for

exhibit 1   Six-Year Summary of Peapod's Financial Performance, 1994–99 ($000s)

Date	Sales	Net Income	Earnings per Share
1999	$73,134	($28,450)	($1.62)
1998	69,265	(21,565)	(1.27)
1997	56,943	(12,979)	(0.87)
1996	27,642	(9,566)	(0.82)
1995	15,209	(6,592)	(0.79)
1994	8,005	(4,437)	(0.75)

grocery products sold online.[1] The eight market areas where the company presently operated had an estimated 6.6 million households, representing approximately 7 percent of total U.S. households. Delivery operations in these areas were conducted out of 22 order fulfillment locations. Exhibit 2 shows the company's eight metropolitan markets, the number of households represented in each market, and the company's local retail supermarket partners. Peapod processed an average of 2,000 orders daily; the average order size was $110–$115 but ran a bit lower in areas where the company used central distribution warehouses—Peapod stocked fewer items at its warehouses than its supermarket partners stocked at their stores. Management believed that Peapod's average order size was about five times the in-store average of supermarkets and convenience stores.

Management's vision for the company was expressed in three statements:

- *Our Dream*—To fundamentally improve people's lives by bringing interactive shopping to a broad consumer market.
- *Our Mission*—To be the world's leading and preferred provider of interactive grocery shopping services.
- *Our Passion*—To amaze and delight each one of our customers.

Peapod's recent income statements and balance sheets are shown in Exhibits 3 and 4.

Peapod's Customers

Peapod's target market was a middle- and upper-income household with PC-savvy adults who were stressed for time and didn't particularly enjoy grocery shopping. This was the basis for its tag line, "Smart Shopping for Busy People." The company's market research indicated that its typical customers were women between the ages of 30 and 54 who lived in dual-income households and had children. The incomes of customers covered a wide range, with a median annual income exceeding $60,000.

Peapod's Strategy

Peapod's strategy was to provide customers with a convenient, user-friendly, personalized way of shopping for grocery items online 24 hours a day, seven days a week. Its product offerings consisted of fresh meat, produce, deli and bakery goods, name-brand

---

[1]Peapod, Inc., Investor's Overview, www.peapod.com.

exhibit 2 Peapod's Metropolitan Markets, Household Exposure, and Retail Partners, February 2000

Metropolitan Market Area Served	Estimated Number of Area Households, 1998	Retail Partners	Peapod Distribution Center
Chicago, Illinois	1,732,000	Jewel Food Stores	Yes
Columbus, Ohio	398,000	Kroger	
Houston, Texas	939,000	Randalls Food and Drug	
Boston, Massachusetts	1,242,000	Stop and Shop	Yes
San Francisco and San Jose, California	840,000	Certified Grocers of California, Andronico's, and Walgreens	Yes
Dallas, Texas	995,000	Tom Thumb	
Austin, Texas	257,000	Randalls Food and Drug	
Long Island, New York	226,000	Giant/Edwards Super Foods Stores	Yes

exhibit 3 Peapod's Statements of Income, 1996–99 ($000, Except Per Share Data)

	1999	1998	1997	1996
Revenues				
Net product sales		$57,305	$43,487	$22,015
Member and retailer		9,650	11,234	4,558
Interactive marketing		1,460	2,222	1,069
Licensing		850		
Total revenues	$73,154	$69,265	$56,943	$27,642
Costs and expenses				
Cost of goods sold	$55,585	$53,903	$40,823	$20,485
Fulfillment operations	24,478	17,196	14,469	6,889
General and administrative	9,788	8,029	5,935	3,785
Marketing and selling	7,168	7,545	7,726	4,739
System development and maintenance	3,543	3,386	1,696	1,124
Depreciation and amortization	2,222	3,264	1,234	651
Total costs and expenses	$102,784	$93,323	$71,883	$37,673
Operating loss	($29,650)	($24,058)	($14,940)	($10,031)
Other income (expense)				
Interest income	$1,384	$2,683	$2,044	$537
Interest expense	(187)	(190)	(83)	(72)
Net loss	($28,453)	($21,565)	($12,979)	($9,566)
Net loss per share	($1.62)	($1.27)	($0.87)	($0.82)
Average shares outstanding	17,542,990	16,964,439	14,915,734	11,664,956

Source: Company 10-K and 10-Q filings.

exhibit 4   Peapod's Balance Sheets, 1997–99 ($000)

	1999	1998	1997
Assets			
Current assets			
Cash and cash equivalents	$ 3,343	$ 4,341	$54,079
Marketable securities	4,704	15,836	8,798
Receivables	1,498	2,516	1,195
Prepaid expenses	473	186	444
Other current assets	993	974	228
Total current assets	10,991	23,853	64,744
Property and equipment			
Computer equipment and software	6,737	4,010	4,499
Service equipment and leasehold improvements	4,189	2,147	1,053
Property and equipment, at cost	10,926	6,157	5,552
Accumulated depreciation	4,290	(2,252)	(2,301)
Net property and equipment	6,636	3,905	3,251
Noncurrent marketable securities and restricted cash	3,143	15,213	
Capitalized software development costs	—	—	998
Goodwill	—	—	117
Total assets	$20,780	$42,971	$69,110
Liabilities and stockholders' equity			
Current liabilities			
Accounts payable	$ 6,147	$ 3,442	$ 7,514
Accrued compensation	497	802	1,258
Other accrued liabilities	1,897	2,688	926
Deferred revenue	615	1,000	1,969
Current obligations under capital lease	690	590	727
Total current liabilities	9,846	8,522	12,394
Deferred revenue	95	448	1,212
Obligations under capital lease, less current portion	1,129	395	701
Total liabilities	11,070	9,365	14,307
Stockholders' equity			
Common stock ($.01 par value, 50 million shares authorized; 17,245,828 and 16,852,557 shares issued in 1998 and 1997)	$ 183	$ 172	$ 169
Additional paid-in capital	71,698	64,319	63,148
Note receivable from officer	(2,369)		
Unrealized gain on available-for-sale securities	(118)	83	—
Accumulated deficit	(58,513)	(30,060)	(8,495)
Treasury stock	(1,171)	(908)	(19)
Total stockholders' equity	9,710	33,606	54,803
Total liabilities and stockholders' equity	$20,780	$42,971	$69,110

Source: Company 10-K and 10-Q filings.

exhibit 5   Peapod's Welcome Page at www.peapod.com

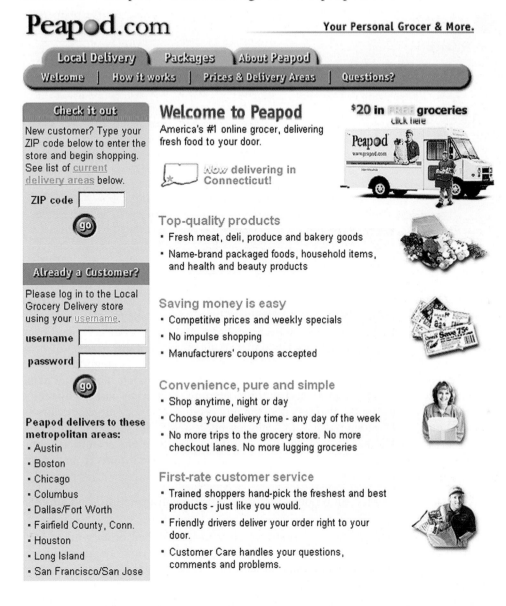

Peapod.com   Your Personal Grocer & More.

Local Delivery | Packages | About Peapod

Welcome | How it works | Prices & Delivery Areas | Questions?

Check it out

New customer? Type your ZIP code below to enter the store and begin shopping. See list of current delivery areas below.

ZIP code [   ]

(go)

Already a Customer?

Please log in to the Local Grocery Delivery store using your username.

username [   ]

password [   ]

(go)

Peapod delivers to these metropolitan areas:
- Austin
- Boston
- Chicago
- Columbus
- Dallas/Fort Worth
- Fairfield County, Conn.
- Houston
- Long Island
- San Francisco/San Jose

Welcome to Peapod

America's #1 online grocer, delivering fresh food to your door.

Now delivering in Connecticut!

Top-quality products
- Fresh meat, deli, produce and bakery goods
- Name-brand packaged foods, household items, and health and beauty products

Saving money is easy
- Competitive prices and weekly specials
- No impulse shopping
- Manufacturers' coupons accepted

Convenience, pure and simple
- Shop anytime, night or day
- Choose your delivery time - any day of the week
- No more trips to the grocery store. No more checkout lanes. No more lugging groceries

First-rate customer service
- Trained shoppers hand-pick the freshest and best products - just like you would.
- Friendly drivers deliver your order right to your door.
- Customer Care handles your questions, comments and problems.

$20 in FREE groceries
click here

canned and packaged goods, household items, and health and beauty products—essentially the same perishable and nonperishable name-brand products typically found in local supermarkets or drugstores. Peapod's prices were competitive, and it had weekly specials; manufacturer's coupons were accepted. Delivery was available seven days a week and could be scheduled for the same day or next day at a time chosen by the customer. Peapod charged a fee for its online order and delivery service that varied by market area. In most markets customers had the option of paying a service charge per order (about $10 per delivery) or a flat rate for unlimited monthly deliveries.

The company's Welcome Page at its Web site is shown in Exhibit 5. The site was accessible to anyone using a Web browser, via personal computers, Web-enabled televisions, high-speed cable services, and wireless devices.

exhibit 6   Ordering Page at Peapod's Web Site

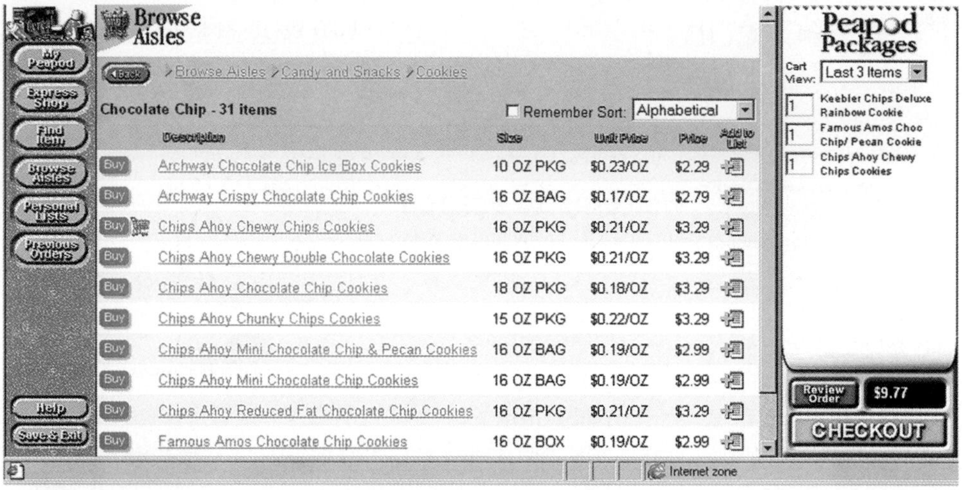

Peapod's Multifeatured, Highly Functional Web Site Technology

Peapod's easy-to-navigate Web site had variety of highly functional features that, management believed, helped encourage repeat purchases and differentiated Peapod from other e-tailers and direct competitors. Customers could shop for items in several ways. One was to browse aisles, moving logically from general product categories to individual items (see Exhibit 6). Another was to conduct product searches by brand name or category, which was particularly useful for redeeming coupons or purchasing recipe ingredients. Shoppers could also sort items in any product category alphabetically or by price, nutritional content (such as fat, calories, cholesterol, and sodium), sale items, and kosher status. Another feature stored a customer's last three grocery orders, eliminating the need to start a shopping list of frequently purchased items from scratch again. Other features included:

- An extensive library of product pictures, nutrition information, and product ingredients.
- An "Express Shop" that helped first-time shoppers build their order without having to browse through the aisles or search for items one at a time. For existing customers, Express Shop, in conjunction with the Previous Orders feature, allowed customers to easily add items to their order.
- A "SmartCart" that displayed a list of the items selected for purchase, as well as a running dollar total of the bill.
- The capability to generate Web pages based on a customer's shopping preferences, buying profile, and other variables so as to provide users with a customized shopping experience.
- A "Buddy E-Mail" function that delivered order confirmations to two different e-mail addresses—something that was useful in households where shopping duties were shared among members.

Gomez Advisors, a leading provider of Internet research and analysis, in September 1999 rated Peapod's Web site first in terms of ease of use among all online grocers.

The company's Web site technology was designed to capture behavioral information from users—mouse clicks, time spent viewing each page, coupon redemptions, and other factors. The tracking data allowed Peapod to generate dozens of metrics to evaluate the quality of its Web site and to identify opportunities to cross-sell additional goods and services.

Marketing and Advertising   Peapod's marketing objectives were to attract more users, to retain the business of current users, to increase the frequency with which users placed orders, to grow average order size, and to enhance awareness of the Peapod brand. To achieve these objectives, the company used radio and newspaper advertising, direct mail, ads on local mass transit systems, Internet advertising, and branding on delivery trucks and employee uniforms (see again Exhibit 5). Company personnel drove attention-getting green Volkswagen "Pod Bugs" with the Peapod insignia to help promote local awareness of the company. In 1999, the company's marketing and advertising budget was about $6 million, the majority of which was focused on growing the customer base and helping the company achieve the operating scale needed for profitability.

One Internet marketing effort the company had come up with to attract new customers was the Peapod Affiliate Program. Peapod started the program in April 1999 as a way of compensating other Web sites for promoting Peapod and providing links to Peapod from their site. Affiliates could earn a $15 commission for each referred visitor who placed an order with Peapod plus an additional $15 for a customer's third order.

To further promote consumer awareness of Peapod, the company had entered into an agreement with Hearst's HomeArts Network, a premier lifestyle site for women on the Web, whereby Peapod would be the exclusive Internet grocery service promoted on the HomeArts Network. The network provided online programming, as well as features from Hearst's 11 women's magazines, including *Redbook, Good Housekeeping, Cosmopolitan,* and *Country Living.* The HomeArts Network had a user base that strongly matched the target Peapod customer. Peapod had also formed a marketing alliance with Excite, Inc., that made Peapod the exclusive online grocer on Excite's Web site. The agreement with Excite gave Peapod exposure to an estimated 35 percent of all Internet users.[2]

Peapod Packages   To help build national presence and awareness of the Peapod brand, the company had begun promoting its "Peapod Packages" for shipment to any location (see Exhibit 7). The company had put together preselected themed product assortments targeting such niche occasions as the Super Bowl, Christmas, Thanksgiving, the arrival of a new baby, or a birthday. There were also care packages for college students and recipe/meal solutions in a box. Shoppers could create their own Peapod Package. Peapod planned to expand the Peapod Package line to include specialty and gourmet foods and gifts.

Distribution Center Operations and Order Fulfillment   Peapod's new $2 million distribution centers each stocked over 12,000 dry grocery, frozen, and dairy products, along with perishable products such as produce, meat, and prepared foods. Items were replenished on a just-in-time basis to optimize space utilization and ensure

---

[2]"Peapod Signs Multi-Year Internet Marketing Deal with Excite," www.peapod.com/v5/Html/Press/ press045.html.

***exhibit* 7**   Examples of Peapod Packages

freshness.[3] While Peapod was opening distribution centers in each of its eight markets, it stated its intention to continue its partnerships with its present retail supermarket allies, albeit on a reduced basis. Until its new central warehousing model was perfected, Peapod was temporarily relying on these partners to stock its central warehouse with perishables, health and beauty aids, and other items it did not currently stock and to fill orders for delivery to those addresses not convenient to its warehouse. Moreover, such alliances gave Peapod an advertising channel for promoting its website at its partners' brick-and-mortar locations.

A major component of Peapod's strategy was to optimize its order fulfillment process from a cost standpoint. As the company began shifting from supermarket partnerships to centralized warehousing, it reengineered its product distribution and order fulfillment practices to reduce costs, minimize stockouts, improve the accuracy of order picking at warehouses, make it economical to accommodate higher order volumes, and ensure that orders were delivered within the scheduled time frame. New warehousing, order picking, and delivery routing software and systems had been designed and put in place.

Order fulfillment was managed by a handheld scanning device that contained pick data for a given metropolitan market area and controlled the order selection process in a manner calculated to minimize the labor time for picking and packing orders. The list of items for a particular order was sorted according to the location of each item in the warehouse, thereby requiring only one pass through the warehouse. The handheld unit displayed each item to be picked and provided a variety of features for assuring accuracy and allowing flexibility for handling exceptions. As individual items appeared on the screen, the picker confirmed the proper item by scanning the item's uniform product code, and was alerted if the wrong item had been scanned. If an item was out of stock, the device noted the out-of-stock status and, if requested by the customer, automatically directed the picker to the customer-designated substitution. A list of out-of-stock items was automatically transmitted to the manager to generate replacement orders.

---

[3]"Peapod Opens Centralized Operations Center in Chicago," Peapod Press Release January 25, 1999.

Delivery logistics were managed by a sophisticated computer program that provided time management information and point-to-point directions throughout the delivery route. The program accounted for traffic conditions, rush-hour volume, road construction, and other variables that could be predicted within the local area. Peapod drivers delivered the packages to each customer's doorstep or unloaded them in the kitchen (if requested) and obtained feedback from customers on the service. To build customer loyalty, Peapod tried to send the same delivery person to the homes of repeat customers. Peapod management was aggressively pursuing ways to fine-tune all of the new systems it had implemented.

So far, order volume had not reached levels that allowed Peapod's warehouse and order fulfillment operation to realize scale economies. The costs of fulfillment operations were 30 percent of sales revenues during the first nine months of 1999, partly because the company was using both central warehouses and the local stores of its retail supermarket partners to fill orders. However, management expected this percentage to decline as the company moved through the period of getting its warehouses up and operating, as experience with the new systems accumulated, and as order volume increased. For the company to become profitable, order fulfillment costs had to drop to a much smaller percentage of revenues.

Nonetheless, Peapod believed that its business model would give it a significant competitive advantage over traditional grocery retailers. By using the Internet to receive orders and central warehouse and distribution facilities to process them, Peapod eliminated the expenses associated with maintaining multiple retail locations in a metropolitan area. Moreover, its use of centralized inventory warehouses and just-in-time deliveries from suppliers led to high inventory turns and reduced stockouts, while at the same time lowering waste and spoilage of perishable goods and reducing the shrinkage associated with store personnel and customer handling of in-store products. Peapod management expected that the efficiencies of its business model would permit competitive pricing and, further, that its sophisticated Web technologies would result in being able to increase sales of high-margin products (private-label goods). Thus, the company expected that, over time, it ought to have higher gross margins and better bottom-line profitability than traditional grocery retailers.

Research and Data Partnerships with Suppliers

Peapod was leveraging the database it was accumulating from tracking user behavior and shopping patterns on its Web site. The company provided advertisers on its Web site with feedback on the effectiveness of marketing programs, and it provided a forum for consumer goods companies to conduct targeted advertising, test electronic couponing, and gather data on online purchasing behavior. The company had created research panels of users at costs that management believed were well below the costs of consumer panels used by Internet research firms. Peapod linked users from its eight markets to form a national online network of panelists and users, enabling the company to collect information on user attitudes, purchasing behavior, and demographics.

Peapod's database and membership profiles permitted it to deliver highly targeted ads and electronic coupons to users, as well as to count the number of Web-page exposures, click-throughs, coupon redemptions, and sales—the data were captured in a manner that allowed the company to measure the impact of a marketing program. Peapod had agreements to provide fee-based online marketing data and research services to a number of national consumer goods companies, resulting in annual revenues of

$1.0 to $1.5 million. Management believed that as Peapod's customer base grew, consumer goods companies would increasingly view Peapod as a powerful advertising venue as well as a valuable research tool, thereby generating additional revenues for Peapod. Participating subscribers included Kellogg's, Kraft, Colgate-Palmolive, Frito-Lay, Coca-Cola, Clorox, Kimberly-Clark, Ralston Purina, and Nestlé U.S.A.

Growth Strategies   Aside from its efforts to build order volume and add new customers in the eight markets where it already operated, Peapod's strategy to grow its business consisted of two major initiatives: (1) expanding into additional market areas and (2) moving beyond groceries and adding altogether new products and services to its lineup. Peapod management planned to use its central warehouse business model and new systems capabilities as the basis for expanding its service into a total of 40 metropolitan areas with 400,000-plus households. The company planned to keep its investment costs down by building economical $2 million distribution centers. Moreover, by establishing a local order fulfillment network with recurring grocery purchases as a foundation, Peapod management believed it would have a pipeline into customer households through which it could provide an increasingly wide range of goods and services at little incremental cost. Peapod management believed that its "last-mile" delivery network for groceries gave it an unparalleled opportunity to build the Peapod brand and to establish personal relationships with individual customers through regular deliveries. Management planned to transform Peapod into a one-stop online shopping site offering home delivery of a host of different products and services, thereby dramatically improving profitability.

As one of the first steps in expanding its product offerings, the company had recently formed a strategic product alliance with Walgreens. Under this agreement, Peapod would begin offering health and beauty products, household hardware and small appliances, electrical supplies, audio- and videotapes, stationery and art supplies, and seasonal items supplied by Walgreens.[4]

The major impediment to Peapod's growth strategies was a potential shortage of capital. The company had nearly $13 million in cash and marketable securities going into the fall of 1999, but the size of the company's losses was creating negative cash flows from operations. The company was depleting its cash reserves to cover the negative cash flow from current operations. Peapod management anticipated that its existing cash and marketable securities would be insufficient to fund the company's operations and capital requirements in 2000 and was therefore currently evaluating financing opportunities. Exhibit 7 shows recent trends in the company's stock price. Analysts following the company forecast that Peapod's losses would amount to $17–$20 million in 2000, equal to a negative $1.10 per share.

Management Changes

Peapod's top management team underwent significant change in 1999. Bill Malloy, brought in as president, chief executive officer, and a member of the board of directors, had established an impressive record of successfully launching new operations and new services while managing rapid growth at AT&T Wireless, and had been one of the key architects of AT&T's Digital One Rate strategy. Cofounder Andrew Parkinson, who stayed on as chairman of the board, began devoting his efforts full-time to Peapod's long-term strategy and business development. Malloy made several top-management

---

[4]"Peapod and Walgreen Co. Announce Product Alliance," Peapod Press Release, March 10, 1999.

changes in the months following his appointment. Michael Brennan was promoted to senior vice president of marketing and product management, George F. Douaire was made senior vice president of Peapod Interactive, and Robert P. Ziegler joined Peapod as director of Chicago operations. The top five officers under Malloy collectively had 36 years of experience in the online grocery business, and several officers had previous experience in packaged foods and consumer products at such companies as Kraft Foods and Procter & Gamble. Peapod employed approximately 475 full-time and 370 part-time employees in early 2000.

THE RETAIL GROCERY INDUSTRY

The U.S. retail grocery industry was a $430 billion business.[5] Sales of health and beauty aids amounted to an additional $200 to $225 billion. Forrester Research estimated that the total sales of grocery and household items, health and beauty items, and beverages in all types of retail outlets amounted to a $720 billion U.S. market.

The top five supermarket chains in 1999 were Kroger, with $43.2 billion in sales; Albertson's, with $35.9 billion; Wal-Mart, with $27 billion from its grocery operations; Safeway, with $26.5 billion; and Ahold, with $20 billion.[6] Slow growth and intense competition were driving supermarket industry consolidation. No supermarket chain had an industry market share much above 10 percent; the top five chains had a combined share under 30 percent. Supermarket sales had grown at an average of just 3.4 percent over the past 10 years, partly because more consumers were shifting some of their purchases to drug chain, wholesale club, and discount chain "supercenter" formats. Traditional grocers' share of total U.S. food sales had dropped from 42 to 40 percent over the last ten years.[7]

Typical supermarkets carried an average of 30,000 items, ranged in size from 20,000 to 40,000 square feet, and averaged $12 million in sales annually. Consumers tended to be price-conscious, and the industry was characterized by fierce price competition.

The supermarket business was a notoriously low-margin business with net profits of only 1 to 2 percent of revenues. Store profits depended heavily on creating a high volume of customer traffic and rapid inventory turnover, especially for perishables such as produce and fresh meat. Competitors had to operate efficiently to make money, and tight control of labor costs and product spoilage was essential. Because capital investment costs were modest, involving mainly the construction of distribution centers and stores, it was not unusual for supermarket chains to realize 15 to 20 percent returns on invested capital.

Supermarket Chains as Potential Competitors in the Online Grocery Segment Most supermarket chains were following developments in the online grocery industry carefully. While some observers believed that existing supermarket chains would be slow to enter into online sales for fear of cannibalizing their existing sales and undermining their brick-and-mortar investments, other industry observers expected supermarket chains to enter the online grocery segment, especially if

---

[5]Ronette King, "Grocery Mergers Are Part of the Growing U.S. Trend," *Times-Picayune,* October 13, 1999, p. A4.

[6]Joan Bergmann, "Food for Thought: Going into the Grocery Industry," *Discount Merchandiser,* May 1999, p. 36.

[7]Nora Aufretier and Tim McGuire, "Walking Down the Aisles," *Ivey Business Journal,* March–April 1999, p. 49.

online grocery sales took off. However, other supermarket industry analysts believed some existing supermarket chains would definitely not stand by idly and let online grocery companies steal market share without a fight. These analysts saw existing supermarket chains as potentially formidable competitors in the online segment because they had well-established supply chains, bought in volumes that gave them bargaining power with food and household product suppliers, had well-known brand names, knew local markets, and could use their distribution centers and neighborhood stores as bases from which to make home deliveries. As many as one-third of U.S. grocery chains were said to have experimented with some type of delivery service.[8]

Albertson's had recently begun testing the market by offering online shopping to customers in the Dallas/Fort Worth, Texas, area. Albertson's was well established in the Dallas/Fort Worth area, with numerous stores and a sizable share of the supermarket business. Management indicated that if its online venture in the Dallas/Fort Worth area was deemed successful, it would expand its online grocery service to other areas.

Clark's Supermarkets, a small, family-owned Colorado chain, announced plans in early 2000 to experiment with online grocery sales at its stores. Clark's intended to put the items stocked in its stores online, allowing customers to log on to its Web site and select the items they wanted. The company had designed a special cart that allowed store personnel to cruise store aisles and pick five orders simultaneously. Clark's strategy was to run the items through its checkout counters, pack them, and have them ready for customer pickup at a time chosen by customers. For the time being, Clark's did not plan to deliver orders to customers' homes. Clark's store in Steamboat Springs was selected to be the pilot for the online experiment; if the service proved popular and successful, Clark's intended to make it available at other Colorado store locations. Clark's saw online ordering as a time-saving service to customers; management did not expect the service to add substantially to the company's profitability.

THE ONLINE GROCERY SEGMENT

The online grocery shopping business was in its infancy in 2000. Analysts believed that online grocery sales amounted to about $235 million in 1999, less than 0.25 percent of total supermarket industry sales. There were 45 companies in the online market, and none were profitable yet.[9] So far, online grocery shopping had been slow to catch on, and industry newcomers had encountered high start-up and operating costs. Sales volumes were too small to permit profitability. The problem, according to industry analysts, was that consumers had been largely disappointed in the service, selection, and prices that they had so far gotten from industry members.

However, some analysts expected online grocery sales to grow at a rapid pace as companies improved their service and selection, PC penetration of households rose, and consumers became more accustomed to making purchases online.[10] Forrester Research forecast that online grocery sales could reach $3 billion by 2003 and as much as $85 billion by 2007. A two-year study by Consumer Direct Cooperative (CDC) concluded that online, consumer-direct grocery sales would account for between 8 and 12 percent of the total grocery market share by 2010.[11] CDC had also done a study of the types of online shoppers (see Exhibit 8). Most online grocery customers were believed to be either starved for time or averse to grocery store visits.

---

[8]Laurent Belise, "A Mouse in the Bakery Aisle," *Christian Science Monitor,* September 8, 1998, p. 11.

[9]Sharon Machlis, "Filling Up Grocery Carts Online," *Computerworld,* July 27, 1998, p. 4.

[10]Ibid.

[11]Terry Hennessy, "Sense of Sell," *Progressive Grocer,* August 1998, pp. 107–10.

exhibit 8 Types of Online Shoppers

Types of Online Shoppers	Comments
Shopping avoiders	Dislike going to the grocery; prime candidate for online grocery shopping
Necessity users	Have limited ability to go to the grocery store; strong candidate for using online grocery shopping as a substitute for in-store shopping
New technologists	Young and comfortable with technology; certain to experiment with buying products online; amenable to online grocery shopping if it is a pleasant and satisfying experience
Time-starved shoppers	Insensitive to price; don't mind paying extra to save time
Responsibles	Have available time; get an enhanced sense of self-worth from grocery shopping
Traditional shoppers	Older; may want to avoid technology and buying products online; very likely to prefer "touch and inspect" shopping in a grocery store

Source: A study by Consumer Direct Cooperative cited in Michael McGovern, "One Stop Shopping," *Transportation & Distribution* 39 (May 1998).

A MARC Group study concluded that "consumers who buy groceries online are likely to be more loyal to their electronic supermarkets, spend more per store 'visit,' and take greater advantage of coupons and premiums than traditional customers."[12] Another study found higher demand for produce online. Edward McLaughlin, head of the Food Industry Management Program at Cornell University, found that 12 to 16 percent of grocery expenditures through Peapod were for fresh produce, compared to the supermarket average of about 10 percent.[13] He reasoned that this outcome was because "decisions made through a computer are more rational, and choices are for healthier foods."

One of the problems with online grocery shopping was that consumers were extremely price-sensitive when it came to buying groceries. The prices of many online grocers were above those of supermarkets, and shoppers in many cases were unwilling to pay extra for the convenience of home delivery. Consumer price sensitivity meant that online grocers had to achieve a cost structure that would allow them to (1) price competitively, (2) cover the costs of picking and delivering individual grocery orders, and (3) have sufficient margins to earn attractive profits and returns on investment. Some analysts estimated that online grocers had to do 10 times the volume of a traditional grocer in order to be successful.[14] However, other analysts and several online grocers believed that the value chain of online grocers was more cost-effective than that of traditional supermarkets (see Exhibit 9).

Gomez Advisor's Ratings of Online Grocers

Gomez Advisors provided user-oriented ratings of numerous types of online companies, ranging from banks to auction sites to travel agents to sellers of sporting goods.

---

[12]Bob Woods, "America Online Goes Grocery Shopping for E-Commerce Bargains," *Computer News,* August 10, 1998, p. 42.

[13]"Net Profits: Making the Internet Work for You and Your Business," *Fortune,* Summer 1999, pp. 240–43.

[14]Lawrence M. Fisher, "On-Line Grocer Is Setting Up Delivery System for $1 Billion," *New York Times,* July 10, 1999, p. 1.

exhibit 9   Comparative Logistics for Traditional Supermarket versus Online Grocer

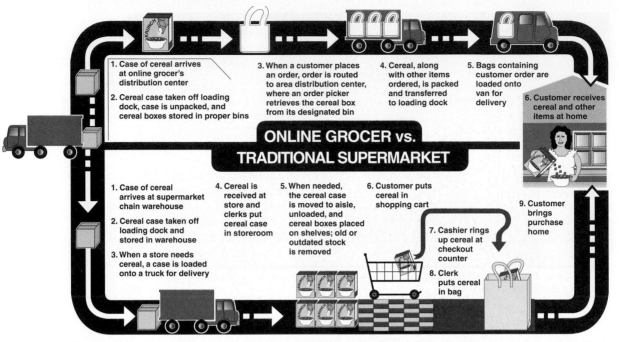

Source: Adopted and revised from E.81Z section of *Business Week,* July 26, 1999, p. EB46.

Many online shoppers were using the Gomez ratings to help them select which Internet providers to do business with. Gomez evaluated online grocers on five aspects:

- *Ease of use*—whether the Web site had well-integrated features that minimized order time and that gave shoppers product comparison capabilities.

- *Onsite resources*—the breadth of product selection and the quality of information resources provided to users.

- *Relationship services*—whether the grocer provided such "extras" as in-home visits with first-time customers, account representatives to answer questions, and willingness to fill unique orders.

- *Overall cost*—product costs (based on nonpromoted prices of a market basket of commonly purchased items), delivery charges, length and frequency of price promotions, and membership fees (including whether there were free trial periods for new members).

- *Customer confidence*—financial stability, reliability of customer service, and guarantees for what was sold.

Gomez also determined on the basis of its ratings which online grocers were most suitable for selective shoppers, bargain-hunting shoppers, time-constrained shoppers, and meal solution shoppers. Exhibit 10 reports the fall 1999 Gomez ratings of the top 10 online grocers.

PROFILES OF SELECTED PEAPOD COMPETITORS

Peapod management anticipated that the company would experience increasing competitive pressures in the online grocery segment. Competition was expected to come

exhibit 10   Gomez Ratings of the Top 10 Online Grocers, Fall 1999

Company	Ease of Use	Overall Cost	Customer Confidence	Onsite Resources	Relationship Services	Overall Score	Comments
Peapod	9.07	7.96	5.41	7.90	3.75	6.97	Rated third (score of 6.17) for time-short shoppers looking for the best deal with the least hassle
HomeGrocer.com	7.33	7.41	4.82	7.74	5.00	6.67	Rated second best (score of 7.02) for selective shoppers wanting *the* best products and delivery service; also rated second best (score of 6.80) for shoppers looking for specific meal solutions (recipes, seasonal foods, and prepared foods)
Webvan	8.22	7.16	2.63	7.32	5.00	6.36	Rated best (score of 7.23) for selective shoppers and best (score of 7.14) for shoppers looking for specific meal solutions
Streamline	4.62	5.93	5.16	7.47	7.50	6.31	Rated best (score of 6.92) for time-short shoppers
ShopLink	6.36	6.98	5.33	5.93	6.25	6.26	Rated second best for time-short shoppers (score of 6.70)
HomeRuns	5.56	8.75	4.97	3.41	2.50	5.18	Ranked best (score of 8.68) for bargain shoppers who love to browse and the thrill of shopping for the best deal
NetGrocer.com	8.22	3.33	2.97	5.49	3.75	4.70	
Albertson's	4.67	8.16	3.99	0.90	2.50	4.13	Ranked second (score of 7.54) for bargain shoppers
Grocer Online	5.42	3.46	6.64	0.36	2.50	3.73	
Your Grocer	4.53	3.84	5.91	2.70	5.00	3.68	

Source: www.gomez.com, February 6, 2000.

exhibit 11   Comparative Prices of Selected Online Grocers, February 2000

Grocery Item	Peapod's Price	Webvan's Price	HomeGrocer.com's Price	NetGrocer.com's Price
Lea & Perrin's Worcestershire sauce (10 oz.)	$2.19	$2.47	$2.25	$2.39
Campbell's Chunky Classic chicken noodle soup (19 oz.)	$2.45	$2.44	$2.19	$2.29
Bunch of green onions (scallions)	$0.50	$0.50	$0.49	Fresh produce not available
French's mustard squeeze (8 oz.)	$0.97	$0.97	$0.95	$0.99
Maxwell House Instant Crystals (8 oz.)	$4.89	$4.92	$5.49	$5.49
Kraft Macaroni and Cheese Deluxe (14 oz.)	$2.39	$2.47	$2.29	$2.49

Source: Company Web sites.

from (1) supermarket chains adopting "click-and-mortar" strategies and pursuing online sales as a new distribution channel to complement their traditional chain of retail outlets and (2) the aggressive market expansion efforts of the 45 companies already in the online segment. This section provides a brief look at three of Peapod's competitors in the online grocery business. Exhibit 11 provides a comparison of Peapod's prices for six selected items with those of Webvan, HomeGrocer.com, and NetGrocer.com.

Webvan Group, Inc.

Webvan's strategic intent was to become the market leader in the full-service online grocery and drugstore business. Louis H. Borders, a founder of the Borders Group who left the bookstore chain in 1992 to form his own investment firm, launched Webvan in Foster City, California, in June 1999 as one of the most ambitious e-commerce enterprises to date. Before going public, Webvan had attracted $122 million in investment capital from CBS, Yahoo!, Softbank, Sequoia Capital, Benchmark Capital, and Knight-Ridder and had recruited the head of Andersen Consulting, George Shaheen, to be its president and CEO.[15] Webvan completed an initial public offering of its stock in November 1999, raising $375 million in capital by selling 9 percent of its shares. The shares, initially priced by Goldman Sachs at $13 to $15 a share, rose to as high as $34 per share before ending the first day's trading at $24.875. The company's prospectus forecast that Webvan would post $11.9 million in revenues in 1999, $120 million in 2000, and $518.2 million in 2001. The prospectus also stated that company expectations were for a $73.8 million loss in 1999, a $154.3 million loss in 2000, and $302 million in losses in 2001.[16] The company shares traded in the $15 to $20 range in early 2000.

Webvan attracted about 10,000 customers in its first six weeks of operation in the San Francisco Bay area. The company had recruited several executives from Federal Express and was using FedEx's hub-and-spoke delivery system as a model for its own distribution system and delivery service. Webvan was using Wal-Mart as its example of

---

[15]Linda Himelstein, "Louis H. Borders," *Business Week,* September 27, 1999, p. 28.

[16]"Webvan Group Files Amended Prospectus for Initial Offering," *The Wall Street Journal,* October 13, 1999, p. A8.

breadth of product selection, Yahoo! as its model for speed, Amazon.com as its model for designing the kind of online shopping experience it wanted to provide, and eBay as its model for "warm-and-fuzzy" feel.[17] It had hired 80 software programmers to create proprietary systems that linked every aspect of its business processes and had recruited managers with expertise in logistics, grocery and drug retailing, and customer service.

Webvan's Strategy and Business Plan   To begin operations, Webvan had constructed a 330,000-square-foot prototype in Oakland, California, to service an area of 40 miles in any direction.[18] The $25 million facility included 4.5 miles of conveyor belts and temperature-controlled rooms to store wine, cigars, produce, meat, and frozen foods. It was designed to serve as many households as 20 to 25 supermarkets. The company planned to eventually stock 50,000 items, including an array of drug-store items, 300 varieties of fresh fruits and vegetables, 750 kinds of cheese, 500 types of cereal, 700 cuts of fresh meat and fish, 700 different wine labels, and chef-prepared meals that could be reheated in the microwave or oven. In the San Francisco market area, Webvan had formed alliances with leading local vendors to provide the freshest produce available; it planned to use such alliances in other markets as well. Webvan claimed that its prices were up to 5 percent less than those of local grocery stores. See Exhibit 12 for Webvan's home page.

Webvan had entered into an agreement with Bechtel Group, one of the world's largest engineering and construction firms, to build Webvan's distribution centers and delivery systems in 26 markets over the next two years. Webvan's projected investment costs for its distribution centers and delivery systems amounted to $1 billion. The company's second distribution center had recently been built in Atlanta.

Webvan's tracking systems monitored customer orders starting with the time they were placed on the company's Web site. Orders were directed from the Web site to the appropriate distribution center. Workers were located at order-picking stations scattered throughout each distribution center; their job was to pick items stocked in their area of the warehouse and put them in color-coded plastic tote bags that signaled whether the items were frozen, refrigerated, or dry. Pickers did not travel up and down aisles but instead moved no more than 20 feet in any direction to reach 8,000 bins of goods that were brought to the picker on rotating carousels. Once pickers completed their portion of a customer's order, the tote was transported on conveyors to other areas of the distribution center where pickers for the remaining items were located. After orders had made the necessary rounds through the warehouse, they were loaded onto trucks refrigerated at 35°F and taken to staging areas located throughout the metropolitan market area. From there, the totes were loaded onto one of the company's 60-plus vans for delivery to customers' homes. Staging areas were located so that Webvan's couriers did not have to travel more than 10 miles in any direction from the staging area to reach a customer's home. The couriers were trained to be courteous and friendly, and to act as customer service professionals and ambassadors for Webvan's service; they were not permitted to accept tips or gratuities. All of the logistics—how many items a tote bag should hold, how far pickers should travel to rotating carousels, how far trucks should travel from staging areas to make deliveries—had been carefully plotted to maximize efficiency.

Webvan management expected that each distribution center would be able to handle 8,000 orders a day (involving more than 225,000 items) and bring in $300 million

[17]Linda Himelstein, "Can You Sell Groceries like Books?" *Business Week,* July 26, 1999, p. EB-44.
[18]Ibid., p. EB-45.

exhibit 12   Webvan's Welcome Page at www.webvan.com

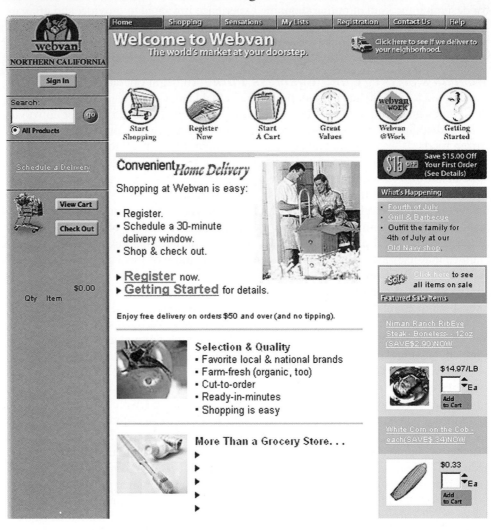

in annual revenues.[19] Louis Borders predicted that Webvan's business model would be so successful and efficient that the company would be able to charge lower prices than both traditional supermarkets and rival online grocers.

Webvan offered free delivery on orders over $50, whereas most other online grocers waived delivery fees only on orders over $75. And the company did not charge a membership fee. Orders were delivered within a 30-minute window selected by the customer. Webvan's Web site offered customers recipes and use of a weekly menu planner.

HomeGrocer.com

Founded in 1997, HomeGrocer.com provided online grocery ordering and delivery service to customers in Seattle, Washington; Portland, Oregon; Orange County, California; and portions of Los Angeles and San Bernardino County. HomeGrocer.com

---

[19]Ibid., p. EB-46.

exhibit 13   HomeGrocer.com's Welcome Page at www.homegrocer.com

offered a broad selection of items, including fresh produce, meats, seafood, dairy products, local specialty foods, health and beauty aids, household items, fresh flowers, pet supplies, best-selling books, video games, and movies. HomeGrocer.com used a distribution center model also; in early 2000, it had four distribution centers and was adding others in the newly entered Los Angeles area. HomeGrocer.com's signature peach-logo delivery trucks had multiple compartments that permitted products to be stored at their appropriate temperatures without affecting the temperatures of the other products.

Customers could order groceries via the Internet until 11 PM and select a 90-minute window for next-day delivery. HomeGrocer.com offered free delivery for all first orders and those $75 or more, in addition to toll-free customer support for its members. To underscore its commitment to quality, the company offered an unconditional 100 percent satisfaction guarantee. HomeGrocer.com had been recognized by Feedback Direct, a leading online customer service authority, as one of the top 50 North American companies to consistently demonstrate superior customer service. Exhibit 13 shows Homegrocer.com's home page.

Although HomeGrocer.com was a fairly small business, with fewer than 25,000 customers, it had ambitious plans to expand into 20 other markets in the near future, aided by a $42.5 million investment from Amazon.com.[20] Amazon's investment gave it a 35 percent stake in the company. Amazon had also recently invested in drugstore.com and Pets.com, and there had been speculation that Amazon might start to use HomeGrocer.com's vans to deliver CDs, books, and prescription drugs to customers' homes. Homegrocer.com had also received funding from the Barksdale Group, an investment firm run by James Barksdale, founder of Netscape, Martha Stewart Living

---

[20]Andrew Marlatt, "Amazon Diversifies Further with $42M Stake in Grocer," *Internet World,* May 24, 1999.

exhibit 14   NetGrocer.com's Welcome Page at www.netgrocer.com

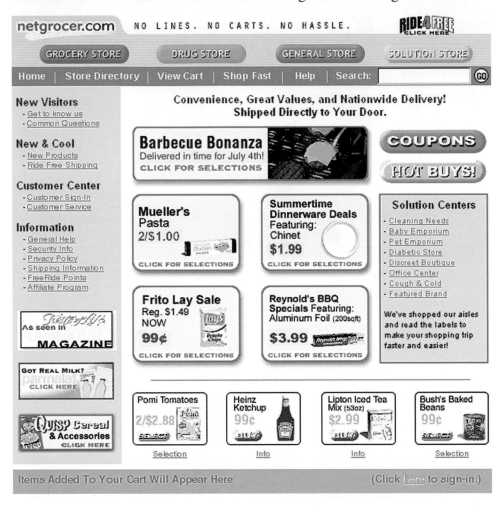

Omnimedia Inc., Hummer Winblad Venture Partners, and Kleiner Perkins Caufield & Byers.[21] The company had filed plans with the Securities and Exchange Commission to issue shares of its common stock to the public in the first half of 2000.

NetGrocer.com

NetGrocer.com began operations in 1995 and offered nationwide distribution through a large central warehouse located in New Jersey. NetGrocer.com's product line included canned and packaged grocery items, paper products, cleaning products, organic and natural foods, international food items, dog and cat foods, laundry items, health and beauty products, dietary supplements, pain relief products, fragrances, baby products, a variety of electronics items (cameras, film, calculators, data organizers, audio accessories, batteries, and video games), CDs, and gifts. It generally offered prices of 10 to 20 percent

---

[21]Rachel Beck, "Online Grocers Work to Build a Market," *Houston Chronicle,* May 30, 1999, p. 7.

less than supermarkets and free delivery for orders over $75. NetGrocer.com's orders were delivered by FedEx on the third business day after the order was received.

In 1999 NetGrocer.com relaunched its Web site following the removal of CEO Daniel Nissan and the firing of 80 percent of its staff. These changes, which occurred shortly after the company shelved its $38 million initial public offering, were attributed to market conditions and expense cuts. Since the launch of the new site, NetGrocer.com's average order size was up 40 percent and time spent on the site had increased dramatically.[22] Exhibit 14 shows NetGrocer.com's home page.

---

[22]Barry Janoff, "Point, Click, Shop," *Progressive Grocer,* June 1999, p. 31.

case | 9 Cannondale Corporation

Romuald A. Stone
Keller Graduate School of Management

John E. Gamble
University of South Alabama

In early 2000 Cannondale Corporation was the world's leading manufacturer and marketer of high-performance aluminum bicycles. The company also marketed CODA bicycle components, HeadShok suspension forks, and a line of bicycle accessories including such items as clothing, packs, and bags. The company's bicycles, which carried its "Handmade in the USA" logo, were known for their innovative designs, light weight, exceptional performance, and durable construction and were sold in the United States and in more than 60 other countries. Since the company's founding in 1971, Cannondale's products had been recognized for their innovation by such publications as *USA Today, Sports Illustrated, Popular Science, Popular Mechanics,* and *Design News.* Cannondale's newest bicycle model, the Jekyll, had been named *Mountain Biking* magazine's "Bike of the Year" for 2000 and dubbed "a manufacturing masterpiece," "a masterful work of art," and "an outstanding achievement in lightweight, dual-suspension performance."[1]

Cannondale achieved success quickly after its founding, recording annual revenues of approximately $8 million by the late 1970s. However, the company's emergence as a major bicycle producer came about only in 1983, when it developed and produced the first affordable aluminum-frame bicycle. Cannondale's aluminum road bikes and its aluminum-frame mountain bike, introduced in 1984, were instant hits and allowed the company's revenues to grow at an annual rate of 30 percent between 1983 and 1985. The company's growth continued at a dramatic rate as the popularity of mountain biking grew exponentially during the late 1980s and early 1990s. In 1982, two years before Cannondale's introduction of its SM 500 mountain bike, there were approximately 200,000 mountain bikers in the United States. By 1992, the number of U.S. mountain bikers had grown to more than 8 million and mountain bikes accounted for 54 percent of U.S. bicycle sales. By 1996 Cannondale had become the leader of the high-performance mountain bike segment and its stock price had appreciated at an annual rate of 32 percent since its initial public offering in 1994.

In early 2000 the company's prospects for spectacular growth appeared to hinge not on the success of its mountain bikes but on its soon-to-be-introduced MX400 off-road motorcycle. The highly innovative aluminum-frame motorcycle was eagerly

---

[1]Cannondale press release, PR Newswire, January 31, 2000.

awaited by motocross enthusiasts and had been described by *Dirt Rider* magazine as "a monumental bike" that had forced "other manufacturers to rethink their current technology."[2] Cannondale remained a leader in the high-performance segment of the mountain bike industry with innovative products like the Jekyll, but its growth during the late 1990s had been severely restricted as the bicycle industry reached maturity during the mid-1990s and grew at an approximate annual rate of 2 percent during the late 1990s. Cannondale's revenue growth had slowed to an annual rate of 9.7 percent between 1995 and 1999 after growing at a compounded annual rate of 22.3 percent between 1991 and 1995. The company's decelerated growth rate was reflected in its stock price, which had steadily declined since its peak of $27 in 1997. As the company prepared to begin shipping the new MX400 in the spring of 2000, Cannondale's founder and CEO Joseph Montgomery hoped that the new motorcycle would be the strategic spark that the company needed to restart the share price growth it had experienced in earlier years. A summary of Cannondale Corporation's financial performance between 1991 and 1999 is shown in Exhibit 1. Exhibit 2 presents a graph of Cannondale's stock performance between 1995 and early 2000.

THE GLOBAL BICYCLE MARKET

With over 1 billion bicycles existing in the world, usage varied considerably, with about 70 percent of all bicycles used as a means of transportation, 29 percent used for recreational purposes, and about 1 percent used solely in racing events. In many countries bicycling was the primary means of land transportation for distances that made walking impractical. In China, for example, traffic controllers saw an average of 10,000 cyclists per hour pass the busiest urban intersections. In the city of Tianjin, with more than 4 million people, there were up to 50,000 cyclists per hour passing through high-traffic intersections. In countries with more developed economies, bicycling was more likely to be a secondary mode of transportation or restricted to recreational use.

Among the world's industrialized nations, Western Europeans were the biggest users of bicycles, with an estimated 115 million bicycle owners. Communities in the Netherlands, Denmark, and Germany were called bicycle-friendly because of their balanced use of bicycles for transport, recreation, and sport. Cycling facilities such as bike lanes and parking sites, along with traffic calming and intermodal transit links, encouraged people to use bicycles for as much as 20 to 50 percent of all urban trips.

In the United States, bicycles were employed mainly for recreation, with only about 5 percent of the country's 100 million bicycles used for transportation. Cycling was the fifth most popular recreational activity in the United States, behind exercise walking, swimming, exercising with equipment, and camping.

In some African and Latin American countries bicycle use was heavy, but governments in those geographic regions tended to stigmatize bicycles as "Third World" means of mobility. While many leaders in government enjoyed the prestige of cars and new highways, their people often relied on walking instead of cycling for essential transport. In countries with developing economies but well-established mass transit systems, such as Russia, bicycles were rare. However, in Eastern European nations such as Hungary, where mass transit was less available and economic conditions made automobile ownership difficult for most, bicycles were used widely and accounted for roughly half of all trips to work.

---

[2]Ibid.

exhibit 1   Consolidated Financial Data for Cannondale Corporation, 1991–99
(In Thousands of Dollars, Except Per Share Data)

	Twelve Months Ended		
	July 3, 1999	June 27, 1998	June 28, 1997
Statement of operations data			
Net sales	$176,819	$171,496	$162,496
Cost of sales	114,627	110,113	101,334
Gross profit	62,192	61,383	61,162
Expenses			
Selling, general and administrative	40,599	39,361	35,707
Research and development	10,222	6,750	3,576
Stock option compensation	—	—	—
Agent and distributor termination costs	—	—	—
Total operating expenses	50,821	46,111	39,283
Operating income (loss)	11,371	15,272	21,879
Other income (expense):			
Interest expense	(4,557)	(1,995)	(1,574)
Foreign exchange and other	1,160	653	843
Total other income (expense)	(3,397)	(1,342)	(731)
Income (loss) before income taxes, minority interest and extraordinary item	7,974	13,930	21,148
Income tax benefit (expense)	(2,051)	(4,578)	(7,642)
Minority interest in net loss (income) of consolidated subsidiary	—	—	—
Income (loss) before extraordinary item	5,923	9,352	13,506
Extraordinary item, net of income taxes[a]	—	—	—
Net income (loss)	5,923	9,352	13,506
Accumulated preferred stock dividends[b]	—	—	—
Income (loss) applicable to common shares and equivalents	$ 5,923	$ 9,352	$ 13,506
Per common share			
Income (loss) before extraordinary item[c]	$0.79	$1.11	$1.56
Income (loss)	$0.79	$1.11	$1.56
Weighted average common and common equivalent shares outstanding[d]	7,518	8,442	8,638
Balance sheet data			
Working capital	$ 74,894	$ 78,975	$ 77,196
Total assets	162,379	152,277	127,284
Total long-term debt, excluding current portion	55,997	40,352	20,319
Total stockholders' equity	75,010	78,238	81,621

[a]Extraordinary items consist of the costs relating to early extinguishment of debt, net of applicable tax benefit, if any.

[b]Reflects preferred stock dividends accumulated during the fiscal period. All cumulative preferred stock dividends were paid in 1995 at the time of the redemption of the preferred stock in connection with the company's initial public offering.

[c]No cash dividends were declared or paid on the common stock during any of these periods.

	Twelve Months Ended		Ten Months Ended		Twelve Months Ended	
	June 29, 1996	July 1, 1995	July 2, 1994	July 3, 1993	September 4, 1992	August 31, 1991
	$145,976	$122,081	$102,084	$80,835	$76,911	$54,544
	92,804	70,816	72,000	59,429	58,927	37,623
	53,172	42,265	30,001	21,406	17,984	16,921
	32,577	27,023	22,290	19,615	18,527	11,993
	2,837	1,751	1,317	1,105	1,314	907
	—		2,046	—	—	—
	—		—	271	1,196	—
	35,414	28,774	25,653	20,991	21,037	12,900
	17,758	13,491	4,348	415	(3,053)	4,021
	(2,224)	(3,929)	(4,460)	(4,177)	(2,990)	(1,976)
	414	24	324	828	(868)	419
	(1,810)	(3,905)	(4,136)	(3,349)	(3,858)	(1,557)
	15,948	9,586	212	(2,934)	(6,911)	2,464
	(5,802)	(1,353)	(791)	(179)	1,422	(959)
	—	—	—	—	850	(343)
	10,146	8,233	(579)	(3,113)	(4,639)	1,162
	—	(685)	—	(464)	—	—
	10,146	7,548	(579)	(3,577)	(4,639)	1,162
	—	(400)	(1,008)	—	—	—
	$ 10,146	$ 7,148	$ (1,587)	$ (3,577)	$ (4,639)	$ 1,162
	$1.23	$1.18	$(.37)	$(.73)	$(1.08)	$0.28
	$1.23	$1.08	$(.37)	$(.83)	$(1.08)	$0.28
	8,216	6,606	4,246	4,291	4,296	4,179
	$ 62,032	$ 22,313	$ 6,366	$ 6,107	$ 3,615	$ 1,903
	109,945	84,008	67,870	65,245	57,877	35,617
	13,114	5,602	6,995	7,872	7,484	6,183
	68,294	36,088	9,640	8,220	4,525	6,893

[d]Shares underlying options granted during fiscal 1994 are treated as outstanding for fiscal 1994 and all prior periods, using the treasury stock method. Weighted average number of shares outstanding in 1995 reflects the issuance of 2,300,000 shares of common stock in connection with the company's initial public offering. Weighted average number of shares outstanding in 1996 reflects the issuance of 1,366,666 shares of common stock in connection with a public offering in fiscal 1996.

Source: Annual reports.

exhibit 2   Monthly Trading Range and Price-Earnings Ratio of Cannondale's Common Stock, 1995–January 2000

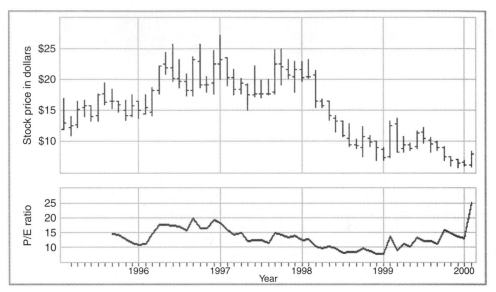

Most of the world's bicycles were made and used in Asia. Seventy-five percent of the world's bicycles were produced in China, India, Taiwan, Japan, and Thailand. With an average annual production of 30 million units, China produced more bicycles than any other nation in the world. In 1999 there were almost 1,000 bicycle parts makers and assembly plants in China, employing approximately 350,000 workers. About 20 million bicycles were produced each year for sale within China, while more than 10 million units were produced each year for export to other countries. The China Bicycle Company (CBC) of Guangzhou was one of the dominant Chinese bike manufacturers. The company was founded by Jerome Sze, a Hong Kong businessman, and began making bicycles for Western firms such as Schwinn in the 1970s. In 1992, CBC was rated as one of the top 10 foreign investment enterprises in China. Taiwan was the world's second largest producer and world's largest exporter of bicycles. During the late 1990s, over 70 percent of the bikes sold in the United States were made in Taiwan. The biggest Taiwanese bikemakers, Giant Manufacturing Company and Merida Industry Company, manufactured bicycles sold in the United States under brand names that included Trek, Schwinn, and Specialized.

THE U.S. BICYCLE INDUSTRY

In 1999 the U.S. bicycle industry was approximately a $5 billion per year industry, counting the retail value of bicycles, related parts, and accessories through all channels of distribution. There were over 100 brands of bicycles sold in the United States and an estimated 2,000 companies involved in either manufacturing or distributing cycling products. Bicycles were sold at nearly all full-line discount stores and sporting goods superstores, at many department stores, and at approximately 6,800 specialty bicycle stores. The annual U.S. sales of bicycles peaked in 1973 at 15.2 million units and averaged nearly 11.5 million units during the 1990s. Exhibit 3 presents annual U.S. bicycle sales between 1981 and 1998.

exhibit 3   U.S. Unit Sales of Bicycles (20-Inch and Larger Wheel
             Sizes), 1981–98 (In Millions)

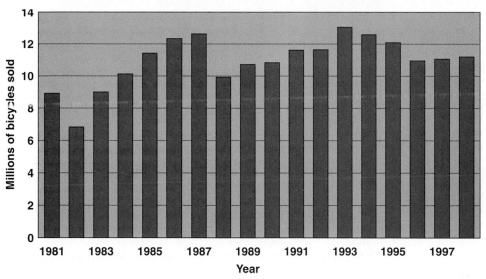

Source: Bicycle Manufacturers Association.

Market Segmentation by Bicycle Category

There were an estimated 54.5 million active adult cyclists in the United States in 1999 who used their bicycles at least once weekly. Adult bicycles fell into five broad categories: mountain, road-racing, multisport, recreational, and specialty. Mountain bikes combined elements from classic balloon-tire bikes with the lightweight alloy components of quality road-racing bikes. These bikes also featured suspension systems, low gears, beefed-up frames, and straight handlebars (allowing a more upright cycling position than road racing or recreational bikes) and were designed for reliable on-road transportation and heavy-duty touring over rugged terrain. Mountain bikes, the largest segment of the adult market, accounted for 63 percent of all bicycles sold in the United States in 1997.

Road-racing bikes were lightweight, with thin tires and drop (curved) handlebars. Multisport bikes, designed for triathlons and other multisport races, were very aerodynamic and typically had smaller diameter wheels than traditional road racers. Recreational bikes, also known as comfort bikes, hybrids, or cross bikes, were typically more comfortable versions of mountain bikes. The specialty bicycle market encompassed various niche products, including tandem bikes, cruisers, and bicycle motocross (BMX) bikes. Cruisers were styled similarly to the venerable Schwinn of the 1950s, with big balloon tires, huge cushy saddles, and swept-back handlebars. BMX bikes, which featured 20-inch wheels, a relatively short but very strong and light frame, and no gears, were originally designed for short races over dirt tracks but were more commonly used by children and adolescents for everyday recreational use.

Factors Affecting Industry Demand

Federal Legislation   During the 1990s the U.S. government enacted legislation that required communities to include cycling in local transit infrastructure planning.

For example, the 1990 Clean Air Act set standards for air quality and required some metropolitan areas to develop methods to reach compliance. One of the recommended approaches involved taking steps to make bicycling a more viable transportation alternative. In addition, the Intermodal Surface Transportation Efficiency Act (ISTEA) of 1991 recognized the transportation value of bicycling and walking and offered mechanisms to increase consideration of bicyclists' and pedestrians' needs within the nation's intermodal transportation system. Federal funding was available from a number of programs, and planning requirements for bicycling were established for states and metropolitan planning organizations. Other provisions of the act included the requirement that states establish and fund a bicycle and pedestrian coordinator in their departments of transportation, and that bicyclist and pedestrian safety continue to be priority areas for highway safety program funding.

However, the provisions of the 1990 Clean Air Act and the 1991 Intermodal Surface Transportation Efficiency Act had done little to create a boom in cycling. Most industry growth during the 1990s was attributable to a growing interest in physical fitness and the popularity of the mountain bike, rather than U.S. government mandates to make cycling an integral part of a balanced intermodal transportation system. There was some belief by industry participants that the 1998 Transportation Equity Act for the 21st Century (TEA-21) would better integrate cycling into mainstream transportation in the United States. TEA-21 would provide as much as $500 million between 1999 and 2003 to create walkable and bicycle-friendly communities that would make cycling and walking safe and practical alternatives to traveling by automobile.

The Appeal of Mountain Biking   The phenomenal growth in mountain biking had been a major factor in the overall growth of the domestic bicycle market during the mid-1980s and early 1990s. The number of mountain bikers in the United States grew from 200,000 in 1982 to approximately 8.5 million in 1997. Only in-line roller skating had grown faster than mountain biking among outdoor recreational and fitness activities between 1987 and 1998. However, by 1999 the mountain bike industry was mature; it remained among the most popular outdoor recreational activities, but its growth rate had slowed considerably (see Exhibit 4).

Three factors contributed to the popularity of mountain bikes: (1) They were more comfortable to ride than typical touring or racing models; (2) the bikes themselves greatly increased the terrain available to bicycles; and (3) more adults were turning toward outdoor activities in their leisure time. The introduction of mountain bike racing as an Olympic sport in 1996 reflected the growth of mountain bike racing as both a participant and spectator sport and created additional exposure for mountain biking. In addition, downhill racing proved to be increasingly popular with spectators, combining high speed and technically advanced equipment with the celebrity of professional athletes and emerging personalities in the sport. During the 1990s the ski resort industry increasingly promoted summer use of ski mountains for biking, with many ski resorts equipping ski lifts to carry bikes and riders uphill.

Factors Influencing Demand for Mountain Bikes in the Late 1990s

Environmental Regulation   The coverage of racing events in mountain bike magazines and the use of racing photos in mountain bike manufacturer advertisements had created a backlash against the industry by hikers and others wishing to preserve the environment. Opponents of mountain biking attempted to portray mountain bikers as

exhibit 4 U.S. Participation Rates of Selected Fitness and Sports Activities, 1998

Activity	Number of U.S. Participation	Annual Change (1997–98)	11-Year Change (1987–98)
Aerobics	21,017,000	−7.9%	−1.0%
Fitness bicycling	13,556,000	n.a.	n.a.
Running/jogging	34,962,000	−4.2	−5.9
Stationary cycling	30,791,000	−3.9	0.1
Treadmill exercise	37,073,000	2.6	743.3
Stair-climbing machine exercise	18,609,000	3.9	777.5
Baseball	12,318,000	−7.2	−18.4
Basketball	42,417,000	−5.9	18.7
In-line roller skating	32,010,000	1.0	581.8
Recreational bicycling	54,575,000	n.a.	n.a.
Golf	29,961,000	−3.4	14.1
Mountain biking	8,612,000	2.1	469.5
Snowboarding	5,461,000	10.5	158.1
Scuba diving	3,448,000	27.7	41.7

n.a. = not available.
Source: Sporting Goods Manufacturers Association, "Sports Participation Trends Report, 1998."

crazed, out-of-control cyclists who destroyed trails and made it unsafe for hikers to enjoy national parks and other government lands. In response to the critics, the U.S. Forest Service had commissioned a survey in 1996 that looked at the impact of bicycles on public lands. The survey found that 98 percent of National Forests reported mountain biking activity that ranged from 50 to 376,000 cyclists per year. Fifty percent of national parks reported annual mountain bike usage by fewer than 4,500 visitors, while 25 percent of national parks reported more than 15,000 mountain bike riders per year. Seventy percent of forest managers reported conflicts between cyclists and hikers, 59 percent were concerned that mountain bikes contributed to park safety problems, 58 percent believed that mountain bikes damaged park resources, and 48 percent witnessed or knew of accidents in the park related to mountain bike usage.

The International Mountain Bike Association (IMBA) noted to its manufacturing and retailing members that industry sales were directly tied to open biking trails. It developed a mantra of "No trails, no sales" and encouraged manufacturers to discontinue ads that depicted racing photographs. The association also encouraged both manufacturers and retailers to take a proactive position in regard to safe and responsible cycling. The IMBA struck an agreement with the Sierra Club that called for wilderness protection, socially responsible mountain biking, restricted trail access, trail user education, and open communication between local mountain biking groups and Sierra Club entities. Additionally, the association maintained an active lobbying effort to ensure that lands regulated by the Bureau of Land Management and the U.S. Forest Service remained open to cycling.

Technological Innovation Technological innovations became increasingly important in the industry as rival mountain bike manufacturers attempted to outpace the modest industry growth rate by introducing technological innovations in frames, components, and suspension systems. Innovations diffused quickly throughout the industry as manufacturers kept adding features in attempts to maintain their historical growth rates. Cannondale was the first to offer affordable large-diameter aluminum-tube bicycles in the early 1980s, but by 1999 aluminum-frame bikes were produced by almost all bike manufacturers, including companies that manufactured inexpensive bicycles sold in discount stores. In 1999, aluminum frames were still found on high-end bikes, but other materials (such as carbon composites and titanium) were also used on more technologically advanced mountain bikes. The appeal of titanium frames was the material's light weight combined with strength. Like titanium frames, carbon composite frames were popular because they were light and strong but also because they could be molded into aerodynamic shapes. Steel- or aluminum-frame bicycle designs were typically bound to the traditional double-triangle shape. Other innovations that had become popular with cycling enthusiasts during the late 1990s included clipless pedals, disc brakes, automatic shifting, and suspension systems.

Front- and full-suspension systems were introduced during the early 1990s and quickly became a popular addition to high-end mountain bikes. The suspension systems provided greater comfort and control than what was available on nonsuspension bikes, and by 1999 suspension systems were found on most mountain bikes at midrange price points over $500. Suspension systems were also available on mountain bikes priced between $200 and $300 in discount stores. However, these lower-priced suspension bikes typically used poorer quality suspension systems and did not offer performance equal to that of higher-end suspension bikes. High-end mountain bike manufacturers sought out innovative features on a regular basis to maintain a comfortable level of differentiation over not only other high-end brands but also lower-priced bicycles that incorporated previous-generation mountain bike technology. K2's computer-chip-activated Smart Shock was an example of a technological innovation that could provide a bicycle manufacturer with the level of differentiation necessary to support premium pricing. The Smart Shock technology sampled the ground conditions and sent damping instructions to the shock 1,000 times per second to maximize tire-to-ground contact. K2 models equipped with the Smart Shock sold at prices between $900 and $2,200.

Market Segmentation by Channel of Distribution

Two primary distribution systems existed in the U.S. bicycle industry—large discount retailers and independent specialty bicycle shops. Department stores, discount stores, and toy stores accounted for about 70 percent of all units sold and about half of the total spent on bikes in 1997. Most of the bikes sold by mass merchandise retailers were offered at prices below $200 and tended to be heavy, without the precision machining or reliable components demanded by cycling enthusiasts. These low-end bikes were fine for cycling around the neighborhood but lacked the durability, reliability, and performance needed for serious biking. The discounters' advantages were price and convenience; their clientele consisted mainly of buyers looking for low-end, low-performance models.

Huffy Corporation, Murray Ohio Manufacturing, and Brunswick Corporation (producer of Roadmaster and Mongoose brands) were the three leading producers of bikes sold by large discounters, department stores, and discount sporting goods superstores. Other brands sold by large discounters were Magna, Pacific, Rand, and Kent. Discount store customers were not particularly brand-loyal and usually made their purchasing decisions based on price and some modest product preferences like bicycle type, color, and size. Competition among manufacturers of less-expensive bicycles, although always strong, had intensified during the 1990s as the discount retail industry had consolidated and low-priced imports from China and Taiwan had fueled a growing price war. Both domestic and Asian bicycle manufacturers were forced to add features and compete more aggressively on price to consistently win contracts with large retailers like Wal-Mart, Target, and Toys "R" Us. During the mid-1990s as little as 40 percent of the bicycles sold by discount retailers were produced outside the United States, but the growing price competition in the industry had compelled low-end manufacturers to abandon bicycle production in the United States. In 1999 both Huffy and Brunswick anticipated losses from their bicycle operations and closed their remaining U.S. production facilities. Both companies had announced that, following those closings, they would source 100 percent of their frames from Asian contract manufacturers.

About 30 percent of the 11 million bicycles sold in the United States during 1998 were sold by small specialty retailers with annual sales averaging about $500,000. These dealers, numbering about 6,800, typically had one location, were family owned, carried four to six brands of midrange to high-end bicycles, and sold about 500 to 600 bikes per year. The sales of parts, accessories, and service accounted for about 50 percent of specialty retailers' gross sales. About 80 percent of bicycles sold by specialty retailers were imported. High-performance bicycle manufacturers like Trek, Schwinn, Giant, Raleigh, Specialized, Cannondale, and Diamondback marketed their bikes exclusively through independent specialty dealers who could provide after-the-sale service for their products.

Specialty bicycle shops accounted for 30 percent of the industry's unit sales and about 50 percent of total dollar sales. Bicycle dealer brands generally started at prices above $200. The average price of a bicycle sold at a bicycle shop was about $350, though prices could range into the thousands. The independent bicycle dealer's ability to offer light, durable, properly assembled bicycles matched to the individual rider's needs worked to the dealer's advantage. In addition, specialty bike dealers commanded a vast majority of parts and accessories sales and virtually 100 percent of the service market. Dealers dominated the market for bicycles selling for $250 and higher. The growing interest in a total fitness lifestyle had also caught the attention of specialty bicycle dealers. Roughly 25 percent of the bicycle stores in the United States sold some kind of indoor exercise equipment (exercise bikes, weight machines, and all associated accessories).

Mountain bikes (26-inch wheel size) represented 55 percent of the bikes sold through the specialty channel in 1997. Mountain bikes had accounted for as much as 63 percent of independent dealer sales as recently as 1995. Children's bikes (20-inch wheels) were the fastest-growing bicycle category sold by specialty dealers, accounting for 33 percent of sales in 1997 versus 20 percent of specialty dealer unit sales in 1994. Recreational bikes were another rapidly growing category and accounted for 10 percent of dealer sales in 1997. It was expected that recreational comfort bikes would become a larger segment of the market as baby boomers aged and the over-40 age category grew. Most dealers had found that comfort bikes were gaining market share directly at the expense of low-end mountain bikes. Road racers accounted for only 2 percent of specialty retailer sales in 1997.

CANNONDALE'S RIVALS IN THE MOUNTAIN BIKE SEGMENT

Cannondale experienced little competition from the large manufacturers—such as Brunswick Corporation, Huffy Corporation, and Murray Ohio—that sold bicycles to discount retailers. For the most part, discount store brands were not sold by independent dealers and dealer brands were not carried in discount stores. The only exception was Mongoose, which had been a dealer brand until its acquisition by Brunswick in 1997. After the acquisition, Brunswick developed lower-priced Mongoose models for discounters as well as maintaining higher-priced models for its independent dealers. Once Mongoose became available at discount stores, many dealers chose to drop the Mongoose brand because of the difficulty in convincing consumers that the dealers' higher-priced Mongoose models, although similar in appearance, were of better quality than Mongoose models found in discount stores.

The high-performance segment of the bicycle industry was highly competitive in the United States and in many other countries. Competition was based primarily on perceived value, brand image, performance features, product innovation, and price. Competition in foreign markets was affected by duties, tariffs, foreign exchange fluctuations, taxes and the effect of various trade agreements and import restrictions. In 2000 there were several key competing brands in the industry.

In some instances competing brands were actually owned by the same parent corporation or holding company. As growth in the mountain bike segment had slowed during the 1990s and as bicycle manufacturers sought continued growth, a number of mergers and acquisitions involving key brands occurred. Owning more than one brand allowed manufacturers to gain greater coverage in specific geographic locations and communities even though dealers were frequently given some modest assurance of an exclusive territory. For example, Intrepid, Inc. (the parent of Trek bicycles), had acquired two high-end mountain bike manufacturers, Gary Fisher and Klein, which allowed the company to increase its network of retail dealers without alienating its Trek dealers. In addition, even though Trek, Klein, and Gary Fisher manufactured similarly equipped models, Intrepid's dealers were not exposed to the consumer price shopping that was seen by Mongoose dealers after Mongoose became available at discount stores. Other brands involved in mergers or acquisitions included Raleigh, Diamondback, Univega, Mishiski, GT, Dyno, Powerlite, and Robinson.

Cannondale's key competitors in 1999 are discussed in the following sections.

Schwinn Cycling & Fitness

Schwinn was founded in 1895 in Chicago by German bikemaker Ignaz Schwinn. At one time, Schwinn was the most prestigious bicycle company in the industry, with as much as 25 percent of the market and sales of 1.6 million units a year. During its first 100 years, Schwinn sold more than 40 million bicycles. Beginning in the 1970s changing consumer tastes and tough new competitors with lighter, more high-tech products began to slowly erode Schwinn's dominant position.

Rather than innovate, Schwinn became obsessed with cutting costs by moving production overseas. Initially, the company outsourced its bicycles from Japan. But by 1978 Taiwanese manufacturers were beating the Japanese on price. Schwinn shifted gears and began importing Taiwanese-made Giant bikes, on which Schwinn put its nameplate. When Giant became a competitor, Schwinn formed an alliance with the China Bicycle Company, but after a few years CBC also used the knowledge gained through collaborating with Schwinn to launch its own brand in the United States and compete against Schwinn.

To make matters worse, Schwinn made the strategic mistake of ignoring the mountain bike craze for most of the 1980s. By 1992, two-thirds of all bikes sold were mountain bikes. Schwinn managers were not alone in their complacency; many Schwinn retailers failed to notice key market trends or keep up with the technological changes sweeping the industry. The proverbial writing was on the wall, and Schwinn filed for Chapter 11 bankruptcy protection in 1992.

In 1993, what was left of Schwinn was purchased by an investor group for $43 million. Schwinn's new owners moved quickly to rebuild the Schwinn brand. The new owners immediately relocated the company to Boulder, home of the University of Colorado and thousands of outdoor enthusiasts. Historically, Schwinn was viewed as a maker of sturdy low-cost bikes, which was contrary to the 1990s consumer preference for the trendier high-performance mountain bikes. The Boulder culture helped Schwinn designers develop new models that included technological features and performance that better appealed to hardcore cyclists, who often influenced the purchases of less-avid cyclists. Even though Schwinn introduced better-styled and more technologically advanced bikes, its image was a major obstacle in turning around the company. As Greg Bagni, Schwinn's new vice president of marketing and product development, noted, the hardcore cyclists who were key to changing the public's perceptions of Schwinn's performance and quality "wouldn't be caught dead on a Schwinn."[3]

Schwinn's efforts to change its image required what Bagni said was a fundamental shift in strategy. "We've evolved from a marketing-driven company to a market-driven company. A marketing driven company will try to sell a warehouse full of yellow bikes . . . a market-driven company will determine what the consumer wants first."[4] In addition to determining what features consumers wanted, Schwinn also began showing up on the racing circuit, using cross-promotions with such well-known brands as Old Navy, Toyota, and MCI to promote Schwinn bikes and study what features appealed to hardcore cyclists.

Once Schwinn's turnaround was well under way, the company was sold again in 1997. The new owners retained Schwinn's management team and acquired GT Bicycles in 1998 to add complementary models to Schwinn's line and increase Schwinn's network of dealers. GT Bicycle was a leading designer, manufacturer, and marketer of mid- to premium-priced bicycles sold under the company's GT, Powerlite, Robinson, and Dyno brand names. GT Bicycles sold a full line of more than 40 bicycle models but was best known for its popular juvenile bikes. Like other manufacturers, GT promoted its brand through focused promotional efforts such as sponsorship of professional BMX racing teams and national, regional, and local bicycle races, as well as cooperative advertising programs with independent bicycle dealers.

Schwinn's turnaround and its addition of GT bikes put it into contention for a leadership position in the U.S. specialty retail channel. Schwinn and GT were strongest at low-end price points between $250 and $500 and together commanded an estimated market share of 18.8 percent at year-end 1999.

Intrepid, Inc.

Intrepid, Inc., was a privately held company that owned the Trek, Gary Fisher, and Klein mountain bike brands and LeMond road-racing bikes. The combined sales of the company's brands made it among the market share leaders in the specialty retailer channel. Trek was Intrepid's best-selling brand and was a pioneer in carbon-fiber frames. The Waterloo, Wisconsin, firm recorded revenues of about $400 million in 1997. Approximately 35 percent of its total revenue came from international sales. The

---

[3]Nancy Brumback, "Schwinn Cycles Fast to Finish First," *Brandmarketing*, December 1999, p. 6.

[4]L. Loro, "Schwinn Aims to Be a Big Wheel Again," *Advertising Age,* January 1995.

company employed 1,800 people worldwide to build and distribute its five bicycle lines, which included over 100 mountain bike, road-racing, touring, tandem, BMX, and children's models.

Trek began in 1976 by hand-building steel frames in a rented facility in Waterloo, Wisconsin. Pursuing high-quality workmanship, the firm expanded quickly, generating $750,000 in sales after just three years. It soon gained a reputation for quality American-made bicycles. By 1986, sales hit $16 million, but the company's rapid growth did not come without problems. The company sustained losses and accumulated unsold inventory, and employee morale was low. In stepped the founder of Trek, Dick Burke, who quickly took charge and articulated a back-to-basics philosophy that rallied employees and reenergized the company with a new mission statement: "Build a quality product; offer a competitive value; deliver it on time; and create a positive work environment."[5] In addition, Burke revised Trek's marketing strategy, developed new and innovative road bikes, and introduced a new line of mountain bikes. He emphasized quality and efficiency in his plant operations and pushed service excellence as the cornerstone of the sales department. As a result of these initiatives, Trek introduced a number of award-winning bicycles and steadily increased sales every year after 1987. Trek's Y-shaped carbon composite frame was one of the company's more innovative and popular products during the late 1990s and was available on many of its high-end bikes. In 1995, the designers working on Trek's Y-frame mountain bike project were named "Design Engineers of the Year" by *Popular Mechanics* and the Trek 970 Y-frame model was named *Mountain Bike* magazine's "Bike of the Year."

Trek's Y-frame was also available in an aluminum construction and could be outfitted with full suspension or in a hardtail configuration that included front suspension only. Trek's suspension could be adjusted to three positions that matched cross-country, downhill, or general riding or racing conditions. Trek also offered a women's frame with modified geometric proportions to better fit a female rider. Trek cosponsored racing teams with Volkswagen and the U.S. Postal Service and independently sponsored a triathlete team to race-test the company's upcoming generations of products. All three cycling teams won a number of prestigious events during 1999. Trek's most popular models sold at low-end and midrange price points between $250 and $1,200.

Intrepid's Gary Fisher and Klein lines of mountain bikes included a greater proportion of high-end models than its Trek line. The company acquired the Gary Fisher brand in 1993 to help it expand its dealer network further into communities that already carried Trek. Intrepid could offer a new dealer the ability to carry Gary Fisher models without offending its existing Trek dealers. Gary Fisher was a premier brand because of the line's award-winning design and performance and because of the notoriety of the company's founder and namesake. Gary Fisher was an accomplished road racer during the 1960s and 1970s who created the first mountain bike in 1974. In 1994 *Smithsonian Magazine* proclaimed Gary Fisher the "Founding Father of Mountain Bikes." Gary Fisher's mountain bike racing teams were co-sponsored with Saab and boasted a number of Olympic gold medal winners among its members. Gary Fisher models were priced comparably to Trek models although Gary Fisher had fewer low-end models between $250 and $500 than Trek.

While Fisher had fewer low-end models than Trek, Klein was Intrepid's high-end mountain bike brand, with prices beginning at over $1,200. Klein Bicycles began in

---

[5]Taken from "Reinventing the Wheel: A Brief History of the Trek Bicycle Corporation," company document.

1974 as an official MIT Innovation Center project when founder Gary Klein, a competition road racer, was enrolled in the university as an engineering graduate student. Gary Klein, along with three of his classmates and their MIT engineering professor, used a $20,000 grant from the university to develop one of the first aluminum-frame bicycles. The students and their professor built a number of prototypes in 1974 and displayed their refined bikes at an international cycle show in 1975. Upon graduation from MIT, Gary and one of the three classmates moved the operation from MIT to Gary's hometown of Chehalis, Washington, where the company's bicycles were still produced in 2000.

Klein Bicycles was known for its technological innovation and craftsmanship. The company was relatively weak in the midrange category but was among the leaders in high-end mountain bikes. Each Klein bicycle was built by hand, and every component was tested under a stringent quality control process. Klein used only certified aerospace-grade aluminum and custom-made, proprietary production equipment to assemble frames at alignment tolerances as exacting as ±.0002 inches. Klein also produced carbon composite frames that were used on some of its four basic road-racing and mountain bike series, which came in multiple configurations. All Klein mountain bike models were available with either hardtail frames or full-suspension systems. Klein Bicycles and Cadillac jointly sponsored the Team Catera racing team, which included such well-known cyclists as Golden Brainard, the fourth highest ranked American in world rankings.

Specialized Bicycles

Specialized Bicycles was a private firm founded by Mike Sinyard in 1974 in Morgan Hill, California, that got its start importing Italian-made bicycle components. In 1981 the company launched the first mass-produced mountain bike—the Stumpjumper (the original model is at the Smithsonian Institution in Washington, D.C.). Specialized also created the first professional mountain bike racing team in 1983, which Mountain Dew began sponsoring in 1996. The company also created and sponsored the Cactus Cup race series that allowed amateurs to race in events similar to professional races but at a level nonthreatening enough for first-time racers to have plenty of fun. During 1998 and 1999 Specialized Cactus Cup races were held in Canada, France, Japan, Brazil, and various locations throughout the United States.

Specialized's slogan was "Innovate or die," and it had been recognized for developing a number of technologically advanced bicycle materials and components used in the production of its mountain bikes. In 1988 Specialized's Stumpjumper Epic became the first mountain bike with a carbon-fiber frame, and in 1989 the company introduced the first composite-material bicycle wheel through a joint venture with DuPont. In 1990 Specialized began producing frames from its M2 metal matrix composite material of aluminum, silicon, copper, and magnesium. The company introduced advanced full-suspension bikes in 1993, and added an improved M4 metal matrix composite frame material in 1998. Specialized also produced a number of models that were equipped with aluminum frames. Other noteworthy innovations developed by Specialized included its S-works wheel sets, which a German university rated the industry's best in terms of rigidity and weight, and its Ground Control suspension systems, which helped keep the rear wheel on the ground even under bumpy surface conditions.

Specialized management believed that its culture was a key contributor to its success in designing innovative new mountain bikes. The company made a practice of hiring avid cyclists as engineers and managers and invited all of its employees along on its daily Specialized Lunch Rides. Each day Specialized employees at its Morgan Hill plant biked over off-road trails and winding roads with the latest Specialized equipment to relieve stress and test the company's newest products. After an hour or so of riding, the employees would take quick showers and head back to their desks to eat a sandwich and return to their work. The company also created a special S-Works R&D team that was allowed to build "dream bikes" without regard to a budget. Mike Sinyard said that the company had "never been satisfied with existing bicycle technology and S-Works allows us to push the edges of the design envelope. Once we perfect new designs for S-Works bikes we begin seeking ways to make those innovations trickle down to consumer price points, which allows us to offer elite design techniques at non-elite prices."[6]

Specialized also believed that its dealers should be knowledgeable about the latest technological innovations in the bicycle industry. The company's Specialized University offered the company's 5,000 dealers in 35 countries courses on the latest frame materials, frame design geometries, and other technological innovations. Specialized University also offered courses that educated dealers and their staffs on proper bicycle sizing and fitting and repair techniques. Specialized dealers carried a full line of 55 models of bicycles that each came in multiple configurations. Specialized's basic classes of bicycles included a BMX line; a juvenile line; two road bike models; and six low-end, midrange, and high-end mountain bike lines.

Giant Global Group

Giant, which began as a small Taiwanese exporter of bicycles in 1972, was the world's largest bicycle exporter in 1999, with 93 percent of its bicycles sold outside of Taiwan. In 1999 Giant bicycles were sold in 60 countries by more than 10,000 retail dealers across seven continents. The company's 1999 revenues were estimated at approximately $400 million. Giant's growth was made possible in large part by an early alliance with Schwinn, which gave Giant the market savvy and production know-how it needed to be a major competitive force in the industry.

Schwinn began importing a small quantity of bikes from Giant in 1978 when it began looking for a source of low-cost bicycles. Schwinn's sourcing from Giant increased in 1981 when Schwinn's Chicago plant went on strike. Deciding against negotiating a settlement with labor, Schwinn's management closed the plant and moved all its engineers and equipment to Giant's factory in Taiwan. As part of the deal with Giant, Schwinn management handed over everything—technology, engineering, volume—that Giant needed to become a dominant bikemaker. In return Schwinn imported the bikes and marketed them under the Schwinn name. By 1984, Giant was shipping 700,000 bicycles to Schwinn, representing 70 percent of the contract manufacturer's sales. By 1987, Giant was selling its own brand-name bikes in Europe and the United States. To gain market share, Giant told dealers its bikes were Schwinn clones and 10 to 15 percent cheaper. Giant also hired several Schwinn executives to help build up its U.S. distribution capabilities.

Giant's move to establish a brand name and move away from contract manufacturing continued throughout the 1990s, with the company dedicating 2 percent of its annual revenues to research and development and hiring 65 designers to develop features

---

[6]Specialized press release, www.specialized.com.

and performance that cycling enthusiasts demanded. Giant's R&D efforts paid off in the late 1990s as its image in the industry soared and it won numerous awards for design innovation. The company's MCR carbon composite bicycle was named the "Best New Product of 1998" by *Business Week,* and in 1999 its XtC SE1 mountain bike was named *Mountain Biking* magazine's "Bike of the Year." In praising Giant's race-ready mountain bike, the magazine's associate editor commented "I couldn't say enough great things about this bike. First and foremost, we were drawn to every aspect of the bike. A quick glance told us this bike was well thought out and was definitely going to be a contender."[7]

Giant began a racing program to promote the company's name among avid cyclists and signed top mountain bike racers to endorse the company's products. In 1998 the company's race teams were ranked numbers two and three worldwide in road racing, numbers three and four in cross-country mountain bike racing, and numbers two and three in downhill racing. Giant also entered into an agreement with outdoor retailer Eddie Bauer to build special edition bicycles that would be sold by Giant retailers. In 1999 Giant's reliance on contract manufacturing had been reduced to 30 percent of its production. Seventy percent of the bikes produced by the company were sold under the Giant brand at prices that typically ranged between $250 and $800 but went as high as $4,000. The company emphasized a "total best value" design and production approach that attempted to match rivals in terms of frame design, component quality, and finish while beating competing brands on price. Giant's 2000 model year product line included 43 models in the mountain bike, road-racing, BMX, hybrid, and juvenile classes.

The company added two plants in China during 1993 and built a plant in the Netherlands in 1997 to keep up with the increased demand for its bicycles. In 1999 the company produced about 2.5 million bicycles with about 1 million produced in Taiwan, 100,000 produced in the Netherlands, and about 1.4 million produced in China. Giant was expected to increase its production in the Netherlands to 400,000 units per year by 2001 and had discussed building production capacity in North America.

Derby Cycle Corporation

Nottingham, England–based Derby Cycle was among the world's largest designers, manufacturers, and marketers of bicycles, with 1997 sales exceeding $500 million. The company was established in 1986 with the acquisition of Raleigh, Gazelle, and Sturmey-Archer bicycles from Britain's TI Group. Throughout the late 1980s and 1990s Derby continued to add to its portfolio with acquisitions of popular brands like Nishiki, Univega, and Diamondback. The company sold more than 2.1 million bicycles in 1997 and was the largest seller of bicycles in the United Kingdom, the Netherlands, Germany, Canada, Ireland, and South Africa. Derby Bicycle operated manufacturing facilities in the United Kingdom, the Netherlands, Germany, Canada, and the United States. Derby was one of the top five producers of bicycles sold through the U.S. specialty retailer channel of distribution and targeted the low-end market with retail prices ranging from $250 to $500.

Diamondback, Derby Cycle's most popular brand of mountain bike sold in the United States, was among the leading brands in the low-end category and was known for incorporating innovative features at moderate prices. The company's 49 basic models of mountain bikes were equipped with either steel or aluminum frames and various

---

[7]Giant Manufacturing Company press release, www.giant-bicycle.com/aboutgiant/whatsnew.asp.

suspension options that ranged from a rigid frame to full suspension. Diamondback also offered bikes in the youth, BMX, hybrid, road-racer, cruiser, and fitness equipment segments. Diamondback and other Derby brands had lost some dealer orders in 1999 and 2000 because of consistently poor dealer service.

CANNONDALE'S HISTORY AND BACKGROUND

Joseph Montgomery, who grew up on an Ohio peach farm and later dropped out of college three times, began Cannondale Corporation in 1971 after having abandoned careers as a charter boat captain and a securities analyst. Joe Montgomery's first career change occurred after his charter boat sank under his command in shark-infested waters. Montgomery took a less life-threatening but more mundane position as a securities analyst in 1964, but after seven years on Wall Street changed careers again to start Cannondale. Joe Montgomery began Cannondale with the vision of making it the best cycling company in the world. His vision inspired 10 principles that made up the Cannondale philosophy:

1. We care about each other, our shareholders, our customers, and our vendors.
2. We produce a stream of innovative, quality products.
3. We devise flexible manufacturing processes that enable us to deliver those innovative, quality products to the market quickly and then back them with excellent customer service.
4. We limit our distribution to the best specialty retailers in the world.
5. We stay lean, remain competitive and entrepreneurial.
6. We put 90 percent of our profits back into the company to underwrite future growth; the balance we share with all of our employees.
7. We promote from within whenever possible.
8. We concentrate on detail, because the last 5 percent is often the difference between success and failure.
9. We continuously improve everything.
10. We govern our every deed by what is "just and right."

As of 2000 Joseph Montgomery had been Cannondale's only chairperson, president, and chief executive officer. The birth and early history of Cannondale was aptly captured in a 1986 article in *New England Business,* excerpted below.

> "I always wanted to start my own business," says the 46-year-old [Joe] Montgomery; he began the search for opportunities when he started working on Wall Street as an analyst in the 1960s for companies such as Prudential-Bache. His employers were looking for fast-track companies in leisure-time industries such as snowmobiles, but he was looking for less obvious opportunities.
>
> "The bike industry was a sleepy industry," Montgomery said. "The industry had old ideas and designs. Anyone who was really aggressive and designed a functional, quality product could make a go. It was a field ripe for new ideas." In 1972 he had one—a mini-trailer that bike campers could use to tow their gear. He quit his job and on the strength of a contract with a distributor, got a $60,000 loan to finance production.
>
> Sales for the trailer started soft and, working in improvised company offices above a pickle store in Cannondale, Conn., he developed bicycle accessories to expand the line. The timing was good. The 1973 Arab fuel embargo hit, sparking a two-year bike boom, and his sales leapt ahead to $2.3 million by 1974. Then, in 1975, recession hit and the boom

ended. The speed and degree of the drop in bike sales was terrifying. In 1974, 14.1 million units sold. In 1975, 7 million sold. Bike shops all over America closed.

"It was a big washout. A lot of people who were tired of some rat race and figured they'd open a bike shop went under. Our sales were cut in half, and we were stuck with $250,000 in bad debts." Having just gotten started, he wasn't about to file for bankruptcy protection.

"The worst thing you can do in this situation is put your head in the sand. You've got to call the guy and say, 'Look, I know what I owe. Here's my business plan, my cash flow analysis. Not only will I pay you what I owe you, I'll continue to buy from you.'"

His creditors liked his approach, and their cooperation helped the company out of trouble. But Montgomery acknowledges it was a sweat. "Very scary," he said. "Very scary."

Through the 1970s and early 80s, Cannondale quietly achieved steady annual sales at around $8 million and became known for an expanding line of quality bike camping equipment. Montgomery wanted to make a bicycle, though. In 1982, he got a letter from a 25-year-old engineer named David Graham, who felt he was stagnating in the Electric Boat facility in Groton, Conn.

"David wrote, 'I'm an engineer and I want to build an aluminum bike,'" Montgomery remembered. "We'd been working on bikes way back in the 70s, and I was pretty sure I wanted to make an aluminum one. Graham took a 50 percent pay cut to come here."

The first Cannondale aluminum bike came out in 1983. It hadn't been easy. There had been production problems: All the fabrication equipment for the aluminum frame had to be custom designed, and they had trouble getting components that would fit the unusually fat tubing. (Like almost all bike manufacturers, Cannondale makes practically nothing on their own bike except the frame. Gears, shifters, and other components are obtained from outside suppliers. Most of these are from the Far East, which somewhat dilutes current company efforts to position itself as an "American-made" bike.)

Finally, the bike hit dealers' floors. It was weird-looking, expensive at $600, and had a number of bugs still to be worked out. But the equipment nuts, the "spoke sniffers" who permeate the bicycling world and are ever on the lookout for something new, embraced it.

For them, the prime attractions were the technical advantages of aluminum. Aluminum, of course, is light, and in premium bikes, light weight is a vital sales point. Yet Cannondale bikes are not appreciably lighter than comparable steel frame bikes, because Graham took advantage of aluminum and used more of it, making the frame tubing thicker and making the bike structurally stiffer.

Ted Constantino, editor of Bicycle Guide, a Boston-based consumer specialty magazine, explains that a stiff frame without any "give" makes for a more efficient bike. "There's a feeling you get on a Cannondale that every kilowatt of energy you put into the pedal comes out the rear wheel."

As important to sales as what the frame does is its distinctive look. "It doesn't hurt," Montgomery ingenuously acknowledges. "If I'm a spoke sniffer, I am proud you can see that I ride something different."

. . . Cannondale as an American company is bucking prevailing trends in the bike industry. The majority of premium bikes sold in the United States are made in the Far East. European and American companies used to dominate until the mid-70s, when the now familiar one-two punch of high quality and low price from Japan hit the market. During the next ten years, old names such as Raleigh, Motobecane, and Puch ran into deep trouble.

But Cannondale saw sales explode right out to the gate; from 1983 to 1985 it grew at a 30 percent annual rate. They expanded their line from one model to 15. In 1984, Cannondale netted a lucrative contract making private-label bikes for L. L. Bean. Market demand and publicity within the industry helped it to expand its dealer network through North America, and then to Europe. It found itself continually expanding its headquarters in Georgetown, which now employs 80, and its production facility in Bedford, Penn., which now employs 175.

. . . If not the largest, it certainly may be the most talked about bike company. In that great consumer undercurrent of hearsay that can make or break a product, Cannondale has been designated as the "best" bike around. That means it's trendy. Trendy is transitory, and Montgomery knows he'll have to work hard to get beyond it. For now, though, trendy is OK. Trendy is something Joe Montgomery can take to the bank.[8]

CANNONDALE IN 2000

In 2000 Cannondale was a leading manufacturer and marketer of high-performance bicycles and high-performance bicycle components, with an estimated 20 percent share of the U.S. high-performance bicycle market. The company also provided its dealers with a full line of bicycle components, accessories, and men's and women's cycling apparel. The company had also set a spring 2000 launch date for its MX400 motocross motorcycle. Even though Cannondale management expected the MX400 to be an important contributor to its revenue growth in future years, the company's main business was high-performance bicycles. Cannondale was a leader in the use of lightweight aluminum as a material for bicycle frames and was the only bicycle manufacturer not to build bicycles from steel. With the exception of its carbon-fiber Raven model, all of Cannondale's bicycle models offered for the 2000 model year were constructed with hand-welded aluminum frames. The company's bicycles, marketed under the Cannondale brand name and carrying its "Handmade in the USA" logo, were sold through specialty bicycle retailers in the United States and in more than 60 other countries.

Cannondale's corporate headquarters was located in Georgetown, Connecticut, and its manufacturing facilities for bicycles, motorcycles, bicycle components, accessories, and clothing were located in Bedford, Pennsylvania. At the end of July 1999, Cannondale employed a total of 779 full-time workers in the United States, 115 in its European subsidiary, 16 in its Japanese subsidiary, and 6 in its Cannondale Australia subsidiary.

Cannondale's Business Strategy

Cannondale's overall business strategy had a significant vertical integration component. The company manufactured its own frames in the United States, whereas most of its competitors imported their frames from Asia. Cannondale was one of the first companies to concentrate on aluminum frames and enjoyed the premier position in this category, as bicyclists continued to gravitate toward lighter, sturdier high-performance bicycles. In addition, Cannondale developed a proprietary component line under the Cannondale Original Design Application (CODA) brand that was used in a growing portion of its product mix and was becoming more important in the aftermarket. With components such as handlebars, brakes, cranks, and derailleurs comprising a significant portion of a bike's value, Cannondale hoped to gain a competitive advantage over manufacturers who relied on outside component suppliers such as Shimano, SunTour, and Campionolo.

Product Innovation   Cannondale's products were designed for cyclists who wanted high-performance, high-quality bicycles. It differentiated its bicycles through technological innovations that made its bicycles lighter, stronger, faster, and more comfortable than those of rivals. The company had an ongoing commitment to R&D and had continued to expand and develop its aluminum bicycle line with a series of innovations, focusing on proprietary frame designs, suspension systems, and components.

---

[8]R. E. Charm, "Like the Company's Sales, Aluminum Bike of Cannondale Stands Out from the Pack," *New England Business* 8, no. 3 (November 3, 1986), p. 41.

Each new frame or component innovation went through a two-month battery of tests in the company's $1 million-plus Q-Lab that included fatigue testing, impact testing, finite element analysis, computerized field testing, and brittle-coat testing. Cannondale's know-how and manufacturing skills enabled the company to be a first-mover and trendsetter. Its original product, the Bugger bicycle trailer, was an industry first that pioneered an entire product category. Cannondale produced the first-ever large-diameter, aluminum-tube bicycles in 1983. It introduced its first mountain bike in 1984. In 1990, the company led the industry in introducing suspension systems in bicycles and in 1996 created a lightweight thermoplastic carbon-skin frame that was bonded to a magnesium spine for its new Raven mountain bike. In 2000 the second-generation Raven frame was honored as one of the "Best of What's New" products by *Popular Science*. Joe Montgomery described his philosophy toward innovation: "We approach everything we do—and I mean everything—with an eye toward innovation. And to a large extent, it's the innovations we've developed on the design and manufacturing side that allow us to continually bring these exciting new products to market."[9] Exhibit 5 shows a time line of Cannondale's growth and key innovations since 1971.

Manufacturing   The centerpiece of Cannondale's manufacturing strategy was its flexible manufacturing system. The strengths of the system included reduced production time, simultaneous production of various models and small batch sizes without high tooling changeover costs. A patented process employed lasers and other devices to cut the uniquely configured joints of various bicycle models without individual setup or changeover. Patented self-fixturing joint designs and hold devices allowed the parts to interlock without special tools as they were readied for welding. The manufacturing system enabled the cost-effective production of a wide product line and a broad range of models in a single day in order to respond to consumer demands. Cannondale's proprietary manufacturing system had allowed the company to reduce the time to completed bike from 17 days to only 3. Further efficiencies in the development process for other parts were realized through a new prototyping and tooling center with computer-aided design and manufacturing (CAD/CAM) technology. The company was committed to maintaining its competitive position by supporting research into further improvements in its manufacturing process and drastically reducing the time required to design and produce new bike models.

Cannondale's CAD/CAM system, which automatically calculated specific tube lengths, and its computer-guided laser tube cutters allowed the company to offer custom-fitted bicycles. The company had built custom-fitted bikes since 1994 for its professional racing staff, and began to offer consumers in Japan, Europe, Australia, Canada, and the United States custom-fitted bikes in 1999. Cannondale was expected to introduce custom fitting in the remainder of the 60-plus international markets where its bicycles were sold in 2000. Cannondale charged a $400 custom fitting fee and could deliver the custom-made bike to the consumer within six weeks.

Cannondale considered its domestic manufacturing base a key competitive advantage. Whereas the majority of bike companies purchased most, if not all, of their models from huge Far Eastern manufacturers, Cannondale made its bike frames in Pennsylvania. As Montgomery explained, "When you go to Asia to get a new frame design manufactured, the manufacturer makes three bikes for each one you order; one for you, one to sell to another bike company, and one to sell under their own brand

---

[9]M. Sloane, "Cannondale: A Company Built on Innovation," *The Journal of Competitive Cycling* 1 (1995), pp. 7–10.

exhibit 5 25 Years of Cannondale Innovations

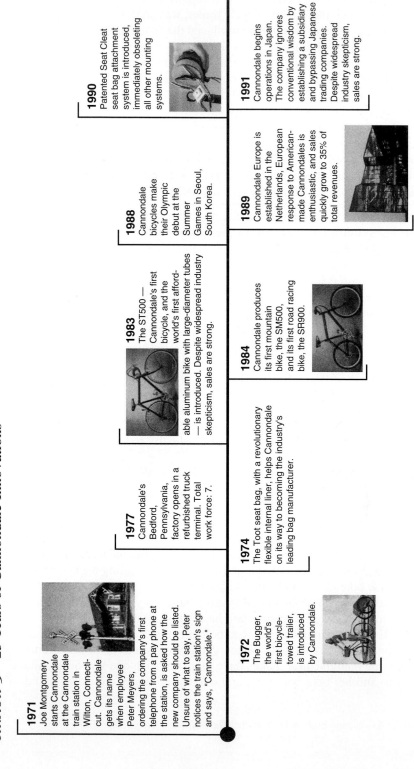

1971
Joe Montgomery starts Cannondale at the Cannondale train station in Wilton, Connecticut. Cannondale gets its name when employee Peter Meyers, ordering the company's first telephone from a pay phone at the station, is asked how the new company should be listed. Unsure of what to say, Peter notices the train station's sign and says, "Cannondale."

1972
The Bugger, the world's first bicycle-towed trailer, is introduced by Cannondale.

1974
The Toot seat bag, with a revolutionary flexible internal liner, helps Cannondale on its way to becoming the industry's leading bag manufacturer.

1977
Cannondale's Bedford, Pennsylvania, factory opens in a refurbished truck terminal. Total work force: 7.

1983
The ST500 — Cannondale's first bicycle, and the world's first afford-able aluminum bike with large-diameter tubes — is introduced. Despite widespread industry skepticism, sales are strong.

1984
Cannondale produces its first mountain bike, the SM500, and its first road racing bike, the SR900.

1988
Cannondale bicycles make their Olympic debut at the Summer Games in Seoul, South Korea.

1989
Cannondale Europe is established in the Netherlands, European response to American-made Cannondales is enthusiastic, and sales quickly grow to 35% of total revenues.

1990
Patented Seat Cleat seat bag attachment system is introduced, immediately obsoleting all other mounting systems.

1991
Cannondale begins operations in Japan. The company ignores conventional wisdom by establishing a subsidiary and bypassing Japanese trading companies. Despite widespread industry skepticism, sales are strong.

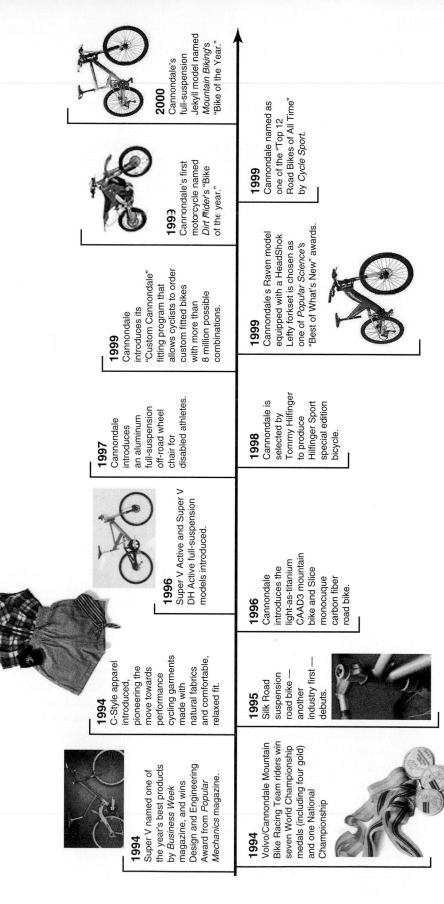

1994
Super V named one of the year's best products by *Business Week* magazine, and wins Design and Engineering Award from *Popular Mechanics* magazine.

1994
C-Style apparel introduced, pioneering the move towards performance cycling garments made with natural fabrics and comfortable, relaxed fit.

1994
Volvo/Cannondale Mountain Bike Racing Team riders win seven World Championship medals (including four gold) and one National Championship

1995
Silk Road suspension road bike — another industry first — debuts.

1996
Super V Active and Super V DH Active full-suspension models introduced.

1996
Cannondale introduces the light-as-titanium CAAD3 mountain bike and Slice monocuque carbon fiber road bike.

1997
Cannondale introduces an aluminum full-suspension off-road wheel chair for disabled athletes.

1998
Cannondale is selected by Tommy Hilfinger to produce Hilfinger Sport special edition bicycle.

1999
Cannondale introduces its "Custom Cannondale" fitting program that allows cyclists to order custom fitted bikes with more than 8 million possible combinations.

1999
Cannondale's Raven model equipped with a HeadShok Lefty forkset is chosen as one of *Popular Science's* "Best of What's New" awards.

1999
Cannondale's first motorcycle named *Dirt Rider's* "Bike of the year."

1999
Cannondale named as one of the "Top 12 Road Bikes of All Time" by *Cycle Sport.*

2000
Cannondale's full-suspension Jekyll model named *Mountain Biking's* "Bike of the Year."

name. By the time your new bike finally makes it into bike shops, the market is flooded with similar designs." He went on to describe the advantage of operating his own factories:

> First off, our factories don't have other customers ahead of us in line. When we make an improvement, or add a model, the reaction is instantaneous. Also, our proprietary designs remain proprietary. And of course, our product doesn't spend an extra six months on the water or stuck in customs, before finally becoming available to customers.[10]

Even though Cannondale's U.S.-based manufacturing facilities were a valuable competitive resource, various equipment problems in its Bedford, Pennsylvania, plant had resulted in unfilled dealer orders during the fall of 1999 and had delayed the introduction of some 2000 models.

Purchasing   Aluminum tubing was the primary material used to manufacture bicycles. Cannondale entered into purchasing agreements with various aluminum suppliers to ensure favorable pricing and delivery terms and certain technical assistance, but believed that termination of its contracts would not have a significant impact on its costs because of aluminum's wide availability. Most of its bicycle components were purchased from Japanese, Taiwanese, and U.S. original equipment manufacturers (OEMs). Its largest component supplier was Shimano, which was the source of approximately 19 percent of total inventory purchases in 1999. Cannondale concentrated buying power among fewer suppliers, which allowed the company to secure higher-volume purchase discounts.

Marketing   The goal of Cannondale's sales and marketing program was to establish the company as the leading high-performance bicycle brand in the specialty bicycle retail channel. The marketing effort focused on promotion of the firm's product innovation, performance, and quality leadership; publicity generated from the Volvo/Cannondale mountain bike racing team; and a media campaign designed to attract consumers to specialty bicycle retailers. Cannondale also maintained an innovative Web site (www.cannondale.com) that averaged more than 25 million hits each month.

Promotion   In 1994, Cannondale formed the Volvo/Cannondale racing team. The team generated considerable publicity in both the cycling press and the general press and through television coverage. Cannondale leveraged the success of its racing team by using photo images of the athletes in print media, point-of-sale literature, banners, product packaging, and product catalogs. Since its inception in 1994, the Volvo/Cannondale team had won four World Championships, six World Cup titles, 28 top finishes in World Cup events, nine National Championships, two Pan Am Games gold medals, and a silver medal at the 1996 Summer Olympic Games in Atlanta, Georgia. In addition, Cannondale supported racing teams in other cycling areas, such as its road-racing team that was cosponsored with Saeco, an Italian firm that was the world's largest manufacturer of espresso machines and its SoBe/HeadShok grassroots squad that provided technical assistance to team riders and held instructional clinics for Cannondale retailers and their staff. SoBe, the leading maker of wellness beverages, also agreed to cosponsor Cannondale's planned MX400 motocross racing team.

Cannondale's print advertising focused on magazines for cycling enthusiasts and general lifestyle magazines to reach upscale adults with an interest in outdoor and leisure activities. In addition, Cannondale entered into a licensing agreement with Tommy Hilfiger in 1998 to produce a special Hilfiger Sport mountain bike that would

---

[10]Ibid.

be sold by Cannondale retailers. Cannondale management believed that the new Hilfiger bikes would draw customers who normally wouldn't shop in a bicycle store.

Sales and Distribution   Cannondale's distribution strategy was to sell its bicycles through specialty bicycle retailers who it believed could provide knowledgeable sales assistance regarding the technical and performance characteristics of its products and offer an ongoing commitment to service. Cannondale bicycles were not available through mass merchandisers, which generally carried lower-priced products and did not have the expertise to sell and support high-performance bikes. The company had not awarded exclusive rights to retailers in any territory. In 2000 the company sold its bicycles through 1,150 specialty retailer locations in the United States and Canada. Cannondale accessories were carried by an additional 500 retail locations in the United States and Canada. Before establishing a new dealer, the company considered such factors as market density in terms of competition, population, and demographics; ability of the retailer to optimize market penetration; commitment to service and the high-performance segment of the market; and dealer creditworthiness.

Research and Development   Cannondale's product development strategy was directed at continually making bicycles lighter, stronger, faster, and more comfortable. Its Volvo/Cannondale mountain bike racing team was closely tied to its R&D process, thus allowing regular testing of both prototypes and finished production models. Cannondale's vice president of R&D explained the company's view of the R&D function and team sponsorships as follows: "Most bike companies view racing as a marketing tool, and while we enjoy the exposure the team provides, for us it's primarily a research and development tool. That's why we continue to support racing so aggressively. We make high-end, high-performance bicycles and we use the athletes' feedback to bring fresh innovations to our bikes. That's why we partially fund the team from our R&D budget, and why you'll always find more Cannondale engineers than marketing people at the races."[11] This collaboration, combined with the racing experience of its engineering staff, produced revisions, new designs, and new product ideas. The company had spent more than $20 million on research and development between 1997 and 1999 and held 35 U.S. patents related to various products, processes, and designs.

Cannondale had developed several proprietary suspension systems and enhancements. Its HeadShok incorporated the suspension and steering mechanisms into one unit built into the head tube of the bicycle. This design provided more accurate steering control than other front-suspension models and also allowed easy adjustability while riding. Cannondale's HeadShok line included 14 models in 2000 and was highlighted by its new Lefty fork, which featured a telescoping blade that reduced weight while delivering 100 millimeters of travel. The Lefty had a distinctive look because of its single fork, which extended down the left side of the bicycle's front wheel.

To ensure structural integrity of its designs, an experimental stress and analysis laboratory was used to collect data on stresses placed on products during actual riding conditions. This information was analyzed and incorporated into the design of new products through its computer-aided design system. In addition, stress analysis testing was conducted during production to verify conformance to design specifications.

International Operations   Cannondale entered the international market in 1989 when it established a European subsidiary, Cannondale Europe, in the Netherlands. Although Cannondale Europe assembled bikes, using imported parts and frames from Cannondale's U.S. facility, it was primarily a selling and distribution organization

---

[11]Cannondale press release, www.cannondale.com/bikepres/19981204.html.

exhibit 6   Selected Financial Data for Cannondale Corporation, by Geographic Area, 1997–99 (In Millions)

	1999	1998	1997
Net sales			
United States	$ 72,413	$ 75,193	$ 80,542
Germany	26,639	25,382	23,569
Other European countries	59,008	52,603	43,478
All other countries	18,759	18,318	14,907
	$176,819	$171,496	$162,496
Identifiable assets			
United States	$ 54,798	$ 37,937	$ 21,905
Netherlands	2,886	3,141	2,949
All other countries	449	380	522
	$ 58,133	$ 41,458	$ 25,376

Source: Cannondale Corporation 1999 10-K.

that reached all of Western Europe directly and served Eastern Europe through distributors. The company sold its bicycles and accessories directly to approximately 1,400 dealers in Austria, Belgium, Denmark, Finland, Germany, Italy, Ireland, Luxembourg, the Netherlands, Norway, Spain, Sweden, Switzerland, and the United Kingdom. Sales growth in Europe, where cycling was second only to soccer in popularity among sports, had averaged a compound growth rate of 12.4 percent between 1993 and 1999.

Cannondale Japan was established in 1992. This subsidiary imported fully assembled bikes and was primarily a selling organization. The company sold bicycles and accessories directly to 300 retailers in Japan and sold accessories only to an additional 27 Japanese retailers. Cannondale's penetration of the Japanese market was estimated to be below 1 percent.

Cannondale Australia was established in 1996 when Cannondale purchased the assets of Beaushan Trading Party Limited. Cannondale's Australian subsidiary imported fully assembled bicycles and a full line of accessories and sold them in Australia and New Zealand to approximately 200 retailers. Exhibit 6 presents Cannondale's net sales contribution and value of identifiable assets by geographic area.

Cannondale's Product Line

Bicycles   In 2000, Cannondale offered 71 models of bicycles, all of which except its carbon-fiber Raven model featured aluminum frames. Cannondale's full-suspension mountain bikes (Super V Raven, Super V, Freeride, and Jekyll) featured front and rear suspension to allow for greater control and comfort at high speeds without sacrificing light frame weight. Cannondale's new Jekyll models included a distinctly different frame design that allowed the geometry of the bike to be customized to the rider's preference by dialing in the head angle and the bottom bracket height. The Jekyll also used the company's new HeadShok Lefty fork that had three times the torsional stiffness of other top forks and weighed just 3.7 pounds. The Jekyll was chosen as *Mountain Biking* magazine's 2000 "Bike of the Year" in its March 2000 issue.

Cannondale's Raven mountain bike was equally innovative. The Raven's frame was made from a carbon composite skin that was stretched over a magnesium spine. The bare frame weighed only 4.7 pounds yet was as rigid as Cannondale's aluminum-frame bicycles. The bike was equipped with Cannondale's HeadShok Lefty fork set and CODA hubs, crank, pedals, saddle, and brakes. The Raven was listed among the four most innovative products, discoveries, or technologies of 1999 by *Popular Science.* The company also offered a variety of front-suspension and rigid-frame mountain bikes among its product line. Cannondale's Smooth Riding Bicycle (SRB) line of mountain bikes was introduced in 1998 and used a mountain bike frame but was outfitted with a wider saddle and tires that were suitable for on-road or off-road use. The SRB also had a more upright riding position that made casual riding more comfortable than a typical mountain bike position. In describing the SRB's place in Cannondale's product line, the company's bicycle product manager said, "Not everyone wants to thrash singletrack or dice it up in the pelotron. But just because a customer wants a more recreational-style bike doesn't mean they want it to be heavy or of poor quality."[12]

Cannondale offered a number of hybrid and comfort bikes to appeal to the cyclist who wanted to cruise around town, get aerobic exercise, commute to work, or occasionally ride off-road trails. Cannondale's comfort bikes were available in full-suspension, front-suspension, or rigid-frame models. Hybrid models were equipped with either front-suspension or rigid frames. Cannondale offered cyclocross bikes for competition in mixed off-road and obstacle races and multisport bikes designed for triathlon and duathlon events.

Cannondale's high-performance road-racing bikes had steep frame angles and a short wheelbase for nimble handling and were equipped with either a front-suspension or rigid frame. In 1999 Cannondale was selected as one of the "Top 12 Road Bikes of All Time" by *Cycle Sport,* a magazine devoted to European road racing. The company's touring bikes included many of the performance features of its other models, but with a longer wheelbase that provided stability when riders were carrying additional gear for camping and touring. Cannondale's flexible manufacturing techniques allowed for small production runs of specialty bicycles such as tandem bikes, which were produced in both mountain bike and road-racing models. Cannondale's product line by category for 2000 is shown in Exhibit 7.

Bicycle Accessories The accessory line helped the company to capitalize more fully on its distribution channels' capability and, at the same time, build brand-name recognition. As with bicycles, Cannondale sought to differentiate its accessories through innovation.

- *Packs and bags*—Cannondale offered a variety of bags and panniers (bags mounted on the sides of the wheels for touring): mountain bike bags, lightweight, moderate-capacity road bike bags; and large capacity touring bags. The company also made fanny packs, duffels, and a backpack designed specifically for cyclists. The patented Seat Cleat bag attachment was honored by *Industrial Design* magazine for its design innovation.

- *Apparel and footwear*—Cannondale offered a complete line of men's and women's cycling apparel, including such garments as shorts, jerseys, jackets, and skinsuits. The company's line consisted of four lines: Vertex, a high-performance,

---

[12]Ibid.

***exhibit* 7**   Cannondale's Number of Models in Each Bicycle Category for 2000

Bicycle Category	Number of Models
Mountain bikes	
Full suspension	11
Front suspension	13
Nonsuspended	3
Road bikes	
Front suspension	3
Nonsuspended	15
Multisport recreational	2
Hybrid	7
Comfort	7
Specialty	
Tandem	5
Touring	3
Cyclocross	2
Total	71

Source: Cannondale Corporation 1999 10-K.

competition-level line; HpX, a versatile line of performance-oriented apparel for riders of all abilities; Terra, a more loosely cut line for off-road riding; and a women's Sport line of tailored, form-fitting garments. Some Cannondale apparel was made from its proprietary Micro-C fabric that forced moisture away from the body. Cannondale's Arago clipless compatible mountain biking shoe was very lightweight and contoured to the foot yet stiff enough to efficiently transfer leg energy to the pedal and crank.

- *Components*—Cannondale's proprietary HeadShok front-suspension forks were an important point of differentiation from other bicycle manufacturers, which virtually all used the same brand of forks produced by one of two independent suppliers. Most of the company's HeadShok forks functioned with the bicycle's frame as part of an integrated system, but the 2000 model HeadShok Lefty was a single-legged suspension system that could be mounted on Cannondale frames or other brands of frames. The Lefty had been recognized for its innovative design by such publications as *Design News, Popular Mechanics,* and the *New York Times.*

  In 1994 Cannondale began sales of CODA components—featuring brakes, handlebars, bar-ends, seat binders, grips, cranksets, and hubs—and began using these components on certain models of its bikes. The company focused its R&D efforts on developing products superior to or more cost-effective than those available from other parts manufacturers. Cannondale's proprietary components like its CODA Competition suspension seatpost not only helped differentiate the company's bikes from brands that used similar components but also provided an additional source of revenue from aftermarket retail sales.

- *Other accessories*—Cannondale's other accessories included tools, pumps, water bottles, and bicycle trailers manufactured by third parties and sold under the Cannondale brand name.

Cannondale's Diversification into Motorcycles

In February 1998 Cannondale founder and CEO Joe Montgomery announced that the company would transfer its bicycle frame design and production skills to the off-road motorcycle industry. Cannondale said that it would bring at least three design innovations to the $700 million market for dirt bikes. Cannondale's new motorcycle would have a radical new engine design, include a unique single-pivot swingarm rear suspension, and be constructed of large-diameter aluminum tubing that would provide greater frame stiffness and lighter weight than a steel frame. Many motorcycle industry observers believed that Cannondale could deliver on its promise to bring new innovations to the industry. The publisher of *Motocross Action Magazine* cautioned skeptics, "Don't discount the bicycle manufacturer's ability to compete in the motorcycle world. Today's mountain bikes far exceed motorcycles in the use of creative metallurgy, CAD-CAM frame design, innovative suspension systems, in the case of Cannondale, an American production facility that can easily produce a high-end product."[13]

MX400 engine innovations included a liquid-cooled, reversed cylinder head, and innovative air intake design, an electric starter, and fuel injection. Cannondale designers said that the reverse cylinder head allowed the engine to have a more upright placement and a lower center of gravity that would aid in the motorcycle's off-road handling. Also, the reverse head allowed the air intake to face the front of the bike and the exhaust to face the rear, away from the water-cooled engine's radiator. The MX400's forward air intake was built into the steering head of the motorcycle's frame and helped supply a flow of debris-free cool air needed for greater power output and a wider powerband. The long air intake also improved low-speed throttle response. The electric starter feature was already available on almost all street bikes but was not usually found on dirt bikes. Cannondale management believed that the electric starter would be a convenience feature that motocrossers would appreciate—starting a dirt bike often took a considerable amount of strenuous kicking because of the very high compression single-cylinder engine designs. The MX400's fuel injection system that provided better throttle response and less maintenance than a carburetor was expected to take much of the engine-failure-related frustration out of motocross.

The MX400's use of fuel injection also allowed Cannondale's design team to create a rear suspension where the shock absorber was positioned at the optimal angle because there was no carburetor blocking the way. The rear suspension was a unique single-pivot linkless design that required less maintenance and provided greater rigidity than traditional motorcycle rear-suspension systems. The entire MX400 frame was built from Cannondale's trademark large-diameter stiff aluminum tubing and was designed to keep the motorcycle's center of gravity low. Commenting on the company's use of large-diameter aluminum tubing and a single-pivot swingarm, Cannondale's director of marketing said, "Flex resistance is every bit as critical to the performance of a motorcycle frame as it is to the performance of a bicycle frame. Whether it's a bicycle or a motorcycle, you want to minimize side-to-side flex in order to preserve steering precision and stability. Wimpy frames and rear suspensions with long, flexible, linkages can't deliver the kind of handling you need in a high-performance vehicle."[14]

By summer 1998 Cannondale began testing 11 different prototypes of the MX400's new engine and frame. The MX400's final test came in November 1999 when the

---

[13]"Bicycle-Maker Cannondale to Unveil New Motorcycle at Indianapolis Trade Show," PR Newswire, February 12, 1999.

[14]Cannondale press release, www.cannondalemotorcycle.com/press/19980501.html.

motorcycle took first place in its racing debut. The MX400 won two 5-lap races on a small 1.25-mile track located near Cannondale's Beford, Pennsylvania, production facility. The MX400 won both races by more than a minute. The MX400 was named *Dirt Rider* magazine's "Bike of the Year" in late 1999. In reviewing the bike's design innovations, the magazine's editor said, "The MX400 looks more like a high-dollar project from a secret division of a major automobile manufacturer than a first attempt from a leader in the pedal power industry."[15] A *Dirt Action* writer concurred with *Dirt Rider*'s assessment of the new Cannondale motorcycle: "The MX400 contains enough innovation to make everything else with knobbies appear quaintly antique. The other manufacturers are going to hate this bike, because it forces them to move motocross machines into a new technological era."[16] The motorcycle was scheduled for a summer 1999 launch, but unforeseen production problems had delayed the MX400's shipment to Cannondale's network of 159 independent motorcycle dealers in 38 states to the spring of 2000. In January 2000 Cannondale's orders for its new MX400 had exceeded its projected sales forecast by more than 80 percent. Cannondale management planned to capitalize on the initial success of the MX400 with the unveiling of several additional motorcycles at the motorcycle industry's 2000 trade show held in Indianapolis, Indiana.

---

[15]As quoted in Cannondale's 1999 annual report.
[16]Ibid.

case 10 Competition in the Retail Brokerage Industry in 2000

Arthur A. Thompson
The University of Alabama

John E. Gamble
University of South Alabama

The competitive structure of the $14 billion U.S. retail brokerage industry was undergoing significant change in early 2000. Prior to the emergence of the online brokerage segment in 1995–96, investors who wanted to buy or sell shares of common stock had to place an order with one of the nearly 600,000 registered brokers who worked at such traditional full-service brokerages as Merrill Lynch, Paine Webber, and Prudential Securities or limited-service discount brokerage firms like Charles Schwab, Quick & Reilly, and Siebert Securities. During the 1996–98 period, the emergence of online trading via the Internet created a three-tier industry structure—full-service brokers, limited-service discount brokers, and new-breed online brokers.

But mushrooming growth in online trading and the competitive effects of investors moving their accounts to online brokerages to take advantage of low-cost commissions and convenient point-and-click investing quickly put full-service brokers and, to a lesser extent, discount brokers in a strategic bind. If full-service brokers began offering online trading options to their customers to counter the market inroads of online brokerages, they undermined the big stream of commission revenues they had historically earned and risked alienating their thousands of professional brokers who delivered services to clients and whose incomes were tied to the size of the commission fees they generated. However, when longtime industry leader Merrill Lynch announced in June 1999 that it would overhaul its full-price/full-service business model and begin offering its customers online trading at $29.95 per trade, the resistance of full-service and discount brokers to online trading crumbled.

By early 2000 virtually all the leading retail brokerage firms in the United States had either added online trading to the list of services they provided to customers or were planning to do so in a matter of months. Full-service brokerages were scrambling behind the scenes to revise their strategies and business models and trying to reassure their brokers that online trading would not wipe out their jobs. The distinction between traditional brokers and online brokers was fading as the Internet came to be seen as a required distribution channel. Competition among retail brokerages of all types, which

exhibit 1   Estimated Market Shares of the Leading Online Brokerage Firms, First Quarter 1998–2000 (Based on Daily Trade Volume)

Brokerage Firm	Estimated Share of Daily Trades		
	Fourth Quarter, 1999	First Quarter, 1999	First Quarter, 1998
Charles Schwab & Co.	22.0%	27.9%	32%
E*Trade	15.3	13.3	12
Waterhouse Securities	13.3	11.7	9
Fidelity (a unit of Fidelity Investments—the leading provider of mutual funds in the United States)	11.4	10.1	8
Datek Online	10.0	10.1	7
Ameritrade	8.8	8.3	6
DLJdirect (a unit of Donaldson Lufkin & Jennrette—a prominent investment banking firm)	3.8	3.8	4
Suretrade/Quick & Reilly (a subsidiary of Fleet Financial—a leading New England bank)	2.0	2.2	4
Morgan Stanley Dean Witter Online (formerly Discover Brokerage Direct)	1.5	2.8	4
All others	11.9	12.6	14
			100%

Source: U.S. Bancorp Piper Jaffray, Inc.

historically had centered on price and breadth of service, was starting to include other areas. And several online brokerage competitors, led by Charles Schwab and E*Trade, were launching a variety of new strategic initiatives to stake out far broader market positions than ever before. Schwab was rapidly transforming itself into a full-service online financial services firm; it could no longer be looked on as a limited-service discount broker with a big stake in online trading. Other brokerages that had pioneered the online trading segment were also branching out to leverage the business potential of the Internet and try to become the financial and investing enterprises of the future.

In addition to adjusting their strategies and business models, many brokerages were rapidly expanding their involvement in electronic communications networks (ECNs), which allowed stock trades to be conducted by computers using software that matched sell orders and buy orders. ECN technology was fast emerging to permit worldwide trading of stocks 24 hours a day, seven days a week. In the past 24 months, eight ECN companies offering automated trading without human intervention had sprung into existence.

The industry landscape was changing fast, and it was unclear how things would play out. Exhibit 1 shows the market shares of the leading online brokerage firms.

INDUSTRY BACKGROUND

"Traditional" Full-Service Brokerages

Historically, full-service brokerage firms had dominated the retail brokerage business, accounting for over 75 percent of investor accounts and assets at retail brokerages. Full-service firms provided an array of financial services to clients—checking accounts;

credit cards; individual retirement accounts (IRAs) and Keogh accounts; retirement planning; mortgages; all kinds of investment advice; and, most recently, online trading services. They functioned as a principal gateway for clients in buying and selling stocks, bonds, mutual funds, options, futures, and other securities. Services were delivered through a network of local offices and highly compensated professional brokers/financial consultants whose job was to woo clients, learn their investment likes and dislikes, provide sound investment advice, execute buy-sell trades, and serve as the principal point of client contact and the marketing of services. Brokers who were good at attracting well-to-do clients, giving attentive personal service, actively helping their clients make a good return on their investments (which generally meant steering them into high-performing stocks, mutual funds, and bonds), and generating a big volume of commission income and fees for the firm typically commanded six-figure compensation packages.

The commissions charged by full-service firms for executing buy-sell orders through a broker varied with the number of shares and with the price of the stock but could exceed $1 per share. For instance, Merrill Lynch's commission schedule resulted in the following charges:

Number of Shares	Price per Share	Commission	Cost as a % of Total Dollar Value of Trade	Cost per Share Traded
100	$ 50	$ 105.00	2.10%	1.05
300	65	236.25	1.21	0.79
500	4	96.74	4.84	0.19
500	10	161.78	3.23	0.32
1,000	114	968.82	0.85	0.97
1,000	20	373.80	1.87	0.37
1,000	30	472.76	1.58	0.47
3,000	114	2,234.96	0.65	0.74
3,000	20	761.25	1.27	0.25

See Exhibit 2 for a comparison of the commissions charged by various types of brokers.

Full-service firms maintained sizable research staffs that generated a stream of ongoing reports on companies, industries, and particular types of investments—all intended to serve as a resource for brokers in furnishing clients with valuable investment information. Full-service firms relied on the proprietary investment information they generated for their clients as a differentiating factor. They believed this information, the full range of services offered, and the personal service rendered by their staffs of professional brokers justified the premium commissions they charged on stock trades.

Starting in the late 1980s and continuing into the late 1990s, the full-service brokerage segment had consolidated through mergers and acquisitions. Going into 2000, the principal full-service brokerage firms were Merrill Lynch, Paine Webber, Morgan Stanley Dean Witter, Salomon Smith Barney, and Prudential Securities, but the segment also included 10 to 15 prominent full-service regional firms such as A. G. Edwards, Robinson-Humphrey, J. C. Bradford, and Edward D. Jones.

Discount Brokerage Firms: The New Breed of Competitors in the 1985–95 Period

In the mid-1980s, Charles Schwab & Co., Quick & Reilly, and several other start-up brokerage enterprises mounted a price-based competitive challenge to the full-service

exhibit 2   Comparative Commissions Charged by Major Types of
Brokerage Firms, Spring 2000

	200 shares at $20	3,000 shares at $10
Full-service brokers		
Average commission	$116.90[a]	$672.59[a]
Discount brokers		
Average commission	66.09[a]	145.05[a]
Online/Internet brokers		
Charles Schwab	29.95	30.00[b]
Morgan Stanley Dean Witter Online	29.95	30.00[c]
DLJdirect	20.00	60.00[d]
E*Trade		74.95
For NYSE-listed stocks	14.95	
For NASDAQ stocks	19.95	
Fidelity	14.95	14.95
Web Street Securities	14.95	Free for stocks listed on the NASDAQ
Waterhouse Securities	12.00	12.00
Datek Online	9.99	9.99
Ameritrade	8.00	8.00
Suretrade	7.95	7.95
Brown & Co.	5.00[e]	5.00[e]

Note: These commission fees are for trades placed at the market price prevailing at the time of execution; orders that specified a limit price often entailed an added fee—equal to $5 at Fidelity, Ameritrade, and Brown & Co.

[a]As of spring 1998.

[b]Schwab's fee structure was a flat $29.95 on all trades up to 1,000 shares or a flat 3 cents per share on all trades of more than 1,000 shares. Active traders were eligible for a special rate of $14.95.

[c]Morgan Stanley Dean Witter Online's fee structure was a flat $29.95 on all trades up to 1,000 shares (telephone orders were $39.95); trades in excess of 1,000 shares were charged at a rate of 3 cents per share for the entire order (telephone orders were 4 cents per share for the entire order).

[d]DLJdirect's fee structure was a flat $20.00 on all trades up to 1,000 shares with a surcharge of 2 cents per share on all shares over 1,000 per trade. Clients with $1 million in DLJdirect accounts paid a fee of $20.00 per trade up to 5,000 shares, with a 2-cent surcharge per share thereafter.

[e]Brown & Co. charged $5.00 on trades up to 5,000 shares; trades greater than 5,000 shares were $5.00 plus a retroactive 1-cent surcharge per share thereafter—hence a trade of 6,000 shares carried a $65 commission; broker-assisted orders were an additional $7.

Source: Credit Suisse First Boston Co. and company advertising and Web sites.

brokers with a limited-service strategy that featured discount commissions. Schwab quickly emerged as the largest and best-known of the discount brokers, using a strategy that stressed heavy media advertising and a comparatively extensive menu of services and product offerings. Because of its reputation and service, Schwab could charge commissions that were only about 30 percent below full-service firms—its fees were the highest of the so-called discount brokers. "Second tier" discount brokers offered much deeper discounts and were content to build their business around serving active traders and bargain hunters and offering minimal services beyond trade execution.

Growing numbers of investors opened accounts with discount brokers during the 1985–95 period. The cut-rate commissions of discount brokers appealed to knowledgeable investors who took very active roles in managing their portfolios, traded stocks frequently (perhaps making a number of trades each business day), and wanted to keep the costs of moving in and out of particular stocks to a bare minimum. Because commissions were a major cost item, active traders were quite interested in locating their accounts at a brokerage that would execute their buy-sell orders at an economical price. Such investors typically used a wide variety of sources to obtain their investment information and were quite willing to forgo the professional advice and proprietary investment research information that were the trademarks of the full-service brokers. The lower fee structure of discount brokers also appealed to economy-minded investors with modest account balances, since lower transactions costs meant they could put a bigger fraction of their limited funds in the investments of their choice.

Discount brokers were able to undercut the commissions of full-service brokers by eliminating the expensive staffs of investment researchers and professional brokers. Trades were executed by salaried customer service representatives who manned phone lines to provide quotes and handle buy-sell orders but who were precluded from giving investment advice. These representatives were hired for their skills in giving courteous, friendly service over the phone and were paid salaries of $28,000 to $40,000 annually; some firms had modest incentive bonuses for representatives based on the number of phone calls they handled daily and the volume of trades they executed. Discount brokers typically provided customers with little, if any, investment information or news updates on companies. A few had a network of local offices to serve walk-in customers in large metropolitan areas, but the majority did business primarily by phone and operated mainly out of a central office with perhaps a few branch offices.

Meanwhile, large national and regional banks, wanting to move a step closer to becoming one-stop financial centers, formed discount brokerage units as an added convenience and service to customers and as a way to attract self-managed IRAs and other retirement plan accounts. Banks with discount brokerage units usually staffed their various banking offices and branches with personnel who were able to answer questions, open brokerage accounts, and in some cases sell mutual funds. However, all stock transactions were normally initiated over the phone with customers speaking directly to brokerage representatives located in a central office. Several mutual fund firms, like Fidelity Investments, also started discount brokerage units, chiefly as a service for the investors who owned some of their mutual funds and to attract new investors. Fidelity already had a number of offices nationwide and toll-free phone lines to serve its mutual fund clients as well as the internal infrastructure to accommodate securities trading; hence, it was simple and inexpensive for Fidelity to piggyback a discount brokerage on top of its existing resource capabilities.

The Emergence of Online Brokerage Firms, 1995–99

Online brokerages began making their appearance in 1995 as use of the Internet exploded and problems of data security were reduced to tolerable levels. By 1998, the online segment had over 60 competitors, versus just 15 in mid-1996. A number of the new entrants were start-up ventures launched by young Internet entrepreneurs—two of the most notable were E*Trade and Web Street Securities. Other online brokerages were established by discount brokerages like Schwab and Quick & Reilly, mutual fund firms like Fidelity, and other financial institutions to provide an additional service for their existing customers and bring in new revenues. The owners and managers of the online trading firms were for the most part convinced that "the Internet was it" and that the future of retail brokerage was in online trading.

The Rapid Growth in Online Trading   While traditional full-service and discount brokerages initially saw online trading as an attraction mainly for computer enthusiasts interested in playing with technology, it didn't take long for online trading to become mainstream. Internet-savvy investors, intrigued with handling their own trades, tracking their portfolios automatically, and saving on commissions, evidenced immediate interest in opening online accounts. Thus, online trading volume climbed swiftly:

Period	Average Number of Trades per Day*
March 1997	95,500
June 1998	228,000
December 1999	807,000

*Estimates provided to case researchers by U.S. Bancorp Piper Jaffray.

A *Fortune* reporter described the appeal of the online trading experience as follows:

> Buying and selling stocks online just feels different, exhilarating even . . . First, it's convenient and private. You can get quotes and research without a broker's assistance, and you don't have a salesman . . . second-guessing your investment decisions. Second, it's fun. The colors, the graphics, the thrill of being connected to the beating heart of capitalism. Place an order for 100 shares of GM, click, and seconds later it's yours . . . Third, your online account comes loaded with useful information: Most online brokers throw in free access to news stories and press releases, stock charts, earnings projections, even analysts' reports.
>
>   And of course, it costs just a fraction of the $125 that a mainline discounter would charge . . . And the price keeps getting lower.[1]

A Florida retiree said, "I can take a position in a stock for, say, $30. At other places, the commission could be $300 to $400. I can sell a stock, then buy it back, and I don't feel like it is costing me an arm and a leg."[2] A 45-year-old female software consultant observed, "The costs have gone way down and it's so easy now."[3] An investor who had switched to an online brokerage from a full-service firm commented, "My broker was so nice, but boy, they were robbing me. All he ever did was place my trades. I can do that for myself."[4]

There were approximately 412,000 online accounts in early 1995; a year later there were over 800,000, and going into 2000 the number was over 13 million—1.8 million new online accounts were added in the fourth quarter of 1999, the largest quarterly jump in the history of the online brokerage business. Assets in online accounts rose 35 percent in 1999, to $900 billion. The percentage of all retail brokerage trades placed online jumped from less than 8 percent in 1996 to 17 percent in 1997 to 25 percent in mid-1998, to 37 percent in the first half of 1999, and to an estimated 48 percent in the second half of 1999.

---

[1]David Whitford, "Trade Fast, Trade Cheap," *Fortune,* February 2, 1998, p. 112.

[2]"The New Stock Traders," *Business Week,* May 4, 1998, p. 134.

[3]Ibid., p. 126.

[4]As quoted in "With the World Wide Web, Who Needs Wall Street?" *Business Week*, April 29, 1996, p. 120.

The Value Chain of Online Brokers   Compared to traditional brokers, Internet brokers used a radically different value chain to deliver services to investors. They kept overhead low by having few offices and no commission-based brokers. While they had small staffs of salaried "financial consultants," registered representatives, and trained customer service personnel answering phones for customers who needed to talk to a "live broker," they relied mainly on the Internet for communicating with customers. Typically, online brokers set up a Web site that interested investors could explore—some parts of the site were free and open to everyone; other parts required that the user have an account and were accessible only by entering the account number and password. It was possible to open up an account by filling out a form online (or else request that new account information and forms be sent through the mail). The Web sites of online brokers allowed customers to obtain delayed and real-time stock quotes, place buy-sell orders, get order confirmations, check account balances, track portfolio performance, view historical charts, check mutual fund data and ratings, peruse industry and company news, and gain access to research reports from a variety of investment research specialists. Customers could access their account information at night and on weekends, and place orders for execution at the next market opening. Some online brokerages developed their own proprietary software for operating their Web sites and maintaining customer account information; others relied on outside vendors for all or most of their requirements and paid a royalty per trade.

Competition among Online Brokers   During the latter half of 1997, aggressive online newcomers led by Ameritrade and Suretrade cut their commission fees and launched multimillion-dollar advertising campaigns to attract new accounts and gain market share. A brief but lively price war ensued, driving average commission fees for leading online brokerages down from just over $50 per trade in early 1996 to about $15 in late 1997. However, since then, prices had stabilized:

Period	Average Commission Charged by Top 10 Online Brokerages
Q1 1996	$52.89
Q1 1997	32.19
Q1 1998	15.53
Q4 1998	15.75
Q4 1999	15.50

Source: Based on data compiled by Credit Suisse First Boston and U.S. Bancorp Piper Jaffray and reported in Theresa W. Carey, "Better, Not Just Bigger," *Barron's Online,* March 13, 2000.

In early 2000, online commission fees per trade ranged from a high of $29.95 at well-known online brokers like Charles Schwab to $14.95 at E*Trade and Fidelity to $8 at Ameritrade and $7.95 at Suretrade to $5 at Brown & Co. and to $1.50 per trade at CyBerCorp (whose customers were hyperactive day traders that often made hundreds or even thousands of trades a day).

Throughout 1996–99, as Web technology progressed, data transfers via modems and servers became faster, and software capabilities were upgraded, competitors in the online segment made their Web pages livelier, easier to navigate, and more informational. Exhibit 3 shows the variety of features and services being offered by online brokerages during the 1997–99 period. To differentiate themselves and attract customers,

exhibit 3   Features and Services Offered by Online Brokerages, 1998–99

- Ability to open an account online or via mail-in forms; account demos; tutorials for using account software.
- Technical support via e-mail or a toll-free line during business hours Monday through Friday. A few firms had tech-support hot lines open 24 hours a day, seven days a week. Response times varied from firm to firm, running from under a minute on average to as much as 15 minutes on average.
- Account information—ability to log on to the account and get price updates on each holding in the portfolio. Most brokerages updated the prices at the close of each trading day; several updated prices and account balances every 15 to 20 minutes; and a few brokerages had invested in the capability to provide updates instantly as stock prices changed.
- Account security.
- Free, unlimited delayed quotes (usually 15 or 20 minutes behind the latest executed trade).
- A limited number (usually 100) of free real-time quotes per transaction. A fee was charged for real-time quotes in excess of the specified number. To deliver real-time quotes, the broker had to have software capability to update stock prices directly on the screen each time they changed and then have a source from which to obtain the real-time quotes (often an outside vendor such as Thomson Financial—a primary provider of real-time quotes to many brokerages).
- Full customer control over placing buy-sell orders.
- Confirmations of trades, usually within a few seconds of placing the order.
- A variety of investment products available online—stocks, bonds, options, and mutual funds.
- Access to historical information—charts showing price and trading volume histories, 52-week high-low trading range, dividend histories, price-earnings ratios, charts showing how the stock price has performed versus various market indexes such as the S&P 500 and the Dow-Jones Industrial Average.
- Business news from such sources such as Dow-Jones, CNN, Bloomberg, Reuters, Business Wire, Standard & Poor's, *Fortune,* and *Business Week.*
- Mutual fund ratings from Morningstar and others.
- Daily market news summaries from CBS Market Watch, Briefing.com, and others.
- Press releases from companies.
- A selection of research links to 10-K reports, annual reports, earnings forecasts by First Call or Zack's Research, the latest analysis of various technical indicators, company histories and background, securities analyst recommendations, and investment advice from various sources.
- The ability to talk to a financial consultant or registered representative if the need arose.
- Electronic fund transfer services.
- IRAs and 401(K) retirement accounts.
- Checking accounts.
- Electronic bill payment.
- Credit and debit cards.
- Full disclosure of commission schedules and a list of fees for IRAs, bounced checks, margin loans, and other services (posted on the Web site for convenient review by customers).
- Investment tools to screen stocks based on criteria chosen by the customer.
- Financial planning and portfolio optimization tools.
- Online educational tools to teach do-it-yourself investors about the basics of investing, managing a retirement plan, and the fundamentals of stock analysis.
- Alerts issued to customers if the outlook for one of their stocks changed suddenly or if the price of a stock in their portfolio swung up or down by a sizable amount in the course of daily trading sessions.

Note: This listing is a representative compilation of features and services offered by the various online brokerages. However, the actual mix of features and services offered by any one particular brokerage firm varied from brokerage to brokerage. Features were in a constant state of flux during 1997–98 as brokerages upgraded or redesigned their Web sites; but by late 1999 the fast and furious pace of features changes and new additions had moderated.

online firms competed on the basis of commission fees, the variety of services offered, Web site features, the amount and caliber of information available at their Web sites, and the tools made available to track portfolios and research companies. Rivals were in a continual race to upgrade and add features, improve their services, expand the amount of information available at their websites, and add valuable research links.

To attract investor attention and build market share, the new online brokerage firms in mid-1997 launched multimillion-dollar advertising campaigns, using screen ads on high-traffic Internet sites, TV and radio spots, and print ads in *USA Today, The Wall Street Journal, Business Week, Fortune, Smart Money,* and other business-oriented magazines. The rush of new entrants made it virtually imperative for competitors to use the mass media to establish visibility and quickly build brand-name awareness. Most of the leaders in the online segment continued to advertise heavily through 1998 and 1999, both to attract new customers and to strengthen name recognition. Industry participants had geared up to spend a combined $1.5 billion on ads to attract new customers during 2000.

Alliances between Online Brokers and Information Providers

Most online brokers did not develop their own information content, but rather formed alliances and strategic partnerships with firms in the business of providing investor information via the Internet. Online brokers needed the content of information providers to make their research and data offerings at their Web sites more appealing to customers and competitive with rival brokerages. Information providers were interested in making their services available to online brokers and their customers in order to broaden their user base—information providers made their money either by providing their information for a fee (paid either by the online broker or their customers) and/or by selling advertising space on their Web sites where their information products were delivered. Once an online broker and an information provider agreed on an alliance or contractual fee arrangement, it was a simple, inexpensive task for broker Webmasters to incorporate direct links on their Web pages to the chosen providers of investor information.

The Responses of Full-Service and Discount Brokers to Online Trading, 1996–99

Full-service and discount brokers initially responded to the growing interest in online trading by creating Web sites for their own customers. No online trading was offered, but clients were offered tidbits of current information (daily market commentaries, recent market indexes updated daily or weekly, and perhaps a sample research report) and their attention called to the range of benefits the brokerage offered. Salomon Smith Barney went a step further; in exchange for registering, browsers at the Internet site could get the firm's current top 10 stock picks and click on links to other Web sites with pertinent information. In early 1996, Prudential Securities became the first full-service broker to offer customers Internet access to account balances and to provide delayed stock quotes. Other full-service and discount brokers soon followed Prudential's lead in providing customers an alternative to tracking their stocks from newspaper listings or calling their broker for quotes. But to access their account information online, the customers of full-service brokers first had to sign up with the broker to obtain the needed software (sometimes paying a one-time fee of $25), install the software on their computers, and use a secure browser (either Netscape Navigator or Internet Explorer). In contrast, the software employed by over three-fourths of the online brokers allowed customers to use the Internet to access their accounts without having to install special proprietary software on their computers.

However, with the exception of Morgan Stanley Dean Witter—which set up a separate unit, Discover Brokerage, to pursue the online brokerage business—none of the leading full-service brokerage firms gave clients an online trading option prior to late 1999. Until then, they had taken the position that the new online brokers did not have the financial strength and brand-name credibility to pose a serious competitive challenge. And they expressed confidence that few of their customers would see the Internet as an appealing substitute for the personalized counsel of a flesh-and-blood broker.

As the marketing executive of one full-service brokerage put it in 1996, "It's really not a concern. We find investors want ongoing advice and counsel."[5] Another industry expert predicted, "You'll see more people shifting back to a full-service house because they want hand-holding in a crisis."[6]

On the other hand, several prominent discount brokerages—namely, Charles Schwab, Quick & Reilly, and Fidelity Discount Brokerage—wasted no time in pursuing the opportunities in online trading. Schwab management, believing that the Internet held tremendous potential, moved early and aggressively to make online trading an integral component of its strategy. Having the best-known reputation of the online competitors, Schwab quickly became the market leader in the online segment. Several of the smaller deep-discount brokerages whose clientele consisted of active traders looking to trade at the lowest possible price also set up online units as a way to retain their current customers and attract additional bargain-hunting traders—a prominent example was Ameritrade. But the majority of discount brokers, like their full-service counterparts, were reluctant to embrace online trading and adopted a wait-and-see posture until competitive pressures in 1999 forced them to accept the handwriting on the wall.

COMPETITIVE CONDITIONS IN 2000

Of the approximately 65 million brokerage accounts in the United States in early 2000, roughly 45 million accounts were at traditional full-service brokers like Merrill Lynch, Morgan Stanley Dean Witter, Salomon Smith Barney, PaineWebber, Prudential Securities, and lesser-known regional firms. Discount brokers had an estimated 8 million accounts and online brokerages had an estimated 12 million accounts. Close to 35 million U.S. households had one or more brokerage accounts (often at both full-service or discount brokers and at online brokers), and household participation was rising, due to growing interest in participating in the booming stock market that had characterized the 1996–99 period. A 1999 government survey indicated that 49 percent of U.S. households had investments in the stock market in 1998 compared to 32 percent in 1989. Moreover, at least 6 million U.S. households had a net worth of over $1 million each. More than 3 million households in the United States had investable assets in excess of $1 million, and the number of these households was expected to grow 13 to 14 percent per year during the 2000–2003 period. A number of analysts predicted that over the next three to five years nearly all investors would be using the Internet to access their accounts. A mid-1999 survey by two research firms found that over 16 million people were interested in beginning online trading.

Industry analysts estimated that 55 to 60 percent of all retail brokerage trades would be placed online during 2000, with the percentage continuing to edge upward. Given the recent surge in online trading activity, it seemed likely that online brokers would be executing an average of 900,000 to 1 million trades per day by year-end 2000 and perhaps as many as 1.5 million daily by 2003. In early 2000, daily trading volume on the New York Stock Exchange (NYSE) averaged around 900 million shares, but a daily volume in excess of 1 billion shares was not uncommon; trading volumes on the National Association of Securities Dealers Automated Quotations (NASDAQ) averaged around 1.2 billion shares and on heavy trading days sometimes ranged as high as 1.8 billion shares. On the AMEX the daily trading volume was only about 50 million shares. Currently, an estimated 30 to 40 percent of the total daily trading volume was being handled by online

[5]Ibid., p. 121.
[6]"Schwab Is Fighting on Three Fronts," *Business Week,* March 10, 1997, p. 95.

brokers—traditionally, much of the daily trading volume was accounted for by institutions and mutual funds, which often traded large blocks of shares (5,000 to 20,000 shares or more). But recently the activities of day traders buying and selling small blocks of 100 to 500 shares several hundred times a day had driven up trading volumes and the share of total trading volume handled by online traders.

Industry analysts at Forrester Research were predicting that the $900 billion in assets in online accounts at year-end 1999 would exceed $3 trillion by 2003 and that the number of online accounts would grow from 12 million to 40 or 45 million as investors at full-service firms opted to use the online trading options these firms were putting in place and as online brokerages attracted more accounts. Commission revenues at online brokerages only were expected to reach $2.5 billion in 2000, up from $600 million in 1997. Revenues of online brokerage firms from all sources (commissions on stock trades, fees from mutual fund sales, interest earned from customers' margin accounts, underwriting fees, and other sources) were projected to jump from just over $4 billion in 1999 to around $10 billion in 2002.

Among the 280 firms offering retail brokerage services to investors in 2000, over 160 provided online trading to customers (the actual number varied almost weekly due to new entrants and merger/acquisitions among existing participants). Banks with discount brokerage operations were among those who had moved slowest in instituting online trading; however, in the years to come they were expected to begin providing an online trading option as part of their online banking offering. Goldman Sachs and J. P. Morgan were among the well-known financial services firms to announce they would offer online trading beginning in 2000.

With full-service firms being only in the beginning stages of offering online trading to customers, it was too early to gauge how many of their customers would begin to do part or all of their trading online and what this might do to their revenue streams from commissions. But it was perfectly clear that the livelihoods of professional brokers, whose incomes depended on the stream of commission fees they generated, were going to be increasingly at risk and that there might be a diminishing need for full-service brokers to maintain an extensive network of branch offices. And most observers believed that full-service brokerage firms would need a new business model and new revenue-generating strategies to continue to be profitable.

A survey commissioned by Fidelity Investments revealed that online investors were, for the most part, pleased with their experience. The main regret of 10 percent of the respondents was that they had not begun online trading earlier. The study showed that investors with online accounts increased their trading from 2.7 to 5.5 trades per month during the first 90 days of going online, but then slowed to an average of 4.5 trades per month.

The Dilemma of Full-Service Brokers in Entering the Online Segment

For full-service firms, entering the online brokerage business posed several internal and competitive dilemmas. The biggest was the "channel conflict" between competing in two segments that offered customers different prices and service levels. At the very least, it was awkward for a full-service brokerage firm, on the one hand, to ask customers to pay a $1,000 commission for buying 1,250 shares of Microsoft if the trade was placed through their longtime broker and, on the other hand, give them the option of making the same purchase online for a fee of only $29.95. Furthermore, giving customers a high-commission/low-commission option put a heavy burden on professional

exhibit 4   The Case for Online Investing versus the Case for Using a Full-Service Broker

The Case for Online Investing	The Case for Using a Full-Service Broker
• Cheaper commissions	• Receive professional advice
• No pressure and no cold calls from a broker	• Better execution
• Faster execution	• Trade less, invest more
• Volumes of information and investment tools are available online to provide stock-picking ideas; one does not need a broker to get stock-picking ideas	• Hand-holding in a bear market
• Online investing is more fun	• Have somebody to call and talk to
• A personal relationship with a broker is not particularly valuable—it's mostly chitchat and, if that is what a person wants, it is available for free in a chat room	• Get stock-picking ideas
• The record of brokers in picking stocks for clients is not very inspiring	• It is easier to get orders through by telephone than by computer
• While most brokers are professional, some are slick-talking salespeople who prod clients to trade too much and push high-fee products so they can earn more commissions	• It is good to have a professional broker looking out for your interests

Source: Adapted from Jonathan Clements, "Yes You Should, No You Shouldn't," *The Wall Street Journal,* June 14, 1999, p. R21.

brokers to figure out how they could continue to deliver value-added services that would generate a sustainable stream of commission fees if many of their clients shifted to online trading. As one broker expressed it, "It's much more difficult if I'm a broker and I'm providing this value-added service, and I turn around and my client can get a trade for $16 a share" from the same company.[7] Another dilemma concerned advertising and promotion. Most online brokers touted their low commissions in their ads, the range of services offered, and the "no pressure" freedom that online trading gave individual investors. Such ads conflicted with the persona of a full-service brokerage delivering custom-tailored services and trustworthy advice from professional brokers whose prices were justified by the value being provided. Exhibit 4 provides a comparison of the reasons given to use an online broker versus the reasons given to use a full-service broker.

Morgan Stanley Dean Witter, which had 11,500 professional brokers, had tried to detour the dilemma by setting up a wholly separate subsidiary, Discover Brokerage Direct, believing that a separate brand name, separate offices and operations, and separate strategies and appeals would help contain the channel conflict between the two businesses. The separation was seen as a way to avoid antagonizing the company's professional brokers who prized the names Morgan Stanley and Dean Witter and hated the notion of their own firm offering a low-price trading option under the same brand names. However, in late 1999, as most full-service brokers were making plans to incorporate an online trading option, Morgan Stanley Dean Witter decided to bring Discover's operations under the

---

[7]As quoted in "Channel Conflict," *The Wall Street Journal,* June 14, 1999, p. R9.

umbrella of its full-service brokerage business and renamed the subsidiary Morgan Stanley Dean Witter Online.

THE ECONOMICS OF ONLINE TRADING

Online trading was considered by analysts to be a potentially lucrative business despite the lower commissions per trade. The revenues of online brokerage firms came from four main sources:

- The commission income from executing customer trades.
- The interest earnings on loans to customers who purchased stocks on margin.
- The interest earned on the cash balances in customer accounts.
- The payments for order flow received from the market makers in each NASDAQ-listed stock.

Revenues from Commissions

Online brokers derived between 40 and 70 percent of their revenues from commission fees, depending on their commission structure. While the fee per trade varied anywhere from $5 to $29.95 (see Exhibit 2), a majority of online brokers charged a flat fee per trade on trades up to 1,000 shares, abandoning the practice used by full-service brokerages of basing the commission on the number of shares and the price per share. Fees were frequently higher on trades of more than 1,000 shares. The fees of online brokers were higher for buying or selling options and for orders that specified a limit price than for buying or selling stocks at the market price. The fees for handling mutual funds purchases or sales varied from broker to broker; many charged nothing (partly as a promotion to help attract new accounts and partly because mutual funds companies had waived their charges on sales made through online brokers as a way to attract investors to their mutual fund families). Exhibit 5 shows the fee schedule for Web Street Securities.

Revenues from Margin Loans and Account Balances

A number of active traders financed a portion of their stock purchases with funds borrowed from their broker. Such purchases were called margin purchases and the loans were referred to as margin loans. The interest rate that brokers charged on margin loans depended partly on the going short-term prime rate and partly on the size of the loan. The broker's base interest rate (referred to as the broker's call rate) typically was pegged 1 to 1.25 percent below the prime. The loans to customers were then made at the broker's call rate plus as little as 0.5 percent or as much as 2 percent depending on the size of the loan. (See Exhibit 5 for an example of one online broker's schedule of interest charges on margin loans.) Brokers used the cash balances in customers' accounts as a source of funds for making margin loans. Money market conditions in 1998 allowed brokers to earn a spread of 4 to 5 percent on margin loans, paying roughly 3 to 4 percent on customer cash balances and realizing an average of 8 to 9 percent on margin loans. Margin loans were a major revenue source; according to Ameritrade's CEO, "That's where we really make our money."[8] In early 2000, margin loans made by retail brokerage firms were at an all-time record high of $240 billion; the total value of all stocks traded on U.S. stock exchanges was $17 trillion.

---

[8]Whitford, "Trade Fast, Trade Cheap," p. 112.

exhibit 5   Commission Schedule for Web Street Securities, April 2000

Trades Executed via the Internet

• Any listed stock trade; any size	$14.95
• NASDAQ stock trade under 1,000 shares	$14.95
• NASDAQ stock trade 1,000 shares or more*	Free
• Equity and index options	$14.95 plus $1.75 per contract
• Mutual funds transaction	$25.00

Trades Executed via a Live Representative

• Any listed stock trade, any size	$24.95
• NASDAQ stock trade under 1,000 shares[†]	$24.95
• NASDAQ stock trade 1,000 shares or more[†]	$24.95
• Equity and index options	$24.95 plus $1.75 per contract
• Mutual funds transaction	$25.00
• Bonds—government, municipals, corporate	Contact a Web Street account executive for pricing.

Margin Rates

• $0–$4,999	2% above broker call[‡]
• $5,000–$9,999	1¾% above broker call
• $10,000–$14,999	1½% above broker call
• $15,000–$19,999	1¼% above broker call
• $20,000–$24,999	1% above broker call
• $25,000+	¾% above broker call

*On stocks trading over $2.00 per share. For stocks trading $2.00 and under per share, $14.95

[†]On stocks trading over $2.00 per share. For stocks trading $2.00 and under per share, $24.95 plus one cent per share.

[‡]Broker call as quoted in *The Wall Street Journal* (7.75% as of April 2000).

Source: www.webstreetsecurities.com, April 14, 2000.

Brokers earned additional interest income by investing any cash balances in customer accounts not used to make margin loans in Treasury bills or other short-term securities. Such short-term investments tended to yield brokers a net margin of 1 to 2 percentage points between the yield on short-term securities and the rate brokers paid customers on account cash balances.

Net interest income from both margin loans and short-term investments was said to average between $8 and $10 per trade.[9] Brokers could also obtain a small amount of revenue from fees earned in lending the shares in customer accounts to traders wishing to sell a stock short.

Order Flow Payments from Market Makers

Payments for order flow originated with firms that specialized in "making a market" for over-the-counter stocks (such as those listed on the NASDAQ, which were not traded on a central trading floor, giving brokers flexibility on where to send investors' incoming orders for execution). A market maker had responsibility for actually executing trades and, in accord with NASDAQ rules, posting the price within 90 seconds

---

[9]Suzanne Wooley, "Do I Hear Two Bits a Trade?" *Business Week,* December 8, 1997, p. 113.

of the trade. Market makers bought a stock at the bid price and sold a stock at the asking price; they executed trades for both investors and their own accounts. The spread between the bid and asking prices on over-the-counter stocks was typically one-eighth of a point or $0.125 per share. Market makers made their money on the spread, buying at the bid price and selling at the asking price and also on trading shares for their own account. The market maker adjusted the bid-ask range up or down in response to the changing balance of incoming orders to buy or sell and in response to changing bid-ask prices.[10] To keep the number of shares being bought or sold in close balance, market makers adjusted the asking price upward when buy orders exceeded sell orders at the prevailing price or when eager buyers were upping their bid prices. Similarly, market makers lowered the asking price when sell orders exceeded buy orders and when bid prices were weakening. Thus the trades being executed by market makers always reflected demand-supply conditions at that point in time.

When the stock markets were closed (normal business hours were 9 AM to 4 PM Eastern time, Monday through Friday), brokers could execute trades for investors on electronic communications networks (ECNs) such as Reuter's Instinet. Also, NASDAQ allowed firms to execute trades on its electronic system, called SelectNet, during regular business hours.

Because there were several market makers or specialists for each stock listed on the NASDAQ, specialists competed against each other for business in executing the trades for those stocks in which they were market makers. To give brokers an incentive and a reward for sending trades their way, market makers typically paid brokers a piece of the spread between the bid price and the asking price of the shares traded.[11] The "kickbacks" from market makers were said to account for about 20 percent of an online broker's overall revenues.[12] Such payments could range from $1 to $2 on a 100-share trade of a $10 stock to perhaps $20 on a 1,000-share trade of a $50 stock or even $100 on a 5,000-share trade of a $75 stock. It was the payments on order flow from market makers that allowed Web Street Securities to execute large trades on the NASDAQ for "free."

Both margin loans and payments from market makers for order flow were a bigger percentage of overall revenues for online brokers than for discount and full-service brokers. One top Ameritrade official said, "I can see a time when, for a customer with a certain size margin account, we won't charge commissions. We might even pay a customer, on a per trade basis, to bring the account to us."

Recently, order flow payments had come under criticism because of the potential they had for ethics problems. Arthur Levitt, chairman of the Securities and Exchange Commission, argued that order flow payments induced brokerages to direct trades to those market makers offering the best order flow payments, a practice that conflicted with a broker's responsibility to get the best price execution for its customers. SEC commissioner Laura Unger had taken the position that online brokers should be required to give out information on their order-routing practices, revealing to customers

---

[10]Investors wanting to sell shares could either indicate a lower limit price they would accept or could place an order to sell at the market price. Likewise, buyers could either specify a maximum or limit price they were willing to pay or could agree to pay the market price at the time the trade was executed. Most buyers and sellers placed their orders "at the market" since they could get the price at which the last few trades were made and since their order would be executed within less than a minute—the orders of Internet traders were usually confirmed within 30 seconds.

[11]The size of the spread between the bid and asking prices came under scrutiny by the National Association of Securities Dealers and federal government officials in 1997–98. Pressure to lower the spread to one-sixteenth of a point resulted.

[12]Cited in Whitford, "Trade Fast, Trade Cheap," p. 112.

the amount of the payments they got by routing orders to market makers. Harsher critics maintained that order flow payments were nothing other than bribes.

The Cost Structure of Online Trading

The current overall cost per trade at an online brokerage was said to average about $5 once a firm's trading volume reached levels that allowed it to fully utilize technology and front-end investments to put the necessary systems in place. The key operating-cost items were the software and the network of servers to allow customers to log on to the trading system, place and confirm orders, execute trades, and track account balances. Once a firm had the required software package and internal support systems to track account balances and clear trades, it could simply add server capacity and customer service personnel as trading volumes grew. As a result, online brokerages could achieve profitability at much lower trading volumes than traditional full-service and discount brokerages whose operations and processes were more labor intensive and who had to spread the fixed costs of their employees and branch office networks over many trades to achieve low unit costs.

Some online brokers had in-house capability to develop and upgrade their own proprietary software and self-clear the transactions of customers; others paid external software developers and related data processing providers fees amounting to $1 to $3 per trade. The reliance on computers and the Internet for interfacing with customers greatly reduced labor costs and the need for walk-in offices. Having customers log on to their accounts and place their own orders also eliminated most order-entry errors, which were often quite expensive for traditional full-service and discount brokerage firms to untangle. Customer trades were usually executed and confirmed within 15 to 30 seconds of placing the order; many customers stayed at the site long enough to get confirmation. Traditional brokers printed and mailed order confirmations to customers. Use of the Internet to provide customers with information further meant much lower costs for telephones, postage, brochures, and other printed materials (research reports, copies of company news releases, and other information of interest).

Extensive advertising and marketing campaigns were deemed necessary at many online brokerages to establish the company's name firmly in the minds of investors who were thinking of opening an online account, to build the size of their account base to more economic levels and spread out fixed costs, and to convey to mainstream investors that online trading was simple, economical, convenient, and fun. Whereas discount brokers spent about 4 to 7 percent of revenues on advertising, the advertising budgets of online brokers were currently running 15 to 20 percent of revenues. Ameritrade spent $40 to $50 million on a 1998 media campaign promoting its low $8 fee on most trades. Suretrade reportedly spent $30 million on its 1997–98 campaign to advertise its $7.95 commission and trading services. E*Trade in 2000 was in the midst of a $350 million, 18-month marketing campaign.

In addition to data processing software, Web page construction, and marketing, online brokers had to maintain ample capacity to handle trading volume. On a number of occasions in 1997 and 1998, customers of several online brokerages experienced delays in logging on to their accounts to make trades because brokers did not have the server capacity to handle the volume of traffic on their Web sites. By mid-1998 most online brokers had added sufficient capacity to handle peak demands on their systems; logjams were a rare occurrence in 2000. However, from time to time, online brokers' systems went down due to equipment or software failures, causing temporary annoyances to customers and generating embarrassing publicity in the media.

Cost-Sharing Synergies with Sister Businesses   Although industry analysts believed that online brokerage firms could, in time, realize profit margins of 15 to 20 percent of revenues, heavy expenditures for advertising and front-end technology costs had crimped profitability. *The Wall Street Journal* reported in March 1998 that only 30 percent of the 50 online brokerages interviewed were profitable and just 20 percent were breaking even.[13] Analysts estimated that an online brokerage operation could make money at commissions as low as $5 a trade if (1) they were a subsidiary of a discount or full-service brokerage and already had their own clearing operations and other supporting infrastructure in place or (2) they were part of an investment firm affiliated with a stock exchange that also had the back-office capability to handle the settlement of securities transactions and take care of other essential customer accounting and data processing operations.[14] The economies of an online brokerage being able to share the costs of such back-office operations with a sister discount or full-service brokerage (or another investment firm with back-office infrastructure) were said to be substantial. Likewise, an online brokerage unit could realize cost savings if it could draw on the offices, customer service personnel, or registered representatives of a sister full-service or discount brokerage to help service the needs of its online customers.

THE RISE OF ELECTRONIC COMMUNICATION NETWORKS

One of the most profound brokerage-related developments of 1999 was the astonishing growth of electronic communication networks (ECNs), which used computers to match buy and sell orders and execute trades without going through traditional market makers. An investor could place an order through an online broker, and if the broker's computer could find a seller at a matching price in an ECN, the order could be executed with no human intervention, at a fraction of the cost of using brokers and market makers. At year-end 1999, ECNs accounted for 33 percent of NASDAQ volume; Rule 390 of the New York Stock Exchange prohibited many NYSE-listed blue-chip stocks from being traded outside the NYSE and regional exchanges. However, bowing to pressure from the Securities and Exchange Commission to open up the trading of NYSE-listed stocks to competition, the NYSE indicated that it planned to withdraw Rule 390 sometime in 2000.

There were 10 ECNs operating in early 2000, several of which were owned wholly or partly by online brokers—E*Trade was an 18 percent owner of Archipelago; Datek Online was the owner of Island ECN, and Schwab, Fidelity, and DLJdirect were involved in REDIbook. Instinet, owned by Reuters, was by far the largest of the ECNs, with revenues of around $850 million in 1999 and a pretax profit margin of around 31 percent. Island was said to execute trades involving as many as 100 million shares per day but had generated revenues of just $14 million in the first nine months of 1999 based on its typical net fee of $1.50 per 1,000 shares (a fee far below what Instinet charged). REDIbook executed orders averaging about 70 million shares daily. Most of the ECNs were losing money due to expanding payroll and marketing costs associated

---

[13]Daisy Maxey, "Analyst Sees On-Line Brokers Expanding Range of Services," *The Wall Street Journal Interactive Edition,* March 9, 1998.

[14]Wooley, "Do I Hear Two Bits a Trade?" p. 112.

with gearing up for higher trading volumes; to be profitable, the network companies needed large-scale volumes.

Moreover, the competing ECNs were not connected as of early 2000, resulting in fragmentation of buy-sell orders and occasional failure to execute a customer's order promptly due to lack of a buy-sell match in a particular ECN. To rectify this situation and respond to pressures from the Securities Exchange Commission (SEC) to create maximum liquidity for all NASDAQ-listed stocks, officials at NASDAQ had initiated efforts to connect the ECNs and, further, to link them to NASDAQ trading to create a single comprehensive electronic central order book accessible to all market makers and ECNs. The central NASDAQ Order Display or "window" would collect and display all quotes and orders to buy the 5,000-plus NASDAQ stocks. To win the cooperation of market makers and ECNs, NASDAQ proposed allowing market makers and ECNs to retain ownership of their orders displayed in the aggregated NASDAQ system. Moreover, investors everywhere could tap into the system to view trades as they were executed and to see the number of shares available at various bid and ask prices. SEC chairman Arthur Levitt saw a single electronic trading system linking all buyers and sellers as a means of boosting competition among market makers and ECNs, executing trades faster, improving service, and lowering trading fees. Levitt believed that Rule 390 blocked competition in stock trading, and he had pushed the NYSE into agreeing to modify Rule 390 as part of his push to establish a central trading system.

ECNs had the potential for saving investors money on each NASDAQ trade by bypassing market makers, who made money off each trade by maintaining a spread between bid (buy) and asked (sell) prices. Most analysts and SEC officials expected that the ECNs would consolidate or be acquired by the major exchanges. According to one analyst, "It is inconceivable . . . that the current environment of nine or ten ECNs is tenable"; he predicted that the total would soon fall to one or two. Some analysts believed that two or three ECNs might attract enough volume to emerge as exchanges in competition with the NYSE and NASDAQ. REDIbook ECN in March 2000 had completed linkage of its system to those of Archipelago, Island Trading, and MarketXT for distribution of after-hours prices and orders.

ECNs also paved the way to trade stocks 24 hours a day, seven days a week on a global scale. According to an Archipelago executive:

> The end game here is, off a platform in America, Europe, and Asia, having a 7x24 electronic stock exchange. In terms of how we get there, I can give you all kinds of scenarios— it changes by the half-hour . . . Step one is to create one book [of quotes]. But in terms of the big picture, anyone who claims to know where this is going is lying to you.

As an initial response to recent developments, both the NYSE and NASDAQ were readying plans to become public companies and to begin offering after-hours trading. The NYSE was also moving on plans to set up an electronic trading network and abandon its long-standing practice of having trades handled by people on the floor of the exchange.

GOMEZ RATINGS OF THE ONLINE BROKERAGE FIRMS

One independent industry authority, Gomez Advisors, ranked over 50 of the estimated 160-plus online brokerage services on a variety of factors to determine who was "best." Gomez had created a scorecard rating each brokerage service on a scale of 1 to 10 on five criteria:

- *Ease of use*—such factors as availability of tutorials, well-integrated features, and ability to customize use.
- *Customer confidence*—including size of capital base, phone response times, tracking of Web site availability, and disclosure of fees and key information about trading rules.
- *On-site resources*—including real-time quotes, charts, news updates, editorial content, and screening tools for stocks and mutual funds.
- *Relationship services*—such factors as real-time updating of stock holdings and account balances, educational content, site security, sophisticated alerts for stock price changes or special news.
- *Overall cost*—commissions, fees, and margin rates.

There were subcategories for each of the five criteria, resulting in consideration of as many as 100 factors to determine a company's rating. Gomez arrived at its ratings by means of direct examination, trial sampling e-mail and telephone support services, a broker's Web site and customer support, a questionnaire, and a telephone interview. Gomez then used a proprietary process to weight the scores to determine which firms were best suited for (1) life-goal planners managing their own individual retirement portfolio of mutual funds, (2) hyperactive traders looking for low commissions and fast execution, (3) serious investors looking for high-quality information, investment tools, and research, and (4) one-stop shoppers interested in a comprehensive package of financial services. Exhibit 6 shows the Gomez rating for the 15 highest rated firms as of late 1999—the latest Gomez ratings of online brokerages can be seen at www.gomez.com.

Numerous publications, including *Barron's, Money, PC World,* and *SmartMoney,* also published ratings of online brokers using their own particular methodology and criteria; while the ratings of who was best and why varied from publication to publication, many of the same brokerages tended to appear on all of the top 10 lists. *Barron's* 1998 survey revealed that during the past 12 months the entire group of online brokers studied had made tremendous strides in upgrading the quality of their Web sites, citing the availability of more research information and more online help. *Barron's* March 2000 survey found even bigger strides in the quality of online brokerages; *Barron's* gave its highest rating (four stars) to DLJdirect, Merrill Lynch Direct, and National Discount Brokers based on trade execution, ease of use, reliability, amenities, and commissions. The high ratings for Merrill Lynch and DLJdirect were primarily due to the research and reports they made available to customers.

Exhibit 7 provides comparative fourth-quarter 1999 statistics for the leading online brokers. Profiles of selected online, discount, and full-service brokers are presented below.

Charles Schwab & Co., Inc. (www.schwab.com)

Charles Schwab & Co. was the fourth largest U.S. financial services company, with 6.7 million active accounts, $765 billion in customer assets (as of February 2000), and 1999 revenues of $3.9 billion and net profits of $589 million. It had an estimated 35 percent market share in the discount brokerage segment and a 22 percent share in the online brokerage segment. Schwab opened 1.5 million new accounts in 1999, helping boost its commission revenues from $1.31 billion in 1998 to $1.86 billion in 1999. Schwab's earnings had grown at a compound rate of nearly 35 percent since 1992 and its stock price had outperformed other major brokerage stocks. About 30 percent of Schwab's customer assets and 10 percent of its customer accounts were managed by 5,800 independent, fee-based investment advisers; these advisers opened Schwab ac-

exbibit 6 Gomez Advisors' Ratings of 15 Leading Online Brokers, Winter 1999

Online Brokerage	Ease of Use	Customer Confidence	On-Site Resources	Relationship Services	Overall Cost	Overall Score	Comments
1. Charles Schwab	7.39	6.91	8.54	8.84	4.35	7.64	Rated first for life-goal planners and one-stop shoppers and second for serious investors; has a comparatively high commission structure
2. E*Trade	8.10	6.15	8.90	7.67	6.62	7.63	Rated first for hyperactive traders and serious investors; rated second for life-goal planners
3. DLJdirect	7.46	8.35	8.35	5.62	6.21	7.28	One of the more expensive online brokers; only clients with over $100,000 in assets have access to DLJ research and IPO stocks
4. Fidelity Investments	5.63	5.71	8.94	8.23	4.61	7.06	Rated third for one-stop shoppers
5. National Discount Brokers	7.18	6.40	7.72	5.82	6.49	6.73	
6. A. B. Watley	5.44	8.10	6.49	4.90	8.48	6.45	Rated second for active traders; excellent site performance and excellent telephone and e-mail customer service
7. My Discount Broker	6.14	6.55	6.41	4.91	8.18	6.19	Excellent 24x7 telephone and e-mail customer service
8. American Express Brokerage	5.04	6.15	6.06	6.62	7.02	6.15	
9. Suretrade	4.92	6.84	6.59	4.44	9.89	6.14	Rated third for active traders; has knowledgeable and timely telephone and e-mail customer service
10. Morgan Stanley Dean Witter Online	7.56	5.63	6.46	5.35	3.95	5.93	An expensive commission schedule
11. Waterhouse Securities	1.60	7.16	7.26	5.43	8.44	5.92	Does not provide real-time account balances and holdings
12. Datek Online	6.49	7.32	4.32	4.18	9.41	5.82	
13. Ameritrade	3.35	7.69	5.65	4.30	8.90	5.68	
14. Quick & Reilly	5.10	7.42	6.40	3.40	6.88	5.67	
15. Web Street Securities	4.47	6.80	5.76	4.33	8.37	5.66	

Source: Web site for Gomez Advisors (www.gomez.com), February 14, 2000.

exhibit 7   Comparative Statistics for the Leading Online Brokers, Fourth Quarter 1999*

Online Broker	Average Number of Trades per Day	Number of Customer Accounts	Assets in Customer Accounts	Assets per Customer Account
Charles Schwab	177,400	3,300,000	$348,000,000	$105,500
E*Trade	123,250	1,881,000	44,000,000	23,400
Waterhouse Securities	107,140	1,300,000	88,000,000	67,700
Fidelity	92,354	3,466,000	269,000,000	77,600
Datek Online	81,040	340,000	10,600,000	31,200
Ameritrade	71,269	686,000	31,600,000	46,100
DLJdirect	30,500	347,000	21,700,000	62,500
Scottrade	22,050	201,000	5,252,000	26,100
CyBerCorp	14,213	3,000	202,000	67,300
Suretrade	13,200	158,000	2,400,000	15,200
Morgan Stanley Dean Witter Online	12,500	193,000	9,500,000	49,200
National Discount Brokers	11,703	196,000	10,830,000	55,300
Dreyfus	10,125	44,000	7,225,000	164,200
Web Street Securities	4,535	88,000	800,000	9,100
Quick & Reilly	3,300	86,000	3,962,000	46,100
All others	32,375	700,000	46,200,000	66,000
Total/Average	806,961	12,987,000	$899,970,000	$69,300

*Data represent domestic online trading activity and do not include broker-assisted trades.
Source: U.S. Bancorp Piper Jaffray and company documents.

counts for their clients and used Schwab's Institutional division to execute buy and sell orders for their clients at the online rate of $29.95 per trade.[15]

According to co-CEO Charles Schwab, the company's mission was "to coach people on investing."[16] Schwab's strategy was geared to service and product variety, innovation, value pricing, and its own unique style of "full-service investing" in which information flowed freely and investors made their own decisions with objective help and advice when they needed it.

Service and Product Variety   Schwab made its services available to customers via a multichannel delivery system that included the Internet, branch offices, a voice recognition quote and trading service, a Touch-Tone telephone quote and trading service, e-mail and wireless technologies, multilingual and international services, and direct access to Schwab professionals day or night. Schwab had been especially successful in catering to small investors. The company had recently retooled its customer service program after studying the practices of such companies as McDonald's and FedEx; a top official explained, "Our current push is to make sure that our customers who need help get it and that our customers who don't, don't get it—and don't have to pay for it."[17]

---

[15]By utilizing Schwab's customer account and trading services, these outside investment advisers avoided the costs of having to design and operate systems to handle transactions and account tracking functions for their clients. Schwab also acted as the custodial agent for the assets in these accounts.

[16]As quoted in *Business Week,* May 25, 1998, p. 123.

[17]"Schwab Is Fighting on Three Fronts," p. 95.

Schwab offered customers a very broad lineup of products that included stock trading, the usual variety of checking account and credit card services, IRA and Keogh retirement plans, and the ability to invest in a broad selection of mutual funds.

Innovation   Schwab was regarded as an industry innovator and the company that had pioneered the marriage of technology and investment advice. In 1974, Schwab became the first brokerage firm to discount its commissions, thus triggering the advent of the discount brokerage segment. In 1984, the firm started a new trend in how mutual funds were sold, launching its innovative OneSource and Mutual Fund Marketplace programs, which by 1998 provided customers with the ability to purchase 1,400 mutual funds through their Schwab account without having to open an account directly with mutual fund providers. Schwab's supermarket approach, which let customers choose among many mutual funds and consolidate their holdings in one account, proved extremely popular among small investors building a retirement nest egg and managing their own IRAs and Keogh plans. Schwab's fees from mutual fund sales accounted for 20 percent of revenues.

The company had built a reputation as an aggressive user of new technology to cut costs and pass the savings on to customers. The company spent about 13 percent of its revenues for new technology. When online trading first made its appearance in 1995, Schwab quickly set its sights on being a leader in electronic brokerage—by year-end 1995 its electronic brokerage unit had 336,000 accounts with $23 billion in assets utilizing the firm's proprietary e.Schwab electronic trading software. Schwab launched trading on the Internet at its Web site in May 1996.

Schwab had made the Internet a centerpiece of its strategy for delivering research, information, and services to account holders. In January 1998, Schwab began offering online trading seminars and providing walk-in customers access to the Internet at its branch offices. It also launched an Analyst Center on its Web site that gave all online customers access to research information from Dow Jones, Standard & Poor's, First Call, and Big Charts at no cost. Customers could receive security analyst reports and consensus opinions on stocks and industries. Customers who had $50,000 or more in their accounts and averaged four trades monthly had access to their own Web pages, a software tool for identifying stocks meeting whatever criteria the investor specified, online interviews with top executives, a one-page report card on 7,000 mutual funds, and a customized one-page comparison of the investor's mutual funds against the performance of major stock indexes.

Because the online brokerage business had become so competitive, with the relatively similar offerings among most of the firms, many analysts believed that Schwab might pursue another reinvention of the business model for brokerage firms. In late 1999, Schwab had partnered with Ameritrade and TD Waterhouse to invest in an online investment bank that would give their customers big allocations of hot initial public offerings of stock of new dot-com companies. The company had recently purchased CyBerCorp, the leading online firm catering to active traders and day traders, and U.S. Trust, a wealth management firm serving affluent individuals and families through 24 offices in nine states. Schwab co-CEO David Pottruck explained the reason for the acquisition of U.S. Trust as follows:

> The baby boomers are emerging as a dominant wealth segment in the United States. They bring with them a desire for a high degree of control, a willingness to embrace technology for their investing needs and an unwillingness to compromise. Many of these investors will demand wealth management services—supported by the unique strengths of the Internet—that offer them more control and information than has ever been available before. At the same time, we believe that these investors are underserved—no one has garnered a truly

significant share of this expanding market; no one has developed a comprehensive wealth management service especially for the needs of the emerging affluent investor.

Through U.S. Trust, we will be able to provide the trust, financial and estate planning, and private banking services that are so crucial to wealth management. Our investment manager clients have told us repeatedly that trust and private banking services are absolutely essential in order to serve affluent clients well.

Value Pricing   Because of its strong reputation among middle-income and value-conscious investors and its comparatively wide range of products and services, Schwab had been successful in maintaining a higher commission structure than other discount and online firms. Schwab management was opposed to attracting business solely on the basis of low price, believing that the range and quality of its services and products justified a price premium over the fees of deep discounters. One executive was quoted as saying, "We have no intention of doing $7 trades."[18] However, in February 2000, Schwab moved to become more price-competitive by cutting its online commissions from $29.95 per trade to a low of $14.95 for customers making 60 or more trades in a quarter.

Online Trading   As the leading electronic brokerage, Schwab had 3.3 million online accounts as of March 2000, up from 1.5 million accounts in May 1998, and 638,000 in early 1997. Online customer assets were nearly $350 billion, compared to $103 billion in April 1998 and $80 billion in December 1997. In February 2000 Schwab handled an average of 280,000 online trades daily. The company's Web site averaged 40 million hits a day in January 1999 versus 20 million in October 1998. Schwab had invested heavily to make its Web site user-friendly and multifeatured. The site, anchored around Schwab's Analyst Center, reflected the firm's strategic direction for its online service—offering retail investors access to "full-service" online investing. Top management believed Schwab offered online investors a combination of multiple service options, technology, access to information and guidance, and value pricing that was unequaled in the brokerage industry. Schwab's latest Web site feature, introduced in early 2000, was Stock Analyzer, a proprietary, step-by-step guide designed to help Schwab customers evaluate individual stocks and make better-informed, more intelligent investing decisions. Designed as both an education and research tool, Schwab's Stock Analyzer walked investors through the stock research process and provided access to current securities analyst recommendations and earnings projections on over 10,000 stocks. Schwab management saw Stock Analyzer as a one-stop destination for both stock research and interpretation and a tool "to make 'smart investing' easier than ever before." Schwab also offered its customers research reports on individual companies from analysts at Credit Suisse First Boston.

In the late 1970s about 95 percent of Schwab's business was done through branch walk-ins or telephone calls to branch office personnel; in 1998, only 5 percent of the firm's business was done in branch offices. In early 2000, close to 75 percent of the trades executed for the company's 6.7 million accounts were done via the firm's online trading service, compared to 48 percent in 1998 and 28 percent in 1997. The balance was done by customers telephoning their orders to personnel in the company's central call centers.

The growth in Schwab's online trading volume had cut its average commission per trade from $68.50 in 1996 to $49 in early 1998 and $40 in early 2000. This had resulted in the duties of its salaried customer representatives shifting from taking orders for trades to talking with clients about financial planning, estate planning, mutual fund

---

[18]Ibid.

selection, the pros and cons of variable annuities, retirement planning, fixed-income investing, and insurance.

Recent Developments at Schwab   Schwab president and co-CEO David S. Pottruck described the company's strategy and recent accomplishments as follows:

> Competitive responses during 1999 highlighted both the power of our vision for redefining full-service investing and the importance of our relentless focus on finding better ways of serving our customers. Our leadership in providing Clicks and Mortar access—combining people and technology—was very much in evidence throughout the year, starting with the introduction of our Schwab Signature Services program. This program provides enhanced personal and online services for customers with higher asset balances or trading volumes with Schwab. We increased our full-time equivalent employees by 4,800 in 1999, including an increase of 2,200, or 47 percent, in customer contact staff. We also opened 49 branches, bringing our year-end total to 340.
>
> Our advances in leveraging technology to improve customer service during 1999 included the launch of SchwabAlerts, which delivers investment and market activity news to customers via both wireless and e-mail. We also started providing our customers with eConfirms, a service that delivers trade confirms electronically. In addition, we have moved many administrative services, including new account openings, contact information updates and check requests, to fully automated Web-based processes. We worked with Excite, Inc., to introduce MySchwab, which enables users to customize a personal home page with their choice of news and information. Other achievements during the year included the introduction of two research tools for mutual funds—Advanced Mutual Fund Screener and Fund Details, which enable customers to access detailed information on all Morningstar, Inc., rated funds. Additionally, for our more active customers we launched and then enhanced Velocity, our desktop trading system.
>
> We made more than a thousand changes to our Web site during the course of 1999 to improve its content and functionality, including enhancements to the Analyst Center research function and the introduction of MyResearch report, which enables customers to design research reports with the information they find most useful. We believe that our leadership in online financial services is reflected in the continued growth in customer use of this channel at Schwab—during the fourth quarter of 1999, online trades made up 73 percent of all trades at Schwab, up from 61 percent during the fourth quarter of 1998. At year-end 1999, we had 3.3 million online accounts with $349 billion in assets, up 50 percent and 100 percent, respectively, from year-end 1998. Our online industry leadership is also reflected in the awards we earned during the year. We swept many of the number one online broker rankings, being recognized as the world's leader by Gomez Advisors, Inc.; Forrester Research, Inc.; Money, SmartMoney, and PC World magazines; and J. D. Power and Associates. Our investment in systems capacity, which totaled $126 million for the year, doubled our trade processing capabilities over the past 12 months, and enabled us to accommodate single-day records of 78 million Web site hits, 62,000 simultaneous customer Web sessions, and 228,000 online trades during December.
>
> Securities market access is another area where we have continued to harness technology to improve customer service. In September 1999, we announced our participation in the REDIbook ECN LLC electronic communications network, which has subsequently enabled Schwab to launch an extended-hours trading session for certain NASDAQ and selected exchange-listed stocks. In order to enhance customer access to initial public offerings we worked with TD Waterhouse Group, Inc., Ameritrade, Inc., and three leading venture capital firms to form a new online investment bank that will focus on information technology and Internet companies. In addition, a precedent-setting no-action letter from the Securities and Exchange Commission will enable us to be the first brokerage firm to provide customers with access to Internet-based presentations by companies in the process of going public. We've also teamed up with OffRoad Capital to provide improved access to private equity investment opportunities.

We moved to expand our international presence through several transactions during the year, including the acquisition of Priority Brokerage Inc. and Porthmeor Securities Inc. of Toronto to form Charles Schwab Canada, Co. We also initiated a joint venture with the Tokio Marine and Fire Insurance Co., Ltd., to develop a full-service brokerage operation for Japanese investors. We extended online and telephonic brokerage services to Swiss investors through our UK operation, and we also formed a joint venture with ecorp Limited to bring Schwab-style service to Australia. Revenues from our international operations rose 68 percent to over $250 million in 1999.

We built our mutual fund offering during 1999 by adding 5 new proprietary Schwab-Funds and 412 new third-party funds to our Mutual Fund Marketplace. Our customers now have access to almost 2,000 funds from 316 families, including 1,143 Mutual Fund One-Source funds. Customer assets in OneSource funds topped $100 billion during December 1999, ending the year at $102 billion, while customer assets in SchwabFunds passed $100 billion earlier in the year and ended 1999 at $108 billion. Overall, customer asset balances in mutual funds totaled $285 billion at month-end December, up 35 percent from December 1998.

Charles Schwab was ranked eighth on *Fortune*'s list of the 100 best companies to work for in America and was rated number two in *Working Woman* magazine's list of the top 25 companies for executive women. Schwab was also named a 1999 Catalyst Award winner as one of the three firms that had done the most to advance women in business.

E*Trade Group (www.etrade.com)

E*Trade had grown rapidly into one of the best-known online personal financial services firms. It operated the world's most visited online investing site (with 300 million page views per month) and served customers at sites in the United States, Japan, Great Britain, Sweden, France, Australia, New Zealand, Korea, and Canada. E*Trade was building the first global cross-border trading network for online investors in an effort to make trading in foreign securities accessible to retail, corporate, and institutional investors alike. E*Trade had been ranked the number one online brokerage by Gomez Advisors in four of the past five quarters and been rated the top online brokerage by Lafferty Information and Research Group, *PC Magazine,* and *Smart Computing Magazine.* According to an August 1999 poll by Opinion Research Corp., E*Trade was one of the top four most recognized e-commerce brands among U.S. adults.

Company Background   E*Trade was formed in 1982 to develop automated trading services for Charles Schwab & Co. and Fidelity Investments. E*Trade began its online trading service in 1992, surviving as a fledgling pioneer until the industry began to take off in 1995. In the first five months of 1996, E*Trade's active accounts grew from 38,000 to 65,000 and its monthly trading volume jumped from 50 million to 170 million shares. Led by 51-year-old Christos Cotsakos, who became CEO in March 1996 after career stints at FedEx and Dun & Bradstreet, E*Trade went public in August 1996, raising $46 million from its initial public offering of stock to fund expansion and build a leadership position in the online trading industry. By early 1997, E*Trade was opening 500 accounts and bringing in $8 to $10 million in assets a day; its customers were placing about 6,000 online trades daily. In late 1997, E*Trade opened a Mutual Fund Center that allowed customers to select from among 4,600 mutual funds at a flat sales commission of $24.95 and, with its acquisition of OptionsLink from Hambrecht & Quist, it began providing stock-option management services for 94,000 employees at 79 companies. The company had $7.8 billion in customer assets in 325,000 accounts and 600 employees as of January 1998; it handled an average of 23,200 trades a day in the first quarter of 1998.[19]

In the summer of 1998, Cotsakos got approval from the company's board of directors to quadruple E*Trade's advertising budget to $175 million a year for each of the next two years (spending a total of $350 million through mid-2000), a move that would wipe out the company's small profits and make it unprofitable until the number of customer accounts and the firm's trading volume grew substantially. In addition, E*Trade allocated around $100 million (about 12 percent of revenues) to upgrade its technology, its Web site capacity, and its operating systems over the next 18 months. To make the company more price-competitive, E*Trade cut its commission rates seven times before arriving at its present $14.95 fee for stocks listed on the NYSE and $19.95 for stocks listed on the NASDAQ. Lower commissions and heavy marketing boosted the number of customer accounts to over 1 million in early 1999.

Recent Developments   While the company had reported a small profit in 1996, 1997, and 1998, E*Trade lost $54.4 million on revenues of $621 million in the fiscal year ending September 30, 1999. In the first quarter of fiscal year 2000 ending December 31, 1999, E*Trade reported after-tax losses from ongoing operations of $38 million on revenues of $246 million. The company's stock price had performed well for shareholders until recent months. It split two-for-one twice in early 1999, rising to an all-time split-adjusted high of $72 in April 1999 before falling back to trade in the mid-30s in early 2000, when the company's losses mounted and traditional full-service brokers moved to institute online trading options for their customers.

E*Trade acquired 330,000 net new accounts during the last three months of 1999, bringing its total active accounts to nearly 1.9 million and customer assets to $44 billion (an average of just over $22,000 per account, but far below the average of $115,000 per account at Schwab and the more than $400,000 per account at Merrill Lynch). The company spent nearly $80 million on marketing in the third quarter of 1999 to add 310,000 new accounts—$238 per new account, reportedly one of the lowest acquisition costs per net new account in the industry. Average transactions per day were in the 130,000 to 140,000 range in the first quarter of 2000, up from 43,000 in the last quarter of 1998. Starting in August 1999, E*Trade cut its commissions on active traders' transactions to $4.95 per trade from $14.95 per trade.

In late 1999, E*trade moved to further expand its customer base and diversify its revenue stream by acquiring Telebanc Financial, the largest online-only bank in the United States, for $1.8 billion; through Telebanc, E*Trade provided customers with online checking accounts, ATM cards, printed checks, and bill-paying services. Also during 1999, E*Trade acquired a 28 percent ownership of E*Offering, an online investment bank; 2 percent of E-Loan, an online loan service that matched borrowers with willing bank lenders; 18 percent of Archipelago ECN; and 100 percent of ClearStation, a Web site with original financial news and 250,000 users. The company had started an E*Trade family of mutual funds, added bond trading to its site, and developed plans to launch Web sites in over a dozen additional countries. E*Trade had entered into strategic alliances with Bond Exchange (to provide bond trading services), First USA (to provide credit cards), InsWeb (an online insurance provider), TheStreet.com and Bridge Information (financial news providers), and Briefing.com and Banc Boston Robertson Stephens (to provide investment research).

---

[19]*The Wall Street Journal,* June 2, 1998, p. C20.

E*Trade management saw these acquisitions and alliances as providing substantial cross-selling opportunities. The day after the Telebanc deal was announced, for example, E*Trade and Telebanc put together a package deal where Telebanc offered a one-year 6.5 percent certificate of deposit—a hefty 208 basis-point premium over the national average—exclusively to E*Trade customers. The promotion attracted 6,000 responses within three weeks.

E*Trade's Strategic Vision   Chris Cotsakos was regarded as an energetic evangelist for online trading who had innovative ideas for making E*Trade a market leader. Cotsakos said, "When the business was just getting started, we went after the early adopters, people who were techno-savvy. Now we're after the mainstream."[20] He believed the handwriting was on the wall for the army of brokers employed at full-service firms: "The days of the $100,000 broker are coming to an end."[21] In an interview published in *Leaders* in 1997, Cotsakos said, "I believe the brokers will have to migrate to a different type of position, like an advisor or consultant to the individual investor. I believe the days of the huge commissions and huge salaries are numbered . . . Brokerage is not a field I would recommend my daughter go into." He foresaw online brokerages outcompeting full-service firms and evolving into one-stop financial services enterprises:

> What we really see ourselves migrating to is a financial services gateway, where people can have access to our proprietary information as well as other content we can aggregate. That way, they can have one-stop shopping with a customized, personalized screen that meets all their financial needs, whether it's banking, buying flowers, viewing their stock portfolio, downloading information to their tax advisors, or doing a transaction.[22]

By early 2000, Cotsakos's vision of having E*Trade's Web site function as a financial online hub where consumers went for self-service investing, banking, insurance, loans, and financial planning was taking on some new twists. Cotsakos's latest idea was to add an array of multimedia features to the E*Trade Web site that would position E*Trade as a "digital financial media" provider. In early 2000, E*Trade launched the first phase of a $100 million initiative that would:

- Permit customers to have personalized Web pages.

- Give E*Trade the capability to broadcast live TV-quality video feeds of news and interviews with company CEOs.

- Permit online chats with financial advisers, loan agents, and investment analysts who had researched particular companies and industries.

- Enable E*Trade to run ads and promotions on personalized Web pages that were tailored to individual interests (such as the latest airline discounts for frequent travelers).

- Provide customers with an electronic calendar that alerted them by e-mail or notices on the Web site of upcoming news and earnings release dates of companies in their portfolio.

- Provide E*Trade's services over handheld devices, cable-TV boxes, and satellite-TV systems as well as PCs.

---

[20] As quoted in Whitford, "Trade Fast, Trade Cheap," p. 112.

[21] As quoted in *Institutional Investor,* January 1997, p. 23.

[22] As quoted in "Declaring War On Brokerage Fees," *Leaders,* April–May–June 1997.

As one E*Trade executive put it, "E*Trade is all about empowering individuals with the right tools and information to take control of their financial lives."

Cotsakos believed that E*Trade needed a remarkable and distinctive corporate culture to propel the company to success. He spent considerable time on culture-building activities, seeking to build a company with wildly creative, hypercompetitive people who were closely knit into a family. To emphasize the need for speed, he organized a day where employees raced Formula One racing cars at speeds of up to 150 miles an hour; to create a loose atmosphere, he encouraged employees to carry around rubber chickens and wear propeller beanies; to promote employee bonding and a team spirit, he had managers attend a cooking school where they had to work closely with one another to prepare a gourmet dinner. To help develop the capabilities to beat out other dot-com rivals, he stressed inventiveness, moving at Internet speed, and bold, aggressive action. The following two quotes represent Cotsakos's ideas:

> We pay big money for intellectual capital and speed. One of the things I learned from my experiences in Vietnam is that if you go in half-way, you can't win. You've got to have not only ground cover but air cover. You've got to bring in the heavy artillery. You've got to go out and say, "I'm here, I've arrived, and I'm not going to be messed with."[23]

> At E*Trade, we're predatory. We believe we have a God-given right to market share.[24]

In a feature article on Chris Cotsakos and E*Trade a *Business Week* reporter observed:

> E*Trade has to be on the offensive, given Cotsakos's ambitions. His dream is to assemble a financial services empire that not only overtakes online rival Charles Schwab but also matches the breadth of brick-and-mortar giants such as Merrill Lynch & Co. and Citigroup. The competition is intense. Schwab is in the lead—and a handful of feisty, barebones Net brokers are doing trades at $8 a pop, compared with $14.95 for E*Trade. Cotsakos has to beat back the Net players and grow fast before Merrill Lynch and others bring all their marketing muscle to bear on the Web.[25]

Ameritrade (www.ameritrade.com)

Ameritrade Holding Corp. was an Omaha-based firm with four subsidiaries: Ameritrade and Accutrade—both deep-discount brokerages with online trading units; AmeriTrade Clearing, which provided securities clearing services for its two sister brokerages, banks, and other brokers and securities dealers; and AmeriVest, which provided discount brokerage services to banks, savings and loan associations, and credit unions. The company successfully completed an initial public offering of common stock in March 1997 and its shares were traded on the NASDAQ. Over the past four years, Ameritrade had transformed itself from a small midwestern discount brokerage into a well-known national brand with 560,000 accounts, over $20 billion in customer assets, 1999 revenues of $268 million and net earnings of $11.5 million. It was the fifth largest online broker in terms of accounts. Its extensive advertising campaigns had given it one of the best-known brand names in the online brokerage segment.

Ameritrade Holding Corp. launched its Ameritrade deep-discount brokerage and no-frills online service in the fall of 1997. The Ameritrade brokerage subsidiary was formed by consolidating three small company-owned brokerages—Ceres Securities (a deep-discount brokerage the company started in 1994); K. Aufhauser (a New York firm acquired in 1995 that had launched the first Internet trading site in August 1994); and

---

[23]As quoted in Daniel Roth, "E*Trade's Plan for World Domination," *Fortune,* August 2, 1999, p. 96.

[24]As quoted in Louise Lee, "Tricks of E*Trade," *Business Week,* February 7, 2000, p. EB-21.

[25]Ibid.

eBroker (a deep-discount online brokerage formed in 1996 to target the most price-sensitive online traders). Ameritrade immediately attracted the attention of online investors with its fees of $8 for Internet trades and a $25 million ad campaign consisting of TV spots, print ads in *USA Today* and *The Wall Street Journal,* radio ads, and direct mail. Ameritrade's primary market target was investors who were comfortable with computers, knowledgeable about how to find investment-related information on the Internet on their own, didn't like going through a broker, and were looking to execute their trades at a very low cost. To help build its customer base and increase brand awareness, Ameritrade had entered into strategic marketing agreements for services and content with America Online, CompuServe, Excite, Intuit, Infoseek, the Microsoft Network, Yahoo!, The Motley Fool, and the *USA Today* Information Network. These agreements gave Ameritrade valuable exposure and gave Ameritrade customers access to a wider range of information and resources and improved trading experiences. By year-end 1997 Ameritrade had added 51,000 new accounts, bringing its account total to 147,000.

In 1998 Ameritrade introduced a new computer game called Darwin, distributed free on CD-ROM, as an educational tool for novice investors who wanted to learn about the Black/Scholes model, butterfly spreads, and other tricks of options trading in a setting with the excitement and features of the popular video game Doom.[26] Ameritrade executives, having spent time in investor chat rooms on the Internet, could tell from the comments and complaints that investor losses on options trading were often the result of the trader's own lack of understanding and know-how.

Ameritrade had been a consistent leader in innovation and was the first brokerage to see the value of aggressive advertising. Ameritrade spent 100 percent of its revenues on advertising and marketing in the fourth quarter of 1997, producing 50 percent account growth in 90 days and a tripling of accounts over the next year. The company spent $44 million on advertising in 1998 and $60 million in 1999, boosting its account total to 560,000 and helping grow revenues by 250 percent. Until mid-1999 Ameritrade had turned its growth into premarketing operating income of roughly $10 per transaction, a 40 percent margin. (See the analysis in Exhibit 8 for a breakdown of Ameritrade's revenues, costs and profits per transaction by quarter and by year.) However, in the second and third quarters of 1999 the company's nonmarketing expenses increased dramatically, from $38 million in the first quarter to $62 million in the third quarter, pushing premarketing operating income down to $4 per transaction (Exhibit 8). Ameritrade had ambitious plans to spend close to $200 million on marketing and advertising starting in the fourth quarter of 1999 and continuing through the first quarter of 2001 to build its accounts and trading volume to levels that would cover the increased expenses and restore its margins. As shown in Exhibit 8, analysts at Credit Suisse First Boston expected that the increase in marketing expenditures would result in Ameritrade incurring a loss in 2000.

The Quick & Reilly Group/Suretrade

The Quick & Reilly Group was a subsidiary of FleetBoston Financial Inc., the largest bank in New England. It consisted of Quick & Reilly, Inc., the third largest discount brokerage in the United States, with 1 million accounts and 120 branch offices; U.S. Clearing, a clearing and trade execution service for more than 350 brokerage and banking firms; JJC Specialist, the second largest specialist on the floor of the NYSE, which made a market in the stocks and securities for 229 NYSE-listed companies; Nash Weiss, which made a market in 3,500 over-the-counter stocks; and Suretrade, a deep

---

[26]Whitford, "Trade Fast, Trade Cheap," p. 114.

	1998 Fiscal Year				1999 Fiscal Year				2000 Fiscal Year Estimates				1998	1999	Est. 2000
	Dec-97	Mar-98	Jun-98	Sep-98	Dec-98	Mar-99	Jun-99	Sep-99	Dec-99	Mar-00	Jun-00	Sep-00	1998	1999	2000
Commissions	$ 22.51	$18.73	$17.82	$17.22	$16.36	$15.47	$14.92	$14.72	$14.65	$14.50	$14.40	$14.25	$18.54	$15.26	$14.43
Interest income	$ 18.71	$14.26	$13.97	$13.02	$10.27	$ 8.15	$ 8.30	$11.13	$10.00	$10.83	$10.83	$10.83	$14.44	$ 9.39	$10.66
Less interest expense	$ 8.12	$ 6.44	$ 6.17	$ 5.60	$ 4.39	$ 3.39	$ 3.21	$ 4.40	$ 3.69	$ 4.83	$ 4.17	$ 4.50	$ 6.34	$ 3.79	$ 4.32
Net interest income	$ 10.59	$ 7.82	$ 7.81	$ 7.42	$ 5.87	$ 4.76	$ 5.10	$ 6.73	$ 6.31	$ 6.00	$ 6.67	$ 6.33	$ 8.10	$ 5.60	$ 6.34
Equity income from investments	$ 1.89	$ 1.16	$ 1.84	$ 0.05	$ —	$ —	$ —	$ —	$ —	$ —	$ —	$ —	$ 1.10	$ —	$ —
Other income	$ 1.65	$ 1.28	$ 1.31	$ 1.12	$ 0.99	$ 0.79	$ 0.76	$ 0.82	$ 0.72	$ 0.65	$ 0.61	$ 0.57	$ 1.29	$ 0.83	$ 0.63
Net revenues	$ 36.63	$28.98	$28.77	$25.81	$23.23	$21.02	$20.78	$22.26	$21.68	$21.15	$21.68	$21.15	$29.03	$21.68	$21.40
Compensation and benefits	$ 9.65	$ 7.64	$ 7.92	$ 6.99	$ 5.99	$ 4.93	$ 5.58	$ 7.48	$ 6.75	$ 6.25	$ 6.00	$ 5.50	$ 7.81	$ 6.01	$ 6.06
Commissions and clearing	$ 1.39	$ 1.25	$ 1.29	$ 1.14	$ 0.83	$ 0.72	$ 0.52	$ 0.61	$ 0.56	$ 0.55	$ 0.54	$ 0.53	$ 1.25	$ 0.65	$ 0.54
Communications	$ 4.46	$ 3.21	$ 2.61	$ 1.93	$ 1.54	$ 1.49	$ 1.37	$ 1.63	$ 1.52	$ 1.44	$ 1.43	$ 1.35	$ 2.80	$ 1.50	$ 1.43
Occupancy and equipment	$ 2.77	$ 2.19	$ 2.03	$ 2.39	$ 1.84	$ 1.52	$ 1.54	$ 2.05	$ 1.80	$ 1.67	$1.60	$ 1.52	$ 2.30	$ 1.73	$ 1.64
Other expense	$ 7.61	$ 5.69	$ 4.69	$ 3.95	$ 3.80	$ 3.85	$ 4.85	$ 6.73	$ 6.64	$ 6.84	$ 6.41	$ 6.13	$ 5.11	$ 4.92	$ 6.47
Operating expense	$ 25.88	$19.98	$18.54	$16.39	$13.99	$12.51	$13.86	$18.49	$17.27	$16.75	$15.99	$15.04	$19.26	$14.81	$16.14
Pre-marketing operating income	$ 10.75	$ 9.01	$10.23	$ 9.42	$ 9.24	$ 8.51	$ 6.92	$ 3.77	$ 4.41	$ 4.40	$ 5.69	$ 6.11	$ 9.76	$ 6.88	$ 5.26
Advertising and promotion	$ 35.59	$ 9.22	$ 3.89	$ 2.52	$ 4.30	$ 4.34	$ 3.21	$ 7.42	$ 9.72	$ 8.24	$ 7.51	$ 3.71	$ 9.44	$ 4.82	$ 6.99
Pre-tax operating income	$(24.83)	$ (0.22)	$ 6.34	$ 6.90	$ 4.94	$ 4.17	$ 3.71	$ (3.65)	$ (5.31)	$ (3.84)	$ (1.81)	$ 2.40	$ 0.32	$ 2.06	$(1.73)
Amortization	$ 0.13	$ 0.09	$ 0.07	$ 0.06	$ 0.04	$ 0.03	$ 0.02	$ 0.03	$ 0.02	$ 0.02	$ 0.02	$ 0.02	$ 0.08	$ 0.03	$ 0.02
Nonrecurring items	$ —	$ 0.59	$ 0.59	$ (0.91)	$ (2.27)	$ —	$ —	$ (0.63)	$ —	$ —	$ —	$ —	$(0.13)	$(0.58)	$ —
Net income before taxes	$(24.70)	$ (0.13)	$ 7.00	$ 6.05	$ 2.71	$ 4.20	$ 3.74	$ (4.25)	$ (5.29)	$(3.82)	$ (1.79)	$ 2.42	$ 0.27	$ 1.50	$(1.71)
Taxes	$ (8.91)	$ (0.04)	$ 2.46	$ 2.15	$ 0.96	$ 1.50	$ 1.32	$ (1.53)	$ (1.90)	$ (1.37)	$ (0.64)	$ 0.87	$ 0.07	$ 0.53	$(0.61)
Extraordinary items	$ —	$ —	$ —	$ —	$ —	$ —	$ —	$ —	$ —	$ —	$ —	$ —	$ —	$ —	$ —
Net income	$(15.79)	$ (0.09)	$ 4.54	$ 3.90	$ 1.75	$ 2.70	$ 2.41	$ (2.72)	$ (3.39)	$ (2.45)	$ (1.15)	$ 1.55	$ 0.20	$ 0.97	$ (1.09)

Source: Equity Research, Credit Suisse First Boston Corp., November 5, 1999. Used with permission.

discount Internet brokerage that began doing business in November 1997. When Quick & Reilly was acquired by FleetBoston in early 1998, FleetBoston immediately moved to make Quick & Reilly products available to Fleet's customers and to market Fleet's products to Quick & Reilly customers; the cross-selling was immediately apparent at Quick & Reilly's Web site (www.quick-reilly.com).

Quick & Reilly was the first NYSE member firm to offer discount commissions to individuals in 1975. It launched its Internet trading system in November 1996 and gained a reputation as one of the fastest, easiest-to-use, and most comprehensive trading systems on the Internet. The company's Web site had been continuously enhanced since its introduction.

Suretrade (www.suretrade.com)   Since its launch in 1997 Suretrade has grown to over 360,000 customer accounts and nearly $2 billion in customer assets. It was considered the Wal-Mart of the online brokerage industry. Suretrade's $7.95 commission fee for market orders was among the lowest in the online brokerage segment (limit orders carried a $9.95 fee). It had one of the lowest margin rate schedules and offered a wealth of free research, real-time quotes, news, charting, portfolio and life planners, stock and mutual fund screeners, and 24-hour online broker-assisted help. Customers could choose to invest in over 3,000 mutual funds. Suretrade had a reputation for fast, accurate trade execution and its Web site was considered easy to navigate. It was recognized as one of the leading online brokerages, earning strong rankings in *Smart Money, Time, Business Week, Money,* and *Kiplinger's.*

At its Web site Suretrade was up front with customers about what they could expect:

> How can we bring you such an extraordinary value, combining excellent Internet trading functionality, content and security, along with a fantastic low commission structure? Our relationship will be an electronic one. It costs us less to answer e-mails than it costs us to answer phone calls. Remember, our great prices aren't for everyone. They are for brokerage clients ready to conduct their affairs electronically. Our low commissions are the reward for clients who are committed to electronic brokerage.[27]

Morgan Stanley Dean Witter Online (www.msdw.com)

Morgan Stanley Dean Witter Online (formerly Discover Brokerage Direct) got its start in electronic brokerage as Lombard Institutional Brokerage, a small discount firm in San Francisco that began offering online trading in September 1995. Lombard was acquired by Dean Witter Discover in January 1997 to serve as its online entry, which changed Lombard's name to Discover Brokerage Direct to create a stronger association with the 40 million holders of the Discover Card. Dean Witter Discover then acquired the Morgan Stanley Group (a leading Wall Street investment banking firm) in May 1997. The new company, Morgan Stanley Dean Witter, had 1999 revenues of $34 billion and earnings of $4.7 billion. The company had three core businesses—securities, asset management, and its Discover Card credit services—creating a company with great financial strength, global scope, and market leadership in a variety of financial service businesses. Dean Witter was the third largest full-service brokerage, with over 450 U.S. branch offices, over 12,600 brokers, 4 million customer accounts, and $425 billion in customer assets.

[27]Company Web site, April 17, 1998.

The company's strategy during the Discover Brokerage era was to compete on value and service. Top management saw price cutting as "a dangerous strategy."[28] Discover Brokerage began an extensive marketing campaign in January 1998 to build a bigger customer base; its campaign included a direct mail appeal to the more than 40 million holders of the Discover card. The company's ads in 1998–99 featured its number one ratings by *Barron's* and *Smart Money*. Discover Brokerage featured commissions as low as $14.95 a trade, 24-hour customer support, and access to over 3,500 mutual funds (many with no loads or transaction fees); customers could also place trades with a registered professional or by Touch-Tone phone. Discover's Web site provided customers with numerous data and research options and featured up-to-the-minute account information—customers could watch the prices change for their holdings as trades were executed. Discover also offered extensive customizing ability so clients could design their own investment-information centers according to their own interests. Discover Brokerage was the only online brokerage to win *a Barron's* four-star rating four years in a row; it also earned a top five-star rating in *Kiplinger's* 1999 survey of online brokerages and a 1998 top rating from *Smart Money*. However, Discover Brokerage achieved only modest success in the marketplace, having attracted about 180,000 accounts and generating an average of 11,000 trades per day when it was renamed Morgan Stanley Dean Witter Online in October 1999.

Morgan Stanley Dean Witter Online charged customers $29.95 for online trades and $39.95 for broker-assisted trades for orders of 1,000 shares or less. For orders over 1,000, online trades were 3 cents per share and broker-assisted trades were 4 cents per share. Customers had access to Morgan Stanley Dean Witter analyst research, electronic funds transfer, check writing, money market funds, extended hours trading, wireless trading (through TradeRunner, a wireless investing service), and a product where they could purchase a "blue-chip" basket of 10 selected stocks for a flat $49.95 commission price. Customers could also choose a plan in which they got unlimited free trades for a single asset-based fee that decreased from 2.25 percent for accounts under $100,000 to 0.30 percent for accounts over $10 million.

Web Street Securities (www.webstreet.com)

Web Street Securities was small, privately held brokerage formed by two entrepreneurs, Joe and Avi Fox, both in their 30s, whose prior venture was a failed international investment banking firm they had founded. After a month and a half of research into online trading during the summer of 1996, the two brothers decided to cast their future with online brokerage. Web Street opened its doors for business in August 1997. It launched its bid for investor attention and market share in early 1998 with a $20 million national advertising campaign featuring attention-getting TV spots (that intoned "You're a player now" when the head of the household portrayed in the ad opened an account online), and full-page media ads in *USA Today* and other publications

Web Street had pioneered several innovations—streaming real-time quotes, pop-up order confirmation messages, and an exclusive one-page "Trading Pit" screen that displayed all the needed information to place a trade and provided customers with access to their positions, real-time account balances, order status, and links to research and news all on one page (see Exhibit 9). Customers could customize their Trading Pit screen to display streaming real-time quotes for designated stocks on their watch lists.

---

[28]"Wooley, Do I Hear Two Bits a Trade?" p. 96.

exhibit 9   Web Street Securities' Innovative Trading Pit Screen

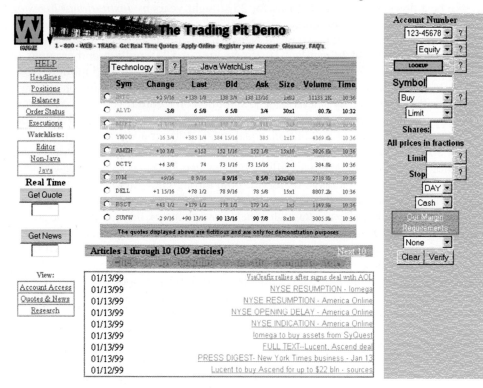

The one-page Trading Pit screen permitted customers to buy and sell with just one click, keep an eye on the streaming quotes of watch-listed stocks, and watch their holdings being updated on the screen as trades occurred. At the Trading Pit customers could, in addition, get real-time updates of account information (customers could watch their holdings being updated on the screen as trades occurred) and click on news updates and research sources. Customers could place broker-assisted trades at $24.95. They could also purchase bonds (corporate, municipal, state, or federal) and any of 4,000 mutual funds from 250 mutual fund families; no commissions were charged on mutual fund purchases. Registered brokers and customer service representatives were on duty 24 hours a day, seven days a week.

However, Web Street had grown more slowly than anticipated during the 1998–99 period and was not believed to be profitable given its present scale of operation.

DLJdirect (www.dljdirect.com)

DLJdirect was the online trading service of Donaldson Lufkin & Jenrette, a premier investment research house and one of the 10 largest investment banking firms, with 1999 revenues of $7.1 billion and more than 10,000 employees in 17 cities in the United States and 15 cities in Europe, Latin America, and Asia. The firm's businesses included securities underwriting, sales and trading, investment banking, financial advisory services, investment research, online brokerage services, and asset management. It was the fifth largest lead manager of initial public offerings and the largest underwriter of high-yield bonds. DLJ and its affiliates handled about 10 percent of the trading volume of the New York Stock Exchange. DLJ's research operation had been ranked among the five best investment research firms for 25 straight years by *Institutional Investor,* whose research covered 1,100 companies in 80 industries.

Originally launched as PC Financial Network, DLJdirect pioneered online investing in the late 1980s. DLJdirect had 1999 revenues of $238 million and earnings of $6.9 million versus 1998 revenues of $118 million and earnings of $1.5 million. However, in the third quarter of 1999, DLJdirect reported a loss of $3.3 million on revenues of $54.9 million followed by a net loss of $2.0 million on record revenues of $76.3 million in the fourth quarter of 1999. At year-end 1999, DLJdirect had 347,000 active online accounts, with assets of $22 billion, equal to $63,400 per account; it added 40,000 net new accounts in the fourth quarter, with assets of $7.4 billion. DLJdirect executed 5.8 million trades in 1999; average daily trades reached 38,000 in December 1999.

DLJdirect provided access to its service both through the Internet and through the major online services (America Online, Prodigy, and CompuServe); customers could also place trades with brokers or through Touch-Tone phones. Clients could trade stocks, options, bonds, and Treasuries and could select from about 7,000 mutual funds (out of the 9,500 currently available funds). Online clients with account balances of $100,000 or more were provided access to DLJ's proprietary research information on 1,100 companies as well as opportunities to buy initial public offerings of stock in which DLJ was a lead manager or participant. In addition, DLJdirect offered real-time quotes, stock and portfolio alerts, a personal stock ticker, and screening tools.

DLJdirect promoted itself as "a serious company for the serious investor." The company received *Barron's* highest rating (four stars) in a March 13, 2000, article reviewing the top 27 online brokers; *Barron's* evaluation criteria included trade execution process, ease of use, reliability and range of offerings, amenities, and commissions. The Lafferty Group, which rated about 500 Web sites in all sectors of the global financial services industry, gave DLJdirect a five-star rating (46 points out of a possible 50 points) during the fourth quarter of 1999. During 1999, DLJdirect had also been rated the top online brokerage by *Forbes, Time Digital, Worth,* Keynote Web Brokerage Index, and Gomez Advisors.

Datek Online Holdings, Inc. (www.datek.com)

Until September 1999, Datek Online was headed by Jeffrey A. Citron, a 29-year-old who had started working at 17 as an office clerk in a small Brooklyn, New York, brokerage called Datek Securities. By age 20, Citron had earned $1 million trading securities and was driving a Mercedes. A few years later, Citron and co-worker Joshua Levine used their computer skills to automate much of Datek's brokerage operations and started to explore ways to computerize stock trades. When in 1988 NASDAQ ordered securities dealers who were market makers in over-the-counter stocks to execute small orders via a computerized electronic system, Citron and Levine came up with a software trading system that allowed Datek Securities to become the biggest brokerage that executed small trades and to make millions of dollars in trading profits—the company had trading profits of about $95 million in 1996, up from $3.8 million in 1992.[29] Citron and Levine became multimillionaires. Jeffrey Citron was labeled a "technology wizard" by *Forbes* and as "one of the 20 most important players on the financial Web" by *Institutional Investor.* But during the 1991–96 period, various officials at Datek Securities were censured, fined, and suspended by the National Association of Securities Dealers on several occasions for violating trading rules in executing small trading orders on the

---

[29]*New York Times,* May 10, 1998, section 3, p. 4.

NASDAQ. Datek Securities was also on the losing end of numerous customer arbitrations alleging violations such as unauthorized trading or failure to execute customer orders.

In 1992, Citron and Levine founded a company (what is now Island ECN) to function as a computerized stock exchange, utilizing software they had created—the company was quite successful and, by 1998, was handling 4 percent of all NASDAQ trading volume.[30] In 1993, Jeffrey Citron formed his own brokerage firm, which he sold a few months later to Joshua Levine. In 1995, Citron established a company to sell electronic trading software, while Levine formed two companies—Big Think (to supply Datek Securities with new computer technology) and Big J Software, a software consulting company whose principal clients were securities firms. In early 1996, Citron, Levine, and Sheldon Maschler, former chief trader at Datek Securities who was the central figure in many of the firm's trading violations and was later suspended from securities trading for one year beginning in February 1997, formed a company to develop and license trading software to Datek Securities and other online brokerage operations; the new company achieved revenues of nearly $100 million in 1996. In 1997, Datek Securities established Datek Online as an Internet brokerage and Jeffrey Citron became CEO. In early 1998, Datek Securities and Levine's Big Think were merged as Datek Online Holdings; Citron, Levine, Erik Maschler (son of Sheldon Maschler), and several others emerged as the principal owners. In 1998 the old Datek Securities unit was sold in an effort to help disassociate Datek Online from its troubled past, but in 2000 the trading and lending practices at the old Datek Securities were still under investigation by the SEC and the U.S. Attorney's Office in Manhattan.

In early 1997, Datek had 10,000 online accounts; in April 1998, it reportedly had 80,000 accounts, containing $1.5 billion in assets. In mid-1999, Datek had 253,000 online trading accounts containing $6 billion in customer assets. A principal reason for Datek's success was its innovative software programs—it had the fastest execution of electronic stock trades, and it offered customers both streaming quotes and free real-time quotes. The firm's systems were based on superfast trading software technology that it was marketing to day-trading firms. Datek Online's low commissions also appealed to active traders. Aside from having spurred trading innovations with its Island ECN, Datek Online was recognized for setting standards for speed and service in the online brokerage business. In 2000, Datek was the fifth largest online brokerage firm.

Jeffrey Citron and the other investors in Datek Online were forced to scrap plans for taking the company public in mid-1998 amid publicity over the continuing investigations of Datek Securities. A lengthy feature article in the *New York Times* in May 1998 detailed the numerous entanglements of Datek Online's owners with Datek Securities and the many sanctions imposed on Datek Securities. However, the article indicated that Jeffrey Citron had recently tightened management controls at Datek Online Holdings, outlawed certain questionable trading practices, hired a major accounting firm as auditor, and completed the sale of the company's Datek Securities trading unit, the center of most of the questioned practices and the target of several ongoing investigations of securities fraud. The purchasers of the securities trading unit, renamed Heartland Securities, were two of the current owners of Datek Online Holdings, Erik Maschler and Aaron Elbogen; in 1970, Elbogen had been one of the original cofounders of Datek Securities.

In early 1999, Edward Nicoll, a 46-year-old Wall Street executive who had earned a law degree from Yale in 1998 without ever having attended college, was brought in to head Datek Online's operations and work with Citron to turn Datek into a quality

---

[30]Ibid.

firm. Nicoll assumed a significant ownership stake in the firm as part of his agreement to join Datek Online. In July 2000, Groupe Arnault of Paris and TA Associates of Boston contracted to invest $195 million in new capital into Datek, but a third investor, Vulcan Ventures (owned by Microsoft cofounder Paul Allen) backed out of a $50 million commitment at the last minute, citing "due diligence" problems. Vulcan also dropped plans to invest $25 million in Island ECN in return for a 12 percent ownership stake. In an article reporting on the Vulcan withdrawal, the *New York Times,* citing people close to the ongoing investigations into Datek Securities, said that during the period when Jeffrey Citron and Sheldon Maschler were the principal traders at Datek Securities the company was involved in a number of money-laundering operations. In October 1999, TD Waterhouse also stepped back from a $25 million investment in Datek, even though TD Waterhouse was a company that Edward Nicoll had cofounded and helped run for 16 years. Both Vulcan and Waterhouse, while attracted by the company's technological innovativeness and rapid growth, were believed to have had second thoughts about partnering with Datek because of its scandal-plagued background. Datek was expected to use the nearly $300 million in planned capital infusions to upgrade its technology at Datek Online and to help prepare Island ECN to become a full-fledged stock exchange (a petition had been filed with the SEC).

To help polish the firm's tarnished reputation and attract investment capital to upgrade its technology, Jeffrey Citron had resigned as chairman and CEO of Datek in September 1999 and relinquished his seats on the board of directors of both Datek and Island. Edward Nicoll replaced Jeffrey Citron as CEO. While Citron still owned about a third of Datek Online Holding's outstanding shares, he had put his shares into a trust for two years so that they could not be used to influence the board during that time. However, Citron's departure and the appointment of Nicoll as his replacement, which occurred while TD Waterhouse was still considering investing in Datek, were insufficient to keep Waterhouse from backing away from its deal with Datek.

Nicoll hoped that Datek Online's prior history and ties to Datek Securities would fade into the background, allowing the company to go public sometime in 2000.

Merrill Lynch (www.ml.com)

Merrill Lynch was a diversified financial services firm whose principal businesses were in investment banking, full-service brokerage, and asset management. It was the world leader in full-service brokerage, with 950 branch offices in 40 countries, approximately 19,000 brokers and account executives worldwide, 8 million retail customer accounts (covering about 5 million households), and $1.34 trillion in its retail brokerage accounts. The firm had an exceptionally broad range of investment products and services, and the name Merrill Lynch was known to virtually all investors worldwide. Merrill Lynch consistently ranked among the leading research providers in the industry, covering some 3,700 companies in 55 countries with its staff of roughly 680 analysts. Current information on all these companies was available to all retail clients through their brokers and could also be accessed online. In the securities-dealer side of its brokerage business, Merrill Lynch was a market maker for the stocks of 550 U.S. companies and 4,800 foreign companies traded in over-the-counter markets. In 1999, Merrill Lynch had total revenues of $21.9 billion and net income of $2.6 billion. Retail brokerage commissions from stock trading accounted for $3.6 billion of Merrill Lynch's revenues, up from $3.2 billion in 1998 and $1.8 billion in 1995.[31] The company had a total of 67,200 employees.

---

[31]1999 Merrill Lynch Factbook, p. 16.

Top management's vision was for Merrill Lynch to be a world-class company that delivered global products, services, and intelligence of the highest caliber through trusted local relationships and to build leadership positions in securities markets throughout the world. Management was committed to serving clients through personalized advice and guidance, helping to create customized solutions to individualized client problems and expertly implement and execute financial plans for clients.

Because of its strong strategic emphasis on using brokers to deliver personalized client services, Merrill Lynch had held back in pursuing online trading. Prior to its June 1999 announcement that it would give its clients an online trading option, Merrill Lynch's only concession in using online capabilities was to create a software package for clients to install on their own computers that allowed them to access their accounts and review account balances; customers were charged $25 for the software. A Merrill Lynch executive indicated that the reason the firm hadn't rushed to offer online trading was "this is not one of the highest-rated things that our clients are asking for."[32]

In December 1999, Merrill Lynch launched its online trading program, called Merrill Lynch Direct. According to a Merrill Lynch executive:

> Merrill Lynch Direct offers far more than just online trading execution. With features such as real-time account positions, tax-management information, the Global Investor Network for research, banking services and online shopping with an exceptional Visa Signature Rewards program, self-directed investors will be able to use this site to help manage all aspects of their financial lives.

Users of ML Direct could obtain help to make informed investment decisions using such information sources as Merrill Lynch's industry-leading research, S&P stock reports, real-time Dow Jones news stories and headlines; S&P stock, bonds and earnings guides and dividend records; as well as daily news feeds from PR Newswire and Business Wire. Merrill Lynch's Global Investor Network (GIN) provided investment research in streaming video; GIN was updated daily with audio and video reports from Merrill Lynch analysts, economists, mutual fund managers, and financial planning experts who covered markets around the world. Merrill Lynch's online clients also had unlimited access to:

- Real-time stock quotes.
- Stock, mutual fund, and fixed-income scanners.
- Retirement, education, and savings goal calculators.
- Comprehensive investor education information.
- Asset allocation and other extensive charting capabilities.

Clients who used Merrill Lynch Direct did not have access to one-on-one advice from the firm's professional financial consultants; broker-assisted trades were not a part of the Merrill Lynch Direct service. Those who wanted one-on-one professional advice could opt for Merrill Lynch's Unlimited Advantage program, a service that combined unlimited online trading and trading through a personal broker for an annual fee ranging from 0.2 percent to 1.0 percent of the assets under management, subject to an annual minimum of $1,500.

Merrill Lynch had invested in Archipelago ECN and several other electronic trading and marketing systems in order to participate in what management saw as a rapidly changing brokerage and trading environment.

---

[32]As quoted in *The Wall Street Journal,* June 2, 1998, p. C20.

American Express Brokerage
(www.americanexpress.com)

One of the newest industry participants was American Express Brokerage, which launched a new online trading service in the fall of 1999; the new service replaced American Express's Financial Direct, an online brokerage site, introduced in 1996, that never caught on. American Express offered its new brokerage service through its American Express Financial Advisors unit, which had a force of 9,300 advisers. Clients of these advisers were charged an annual fee based on a percentage of the assets in their accounts. American Express Brokerage's commission schedule varied according to how the trade was placed and the size of a customer's account:

Online trades with an account balance of:	
Less than $25,000	$14.95 (for all stock trades up to 3,000 shares/trade)
$25,000 to $99,999	Free unlimited buys, $14.95 sells
$100,000 and above	Free unlimited buys and sells
Voice response/Touch-Tone trading	$19.95 (for all stock trades up to 3,000 shares/trade)
Trades placed with an adviser	$44.95 (for all stock trades up to 3,000 shares/trade)

American Express Brokerage was able to provide free trading on large accounts because of the annual fees charged on the assets in each account and because it was able to defer some of the costs with the order flow fees it received from market makers.

American Express Brokerage offered nearly 2,000 mutual funds from such recognized fund families as Janus, American Century, Scudder, and T. Rowe Price. Customers could also purchase certificates of deposit and buy insurance. All account holders had access to unlimited check writing, ATM privileges, and bill-paying options. In August 1999, American Express had launched an online bank, and in September 1999 it had introduced a credit card, aimed at active Internet shoppers, that used a chip embedded in the card to provide added security features.

case 11 eBay: King of the Online Auction Industry

Louis Marino
The University of Alabama

Patrick Kreiser
The University of Alabama

As Pierre Omidyar (pronounced oh-*mid*-ee-ar), chairman and founder of eBay, set his morning copy of *The Wall Street Journal* down on the desk, he nervously wondered how long eBay's amazing run of success would continue. He had just read an article detailing the explosion in sales of Amazon.com to $650 million during the fourth quarter of 1999, a number that exceeded the company's entire sales for the year of 1998. Even more disconcerting to Pierre was that online auctions were the fastest-growing part of Amazon's business in 1999. Competition from Amazon.com, Yahoo!, and several other enterprising dot-com companies that had started holding auctions at their Web sites had reduced eBay's dominant market share from 80 percent to 60 percent during 1999. Other outsiders, including Microsoft and Dell, had announced plans to fund new ventures to enter the online auction business.

When Pierre formed eBay in 1995, he had never imagined the company would become so successful. He had continued to work at his old job even after forming eBay. Soon, however, he realized that the online auction industry represented a tremendous market opportunity—eBay gave hobbyists and collectors a convenient way to locate items of interest, a way for sellers to generate income, and a means for bargain hunters to pick up a wanted item at less than they might have paid in a retail store. Still, the rapid growth of eBay had surprised almost everyone (see Exhibit 1).

By 1999, when people thought about online auctions, the first name that popped into their heads was eBay. Going into 2000, eBay had created the world's largest Web-based community of consumer-to-consumer auctions using an entertaining format that allowed people to buy and sell collectibles, automobiles, jewelry, high-end and premium art items, antiques, coins and stamps, dolls and figures, pottery and glass, sports memorabilia, toys, consumer electronics products, and a host of other practical and miscellaneous items. At year-end 1999, eBay had listed over 3 million items in over 3,000 categories; browsers and buyers could search listings by item, category, key word, seller name, or auction dates. The company Web site had approximately 10 million registered users and,

exhibit 1   Selected Indicators of eBay's Growth, 1996–99

	1996	1997	1998	1999
Number of registered users	41,000	341,000	2,181,000	10,006,000
Gross merchandise sales	$7 million	$95 million	$745 million	$2.8 billion
Number of auctions listed	289,000	4,394,000	33,668,000	129,560,000

on average, attracted 1.8 million unique visitors daily. EBay members listed more than 375,000 items on the site every day.

However, Pierre Omidyar, Margaret Whitman (eBay's president and CEO), and other eBay executives were well aware that eBay needed to address a myriad of emerging market challenges. The complexion of the online auction industry was changing almost daily. While eBay's management team had met past challenges successfully, it wasn't going to be easy to hurdle the competitive and market challenges ahead.

THE GROWTH OF E-COMMERCE AND ONLINE AUCTIONS

Although the ideas behind the Internet were first conceived in the 1960s, it wasn't until the 1990s that the Internet garnered widespread use and became a part of everyday life. The real beginning of the Internet economy took place in 1991, when the National Science Foundation (NSF) lifted a restriction on commercial use of the Internet, making electronic commerce, or business conducted over the Internet, a possibility for the first time. By 1996, there were Internet users in almost 150 countries worldwide, and the number of computer hosts was close to 10 million. International Data Corporation (IDC) estimated there would be 320 million Internet users worldwide by 2002 and 500 million by year-end 2003.

The GartnerGroup forecast that business-to-business e-commerce would grow from $145 billion in 1999 to $7.29 trillion in 2004, while business-to-consumer revenues would climb from $31.2 billion in 1999 to over $380 billion in 2003. Within the business-to-consumer segment, where eBay operated, U.S. e-commerce accounted for over 65 percent of all Internet transactions in 1999 but was expected to account for only about 38 percent in 2003, due to rapid expansion in other parts of the world.

Business-to-consumer e-commerce in Europe was projected to grow from $5.4 billion in 1999 (17.3 percent of the world total) to over $115 billion (more than 30 percent of the world total) by 2003. As can be seen from Exhibit 2, online auction sales of collectibles and personal merchandise was expected to represent an $18.7 billion market in 2002.

Key Success Factors in Online Retailing

While it was relatively easy to create a Web site that functioned like a retail store, the big challenge was for an online retailer to generate traffic to the site in the form of both new and returning customers. Most online retailers strived to provide extensive product information, include pictures of the merchandise, make the site easily navigable, and have enough new things happening at the site to keep customers coming back. (A site's ability to generate repeat visitors was known as "stickiness.") Retailers also had

exhibit 2   Estimated Growth in Global E-Commerce and Online Auction Sales, 1999–2004

	1999	2000	2001	2002	2003	2004
Estimated business-to-business sales	$145 billion	$403 billion	$953 billion	$2.18 trillion	$3.95 trillion	$7.29 trillion

Source: GartnerGroup.

Estimated Growth in Global Business-to-Business E-Commerce

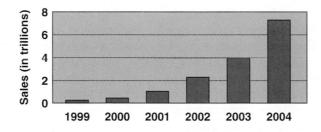

Online Auction Sales of Collectibles and Personal Merchandise
(Sales in billions of dollars)

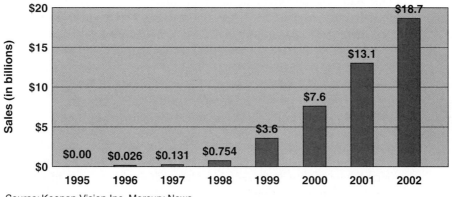

Source: Keenan Vision Inc. Mercury News.

to overcome users' nervousness about using the Internet itself to shop for items they generally bought at stores and their wariness about entering their credit card numbers over the Internet. Online retailing had severe limitations in the case of those goods and services people wanted to see in person to verify their quality. From the retailer's perspective, there was the issue of collecting payment from buyers who wanted to use checks or money orders instead of a credit card.

HISTORY OF AUCTIONS

An auction is a method of buying and selling goods to the highest bidder. A seller offers a particular product or service for sale, and the buyer who makes the highest offer for it is considered the auction winner. As the demand for a particular good rises among the buyers (typically due to its scarcity or desirability), the price also rises. Competition among bidders for a desirable good drives up the price. Sometimes the highest bid will exceed the generally accepted market value of the good, a phenomenon known as the "winner's curse." In this situation, the buyer becomes so emotionally attached to the good or to placing the highest bid that he or she ends up bidding more than the good would cost in a nonauction setting.

The first known auctions were held in Babylon around 500 BC. In these auctions, women were sold to the highest bidder on the condition that they marry the auction winner. In ancient Rome, soldiers would auction the spoils of their victories and wealthy citizens would auction their expensive belongings and prized possessions. In 193 AD, the entire Roman Empire was put up for auction after the emperor Pertinax was executed. Didius Julianus bid 6,250 drachmas per royal guard and was immediately named emperor of Rome. However, Julianus was executed only two months later, indicating that he may have been the first-ever victim of the winner's curse.

Since that time, auctions have been conducted in every corner of the globe. The possessions of deceased Buddhist monks were auctioned off as early as the seventh century. In the late 16th century, auctions began to be held in taverns and alehouses in Great Britain. Sotheby's was founded in 1744, and Christie's was established in 1766; both have now become world-renowned auction houses for rare and valuable items. Auctions for tobacco, horses, and other domestic animals were commonplace in colonial America.

Auctions have endured throughout history for several reasons. First, they give sellers a convenient way to find a buyer for something they would like to dispose of. Second, auctions are an excellent way for people to collect difficult-to-find items, such as Beanie Babies or historical memorabilia, that have a high value to them personally. Finally, auctions are one of the "purest" markets that exist for goods, in that they bring buyers and sellers into contact to arrive at a mutually agreeable price. Experts estimated that the national market for auctions, garage sales, flea markets, and classified purchases was greater than $100 billion in 1999.

ONLINE AUCTIONS

Online auctions worked in essentially the same way as traditional auctions, the difference being that the auction process occurred over the Internet rather than at a specific geographic location with buyers and sellers physically present. In 2000, there were three categories of online auctions:

1. Business-to-business auctions, which accounted for $2.5 billion in sales in 1998 and involved such items as computers, used equipment, and surplus merchandise.
2. Business-to-consumer auctions, in which businesses sold goods and services to consumers via the Internet. Many such auctions involved companies interested in selling used or discontinued goods, or liquidating unwanted inventory.
3. Person-to-person auctions, which gave interested sellers and buyers the opportunity to engage in competitive bidding.

Since eBay's pioneering of the person-to-person online auction process in 1995, the number of online auction sites on the Internet had grown to well over 1,600 by the end of 1999. Forrester Research predicted that 6.5 million customers would use online auctions in 2002. In 1999 an estimated 8.2 percent of Internet users registered at an auction site; the percentage was expected to be 14.5 percent by 2002.

Online auction operators could generate revenue in four principal ways:

1. Charging sellers for listing their good or service.
2. Charging a commission on all sales.

3. Selling advertising on their Web sites.

4. Selling their own new or used merchandise via the online auction format.

Most sites charged sellers either a fee or a commission and sold advertising to companies interested in promoting their goods or services to users of the auction site.

Auction Software Packages

In 1996, OpenSite Technologies began to offer packaged software applications to firms interested in creating their own online auction Web sites. Moai Technologies and Ariba, Inc., were other sources for auction software. The ready availability of commercial software packages made it easy for firms to create and operate online auction sites. OpenSite had marketed over 600 auction packages to such companies as The Sharper Image, CNET, and John Deere. OpenSite claimed that its purpose was to bring together "buyers and sellers, helping businesses dynamically manage inventory, create sales channels, attract customers, and test market new products, to create efficient markets for goods and services."

Providers of Site Hosting and Online Auction Services

Auction firms could, if they wished, outsource all the hosting functions associated with online auctions to independent site-hosting enterprises and could even turn the entire auction process over to an independent online auction specialist. FairMarket, the leader in auction outsourcing in 1999, provided companies such as ZDNet, MicroWarehouse, and CollegeBytes.com with a means of selling their goods at online auction at FairMarket's Web site. The use of site hosts and independent online auction services was a particularly appealing option for companies that wanted to use online auctions as a distribution channel but preferred to devote only minimal time and energy to site construction and upkeep. By paying FairMarket an annual hosting fee between $2,000 and $10,000, as well as a percentage fee on all transactions, firms were able to have an auction site without having to worry about the hassle of site upkeep.

Online Auction Users

Participants in online auctions could be grouped into three categories: (1) bargain hunters, (2) hobbyists/collectors, and (3) sellers.

Bargain Hunters   Bargain hunters viewed online auctions primarily as a form of entertainment; their objective usually was to find a great deal. One bargain hunter described the eBay experience as follows:

> A friend and I would spend one day a week going flea marketing and auctioning. Since school has started again, time has become a hot commodity. We've found that we can use eBay to fill that flea marketing, auctioning need. We'll call each other, then get on eBay and hunt and find things together even though we can't be together. EBay has definitely been a great way to spend quality time together!

Bargain hunters were thought to make up only 8 percent of active online users but 52 percent of eBay visitors. To attract repeat visits from bargain hunters, industry observers said, sites must appeal to them on both rational and emotional levels, satisfying their need for competitive pricing, the excitement of the search, and the desire for community.[1]

Hobbyists and Collectors   Hobbyists and collectors used auctions to search for specific goods that had a high value to them personally. They were very concerned with both price and quality. Collectors prized eBay for its wide variety of product offerings. One user commented:

> My sister collects Princess House hand-blown ornaments. She needed the first three to complete her series. I posted to the Wanted Board several times, and also put a note on my About Me page. Well, we have now successfully completed her series. We could never have done this without eBay because the first one is so hard to find. Thanks eBay!

Sellers   Those in the sellers category could be further differentiated into at least three types: casual sellers, hobbyists/collectors, and power sellers. Casual sellers included individuals who used eBay as a substitute for a classified ad listing or a garage sale to dispose of items they no longer wanted. While many casual sellers listed only a few items, some used eBay to raise money for some new project. One such seller stated:

> Thank you! After just starting to use your site less than a month ago, I have increased my earnings by over $1,000. I have not yet received all the cash, but so far the response has been fantastic. This all started with a Kool-Aid container and four cups I had that were collecting dust in a box in the attic. I was "browsing for bargains" and saw someone else had made $29.00 from those plastic things! I was AMAZED! Needless to say, I listed them. I only made $8.00, but I received my first positive feedback. Since then I am listing daily.
>
> My wife and I are scrimping to save for an adoption of a baby. The fees are much more than our modest income can afford, and this extra cash will come in handy. My wife and I sincerely thank you and your company for the opportunity to be a part of eBay.

Sellers who were hobbyists or collectors typically dealt in a limited category of goods and looked to eBay as a way to sell selected items in their collections to others who might want them. Power sellers were typically small to medium-sized businesses that favored eBay as a primary distribution channel for their goods and often sold tens of thousands of dollars' worth of goods every month on the site. One estimate suggested that while these power sellers accounted for only 4 percent of eBay's population, they were responsible for 80 percent of eBay's total business.[2]

Concerns about Buyer Addiction to Online Auctions

Some members of the online auction community reportedly found the experience so intriguing that they became addicted. According to the Center for Online Addiction, symptoms of online auction addiction ranged from "using online auctions as a way of escaping from problems or relieving feelings of helplessness, guilt, anxiety, or depression" to "needing to bid with increasing amounts of money in order to achieve the desired excitement."[3] The center predicted that "online auction houses will be the next frenzy leading to shopping addiction" and had treated online auction addicts who had to take out a second mortgage or file bankruptcy as a result of their excessive online purchases.[4] One online auction addict told of his experience as follows:

---

[1]"Internet Consumer Segments Identified for First Time," PR Newswire, April 17, 2000.

[2]Claire Tristram, "'Amazoning' Amazon," www.contextmag.com, November 1999.

[3]www.netaddiction.com, April 16, 2000.

[4]Ibid.

It became critical when my boss confronted me. [My employer] had monitored my Internet use, and it was even more than I was aware of. My boss told me he had no choice but to terminate me. I've been at this job almost five years, have achieved recognition at the national level for the program, and have previously been a very capable employee. How can I [justify] throwing all that away? There is no doubt, though, that my productivity had really begun to suffer.

I was truthful with my boss about how this had become a compulsion I just could not control. I attributed it to some real stresses in my personal life, and kept telling myself that when things settled down, I would get a handle on it. He has put me on [administrative] leave while he thinks things over.[5]

PIERRE OMIDYAR AND THE FOUNDING OF EBAY

Pierre Omidyar was born in Paris, France, to parents who had left Iran decades earlier. The family emigrated to the United States when Pierre's father began a residency at Johns Hopkins University Medical Center. Pierre grew up in modest circumstances; his parents divorced when he was two but remained near each other so he could be with both of them. Pierre's passion for computers began at an early age; he would sneak out of gym class in high school to play with computers. While still in high school, at age 14 he took his first computer-related job in the school's library, where he was hired for $6.00 an hour to write a program to print catalog cards.[6] After high school Pierre attended Tufts University, where he met his future wife, Pamela Wesley, who came to Tufts from Hawaii to get a degree in biology. Upon graduating in 1988, the couple moved to California, where Pierre, who had earned a BS in computer science, joined Claris, an Apple Computer subsidiary in Silicon Valley, and wrote a widely used graphics application, MacDraw. In 1991, Omidyar left Claris and cofounded Ink Development (later renamed eShop), which became a pioneer in online shopping and was eventually sold to Microsoft in 1996. In 1994 Omidyar joined General Magic as a developer services engineer and remained there until mid-1996, when he left to pursue full-time development of eBay.

Internet folklore has it that eBay was founded solely to allow Pamela to trade Pez dispensers with other collectors. While Pamela was certainly a driving force in launching the initial Web site, Pierre had long been interested in how one could establish a marketplace to bring together a fragmented market. Pierre saw eBay as a way to create a person-to-person trading community based on a democratized, efficient market where everyone could have equal access through the same medium, the Internet. Pierre set out to develop his marketplace and to meet both his and Pamela's goals. In 1995 he launched the first online auction under the name of Auctionwatch at the domain name of www.eBay.com. The name eBay stood for "electronic Bay area," coined because Pierre's initial concept was to attract neighbors and other interested San Francisco Bay area residents to the site to buy and sell items of mutual interest. The first auctions charged no fees to either buyers or sellers and contained mostly computer equipment (and no Pez dispensers). Pierre's fledgling venture generated $1,000 in revenue the first month and an additional $2,000 the second. Traffic grew rapidly, however, as word about the site spread in the Bay area; a community of collectors emerged, using the site to trade and chat—some marriages resulted from exchanges in eBay chat rooms.[7]

---

[5]www.auctionwatch.com, April 16, 2000.

[6]tbwt.com/interaction/1pomid/1pomid.htm.

[7]Quentin Hardy, "The Radical Philanthropist," *Forbes,* May 1, 2000, p. 118.

exhibit 3   eBay's Income Statements, 1996–99 ($000, Except Per Share Figures)

	1996	1997	1998	1999
Net revenues	$32,051	$41,370	$86,129	$224,724
Cost of net revenues	6,803	8,404	16,094	57,588
Gross profit	25,248	32,966	70,035	167,136
Operating expenses				
Sales and marketing	13,139	15,618	35,976	95,956
Product development	28	831	4,640	23,785
General and administrative	5,661	6,534	15,849	43,055
Amortization of acquired intangibles	—	—	805	1,145
Merger related costs		—	—	4,359
Total operating expenses	18,828	22,983	57,270	168,300
Income (loss) from operations	6,420	9,983	12,765	(1,164)
Interest and other income (expense), net	(2,607)	(1,951)	(703)	21,377
Income before income taxes	3,813	8,032	12,062	20,213
Provision for income taxes	(475)	(971)	(4,789)	(9,385)
Net income	$ 3,338	$ 7,061	$ 7,273	$ 10,828
Net income per share				
Basic	$0.39	$0.29	$0.14	$0.10
Diluted	.07	0.08	0.06	0.08
Weighted average shares				
Basic	8,490	24,428	52,064	108,235
Diluted	45,060	84,775	116,759	135,910

Source: Company financial documents.

By February 1996, the traffic at Pierre Omidyar's site had grown so much that his Internet service provider informed him that he would have to upgrade his service. When Pierre compensated for this by charging a listing fee for the auction, and saw no decrease in the number of items listed, he knew he was on to something. Although he was still working out of his home, Pierre began looking for a partner and in May asked his friend Jeffrey Skoll to join him in the venture. While Jeff had never cared much about money, his Stanford MBA degree provided the firm with the business background that Pierre lacked.[8] With Pierre as the visionary and Jeff as the strategist, the company embarked on a mission to "help people trade practically anything on earth." Their concept for eBay was to "create a place where people could do business just like in the old days—when everyone got to know each other personally, and we all felt we were dealing on a one-to-one basis with individuals we could trust."

In eBay's early days, Pierre and Jeff ran the operation alone, using a single computer to serve all of the pages. Pierre served as CEO, chief financial officer, and president, while Jeff functioned as co-president and director. It was not long until Pierre and Jeff grew the company to a size that forced them to move out of Pierre's living room, due to the objections of Pamela, and into Jeff's living room. Shortly thereafter, the operations moved into the facilities of a Silicon Valley business incubator for a time until the company settled in its current facilities in San Jose, California.

Exhibits 3 and 4 present eBay's recent financial statements.

---

[8]Adam Cohen, "The eBay Revolution," www.time.com.

exhibit 4   eBay's Consolidated Balance Sheets, 1997–99 ($000)

	December 31, 1997	December 31, 1998	December 31, 1999
Assets			
Current assets			
Cash and cash equivalents	$3,723	$ 37,285	$219,679
Short-term investments	—	40,401	181,086
Accounts receivable, net	1,024	12,425	36,538
Other current assets	220	7,479	22,531
Total current assets	4,967	97,590	459,834
Property and equipment, net	652	44,062	111,806
Investments	—	—	373,988
Deferred tax asset	—	—	5,639
Intangible and other assets, net	—	7,884	12,675
Total assets	$5,619	$149,536	$963,942
Liabilities and Stockholders' Equity			
Current liabilities			
Accounts payable	$ 252	$ 9,997	$ 31,538
Accrued expenses and other current liabilities	—	6,577	32,550
Deferred revenue and customer advances	128	973	5,997
Debt and leases, current portion	258	4,047	12,285
Income taxes payable	169	1,380	6,455
Deferred tax liabilities	—	1,682	—
Other current liabilities	128	5,981	7,632
Total current liabilities	1,124	24,656	88,825
Debt and leases, long-term portion	305	18,361	15,018
Other liabilities	157		
Total liabilities	1,586	48,998	111,475
Series B mandatorily redeemable convertible preferred stock and Series B warrants	3,018	—	—
Total stockholders' equity	1,015	100,538	852,467
Total liabilities and stockholders' equity	$5,619	$149,536	$963,942

Source: Company financial documents.

EBAY'S TRANSITION TO PROFESSIONAL MANAGEMENT

From the beginning Pierre Omidyar intended to hire a professional manager to serve as the president of eBay: "[I would] let him or her run the company so . . . [I could] go play."[9] In 1997 both Omidyar and Skoll agreed that it was time to locate an experienced professional to function as CEO and president. In late 1997 eBay's headhunters came up with a candidate for the job: Margaret Whitman, then general manager for Hasbro Inc.'s preschool division. Whitman had received her BA in economics from Princeton and her MBA from the Harvard Business School; her first job was in brand

[9]*Business 2.0,* "Billionaires of the Web," The Candyman, June 1999.

management at Procter & Gamble. Her experience also included serving as the president and CEO of FTD, the president of Stride Rite Corporation's Stride Rite Division, and as the senior vice president of marketing for the Walt Disney Company's consumer product division.[10]

When first approached by eBay, Whitman was not especially interested in joining a company that had fewer than 40 employees and less than $6 million in revenues the previous year. It was only after repeated pleas that Whitman agreed to meet with Omidyar in Silicon Valley. After a second meeting, Whitman realized the company's enormous growth potential and agreed to give eBay a try. According to Omidyar, Meg Whitman's experience in global marketing with Hasbro's Teletubbies, Playskool, and Mr. Potato Head brands made her "the ideal choice to build upon eBay's leadership position in the one-to-one online trading market without sacrificing the quality and personal touch our users have grown to expect."[11] In addition to convincing Margaret Whitman to head eBay's operations, Omidyar had been instrumental in helping bring in other talented senior executives and in assembling a capable board of directors. Notable members of eBay's board of directors included Scott Cook, the founder of Intuit, a highly successful financial software company, and Howard Schultz, the founder and CEO of Starbucks. (For a profile of eBay's senior management team, check out the Company Overview section at www.ebay.com.)

Whitman ran the operation from the time she came on board. Omidyar, who owned 27.9 percent of eBay's stock (worth approximately $6 billion as of March 2000), spent considerable time in Paris. He and Pamela, still in their mid-30s and concerned about the vast wealth they had accumulated in such a short period of time, were devoting a substantial amount of their energy to exploring philanthropic causes.[12] They had decided to give most of their fortune to charity and were scrutinizing alternative ways to maximize the impact of their philanthropic contributions on the overall well-being of society. Jeffrey Skoll owned 16.7 percent of eBay's shares (worth about $3.6 billion), and Margaret Whitman owned 5.2 percent (worth about $1 billion).

HOW AN EBAY AUCTION WORKED

EBay endeavored to make it very simple to buy and sell goods (see Exhibits 5 and 6). In order to sell or bid on goods, users first had to register at the site. Once they registered, users selected both a user name and a password. Nonregistered users were able to browse the Web site but were not permitted to bid on any goods or list any items for auction. On the Web site, search engines helped customers determine what goods were currently available. When registered users found an item they desired, they could choose to enter a single bid or to use automatic bidding. In automatic bidding the customer entered an initial bid sufficient to make him or her the high bidder and then the bid would be automatically increased as others bid for the same object until the auction ended and either the bidder won or another bidder surpassed the original customer's maximum specified bid. Regardless of which bidding method they chose, users could check bids at any time and either bid again, if they had been outbid, or increase their maximum amount in the automatic bid. Users could choose to receive e-mail notification if they were outbid. Once the auction had ended, the buyer and seller were each notified of the winning bid

---

[10]www.ebay.com, Company Overview page.

[11]eBay press release, May 7, 1998.

[12]Hardy, "The Radical Philanthropist."

exhibit 5 eBay's Instructions for Becoming a New Bidder

Source: pages.eBay.com/help/basics/n-bidding.html.

and were given each other's e-mail address. The parties to the auction would then privately arrange for payment and delivery of the good.

Fees and Procedures for Sellers EBayers were not charged a fee for bidding on items on the site, but sellers were charged an insertion fee and a "final value" fee; they could also elect to pay additional fees to promote their listing. Listing, or insertion, fees ranged from 25 cents for auctions with opening bids between $0.01 and $9.99, to $2.00 for auctions with opening bids of $50.00 and up. Final value fees ranged from 1.25 to 5 percent of the final sale price and were computed based on a graduated fee schedule in which the percentage fell as the final sales price rose. As an example, in a basic auction with no promotion, if the item had brought an opening bid of $100 and eventually sold for $1,500, the total fee paid by the seller, would be $33.88—the $2.00 insertion fee plus $31.88. The $31.88 is based on a fee structure of 5 percent of the first $25.00 (or $1.25), 2.5 percent of the additional amount between $25.01 and $1,000.00 (or $24.38), and 1.25 percent of the additional amount between $1,000.01 and $1,500.00 (or $6.25).

A seller who wished to promote an item could choose a bold heading for an additional fee of $2.00. A seller with a favorable feedback rating (discussed below) could have his or her auction listed either as a "Featured Auction" for $99.95, which allowed the seller's item to be rotated on the eBay home page, or as a "Category Featured Auction" for $14.95, which allowed the item to be featured within a particular eBay category.

exhibit 6   eBay's Instructions for Becoming a New Seller

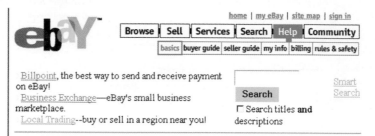

New to Selling?

It's so easy—you'll love it! Here's what to do...

1. First, you'll need to register, if you haven't done so already.

2. **Set up your selling account.** Place your credit card on file with eBay and you're ready to sell! If you'd like to accept credit card payments from winning bidders, sign up for Billpoint online payments.

3. **Gather the info** you'll need before you prepare your listing:
    - your item description
    - the URL (web site address) for any photos (see the photo tutorial)
    - the category you'll list under

4. Go to the Sell Your Item form, **fill in the info**, and review your listing. Be sure to check the information carefully, then click on Submit My Listing.

5. You'll see a confirmation page; **jot down the info**, such as your item number. This will be helpful if you want to update your listing, and to keep track of your item's status as your very own auction progresses!

6. When your auction closes, **contact your winning bidder** or bidders within three business days. You'll want to confirm the final cost, including any shipping charges, and tell them where to send payment. When the bidder meets your payment terms, you fulfill your end of the agreement by sending them your item. Your auction forms a binding contract between you and the winning bidder or bidders.

And then that's it—your item is sold!

Source: pages.eBay.com/help/basics/n-selling.html.

For $1.00, a seller could choose to place a seasonal icon (such as a shamrock in connection with St. Patrick's Day) next to his or her listing. A seller could also include a description of the product with links to the seller's Web site. In addition, a seller could indicate a photograph in the item's description if the seller posted the photograph on a Web site and provided eBay with the appropriate Web address. Items could be showcased in the Gallery section with a catalog of pictures rather than text. A seller who used a photograph in his or her listing could have this photograph included in the Gallery section for 25 cents or featured there for $19.95. A Gallery section was available in all categories of eBay. Certain categories of items—such as real estate, automobiles, and "Great Collections"—had special promotion rates.

New sellers were required to file a credit card number with eBay for automatic monthly billing, while sellers who had opened accounts prior to October 22, 1999, could alternatively choose a pay-as-you-go method. The latter option, however, was relatively unattractive since it allowed eBay to block any account whose balance due reached $25.00. The block was removed once the fee was paid, or once the seller had registered a credit card with eBay.

How Transactions Are Completed   When an auction ended, the eBay system validated that the bid fell within the acceptable price range. If the sale was successful, eBay automatically notified the buyer and seller via e-mail; the buyer and seller could then work out the transaction details independent of eBay. At no point during the process did eBay take possession of either the item being sold or the buyer's payment. Rather, the buyer and seller had to independently arrange for the shipment of and payment for the item; buyers typically paid for shipping. A seller could view a buyer's feedback rating (discussed below) and then determine the manner of payment, such as personal check, cashier's check, or credit card, and also whether to ship the item before or after receiving payment. Under the terms of eBay's user agreement, if a seller received one or more bids above the stated minimum, or reserve, price, the seller was obligated to complete the transaction, although eBay had no enforcement power beyond suspending a noncompliant buyer or seller from using eBay's service. In the event the buyer and seller were unable to complete the transaction, the seller notified eBay, which then credited the seller the amount of the final value fee. When items carrying a reserve price sold, sellers were credited the $1.00 reserve fee. Invoices for placement fees, additional listing fees, and final value fees were sent via e-mail to sellers on a monthly basis.

Feedback Forum   In early 1996 eBay pioneered a feature called Feedback Forum to build trust among buyers and sellers and to facilitate the establishment of reputations within its community. Feedback Forum encouraged individuals to record comments about their trading partners. At the completion of each auction, both the buyer and seller were allowed to leave positive, negative, or neutral comments about each other. Individuals could dispute feedback left about them by annotating comment in question. By assigning values of $+1$ for a positive comment, 0 for a neutral comment, and -1 for a negative comment, each trader earned a ranking that was attached to their user name. A user who had developed a positive reputation over time had a color-coded star symbol displayed next to his or her user name to indicate the amount of positive feedback. The highest ranking a trader could receive was "over 10,000," indicated by a shooting star. Well-respected high-volume traders could have rankings well into the thousands. Users who received a sufficiently negative net feedback rating (typically a -4) had their registrations suspended and were thus unable to bid on or list items for sale. EBay users could review a person's feedback profile before deciding to bid on an item listed by that person or before choosing payment and delivery methods. A sample user profile is shown in Exhibit 7.

The terms of eBay's user agreement prohibited actions that would undermine the integrity of the Feedback Forum, such as leaving positive feedback about oneself through other accounts or leaving multiple negative comments about someone else through other accounts. EBay's Feedback Forum system had several automated features designed to detect and prevent some forms of abuse. For example, feedback posted from the same account, positive or negative, could not affect a user's net feedback rating by more than one point, no matter how many comments an individual made. Furthermore, a user could only make comments about his or her trading partners in completed transactions.

exhibit 7 A Sample Feedback Forum Profile

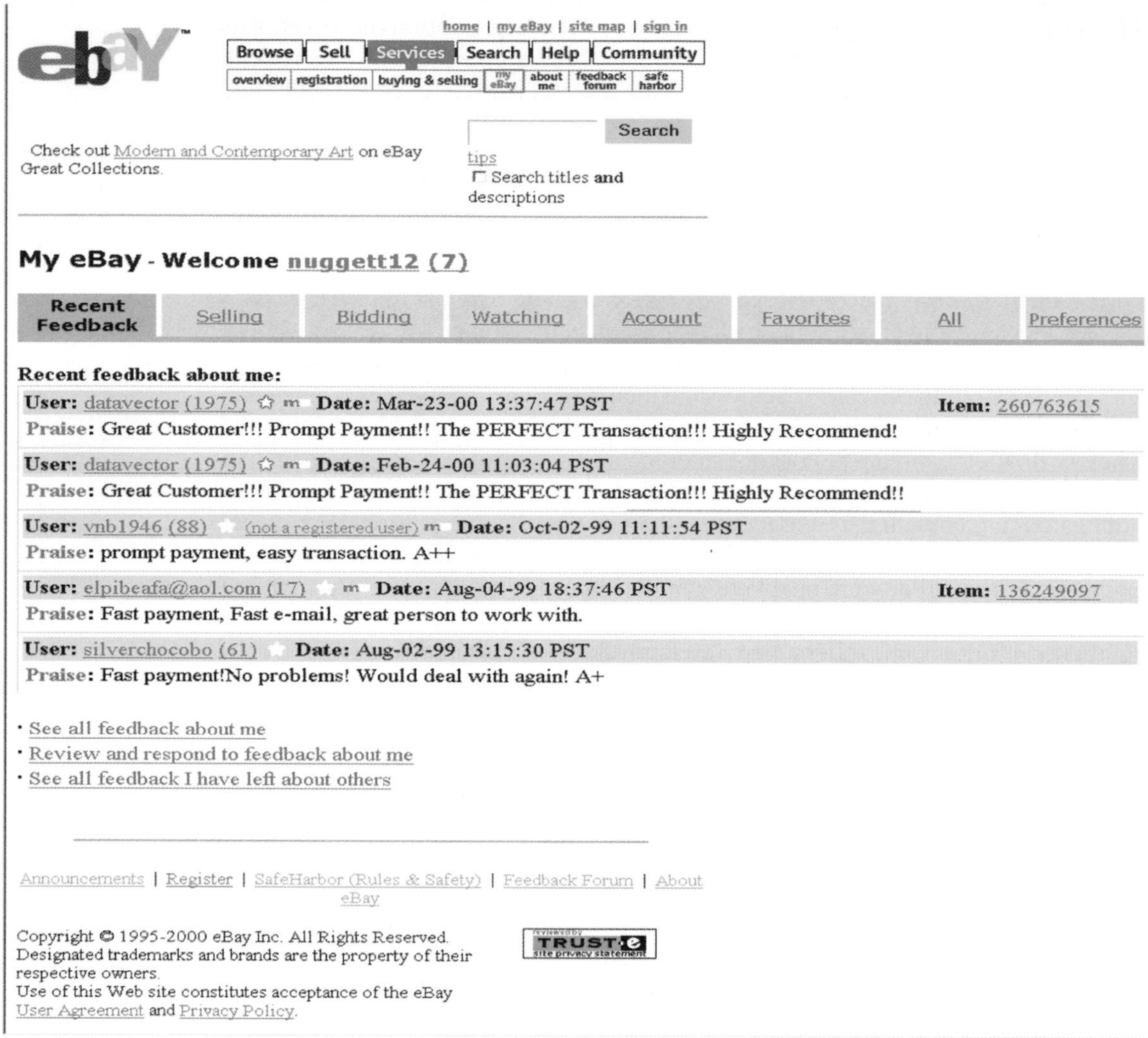

Source: www.ebay.com, April 14, 2000.

The company believed its Feedback Forum was extremely useful in overcoming users' initial hesitancy about trading over the Internet, since it reduced the uncertainty of dealing with an unknown trading partner.

EBAY'S STRATEGY TO SUSTAIN ITS MARKET DOMINANCE

Meg Whitman assumed the helm of eBay in February 1998 and began acting as the public face of the company. Pierre Omidyar stepped back to become chairman of eBay's board of directors and focused his time and energy on overseeing eBay's strategic direction and growth, business model and site development, and community advocacy. Jeff Skoll, who became the vice president of strategic planning and analysis, concentrated on competitive analysis, new business planning and incubation, the development of the organization's overall strategic direction, and supervision of customer support operations.

The Move to Go Public

Within months of assuming the presidency of eBay, Whitman took on the challenge of preparing the company to raise capital for expansion through an initial public offering (IPO) of common stock. Through a series of road shows designed to convince investors of the potential of eBay's business model, Whitman and her team generated significant interest in eBay's IPO. When the shares opened for trading on September 24, 1998, eBay's executives had high hopes for the offering, but none of them dreamed that it would close the day at $47, or 160 percent over the initial offering of $18 per share. The IPO generated $66 million in new capital for the company and was so successful that *Bloomberg Personal* magazine designated eBay as the "Hot IPO of 1998"; *Euromoney* magazine named eBay as the best IPO in the U.S. market in January 1999. The success of the September 1998 offering led eBay to issue a follow-up offering in April 1999 that raised an additional $600 million. As a qualification to the IPOs, eBay's board of directors retained the right to issue as many as 5 million additional shares of preferred stock with no further input from the current shareholders in case of a hostile takeover attempt.

With the funds received from the IPOs, eBay launched strategic initiatives aimed at six specific objectives:[13]

1. Growing the eBay community and strengthening our brand, both to attract new members and to maintain the vitality of the eBay community;
2. Broadening the company's trading platform by growing existing product categories, promoting new product categories, and offering services for specific regions;
3. Fostering eBay community affinity and increasing community trust and safety through services such as user verification and insurance;
4. Enhancing Web site features and functionality through the introduction of personalization features such as About Me, which permits users to create their own home page free of charge, and the Gallery, an opportunity for sellers to showcase their items as pictures in a photo catalog;
5. Expanding pre- and post-trade value-added services, such as assistance with scanning and uploading photographs of listed items, third-party escrow services and arrangements to make shipping of purchased items easier;
6. Developing international markets by actively marketing and promoting our Web site in selected countries.

To pursue these objectives, eBay employed three main competitive tactics. First, it sought to build strategic partnerships in all stages of its value chain, creating an impressive portfolio of over 250 strategic alliances with companies such as America Online (AOL), Yahoo!, Lycos, Compaq, and Warner Brothers. Second, it actively sought customer feedback and made improvements based on this information. Third, it actively monitored the external environment for developing opportunities.

eBay's Business Model

EBay's business model was based on creating and maintaining a person-to-person trading community where buyers and sellers could readily and conveniently exchange information and goods. EBay's role was to function as a value-added facilitator of online buyer-seller transactions by providing a supportive infrastructure that enabled buyers and sellers to come together in an efficient and effective manner. Success depended not only on the quality of eBay's infrastructure but also on the quality and quantity of buyers and

---

[13]Company S-1 filing with the Securities and Exchange Commission, March 25, 1999, p. 4.

sellers attracted to the site; in management's view, this entailed maintaining a compelling trading environment, a number of trust and safety programs, a cost-effective and convenient trading experience, and strong community affinity. By developing the eBay brand name and increasing the customer base, eBay endeavored to attract a sufficient number of high-quality buyers and sellers necessary to meet the organization's goals. The online auction format meant that eBay carried zero inventory and could operate a marketplace without the need for a traditional sales force.

Growing the eBay Community and Strengthening the Brand

In developing the eBay brand name and attracting new users, the company initially relied largely on word-of-mouth advertising, supplemented by public relations initiatives such as executive interviews and speaking engagements, special online events, and astute management of the public press. Then, with funds from the public offerings of common stock, eBay expanded its marketing activities to include advertising online as well as in traditional media, such as national magazines like *Parade, People, Entertainment Weekly, Newsweek,* and *Sports Illustrated.* A cornerstone of the strategy to increase eBay's exposure was the formation of alliances with a variety of partners, including Kinko's, First Auction, and Z Auction as well as Internet portals AOL, Netscape, and GO.com.

The Alliance with First Auction   In January 1998, eBay entered into a marketing agreement with First Auction, the auction division of the Internet Shopping Network. The terms of this agreement allowed both companies to advertise their services on each other's sites. While both organizations offered online auctions, eBay featured person-to-person trading, and First Auction engaged in business-to-consumer transactions, which eBay did not consider direct competition. A similar agreement was formed in February 1998 with Z Auction, another vendor-based auction site.

Alliance with America Online   EBay's initial alliance with AOL, announced in February 1998, was limited to eBay's providing a person-to-person online auction service in AOL's classifieds section. However, in September 1998 this agreement was expanded. In return for $12 million in payments over three years, AOL made eBay the preferred provider of personal trading services to AOL's 13 million members and the 2 million members of AOL's affiliate CompuServe. In 1998 eBay also became a "distinguished partner" of Netscape's Netcenter. In February 1999 eBay's relationship with Netscape was broadened to include banner ads and bookmarks. In March 1999 eBay's arrangement with AOL was expanded to feature eBay as the preferred provider of personal trading services on all of AOL's proprietary services, including Digital Cities, ICQ, CompuServe (both international and domestic), Netscape, and AOL.com. In return for this four-year arrangement, eBay agreed to pay CompuServe $75 million and to develop a co-branded version of its services for each of AOL's properties involved in the agreement, with AOL receiving all of the advertising revenues from these co-branded sites.[14]

The Alliance with Kinko's   In February 2000, eBay formed strategic marketing agreements with Kinko's, a global retail provider of document copying and business services, and GO.com, the Internet arm of Walt Disney Company. EBay's alliance

[14]eBay's 1999 10-K report.

with Kinko's allowed eBay to place signage in Kinko's stores across the country, and to offer its users 15 minutes of free computing rental at Kinko's locations. In return, eBay featured Web links to Kinko's Web pages in eBay's Computer, Business/Office, and Big Ticket categories, and encouraged users to go to Kinko's for photo scanning, e-mail, document faxing, and teleconferencing services.

The Alliance with GO.com   The long-term intention for the cooperative agreement with GO.com was for eBay to eventually become the exclusive online trading service across all of Disney's Internet properties. In the initial stages of the agreement, however, eBay was only to market and develop co-branded person-to-person and merchant-to-person sites on behalf of the Walt Disney company.[15]

Broadening the Trading Platform

Efforts intended to broaden the eBay trading platform concentrated on growing the content within current categories, on broadening the range of products offered according to user preferences, and on developing regionally targeted offerings. Growth in existing product categories was facilitated by deepening the content within the categories through the use of content-specific chat rooms and bulletin boards as well as targeted advertising at trade shows and in industry-specific publications. Further, in April 1998, custom home pages were created for each category so collectors could search for their next treasured acquisition without having to sort through the entirety of eBay's offerings.

In June 1999 eBay formed a collaborative relationship with the Collecting Channel, a portal owned by ChannelSpace Entertainment, Inc. The Collecting Channel was a premier Internet information source for virtually every conceivable category of collectibles. It delivered content in ways ranging from original audio/video programming to live chats to live video conferencing. EBay's agreement called for The Collecting Channel to provide in-depth content to eBay collectors and for eBay, in return, to provide links to The Collecting Channel's Web site.

Part of eBay's strategy to broaden its user base was to establish regional auctions. In 1999 eBay launched 53 regional auction sites focused on the 50 largest metropolitan areas in the United States. Management believed that having regional auction sites would encourage the sale of items that were prohibitively expensive to ship, items that tended to have only a local appeal, and items that people preferred to view before purchasing. EBay had also done several promotional or feature auctions, partnering with Guernsey to sell home-run balls hit by baseball stars Mark McGwire and Sammy Sosa in their 1998 home-run race and partnering with BMW in 1999 to auction the first BMW X5 sports activity vehicle to be delivered, with the proceeds going to the Susan G. Komen Breast Cancer Foundation.

Additional efforts to broaden the trading platform involved the development of new product categories. Over 2,000 new categories were added between 1998 and 2000, bringing the total to 3,000 categories (greatly expanded from the original 10 categories in 1995). One of the most significant new categories was eBay Great Collections, a showcasing of rare collectibles such as coins, stamps, jewelry, and timepieces as well as fine art and antiques from leading auction houses around the world. This category came from eBay's April 1999 acquisition of Butterfield and Butterfield, one of the world's largest and most prestigious auction houses.

---

[15]eBay press release, www.ebay.com, February 8, 2000.

The growing popularity of automobile trading on the eBay Web site prompted the creation of a special automotive category supported by Kruse International, one of the world's most respected organizations for automobile collectors. The automotive category was further expanded in March 2000 through a partnership with AutoTrader.com, the world's largest used-car marketplace, that established a co-branded auction site for consumers and dealers to buy and sell used cars.

Fostering eBay Community Affinity and Building Trust

Since its founding in 1995, eBay had considered developing a loyal, vivacious trading community to be a cornerstone of its business model. To foster a sense of community among eBay users, the company employed tools and tactics designed to promote both business and personal interactions between consumers, to foster trust between bidders and sellers, and to instill a sense of security among traders.

Interactions between community members were facilitated through the creation of chat rooms based on personal interests. These chat rooms allowed individuals to learn about their chosen collectibles and to exchange information about items they collected. To manage the flow of information in the chat rooms, eBay employees went to trade shows and conventions to seek out individuals who had both knowledge about and a passion for either a specific collectible or a category of goods. These enthusiasts would act as community leaders or ambassadors; they were never referred to as employees but were compensated $1,000 a month to host online discussions with experts.

Although personal communication between members fostered a sense of community, as eBay's community grew from "the size of a small village to a large city"[16] additional measures were necessary to ensure a continued sense of trust and honesty among users. One of eBay's earliest trust-building efforts was the 1996 creation of the Feedback Forum, described earlier.

Unfortunately, the Feedback Forum was not always sufficient to ensure honesty and integrity among traders. While eBay estimated that far less than 1 percent of the millions of auctions completed on the site involved some sort of fraud or illegal activity, some users would agree with Clay Monroe, a Seattle-area trader of computer equipment, who estimated that while "ninety percent of the time everybody is on the up and up . . . ten percent of the time you get some jerk who wants to cheat you."[17] Fraudulent or illegal acts perpetrated by sellers included misrepresentation of goods; trading in counterfeit goods or pirated goods that infringed on others' intellectual property rights; failure to deliver goods paid for by buyers; and shill bidding, whereby sellers would use a false bidder to artificially drive up the price of a good. Buyers could manipulate bids by placing an unrealistically high bid on a good to discourage other bidders and then withdraw their bid at the last moment to allow an ally to win the auction at a bargain price. Buyers could also fail to deliver payment on a completed auction.

Recognizing that fraudulent activities represented a significant danger to eBay's future, management took the Feedback Forum a step further in 1998 by launching the SafeHarbor program to provide guidelines for trade, provide information to help resolve user disputes, and respond to reports of misuse of the eBay service.[18] The SafeHarbor

---

[16]Tristram, "'Amazoning' Amazon."

[17]Stephen Buel, "eBay Inc. Feeling Growing Pains," *San Jose Mercury News,* December 26, 1998.

[18]eBay 10-K, filed July 15, 1998.

initiative was expanded in 1999 to provide additional safeguards and to actively work with law enforcement agencies and members of the trading community to make eBay more secure. New elements of SafeHarbor included free insurance, with a $25.00 deductible, through Lloyd's of London for transactions under $200.00; enhancements to the Feedback Forum; a new class of verified eBay users with an accompanying icon; easy access to escrow services; tougher policies relating to nonpaying bidders and shill bidders; clarification of which items were not permissible to list for sale; and a strengthened anti-piracy and anti-infringement program. The use of verified buyer and seller accounts was viewed as especially significant because it allowed eBay to ensure that suspended users did not open new eBay accounts under different names. User information was verified through Atlanta-based Equifax Inc.

To implement these new initiatives between 1999 and 2000, eBay increased the number of positions in its SafeHarbor department from 24 to 182, including full-time employees and independent contractors. It also organized the department around the functions of investigations, community watch, and fraud prevention. The investigations group was responsible for examining reported trading violations and possible misuses of eBay. The fraud prevention group mediated customer disputes over such things as the quality of the goods sold. If a written complaint of fraud was filed against a user, eBay generally suspended the alleged offender's account, pending an investigation. The community watch group worked with over 100 industry-leading companies, ranging from software publishers to toy manufactures to apparel makers, to protect intellectual property rights. To ensure that illegal items were not being sold and sale items listed did not violate intellectual property rights, this SafeHarbor group automated daily keyword searches on auction content. Offending auctions were closed and the seller was notified of the violation. Repeated violations resulted in suspension of the seller's account.

As eBay expanded its categories to include Great Collections and the new automobile categories, new safeguards were introduced to meet the unique needs of these areas. In the eBay Great Collections category, the company partnered with Collector's Universe to offer authentication and grading services for specific products such as trading cards, coins, and autographs. In the automobile area, eBay partnered with carclub.com to provide users with access to carclub.com's inspection and warranty service.

Enhancing Web Site Features and Functionality

In designing its Web site, eBay went to great lengths to make it intuitive, easy to use by both buyers and sellers, and reliable. Efforts to ensure ease of use ranged from narrowly defining categories (to allow users to quickly locate desired products) to introducing services designed to personalize a user's eBay experience. Two specific services developed by eBay to increase personalization were "My eBay" and "About Me."

My eBay was launched in May 1998 to give users centralized access to confidential, current information regarding their trading activities. From his or her My eBay page a user could view information pertaining to his or her current account balances with eBay; feedback rating; the status of any auctions in which he or she was participating, as either a buyer or a seller; and auctions in favorite categories. In October of the same year, eBay introduced the About Me service, which allowed users to create customized home pages that could be viewed by all other eBay members. These pages could include elements from the My eBay page such as user ratings or items the user had listed for auction, as well as personal information and pictures. This service not only increased customer ease of use but also contributed to the sense of community among the traders; one seller stated that the About Me service "made it easier and more rewarding for me to do business with others."[19]

When eBay first initiated service, the only computer resource it had was a single Sun Microsystems setup with no backup capabilities. By 1999 eBay's explosive growth required 200 Windows NT servers and a Sun Microsystems server to manage the flow of users on the site, process new members, accept bids, and manage the huge database containing the list of all items sold on the site. On June 10, 1999, the strain of managing these processes while attempting to integrate new product and service offerings proved too much for the system and the eBay site crashed. It stayed down for 22 hours. The outage not only seriously shook user confidence in eBay's reliability but also cost the company some $4 million in fees; the company's stock price reacted to the outage by falling from $180 to $136.[20]

Unfortunately, the June 10 site crash proved to be the first in a string of outages. While none of them was as significant as the first (most lasted only one to four hours), confidence in eBay continued to decline in both the online community and on Wall Street as eBay's stock fell to 87$^{11}\!/_{16}$ in August 1999. To counter these problems, eBay sought out Maynard Webb, a premier software engineer and troubleshooter who was working at Gateway Computer.

Webb put a moratorium on new features until system stability was restored. Webb believed that it was virtually impossible to completely eliminate outages, so he set a goal of reducing system downtime and limiting outages to one hour.[21] To achieve this goal Webb believed he would need a backup for the 200 Windows NT servers, another for the Sun Microsystems unit, and a better system for managing communications between the Windows NT and Sun systems. In attacking these challenges, eBay acquired seven new Sun servers, each valued at $1 million, and outsourced its technology and Web site operations to Exodus Communications and Abovenet. These outsourcing agreements were intended to allow Exodus and Abovenet to "manage network capacity and provide a more robust backbone" while eBay focused on its core business.[22] While eBay still experienced minor outages when it changed or expanded services (for example, a system crash coincided with the introduction of the 22 regional Web sites), system downtime decreased. However, the stability of the system under eBay's explosive growth and continuous introduction of new features and services was a major and continuing management concern.

Expanding Value-Added Services

To make it easier for eBay's sellers and buyers to transact business, in 1998 the company announced that it would offer an "'end-to-end' person-to-person trading service . . . [by providing] a variety of pre- and post-trade services to enhance the user experience."[23] Pretrade services that eBay planned to offer included authentication and appraisal services, while planned post-trade services included third-party escrow services as well as shipping and payment services.

---

[19]Ann Pearson, in an eBay press release dated October 15, 1998.

[20]Julie Pita, "Webb Master," *Forbes,* December 13, 1999.

[21]Ibid.

[22]eBay press release, October 8, 1999.

[23]eBay S-1 filed July 15, 1998, p. 46.

In preparation for Christmas 1998, eBay formed alliances with Parcel Plus, a leading shipping service, and with Tradesafe, and I-Escrow, both of which guaranteed that buyers would get what they paid for. According to eBay's agreement with I-Escrow, monies paid to the seller were held in an escrow account until the buyer received and approved the merchandise. EBay's arrangement with Tradesafe called for the seller to register a credit card with Tradesafe to guarantee funds up to $1,200; proceeds of a sale were deposited directly into the seller's bank account. If the buyer was not satisfied with the transaction, all or part of the money was refunded. Both I-Escrow and Tradesafe charged a small percentage of the purchase price for their services.

In April 1999, eBay entered into a five-year partnership with Mail Boxes, Etc. (the world's largest franchiser of retail business, communications, and postal service centers), and iShip.com (the leader in multicarrier Web-based shipping services for e-commerce) to offer person-to-person e-commerce shipping solutions.[24] EBay's agreement with iShip gave eBay users access to accurate zip-code-to-zip-code shipping rates with various shipping services and allowed users to track packages. The agreement with Mail Boxes, Etc. (MBE), required eBay to promote MBE's retail locations as a place where sellers could pack and ship their goods; eBay and MBE were contemplating expanding their agreement to allow buyers to open and inspect their newly purchased goods at MBE retail stores prior to accepting the shipment.

To facilitate person-to-person credit card payments, eBay acquired Billpoint, a company that specialized in transferring money from one cardholder to another. Using the newly acquired capabilities of Billpoint, eBay was able to offer sellers the option of accepting credit card payments from other eBay users; for this service, eBay charged sellers a small percentage of the transaction. EBay's objective was to make credit card payment a "seamless and integrated part of the trading experience."[25] In March 2000, eBay and Wells Fargo, the owner-operator of the largest Internet bank, entered into an arrangement whereby Wells Fargo would purchase a minority stake in Billpoint and Billpoint would use Wells Fargo's extensive customer care and payment processing infrastructure to process credit card payments from eBay buyers to eBay sellers.

In January 2000, eBay entered into an exclusive agreement with E-Stamp that allowed E-Stamp to become the exclusive provider of Internet postage from the U.S. Postal Service on eBay's Web site. In return for being prominently featured on eBay's website, E-Stamp gave eBay users easy access to its Web site, offered them reduced fees for its service, and gave them a significant discount on the E-Stamp Internet postage starter kit. According to sources close to the deal, E-Stamp paid eBay close to $10 million a year for gaining such access to eBay's customers.[26]

Developing International Markets

As competition increased in the online auction industry, eBay began to seek growth opportunities in international markets in an effort to create a global trading community. While international buyers and sellers had been trading on eBay for some time, there were no facilities designed especially for the needs of these community members. In entering international markets, eBay considered three options. It could build a new

---

[24]eBay press release, April 8, 1999.

[25]eBay press release, May 18, 1999.

[26]Jane Weaver, "eBay: Can It Keep Customers Loyal?" www.zdnet.com, May 13, 2000.

user community from the ground up, acquire a local organization, or form a partnership with a strong local company. In realizing its goals of international growth, eBay employed all three strategies.

In late 1998, eBay's initial efforts at international expansion into Canada and the United Kingdom relied on building new user communities. The first step in establishing these communities was creating customized home pages for users in those countries. These home pages were designed to provide content and categories locally customized to the needs of users in specific countries, while providing them with access to a global trading community. Local customization in the United Kingdom was facilitated through the use of local management, grassroots and online marketing, and participation in local events.[27]

In February 1999, eBay partnered with PBL Online, a leading Internet company in Australia, to offer a customized Australian and New Zealand eBay home page. When the site went live in October 1999, transactions were denominated in Australian dollars and, while buyers could bid on auctions anywhere in the world, they could also search for items located exclusively in Australia. Further, local chat boards were designed to facilitate interaction between Australian users, and country-specific categories, such as Australian coins and stamps as well as cricket and rugby memorabilia, were offered.

To further expand its global reach, eBay acquired Germany's largest online person-to-person trading site, alando.de AG, in June 1999. EBay's management handled the transition of service in a manner calculated to be smooth and painless for alando.de AG's users. While users would have to comply with eBay rules and regulations, the only significant change for alando.de AG's 50,000 registered users was that they would have to go to a new URL to transact their business.

To establish an Asian presence, in February 2000 eBay formed a joint venture with NEC to launch eBay Japan. According to the new CEO of eBay Japan, Merle Okawara, an internationally renowned executive, NEC was pleased to help eBay in leveraging the tried-and-trusted eBay business model to provide Japanese consumers with access to a global community of active online buyers and sellers. In customizing the site to the needs of Japanese users, eBay wrote the content exclusively in Japanese and allowed users to bid in yen. The site had over 800 categories ranging from internationally popular categories (such as computers, electronics, and Asian antiques) to categories with a local flavor (such as Hello Kitty, Pokémon and pottery). The eBay Japan site also debuted a new merchant-to-person concept known as Supershops, which allowed consumers to bid on items listed by companies.

Honors and Awards

As a result of the relentless implementation of its business model, eBay had met with significant success. Not only was the company financially profitable from its first days (see again Exhibits 3 and 4), but it had won many prestigious honors and awards in 1998 and 1999. Among the most significant were Best Internet Auction Site (*San Francisco Bay Guardian,* July 1998); Electronic Commerce Excellence (CommerceNet, October 1998); Top E-Commerce Program/Service (Computer Currents Readers' Choice Awards, February 1999); Editor's Choice Award (*PC* magazine, March 1999), and Top 50 CEOs (*Worth* magazine, May 1999).

---

[27]eBay 10K filed March 30, 2000.

HOW EBAY'S AUCTION SITE COMPARED WITH THAT OF RIVALS

Auction sites varied in a number of respects: site design and ease of use, the range of items up for auction, number of simultaneous auctions, duration of the bidding process, and fees. Gomez Advisors, a company designed to help Internet users select which online enterprises to do business with, had developed rankings for the leading online auction sites as a basis for recommending which sites were best for bargain hunters, hobbyists/collectors, and sellers. To be considered in the Gomez ratings, an auction site had to (1) have more than 500 lots of original content; (2) conduct auctions for items in at least three of the following six categories: collectibles, computers/electronics, jewelry, sports, stamps/coins, and toys; (3) have more than five lots in each qualifying category; and (4) have sustained bidding activity in each category. Exhibit 8 shows the winter 1999 Gomez ratings of online auction competitors—the latest ratings can be viewed at www.gomez.com.

EBAY'S MAIN COMPETITORS

In the broadest sense, eBay competed with classified advertisements in newspapers, garage sales, flea markets, collectibles shows, and other venues such as local auction houses and liquidators. As eBay's product mix broadened beyond collectibles to include practical household items, office equipment, toys, and so on, the company's competitors broadened to include brick-and-mortar retailers, import/export companies, and catalog and mail order companies. Management saw these traditional competitors as inefficient because their fragmented local and regional nature made it expensive and time-consuming for buyers and sellers to meet, exchange information, and complete transactions. Moreover, they suffered from three other deficiencies: (1) they tended to offer limited variety and breadth of selection as compared to the millions of items available on eBay, (2) they often had high transactions costs, and (3) they were "information inefficient" in the sense that buyers and sellers lacked a reliable and convenient means of setting prices for sales or purchases. Thus, eBay's management saw its online auction format as competitively superior to these rivals because it (1) facilitated buyers and sellers meeting, exchanging information, and conducting transactions; (2) allowed buyers and sellers to bypass traditional intermediaries and trade directly, thus lowering costs; (3) provided global reach, greater selection, and a broader base of participants; (4) permitted trading at all hours and provided continuously updated information; and (5) fostered a sense of community among individuals with mutual interests.

From an e-commerce perspective, Amazon.com and Yahoo! Auctions had emerged as eBay's main competitors going into 2000, but FairMarket, AuctionWatch, GO Network Auctions, and Auctions.com were beginning to make market inroads and contribute to erosion of eBay's share of the online auction business. Moreover, the prospects of attractive profitability and low barriers to entry were stimulating more firms to enter the online auction industry and imitate eBay's business model. EBay management saw competition in the online auction industry as revolving around 10 factors: the volume and selection of goods, the population of buyers and sellers, community interaction, customer service, reliability of delivery and payment by users, brand image, Web site construction, fees and prices, and quality of search tools.

exhibit 8 Comparative Gomez Advisors' Ratings of Leading Online Auction Sites

A. Ratings Based on Site Characteristics (Rating scale: 0 = lowest; 10 = highest)					
Auction Site	Ease of Use[a]	Customer Confidence[b]	On-Site Resources[c]	Relationship Services[d]	Overall Score
1. eBay	9.07	6.99	8.40	8.40	7.97
2. Amazon.com	9.05	8.49	7.03	6.17	7.67
3. Yahoo! Auctions	8.69	6.91	4.18	8.62	7.11
4. GO Network Auctions	9.14	7.44	6.49	5.89	7.00
5. FairMarket Network	7.97	6.89	6.73	5.17	6.42
6. Auctions.com	8.22	6.78	5.50	5.10	6.41
7. utrade	8.87	4.60	2.43	6.57	5.65
8. Boxlot	7.20	7.83	3.19	4.09	5.63
9. Haggle Online	7.62	4.65	4.80	4.72	5.29
10. edeal	8.05	4.04	2.35	5.83	5.17
11. ehammer	7.59	5.35	4.21	3.15	5.09

[a]Based on such factors as screen layout, tightly integrated content, functionality, useful demos, and the extensiveness of online help.
[b]Includes the reliability and security of the online auction site, knowledgeable and accessible customer service, and quality guarantees.
[c]Based on the range of products, services, and information offered, information look-up tools, and transactions data.
[d]Based on personalization options, programs and perks that build a sense of community and customer loyalty to the site.

B. Ratings Based on Type of Auction Site User (Rating scale: 0 = lowest; 10 = highest)*			
Auction Site	Bargain Hunters	Hobbyists/Collectors	Sellers
1. eBay	8.43	7.98	7.94
2. Amazon.com	7.46	7.71	6.87
3. Yahoo! Auctions	7.37	6.67	6.96
4. GO Network Auctions	6.84	6.72	6.54
5. FairMarket Network	6.16	6.44	6.10
6. Auctions.com	5.94	6.31	5.47
7. utrade	5.65	5.01	5.34
8. edeal	5.61	4.83	4.89
9. ehammer	5.05	5.27	4.60
10. Haggle Online	5.00	4.88	5.07
11. Boxlot	4.79	5.57	4.57

*Each of the four criteria in part A above were weighted according to their perceived importance to bargain hunters, hobbyists/collectors, and sellers. These criteria were then averaged together to develop a score for each of the three types of online auction site users.
Source: Gomez Advisors, www.gomez.com, March 2, 2000.

Exhibit 9 provides selected statistics for the leading competitors in the online auction market. Exhibit 10 provides comparative financial data, and Exhibit 11 provides comparative Web site traffic.

Amazon.com

At the end of 1999, Gomez.com ranked Amazon.com as the second best online auction Web site. Amazon.com, created in July 1995 as an online bookseller, had rapidly

exhibit 9   Selected Auction Statistics for eBay, Amazon, and Yahoo!,
December 1999

	eBay	Yahoo! Auctions	Amazon.com
Number of items listed for auction	3.8 million	1.3 million	415,000
Percentage of listed auctions closing with a sale	65%	14%	11%
Average number of bids per item	3.03	0.59	0.33
Average selling price for completed auctions	$65.19	$31.09	$25.77

Source: Taken from "Internet: eBay: Crushing the Competition," *Individual Investor,* January 21, 2000.

exhibit 10   Comparative 1999 Financial Statistics for eBay, Amazon,
and Yahoo!*

	eBay	Amazon.com	Yahoo.com
Net revenues	$224,724,000	$1,639,839,000	$588,608,000
Cost of goods sold	57,588,000	1,349,194,000	92,334,000
Net income	10,828,000	(719,968,000)	61,133,000
Net income per share	0.04	(2.20)	0.20

*Includes all business areas for Amazon.com and Yahoo!, not just online auctions.
Source: 1999 Company financial statements.

exhibit 11   Number of Unique Visitors during December 1999

Web Site	Total Number of Unique Visitors
Yahoo! sites	42,361,000
GO Network	21,348,000
Amazon.com	16,631,000
eBay.com	10,388,000

Source: www.mediametrix.com.

turned into a full-line, one-stop-shopping retailer with a product offering that included books, music, toys, electronics, tools and hardware, lawn and patio products, video games, software, and a mall of boutiques (called z-shops)—some 18 million items at last count. Amazon.com was the Internet's number one music, video, and book retailer. The company's 1999 revenues of $1.64 billion were up 169 percent over 1998, but despite the company's rapid revenue growth it was incurring huge losses due to the expenses of (1) establishing an infrastructure to support its sales (the company expanded its worldwide distribution capacity from 300,000 square feet to over 5 million square feet in 1999) and (2) attracting customers via advertising and online:

Year	Net Loss
1996	$ 6.2 million
1997	31.0 million
1998	124.5 million
1999	720.0 million

While Amazon's management was under mounting pressure to control expenses and prove to investors that its business model and strategy were capable of generating good bottom-line profitability, it was clear that management's decisions and strategy were focused on the long term and on solidifying Amazon's current position as a market leader. Management believed that its business model was inherently capital efficient, citing the fact that going into 2000 the company had achieved annualized sales of $2 billion with just $220 million in inventory and $318 million in fixed assets. The company's customer base rose from 6.2 million to 16.9 million during 1999. The company invested more than $300 million in infrastructure in 1999 and opened two international sites, Amazon.co.uk and Amazon.de. These two sites, along with Amazon.com, were the three most popular online retail domains in Europe. Amazon also entered into a number of strategic alliances. During the fourth quarter of 1999 and the first month of 2000, the company announced partnerships with NextCard, Ashford.com, Greenlight.com, Audible, and living.com, as well as an expanded partnership with drugstore.com. It already had e-commerce partnerships with Gear.com; Homegrocer.com; Della.com (an online service for gift registry, gift advice, and personalized gift suggestions); Pets.com; and Sotheby's (a leading auction house for art, artiques, and collectibles).

With its customer base of almost 17 million users in over 150 countries and a very well-known brand name, Amazon.com was considered an imposing competitive threat to eBay. Amazon.com launched its online auction site in March 1999. The site charged sellers for listing their products and also charged a commission on sales. Although Amazon's selection of auctions did not match the one offered by eBay, the company reported that online auctions were the fastest-growing part of its business. The number of auctions on Amazon grew from 140,000 to 415,000 during the second half of 1999. Amazon.com offered three major marketplaces for its users: Auctions, zShops, and sothebys.amazon.com. Its auction site formed partnerships with DreamWorks to promote that company's films *Stuart Little* and *American Beauty* (72 auctions, averaging 27 bids per auction, total gross merchandise sales of over $25,000, yielding an average of over $400 per item) and with television celebrity Oprah Winfrey (25 auctions, averaging 38 bids per auction, total gross merchandise sales of over $130,000, yielding an average of over $6,000 per item).[28] An example of an auction from the Amazon.com Web site is shown in Exhibit 12.

Yahoo! Auctions

Yahoo.com, the first online navigational guide to the Web, launched Yahoo! Auctions in 1997. Yahoo.com offered services to nearly 120 million users every month and the Yahoo! Network operated in North America, Europe, Asia, and Latin America. Yahoo! reported net revenues of $588 million in 1999 (up 140 percent from 1998) and net income

---

[28]Amazon.com press release, February 2, 2000.

exhibit 12   Representative Screen from an Amazon.com Auction

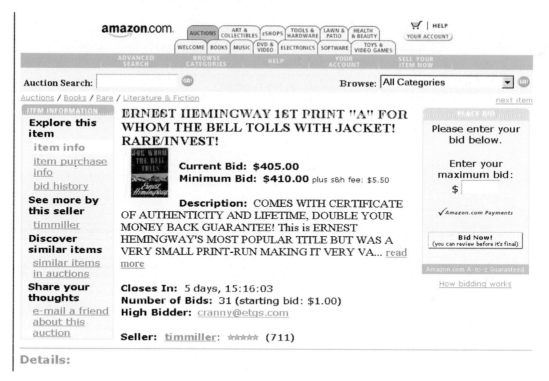

of $142 million. Yahoo's user base grew from 60 million to 120 million during 1999, and 40 million of these users were outside the United States. In December 1999, Yahoo's traffic increased to an average of 465 million page views per day. Yahoo! had entered into numerous alliances and marketing agreements to generate additional site traffic and was investing in new technology to improve the site's performance and attractiveness.

Its auction services were provided to users free of charge, and the number of auctions listed on Yahoo! increased from 670,000 to 1.3 million during the second half of 1999. Yahoo! Auctions was expanded to include Hong Kong, Taiwan, Korea, Mexico, Brazil, and Denmark at the end of 1999. Localized Yahoo! auctions outside the United States were being conducted in 16 countries in 11 different languages. Yahoo! Japan Auctions was the largest localized online auction service in Japan. At the end of 1999, Yahoo! launched Yahoo! Merchant Auctions and Featured Auctions in order to allow retailers and sellers to promote their auctions. Yahoo! Auctions also offered many extra services to its users. Gomez.com rated Yahoo! Auctions as the number one online auction site in the Relationship Services category. An example of a screen from Yahoo! Auctions is shown in Exhibit 13.

FairMarket

FairMarket, a new online auction provider that went online in September 1999, had quickly emerged as one of the leading providers of private-label, outsourced, networked auction services for business clients. It offered a number of formats: hosted auctions, fixed-price auctions, declining-price or markdown auctions for merchants wishing to dispose of overstocked merchandise, and shopping-by-request services. The company was

exhibit 13   Example of a Screen from a Yahoo! Auction

formed through an alliance of Microsoft, Dell Computer, Lycos, Excite, CBS Sportsline, CompUSA, and several others. The FairMarket network of auctions included Alta Vista Auctions, CityAuction, Excite Auctions, GO Auction, Lycos Auctions, and MSN Auctions. The company went public in early 2000, raising approximately $75 million to support expansion.

FairMarket managed and maintained online auctions for such customers as JCPenney (which had auctions that allowed customers to purchase new, quality merchandise and auctions that incorporated an automatic markdown format for overstocked merchandise from JCPenney retail store and catalog operations); the Times Digital Company (which conducted local auctions in New York City and other locations); Dell Computer (which held auctions for customers wishing to sell their used computers and for equipment coming off lease); Ritz Camera (which used auctions to sell end-of-life camera equipment); Outpost.com (which auctioned a mix of new and refurbished computer and computer accessory items); and SportingAuction (which used FairMarket's network systems to auction an extensive selection of high-quality sporting goods).

FairMarket received a percentage fee of all the items sold on auctions it conducted for its customer-sellers.

AuctionWatch

AuctionWatch.com was formed in July 1998 and incorporated in January 1999 as a privately held company backed by several venture capital firms and private investors. The company, a very small online auction site originally, had raised $10 million in capital in August 1999 to expand both its site and its available features. The AuctionWatch site was designed to model eBay, and had many of the same types of offerings. By the end of 1999, AuctionWatch.com was conducting over 25,000 auctions daily, had served over 2 million auction images per day, and received over 20,000 posts each month in its visitor center. AuctionWatch catered to businesses looking to use online auctions as a new distribution channel and to attract new customers. One of the unique features at Auction-Watch was a content service that allowed users to compare and contrast the fee structures of the top consumer-to-consumer, business-to-consumer, and business-to-business auction sites; the information was updated monthly.

As of April 2000, AuctionWatch had over 250,000 registered users and was conducting about 1 million auctions monthly. AuctionWatch attracted 1.7 million unique visitors in March 2000, an increase of over 100 percent from February and over 500 percent from December 1999. In the first quarter of 2000, businesses and auction enthusiasts used AuctionWatch to sell over $120 million worth of merchandise.

GO Network Auctions

GO.com was the result of a November 1999 merger between Walt Disney's online unit, the Buena Vista Internet Group (BVIG), and Infoseek Corporation. The company oversaw ABC.com, ESPN.com, and Disney.com, as well as several other popular Web sites; its chief activity was serving as the Internet business arm of the Walt Disney Company. The GO.com portal focused on entertainment, leisure, and recreation activities. The online auction section of the GO Network, auction.go.com, was experiencing rapid growth. GO Network Auctions offered over 100 product categories and provided users with a guarantee against fraudulent listings; one of its main features was auctioning Disney products, including movie sets, props, and memorabilia from movies from Walt Disney Studios and from ABC-produced shows. The Web site was also considered extremely easy to navigate. Gomez.com ranked GO Network Auctions number one in the Ease of Use category among online auctions.

In February 2000, GO.com and eBay announced a four-year agreement to develop and market online trading and auction experiences in a co-branded person-to-person site and new merchant-to-person sites. According to terms of the agreement, eBay would ultimately become the online trading and auction service for all of Disney's Internet properties, including the GO Network portal, and would collaborate on merchant-to-person auctions for authenticated products, props, and memorabilia from throughout the Walt Disney Company.

Auctions.com

Auctions.com was originally launched as Auction Universe in November 1997. After being acquired by Classified Ventures in 1998, the site was relaunched as Auctions.com on December 13, 1999. The company claimed to be "the world's fastest growing online auction network" at the beginning of 2000.[29] Auctions.com had hundreds of categories and several thousand product listings available for users. Not only did the company's Web site offer 24-hour customer service support, but it also had the premier online transaction security program (Bid$afe). The Federal Trade Commission claimed that Bid$afe was one of the "best fraud protection programs on the Web."[30]

Formed in 1997 and headquartered in London, QXL.com was moving rapidly to try to dominate the online auction market in Europe. Rather than create one Web site for Europe, QXL's strategy was to methodically enter one European country after another, launching its own new sites in some countries and acquiring already established players in others. While QXL was thinking globally, it was acting locally, operating in 12 different languages, accommodating 12 different currencies (until use of the euro), and tailoring its merchandise features to the preferences of users in each country, QXL's market reach included Great Britain, Germany, France, Italy, Spain, the Netherlands, Denmark, Finland, Poland, Norway, and Sweden. QXL was developing technology so that it could quickly and economically customize its sites for each country. Currently, however, its sites were slow and antiquated compared to eBay.

In 2000, the online aution market in Europe was much less developed than in the U.S.; there were not as many Internet users and many European Web surfers were leery of entering bids to purchase an item online. To combat the wariness of online auctions exhibited by actual and prospective visitors to its online auction site, QXL was conducting a number of auctions for goods put up for sale by retail merchants. QXL management reasoned that site visitors who were reluctant to buy items from a stranger would feel comfortable enough to enter bids to buy merchandise from an established retailer.

NICHE AUCTIONS

Many new competitors had also begun offering auctions targeted at smaller segments of the online auction industry. These auctions primarily specialized in one product or service type, such as computers/electronics, fine art, industrial products, music-related goods, international auctions, and just about any other product or service imaginable. There were sites offering laptop computers (AuctionLaptops.com), guitars (Guitarauction.com), German wines (Koppe and Partner Wine Auctions), and even a site that auctioned nothing but racing pigeons (ipigeon.com). There were several significant companies conducting niche auctions:

● *Outpost.com*—Outpost.com was founded in 1995 to service primarily the small-office/home-office market. By the end of 1999, the company offered over 170,000 products online, primarily in the computer/electronics area. Bizrate.com rated Outpost.com the number one consumer shopping experience on the Web, and Forrester Research awarded the company the 1999 number one PowerRanking for Computing. The company had half a million customers and 4 million monthly visitors. In 2000, the company announced separate partnerships with Golf Galaxy and Computer.com. Outpost claimed to differentiate itself from other online auction sites "by focusing on the needs of the customer and delivering its services with reliability,

---

[29]www.auctions.com/backgrounder.asp, April 20, 2000.
[30]Ibid.

fully encrypted secure servers, depth of product selection and building a team of dedicated and knowledgeable professionals that support all efforts of the business."[31]

- *eWanted.com*—eWanted.com pioneered the idea of the "backward auction" in October 1998. A backward auction was the exact opposite of a traditional online auction. Buyers would place ads specifying the item they wanted, as well as the product's primary characteristics. Then sellers would browse these ads and submit offers to the buyers. The theory was that sellers would compete with each other for a particular buyer, thus driving the auction price down. In return, sellers entered a marketplace where they knew that buyers existed for their particular product or service.

- *eRock.com*—eRock.com specialized in offering rock-and-roll memorabilia to "serious die-hard fans, collectors, and dealers."[32] The site had 12 different categories of music auctions available, and also offered a chat room for users to talk about their musical interests and links to the Web pages of several popular rock groups.

THE FUTURE

As eBay headed into the second quarter of 2000, it was looking for new avenues to expand its services. According to Brian Swette, eBay's chief operating officer, the company was "at the five yard line with its core business."[33] The next driver of the company's growth was expected to be international expansion, followed by business-to-business and automobile and regional sites.[34] Swette predicted that each of these areas could wind up "as large as the core eBay."[35]

In response to the increasing opportunities in the business-to-business auction segment, and the number of small companies trading on eBay, the company developed the eBay Business Exchange in March 2000. To avoid head-on competition with other auction sites in this market segment, eBay was focusing on businesses with fewer than 100 employees. Swette saw Business Exchange as a natural evolution of eBay's business model and expected that larger companies would eventually participate. Specific categories offered in the new eBay Business Exchange included computer hardware, software, electronics, industrial equipment, office equipment, and professional tools.

EBay had recently announced plans to enter France, Europe's third largest online commerce market. EBay management viewed France as critical in capturing the European market. However, well-established competition existed in the French market in the form of QXL.com, the leading British online auctioneer, and the I-Bazar Group, a France-based corporation that had anticipated eBay's arrival in 1998 and purchased the domain name eBay.fr.

While the number of concurrently active eBay auctions soared from approximately 1 million to 4.5 million between 1998 and year-end 1999, from January 2000 to March 2000 the number of auctions was holding at a relatively constant 4.2 to 4.4 million. EBay spokesperson Kevin Pursglove dismissed the flat trend, stating, "Listings are an

---

[31]www.outpost.com, Investor Relations, April 20, 2000.

[32]www.erock.com, April 20, 2000.

[33]"The One Thing Not for Sale on eBay," www.thestandard.com, April 20, 2000.

[34]Ibid.

[35]Ibid.

exhibit 14   eBay's Stock Price Performance, September 1998–
April 2000

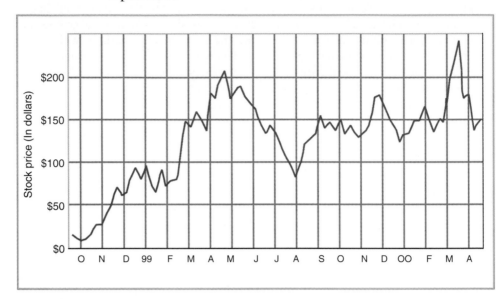

interesting thing to look at, but sellers are more interested in selling their merchandise."[36] Wall Street analysts, however, saw the lack of growth in the number of auctions as signaling a coming slowdown in eBay's revenue and profit growth and an indication of market share erosion.

Pierre Omidyar folded his newspaper to prepare for a meeting with Meg Whitman and Jeff Skoll to discuss two developing situations. The first topic on the list was to review the possibility of a cross-marketing strategic alliance with competitor Yahoo! to gain broader exposure to Yahoo's broad customer base. Partnering with a competitor that also offered auction services seemed to have pluses and minuses. The second item on the agenda involved the potential of launching storefront operations where eBayers could purchase goods at a fixed price, much like Amazon. As he headed down the hall to the meeting, Pierre recalled a statement that Meg Whitman had made in a recent interview: "I have this philosophy that you really need to do things 100 percent. Better to do 5 things at 100 percent than 10 things at 80 percent. Because the devil in so much of this is in the detail and while we have to move very, very fast, I think you are not well served by moving incredibly rapidly and not doing things that well."[37] Given recent developments, Pierre was forced to wonder if they were operating at 100 percent. Also, if Forrester Research was correct in their recent prediction that the majority of online retailers would be out of business by the end of 2000, would 100 percent be enough?[38] The recent drop in the company's stock price had been troubling (see Exhibit 14), and the company needed to launch strategic initiatives that would sustain rapid growth and get it back on the road to market dominance.

---

[36]"Auction Growth Slows at eBay, Can Earnings' Growth be Far Behind?" *Barron's Online,* April 17, 2000.

[37]"What's behind the Boom at eBay?" *Business Week Online,* May 21, 1999.

[38]Forrester.com press release, April 11, 2000.

case 12 | CDnow in the Online Music Business

Alan B. Eisner
Pace University

Nicole Belmont
Pace University

CDnow was one of the world's largest e-commerce retailers of music products, with 1999 sales of $147 million, up from $56 million in 1998. Visitors to its Web site (www.cdnow.com) could choose from a lineup of more than 500,000 items that included music CDs and DVDs, videotapes, cassettes, traditional vinyl albums, custom CDs, 650,000 sample sound clips, and music downloads. CDnow was one of the first sites to offer the sale of music downloads and currently offered both free and purchasable music downloads. The site also featured daily news about developments in the music industry, feature stories, exclusive interviews with artists, and a list of bestsellers. In addition, site users could obtain a list of selections and recommendations tailored to their individual music preferences.

CDnow's Web site was one of the best-known and most-visited online music destinations, with an average daily audience of over 800,000 people. Over 3.2 million customers had made purchases since the inception of CDnow in August 1994; 1.6 million of these made their first purchase in 1999. The company's vision was to create an online music destination with unprecedented access to and coverage of the world of music. Part of the CDnow vision was "to make every visit to the site, whether for browsing or buying, a valuable and rewarding experience." CDnow catered to Internet users in the United States, Europe, and the Middle East; visitors could browse the contents of CDnow's site in any of eight languages—English, French, Spanish, Portuguese, Dutch, German, Italian, and Japanese.

COMPANY BACKGROUND

CDnow, based in suburban Philadelphia, was founded by twin brothers Jason and Matthew Olim in 1994. Their goal was to "build a better music store through intelligent album recommendations, custom CDs, music samples, a vast library of reviews and fea-

---

exhibit 1   Six-Year Financial Summary for CDnow, 1994–99

Year	Revenues	Net Income	Earnings per Share
1999	$147,189,000	($121,527,000)	($4.32)
1998	56,395,000	(43,769,000)	(2.79)
1997	17,373,000	(10,747,000)	(1.42)
1996	6,300,000	(1,810,000)	(0.29)
1995	2,176,000	(201,000)	(0.03)
1994	103,000	(58,000)	(0.01)

Sources: CDnow Corporate Web site, SEC filings, and disclosure.

tures from top music writers and exclusive editorial content."[1] The Olim brothers formed a company that prided itself on broad selection, informative content, easy-to-use Web site navigation and search capabilities, a high level of customer service, competitive pricing, and personalized merchandising and recommendations.

The concept for CDnow came to Jason Olim while he was looking through a stack of albums in a record store. Jason had stopped asking clerks for advice because of their lack of knowledge and instead brought music encyclopedias with him on music-buying trips. Jason Olim said, "It suddenly occurred to me one day that I could take the information in guide books . . . put it in a database, and with that database I could take the products that were also available for sale . . . and I could merge it together and make it available on the Internet."[2]

Within 24 hours, Jason had formulated a business plan, which he quickly showed to his brother Matthew, who was studying astrophysics at Columbia University. CDnow was born through the combination of Matthew's expert computer-programming skills and Jason's business skills. The company began in their parents' basement with a $20,000 initial investment. Sales were $14 their first month.

The company went public in February 1998 at a price of $16 per share, raising $88.5 million in equity capital. The shares had traded as high as $39 in 1998, but since then had lost favor with investors. During 1999, the stock traded in the range of $10 to $25. Jason Olim was president and CEO of the company; his brother Matthew was principal software engineer and a member of the company's board of directors. The two brothers each owned 9 percent (or 2,960,000 shares) of the company's outstanding stock. In February 2000, Michael Krupit, formerly the company's vice president of technology, was named chief operating officer and assigned responsibility for day-to-day operations and the company's organizational structure. The company had just over 500 employees.

Since the launch of the company's Web site, CDnow's revenues had expanded rapidly, growing at an average annual compound rate of 187 percent during the 1995–99 period (see Exhibit 1). But the company had yet to earn a profit; in fact, losses were mounting, as shown in Exhibit 2. The company was financing its expansion and covering negative cash flows with capital raised from its public sale of stock in February 1998, but cash reserves were dwindling. The company had cash and cash equivalents of

---

[1]"CDnow Breaks New Ground for Online Shopping with Personalization Technology," PR Newswire, September 16, 1998, p. 916.

[2]John Wilen, "Going for Miles Inspires CDnow," *Philadelphia Business Journal,* October 17, 1997, p. 16.

exhibit 2   Consolidated Statements of Income for CDnow, 1995–99

	1999	1998	1997	1996	1995
Net sales	$147,189,405	$56,394,606	$17,372,795	$6,300,294	$2,176,474
Cost of sales	118,037,621	45,250,328	13,847,773	5,074,087	1,815,672
Gross profit	29,151,784	11,144,278	3,525,022	1,226,207	360,672
Operating expenses					
Operating and development	23,421,062	8,000,023	2,541,434	669,280	149,982
Sales and marketing	89,734,790	44,572,304	9,607,603	765,156	229,912
General and administrative	11,736,503	4,244,194	1,953,078	563,593	180,573
Amortization of goodwill	25,786,261	202,801			
Other operating charges				1,024,030	
Total operating expenses	150,678,616	57,019,322	14,102,115	3,022,059	560,467
Operating loss	(121,526,832)	(45,875,044)	(10,577,093)	(1,795,852)	(199,665)
Interest and other income	2,688,882	2,742,581	201,650		
Interest expense	(391,075)	(636,458)	(371,962)	(14,556)	(1,248)
Net loss	($119,229,025)	($43,768,921)	($10,747,405)	($1,810,408)	($200,913)
Net loss per share	($4.32)	($2.79)	($1.42)	($0.29)	($0.03)
Weighted average number of shares outstanding	27,618,917	15,712,857	7,845,684	6,139,072	6,000,000

Source: CDnow's 1999 10-K report to the SEC.

$20.6 million as of December 31, 1999, compared to $49.0 million as of December 31, 1998 (see Exhibit 3). However, at year-end 1999, CDnow had a working capital deficit of $37.2 million, owing to a sharp climb in accounts payable and the company's eroding cash position.[3]

THE ONLINE MUSIC INDUSTRY

Exhibit 4 shows the structure of the overall music industry. Exhibit 5 presents the sales of prerecorded music by category. In 1998, U.S. online music sales were an estimated $152 million, equal to about 1 percent of recorded music sales (see Exhibit 6).[4] Preliminary estimates were that sales in 1999 reached $375 million.[5] Internet sales of music, however, were predicted to grow to $2.6 billion annually by 2003 and account for close to 14 percent of all U.S. retail music sales (Exhibit 7).[6] According to a survey conducted by Strategic Record Research, 38.4 percent of consumers were expected to spend more on music in 1999 than in 1998 (see Exhibit 8).[7] This online spending was predicted to come from an increasingly Internet-enabled generation of consumers.

---

[3]A company's working capital is defined as current assets minus current liabilities.

[4]"Recorded Music Market Healthy as Current Releases and CD Albums Gain," *Research Alert,* August 6, 1999, p. 1.

[5]Patrick M. Reilly, "Barnesandnoble.com to Join a Crowd of Firms Offering 'Online Music Stores,'" *The Wall Street Journal,* July 7, 1999, p. B2.

[6]"Record Stores Face New Era Personal Touch Called Key to Staying in Sync as Online Sales Pick Up," *Bloomberg News,* July 22, 1999, p. C3.

[7]"Clothes and Home Goods Give Music a Run for the Money," *Billboard,* May 16, 1998, p. 110.

exhibit 3   Condensed Balance Sheet Data for CDnow, 1998–99

	1999	1998
Assets		
Current assets		
Cash and cash equivalents	$ 20,612,706	$49,041,370
Accounts receivable, net	4,068,700	839,672
Prepaid expenses and other	5,580,241	8,322,889
Total current assets	30,261,647	58,203,931
Property and equipment	17,216,980	6,643,995
Goodwill and other intangibles	70,121,321	833,735
Other assets	1,201,809	3,361,982
Total assets	$118,801,757	$69,043,643
Liabilities and Stockholders' Equity		
Current liabilities		
Current portion of long-term debt	$ 1,670,838	$ 822,043
Accounts payable	46,431,122	10,306,323
Accrued merger costs	1,384,679	—
Accrued expenses	17,927,779	4,667,395
Total current liabilities	67,414,418	15,795,761
Long-term debt	2,629,359	1,750,892
Common stock subject to put rights	2,999,995	—
Deferred rent liabilities	992,696	358,053
Common stock	204,573,908	102,137,536
Additional paid-in capital	14,589,814	4,325,817
Deferred compensation	(61,905)	(216,913)
Accumulated deficit	(174,336,528)	(55,107,503)
Total stockholders' equity	44,765,289	51,138,937
Total liabilities and stockholders' equity	$118,801,757	$69,043,643

Source: CDnow 1999 10-K report.

The Attractiveness of Online Music Retailing

Several factors made the online music retailing business attractive relative to traditional retail stores. Online technology featured many multimedia options that enabled consumers to listen to sound samples; search for music by genre, title, or artist; and access a wealth of information and events, including reviews, related articles, music history, news, and recommendations. Online retailers could more easily obtain extensive demographic and behavioral data about their customers, providing them with greater direct marketing opportunities and the ability to offer a more personalized shopping experience. In addition, online retailers could offer consumers significantly broader product selection, the convenience of home shopping, and 24-hour-a-day, seven-day-a-week operations available to any foreign or domestic location with access to the Internet. Typical retail music stores stocked around 12,000 items, but the total could range as high as 50,000 items for megastores. According to Jupiter Communications, a marketing research firm, approximately 80 percent of unit sales at traditional retail stores came from roughly 20 percent of the available titles.

exhibit 4 Music Industry Market Structure

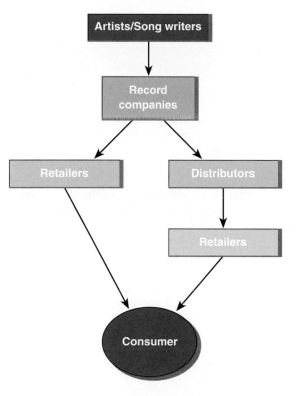

exhibit 5 Percentage of Music Sales by Category

Music Category	1998 Recording Sales by Genre
Rock	25.7%
Country	14.1
R&B	12.8
Pop	10.0
Rap/Hip Hop	9.7
Gospel	6.3
Classical	3.3
Jazz	1.9
Other	11.3
	100.1%

Source: Research Alert, August 6, 1999.

Physical-store-based retailers had to make significant investments in real estate, inventory, and personnel for each store location. Online retailers generally incurred a fraction of these costs due to centralized distribution and virtually unlimited merchandising space. It was cost-effective for online retailers to offer a broader range of titles and information than brick-and-mortar music retailers, especially titles issued by independent

exhibit 6   Percentage of 1998 Music Sales by Type of Retailer

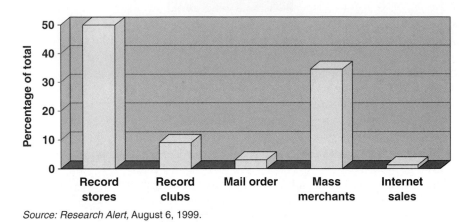

Source: *Research Alert,* August 6, 1999.

exhibit 7   Online Music Sales Estimates

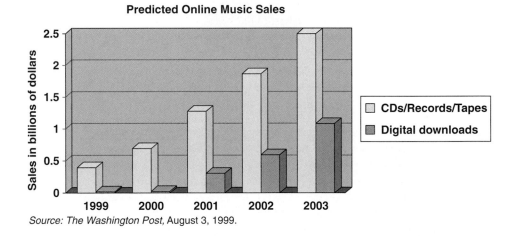

Source: *The Washington Post,* August 3, 1999.

exhibit 8   Population Groups Most Likely to Increase Music Spending

Population Groups Most Likely to Spend More	Percentage Indicating a Desire to Increase Music Spending
Males 18–25	11.6%
Males 12–17	11.5
Females 12–17	11.6
Females 35–44	11.6

Source: *Billboard Magazine* survey, May 16, 1998.

labels, which accounted for a growing percentage of new titles. Independent labels accounted for 21 percent of the total music market in 1996 versus only 12 percent in 1992, and they released 66 percent of the titles in 1996. It was burdensome for brick-and-mortar music retailers to stock and promote more than a few of the independent labels, creating a gap that online retailers could economically fill. Online retailers, however, faced significant technology costs associated with operating a cutting-edge online store and sizable marketing and promotion costs to build site traffic, which offset many of their cost advantages over brick-and-mortar retailers.

From a demographic standpoint, persons over 30 years old were accounting for a growing percentage of music sales—48 percent of total sales in 1997 versus 34 percent in 1996. Online retailers saw the Internet as a particularly attractive medium for marketing music titles to middle- and upper-income customers in the over-30 age group because their purchases were less likely to be "hits-driven." A bigger fraction of this population group had diverse music interests, which made them more likely to shop online, where they could select from hundreds or thousands of titles. Moreover, they could afford to buy more titles at one time, were likely to have access to computers, and had credit cards with which to make electronic payments.

Competitive Threats to Online Music Retailing

Online music retailers saw record clubs as a potentially serious competitive threat. After experiencing declining sales and buyer interest during the 1995–97 period, record clubs had rejuvenated their business by relaxing their membership policies. "Hassle-free memberships" gave customers up to two years to purchase a minimum of six titles, and clubs had abandoned the annoying practice of automatically shipping a club-designated CD if subscribers did not reply in time.[8] Record clubs had also improved their customer service and were putting substantially more resources into advertising and marketing.

Another potential threat to online music retailers (and music retailers in general) was the rapidly rising popularity of direct digital distribution, which allowed consumers to download individual songs from the Internet and copy them directly onto CDs, a practice that many observers saw as having the potential to revolutionize the whole music industry.[9] Recording studios saw digital downloads as a major threat to their role because artists could make their own recordings, distribute them directly over the Internet, and thus earn well above what they received in royalties from the record companies. (See Illustration Capsule 16 in Chapter 4 of the text for a breakdown of the recording industry value chain.) Such a move—said to be under consideration by some artists, especially those who were unsigned by the major recording studios—held the potential for cutting the record producers and brick-and-mortar retailers out of the industry value chain entirely. Sales of digital music downloads, estimated at a meager $1 million in 1999, were predicted to reach $1.1 billion by 2003.[10] To capitalize on growing buyer

---

[8]Michael Christman, "Record Clubs Utilize New Strategies," *Billboard,* January 30, 1999.

[9]"On-line Retailing Expands but Has Yet to Come of Age," *Music Business International,* August 1998.

[10]Stephanie Stoughton, "The Score on Downloads: Analysts Sing Praises of Online Music Trend," *Washington Post,* August 3, 1999, p. E1.

exhibit 9   Market Reach of the Most Popular Internet Portals

	Percent of the Online Population Reached
America Online	48.3%
Yahoo!	44.4
Microsoft Network	35.4
Netscape	27.7
Excite	26.2

Source: Newsbytes News Network, April 21, 1998.

interest in digital downloads and counter the competitive threat to their business, Sony, Universal Music, and BMG Entertainment had announced plans to begin selling downloadable CDs directly to online shoppers.

Price discounting was becoming a bigger factor in the online music segment's competitive environment. Online retailers were more aggressive in discounting their prices and running special promotions than were traditional store retailers, record clubs, and record companies with online stores. For example, most record companies had established online sites to sell directly to the consumer, but their prices were generally higher than those of online music retailers like CDnow and Amazon.com; this was partly to avoid creating channel conflict and angering the traditional brick-and-mortar music retailers on whom the record companies depended for most of their sales. Online retailers could offset the revenue loss from price discounting with the fees they earned from selling advertising space on their Web sites.

Profit Margins of Online Music Retailers

Online music retailers were struggling to make a success of their business model. Most were plagued with losses, owing to capital expenditures for state-of-the-art Web site technology and very large marketing and advertising expenditures to build site traffic. To turn losses into profits, online retailers had to achieve a large volume of sales and, at the same time, keep a tight rein on marketing costs. According to one observer, "Everyone is losing money because the margins are so low. What people are shooting for is an established market share by 2002. It is important that you be No. 1, No. 2, or maybe No. 3." An official with the Association of Internet Professionals said, "You build the name, you build the brand, then you make the money."[11] Jason Olim, CDnow's CEO, believed that "given time, the market will support only three or four brands."

To build sales and market share, online retailers had to build strong brand awareness and generate heavy site traffic. One way of doing this was by allying with Yahoo!, America Online, and the other portals that Web surfers used as gateways for sessions on the Internet and paying them substantial sums for advertising space. Getting lots of exposure on the major portals (see Exhibit 9) was deemed critical to building traffic, since it was difficult for online music retailers to differentiate on the basis of product selection (most of the major online music retailers had extensive selections to choose

---

[11]Associated Press, "Music Retailer Is Attempting to Build a Noteworthy Company," *Buffalo News,* June 9, 1998, p. 7D.

from). The big Internet retailers were willing to pay to lock up advertising space and Web links on the leading portals for as long as two to four years. To counter the exclusive promotional arrangements that several of the online music retailers had negotiated with prominent portals, rivals were shifting more money to traditional media advertising. CDnow had run advertisements on the Howard Stern show, placed print advertisements in such music publications as *Spin* and *Variety,* and negotiated promotional deals with MTV and the Rolling Stone Network.

CDNOW IN 2000

CDnow was a major player in the online music industry, with a 33 percent market share in 1999. CDnow faced competition from many different kinds of competitors entering the online music industry. Competitors included online music retailers, in-line music retailers, book retailers, movie retailers, book and music clubs, and record companies. Notable competitors included such online retailers as Amazon.com, Borders.com, Barnesandnoble.com, MuZic.com, Rock.com, Buy.com, and CD Universe; brick-and-mortar retailers like Tower Records, Musicland, and Sam Goody's; Columbia House and other record clubs; and record companies Sony and BMG (which were launching online sites). In the online segment, rivalry revolved around brand recognition, selection, price, the effectiveness of advertising and customer acquisition efforts, the variety of value-added services provided on company Web sites, ease of site use, site content, quality of customer service, and technical expertise. Several of CDnow's online rivals had longer operating histories, a larger customer base, greater brand recognition, and significantly greater financial, marketing, and technological resources. CDnow's executives viewed entry barriers as minimal because an online retailer could launch a new site at relatively low cost. They saw competition in the overall retail music business as being intense and evolving rapidly because of spreading consumer interest in digital downloading of music recordings (as opposed to purchasing CDs and cassettes).

Management believed that, as digital downloading of music grew in popularity, CDnow's broad base of music buyers, its relationships with record labels, and use of the most advanced Web technology would position the company as a leader in offering music fans secure, speedy, high-quality downloads. The company's interactive media division developed content for the Web site that included news about music artists, artist interviews and reviews, and a community where unsigned bands could promote their recordings.

CDnow strived to make its online store appealing, informative, and authoritative. Exhibit 10 shows CDnow's home page. CDnow had designed its Web site to be intuitive and easy to use, endeavoring to allow customers to learn about, find, and order CDs and other music-related products with a minimum of effort. Customers could focus their searches with a "fast-find" search engine, browse among top sellers and other featured titles, read reviews, listen to music samples, participate in promotions, and check the status of their orders. New users could access an information page designed to give shoppers a quick understanding of the site and its many features. To encourage purchases, CDnow rotated promotions among items throughout the store; it frequently discounted recent releases and popular titles. To encourage the purchase of multiple titles, CDnow lowered shipping costs for larger orders. Customers could pay for orders with a credit card, check, or money order.

As the result of the acquisition of superSonic Boom, Inc., CDnow had the technology to allow customers to build customized CDs from a collection of 60,000 individual

exhibit 10   CDnow's Home Page, April 2000

songs by various artists. Buyers selected their favorite songs to create a full-length CD, added a personalized title, and wrote their own liner notes. Custom CDs were an especially popular item for Valentine's Day gifts and for Christmas and other holidays. In addition, CDnow sold branded custom CDs to other companies for corporate promotions, in volume as well as on demand. CDnow manufactured and shipped each custom CD from its Fort Washington facility and, on occasion, used third parties to provide manufacturing and shipping.

exhibit 11 CDnow's Order Fulfillment Process

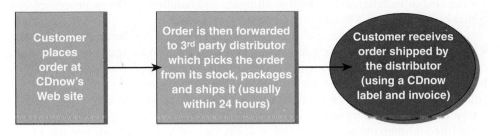

Recent Traffic at CDnow's Web Site

In February 2000, CDnow attracted a record 5.7 million unique visitors to its Web site, making it the 33rd most visited domain according to data compiled by Media Metrix. The company's February audience was larger than either MP3.com's or MTV.com's. CDnow was the fifth largest Internet shopping site, with an 8.1 percent reach among all Web users; it was the only music destination among Media Metrix's list of the top 10 shopping sites. CDnow's unique customer count increased to 3.5 million in February 2000, up from 3.2 million in December 1999. Average page views per visit reached a high of 9.9 pages, and visitors spent an average of 1 minute 48 seconds viewing each page, well above CDnow's typical average of 1 minute 20 seconds per page. According to PCData's February list of Internet buyers, CDnow ranked first by completing over 1 million transactions, ahead of Amazon.com. However, CDnow's February 2000 transactions were boosted by redemption of coupons for free custom CDs in a promotional campaign cosponsored by Pizza Hut. CDnow included the amount of coupons redeemed to purchase merchandise in its reported revenues (coupons redeemed accounted for 4.9 percent of CDnow's reported revenues in 1999 and 3.2 percent in 1998). Site-tracking data revealed that 63 percent of CDnow's retail sales revenues were generated by repeat customers, a statistic that management believed confirmed the attractiveness of the content of CDnow's Web site.

These traffic statistics were instrumental in helping CDnow sell advertising on its Web site and gain sponsors for product promotions. Part of CDnow's revenue-generating strategy was to leverage its site traffic and paying customer base by selling advertising and sponsorships to companies interested in promoting their own goods and services to CDnow's customer base and daily Web site audience. Recent advertisers included Oracle, Oldsmobile, and United Airlines. Advertising revenues totaled $8.8 million in 1999, up 626 percent over 1998.

CDnow's Order Fulfillment Process

CDnow's inventory was owned and held by outside vendors who shipped directly to CDnow's customers. The breadth of inventory maintained by these vendors provided CDnow with the ability to maintain high order-fill rates. CDnow updated the items available on its site daily, using inventory information supplied by its vendors; this feature enabled customers to check availability before placing an order. Orders were transmitted to the appropriate vendor at least once daily (usually more often); vendors shipped orders using a CDnow label and invoice normally within one business day after the order was placed with CDnow (see Exhibit 11). Shipping fees were $2.99 for the first CD and 99 cents for each additional CD up to a maximum of $4.97.

For an added fee, customers could request next-day delivery. Vendors billed CDnow for the cost of merchandise as well as shipping and handling. CDnow processed customer billing through a third-party credit card processor.

CDnow's primary order fulfillment vendor was Valley Media, the second largest U.S. wholesaler of records, cassettes, and compact discs and a specialist in handling order fulfillment activities for most online music retailers.[12] Although Valley Media handled about 85 percent of CDnow's orders, the music seller also used the order fulfillment services of Alliance OneStop Group to provide greater breadth of selection to customers and deeper inventories of fast-selling items. Orders for videos and DVDs were filled through the services of Baker & Taylor, and MSI of Miami was used to fill orders produced by foreign record companies, including 60,000 international titles from an order fulfillment center in the Netherlands that serviced European markets. Valley Media offered customers (online music companies and retailers) the widest selection of music titles and had a state-of-the-art inventory, order-filling, and shipping system that allowed it to provide customers with next-day delivery service.[13]

In order to preserve their relationships with the traditional brick-and-mortar music retailers, most record companies were very reluctant to do business directly with online retailers. Thus, Amazon.com was the only major online music retailer that bought products directly from record companies, stocked them in company-owned warehouses, and had internal systems for filling, packing, and shipping customer orders.[14] However, Amazon, still working to develop its own next-day delivery capabilities, used the services of Valley Media for customers who requested next-day delivery.

CDnow's Strategic Marketing Alliances

CDnow's biggest promotional and marketing alliance was with America Online. Under the marketing agreement with AOL, CDnow and AOL shared revenues generated from the sale of advertising, sponsorships, CDs, and related merchandise derived from CDnow's being featured as the exclusive online music retailer within AOL's Music Space Channel and its featured position on AOL's Shopping Channel. CDnow could take advantage of banner advertising opportunities on AOL and was assigned specific keywords on AOL's search engine. Its agreement with AOL continued through August 31, 2000. CDnow had also entered into promotional alliances with Yahoo!, Excite, Lycos, Webcrawler, Tripod, and Geocities in an effort to extend its reach and gain a presence on the sites of the major portals and search engines. The company's agreement to be the exclusive retailer of CDs and other music-related products on the Lycos and Tripod Web sites, however, became the subject of litigation in July 1999, when CDnow filed a lawsuit alleging breach of contract with regard to the Web site linking arrangements.

Most recently, CDnow had entered into a multiyear integrated marketing agreement with MTV Networks whereby CDnow, MTV, and VH1 instituted cross-promotions through online retailing and content, event sponsorships, and on-air advertising.[15] MTV and VH1's online sites provided links to CDnow, and CDnow offered music news

---

[12]Don Jeffery, "Cyber Selling," *Billboard,* July 18, 1998, p. 29.

[13]"California-based Music, Video Distributor Enjoying Good Growth," *Tribune Business News,* November 10, 1997, p. 1110.

[14]Ed Christman, "Amazon.com Buys Directly from a Major," *Billboard,* October 17, 1998, p. 10.

[15]Carla Hay, "MTV Networks, CDnow Make Marketing Deal," *Billboard,* June 6, 1998, p. 71.

provided by MTV and VH1, as well as a "Now Playing" ticker highlighting each channel's programming schedule. CDnow also was the exclusive online retailer for the MTV Music Awards. Both CDnow and MTV had very high expectations for the marketing alliance. Jason Olim said, "This alliance with MTV and VH1 affords CDnow the opportunity to take its integrated marketing strategy to the next level. They are the only brands that have the true horsepower to move consumers from their televisions to their computers, and that's what marketing convergence is all about." Matt Farber, MTV/VH1's senior vice president of programming enterprises, was equally enthusiastic, saying, "We chose CDnow because their sole business is the music transaction business online, and they've created a leading brand name in their field, just as MTV and VH1 have. CDnow's marketing strategies also mutually complement MTV and VH1's strategies."

Another multiyear marketing alliance had been negotiated with the Rolling Stone Network. Visitors to the CDnow site were provided access to over 30 years of Rolling Stone music coverage, and visitors to the Rolling Stone Network were provided a link to CDnow's music products. The Rolling Stone's content available through CDnow included landmark covers, cover story excerpts, reviews, award-winning features, and the magazine's "Random Notes," "Grapevine," and "The Industry" columns.

The payments made by CDnow to its marketing alliance partners were much of the reason the company's sales and marketing expenses had risen from $44.6 million in 1998 to $89.7 million in 1999 and were a principal contributor to the company's reported 1999 losses of $119 million.

CDnow's Efforts to Employ New Technologies at Its Web Site

CDnow was making an effort to keep its Web site on the cutting edge of technology. The company's operating and development expenses of $23.4 million in 1999 (versus $8.0 million in 1998) reflected increased spending for the systems and telecommunications infrastructure necessary to support increased traffic and transactions volume. Management saw site and systems improvements as necessary to avoid losing out to other online competitors, but in early 2000 several competitors—Amazon.com in particular—were devoting substantially more resources to site and systems development than CDnow. CDnow had deployed systems for online content dissemination, online transactions processing, customer service, market analysis, and electronic data interchange. Much of its software was proprietary and had been developed both to minimize the engineering required to maintain a growing array of merchandise items and content and to reduce the effort it took to make changes and updates to CDnow's site. The company used redundant data storage systems, multiple servers, and multiple dedicated Internet connections to maintain round-the-clock operations.

In years past, CDnow's pioneering use of technology had proved a key element in its climb into the ranks of leading online music retailers. CDnow's Web site employed such popular online shopping features as shopping cart software, buy-Web links, intelligent album recommendations, and RealAudio samples.[16] Picking up on the popularity of personalized services among Internet users, CDnow had developed My CDnow and Album Advisor as service features to help visitors find the music selections they liked. CDnow's Jason Olim said, "My CDnow is the most important innovation since

---

[16]Brett Atwood, "Music Site Masters Get Cosmic Credit," *Billboard,* April 19, 1997, p. 81.

my brother and I launched the store four years ago. This ground-breaking tool enables each of our customers to create their own music store."[17] My CDnow features included a Wish List, which allowed customers to keep a list of music products for future visits, a Gift Registry and a personal music consultant through Recommends and Favorite Artists. This service kept customers in touch with their favorite artists and provided features such as a music rating system and a personal order history.

Album Advisor asked customers to name three artists they liked or were interested in; it then made recommendations based on which albums by these artists had been bought the most frequently by other CDnow customers. Customers could then listen to RealAudio clips of selections from the recommended albums. Research indicated that people were 82 percent more likely to purchase music online if they were first able to hear a selection or two from an album.[18] According to CDnow's vice president of technology and creative services, "Intelligent recommendations are critical for operating a virtual store that combines content and commerce. Customers are getting better judgment from artificial intelligence than they would from the human intelligence of most clerks at a retail store."[19]

CDnow's Affiliate Program

To encourage grassroots Web sites to sell CDnow merchandise and provide a link to CDnow, management had come up with an incentive program it called Cosmic Credit. Through this plan, CDnow reached out to those Web sites that were developed by independent artists and musicians and fan sites devoted to particular music artists. Since inception of the program, 230,000 Web sites had agreed to participate and were provided with embedded hyperlinks through which potential customers could be immediately connected to the CDnow site; 85,000 new Web sites had been added as participants during 1999. CDnow's goal for this program was to build a community among fan sites. Member sites received commissions in store credit or cash based on the dollar purchases made by people using the link. The credit incentives ranged from 7 to 15 percent, and member sites could opt for quarterly cash payments when they accumulated credits of $100 or more; there were also monthly bonuses for sites that generated the highest volumes of sales. The 230,000 affiliate sites were a significant source of traffic and new customers for CDnow.

Sales and Marketing Strategies

In addition to the strategic alliances and marketing agreements described earlier, CDnow used "co-marketing advertising" to help build brand awareness and drive traffic to its Web site. In January 2000, for example, CDnow joined with Pizza Hut in an integrated promotion whereby Pizza Hut customers who purchased a Big New Yorker Pizza received an access code to make their own custom CD at www.cdnow.com. The promotion was advertised via signs and placards in participating Pizza Huts, radio spots, and network TV commercials that aired in January and February (including one Super Bowl spot in January). The success of this promotion was a big factor in the record high traffic at CDnow's site in February 2000. Management planned to continue its use of such promotions.

---

[17]"CDnow Breaks New Ground for Online Shopping with Personalization Technology."

[18]"Internet Audio Clips Bolster Online Sales," *Music Week,* September 19, 1998, p. 10.

[19]Lynda Radosevich, "AI Wises Up," *InfoWorld,* August 3, 1998, p. 60.

Another marketing strategy was the use of personalized e-mails to target prospective and existing customers with messages and special promotions. The e-mails contained such information as purchase recommendations based on the customer's indicated interests and prior purchases, information concerning new releases, and announcements of special merchandise promotions. Directed e-mails were sent to visitors who had registered at CDnow's site but had not yet made a purchase and to previous buyers who had not made a recent purchase.

Customer Service

CDnow management believed that attentive customer service was critical to retaining and expanding its customer base. Customer service representatives were available 24 hours a day, seven days a week to provide assistance via e-mail, phone, or fax. Customer service representatives handled questions about orders, took credit card information over the phone, and helped customers find music titles. The company strived to answer all e-mails within 24 hours. It had 140 customer service representatives. CDnow offered seven foreign language versions of its Web site (in addition to English) that contained translations of account registration and ordering instructions. It supported its international sales efforts with customer service representatives fluent in nine languages.

Growth and Expansion Strategies

CDnow was aggressively attempting to grow sales and strengthen its competitive presence by expanding into foreign markets, diversifying its product line, and making new acquisitions.

CDnow Europe CDnow was boosting its presence in the European market as fast as resources permitted. A European warehouse was being opened to handle order fulfillment for consumers in Europe and the Middle East. CDnow expected this move to lower shipping costs and reduce delivery delays to buyers in 37 countries in Europe and the Middle East. To broaden its appeal to foreign buyers, CDnow had added 100,000 international selections to its product offerings and opened a multilingual customer service center. Jason Olim explained, "CDnow is building a better music store for our European and Middle Eastern customers, who can now enjoy one-stop shopping for local and U.S. product which is shipped from a centralized location."[20] International sales accounted for 20 percent of CDnow's total revenue in 1999.

To give it better exposure to European users of the Internet, in 1998 CDnow entered into a promotional arrangement with search engine Lycos Bertelsmann in what was claimed to be Europe's biggest e-commerce deal to date. Jason Olim saw the agreement as key to CDnow's European strategy: "This deal initiates CDnow's international marketing efforts. In Europe, we needed a company that would enable us to target each country."[21] The agreement called for CDnow to become the exclusive music retailer for Lycos Bertelsmann in 11 European countries including Britain, France, Germany, Italy, Spain, Switzerland, and the Benelux countries. (The fees CDnow paid Lycos Bertelsmann for the exclusive promotional arrangement were not fully disclosed.) The Internet exposure that CDnow received in Europe as a result of its agreement with Bertelsmann paved the way for CDnow to sell CDs in Britain at U.S. prices, providing customers a saving of up to 50 percent on recommended retail prices for

[20]"CDnow Announces Launch of CDnow Europe," CDnow press release, August 17, 1998.

[21]"U.S. CD Firm Nets Online Deal for European Outlet," *Marketing,* April 16, 1998, p. 8.

CDs in Britain. CDnow was featured on all Lycos sites in Europe and potential customers were delivered to CDnow's Web site through banner ads, links, and Keyword Interactive Text Insertion software.

To further strengthen its ability to attract foreign customers, CDnow contracted with Yahoo! to be the premier music retailer of many of Yahoo's World Sites. CDnow was featured on Yahoo UK, New Zealand, Korea, Singapore, Yahoo Chinese, Yahoo en Español, and Yahoo's Chinese- and Spanish-language Web guides. The agreement expanded CDnow's previous agreement with Yahoo! that made CDnow the exclusive music retailer on Yahoo's main directory in the United States.

Product Line Expansion   To broaden its appeal to site visitors, CDnow began selling movies and music videos in both VHS and DVD formats in December 1999. It also began merchandising T-shirts and music accessories. From time to time, the company ran special promotions of audio and video equipment, such as DVD players and CD recorders. Management expected to continue to widen the range of the company's product offerings.

Acquisition of SuperSonic Boom   In early 1999, CDnow acquired superSonic Boom, the first company to offer custom CDs on the Internet. SuperSonic Boom offered 12,000 titles in its catalog and had over 60,000 titles licensed. Customers could make selections from the company's collection of recordings, choose the playing sequence, create an album title, and build custom CDs. CDnow management believed superSonic's technological capabilities in custom CDs represented a valuable way to enhance and differentiate the company's product lineup. Jason Olim explained, "SuperSonic Boom provides us with a talented management team and custom digital capabilities that will significantly expand the level of personalization in the CDnow shopping experience. We believe this technology empowers our customers to create unique products for gifts, as well as their own listening pleasure."[22]

Merger with N2K, Inc.   In 1998, CDnow merged with its largest competitor, N2K, which operated an online music store called Music Boulevard. At the time, this move created the industry's largest e-commerce site devoted to music and music-related products and the third largest online retailer in terms of sales revenues.[23] Jon Diamond, cofounder and vice chairman of N2K, commented:

> The merger of CDnow and N2K unites the two leading brands in online music, creating the most powerful franchise in our marketplace, and one of the clear leaders among Internet companies. Our respective companies are coming together at a uniquely opportune time, having already made the necessary investments to develop solid technology platforms, key alliances, and organizations of talented executives and relationships of trust with music consumers. This is a "win/win" providing customers with a truly superior music experience online and enhancing the value of the companies.

As part of the merger arrangement, a new publicly traded company, also called CDnow, Inc., was formed. Existing CDnow shareholders received 1.0 shares of common stock in the new company for each share they owned, and N2K existing shareholders received 0.83 shares in the new company. Jon Diamond, N2K's CEO, became chairman of CDnow's board of directors.

The merger gave the new CDnow the largest selection of music items available anywhere, combined the two original companies' musical expertise, and gave the new company a broader Internet presence. N2K had specialized in classical, jazz, and country

---

[22]"CDnow Acquires superSonic Boom," CDnow press release.

[23]"N2K Inc. and CDnow, Inc., Announce Merger Plans," CDnow press release, October 23, 1998.

exhibit 12 Amazon.com Music Store Features Added in 1999

Free digital downloads that enable customers to try before they buy
Amazon.com's Music Store dedicated an area of its store to free, full-length song downloads from established artists, major-label performers, and independent artists.

Expanded selection of music from independent artists unavailable in most stores
Customers could find thousands of noteworthy CDs by independent artists and labels. With these features, customers could easily explore and discover great new music from independent artists in any genre.

Classical music center
No other music store—physical or online—offered classical music experts and novices a greater selection of classical music or more ways to discover excellent classical recordings.

Information on new titles—before they are released
At Amazon.com, customers could order CDs before they were released and receive them on the day of release.

Source: Adapted from "No. 1 Online Music Retailer Amazon.com," Amazon.com press release, February 2, 2000.

music, while CDnow had previously specialized in rock and pop music. In the years leading up to the merger, the two companies had been battling for market share. Additionally, it created opportunities for cost reductions and new efficiencies. A major benefit of the merger, from CDnow's perspective, was the $27.8 million in cash that N2K had at the time of the merger. Without this cash, CDnow would have had a negative cash balance at the end of 1999 (see again exhibit 3).

However, a major driver of the merger was the need to counter Amazon.com's entry into the online music segment. Amazon became a major player in the online music industry overnight. Although it began selling music only in June 1998, Amazon's revenues from music product sales in the fourth quarter of 1998 totaled $50 million (CDnow's revenues totaled $56 million for all of 1998).[24] Amazon.com's instant success was attributed to its strong brand-name recognition among Internet users, the size and makeup of its customer base, and the fact that many buyers of books were also buyers of music—at Amazon, they could now purchase both.

AMAZON.COM

Amazon began operations on the Web in July 1995 as a bookstore. However, by the beginning of 2000, Amazon had diversified its product offerings to include more than 18 million unique items in such categories as books, CDs, toys, electronics, videos, DVDs, home improvement products, software, and video games. Amazon's strategy was to become a dominant online retailer by continually adding new product categories. Amazon.com, considered the "number one place to save money on the Internet," had more than 1 million registered users. Amazon's strategic vision was to be the premier "customer-centric company, where customers could find and discover anything they may want to buy online."[25] Amazon offered basically the same customer service and ease-of-use features as CDnow and was willing to match any new features that CDnow developed (see Exhibit 12). Amazon also invested heavily in a network of

---

[24]Richard Tedesco, "Amazon Gets More Tuneful," *Broadcasting & Cable,* June 14, 1999, p. 108.

[25]"Amazon.com Announces Profitability in U.S.-based Book Sales," Amazon.com press release, February 2, 2000.

company-owned warehousing and distribution centers to reduce its dependence on ful-fillment houses.

CDNOW'S MERGER WITH COLUMBIA HOUSE

On July 13, 1999, CDnow reached an agreement with Time Warner and Sony Corporation to merge their jointly owned Columbia House with CDnow to form a new company by the first quarter of 2000. Scott Flanders, formerly CEO of wireless products vendor Telestreet.com, was designated to serve as CEO of the new company.[26] According to terms of the merger agreement, Sony and Time Warner would each own 37 percent of the new company and CDnow shareholders would own the remaining 26 percent.

The plan was for CDnow to continue as an online music retailer with a wider product selection and for Columbia House to continue to operate as a membership-based club. The merger offered significant advantages for all parties involved. CDnow would receive financial backing and cheaper access to prerecorded music products marketed by Sony and Time Warner, plus it would gain access to Columbia House's database of 16 million active music customers and 45 years of direct marketing experience. Sony and Time Warner would gain a solid foothold in online music sales and an online vehicle for selling music via digital downloading. Also, the new company would be able to negotiate promotion and marketing arrangements with Time Warner's Warner Music Group and other media holdings.

An Unexpected Turn of Events

On March 13, 2000, CDnow, Time Warner Inc., and Sony Corporation abruptly announced cancellation of their merger plans, raising questions about the immediate future of both CDnow and Columbia House. The merger died because of a sharper-than-expected decline in Columbia House's performance since early fall 1999. According to Jason Olim, the merger fell apart because Columbia House's projections for 2000 were lower than expected; a major motivation for the merger from CDnow's perspective was that Columbia House's cash flows would support CDnow's growth and expansion until it reached profitability. Olim indicated that the latest Columbia House projections showed its cash flows would be insufficient to support CDnow, plus it had a higher debt load than CDnow executives had anticipated. While Time Warner officials admitted that Columbia House's 1999 results were below expectations and thus a major factor in the merger abandonment, they noted that CDnow's results were also weaker than expected and that a main reason for calling the merger off was the difficulty of gaining Federal Trade Commission approval for the merger. Another complicating factor was said to be the pending merger of America Online and Time Warner.

As part of the merger termination agreement, Time Warner and Sony agreed to invest $21 million in CDnow through the purchase of 2.4 million additional shares of CDnow's common stock and to convert an existing $30 million loan commitment to CDnow into long-term convertible debt. Jason Olim indicated that only half of the loan had been used, giving the company a net infusion of $36 million in new capital in addition to the company's existing cash balance.

---

[26]Ed Christman, "CDnow/Col. House Co. Takes Shape," *Billboard,* October 2, 1999, p. 12.

As part of its announcement of the merger termination, CDnow said that it had retained Allen & Company, an investment bank, to explore its strategic options. Nancy Peretsman, an Allen & Company executive, said, "Based on CDnow's position in the marketplace, Allen & Company is very optimistic about finding interest in attractive strategic transactions."[27] CDnow also announced that the company's operating goals for 2000 included significant reduction of operating expenses by lowering marketing expenses. However, the company said it did not plan any layoffs of personnel.

During the next several days, CDnow's stock price dropped from around $9 per share to trade in the $3 to $4 range. In the company's 1999 annual report, released March 29, 2000, Arthur Andersen, the company's auditor, expressed "substantial doubt" about the company's ability to stay in business due to a shortage of working capital, losses from operations, and significant payments due in 2000 for its marketing agreements with Internet portals and other allies. However, company officials stated that CDnow had cash and other sources of liquidity totaling $40 million and that it had sufficient cash flows to meet its obligations through September 2000. Jason Olim said,

> Our business is one that is fundable. We are confident we will be able to close a strategic transaction with a strategic investor in the next few months that will give the company the liquidity to get through to profitability.

There was considerable speculation as to who might be interested in partnering with, acquiring, or merging with CDnow. One potential was to find a music retailer that did not have significant online retailing operations, such as Musicland or Trans World Entertainment Corp., whose chains included Camelot Music and The Wall. Another possibility was Viacom, the owner of MTV and VH1, which already had a relationship with CDnow.

---

[27]"CDnow Retains Allen & Company to Explore Strategic Options," CDnow press release, March 13, 2000.

case 13 Callaway Golf Company

John E. Gamble
University of South Alabama

As Ely Callaway walked through the sea of drivers, irons, putters, golf apparel, golf bags, and training devices displayed at the 2000 PGA Merchandise Show in Orlando, Florida, and toward Callaway Golf Company's booth, he noted that the eyes cast toward him seemed to express a greater sense of anticipation and curiosity than usual. As one of the most recognizable figures in the golf equipment industry, he had grown accustomed to his celebrity status among the golfing world and was aware that both rivals and retailers alike anxiously awaited the new products his company typically launched at the industry's premier annual trade show. However, the drama and suspense surrounding Callaway's new products at the February 2000 show were very different from usual. Callaway had gone ahead and introduced its innovative Big Bertha X-14 irons and Big Bertha Steelhead Plus metal woods in January. The PGA Merchandise Show had been saved for the introduction of the company's highly touted and much-anticipated Callaway golf ball.

Callaway Golf Company had become the leader in the golf equipment industry by developing technologically advanced golf clubs that compensated for the poor swing characteristics of most amateur golfers. During a golf swing, the clubhead travels in an arc around the golfer's body, making contact with the ball for 300 to 500 milliseconds. During this very brief period of contact, inertia is transferred from the clubhead to the ball, and the ball is propelled forward at a speed of up to 150 miles per hour. There are an infinite number of variations in a golfer's swing that can alter the swing path, causing the clubhead to strike the ball not squarely but somewhat off-center, at an angle. The more that a golfer's swing path deviates from square contact with the ball, the greater the loss of accuracy and distance. A golfer loses approximately 12.5 yards of distance for every millimeter that the ball is struck off the clubhead's center.

Ely Callaway, the founder of Callaway Golf Company, understood the importance of the physics of golf, so much so that he made the phrase, "You can't argue with physics," an early company slogan. Callaway Golf revolutionized the golf industry in 1990 by introducing an oversized clubhead called the Big Bertha that was more forgiving of golfers' swing imperfections. A Callaway executive stated in a 1995 *Fortune* interview that the company's objective was to design a club that would allow golfers to "miss [the center of the clubhead] by an inch" and still achieve distance and accuracy.

The company's high-tech golf clubs became so popular with golfers in the 1990s that Callaway Golf's revenues and profits grew by 1,239 percent and 1,907 percent, respectively, between 1991 and year-end 1996. With the company's competitive position securely rooted and a line of innovative new clubs ready for a 1997 launch, Ely Callaway retired as CEO in mid-1996 and turned to Callaway Golf Company president Donald Dye to become the new CEO. Soon after Ely Callaway's retirement, Callaway Golf Company's fortunes reversed due to a variety of factors, including the Asian financial crisis, poor global weather conditions, strategic miscues on the part of Callaway's executives, and the introduction of innovative clubs by rivals. The reversal led to nearly an 18 percent sales decline in 1998. Callaway Golf also broke its string of 24 consecutive quarters of growth in net income in early 1998 and went on to record a net loss of $26.5 million for the entire 1998 fiscal year.

Ely Callaway returned as CEO in November 1998 to launch a vast turnaround effort that included the development of new models of golf clubs and a $54.2 million restructuring program, which brought a number of operational improvements and cost-reduction initiatives. Callaway Golf Company returned to profitability and recaptured a great deal of its lost market share in 1999, but on February 4, 2000, the entire golf industry watched intently as Ely Callaway launched the company's new Rule 35 golf ball. Callaway's entry into the golf ball market had been vigilantly anticipated since mid-1996 when Ely Callaway announced the formation of the Callaway Golf Ball Company, and was considered by many industry participants to be the biggest event in the golf equipment industry since the debut of the Big Bertha. Callaway's managers and investors expected the entry to become a catalyst for the company's future growth. Exhibit 1 presents a summary of Callaway Golf Company's financial performance between 1989 and 1999.

COMPANY HISTORY

When Ely (rhymes with *feely*) Reeves Callaway Jr. graduated from Emory University in Atlanta, his father said, "Don't go to work for the family."[1] Ely Callaway Sr. and almost everyone else in La Grange, Georgia, worked for the younger Callaway's uncle, Fuller Callaway. Fuller Callaway owned a number of farms, 23 cotton mills, the local bank, and the local department store. Heeding his father's advice, Ely Callaway Jr. decided to join the army just prior to World War II. By the age of 24, he had achieved the rank of major and had become one of the army's top five procurement officers responsible for purchasing cotton clothing for the U.S. armed forces. At the peak of World War II, Callaway's apparel procurement division of the U.S. Army purchased 70 percent of all cotton clothing manufactured by the U.S. apparel industry.

After the war, Callaway was hired as a sales representative with textile manufacturer Deering, Millikin & Company. He rose quickly through the company's ranks by selling textiles to the manufacturers from which he had purchased apparel while in the Army. Callaway was later hired away from Deering, Millikin by Textron, which subsequently sold its textile business to Burlington Industries—at that time the largest textile manufacturer in the world. Ely Callaway was promoted to president and director of Burlington Industries, but he left the company in 1973 after losing a bid to become its chief executive officer.

Callaway had long believed that Burlington Industries' success was a result of its ability to provide customers with unique, superior-quality products. When Callaway left Burlington and the textile industry, he decided to launch his own business founded on that same philosophy. In 1974 he established Callaway Vineyard and Winery outside of

---

[1]*Inc.*, December 1994, p. 62.

exhibit 1 Callaway Golf Company, Financial Summary, 1989–96 (In thousands, except per share amounts)

	1999	1998	1997	1996	1995	1994	1993	1992	1991	1990	1989
Net sales	$714,471	$697,621	$842,927	$678,512	$553,287	$448,729	$254,645	$132,058	$54,753	$21,518	$10,380
Pretax income	$85,497	($38,899)	$213,765	$195,595	$158,401	$129,405	$69,600	$33,175	$10,771	$2,185	$329
Estimated ranking within industry—sales	1st	1st	1st	1st	1st	1st	1st	2nd	6th	14th	23rd
Pretax income as a percent of sales	12%	–6%	25%	29%	29%	29%	27%	25%	20%	10%	3%
Net income	$55,322	($25,564)	$132,704	$122,337	$97,736	$78,022	$42,862[a]	$19,280	$6,416	$1,842	$329
Net income as a percent of sales	8%	–4%	16%	18%	18%	17%	17%[a]	15%	12%	9%	3%
Fully diluted earnings per share[c]	$0.78	($0.38)	$1.85	$1.73	$1.40	$1.07	$0.62	$0.32	$0.11	$0.04	$0.01
Shareholders' equity	$499,934	$453,096	$481,425	$362,267	$224,934	$186,414	$116,577	$49,750	$15,227	$8,718	$6,424
Market capitalization at Dec. 31	$1,349,595	$769,725	$2,120,813	$2,094,588	$1,604,741	$1,127,823	$901,910	$245,254	—[b]	—[b]	—[b]

[a]Includes cumulative effect of an accounting change of $1,658,000.

[b]The company's stock was not publicly traded until February 1992.

[c]Adjusted for all stock splits through February 10, 1995, not adjusted for February 10, 1995, stock split.

Source: Callaway Golf Company annual reports.

San Diego. The well-known northern California vineyards scoffed at Callaway's entry into the industry and predicted a rapid failure of the venture. Not only did Callaway have no experience running a winery but, additionally, no vineyard had ever been successful in the San Diego area. Ely Callaway understood the risks involved and was much better prepared to run a start-up vineyard than skeptics believed. He began by transplanting the very best grape vines from Italy to California and hired winemaking experts to manage the day-to-day operations of the vineyard. Callaway's strategy was to focus on a narrow segment of the wine market where competition with the established wineries was not as strong and barriers to entry were relatively low. Callaway Vineyard and Winery limited distribution of its products to exclusive restaurants that chose to stock only the highest-quality wines. The company made no attempt to distribute its high-quality wines through traditional retail channels. In 1981, Ely Callaway sold the company to Hiram Walker & Sons, Inc., for a $14 million profit.

In late 1982, Ely Callaway decided to enter the golf club industry and, once again, apply his concept of "providing a product that is demonstrably superior to what's available in significant ways and, most importantly, pleasingly different."[2] Callaway purchased Hickory Stick USA, a manufacturer and marketer of replicas of old-fashioned hickory-shafted clubs, for $400,000. From the outset, Callaway grasped the limitations of the company's hickory-shafted product line and realized that the company would have to extend its offerings beyond replicas of antique golf clubs to provide an acceptable return on his investment.

Callaway noticed that most golf equipment had changed very little since the 1920s and believed that many golfers would purchase technologically advanced golf equipment if it would improve their game. Ely Callaway and Richard C. Helmstetter—Callaway Golf's senior executive vice president and chief club designer—put together a team of five aerospace and metallurgical engineers to develop the S2H2 (short, straight, hollow hosel) line of irons. The S2H2 line was introduced in 1988 and was well received by golfers. The following year the company introduced S2H2 traditional-sized metal woods, and in 1990 it introduced the Big Bertha driver—named after the World War I German long-distance cannon. The Big Bertha was revolutionary in that it was much larger than conventional woods and lacked a hosel so that the weight could be better distributed throughout the clubhead. This innovative design gave the clubhead a larger sweet spot, which allowed a player to mis-hit or strike the golf ball off-center of the clubhead and not suffer much loss of distance or accuracy. By 1992 Big Bertha drivers were number one on the Senior PGA, the LPGA, and Hogan Tours. Callaway Golf Company became a public company on February 28, 1992. By year-end 1992 its annual revenues had doubled to $132 million, and by 1996 Callaway Golf had become the world's largest manufacturer and marketer of golf clubs, with annual sales of more than $678 million.

Ely Callaway's 1996 Retirement and the Formation of the Callaway Golf Ball Company

Callaway Golf continued to lead the golf equipment industry through the mid-1990s with innovative new lines of clubs. The company also introduced a line of golf apparel in 1996 that was available to golfers through an exclusive licensing agreement with Nordstrom. In May 1996, Ely Callaway announced that even though he would remain

---

[2]*Business Week,* September 16, 1991, p. 71.

involved in the promotion of the Callaway Golf products, he was transferring his position as chief executive officer to the company's president, Donald Dye. Dye had been a business associate of Ely Callaway since 1974, when Callaway was in the wine business. Ely Callaway simultaneously announced that he and Charles Yash, Taylor Made Golf Company's CEO and president, would launch Callaway Golf Ball Company as a subsidiary of Callaway Golf. "We believe that there is a good and reasonable opportunity for Callaway Golf Ball Company, in due time, to create, produce and merchandise a golf ball that will be demonstrably superior to, and pleasingly different from, any other golf ball we know of," said Callaway.[3] Yash, who had been the general manager of Spalding's golf ball business and who turned around Taylor Made with the introduction of the Burner Bubble driver, resigned his post at Taylor Made to become president and CEO of the new venture. Upon announcing his decision to work with Callaway, Yash commented, "This is an exciting and most unusual opportunity to develop a new and important golf ball franchise with Ely Callaway for Callaway Golf Company. As a competitor, I have been in awe of Callaway's accomplishments. As his partner, I look forward to the exciting opportunities and challenges Ely and I are sure to find in this new venture."[4]

Callaway Golf Company's 1998 Performance and the Return of Ely Callaway as CEO

A variety of events occurred shortly after Ely Callaway's retirement that resulted in Callaway Golf's loss of market share in fairway woods and its poor financial and market performance in 1998. The U.S. and international markets for golf clubs moved from rapid growth to maturity during 1997 and 1998 after a large percentage of avid golfers purchased titanium drivers and saw little reason to upgrade again until dramatic innovations were available. Global market maturity was compounded by the Asian financial crisis that began in late 1997 and made the export of U.S.-made products, especially expensive luxury goods like Callaway golf clubs, unaffordable for many Asians. Also, heavy global rainfall caused by El Niño contributed to an overall decline in the number of rounds played around the world in 1998. In addition, many club manufacturers believed that the United States Golf Association's (USGA) discussions during 1998 to limit innovations in golf club design caused many golfers to postpone club purchases. The USGA had considered a number of limitations on club design, but ultimately decided to bar only a "spring-like effect" in golf clubs. The USGA advised Callaway Golf that none of its products violated the new regulation.

The emergence of shallow-faced fairway woods had as much to do with Callaway's downturn as any other single event. Callaway had dominated the market for fairway woods since the early 1990s, when the Big Bertha line gained in popularity. By 1996 no other manufacturer came close to Callaway in building a loyal following among fairway woods customers. Even when Callaway users experimented with a rival's new driver, they frequently stayed with Callaway for their fairway woods. However, Callaway's dominance in fairway woods was severely challenged in 1997 when relatively unknown golf manufacturers Adams Golf and Orlimar Golf each heavily

---

[3]"Donald H. Dye Given CEO Duties at Callaway Golf Company." *Two-Ten Communications, Ltd.,* 1996. www.twoten.press.net:80/stories/96/05/13/headlines/appointments_callaway.html, February 6, 1997.

[4]"Keeping His Eye On the Ball," *ParValu Stock Update,* 1996. www.golfweb.com:80/gi/parvalu/updates/03.html, February 6, 1997.

promoted a line of shallow-faced fairway woods that they claimed made it easier for golfers to hit a ball off the fairway or from a poor lie. The two challengers each ran a series of highly successful infomercials that demonstrated the clubs' performance and led to phenomenal sales growth for both companies. Adams' and Orlimar's success came more or less directly at the expense of Callaway. No other golf club manufacturer sold large volumes of fairway woods, so when golfers purchased the new clubs offered by Adams and Orlimar, it was typically Callaway that lost sales and market share.

Callaway CEO Donald Dye took much of the blame for Callaway's failure to predict the popularity of shallow-faced woods and was also ultimately responsible for initiatives that took management's focus off of golf clubs. Under Dye, Callaway Golf began new ventures in golf course and driving range management, opened interactive golf sites, created a new player development project, and launched a golf publishing business with Nicholas Callaway, the youngest son of Ely Callaway and a successful publisher of tabletop books. After a record year in 1997, the company's financial and market performance suffered immensely during 1998. In October 1998, Donald Dye resigned as Callaway's CEO and Ely Callaway returned to rebuild the company.

Ely Callaway's first efforts on his return to active management at Callaway Golf were to "direct [the company's] resources—talent, energy, and money—in an ever-increasing degree toward the creation, design, production, sale and service of new and better products."[5] As part of his turnaround strategy, Ely Callaway also initiated a $54.2 million restructuring program that involved a number of cost-reduction actions and operational improvements. During 1997 and 1998 the company had built up a large inventory of older model clubs that were not sold before the latest clubs were shipped to retailers. Callaway management liquidated the inventory of older generation clubs to generate cash flow and improve the company's financial position. In addition, the company divested its interest in noncore businesses began under Dye and combined the administrative and manufacturing functions of Odyssey Golf and Callaway Golf. Callaway's business restructuring eliminated a variety of job responsibilities and thus resulted in the loss of 750 positions from all functional areas of the company. Callaway Golf Company's income statements for 1993 through 1999 are presented in Exhibit 2. Exhibit 3 presents the company's balance sheets for 1993–99. The company's market performance is graphed in Exhibit 4.

THE GOLF EQUIPMENT INDUSTRY

In 1999, more than 26 million Americans played golf. Of these, 5.4 million were considered avid golfers, playing more than 25 rounds of golf annually. The number of U.S. golfers was expected to grow 1 to 2 percent annually through 2010 as the baby boom generation aged and had more free time and disposable income. In 1999 the typical golfer was a 39-year-old male with a household income of $66,000 who played golf about twice a month. Many women, juniors, and senior citizens also enjoyed the sport. In 1999 there were 5.7 million women and 2.1 million junior golfers aged 12 to 17 in the United States. Seniors accounted for 25 percent of all U.S. golfers in 1999. The average golf score was 97 for men and 114 for women. Only 6 percent of men and 1 percent of women golfers regularly broke a score of 80. Exhibit 5 provides the number of U.S. golfers during various years between 1986 and 1999.

---

[5]Callaway Golf Company 1998 annual report.

exhibit 2   Callaway Golf Company, Income Statements, 1993–99 ($000, except per share amounts)

	1999	1998	1997	1996	1995	1994	1993
Net sales	$714,471	$697,621	$842,927	$678,512	$553,287	$448,729	$254,645
Cost of goods sold	376,405	401,607	400,127	317,353	270,125	208,906	115,458
Gross profit	338,086	296,014	442,800	361,159	283,162	239,823	139,187
Selling, general, and administrative expenses	224,336	245,070	191,313	155,177	120,201	106,913	—
Research and development costs	34,002	36,848	30,298	16,154	8,577	6,380	3,653
Restructuring and transition costs	(181)	54,235	—	—	—	—	—
Litigation settlement	—	—	12,000	—	—	—	—
Income (loss) from operations	79,909	(40,139)	209,189	189,828	154,384	126,530	68,416
Interest & other income, net	9,182	3,911	4,586	5,804	4,038	2,879	1,184
Interest expense	(3,594)	(2,671)	(10)	(37)	(21)	(4)	—
Income before income taxes and cumulative effect of accounting change	85,497	(38,899)	213,765	195,595	158,401	129,405	69,600
Provision for income taxes (benefit)	30,175	(12,335)	81,061	73,258	60,665	51,383	28,396
Cumulative effect of accounting change	n/a	n/a	n/a	n/a	n/a	n/a	(1,658)
Net income	$55,322	($26,564)	$132,704	$122,337	$97,736	$78,022	$42,862
Primary earnings per share	$0.79	($0.38)	$1.94	$1.83	$1.47	$1.14	$0.62
Fully diluted earnings per share	$0.78	($0.38)	$1.85	$1.73	$1.40	$1.07	$0.60
Common equivalent shares	71,214	69,463	71,698	70,661	69,855	73,104	68,964

Source: Callaway Golf Company annual reports.

Golf was popular in developed countries worldwide—especially so in Asia, where there were over 3,500 courses and 16 million golfers. Most of Europe's 2 million-plus golfers resided in England, France, Germany, Scotland, Ireland, and Sweden. The sport was becoming popular in former Soviet-bloc countries—such as Croatia, Slovenia, the Czech Republic, Poland, and Russia—but was not expected to grow dramatically until the economies of those countries stabilized. Russia's first country club opened in Moscow in 1993; by 2000, it had 550 members, who had each paid a $28,000 membership fee for the privilege to play the Robert Trent Jones–designed course. However, only 70 of the club's members were Russian. Some teaching professionals working in Russia projected that there could be 100,000 golfers in Russia by 2025, but in 2000 there were fewer than 500 Russians who could be called avid golfers.

The wholesale value of golf equipment sales in the United States had increased from $740 million in 1986 to over $2.7 billion in 1999. In 1999 the U.S. market for golf balls accounted for about 25 percent of the industry's wholesale sales. The wholesale

exhibit 3   Callaway Golf Company, Balance Sheets, 1993–99 ($000)

	1999	1998	1997	1996	1995	1994	1993
Assets							
Current assets							
Cash and cash equivalents	$112,602	$ 45,618	$ 26,204	$108,457	$ 59,157	$ 54,356	$ 48,996
Accounts receivable, net	54,525	73,466	124,470	74,477	73,906	30,052	17,546
Inventories, net	97,938	149,192	97,094	98,333	51,584	74,151	29,029
Deferred taxes	32,558	51,029	23,810	25,948	22,688	25,596	13,859
Other current assets	13,122	4,310	10,208	4,298	2,370	3,235	2,036
Total current assets	310,472	323,606	281,786	311,513	209,705	187,390	111,466
Property, plant, and equipment, net	142,214	172,794	142,503	91,346	69,034	50,619	30,661
Other assets	120,143	127,779	112,141	25,569	11,236	5,613	2,233
Total assets	$616,783	$665,827	$561,714	$428,428	$289,975	$243,622	$144,360
Liabilities and shareholders' equity							
Current liabilities							
Accounts payable and accrued expenses	$ 46,664	$ 35,928	$ 30,063	$ 14,996	$ 26,894	$ 17,678	$ 11,949
Accrued employee compensation and benefits	21,126	11,083	14,262	16,195	10,680	9,364	6,104
Accrued warranty expense	36,105	35,815	28,059	27,303	23,769	18,182	9,730
Accrued restructuring cost	1,379	7,389	—	—	—	—	—
Income taxes payable	—	9,903	—	2,558	1,491	11,374	n/a
Total current liabilities	105,274	184,008	72,384	61,052	62,834	56,598	27,783
Long-term liabilities	11,575	18,823	7,905	5,109	2,207	610	n/a
Shareholders' equity							
Common stock	763	751	743	729	709	680	676
Paid-in-capital	307,329	258,015	337,403	278,669	214,846	75,022	60,398
Unearned compensation	(2,784)	(5,653)	(3,575)	(3,105)	(2,420)	(3,670)	(2,591)
Retained earnings	288,090	252,528	298,728	238,349	131,712	114,402	58,094
Less grantor stock trust*	(93,744)	(54,325)	(151,315)	(152,375)	(119,913)	—	—
Total shareholders' equity	499,934	453,096	481,425	362,267	224,934	186,414	116,577
Total liabilities and shareholders' equity	$616,783	$655,827	$561,714	$428,428	$289,975	$243,622	$144,360

*The sale of 5,300,000 shares to the grantor stock trust had no net impact to shareholders' equity. The shares in the GST may be used to fund the company's obligations with respect to one or more of the company's nonqualified employee benefit plans.

Source: Callaway Golf Company annual reports.

value of the international golf ball market was estimated at $1.5 billion. Exhibit 6 provides wholesale sporting goods equipment sales for selected years during the 1986–99 period. The growth in golf equipment sales during the early 1990s was attributable not so much to an increase in the number of golfers as to the introduction of technologically advanced equipment offered by Callaway Golf and other manufacturers like Ping and Taylor Made. Many of these technological advances made the game much easier for be-

exhibit 4 Monthly Performance of Callaway Golf Company's Stock Price, 1992–March 2000

(a) Trend in Callaway Golf Company's Common Stock Price

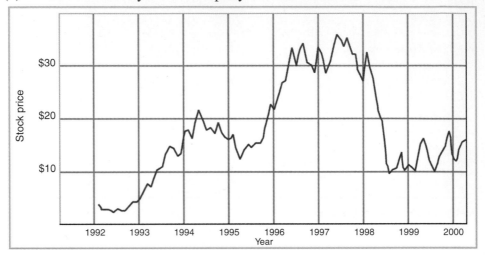

(b) Performance of Callaway Golf Company's Stock Price versus the S&P 500 Index

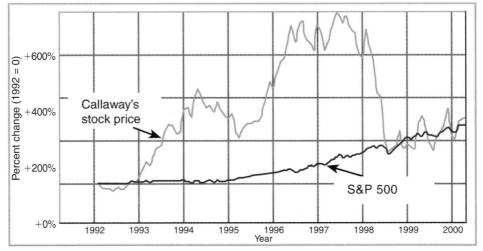

ginners to learn than was possible with older equipment. Additionally, experienced players frequently looked for equipment that could help them improve their game. However, it was expected that in the early 2000s the sales of golf equipment would grow only modestly since most avid golfers had already upgraded their equipment and were unlikely to do so again unless major new innovations came about.

Key Technological Innovations

The golfing industry had come up with four major innovations that made it easier for golfers to hit better shots and improve their scores: (1) perimeter weighting in the late

exhibit 5   Number of U.S. Golfers, 1986, 1991, 1993, 1995, 1997, 1999

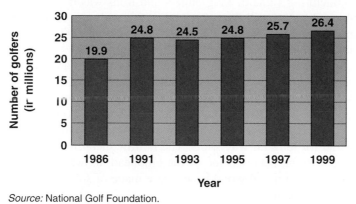

Source: National Golf Foundation.

exhibit 6   Wholesale Sales of Sporting Goods Equipment, 1986, 1993–99 (In Millions of Dollars)

Type of Equipment	1999*	1998	1997	1996	1995	1994	1993	1986
Exercise	$ 3,635	$ 3,400	$ 3,180	$ 2,890	$ 2,510	$ 1,825	$ 1,755	$ 680
Golf	2,770	2,800	2,749	2,463	2,130	1,793	1,490	740
Camping	1,700	1,620	1,590	1,500	1,508	1,275	1,225	580
Baseball/softball	340	340	338	350	349	348	328	240
Soccer	230	220	208	200	185	175	155	90
Tennis	220	215	235	240	235	259	380	255
Total sports equipment	$17,805	$17,350	$17,064	$16,395	$15,379	$13,877	$12,433	$8,250

*Estimated

Source: Sporting Goods Manufacturers Association, *1997–1999 State of the Industry Reports.*

1960s, (2) metal woods in the early 1980s, (3) graphite shafts in the late 1980s, and (4) oversized clubheads in the early 1990s. Perimeter weighting came about due to the poor putting of Karsten Solheim, a General Electric mechanical engineer, who took up golf at the age of 47 in 1954. Solheim designed a putter for himself that he found provided more "feel" when he struck the ball. Solheim moved much of the clubhead weight to the heel and toe, leaving a cavity at the rear and center of the club. Perimeter-weighted or cavity-back clubs had a larger "sweet spot" because of a higher moment of inertia or resistance to twisting. The resistance to twisting reduced the gear effect of the clubhead and resulted in straighter, longer shots with irons. In addition to perimeter weighting, Karsten Solheim also developed the investment-casting manufacturing process. This process allowed clubheads to be formed from molds, rather than forged from steel—the traditional manufacturing process.

Solheim made his putters by hand from 1959 until 1967, when he left GE and founded Karsten Manufacturing. By the 1970s, Karsten was manufacturing a full line of perimeter-weighted putters and irons that carried the Ping brand name. Solheim chose this name because of the sound the cavity-back clubhead made when it struck the ball. Karsten Manufacturing's line of Ping putters and irons was thought to be among the most technologically advanced throughout the 1980s and reigned as the market leader. Karsten Manufacturing was renamed Ping, Inc., in 1999. In 2000, over 95 percent of all irons and putters sold worldwide were perimeter-weighted.

Ping's investment-casting manufacturing process also made the manufacture of perimeter-weighted "metal woods" possible. Taylor Made designed the first metal wood which, like the perimeter-weighted irons, had the advantage of a larger sweet spot than traditional clubs. Although they actually had no wood components, metal woods were so named because it had been traditional to use wooden clubs for driving from the tee and for long fairway shots. The hollow metal head made it possible to move the weight to the heel and toe of the clubhead, as was done with perimeter-weighted irons. Conventional wood heads were made of solid persimmon and had a uniform weight distribution.

The characteristics of the golf club shaft affected a club's performance almost as much as the clubhead did. Distance and accuracy were largely a function of shaft characteristics. Weak or overly flexible shafts could torque as a result of the swinging action and the weight of the clubhead. The torquing of the shaft created a gear effect that resulted in a mis-hit golf ball. Additionally, the flex of the shaft had the ability to increase clubhead speed and improve accuracy. Shafts with greater flex at the tip or clubhead end were advantageous to high handicappers because they helped produce greater clubhead speed at the point of contact with the golf ball, caused the ball to have a higher trajectory, and promoted greater distance. Professional and low-handicap golfers preferred shafts that flexed a few inches higher or nearer the grip because a higher flex point produced added control of the shot.

Graphite shafts were introduced in 1969 by Shakespeare, but were not accepted by golfers because they flexed too much and overly dampened the feel of the club striking the ball. By the early 1990s, technological advances in graphite materials, shaft design, and production had eliminated the previous torsion problems, and graphite shafts quickly gained acceptance by both amateur and professional golfers. Shaft manufacturers were using aerospace technology to improve graphite shafts that had as many as 14 to 16 layers of composite materials (carbon fibers, Kevlar, boron, glass-fiber-reinforced epoxy resins, and synthetic fibers). In 1998, graphite shafts were used in 86 percent of drivers, 77 percent of fairway woods, and 46 percent of irons. Because of the higher prices commanded by graphite, the dollar volume of graphite shaft sales exceeded that of steel alloy shafts by a greater margin than the unit volume differential.

Callaway Golf was the first golf club manufacturer to actually increase the size of the hollow metal wood and make the size of the sweet spot bigger. The larger the clubhead, the bigger the sweet spot, but weight was the primary constraint in increasing clubhead size. If oversized clubheads were too heavy, golfers could not achieve as much speed as they could with lighter clubheads. Slower clubhead speeds resulted in shorter flight distances. The vice president of research and development for a golf club manufacturer described the challenge of trying to increase the size of metal wood clubheads as follows:

> The problem with a big driver is that you have to keep the total weight about the same as a normal-sized driver in order to give the same feel to the golfer. You can't build an overweight club or one that you can't swing at the same speed. A slightly bigger head pulls a little more drag through the air, but it's negligible. Making a bigger head is like blowing

bubble gum. You have the same amount of gum but you've got to make a bigger bubble, so the metal walls will be thinner.[6]

Companies experimented with a number of materials, including stainless steel, titanium, silicon aluminum carbide, and thermoplastics, to find a way of increasing clubhead size without adding weight to the clubhead or diminishing its structural integrity. By 1992, most manufacturers had discovered that titanium was the best material for oversized drivers because the material was 20 percent lighter and 40 percent stronger than stainless steel. By using titanium, club manufacturers were able to increase the size of oversized drivers by about 30 percent. A golf club design engineer explained why material selection was vital to the structural integrity of the clubhead:

> Keeping weight to a minimum is the single biggest aggravation. Once you have a shape you're comfortable with, the challenge is to design a driver that will meet your weight standards. Everybody wants to go bigger, bigger, and bigger in drivers, but as you go bigger, your wall gets thinner. You could make a driver three times the normal size, but it would be like tinfoil. It would fold up and crush on impact.[7]

During the late 1990s, innovators like Callaway Golf and Taylor Made began to use combinations of metals in the design of oversized metal woods and irons. In 1997 Callaway introduced a line of irons that were 85 percent titanium and 15 percent tungsten. A tungsten insert was placed directly at the center of the enlarged sweet spot of the titanium clubface to add weight to the portion of the clubhead that should actually strike the ball. The addition of tungsten to the clubhead concentrated 40 percent of the clubhead weight directly at the sweet spot and made it possible to create an oversized clubhead with a weight concentration designed to maximize the energy transfer from the clubhead to the ball. Taylor Made introduced tungsten-titanium oversized clubs shortly after Callaway's introduction of its tungsten-titanium Great Big Bertha irons. In 1998 Callaway and Taylor Made introduced tungsten-titanium woods and Orlimar boasted clubheads that were made from three different metals. Cleveland Golf introduced a four-metal oversized clubhead design in 1999. In 2000 all major golf club manufacturers had at least one oversized exotic metal driver with a graphite shaft in its product line.

Competitive Rivalry in the Golf Equipment Industry

For decades, the golf equipment industry had been dominated by Wilson Sporting Goods, MacGregor Golf, Inc., and Spalding Sporting Goods. All three companies were very conservative in their approach to new product development, sticking to lines of the standard steel-shafted, forged-steel clubs that had been popular since the 1920s. They were caught completely off guard by the success of companies like Ping, Taylor Made, and Callaway Golf. Amateur golfers readily accepted the technological advances offered by the new golf companies and the market shares of the established brands of the three traditional industry leaders quickly eroded. An executive for one of the new manufacturers stated that Wilson's inability to introduce innovative products of its own had resulted in the company's market share diminishing to a "rounding error."[8]

---

[6]*Machine Design,* April 23, 1992, p. 32.

[7]Ibid.

[8]*Fortune,* June 12, 1995, p. 110.

In the late 1980s as many as 20 manufacturers accounted for about 80 percent of all golf equipment sales, but by 1997 the industry had already consolidated to the point where 6 companies commanded over 80 percent of the market for golf equipment. It was estimated that, of the more than 350 manufacturers in existence, only those 6 were profitable. During the late 1990s industry consolidation stimulated attrition as many smaller club manufacturers exited the industry. Even though longtime industry partic- ipants like Wilson, MacGregor, and Spalding were still in business and had attempted to introduce technologically advanced lines of clubs, they had all largely failed in re- gaining lost market share.

Manufacturing   Most club makers' manufacturing activities were restricted to club assembly, since clubhead production was contracted out to investment casting houses and shafts and grips were usually purchased from third-party suppliers. Most golf club companies offered two to four general models of irons and woods built around proprietary heads that were internally developed. Each clubhead model line was equipped with shafts of varying flex that were either proprietary designs or standard models purchased from shaft manufacturers. Grip manufacturers such as Eaton/Golf Pride and Lamkin offered a number of models, but club manufacturers usually chose to purchase a limited variety of grips from a single source, since most golfers did not have strong preferences for one brand of grip over another. Some club manufacturers used custom grips bearing the company name and logo, while others used standard grips.

The brand and type of shaft had a relatively important influence over golfers' per- ceptions of club quality and performance. Most golfers had a strong preference for ei- ther steel or graphite and some preference for certain manufacturers. True Temper had one of the best reputations in steel shafts and had dominated that segment of the in- dustry ever since it introduced the steel shaft in 1924. Most club manufacturers pur- chased standard steel shafts from a sole supplier rather than developing proprietary steel shafts or using a multiple sourcing strategy.

As the 1990s progressed, a larger and larger percentage of golfers' preferences shifted to graphite shafts for both drivers and irons. Graphite shaft manufacturers could easily produce a broad line of shafts with varying degrees of flex at a number of flex- points. Many golfers were persuaded that the unique characteristics of graphite con- tributed to game improvement. Companies such as Aldila, United Sports Technologies, HST, Unifiber, and Graman USA were competent manufacturers of high-quality graphite shafts and had made it difficult for True Temper to build a dominant market share in the graphite segment as it had done in steel.

Some companies such as Callaway Golf independently designed their shafts, while others collaborated with shaft manufacturers to develop proprietary graphite shafts. Taylor Made's innovative "bubble shaft" was co-designed and manufactured by respected graphite shaft producer HST. Cobra Golf was the only golf manufacturer to vertically integrate into shaft production and produce 100 percent of its shafts in- house. Cobra Golf was acquired by American Brands (renamed Fortune Brands in 1998 when its cigarette business was divested), which also owned Foot-Joy (a leading maker of golf shoes) and Titleist (the maker of the most popular brand of golf balls and also a producer of golf clubs and other golf equipment). Cobra's golf club shaft facili- ties were used to produce a portion of the shafts needed for Fortune's Titleist golf clubs.

Marketing   As television networks aired increasing numbers of professional golf tournaments, endorsements by professional golfers started to play a major role in the marketing of golf equipment. The dollar volume of player endorsements was estimated to be three times greater than the projected total Professional Golfers Association (PGA) year 2000 prize money payout of $132 million.

Professional golfer endorsements had been instrumental in the success of some fledgling companies. In 1990, Cobra Golf offered Greg Norman shares of stock and Australian distribution rights to the new company's products in return for the golfer's use and endorsement of Cobra equipment. Norman accepted the offer and, after the company went public, sold 450,000 Cobra shares for $12 million. Norman received an additional $30 million from the sale of his remaining Cobra Golf shares when American Brands acquired Cobra in 1996. Norman's endorsement of Cobra golf clubs helped make Cobra Golf an almost immediately identifiable brand in the golf equipment industry and an attractive acquisition target. Fortune Brand's belief in endorsements led the company to offer Tiger Woods a $20 million five-year contract upon his professional debut in 1996 to endorse Titleist drivers, irons, and balls. Woods's endorsement of the company's newly designed lines of clubs resurrected the brand's presence in clubs, particularly so in woods, where its new 975D driver became one of the top-selling clubs of 1999. Prior to Woods's endorsement of Titleist clubs, the company was primarily thought of as a golf ball company.

Tiger Woods's entry into the PGA set a new standard for endorsement contracts— the $20 million Woods received in 1996 for endorsing Titleist golf clubs and balls was surpassed by the $40 million he received for endorsing Nike apparel and footwear for a five-year period. In 1999 Woods signed a five-year renewal with Nike for $90 million. Tiger Woods also signed a two-year, $10 to 15 million deal with Buick to appear in Buick ads and carry the Buick logo on his golf bag. Woods's five-year renewal with Titleist provided a $2 million annual fee to use Titleist balls and clubs in PGA tournaments; this contract was primarily a defensive measure for Fortune Brands since Woods's Nike and Buick contracts prevented him from appearing in Titleist advertisements or displaying the Titleist logo on his golf bag. Tiger Woods's success in landing large endorsement contracts had spilled over to other professional golfers to some degree, but in 2000 no other golfer had been able to garner contracts in the same range as those signed by Woods.

Most pro-line or high-quality golf equipment manufacturers distributed their products through on-course pro shops and a select number of off-course pro shops, such as Edwin Watts and Nevada Bob's. The off-course pro shops were quickly accounting for the largest portion of retail golf club sales because they carried a wider variety of brands and marketed more aggressively than on-course shops. Most on-course pro shops sold only to members and carried few clubs since their members purchased golf clubs less frequently than apparel and footwear. In 1997 on-course pro shops carried, on average, 4 brands of drivers, 4 brands of irons, and 6 brands of putters, while off-course pro shops carried, on average, 12 brands of drivers, 18 brands of irons, and 17 brands of putters.

Pro-line manufacturers chose to limit their channels of distribution to on-course and off-course pro shops because they believed that PGA professionals had the training necessary to properly match equipment to the customer. Manufacturers such as Taylor Made, Callaway, and Ping all provided the pro shops with inexpensive devices that gave an estimate of the golfer's swing characteristics. The pro could take the readings from these devices and then custom-fit the golfer with the proper clubs. Custom fitting could be done more precisely with more expensive, specialized computer equipment, but most pro shops had not invested in the new technology. The Sportech Swing Analyzer aided in custom fitting by recording 12 swing variables, such as clubhead speed and path, club face angle at impact, ball position, the golfer's weight distribution, ball flight pattern, and ball flight distance. The pro could use the fit data provided by the Swing Analyzer to select the appropriate club for the customer. Golf equipment manufacturers expected a larger percentage of golfers to demand more precise custom fitting from retailers in the future.

Pro shops generally chose to stock only pro-line equipment and did not carry less expensive, less technologically advanced equipment. Low-end manufacturers such as Spalding, MacGregor, and Dunlop sold their products mainly through discounters, mass merchandisers, and large sporting goods stores. These retailers had no custom-fitting capabilities and rarely had sales personnel who were knowledgeable about the performance features of the different brands and models of golf equipment carried in the store. The appeal of such retail outlets was low price, and they mainly attracted beginning golfers and occasional golfers who were unwilling to invest in more expensive equipment.

CALLAWAY GOLF COMPANY

Callaway Golf Company's competitive strategy was rooted in Ely Callaway's philosophy that true long-term success comes from innovative products that are "demonstrably superior to, and pleasingly different from" the products offered by industry rivals. Ely Callaway believed that due to the difficulty of the game of golf (there was tremendous room for variation in *each* swing of the club and for off-center contact with the ball), serious golfers would be willing to invest in high-quality, premium-priced equipment, like the Big Bertha driver and the titanium Great Big Bertha driver, if such clubs could improve their game by being more forgiving of a less-than-optimum swing. Since the introduction of Callaway's S2H2 line of irons in 1988, the company had sought to develop, manufacture, and market the most technologically advanced golf clubs available. In addition, Richard Helmstetter and his team of engineers sought quantum leaps in club performance, rather than incremental improvements, with each new line of clubs introduced by the company.

Callaway's "Demonstrably Superior and Pleasingly Different" Value Chain

Callaway Golf Company's ability to develop "demonstrably superior and pleasingly different" golf clubs was a result of activities performed by the company throughout its value chain. Callaway's differentiation was achieved through both its unique value chain and through its ability to out-execute its rivals where value chain similarities existed.

Product Development and the Helmstetter Test Center When Ely Callaway purchased Hickory Stick USA he believed strongly that developing "demonstrably superior and pleasingly different" golf clubs would be more closely related to the company's physics-oriented R&D than would a focus on cosmetics. Richard Helmstetter and his engineering team were critical to the execution of Callaway's competitive strategy. As of 2000 Callaway Golf had consistently outspent its rivals on R&D. In 1999 alone, the company spent $27 million on research and development related to its golf club business—more than most of its key rivals' combined R&D budgets. The company's R&D efforts allowed it to continually beat its competitors to the market with new innovations. Callaway's engineers developed the first oversize driver in

1990, were the first to make clubheads even larger by using titanium, and were the first to use a combination of materials (titanium and tungsten) in clubhead design.

Callaway Golf opened the Richard C. Helmstetter Test Center in 1994 to support its research and product development efforts. The test center was located about a mile from Callaway's main campus and included a laboratory and a golfing area. The test center laboratory was home to Helmstetter's engineers, who worked both on teams and individually to develop new models of clubheads and shafts. Callaway's products were designed on powerful workstations running computer-aided design (CAD) software similar to that used in the aerospace industry. The CAD software allowed engineers not only to design new clubheads and shafts but also to conduct aerodynamic and strength testing in a simulated environment. Actual physical models could be created from the computer-generated images through the use of numerically controlled systems. The center's "destruction and durability" laboratory used robots and air cannons to establish minimum thresholds of strength and durability for prototypes of new models of clubheads and shafts.

The club-fitting and specifications area of the test center used the company's Callaway Performance Analysis System to match equipment to a golfer's swing characteristics. The internally developed proprietary video and computer system used stereo imaging techniques to capture a sequence of eight multiple exposures of the clubhead and ball at various time intervals immediately before and after a golfer hit the ball into a net approximately 10 feet from where it was struck. Callaway's proprietary computer software analyzed the video images of the clubhead's approach to the ball and the ball's rotational patterns over its first few feet of flight to make a variety of calculations needed to project the ball's ultimate path. The projected path was displayed on a six-foot video screen that showed the ball's flight along the 18th fairway at Pebble Beach. The computer system also recorded the clubhead speed, ball velocity, side spin, back spin, attack angle, and launch angle to calculate the efficiency rating, carry, roll, total distance, and dispersion (deviation from a straight path). All of these statistics were projected on the screen, along with the image of ball's flight down the fairway. The equipment allowed the company to build a set of clubs for the touring professional that had the perfect swing weight, frequency, loft, lie, and length to maximize distance and accuracy.

The Helmstetter Test Center's golfing area was an 8.1-acre outdoor testing facility that included three putting and chipping greens, a deep pot bunker, a shallow fairway bunker, and a 310-yard fairway that was 80 yards wide at its narrowest point. Sensors located along the fairway recorded the distance and dispersion of any ball landing in the test area. Atmospheric conditions, such as wind speed, direction, temperature, barometric pressure, humidity, and dew point were recorded by three weather stations located around the test site. The facility also included an artificial tee box and green that accurately simulated a real green. Ball reaction on the simulated green was almost identical to that on the other three greens and allowed the company to continue testing while the natural test site was being irrigated or mowed.

The Helmstetter Test Center had two primary uses: It provided an ideal place to custom-fit clubs for the touring pros who used Callaway equipment, and it allowed Callaway R&D staff to test new products during their developmental stage. Once a professional's new clubs were fitted using the video and computer capabilities of the Callaway Performance Analysis System, the touring pro could then use the golfing area to hit balls and fine-tune his or her clubs by requesting minor modifications to the clubhead or shaft. Callaway included nontouring professionals in addition to engineers among its R&D staff. The golfing staff was critical to the product development process since engineers were able to refine new prototypes based on the feedback and recom-mendations of Callaway's R&D staff golfers. Callaway's engineers also tested proto-types with robots to evaluate the distance and accuracy of the club, but only a human could evaluate the feel of a golf club striking a ball.

Callaway's Purchasing and Production Processes   Once its clubheads were designed on a CAD system and tested in the Helmstetter Center, stainless-steel master plates were cut by Callaway to the exact specifications called for by the system. Each clubhead mold was made by pouring liquid wax between the stainless-steel mas-ter plates. The wax clubheads were removed from the master plates and sprayed with a mixture of highly heat resistant material. The wax was melted out of these heat-resistant molds, leaving a hollow core. The hollow molds were then sent to an invest-ment casting house, where either stainless steel or titanium was poured into the molds. The casting house then broke away the mold and welded, sanded, and painted the club-heads before sending them to Callaway for further assembly.

Callaway Golf used five investment casting houses, all of which underwent exten-sive screening and were closely monitored during the casting process. Callaway man-agement believed that it was particularly important to supervise the casting process since poor casting could produce clubhead inconsistencies that could lead to poor per-formance or product failures. Callaway had entered into a joint venture with Sturm, Ruger & Company in 1995 to produce its clubheads but had since recognized that qual-ity clubheads could be obtained through outsourcing. Even though Callaway Golf was certain it would obtain high-quality clubheads through its sourcing agreements, it made daily inspections of incoming clubhead shipments using the materials analysis and durability-testing capabilities of the Helmstetter Center.

Like Callaway's clubheads, all of its shafts were designed and tested at the Helm-stetter Center. Callaway manufactured all prototype shafts by hand at the testing cen-ter but contracted shaft production out to independent shaft manufacturers once specifications were established for the various graphite shafts used in its product line. As with clubheads, shafts were drawn from incoming shipments and tested at the com-pany's R&D facility. Steel shafts were contracted out and inspected in a similar fash-ion. Callaway had produced as much as 50 percent of its graphite shafts internally during the late 1990s but outsourced 100 percent of its shaft requirements in 2000.

Callaway Golf's cell manufacturing process allowed the company to include qual-ity control inspections throughout each club's assembly. In addition, the assembly plant was highly automated, with all processes requiring very tight tolerances performed by computer-controlled machinery. For example, the drilling necessary to produce Call-away's tapered bore-thru hosels was done by a series of precision drill presses that en-sured that each hosel was drilled at the correct angle. Once the hosel had been drilled through, the clubhead moved to a production station that checked the lie and loft angles of the club and made any necessary corrections by slightly bending the clubhead to the proper angle.

Each shaft was inspected for fractures prior to insertion into the clubhead, and then the entire assembled club was weighed to assess the swing weight. Callaway produc-tion workers could choose between medallions of four different weights to bring a fin-ished iron to the exact specified swing weight. The chosen medallion was permanently affixed to the back of the clubhead with a press. Swing weights for assembled woods were brought to their specifications by inserting epoxy through a small hole in the rear of the clubhead.

After undergoing a baking process that dried the glue used to attach the shaft to the clubhead, each club was fitted with a grip using a laser alignment device, airbrushed with details like the club number and Callaway trademarks, and then visually inspected for blemishes or other imperfections. Each finished club was wrapped by hand to protect its finish during shipping.

Sales and Customer Service   New product development at Callaway Golf Company was a cross-functional effort that included not only the R&D staff but also the company's sales and advertising staffs. Callaway sales and advertising personnel would evaluate new designs created by the company's aerospace engineers and recommend design changes based on their knowledge of the market. Once a new design was settled on, Callaway's sales force and internal advertising staff would create a name for the new product line, an advertising campaign, and promotional materials that would accompany the product launch in parallel with the R&D staff's developmental and testing processes.

Callaway's customer service department was viewed as a critical component of the company's overall level of differentiation. The customer service staff was made up of experienced employees who were offered a generous compensation package that included commissions for superior performance in meeting the needs of Callaway's retailers and consumers. Many of Callaway's rivals viewed customer service as a low-value-adding activity and typically made customer service a place for entry-level employees to become acquainted with the business. Each of Callaway Golf's customer service representatives received eight weeks of training before being allowed to handle a customer service inquiry. No other company in the industry provided more than three weeks of training to its customer service personnel. In addition to providing extensive training, Callaway promoted a team-oriented atmosphere that allowed the company's knowledge base to expand through the mentoring of newer employees by longtime customer service employees.

The entire customer service staff was empowered to make a final decision regarding a consumer or retailer complaint or warranty claim. Callaway customer service personnel were allowed to make decisions that might be pushed to the CEO at some other golf equipment companies. For example, if a golfer was vacationing and had a problem with a club, a customer service staff member could instruct the consumer to visit a local retailer to pick up a replacement club. If the consumer was out of the country and was not near a Callaway retailer, the Callaway employee was allowed to send a new club to the customer via Federal Express. Callaway customer service staff members were also known to send a gift to club owners who had experienced problems with Callaway equipment. Callaway's two-year warranty on all of its products entitled the owner to replace any defective product with a new product rather than return the product for a repair. In addition, Callaway generally chose to replace defective or broken clubs for the life of the club rather than stick to its two-year warranty period. A Callaway sales executive remarked, "A bad experience with a Callaway product usually winds up making someone a Callaway customer for life."

Callaway Golf's Product Line

Metal Woods   Callaway Golf's Big Bertha driver was the most innovative club in the industry when it was introduced in 1990. Its key features were a bigger clubhead, a bigger sweet spot, and a longer shaft, all of which helped to improve the consistency with which a golfer could drive the ball off the tee. Callaway wasted no time in capitalizing on the explosive popularity of its new driver; company managers understood that once a driver developed a following among golfers, these golfers usually wanted other woods to match it. The company subsequently introduced a series of fairway woods—a 2 wood, a

3 wood, a 5 wood, two styles of 7 woods, a 9 wood, and an 11 wood—to complement the Big Bertha driver. Many golfers rushed to buy not only the Big Bertha driver but also the company's other Big Bertha metal woods; it was common for Big Bertha enthusiasts to have three or four of the Big Bertha fairway woods in their bag.

Four years later, the company again moved to set itself apart from rival equipment makers (most of whom had by then come out with imitative versions of the Big Bertha line) by introducing the Great Big Bertha driver, made out of strong, lightweight titanium. The driver had a clubhead 30 percent larger than the original Big Bertha driver but was still just as light because of the substitution of titanium for stainless steel in the clubhead and the use of a graphite shaft; the Great Big Bertha (GBB) was the industry's most technologically advanced golf club and retailed for $500 (a heretofore unheard-of price for a single golf club).

Callaway's introduction of its titanium Biggest Big Bertha in 1997 again caught industry rivals off guard as they moved to match the size of the GBB. The Biggest Big Bertha (BBB) was 15 percent larger than the titanium Great Big Bertha (and the titanium clubs produced by Callaway's rivals) and was equipped with a 46-inch lightweight shaft. The total weight of the BBB was less than the total weight of the titanium GBB and the stainless steel Big Bertha drivers, which had 45- and 44-inch shafts, respectively.

The size of Callaway woods began to decrease with the introduction of its Big Bertha (BB) Steelhead metal woods in 1998 and Hawk Eye titanium metal woods in 1999. The BB Steelhead line was created in response to the popularity of the shallow-faced woods introduced by Orlimar and Adams in 1998. BB Steelhead drivers and fairway woods had a lower center of gravity than GBB and BBB woods, but had a higher profile than Adams and Orlimar woods. The BB Steelhead line incorporated the best features of both competing club designs by maintaining a very low center of gravity but having a larger clubface, which prevented the golfer from hitting below the ball, as was frequently done by amateur golfers using shallow-faced woods.

The BB Steelhead Plus was introduced in January 2000 as an improvement to the BB Steelhead line of drivers and fairway woods. Like the BB Steelhead line, the BB Steelhead Plus included a precision-cast steel chip to lower the club's center of gravity but featured variable clubface thickness that optimized energy transfer between the clubhead and the ball. Callaway's Variable Face Thickness Technology, developed through computer modeling and player testing, allowed the company to vary the clubface thickness to maximize perimeter weighting while keeping an elliptical area near the center of the clubface relatively thick. This thickness directly at the sweet spot of the clubface provided more energy transfer when a ball was well struck, while the perimeter weighting and thin walls near the outside edges of the clubface provided more forgiveness if a ball was mis-hit. Callaway's BB Steelhead Plus metal woods and its Variable Face Thickness Technology are described in the Callaway print ad shown in Exhibit 7. Callaway's Great Big Bertha Hawk Eye titanium drivers and fairway woods featured a titanium body and crown plate and Callaway's exclusive tungsten gravity screw, which accounted for only 2 percent of the clubhead volume but 25 percent of its overall weight. The lightweight titanium clubhead body and crown plate allowed Callaway to increase the overall size of the driver and the sweet spot, while the tungsten screw performed a number of functions. First, the use of tungsten low in the club created a low center of gravity, which helped the golfer produce a high trajectory. The tungsten screw also was strategically positioned in the sole of the clubhead to create Callaway's Draw Bias Technology, which drew the clubhead square at impact and reduced the likelihood of a slice. The tungsten screw also increased backspin, which helped produce greater distance. Exhibit 8 presents a print ad for Callaway's line of GBB Hawk Eye metal woods.

***exhibit* 7**   Sample Ad for Callaway Golf's New Big Bertha Steelhead Plus Metal Woods

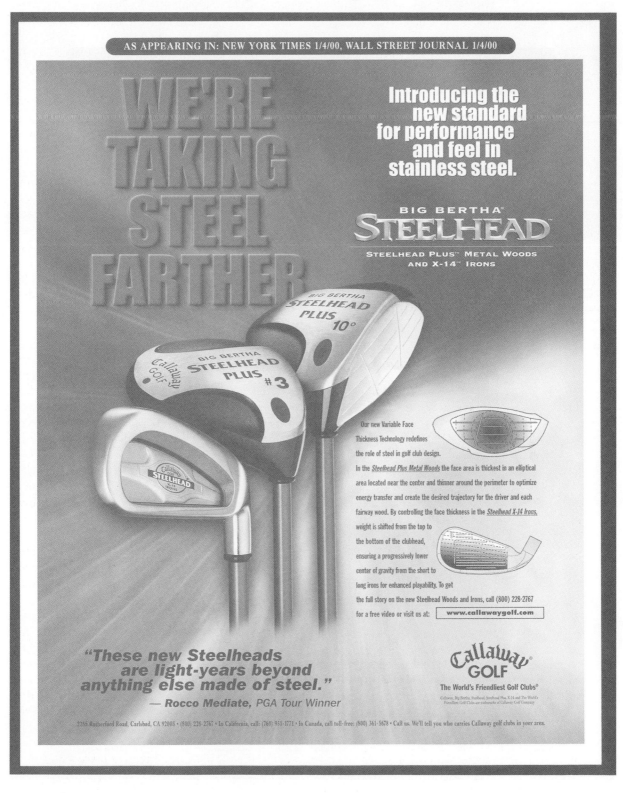

exhibit 8   Sample Ad for Callaway Golf's New Hawk Eye Metal Woods

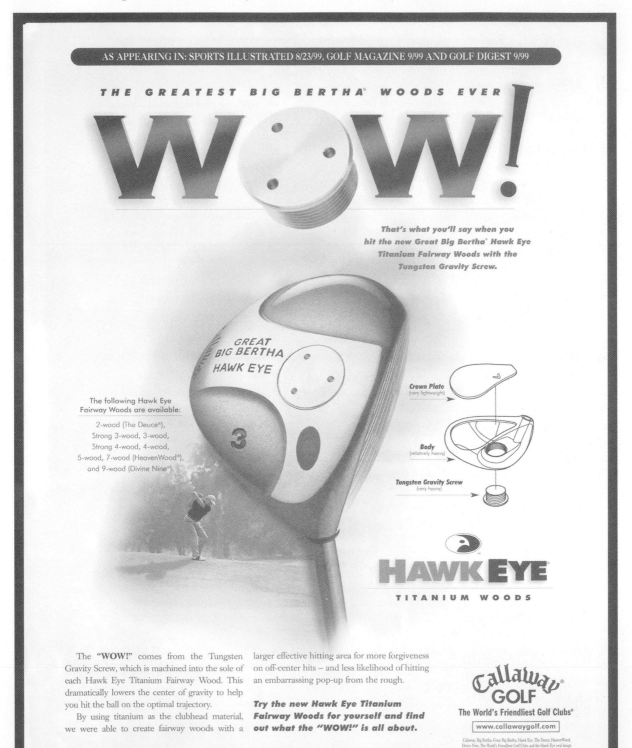

Irons   To capitalize on the initial popularity of the Big Bertha metal woods, Callaway Golf introduced lines of stainless-steel and graphite-shafted Big Bertha irons in 1994. In 1997 the company introduced Great Big Bertha tungsten-titanium irons, which included a tungsten insert located in the sole of the club that lowered the club-head's center of gravity. The use of titanium allowed Callaway to increase the overall size of the clubface, creating a larger sweet spot, while the tungsten insert allowed Callaway to keep the center of gravity low and add weight to the sweet spot. This low center of gravity and concentration of weight in the sweet spot allowed the irons to hit higher, straighter shots.

Callaway's Hawk Eye tungsten-injected titanium irons, introduced in 1999, included innovative design improvements over the original GBB tungsten-titanium irons. The Hawk Eye titanium irons included a hidden cavity that ran the length of the club-head and extended upward behind the hitting area. Small, uniform tungsten spheres were added by a computer weigh station to the cavity through a port and then covered with a dense molten metal to permanently lock them into place. Each iron contained a different number of spheres depending on the optimal center of gravity for the loft of the club. Once the appropriate number of tungsten spheres and the molten metal were added to the clubhead, the weight port was hidden by a Hawk Eye medallion. The Tungsten Weight Matrix that resulted from the addition of the spheres occupied only 27 percent of the volume of a Callaway Hawk Eye 5-iron yet accounted for 45 percent of the club-head's weight. The weight matrix created a low center of gravity that acted much like the gravity screw used in Hawk Eye metal woods and allowed golfers to create a high shot likely to maintain a straight path.

Callaway Golf replaced its stainless-steel Big Bertha irons in 1998 with its Big Bertha X-12 irons. The X-12 line of irons included a number of improvements over the Big Bertha irons and became the best-selling iron in the company's history. The X-12 line featured a narrower sole than Big Bertha irons, which made it easier to hit shots out of the rough. Big Bertha X-12 irons also had a multilayer design effect on the back of the clubface that allowed Callaway designers to locate the center of gravity at the ideal location for each length iron. The introduction of a variable 360-degree undercut channel also aided Callaway engineers in placing the center of gravity at the best possible location on the clubhead.

Callaway replaced the X-12 line of irons in 2000 with the Big Bertha X-14 Steel-head line. The X-14 featured Callaway's Variable Face Thickness Technology, which tapered the clubface from top to bottom and from heel to toe to create better perimeter weighting than previous generations of Callaway irons. The technology also allowed Callaway engineers to move the center of gravity to the ideal location on each iron. For example, the X-14 short irons had a higher center of gravity to provide extra control on approach shots, while the midlength irons and long irons had a lower center of gravity to produce a higher ball flight. Exhibit 9 shows a sample ad for Callaway Golf's X-14 irons.

Putters   Callaway Golf Company manufactured and marketed Bobby Jones, Carlsbad, and Tuttle lines of putters and the Odyssey brand of putters. Callaway had moderate success with its own Callaway putter lines, but its acquisition of Odyssey in 1997 made it the leading producer of putters in 2000. The 12 Bobby Jones putters and four Carlsbad putters were all made from stainless steel and came in blade and mallet styles. The Tuttle putter came in one model, which was unique in that it actually resembled a Big Bertha driver but was the size of a putter. Odyssey became known as an innovator in putters when it became one of the first companies to introduce polymer clubface inserts. Many golfers preferred putters with an insert since the soft material

exhibit 9   Sample Ad for Callaway Golf's New Big Bertha Steelhead X-14 Irons

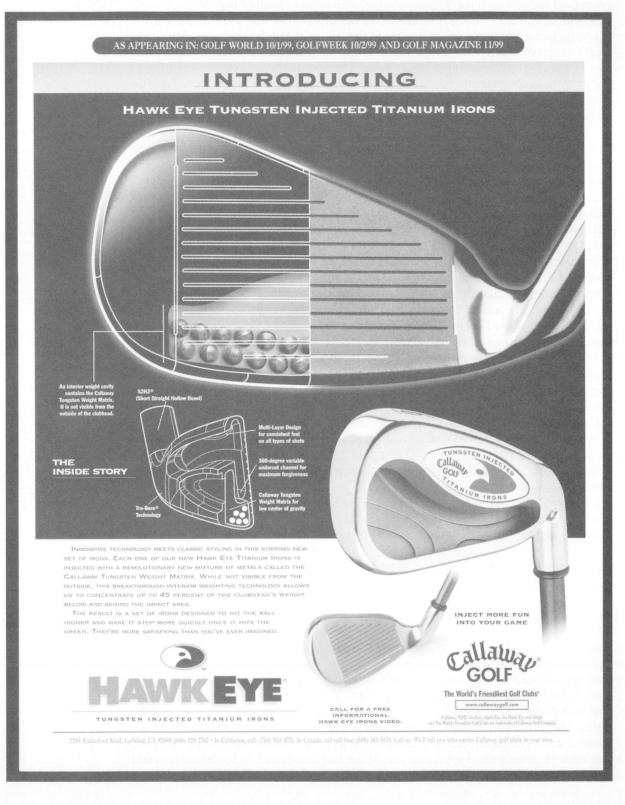

created a softer noise and provided more feel when putting a ball. Callaway's Odyssey putter was one of the two leading brands of putter in 2000 (Ping and Odyssey regularly exchanged the number one title) and was available in 26 different blade and mallet designs. Each of Odyssey's 26 models of putters featured its Stronomic polymer insert, available in three degrees of softness. In early 2000, Odyssey introduced its White Hot line of putters, which used Callaway's golf ball material as a clubface insert.

Callaway's Battle against Patent and Trademark Infringement

Ever since the Big Bertha driver had gained mass acceptance by professional and amateur golfers, Callaway Golf had been attacked by small golf companies offering clubs that were so similar in design and appearance that they infringed on Callaway's patents and trademarks. Although they looked like the branded clubs, the knockoff clubs were of inferior quality and typically sold for as much as 75 percent less than name-brand clubs. Some knockoff brands outsold the brands offered by such well-known makers as Hogan, Cleveland, and MacGregor. Callaway Golf was extremely committed to battling the makers of knockoff and counterfeit clubs. The company hired a retired U.S. Army counterintelligence expert to investigate trademark infringement cases and also worked in this area with private investigators, U.S. Customs, and U.S. marshals. In early 2000, Callaway Golf carried out a four-state sweep against illegal club makers that netted $65,000 worth of Callaway golf clubs that had been stolen and were being sold over the Internet; officials seized 5,800 golf clubs, including Canterbury Big Bursar V-17 irons and Connection Golf Big Bernard Steelclad metal woods. However, even when patent infringers and counterfeiters were caught and convicted, it was difficult to collect damages because such companies usually had minimal assets to seize.

Callaway Golf also aggressively protected its legal rights when it believed that a branded rival infringed on its patents or made false claims about either its own products or Callaway's products. In 1998 Callaway brought a suit against Spalding Sports Worldwide for trademark violation after Spalding created a line of System C golf balls and claimed they were specifically designed for Callaway clubs. The two parties settled in 1999, with Spalding agreeing to pull the line of golf balls. In addition, after a legal challenge from Callaway, Orlimar Golf was ordered by the court to retract advertisements falsely claiming that it was the number one metal wood used on the PGA tour. In 1999 Callaway Golf saw that the vice president of Callaway Golf Ball Company could in no way be involved with Taylor Made's golf ball operations after the Callaway employee left with company trade secrets to become Taylor Made's president and CEO. Callaway Golf also forced an apology from the CEO of La Jolla Golf after Callaway found that La Jolla's chief executive had used a fictitious name to make untrue and disparaging remarks about Callaway golf clubs on the Internet.

Endorsements and Use of Callaway Products by Golf Professionals

Callaway golf clubs were popular with both professionals and amateurs alike. Callaway drivers were endorsed by the professional golfers listed in Exhibit 10. However, many professional golfers used Callaway equipment even though they were not paid to endorse the company's products. In 1999 Callaway drivers were used in 61 wins,

exhibit 10   Callaway Golf Company Staff Professionals, 2000

Tour	Staff Players
Professional Golfers Association	Stephen Ames
	Paul Azinger
	Oline Browne
	Carlos Franco
	Brian Henninger
	Rocco Mediate
	Jesper Parnevik
	Paul Stankowski
Senior Professional Golfers Association	Bob Charles
	Jim Colbert
	Jim Dent
	Dave Eichelberger
	Bruce Fleisher
	David Graham
	Orville Moody
	Walter Morgan
	Bob Murphy
Ladies Professional Golfers Association	Jane Geddes
	Rachel Hetherington
	Rosie Jones
	Emilee Klein
	Leta Lindley
	Cindy McCurdy
	Liselotte Neumann
	Alison Nicholas
	Annika Sorenstam
European Professional Golfers Association	Mark McNulty
	Colin Montgomerie
	Eduardo Romero

Source: Callaway Golf 2000 catalog.

Callaway irons were used in 37 wins, and Odyssey putters produced 36 wins in a total of 186 PGA, LPGA, Senior PGA, Nike, and European PGA professional tournaments. A comparison of clubs used by professionals in all five tournaments is presented in Exhibit 11.

CALLAWAY GOLF'S MAJOR COMPETITORS

Callaway management considered its strongest competitive rivals to be Ping and Taylor Made because of those companies' track records in product innovation and their strong brand-name recognition: Ping irons had dominated the industry during much of the 1980s and 1990s (the perimeter-weighting feature pioneered by Karsten was a major technological breakthrough and had since become the industry standard in designing irons), while Taylor Made's distinctive bubble shaft was also considered to be a high-tech innovation. Other key rivals of Callaway Golf Company were Titleist, Adams Golf, and Orlimar Golf. Exhibit 12 presents a price comparison of golf equipment produced by Callaway Golf Company and its key rivals.

exhibit 11   Golf Club Use Comparison among Professional Golfers
(All tours combined), 1998–99

	1999	1998
Drivers		
Callaway	38.5%	55.2%
Titleist	24.2	16.9
Ping	13.4	n.a.
Taylor Made	5.3	8.0
Orlimar	3.0	0.1
All others	15.6	17.5
Total drivers	100.0%	100.0%
Fairway woods		
Callaway	52.1%	48.3%
Orlimar	17.9	10.5
Taylor Made	8.8	13.3
Titleist	4.5	5.1
Cleveland	3.1	n.a.
All others	13.6	20.3
Total fairway woods	100.0%	100.0%
Irons		
Callaway	18.3%	19.4%
Ping	15.0	15.3
Mizuno	15.0	14.1
Titleist	14.5	12.6
Taylor Made	4.4	4.7
All others	32.8	33.9
Total irons	100.0%	100.0%
Putters		
Odyssey	28.9%	31.0%
Ping	21.8	24.8
Titleist	19.8	18.7
Never Compromise	11.2	3.7
Tear Drop	4.0	n.a.
All others	14.3	16.0
Total putters	100.0%	100.0%

n.a. = Not available.

Source: Callaway Golf Company annual reports and Darrell Survey.

Ping

Ping had not been well known for its drivers but had been one of the industry's premier manufacturers of irons since its Ping Eye 2-irons were introduced in the mid-1980s. The company's Ping Eye 3-irons that were introduced in 1999 were among the most popular irons with both professionals and amateurs. Ping Eye 3-irons were one of the two leading brands of irons sold in the United States and were frequently the most-used iron in various professional tournaments. Ping Eye 3s were available with a compact

exhibit 12   Retail Price Comparison of Equipment Produced by
Leading Golf Equipment Companies, March 2000

Brand	Titanium Drivers	Graphite-Shafted Stainless-Steel Irons (Set of 8)	Putters (Price Range of Most Popular Models)	Golf Balls (Price per Ball—Based on Single Sleeve)
Callaway Golf/Odyssey	$400	$900	$90–$200	$3.60
Ping	$400	$850	$80–$140	n.a.
Taylor Made	$300	$750	$100	$3.33
Titleist	$400	$870	$270	$3.33
Adams Golf	$300	Not carried	n.a.	n.a.
Orlimar Golf	$300	$800	n.a.	n.a.

n.a. = Not applicable.
Source: Edwin Watts Golf Shops and International Golf Discount, March 11, 2000.

blade-style clubhead designed for low-handicap golfers and with an oversized clubhead
that had greater perimeter weighting for more forgiveness. All Ping Eye 3-irons featured a custom tuning port that was very similar in appearance to Callaway's tungsten
weight matrix port, but functioned differently. Rather than acting as a port to add tungsten weights, Ping's custom tuning port allowed the company to make minor adjustments to the loft and lie of the club during custom fitting.

Ping had elected not to introduce a titanium driver until 1998, because the company's engineers believed that the material provided no advantage over stainless steel.
However, in 2000 its 323-cc displacement TiSI titanium driver was actually the largest
custom-fit driver available. Ping also offered Ti3 titanium fairway woods that featured
a zirconium soleplate and a tungsten bottom weight that were both intended to lower
the club's center of gravity. Ping also offered an i3 line of stainless-steel fairway woods
in five different lofts.

Ping's greatest strength was in putters, where it alternated every quarter or so with
Odyssey as the number one brand of putters in the U.S. and international markets. Depending on the tournament, Ping putters were often used by professional golfers more
than any other brand. Ping had 46 models of putters that were made from either an-
tiqued manganese bronze, stainless steel, or laminated maple. Certain Ping putters featured inserts made from an elastomer compound, aluminum pixels, or copper pixels.
Ping began offering custom-fit clubs in the 1960s, and in 2000 all Ping metal woods,
irons, and putters could be custom-fitted to golfers who desired that service.

Taylor Made–Adidas Golf

Taylor Made was founded in 1979 by Gary Adams, who mortgaged his home and began
production of his metal woods in an abandoned car dealership building in McHenry,
Illinois. Both touring pros and golf retailers were skeptical of the new club design until
they found that the metal woods actually hit the ball higher and farther than persimmon
woods. By 1984, Taylor Made metal woods were the number one wood on the PGA
tour and the company had grown to be the third largest golf equipment company in the

United States. In 1984 the company was acquired by France-based Salomon SA, which provided the capital necessary for the company to continue to develop innovative new lines of clubs. The company's sales had stalled during the late 1980s and early 1990s until it introduced its Burner Bubble drivers in 1994. The bubble shaft design allowed some of the shaft weight to be moved from underneath the grip to just below the grip. Taylor Made management claimed that this weight relocation decreased the club's inertia, which resulted in faster clubhead acceleration. The bubble shaft also featured a reinforced midsection, said to minimize any twisting of the clubhead during the swing.

Many of the company's innovations in drivers and fairway woods mirrored those of Callaway Golf. In 1996, shortly after Callaway's introduction of the Great Big Bertha, Taylor Made had come out with an oversized titanium driver that had its differentiating bubble shaft and copper-colored clubhead. Taylor Made also produced and marketed a line of irons with its patented bubble shafts and introduced a line of bubble-shafted tungsten-titanium irons and a new titanium bubble-shafted T2 driver in 1997. The T2 and Taylor Made's tungsten-titanium irons appeared in retail locations at approximately the same time that the Biggest Big Bertha and the Big Bertha tungsten-titanium irons made their debut. Also in 1997, Taylor Made and its parent were both acquired by the Germany-based sports conglomerate Adidas.

In 2000 Taylor Made offered titanium FireSole metal woods and irons that featured a tungsten sole plug and SuperSteel stainless-steel metal woods and irons. The FireSole was Taylor Made's answer to Callaway's Hawk Eye lines of metal woods and irons, while its promotion of its SuperSteel line touted many of the same benefits as Callaway's BB SteelHead Plus metal woods and X-14 irons. Taylor Made also offered FireSole Rescue clubs, which had a large tungsten sole attached to a reduced-size titanium clubhead that placed 75 percent of the clubhead's weight below the equator of the ball. The rescue woods had an ultralow center of gravity and could be used on either the fairway or the rough. In early 2000 Taylor Made's Rescue fairway woods were unique; no products of similar appearance were offered by other major club manufacturers. Taylor Made also had a line of putters that featured a polymer clubface. Taylor Made introduced its InterGel line of golf balls in 1999.

Fortune Brands/Acushnet (Titleist and Cobra Golf)

The Acushnet Company was a rubber deresinating company founded in 1910 in Acushnet, Massachusetts. The company opened a golf ball division in 1932 when founder Phil Young believed that a bad putt during a round of golf he was playing was a result of a faulty ball rather than his poor putting. Young took the ball to a dentist's office to have it X-rayed and found that the core of the ball was indeed off-center. Young believed that Acushnet could develop and manufacture high-quality golf balls and teamed with a fellow MIT graduate, Fred Bommer, to create the Titleist line of balls. Young and Bommer introduced their first Titleist golf ball in 1935, and by 1949 Titleist had become the most-played ball on the PGA. In 2000, Titleist was still the number one golf ball on the PGA, being used by more than 75 percent of all professional golfers in tournament play. Acushnet also manufactured and marketed a Pinnacle line of golf balls, developed in 1980 as a lower-priced alternative to Titleist branded golf balls.

Acushnet's acquisition of John Reuter, Jr., Inc., in 1958 and Golfcraft, Inc., in 1969 put Titleist into the golf club business. Titleist's Reuter Bull's Eye putter became a favorite on the PGA tour during the 1960s, and its AC-108 heel-toe weighted irons were among the most popular brands of irons during the early 1970s. In 1996 the Acushnet Company was acquired by American Brands, which had increased its presence in the golf equipment industry in 1985 when it acquired Foot-Joy, the number one seller of golf gloves and shoes. Also in 1996 American Brands acquired Cobra Golf for $715 million. The company's golf and leisure products division had an operating profit of $147 million on sales of $965 million in 1999.

Acushnet's two golf club brands maintained separate sales forces, but every other value chain activity was combined for overall cost savings whenever possible. The Titleist brand of clubs had achieved only moderate success after Ping's perimeter-weighted clubs became popular in the 1980s, but Titleist had become much more successful during the late 1990s due to Tiger Woods's endorsement of the company's irons and metal woods. In 2000 Titleist's 975D driver, used by Tiger Woods, was among the more popular drivers with both professionals and amateurs. The 975D was an oversized titanium driver designed for a flatter ball flight to help a golfer achieve greater roll once the ball hit the ground. The Titleist titanium 975R was a variation of the 975D, which had a more shallow face and a slightly smaller clubhead. Titleist also offered a line of 975F stainless-steel fairway woods in 2000.

Titleist had two lines of stainless steel irons: the DCI 990 and DCI 981. The DCI 990 was intended for low-handicap golfers and had a reduced clubface offset and more weight toward the lower portion of the heel, where better golfers were more prone to mis-hit a golf ball. The DCI 981 line, designed for higher-handicap golfers, had an offset clubface, a low center of gravity, and more weight toward the toe of the clubface of short irons. The overall design objectives of the 981 line were to produce higher trajectories and more forgiveness. The DCI 981 also was available in an SL series intended for seniors or other golfers with less clubhead speed. All Titleist irons and metal woods were available with either steel or graphite shafts. Titleist also marketed a line of 17 different Scotty Cameron putters in stainless steel, teryllium, or platinum finishes. Some Scotty Cameron putters included an elastomer membrane covering the clubface.

In 1996, Cobra Golf held the industry's number two spot in irons and was number three in drivers and fairway woods (behind Callaway and Taylor Made). Cobra's popularity was a result of Greg Norman's endorsement of the clubs and the company's strategy of reducing the loft of its irons. The reduced loft added considerable distance to each club. For example, a golfer switching to King Cobra irons might pick up 20 yards or more on each club. Cobra Golf's King Cobra drivers were also considered a long-distance club.

After its acquisition by Acushnet, Cobra began to rapidly lose market share in both irons and metal woods. The company was forced to change its marketing approach since its high-profile, aggressive marketing practices clashed with the wishes of Acushnet's managers, who preferred a conservative approach to marketing. In addition, Acushnet management believed that Cobra should redesign its clubs to promote forgiveness at the expense of distance. Loyal Cobra customers were disappointed when they found that Cobra new models of clubs did not offer any greater distance than other brands. The decline in demand forced Cobra into a practice of deep discounting, which encouraged golfers to wait for the company to cut prices before they purchased the latest Cobra products. Cobra Golf also lost a considerable number of retailers during the later 1990s. The combination of missteps by Acushnet and Cobra Golf managers had all but made Cobra an afterthought by 1999.

Cobra struggled to rebuild its image and market presence after its strategic gaffes of the late 1990s. In 1999 the company launched a Web site and print ads that promoted its products as hip, nonconformist alternatives to the more technology-based golf clubs on the market. In early 2000 Cobra had abandoned this new image and recast itself as a more mainstream golf company.

Cobra's new products for 2000 included its Gravity Back drivers and fairway metal woods, which featured a titanium clubhead with a bronze alloy backweight placed at the rear of the clubhead. The bronze alloy backweight was designed to give the club a lower center of gravity. The Gravity Back fairway woods also featured a copper-tungsten sole weight to further lower the center of gravity. Cobra's CXI stainless-steel irons featured an *X*-like design on the backside of the clubface to more evenly disperse weight throughout the rear of the cavity back club. In 1999 Cobra Golf introduced Cobra Dista golf balls, which came in four models.

Adams Golf

Barney Adams founded Adams Golf in 1987 in Plano, Texas, as a golf club components supplier and contract manufacturer. In 1995 the company introduced its Tight Lies line of fairway woods, which featured an innovative low-profile clubface with a very low center of gravity. The shallow clubface and low center of gravity enlarged the effective hitting area of the clubface and created shots with a higher trajectory than shots with traditional-sized metal woods of the same loft. Tight Lies fairway woods were named the "Breakthrough Product of the Year" in 1997 by the Golf Market Research Institute and were rated the "Best of the Best" fairway woods in an independent real-golfer comparison in 1998. Adams Golf went public in July 1998 at an initial offering price of $16.00. The company recorded 1998 sales and earnings of $85 million and $13 million, respectively. In 1997 Adams had revenues of $37 million and a net loss of $5 million.

Adams's success became more difficult to maintain after other leading golf club manufacturers offered new lines of fairway woods with a shallower face than their previous models. In 1999 Adams Golf's revenues had declined to $54 million and the company recorded a net loss of $11 million. The company's stock traded below $2.00 during the first three months of 2000. Adams Golf's product line for 2000 included its Tight Lies^2 fairway woods, which had a deeper clubface than the original Tight Lies fairway woods. The new Tight Lies^2 retained the key features of the original Tight Lies line, but its deeper clubface made it easier to hit from the rough. In 1999 Adams introduced a line of SC series drivers, which were available in four different clubface curvatures designed to correct either a slice, a fade, or a hook. One SC driver featured a neutral clubface curvature for golfers without swing path problems. Adams also offered Assault VMI (variable moment of inertia) irons, which were heavier than most other brands of irons and used a patented mathematical formula to determine the ideal weight of the club based on the overall club length, shaft length, grip weight, and shaft weight.

Orlimar Golf Company

Orlimar Golf Company was founded in 1960 by Lou Ortiz in the basement of a converted stable in San Francisco. The company was a little-known maker of custom clubs primarily used by professionals and had annual sales of under $1 million in 1996. The company exploded onto the broad market for golf clubs in 1998 when it introduced its Tri-Metal fairway woods. Orlimar's Tri-Metal woods were made of stainless steel, copper, and tungsten and featured a low center of gravity and a shallower clubface than Callaway's GBB fairway woods. The combination of three metals and the low profile made the Tri-Metal instantly popular with professionals and amateurs alike. By year-end 1998 the company's sales had grown to more than $50 million and it was named as the fastest-growing private company in the San Francisco Bay area.

The company added drivers and irons to its product line in 1999 as its sales of fairway woods began to decline after Callaway's fairway woods began to recapture market share lost in 1997 and 1998. Orlimar's 2000 lineup of new products included its Tri-Metal Plus fairway woods and drivers and Tri-Metal irons. Like Orlimar's original Tri-Metal woods, Tri-Metal Plus fairway woods and drivers were made from stainless steel and included a copper tungsten sole plate to lower their center of gravity, but the Plus line had a deeper clubface than the original Tri-Metals. The clubface of the Tri-Metal Plus metal woods was coated with an Alpha Maraging Face material that the company claimed was harder than titanium. Orlimar's Tri-Metal irons were made from the same materials as the company's metal woods and were designed to produce high trajectories and longer distance than competing clubs.

Callaway's Prospects for Growth and the February 2000 Launch of the Callaway Golf Ball

Callaway's introduction of its new Rule 35 golf ball had been eagerly awaited since mid-1996, when Ely Callaway announced the formation of Callaway Golf Ball Company and the move of Charles Yash from Taylor Made to the new company. Whereas Nike had entered the golf ball industry in 1999 by outsourcing its production to Bridgestone and Taylor Made chose its mode of entry by purchasing an existing plant from a competitor, Ely Callaway had chosen a more time-consuming route to enter market for golf balls by electing to construct a new golf ball facility and internally develop an all-new ball. He noted: "This is the first time in the modern history of the industry, to our knowledge, that anyone has built a major-production golf ball business from scratch. After analyzing all of our other options, which included buying an existing company, buying an existing plant or buying a golf ball from another manufacturer and merely stamping our name on it, we decided this was the best way to go in order to create a superior product now and for the future."[9]

Callaway Golf spent three years developing in parallel its new golf ball and its state-of-the-art production facility. The company's entry into the market represented a $170 million investment in the research and development of the ball, construction of the 225,000-square-foot production facility, and development and purchase of special manufacturing equipment. Callaway's manufacturing facility and its equipment were designed specifically for the unique production requirements for the new ball.

Ely Callaway believed that the company's custom-designed manufacturing equipment and facility would contribute to the company's competitive strength and the ball's success: "No one else has the collection of late 90s equipment that we have, everything you need to make a better ball. No one has put it together and purchased it all the way we have. Some of the companies, because of the age of some of their equipment, just can't utilize the latest equipment without going outside."[10] Callaway's competitors were so interested in the company's new golf ball facility that they took aerial photographs of the plant's foundation as it was under construction.

Callaway Golf Ball Company engineers, recruited from Du Pont and Boeing, used aerodynamic computer programs (first used by Boeing and General Electric) to evaluate more than 300 dimple patterns and more than 1,000 variations of ball cores, boundary layers, and cover materials to create the new Rule 35 ball. Callaway engineers

---

[9]"Play Ball: Callaway Introduces the Rule 35," www.pgatour.com.

[10]"Long on Promises, Short on Explanation," *Golfweek,* February 5, 2000.

designed only two models of the Rule 35 ball—choosing to develop a "complete-performance" ball rather than separate balls developed for spin, control, distance, and durability. Ely Callaway explained the company's product development objectives as follows: "We have combined all of the performance benefits into one ball so players no longer need to sacrifice control for distance, or feel, or durability. Each Rule 35 ball contains a unique synergy of distance, control, spin, feel and durability characteristics. This eliminates confusion and guesswork in trying to identify the golf ball that is right for each individual golfer."[11]

Callaway's production process used computers to mill the rubber core, control injection molding of a boundary layer, and deposit a proprietary urethane coating to golf balls as they were assembled. The golf balls then moved through a transparent tube to a battery of diagnostic machines that ensured that each ball was exactly the same. A laser was then used to twice measure the depth of each of the ball's 382 dimples, and an electrical process was used to bond paint to the ball securely and evenly. Each ball was then X-rayed and machine-inspected before being packed or rejected. Callaway's production process included 16,000 quality assurance checkpoints, and Callaway employees were allowed to stop the flow of balls at the first sign of defects.

Callaway's Rule 35 balls were differentiated from competing brands in a large number of ways. The name Rule 35 was a play on the 34 long-standing rules of golf published by the USGA and the Royal & Ancient Golf Club of St. Andrews. Ely Callaway suggested that there should be a 35th rule of golf—"Enjoy the game."[12] The complete-performance balls came in only two variations, whereas the golf balls offered by competitors came in as many as 10 models. The blue-logo Callaway ball was called the Softfeel and had all of the same characteristics as its red-logo Firmfeel ball but had a slightly softer feel. Ely Callaway believed the availability of only two complete-performance balls and the avoidance of a discussion of the technical aspects of the balls' design and construction would make it easier for golfers to purchase golf balls: "We know there is a lot of complex science that goes into making a golf ball, but we don't think there should be a lot of complexity to buying one."[13] Callaway later commented, "We've come up with two balls. That's it. We're not gonna tell you much about them. We have only two, you make the choice. If you like a soft feel, you try this one (blue). If you like a firm feel, you try this one (red). We don't say a damn thing about how far they go. We don't say a word about compression or the construction or the details of the cover. We just say, 'Try them.' We believe that either one of them will give you more of what you've been looking for in one ball than anything else."[14]

Callaway Golf Ball Company's CEO, Chuck Yash, discussed the company's philosophy behind offering only two models of the Rule 35 and why the company refused to comment on the ball's technology: "Our basic aim in this process was to make a ball that reflects the parent company's philosophy and vision of creating a 'demonstrably superior and pleasingly different' product. We also set out to cut through the noise regarding the performance claims by most of the competitors' products, and all of the techno-babble about various polymers and compressions and dimple patterns and claims regarding the longest distance balls. What we have in Rule 35 is a very clear

---

[11]"Callaway Enters the Ball Game," *Show News,* February 5, 2000.

[12]"Play Ball: Callaway Introduces the Rule 35."

[13]"Callaway Enters the Ball Game."

[14]"Long on Promises, Short on Explanation."

exhibit 13   Estimated Manufacturing Shares of the Leading Producers
of Golf Balls, 12 Months Ending September 30, 1999

	Dollars	Units
Titleist	36%	29%
Top-Flite/Spalding	23	27
Pinnacle	11	14
Maxfli	8	7
Wilson	7	8
Slazenger	5	3
Precept	3	2
Dunlop	2	3
Taylor Made	1	1
All others	4	6
Total	100%	100%

Source: Callaway Golf Company

message. If you prefer a firm feel, our Firmfeel ball has everything you need in performance. If you prefer a softer feel, our Softfeel ball is the choice. It's that easy."[15]

Callaway golf balls were further differentiated by their logo and packaging. The Callaway name used a stylized script rather than the Old English script used on Callaway golf clubs, and the company's logo was comprised of a letter *C* created from a rendering of the bottom of a golf cup. The balls were also packaged in sleeves of 5 and packs of 10 rather than sleeves of 3 or packs of 12 like other brands. Callaway Golf Ball Company's national sales manager explained why Callaway chose unique packaging for its golf balls: "When we were doing our research, we couldn't find a single person who could tell us why golf balls were packaged in sleeves of three or in dozens. When we discovered that the average golfer uses 4.5 balls per round, we decided the five-ball sleeve was the right way to go with packaging."[16] In addition, unlike the packaging of other brands of balls, Callaway's packaging included only the name and logo printed on a translucent plastic box rather than the name and product performance characteristics printed on a cardboard box. Callaway's use of a five-ball sleeve also allowed its golf balls to be placed away from other brands of balls since most retailers' display cases were designed for three-ball sleeves.

Even though the industry had long been dominated by Titleist and Spalding (see Exhibit 13), many analysts believed that Callaway's ability to develop technologically advanced products, its marketing expertise, and its established retailer network would allow the company to quickly gain a 2 to 3 percent share of the market and achieve $60 to $70 million in sales during 2000. Analysts also speculated that Callaway Golf Ball Company could hit sales of over $200 million within two years of the ball's launch. It was expected that Callaway's golf ball operations would considerably impact the company's net profit since profit margins in the premium segment of the golf ball market ranged between 60 and 75 percent. In addition, golf ball sales were less seasonal since

[15]Callaway press release, February 4, 2000.
[16]"Callaway Enters the Ball Game."

they were consumable items that were purchased throughout the year. Also, unlike a $500 driver, golfers could not delay the purchase of golf balls until they felt financially ready to make a large purchase. The company's objective was for the Rule 35 to capture a 10 percent share of the market within two years and ultimately become one of the two top brands of golf balls. "We have 7 million people out their playing our products, and 80 percent of them think they're the best clubs in the world," said Ely Callaway. "We have almost a guaranteed 'try' on our new products."[17] Callaway further commented, "We're going to sell a lot of balls."[18] An advertisement for the Rule 35 golf ball is shown in Exhibit 14 on the following page.

In February 2000 a survey of golf equipment company executives voted Callaway's Big Bertha driver the best golf product of the century by a 2-to-1 margin. The same group of executives called Ely Callaway the most influential golf trade person of the 1990s. As he approached his 81st birthday, Ely Callaway had vowed to retire by December 31, 2000, and make Chuck Yash the new CEO and president of Callaway Golf Company as well as Callaway Golf Ball Company. Just prior to the PGA Merchandise Show, Chuck Yash commented on his growing responsibility at Callaway Golf Company and the importance of its golf ball operations to the company's future growth: "The trust and faith Ely and the board of directors and the shareholders have shown in us is extraordinary. It has allowed me to use my 20 years of golf experience to build an organization and a team that, we believe, can have a significant impact. That is the way we are looking at things now, as a long-term commitment. It will take years before we feel we can compete with the leading companies in the golf ball market. But that is our objective. If we do that right, we have the potential to continue to grow."[19]

·

[17]"Rule 35 Tees Off," *San Deigo Union-Tribune,* February 4, 2000.
[18]"Play Ball: Callaway Introduces the Rule 35."
[19]"On the Spot: Chuck Yash," *Golf Product News,* January/February 2000.

exhibit 14   Sample Ad for Callaway Golf's Rule 35 Golf Ball

case 14 drkoop.com

Nicole Herskowitz
University of Michigan

Michael Iverson
University of Michigan

Fred Howard
University of Michigan

Janet Mehlhop
University of Michigan

Pilar Speer
University of Michigan

As Dennis Upah, cofounder of drkoop.com, sat in his small, dimly lit office sipping a glass of water, he thought back to an earlier conversation with his partner, C. Everett Koop, former surgeon general of the United States. He kept coming back to the comment that Dr. Koop had made: "I am excited about how the Web has greatly enhanced consumers' abilities to access health care information. I firmly believe that empowered consumers make better, more informed decisions with their physicians. Our new Web site gives Americans one premier location on the Net to find trusted, quality health care information."[1]

Since the drkoop.com launch in late 1998, the company had quickly grown to be the largest Web-based health information service, but revenues were far short of what was needed to make the new company profitable. Although the new company was focused on providing health care information, Dennis knew the site had to make a profit to keep shareholders happy and to ensure that the business would survive. He thought idly, "This tap water is terrible. I hope we soon turn a profit so we can afford a water cooler!" But he quickly jumped back to the issue that was troubling him: What strategy did drkoop.com need to pursue to sustain its early success? Sites offering medical advice were proliferating, and several competitors were mounting offensives to challenge drkoop.com.

THE HISTORY OF MEDICAL ADVICE

People have sought knowledge about their ailments as far back as ancient times, when medicine men performed spells and advised people on their spiritual and mental health. In modern times, people have come to rely on their personal physicians for medical advice. For sicknesses like the flu or the common cold, there is a lot of information available from local pharmacists, the media, and friends, not to mention each individual's own personal experience with various remedies. For those who want detailed information or want to doctor themselves with assorted natural herbs, vitamin supplements, and

---

[1]"Dr. Koop's Community," 1998 Business Wire, Inc., July 20, 1998.

This case was prepared under the supervision of Professor Alan Afuah, University of Michigan, for purposes of class discussion © 1999 by the case authors. All rights reserved.

other remedies available without a prescription, there are also numerous books, magazines, and health foods advisories. Numerous support organizations have sprung up in recent years to help people afflicted with cancer, diabetes, and other serious illnesses.

In addition to conducting its own R&D efforts to discover new prescription drugs to cure or prevent ailments of all types, the pharmaceutical industry contributes to health research organizations. Bristol-Myers Squibb, for example, donated $23 million through the Bristol-Myers Squibb foundation in 1997. A large portion of this money went to organizations such as the National Cancer Foundation and the National Diabetes Foundation. Pharmaceutical firms also help inform patients of new treatment options through media advertising, Web sites, other forms of publications, and extensive collaboration with patient support and prevention groups.

In late 1999, all pharmaceutical companies had extensive Web sites with numerous links and information options that addressed their primary treatment areas. Companies like Medtronic and Guidant had Web sites with specific areas dedicated to various types of cardiovascular problems. On Medtronic's site, for example, there were pages dedicated to ventricular fibrillation that not only featured medical advice but also contained many links to associated sites such as that of the American Heart Association.

MEDICAL ADVICE ON THE INTERNET

The first Web sites pertaining to health care were created by pharmaceutical firms as part of their efforts to begin conducting business-to-business e-commerce with pharmaceutical distributors, drugstore chains, and physicians who wrote prescriptions. In the beginning, most pharmaceutical firms used their Web sites to advertise their products and services. However, they soon discovered that the aspect of the Internet that attracted the most users was information. Sites providing a wealth of free, informative, interesting, and valuable content began seeing thousands and then millions of unique hits each quarter. The appeal of good information quickly caught the attention of entrepreneurs who seized on the potential for providing medical information via the Internet.

Medical information Web sites were launched to provide the public with readily accessible and accurate information on a broad variety of health-related topics, curtailing the need for people to rely totally on a physician or medical specialist for answers to their questions or concerns. Site founders, recognizing "the value of the Internet as a viable tool for educating the public," saw themselves as performing a valuable public service by creating open access to tens of thousands of pages of reliable and trustworthy health care information.[2] The information on their sites was compiled from books and articles by well-known physicians, journals reporting medical research and the latest studies, information-providing partners, a medical advisory board, and various other medical experts.

Medical information Web sites began popping up left and right in the 1997–99 period. With competition on the rise, medical information providers were forced to add services to their sites in order to maintain growth in number of hits and unique viewers. Following the business models from other content provider Internet companies, the idea of "chat rooms" quickly found its way into the online health care scene. But to combat the potential for misleading or inaccurate information to be dispensed in chat rooms, most medical sites developed an "Ask the Expert" feature to help site users get accurate, timely answers to their questions. Several medical information providers had recruited experts, including physicians and specialists, to give advice to site users and respond to specific questions. Additionally, most medical sites, concerned with maintaining the

---

[2]www.drkoop.com/aboutus/koop.

integrity and objectivity of the information being provided, set up "stringent rules governing the ethics of the sites, including how advertising and editorial content should be addressed."[3]

WHO IS DR. KOOP?

Dr. C. Everett Koop became a well-known public figure while serving as surgeon general in the Reagan administration. He played a prominent role in building public awareness of the acquired immune deficiency syndrome (AIDS) and was often in the public limelight crusading against the destructive effects of tobacco. As surgeon general, he was a strong proponent of tough antismoking regulations. Following his tenure as surgeon general, Dr. Koop continued his mission of encouraging good health. His latest effort was to help found and launch drkoop.com as a provider of medical information.

Dr. Koop was born in Brooklyn, New York, in 1916. After earning his M.D. from Cornell University in 1941, he worked at Children's Hospital at the University of Pennsylvania for 35 years. During his tenure there, he built a reputation as one of the nation's best pediatric surgeons. From 1981 to 1989, Dr. Koop served as surgeon general of the U.S. Public Health Service and director of international health. In 1999, Dr. Koop continued to lead an active role in the health community and health education through writings, electronic media, public appearances, and personal contacts. He taught medical students at Dartmouth College, where the Koop Institute was based. He was chairman of the National Safe Kids Campaign, Washington, D.C., and produced 75 point-of-diagnosis videos during 1999–2001 for Time-Life Medical, of which he was chairman of the board.

The Web site was named after its 83-year-old cofounder to provide credibility and to give the site a competitive edge over rival medical information providers. Cofounder Dennis Upah believed Dr. Koop's name was an incredible asset. Upah said, "He's the most trusted man in health care. He's an icon. With that comes a tremendous responsibility and scrutiny."[4] In a recent survey by Bruskin-Goldring, almost 60 percent of consumers recognized Dr. Koop, and of that percentage, nearly half believed him to be a top authority on health care issues.[5] In return for use of his name, Dr. Koop agreed to receive a royalty equal to 2 percent of revenues from sales of the company's current products and up to 4 percent of revenues derived from sales of new products. However, this agreement was later modified; the royalty payments were eliminated and in their place Dr. Koop was granted rights to purchase 214,000 shares of drkoop.com's stock at an exercise price of $17.84. The rights vested at the rate of 8,900 shares per month.

DRKOOP.COM IS BORN

After incorporating in July 1997, Empower Health Corporation launched the drkoop.com Web site on July 20, 1998, as a comprehensive consumer health care portal providing information on acute ailments, chronic illnesses, nutrition, and fitness and wellness, as well as access to medical databases, publications, and real-time medical news. The company said its mission was to "empower consumers with the information and resources they need to become active participants in the management of their own

---

[3]Ibid.

[4]"i:20 drkoop.com's Dennis Upah," *Crain Communications,* November 1999.

[5]PR Newswire Association, Inc., March 29, 1999.

health." At the time, Dr. C. Everett Koop, the chairman of Empower, said, "I am excited about how the Web has greatly enhanced consumers' abilities to access health care information. I firmly believe that empowered consumers make better, more informed decisions with their physicians. Our new website gives Americans one premier location on the Net to find trusted, quality health care information."[6] The company went public in June 1999 at a price of $9; the stock price jumped to as high as $40 in July 1999 but then declined and traded in the $11–20 range during the last quarter of 1999 and in early 2000. The company's initial public offering raised about $85 million in new capital.

To build drkoop.com brand awareness, Empower Health partnered with USWeb Corporation, a specialist in Web audience development. Together, they devised a strategy built around innovative banner advertising and media placement of ads, search engine optimization, and online public relations and promotions.[7] In its first 90 days, the site attracted more than 1 million visitors. By June 1, 1999, the company had attracted 6 million unique users and signed up 280,000 registered members.

The initial success continued on into the second half of 1999, drawing over 15 million page views in October 1999.[8] In November 1999, Media Metrix ranked the site as the number one health Web site, and PC Data noted that it was the number one health Web site from March 1999 through November 1999. Media Metrix ranked drkoop.com as 25th in its News/Information/Entertainment category. During the fourth quarter of 1999, drkoop.com attracted 11.8 million unique visitors, who viewed 49.4 million pages. By January 2000, the company had 1 million registered users.

THE MARKET OPPORTUNITY FOR DRKOOP.COM

Health care was the largest segment of the U.S. economy in the late 1990s, accounting for annual expenditures of roughly $1 trillion.[9] Health and medical information was one of the fastest-growing areas of interest on the Internet. According to Cyber Dialogue, an industry research firm, during the 12-month period ended July 1998, approximately 17 million adults in the United States searched online for health and medical information, and approximately 50 percent of these individuals made offline purchases after seeking information on the Internet. Cyber Dialogue estimated that approximately 70 percent of the persons searching for health and medical information online believed the Internet empowered them by providing them with information before and after they went to a doctor's office. Cyber Dialogue also estimated that the number of adults in the United States searching for online health and medical information would grow to approximately 30 million in the year 2000, and they would spend approximately $150 billion for all types of health-related products and services offline.[10] Exhibit 1 shows the size of the various U.S. health care market segments. Medical information providers hoped to tap into a piece of this business.[11]

---

[6]"Dr. Koop's Community."

[7]"USWeb Audience Development Practice Helps Establish Success of Leading Consumer Healthcare Site," 1998 Business Wire, Inc., November 19, 1998.

[8]"drkoop.com Breaks 15 Million Page Views for October," PR Newswire, November 22, 1999.

[9]See Hoover's online database (www.hoovers.com/industry/snapshot/0,2204,23,00.html). See also Thomas E. Miller and Scott Reents, "The Health Care Industry in Transition," Cyber Dialogue, 1998.

[10]Miller and Reents, "The Health Care Industry in Transition."

[11]Ibid.

exhibit 1   Size of the U.S. Health Care Market, 1997

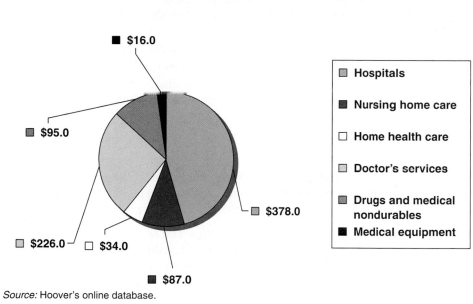

1997 Annual Market Size (in $ billions)

- ■ $16.0
- ■ $95.0
- ■ $378.0
- □ $226.0
- □ $34.0
- ■ $87.0

Legend:
- ◻ Hospitals
- ■ Nursing home care
- ☐ Home health care
- ◻ Doctor's services
- ◻ Drugs and medical nondurables
- ■ Medical equipment

Source: Hoover's online database.

DRKOOP.COM'S BUSINESS MODEL AND STRATEGY

In the company's prospectus for its common stock offering in mid-1999, management described the objective and business model for drkoop.com:

> Our objective is to establish the drkoop.com network as the most trusted and comprehensive source of consumer health care information and services on the Internet. Our business model is to earn advertising and subscription revenues from advertisers, merchants, manufacturers, and health care organizations who desire to reach a highly targeted community of health care consumers on the Internet. We also earn revenues by facilitating e-commerce transactions, such as sales of prescription refills, vitamins and nutritional supplements, and insurance services offered by outside parties.

Drkoop.com's strategy incorporated the following key elements:

- Establish the drkoop.com brand so that consumers associate the trustworthiness and credibility of Dr. C. Everett Koop with the company.
- Provide consumers with high-quality health care content to attract users to www.drkoop.com and promote their loyalty to the company's Web site.
- Distribute drkoop.com content to affiliated portals and other Web sites that (1) have established themselves as pathways for a broad variety of information and (2) have the potential to drive traffic to drkoop.com and provide broad exposure to the drkoop.com brand.
- Develop and expand online health care communities to allow users with similar health-related experiences to exchange information and gather news and knowledge in a secure, anonymous environment.

- Provide consumers with unique tools, such as one that educates consumers on the interaction among various drugs and other substances.
- Deploy a comprehensive personal medical record that will allow users to establish and maintain a lifelong record of their health and medical information in a secure portion of the company's database.
- Provide an attractive Web site that can deliver advertising in a highly targeted manner, thereby commanding higher advertising rates.
- Facilitate e-commerce transactions offered by merchants, manufacturers, and service providers to a highly targeted community of health-conscious consumers.

Strategic Partnerships

A chief component of drkoop.com's strategy was to partner with organizations that would add to its content and service offerings, further expand its business model into traditional areas of the health care industry, and grow its viewing base. To develop content for its Web site, drkoop.com had partnered with the following eight organizations:

- *The American Council on Science and Health*—The ACSH was an independent, nonprofit, tax-exempt organization that conducted studies and did research in such areas as food, nutrition, chemicals, pharmaceuticals, lifestyles, the environment, and health. A board of 300 physicians, scientists, and policy advisers peer-reviewed all reports and published papers.
- *Cleveland Clinic Foundation*—The Cleveland Clinic integrated hospital patient care, research, and medical education in a private, nonprofit group practice with 1,000 salaried physicians. In 1999, *U.S. News and World Report* ranked the Cleveland Clinic best in the country for cardiac care and the fourth best hospital overall.
- Dartmouth Medical School—The Dartmouth Medical School provided consumer health and medical information on more than 60 medical topics along with analysis on leading medical research and trends written by staff and experts.
- *Lifescape.com*—Lifescape provided timely news articles, clinical information, and state-of-the-art assessment tools in areas relating to family, relationships, emotional health, and mental well-being.
- *Multum Information Services*—Multum provided drkoop.com with a comprehensive and up-to-date database of drug information that was the basis for drkoop.com's trademarked DrugChecker tool.
- *Screaming Media*—Screaming Media provided drkoop.com with late-breaking, real-time news and editorials on health and health care issues from over 50 wire services.
- *World Book*—World Book contributed use of its trusted and thorough World Book Rush–Presbyterian–St. Luke's Medical Center Medical Encyclopedia.
- *Shared Medical Systems*—SMS was a provider of software that enabled secure online data exchanges between patients, their physicians, and local health care organizations.

Going into 2000, drkoop.com had over one dozen agreements to be the exclusive or preferred provider of health care information for particular Web sites. The major ones were as follows:

- *Infoseek and Buena Vista Internet*—To enhance brand awareness and increase traffic on its Web site, drkoop.com entered into agreements with Infoseek Corporation and the Buena Vista Internet Group, a unit of the Walt Disney Company, to be the exclusive provider of health and related content on three Web sites of the Go Network: Go.com Health Center, ESPN.com Training Room, and the Family.com Health Channel. In addition, drkoop.com became the exclusive pharmacy and drugstore, health insurance, and clinical trials partner in the Go.com Health Center. Under the Infoseek agreement, drkoop.com was also the premier health content provider for ABCnews.com. The agreement was for the period April 1999 to April 2002 and called for drkoop.com to pay Infoseek and Buena Vista approximately $58 million in total consideration.

- *Adventist Health System*—In January 1999, drkoop.com exchanged 2,615,677 shares of preferred stock for $3.5 million in cash plus a 10 percent share of Health-Magic. HealthMagic was a subsidiary of Adventist Health Systems and a developer of a personal medical record application.[12] This partnership gave the company access to and use of a personal medical record application and secured Adventist as a customer in the Community Partner program.

- *FHC Internet*—FHC purchased 1.1 shares of drkoop.com common stock at the offering price of $9 as part of an agreement for FHC to sponsor drkoop.com's mental health center.[13] FHC Internet was a subsidiary of Foundation Health Systems that specialized in the outsourcing of disease management programs for local health care organizations.

- *Quintiles International*—Quintiles entered into an agreement with drkoop.com to jointly develop a clinical trials information center. Quintiles was the world's largest provider of clinical research services to pharmaceutical companies and, as part of the agreement, purchased $5 million worth of shares of drkoop.com at the IPO price of $9. The clinical trials center provided visitors to the drkoop.com site with information about clinical trials that were currently going on across the country. Visitors could fill out an online prescreen form for various clinical trials, which was then forwarded to study sites. Drkoop.com received approximately $100 for each referral. Quintiles expected the agreement to help it speed recruit of candidates for clinical trials, lower prescreening costs, and create a larger pool of potential candidates for participation in clinical trials.[14]

- *America Online*—Drkoop.com's agreement called for it to provide medical information services to America Online and CompuServe members as well as to AOL's Internet portals—AOL.com, Netscape.com, and DigitalCity.com. To gain exposure to the 70-plus million users from the five entities combined and the benefits of AOL's sales force, drkoop.com agreed to pay AOL $89 million over the next four years and also to give AOL warrants to purchase 1.6 million shares of drkoop.com's stock at an exercise price of $15.94. Drkoop.com received an $8 million license fee for the use of a co-developed personal medical record.

- *Phar-Mor*—Drkoop.com's partnership with Phar-Mor, an online drugstore, involved Phar-Mor's sponsoring a monthly drkoop.com pharmacy newsletter. Users of Phar-Mor's Web site were directed to drkoop.com to gain necessary medical information, while visitors to drkoop.com could click on links to Phar-Mor's Web site.

- *DrugEmporium*—DrugEmporium and drkoop.com signed an agreement in October 1999 whereby drkoop.com visitors could purchase over 20,000 discounted products sold by DrugEmporium. Shoppers at DrugEmporium could go directly to

---

[12]Bear Stearns Equity Research, Health Care Industry, July 27, 1999.
[13]Ibid.
[14]Ibid.

drkoop.com for further information on products they were considering. Further, drkoop.com's DrugChecker was integrated into the purchase of all prescription drugs at DrugEmporium, automatically checking for any potential problems.

- *Other Alliances and Comarketing Partnerships*—drkoop.com had partnered with such health care providers and HMOs as Highmark (one of the 10 largest insurers in the United States); MemorialCare (a large health care system serving more than 14 million residents in Los Angeles and Orange County); Scott and White Hospital and Clinic (one of the largest multispecialty hospitals in the United States); Promina Health Systems (a nonprofit health care organization serving 4.3 million residents in the Atlanta area); the Cleveland Clinic (with a staff of over 850 physicians); and the Baptist Health System (serving 3.5 million residents in the Miami, Florida, area). In addition to these agreements, drkoop.com had agreements to provide content, establish direct links to each other Web sites, or otherwise gain market exposure with The Weather Channel, Physicians' Online, Salon.com Health & Body, SeniorNet, @Home, Roadrunner (the cable-based Internet service provider of Time Warner and Media One cable systems), Tallahassee Memorial HealthCare, and Yahoo Health.

Community Partners and Television Partners   Through the Community Partner Program, drkoop.com enrolled hospitals and health systems as local affiliates, allowing them to integrate the drkoop.com brand and content into their online initiatives. Participating health care organizations could draw on the content and resources at the drkoop.com Web site to supply their patients with online health care information and interactive capabilities, thus helping patients to educate themselves and make more informed decisions. In February 2000, there were more than 300 local health care facilities participating in the Community Partner Program. In recent months, drkoop.com had also begun a Television Partner Program and was supplying content to 18 local television stations.

Using the Partnerships to Build a "Network"   The company saw all these content and affiliate partnerships as a central part of its strategy to create

> an Internet-based consumer health care network that . . . provides individuals with trusted health care content, services, and tools to empower them to better manage their health. Our network affiliates include other Internet portals, Web sites, health care organizations, and traditional sources of health and medical news. Establishing affiliations with traditional media outlets allows us to deliver quality health care content to a targeted audience. Affiliates provide local, relevant information directly to a local audience. Through this unique means of distribution, drkoop.com is building a leading network of health content and editorial-based, breaking health news on the Internet.[15]

drkoop.com's Recent Marketing and Promotion Efforts

To build brand awareness and traffic, drkoop.com advertised on high-frequency Web sites such as Yahoo! Competitors were pursuing much the same approach. WebMD.com advertised on NetZero, a free Internet service provider for consumers, and Onhealth.com also advertised on Yahoo! Also, drkoop.com had entered into arrangements with local TV stations to give the stations content for health-related news stories in exchange for a drkoop.com "plug" at the end of a news story on a health issue.

---

[15]Company documents.

In late 1999, drkoop.com launched a $10–$15 million advertising campaign to build brand recognition.[16] Management believed that growing competition among medical information providers on the Internet made higher levels of advertising necessary. The company had also employed Creative Artists Agency (CAA) to help build awareness and use of its Web site.[17]

drkoop.com's Revenue Sources

The company generated revenue from selling advertising on its site, licensing its content to others, and partnerships with others. The big revenue generator was selling Web site ads. DrugEmporium was the only sponsor of the Web site. The site was covered with DrugEmporium advertisements and direct links to facilitate over-the-counter medication purchases. Advertising was also being sold to the company's Community Partners (local hospitals) and health insurance companies. Actual and projected financial statements for drkoop.com are shown in Exhibits 2, 3, and 4.

INFORMATION AND CONTENT AT THE DRKOOP.COM WEB SITE

The drkoop.com Web site contained over 70,000 pages of health information and tools for users. The tag line for the site mirrored Dr. Koop's belief that "the best prescription is knowledge." Going into 2000, the site served as a content and community portal with links to other information sources. Information at the site was organized around six categories:

- News
- Family
- Resources
- Wellness
- Community
- Conditions

Users could sign up to become drkoop.com members; membership enabled them to access interactive tools, community bulletin boards, and chat rooms. The site allowed members to customize their own drkoop.com homepage to cover whatever topics, health issues, and diseases that interested them.

News

The drkoop.com News section provided the latest and most critical information about health. Users could review recent and late-breaking information about product recalls, health-related editorials, health events, polls, special reports, and sports medicine. The site included reports and press releases from such sources as the American Council on Science and Health (ACSH) and the Occupational Safety and Health Administration (OSHA). Using drkoop.com's HealthSearch feature, members could readily locate

---

[16]"i:20 drkoop.com's Dennis Upah."

[17]CAA provides strategic consulting services in marketing and technology areas and holds alliances with Internet incubator, idealab! and communications consulting and advertising company, Shepardson, Stern and Kaminsky.

exhibit 2 Actual and Projected Income Statements for drkoop.com, 1997–2001
(In Millions of $, Except for Per Share Data)

	Income Statement Data					Revenue-Cost-Margin Analysis				
	1997	1998	1999	2000*	2001*	1997	1998	1999	2000*	2001*
Revenues										
Advertising	—	—	$ 7.7	$ 23.3	$42.3	N/A	N/A	81.1%	72.7%	63.4%
Content licensing	—	—	1.7	6.7	17.1	N/A	N/A	17.9	20.8	25.6
Other	—	—	0.1	2.1	7.4	N/A	N/A	1.1	6.5	11.0
Total revenues	—	$0.04	$ 9.5	$ 32.1	$66.7	N/A	N/A	100.0%	100.0%	100.0%
Cost of operations										
Production, content, and product development	$ 0.5	$ 4.4	$ 9.4	$ 20.8	$23.5	N/A	N/A	98.9%	64.9%	35.2%
Sales and marketing	—	2.0	45.6	34.6	35.8	N/A	N/A	480.0	107.7	53.6
Total cost of sales	$ 0.5	$ 6.4	$55.0	$ 55.4	$59.3	N/A	N/A	578.9%	172.6%	88.8%
Gross income	($ 0.5)	($ 6.4)	($47.9)	($ 23.3)	$ 7.4					
Gross margin %	NM	NM	NM	(72.6%)	11.1%					
General and administrative expense	$ 0.2	$ 2.6	$ 9.5	$ 10.6	$12.2	N/A	N/A	100.0%	33.0%	18.3%
Operating income	($ 0.6)	($ 9.0)	($57.4)	($ 33.9)	($ 4.8)					
Operating margin	NM	NM	NM	(105.6%)	(7.2%)					
Nonoperating income and expenses										
Interest (net)	—	—	$ 1.3	$ 1.7	$ 1.7	N/A	N/A	13.7%	5.3%	2.5%
Other	—	—	—	—	—	N/A	N/A	0.0	0.0	0.0
Pretax income	($ 0.6)	($ 9.0)	($56.1)	($ 32.2)	($ 3.1)	N/A	N/A	(590.5%)	(100.3%)	(4.6%)
Pretax margin	NM	NM	NM	(100.3%)	(4.6%)					
Provision for income taxes	—	—	—	—	$ 0.6					
Tax rate	0%	0%	0%	0%	(18%)					
Income before nonrecurring items	($ 0.6)	($ 9.0)	($56.1)	($ 32.2)	($ 3.6)	N/A	N/A	(590.5%)	(100.3%)	(5.4%)
Nonrecurring items	—	—	—	—	—					
Net income	($ 0.6)	($ 9.0)	($56.1)	($ 32.2)	($ 3.6)	N/A	N/A	(590.5%)	(100.3%)	(5.4%)

*Estimated.

NM = Not meaningful. N/A = Not applicable.

Source: Company reports; Bear, Stearns & Co. Inc. estimates.

exhibit 3   drkoop.com's Balance Sheet Data, 1998–1999, with Estimates for 2000–2001*
($ In Millions, Except for Share Data)

	December 1998	December 1999	December 2000*	December 2001*
Assets				
Current assets				
Cash and equivalents	—	$ 35.7	$ 19.9	$ 11.1
Accounts receivable		10.5	9.6	14.5
Other	—	22.6	5.9	5.9
Total current assets	$ 0.1	$ 68.9	$ 35.4	$ 31.5
Property, plant, and equipment	$ 0.3	$ 10.4	$ 1.0	$ 2.2
Investment	—	$ 5.0	$ 5.0	$ 5.0
Licenses	—	2.8	2.1	1.2
Other	—	12.4	—	—
Total assets	$ 0.4	$ 99.5	$ 43.6	$ 39.9
Liabilities and stockholders' equity				
Current liabilities				
Accounts payable	$ 0.8	$ 8.2	$ 5.0	$ 5.0
Accrued liabilities	0.5	9.6	2.7	2.7
Deferred revenue	—	3.4	0.7	0.7
Notes payable	0.5	—	0.3	0.3
Total current liabilities	$ 3.0	$ 23.2	$ 8.7	$ 8.7
Other	—	—	—	—
Redeemable preferred stock	$18.4	—	—	—
Preferred stock	—	—	—	—
Common stock	—	—	—	—
Capital in excess of par	—	$149.4	$133.5	$129.9
Retained earnings (deficit)	(19.6)	(75.7)	(94.9)	(94.9)
Other	(1.4)	(2.4)	(3.9)	(3.9)
Total stockholders' equity	($21.0)	$ 71.3	$ 34.8	$ 31.2
Total liabilities and stockholders' equity	$ 0.4	$ 99.5	$ 43.6	$ 39.9
Selected financial statistics				
Current ratio	0	7.7	4.1	3.6
Days sales outstanding	N/A	94	80.4	65.2
Book value/share	N/A	$ 2.23	$ 1.14	$ 0.99
Return on equity	N/A	N/A	N/A	N/A
Cash flow per share	($0.32)	($ 0.41)	($1.00)	($ 0.06)
Free cash flow per share	($0.33)	($ 0.41)	($1.04)	($ 0.12)
Long-term debt/total capital	0%	0%	0%	0%

*Estimated.

Source: Company reports; Bear, Stearns & Co. Inc. estimates.

archived articles relating to all types of health concerns. The search function not only scanned the drkoop.com site but also searched the MedLine database of medical journals and the National Cancer Institute's bibliographic database for relevant articles or abstracts.

exhibit 4   drkoop.com's Statement of Cash Flows, 1998–1999, with Projections for 2000–2001 ($ in Millions, Except for Share Data)

	1998	1999	2000*	2001*
Cash flows from operating activities				
Net income	($9.0)	($ 68.2)	($32.2)	($ 3.6)
Depreciation and amortization	0.1	1.4	1.8	1.8
Other	0.1	26.5	—	—
Change in current account				
Accounts receivable	—	(4.7)	(4.9)	(4.9)
Increase in other assets	—	—	—	—
Accounts payable	2.1	(0.1)	—	—
Accrued liabilities and other assets	—	(0.2)	—	—
Deferred revenue	—	(0.5)	—	—
Other	—	(6.0)	—	—
Cash provided by operating activities	($6.8)	($ 50.7)	($35.4)	($ 6.7)
Cash flows from investing activities				
Capital expenditures	($0.3)	($ 0.6)	($ 1.3)	($ 2.1)
Net cash used in investing activities	($0.3)	($ 0.6)	($ 1.3)	($ 2.1)
Cash flows from financing activities				
Net long-term financing	$0.5	—	—	—
Preferred stock issuances	6.6	$ 5.8	—	—
Common stock issuances	—	90.0	—	—
Other	—	12.0	—	—
Net cash provided in financing activities	$7.1	$107.8	—	—
Net increase (decrease) in cash	—	$ 56.6	($36.7)	($ 8.8)
Cash beginning of year	—	—	56.6	19.9
End of year	—	$ 56.6	$19.9	$11.1
Cash flow/share	($0.3)	($ 2.25)	($1.00)	($0.06)
Free cash flow (FCF) per share	($0.3)	($ 2.27)	($1.04)	($0.12)

	1998	1999	2000*	2001*
Cash flow from operations minus net loss (income)	$2.2	$ 17.5	($ 3.1)	($ 3.1)
EBITDA*	(9.0)	(41.6)	(32.1)	(3.0)
Free cash flow (FCF)	(6.5)	(50.1)	(34.1)	(4.6)

*Estimated.

* Earnings before interest, taxes, depreciation, and amortization.

Source: Company reports; Bear, Stearns & Co. Inc. estimates.

Family

The Family section of the drkoop.com Web site was divided into subcategories, including Children, Men, Women, and Elderly. The Web site had received accolades as a superior health care destination for women and children. On November 8, 1999, eHealthCare World awarded drkoop.com a gold medal in the category "Best Site for Women" based on meeting women's needs for its health and medical news, information, education, advice, support, and community events.[18]

---

[18]"drkoop.com Web Site Dominates Awards at eHealthcare World," PR Newswire, November 8, 1999.

Resources

Drkoop.com provided users with a variety of content and tools for users to personalize their experience at the Web site. Drkoop.com's Personal Drugstore was a central location where consumers could find information about prescription drugs and check drug interactions. DrugChecker, a proprietary drkoop.com technology, enabled consumers to ensure that their medications did not interact with each other or with food to cause adverse reactions. Such information was considered vital information, considering that the American Medical Association reported adverse drug interactions were the fourth leading cause of death in the United States. Over 100,000 deaths in 1997 were attributed to the adverse affects of prescription drugs.[19] Drkoop.com's DrugChecker technology received a gold medal as the "Best Interactive Assessment Tool" in the eHealthcare World awards.[20] Members could download the DrugChecker tool and add it to their personal Web site, free of charge. In late 1999, over 9,500 Web sites were making DrugChecker available.[21]

Drkoop.com's Personal Insurance Center helped consumers evaluate insurance plans through access to an insurance library, a glossary of terms, and expert advice. Users could review frequently asked questions, search archived questions, and send their questions to insurance expert Jim Perry, the director of state affairs for the Council for Affordable Health Insurance. The Personal Insurance Center pages contained advertisements with direct links to several health insurance sites, including eHealthInsurance.com and Quotesmith.com, that provided online policy information and premium quotes. This section of the site was recognized for its extensive library of insurance articles, information on insurance programs by state, Medicare and Medicaid information, and tools for choosing an insurance policy.[22] Drkoop.com won a silver medal at the eHealthcare World Awards as the "Best Managed Care Site."

Prior to proliferating use of the Internet, information about clinical trial results and registration was limited for patients. Drkoop.com had recently begun disseminating information about clinical studies; this included such things as patient information, trial procedures, how research was conducted, and how consumers could participate in a Quintiles clinical study. Drkoop.com had formed a partnership with Quintiles, the world's leading provider of health care services to the pharmaceutical industry and largest clinical trials management organization, whereby drkoop.com was compensated for successfully recruiting qualified participants into clinical trials.

Drkoop.com had a database and directory of health resources in local communities. A regional directory helped consumers locate hospitals; however, the directory listings were limited to hospitals that participated in the drkoop.com Community Partner Program.[23] A Physician Locator tool, provided by the American Board of Medical Specialties (ABMS), allowed members to search and verify the location and specialty of any physician certified by the member boards of the ABMS. When members clicked on the Physician Locator service, they were automatically transferred to the ABMS site. The Resources section also provided links to pharmacy sites where consumers could order and reorder their prescriptions with doctor approval. When asked if prescriptions

---

[19]"Dr. Koop's Community."

[20]"drkoop.com Web Site Dominates Awards at eHealthcareWorld."

[21]Ibid.

[22]Ibid.

[23]Hospitals that participate in the Community Partner Program pay $50,000 to $100,000 per year to license drkoop.com health care information to use on their Web sites. In addition, direct links are provided from the drkoop.com site to their individual Web sites.

will be given almost exclusively online, Donald Hackett, president and CEO of drkoop.com, did not expect the Internet to become the chief vehicle for providing prescriptions to patients. He said:

> Although I'm a technologist at heart, there's a tremendous amount of human interaction that needs to take place. But even when the consumer needs to schedule the appointment, you can eliminate waste from the system with new technology. This technology is about streamlining the screening process.[24]

Other resources included drkoop.com's rankings of other health sites (not including major competitors such as WebMD and onhealth.com) and a list of books recommended by drkoop.com experts and community leaders. Through an alliance with Amazon.com, users wishing to purchase any of the recommended books were automatically sent the Amazon.com site.

Wellness

The primary topics in the Wellness section were fitness and prevention. There was advice on weight loss, along with diet-oriented chat rooms and recipes for diet foods. Consumers could use this section to plan a workout routine that matched diet and time constraints. The section's theme was that by staying healthy and fit, people could prevent many illnesses.

In further support of the wellness theme, there were pages devoted to one of Dr. C. Everett Koop's favorite subjects: the evils of smoking. In addition to extensive information on the effects of smoking on the body, there was information on quitting programs and support groups. Much of the information concerning smoking reflected Dr. Koop's strong personal views.

Community

Drkoop.com's underlying philosophy of getting people together and giving them the tools and information to improve their health was much in evidence in the Community section of the Web site, which had more than 130 interactive chat rooms and message boards devoted to specific afflictions and health problems. Users could click on any of the 130-plus topics and join in on chat room discussions, read message board postings, and post messages sharing their own experiences and views. In addition, there were daily topics of discussion where participants could "listen in" on discussions not only with other patients, but also with doctors.

The Community section had a constant stream of banner ads and large sidebar ads from sites such as DrugEmporium.com; links to these sites made it convenient for site users to purchase health care products and services online. The ads often focused on the particular disease that the user was currently examining.

Conditions

The Conditions section was an online encyclopedia of medical advice. Visitors could research almost any disease or mental health issue they had questions about. It also offered shortcuts to advice pages for first aid and for common symptoms such as back

---

[24]"Posts," *The Standard,* June 28, 1999.

pain or insomnia. The first-aid pages provided advice on a wide variety of topics, from animal bites to sunburn.

Site Disclaimer/Liability

The drkoop.com site had a disclaimer on every Web page that stated, "This information is not intended to be a substitute for professional medical advice. You should not use this information to diagnose or treat a health problem or disease without consulting with a qualified health care provider. Please consult your health care provider with any questions or concerns you may have regarding your condition."[25]

Site Awards

On November 4, 1999, drkoop.com won more awards than any other health care Web site at eHealthcare World Awards in New York. The site received two Gold and two Silver awards, in recognition of its trusted content and health care information for consumers. However, the drkoop.com Web site had been criticized by the American Medical Association for not providing sufficient information related to sponsorship and commerce relationships.

DRKOOP.COM'S MEDICAL ADVISORY BOARD

To help develop the content of the medical information and resources available at its website, drkoop.com had created a Medical Advisory Board consisting of Dr. C. Everett Koop and five others:

- Dr. Nancy Snyderman—a member of the company's board of directors, the medical correspondent for ABC (who made frequent appearances on *Good Morning America, 20/20,* and the *ABC Evening News*), a monthly columnist for *Good Housekeeping,* the author of a book on health care for women over 40, the author of several published papers and an associate clinical professor at the California Pacific Medical Center and the University of California–San Francisco.

- Dr. James F. Dickson III—a former deputy assistant secretary of health and assistant surgeon general, the author of over 50 published papers on surgery and biomedical research, the editor of six books, and a fellow of the American College of Surgeons.

- Dr. Bruce Hensel—an Emmy Award–winning medical, health, and science editor/reporter for NBC4's *Channel 4 News;* the host of *4 Your Health!*; a local Emmy Award–winning series of half-hour specials featuring the latest in medical breakthroughs, information, and technology; an associate professor of medicine at UCLA; and the winner of several other awards for medical education.

- Dr. Stanley Joel Reiser—a professor of humanities and technology in health care at the University of Texas–Houston Health Care Center, the author of over 120 articles and books, a noted speaker on medical topics, and recognized authority on medical ethics, the assessment of medical technologies, the role of values in governing health care organizations, and public health care policy.

- Dr. Michael Seth Shaw—president of Health Science Media (a health care education, communications, and media company in Atlanta, Georgia) since 1979; a

---

[25]Disclaimer present on every page of the drkoop.com Web site.

graduate of Emory University School of Medicine; and a member of several medical organizations.

COMPETITION AND PROFILES OF SELECTED RIVALS

Competition in the online medical information provider industry was strong and getting stronger. Hundreds of sites providing various kinds of medical information had emerged over the past two years. All of the most popular sites provided extensive consumer health information, chat rooms, expert advice, links to products and comprehensive and fully tailored health care publications for professionals of all specialties.

In addition to the companies that specialized primarily in online health and medical information, large medical and health care companies were establishing an Internet presence. Some provided medical information, but the primary focus of most such companies was on marketing health insurance and/or over-the-counter drug products. Most pharmaceutical companies had portions of their corporate Web sites dedicated to consumer health information. One big player in this area was Merck, which published an online "medical bible." The pharmaceutical companies were not direct competitors of medical information providers like drkoop.com because their main focus was to sell pharmaceutical products, but they were still players in the online medical information market.

Drkoop.com's management expected that competition among these sites to obtain content would likely increase the fees charged by high-quality content providers, perhaps driving up costs significantly. In addition, competition was forcing all medical information providers to try to set themselves apart on the basis of differentiating Web site features. The addition of new features required rivals to continue to improve the technology underlying their Web sites, also driving up costs significantly.

In October 1999, PC Data ranked drkoop.com as the number one dedicated health care site, based on Web site traffic, for the seventh consecutive month (see Exhibit 5).[26] According to PC Data, the site was the 43rd most popular site on the Internet overall.

Brief profiles of selected leading online medical information providers are presented below.

Healtheon/WebMD.com

Drkoop.com's strongest competitor was Healtheon/WebMD Corporation, which claimed to be the first comprehensive online health care portal.[27] The company was formed by a merger of Healtheon and WebMD in May 1999. Following the merger, the companies combined their consumer Web sites, MyHealtheon.com and MyWebMD.com, into one site (www.webmd.com). Healtheon/WebMD was building a system of software and services to automate such tasks as HMO enrollment, referrals, data retrieval, and claims processing for use by insurers, doctors, pharmacies, and consumers. The site also offered physician communications services, physician references, medical information and news, and personalized content to its users. Healtheon/WebMD had revenues of $28.7 million in the quarter ending September 1999.

In early December 1999, Rupert Murdoch's News Corp. formed a $1 billion partnership with Healtheon/WebMD in one of the largest media and Internet deals to date.[28]

---

[26]PR Newswire Association, October 7, 1999, Financial News section.

[27]www.ixl.com/success/webmd/index.html.

[28]www.thestandard.com/article/display/0,1151,6224,00.html.

exhibit 5   Traffic Statistics on Medical Information Provider Web Sites, September 1999

Company	Number of Unique Hits, September 1999
drkoop.com	5,539,000
onhealth.com	2,262,000
discoveryhealth.com	1,077,000
webmd.com	765,000
thriveonline.com	753,000
healthyideas.com	714,000
intelihealth.com	675,000
allhealth.com	596,000
AOLhealth.com	568,000
Healthcentral.com	532,000
medscape.com	415,000
ama-assn.org	404,000
mediconsult.com	225,000

News Corp. became a 10.8 percent owner of Healtheon/WebMD, providing $700 million in "branding services" over 10 years, purchasing $100 million of Healtheon/WebMD's stock, investing $100 million cash in the Internet company, and signing a $62.5 million five-year licensing deal to syndicate WebMD's daily broadcast content. In describing the partnership, News Corp. president and COO Peter Chernin said, "Companies traditionally re-purpose print or broadcast content for the Web. With this deal, we're using the Web as a source for original, unique programming which will be leveraged across all media owned by News Corp."[29] The goal of this partnership was to drive television viewers to medical Web sites and vice versa, creating single health care information brands across all media. Industry observers speculated that the News Corp. partnership could give Healtheon/WebMD an advantage in internationalizing online health care.

Mediconsult.com

Mediconsult's mission was to provide timely, comprehensive, and accessible information on chronic medical conditions, using the latest available technology to deliver information efficiently. Its Web site featured a fee-based service, *MediXpert,* which let visitors present a case to a medical specialist who responded with a confidential report. Mediconsult had no affiliation with any HMO, hospital, or other health care organization in order to ensure unbiased, objective, credible information. Management insisted that all information on its site "pass a rigorous clinical review process before we deem it worthy" of the consumer.[30] The site also had a powerful search engine, Medisearch, which allowed quick keyword inquiries. Mediconsult reported revenues of $3.1 million for the quarter ending September 1999.

---

[29]thestandard.com.

[30]www.mediconsult.com.

In September 1999, Mediconsult.com acquired Physicians Online in a stock deal valued at $180 million. The acquisition was expected to help Mediconsult.com take advantage of the recent introduction of online medical records and other services designed to connect doctors and patients and deliver health care.[31]

The Health Network.com

The Health Network was a 50/50 partnership between FOX Entertainment Group and AHN Partners, LP, that combined the leading health cable television channel (The Health Network) with one of the most visited health information sites on the Internet (ahn.com, recently renamed TheHealthNetwork.com). The partnership promoted itself as a one-stop television and Internet site where consumers could find information, support, and the motivation needed to make decisions about leading a healthy life. The Health Network reached more than 17 million households in all 50 states through cable and satellite and could be seen via the Internet with live streaming video. Its Web site was the premier source of live medical events, such as the first live Internet birth and the first live Internet triplet birth.

Viewers, whether online or watching on television, were provided information by doctors and other experts in a clear, interesting, and easy-to-understand manner. In addition, the online site provided original programming, breaking news, exercise and nutrition guides, expert medical advice, and in-depth information. Online users could connect directly with both credible medical professionals and people who had similar interests in specific health categories such as women's health, parenting, and heart health.

Medscape

Medscape's home page was comprehensive, well organized, and user-friendly. It featured the Medscape Network (for student, nurses, physicians), Medscape Resources, My Medscape (records personalized info from previous visits) and an Editorial Board. In addition, Medscape published *Medscape General Medicine,* an online, peer-reviewed medical journal, and it offered a database of continuing medical education programs, an online bookstore, and physician Web sites for its members.

Medscape produced the consumer-oriented CBS *HealthWatch.* In July 1999, CBS acquired a 35 percent stake in Medscape in exchange for $157 million in advertising and branding services. The company had recently announced a content agreement with America Online. The three-year arrangement called for Medscape to develop co-branded health sites for AOL's 18 million subscribers. In exchange, Medscape will pay AOL $33 million for two years.

Medscape reported revenues of $3.1 million for the quarter ending September 1999.

The American Medical Association Web Site (www.ama-assn.org)

The American Medical Association (AMA) represented about 35 percent of U.S. doctors (down from 50 percent in 1975). A core objective of the AMA was to be the world leader in obtaining, synthesizing, integrating, and disseminating information on health and

---

[31]www.thestandard.com/article/display/0,1151,6224,00.html.

medical practice. The AMA published numerous journals, and its corporate Web site, a portion of which was accessible to members only, provided valuable online information. The general public could use the site to look for medical group and physician locators; to get medical advice about injuries, illnesses, and specific conditions; and to read about general health information. Consumers could also learn about the association's advocacy and legislative initiatives and read about topics on medical ethics and education.

Revenue erosion from declining membership was expected to cause the AMA to devote time and resources to enhancing and promoting the public part of its Web site as a way of rejuvenating its revenue stream.

OnHealth.com

OnHealth Network Company was a consumer health information company based in Seattle. Its Web site was not tied to a particular doctor group, health system, or insurance company. OnHealth.com offered both proprietary and syndicated content. Most information came from the *New England Journal of Medicine,* Cleveland Clinic, Beth Israel Deaconess Medical Center, and physicians who taught at Harvard, Columbia, and Stanford. A unique feature on the site's home page was the Herbal Index, which contained 140 descriptions of alternative health remedies. About 80 percent of OnHealth's audience was female.

The company had negotiated agreements to provide content to several Web sites, including America Online and WebTV. In December 1999, OnHealth.com signed an agreement with Ask Jeeves, Inc., a leading provider of natural-language question-answering services on the Web for consumers and businesses. This deal will provide OnHealth with prominent brand positioning.[32]

The site was supported by advertising. Advertisers included Johnson & Johnson and Pfizer. Site operators claimed that the information about a topic was not influenced by the advertisements displayed on that page, indicating, "If it ever appears otherwise to you, please let us know."[33]

Affiliates of Van Wagoner Capital Management owned about 39 percent of the company. OnHealth reported revenues of $1 million for the quarter ending September 1999.

iVillage's www.allHealth.com

iVillage's Web site targeted women aged 25 to 49 through more than 15 "channels" focusing on topics such as health, food, parenting, relationships, and shopping. The health sections of the site were at betterhealth.com or allhealth.com. The sites used the tag lines "Take Charge of Your Health!" and "Information you need from a Community you can trust."[34] Site features included extensive chat rooms, weekly polls, and shopping. iVillage members could "ask the experts" for medical advice. iVillage generated more than 80 percent of its revenue from advertising, but the company was looking to enlarge its online product offerings; its first step in this direction was a line of baby products offered at iBaby.com. In the quarter ending September 1999, iVillage reported revenues of $10.7 million.

---

[32]www.askjeeves.com. Investor Relations.

[33]onhealth.com/chl/info/item.asp.

[34]www.allhealth.com.

Candice Carpenter, iVillage's CEO, commenting on the recent merger between Healtheon and WebMD, said, "I think it's pretty obvious there needs to be some (more) consolidation. We've got to clean this up a little. I don't know who's going to do it, but somebody should step up to the plate to do that job."[35]

CONFLICTS OF INTEREST AND ETHICS CONCERNS

There vas a growing concern among many medical information providers about the potential for conflicts of interests and potential liability in providing inaccurate information, diagnosis, and prescribing drugs online. In a proactive attempt to address such issues, Dr. C. Everett Koop initiated a meeting of interested parties. The meeting resulted in the formation of a coalition of 16 companies, including Healtheon/WebMD, Medscape Inc., America Online Inc., and drkoop.com, to develop an ethical code of conduct for Internet-based medical information providers. Alliance members accounted for 27 percent of total Internet audience traffic.[36] The group was working to create a set of recommended policies and practices for advertising, privacy, and content that would ensure the reliability of health information that consumers accessed through e-health providers. Donald Kemper, the chairperson of Hi-Ethics, stated that "our ultimate goal is to guide a future of consumer confidence in health care information."[37]

FUTURE OUTLOOK FOR DRKOOP.COM

Donald W. Hackett, president and CEO of drkoop.com, believed the company had a promising future:

> The successful execution of our business strategy has firmly positioned the company for growth. Our registered users are growing at a healthy pace, we are rapidly extending our reach, our advertising and sponsorship pipeline is strong, and the drkoop.com brand name continues to be recognized as an industry leader. Looking ahead, we intend to leverage the strength of our domestic business to accelerate expansion into international markets. We recently announced our first alliance with Australia's Medweb and anticipate continued international expansion in the first half of 2000.

Nonetheless, Hackett and company cofounder Dennis Upah knew the challenges ahead were formidable. Medical sites on the Internet were proliferating. Competition was becoming stronger. WebMD and Rupert Murdoch's News Corp. had announced plans to put more than $1 billion into developing their medical information site. Companies like Healtheon/WebMD were partnering with hospitals to provide services other than medical information. While there were many opportunities for medical information providers, it was far from clear which business model and strategy made the most sense for drkoop.com. And even more important, drkoop.com was "burning" through its cash reserves and looking at negative cash flows for some time to come. A number of investors were becoming increasingly concerned about the company's financial position and the viability of its business model.

---

[35]www.thestandard.com/article/display/0,1151,4839,00.html.

[36]"Leading E-Healthware Companies Form Alliance to Benefit Internet Consumers," Business Wire, November 4, 1999.

[37]Ibid.

case 15 WingspanBank.com

Laura Cooke
University of Michigan

Hyung Kim
University of Michigan

Liza Hovey
University of Michigan

Paul Rakowski
University of Michigan

[WingspanBank] cannibalize[s] existing business to build new business.[1]

—John B. McCoy, President and CEO, Bank One Corporation

It was Monday, November 15, 1999, and John B. McCoy already felt like it had been a long week. *The Wall Street Journal* had announced the impending departure of James Stewart,[2] chief executive of Wingspan, and investors and media hounds alike were clamoring for more details.

McCoy remembered Wingspan's first days, when he worried about the many Internet start-ups beginning to offer a wide array of financial services. Reasoning that bankone.com was insufficient to stem the tide, he launched WingspanBank.com as a freestanding Internet bank.[3] After all, he thought, if customers were going to abandon brick-and-mortar banks in favor of Internet banks, Bank One should offer the best choice: WingspanBank.com.

Thus, WingspanBank.com was launched on June 24, 1999, under the auspices of the First USA division of Bank One. Unfortunately, the First USA division had performed poorly since then, and analysts had been questioning whether the excitement of launching WingspanBank.com had distracted management from its core business—credit cards.[4]

As McCoy considered the situation, several questions came to mind: Had he been right about permitting cannibalization? What is the role of Wingspan at Bank One? What is the future of Bank One in the era of e-commerce?

BACKGROUND

There was a lot for McCoy to consider. The final decades of the 20th century had brought changes to every possible dimension of banking. From changes in government

---

Prepared under the supervision of Professor Allan Afuah. University of Michigan. Some data, names and situations have been disguised to maintain confidentiality.

[1]"Internet Defense Strategy: Cannibalize Yourself," *Fortune,* September 6, 1999, p. 122.

[2]"Bank One Says CEO of Internet Venture, Wingspan, Will Resign at Year's End," *The Wall Street Journal,* November 15, 1999, p. B11.

[3]"Internet Defense Strategy: Cannibalize Yourself," pp. 121–34.

[4]"WingspanBank: Losing Its Wings?" *The Industry Standard* (www.thestandard.com/article/display/0,1151,7658,00.html?05).

exhibit 1   Bank One Milestones

1868	F. C. Session founds Commercial National Bank in Columbus, Ohio.
1929	Commercial National and National Bank of Commerce combine to form City National Bank and Trust.
1935	First John (H.) McCoy becomes bank president.
1958	Second John (G.) McCoy becomes bank president.
1966	City National Bank introduces first Visa (then Bank.Americard) credit card outside California.
1967	First Banc Group of Ohio formed as holding company for City National Bank; First Banc buys Farmers Savings and Trust of Mansfield, Ohio.
1977	First Bank introduces first cash management account in partnership with Merrill Lynch.
1979	Company changes name to Banc One; all affiliated banks renamed Bank One.
1984	Third (and present) John (B.) McCoy becomes bank president; federal government relaxes restrictions on interstate banking; and Banc One expands into Indiana, Kentucky, Michigan, and Wisconsin.
1989	Banc One enters Texas market with acquisition of 20 failed Mcorp and other banks.
1991	Banc One enters Illinois.
1992	Banc One enters Arizona and Utah.
1994	Banc One begins major consolidation effort.
1996	Banc One buys Premier Bancorp., Louisiana's number three bank.
1997	Banc One acquires number four card issuer, First USA, and buys Liberty Bancorp of Oklahoma.
1998	Banc One acquires First Chicago NBD in $30 billion stock swap and changes name to Bank One Corporation, based in Chicago, Illinois; Bank One is number four banking company in United States. The company launches bankone.com, which offers traditional banking services to current customers (and general information about Bank One Corporation).
1999	Bank One becomes world's largest issuer of Visa credit cards; it also launches WingspanBank.com (as unit of First USA division), which offers wide array of financial services—including insurance, mortgage, and mutual fund services.

Sources: Bank One Corporation 1998 annual report; Hoover's Company Capsules; and WingspanBank Marketing.

regulations to the emergence of the Internet, the ever-changing landscape for financial service companies brought difficult challenges and uncertain opportunities.

History of Bank One

Just as its official all-capital-letter name BANK ONE CORPORATION (hereinafter Bank One) proclaims, this financial institution thinks big, and its recent history (see Exhibit 1) shows that it embraces innovations. Among them are the first Visa (then called BankAmericard) credit card service outside California in 1966, and the first cash management account in 1977, which combined the higher interest rates of a brokerage account with the flexibility of checking services.

The bank—founded in 1868 and called City National Bank after the merger of two Columbus, Ohio, banks in 1929—also has a strong history of acquisitions. In 1967, its management created a holding company to enable expansion and named it First Banc Group of Ohio to skirt legal restrictions on the use of the word *bank.* Its acquisition of a bank in neighboring Mansfield, Ohio, initiated a string of intrastate acquisitions.

exhibit 2 Summary Balance Sheet for Bank One, 1997–1998
(In Millions of $)

	Year Ended December 31st	
	1998	1997
Assets		
Cash and due from banks	$ 10,878	$ 10,000
Interest-bearing due from banks	4,642	6,910
Funds and securities under resale agreements	9,862	9,168
Trading and derivative products	12,299	9,869
Investment securities	44,852	26,039
Loans, net	153,127	156,762
Bank premises and equipment, net	3,340	3,426
Other assets	13,496	11,818
Total assets	$261,496	$239,372
Liabilities and stockholders' equity		
Deposits, total	$161,542	$153,726
Short-term borrowings, total	40,101	33,152
Long-term debt	21,295	20,543
Other liabilities	17,998	12,901
Total liabilities	$240,936	$220,322
Stockholders' equity		
Preferred stock	$ 190	$ 326
Common stock, $0.01 par value	12	12
Surplus	10,769	12,584
Retained earnings	9,528	8,063
Other	61	(1,935)
Total stockholders' equity	$ 20,560	$ 19,050
Total liabilities and stockholders' equity	$261,496	$239,372

Source: Bank One Corporation 1998 annual report.

When restrictions on interstate banking were removed in 1984, Banc One (changed from First Banc in 1979) expanded into Arizona, Illinois, Indiana, Kentucky, Michigan, Texas, Utah and Wisconsin—primarily through stock swaps.

Following its "merger of equals" (under Banc One leadership) with First Chicago NBD in 1998, Bank One (so renamed after the merger) was the fourth largest banking company in the United States (see Exhibits 2 and 3). In addition, the recent acquisition of credit card issuer First USA made Bank One, already the number three issuer, the largest issuer of Visa credit cards in the world.

First USA featured a more entrepreneurial culture than Bank One and also brought significant e-commerce expertise in the form of its Internet Marketing Group. In its efforts to develop an e-commerce strategy for First USA and implement firstusa.com, this group had learned important lessons and forged useful relationships. The Internet Marketing Group made it possible for Bank One to take fuller advantage of the mounting Internet explosion than its current presence. BankOne.com (see Exhibit 4) was

exhibit 3   Summary Income Statement for Bank One, 1997–1998
(In Millions, except for Per Share Data)

	Year Ended December 31st	
	1998	1997
Interest income		
Interest income, total	$17,524	$17,545
Interest expense, total	8,177	8,084
Less provision for credit losses	1,408	1,988
Net interest income after credit losses	$ 7,939	$ 7,374
Noninterest revenue		
Market-driven revenue	$ 546	$ 552
Fee-based revenue	6,728	5,645
Other	797	497
Total noninterest revenue	$ 8,071	$ 6,694
Noninterest expense		
Salaries and benefits	$ 4,477	$ 4,224
Net occupancy and equipment	845	739
Depreciation and amortization	680	693
Outside service fees and processing	1,349	1,145
Marketing and development	1,024	837
Communication and transportation	781	711
Merger-related and restructuring charges	1,062	337
Other	1,327	1,054
Total	$11,545	$ 9,740
Earnings before income taxes	$ 4,465	$ 4,427
Applicable income taxes	1,357	1,467
Net income	$ 3,108	$ 2,960
Earnings per share, basic	$ 2.65	$ 2.48
Earnings per share, diluted	$ 2.61	$ 2.43

Source: Bank One Corporation 1998 annual report.

meant simply to offer online services to current customers of Bank One and to serve as the corporation's online information presence.

Explosion of the Internet

By the late 1990s, the Internet had already transformed itself from a convenience for academics and curiosity for intellectuals to a viable commercial force and powerful business tool. Three primary phenomena converged to spur this emergence:

- *More people had access to the Internet.* Personal computers (PCs) and Internet access became increasingly affordable and reliable. Frenetic competition, learning effects, and scale economies in the PC and Internet industries even made it possible

exhibit 4   BankOne.com Start Page

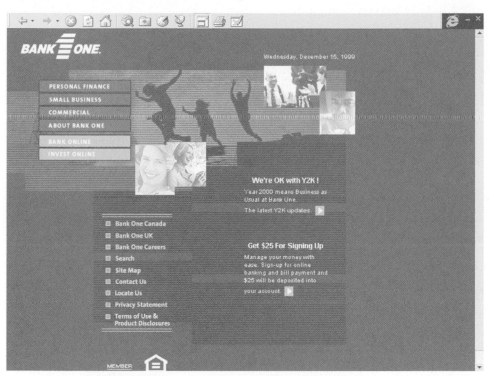

Source: www.bankone.com.

for some companies to offer free PCs to consumers willing to purchase Internet access (and vice versa). In addition, the network software offered security and ease of use. By 1998, over 50 percent of U.S. households had personal computers (PCs), and over 30 percent had Internet access (see Exhibit 5).

- *The Internet offered something for everyone.* Internet companies were enjoying extraordinary market valuations, and no one wanted to be left out. For instance, the market value of online toy merchant eToys surpassed the market value of Toys "R" Us within its first day of trading. As a result, seemingly every business looked for ways to offer its products and services on the Internet, and consumers invested what they could. With this infusion of capital and labor, the Internet grew, and the number of online destinations grew sixfold between 1996 and 1999.[5]

- *People became comfortable with e-commerce.* Consumers were doing more and more business on the Internet. Advances in Internet security assuaged fears, and as the Internet became more familiar and affordable, people could and would spend more time "surfing" and buying. As a result, the $7.8 billion online retail market of 1998 is projected to reach $108 billion by 2003 (see Exhibit 6).

With the longest economic expansion in the history of the United States as a backdrop, the Internet was real, and e-commerce an undeniable force.

---

[5]Forrester.com, October 15, 1999.

exhibit 5   Number of U.S. Consumers with PCs and Internet Access

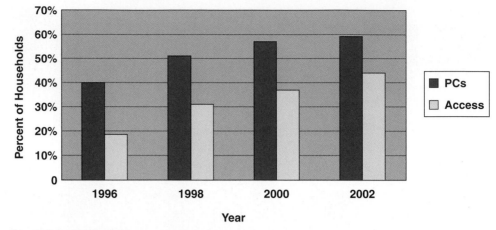

Source: Forrester Research.

exhibit 6   U.S. Online Retail Spending

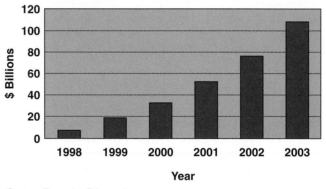

Source: Forrester Research.

Internet Banking

As the Internet achieved greater prominence, online banking emerged. Early Internet-only entrants included Telebank, Net.B@nk (see Exhibits 7 and 8) and Security First Network Bank. Offering cost savings to suppliers and convenience to consumers, Internet banking appeared poised for tremendous growth. Not only did Internet-only banks avoid the overhead expenses incurred by brick-and-mortar locations, but an online transaction cost only 1 cent, compared to $1.07 for a traditional face-to-face transaction (see Exhibit 9). Internet banks could pass these cost savings on to customers in the form of higher interest rates and lower service fees (see Exhibits 10 and 11).

In the mid-1990s the industry began its climb, despite federal banking regulations that limited its growth. For instance, unlike other Internet ventures, online banks had to generate sufficient revenue to cover such expenses as marketing and administration. Nevertheless, pure Internet banks continued to appear, and in October 1998, Compu-Bank became the first national virtual bank to receive a charter from the Office of the

exhibit 7   Net.B@nk.com Start Page

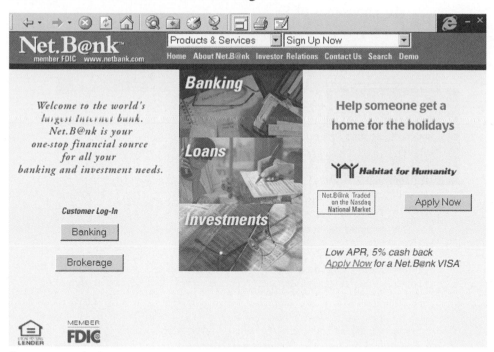

Source: www.netbank.com.

Comptroller of the Currency and approval from the Federal Deposit Insurance Corporation (FDIC).

With interest rates rising and fees falling at online banks, Internet banking burgeoned in the late 1990s. In 1998 alone, the number of households using online banking nearly doubled, to 7 million, and estimates suggest that this number will reach 24 million by 2002.[6] Ominously, this growth, while rapid, pales in comparison to that of other financial services like online brokerage.

Witnessing this growth, traditional brick-and-mortar banks began to acknowledge the importance of this new channel and worked to develop Internet strategies. Among the first were large national banks like Bank of America, Citibank, and Wells Fargo. Their initial Internet attempts meant limited services such as the ability to check balances and transfer funds. The primary purpose of their Internet sites was to retain existing customers and provide information about retail products at brick-and-mortar locations. Soon, however, such other banking giants as Citibank, American Express, and Bank One would work to create separate entities under which to develop true online offerings (see Exhibit 12).

Traditional banks had many assets to leverage in developing Internet products. Customers could use pre-existing ATM networks without per-use transaction fees. In addition, individuals could make deposits at bank locations, electronically or by "snail

---

[6]"Take Your Banking Online" (cnnfn.com/1999/05/21/banking/q_online_banks/), May 21, 1999.

exhibit 8   Net.B@nk Summary Income Statement, 1998–1999
             (In Thousands of $)

	Six Months Ended June 30th	
	1999	1998
Interest income		
Interest income, total	$17,979	$6,459
Interest expense, total	10,290	4,017
Net interest income	$ 7,689	$2,442
Noninterest income		
Noninterest income, total	$ 477	$ 226
Noninterest expense, total	5,851	2,570
Net noninterest income	($ 5,374)	($2,344)
Provision for loan loss	$ 105	$ 10
Earnings before income taxes	$ 2,210	$ 88
Income tax (expense) benefit	(751)	(30)
Tax benefit of loss	—	3,059
Net income	$ 1,459	$3,117

Source: NetBank Investor Relations.

exhibit 9   Estimated Banking Transaction Costs

Transaction Type	Per Unit Cost
Face-to-face (with teller)	$1.07
Mail-in	0.73
Telephone*	0.54
Automated teller machine	0.27
Internet	0.01

*Balance inquiry or money transfer.
Source: "Cyber-Banking Breaks New Ground, Expands towards Mainstream," *Bank Rate Monitor,* January 12, 1999.

mail." Finally, traditional banks' strong brand recognition meant virtually instant trust with potential online clientele.

Established banks faced special challenges, too. General concerns about online privacy and security took on heightened importance when considering individuals' finances. In addition, the considerable investments were unlikely to bring short-term returns. Indeed, this new channel could cannibalize existing business. Furthermore, their conservative outlook coaxed most traditional banks to view the Internet as a revenue source—not as another branch location—and many actually charged customers for online transactions.

Quickly, however, online banks began to recognize that banking services—not venue—would continue to provide most of the revenue. Pete Kight, CEO of CheckFree

exhibit 10   Comparative Interest Rates of Selected Banks, December 1999

Bank	Checking*	Savings*
AmEx Membership Bank	2.00%	2.00%
Bank One	1.49%	1.49%
Bank of America	0%	1.00%
Chase.com	0.76%	2.13%
Citif/i	0%	2.47%
CompuBank	3.00%	3.50%
NetB@nk	Up to 3.93%	N/A
Telebank	Up to 3.68%	Up to 4.88%
WingspanBank.com	Up to 4.5%	N/A
Mean	0.84%	2.13%

*For balances of $0–$15,000.
Source: Company Web sites as of December 13, 1999.

exhibit 11   Comparative Fees of Online Banks, December 1999

	Savings Account	Bill Payment Services	Out-network ATM	Monthly Service Fee	Minimum Account Balance	Online Brokerage Link	Instant Credit Access
AmEx Membership B@nking	Free	Free	Free[1]	None	Yes	Yes	
bankofamerica.com	Free				Yes		
bankone.com	Free						Yes
citif/i	Free	Free	Free	None		Yes	
chase.com	Free						Yes
CompuBank	Free	Free	Free[1]	None	Yes		
NetB@nk		Free		None		Yes	
Telebank	Free	Free		None	Yes[2]	Yes	
wellsfargo.com	Free	Free[3]			Yes	Yes	
WingspanBank.com		Free	Free[4]	None		Yes	Yes

All offer free interest checking and in-network ATM use.
[1]Maximum 4 surcharges per month reimbursed.
[2]Interest not paid on balance below $1,000.
[3]With minimum balance.
[4]Up to $5 per month.
Source: Company Web sites as of December 6, 1999.

Corporation, the premier bill payment and presentment service for online banks, summed it up: "You don't open a new branch and ask your customers to pay to bank there. You need to open a branch online because that's where your customers are."

By November 1999, the landscape looked fragmented, and the competition fierce. Already there were more than 500 online banks,[7] and another 1,000 were predicted

---

[7]"True U.S. Internet Banks," *Online Banking Report,* November 29, 1999.

exhibit 12   Internet-only Divisions of Established Banks

	Internet-only Division	Launch Date
Bank One	Wingspan.com	June 1999
Citibank	Citif/i	August 1999
American Express	Membership B@nking	July 1999
Central Bank USA	USAccess Bank	Pending
Texas Capital Bank	BankDirect	Pending

Source: Team Research.

to launch in the next year. The Federal government further spurred competition in November with the repeal of the Glass-Steagall Act, removing barriers among banks, brokerages and insurance companies (see Exhibit 13). E*Trade quickly announced its intention to purchase Telebank, an early Internet-only bank. Bill Wallace, CIO of Wingspan, describes an even more chaotic scenario: "The other potential competitors that keep me up at night are the Yahoos and AOLs of the world. They have the customer base, but currently face a barrier to entry in being unable to secure charters. If this [barrier] opens up . . ."

To finish Wallace's thought: new entrants vying for space would simply overrun the online banking industry.

WINGSPANBANK.COM

Completing 119 acquisitions in the past 15 years had helped make Bank One the fourth largest bank in the United States. For the 21st century, however, CEO John McCoy looked to another avenue for growth—the Internet.[8]

The Decision to Launch

This fundamental shift in strategy came during a trip in the fall of 1998 that McCoy took with Dick Vague, then head of the First USA Division and a Bank One executive vice president. McCoy and Vague visited Internet companies like Yahoo!, Excite, and America Online. The ostensible purpose was for Vague to negotiate marketing deals for First USA's credit cards.[9] Significantly, however, McCoy began to see the power of the Internet in general and of online banking in particular.

This exposure served as the foundation for a new type of bank within Bank One and a new growth strategy. McCoy quipped that Bank One might never buy another bank because of the tremendous growth potential he saw in the Internet.

In February 1999 McCoy gathered key Bank One executives to discuss what type of online bank to create. The result was WingspanBank.com—a broad-based, Internet-only bank that met all of a customer's financial service needs through one integrated user ID.

---

[8]"Taking Flight with Wingspan," *Crain's Chicago Business,* August 2, 1999.
[9]"Bank One: Nothing but Net," *Business Week,* August 2, 1999.

exhibit 13   Glass-Steagall Act

On November 12, 1999, United States President Bill Clinton signed a new financial modernization bill into law, the Gramm-Leach Act, thus repealing the significant restrictions that had been placed on financial institutions in the United States by the Depression-era legislation, the Glass-Steagall Act. That bill had regulated the industry by preventing banks, insurance companies and brokerage firms from entering into each other's lines of business.

The essence of the Glass-Steagall Act had been to separate commercial and investment banking. Its intention was to protect the commercial customers since it was born out of the concept that the investing activities of bankers in the 1920s had led to the stock market crash and resulting Great Depression of the 1930s. As financial markets have become more accessible to the consumer through such means as the Internet and the Securities and Exchange Commission has been diligent in keeping the markets transparent, such protection no longer was relevant.

While for the most part individual consumers were unaware of the restrictions caused by Glass-Steagall, much infighting had resulted over the years between various financial institutions desiring to offer a wider variety of services to their customers. It is anticipated that with the Act's repeal, many mergers will take place in the financial services industry and that competition will increase significantly. The lines between banks, brokerage firms and insurance companies has certainly been blurred.

Source: Dee DePass, *The Minneapolis Star Tribune,* November 13, 1999.

The Vision

> *If your bank could start over, this is what it would be.*
> —WingspanBank.com slogan

To herald this new Internet-only bank, senior management wanted to create a new brand. James Stewart, the original CEO of Wingspan, explained:

> We wanted something that was unique to online and financial services. We wanted a name that was not necessarily a literal name like Internet bank.com but something that could ultimately come to mean something. Like Amazon didn't mean "books online" and Excite didn't mean "search engine"—but now they do.[10]

The team looked to the market for this new name. After a series of focus groups, potential customers and senior management agreed upon Wingspan. Wingspan symbolized the breadth of new products and emphasized the fresh start. With their early entry into the market, the team hoped that WingspanBank would soon become synonymous with "Internet banking."

WingspanBank should be more than simply Bank One online—indeed, bankone.com already existed. WingspanBank should be a "one-stop shop" for financial services: checking, savings, direct deposit, credit cards, installment and other loans, investments, bill payment, financial planning, CDs, mortgages, insurance, and more. Multiple "best-in-class" vendors would provide these services, permitting Wingspan-Bank customers to use a variety of financial institutions through one channel.

Michael Cleary, president of Wingspan commented:

> Bank One has a multibrand strategy on the Internet. Our goal is to create different products for different customers with different needs. Bank One is for the brick-and-mortar customer

---

[10]*Crain's Chicago Business,* August 2, 1999.

with a regional focus. Wingspan is for an Internet customer with a national focus. To make a consumer products analogy, you may not know whether a customer wants Tide or Wisk, but either way, P&G will make sure to provide it.

The essence of WingspanBank, however, would be convenient, comprehensive, and objective solutions to customers' problems at competitive prices—not merely products. Wingspan committed to becoming a "trusted adviser" to its customers. Cleary noted:

> Offline banks have promised for years to be the trusted adviser for customers. The Internet provides us with the tools to do that. [But] only time will tell whether people will provide the information we need to deliver that value.

The scope was national—extending beyond the 14 states where Bank One operated. The primary target market for WingspanBank.com was a segment that bankone.com could not reach—the growing core group of Internet users who disdain traditional banks. Wingspan wanted both present and future users of Internet banks, especially those who currently bank with Bank One competitors. Even taking Bank One's own customers was deemed acceptable.

Implementation

Jim Stewart was selected to be CEO of Wingspan and an "iBoard of Directors" of technology leaders was created. Together, they set a time frame of 90 days to launch, but where should WingspanBank be born in order to foster creativity, innovation, and speed to market?

The answer was First USA. According to Cleary:

> Bank One bought First USA for its speed and marketing savvy. First USA has the entrepreneurial spirit and acts quickly. I never thought it could move so fast, but indeed it is a fast company.

First USA understood direct marketing and lived to "test and learn." In addition, its Internet Marketing Group had recent experience in the Internet world, and its culture appeared to align well with the goals of Wingspan.

Around 30 external vendors were selected to speed launch and expand product offerings in keeping with the Wingspan vision. These partners comprised the best service providers for each product area. Though invisible in most cases to WingspanBank customers, they directly represented the brand and were thus crucial to the success of the venture. All partners began work based on verbal agreements—time constraints prevented legal negotiations. The work required to implement so much functionality in so little time meant 18-hour days for Wingspan employees and partner staff alike.

Meanwhile Carol Knight, a former First USA consultant, had been selected to head up the marketing and PR efforts. Within the first month, her group conducted over 60 focus groups! These groups clarified what consumers wanted from an Internet bank and helped refine Wingspan's goals.

For instance, consumers' main concern was trustworthiness of the site, followed closely by price. Ease of use and customer service became paramount, increasing the importance of site design and seamless integration of the multiple vendors. Thorough testing before launch was essential—any technical difficulty with the site could sabotage the new brand. A customer's first impression of WingspanBank.com was critical.

Customers also believed putting all of their assets in one place was risky, but using multiple vendors made them feel more secure. This sentiment reassured Wingspan management that partnerships and offerings of non–Bank One products on the site were keys to success. Customers also desired personal financial management (PFM). Although these checking and bill-payment services offered no profit margin, customized PFM could ultimately generate revenue by permitting targeted products such as loans to be "pushed" to consumers.

The marketing team of 30—including Wingspan's advertising and public relations agencies, First USA staff and external consultants—was also developing a plan in keeping with the Wingspan vision. The perceived importance of marketing shows in the nearly $100 million allocated from a total annual operating budget for Wingspan of approximately $150 million.[11] The plan included network TV spots, radio ads, celebrity personalities, press releases, and news features. Each of these activities was critical to the establishment of a stand-alone brand.

Unlike traditional Bank One advertising, which was regional, this campaign demanded national exposure, especially in markets where Bank One did not have a presence (to minimize cannibalization). Cities such as Boston, Seattle, and Philadelphia were ideal. However, the campaign also had a presence in California and Texas, which were existing Bank One markets.

The timeliness was critical to the plan:

> The ad agency had eight weeks to design a campaign and shoot a commercial. The actors practiced a script with no bank name because it was not yet determined. The day of the commercial shoot when the name was revealed, the biggest concern was whether the actors would be able to make this change.[12]

WingspanBank.com was launched on June 24, 1999 (see Exhibit 14)—just 123 days from kickoff. McCoy was very visible during this time, including an interview for *The Wall Street Journal* during which he announced the financial impact to Bank One. In the first year, WingspanBank was expected to dilute the value of Bank One's stock by 5 cents per share; in the second year, to add 5 cents per share; and in the third year, to add 20 cents per share.

Current State

By most measures, Wingspan succeeded in meeting its goals.

Culture   Being an Internet start-up within a larger organization offers both opportunities and challenges. Kevin Watters, Wingspan's senior vice president of marketing, summarized the advantages:

> Compared to other Internet banks Wingspan has the cash resources of Bank One and First USA, which means enormous marketing dollars. In addition, we are able to mine data from First USA to provide better offers via direct mail and email than competitors. That's a 70-million-cardholder database to pull from. There is also shared learning across the three organizations (Bank One, First USA and Wingspan).

Cleary noted the challenges:

> It's sometimes hard to act like an Internet company. There is no currency like an e-trade—currency for marketing deals, advertising, and talent. Businesses are about people and if we don't have what Internet-savvy people want, we're handcuffed. We're also responsible for

---

[11]"Bank One Says CEO of Internet Venture, Wingspan, Will Resign at Year's End."
[12]Telephone interview with Michael Cleary, President, Wingspan, December 6, 1999.

exhibit 14   WingspanBank.com Start Page

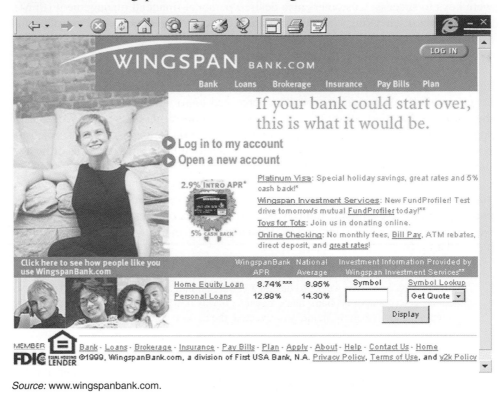

Source: www.wingspanbank.com.

part of an earnings stream at Bank One, and we all know that at Internet start-ups, earnings don't drive success. We're forced to look at profitability [earlier].

Customer Base   Within its first 90 days of operations, Wingspan had signed up 50,000 customer accounts. By comparison, Net.B@nk, which had been operating for over three years, had only 35,000 customers. On the other hand, bankone.com had 350,000 customers, nearly 8 million people were online, and 200,000 of them used Internet-only banks.

Wingspan wants to know whether their customers will switch among banks or remain loyal. Wingspan's "stickiest" products so far include online bill payment and direct deposit. With these products, customers spend a great deal of time and provide specific information to the bank, thus increasing their switching costs. In fact, Wells Fargo research indicates that online customers using bill payment services are 16 times more likely than brick-and-mortar customers to stay with the bank and be profitable.[13]

In terms of "mindshare" and general awareness, Wingspan has hit its goals but still hopes to target better the core Internet banking consumer through both traditional and Internet advertising. In addition, a recent alliance with Lycos through which Lycos customers can bank through a co-branded Wingspan-and-Lycos site may represent future direction.

Services   Customers can use Bank One's ATMs for free—but not the tellers and other face-to-face branch services. Customers can complete applications online, get

---

[13]Telephone interview with Peter Kight, Chief Executive Officer, CheckFree Corporation, December 1, 1999.

approved, and start banking in the same online session, which is unusual—most online banks make customers wait for passwords received via e-mail. Customers can also receive virtually instant decisions on products ranging from credit cards to installment loans—the response to an online home equity loan application takes only 50 seconds! Many WingspanBank services and rates are not available to Bank One customers. For example, Bank One customers pay $4.95 per month for the same bill-payment services Wingspan customers get for free.

Since the launch, Wingspan had continued to demonstrate its commitment to its vision through continual spending and maintenance of product quality. For example, in its commitment to maintain the best portfolio of products and services, management added CheckFree Corporation, the leading supplier of bill payment services, to the list of vendors. According to CIO Wallace, "Wingspan will continue to look at all vendors in the marketplace and select the best ones."

The original plan added novel, meaningful functionality to the site every four to six weeks. Wingspan currently was making site changes over a six-to-eight-week time frame, but it continued to innovate. According to Cleary, there was still much to do:

> We launched quickly to beat Citibank and American Express, to test and to learn. There are many things not done at launch that we must complete in order to reach our goals. For example, we have not yet implemented many of our cross-selling techniques. Wingspan needs to recognize customers when they come to the site using CRM [customer relationship management] tools to deepen the relationship.

Wallace reflected on the future as well:

> The model for Wingspan must change from product- to relationship-focused. In the past 25 years, banks created complicated views of banking and took away customers' control over their finances. Wingspan can erase the complexity and give customers back this control. For example, if there is $10,000 in a checking account, we can automatically issue a CD for the unused portion so that customer earns an extra $25. This adds value to the relationship.

Wingspan was expected to continue its furious growth and use its flexibility and size to its advantage. Relative to other Internet banks, Wingspan had higher brand awareness, better prices, and leaner operations, allowing it to provide customer enhancements that other companies could not readily match.

THE DILEMMA

John McCoy liked what Wingspan had achieved, but he was concerned. Shares of Bank One had fallen more than 40 percent since May. The First USA division suffered $70 billion in outstanding receivables, and expensive advertising campaigns had yet to deliver predicted returns.[14] Furthermore, the press unrelentingly included Wingspan in its criticism of Bank One even though Wingspan revenues meant little to a banking behemoth with $260 billion in assets. Was it because several executives at Wingspan—including Dick Vague and now James Stewart—had departed?

It was ironic, McCoy thought, that Wingspan had met virtually all of it goals and led the industry, yet remained underappreciated outside—and maybe even inside—Bank One. Given all this, he had to ask himself: Now what?

---

[14]Ibid.

case 16 Ben & Jerry's— Japan

James M. Hagen
Cornell University

On an autumn evening in Tokyo in 1997, Perry Odak, Angelo Pezzani, Bruce Bowman, and Riv Hight gratefully accepted the steaming hot oshibori towels that their kimono-bedecked waitress quietly offered. After a full day of meetings with Masahiko Iida and his lieutenants at the Seven-Eleven Japan headquarters, the men from Ben & Jerry's welcomed the chance to refresh their hands and faces before turning to the business at hand. It had been just over nine months since Odak had committed to resolving the conundrum of whether to introduce Ben & Jerry's ice cream to the Japan market and, if so, how. The next morning would be their last chance to hammer out the details for a market entry through Seven-Eleven's 7,000 stores in Japan or to give the go-ahead to Ken Yamada, a prospective licensee who would manage the Japan market for Ben & Jerry's. Any delay in reaching a decision would mean missing the summer 1998 ice cream season, but with Japan's economy continuing to contract, perhaps passing on the Japanese market would not be a bad idea.

Perry Odak was just entering his 11th month as CEO of the famous ice cream company, named for its offbeat founders. He knew that the Seven-Eleven deal could represent a sudden boost in the company's flagging sales of the past several years. He also knew that a company with the tremendous brand recognition Ben & Jerry's enjoyed needed to approach new market opportunities from a strategic, not an opportunistic, perspective. Since meeting Masahiko Iida, the president of Seven-Eleven Japan, just 10 months earlier, Odak had been anxious to resolve the question of whether entering the huge Japanese market via Seven-Eleven was the right move or not.

BEN & JERRY'S BACKGROUND: 1978 TO 1997

1978 to 1994: Growth from Renovated Gas Station to $160 Million in Sales[1]

Brooklyn, New York, schoolmates Ben Cohen and Jerry Greenfield started their ice cream company in a defunct gas station in Burlington, Vermont, in 1978, when both were in their mid-20s. The combination of their anticorporate style, the high fat content of their ice cream, the addition of chunky ingredients, and catchy flavor names like Cherry Garcia found a following. In addition to selling by the scoop, they began selling

[1]Monetary values are in U.S. dollars unless otherwise noted.

pints over the counter, and the business grew. With the help of less visible team members Jeff Furman and Fred (Chico) Lager, the founders took the company public to Vermont stockholders in 1984, later registering with the Securities and Exchange Commission (SEC) for nationwide sale of stock. The company name was Ben & Jerry's Homemade, Inc., and it began trading over the counter with the symbol BJICA.

Stockholder meetings were outdoor festivals where standard attire included cutoffs and tie-dyed T-shirts and where Cohen was liable to call the meeting to order in song. Cohen and Greenfield determined that in addition to being fun to work for, the company would be socially responsible, known for its "caring capitalism." Highlighting its community roots, Ben & Jerry's would buy its cream only from Vermont dairies. In the case of one of its early nut flavors, Rain Forest Crunch, the nuts would be sourced from tribal cooperatives in South American rain forests where nut harvesting would offer a renewable alternative to strip-cutting the land for wood products, and where the co-op members would, hopefully, get an uncommonly large share of the proceeds. As another part of its objective of caring capitalism, Ben & Jerry's gave 7.5 percent of pretax profits to social causes like Healing Our Mother Earth, which protected community members from local health risks, and the Center for Better Living, which assisted the homeless.

The product Cohen and Greenfield were selling was exceptionally rich (at least 12 percent butterfat, compared with about 6 to 10 percent for most ice creams). It was also very dense, due to a low overrun (low ratio of air to ice cream in the finished product). This richness and density qualified it as a superpremium ice cream. Häagen-Dazs (founded in New Jersey in 1961) was the only major competitor in the superpremium market. While Häagen-Dazs promoted a sophisticated image, Ben & Jerry's promoted a funky, caring image.

As Ben & Jerry's began to expand distribution throughout the Northeast, it found it increasing difficult to obtain shelf space in supermarkets. Charging Häagen-Dazs with unfairly pressuring distributors to keep Ben & Jerry's off their trucks, Greenfield drove to Minneapolis and gained national press coverage by picketing in front of the headquarters building of food giant Pillsbury, which had earlier acquired Häagen-Dazs. His homemade sign read, "What is the Doughboy afraid of?"—a reference to Pillsbury's mascot and to the company's apparent efforts against the underdog ice cream makers from Vermont. This David versus Goliath campaign earned Ben & Jerry's national publicity and, when combined with some high-powered legal action, gave the company freer access to grocery store freezer compartments.

A policy at Ben & Jerry's was that the highest-paid employee would not be paid more than seven times what the lowest-paid worker earned. Part of the anticorporate culture of the company was a policy that allowed each employee to make up his or her own job title. The person who might otherwise have been called the public relations manager took the title "Info Queen." Cohen and Greenfield took turns running the company. Whether despite or because of these and other unusual policies, the company continued to grow (see Exhibit 1). In 1985 the company bought a second production plant, this one in nearby Springfield, Vermont. A third plant was later built in St. Albans, Vermont. By the late 1980s, Ben & Jerry's ice cream had become available in every state of the union.

1994 to 1997: Responding to Fallen Profits

By 1994, sales exceeded $150 million, distribution had extended beyond the U.S. borders, and the company had over 600 employees. The future was not encouraging, though, with 1994 actually bringing in a loss. While Ben & Jerry's unquestionably held the second largest market share (at 34 percent compared to Häagen-Dazs's 44 percent)

exhibit 1   Ben & Jerry's Annual Sales, 1983–97 (In Millions)

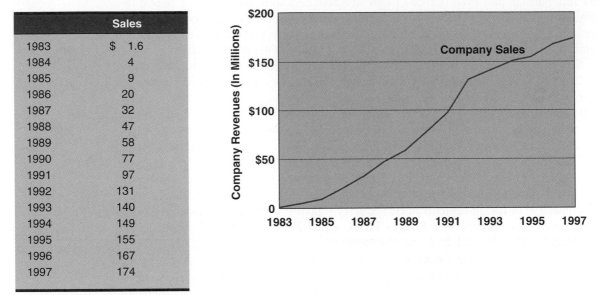

	Sales
1983	$ 1.6
1984	4
1985	9
1986	20
1987	32
1988	47
1989	58
1990	77
1991	97
1992	131
1993	140
1994	149
1995	155
1996	167
1997	174

Source: Ben & Jerry's annual reports.

of the American superpremium market, the company had started to lose its place. Net income had also suffered badly since reaching a high in of $7.2 million in 1993 (see Exhibit 2). While Cohen was most often the company's CEO, much of the company's growth occurred while Chico Lager was either general manager or CEO between 1982 and 1990. Cohen was particularly engaged in efforts to further the cause of social justice by such activities as attending meetings of similarly minded CEOs from around the world. Board member Chuck Lacy had taken a turn at the helm, but he lacked aspirations for a career as a CEO, just as the company's namesakes did. The slowdown in growth and retreat in market share comprised a threat to the company's survival and to the continuation of its actions and contributions for social responsibility.

The company had never had a professional CEO and had avoided commercial advertising, relying for publicity on press coverage of its founders' antics and social interest causes. This approach was apparently losing its effectiveness, and the company could no longer feature an underdog image in its appeals for customer support. Relaxing the rule on executive compensation, the company launched a highly publicized search for a CEO, inviting would-be CEOs to submit a 100-word essay explaining why they would like the job. In 1996, Bob Holland, a former consultant with McKenzie Corporation, took the presidency, bringing a small cadre of fellow consultants with him. All of Holland's highly schooled management sensibilities were put to the test as he took over a company that had lacked effective management in recent years, commencing employment for a board of directors that was suspicious of traditional corporate culture. By this time, Cohen, Greenfield, and Furman still had considerable influence over the company, controlling about 45 percent of the shares. This permitted them, as a practical matter, to elect all members of the board of directors and thereby effectively control the policies and management of the firm. Holland's relationship with the board didn't work, and 18 months later he was out, the company's decline had not been reversed, and morale among the employees was at a low.

While the board was willing to pay a corporate-scale salary to its CEO, it was unwilling to let go of the company's tradition of donating 7.5 percent of before-tax profits to not-for-profit social causes. A spirit of socially responsible business management

exhibit 2 Ben & Jerry's Net Income, 1990–97 (In Millions)

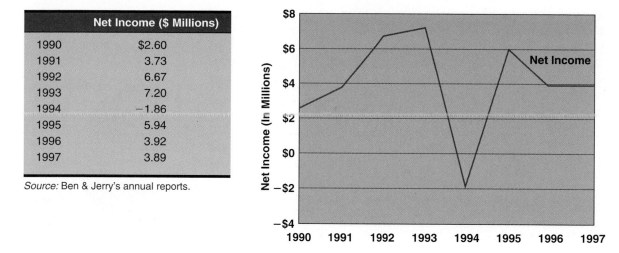

	Net Income ($ Millions)
1990	$2.60
1991	3.73
1992	6.67
1993	7.20
1994	−1.86
1995	5.94
1996	3.92
1997	3.89

Source: Ben & Jerry's annual reports.

would need to continue, as that was still the company's stock in trade as much as the ice cream was. With this, as well as the need to survive, in mind, the board hired Perry Odak at the recommendation of one of its members. Odak was offered a base salary of $300,000, with a start date in January 1997.

While Odak had grown up on a dairy farm in upstate New York, it was not his dairy background that landed him the job as CEO of Ben & Jerry's. His experience at turning around troubled companies was far more important. Odak was recruited away from a consultancy assignment at U.S. Repeating Arms Company, which he had been instrumental in turning around from its decline into red ink. That position had followed a diverse series of others ranging from senior vice president of worldwide operations of Armour-Dial, Inc., to president of Atari Consumer Products, along with numerous consultancies and entrepreneurial activities that included the start-up team and management of Jovan, a fragrance and cosmetic company. A professional manager who thrived on challenges and abhorred mere maintenance of a company, Odak had entered the business world with a degree in agricultural economics from Cornell University, topped with graduate coursework in business.

THE MARKET FOR SUPERPREMIUM ICE CREAM

Ice cream is noted as far back as the days of Alexander the Great, though it was first commercially manufactured in the United States in 1851. By 1997, almost 10 percent of U.S. milk production went into ice cream, a $3.34 billion market. The ice cream brands that dominated American supermarket freezer cases are listed in Exhibit 3 and Exhibit 4. National (as opposed to regional) branding of dairy products, including ice cream, was a recent phenomenon. Dreyer's (owned in part by the Swiss food giant Nestlé and branded Edy's on the East Coast) was the biggest brand, at 13.9 percent of the U.S. market, in terms of value. The next biggest was Breyer's, a unit of the Dutch-English firm Unilever, at 12 percent. Blue Bell (from Texas) was fourth biggest at 5.2 percent, and Häagen-Dazs (owned by the UK beverage and food company then known as Grand Metropolitan) was at 4.6 percent. Ben & Jerry's came in at about 3.6 percent of the market. Healthy Choice Premium ice cream (owned by the agribusiness and consumer food firm ConAgra) was close behind, with 3.2 percent. Starbucks (one of Dreyer's brands) had 1.0 percent. The

exhibit 3   Top U.S. Ice Cream Brands, 1996–97

	Sales ($ Millions)
All brands	$3.34
Store brands	1.00
Dreyer's/Edy's premium	0.46
Breyer's premium	0.40
Blue Bell premium	0.17
Häagen-Dazs	0.15
Ben & Jerry's	**0.12**
Healthy Choice premium	0.10
Starbucks premium	0.03
Homemade premium	0.02
Breyer's Free premium	0.02

Source: Ben & Jerry's.

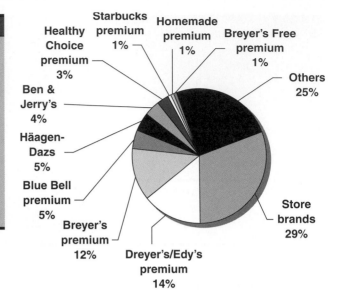

biggest share of the market (some 30.2 percent) came from retailers' private-label products, and a number of economy brands (with which Ben & Jerry's did not regard itself to be competing) made up the balance.

There are considerable economies of scale in ice cream production, so despite the advantages of having dispersed production in order to reduce costs of transporting the frozen finished product or the highly perishable cream, milk, and egg yolks that are principal raw ingredients, each major manufacturer generally had only a few plants to serve vast markets. Market leader Häagen-Dazs had just two plants in the United States, while Ben & Jerry's had three. Even with relatively few plants, Ben & Jerry's was operating at only about half of plant capacity in 1997.

While the Ben & Jerry's brand had the country's fifth highest share of the ice cream market (in terms of value), it still accounted for only a small 3.6 percent of the market. Ben & Jerry's, though, measured its competitive strength not in general ice cream sales (including many store brands and economy ice creams), but rather in sales of superpremium (high-fat-content) ice cream. The market for this product was much less fragmented, with Häagen-Dazs getting 44 percent and Ben & Jerry's getting 34 percent of the $361 million of supermarket (excluding convenience store and food service) sales measured and monitored by scanner data. If the two companies' frozen yogurts and sorbets were included, their market shares would be 36 percent for Ben & Jerry's and 42 percent for Häagen-Dazs. Both companies specialized in superpremium products, with additional sales being derived from sorbets, frozen yogurts, and novelties. Häagen-Dazs had really pioneered the category back in 1961 when Reuben Mattus founded the company in New Jersey. The company was later acquired by the giant food company Pillsbury, which in turn was bought in 1989 by the UK liquor and food giant Grand Metropolitan.

Both Ben & Jerry's and Häagen-Dazs had achieved national distribution, primarily selling their product in supermarkets and convenience stores. Ben & Jerry's had 163 scoop shops, compared to 230 Häagen-Dazs shops. Dairy Queen (with 5,790 shops worldwide) and Baskin Robbins dominated the scoop-shop business, though their products were not superpremium. Prices for Ben & Jerry's and Häagen-Dazs would range from $2.89 to $3.15 per pint, often more than twice as expensive as conventional (high-overrun/lower-butterfat) ice cream and premium brands. Starbucks and

exhibit 4   U.S. Market Share of Superpremium Brands, 1997

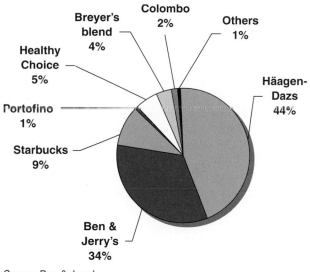

Source: Ben & Jerry's.

Portofino ice creams were other, much smaller contenders in the United States, with their "premium plus" products characterized by a butterfat content slightly under that of the superpremium category.

Statistical evidence indicated that ice cream consumption increased with income and education. Starting in the mid-1990s, though, sales growth started to fall off and Ben & Jerry's experienced a decline in profits, even suffering a loss in 1994. Häagen-Dazs and Ben & Jerry's product sales were very widely available across the entire U.S. market, and it was clear that future growth would have to come from new products or from new (non-U.S.) markets. More troubling was that Ben & Jerry's was beginning to lose market share in both the total ice cream market and, more important, the super-premium market.

BEN & JERRY'S INTERNATIONAL SALES

Ben & Jerry's was intentionally slow to embrace foreign markets. Cohen was opposed to growth for growth's sake, so the company's few adventures overseas were limited to opportunistic arrangements that came along, primarily with friends of the founders. Meanwhile Häagen-Dazs had no such hesitation. By 1997, it was in 28 countries with 850 dipping shops around the world. Its non-U.S. sales were about $700 million, compared to about $400 million of domestic sales. Ben & Jerry's, on the other hand, had foreign sales of just $6 million, with total sales of $174 million. In terms of non-U.S. superpremium ice cream sales, Häagen-Dazs and Ben & Jerry's were still the leading brands, but Häagen-Dazs was trouncing Ben & Jerry's.

Canada

Ben & Jerry's first foreign entry was in Canada in 1986, when the company gave a Canadian firm all Canadian rights for the manufacture and sale of ice cream through a licensing agreement. While about one-third of the product was exported from the United States, high Canadian tariffs (15.5 percent) and particularly quotas (only 347 tons annually) made export impractical. In 1992 Ben & Jerry's repurchased the Canadian license and as of 1997 there were just four scoop shops in Quebec. The Canadian dairy industry remained highly protective even after enactment of the North American Free Trade Agreement.

Israel

Avi Zinger, a friend of Ben Cohen's, was given a license, including manufacturing rights, for the Israel market in 1988. His 1997 sales totaled about $5 million, but the only revenue accruing to Ben & Jerry's Homemade, Inc., would be licensing income, and this amount was negligible. To ensure quality coming from the plant in Yavne, Israel, Zinger and his staff received training at the Waterbury factory. As of fall 1997, there were 14 Ben & Jerry's scoop shops in Israel, with the shops selling such items as gifts, baked goods, and beverages in addition to the ice cream. Zinger also sold Ben & Jerry's products through supermarkets, hotels, delis, and restaurants.

Russia

The company entered into its first foreign joint venture in 1990 by establishing the firm Iceverk in the Russian republic of Karelia, which is Vermont's sister state. This grew out of Cohen's travel to Karelia as part of a sister-state delegation in 1988. A goal of the joint venture was to promote understanding and communication between the peoples of these two countries. The joint venture agreement specified the following division of ownership shares: Ben & Jerry's, 50 percent; the Intercentre cooperative, 27 percent; Petro Bank, 20 percent; and Pioneer Palace (a facility similar to a YMCA that provided the location), 3 percent. Half of any profits would stay with Iceverk, and the balance would be divided among the partners. Ben & Jerry's contributed equipment and know-how to the venture, while the local partners provided the facilities for the factory and for two scoop shops. After considerable, mostly bureaucratic, delays, the shops opened in July 1992. By 1993, there were three scoop shops and about 100 employees. Iceverk opened several more scoop shops, and the venture began to sell pints in supermarkets locally, as well as in Moscow. Ben & Jerry's hired James Flynn to put his University of New Hampshire marketing degree to good use by serving as marketing rep in Moscow. Sales improved as food-service customers increasingly bought the product. In 1996, Ben & Jerry's terminated the joint venture, giving its equity and equipment at no cost to its joint venture partners. A retrospective view of that decision is that the company felt that the management time needed to keep the partnership going was too demanding, given the perceived potential. Iceverk no longer uses the Ben & Jerry's name, though it does continue to make ice cream in Petrozavodsk, Karelia's capital.

United Kingdom

In 1994 there was much discussion at Ben & Jerry's headquarters in Burlington about whether the company was ready to strategically (rather than just opportunistically) move into international markets. Susan Renaud recalled the consensus being that no, they were not, but just three months later the company shipped a container of product to Sainsbury, an upscale supermarket chain in the United Kingdom. Cohen had met a Sainsbury executive at a meeting of the Social Venture Network, and the executive had encouraged him to ship over some product. This launch was made with no idea of what the pricing would be and no knowledge of what kind of packaging and ingredients were acceptable in that market. The company was shipping a 473-milliliter package, while the standard was 500 milliliters. With its foot in the door, the company thought it best to try other outlets in England, as well. It tried out one distributor, which had agreed to donate 1 percent of its Ben & Jerry's turnover to charity. Sales did not materialize, and another distributor was tried, this time without the charity constraint. The product had a distinctive market position, with one radio commentator alleged to have said, "If Häagen-Dazs is the ice cream you have after sex, Ben & Jerry's is the ice cream you have instead of sex." By 1997, UK sales totaled $4 million.

France

In 1995, the company entered France with great ambivalence. CEO Bob Holland was all for entering the French market, and the company sent off a container of product to Auchan, a major retailer to which Cohen was introduced through Social Venture Network ties. As global protests grew over French nuclear testing, though, there were discussions in the company about withdrawing from the French market or vocally protesting against the French government. With this internal disagreement concerning the French market, there was no marketing plan, no promotional support, and no attempt to address French labeling laws. The company hired a French public relations firm, noted for its alternative media and social mission work, and separately contracted with a sales and distribution company. But there was no plan and nobody from Ben & Jerry's to coordinate the French effort. In 1997, sales in France were just over $1 million.

Benelux

Ben & Jerry's entry into the Benelux market was also without strategic planning. In this case, a wealthy individual who had admired the company's social mission asked to open scoop shops, with partial ownership by the Human Rights Watch. By 1997, there were three scoop shops in Holland. Sales totaled a mere $287,000, but there was the prospect of using the product reputation from the scoop shops to launch supermarket and convenience store sales.

Summary of International Sales

In short, Ben & Jerry's fell into several foreign markets opportunistically, but without the consensus of the board and without the necessary headquarters staff to put together any kind of comprehensive plan. As the company had never developed a conventional marketing plan in the United States, it lacked the managerial skill to put together a marketing campaign for entering the foreign markets.

As a result, by 1997, Ben & Jerry's international sales totaled just 3 percent of total sales. While the company had nearly caught up with Häagen-Dazs in U.S. market share, Häagen-Dazs was light years ahead in the non-U.S. markets. With declining profits and domestic market share at Ben & Jerry's, it was beginning to seem time to give serious attention to international market opportunities.

FOCUS ON MARKET OPPORTUNITIES IN JAPAN

Background on the Market for Superpremium Ice Cream in Japan

In the 1994–96 period, when Ben & Jerry's was having its first taste of a hired professional CEO (Bob Holland), the company struggled with the prospects of strategically targeting a foreign market and developing a marketing plan for its fledgling overseas operations. In particular, the company made inquiries about opportunities in Japan, the

exhibit 5   Size of Japan's Ice Cream Market

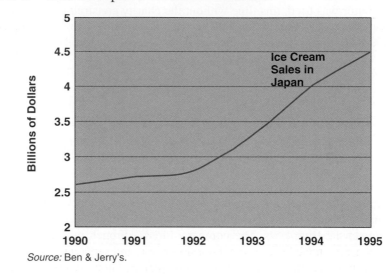

Source: Ben & Jerry's.

second largest ice cream market in the world, with annual sales of approximately $4.5 billion (see Exhibit 5). While the market was big, it was also daunting. Japan was known to have a highly complex distribution system driven by manufacturers, its barriers to foreign products were high, and the distance for shipping a frozen product was immense. Ben & Jerry's would be a late entrant, more than 10 years behind Häagen-Dazs in gaining a foothold in the market. In addition, there were at least six Japanese ice cream manufacturers selling a superpremium product. A major Japanese frozen desserts company, Morinaga Seika, had made proposals to Ben & Jerry's on two different occasions in 1995. In both cases the proposals were rejected. In January 1996, Morinaga actually conducted focus groups to evaluate Ben & Jerry's products. It was beginning to seem appropriate to take a closer look at the Morinaga proposals and other options.

Despite the challenges of entering Japan, that market had several compelling features. Japan was arguably the most affluent country in the world, Japanese consumers were known for demanding high-quality products with great varieties of styles and flavors (which practically defined Ben & Jerry's) and it seemed that the dietary shift toward more animal products was still under way. By 1994, Japan's 42-kilogram annual per capita consumption of milk was less than half that (103 kilograms) of the United States, and cheese consumption was about one-tenth that of the United States. Commercial dairy sales had really only taken off after World War II, when school lunch programs were initiated with milk as a regular component. Incomes in Japan increased dramatically from the 1950s to the 1980s so that animal-based food products and home refrigerators were affordable to a large number of people.

Though Häagen-Dazs's financial figures were not published by its parent, Grand Metropolitan, market intelligence suggested that the ice cream maker had Japanese sales of about $300 million, with Japan providing the highest margins of any of its markets. Häagen-Dazs had managed to capture nearly half the superpremium market in Japan. It entered the market as an imported product and later began production in Japan at a plant owned jointly by Häagen-Dazs, Sentry, and Takanashi Milk Products. About 25 percent of Häagen-Dazs's sales there appeared to be from scoop shops. In addition to gaining visibility through scoop shops, Häagen-Dazs operated a fleet of ice cream parlor buses (with upper-deck café tables) at exhibitions and other public gatherings. On the one hand, Häagen-Dazs would be a formidable competitor that would likely guard its market share. On the other hand, there would be no apparent need for Ben & Jerry's to teach the local

exhibit 6   Japanese Superpremium and Premium Sales by Package

	Brand	Size (ml)	Price (Yen)
Home cup	Bleuge	950	950
Pint	Häagen-Dazs	474	850
	Lotte	470	850
	Meiji	470	950
Personal cup	Häagen-Dazs	120	250
	Meiji	145	250

Source: Fuji Keizai Co.

market about superpremium ice cream. The market seemed to welcome imported ice cream, and expectations of falling tariffs on dairy products suggested new opportunities for ice cream imports from abroad. Häagen-Dazs's flavors in Japan were generally the same as those in the United States, with some modifications, such as reduced sweetness. While prices were attractive in Japan, about $6 per pint, it was unclear how much of that would go into the pockets of the manufacturer versus various distributors.

In contemplating an entry into the Japanese market, it was hard to avoid thinking about the case of Borden Japan. Borden introduced a premium ice cream to the market in 1971 through a joint venture with Meiji Milk. The product was highly successful, and Borden was leader of the category. In 1991, the Borden-Meiji alliance came to an end and Borden had extreme difficulty gaining effective distribution. Borden did not follow industry trends toward single-serving cups of ice cream, and it suffered greatly when distributors started lowering the price of the product, sending the signal to consumers that Borden was an inferior product. After sales had fallen by more than two-thirds in just two years, Borden withdrew from the Japanese market. Desserts were uncommon in Japan, leaving ice cream primarily for the snack market. Thus, single-serving cups (about 120 milliliters) became popular, accounting for about 45 percent of sales (see Exhibit 6), and ice cream came to be sold increasingly in convenience stores. By 1993, about a quarter of all ice cream sales were in convenience stores, compared to 29 percent in supermarkets (see Exhibit 7).

One concern at Ben & Jerry's was its size. With total worldwide sales of just over $150 million, it was very small in comparison to Häagen-Dazs, which had estimated sales of $300 million in Japan alone. At least five Japanese companies already in the superpremium market were larger than Ben & Jerry's, with leaders Glico, Morinaga, Meiji, and Snow Brand all having total ice cream sales three to four times that of Ben & Jerry's, and in each case ice cream was just part of the company's product line.

Cohen was not very enthusiastic about the sort of financial or managerial commitment that was apparently required to enter the Japanese market, and he couldn't see how entering that market fit in with the company's social mission. Others on the board shared his attitude. Two immediate problems were that entering Japan would not be the result of any social mission (the concepts of social mission and corporate charity being very foreign in Japan), and the company's lack of international success suggested that it may already have been spread too thin in too many countries. Jerry Greenfield, however, was interested enough to visit Japan on a market research tour in early 1996. The purpose was to see just how Ben & Jerry's might gain distribution if the company were to enter the Japanese market. Valerie Brown of Ben & Jerry's fledgling marketing department accompanied Greenfield. Contacts for the visit came primarily from Valerie's classmates at Harvard Business School, from a consulting company, and from the Japan External Trade Organization.

***exhibit* 7**   Japanese Ice Cream Market by Channel

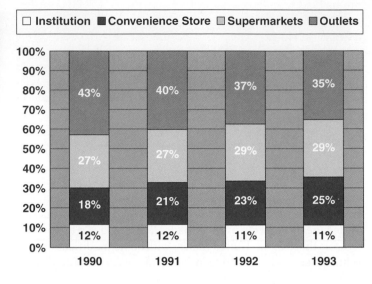

	Cumulative Annual Growth, 1990–93
Institution	−1.7%
Convenience stores	8.3
Supermarkets	1.8
Outlets	−4.4

Source: Ice Cream Data Book (Morinaga).

Alternative Strategies for a Ben & Jerry's Entry into Japan

In his visit to Japan, Greenfield was willing to consider entry into Japan through such diverse distribution channels as Amway Japan, Domino's Pizza, and department stores. One of his meetings was with the Japanese distributor of Dreyer's, the American company with partial ownership by the Swiss food giant Nestlé. Dreyer's, not being perceived as a direct competitor, was Ben & Jerry's largest distributor in the United States. Dreyer's had licensed its trademark with a joint venture operation in Japan in 1990. Sales had since fallen, and the joint venture seemed to have had difficulty with its biggest customer, Seven-Eleven Japan. The retailer's demands for just-in-time delivery required Dreyer's to maintain large inventories, and the retailer demanded the right to rapidly drop flavors that did not meet sales expectations.

Another meeting was with a high-level team of Seven-Eleven executives, including Masahiko Iida, the senior managing director, and Yasayuki Nakanishi, the merchandiser of the foods division. Iida expressed interest in selling Ben & Jerry's ice cream, suggesting that Ben & Jerry's could sell directly to Seven-Eleven, avoiding some of the distribution costs that are typical of the usual multilayer distribution system in Japan. On the other hand, a major American beverage distributor in Japan warned that it would be the kiss of death to enter the market through some kind of exclusive arrangement with a huge convenience store chain like Seven-Eleven. The balance of power would be overwhelmingly in the retailer's favor.

Meiji Milk Products (with $447 million of ice cream sales), in combination with its importer, the giant Mitsubishi Trading Company, expressed interest in distributing Ben & Jerry's products. This team clearly had very strong distribution resources, including an exclusive supply contract for Tokyo Disneyland. One concern was that Meiji already had a superpremium brand called Aya. Despite Meiji's strong interest, though, this option had probably become a long shot on account of earlier protests by Ben & Jerry's leadership of deforestation practices by another division of Mitsubishi.

Other marketing possibilities that had surfaced in 1996 included an arrangement with the advertising agency that had charge of Japan Airlines' in-flight entertainment, as well as a chance to open a scoop shop at a highly visible new retail development about to be built at Tokyo Disneyland. If anything, the many options, focus groups, and proposals made the decision about what to do with Japan even more difficult. The fact that the Ben & Jerry's board was divided on whether the company even had any business in a Japanese launch discouraged further action. By late 1996, Holland was following up discussions with a well-recommended Japanese American who was available to oversee marketing and distribution of Ben & Jerry's products in Japan. Ken Yamada, a third-generation Japanese American from Hawaii, had obtained the Domino's Pizza franchise for Japan. His compensation would be a margin on all sales in Japan. When Bob Holland's employment with Ben & Jerry's ended later in the year, Holland was still in discussion with Yamada, but he was still lacking the enthusiastic support of the board of directors for a possible entry into Japan.

A Fresh Look at the Options in Japan

Perry Odak assumed leadership of Ben & Jerry's in January 1997, inheriting the file of reports on possible strategies for entering the Japanese market. Neither the file nor institutional memory indicated much momentum leading toward any one of the Japanese strategies. In being hired, however, Odak had the board's agreement that the company's sales (and especially profits) must grow and that non-U.S. markets were the most likely key to that growth.

In February 1997, Odak added a business-related detour to a scheduled trip to Thailand with his wife. He stopped by Tokyo for a courtesy call to Mr. Iida, the president of Seven-Eleven Japan, a controlling parent company of Seven-Eleven U.S.[2] This was to more or less make up for Ben & Jerry's inability to send a CEO to a January "summit" meeting in Dallas at which Mr. Iida and the head of the U.S. Seven-Eleven operations had wished to meet face to face with the leaders of its major suppliers. Seven-Eleven U.S. was, in fact, Ben & Jerry's biggest retail outlet and Ben & Jerry's was a major supplier to Seven-Eleven.

After about 10 minutes of pleasantries at this introductory meeting at the Seven-Eleven headquarters in Tokyo, Iida asked Odak point blank: "Is there anyone at Ben & Jerry's who can make a marketing decision? We'd like to sell your product, but don't know how to proceed or with whom." Rather taken aback at this surprisingly direct inquiry, Odak replied that he could indeed make a decision and he resolved to sort through the options and get back to Iida in short order.

Back in Burlington, Odak installed Angelo Pezzani as the new international director for Ben & Jerry's Homemade. Odak had known Pezzani since 1982 when they both started work at Atari on the same day. Pezzani's position was then general consul of Atari Consumer Products Worldwide. Going over the options with Pezzani, it appeared that partnering with Yamada was still the strongest option for entering Japan, but the Seven-Eleven option had not yet been well developed for consideration. Yamada represented considerable strength with his Domino's success and with the fact that Domino's

[2]A brief explanation of the relationship between the Japan Seven-Eleven organization and the U.S. 7-Eleven organization is in order. 7-Eleven convenience stores originated in Texas in 1927 as a retail concept of Southland Corporation, which had been in the ice business. Southland began using the 7-Eleven banner in the 1950s because the stores would be open from 7 AM to 11 PM. The business grew through company-owned and franchised stores. Southland gave a master franchise for Japan to the Ito Yokado Company, a large supermarket operator there, which in turn established Seven-Eleven Japan to conduct the 7-Eleven business in Japan through company-owned and franchised stores. In the 1980s, Southland was in financial distress and Ito Yokado, along with its subsidiary, Seven-Eleven Japan, bailed out Southland, acquiring a controlling interest in the company. In this light, Odak's dinner with Iida in Japan constituted a sort of executive summit between Ben & Jerry's and its largest customer.

already offered ice cream cups as part of its delivery service in Japan. Possible draw-backs were his insistence on having exclusive rights to the entire Japanese market, with full control of all branding and marketing efforts there.

Pezzani and Odak decided to continue negotiations with Yamada, keeping that option alive, and to simultaneously let Iida know that they wanted to explore options with Seven-Eleven. They requested an April meeting with Iida in Japan to move things along. The April meeting would include Mr. Nakanishi, the head of frozen ice desserts for Seven-Eleven Japan, and Bruce Bowman, Ben & Jerry's head of operations. To work out ground arrangements for the meeting, Odak and Pezzani needed someone on the ground in Japan. They called on Rivington Hight, an American who had learned Japanese in the U.S. intelligence service, married a Japanese woman, and lived in Japan for much of the past 30 years. No stranger to Odak or Pezzani, Hight had also worked for Atari in 1982 as president of Atari Japan. Like Odak and Pezzani, he had held a variety of management positions and consultancies in the years since.

The April meeting in Japan was basically intended to lay the framework to begin hashing out the many details that would be involved if Ben & Jerry's were to enter the Japan market through Seven-Eleven. It was a chance for the critical players in each company to get together. Perry brought Pezzani, Bowman, and Hight. Arriving at the Ito-Yokado/Seven-Eleven headquarters building at the foot of Tokyo Tower, the Ben & Jerry's team walked into a lobby full of sample-laden salespeople and manufacturers nervously awaiting their chance to put their products on the shelves of some 7,000 stores. The receptionist quickly identified Odak and company and immediately put VIP pins on their dark lapels, directing them to the VIP elevator that went straight to the executive suite on the 12th floor. A hostess there immediately guided the group across the plush white carpeting to a spacious meeting room, where they were served tea while awaiting Iida and Nakanishi. Odak arrived with more questions than answers, but he was determined that any product Ben & Jerry's might sell in Japan would be manufactured in Vermont, where the company had considerable excess capacity. Also, the costs of labor and raw dairy products were higher in Japan than the United States, so the 23.3 percent tariff and cost of shipping seemed not to be prohibitive. As a result of the Uruguay Round of the General Agreement on Tariffs and Trade (the former name of the World Trade Organization), the tariff would be reduced to 21 percent in the year 2000. The introductory meeting went well, but they had not yet addressed any of the difficult issues except to establish that it would be possible to export the product from Vermont to Japan.

Wrestling with the Details of the Seven-Eleven Option

Odak, Pezzani, and Bowman had a full plate of issues to resolve. The first question was market. Iida had said he was interested in Ben & Jerry's product because it was something new to Japan and particularly unique with its chunks. Seven-Eleven had even tried to get a Japanese company to co-pack a chunky superpremium ice cream, but the Japanese packer was unsuccessful with its production processes. Research supporting a clear market for this novel product in Japan was scant, though it seemed unlikely that Seven-Eleven would commit shelf space to a product it had any doubt about and both Iida and Nakanishi certainly knew their market. A skeptical view of Seven-Eleven's interest in bringing Ben & Jerry's to Japan was that Seven-Eleven's combined U.S. and Japanese operations would become so important to Ben & Jerry's (potentially accounting for a substantial portion of its sales) that Seven-Eleven could, in some fashion, control the ice cream maker. Even if that were not part of Seven-Eleven's motivation, it could be a concern.

While Ben & Jerry's management was leaning toward an entry into Japan, it was not a foregone conclusion. The entry would require a commitment of capital and managerial attention. As the product would be exported from the United States, there would be the risk of negative exchange rate movements that could make exports to Japan no longer feasible, thus making Ben & Jerry's financial picture less predictable. Commodity risk was also a serious concern in that the price of milk could rise in the United States, hurting Ben & Jerry's relative to competitors producing ice cream in Japan.

Assuming that an entry into the Japanese market was desirable, there were a number of apparent options for gaining distribution there, making it necessary to seriously consider the pros and cons of entering by way of Seven-Eleven. The most obvious pro was immediate placement in the freezer compartments of over 7,000 convenience stores in that country. In the early 1990s, the convenience store share of the ice cream market had increased and it appeared that these stores were now accounting for at least 40 percent of superpremium ice cream sales in Japan. Equally positive was the fact that Seven-Eleven had taken advantage of its size and its state-of-the art logistics systems by buying product directly from suppliers, avoiding the several layers of middlemen that stood between most suppliers and Japanese retailers. These cost savings could make the product more affordable and/or allow a wider margin to protect against such risks as currency fluctuation.

On the negative side, if the product was introduced to the market through a convenience store and it was just one of many brands there, would it be able to build its own brand capital in Japan as Häagen-Dazs had? Would the product essentially become a store brand? Without brand capital it could be difficult to distribute the product beyond the Seven-Eleven chain. An alternative approach of setting up well-located scoop shops, along with an effective marketing or publicity campaign, could give the product cachet, resulting in consumer pull that could give Ben & Jerry's a price premium as well as a range of marketing channels. Would committing to one huge retail chain be a case of putting too many eggs in one basket? A falling out between Ben & Jerry's and Seven-Eleven Japan could leave the ice cream maker with nothing in Japan. Even during discussions with Ben & Jerry's, the retailer was known to be terminating its supply agreement with the French ice cream manufacturer Rolland due to allegedly inadequate sales. Presumably Seven-Eleven could similarly cut off Ben & Jerry's at some future date.

While weighing the pros and cons of the business arrangement, there were also production issues Ben & Jerry's had to consider. Nakanishi insisted the ice cream be packaged only in personal cups (120 milliliters) and not the 473 milliliter (pint) size that Ben & Jerry's currently packed. The main argument for the small cups was that ice cream is seldom consumed as a family dessert in Japan, but rather is consumed as a snack item. A secondary argument was that, for sanitation purposes, customers liked their own individual servings. Cake, for example, was generally served in restaurants with each slice individually wrapped. Nakanishi's insistence was despite the fact that Seven-Eleven stocked Häagen-Dazs and some of its local competitors in both sizes.

Bruce Bowman embraced the challenge of designing a production system that would accommodate small cups that the company had never packed before. It seemed that about $2 million of new equipment would be needed, though it could be installed in the existing buildings. The sizes of some of the chunks would have to be reduced in order for them to not overwhelm the small cups. Besides requiring these known adjustments to production operations, Seven-Eleven might be expected to request other product changes. Japanese buyers were known for being particularly demanding in their specifications.

Ben & Jerry's had long been shipping ice cream to the West Coast and to Europe in freezer containers. Shipments to Japan were feasible, though the Seven-Eleven approach to just-in-time inventory procedures would make delivery reliability especially key and, of course, costs would have to be minimized. Logistics research indicated it would likely take at least three weeks' shipping time from the plant in Vermont (the St. Albans plant would be used if the Japanese plan was implemented) to the warehouse in Japan. Because of the Japanese label needed in Japan, production would have to carefully meet the orders from Seven-Eleven. The product could not be shifted to another customer, nor could another customer's product be shifted to Japan.

A number of sticky points needed to be resolved. In addition to changing the package size, Seven-Eleven wanted to provide its own design for the package art, and the design would definitely not include a photo of Ben and Jerry. Packaging had always been an important part of the Ben & Jerry's product. Funky lettering and the images of Ben and Jerry are part of what made the product unique. If Seven-Eleven were given control over the package art, what would that do to the benefits of developing a global branded product? Would consumers be confused about the placement of the product as they traveled? On the other hand, the carton designs had already been evolving somewhat and maybe a bit more evolution would satisfy Seven-Eleven. In fact, the earlier focus groups by Morinaga brought out the concern that it was too bad the "strange Ben & Jerry's packaging" had to detract from the good ice cream.

Ben & Jerry's sent a number of samples to consider and Nakanishi developed a short list that would be tested (if the deal went forward) in a couple dozen Seven-Eleven stores so that the top five flavors could be identified for the market entry. Chunky Monkey was near the top of Nakanishi's list, though the name absolutely had to change, he said. It turned out that only minor ingredient modifications would be needed to reduce the sweetness and to replace "vegetable gum" with "protein solids."

Through numerous communications and several meetings during the summer of 1997, a number of issues were discussed and resolved. For example, Seven-Eleven would acquire only a six-month exclusive right to Ben & Jerry's, and even that would be only for the specific flavors being sold to Seven-Eleven. Because of its relatively small size and inability to cover a loss, Ben & Jerry's was asking for sale terms that would transfer title (and all risk) for the product at the plant gate. It also was asking for 12 weeks' lead time on any order to allow for sourcing of ingredients, as well as efficient production scheduling. It appeared that these requests would not be too burdensome for Seven-Eleven. The sensitive issue of price was intentionally left until late in the discussions. Häagen-Dazs was being sold for 250 yen per 120 milliliter cup, and Seven-Eleven wanted to position Ben & Jerry's at a slightly lower price point. This would be problematic for Odak, who had recently increased the domestic price for Ben & Jerry's ice cream in part to support the product's position as equal or superior in quality to Häagen-Dazs.

A concern yet lurking in the boardroom in Burlington, Vermont, was what the company's social mission in Japan would be. Since the early 1990s, the company had moved beyond using its profit to fund philanthropy. The new imperative was to better the workplace, community, and world through regular day-to-day operations. On the other hand, profits were still needed in order to even have day-to-day operations, and a new market (such as that in Japan) could be the ticket to those profits. In the meantime, no particular social mission had emerged from the summer discussions of entering the Japanese market.

The Approaching Deadline for a Summer 1998 Launch in Japan

Odak and his staff had made steady progress narrowing and developing their Japanese options during the summer of 1997. If they were to enter the Japanese market for the summer 1998 season, though, they would have to commit to one plan or another no later than autumn 1997. Two distinct entry options had emerged.

The Yamada option was largely the same as it had been at the beginning of the year. His proposal was to have full control of marketing and sales for Ben & Jerry's in Japan. He would position the brand, devise and orchestrate the initial launch, and take care of marketing and distribution well into the future. He would earn a royalty on all sales in the market. By giving Yamada full control of the Japan market, Ben & Jerry's would have instant expertise in an otherwise unfamiliar market, as well as relief from having to address the many issues involved in putting together an entry strategy and in ongoing market management. Yamada knew frozen foods and had an entrepreneurial spirit and marketing savvy, evidenced by his success in launching and building up the Domino's Pizza chain in Japan. Giving up control of a potentially major market, though, could not be taken lightly. Because Yamada would invest his time in fleshing out and executing a marketing plan only after reaching agreement with Ben & Jerry's, there was no specific plan available for consideration. Even if there were, Yamada would retain the rights to change it. For the near term, however, Yamada would expect to add selected flavors of Ben & Jerry's ice cream cups to the Domino's delivery menu, providing an opportunity to collect market data based on customer response.

The Seven-Eleven option would leave Ben & Jerry's in control of whatever market development it might want to pursue beyond supplying Seven-Eleven in Japan. While Seven-Eleven would provide an instant entry to the market, the company would not be in a position to help Ben & Jerry's develop other distribution channels in Japan. The retailer thought it could sell at least six cups per day at each store, which would be the minimum to justify continuing to stock Ben & Jerry's. Looking at the size of Seven-Eleven's ice cream freezer cases suggested that this would require approximately 10 percent of Seven-Eleven's cup ice cream sales to be Ben & Jerry's products. Ben & Jerry's was as yet unknown in Japan, and it did not have the budget for a marketing campaign there. Sales would have to rely primarily on promotional efforts by Seven-Eleven, but the company was making no specific commitment for such efforts.

Another option was increasingly compelling—that of holding off on the market entry. Japan's economy was continuing to languish, with increasing talk that it could be years before recovery. A financial crisis that had commenced with a devaluation of Thailand's currency in July 1997 seemed to be spreading across Asia. If the pending Asian crisis hit an already weakened Japanese economy, the economics of exporting ice cream from Vermont to Japan could become infeasible.

Though the value of the yen had recently fallen to 125 yen to the dollar, Ben & Jerry's could still sell the product at the plant gate at an acceptable profit with room for both shipping expense and satisfactory margins for Seven-Eleven and its franchisees. If the rate went as high as 160 yen to the dollar, then the price in Japan would have to be raised to a level that might seriously cut into demand, especially relative to Häagen-Dazs, which had manufacturing facilities in Japan.

It would be a long evening meal as Odak, Pezzani, Bowman, and Hight gave their final thoughts to the decision before them. Not only had Odak promised Iida that he could make a decision, but Yamada needed an answer to his proposal as well. In any event, Ben & Jerry's had to proceed with one plan or another if it was going to have any Japanese sales in its 1998 income statement.

case 17 Viña San Pedro

David Wylie

Babson College

Viña San Pedro (VSP) was the third largest winery in Chile, with 1998 sales of 37 billion Chilean pesos (CP). Bonifacio Correa had planted the original vines with French stock in 1865 on the farm in Molina that the family had owned since 1701. For years, VSP wines enjoyed a reputation of being one of the finest in the country, and the vineyard remained in the Correa family until 1941. New owners expanded the vineyard so that by 1994, 1,150 hectares[1] were in production, making it the largest single-site vineyard in the country. It was, however, barely profitable and survived primarily by producing inexpensive wines for the domestic market.

COMPAÑA CERVECERIAS UNIDAS

In 1994, Compaña Cervecerias Unidas S.A. (CCU), a diversified beverage company that operated primarily in Chile and Argentina, purchased a 48.4 percent share of VSP stock for CP 7.8 billion. In 1992, CCU issued 4,520,582 American depository shares (ADSs) in an international American depository receipt (ADR) listed on the NASDAQ.[2] In 1996, it completed another ADR, thereby raising U.S. $155 million in additional capital. CCU shares also traded on the Chilean stock exchange. In 1998, CCU had sales of CP 280 billion and was the dominant player in the domestic beer market with a 91 percent market share. (See Exhibit 1 for CCU financial statements, Exhibit 2 for exchange rate information, and Exhibit 3 for inflation rates.) It was also the second largest beer seller in the Argentine beer market; the second largest Chilean soft-drink producer; the largest Chilean mineral water producer; and, with the acquisition of VSP, the third largest producer of wine in Chile. The management of CCU recognized VSP as a diamond in the rough.

CCU had been established in 1902 following the merger of two existing brewers. By 1916, it owned and operated the largest brewing facilities in Chile. It had also expanded its operations to include the production and marketing of soft drinks in 1907 and began bottling and selling mineral water products in 1960.

In 1986, following an economic crisis in Chile, Inversiones y Rentas was formed as a closed corporation to purchase the company out of receivership, and it still held 63 percent of the company. Inversiones y Rentas was owned 50 percent by Quiñenco S.A., a holding company beneficially owned by the Luksic family, and 50 percent by

---

Prepared under the supervision of Professors U. Srinivasa Rangan and Steve Allen of Babson College. The authors would like to thank the Institute for Latin American Studies at Babson College for its contribution to this effort.

[1]A hectare is 100 meters square, or about 2.5 acres.

[2]CCU traded on the NASDAQ under the symbol CCUUY.

exhibit 1   CCU Financial Statements (In Millions of Chilean Pesos as of December 31, 1998)

	Consolidated Income Statement		
	1996	1997	1998
Revenues	252,019	272,477	280,111
Cost of goods sold	(122,694)	(126,200)	(127,643)
Selling, general, and administrative expenses	(98,366)	(103,076)	(107,849)
Operating income	30,959	43,202	44,618
Operating margin	*72.3%*	*15.9%*	*15.9%*
Nonoperating result	(4,823)	5,777	4,777
Taxes	(2,570)	(4,303)	(4,644)
Minority interest and others	(3,417)	(5,678)	(5,437)
Net income	20,149	38,998	39,315

	Consolidated Balance Sheet		
	1996	1997	1998
Current assets	152,487	208,932	217,493
Fixed assets	263,931	276,000	287,164
Other assets	44,404	50,656	62,726
Total assets	460,822	535,588	567,384
Current liabilities	79,136	89,830	82,334
Long-term liabilities	113,097	98,827	102,282
Minority interest	38,072	42,086	49,164
Shareholder equity	230,517	304,845	333,604
Total liabilities and shareholders' equity	460,822	535,588	567,384

	Segment Performance		
Consolidated Results	1996	1997	1998
Net revenues			
Beer Chile	113,794	117,972	117,081
Beer Argentina	24,868	35,213	37,746
Soft drinks & mineral water	92,718	90,699	88,063
Wine	20,024	28,237	36,825
Others	10,911	8,641	10,780
Intercompany transactions	(10,296)	(8,284)	(10,383)
Total	252,019	272,477	280,111

(continued)

Paulaner-Salvator Betwiligungs AG, a holding company for the Schörghuber Group. All of the common stock was owned by private parties but was listed on the Chilean Stock Exchange.

Quiñenco S.A. was engaged in a wide variety of businesses in Chile and Argentina. It controlled more than 50 companies engaged in telecommunications, manufacturing,

exhibit 1   (*continued*)

Consolidated Results	Segment Performance		
	1996	1997	1998
Cost of goods sold			
Beer Chile	47,309	45,750	42,387
Beer Argentina	13,814	19,760	19,927
Soft drinks & mineral water	49,271	43,504	42,954
Wine	12,699	17,502	24,180
Others	9,898	7,968	8,577
Intercompany transactions	(10,296)	(8,284)	(10,383)
Total	122,694	126,200	127,643
Selling, general, and administrative expenses			
Beer Chile	42,307	42,345	40,931
Beer Argentina	11,510	15,033	20,218
Soft drinks & mineral water	36,327	36,323	36,056
Wine	6,884	8,168	9,400
Others	1,338	1,207	1,245
Total	98,366	103,076	107,849
Operating income			
Beer Chile	24,179	29,878	33,763
Beer Argentina	(457)	420	(2,399)
Soft drinks & mineral water	7,120	10,872	9,053
Wine	442	2,566	3,244
Others	(324)	(534)	958
Total	30,959	43,202	44,618
Operating margin	*12.3%*	*15.9%*	*15.9%*
Nonoperating results			
Financial income	3,185	8,302	11,577
Income from investments in related companies	2,132	2,142	880
Other nonoperating income	2,313	7,669	7,954
Amortization	(2,583)	(2,590)	(1,143)
Interest expenses	(7,995)	(7,039)	(7,429)
Other nonoperating expenses	(1,443)	(2,315)	(7,054)
Price-level restatement	(432)	(392)	(9)
Total	(4,823)	5,777	4,777
Income tax	(2,570)	(4,303)	(4,644)
Minority interest	(3,417)	(5,704)	(5,464)
Amortization of negative goodwill		26	27
Net income	20,149	38,998	39,315
Other relevant information			
Sales volumes (thousands of hectoliters)	8,681	9,312	9,471
EBITDA (Operating income + Depreciation + Amortization)	57,226	71,674	74,619
EBITDA Margin	*22.7%*	*26.3%*	*26.6%*

Source: CCU annual report, 1998.

exhibit 2   Historical Exchange Rates (Average Annual)

Year	CP$/U.S.$	U.S.$/CP$
1991	326	.00306
1992	346	.00289
1993	375	.00267
1994	418	.00239
1995	410	.00244
1996	412	.00243
1997	420	.00238
1998	455	.00220

Note: Official exchange rates of the Chilean peso were pegged to the U.S. dollar from 1975 to July 3, 1992, at a rate adjusted daily determined by monthly rates of national and world inflation. On January 26, 1992, the Central Bank revalued the peso, reducing the official dollar exchange rate by 5 percent, which meant that it dropped from 395 to 375 pesos. On July 3, 1992, in a move designed to halt currency speculation, Chile announced that the peso would no longer be measured exclusively against the dollar but rather would use a blend of the dollar, the German mark, and the Japanese yen in a 50-30-20 ratio.

exhibit 3   Consumer Price Index (Period Averages, Annual Percentage Rate)

	All Items	Food	Housing	Clothing
1992	15.5	18.0	14.4	15.4
1993	12.7	10.9	13.8	10.5
1994	11.4	9.8	12.2	3.0
1995	8.2	8.3	7.6	(1.2)
1996	7.4	6.1	7.7	(7.1)
1997	6.1	7.1	5.9	(4.7)

food processing and distribution, financial services, cable television, hotels, and commercial printing, altogether controlling approximately 6 percent of the Chilean gross national product. The Schörghuber Group's interests were more concentrated in Europe, with holdings primarily in other beverage companies, real estate, hotels, and aircraft leasing.

In 1994, CCU diversified its operations both in the international and domestic markets. In October, it purchased a 48.4 percent interest in Viña San Pedro. In November, it created the ECUSA joint venture with Argentinean bottler BAESA for the production, bottling, and marketing of soft drinks and mineral water products in Chile. It also acquired a 27 percent interest in a Croatian brewer, an interest that was increased to 43 percent by 1997.

THE EARLY YEARS OF CCU CONTROL

During the first few years of CCU control, management focused on reducing costs, increasing distribution, and increasing the quality of VSP wines. By 1995, debt had been reduced by CP 7.8 billion, CP 864 million had been invested in expanded capacity for aging wines, and CP 178 million had been invested in planting new vineyards for producing premium red wines. As a result of these added investments, CCU's total ownership position increased to 51.2 percent. Since new plantations took several years to become productive and higher quality wine required time to age, delivery of finished wine from its own vineyards remained level at about 11 million liters and was almost exclusively devoted to exports. The balance of 24 million liters was sold domestically and was created from grapes purchased from independent growers.

CCU had also assumed responsibility for the distribution of VSP wines in all but the most remote areas of Chile and quintupled the number of customers to 30,000. Domestic sales increased by 29 percent between 1995 and 1996, although a 5.5 percent rise in the average price for a case of wine sold had contributed to this increase. In 1996, after three years of losses, VSP finally boasted a profit of CP 305 million. (See Exhibit 4 for VSP financial statements.)

In 1997, Matias Elton joined VSP as president. A graduate of Georgetown University and experienced in the U.S. fruit importing industry, he was charged with the task of growing domestic market share, increasing quality to capture higher margin sales, expanding export sales, and achieving further economies of scale.

During Elton's first year, another CP 17.7 billion was invested to further increase capacity. New hectares of vineyards were acquired and planted, storage capacity increased to 36.3 million liters, and bottling capacity expanded from 22,600 to 25,100 bottles per hour. During the year, VSP's total production grew to over 44 million liters of wine, 45 percent of which was from its own vineyards. CP 8.2 billion was invested in vineyard (planting represented CP 4.5 million per hectare), CP 3.0 billion in vinification capacity, CP 819 million in aging capacity, and CP 5.6 billion in bottling capacity. Elton also reorganized the company so that each function had clear reporting responsibilities and to make Wilfred Leigh, the export manager, directly report to him rather than to the individual responsible for domestic sales. (See Exhibit 5 for an organization chart.)

In July of 1998, Patricio Jottar joined CCU as its new president. Armed with a clear vision for the company's future, he saw that while there might be some product cannibalization, further synergies could be gained among the CCU companies. Existing distribution capabilities of CCU could be further leveraged. Administrative expenses (human resources, legal, engineering, accounting, auditing) could be reduced with the use of common resources. Influence on regulatory bodies and lobbying efforts could be enhanced. Finally, knowledge about trends, prices, global markets, and retailers could be shared among all the CCU companies. Meanwhile, Jottar had implemented a new set of objectives for the company based on return on capital employed (ROCE) rather than just on profitability.[3]

THE WINE COUNTRY OF CHILE

Just south of Santiago, Chile, the central plateau opened between the mountains, boasting the perfect soil, drainage, and climate for grapes to flourish.[4] Traveling south along

---

[3]Jottar estimated the weighted average cost of capital to be 12 percent. Capital employed was defined as operating assets less operating liabilities.

[4]Thomas P. McDermott, Michael Amorose, and Gerwin Neuman, *A Catalog of Chilean Wines,* July 1997.

exhibit 4 VSP Financial Statements (Thousands of Chilean Pesos)

Balance Sheet		
	Fiscal Year Ending	
	December 31, 1998	December 31, 1997
Assets		
Cash and equivalents	378,388	1,004,285
Net receivables	9,015,694	5,241,443
Inventory	13,710,656	10,853,815
Prepaid expenses	52,484	75,530
Prepaid taxes	1,922,132	345,218
Other current assets	150,078	2,666,036
Total current assets	25,229,432	19,354,101
Land	5,585,210	3,407,403
Plant and equipment	13,959,211	11,262,972
Accumulated depreciation	5,744,390	4,945,413
Net property, plant, and equipment	13,800,031	9,724,962
Other long-term assets	15,371,155	6,244,174
Revaluation of long-term assets	3,202,659	3,291,692
Intangible assets	3,232,837	3,215,013
Total assets	60,674,472	42,662,168
Liabilities and shareholders' equity		
Accounts payable	4,141,784	3,850,157
Short-term debt and current long-term debt	13,560,048	6,163,769
Allowances and escrow	871,881	877,465
Income taxes payable	55,974	—
Payable to related businesses	3,945,518	8,605
Dividends payable	—	120
Other current liabilities	1,007,160	1,923,078
Total current liabilities	23,582,365	12,823,194
Long-term debt	9,920,870	5,055,874
Provision for risk and other charges	75,562	101,607
Minority interests	510	204
Total liabilities	33,579,307	17,980,879
Common stock	26,006,880	26,006,880
Capital surplus	1,089,436	1,089,436
Retained earnings	(1,151)	(2,415,027)
Common shareholders' equity	27,095,165	24,681,289
Total liabilities and shareholders' equity	60,674,472	42,662,168

(continued)

the Pan American Highway, orchards gave way to vineyards that spread as far as the eye could see until they were interrupted by the snow-capped Andes Mountains on the east and the Cordillera Mountains, which parallel the Pacific ocean, on the west. (See Exhibit 6 for map of South America.) This region, only about 75 miles wide and 200 miles long, was considered to be the source of the choicest wines in Chile. Runoff from

exhibit 4   (*continued*)

Income Statement		
	Fiscal Year Ending	
	December 31, 1998	**December 31, 1997**
Net revenue	34,902,924	25,651,657
Cost of goods sold	24,087,037	16,957,841
Gross margin	10,815,887	8,693,816
Selling and general expenses	6,886,678	5,982,628
Operating income	3,929,209	2,711,188
Interest income	108,112	193,204
Other income and expenses—net	264,980	143,822
Interest expense	1,503,635	1,094,036
Monetary correction	(320,586)	244,392
Pretax income	2,478,080	2,198,570
Income taxes	63,899	5,560
Minority interest	305	43
Net income	2,413,876	2,192,967

Cash Flow Statement		
	Fiscal Year Ending	
	December 31, 1998	**December 31, 1997**
Beginning cash balance	3,670,321	1,673,022
Cash flow from operations	(5,005,034)	(660,308)
Increase in debt—net of payments	9,557,545	6,752,528
Increase in debt to related companies	3,585,581	—
Total cash flow from financing activities	13,143,126	6,752,528
Cash flow from capital expenditures	(11,261,154)	(3,940,222)
Total cash flow	(3,123,062)	2,151,998
Effect of inflation	(18,793)	(154,699)
Net cash flow after inflation	(3,141,855)	1,997,299
Ending cash balance	528,466	3,670,321

Note: The Chilean Cash Flow statement differs from that of the United States.

the snowfields of the Andes provided abundant irrigation, while the mountains along the coast protected the valley from too much direct rainfall. Toward the north, the hills were covered in sagebrush and cactus, and toward the south the climate became too cool and moist to nurture the best grapes. Small vineyards dotted the valley, nestled among dominant giants: Concha y Toro, Santa Rita, and Viña San Pedro.

Wine production in Chile dated back more than 400 years, but quality wines only began to appear in the first half of the 19th century after European vines were introduced. Beginning in 1860, European vineyards were ravaged for almost 30 years by the destructive phylloxera plague. Chile was left unaffected and, indeed, in 1998 was the only country in the world that continued to produce from original rootstock.

exhibit 5   The New VSP Organization

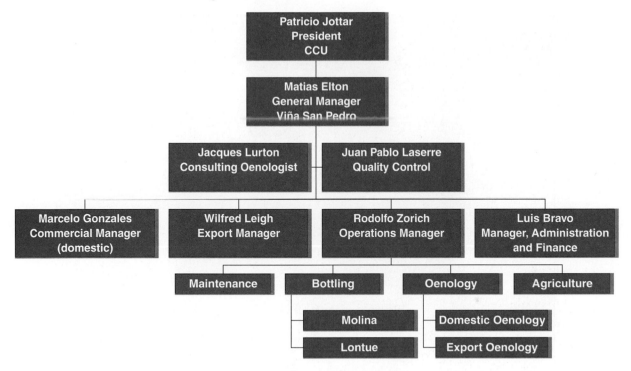

In 1938, new plantings were prohibited in an effort to curb alcoholism in the country, although by 1973, per capita consumption was still high, at 59 liters. The new Augusto Pinochet government, recognizing that wine could become an important export, lifted the ban in 1973, and both the quality and quantity of wine production grew. Better segmentation of grapes and selection practices by producers to create high-end labels allowed the creation of some very top-quality, higher priced labels in addition to the more popularly priced table wines and varietals. By 1997, total Chilean production had risen to 418 million liters, mainly from the introduction of better agricultural practices to enhance productivity and from the introduction of better processing technologies. There were about 61,000 hectares planted in vineyards in Chile by the end of 1997. Concha y Toro had 3,843 hectares, Santa Rita 2,057, and VSP 1,700. They had winemaking capacity of 107 million, 56 million, and 53 million liters, respectively.

While Pinochet had encouraged production in 1973, he also imposed a curfew that contributed to a drop in domestic consumption. By 1985, consumption had declined to 400 million liters, or 36.9 liters per capita, and by 1997 Chile's 15 million inhabitants consumed only 211 million liters of wine each year, or about 14.4 liters per capita. Industry analysts, however, expected consumption to increase by 4 percent per year, to 239 million liters by 2001. The domestic market had thus not offered great opportunities for growth among wineries. This market was extremely price-sensitive, and production became consolidated among the largest wineries that had the greatest economies of scale. Some smaller vineyards focused on producing premium wines. Others sold cheap wines within the very local "informal market," while still others were content to sell their grape production as raw material to the larger producers.

exhibit 6   Map of South America

Chilean wines proved to be a hit in the international market, particularly for lower cost wines. The ideal climate and isolation from those pests that often forced wine-makers to be aggressive with the application of pesticides contributed to quality. High yields and low labor costs provided a lower cost of production than in other countries. Chilean vineyards yielded more than twice the harvest of grapes from each hectare than European vineyards. Since winemaking was so labor-intensive, Chile's indus-try-friendly labor laws, low wages, and a labor union presence that was the lowest in the entire Western Hemisphere reduced the cost of labor. In addition, a strong national health care system allowed temporary labor to be readily available. Also, the seasonal difference from wine regions in the Northern Hemisphere gave Chile a unique advantage in marketing seasonal wines. The result of all this was a lower price for high quality—hence, good value.

By 1987, Chilean wines began attaining a level of quality acceptable by international oenophiles.[5] Exports of wine from Chile had grown from 11 million liters in 1987 to 43 million liters in 1990 to 207 million liters in 1997 as the average price per liter sold rose from $.62 to $1.86.

THE WINES OF VIÑA SAN PEDRO

VSP made a full range of wines, from the Gato brand at the low end to the award-winning Cabo de Hornos at the top end (see Exhibit 7 for a complete list of San Pedro wines). Generally, wines were classified as popular, varietal, and reserve. Like the other large wineries, VSP purchased grapes from local growers to be made into Gato and other popular wines destined for the domestic market. For the export market, however, it used only high-quality grapes from its own vineyards. In addition, it exported some wine in bulk to countries such as France where the cost of production was higher and bulk wine could be mixed with wine of domestic origin to add volume. Most countries allowed up to 10 percent of a wine to be of foreign origin while still being labeled as domestically produced.

The following table shows the VSP product sales mix in 1997 (in millions of liters):

	Popular	Varietal	Reserve	Bulk	Total
Export	.6	15.6	.3	2.0	18.5
Domestic	24.5	.8	.1	0.0	25.4
Total	25.1	16.4	.4	2.0	43.9

Gato

Gato wine was a popularly priced wine that was sold both in the domestic and export markets. For the domestic market, it was produced primarily from purchased "country" grapes and packaged in five-liter jugs, plastic/cardboard containers, and cardboard one-liter Tetra-Packs. Approximately 70 percent of VSP domestic sales were in Gato Tetra-Packs, 15 percent in jugs, and 9 percent in bottles. The remaining 6 percent of domestic sales were bottled varietal and reserve wines.

Gato wine was not aged but rather was packaged and sold as soon as fermentation was complete. For the export market, it was made from high-yield grapes from the company vineyards and packaged in bottles. The red wine was blended from cabernet-sauvignon and Merlot grapes, while the white wine was a combination of sauvignon and chardonnay grapes. An average hectare for the production of Gato wines produced about 17.9 tons of grapes per year, and the company estimated that it required about $1.56 million in working capital for every million liters of Gato wine.

---

[5]Lovers or connoisseurs of wines.

exhibit 7   Viña San Pedro Wines

Name	Category	Brand	Packaging	Size (cc)	Retail Price ($U.S.)
Cabo de Hornos	Premium	San Pedro	Bottle	750	39.10
Castillo de Molina	Reserve		Bottle	750	10.90
Seleccion del Directorio	Reserve	Santa Helena	Bottle	750	7.60
35 Sur	Varietals		Bottle	750	6.50
Siglo de Oro	Varietals	Santa Helena	Bottle	750	4.30
Gato	Year Wine		Bottle	750	3.30
Urmeneta	Year Wine		Bottle	750	3.50
Gran Vino	Year Wine	Santa Helena	Bottle	750	2.20
Gato	Year Wine	San Pedro	Carton	1,000	2.10
Santa Helena	Year Wine	Santa Helena	Carton	1,000	1.60
Etiqueta Dorada	Year Wine	San Pedro	Carton	1,000	1.30
Gato	Year Wine	San Pedro	Jug	5,000	9.80
Santa Helena	Year Wine	Santa Helena	Jug	5,000	7.60
Etiqueta Dorada	Year Wine	San Pedro	Jug	5,000	5.40

Other lines of San Pedro popular wines included Etiqueta Dorada and Santa Helena Gran Vino.

Varietal

Varietal wines were each made from a single variety of grape and aged for up to a year in stainless-steel tanks before being bottled and sold. The grapes used were from VSP's own vineyards that yielded about 12.7 tons per hectare.

VSP varietal wines included Castillo de Molina, 35 Sur, a higher-priced Gato, Siglo de Oro, and a Santa Helena Gran Vino.

Reserve

Reserve wines were often a blend of several different varieties of grapes, and again made only from grapes from VSP's own vineyards. These vineyards received special treatment in order to raise the proportion of grape skins to pulp, since the skins imparted a richness to the flavor of the wine. These grapes, therefore, were stressed at certain intervals to impede growth. Consequently, these vineyards only produced about eight tons per hectare. Reserve grapes were all hand-picked, and those destined for white wine were all picked at night to reduce the added oxidation that occurred with exposure to the sun. To add flavor, the wine was fermented in large oak casks rather than stainless-steel tanks. Reserve wines required a longer aging period, usually in either French or American oak barrels, depending on the flavor desired. The wine was further aged in bottles to allow the tannins to blend into the wine. The wine was not sold for two years after harvest.

Reserve wines in the VSP portfolio included a Castillo de Molina; Las Encinas (a special dry white reserve wine); and the top of the Santa Helena line, Seleccion del Directorio.

Premium Reserve

At the top of the scale was the premium reserve wine, Cabo de Hornos. While very little of this wine was produced, it allowed the winery to boast of its winemaking capabilities, a stature that was frequently confirmed in international wine competitions. The small vineyard dedicated to the premium reserves produced only about 10.7 tons per hectare. Again, these wines were aged in oak barrels and again in bottles, taking three years before being sold.

VINICULTURE

The prevailing sentiment was that while quality was not everything, it remained "number one, two, and three" in importance. Jacques Lonton was the oenologist from France who was brought in to consult in developing broad product definition strategies and to fine-tune final mixing formulas. He told the VSP managers that he thought that the quality of wines was derived 80 percent in the fields in growing the grapes, 15 percent in vintification, and the rest in "art."

Not all vines were treated equally. Growing techniques varied according to subtle variations in soil and irrigation conditions and climatic differences between fields depending on where they lay in the valley floor. Even more important were the kind of grapes being grown and the quality of grapes desired. Certain grapes needed more sunlight than others and might be planted in rows at different angles to the sun, pruned so that the leaves created different shade patterns, or irrigated at varying intervals or intensity according to the amount of water content for the grapes which the oenologist had specified. Some vines might be irrigated frequently and during periods of maximum grape growth in order to maximize volume. Others required more irrigation at peak growth periods for the vines in order to encourage more foliage to protect the grapes from the sun.

Picking grapes was a science unto itself. As the grapes matured, the sugar content of grapes was monitored by Bernard Fresius, the head agriculturist, to help decide exactly when the harvest should occur according to the type of wine desired and the type of grapes. Grapes for the lower grade wines could be harvested mechanically. In contrast, some varieties of grapes and those for the higher grades of wine needed to be picked by hand and indeed might require harvesting in several waves to make sure that only clusters that were at the ideal level of ripeness were harvested.

Fresius was the only employee to actually live at the vineyard. He occupied a renovated farmhouse overlooking the vineyards and mountains with his wife and two young children. While his formal role was to translate the specifications for grapes required for the following season into growing strategies, he constantly monitored the condition of the vines. Usually he patrolled the vineyards in his car, but it was not unusual to find him on horseback, riding down the rows while stopping frequently to examine a shoot, new leaf, or ripening cluster of grapes. He had graduated from agricultural school and, while he only had to take the exam to become a licensed oenologist, he preferred to stay in the vineyards and leave the oenology to the five full-time oenologists who designed the wines and monitored their fermentation, mixing, and aging to assure the required taste, quality, and complexity.

Fresius developed the annual plans for the vineyards, which were then interpreted into monthly plans by the two agronomists who reported to him. Each had responsibility for 600 hectares. Three agrarian technicians reported to each agronomist. They prepared weekly plans for the 200 hectares under their control. Four full-time laborers and four tractor drivers reported to each agrarian technician. These individuals prepared and managed the daily vineyard plans for the 44, on average, seasonal laborers. Seasonal labor worked about 37,000 man days each year, peaking during the three two-month periods devoted to pruning, canopy management, and harvesting. They were paid an average of about $11.25 per day. The total cost to the company was a little more than $17.25 per day after health insurance contributions and administrative costs.

Machines were available and could be used for some of the operations like canopy management and harvesting, but they were expensive: about $130,000 each. They could each handle about 150 hectares, doing the work otherwise done by about 80 laborers, but since the work came in distinct waves, usually it was more cost-effective to rent the machines and pay, on average, $300 per hectare per year in rental fees. Hiring laborers to do the same work, in contrast, cost $650 per hectare per year. The following table shows the growing costs per hectare in 1997 (in thousands of Chilean pesos):

	Reserve Wines	Varietal Wines	Gato Wines
Manual labor	398	379	423
Consumables	121	164	175
Machine	94	163	142
Total	613	706	741
Liters/Hectare	10,684	12,716	17,948

VINIFICATION

After the grapes were harvested in March, they were loaded into bins at the end of each row of vines and trailered in to the winemaking facility. There, a machine de-stemmed and gently crushed the grapes to release the juice, or "must."

For red wines, the must and skins were transferred into fermentation vats made either of stainless steel or wood. For white wines, sulfur dioxide was first added to the must to prevent oxidization that would result in a less fruity wine. Sediment was removed from the must before it was transferred into the fermentation vat.

There, grape sugar was converted into alcohol through the action of natural yeast found in grape skins (or sometimes by the addition of special yeast strains).

Alcoholic fermentation for red wines took place over a period of 5 to 10 days. Most red wines were fermented to complete dryness, with little or no residual sugar remaining. Alcoholic fermentation for white wine lasted longer than for red (12 to 15 days) and at cooler temperatures so that more of the juices' natural aromas were retained. Letting all of the grape sugar turn into alcohol made dry white wines.

Some wines were then "macerated," or left to soak with the skins, pulp, and dead yeast cells (together called "marc") for up to 18 days, during which time the alcohol extracted pigment, tannins, and flavors from the marc.

After fermentation and maceration, if specified, the fermented grape juice (called free-run wine) was separated from the marc. Then the marc was pressed to extract any remaining wine. This wine, called "vin de presse," had highly concentrated flavors, tannins, and colors and could be blended back into the wine to achieve the desired style and flavor.

Sometimes, red wine went through an additional fermentation process known as secondary fermentation, which converted naturally occurring malic acid to lactic acid.

exhibit 8   Sales History of VSP (Volume in Millions of Liters)

Year	Domestic	Export	Total
1995	18.0	9.4	27.4
1996	23.8	11.6	35.4
1997	25.4	18.6	44.0
1998	28.7	23.1	51.8

This lowered a wine's acidity and made it softer and more pleasant to drink. In white wine production, malolactic fermentation risked lowering the wine's acidity too much, so it had to be accomplished with great skill and subtlety.

The next stage was clarification. The wine was filtered and run through a centrifuge to separate the clear wine from any remaining particles.

The final stage of the vinification process was blending, where the winemaker combined wines made from different grape varieties and vats to create the desired bouquet, style, and flavor of wine. This stage was completed in August.

Popularly priced wines were ready to be bottled and sold immediately. The varietal wines were bottled and aged for several months before being sold. Reserve wines, however, required further aging. Red wine could be aged for up to two years in oak barrels to impart structure, additional tannin, and flavor. Finally, it was bottled and stored in cellars for further aging or shipped to distributors. Aging was much shorter for white wines than for reds. Some was aged for up to one year in oak barrels to give it additional structure and flavor; however, most white wines were bottled within a year after harvest.

More complex white wines such as Viña San Pedro "Encinas" required a special treatment. It, like its red counterpart, was aged for up to two years in oak barrels to increase richness before bottling and distribution.

THE MARKET FOR VSP WINES

Historically, VSP's sales had been almost exclusively domestic, but as export sales grew it was becoming very clear that the future for VSP profitability was in that market. In 1998, it had leap-frogged from being the number five exporter to being number two with sales of 23.1 million liters, second only to Concha y Toro (see Exhibit 8). VSP had proven that it could produce wine at a level of quality that was acceptable to the international community. While its Cabo de Hornos wine was the clear leader in terms of quality and price, very little was produced. Its primary purpose was to prove VSP's capabilities. Most of the wine exported was in the lower price range.

The economics of the export market was very different from that of the Chilean market. The greater need for marketing and the higher cost of buying grapes from independent producers drove domestic profitability into negative territory, while the less marketing intensive wines produced from VSP's own grapes were very profitable (see Exhibit 9). For the larger vineyards that purchased much of their grape requirements from independent growers, the inflation-adjusted cost in pesos to purchase grapes for wine production had risen almost 400 percent between 1992 and 1998 from $.50 per liter to $1.25 in just the last two years. In contrast, the actual production cost of grapes

exhibit 9   Cost-profit Economics of VSP Wine Production, as a Percent
of Total Sales Revenues

	Domestic	Export
Sales	100%	100%
Production costs		
Wine	56	25
Packaging	20	20
Labor	4	4
Total production cost	80	49
Gross margin	20	51
Marketing	10	2
Overhead	20	20
Profit (loss)	(10%)	29%

exhibit 10   Grapes Purchased*

	1996	1997	1998	1999	2000	2001	2002	2003
Own grapes used for exported wines	100%	60%	50%	60%	65%	70%	70%	70%
Grapes purchased as % of total production		41%	52%	52%	49%	47%	46%	38%

*Actual 1996–1998, forecast for 1999–2003.

remained at only $.34 per liter. Meanwhile, domestic wine prices did not increase at
the same pace, placing a strong squeeze on margins.

Elton planned to tackle the situation on two fronts. First, the vineyards that were being planted would come into production in the next several years, driving the cost down
and quality up (see Exhibit 10). More aggressive marketing and a more flexible packaging technology would drive domestic promotions to gain market share. This market,
however, did not promise the growth of the export market. In the fast-growing export
market, sales of those wines that could be sold in the same year as the harvest would be
promoted to drive cash flow. Then slowly, higher quality, higher priced, and higher margin wines would be introduced into markets where VSP wines had become accepted.

DOMESTIC MARKET

Domestic sales of wine were dominated by three vineyards with 52.1 percent of the
market: Concha y Toro, Santa Rita, and VSP (see Exhibit 11). The rest of the market
was highly fragmented among a number of smaller wineries. While the so-called formal market paid an 18 percent value-added tax and a 15 percent alcohol excise tax, an
informal market of small vineyards that avoided these tax burdens was about a quarter
the size of the formal market.

The domestic market was less quality-conscious than the export market and was
more sensitive to price. Of all domestically sold wine, 70 percent was sold in cardboard

exhibit 11   Domestic Market Share

Winery	1997	1998
Concha y Toro	23.5%	24.0%
Santa Rita	17.0	21.1
Viña San Pedro	11.6	10.7
Total	52.1%	55.8%

exhibit 12   Prices and Market Share of Major Brands of One-Liter Cardboard Containers of Wine

Brand	Winery	Retail Price (CP)	Market Share*
Santa Rita 120	Santa Rita	1,062	8.3%
Clos Pirque	Concha y Toro	1,012	6.4
Santa Carolina	Santa Carolina	992	0.2
Ochagavia	Santa Carolina	970	0.6
Gato	San Pedro	996	4.7
Fressco	Concha y Toro	819	1.3
Santa Helena	San Pedro	787	4.1
Bodega 1	Santa Rita	783	3.3
Etiqueta Dorada	San Pedro	762	1.5
Planella	Santa Carolina	761	2.6
Santa Rita Carrera	Santa Rita	733	1.3
Fray Leon	C. Vieja	732	1.1
San Jose	Tocornal	711	1.4
Tocornal	Concha y Toro	797	3.9
Grosso	FCO de Aguirrre	669	1.6
Total			42.3%

*Share of total Chilean wine market, September 1998.

containers, 20 percent in five-liter jugs or plastic/cardboard containers, and 10 percent in bottles. The average price for wine in cardboard containers was only $1.75, while only 14 percent of bottled wine sold for less than $2.20. Of bottled wine, 73 percent was sold at prices ranging from $2.20 to $4.40 (see Exhibit 12).

VSP domestic sales were concentrated in cardboard containers with 87.7 percent of sales, with only 4.5 percent in bottles, 5.5 percent in jugs, and 2.3 percent in plastic/cardboard containers. Its average price for wine sold in cardboard containers was CP 952 per liter, about 5 percent lower than the other market leaders. Consumer research revealed, however, that consumers perceived the wines of VSP competitors to be of somewhat better quality than those of VSP, even though VSP was the only winery in the group which produced a full range of wines.

Marketing practices varied among the leaders, with Santa Rita spending about 46 percent of total Chilean wine marketing expense, Concha y Toro 29 percent, and VSP only 3 percent. Marketing expenditures were concentrated in newspaper and magazine advertising, point of purchase, and billboards.

VSP distributed its wine in Chile exclusively through the CCU distribution network except in the most remote regions. CCU maintained a sales force of 500 people, had 20 warehouses around the country, and kept a delivery fleet of 450 trucks. Of its sales, 74 percent were beer, 21 percent soft drinks, and 5 percent wine. Eighty-one percent of the wine sold was on a cash basis, while the remaining 19 percent was sold on a 30-days-payable basis.

The base of VSP customers had grown from about 6,000 to over 30,000 through the efforts of the CCU distribution system. Of its sales, 37 percent were directly to retailers, 23 percent to wholesalers who sold to smaller retailers, 23 percent to supermarkets, and 12 percent to bars and restaurants.

VSP's objective for the domestic market within four years was to capture a 20 percent market share in the cardboard-carton market and an 8 percent share in the bottled-wine market. The net result would be attaining a total domestic market share of 15 percent. This meant an increase of 11 million liters over the next five years.

Clearly this was an aggressive set of goals, but marketing executives were confident that they could pull it off. While one key element of the strategy was to increase the marketing budget to 12 percent of sales with a message promoting the quality of its wines, the primary tool was to differentiate VSP wines with the use of a new cardboard packaging system.

All of the major wineries used a system called Tetra-Pack, which fed rolls of printed cardboard into a machine which created the box, filled it with wine, and sealed it. While the system was inexpensive to operate on a per unit basis, it was quite inflexible. Each machine had to be devoted to a single-size box. VSP had been approached by SIG Combibloc, a German competitor of Tetra-Pack. VSP had negotiated an exclusive agreement for use of the Combibloc system in Chile until 2001. This system allowed a single machine easily to bottle different package sizes. The company would provide the machines at no cost to VSP as long as VSP purchased the collapsed boxes from them. (See Exhibit 13 for description of Combibloc system.)

VSP marketing executives saw the use of the Combibloc system as an innovative approach to differentiating their wines in the marketplace. They hoped that a promotion aimed at increasing the perception of quality and a new program to sell 1.1-liter boxes for the same price as competitors were selling 1.0-liter boxes would net a significant gain in market share.

EXPORT MARKET

In 1998, over 90 Chilean vineyards exported wine, but the 4 largest vineyards accounted for 65 percent of that amount. Most of these vineyards competed on the basis of good value since they had a cost/quality advantage over other producing countries. The smaller vineyards tended to target the higher end of the market, while the larger vineyards targeted the larger part of the market that demanded better quality at lower prices.

Indeed, exports accounted for much of the growth of VSP in recent years. VSP managers were quick to admit that the character of the individual markets were the most important component of exporting, but that finding and maintaining good relationships with importers was crucial. VSP did virtually no advertising in other countries, leaving

exhibit 13   The Combibloc System

The new combibloc filling machine generation: Efficient—compact—easy handling

The new machine generation from SIG Combibloc International GmbH is setting new standards in the aseptic filling sector: With an output of 10,000 to 12,000 beverage cartons per hour—depending on the format—the combibloc system is currently the fastest aseptic filler worldwide.

Four-track operating mode

Speed alone is not everything: The machines also offer high efficiency. Since this is combined with simple operation and maintenance, the new filling machine generation can really help to lower customers' filling costs. The high filling rates are primarily achieved by the four-track operating mode.

The new machine generation, like the old, is suitable for filling a wide variety of products, ranging from juice and milk to water and wine.

Optimized production

A reduction in operating costs is guaranteed, for instance, by shorter preparation and cleaning times and longer production times. For example, the time needed to prepare for production is cut by 30 minutes as a result of simultaneous sterilization of the filling machine (with H_2O_2) and the filling station (with steam) as well as a reduction in the number of parts that have to be installed. Optimization of the cleaning process reduces personnel time by a further 30 minutes. This is due to:

- Easy access for cleaning and operating staff
- Automatic coupling device for CIP and sterilization
- Simultaneous cleaning of filling system and filling machine
- Hygienic design of the aseptic zone

In addition, the new filling technology offers low-foam filling. Consequently there is no need for a defoamer. Depending on the product, continuous production times of more than 44 hours can be achieved in this way.

The lower service costs also make an important contribution towards reducing costs. In spite of its high performance, the new machine generation is less susceptible to wear—because fewer moving parts are used and, of course, on account of the four-track operating mode. Exchangeable modules also lead to shorter maintenance times.

Other advantages of the new filling machine generation from SIG Combibloc are ease of handling, computer-aided control (by touch screen) and, last but not least, the low space requirement of the machines. Carton off-take to one side—in the case of four-track operation—also saves space and simplifies installation of downstream systems such as the tray packer.

Size flexibility

Like all other combibloc machines, the new filling machine generation offers all the well-known advantages of the combibloc system, for instance, size flexibility: This means that each machine can be converted for up to five different carton sizes within just a few minutes.

With the new filling machine generation, SIG Combibloc offers attractive arguments for marketing aseptic products. This is because the new filling machines can optimize production conditions for filling companies and, consequently, improve competitiveness.

Source: www.combibloc.com.

the responsibility for selling to the importers and to the wholesalers who were their customers. In 1998, VSP exported through 64 agents to 49 countries. Typically, importers took a 20 percent markup as did wholesalers. The retailer added a 26 percent markup, on average, to wines (see Exhibit 14 for the economics of export sales). One of the

exhibit 14   Value Chain Economics of Wine Exporting (In U.S. Dollars)

Retail price	**$10.00**	
Retail markup	2.06	26.0% of wholesaler price
Wholesaler price	7.93	
Wholesaler markup	1.32	20.0% of importer price
Importer price	6.61	
Importer markup	1.10	20.0% of vineyard price (revenue)
Gross revenue to vineyard	5.51	
Export cost		
Commissions, freight, duty	0.22	4.0% of vineyard revenue
Foreign marketing	0.11	2.0
Administrative costs—exports	0.11	2.0
Total export cost	0.44	8.0
Net revenue to vineyard	5.07	92.0
Allocated export costs	0.55	10.0
Financial costs and monetary correction	0.22	4.0
Contribution from sales	4.30	78.0
Cost of sales		
Raw material	1.54	28.0
Direct materials	1.65	30.0
Direct labor	0.11	2.0
Depreciation	0.11	2.0
Total cost of sales	3.42	62.0
Net profit from exports	$ 0.88	16.0%

advantages of selling wines in the popular price range was, VSP marketers thought, that there was less need for promotional activity, particularly in a market that was largely driven by price. (See Exhibit 15.)

On the negative side, export sales were subject to the volatility of exchange rates, often making planning more difficult. This was especially critical at VSP since expenses were almost entirely denominated in Chilean Pesos, while export revenues were denominated in a number of different currencies. (See Exhibit 16).

Exports to Japan represented a major opportunity, but was somewhat muted by a recent downturn in economic conditions there. Japanese consumers had begun to appreciate higher quality imported wines and consumption had risen to .5 liters per person per year in 1995. By 1998, it had risen to 1.4 liters, but much of this increase was in lower priced wines. This was the demand that had driven VSP's success in Japan as exports to the Pacific Rim had risen from 4 percent of its total exports in 1996 to 15 percent in 1998. Per capita consumption was expected to increase further by 2001 to 2.2 liters, still below the three-liter world average.

The United States and Canada appeared to be particularly ripe markets for expansion. There, VSP sales had grown to 2.6 million liters in 1998, primarily driven by sales on the West coast of the United States. The strategy was to continue to build

exhibit 19 Still Wine Sales in Major Markets by Value (U.S. $ Billion)

	1992	1993	1994	1995	1996	CAGR† 1992–1996	1997	1998	1999	2000	2001	CAGR† 1997–2001
France	7.81	8.46	8.80	9.01	9.30	4.5%	9.60	9.85	10.08	10.29	10.55	2.4%
United States	5.94	6.51	6.88	7.19	7.40	5.7	7.55	7.70	7.84	7.98	7.61	1.8
United Kingdom	4.06	4.61	5.24	5.54	6.05	10.5	6.42	6.80	7.20	7.61	8.02	5.7
Italy	4.30	4.42	4.50	4.60	4.69	2.2	4.81	4.97	5.13	5.29	5.44	3.1
Germany	3.93	3.65	3.73	3.79	4.26	2.3	4.28	4.34	4.40	4.48	4.55	1.5
Argentina	1.10	1.15	1.35	1.49	1.58	9.6	1.67	1.77	1.89	2.02	2.17	6.8
Austria	1.21	1.29	1.38	1.43	1.48	5.2	1.52	1.57	1.64	1.70	1.78	4.0
Greece	0.71	0.82	0.87	1.11	1.33	17.2	1.45	1.58	1.73	1.88	2.04	8.9
Canada	1.05	1.09	1.20	1.26	1.30	5.5	1.36	1.43	1.50	1.58	1.65	5.0
Australia	0.81	1.01	0.96	1.03	1.16	9.9	1.25	1.34	1.45	1.55	1.66	7.4
Russia*	0.00	0.17	0.35	0.83	0.98	1184.4	1.21	1.46	1.72	1.98	2.24	16.7
Belgium	0.76	0.78	0.78	0.81	0.82	1.9	0.78	0.75	0.72	0.69	0.66	–4.1
Switzerland	0.73	0.73	0.75	0.76	0.77	1.3	0.74	0.73	0.71	0.69	0.67	–2.5
Sweden	0.68	0.68	0.76	0.76	0.74	2.3	0.79	0.84	0.89	0.95	1.01	6.3
Poland	0.29	0.34	0.44	0.50	0.61	20.6	0.69	0.79	0.89	1.00	1.12	12.9
Portugal	0.62	0.56	0.56	0.55	0.55	–2.9	0.54	0.52	0.51	0.50	0.49	–2.4
Spain	0.43	0.48	0.51	0.55	0.55	6.4	0.55	0.56	0.57	0.58	0.59	1.8
Japan	0.46	0.42	0.38	0.36	0.45	0.4	0.47	0.50	0.53	0.55	0.58	5.4
South Africa	0.39	0.40	0.43	0.44	0.45	3.7	0.45	0.46	0.46	0.47	0.48	1.6
Chile	0.37	0.37	0.36	0.33	0.36	–0.5	0.38	0.40	0.42	0.45	0.47	5.5

*Value distorted by currency instability.

†CAGR = Compound average growth rate.

Source: Euromonitor.

exhibit 20   Major Importers and Exporters of Wine, 1995
(In Millions of Liters)

	Imports	Exports
Germany	877	230
United Kingdom	639	0
France	600	1,140
Russia	300	0
United States	275	133
Spain	236	626
Belgium	230	0
Netherlands	188	0
Switzerland	187	0
Canada	148	0
Denmark	130	0
Japan	108	0
Italy	0	1,583
Argentina	0	215
Bulgaria	0	190
Moldova	0	166
Portugal	0	155
Chile	0	129
Hungary	0	127
Australia	0	115

with what products? The big concern was what might happen if the market continued
to grow beyond expectations. If supply were low, VSP might be forced to allocate production among importers and jeopardize carefully nurtured relationships. In addition,
he now had to meet the new ROCE objectives.

case | 18 Campbell Soup Company in 2000

John E. Gamble
University of South Alabama

Arthur A. Thompson, Jr.
University of Alabama

As the new millennium began, Campbell Soup's CEO, Dale Morrison, was wrestling with how to get the company's underperforming business portfolio back on track and satisfy shareholder expectations of a steadily rising stock price. Morrison was the third CEO in recent years to struggle to develop a diversification strategy for Campbell that could produce attractive growth in revenues and profits. Under two prior CEOs, George McGovern and David Johnson, Campbell's business portfolio had been re-vamped, but the gains in performance had proved temporary and the overall results somewhat disappointing. Now the challenge to restore luster to Campbell's business lineup and build shareholder wealth rested with Dale Morrison.

Going into 2000 Campbell Soup Company was one of the world's leading manu-facturers and marketers of branded consumer food products, with approximately 24,500 employees, 1999 revenues of $6.4 billion, 30 manufacturing plants in six nations, and over 2,000 products on the market. Its major brands in the United States were Campbell's flagship red-and-white label canned soups, Prego spaghetti sauces, Godiva chocolates, Pepperidge Farm baked goods, V8 vegetable juices, Swanson broths, Franco-American canned pastas, and Pace Mexican salsas. Arnott's baked goods and Home Pride sauces were the best-selling Campbell brands in various international markets.

COMPANY BACKGROUND

The company was founded in 1869 by Joseph Campbell, a fruit merchant, and Abram Anderson, an icebox maker, and was originally known for its jams and jellies. In 1891 it was incorporated as the Joseph Campbell Preserve Co. in Camden, New Jersey. John T. Dorrance, a brilliant 24-year-old chemist with a PhD from the Massachusetts Insti-tute of Technology, was hired by the company in 1894 and three years later developed a process for canning soup in condensed form. The new process took water out of the soup during the canning process and thus dramatically reduced production and distrib-ution costs. Soups made with the new production process were awarded the gold medal at the 1900 Paris Exhibition and by 1905 were selling at the rate of 40,000 cases per week. John T. Dorrance purchased the company in 1900, and it was entirely owned by his family until 1954. It was reincorporated as the Campbell Soup Company in 1922.

When John Dorrance died in 1930, he left an estate of over $115 million—the nation's third largest at that time. He also left a company devoted to engineering, committed to providing good products (in recessions it would rather shave margins than cut back product quality or raise price), and obsessed with secrecy. His successor, John T. Dorrance Jr., headed the company for the next 24 years (1930–54) and few, if any, important decisions were made at Campbell without his approval. In 1954, the company went public, with the Dorrance family retaining majority control. In 1999, the Dorrance family still owned about 50 percent of Campbell's stock and, despite having relinquished direct management control, still exerted considerable shareholder influence. Four of Campbell Soup's 16 board members were grandchildren of John T. Dorrance Sr.

Over the years Campbell had diversified into a number of businesses—Swanson frozen dinners, Pepperidge Farm bakery products, Vlasic pickles, Franco-American spaghetti products, Recipe pet food, various fast-food restaurant chains, Godiva chocolates, and even retail garden centers. However, canned soup had always remained Campbell's core business. The company had had three chief executive officers over the last 20 years, and its corporate strategy had evolved with each change in leadership. The company's diversification strategy and new investment priorities had shifted as each new CEO pursued a course to build value for Campbell Soup Company's shareholders.

THE GORDON McGOVERN ERA: 1980–89

Gordon McGovern was in business school when Margaret Rudkin, founder of Pepperidge Farm, spoke to his class. She told how she had built her bread company from scratch in an industry dominated by giants. McGovern was impressed. He wrote to Rudkin for a job, received it in 1956, and began his climb through Pepperidge Farm's ranks. When Campbell acquired Pepperidge Farm in 1961, it had sales of $40 million and had only reached $60 million when McGovern became Pepperidge Farm's president in 1968. When McGovern was named president of Campbell in 1980, Pepperidge Farm's annual sales had grown to $300 million under his leadership. McGovern implemented several key elements of Pepperidge Farm's strategy when he took over at Campbell: creativity and a willingness to experiment, emphasis on new product development, and building strong competencies in marketing.

McGovern's Corporate Strategy as Campbell's CEO

During the McGovern years, Campbell's strategic focus was on the consumer. The consumer's "hot buttons" were identified as nutrition, convenience, low sodium, attractive price, good quality, and unique products—and managers were urged to press those buttons. Business unit managers were expected to be responsive to consumer perceptions, needs, and demands regarding nutrition, safety, flavor, and convenience. Key business unit strategies included (1) improving operating efficiency, (2) developing new products to capitalize on consumer trends, (3) updating advertising for new and established products, and (4) continuing Campbell's long-standing emphasis on high production standards and premium-quality products.

Early in his tenure, McGovern developed a five-year plan that featured four financial performance objectives: a 15 percent annual increase in earnings, a 5 percent increase in volume, a 5 percent increase in sales (plus inflation), and an 18 percent return on equity by 1986. The two cornerstones of McGovern's growth strategy were (1) developing and introducing new products and (2) making acquisitions every two years that would bring in $200 million in annual sales. Campbell's acquisition strategy was to look for small, fast-growing food companies strong in product areas where Campbell had no presence and companies on the fast track that were in rapidly growing product categories or industries. Under McGovern, Campbell made a number of acquisitions:

1982

● Mrs. Paul's Kitchens, Inc., a processor and marketer of frozen prepared seafood and vegetable products, with annual sales of approximately $125 million (acquired at a cost of $55 million).

● Snow King Frozen Foods, Inc., engaged in the production and marketing of a line of uncooked frozen specialty meat products, with annual sales of $32 million.

● Juice Bowl Products, Inc., a Florida producer of fruit juices.

● Win Schuler Foods, Inc., a Michigan-based producer and distributor of specialty cheese spreads, flavored melba rounds, food service salad dressings, party dips, and sauces, with annual sales of $6.5 million.

● Costa Apple Products, Inc., a producer of apple juice retailed primarily in the eastern United States, with annual sales of $6 million.

1983

● Several small domestic operations, at a cost of $26 million, including:
  —Annabelle's restaurant chain of 12 units in the southeastern United States.
  —Triangle Manufacturing Corp., a manufacturer of physical fitness and sports medicine products.

1984

● Mendelson-Zeller Co., Inc., a California distributor of fresh produce.

1985

● Continental Foods Company SA and affiliated companies, which produced sauces, confectioneries, and other food products in Belgium and France; the cost of the acquisition was $17 million.

● A 20 percent ownership interest in Arnott's Ltd., an Australian producer of cookies and crackers.

1988

● Freshbake Foods Group, a British producer of baked goods.

Campbell's Business Portfolio under McGovern

During the McGovern era, Campbell Soup Company was organized into six business units—Campbell U.S., Pepperidge Farm, Vlasic Foods, Mrs. Paul's Kitchens, Other United States, and International. Sales and profit performance by division are shown in Exhibit 1.

The Campbell U.S. Business Unit In 1989 the Campbell U.S. division was the company's largest operating unit, accounting for just over 50 percent of corporate revenues. The Campbell U.S. division was divided into eight profit centers: soup, frozen foods, grocery, beverage, food service, poultry, fresh produce, and pet foods.

exbibit 1 Performance of Campbell's Divisions under Gordon McGovern, 1980–89 ($ Millions)

	1989	1988	1987	1986	1985	1984	1983	1982	1981	1980
Campbell U.S.										
Sales	$2,776	$2,584	$2,445	$2,507	$2,500	$2,282	$1,987	$1,773	$1,678	$1,608
Operating earnings	175	272	284	302	292	278	250	211	190	205
Pepperidge Farm										
Sales	548	495	459	420	426	435	433	392	329	283
Operating earnings	54	58	54	46	39	35	43	41	35	29
Vlasic Foods										
Sales	441	353	283	263	199	193	168	149	137	130
Operating earnings	39	30	22	24	16	14	13	12	10	8
Mrs. Paul's Kitchens										
Sales	140	150	153	141	138	126	108	—	—	—
Operating earnings	0.4	(4)	10	8	11	14	10	—	—	—
Other United States*										
Sales	—	—	59	76	81	84	64	56	27	35
Operating earnings	—	—	(2)	(7)	(3)	(2)	(1)	(1)	(1)	1
International										
Sales	1,527	1,037	898	766	716	624	599	643	694	512
Operating earnings	($ 81)	$ 58	$ 69	($ 61)	$ 35	$ 34	$ 33	$ 46	$ 46	$ 33

*Division eliminated in 1988 and replaced with a new division named Campbell Enterprises.

Source: Campbell's annual reports.

Exhibit 2 shows the brands Campbell had in this division and the major competitors each brand faced during most of the 1980s.

The soup business group alone accounted for more than 25 percent of the company's consolidated sales (as compared to around 50 percent in the 1970s). Campbell's flagship brands of soup accounted for 80 percent of the $1 billion–plus annual canned soup market; in 1989, Campbell offered grocery shoppers over 50 varieties of canned soups. Heinz was the second largest soup producer, with 10 percent of the market. Heinz had earlier withdrawn from producing Heinz-label soups and shifted its production over to making soups for sale under the private labels of grocery chains. Heinz was the leading private-label producer of canned soup, holding almost an 80 percent share of the private-label segment.

Although the soup business was relatively mature (McGovern preferred to call it underworked), Campbell's most ambitious consumer research took place in this unit. McGovern opted to grow Campbell's soup sales by turning out a steady flow of new varieties in convenient packages: "Ethnic, dried, refrigerated, frozen, microwave—you name it, we're going to try it."[1] In 1985, Campbell entered the $290 million dry-soup-mix market dominated by Thomas J. Lipton Inc., a business unit of Unilever. Dry-soup sales in the United States were growing faster than sales of canned soup. Lipton's aggressive response to test marketing of an early Campbell dry-soup product resulted in Campbell's rushing a six-flavor line into national distribution ahead of schedule.

In 1982 McGovern caused a stir when he announced publicly that Campbell's Swanson TV-dinner line was "junk food": "It was great in 1950, but in today's world it didn't go into the microwave; it didn't represent any variety or a good eating experience to my palate."[2] Over the past five years, Swanson's sales volume had slipped 16 percent. He maintained that consumers had discovered better-quality options to the TV-dinner concept. Campbell's frozen foods group answered the challenge by creating a new frozen gourmet line, LeMenu. Campbell committed about $50 million in manufacturing, marketing, and trade promotion costs when initial market tests of the LeMenu line proved encouraging.

LeMenu products—packaged on round heatable plates and featuring such selections as chicken cordon bleu, al dente vegetables, and sophisticated wine sauces—produced 21 percent growth in the frozen meal unit, with sales of $150 million during its first year of national distribution (1984), double Campbell's sales projection. In addition, the Swanson line of TV dinners was overhauled to put in less salt and more meat stock in gravies, add new desserts and sauces, and create new packaging and a redesigned logo.

The grocery business unit's star was Prego spaghetti sauce. By 1984 the Prego brand had captured 25 percent of the still-growing spaghetti sauce market, becoming the number two sauce, behind Ragu. A Prego Plus spaghetti sauce line was introduced in 1985.

Pepperidge Farm Pepperidge Farm was Campbell's third largest division in 1989, with 10 percent of the company's consolidated sales. Although the division was one of Campbell's best performers during the late 1970s (with sales rising at an average compound rate of 14 percent), by the mid-1980s growth had slowed and a number of newly introduced products had produced disappointing results (Star Wars cookies, Vegetables in Pastry). To remedy the division's weak performance, a number of steps were taken:

---

[1]As quoted in *Business Week,* December 24, 1984, p. 67.
[2]Ibid.

exhibit 2   The Campbell U.S. Division: Products, Rival Brands, and Competitors as of 1985

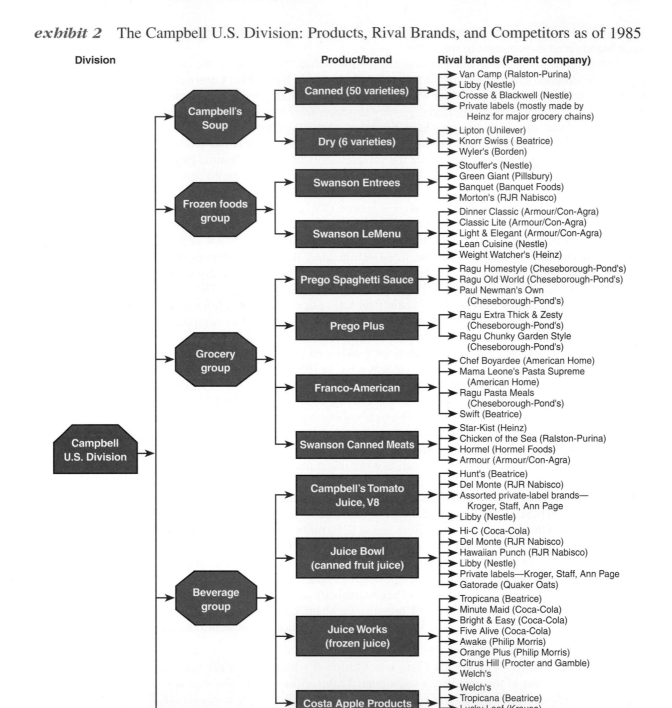

exhibit 3   The Pepperidge Farm Division: Products, Rival Brands, and
                   Competitors in 1985

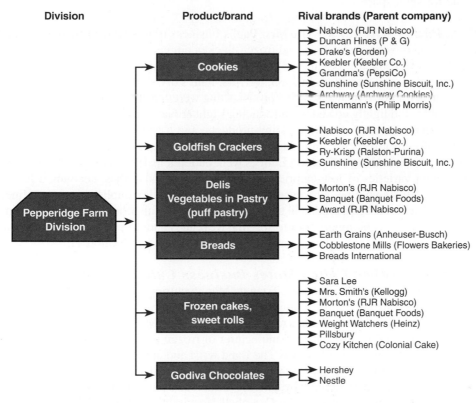

| Division | Product/brand | Rival brands (Parent company) |

- The Costa Apple Products unit, acquired in 1982, was transferred to the Campbell U.S. beverage group.
- Pepperidge Farm divested itself of operations that no longer fit into its strategic plan, including Lexington Gardens, Inc., a garden center chain.
- Deli's Vegetables in Pastry went back into research and development to improve quality.
- A new management team was put in place and a comprehensive review of each product was initiated.

Exhibit 3 shows Pepperidge Farm's product portfolio during the 1980s.

Vlasic Foods   Vlasic, Campbell's fourth largest division, was the leading producer and marketer of pickles and relishes in the United States, with a 31 percent market share. During the 1982–84 period, Vlasic also had responsibility for Win Schuler Foods, a Michigan-based maker of cheese spreads, melba rounds, party dips, sauces, and salad dressings. Win Schuler was purchased in 1982, and its products were marketed in several states in the upper Midwest. When sales of the Win Schuler unit flattened in 1984, partly due to a sagging Midwest economy, McGovern transferred the unit to the refrigerated foods group in the Campbell U.S. business division.

In 1985 Vlasic implemented new labels that used color bands and a new flavor scale to help consumers find their favorite tastes quickly on the supermarket shelf. Following up on marketing research indicating consumer desires for new and interesting flavors, Vlasic had introduced Zesty Dills and Bread and Butter Whole Pickle lines in

1985. Heinz was Campbell's leading national competitor in this area, but there were a number of important regional and private-label brands that competed with Heinz and Vlasic for shelf space.

Mrs. Paul's Kitchens   The Mrs. Paul's business unit produced frozen fish entrees, frozen breaded vegetables, and frozen chicken nuggets. When Campbell acquired Mrs. Paul's in 1982, it was rumored that Heinz and Pillsbury, among others, were considering the same acquisition. In 1983, the Mrs. Paul's division responded to consumer preferences for convenience seafood products that were nutritious, low in calories, microwavable, and lightly coated by introducing Light & Natural Fish Fillets. Quality improvements were also made in existing products, and a promising new product line, Light Seafood Entrees, was introduced in 1984. Market share increased about 25 percent over 1983, and Light Seafood Entrees went national in 1985. This line, which featured seven varieties of low-calorie microwavable seafood dishes, accounted for 11 percent of 1985's volume. However, sales of the company's established product lines of breaded seafood items eroded in the years following acquisition because these items had to be fried in cooking oil prior to serving. Revenues had dropped in both 1988 and 1989, and the division was barely profitable in 1989 (see again Exhibit 1).

Campbell's Other United States Business Unit   Grouped into the Other United States business division were Triangle Manufacturing Corporation, a health-and-fitness products manufacturer; Campbell Hospitality, a restaurant unit that operated 59 Pietro's restaurants, 15 Annabelle's restaurants, and 6 H. T. McDoogal's restaurants; and Snow King Frozen Foods, Inc., a manufacturer of frozen specialty meat products. Triangle's best-known product line was The Band wrist and ankle weights, which had the number two position in its market category, with a market share of 14 percent. Triangle was trying to build on its strength by entering the exercise equipment market and by selling its products internationally. The Campbell Hospitality division struggled through most of the 1980s to sustain sales and earnings growth. Snow King was also a weak performer. In 1988, this division was reorganized and renamed Campbell Enterprises; it included Triangle Manufacturing; Godiva International; V8 and Campbell Juices; Campbell Food Services; Snow King Frozen Foods; and Pietro's, Annabelle's, and H. T. McDoogal's restaurant chains. All three restaurant chains were divested in 1989.

Campbell's International Business Unit   The International business unit was Campbell's second largest division throughout the 1980s and accounted for about one-fifth of corporate revenues in 1989. Campbell International had subsidiaries in about 12 foreign countries as of 1989 and had plans to expand further. The division was reorganized in 1985 to build a more solid base for sales and earnings growth. McGovern's goal was for the International division to contribute 25 percent of Campbell's corporate sales and earnings. His strategy was to develop and strengthen Campbell's presence in international markets and to make Campbell a premier international company.

A number of acquisitions were completed in 1989 to strengthen Campbell's international competitive position. The Habitant soup and pickle brands, the Laura Secord brand of jams, and a refrigerated distribution company were all acquired by Campbell's Canadian subsidiary. In Europe, Campbell acquired a German specialty food importer and an Italian producer of institutional foods. Also during 1989, the company increased its ownership in Australia's leading cookie company, Arnott's Ltd., to 32 percent; acquired 50 percent ownership in an Australian juice manufacturer; and obtained complete ownership of Melbourne Mushrooms. The International division's three biggest profit contributors in 1989 were Campbell Soup Canada, the European food and confectionery group, and the operations in Australia.

Even though the company had a number of successes internationally, Campbell management had encountered some difficulties. Campbell's Italian business suffered losses during 1989 as a result of excessive costs brought on by an aggressive and poorly controlled attempt to build market share. Campbell was also having difficulty with making its recently acquired Freshbake Foods unit profitable. The UK food processing company was struggling to absorb a number of acquisitions it had made prior to its acquisition by Campbell in 1988. Campbell management found it necessary to institute an extensive restructuring process at Freshbake, including closing a number of plants.

McGovern's Approach to Managing Campbell's Business Portfolio

Every Saturday morning McGovern did his family's grocery shopping, stopping to straighten Campbell's displays and inspect those of competitors, studying packages and reading labels, and trying to learn all he could about how and what people were eating. He encouraged his managers to do the same. Several board meetings were held in the backrooms of supermarkets so that afterward directors could roam the store aisles interviewing customers about Campbell products.

McGovern decentralized Campbell management to facilitate entrepreneurial risk taking and new product development, devising a new compensation program to reward these traits. He restructured the company into some 50 autonomous units, each with the leeway to develop new products even if the new product ideas were closely related to another business unit's products. Thus, the Prego spaghetti sauce unit—not the frozen food group—initiated frozen Mexican dinners. And although it wasn't his job, the director of market research created Today's Taste, a line of refrigerated entrees and side dishes. "It's like things are in constant motion," the director said. "We are overloaded but it's fun."[3]

McGovern believed the new structure encouraged managers of business units, who had to compete for corporate funding, to be more creative and venturesome in developing promising products:

> These business divisions allow the company to really get its arms around chunks of the business. The managers are answerable to the bottom line—to their investments, their hiring, their products—and it's a great motivation for performance.[4]

As part of this motivation, Campbell began annually allotting around $30 to $40 million to support new ventures and the creation of new product families; it often took $10 million to develop and test new products. In addition, it took $10 to $15 million in advertising and couponing to launch a new brand. McGovern believed a special new product venture fund was needed to encourage managers to think big in terms of new product development. He emphasized that it was no disgrace to fail if the effort was a good one. High failure rates were common in the industry—only about 20 percent of new products lasted more than one year on the market—but Campbell's failure rate on

---

[3]As quoted in *The Wall Street Journal,* September 17, 1984, p. A10.

[4]*Advertising Age,* January 3, 1983, p. 38.

new product introductions was running even higher. In fact, during the 1980s, only about one out of eight new Campbell products reaching the market was successful.

Every Friday morning McGovern held meetings to discuss new products. The fact-finding sessions were attended by financial, marketing, engineering, and sales personnel. Typical McGovern questions included: "Would you eat something like that?" "Why not?" "Have you tried the competition's product?" "Is there a consumer niche?"[5]

McGovern's New Product Development and Marketing Strategies

McGovern instituted a number of internal changes to make Campbell's product development strategy produce the desired results. Much revolved around efforts to enhance the sophistication of Campbell's corporate marketing strategies and approach to marketing research. Under McGovern, Campbell's market research unearthed several findings and projections that drove the company's product development effort:

● Women comprised 43 percent of the workforce (with a level of 50 percent projected by 1990).

● Two-income marriages represented 60 percent of all U.S. families and accounted for 60 percent of total family income.

● Upper-income households would grow 3.5 times faster than the total household formations.

● More than half of all households consisted of only one or two members; 23 percent of all households contained only one person.

● More and more consumers were exhibiting a growing preference for refrigerated and fresh produce over canned and frozen products.

● The percentage of meals eaten at home was declining.

● Nearly half of the adult meal planners in the United States were watching their weight.

● Poultry consumption had increased 26 percent since 1973.

● Ethnic food preparation at home was increasing, with 40 percent, 21 percent, and 14 percent of households preparing Italian, Mexican, and Oriental foods, respectively, at home from scratch.

● There was a growing consumer concern with food avoidance: sugar, salt, calories, chemicals, cholesterol, and additives.

● The "I am what I eat" philosophy had tied food into lifestyles that embraced exercise machines, hot tubs, jogging, racquetball, backpacking, cross-country skiing, and aerobic dancing.

In response to growing ethnic food demand, Campbell began marketing ethnic selections in regions where consumer interests for particular food types were strong. For instance, it marketed spicy Ranchero Beans only in the South and Southwest, and its newly acquired Puerto Rican foods only in New York City and Florida (which had sizable Puerto Rican populations).

---

[5]*The Wall Street Journal,* September 17, 1984, p. A10.

Campbell's product-development guidelines emphasized convenience, taste, flavor, and texture. The strategic themes McGovern stressed were these:

● Concentrate on products that represent superior value to consumers and constantly strive to improve those values.

● Develop products that help build markets.

● Develop products that yield a fair profit to Campbell.

In pursuing these guidelines, Campbell adopted several operating practices:

● Using ongoing consumer research to determine eating habits; this included checking home menus, recipes, and food preparation techniques to learn which food items were served together.

● Studying meal and snack occasions to learn which household members participated so that preliminary estimates of volume potential could be made for possible new products and product improvement ideas.

● Testing new or improved products in a large enough number of households across the United States that reliable national sales projections could be made. Once a product met pretest standards, testing in a sample of supermarkets and sales outlets was conducted.

● Rolling out the new products on a regional or national plan and using test-market data to establish the sequence in which area markets should be entered.

By 1983 McGovern's strategy had turned Campbell into the biggest generator of new products in the combined food and health-and-beauty aids categories, with a total of 42 new products. Prego spaghetti sauce, LeMenu frozen dinners, Great Starts breakfasts, and Chunky New England Clam Chowder were among the leading products introduced by Campbell Soup during the early 1980s. Meanwhile Campbell's marketing budget grew from $275 million in 1982, to $488 million in 1985, and to $552 million in 1989. Ad expenditures jumped from $67 million in 1980 to $197 million in 1989. Prior to McGovern, Campbell often trimmed ad spending at the end of a quarter to boost earnings.

In 1982 McGovern was named *Advertising Age*'s Adman of the Year for his efforts in transforming Campbell into "one of the most aggressive market-driven companies in the food industry today."[6] *Advertising Age* cited the company's emphasis on nutrition and fitness as opposed to the former "mmm, mmm, good" emphasis on taste. Print ads featured government studies concerning soup's nutritional values and a new slogan, "Soup is good food."

Production, Quality, and Cost Considerations during the McGovern Era

Gordon McGovern also stressed the importance of high production quality; a 1984 article in *Savvy* quoted him as saying, "I want zero defects. If we can't produce quality, we'll get out of the business." That same year, Campbell held its first Worldwide Corporate conference dedicated to quality. Hundreds of Campbell managers from all levels and most company locations spent three days at this conference. Management believed that the ultimate test of quality was consumer satisfaction, and the company's

---

[6]*Advertising Age,* January 3, 1983, p. 38.

goal was to instill a strong quality consciousness among employees in every single operation throughout the company.

Before McGovern took over, Campbell used to adjust the design of new products so that they could be produced with existing equipment and plant facilities. For example, a square omelet was specified for Swanson's breakfasts because it was what the installed machine would make. After McGovern's appointment, although low-cost production was still a strategic factor, market considerations and consumer trends—not existing machinery and production capabilities—were deciding factors in production, packaging, and labeling. Still, the company spent between $150 million and $300 million annually throughout the 1980s for improved equipment, new plants and plant expansions, better packaging technology, and distribution facilities.

Campbell executives believed the company's key strengths during the 1985–89 period were (1) a worldwide system for obtaining ingredients; (2) a broad range of food products that could be used as a launching pad for formulating, producing, and marketing new products; and (3) an emphasis on low-cost production.

Campbell's Performance under Gordon McGovern

McGovern's campaign for renewed growth via new product introduction and acquisition produced good results early on. By year-end 1984 sales were up 31 percent—to $3.7 billion—and earnings had risen by 47 percent—to $191 million. During McGovern's 10-year reign as CEO, Campbell introduced 922 new items—more than any other food-processing company. By the late 1980s however, there were signs that Campbell's brand managers had become so involved in new product development that they had neglected the old stand-by products as well as slighting cost-control and profit margin targets. According to one Campbell executive:

> We became fat cats. We said, "We can't fail." We began to throw things against the marketplace that had long paybacks and were in processes, packaging, and distribution that we didn't understand.[7]

Campbell's growth in operating earnings for fiscal years 1985–89 fell short of McGovern's 15 percent target rate, and McGovern in 1989 initiated several internal restructuring moves to eliminate many of the inefficiencies and cost excesses that had crept into the company's operations and new product development efforts. A summary of Campbell Soup's financial performance between 1989 and 1999 is presented in Exhibit 4.

McGOVERN'S RESIGNATION AND THE RECRUITMENT OF A REPLACEMENT

Beginning in the late 1980s, the heirs of John T. Dorrance began to show frustration with Campbell Soup's industry-lagging performance and began to openly criticize McGovern's approach to running the company. Quaker Oats management believed that the Dorrance family might be interested in a merger between the two companies and approached Campbell's chairman of the board, Robert Vlasic, in March 1989 to explore the issue. The Dorrance heirs were split on the prospect of a merger, with one faction publicly announcing its intent to sell its shares and another vying to block a

---

[7]As quoted in *Financial World,* June 11, 1991, p. 53.

exhibit 4 Financial Summary, Campbell Soup Company, 1989–99 (In Millions, Except Per Share Amounts)

	1999	1998	1997	1996	1995	1994	1993	1992	1991	1990	1989
Net sales	$6,424	$6,696	$7,964	$7,678	$7,250	$6,664	$6,577	$6,263	$6,204	$6,205	$5,672
Earnings before taxes	1,097	1,073	1,107	1,179	1,042	963	520	779	667	179	107
Earnings before cumulative effect of accounting change	1,097	1,062	713	802	698	630	257	491	402	4	13
Net earnings	724	660	713	802	698	630	8	491	402	4	13
Taxes on earnings	373	384	394	395	344	333	263	309	266	175	93
Interest—net	173	175	165	126	115	64	74	87	90	94	56
Earnings per share	1.63	1.46	1.51	1.61	1.40	1.26	0.02	0.97	0.79	0.01	0.03
Dividends per share	0.89	0.82	0.75	0.67	0.61	0.55	0.46	0.36	0.28	0.25	0.23
Wgt. avg. shares outstanding	445	460	472	498	498	501	504	504	508	518	518
Capital expenditures	297	256	331	416	391	421	371	362	371	397	302
Depreciation and amortization	255	261	328	326	294	255	242	216	209	201	192
Assets	5,522	5,633	6,459	6,632	6,315	4,992	4,897	4,353	4,149	4,115	3,932
Stockholders' equity	$ 235	$ 874	$1,420	$2,742	$2,468	$1,989	$1,704	$2,027	$1,793	$1,691	$1,778

Source: Campbell annual reports.

merger at all costs. The heirs supporting Campbell Soup's independence successfully prevented a merger but were unable to bring prompt reconciliation among the family.

Disenchanted with the family squabble and stung by outspoken criticism of his performance by family members, Gordon McGovern resigned as CEO and took early retirement in November 1989. Campbell's search for a replacement, spearheaded by Ippy Dorrance and Robert Vlasic, quickly focused on Gerber's CEO, David Johnson, as best candidate to replace McGovern. A native of Australia, David Johnson had a bachelor's degree in economics from the University of Sydney and an MBA from the University of Chicago. Starting out as a management trainee with the international division of Colgate-Palmolive in Australia, he moved up through the ranks to become managing director of Colgate's South African operations in 1967. In 1973, he moved to Hong Kong as president of Warner-Lambert/Parke Davis Asia; there, exposed to the Orient's fundamentally different customs and approaches, he came to appreciate that if managers were creative enough to look beyond accepted solutions to business problems, it was easy to find innovative answers. Looking back on his Hong Kong experiences, Johnson observed that he gained "an elasticized mind, opened to a greater run of possibilities than I'd ever known before."[8] Warner-Lambert brought Johnson to the United States in 1976 as president of its personal products division; a year later, he was promoted to president of the company's American Chicle division. When Warner-Lambert acquired Entenmann's in 1979, Johnson took over as head; he then moved to General Foods when GF acquired Entenmann's from Warner-Lambert in 1982. As Entenmann's chief executive from 1979 to 1987, he engineered the company's drive from a regional to a national provider of bakery products, more than quadrupling sales and profits. In 1987, Johnson left Entenmann's to become CEO of Gerber Products, a company whose performance had been lackluster for several years. He proceeded to craft a turnaround strategy for Gerber that involved divesting seven business divisions (toys, furniture, trucking) and refocusing Gerber's attention on its core baby-foods business. By 1990, 27 months after Johnson became CEO, Gerber's sales were up 30 percent, profits were up 50 percent, and the stock price had tripled. With the Dorrance family's blessing, Campbell lured Johnson away from Gerber as McGovern's successor.

THE DAVID JOHNSON ERA: 1990–97

When David Johnson became chairman and CEO of Campbell Soup Company in January 1990, he saw his first priority as crafting a strategy for Campbell that would grow earnings and win the confidence of the Dorrance heirs. While at Gerber, Johnson viewed Campbell, a competitor of Gerber's in some product categories, as an underperforming company that was a likely target for corporate raiders, once even commenting, "Boy, that's a troubled company. I could really run that one."[9] In interviewing for the job at Campbell, Johnson determined that the arguments and differences between the Dorrance family and Campbell's prior management were more a function of "poor results" than of activist family members wanting to meddle in company affairs or the desire of some to sell out their stake and invest their inheritance elsewhere. Johnson deemed the challenge worthy for several reasons:

---

[8]Jeffrey Zygmont, "In Command at Campbell," *Sky Magazine,* March 1993, p. 60.
[9]As quoted in *Fortune,* September 9, 1991, p. 143.

It was a company that was founded on incredible strength on which you could build. I knew that it had excellent R&D. I knew it had terrific brands. It had lost its direction, lost its focus, was underperforming, and I knew that it could be refocused and reorganized within six months, and that we could really get it going very quickly.[10]

Johnson immediately embarked on a course of boosting Campbell's performance quickly, not only to pacify disgruntled shareholders but also to get the company's stock price high enough to discourage would-be acquirers from launching a takeover attempt:

> Under those circumstances, when you come in, it's not the pretties of "Here is my vision. Let me explain the principles from the book." When you move in, you've got to do it in an exciting fashion, lay down the challenge—Boom! Strike! Crash! It's short-term focus. You know that dirty word we're all accused of? "Short term." Isn't it terrible? Under those circumstances, if you don't win the first year, if you don't win in the short term, you're dead.[11]

Johnson's Turnaround Strategy

To spur Campbell's managers and give them something to shoot for in rejuvenating the company's performance, Johnson set financial objectives of 20 percent earnings growth, 20 percent return on equity, and 20 percent cash return on assets: "I used to say, if perfect human vision is 20-20, then perfect business vision is 20-20-20, which was shorthand for earnings, return and cash."[12] This was followed by the establishment of four corporate-level strategic principles to guide the creation of business and functional strategies in each divisional unit:

- The primary purpose of the corporation is to *build shareholder wealth.* It is imperative to provide dividend growth and long-term stock appreciation to reward the stockholders of the corporation.

- Campbell must exploit its *brand power.* Campbell's strong brands have been the basis of the company's strength's over the past 90 years and should be the focal point for the future.

- Campbell's ability to sustain its brand power and build on its powerful brands is only possible through *people power.* The company's employees have to be responsible for maintaining the existing brands, for building on these brands, and for finding new markets for these brands. Campbell should encourage individual risk-bearing and teamwork with rewards linked to results.

- It is important to *preserve the company's independence.* Management needs to preserve the heritage of Campbell Soup Company and resist any outside thrust for control through delivery of superior performance on building long-term shareholder wealth.

Johnson disagreed with McGovern's view that Campbell's growth should come primarily from the acquisition of small, fast-growing food companies and from the introduction of new products that served some niche of the food industry. Instead, Johnson believed that Campbell Soup should concentrate on growing sales of its best-known brands—the red-and-white soup line, Prego, Pepperidge Farm, Vlasic, and Swanson—and to increase its U.S. market share in these product categories. During the 1980s, for

---

[10]As quoted in *Sky Magazine,* March 1993, p. 54.

[11]As quoted in *Fortune,* December 14, 1992, p. 112.

[12]Ibid.

example, Campbell's tonnage in canned soups had risen a paltry 1 percent annually and Campbell's market share of the U.S. soup market, according to Wall Street estimates, had slipped from a lofty 80 percent in the 1950s and 1960s to 70 percent in the mid-1980s to around 65 percent in 1990. Johnson also decided to press harder and faster than McGovern had to gain increased penetration of foreign markets.

While McGovern had pursued ways to reduce costs and eliminate inefficiencies during his 1989 restructuring, Johnson saw opportunities to achieve further economies and better profit margins, principally by eliminating unprofitable and slow-selling items from Campbell's product lineup and by divesting peripheral lines of businesses that did not complement the company's strengths or bolster the market power of its flagship brands. Consequently, the strategy Johnson crafted to boost Campbell's performance incorporated six major initiatives:

- Divesting poorly performing and nonstrategic business units and reorganizing Campbell's six divisions.
- Eliminating weak items from the company's product lineup.
- Requiring that new product introductions exploit Campbell Soup's strengths, core competencies, and organizational capabilities as well as have the potential to achieve the three 20-20-20 financial performance targets.
- Focusing on the global marketing of the company's competencies and capabilities.
- Installing and expanding low-cost business systems at the corporate level to support the operations of the business divisions.
- Improving utilization of assets to maximize the return to stockholders.

Exhibit 5 shows the business lines that were divested—Johnson saw all of them as either nonstrategic and unrelated to Campbell's core competencies or as chronic money losers or low-return businesses. This pruning of Campbell's portfolio resulted in the sale of 8 plants and the shutdown of 12 plants worldwide plus a workforce reduction of 8,000 people during Johnson's first 18 months as CEO. As the remaining plants bid to absorb the production of the closed plants, overall capacity utilization rose from 60 to 80 percent; Campbell's Maxton, North Carolina, plant was able to increase its output 50 percent and become Campbell's first canned-soup plant to drive manufacturing costs below 50 percent of the retail price of its products. Included among the initial plant closings was the company's 131-year-old Camden, New Jersey, plant with its distinctive water towers painted to look like giant Campbell Soup cans.

Johnson's restructuring continued throughout his tenure, with major initiatives approved by the board in 1993 and 1996. The 1993 restructuring program identified six plants and 14 businesses that were to be sold. In 1996 the board approved an additional restructuring that eliminated not only additional plants and businesses but also 2,100 administrative and operational positions at various Campbell Soup facilities. Both restructuring programs were intended to shift production from underutilized or inefficient production facilities to more cost-effective locations and eliminate nonstrategic poor-performing businesses from the portfolio. Under Johnson, Campbell Soup went on to divest a total of 26 businesses that had an average net profit margin of 1 percent. Campbell Soup also closed a total of 10 older and inefficient plants between 1990 and 1997 to boost capacity utilization.

Once Johnson assessed that the turnaround was well under way, he complemented the divestitures with 20 acquisitions of higher-margin business with ample growth potential to complete the portfolio restructuring initiative. In 1996 David Johnson commented on the strategy of moving Campbell from a position of "best in class" to "best

exhibit 5   Divested Campbell Soup Company Businesses, 1990–96

- Fried chicken plant in Sumpter, South Carolina
- Salmon Farms
- Snow King Frozen Foods—frozen meat products
- Triangle Manufacturing Corporation—a health-and-fitness products manufacturer
- Mushroom farms
- Menderson-Zeller, Inc.
- Recipe Pet Food
- D. Lazzaroni Cookie Company (Italy)
- Win Schuler Foods, Inc.
- Juice Bowl
- Juice Works
- The fresh produce and frozen vegetable portions of the UK Freshbake Foods Group—the frozen entree portion of Freshbake was retained.
- Campbell Chilled Foods, Ltd. (United Kingdom)
- Mrs. Paul's frozen seafood
- Poultry processing operations
- Marie's salad dressings
- Beeck-Feinkost GmbH chilled foods (Germany)
- Beef farms in Argentina
- Durkee and Early California olives
- Groko BV frozen vegetable processing (Holland)

Source: Campbell annual reports and 10-Ks.

in show," the contribution of the newly acquired businesses, and the company's prospects for growth:

> We begin this new attack from a position of great strength. Our balance sheet and cash flow are strong. Since 1990, we have divested non-strategic and low-margin businesses with approximately $800 million in sales and acquired strategic, higher-margin businesses with more than $1.2 billion in sales, including Mexican sauce leader Pace Foods. Our management team has transformed Campbell into a place where results count and where the bar is constantly raised . . . We are poised for breaking away from our competitors in the food industry. This strategic growth plan is designed to vault our company into the ranks of the world's renowned consumer goods companies, in terms of financial profile and market multiple.[13]

Exhibit 6 presents a listing and description of business acquisitions initiated by David Johnson. By year-end 1996 the new businesses Johnson had added to Campbell's portfolio achieved an average net profit margin of 12 percent.

Many of Johnson's acquisitions were intended to add brands and infrastructure that were necessary for the growth of Campbell's international business. The acquisition of Pace Foods was one of the few acquisitions not specifically aimed at growing international food sales. Pace Foods, the leading U.S. producer and marketer of Mexican salsa, was Campbell's biggest acquisition ever. The $1.12 billion purchase price represented five times Pace's sales and 20 times its earnings. A number of companies, including Heinz and Lea & Perrin, had been attempting to buy Pace for a number of

---

[13]As quoted in PR Newswire, September 5, 1996.

exhibit 6   Businesses Acquired by Campbell Soup, 1994–97

1994 (Acquisitions totaled $14 million)
- Dandy mushrooms (Australia)
- Fray Bentos canned meats (Australia)

1995 (Acquisitions totaled $1.26 billion)
- Pace Foods—the leading salsa brand in the United States, with annual sales of $700 million. The company was purchased for $1.12 billion.
- Increase in share ownership of Arnott's Ltd. to 65 percent.
- Fresh Start Bakeries—maker of buns and English muffins for quick-service restaurants in the United States, Europe, and South America. At the time of the acquisition, the company had approximate annual sales of $75 million, 480 employees, and had been a supplier to McDonald's for more than 30 years. The business was integrated into Campbell's Food Service unit.
- Stratford-upon-Avon Foods—a food-service company operating in the United Kingdom with annual sales of $60 million. The business manufactured, marketed, and distributed canned baked beans, vegetable and fruit products, and branded and private-label pickles.
- Greenfield Healthy Foods—U.S. manufacturer of all-natural, low-fat cakes and cookies. The company provided Pepperidge Farm with new resources to enter the $800 million healthy-snack category.
- Homepride sauces—the best-selling cooking sauce in the United Kingdom. The business, purchased for an estimated $93 million, allowed Campbell to build gravy and sauce sales in the United Kingdom.

1996 (Acquisitions totaled $186 million)
- Joint venture began between Arnott's Ltd. and Helios Foods, one of Indonesia's most prominent food companies—thereby providing Arnott's with biscuit manufacturing capability in Asia.
- Joint venture began in Malaysia with Cheong Chan that provided manufacturing facilities for canned soups, ketchup, and soy sauces in Southeast Asia. Campbell Soup also acquired a minority interest in Cheong Chan.
- Joint venture between Godiva and J. Osawa Ltd. to immediately open 33 retail stores and outlets for Godiva chocolates. An additional 20 stores were planned to open by the year 2000.
- Increase in share ownership of Arnott's Ltd. to 70 percent.

1997 (Acquisitions totaled $228 million)
- Erasco Group—the leading wet-soup brand in Germany, with annual sales of $223 million and 900 employees. The business was purchased for approximately $210 million. Campbell management believed that the acquisition would accelerate the company's growth throughout Germany and the European Union.
- Kettle Chip Company—salty-snack company operating in Australia and acquired for $18 million.

years, but owner Kit Goldsbury was not interested. The chief operating officer of Pace Foods stated that Goldsbury agreed to the sale to Campbell because Goldsbury could identify with and liked Campbell's management team.[14]

As a product category, salsa (a spicy blend of jalapeños, tomatoes, onion, and garlic) surpassed ketchup in 1991 as the nation's best-selling condiment. The salsa category grew at just under a 13 percent compound annual growth rate from 1988 to 1993

---

[14]*The Wall Street Journal,* November 29, 1994, p. A3.

as sales increased from $325 million to $700 million. The rapid growth in sales of salsa products was attributed to its spicy flavor and low fat content (a jar of Pace salsa contained no fat and only 70 calories), to the excellent way it complemented such snack foods as tortilla chips, to growing consumer popularity of Mexican dishes, and to a fast-increasing Hispanic population.

Johnson's Revised New Product Development and Marketing Strategies

David Johnson instituted a more cautious approach to new product development and challenged Campbell marketers to become more aggressive in marketing the company's products. Johnson was quick to comment, "There's no such thing as mature markets, only tired marketers,"[15] when told that low industry growth rates were obstacles to growth. New product ideas were more heavily researched and tested before they were put on the market. Moreover, new products were expected to provide quicker paybacks on investment; potential products that held little promise for near-term profitability and for meeting the 20-20-20 financial performance standards were tabled.

The search for new product ideas was limited to areas where Campbell had production and marketing expertise; as one executive put it, "We want to be in areas we know we are good at and in processes we are good at."[16] Despite the more conservative approach to new product development, Campbell introduced nearly 300 new products during Johnson's first three years as the company's chief executive. Johnson committed between $77 million and $88 million annually to R&D during his last three years as CEO to improve existing products and to develop new products that would be successful in U.S. and international markets. New items included cream of broccoli soup (which became the first new soup since 1935 to rank in the top five best-selling soups), Joseph A. Campbell premium-quality ready-to-serve soups, cheese tortellini soup, Light 'n Tangy V8, Swanson Kids Fun Feast frozen dinners, Vlasic Sandwich Stackers, Prego pizza sauce, and more varieties of Pepperidge Farm products. Johnson suggested that the company's new approach to product development had been successful in developing products that consumers desired and had allowed the company to achieve sales growth in traditionally mature markets: "Innovations and breakthroughs are so simple, but they come only if you're immersed in your field and determined to make the necessary connections. For instance, take our Stackers, which are pickles sliced to lay flat on a sandwich. A simple idea, but it took off: The overall Stackers market grew 55% last year. In addition, we're tapping into growing consumer segments, such as the healthy food category. For example, our new line of cream soups is 98% fat free."[17]

Johnson's Corporate Reorganization

Johnson's reorganization effort aimed at capturing strategic-fit benefits among related products and product families Johnson concluded that McGovern's 50 autonomous units had resulted in lack of communication and cooperation between the different business units. For example, the U.S. soup division once ran a promotion with Nabisco

---

[15]As quoted in *Chief Executive,* November 1996.

[16]As quoted in *Financial World,* June 11, 1991, p. 53.

[17]As quoted in *Chief Executive,* November 1996.

crackers even though Pepperidge Farm produced a competing product. Also, U.S. tomato paste plants did not share technology with Mexican tomato paste plants since the Mexican plants were in a different division. A three-division structure was established during Johnson's first year as Campbell CEO to improve communication and technology sharing between businesses in similar product categories and geographies (see Exhibit 7). This initial structure was modified three times over the next five years. Each shuffling of businesses within the three-division structure was directed at improving the strategic fit within the portfolio of businesses. The series of new alignments also helped Campbell Soup put more emphasis on the company's international businesses.

Johnson's International Push

Johnson was convinced that a sizable fraction of Campbell Soup's growth should come from international expansion because the world market for processed food products was projected to grow over twice as fast as the 1 percent growth rate projected for the $200 billion U.S. food-processing industry. By 2000, Johnson wanted at least one-third of Campbell's revenues to come from outside of the United States. Johnson saw such companies as Coca-Cola and Gillette, whose international operations contributed 70 to 80 percent of total sales, as prototypes for Campbell Soup's future:

> Clearly, we're not going to be a Coca-Cola or Gillette in two years, but we're inching toward that aim as we go into the next century . . . We're expanding in the United Kingdom, Canada, and Australia, and trying to establish more beachheads in Asia Pacific. Our acquisition of Germany's Erasco increases our total international soup sales to 21 percent of total soup sales. We bought an operation in Malaysia called Cheong Chan, where we're now making the investments that will enable us to produce soup instead of importing it. We're looking for ventures in China and growing in Taiwan.

Campbell marketed its soups in Mexico, Canada, Argentina, Poland, Hong Kong, and China, and its baked goods in Europe and Asia Pacific. In 1993 Campbell increased its 33 percent share of Australia's Arnott's Ltd. to 58 percent to gain an organizational base for increasing its long-term presence in baked goods in the Pacific Rim and Asia. Johnson increased Campbell's ownership of Arnott's further to 65 percent in 1995 and to 70 percent in 1996. To help familiarize himself with Campbell's international operations and to better gauge the company's potential for foreign expansion, Johnson had all of Campbell's top international executives report directly to him for the first 12 months he was at Campbell.

International marketing of prepared foods was not easy. Taste preferences varied significantly from country to country (and sometimes within countries), prompting international producers to employ multicountry strategies to gear product characteristics to local preferences and eating habits. Campbell's 1988 acquisition of Britain's Freshbake Foods Group never performed up to expectations partly because Campbell management didn't cater adequately to the taste preferences of British consumers. Also, Campbell's penetration of the European soup market had proved more difficult than originally expected because the predominant forms of store-bought soups on the continent were dry soups and ready-to-serve soups; demand for Campbell's mainstay condensed soups was virtually nonexistent in Europe, and consumers had to be persuaded of the merits of switching to a different preparation technique.

Campbell management opened a Hong Kong taste kitchen as part of the company's effort to ensure that the products it introduced would appeal to Asia's 2 billion consumers, whose average per capita soup consumption averaged six bowls per week. The Hong Kong kitchen proved to be a success, having a role in creating such popular

exhibit 7 Comparison of Campbell's Business Unit Structure under Gordon McGovern and David Johnson

Campbell's Structure under Gordon McGovern		Campbell's Structure under David Johnson		Campbell's Structure under Dale Morrison	
Division	Example Brands/Services	Division	Example Brands/Services	Division	Example Brands/Services
Campbell U.S.		**U.S.A.**		**Soups and Sauces**	All worldwide dry and canned soups, Franco American pastas, V8, Campbell's tomato juice
• Soup Group	Red-and-white, Healthy Request, Chunky	• U.S. Soup Group	Dry and canned soup, Franco-American		
					Prego spaghetti sauces, Pace salsas, Swanson broths,
• Frozen Food Group	Swanson, LeMenu	• Beverage Group	V8, Campbell's tomato juice		Erasco, Cheong Chan, Home Pride, Leibig, Stockpot
• Grocery Group	Prego, Franco-American, Swanson canned meats	• Meal Enhancement Group	Open Pit barbecue sauce, Pace salsas, Vlasic, Prego, food service		
• Beverage Group	Campbell's tomato juice, V8, Juice Bowl, Juice Works	• Frozen Foods Group	Swanson		
• Pet Food Group	Recipe				
Pepperidge Farm	Pepperidge Farm breads, cookies, Godiva chocolates, Costa apple juice, Deli's frozen entrees	**Bakery and Confectionery**	Arnott's Ltd., Pepperidge Farm, Delacre, Godiva Chocolatier, Lami Lutti confections, Kettle Chips	**Biscuit and Confectionery**	Arnott's Ltd., Pepperidge Farm, Godiva Chocolatier, Kettle Chips
Vlasic	Pickles and relishes				
Mrs. Paul's	Frozen fish, frozen chicken, frozen vegetables				
Other U.S.	Triangle Manufacturing Corp.—fitness products				
	Campbell Hospitality—restaurants				
	Snow King Frozen Foods—frozen meats			**Away from Home**	Distribution and Campbell soups, Pace salsas, and specialty kitchen entrees to food-service markets
Campbell International	Soup—Canada and Mexico	**International Grocery**			
	Fresh Bake Foods Group (Britain)—baked goods	• International Soup Group	Red-and-white canned soup, Erasco, Cheong Chan, Home Pride		
		• International Specialty Foods	Stratford-upon-Avon, Fray Bentos, Swift		

Source: Campbell annual reports.

exhibit 8   Sales and Earnings of Campbell Soup Company, by Geographic Region, 1991–99 ($ Millions)

	1999	1998	1997	1996	1995	1994	1993	1992	1991
United States									
Net sales	$4,808	$4,850	$5,495	$5,332	$5,012	$4,639	$4,744	$4,649	$4,496
Earnings before taxes	1,196	1,124	1,155	1,123	957	854	715	809	695
Europe									
Net sales	630	859	1,201	1,122	1,143	1,041	1,050	1,043	1,149
Earnings before taxes	32*	36*	50	71	74	64	(170)	45	49
Other countries									
Net sales	1,054	1,044	1,408	1,347	1,179	1,011	917	652	656
Earnings before taxes	$ 121	$ 123	$ 122	$ 172	$ 171	$ 154	$ 99	$ 70	$ 55

*Earnings before interest and taxes

Source: Campbell annual reports.

sellers as scallop, watercress, duck-gizzard, and ham soups. The kitchen was experimenting with other soup varieties made from pork, dates, figs, and snake.

Campbell had been successful in Mexico with spicy soups such as Creama de Chile Poblano and had captured 10 percent of Argentina's $50 million soup market within one year of introducing nine varieties of its red-and-white canned soup. A summary of Campbell Soup's geographic performance between 1991 and 1998 is displayed in Exhibit 8.

THE DALE MORRISON ERA BEGINS: MID-1997 TO PRESENT

When David Johnson's five-year contract expired and he elected to step aside as Campbell Soup Company's CEO in July 1997, the company announced that 48-year-old Dale Morrison would become its new chief executive officer effective July 15, 1997. Morrison joined Campbell Soup in June 1995 as president of Pepperidge Farm, where he was largely responsible for a turnaround of the business that had averaged 2 to 3 percent sales growth between 1990 and 1995. Prior to joining Campbell Soup's management, Morrison spent 14 years with PepsiCo, where he held management positions with both Frito-Lay and Pepsi-Cola. Dale Morrison also coordinated the merger of British snack foods companies while at Frito-Lay. Morrison held a number of positions with General Foods from 1972 to 1981, marketing such brands as Tang, Post cereals, and Kool-Aid.

David Johnson agreed to remain on as chairman of Campbell's board of directors through July 1999 from which he could aid Morrison in an advisory role. Johnson announced, "My priority is to ensure that we continue our relentless commitment to building shareowner wealth. I will assist Dale in exploring the strategies needed to achieve Campbell's vision of becoming the best consumer products company in the world."[18]

---

[18]As quoted in *Milling & Baking News,* July 8, 1997, p. 14.

Morrison's Accomplishments at Campbell Soup Prior to His Appointment as CEO

When he arrived at Pepperidge Farm, Dale Morrison initiated a number of cost-cutting programs that freed up resources and gave the division enough gross margin leeway to spend additional sums on marketing and product promotion. Such products as Pepperidge Farm Goldfish crackers and Milano cookies benefited from increased advertising and marketing innovations like Goldfish milk-carton-style packaging, which was easier for children to manage than the previous paper-bag-style packaging. Morrison also made a point of visiting all Pepperidge Farm plants and met with the company's independent distributors, whom Morrison reclassified as sales development associates. Morrison's strategies resulted in a 10 percent sales increase in 1996, a 13 percent sales increase in 1997, and a 20 percent earnings increase in both years.

In recognition of his success at Pepperidge Farm, David Johnson gave Morrison added responsibilities at Campbell Soup. Morrison was appointed president of Campbell's International Specialty Foods in November 1996, putting him in charge of Campbell's international grocery, food-service, frozen and specialty foods, and bakery and confectionery businesses.

Recent Trends in the Performance of Campbell Soup's Stock Price, 1990–2000

Exhibit 9 shows Campbell Soup's market performance relative to the Dow Jones Industrial Index and the Dow Jones composite of other food-processing companies since 1990. The company's stock performance mirrored that of many of its processed food competitors, which averaged a 30 percent decline in their share prices and had collectively seen over $160 billion in market value disappear during 1999. Some of Campbell Soup's share price decline after January 2000 was attributable to a number of class-action lawsuits brought against Campbell Soup that claimed the company misrepresented its revenue from its condensed soup sales between November 1997 and January 1999. The complaints alleged that, in an attempt to meet analysts' quarterly earnings estimates, the company claimed to have sold product to major distributors and resellers when in actuality Campbell never shipped the product to customers. When asked about the suits' allegations by a *Wall Street Journal* reporter, Campbell's chief financial officer retorted, "Campbell Soup does not make and has not made sham shipments of its products. We do not make and have not made false or misleading statements."[19]

Morrison's Strategy for Campbell Soup

Morrison's strategies to improve Campbell Soup's performance were, for the most part, a continuation and refinement of Johnson's initiatives. Morrison agreed with David Johnson that Campbell Soup should become more like Coca-Cola, with faster sales growth in international markets and a tighter focus on the core business. Morrison wanted to increase Campbell Soup Company's annual sales growth to 8 to 10 percent and believed that the company's greatest opportunity for rapid growth lay in focusing on its premium brands, which were differentiated from competing brands in terms of taste, perceived quality, and image. Morrison wanted growth to come more

---

[19]As quoted in *The Wall Street Journal Interactive Edition,* February 17, 2000.

exhibit 9   Campbell Soup Company's Stock Performance, 1990–March 2000

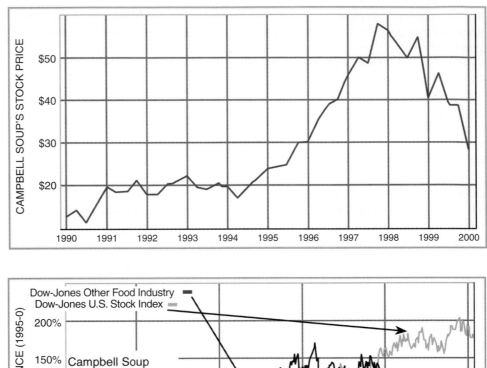

from volume increases rather than price increases and intended to allocate greater resources to advertising some of the company's more highly differentiated brands like Joseph A. Campbell premium-quality ready-to-serve soups, Pepperidge Farm Goldfish crackers, and Milano cookies. The centerpiece of Morrison's plan for boosting unit sales was to increase advertising expenditures from 3.5 percent of sales to 8 percent of sales. Morrison also launched initiatives to enhance Campbell products' differentiated image in international markets. In Japan, for example, the decision was made to upgrade the quality of its soup cans and to redesign the labels on the cans; Japanese consumers were drawn to products with high-quality packaging.

Morrison's Portfolio Restructuring Efforts   In September 1997 Dale Morrison announced the spinoff of seven low-growth businesses with combined sales of $1.4 billion—about 18 percent of Campbell Soup Company's 1997 sales. The spinoff was a carryover of strategic initiatives that David Johnson had announced in September

1996. Under the plan, Vlasic Foods International would become a stand-alone company with operations in the United States, Europe, and South America and over 9,000 employees. The new company's shares would be distributed tax-free to Campbell shareholders, and upon the completion of the spinoff the new company would be ranked 21st among 32 publicly traded food companies. Campbell's Swanson frozen food business in the United States and Canada and its frozen food lines in the United Kingdom would make up Vlasic Foods International's frozen food division. The grocery division would include Campbell's Vlasic retail and food-service products, Swift Armour meats in Argentina, Open Pit barbecue sauces, Stratford-upon-Avon's retail and food-service pickle and canned vegetable businesses in the United Kingdom, Gourmet Specialty Foods in Germany, and the U.S. fresh mushroom business.

Morrison commented at the time of the announced spinoff that shareholders would benefit greatly by a separation of Campbell Soup businesses:

> This is a watershed day for Campbell Soup Company and its shareowners. Spinning off these businesses allows us to focus on our most profitable businesses with the highest growth potential. Our core businesses have gross margins in excess of 45%. Net sales for these businesses grew 10% and earnings grew 15% in fiscal 1997. This is an outstanding platform to drive significant volume growth while continuing to deliver top-quartile earnings. The creation of this new company gives great brands like Vlasic and Swanson tremendous opportunities for growth under a dedicated management team. In both cases, shareowners will reap the rewards of highly focused companies.[20]

Some Wall Street analysts were not as optimistic that the new company would become a strong competitor in the processed-food industry. One portfolio manager suggested that the spinoff would allow Campbell to achieve higher growth rates in terms of sales and earnings, but Vlasic Foods International would find growth difficult: "Whenever a company spins off the crummy parts, it's always good for what's left. What they're spinning off didn't have the value or the growth rate of the other divisions."[21] Another analyst commented on the attractiveness of frozen food, where over the last 10 years the size of the market had declined and margin points were gained only through price cuts: "There is not going to be a mad rush to own this [new] food company. Swanson has been a stagnant brand at best, though I suppose it's a bit better than Schlitz beer."[22]

Even though the frozen foods category was highly competitive and had become commodity-like after the 1980s, Vlasic Foods International did include a number of popular brands and products. Swanson was the originator of the TV dinner in 1954 and continued to maintain category leadership with products like Hungry Man dinners, Great Start breakfasts, and Fun Feast kids' meals. Vlasic was the leader in U.S. pickle sales, with a 36 percent market share, and approximately 35 percent of Vlasic's sales came from products introduced within the previous five years. In addition, Swift was Argentina's largest exporter of beef, Open Pit was the number one barbecue sauce in the midwestern United States, Gourmet Specialty Foods was Germany's number one specialty foods company, and the company's mushroom business was the largest in the world. The new company's third- and fourth-quarter sales and earnings fell below projections, and sales of pickles and frozen foods were down about 10 percent for the year. The company's stock closed at $22¾ on the first day of trading in March 1998, but was trading in the $13 to $15 range within four months of the spinoff. The

[20]Securities and Exchange Commission, Form 8-K, September 9, 1997.

[21]*Knight-Ridder/Tribune Business News,* September 10, 1997.

[22]As quoted in *The New York Times,* September 10, 1997, p. D1.

exhibit 10   Vlasic Foods International's Stock Performance, by Week, March 1998–March 2000

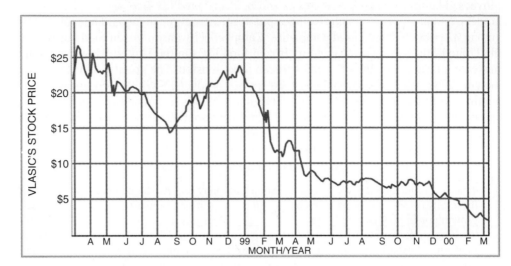

market performance of Vlasic Foods' common stock following its spinoff is depicted in Exhibit 10.

Morrison continued to restructure Campbell's portfolio during 1998 and 1999 to allow the company to focus on core brands and activities directly related to either product quality or image. Continental Sweets was sold to a Dutch venture capital fund in 1998. Continental Sweets made and distributed sugar and chocolate confectionery; its facilities were located in France and Belgium. Campbell Soup also sold its European-based Delacre premium biscuit business and Australian-based Melbourne Mushrooms and Spring Valley beverages in 1998.

The company's Fresh Start Bakeries, a supplier of English muffins and buns to quick-service restaurants, was sold to a joint venture between Berkshire Partners and Fresh Start's management in May 1999. Morrison also chose to divest the company's can-making assets to Silgan Holdings—a supplier of food cans with annual sales of approximately $1.5 billion. The can-making operations were sold for $123 million, and the transaction included a 10-year supply agreement between Campbell Soup and Silgan that called for can purchases by Campbell totaling over $200 million each year. The company also took restructuring charges of $262 million and $41 million in 1998 and 1999, respectively, related to streamlining its production and administrative facilities in North America and Europe. The restructuring programs merged certain Canadian and U.S. administrative functions and attempted to maximize capacity utilization among its production facilities by combining operations whenever possible. For example, Campbell closed its Pace salsa plant in San Antonio, Texas, and shifted production of Pace products to Campbell's Paris, Texas, plant, which produced Prego spaghetti sauce, Franco-American gravies, and an assortment of soups. Campbell Soup management expected the restructuring program to reduce the company's operating expenses by $221 million annually.

The spinoff and divestitures allowed Campbell Soup to implement a $2 billion share buyback plan to repurchase 8 percent of the company's 451 million outstanding shares of stock between 1999 and 2001. The strategy to boost earnings per share and return on stockholders' equity was a continuation of an ongoing Johnson strategy of repurchasing 2 percent of the company's outstanding shares annually. Morrison also retained a Johnson-devised strategy of repurchasing shares in addition to the $2 billion buyback plan to offset per share dilution resulting from incentive compensation programs.

To boost Campbell's growth potential, Morrison initiated a number of new acquisitions during 1997 and 1998. In 1997 the company purchased the remaining 30 percent of Arnott's outstanding shares for $290 million, giving Campbell 100 percent ownership of the Australian biscuit company. The company also acquired Leibig soups in 1997 for $180 million. Leibig was France's leading producer of wet soups, with annual sales of approximately $75 million. In June 1998 Campbell Soup acquired privately held Fortun Foods for $105 million. Fortun's Stockpot brand of fresh, chilled soup was distributed to restaurants, supermarkets, and convenience stores in over 20 countries and was the market leader in premium refrigerated soups, with about 50 percent market share of the rapidly growing category and annual sales of $40 million. Campbell Soup had tried unsuccessfully a number of times since the 1980s to develop freshly made chilled soup without preservatives. Fortun's manufacturing process transferred hot soup from the kettle to a vacuum-sealed bag that was then immediately refrigerated. The company's proprietary process allowed Stockpot soups to stay fresh for about 120 days.

Morrison's acquisitions and divestitures prompted a realignment of Campbell Soup divisions and business units. Morrison created a Soups and Sauces division, which included all soup and sauce brands marketed globally. The Biscuit and Confectionery division was reorganized to include all global brands of baked goods, and the makeup of the Away from Home food-service division was adjusted to include all businesses that were dedicated to supplying the growing quick-service restaurant industry. A special division titled Campbell's Other was temporarily formed to handle the details of transferring the divested businesses to the new owners and report the historical performance of divested businesses.

Morrison believed that cross-business skills transfer would be more readily achieved by abandoning Campbell's previous geographically based divisions and placing all businesses sharing common R&D, production, and marketing activities in a common division (see again Exhibit 7, which presents a comparison of business divisions and units under Gordon McGovern, David Johnson, and Dale Morrison). Exhibit 11 provides the sales and operating earnings for Morrison's divisions from 1995 to 1999. The 1995 and 1996 financial data shown in the exhibit have been reorganized to match Campbell Soup Company's divisional structure in 1997–99.

CAMPBELL SOUP IN 2000

Soups and Sauces Group

The Soups and Sauces division was Campbell's largest operating unit, accounting for about two-thirds of the company's total consolidated sales. The U.S. and international markets for canned soup were mature and possibly entering into a declining stage. The U.S. wet-soup category had grown at low single-digit rates during the late 1990s and was not expected to grow at a faster rate during 2000–2001. The maturity of the U.S. soup segment was attributable to the increased popularity of fresh foods, a 40 percent decrease in the usage of cooking soups in recipes, and an overall reduced tendency of consumers to purchase canned products. The slow growth in international markets was

exhibit 11   Sales and Earnings of Campbell Soup Company, by
                    Division, 1995–99 ($ Millions)

	1999	1998	1997	1996	1995
Soups and Sauces					
Sales	$4,423	$4,434	$4,156	$3,742	$3,415
Operating earnings	1,082	1,109	1,012	978	863
Biscuits and Confectionery					
Sales	1,430	1,522	1,546	1,459	1,348
Operating earnings	215	206	154	183	164
Away from Home					
Sales	507	453	459	418	345
Operating earnings	57	53	62	55	40
Other					
Sales	126	334	1,904	2,149	2,204
Operating earnings	(5)	(85)	99	150	135
Interdivision					
Sales	($ 62)	($ 49)	($ 101)	($ 90)	($ 62)

Source: Campbell annual reports.

primarily related to the preference for homemade soups in many regions. During most of the 1990s consumption of Campbell's soups grew at 2 to 3 percent annually, but U.S. consumption of Campbell's wet soups declined by about 1 percent in 1998 and by 8 percent in 1999. Campbell's worldwide soup sales grew by 3 percent during 1998, but declined by 4 percent in 1999. The company's 1997 acquisition of Liebig helped Campbell Soup increase its international wet-soup volume by 7 percent in 1999.

Campbell's market share in the condensed soup category had declined from 80 percent in 1993 to 74 percent in 1997. In an attempt to regain lost market share, the company forwent its usual 3 to 7 percent annual price increases in 1998 since much of its lost market share was being captured by lower-priced private-label brands. The level pricing failed to recapture enough lost market share to offset the impact of smaller margins on the division's 1998 revenues. In 1999 the company's U.S. sales of canned soup declined by 8 percent after Campbell management eliminated quarter-end promotions to retailers.

The division implemented a plan to increase advertising spending by 18 percent in 1998 and intended to eventually increase the advertising budget for Campbell soups and sauces from 3.5 percent of sales to 8 percent of sales. Dale Morrison believed that increased advertising was necessary to support new products and newly packaged products and to promote soup in appealing ways to children. Campbell's fastest growing soup and sauce products during the late 1990s were Swanson broths and V8 Splash juices. Swanson's 20 percent annual growth was in large part a result of new 32-ounce recloseable aseptic packaging and its positioning as a 100 percent fat-free seasoning alternative that could be used in a number of recipes. Recent product introduction V8 Splash, a beverage combining carrot and tropical fruit juices, helped the V8 brand grow by more than 10 percent in 1998, and the 1999 introduction of new packaging (e.g., kid-sized juice boxes), new flavors, and a greater availability throughout the world helped V8 Splash become Campbell's most successful new product introduction in more than a decade.

Campbell introduced additional products after Morrison became the company's CEO to improve the sales volumes of products like tomato soup. Its new 32-ounce recloseable plastic ready-to-serve Campbell Tomato Soup allowed consumers to pour a single serving or use what was called for by a recipe and then store the remaining portion in the refrigerator for later use. Campbell marketers believed that having soup in the refrigerator would lead to higher consumption since most people opened the refrigerator more often than the pantry. Campbell Soup added a line of Select Soups, packaged in metal cans, as was the company's Classic line of soups that included tomato, cream of broccoli, and cream of mushroom, but the Select Soups line included more unique varieties of soups. Select Soups used distinctive combinations of ingredients to create flavorful soups like chicken and pasta with roasted garlic—a blend of chicken, penne and rotini pasta, and vegetables with roasted garlic in a chicken broth. Campbell Soup also introduced a Soups-to-Go line of ready-to-serve microwavable single-serving bowls that achieved volume gains in 1999. Joseph A. Campbell premium-quality soups had not experienced the sales gains expected by Campbell management; the line was rebranded Simply Home in 1998 and achieved volume gains in 1999. Campbell's Chunky line was also one of the company's faster-growing lines of canned soup in the late 1990s.

Even though the company had been largely successful with its new product introductions in recent years, Campbell management still believed in David Johnson's commitment to thoroughly assessing a product's potential on the market prior to its launch. Robert Bernstock, president of Campbell's U.S. Grocery division, explained, "In the early 1990s we were launching two new, single SKU products with more than $10 million in sales a year. We're now launching more than 20 a year. Tremendous upfront discipline is the key. We spend 12–18 months in rigorous testing."[23]

Biscuits and Confectionery Group

Campbell's Biscuits and Confectionery business unit had 1999 sales of $1.4 billion and operating earnings of $215 million. The division included Pepperidge Farm in North America; Godiva chocolates in North America, Europe, and Asia; Arnott's in the Pacific Rim/Asia; and Kettle Chips in Australia. Such products as Goldfish crackers, Swirl bread, and Milano cookies helped the Biscuits and Confectionery division achieve a sales increase of 5 percent in 1998 prior to the impact of exchange rates. The division had a sales decline of 6 percent in 1999, but Godiva grew its U.S. sales volume by more than 10 percent in 1998 and made some headway in increasing penetration of European and Asian markets. Campbell management expected the business to continue to increase its strength in Asia as more Godiva retail outlets were opened in the region. The company also opened additional freestanding boutiques in shopping malls and Godiva departments in upscale department stores throughout the United States.

Pepperidge Farm continued the transformation begun by Dale Morrison in 1995 with continued increases in sales volume. The company's increased promotion of Goldfish crackers allowed sales of the product to grow 25 percent in 1996 and 40 percent in 1997. New varieties such as Goldfish Grahams contributed to sales volume increases for Goldfish products in 1999. Other market-leading Pepperidge Farm products included Milano cookies, which grew by 35 percent in 1997, Dessert Classics frozen cakes, and

---

[23]As quoted in *Prepared Foods,* September 1997, p. 14.

frozen garlic bread, which grew more than 40 percent after being moved adjacent to frozen pasta in grocery freezers. Pepperidge Farm management had established a "2 × 2" program with the objective of doubling sales between 1997 and 2000. The program called for Pepperidge Farm to achieve its growth objective by developing several innovative new products, lowering operating costs by eliminating costs that did not provide value to the customer, and purging waste.

Campbell management believed that a controlling interest in Arnott's Ltd. would yield a competitive advantage in the $3 billion Asian cookie-and-cracker market. The 132-year-old Arnott's was one of Australia's best-known food companies, had access to low-cost ingredients, and had efficient manufacturing processes. Arnott's Australian location also provided a shipping-cost advantage for products exported to the entire Asian/Pacific Rim region. The biscuit and confectionery division introduced popular Pepperidge Farm products to international markets in 1999 when Arnott's Goldfish were launched in Australia.

Away from Home Group

Dale Morrison, like David Johnson, realized the importance of Campbell's food-service unit, Away from Home, in growing corporate sales and earnings. In 2000, U.S. consumers were projected to eat approximately 46 percent of all meals away from home and spend an estimated $342 billion in restaurants. On an average day, almost 140 million meals were eaten in U.S. restaurants and cafeterias. In addition, nearly 21 percent of U.S. households used some form of takeout or delivery each day. Campbell Soup management intended for the company to make Campbell products readily available to both consumers who purchased food for home preparation and those who chose to dine away from home. Morrison believed that Campbell Soup should position itself to provide soups and other processed foods to consumers in their homes and other locations: "If you look at the U.S. soup business, you could say we have an 80% share of the condensed and ready-to-serve market, and where do we go from there? But if you look at soup consumption in total . . . we really have a 38% share. Under that frame of reference, there's real opportunity."[24]

In 1999 the sales of the Away from Home division reached $507 million—a 12 percent increase over 1998. The division provided pot pies to Kentucky Fried Chicken, soups to roughly one-third of McDonald's restaurants, and a wide variety of Prego entrees and Campbell soups to various restaurants and cafeterias. V8 Splash beverages and Pace Mexican salsas were also distributed to restaurants, delicatessens, and cafeterias. The company had introduced serve-your-own soup vending machines in convenience stores and soup kettles in college cafeterias and had also provided complete meals to supermarket delis and cafeterias that included entrees and side dishes packaged in 5.5- and 2.5-pound aluminum trays. The company also tested the popularity of soup kiosks in airports and sports arenas. Campbell's 1998 acquisition of Stockpot soups allowed the company to expand its branded soup presence in the food-service market for soups because of Stockpot's proprietary manufacturing process that allowed soups to be shipped fresh and without preservatives.

Events at Campbell Soup in Early 2000

Campbell Soup Company was ranked number four among *Fortune* magazine's 1999 and 2000 listings of the most admired food companies; it also was ranked as the third

---

[24]Ibid.

most profitable food company among the Fortune 500. However, Campbell Soup's financial and market performance fell considerably short of being rated "best in show" (a David Johnson objective). In his letter to the stockholders in the company's 1999 annual report, Dale Morrison stated his belief that even though the processed-food industry was confronted by a variety of challenges and Campbell Soup had failed to outperform the overall stock market, it was still feasible for Campbell Soup to deliver an attractive return to its shareholders:

> Campbell Soup Company's primary commitment has been, and always will be, to build shareowner wealth. For many years, we succeeded brilliantly in doing so. Lately, however, much has been said and written about the challenges facing our industry and our company—challenges relating, for example, to changing consumer habits and the pace and prospects for growth. Over the past several years, the food industry has underperformed the overall market. And as we are all aware, this year, in a painful departure from our recent track record, Campbell disappointed our investors as well. Our stock price declined 19 percent in the [1999] fiscal year. So I believe our shareowners today are entitled to ask, "What does the future hold for Campbell Soup Company?"
>
> The answer begins with our central business—soup. For millions of people, the Campbell's name is synonymous with quality, wholesomeness, and the best moments of family life.
>
> Beyond soup, we compete in categories that offer abundant opportunities to grow with changing consumer preferences and lifestyles—sauces, beverages, biscuits and confectionery. Campbell brings significant brand power to these categories with favorites like V8 and V8 Splash, Pace, Prego, Franco-American, Pepperidge Farm, Arnott's and Godiva.[25]

Mounting Problems

Despite Morrison's optimism about the company's growth prospects, Campbell's stock price continued to slide from its all-time high of $63 per share in early 1998. During the first nine months of 1999, the stock price traded mostly in the $40 to $45 per share range. Then in late fall of 1999 it began a steep slide, falling below $30 as the company was hit by (1) a series of shareholder lawsuits alleging that company documents misled shareholders about revenues, (2) a February 2000 recall of 109,000 pounds of canned vegetable soup in 13 states after consumers found long pieces of metal in the soup, and (3) forecasts of slow growth for Campbell's brands by both Wall Street analysts and Campbell's executives. Campbell Soup had reported slightly better-than-expected second-quarter earnings for the period ending December 1999, but several Wall Street analysts expected full-year earnings for fiscal year 2000 (ending July) to be $1.86, rising to perhaps $1.99 at the end of fiscal year 2001.

On March 22, 2000, Dale Morrison resigned as president, CEO, and a director of the company. He was replaced by David Johnson, the company's previous CEO, who agreed to serve while the company's board of directors searched for a permanent replacement. The closing stock price on March 22, 2000, was $29^{11}/₁₆, off $1^{7}/₁₆.

---

[25]Campbell Soup Company 1999 annual report.

19 The Black & Decker Corporation in 2000

John E. Gamble
University of South Alabama

Arthur A. Thompson
University of Alabama

In 2000 Black & Decker Corporation was still struggling to get out from under the array of financial and strategic problems stemming from the company's $2.8 billion acquisition of Emhart Corporation in 1989. Black & Decker had long been the world's leading producer and marketer of power tools and power tool accessories. But it had begun a program of diversification in the 1980s that had produced mixed results for shareholders. The company's foray into small household appliances had been a success originally, but the small-appliance division acquired from General Electric in the early 1980s had recently been divested because of its drag on B&D's growth. The follow-on acquisition of Emhart, a conglomerate with very diverse business interests, had proved to be a significant impairment to the company's earnings and cash flow as well as a management burden, and during the past 11 years Black & Decker had achieved success in only a few of the businesses it obtained in the Emhart acquisition.

Black & Decker described itself as a diversified global manufacturer and marketer of household, commercial, and industrial products. Going into 2000, the company was the world's largest producer of power tools, power tool accessories, security hardware, and electric lawn and garden products. The company's Price Pfister kitchen and bathroom faucets subsidiary, a business acquired in the Emhart deal, had gained market share for 11 consecutive years to become the third largest brand of plumbing fixtures in North America. Black & Decker was also the worldwide leader in the market for certain types of mechanical fastening systems used in automobile assembly and in other industrial applications—fasteners had been one of Emhart's businesses as well. But while Black & Decker's business portfolio included a lineup of several competitively strong brands, the company's stock price had been a ho-hum performer

exhibit 1   Market Performance of Black & Decker's Common Stock,
by Quarter, 1985–January 2000

(a) Trend in Black & Decker's Common Stock Price

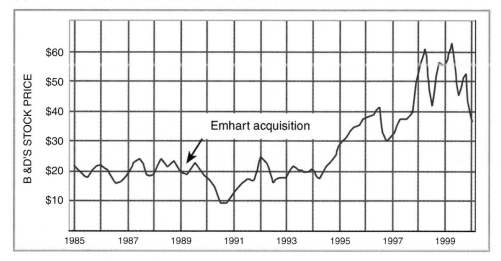

(b) Performance of Black & Decker's Stock Price versus the
S&P 500 Index

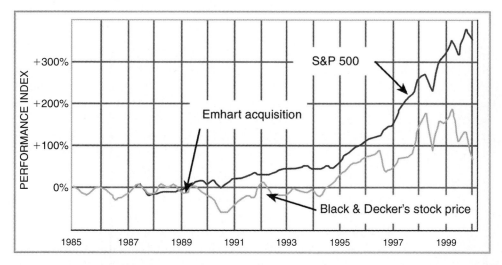

throughout the unprecedented bull market of the 1990s, substantially lagging behind
the performance of well-known indexes like the Dow Jones Industrials Average and
the Standard & Poor's 500 Index. A graph of Black & Decker's stock performance between 1985 and January 2000 is presented in Exhibit 1. Exhibit 2 provides an 11-year
summary of Black & Decker's financial performance.

exhibit 2 Summary of Black & Decker's Financial and Operating Performance, 1989–99 (In Millions of Dollars Except Per Share and Employee Data)

	1999	1998	1997	1996	1995	1994	1993	1992	1991	1990	1989
Sales	$4,520.5	$4,559.9	$4,940.5	$4,914.4	$4,766.1	$4,365.2	$4,121.5	$4,045.7	$3,952.6	$4,313.2	$3,172.5
Operating income	536.3	(466.2)	489.3	356.9	426.1	351.9	302.7	177.1	365.2	458.1	259.2
Operating income excluding restructuring and goodwill amortization*	536.3	509.2	552.6	514.5	494.5	424.9	364.4	391.3	436.0	524.1	284.5
Income taxes	141.0	166.5	122.3	43.5	9.0	62.7	60.7	44.3	54.5	72.4	32.9
Earnings data:											
Earnings (loss) from continuing operations	300.3	(754.8)	227.2	159.2	216.5	89.9	64.1	(95.3)	16.1	19.7	30.0
Discontinued operations	—	—	—	70.4	38.4	37.5	31.1	22.0	36.9	31.4	—
Extraordinary item	—	—	—	—	(30.9)	—	—	(22.7)	—	—	—
Cumulative effects of accounting change	—	—	—	—	—	127.4	(29.2)	(237.6)	—	—	—
Net earnings (loss)	300.3	(754.8)	227.2	229.6	224.0	254.8	66.0	(333.6)	53.0	51.1	30.0
Total assets	4,012.7	3,852.5	5,360.7	5,153.5	5,545.3	5,264.3	5,166.8	5,295.0	5,456.8	5,829.7	6,258.1
Long-term debt	847.1	1,148.9	1,623.7	1,415.8	1,704.5	1,723.2	2,069.2	2,108.5	2,625.8	2,754.7	2,629.7
Total debt	1,243.5	1,360.6	1,862.5	1,705.8	2,351.7	2,393.3	2,564.6	2,563.8	2,870.3	3,266.2	4,057.5
Stockholders' equity	801.1	574.0	1,791.4	1,632.4	1,423.2	1,169.4	1,048.9	1,074.0	1,027.1	920.7	720.7
Capital expenditures	171.1	146.0	203.1	196.3	203.1	181.5	190.3	167.7	94.9	103.1	112.1
Depreciation and amortization	160.0	155.2	214.2	214.6	206.7	195.4	182.4	188.3	187.1	197.8	131.0
Number of employees	22,100	21,800	28,600	29,200	29,300	29,200	30,500	32,300	31,900	35,900	38,600
Number of shares outstanding	88.4	91.8	96.5	96.1	94.4	85.3	84.5	76.3	62.6	61.4	59.6
Dividends per share	$ 0.48	$ 0.48	$ 0.48	$ 0.48	$ 0.40	$ 0.40	$ 0.40	$ 0.40	$ 0.40	$ 0.40	$ 0.40

*For 1998 this figure also excludes goodwill write-off and gain on sale of businesses.

Source: The Black & Decker Corporation annual reports.

THE EXPECTATION OF BETTER TIMES FOR BLACK & DECKER

In late 1998 Black & Decker management celebrated the completion of an almost decade-long effort to divest nonstrategic businesses gained through its 1989 acquisition of Emhart Corporation and expected the company to enter a long-awaited period of growth as its entire management attention was refocused on its core power tools, plumbing, and security hardware businesses. Black & Decker's CEO, Nolan Archibald, told Wall Street analysts in early 1998 that the pending elimination of nonstrategic businesses that manufactured and marketed such products as True Temper golf club shafts and Emhart glass-making machinery would allow the company to position itself for greater growth in 1999 and 2000. "This [portfolio restructuring] will allow us to focus on core operations that can deliver dependable and superior operating and financial results."[1] However, with the exception of a brief run up to $60 per share in mid-1999, the portfolio restructuring had done little to improve the market performance of the company's securities. In January 2000 Black & Decker's common shares traded at a 52-week low and at a price below the high for 1996 and 1997. Nevertheless, management continued to express confidence that the company's streamlined business portfolio would allow Black & Decker to achieve revenue and earnings growth that the market would find impressive. In commenting on the company's year-end 1999 financial performance, Nolan Archibald said, "We are extremely pleased with Black & Decker's performance this past year, which resulted in record earnings and clearly indicates that the strategic repositioning we undertook in 1998 has been successful."[2]

COMPANY BACKGROUND

Black & Decker was incorporated by Duncan Black and Alonzo Decker in 1910 and initially produced milk cap machines and candy dippers. In 1916 the company introduced its first power tool—a portable half-inch electric drill that was eventually placed on display in the Smithsonian Institution. Over the next 40 years, Duncan Black and Alonzo Decker undertook a number of actions that established the company as the dominant name in power tools and accessories. Black & Decker introduced the first portable screwdriver in 1922, the first electric hammer in 1936, finishing sanders and jigsaws in 1953, and the Dustbuster handheld vacuum in 1978. The company expanded internationally in 1919 when it began sales operations in Russia, Japan, and Australia and opened a production facility in Canada in 1922. The company eventually became known worldwide for its power tools, particularly so in Europe. Black & Decker was managed by the two partners until they died—Black in 1951 and Decker in 1956. As managers, Black and Decker achieved growth by adding to the company's lineup of power tools and accessories and by increasing its penetration of more and more foreign markets. The company maintained a corporate growth strategy tied exclusively to product-line extensions and international expansion until the mid-1980s.

Diversification into Small Household Appliances

Black & Decker began to pursue diversification in the 1980s because of growing maturity of its core power tools business. In 1984 Black & Decker acquired General Electric's

---

[1]As quoted in *Knight-Ridder/Tribune Business News,* January 28, 1998.

[2]As quoted in PR Newswire, January 27, 2000.

housewares business for $300 million. GE's brands had about a 25 percent share of the small-appliance market and generated annual revenues of about $500 million. GE sold its small-appliance division, despite its number one market position, because of the division's low profitability. GE's strong suit was in irons and toaster ovens, where its share was close to 50 percent; sales of GE irons alone totaled about $250 million. Among the other 150 GE products acquired by Black & Decker were coffeemakers, hair dryers and hair curlers, food mixers and processors, toasters, electric skillets, can openers, waffle irons, and blenders. Also in 1984, Black & Decker purchased three European tool manufacturers to fill in product gaps and strengthen its manufacturing base; the acquisition involved a Swiss manufacturer of portable electric woodworking tools for professional users, the leading European manufacturer of drill bits, and a German producer of hobby and precision power tools.

The acquisition of GE's housewares division launched Black & Decker on a course to transform the company from a power tools manufacturer into a consumer products company. In early 1985, the firm changed its name from Black & Decker Manufacturing Company to Black & Decker Corporation to reflect its new emphasis on "being more marketing driven" rather than being merely engaged in manufacturing.

Black & Decker's CEO—Nolan D. Archibald

The chief architect of Black & Decker's foray into diversification was Nolan D. Archibald. Black & Decker hired Archibald as president and chief operating officer in 1985, shortly after the acquisition of GE's small household appliance business. Prior to joining Black & Decker, Archibald was president of the $1.7 billion consumer durables group at Beatrice Companies, where he was responsible for such business units as Samsonite luggage, Culligan water treatment products, Del Mar window coverings, Stiffel lamps, and Aristocraft kitchen cabinets. At the time he was hired, Archibald was 42 years old; he was chosen from a pool of some 50 candidates for the position and turned down offers to be president at two other companies to take the B&D job. Archibald had been at Beatrice since 1977 and was successful in engineering turnarounds in three of Beatrice's businesses. Prior to that, he had headed a turnaround of Conroy Inc.'s Sno-Jet Snowmobile business. Archibald spent two years of his youth winning converts as a Mormon missionary, was an All-American basketball player at Utah's Dixie College, became a standout player at Weber State College in Utah, earned his MBA degree at Harvard Business School, and tried out (unsuccessfully) for the Chicago Bulls professional basketball team. Corporate headhunters rated Archibald as a good strategic thinker who was personable, versatile, and sensitive to people.

Archibald's Early Successes at B&D   According to one Black & Decker dealer, prior to when Archibald took over as president in September 1985 "Black & Decker had been coasting along for quite a few years like a ship without a captain."[3] Archibald wasted little time in reorganizing Black & Decker's worldwide manufacturing operations. Within three months, Archibald initiated a restructuring plan to close older, inefficient plants and boost factory utilization rates by consolidating production within B&D's newest and biggest plants. Approximately 3,000 jobs were eliminated, including a number of high-level managerial jobs. In 1985, B&D took a $215 million write-off for plant shutdowns and other cost-saving reorganization efforts.

---

[3]As quoted in *Business Week,* July 13, 1987, p. 90.

Prior to 1985, the company had pursued a decentralized, multicountry strategy. Each geographic area had its own production facilities, its own product-design centers, and its own marketing and sales organizations to better cater to local market conditions. Over the years, this had resulted in short production runs at scattered production sites, reduced overall manufacturing efficiency, and prevented achievement of scale economies—for example, there were about 100 different motor sizes in B&D's product line. Archibald set the company on a more globalized approach to product design and manufacturing, with much greater communication and coordination between geographic operating units. Production at plants was organized around motor sizes, the number of product variations was reduced, and production runs were lengthened. From 1984 to 1989 seven plants were closed and nearly 3,000 employees were let go. Archibald also insisted more emphasis be put on quality control—during the early 1980s, B&D's reputation in power tools had been tarnished by shoddy product quality.

Meanwhile, Archibald put additional resources into new product development and redesign of the company's power tools and small-appliance lines. Archibald set a goal for the tool division to come up with more than a dozen new products each year—more than B&D had introduced in the five years before his arrival. He also created panels of dealers to suggest new products and features that consumers desired. The company introduced a number of highly successful products such as its Snakelight flashlights; a line of cordless power tools; Macho rotary hammers that could punch holes in stone, brick, and concrete; DeWalt professional power tools; and VersaPak rechargeable batteries that fit both Black & Decker power tools and household appliances.

One of Archibald's biggest marketing challenges was transferring consumers' brand loyalty for GE small appliances over to Black & Decker. Some observers believed Black & Decker would have trouble because B&D's traditional customers were men, and buyers of houseware products were usually women—as a *Wall Street Journal* article headline put it, "Would You Buy a Toaster from a Drillmaker?" B&D executives believed, however, that many women were familiar with the Black & Decker name because they bought power tools as gifts for men and because B&D had pioneered the development of household appliances powered by rechargeable batteries. Black & Decker's handheld DustBuster vacuum cleaner was the market leader, with a 45 percent share. B&D also had been marketing a cordless rotary scrub brush, a cordless rechargeable shoe shiner, and a rechargeable flashlight. Even before acquiring GE's housewares business, B&D had planned to introduce a line of cordless kitchen appliances, but gaining ample retail shelf space was often a hit-or-miss proposition. What made the GE acquisition attractive to B&D was the extra clout that being able to offer retailers a full line of housewares would have in competing for shelf space.

Black & Decker's competitors in small appliances saw the brand-name transition from GE to Black & Decker as an opportunity to gain market share that once was GE's. Sunbeam Appliance quadrupled its 1985 ad budget to $42 million because it wanted to replace GE as the best-known brand in small appliances. Norelco launched a new line of irons and a handheld can opener powered by rechargeable batteries to wrest share away from GE/Black & Decker. Hamilton Beach introduced a battery-operated carving knife. Nearly all small-appliance producers were rumored to be trying to develop cordless adaptations of irons, coffee makers, handheld mixers, and electric carving knives.

Archibald responded to the brand transfer challenge with a series of actions. Since Black & Decker had until 1987 to put its own name on all the GE products it acquired, it led off the transfer process by first putting its name on GE's innovative, expensive, high-margin Spacemaker products, which were designed to be mounted under kitchen cabinets—a line that was not as strongly identified with the GE name. Then B&D introduced a new iron (invented by GE) that shut off automatically when it sat too long or was tipped over; B&D's TV ads for the iron showed an elephant walking away from an iron that had been left on, with a tag line: "Even elephants forget." The brand transfer was accomplished product by product, in each case accompanied by heavy advertising. Under Archibald, Black & Decker spent approximately $100 million during the 1985–87 period to promote the brand transition. The company also organized a large team of brand transition assistants to hang paper tags on display models of newly rebranded products in about 10,000 retail stores across the United States—the tags stated that GE previously sold products now made by Black & Decker. Most analysts regarded Archibald's brand transfer program as successful; a Harvard Business School professor stated, "It is almost a textbook example of how to manage a brand transition."[4]

Archibald was promoted to chairman, president, and chief executive officer in 1986. He was listed among *Fortune* magazine's 10 Most Wanted Executives that year and was named as one of the Six Best Managers of 1987 by *Business Week.* By year-end 1988, Archibald was widely credited with engineering another impressive turnaround, having boosted Black & Decker's profits to $97.1 million—up sharply from the loss of $158.4 million posted in 1985. Archibald was also the recipient of the American Marketing Association's 1996 Edison Achievement Award for his accomplishments as Black & Decker chief executive.

Failed Acquisition Attempts

In early 1988 Black & Decker began an unsolicited takeover bid for American Standard Inc., a diversified manufacturer of bathroom fixtures, air conditioning products, and braking systems for rail and automotive vehicles. American Standard had revenues of $3.4 billion and earnings of $127 million in 1987 (compared to revenues of $1.9 billion and earnings of almost $70 million for Black & Decker). After several months of negotiations, the takeover effort failed and B&D withdrew from the battle.

In January 1989, Black & Decker negotiated a deal with Allegheny International to purchase its Oster/Sunbeam appliance division for about $260 million. Oster/Sunbeam was a leading manufacturer and marketer of small household appliances—blenders, can openers, food mixers, electric skillets, steam irons, and other kitchen items. However, in February, Allegheny International backed out of the sale and merged with another company instead.

The Emhart Acquisition

A month later, in March 1989, Black & Decker agreed to acquire Emhart Corporation for $2.8 billion, rescuing the firm from a hostile takeover bid. Emhart had 1988 sales of $2.8 billion, earnings of $127 million, assets of $2.4 billion, and shareholders' equity of $971 million. Emhart was a diversified manufacturer of industrial products (1988 sales of $1.6 billion), information and electronic systems (1988 sales of $654 million), and consumer products (1988 sales of $547 million). Approximately 40 percent of Emhart's sales and earnings came from foreign operations, the majority of which were concentrated in Europe. Exhibit 3 provides a profile of Emhart's business portfolio. Exhibit 4 provides data on the financial performance of Emhart's business units.

---

[4]Ibid.

exhibit 3   Emhart Corporation's Business Portfolio in 1989 (At the Time of the Company's Acquisition by Black & Decker)

Business and Product Categories	Trademarks/Names	Primary Markets/ Customers
Industrial businesses (1988 sales of $1.6 billion)		
Capacitors, audible signal devices	Emhart, Mallory, Sonalert, Arcotronica	Telecommunications, computer, automotive, and electronic components industries
Electromechanical devices, solid-state control systems, hydrocarbon leak detection systems	Emhart, Mallory, Pollulert	Appliance, automotive, and environmental controls manufacturers
Commercial door hardware, electronic locking systems	Emhart, Carbin, Russwin	Commercial, institutional building construction, and original equipment manufacturers
Footwear materials (insoles, toe puffs, shanks, eyelets, tacks, and nails)	Emhart, Texon, Aquiline	Manufacturers of footwear
Fastening systems (rivets, locknuts, screw anchors, adhesive systems, sealants, and grouts)	Emhart, Molly, Warren, Gripco, Bostik, Kelox, Dodge, Heli-Coil, POP	Appliance, construction, electronics, furniture/ woodwork, packaging, automotive, and other transportation industries
Glass container machinery	Emhart, Hartford, Powers, Sundsvalls	Producers of glass containers for beverage, food, household, and pharmaceutical products
Printed circuit board assembling machinery	Emhart, Dynapert	Electronics industry
Information and electronic systems (1988 sales of $654 million)		
Technology-based systems and services (including computer-based systems), scientific research services, program management	Emhart, PRC, Planning Research Corp., PRC System Services, PRC Environmental Management, PRC Medic Computer Systems, Nova, Stellar	Governmental units and agencies, real estate multiple listing services, group medical practices, and public utilities
Consumer products businesses (1988 sales of $547 million)		
Door hardware, including lock sets, high-security locks, and locking devices	Emhart, Kwikset	Residential construction
Nonpowered lawn and garden equipment, landscape lighting	Garden America, True Temper	Do-it-yourself homeowners
Underground sprinkling and watering systems	Lawn Genie, Drip Mist, Irri-trol	Landscape specialists, do-it-yourself consumers
Golf club shafts, bicycle-frame tubing	True Temper, Dynamic Gold, Black Gold	Golf club manufacturers
Bathroom and kitchen faucets	Price Pfister, The Pfabulous Pfaucet with the Pfunny Name	Residential and commercial construction
Adhesive, sealants	Bostik, Thermogrip	Residential and commercial construction, do-it-yourself consumers
Fasteners, staplers, nailers	Blue-Tack, POP, Molly	Residential and commercial construction

exhibit 4 Financial Performance of Emhart's Business Groups, 1986–88 (In Millions of Dollars)

	1988	1987	1986A*	1986B
Revenues				
Industrial				
Components	$ 641.8	$ 671.9		$ 653.9
Fastening systems	640.5	638.8		576.3
Machinery	279.0	291.1		419.2
	$1,561.3	$1,601.8		$1,649.4
Information and electronic systems	653.7	438.3		39.3
Consumer	547.5	414.4		405.6
Total	$2,762.5	$2,454.5		$2,094.3
Operating Income (Loss)				
Industrial				
Components	$ 63.8	$ 65.7	$ 48.2	$ (5.4)
Fastening systems	74.8	78.7	68.3	24.8
Machinery	42.7	34.1	44.4	3.9
	$ 181.3	$ 178.5	$160.9	$ 23.3
Information and electronic systems	37.2	22.3	2.0	2.0
Consumer	84.8	68.3	60.4	51.7
	$ 303.3	$ 269.1	$223.3	$ 77.0
Corporate expense	(35.0)	(32.9)	(30.3)	(34.0)
Total	$ 268.3	$ 236.2	$193.0	$ 43.0
Identifiable Assets				
Industrial				
Components	$ 457.8	$ 472.0		$ 400.3
Fastening systems	428.4	428.2		409.7
Machinery	167.8	164.8		297.2
	$1,054.0	$1,065.0		$1,107.2
Information and electronic systems	546.7	361.3		334.5
Consumer	702.7	225.1		266.1
	$2,303.4	$1,651.4		$1,707.8
Corporate	123.2	378.5		148.9
Total	$2,426.6	$2,029.9	$000.0	$1,856.7

*1986 before provision for restructuring.
Source: Emhart 1988 annual report.

In the days following the announcement of Black & Decker's friendly plan to acquire Emhart, B&D's stock price dropped about 15 percent. There was considerable skepticism over the wisdom of the acquisition, both from the standpoint of whether Emhart's businesses had attractive strategic fit with B&D's businesses and whether B&D could handle the financial strain of making such a large acquisition. Emhart was significantly larger than Black & Decker:

1988 Financials	Emhart	Black & Decker
Sales revenues	$2.76 billion	$2.28 billion
Net earnings	126.6 million	97.1 million
Assets	2.43 billion	1.83 billion
Stockholders' equity	970.9 million	724.9 million
Long-term debt	$674.3 million	$277.1 million

The acquisition agreement called for Black & Decker to purchase 59.5 million shares (95 percent) of Emhart Corporation common stock at $40 per share—a price almost three times book value per share ($14.32). Altogether, Black & Decker had to secure $2.7 billion in financing to acquire Emhart. To come up with the funds, Black & Decker entered into a credit agreement with a group of banks that consisted of term loans due 1992 through 1997 and an unsecured revolving credit loan of up to $575 million. The loans carried an interest rate of ¼ percent above whatever the prevailing prime rate was. Scheduled principal payments on the term loans were as follows:

1992	$201,217,000
1993	274,287,000
1994	275,221,000
1995	743,923,000
1996	401,318,000

The credit agreement included covenants that required Black & Decker to achieve certain minimum levels of cash flow coverage of its interest obligations and not to exceed specified leverage (debt-to-equity) ratios during the term of the loan:

Fiscal Year	Maximum Leverage Ratio	Minimum Cash Flow Coverage Ratio
1992	3.25	1.35
1993	2.75	1.50
1994	2.25	1.55
1995 and thereafter	1.50	1.60

Note: The leverage ratio was calculated by dividing indebtedness, as defined by the credit agreement, by consolidated net stockholders' equity. The cash flow coverage ratio was calculated by dividing earnings before interest, taxes, depreciation, and amortization of goodwill minus capital expenditures by net interest expense plus cash income tax payments and dividends declared.

Other covenants in the credit agreement limited Black & Decker's ability to incur additional indebtedness and to acquire businesses or sell assets.

Black & Decker also entered into factoring agreements with financial institutions where it sold its receivables at a discounted rate to avoid waiting 30 to 60 days to collect on its invoices. The company ended its sale of receivables program in December 1997 when it became able to meet its liquidity requirements without factoring receivables.

Black & Decker recorded the excess amount of its purchase price for Emhart over the book value of Emhart's net assets as goodwill to be amortized on a straight-line basis over 40 years. This resulted in Black & Decker's having increased depreciation and amortization charges of about $45 million annually.

Initial Divestitures of Emhart Businesses

Senior management at Black & Decker realized early on that as much as $1 billion of Emhart's business assets would have to be sold to reduce B&D's interest expenses and debt obligations and enable it to meet its covenant agreements. According to accounting rules, these assets had to either be sold within a year or be consolidated with the rest of B&D assets—a move that could cause B&D to fail to meet its maximum leverage covenant. The Emhart businesses that were identified for sale within one year from the acquisition date included footwear materials, printed circuit board assembly equipment (Dynapert), capacitors, chemical adhesives (Bostik), and the entire information and electronic systems business unit (PRC). During 1989 and early 1990, Black & Decker sold the Bostik chemical adhesives division to a French company for $345 million, the footwear materials business to the United Machinery Group for approximately $125 million, and its Arcotronics capacitors business to Nissei Electric of Tokyo for about $80 million; the net proceeds from these sales were used to reduce debt. In early 1990, when the one-year period expired, Black & Decker was forced to consolidate about $566 million of the unsold assets, boosting the goodwill on its balance sheet by $560 million, raising annual amortization charges by $14 million. To keep from violating the maximum debt/equity ratio allowed under its credit schedule, Black & Decker was forced to issue $150 million in new preferred stock, $47 million of which was purchased from its 401(K) employee thrift plan when no other buyers came forward.

Throughout 1991 Black & Decker continued to struggle to meet its covenant agreements. The company divested Emhart's Garden America business unit and the Mallory Controls operations in North America and Brazil for a combined total of about $140 million. The company also sold its True Temper Hardware unit, its PRC Medic unit, and its U.S. Capacitors business for a combined total of nearly $110 million. The prices B&D got for the Emhart businesses it sold were generally below management's expectations, partly because oncoming recessionary effects reduced what buyers were willing to pay.

Nonetheless, these divestitures (described by B&D management as "nonstrategic assets") and the sale of $150 million in preferred stock, allowed Black & Decker to reduce its total debt from a peak of $4 billion following the Emhart acquisition in April 1989 to $2.9 billion at year-end 1991. Even so, Black & Decker was still hard pressed to generate enough cash to meet its debt repayment schedule, a problem compounded by the 1990–91 recession, which hit the company's tool and household goods businesses fairly hard. The company's stock price fell from the mid-20s at the time of the Emhart acquisition to a low of $11–$12 in early 1991—many observers believed that the fundamental cause of B&D's financial plight was that it had paid too much for Emhart. There was also concern about whether there was enough strategic fit between Emhart and B&D. By early 1992, the stock price had recovered to the low 20s, partly because a decline in the prime rate from 10 percent to 6.5 percent had lowered B&D's interest burden substantially. (The credit agreement pegged the interest rate B&D paid at ¼ percent above the prevailing prime rate.)

Subsequent Divestitures: 1993–96

During the next six years, Black & Decker's corporate management sought to find buyers for several nonstrategic businesses acquired as part of the Emhart deal. Three were sold between 1993 and 1996.

Dynapert   The Dynapert business unit provided automated equipment for assembling printed circuit boards to electronics customers around the world. The equipment was among the most complex computer-controlled machinery being used in any industrial application. Dynapert had two manufacturing plants (one in the United States and one in England) and sales and service facilities throughout the world. The unit had launched a total quality program and implemented just-in-time manufacturing techniques.

Sales were made directly to users by an employee sales force and independent sales representatives. Dynapert faced competition from both U.S. and foreign manufacturers. Competition centered on technological and machine performance features, price, delivery terms, and provision of technical services. The Dynapert division, which generated 1991 sales of about $180 million, had been put on the market shortly after the Emhart acquisition, and was sold two years later to Dover Corporation's Universal Instrument division for an undisclosed amount.

Corbin Russwin   Emhart's Corbin Russwin manufactured locks and door hardware for the European commercial security hardware market. The unit employed 550 people at its plant in Berlin, Germany. Yale and Valour, Inc., the British manufacturer of Yale locks, purchased the Corbin Russwin unit from Black & Decker in 1994 for $80 million. Black & Decker recorded a gain of $18 million on the combined sales of the Corbin Russwin and Dynapert units.

PRC Information Systems and Services   This segment consisted of a single business unit known as PRC, Inc., headquartered in McLean, Virginia. PRC and its predecessors had been in business since the mid-1970s. A majority of PRC's business came from contracts with various agencies and units of the federal government. Approximately 40 percent of PRC's 1991 revenues were from contracts with the Department of Defense. In addition, PRC was the leading provider of (1) online printed residential real estate multiple listing systems and (2) computer-aided emergency dispatch systems. The types of services PRC provided were highly competitive, and strategic defense expenditures were expected to decline given the improvement of foreign relations. Many of PRC's competitors were large defense contractors with significantly greater financial resources. As the Department of Defense's expenditures for weapons programs continued to decline, these large contractors were expected to bid more aggressively for the types of contract work done by PRC. PRC had also been put on the market for sale following the Emhart acquisition. In 1991, PRC had sales of $684 million and pretax operating earnings of $32.3 million. In mid-1991 B&D appointed a new person to head PRC; shortly thereafter, PRC launched an initiative to pursue new markets. The objective was to shift PRC's business mix so that half came from U.S. customers and half from overseas customers. However, PRC management had great difficulty developing new nongovernment customers and was only growing at about one-third the rate of its closest competitors under Black & Decker ownership.

Black & Decker had little success in locating interested buyers for the PRC unit until 1995, when PRC Realty Systems and PRC Environmental Management, Inc., were sold for $60 and $35.5 million, respectively. Litton Industries agreed to purchase the remaining PRC operations in 1996 for $425 million. Prior to its sale to Litton, when it appeared that finding a buyer was becoming increasingly unlikely, Black & Decker management had considered a spinoff of the unit in 1992. The spinoff was never finalized because Wall Street showed little interest in a $350 million public offering of PRC stock. PRC's 1995 sales and after-tax earnings were $800 million and $38.4 million, respectively.

Black & Decker's 1998 Divestitures

Black & Decker again initiated portfolio restructuring in 1998 when it divested its household products business and two businesses gained through the Emhart acquisition.

Household Products   Black & Decker's household products business had established itself as a worldwide leader in products used for home cleaning, garment care, cooking, and food and beverage preparation by 1990. It had the largest market share of any full-line producer of household appliance products in the United States, Canada, Mexico, and Australia and a growing presence in Europe, Southeast Asia, and Latin America. The household products division was using the worldwide distribution network and brand-name recognition that had been established by the tools division to gain greater global penetration in household appliances. However, by 1996, the company had lost substantial market share in almost every housewares product category. Its Toast-R-Ovens and irons were the only remaining Black & Decker products that held leading shares of their respective markets. (See Exhibit 5 for market shares of the major competitors by product category for 1990, 1993, and 1996.)

Like the market for power tools, the market for small household appliances was both mature and cyclical. Growth opportunities existed mainly in the form of creating innovative new products and in increasing market penetration in the countries of Eastern Europe and other developing nations where household appliance saturation rates were low. It was difficult to grow sales in the United States without introducing innovative new products since most small appliances had very high household saturation rates. In 1996 blenders were found in 80 percent of U.S. households, coffeemakers had a 74 percent saturation rate, and toasters were found in 90 percent of U.S. households. Many consumers clearly had both a toaster and toaster oven, since toaster ovens had a 42 percent U.S. household saturation rate.

Black & Decker's housewares business unit had been successful at launching new products that might entice a consumer into replacing an existing small appliance for one offering more features or better performance. The company's SnakeLight flexible flashlight was introduced in 1994 and quickly became one of the most popular small appliances ever developed by the company. In 1996 the company introduced a revamped Quick 'N Easy line of irons with a new Sure Steam system, and in 1998 it improved the glideability of its irons with a new proprietary coated soleplate. The company also introduced cordless products such as the ScumBuster, a submersible scourer and scrubber, and the FloorBuster, an upright vacuum cleaner that achieved rapid sales increases.

In late 1997 the company launched a designer line of small kitchen appliances, Kitchentools, which won five Industrial Design Excellence Awards in 1998. The Kitchentools line carried premium pricing; the stand mixer had a suggested retail price of $289.99, the thermal coffeemaker listed at $159.99, the blender was priced at $139.99, the food processor was priced at $229.99, the hand mixer's retail price was $69.00, and the Kitchentools can opener carried a suggested retail price of $34.99. Even though the Kitchentools line was praised for its quality and innovative styling, it did not sell as well as Black & Decker management had expected. The company also had some difficulty manufacturing the products and getting them to market by the planned launch date.

Black & Decker had lost substantial market share in recent years and had seen its profit margins erode despite its best efforts to maintain efficient operations. Between 1995 and 1997 the company had completely overhauled its supply chain management

exhibit 5   Unit Volume for Selected Small Appliances and Market
Shares of Leading Producers, 1990, 1993, and 1996
(Unit Volume in Thousands)

Product/Leading Brands	1990	1993	1996
Can openers	6,200	6,380	6,910
Rival	33%	27%	26%
Hamilton Beach/Proctor Silex	13	15	24
Black & Decker	26	28	13
Oster/Sunbeam	11	13	13
Coffeemakers	17,740	14,390	15,000
Mr. Coffee	28%	31%	32%
Hamilton Beach/Proctor Silex	19	18	24
West Bend	—	3	9
Black & Decker	20	17	8
Food processors	4,760	1,916	1,525
Hamilton Beach/Proctor Silex	21%	19%	40%
Cuisinart	Unknown	13	18
Black & Decker	25	21	10
Oster/Sunbeam	18	19	8
Hand mixers	4,400	5,060	5,280
Hamilton Beach/Proctor Silex	14%	18%	24%
Black & Decker	34	28	15
Oster/Sunbeam	25	18	13
HPA/Betty Crocker	—	—	11
Irons	16,950	17,460	15,600
Black & Decker	50%	50%	38%
Hamilton Beach/Proctor Silex	24	30	29
Oster/Sunbeam	17	10	17
Rowenta	—	—	7
Toaster ovens	2,800	3,340	3,670
Black & Decker	57%	56%	56%
Toastmaster	13	16	17
Hamilton Beach/Proctor Silex	19	20	11
HPA/Betty Crocker	—	—	6
Toasters	8,900	9,850	10,760
Hamilton Beach/Proctor Silex	35%	50%	37%
Toastmaster	27	31	30
Rival	—	—	17
HPA/Betty Crocker	—	—	5
Black & Decker	16	13	4

Source: Compiled by case researchers from data presented in *Appliance,* April 1991 and April 1997.

to reduce finished goods inventory and improve customer service and production planning. The company had eliminated $150 million from logistics costs during that time period but still only averaged about 2 percent profit margins on its housewares products. The business unit was identified for divestiture by Nolan Archibald in January 1998 and was sold to Windmere-Durable in May 1998 for $315 million. The agreement allowed

Black & Decker to retain its DustBuster, FloorBuster, ScumBuster, and SnakeLight product lines. In June 1998 Black & Decker announced the sale of its housewares operations in New Zealand and Australia to Gerard Industries, an Australian electrical products manufacturer. The company had also sold its consumer glue gun and stapler business to Longwood Industries for an undisclosed amount in July 1998.

Recreational Outdoor Products   In 1998 B&D's True Temper Sports business unit was the leading global designer, manufacturer, and marketer of steel golf club shafts; with over a 60 percent market share in the steel shaft segment, it was three times as large as its closest rival. True Temper also manufactured graphite shafts but had a very limited market share in that segment since it focused on the premium end of the market. The division supplied more than 800 golf club manufacturers around the world, including such industry leaders as Callaway Golf, Ping, Titleist, and Taylor Made. The sales of this unit had grown at a compounded annual rate of 12 percent between 1995 and 1997. True Temper Sport's growth rate reflected the overall growth in the golf equipment industry. The unit also manufactured specialty tubing for the bicycle and sporting goods industries. Many of the bicycles and kayak paddles used by U.S. Olympians were manufactured from True Temper precision tubing.

Black & Decker sold the business to Cornerstone Equity Investors in June 1998 for $178 million. The new owners stated that they intended for True Temper to remain the leader in golf club shafts and that they intended to expand into new product categories requiring specialty tubing. True Temper's president said that the new company would develop precision tubing products for such sporting goods industries as downhill skiing and archery.

Glass-Container-Forming Machinery   In 1998 B&D's Emhart glass-container-forming machinery division was considered the global leader and offered the world's most complete line of glass-container-making equipment. Important competitive factors were price, technological and machine performance features, product reliability, and technical and engineering services. An increasing worldwide preference for plastic and other nonglass containers had led to a slowing growth rate for glass-container-forming equipment and inspection equipment. There was little seasonal variation in industry demand. Glass-container-making equipment was in 24-hour use in virtually all plants worldwide, creating a predictable need for servicing and rebuilding; nearly two-thirds of the unit's revenues came from rebuilding and repair services and technology upgrades. In January 1998 the business was identified as a nonstrategic asset that was to be divested; it was sold to Bucher Holding AG of Switzerland in September 1998 for $178 million.

BLACK & DECKER'S BUSINESS PORTFOLIO IN 2000

In 2000 Black & Decker Corporation was a diversified multinational enterprise with a business portfolio consisting of:

- Power tools and accessories for both do-it-yourselfers and professional tradespeople.
- Lawn and garden equipment.
- Security hardware for residential markets in the United States and residential and commercial hardware in certain European countries.
- Cleaning and lighting products.

exhibit 6 Black & Decker's Business Portfolio at Year-end 1999

Power tools and accessories (1999 sales: $3.21 billion)	• Master keying systems • Faucets and fixtures • Lawn and garden care products
• Drills • Screwdrivers • Saws • Sanders • Grinders • Tabletop saws • Drill bits • Screwdriver bit • Saw blades • Cleaning and lighting products	**Fastening and assembly systems (1999 sales: $498 million)** • Rivets and riveting tools • Threaded inserts • Stud welding fastening systems • Lock nuts • Self-drilling screws • Construction anchors
Hardware and home improvement (1999 sales: $882 million)	
• Lock sets • Deadbolts	

- Plumbing products.
- Commercial fastening systems.

Exhibit 6 provides a detailed listing of the products produced and marketed by B&D in these business areas. Exhibit 7 provides 1997–99 financial performance data by business group. A brief description of each business group follows.

Power Tools and Accessories

Black & Decker was the world's largest manufacturer, marketer, and servicer of power tools and accessories. The company's products were available at almost all retail outlets that sold power tools in the United States, Europe, and other developed countries. In fact, Black & Decker products were so popular in the United Kingdom that many British do-it-yourselfers referred to home improvement projects as "Black & Decker-ing." Black & Decker was named as the top-performing hardware brand by 6 out of every 10 U.S. retailers included in a 1997 survey conducted by *Discount Store News.* Other brands that were highly rated by hardware retailers were Stanley, General Electric, Skil, Rubbermaid, Makita, and Dutch Boy. Black & Decker's products were also highly rated in terms of performance by consumers, and most of its products carried a two-year warranty.

Industry Growth and Competition Demand for power tools and accessories was regarded as mature and cyclical. Volume was influenced by residential and commercial construction activity, by consumer expenditures for home improvement, and by the overall level of manufacturing activity. (A number of manufacturers used power tools in performing certain production tasks—automotive and aerospace firms, for example, were heavy users of power tools.) Worldwide sales of power tools were an estimated $10 billion in 1999. The North American market for power tools was estimated at $3.5 billion, European sales were estimated at $4.0 billion, Asia/Pacific sales were an estimated $2.0 billion, and Latin American sales of power tools were approximately $500

exhibit 7 Black & Decker's Financial Performance by Business Segment, 1997–99

	Power Tools and Accessories	Hardware and Home Improvement	Fastening and Assembly Systems	All Others	Currency Translation Adjustments	Corporate Adjustments and Eliminations	Consolidated
1999							
Sales to unaffiliated customers	$3,209.3	$881.8	$497.7	—	($ 68.3)	$ —	$4,520.5
Operating income before restructuring and exit costs, write-off of goodwill, and gain on sales of businesses	377.3	124.0	84.3	—	(6.9)	(42.4)	536.3
Depreciation and amortization	87.7	31.1	15.4	—	(1.8)	27.6	160.0
Identifiable assets	1,836.0	508.2	273.2	—	2,617.4	1,395.3	4,012.7
Capital expenditures	$ 109.1	$ 38.3	$ 26.9	—	($ 3.5)	$ 0.3	$ 171.1
1998							
Sales to unaffiliated customers	$2,946.4	$851.1	$463.0	$333.6	($ 34.2)	$ —	$4,559.9
Operating income before restructuring and exit costs, write-off of goodwill, and gain on sales of businesses	293.4	125.2	76.6	16.5	(4.4)	(23.3)	484.0
Depreciation and amortization	88.2	27.1	13.4	—	(1.1)	27.6	155.2
Identifiable assets	1,631.3	507.8	246.7	13.3	(4.6)	1,471.3	3,852.5
Capital expenditures	$ 79.1	$ 36.5	$ 16.2	$ 13.3	($ 1.1)	$ 2.0	$ 146.0
1997							
Sales to unaffiliated customers	$2,936.4	$804.8	$451.3	$718.1	$ 29.9	$ —	$4,940.5
Operating income before restructuring and exit costs, write-off of goodwill, and gain on sales of businesses	290.7	121.3	69.7	61.7	(2.3)	(51.8)	489.3
Depreciation and amortization	87.5	24.7	11.9	24.4	(0.3)	66.0	214.2
Identifiable assets	1,635.4	476.5	248.2	438.6	8.0	2,554.0	5,360.7
Capital expenditures	$ 113.2	$ 47.3	$ 15.4	$ 25.3	($ 0.2)	$ 2.1	$ 203.1

Source: Black & Decker annual reports.

million. The global market for power tools failed to grow significantly between 1997 and 1999, but was expected to grow at low- to mid-single-digit annual rates between 2000 and 2002. The industry's worldwide demand plateau during the late 1990s was attributable in large part to Asian financial and economic troubles. During 1998 and 1999 North America was the fastest-growing market for power tools as cordless and professional-grade power tools gained in popularity with consumers. Demand in Europe grew more slowly than in the United States during the late 1990s and was expected to continue to lag behind U.S. demand in the near future. Worldwide, the biggest percentage growth during the early and mid-1990s occurred in emerging Asian countries, where the use of power tools was quickly replacing the use of hand tools. Healthy demand for power tools was expected to return to Asian markets once the region had fully recovered from the effects of financial and economic instability that began in late 1997.

Market Segments　　There were two distinct groups of buyers for power tools: professional users and do-it-yourselfers. Professional users included construction workers, electricians, plumbers, repair and maintenance workers, auto mechanics, and manufacturing workers. Professional users were very conscious of quality and features; they tended to buy only those tools that were durable, functional, dependable, and capable of precision. They also tended to be very knowledgeable compared to do-it-yourselfers, many of whom were first-time buyers and used power tools infrequently.

Because the needs of professional users and do-it-yourself consumers tended to be sharply different, some manufacturers had a heavy-duty professional line and a consumer/do-it-yourself line and others catered to just one of the two segments. Professional users tended to purchase their tools through jobbers, contractor supply firms, industrial supply houses, building supply centers, and some home improvement centers. Tools for the consumer segment were sold at home improvement centers, building materials centers, mass merchandisers (Sears), discount chains (Wal-Mart, Kmart), and hardware stores.

Until the late 1980s, the consumer tool segment was growing at a faster clip than the professional segment. But narrowing price differentials and a rising interest on the part of gung-ho do-it-yourselfers in professional-quality tools had, in the U.S. market, spurred demand for heavy-duty professional tools. The sales of both consumer-grade and professional-grade cordless products were also becoming increasingly popular, with a compound annual growth rate of over 10 percent during the mid- and late 1990s.

Competition　　Power tool manufacturers competed on such variables as price, quality, product design, product innovation, brand-name reputation, size and strength of retail dealer networks, and after-sale service. All makers were working to bring out new products that were lightweight, compact, cordless, quiet, less prone to vibration, strong, and easy to manipulate. The major manufacturers had sales forces whose main task was to expand and strengthen the network of retail dealers carrying their line of tools. Salespeople signed on new dealers and called on major accounts—wholesale distributors, discount chains, home improvement centers, and other mass merchandisers—to win better access to shelf space in their retail outlets, help with promotion and display activities, and upgrade dealers' product knowledge and sales skills. Some manufacturers offered training seminars and provided training videos to dealers/distributors. Manufacturers that concentrated on the professional segment engaged in limited advertising and promotion activities, spending their dollars for trade magazine ads, trade shows, and in-store displays. Those that concentrated on the consumer segment, like Black & Decker, spent comparatively heavily for TV and magazine ads and also for co-op ad programs with dealers.

exhibit 8   Estimated U.S. Sales and Market Shares of Power Tool Manufacturers, 1979, 1991, and 1997 ($ Millions)

	1979		1991		1997	
	Dollar Sales	**Percent Share**	**Dollar Sales**	**Percent Share**	**Dollar Sales**	**Percent Share**
Consumer tools						
Black & Decker	$169	44.5%	$ 325	39.7	$ 460	43.1%
Sears/Ryobi	107	28.2	280	34.0	305	28.5
Milwaukee	6	1.5	4	0.5	6	0.6
Makita	2	0.5	43	5.2	32	3.0
Porter Cable	—	—	—	—	—	—
Delta	—	—	—	—	—	—
Skil	52	13.7	82	10.0	165	15.4
Others	44	11.6	86	10.6	102	9.4
Total	$380	100.0%	$ 820	100.0%	$1,070	100.0%
Professional tools						
Black & Decker	$205	42.1%	$ 125	17.9%	$ 918	36.7%
Sears/Ryobi	9	1.8	50	7.1	285	11.4
Milwaukee	89	18.2	145	20.7	436	17.4
Makita	22	4.5	160	22.9	304	12.2
Porter Cable	NA	NA	50	7.1	240	9.6
Delta	NA	NA	40	5.7	209	8.4
Skil	54	11.1	40	5.7	32	1.3
Others	109	22.3	90	12.9	76	3.0
Total	$488	100.0%	$ 700	100.0%	$2,500	100.0%
Total tools						
Black & Decker	$374	43.1%	$ 450	29.6%	$1,378	38.6%
Sears/Ryobi	116	13.4	330	21.7	590	16.5
Milwaukee	95	10.9	149	9.8	442	12.4
Makita	24	2.8	203	13.4	336	9.4
Porter Cable	NA	NA	50	3.3	240	6.7
Delta	NA	NA	40	2.6	209	5.9
Skil	106	12.2	122	8.0	197	5.5
Others	153	17.6	176	11.6	210	9.4
Total	$868	100.0%	$1,520	100.0%	$3,570	100.0%

NA = not available

Source: Compiled by the case researchers from a variety of sources, including telephone interviews with company personnel; data for 1979 are based on information in Skil Corporation, Harvard Business School, case #9-389-005.

Black & Decker's Global Competitive Position in Power Tools   In 2000 Black & Decker was the overall world leader in the world power tool industry, followed by Bosch/Skil Power Tools, a division of Robert Bosch Corporation (one of Germany's leading companies), and Japanese brands Makita and Hitachi. Other competitors were Atlas/Copco, Delta/Porter Cable, Hilti, Ryobi, and Electrolux. For most of the company's history, Black & Decker's greatest strength was in the consumer tools segment (see Exhibit 8); it was the market leader in the United States, Europe (where it had had a presence since the 1920s), and many other countries outside Europe. No other manufacturer came close to matching B&D's global distribution capabilities in the do-it-yourself segment. Makita and Ryobi were the leaders in Japan and several other Asian countries. Bosch was strongest in Europe.

In consumer tools Black & Decker's strongest U.S. competitor was Sears, which marketed tools under the Sears Craftsman label. Sears's longtime supplier of tools was Ryobi, which supplied Sears with 75 percent of its tool requirements. Skil's strength was in power saws; its 1992 joint venture with Robert Bosch Power Tools was contrived to give the two brands more clout in gaining shelf space and greater global coverage capabilities. Black & Decker's consumer-grade power tools were also carried by Sears, and the company had developed a new Quantum line of power tools sold exclusively by Wal-Mart. Quantum was an intermediate line that was more durable than typical consumer lines but did not meet the performance of the company's professional power tools. Black & Decker's Mouse sander, WoodHawk circular saws, and FireStorm drills, along with its products that used the VersaPak interchangeable battery, were among the company's best-selling consumer tools.

Although surveys showed that consumers associated the Black & Decker name with durable power tools, trade professionals viewed Black & Decker products as products for do-it-yourselfers. During the late 1980s, the company's charcoal-gray professional tools line was not seen by professional users as sufficiently differentiated from B&D's traditional black line of consumer tools. Professionals preferred tools made by Makita, Skil, and Milwaukee (a U.S. tool manufacturer with a reputation for quality, heavy-duty tools). During the 1970s and 1980s, Makita had steadily increased its share of the professional segment and by 1991 had captured 53 percent of the U.S. professional handheld power tool segment.

In 1991 B&D executives formed a team, headed by the president of B&D's power tools division, to come up with a new strategy for the professional market segment. The team elected to create an entirely new line of industrial-grade tools for professional users under the DeWalt brand, a name borrowed from a 65-year-old maker of high-quality stationary saws acquired by B&D in 1960. The team changed the tools' color from gray to industrial yellow because the latter was easy to see, signaled safety, and was distinct from other leading brands of professional power tools. Every product in B&D's professional line was redesigned based on input from professionals, dealers, and B&D engineers. The redesigned versions were all tested by professional users; every item had to meet or beat Makita's tools in user tests before going into production. The new DeWalt line was introduced in March 1992. As part of the introduction of the DeWalt line, B&D created "swarm teams" of 120 young, high-energy marketers that visited construction sites to demonstrate DeWalt tools in their bright yellow-and-black Chevy Blazers. DeWalt swarm teams also promoted DeWalt tools at NASCAR events, vocational clubs, union apprenticeship programs, and retail locations. The company intended to double the number of swarm team members in the United States between 1998 and 1999. In 1996 DeWalt swarm teams invaded Europe with a fleet of yellow-and-black Range Rover Defenders with the charge of making DeWalt a leading brand on that continent. The company also instituted a policy of offering professional users the loan of a DeWalt power tool when waiting for their equipment to be fixed at any of the company's 135 U.S. service centers. There were also DeWalt demonstration booths at each of the service centers.

Initial response to the DeWalt line was excellent. As the brand began to gain in popularity with professional users, Black & Decker developed additional DeWalt tools. In 1997, newly introduced DeWalt products were awarded two Industrial Design Excellence Awards from the Industrial Designers Society of America. The success of the new DeWalt line exceeded Black & Decker management's expectations and surpassed its

$200 million sales volume objective for 1995 by over $100 million. In 1999 DeWalt was one of the leading power tool brands for professionals and serious do-it-yourselfers.

Black & Decker was also the world leader in the market for such accessories as drill bits, saw blades, and screwdriver bits. Vermont American, Irwin Hanson/American Tool, Bosch, Freud, and Wolfcraft were B&D's closest competitors in the accessories market, but no other company had as broad a product line or geographic coverage as Black & Decker. Most of the company's growth in accessory sales was accounted for by accessory lines developed for the DeWalt brand and a line of new premium woodworking saw blades. The company intended to maintain its market leadership by expanding into more woodworking supply and industrial/construction distribution channels and continuing to introduce innovative products.

In 1998 Black & Decker launched a series of initiatives intended to strengthen its competitive position in power tools and accessories. First, it introduced a corporatewide six sigma quality program to bring about improvements in costs, defect rates, product quality, and customer satisfaction. Second, the company took a $164 million restructuring charge that involved the elimination of 2,900 positions; worldwide plant rationalization that resulted in plant closings in Canada, Singapore, and Italy; a reorganization of its European operations; and various reengineering projects in all plants. Third, it initiated a restructuring of its supply chain management to improve customer service while reducing inventories. Although Black & Decker's restructuring program cut across all business units, it was primarily focused on its global power tools business and was expected to yield more than $100 million annually in cost savings. Additional cost savings were achieved through the integration of Black & Decker's cleaning and lighting products like its DustBuster vacuum cleaner, ScumBuster wet scrubber, and SnakeLight flashlight with its power tool businesses after the sale of the housewares division to Windmere in 1998.

The April 21, 1999, exit of Joseph Galli, Black & Decker's president of its Worldwide Power Tools and Accessories group, shocked analysts and investors and caused a one-day 8 percent decline in the company's share price. Galli, age 41, was a rising star at Black & Decker and was thought to be the leading candidate to succeed Archibald as CEO. There was a widely held belief in the power tools industry that much of the DeWalt brand's success was attributable to Galli's strategic leadership and that Galli had been forced out of B&D as a result of his desire to become the company's CEO within the near future. Archibald, who had no immediate retirement plans, commented that Galli had "expressed an interest in advancing his management career to a higher level, and we have agreed it makes sense for him to pursue this goal outside of Black & Decker."[5] In June 1999 Joe Galli become president and chief operating officer of Amazon.com. Even though there was some initial concern by investors over Galli's departure, B&D's Power Tools and Accessories group continued to perform well in his absence; its sales increased by 11 percent and operating profit increased by 27 percent during the fourth quarter of 1999. The business unit's annual sales and operating profits increased by 9 percent and 29 percent, respectively, over 1998 sales and operating profits.

Lawn and Garden Equipment

Black & Decker's lawn and garden tools like Groom 'N' Edge, Vac 'N' Mulch, and LeafBuster were distributed through the same channels as the company's power tools. In addition, the buyers of B&D's hedge trimmers, string trimmers, lawn mowers, edgers, and blower/vacuums could get the items repaired at B&D's 150 company-owned service

[5]As quoted in the *Baltimore Sun,* April 22, 1999.

centers worldwide and several hundred other authorized service centers operated by independent owners. Where feasible, B&D's lawn and garden products had a global design. The company had recently begun to offer cordless electric string trimmers and hedge trimmers in North America and Europe. The cordless hedge trimmer could run continuously for about 30 minutes, and the cordless string trimmer could trim hard-to-reach areas from a half-acre lawn on a single battery charge. As of 2000, Black & Decker marketed its cordless lawn mowers only in Europe.

Security Hardware

B&D's security hardware business was the leader in the $2 billion global market for door hardware for homes and businesses. The company had developed good-better-best product lines that covered all major residential price points. The Kwikset brand was positioned as an affordable product targeted to do-it-yourselfers; B&D had boosted Kwikset's sales by providing retailers with a videotape that took the mystery out of changing household locks. Kwikset Plus was a midrange product, and the company's TITAN products were designed for the fine home market. TITAN NightSight handsets and deadbolts featured lighted keyways, and the TITAN AccessOne keyless entry deadbolt and handset systems allowed homeowners to use a remote control to unlock the door from as far away as 30 feet. The TITAN line also included the Society Brass Collection of solid brass designer door hardware. All TITAN products boasted a lifetime finish that was protected against tarnishing, rust, and corrosion.

This business, acquired from Emhart, had achieved significant cost savings by integrating its purchasing, distribution, and marketing activities with B&D's other consumer products businesses. B&D's worldwide distribution network was also providing the hardware group wider geographic sales opportunities. In many instances, door hardware was sold in the same retail channels as B&D's power tools and accessories. Black & Decker's restructuring and six sigma quality initiatives, begun in 1998, also affected its security hardware business—products and facilities were rationalized, high-cost operations were restructured, and automation was used where feasible. Black & Decker's major competitors in the North American security hardware market included Schlage, Weiser, Weslock, and a variety of Asian exporters. Major competitors in Europe included Williams, Assa Abloy, Cisa, Keso, and Abus.

Plumbing Products

B&D's plumbing products business, Price Pfister, had gained market share since the Emhart acquisition to become the third largest manufacturer and marketer of plumbing fixtures in North America by 2000. Price Pfister had benefited from access to B&D's retail distribution network by gaining more shelf space in home improvement centers. Price Pfister had also introduced fashionable, but affordably priced, new designs and new lines that had become popular with plumbing wholesalers and plumbing contractors. Price Pfister had increased its brand recognition through in-store merchandising activities and with TV ads using the theme "The Pfabulous Pfaucet with the Pfunny Name" in the early 1990s and "The Pfabulous Pfaucet. Pforever. No Drips, No Tarnish, No Worries" theme in the late 1990s.

Price Pfister's major competitors in the $1.9 billion North American market for sink, tub, shower, and lavatory plumbing hardware were American Standard, Kohler, Delta, and Moen. The industry had grown at a slow rate of 2 to 3 percent since 1995 and was expected to grow at a comparable rate over the next few years. Plumbing products with new styles and features were in the highest demand. Black & Decker expected new decorative faucets like Price Pfister's Georgetown and Roman lines, introduced during the late 1990s, to account for 20 percent of the unit's annual sales. Price Pfister expected to improve its performance with the addition of innovative and attractive new lines, better in-store merchandising, improved manufacturing efficiency, and better supply chain management.

Commercial Fastening Systems

Black & Decker was among the global leaders in the $2 billion fastening and assembly systems market. This business unit marketed fastening products under 26 different brands and trademarks to automotive, electronics, aerospace, machine tool, and appliance companies in the United States, Europe, and the Far East. The industry's recent growth rate had ranged between 3 and 5 percent, and future growth was expected to remain within that range. Some emerging markets did generate higher growth rates as new industries and companies emerged and plant capacity was added.

Products were sold directly to users and also through distributors and manufacturers' representatives. Competition centered on product quality, performance, reliability, price, delivery, and ability to provide customers with technical and engineering services. Competition came from many manufacturers in several countries. Major competitors included Textron, TRW, Eaton, and such regional companies as Raymond, Gesipa, Huck, and Fukui. Black & Decker was the global leader in commercial blind riveting and automotive stud welding systems, and its other fastening system categories held strong positions in various geographic regions. Black & Decker management intended to maintain its leadership in the automotive stud welding category with new product innovations. More than 30 percent of the unit's 1999 sales were accounted for by products introduced within the past five years. Black & Decker intended to improve the performance of the division through implementation of its six sigma quality initiative, reengineered operations, and plant rationalizations.

BLACK & DECKER'S FUTURE PROSPECTS

The year 2000 marked the beginning of Black & Decker's second year of operations with its streamlined portfolio of businesses following the 1998 divestiture of its small-appliance, True Temper recreational products, and Emhart glass-forming machinery businesses. Black & Decker had sold the three businesses for more than management's expected $500 million and was able to reduce operating expenses by more than $100 million annually, primarily as a result of the elimination of 3,000 jobs from its payroll. In addition, the series of divestitures had cut the company's amortization of goodwill associated with the Emhart acquisition by about $30 million annually for the next 30 years.

This last round of divestitures, coupled with the sale of businesses in earlier years, completed the divestiture of the nonstrategic Emhart assets gained in the 1989 acquisition. Price Pfister and Kwikset were two of the Emhart businesses that initially captured the attention of Black & Decker management and were now among the three remaining Emhart businesses still included in Black & Decker's portfolio. So far, the 1998 divestitures had not produced steady increases in the company's stock price, but Nolan Archibald was confident that the company's ability to focus solely on power tools and other closely aligned businesses would allow the company to begin to provide its shareholders with above-average returns.

case 20 Robin Hood

Joseph Lampel
New York University

It was in the spring of the second year of his insurrection against the High Sheriff of Nottingham that Robin Hood took a walk in Sherwood Forest. As he walked he pondered the progress of the campaign, the disposition of his forces, the Sheriff's recent moves, and the options that confronted him.

The revolt against the Sheriff had begun as a personal crusade. It erupted out of Robin's conflict with the Sheriff and his administration. However, alone Robin Hood could do little. He therefore sought allies, men with grievances and a deep sense of justice. Later he welcomed all who came, asking few questions and demanding only a willingness to serve. Strength, he believed, lay in numbers.

He spent the first year forging the group into a disciplined band, united in enmity against the Sheriff and willing to live outside the law. The band's organization was simple. Robin ruled supreme, making all important decisions. He delegated specific tasks to his lieutenants. Will Scarlett was in charge of intelligence and scouting. His main job was to shadow the Sheriff and his men, always alert to their next move. He also collected information on the travel plans of rich merchants and tax collectors. Little John kept discipline among the men and saw to it that their archery was at the high peak that their profession demanded. Scarlock took care of the finances, converting loot to cash, paying shares of the take, and finding suitable hiding places for the surplus. Finally, Much the Miller's son had the difficult task of provisioning the ever-increasing band of Merrymen.

The increasing size of the band was a source of satisfaction for Robin, but also a source of concern. The fame of his Merrymen was spreading, and new recruits were pouring in from every corner of England. As the band grew larger, their small bivouac became a major encampment. Between raids the men milled about, talking and playing games. Vigilance was in decline, and discipline was becoming harder to enforce. "Why," Robin reflected, "I don't know half the men I run into these days."

The growing band was also beginning to exceed the food capacity of the forest. Game was becoming scarce, and supplies had to be obtained from outlying villages. The cost of buying food was beginning to drain the band's financial reserves at the very moment when revenues were in decline. Travelers, especially those with the most to lose, were now giving the forest a wide berth. This was costly and inconvenient to them, but it was preferable to having all their goods confiscated.

Robin believed that the time had come for the Merrymen to change their policy of outright confiscation of goods to one of a fixed transit tax. His lieutenants strongly resisted this idea. They were proud of the Merrymen's famous motto: "Rob the rich and give to the poor." "The farmers and the townspeople," they argued, "are our most important allies. How can we tax them, and still hope for their help in our fight against the Sheriff?"

Robin wondered how long the Merrymen could keep to the ways and methods of their early days. The Sheriff was growing stronger and becoming better organized. He now had the money and the men and was beginning to harass the band, probing for its weaknesses. The tide of events was beginning to turn against the Merrymen. Robin felt that the campaign must be decisively concluded before the Sheriff had a chance to deliver a mortal blow. "But how," he wondered, "could this be done?"

Robin had often entertained the possibility of killing the Sheriff, but the chances for this seemed increasingly remote. Besides, killing the Sheriff might satisfy his personal thirst for revenge, but it would not improve the situation. Robin had hoped that the perpetual state of unrest, and the Sheriff's failure to collect taxes, would lead to his removal from office. Instead, the Sheriff used his political connections to obtain reinforcement. He had powerful friends at court and was well regarded by the regent, Prince John.

Prince John was vicious and volatile. He was consumed by his unpopularity among the people, who wanted the imprisoned King Richard back. He also lived in constant fear of the barons, who had first given him the regency but were now beginning to dispute his claim to the throne. Several of these barons had set out to collect the ransom that would release King Richard the Lionheart from his jail in Austria. Robin was invited to join the conspiracy in return for future amnesty. It was a dangerous proposition. Provincial banditry was one thing, court intrigue another. Prince John had spies everywhere, and he was known for his vindictiveness. If the conspirators' plan failed, the pursuit would be relentless, and retributions swift.

The sound of the supper horn startled Robin from his thoughts. There was the smell of roasting venison in the air. Nothing was resolved or settled. Robin headed for camp promising himself that he would give these problems his utmost attention after tomorrow's raid.

case 21 Replacements, Ltd.: Replacing the Irreplaceable

Lew G. Brown   Kevin B. Lowe

Tony R. Wingler   Don K. Sowers

Vidya Gargeya   Kristen M. Cashman

John H. Lundin   Charles A. Kivett

All of The University of North Carolina at Greensboro

On September 5, 1997, just a little before 1:30 PM, a group of faculty members and an undergraduate research fellow from The University of North Carolina at Greensboro assembled outside the front entrance to Replacements, Ltd. The company's headquarters was located just off Interstate highways 85 and 40 on Greensboro's eastern edge. As the group waited for everyone to arrive, a steady stream of customers entered and left the company's large, first-floor showroom.

Once everyone was present, the group entered the building, and Doug Anderson, executive vice president, escorted the visitors to the second floor conference room. Waiting there was Ron Swanson, chief information officer; Scott Fleming, vice president of operations; and Kelly Smith, chief financial officer (see Exhibit 1 for Organizational Chart).

A few minutes later, Bob Page, the company's president, entered the conference room. He was casually dressed, as were all the other officers, wearing a dark blue knit shirt that bore the Replacements, Ltd., logo. Following closely behind Bob were his two miniature black and tan dachshunds, Trudy and Toby. Bob always had the two dogs with him at work, and they had free run of the executive office area. It was not unusual for them to enter and leave meetings, perhaps carrying chew-toys with them.

After introductions, Bob Page began. "I'm not comfortable making speeches, but I do like to talk about the company's history. So, I thought I would just do that as a way of helping you begin gathering information for your case."

> I was born on a small tobacco farm in Rockingham County, near the city of Reidsville. I have two brothers and a sister. We grew up working on the farm. When the time came, I went to North Carolina State University. After two years, I decided to transfer to UNC

exhibit 1 Replacements, Ltd., Organizational Chart

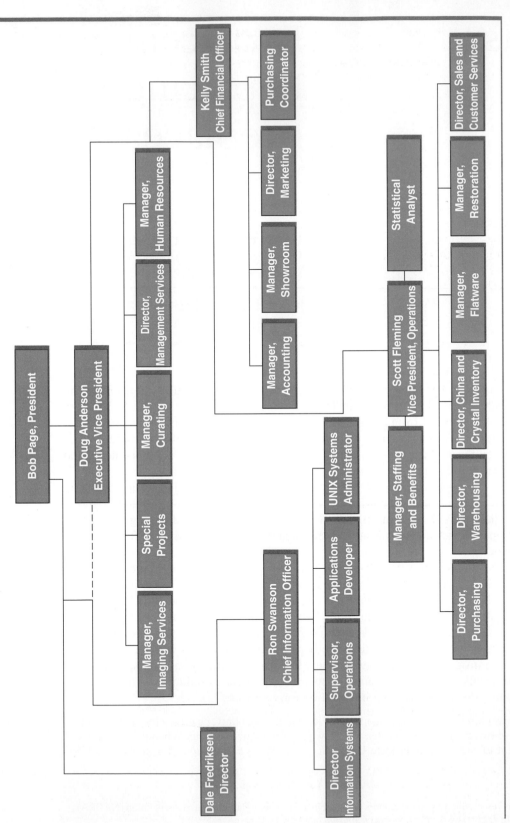

Source: Replacements, Ltd.

Chapel Hill, where I majored in accounting. After graduation, the Army drafted me. I got out in 1970, went to work for an accounting firm, and later earned my CPA.

After about four years, for some reason, I took a job as an auditor with the state of North Carolina. From the first day, I hated the job. I just didn't like politics and all the rules and regulations. I was very unhappy.

About this time, I guess to get away from my unhappiness at work, I started going to flea markets, buying and selling things on consignment. It was not unusual for me to leave work on a Friday afternoon and drive all night in order to be at a flea market, say, in Nashville, Tennessee, the next morning.

People learned about my hobby and began to ask me to keep an eye out for various things, especially china patterns. Perhaps they had broken a piece of their china and found that the manufacturer no longer made that pattern. Or, perhaps they had never had a full set and now wanted to complete it. When I got a request, I'd make a note on a 3-by-5 index card and put it in an old recipe box. When I was at a flea market and found a china pattern that someone needed, I'd buy it. When I got home, I'd drop them a line or give them a call.

I was still working for the state at this time. Word of my hobby spread, and I found myself getting more and more requests. I'd come home at night and find lots of mail and phone messages. I set up a card table in my bedroom to keep up with the paperwork. I packed orders for mailing on my kitchen floor.

By 1981, I was working late almost every night. I'd sold about $53,000 worth of china, etc., the previous year. I finally got up the nerve to quit my job with the state in March and to try to make a go of my hobby. My friends thought I was crazy to leave a good job with the state in order to sell used "dishes." But I wanted to do something enjoyable and fun. I thought I'd be better off in the long run.

The first thing I needed was more space, because I'd filled up my apartment. I rented about 500–600 square feet in a building in Greensboro. I needed some way to haul all the stuff I bought around, so I bought a used van for $3,000. Funny, I had to put up my old Toyota as collateral to buy the van. I hired a part-time college student to pack orders for me, and I did the rest. I still went on buying trips every weekend.

By September that year, 1981, I had incorporated the business as "Replacements" and bought a 2,000-square-foot building that the owner financed for me. I had several part-time employees by then, and it didn't take long to run out of space. So I started looking for another location. Zoning regulations were a real problem.

I found a place with 4,000 square feet. We filled it up in a year. This was sometime in 1982. I got two more adjoining lots, and we built a 15,000-square-foot building.

Sometime around 1986, we moved again. This time to a place with 40,000 square feet, and the company was up to 50 employees. That same year, I was nearly killed in a car wreck while on one of my trips and had to spend nearly five months in a wheelchair.

By 1989, I realized we needed more space. This time I was going to look around to find a piece of land that was big enough so that we wouldn't have to move again. Moving is such a nightmare. A friend happened to see this 87-acre parcel where we are now. I bought it, and we built 105,000 square feet. It took two teams four months to move the inventory. It was 20 miles one way from the old place. Operating during that period was also a nightmare, because you were never sure where anything was. Often a piece you needed was still at the old place, and we'd have to make a special trip just to get it.

In 1994, we expanded, adding 120,000 square feet this time. As you'll see when you tour the building, we're about full again.

Today, we have about 500 employees here and about 1,500 dealers out scouring flea markets, auctions, etc., looking for stuff they can buy and then sell to Replacements so we can then sell it to our customers. We publish a quarterly index that lists 95,000 patterns and what we will pay a dealer, or an individual, for any of the pieces in those patterns. We have four million pieces in our inventory. We also buy from manufacturers when they discontinue a pattern, and we handle current lines. We also buy silverware and flatware, collectibles, and crystal. We now get about 26,000 calls in an average week. Our sales this

exhibit 2   Replacements, Ltd., Total Sales vs. Employees

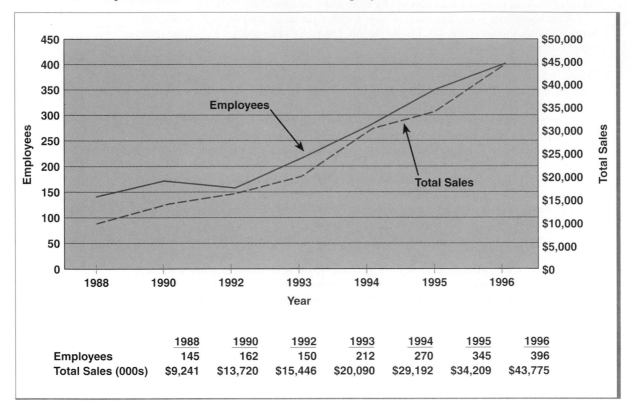

	1988	1990	1992	1993	1994	1995	1996
Employees	145	162	150	212	270	345	396
Total Sales (000s)	$9,241	$13,720	$15,446	$20,090	$29,192	$34,209	$43,775

year will be about $60 million. (See Exhibit 2.) Not bad for selling used "dishes." And we're the largest company like this in the world. Our nearest competitor has less than $3 million sales and 10 employees. We really don't have any competition.

And, I'm happy. I'm the sole owner of this business, yet I still live in the same 1,300-square-foot house I have lived in since I bought it for $55,000 fourteen years ago. I drive a seven-year-old Ford Explorer. I really enjoy helping folks find and replace that piece that broke. China, crystal, and all that is so personal. We have people come in here and bring their entire set of china and crystal. They may be going into a retirement home and don't have room for it and don't have family to give it to. They ask us to find one buyer so the set won't be broken up. And we do. I take customer calls every day. This business is all about helping people out and making them happy.

I know you folks are from the business school. We're glad you're here. We're always looking for new ideas. But, you need to understand, we don't have a business plan. We don't have a strategy. We don't have a marketing plan. We don't have budgets. We don't have much of that stuff you teach, but we've been pretty successful.

MARKETING

The Tabletop Market

Bob Page had obviously identified a large, untapped market, but no one knew just how large the market for used china, crystal, and flatware was. There were no market studies or market research reports on the market.

However, information was available on the retail "tabletop" market. *HFN* Magazine presented an analysis of the industry in its September 1997 issue. Exhibit 3 presents summary statistics from that report and information on the major manufacturers in the tabletop market. The tabletop market included dinnerware, glassware and crystal, and flatware. The dinnerware market included housewares sold by mass merchandisers (so-called "everyday" or casual dinnerware), upstairs casual (casual or everyday dinnerware with somewhat higher prices than mass market prices), and upstairs formal (including formal china). The term *upstairs* implies a higher priced, more formal item. Crystal included stemware—crystal pieces that included a base and a stem supporting the portion that held the beverage, such as a wine glass. Flatware included sterling silver, silverplate (utensils that were plated with silver), and stainless steel pieces.

The *HFN* article noted several industry trends:

● Lifestyle stores and home superstores like Linens and Things and Bed, Bath, and Beyond were responsible for much of the industry's growth.

● A move to "open stock" selling, that is, allowing customers to buy individual items rather than requiring that they buy full place settings or sets of items. Some brides, for example, were requesting just dinner plates. Some consumers were mixing formal and casual tableware.

● A continued movement from formal to casual, as evidenced by the move to more casual dress in business settings. Color had become more important in casual china.

● Baby boomers were saving for retirement and at the same time, to deal with stressful lifestyles, were eating out more often and spending more on leisure.

● In upstairs tabletop, upstairs casual dinnerware and crystal stemware were doing well, but analysts did not regard formal china as a growth opportunity. Noritake, the second largest formal china manufacturer, had targeted the self-purchase customer and the "encore" bride. Although manufacturers of formal tableware were responding to the casual trend, they were not neglecting the formal.

Marketing at Replacements

"As Bob Page often says, 'We'll try anything—once,'" Kelly Smith observed as he discussed Replacements' marketing strategy. Kelly served as the company's chief financial officer and also headed its marketing efforts. Kelly joined Replacements in 1995 after graduating from Wake Forest University with a degree in accounting, getting his CPA, and working with Arthur Andersen, Kayser Roth (a textile firm), and NationsBank.

> For example, in June 1994, the company decided to try advertising in *Parade Magazine,* the magazine that's inserted in Sunday newspapers all across the country. The people at *Parade* had been trying to get us to advertise. So, we advertised only in the west-coast edition, thinking there'd be consumers, especially in California, who'd be interested in our service; and advertising in one region would give us a chance to see how *Parade* worked. It so happened that the first ad followed a major California earthquake by only a couple of months. Apparently there were a lot of people who'd lost some or all of their china and crystal in the quake. The Monday morning following the Sunday ad, our telephones rang off the hook. We had over 3,000 phone calls that day, which at that time was really a huge volume of calls for one day. It was by far our record day. And for a long time that record stood.
>
> Just to give you an idea of how we have grown, yesterday we had—let me look at my daily call record a second—yes, we had 4,800 calls yesterday. That's a pretty normal day now.

exhibit 3   The Tabletop Industry, 1996

A. Total Market:

Category	Retail Dollar Volume	Percent of Total
Dinnerware	$1.659 billion	40.3%
Glassware and Crystal	1.706 billion	41.4%
Flatware	753 billion	18.3%
Total Market	$4.118 billion	100% +3.3% from 1995

B. Dinnerware Analysis:

Category	Retail Dollar Volume	Percent of Total
Housewares, Mass Market	$934.2 million	56.3%
Upstairs Formal	431.2 million	26.0% −2% from 1995
Upstairs Casual	293.6 million	17.7%
Total Dinnerware	$1.659 million	100% +2% from 1995

C. Crystal Analysis:

Category	Retail Dollar Volume	Percent of Total
Crystal Giftware	$455.7 million	68.1%
Crystal Stemware	175.3 million	26.2% +1.92% from 1995
Crystal Barware	38.1 million	5.7%
Total Crystal	$669.1 million	100% +5% from 1995

D. Flatware Analysis:

Category	Retail Dollar Volume	Percent of Total
Stainless Steel	$535.9 million	72%
Sterling Silver	152.0 million	20% No Change from 1995
Silverplate	65.0 million	8%
Total Flatware	$752.9 million	100% +5% from 1995

Major Manufacturers of Upstairs Tableware

1. **Lenox, Inc.** Estimated 1996 sales: $370 million. Parent: Brown-Forman, Corp. Subsidiaries: Dansk International Designs, Ltd.; Gorham, Inc.; Kirk Stieff Company.
2. **Mikasa, Inc.** Estimated 1996 sales: $372.3 million. Public company with headquarters in London.
3. **Noritake Company, Inc.** Estimated 1996 sales: $51 million. Parent: Noritake Company, Ltd. Headquarters in London.
4. **Royal China and Porcelain Companies, Inc.** Estimated 1993 sales: $30 million. Parent: Royal Worcester Spode, Ltd.; Gorham, Inc. Headquarters in London.
5. **Royal Doulton USA, Inc.** Estimated 1992 sales: $8.4 million. Parent: Pearson, Inc. Headquarters in London.
6. **Waterford Wedgwood PLC., Inc.** Estimated 1996 sales: $636.7 million. [Wedgwood Group (china) = $378 million, Waterford Crystal = $259 million.]
7. **Oneida Silversmiths Division.** Estimated 1996 sales: $270 million. Parent: Oneida Ltd. (Oneida Ltd. 1997 sales = $376.9 million, 54% of sales from consumer tableware.)
8. **Reed and Barton Corporation.** Estimated 1995 sales: $43 million. Private company with headquarters in London.
9. **Syratech Corporation.** Estimated 1996 sales: $270.9 million. Silver, silverplated, and sterling brands marketed under Wallace, International Silver, and Westmoreland brand names. Wallace Silversmiths, Inc., 1996 sales estimated at $75 million. Corporate revenues include sale of casual furniture.
10. **Durand International.** Estimated 1994 sales: $24 million. Manufactures lead crystal. Private subsidiary with headquarters in London.

Source: HFN magazine, September 1997, pp. 5–29.

I know you're interested in what I think the big issues are from a marketing perspective. Well, the first issue is how we can continue to find the right media to generate new leads, new customers. Historically, we've been space-ad driven. We've not done a lot of prospecting, direct mailing, buying lists, like a lot of direct marketing companies do. What little we've done we've found to be unsuccessful if we didn't have the names of patterns associated with customer names; that is, we know what particular patterns each customer on the list owns. We've talked to bridal stores to try to get the list of clients who bought a certain pattern when we learn that a manufacturer has discontinued that particular pattern, but we really haven't had much luck with that. The big challenge is finding the right media to help us sustain our growth rate. We know it's out there; it's just a question of finding it.

A second problem we face is having a more defined customer contact strategy. Once we get a name on file, we tend to send them quotes several times a year. We have seasonal sales and sales on select patterns. We've some general controls on this; but in theory, we could send out lots of quotes for just a little bit of inventory. We don't do any analysis of our customers' buying histories, and we rarely purge our database. We need to come up with a strategy to generate sales without spewing quotes out of our building. But, we know how important quoting is. In July 1995, we stopped quoting for a month while we converted to a new computer system; and sales plummeted. We all became sensitized to how important the quoting process is to maintaining sales growth. But I was doing some estimating just last week. If you're on file with one pattern, you'll probably get four to six mailings a year from us. If you, however, had eight patterns, you might get 48 mailings a year—and they'd all come in the same old, nice-looking envelope. So we've got to figure out what we call "smart quoting."

Target Market

Our target market is anyone who has china, crystal, sterling, or flatware patterns where they need to replace a broken or missing piece or just want to complete their set but the pattern is no longer produced. We also offer collectible items, like Hummel figurines, for people who like to collect those kinds of things.

We had a study several years ago. We determined that our typical customer was between 45 and 75 years old and was generally an affluent female. I wish I could find that study, but I can't seem to put my hands on it.

Product

I guess the first question a lot of people have is how do we get all the things we have to sell. Well, I said this is an unusual business. Unlike other retailers, we can't call up the manufacturer and say, "Send us 100 suits in assorted sizes."

The primary source of our product is the 1,500 or so active independent, individual suppliers who buy china, etc., anywhere they can find it. It might be at a flea market, an estate auction, or an antique store. The supplier can look up a particular pattern and piece in that pattern in our index to see what we'll pay for it (see Exhibit 4). Then the supplier can buy the piece for something less than what we will pay. The supplier makes money on the spread, just as we do when we sell the piece for more than we paid the supplier.

That supplier then boxes up any pieces he/she may have and sends them to us. Each morning we'll get from 300 to 500 boxes delivered to us in Greensboro—about 250,000 pieces a month. It's like Christmas every day. We never know what's coming until we open the boxes.

Once we open the box, we inspect the contents and compare them to the paperwork the supplier has completed and included with the shipment. That paperwork includes the supplier's statement as to what he/she expects us to pay. We grade the merchandise, enter it in the computer, and send it to inventory. The paperwork then goes to accounting so that we can pay the supplier. We pay the suppliers within 14 days, and sometimes sooner. Some of the suppliers just do this as a hobby. For others, it's their job. Last year we paid 61 different

exhibit 4 Sample Line from Page in Replacements' Supplier Index*

China Pattern: Noritake	N	PLA	CS	DP	LP	SP	BB	CR
Lilac Time	2483	13.5	1	11	9	1	.50	3
		SU	OV	RV	PL1	PL2	PL3	FR
Lilac Time (cont.)		4	2	21	24	1	41	6
		CER	SO	CSS	GR	BD	S/P	TP
Lilac Time (cont.)		7	10	17	27	23	15	45
		CP	CV	DE	CH	REL	MUG	BOU
Lilac Time (cont.)		45	49	9	33	10	10	12

Code Key

Code	Description	Code	Description
PLA	Place setting, consisting of:	CER	Cereal bowl (rim or coupe)
CS	Cup and saucer	SO	Soup bowl (rim or coupe, 7″ to 9″)
DP	Dinner plate (10″ to 10¾″)	CSS	Cream soup and saucer
SP	Salad plate (round, 8″ to 8¾″)	GR	Gravy boat with stand (1 or 2 pieces)
BB	Bread and butter (6″ to 7¾″)	BD	Butter dish with lid
LP	Luncheon plate (round, 9″ to 9½″)	S/P	Salt and pepper set
CR	Creamer	TP	Tea pot with lid (short and stout)
SU	Sugar bowl with lid	CP	Coffee pot with lid (tall and thin)
OV	Oval vegetable bowl (9″ to 11″)	CV	Covered vegetable (oval or round)
RV	Round vegetable bowl (8″ to 11″)	DE	Demitasse cup and saucer
PL1	Platter One (10″ to 13⅞″))	CH	Chop plate (round platter, 12″ to 14″)
PL2	Platter Two (14″ to 15⅞″))	REL	Relish (7″ to 10″)
PL3	Platter Three (16″ to 18″)	MUG	Mug
FR	Fruit/Dessert bowl (4″ to 5¾″)	BOU	Bouillon soup and saucer

*Figures listed under the codes for type of piece are in dollars. For example, 13.5 listed for a place setting of Noritake Lilac Time means that Replacements will pay $13.50 for a four-piece place setting consisting of a cup and saucer, dinner plate, salad plate, and bread and butter plate.

suppliers more than $20,000 each, with a few earning in the six-figure range. We want being a supplier to be a reliable and stable source of income.

One problem is that, as in any business, about 20 percent of the suppliers produce about 80 percent of the product. We have a lot of inactive suppliers. We had about 3,000 suppliers two years ago. All it cost was $15 a year to be a supplier and get our index, which we publish four times a year. But it cost us $25 a year just to publish the indexes for that supplier. The index contains general information for our suppliers and lists what we will pay for every piece of every china, crystal and glassware, flatware, and collectible item. The index is about two inches thick.

So, in January 1996, we started the STAR supplier program. We raised the annual membership fee to $100. For this, the member got the indexes free, access to a special 800 number, 24-hour turnaround on quotes, electronic payment to the supplier's bank account, and a one-percent rebate on all sales to us once the supplier passed $5,000 in a year. The one percent rebate applied to all $5,000 plus the amount above that level. That program helped a little, but we still had too many people who didn't sell anything to us.

So we've just revised the program again. Now, you have to sell us at least $2,000 in the prior year in order to be a STAR supplier. If you sold less than $500, it will cost you $400 to be a member. We're probably down to about 1,500 suppliers now. They account for about 85 percent of our supply.

exhibit 5 Replacements, Ltd., Sales by Product Type

Product Type	1995	1996	1997
China	$23,280,361	$29,180,113	$34,107,173
Crystal	2,911,824	3,594,419	4,134,168
Flatware	4,986,811	6,778,454	9,097,704
Collectibles	365,474	676,207	884,495
Showroom	1,128,235	1,665,924	1,573,174
Totals	$32,672,705	$41,895,117	$49,796,714

Source: Replacements, Ltd.

About 8 to 10 percent of our supply comes from manufacturers. When a manufacturer decides to discontinue a pattern, we will buy its inventory of that pattern. The manufacturers decided about five years ago that it was cheaper to let us handle the small orders for remnants. They'll also often sell active patterns to us as they would to any other dealer with us getting a standard discount from their recommended retail price. We have active accounts with most manufacturers now. In fact, we are Noritake's biggest customer.

The final 5 to 7 percent of our supply comes from individuals. (Exhibit 5 summarizes sales by product type.) People may just walk into our showroom and sell to us. Sometimes they have inherited the items and don't want them or would rather have the money. Other times, the person is going through a divorce and wants to sell the items.

We estimate that we have about 95,000 patterns and over four million pieces of inventory. We also offer collectibles like rare figures, collectible plates, past Christmas ornaments, etc. For all our products, we offer a 30-day, money-back, satisfaction guarantee.

We also have a couple of other "products." We offer a free-pattern identification service. We have several curators who work with customers to identify patterns. Often a person doesn't know the manufacturer's or the pattern's name. They can send us a picture, tracing, or an actual piece; and our staff will conduct the research to identify the pattern and manufacturer. We also offer a flatware restoration and cleaning service and have considered offering a china repair service. We repair china now for resale, but we have never offered that service to our customers.

Price

Bob understands supply and demand so well. From the very beginning he was developing his buying-pricing model so we can buy the inventory we need, not buy the inventory we don't need, and move the inventory that we have.

Bob uses a pricing matrix that has customer groups down one axis, that is, the number of customers we have for a pattern. For example, do we have 1 to 10 customers or 11 to 20, and so forth. The other axis is the number of pieces we have in stock. At the intersection of each row and column is the percentage of the retail price that we're willing to pay for an item. So if we have a lot of customers for a pattern and not much inventory, we'll pay 50 percent of retail, which is the most we'll pay for anything. At the other end of the scale, if we have lots of inventory and not many customers, we'll only pay five percent of retail. Bob set up these parameters years ago. We continue to find ways to add layers of screening to make pricing more advantageous for us. We have minimum/maximum/absolute pricing we set for particular patterns that can override the matrix based on all sorts of factors. There may be a particular pattern that we really want, and we'll pay a certain price for items in that pattern regardless of what the matrix might say.

Pricing is a continuous process. Literally every day, Bob's setting up special pricing scales for certain patterns or groups of patterns. By changing the retail prices, we automatically change the buying prices by action of the matrix. So, if we need more dinner plates in a pattern, we can raise the retail price to reflect demand. This increases the buying price. At some price point, our buyers will seek out that pattern; or if they or others are holding that pattern, at some price they'll be willing to sell. We started getting away from the standardized pricing scales to more customized pricing about 1½ to 2 years ago. This is Bob's biggest time consumer and his most important job.

Although there'll always need to be judgment in this, we need to systematize our pricing in order to reduce the amount of fine tuning or tweaking we do now.

Place

In addition to selling directly to our customers by mail, we also operate a showroom here so customers can stop by and make purchases. Bob started a showroom several years ago. It was probably only about 200 square feet—pretty much of an afterthought. But more and more people kept stopping by, so the showroom had to grow. Now it takes 12,000 square feet, and we have about 100,000 people per month visiting it. We also offer guided tours every half hour from 8:30 AM to 8:00 PM, seven days a week, year round. Part of our showroom is our museum, which has over 2,000 unique pieces of china, crystal, and silver on display.

Promotion

I've asked Mark Klein to join us. Mark serves as our director of marketing. He's responsible for all our communications work. He directs a graphic artist, a media placement coordinator, a manufacturer's liaison, and a senior merchandising analyst who takes care of developing and placing all our ads. He also supervises our mailing operation, which involves a manager and seven employees. Before joining us last September, Mark worked 10 years with Hecht's Department Stores as a buyer of housewares, china, and furniture, and then served as a field sales representative for a furniture company for six years. He has a degree in marketing and management from Virginia Tech.

Mark, perhaps you could discuss our advertising program.

Advertising

Okay, Kelly. Our advertising's obviously very important in generating leads. We track our advertising very carefully so we can determine which are the best magazines to use for advertising.

I guess it'd be good to start by summarizing our print advertising program. I've prepared for you this table, which summarizes our print advertising program for September 1996 through August 1997 (see Exhibit 6). During this period, we advertised in 84 magazines. This table summarizes the top 14 magazines in terms of the sales dollars the advertising generated. It shows basic information on the magazine and our ad, the code our telemarketers use when they record that magazine as the source of a new customer, the "return on investment" from the ad, the cost of the ad, and the number of new sales and clients it generated in the period. We calculate the ROI measure by taking 50 percent of the total sales amount (which assumes an average 50 percent gross margin on sales) and dividing that by the cost of the ad. This figure then gives us the gross margin dollars generated for each dollar of ad cost. If this number drops below 1.0, then we drop that magazine unless there's some other factor working.

We also track sales for magazines in which we didn't advertise during the past 12 months. You see, once a person becomes a client and we include the client in our database, we designate the source of that client. Our operators ask the clients on their first call how they heard about Replacements. If a client says he/she saw our ad in the *New York Times Magazine,* then we put that code in the client's file. From then one, we credit all purchases

exhibit 6　　Advertising Analysis for Publications Where Ads Were Placed in 9/96–8/97 Period

Publication*	Code	ROI	Ad Cost	Total Sales	New Clients
Better Homes & Gardens Ad-Monthly　Pub-Monthly 1½″ Listing　⅓ pg in 3/96	GB	$ 7.76	$ 62,295	$ 966,862	8,801
Colonial Homes Ad-Bimonthly　Pub-Monthly ½ Pg DW	CH	$ 13.75	$ 8,444	$ 232,280	1,942
Country Living Ad-Monthly　Pub-Bimonthly ⅓ Pg Masthead out May 96, 16M Classified Word Ad	CL	$ 35.40	$ 7,166	$ 507,273	4,208
Good Housekeeping Ad-Monthly　Pub-Monthly 1″ Listing Remnant 7/96, 25M	GH	$ 7.91	$ 27,437	$ 433,917	3,735
Gourmet Ad-Monthly　Pub-Monthly STF Calico blue starting in Dec 96 ½ Page, BW	GT	$ 6.60	$ 23,099	$ 305,065	2,002
House Beautiful Ad-Monthly　Pub-Monthly ½ Page 4-C	HB	$ 8.18	$ 41,889	$ 685,364	4,526
Martha Stewart Living Ad-Monthly　Pub-Monthly Vil Holly in Dec 96 issue ½ Page 4/C, 10x/yr.	MS	$ 6.27	$ 30,490	$ 382,570	5,403
New Yorker Ad-Weekly　Pub-Weekly 1½″ weekly 1/6 thru 7/7/97	YO	$ 3.30	$ 54,137	$ 357,708	1,857
Smithsonian Ad-Monthly　Pub-Monthly 2″ Listing/makegood 3/97	SM	$ 5.71	$ 23,709	$ 270,819	1,605
Southern Living Ad-Monthly　Pub-Monthly 39 words, Prepaid Oct-Dec 97 Prepay 3 mos. 10% discount	SL	$106.87	$ 9,567	$ 2,044,962	12,122
Sunset Ad-Monthly　Pub-Monthly 4-C Test ad Oct, Nov, Dec 96, JB BW ¹⁄₁₂ pg ¹⁄₁₂ Page, 2/97 Coach Scenes	TU	$ 10.77	$ 18,117	$ 390,238	2,668
Victoria Ad-Monthly　Pub-Monthly ½ 4C in 3/96, 12M	VI	$ 6.94	$ 24,345	$ 337,898	5,286
Yankee Ad-Monthly Pub-Monthly	YA	$ 5.27	$ 27,417	$ 289,030	2,320
SUBTOTAL—All but *Parade*		$ 8.39	$ 552,346	$ 9,265,633	75,286
Parade Ad-Monthly Pub-Monthly	—	$ 2.58	$1,049,263	$ 6,246,195	89,572
TOTAL—All publications		$ 4.84	$1,601,609	$15,511,828	164,858

*Specific publications listed are the top 14 in terms of total sales. Subtotal and total figures include *all* publications.
Source: Replacements, Ltd.

exhibit 7   Source of Clients—Non-Publications 9/96–8/97

Client Source	Code	Total Sales
Antique Clubs	LZ	$ 3,380
Antique Shop	AS	462,533
C. C. M. List	GP	253,791
C. C. Lists	IQ	290,353
Department Store Referral	DQ	2,305,730
Discovery Channel—*Start to Finish*	DC	214,899
Friend or Relative Referral	FR	11,950,129
Jewelry Store—Referral	JS	613,540
Magazine Article	MG	1,456,009
Manufacturer	MF	1,880,817
M. C. C. List	MK	367,566
9/96 List	QS	537,744
NO CODE—Mail In's Letter	NC	2,452,630
Old Code—Absolute Codes	OC	2,287,369
Competition Referral	OS	841,373
Previous Customer—dropped off & came back	PC	985,375
Signs—Front of Building & Billboard	SI	1,889,706
W. D. C. List	WA	$ 1,288,942

Source: Replacements, Ltd.

that client may make to that magazine. Sometimes we may have discontinued our ads in that magazine, but we still track our sales for those customers by that magazine.

Many of these magazines also have sections where they list the advertisers in that edition and allow readers to circle a number on a card to request information from that advertiser. This information comes to us from the magazines, and we have to enter the information manually and then mail the person a Replacements' brochure. We track these inquiries and sales from the inquiries also.

"Although it's not advertising, Mark, this might be a good time to mention how we track our other client sources," Kelly interjected.

Good point. I also prepared a list of our top 16 client sources from other than publications. I took these from an overall list of about 150 such sources (see Exhibit 7). For example, if a customer calls in and says he/she was referred to us by an antique store, we would code that customer as "AS." The exhibit shows that in the past 12 months we had over $462,000 in sales to such customers. This table also shows the sales we credit to our lists, that is, lists of customers we've purchased over the years. You'll see on the exhibit a listing for the "C. C. M. List" or the "W. D. C. List." You'll notice also the listing for "Department Store Referral." Many people will go to a department store if they break a piece of china or need additional pieces. If the store doesn't carry that pattern or if it's discontinued, often the store personnel will refer the customer to us. The Discovery Channel has a show called *Start to Finish* that runs about a five-minute segment on Replacements. It's run the segment about 12–15 times over the past two years. Every time it runs, we get a burst of telephone calls. In fact, you can "see" the calls move across the country as the show airs in different time zones.

The largest total sales dollar item is the "friend or relative" entry. You can see the importance of word of mouth; but, frankly, we wonder if this entry isn't just a catch-all when our operators are busy. For example, when someone calls and indicates that she saw our ad in *American Country Collectibles* magazine, the operator may not know the code for that magazine. If not, he/she must go to another screen and scroll through a list to find the code. This takes time, and our operators are very busy. We think that in such a case it is easy just to enter the code for friend or relative (FR) and save the time and trouble of looking.

"That's right," Kelly noted. "Having our operators get accurate information is one of our biggest concerns. If they only realized how critical this information is to all our tracking."

You'll also notice (in Exhibit 7) the listings for "No Code" and "Old Code." These categories represent customers who write a letter to place an order and technically there's no other source or the customer had an obsolete (old) code. "Competition referral" represents customers who were referred to us by a competitor who could not meet their needs. "Previous customer" represents customers who at some time asked us to take their names off our lists so they wouldn't get our mailings but who subsequently called to place an order. And "Signs" represents customers who stop in our showroom because they saw one of our billboards or the signs in front of the building as they drove by.

One of the items on that exhibit listed "department store referrals." We have what we call our "Partners in Business" program. For stores that refer customers to us as a policy, we pay that store a 5 percent referral rebate based on the sales to clients it refers. We pay these rebates quarterly as long as the rebate is greater than $25. As you can imagine, however, this is another coding problem for our operators because we have about 130 of these partners.

To summarize all this, I also have a table that shows the number of phone and mail inquiries, the number of inquiries from our customer lists, the number of sales transactions from those inquiries, and the conversion ratio (see Exhibit 8). This ratio is the total number of inquiries divided by the number of sales transactions. The numbers on this exhibit represent the monthly averages for each of the last six years. The category "Customer List Inquiries" is not broken down into mail or phone, but as you can see, the great majority of our inquiries are by phone. The monthly average for customer list inquiries has grown significantly in the last two years due to several acquisitions of customer lists. When we acquire a list we also get information on the patterns each customer on the list has. Then we send each customer a quote that lists their patterns and the items we have in those patterns and lets them know that Replacements will be their new source. These mailings generate many inquiries.

When we speak of acquisitions here, we mean that we have acquired the company's mailing list and in some cases its inventory if the company is going out of business. Because of the importance of acquisitions, I also prepared this table that lists our acquisitions by year along with other information about the purchase (see Exhibit 9).

I think Kelly mentioned earlier that we are space-ad driven. We've tried a little television and radio advertising, but they just don't seem to work very well for us. We've too much information we need to communicate, and we can't seem to do it effectively in 30 seconds or a minute. Plus, we find that people need to see sample items in the ad.

For example, here's a sample ad from *Parade* (see Exhibit 10). You'll notice the line of plates across the bottom. One might assume that we just pick some sample plates for the ad, but we select each individual plate/pattern very carefully based on our inventory and the number of customers who might want that pattern. We'll have people call in who'll say that they recognize their pattern as being the fifth plate from the left in the ad. So our operators must have copies of the ads with pattern names noted so they can help the customers.

Our staff does all of the creative work in developing our ads. Until 1995, we used outside companies to do this. We think we can do it just as well; and by placing the ads ourselves, we save the 15 percent fee we'd have paid an advertising agency to do that.

Despite our focus on print ads, we're trying to get a TV ad with VISA, the credit card folks. You may remember that VISA has these ads in which it features unique or unusual businesses and notes that the establishments don't take American Express. We think we fit

exhibit 8 Average Monthly Inquiries, 1992–97 Fiscal Years

	Phone Inquiries		Mail Inquiries		Subtotal Inquiries w/o Customer List	Customer List Inquiries		Total Inquiries	New Leads Sales Transactions	Conversion Ratio
	#	% of Total	#	% of Total		#	% of Total			
1992 Monthly Average	3,815	41%	5,546	59%	9,361	—	—	9,361	4,537	2.06
1993 Monthly Average	3,968	17%	6,845	30%	10,813	11,900	52%	22,713	6,602	3.44
1994 Monthly Average	13,522	80%	3,403	20%	16,295	21	0%	16,946	8,947	1.89
1995 Monthly Average	21,249	66%	4,639	14%	25,889	6,470	20%	32,359	11,164	2.90
1996 Monthly Average	32,300	57%	4,655	8%	36,955	19,845	35%	56,800	13,234	4.29
1997 Monthly Average	29,734	46%	2,976	5%	32,710	31,755	49%	64,465	15,794	4.08

Source: Replacements Ltd.

exhibit 9   Replacements' Assets Acquisitions

Acquisition	Cost	What Purchased	Total Sales to 8/97	Number of Customers	Sales per Customer
Pre-1992					
C. H.	$ 4,500	List & Inventory	$ 128,919	2,727	$ 47.28
F. D.	4,000	List & Inventory	20,073	464	43.26
II.	Free	List	61,099	5,338	11.45
M. Z.	Unk.	List & Inventory	46,979	598	78.56
V. H.	325,000	List & Inventory	651,583	15	43,439
1993					
Mgs.	$ 25,000	List & Inventory	$ 165,371	3,562	$ 46.43
W. D. C.	14,300	List	8,904,106	123,741	71.96
C.A.	10,000	List & Inventory	124,138	3,599	34.49
1994					
Ab.	$ 125,000	List & Inventory	$ 272,331	6,859	$ 39.70
Gu.	4,500	List	44,583	2,787	16.00
C. T.	65,000	List & Inventory	419,279	11,326	37.02
1995					
C. C.	$ 10,000	List	$ 911,620	29,261	$ 31.15
A. S. G.	5,000	List	196,020	3,683	53.22
C. C. M.	240,000	List & Inventory	755,368	39,322	19.21
1996					
A. W.	$ 25,000	List & Inventory	$ 45,796	1,589	$ 28.82
He.	1,750	List	3,442	928	3.71
C. S.	683	List	53,497	2,746	19.48
C. C. X.	5,033	List & 800#	94,207	5,570	16.91
F. G.	165	List	765	659	1.16
S. H. List	11,000	List	585,178	114,348	5.12
1997					
M. C. C.	$ 200,000	List & Inventory	$ 395,539	34,548	$ 11.45
P.S.	9,000	List	42,263	4,648	9.09
W. D. S.	900,000	List & Inventory	1,450,570	82,915	17.49
P. P.	60,000	List & Inventory	35,523	1,794	19.80
TOTALS	$2,044,931		$15,408,249	483,027	$ 31.90

Source: Replacements, Ltd.

VISA's criteria, and Bob has a personal goal of getting Replacements in one of those ads. We even filmed a sample ad to show VISA. We haven't had any luck yet. VISA is also developing some radio ads with the same theme, but we're not sure Replacements will work as well on radio.

We're always looking for new home-and-shelter-type publications in which to advertise. Bob encourages us to try anything. One of the greatest things about working here is that we don't have an ad budget—so if we come up with an idea we like, we just try it. Although we don't have a budget, we spend about 3 to 4 percent of revenue on advertising. We just seem to hit that range. We could certainly spend more, but we find there is a "wear-out" factor with our advertising. For example, we only advertise once a month in *Parade*. Our ad is on the page with the "Intelligence Report" feature, the second-most-read page in

exhibit 10   Sample *Parade* Ad

Source: Replacements, Ltd.

the magazine. But our space is always the same size and our ads look alike even though we change them. If we advertised every week, we'd just speed up the wear-out factor.

Personal Selling

I've mentioned our telemarketing staff several times, so perhaps I should discuss this process in more detail. We've about 70 full-time staff in this area who operate from 8 AM to 10 PM daily, year round. When we're not open, we record messages by voice mail and return the calls the next day. About 90 percent of our sales are by telephone with the remaining 10 percent occurring in our showroom. Our operators will handle about 26,000 calls a week. We have five T-1 lines into the building, each T-1 being 24 lines. Even though you have to add 24 lines at a time, we'll add a T-1 before we really need it because we want customers to be able to get in. It is rare that all of our lines are busy, but it has happened. People can also e-mail us at **ReplaceLtd@aol.com**.

The first time a customer calls our 1-800-Replace number, he/she's typically seen one of our ads and is interested in getting a free list of patterns we carry and other basic information. Our operators try to establish rapport. Our goal in that first call is to get the customer's name and address and the names of any patterns he/she owns and a particular piece request. This is critical to us knowing how to price and how to adjust our pricing matrix. As I've noted, we also record how the customer came to call us, through an ad, a referral, or however. So our goal is to get that customer on file with as much specific information as possible. Finally, our operators are supposed to conclude the call by asking if the customer has any other china, crystal, silver, flatware, glassware, everyday stoneware, etc., needs that we can help them with. This is a way to educate the customer about our other offerings. So many customers think we only carry china.

We have over 2½ million customers on file. However, one problem is that many records are so old that we are not sure if the information, such as which pieces they want, is still valid. If a customer calls in who is already on our system, the operator just punches in the customer's phone number to call up his/her information.

So, we have a standard format that our operators follow. The typical operator will take 70 to 110 calls per day. We try to hire people with telephone experience. They need the ability to sit at a desk all day and take calls. We put them through a month's training. New employees can take monitored calls in about two weeks. They have to learn the computer screens and how to work them. They'll sit and listen as an experienced person takes calls.

Because we can get bursts of calls from time to time, we've developed a system so that other staff members working in other functional areas are trained to handle phone calls and take orders. Even our managers, including Bob, do this. When someone calls, our automatic system answers before the first ring and delivers a prerecorded message. At the end of the message, the call goes to an operator, depending on which number the customer selects from the menu. The computer monitors incoming traffic, and whenever there are more than two calls in the queue, the queue beginning whenever the system answers a call, we have bells that ring in certain offices. For example, bells will ring in the accounting office, the mailroom, and other support departments. The bells also ring in several of the managers' offices like Kelly's and Bob's. A light in the telephone operators' room goes on so that an operator who's getting ready to go on a break, for example, knows to wait.

That's our standard system. We also have what we call a "Code 2." Anyone who is involved in the system can call a Code 2. They do this by announcing over the intercom that we have a Code 2.

We don't have any specific rules about when to do this. For example, we've a display on our phones that tells us how many calls are in queue and what the maximum wait time is. If I notice that there are more than three calls in the queue and wait time is 20 seconds, I'll call a Code 2. We do this over the intercom rather than with bells so that back-up staff will hear it even if they aren't at their desks.

As a result of this system, we can handle the peak-call periods. Our average wait time is *eight seconds.* If we do have calls that are blocked due to our lines being busy or customers abandon a call, we have a system that captures their phone numbers; and we'll call them the next day to see if we can help them.

We've five supervisors who monitor calls for quality-control purposes, and we produce daily reports that keep up with every detail. We know how many calls each person takes, the average talk time, and lots of other information. I noted that managers serve as Code 2 backups. Bob Page, for example, took 69 calls yesterday. That's high, but he enjoys taking the calls. It allows him, and all of us, to keep in touch with customers.

We also have a similar phone system with 20 operators in our purchasing department. These folks deal with our suppliers. We have 12 people in our customer service area, handling questions, returns, or problem orders. We're considering consolidating all three groups and using the phone system to route calls to each operator based on that operator's skills and responsibilities.

Now once a person has called, talked to an operator, and been added to the system as a new client, we'll have their patterns on file. The next day, we send that person a quote that lists his/her patterns and the prices for the pieces that we have in stock (see Exhibit 11). We send these letters first class because we found that bulk mail was too slow. We also can send just a brochure.

If the person calling wants a dinner plate in a certain pattern and we don't have that pattern in stock, we ask the customer if he/she would like to be in our "call collect first" program. That means the customer says he/she'll accept a collect call if the piece he/she is looking for comes in. We'll call them before we send out letters to other customers who're looking for that same pattern or piece. This used to be an actual collect call; but we found we were spending so much time trying to complete the collect call, so we just started paying for it ourselves. But by the customer saying he/she'll accept a collect call, we know we have a more serious customer.

When we get more pieces in on a pattern than we need to satisfy our "call collect" customers, we send out a mailing to others in the database who are looking for that pattern. These and all the other quotes we mail, with the exception of that first quote, go 3rd class bulk with about a 10-day delivery time. We have some decision rules that determine when and if we do a wider mailing.

Independent of these mailings are our "sales runs." These account for the bulk of our mailings. We group patterns into various groups to balance the size of our mailings. Based on our sales history and inventory, the computer will calculate a discount and generate sales quotes. We go through that sales cycle about five times a year with each cycle being about three weeks and each mailing ranging from 240,000 to 375,000 letters. If we still have inventory after a sales run, we may discount the item even more the next time. One to two times a year, we go through the process of quoting everybody at full price (see Exhibit 12).

exhibit 11   Sample Quote

REPLACEMENTS, LTD.
China, Crystal & Flatware • Discontinued & Active
1089 Knox Road, PO Box 26029, Greensboro, NC 27420
1-800-REPLACE (1-800-737-5223) • ReplaceLtd@aol.com

10/02/97 R01 SHEDUCR   1952

PLEASE COMPARE THIS PATTERN NUMBER AND OTHER DESCRIPTIVE INFORMATION WITH PIECES IN YOUR PATTERN. IF INFORMATION DOES NOT MATCH PLEASE ADVISE US SO WE MAY CORRECT OUR FILES.

#BWNDFCX   SHEDUCR   T010
BAHAMA SHORES DR S
SAINT PETERSBURG , FL 33705

PATTERN DUCHESS
COMPANY SHELLEY
PATTERN NUMBER 13401
DESCRIPTION RED, FLORAL BORDER
AND CENTER

THE FOLLOWING IS A LIST OF THE PIECES WE NOW HAVE AVAILABLE IN YOUR PATTERN. All pieces are subject to prior sale. For this reason, WE ENCOURAGE YOU TO ORDER BY PHONE. If ordering by mail, please fill out the quantity requested and total amount for each piece ordered in the area below, and follow the instructions found on the back of this page. Please allow 2-3 weeks for delivery.

QUANTITY AVAILABLE	PIECE DESCRIPTION	SIZE (IN INCHES)	PRICE (PER PIECE OR SET)	ENTER ORDER HERE	
				QUANTITY ORDERED	TOTAL AMOUNT
7	CUP AND SAUCER SET (FOOTED)	2 1/2	$71.95		
3	PLATE-SALAD	8 1/8	$49.95		
8	PLATE-BREAD AND BUTTER	6	$36.95		
1	CUP ONLY-(FOOTED)	2 1/2	$67.95		
7	CREAM SOUP AND SAUCER SET		$108.95		
9	CUP AND SAUCER SET-DEMI TASSE		$62.95		
1	SAUCER ONLY-DEMI TASSE		$20.95		
8	BOWL-SOUP/RIM	8 1/4	$62.95		
2	VEGETABLE-OVAL	9 1/2	$137.00		

***   SPECIAL DISCOUNTED PIECES   ***
*** Pieces below are discounted due to slight imperfections - discounts are ***
*** based on the condition of each piece and are taken off of our full ***
*** retail price. They are noted by the following symbols: #=25% discount; ***
*** *=50% discount; &=75% discount. These pieces have our full guarantee to ***
*** have NO cracks or chips and can be returned within 30 days of receipt. ***

2	CUP AND SAUCER SET (FOOTED)	#2 1/2	$35.98		
6	PLATE-SALAD	#8 1/8	$24.98		
5	PLATE-BREAD AND BUTTER	#6	$18.48		
1	PLATTER-OVAL SERVING	#16 1/2	$147.50		

*** Looking for pieces not shown above? ***
*** Ask about our Can Not Find Program ***

IF YOU ARE RECEIVING MAILINGS PERTAINING TO PATTERN(S) THAT ARE NO LONGER OF INTEREST TO YOU, OR IF YOU ARE RECEIVING INFORMATION ON INCORRECT PATTERNS, PLEASE NOTIFY US.

SEE REVERSE SIDE FOR TERMS AND CONDITIONS

PLEASE PROVIDE SHIPPING ADDRESS IF DIFFERENT FROM ABOVE

Name

Street Address
(No PO Box)

City   State   Zip

PAYMENT METHOD ☐ PERSONAL CHECK (make check payable to Replacements, Ltd.)
☐ CREDIT CARD (Check One) ☐ MASTERCARD ☐ VISA ☐ DISCOVER

Account #   Exp. Date ___/___
                     Month Year

Cardholder's Signature

SO WE MAY SERVE YOU BETTER, PLEASE PROVIDE THE FOLLOWING

Day Phone ( )
FAX ( )

SHIPPING, HANDLING & INSURANCE

CONTINENTAL USA (PER TOTAL ORDERED):
$1 - $50 $7.50 $200.01 - $300 $16.00
$50.01 - $100 $9.50 $300.01 - $400 $18.00
$100.01 - $200 $13.00   over $400 $24.00
CANADA and PARCEL POST orders: double above rates. International shipping rates quoted upon request. Duty extra.

SUBTOTAL	
NC RESIDENTS PLEASE ADD 6% SALES TAX	
SHIPPING, HANDLING & INSURANCE	
TOTAL	

exhibit 12   1997 Sales Cycle 4—Sales Run Work Process Schedule

Group	Group's Previous Sale Ends	Sale Dates	Begin Process	Greenbar to Bob	Greenbar from Bob	Start Printing	Finish Printing	Finish Mailing	Number of Customers
11&13	6/18/97	7/16–8/7	6/24	6/25	6/27	6/30	7/6	7/7	271,568
15&2	6/25/97	7/23–8/14	6/26	6/27	6/30	7/7	7/12	7/13	239,821
1&3	7/2/97	7/30–8/20	6/27	6/30	7/1	7/13	7/19	7/21	261,169
4&5	7/9/97	8/6–8/27	7/1	7/2	7/3	7/20	7/26	7/28	313,466
6&7	7/16/97	8/13–9/3	7/21	7/22	7/24	7/27	8/2	8/4	314,709
8&9	7/23/97	8/20–9/10	7/28	7/29	8/1	8/3	8/9	8/11	317,805
10&11	7/30/97	8/27–9/17	8/4	8/5	8/7	8/10	8/16	8/18	360,137
16	8/6/97	9/3–9/24	8/11	8/12	8/14	8/17	8/23	8/25	371,760
17&14	8/13/97	9/10–10/1	8/18	8/19	8/21	8/24	8/31	9/1	375,468

Group II	Hutchenreuter Crystal—Kaysons Lenox Crystal
Group 13	Ken Kraft China—Mauser Mfg. Co. Silver (omit Mikasa & Metlox China) International Silver (Lufberry—Zephyr)
Group 15	Moncrief—Oscar de la Renta Silver
Group 2	Royal Dalton Red Wing China—Royal Saxony Gorham Silver (252H—Imperial Chrysanthemum)
Group 1	Old Abbey—Rewcrest (omit Royal Doulton) Oneida (Modjeska)—Oneida (Young Love) Rosenthal
Group 3	Royal Sealy—Sheffield (omit RW)
Group 4	Shafford—Warwick China (omit Syracuse) (omit Towle)
Group 5	Gorham Silver (Imperial—Zodiac) Waterford—Zylstra (omit Wedgwood China) Allan Adler Silver—Booths
Group 6	Wedgwood Borsumy Fine Chila—Crown Empire (omit Castleton)
Group 7	Castleton Towle Ceralene Raynaud—Englishtown Crafts
Group 8	Enesco China—Freeman (omit Fostoria)
Group 9	Fostoria Frigast Silver—Hibbard, Spencer, Bart (omit Haviland)
Group 10	International Silver (1810—Lovelace) Haviland Johnson Brothers
Group 12	Lenox China
Group 16	Noritake, Wallace Silver
Group 17	Metlox, Royal Worcester, Syracuse Oneida/Heirloom Silver (Abington)—Oneida/Heirloom Monte Carlo
Group 14	Mikasa Spode China

Source: Replacements, Ltd.

exhibit 13   Replacements, Ltd.—First Year Results of Acquisitions

Acquisition Year	Total Cost	Total New Revenue in Acquisition Year	Total New Customers in Acquisition Year
Pre-1992 (cumulative)	$ 333,500	$ 172,380	8,427
1993	49,300	2,564,436	129,045
1994	194,500	107,495	16,418
1995	255,000	434,655	66,103
1996	43,631	123,203	123,067
1997	1,169,000	1,923,895	123,905
Totals	$2,044,931	$5,326,064	466,965

Source: Replacements, Ltd.

"So you can see," Kelly concluded, "how, as I mentioned earlier, someone could get lots of mailings from us over the period of a year. This can get expensive, and we don't want to overwhelm people with quotes. So we have to work constantly on and think about our customer-contact strategy. Are there more efficient and effective ways to contact customers once we find them and get them on our system?"

FINANCE

Watching the Flow

Later, after the UNCG faculty members had left, Kelly's attention returned to the financial data on his desk. The company faced many questions ranging from how to meet space and staffing needs to the more basic question the management team had discussed informally over the past three years: Should the company plan and control its growth in a more deliberative fashion? Because Replacements' preeminent market position offered some relief from competitive pressures, the discussions focused on the market's potential and the implications of growth for various areas of the firm.

Kelly had contemplated the issue of planning growth for some time. His nature, experience, and education led him to see planned growth as essential for longer-term survival. In his professional experience, Kelly had been associated with firms that had elected to react to changing situations instead of anticipating change and identifying alternative courses of action. These "flying-blind" experiences had impressed on him the importance of proactive planning.

Though his experience with growth planning was not extensive, Kelly sensed the need for a guiding philosophy to frame the issue. Much of Replacements' recent growth had come from acquiring customer lists. As he studied the data on acquisitions (see Exhibits 13 and 14), he wondered about the benefits of growth through acquisitions—had they been good uses of the firm's resources? Given the market potential, the issue of whether to focus efforts on product and market development or on growth through acquisitions was a relevant one.

The issue of how to finance operations was also an important factor in the larger issue of long-term planning. Replacements' profit margins and healthy cash flow suggested it could benefit from including debt in the financing mix. Despite the potential of debt financing for increasing profits and performance measures such as return on

exhibit 14   Replacements, Ltd.—Sales in Subsequent Years Derived from Acquired Lists

Year Acquired	1993	1994	1995	1996	1997	Total Sales Including Acquisition Year
Pre-1992 cumulative sales	$121,903	$ 169,218	$ 139,020	$ 150,982	$ 155,150	$ 908,653
1993		2,239,767	1,537,437	1,511,463	1,340,515	9,193,615
1994			249,040	203,070	102,402	700,100
1995				803,525	624,828	1,863,008
1996					659,682	782,885
1997					1,923,895	1,923,895
Totals by year	$121,903	$2,408,985	$1,926,297	$2,669,348	$4,886,472	

Source: Replacements, Ltd.

equity, Bob Page had consistently shunned long-term debt. The company used bank lines of credit as necessary, but the financing policy had been to be "out of the bank" as soon as possible. The aversion to debt was based on the desire to avoid outside influence and oversight regardless of the potential for boosting earnings.

Kelly felt a deliberative and integrative approach to the growth issues was integral to the firm's continued development. Members of the management team had discussed a manageable rate of growth informally, and Kelly felt it appropriate to provide specifics on the growth rate Replacements could sustain from a financial perspective (see Exhibits 15 and 16 for Replacements' financial data). Additionally, Kelly felt detailing the sustainable growth rate could motivate discussions of the benefits of using long-term debt in the financing mix. He saw contrasting the current level of sustainable growth with that provided by including some prudent levels of debt as an effective means of directing the discussions.

OPERATIONS MANAGEMENT AND INFORMATION SYSTEMS

Taking Inventory

Scott Fleming, Replacements' vice president for operations, had just left the inventory area and entered the company's first floor showroom on his way back to his second floor office. He noticed Ron Swanson, chief information officer, who had just finished talking to one of the sales associates who helped showroom customers. In the background, another group of visitors was departing on a Replacements' tour—as groups did every thirty minutes.

Scott had worked for Replacements for seven years during the 1980s. He left the company for four years before returning in 1994. Ron had joined Replacements in early 1996 as chief information officer. He brought 27 years of experience, including 20 years with county government in Iowa; 5 years with Sara Lee; and 2 years with CMI, a textile manufacturer.

"Hey, Ron!" Scott called as he waved his hand at Ron. "I was just on the way up to see if I could catch you. I've just been back in the inventory area. As you know, we had a tremendous

exhibit 15   Replacements, Ltd.—Income Statements, 1994–1997 (Fiscal Years Ending September 30th)

	Fiscal Year 1994	Percent of Sales	Fiscal Year 1995	Percent of Sales	Fiscal Year 1996	Percent of Sales	Fiscal Year 1997	Percent of Sales
GROSS SALES	$29,191,925		$34,209,290		$43,775,216		$52,150,998	
Returns and Allowances	1,327,429		1,536,585		1,880,099		2,354,284	
NET SALES	27,864,496	100%	32,672,705	100%	41,895,117	100%	49,796,714	100%
Cost of Sales	9,467,876	34%	11,387,459	35%	13,701,095	33%	16,345,752	33%
GROSS PROFIT	18,396,620	66%	21,285,246	65%	28,194,022	67%	33,450,962	67%
Salaries	1,730,479	6%	2,403,150	7%	2,905,275	7%	2,744,300	6%
Wages	3,477,359	12%	4,647,444	14%	5,789,083	14%	7,755,830	16%
Overtime	723,801	3%	940,017	3%	1,338,198	3%	1,911,367	4%
Accrued Leave	64,854	0%	111,201	0%	111,658	0%	94,095	0%
Commissions	101,989	0%	225,787	1%	41,791	0%	51,365	0%
Bonuses	96,604	0%	167,976	1%	202,032	0%	244,339	0%
Total Compensation	6,195,086	21%	8,495,575	26%	10,388,037	24%	12,801,296	26%
Unemployment Taxes	35,310	0%	40,630	0%	28,332	0%	79,233	2%
FICA	452,775	2%	615,470	2%	794,884	2%	922,148	1%
1(k) Employer Contribution	170,761	1%	217,378	1%	240,505	1%	350,655	0%
Workers Compensation	136,926	0%	148,563	0%	143,009	0%	164,507	2%
Group Insurance	643,607	2%	949,400	3%	827,184	2%	1,151,450	0%
401 K Admin. Expenses			8,660	0%	5,171	0%	3,312	0%
Section 125 Admin. Expenses			7,189	0%	2,463	0%	71,710	0%
Total Benefits	1,439,379	5%	1,987,290	6%	2,041,548	5%	2,743,015	5%
Total Benefits and Compensation	7,634,465	27%	10,482,865	32%	12,429,585	30%	15,544,310	31%

exhibit 15 (*continued*)

	Fiscal Year 1994	Percent of Sales	Fiscal Year 1995	Percent of Sales	Fiscal Year 1996	Percent of Sales	Fiscal Year 1997	Percent of Sales
Advertising Expense	1,110,577	4%	1,144,408	4%	1,732,440	4%	1,832,064	4%
Postage/Mailing	984,218	4%	1,551,568	5%	2,369,697	6%	2,797,134	6%
Telephone	477,404	2%	840,808	3%	804,964	2%	812,221	2%
Building Rent	400,165	1%	817,415	3%	900,000	2%	900,000	2%
Credit Card Fees	498,678	2%	590,588	2%	785,570	2%	954,801	
Depreciation	458,234	2%	614,112	2%	641,966	2%	789,686	2%
Operating Supplies	308,376	1%	370,575	1%	411,809	1%	473,746	1%
Utilities	160,891	1%	231,073	1%	227,696	1%	255,811	1%
Property Taxes	33,354	0%	54,262	0%	63,179	0%	67,695	0%
Packaging Materials	214,075	1%	262,546	1%	449,437	1%	595,873	1%
Printed Forms	408,916	1%	444,797	1%	488,449	1%	587,632	1%
Equipment Rent	8,701	0%	191,204	1%	342,034	1%	573,204	1%
Handling, Net	(2,105,453)	(8%)	(2,723,618)	(8%)	(1,723,072)	(4%)	(2,096,806)	
Interest Expense	17,954	0%	131,401	0%	22,936	0%	78,237	
Professional Fees							630,252	
All Other	1,615,101	6%	1,968,864	6%	652,204	2%	595,779	1%
Total Operating Income	$ 3,590,179	14%	$ 5,619,610	17%	$ 6,656,260	16%	$ 9,847,614	20%
OPERATING INCOME	7,171,976	26%	5,182,771	16%	9,108,177	22%	8,059,035	16%
Other (Income) Expense	(17,974)	0%	(1,629)	0%	33,645	0%	(92,812)	0%
Lower of Cost or Market Adjustment*	(1,819,417)	(7%)	(2,072,436)	(6%)	(3,034,060)	(7%)	1,980,476	4%
Taxes**	$ 5,334,585	19%	$ 3,108,706	10%	$ 6,107,762	15%	$ 6,171,371	12%

*Adjustment to reflect changing cost of replacing inventory.

**Replacements is a Subchapter S corp., owner pays taxes.

Source: Replacements, Ltd.

exhibit 16   Replacements, Ltd.—Balance Sheets, 1994–97

	September 30, 1994	September 30, 1995	September 30, 1996	September 30, 1997
Assets				
Cash	($ 375,198)	($ 1,447,148)	($ 104,738)	($ 437,934)
Accounts Receivable	211,687	55,580	296,872	366,892
Inventory, Net of Adjustment	9,412,126	10,484,204	13,123,100	18,156,111
Prepaid Expenses	589,364	785,119	798,343	1,066,523
Deposits	63,516	614,951	296,053	200,052
Total Current Assets	$ 9,901,495	$10,492,706	$14,409,630	$19,351,644
Computer Equipment and Software	1,495,687	1,441,437	1,604,709	1,785,108
Leasehold Improvements	1,139,830	1,332,881	1,717,359	1,817,643
Office Furniture and Equipment	733,000	1,125,775	980,615	835,647
Operations Equipment	801,168	895,837	871,504	916,524
Total Capital Assets	$ 4,169,685	$ 4,795,930	$ 5,174,187	$ 5,354,992
Accumulated Depreciation	2,392,598	(2,421,183)	2,685,836	3,052,968
Net Capital Assets	1,777,087	2,374,747	2,488,351	2,301,954
Cash Surrender Value of Insurance	93,676	115,069	133,843	176,173
Long-Term Investments	(36,996)	(39,021)	(12,236)	35,212
Fine Art Items	7,173	7,173	7,173	7,173
Total Other Assets	$ 63,853	$ 83,221	$ 128,780	$ 218,558
Total Assets	$11,742,435	$12,950,674	$17,026,761	$21,872,156
Credit Lines	$ 886,000	$ 973,000		$ 2,325,000
Accounts Payable, Trade	388,208	908,607	$ 1,389,684	1,450,395
Deferred Revenue	45	113,290	1,070,458	1,623,969
Accrued Compensation and Benefits	889,715	1,272,937	1,592,571	1,682,270
Other Accrued Expenses	51,455	9,625	6,539	102,180
Total Current Liabilities	$ 2,215,423	$ 3,277,459	$ 4,059,252	$ 7,183,814
Common Stock	20,000	20,000	20,000	20,000
Paid-In Capital	73,568	73,568	73,568	73,568
Retained Earnings	6,926,687	9,433,444	9,579,647	12,873,941
Distributions to Owner	(2,827,828)	(2,962,503)	(2,813,468)	(4,450,469)
Year-to-Date Net Income	5,334,585	3,108,706	6,107,762	6,171,371
Total Equity	$ 9,527,012	$ 9,673,215	$12,967,509	$14,688,411
Total Liabilities and Equity	$11,742,435	$12,950,674	$17,026,761	$21,872,156

Source: Replacements, Ltd.

number of shipments come in yesterday, and the pieces are beginning to work their way back to inventory. The staff is really pushed. Bob has always believed that the more inventory we have the more we can sell. But no matter how fast we grow, it seems that the inventory grows faster. I'm concerned that we need to tackle this problem strategically. I think keeping track of inventory is taxing our information system."

On an average day, Replacements' supplier network shipped 300–400 boxes via surface carriers (like UPS), resulting in the company receiving more than 50,000 pieces in an average week. In turn, the company shipped about 35,000 pieces a week to meet customer orders (see Exhibit 17).

exhibit 17   Facility Layouts at Replacements, Ltd.

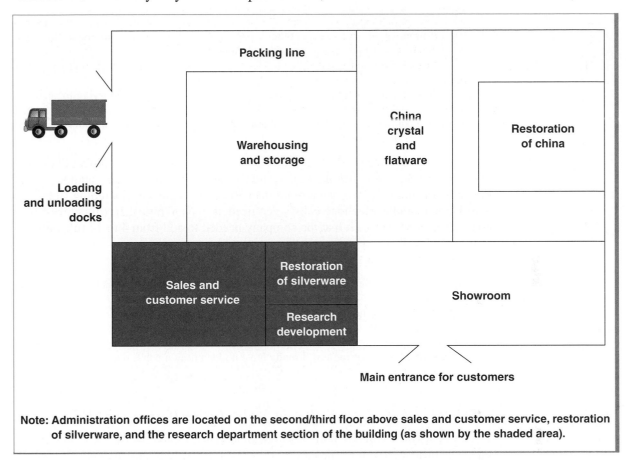

Note: Administration offices are located on the second/third floor above sales and customer service, restoration of silverware, and the research department section of the building (as shown by the shaded area).

At the beginning of any given day, the company had no listing of the items that would be delivered to its docks that day. A shipment's contents were known only after warehouse employees opened the box. Once employees opened the boxes, they used computer terminals to enter data on the pieces received. They then sent the pieces to the appropriate area (china, crystal, or flatware), where other employees carefully inspected each piece and determined the amount that Replacements would pay to the supplier for each piece. Employees then issued payment orders and sent them to the accounting department. They also assigned each piece to a specific location in one of more than 59,000 bins arranged in 16-foot-high shelves and then transferred the piece to inventory. Defective items were sent to appropriate areas for restoration and then placed in inventory.

The company stocked about 73,000 china patterns from 1,300 manufacturers; 12,500 crystal patterns from 265 manufacturers; and 9,600 flatware patterns from 439 manufacturers. The total inventory amounted to more than 4 million individual pieces.

Scott continued,

One of my concerns is that we have so many new people. They're good employees, but they don't yet know the patterns. Although they can quickly learn to find the more commonly ordered patterns, it's hard for them to find the rarer, less frequently ordered patterns. Further, I'm concerned that it is easy for a new employee who is working hard to put a piece in the wrong place. As a result, it could be lost forever! There's no telling how much lost inventory we have floating around on those shelves.

And on top of that, we estimate that about 7 percent of the items we receive are broken in shipment; and we break another 2 percent while we are handling them. So, we've got a quality problem on top of an information problem.

"I can tell you're frustrated, Scott," Ron answered. "Do you have any ideas as to how my department can help you?"

I wish I had some new ideas, Ron. Frankly, I am at my wit's end trying to solve this inventory/quality management problem without an accurate information system. And, to add to the confusion, we're unable to handle all the calls we receive from both our suppliers and customers.

Replacements received about 5,000 calls from customers and suppliers in a typical 14-hour day. About 56 salespeople and 61 purchasing employees handled most of the calls. In addition, there were more than 80 other employees, including Bob Page, who helped handle telephone calls when needed. Jack Whitley, Jr. (director of sales and customer service) felt that the company needed to add from 4 to 14 full-time employees to handle the telephone calls.

Scott lamented,

Our phone records tell us that customers abandon about 1 percent of all calls. I wish we could do something about that. That translates to more than a half million dollars in revenue! Also, many times we find that a particular item sought by a customer is not available in our inventory. However, in all likelihood a supplier could find that item within a few months. But, we have no system in place by which we can correlate the receipt of that item to the earlier customer request. I really have no idea how much money we may be losing on that account.

History of Replacements' Information Systems

The earliest system used to remember customers' names and patterns was simply Bob Page's handwritten 3-by-5 file cards. After about three years, the manual system was unable to keep up with the growth in customers and inventory.

In 1985, Replacements purchased a Data General (DG) minicomputer. The installation automated both the china and flatware inventory and the customer list.

In 1987, Replacements hired an internal programming staff to develop both batch and data-entry functions to support the company's operations. This group subsequently developed the first online systems, which were referred to as "green screen-COBOL-interactive" systems.

In 1993, the company installed the first local area networks (LANs), and PCs began to replace the terminals. Even though the PCs possessed computing capability, they employed a "terminal emulation" interface that used only a small portion of their total capability. Eventually, the DG system grew to 300 terminals, with 220 of them being PCs.

Later in 1993, the DG system's scalability (the ability to increase the system to meet demand) became an issue. Replacements' management decided to look into two alternative solutions:

1. Expand the existing, proprietary DG platform by changing to the UNIX operating system using Oracle database software.

2. Move to a more "open" system of Hewlett-Packard hardware with the UNIX operating system and Sybase database software.

Both options required a database conversion from the old INFOS database management system. Replacements hired an independent consulting firm to supply the project manager for the projected conversion. The task of translating the database structure from the hierarchical INFOS database to the relational Oracle database proved more difficult than the consulting firm had projected. The initial implementation date was delayed over nine months. During this period, many of the development staff left Replacements. After eighteen months of working to convert the database, the management team decided to implement the new system immediately. Managers had considered different cut-over approaches; but the main problem was that only one computer was available, and it could only run one operating system and database at a time. The team decided that an immediate cut-over from the old to the new system would happen over a long holiday weekend—"Tomorrow we go live!" That holiday weekend was the July 4th weekend, 1995.

Problems riddled the changeover from the start. The new systems lost recently entered orders. Critical inventory updates failed. Important data was lost somewhere in the system. The new system "came apart," and system users rapidly lost confidence in its precision and reliability. In some instances, when a customer called to place an order, the order taker would frequently run back into the warehouse to verify the existence of the inventory before confirming the order. Because of the problems with lost orders, some orders were handwritten and hand filled to insure inventory availability and delivery. One executive remarked, "This came as close as anything to completely destroying the business."

Eventually the new system became more reliable, and the employees became more confident in its ability to reflect inventory and to execute necessary transactions accurately. During this period, Replacements' programmers found lots of errors in the programming modules. This revelation made the managers realize that they needed to be more proactive in their system's design and development.

It took the internal programmers almost a year to repair the system installed on July 4, 1995. By then, they had also implemented a limited fail-safe system that provided redundancy in the system by providing for the operation of major functions if the primary system failed. The backup system did not have the capability to run the entire operation, but it would prevent a total shutdown. In order to keep the vital operations functioning, the group decided that the system would suspend noncritical operations in the event of a primary computer failure.

Toward the end of 1995, managers decided that they needed to take a more strategic view in the information systems area. A six-month search ensued to select a chief information officer (CIO). The search resulted in the hiring of Ron Swanson as Replacements' first CIO in May 1996. At this time, most of the information systems' staff were new on the job also. The information services provided consisted of basic maintenance only (keeping what was running operational).

After five months on the job, CIO Swanson submitted his initial vision of what was needed. The report, entitled, "A Proposal for Strategic Direction," recommended a change in hardware platform, a change to a new financial system, a change to database servers, and a change in application development tools. As a result, Replacements developed a new financial system on the IBM AS400; moved to a Microsoft NT Server on a 10/100 megabit local area network to provide access to data and images pertaining to china and flatware; and implemented Powerbuilder, a comprehensive application development tool. A new call center was implemented to enhance the capacity for handling incoming calls. Replacements also began leasing rather than purchasing hardware.

Systems in Place—Late 1997

Replacements' information systems fell into two categories: processing equipment and telecommunications equipment. The processing equipment included the following hardware and applications: (see Exhibit 18).

exhibit 18   Replacements, Ltd., Network Diagram

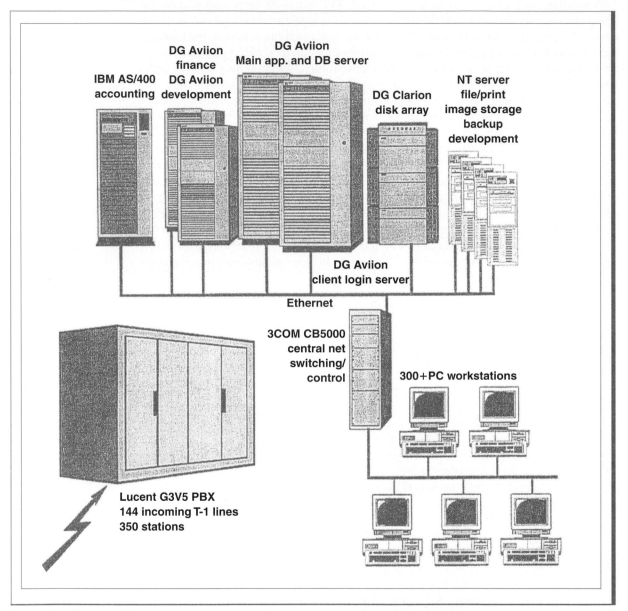

Source: Replacements, Ltd.

- Two Data General (DG) Aviion 9500s configured with multisymetric arrays of processors (12 ea. 50 mhz Motorola CPUs), 1 gigabyte of RAM, sharing a 72 gigabyte Clarion Disk Array (RAID) configured as servers in a client/server architecture. One DG was dedicated as an Oracle database server handling the customer, supplier, and inventory databases; the other DG was used as an application server doing the "workhorse" applications: retail sales and quoting, customer service, purchasing, inventory receiving, and operations tasks. Both systems were rapidly approaching their functional limits. Management needed to decide on future upgrades of and applications for these systems.

- One IBM AS400 operating J. D. Edwards financial systems, which interfaced with the Oracle database server once per day to update the open purchase orders to the large corporate china and flatware suppliers.
- Two NT workstations operating the shipping–package processing. The system weighed the parcel, calculated the shipping, and sent the data to a printer to create a label and to a COBOL application that generated manifests for both UPS and the U.S. Post Office.

Replacements relied on MicroFocus COBOL for its applications and had in excess of 1,000,000 lines of COBOL code. Some managers wanted to replace COBOL programming with something more effective.

The telecommunications equipment handled both voice and data communication with customers and suppliers. The communication equipment included:

- Lucent Technologies Definity G3 PBX, which operated call management, call accounting, Audix (voice mail and internal call switching), and CMS (call management system) software to handle the call volume.
- A switched Ethernet 10/100 megabit data communications network employing a fiber backbone between the wiring closets and Category 5 copper cabling from the closets to the desktop.
- One NT server that operated OnTool fax server software. Incoming faxes were viewed and forwarded via e-mail, and outbound faxes were generated at each individual's workstation.

IS Challenges

Replacements faced many questions and challenges in the information systems area. How could the functional areas integrate their operations, and how could the systems insure the data collected was current and accurate? What upgrade path should the company take to enhance the performance of the major processors (DGs and IBM)? Could operations and marketing help to design a more effective system to support their needs? Did Replacements have the information architecture to guide its processing and application decisions into the 21st century? In which IS competencies should Replacements invest? Should IS merely support the other functional areas at Replacements, or were there some areas where IS should take the lead?

HUMAN RESOURCES AND ORGANIZATIONAL BEHAVIOR

Waiting in Line

Doug Anderson was standing in a *slow*-moving line at a "fast-food" restaurant. As the line inched along, his shoes disconcertingly sticking to the gummy floor, he watched the employees' apparent ambivalence toward their customers. Doug reflected on how far the service ideals of these employees were from those espoused in the restaurant founder's autobiography. He pondered the problem of increased organizational size and the role of human resource policies in creating this distance between vision and reality. He resolved that his company must maintain the "Spirit of Replacements" despite tripling the number of employees in the past four years and despite the coming growth.

Doug had been with Replacements for four years. As executive vice president, he was Bob Page's "right-hand man," charged with seeing that what Bob wanted got done. Doug had earned a business degree in 1969 from The University of North Carolina at Chapel Hill and had worked for Blue Bell Corporation, now VF Corporation, for 17 years in human resources. Following a series of leveraged-buyout-driven, downsizing initiatives at Blue Bell, he accepted a position as the first American that the Japanese firm Konica hired for its U.S.-based film-manufacturing operations. There, he served as head of human resources and public relations. After four years with Konica, he chose to open his own consulting firm. Replacements hired Doug to perform an executive salary survey; and a few months later, he joined the firm.

As Doug reflected on his experience in the fast-food restaurant, he wondered,

> When I came, we had 150 employees. Everybody knew everybody, and you really didn't worry much about a system. But when you get in the 450 range, communication gets difficult. If everyone had the same wage grade, 450 employees would still not be too much of a problem. But with 450 employees, 80 of those taking sales calls alone, and prospects for continued rapid growth, I am no longer sure if the current approach is appropriate. When in a company's growth do you need to get more procedural? How do you institute new work systems in an organization where department heads recoil at the mere mention of a process that has even a hint of bureaucracy? If we believe in documenting performance, and clearly we do, then why not document how we handle a call, certify an employee skill, or determine compensation increases?

The "Spirit of Replacements"

Employees used the phrase "Spirit of Replacements" to capture the attitude that serving the customer was more important than mechanistic operating procedures, job titles, or organizational turf battles. The company did not define customers as dollars but as individuals who each deserved the highest service level possible. Day-to-day resource allocations were driven by what was fair, what was logical, and what made sense for the customer in the context of the moment.

Doug Anderson summarized the philosophy by noting that, "Values drive the system, the system does not drive the values, but common sense supersedes the values. The customer does rule here. We are about *actions,* not plaques and mission statements. The Spirit is the meat, the glue. People know if you are sullen. I don't care how many units you produce, we want people who care and that this caring flows through to the customer's impression of the company. Some people come in with the expectation that if they do not violate a handbook regulation, then you can't talk to them about their actions. We do not believe in that here."

Making the spirit operational required a high energy level and a highly flexible workforce. It also required a very high level of workforce commitment. The company asked employees to "see" when extra work was required and to step up to that need. Replacements operated 365 days a year because it was often on holidays or weekends that customers had the opportunity to think about their need for replacement pieces, or additional china, or their desire to complete a silver service. Thus, Replacements often experienced peak demand at times when many businesses did not operate. It was at these peak times that the spirit was most prevalent.

Doug continued,

> We do not want to be like other companies. We do not use terms like *organization* or *company,* or *report to.* We do not want to say, "Attention shoppers! It is time to go home." We want people to see the work and step up to do it. Everyone does not work every holiday, but

we are always asking managers to volunteer. Every holiday that I have been away, I have this nagging feeling that I have in some way let Bob down. When there is a forecast of snow, you look for who hangs in there the rest of the day and who gets up early the next day to insure he/she arrives on time. Because, you know what? It's not snowing in California, and that customer expects to be served. We never forget these things [committed employee actions].

But for the true believers, this high commitment, high involvement workplace was highly motivating. One employee referred to working at Replacements as "like playing on the Internet—you sit down to do one thing and three hours later you look at your watch and way, 'Wow, is it that late already?'"

Recruitment, Selection, Training, Compensation, and Turnover

Recruitment Replacements recruited primarily through local newspaper advertisements and word of mouth. The company had no nepotism rules beyond the prohibition of direct-report relationships. It made every effort to place employee relatives in separate departments, although this was not always possible. The company's reputation for paying above-average wages, providing a high involvement workplace, and having progressive policies toward same-sex domestic relationships was an asset to its recruiting efforts.

Selection Replacements primarily used the interview process and an assessment of prior work history in making its selection decisions. It used the interview method extensively because most employees came with little or no job knowledge, making attitude an important selection variable. The company did not have the luxury of hiring trained employees away from competitors, because there weren't any competitors. Though there were a number of entrepreneurs with some relevant knowledge, their importance as suppliers precluded bringing them in house. Hiring clerks who sold china in retail stores was also of limited value because they were generally only familiar with 100 or so current patterns of the 95,000 patterns that Replacements sold.

The interview included a realistic job preview for the applicant. Doug believed job previews served the candidate well because no one ever left saying, "I didn't know it would be this way."

Interviewers focused on identifying enthusiastic employees who were willing to be flexible. The company valued enthusiasm because, although the technical side of the business was not complex, the volume of products required a passion for the business. Experience indicated that employees who lacked enthusiasm were probably going to leave, whereas an enthusiastic worker had a much higher probability of achieving high performance.

Doug observed that,

The catalyst for the effectiveness of the training is whether people care about the business or not. If you are interested in baseball cards you will learn baseball cards. If you don't care, it's going to be a struggle. We kind of like what we do, or at least those who do well here do. If this is nothing more than a job, nothing more than *dishes,* then they can memorize some things, but they are not what we want. That is where we have turnover.

The challenge of selecting those who would adopt and embody Replacements' values was vexing. The company found that a business that needed to operate day and night and on holidays and weekends required a level of employee commitment that many employees in the 1990s did not have. Yet this level of commitment was what the customer expected. Finding employees who would place customer needs above their own was difficult.

> If I could find a consultant who could help me measure, give me the formula . . . not for whether people care, I can determine that, it may take a week but I can determine that . . . but who will take the values that we believe in and carry those out to 200 calls. We don't set rules here, every case is so different. . . . Bob values flexibility deeply and values are what allow for consistent service delivery under flexible conditions. . . . So [in selection decisions] . . . *How do I know that you are the one?* . . . Finding people who want a piece of this, who will be on fire here, is the greatest challenge . . . deciding *whom* to hire is just critical.

Training   Replacements trained new employees intensively during a 90-day probationary period. Supervisors met with new employees weekly and gave formal feedback. At 30, 60, and 90 days, the company provided employees with quantitative performance indicators. Training emphasized "training them our way" with a focus on serving the customer and continuous improvement. One element of the continuous improvement approach was an emphasis on providing feedback, both positive and negative. The feedback process permeated the organization as a training mechanism, and Bob Page drove the process by declaring that he was never satisfied with how well Replacements served its customers. Though negative feedback might occasionally engender conflict, Doug pointed out that the attitude toward the importance of feedback was simply that, "Conflict or not, the company must excel in serving the customer, so we will do what needs to be done. We simply have got to fix it [what is wrong]."

Replacements adopted a policy of cross-training employees in order to avoid service delays or peak-period staffing problems in each department. The flow of work through the organization was often referred to as "chasing the bubble." If incoming shipments were especially large for several days, "bubbles" occurred in receiving, then grading, and then inventory stocking. If sales were especially strong for several days, the "bubble" appeared in customer service (answering phones), then pulling inventory, then packing, and then shipping.

Volunteerism was one method for cross-training. Because of the "bubble," employees volunteered to help out in departments experiencing a bottleneck and effectively became cross-trained. Supervisors using volunteers were counseled to give those employees work at which they could be successful so as to encourage future volunteerism and to make their cross-training experience a positive one.

> Eighty percent of what we do can be done with manual skills and enthusiasm for learning. About 20 percent requires some specialized knowledge. So give the volunteers the 80 not the 20. Because we give feedback, we need to make sure that feedback is given in something that they have a chance to succeed in. Otherwise volunteerism will be avoided because people won't seek opportunities for lots of negative feedback. Thus the manager has an incentive to make sure that it is a good experience.

Supervisors conducted appraisals for compensation purposes annually with occasional six-month review for employees who were really "showing us some stuff." Seeing job descriptions as too constraining, the company measured performance against job guides consisting of three or four "bullet" statements that outlined the major job requirements. Supervisors gave informal developmental appraisals daily or weekly through the emphasis on feedback.

Supervisors provided a global rating of performance and then ranked their employees from highest performer to lowest performer with rationales for why they ranked them where they did. Though supervisors used a traditional dimensional performance appraisal instrument for feedback, the global rating/ranking system drove the compensation decisions Bob Page made (a process described in more detail later). Bob's perspective was that you could write all you wanted on an appraisal instrument, but what is a "3" versus a "4," anyway? Bob wanted to know which employee was best and why. He simply did not have the time to read ratings and rationales for multiple dimensions of each employee's performance. Bob then directly linked this rating to rewards asking: If he/she is the best, why isn't he/she making the most?

Replacements informed employees of their ranking within quartiles, but it did not provide feedback in any formal way as to what the employee needed to do to move into the next quartile. Supervisors often "power ranked" the dimensions of quantitative performance with qualitative measures prior to determining global ratings. These qualitative categories included company commitment, concern and respect for others, cooperation/adaptability, and problem solving/initiative. Ultimately, however, to satisfy his analytical bent, Bob Page wanted hard data. He then would apply his own power ranking to the intangibles, as a way of acknowledging that "attitude is half the battle."

Compensation   Replacements' policy was to pay above-average wages at lower organizational levels and competitive or above-average salaries at upper-management levels. Above-average wage levels increased the selection pool and reflected the desire to select and retain employees who would embody the "Spirit of Replacements" and reach higher productivity levels.

"Our expectations are up here," Doug emphasized, raising his hand above his head. "Our reward system is up here [again, raising his hand]. We don't expect people to perform miracles, we just expect them to care enough to give more than most people choose to give their employers."

To encourage employee flexibility, Replacements' compensation system incorporated the notion of skill-based pay. The company regarded an employee who could perform multiple jobs as being much more valuable and added an additional $.25 to $.50 *per skill* to hourly pay rates for those employees. Because the employee acquired these skills through the volunteer system, the method for determining whether the employee had acquired the new skill was relatively informal. Basically, the employee earned a skill-based pay increase when the department head in a particular area said, "Hey, that guy Kevin does a good job when he comes over to help us out with [skill]."

Acknowledging the informality of the system, Doug observed,

> Employee compensation for skills is somewhat like most of the business—we take an honest appraisal and run with it. We do not have a very sophisticated instrument. An employee could say, how do you know if I have the skills or not. . . . We may be too subjective about that. But we do have a tracking report, who can do what . . . so people at least know that we value skill acquisition and that we try to keep up with it. Still, once the employee is designated as having acquired the skill, it's not clear how often they would have to use it to continue to have it incorporated into their hourly wage. . . . We would welcome some wage and salary guidance along those lines.

Informal rewards were also an important motivator. Given Bob's strong persona, many employees coveted his attention, Doug noted.

> Bob is the star, the Michael Jordan of Replacements, and the reward structure includes the level of interaction with Bob. One VP left because it ate at him that he had less access to Bob than some other employees. But one does not gain Bob's favor by trying to gain Bob's favor. Bob's favor is gained by exemplary commitment to the customer and only by extension to Replacements, Ltd.

Some who did not get an above-average level of interaction with Bob and other senior management employees charged favoritism. On the charge of favoritism, Doug readily admitted,

Yes, we do [play favorites]. Who upper management speaks to are those that love to be here. They are the ones we interact with the most. I think that is only natural. This combination of monetary compensation and informal rewards serves as a powerful motivator for the "right type" of employee. . . . We say thank you a lot. But at the end of the day, you still have to put the money where your mouth is.

Management reviewed salaries each October. Supervisors presented quartile rankings with supporting quantitative data to Bob. Bob reviewed each of the 450 salary increases personally, adjusting them upward or downward based on his interpretation of the supervisor's appraisal and his personal assessment of that employee's performance. Replacements' employees also received a Christmas bonus, generally ranging from $1,000 to an amount known only to Bob. These Christmas bonuses were solely subjective on Bob's part, determined without formal supervisor input. Occasionally, some employees would argue that this procedure for determining merit and Christmas bonuses was not fair. It then fell to Doug Anderson and other senior managers to educate them on how they might be misinformed regarding the fairness issue. Most senior managers were comfortable with this "education" responsibility because they believed Bob was extremely fair and logical in his decision processes.

Turnover Turnover rates had been a consistent source of concern. Despite requiring little or not industry experience, paying above-average wages, and offering considerable opportunity for increasing task variety through a high involvement volunteerism culture, Replacements experienced "more turnover than you might predict."[1] For some, learning the breadth of product line might be a barrier. For others, the level of commitment required to embody the "Spirit of Replacements" might cause them to leave. The most frequently given reason for leaving in exit interviews was, "Well, I'm leaving because you are never satisfied—no matter what I do, it is just never enough!" It seemed to Replacements' long-term employees that people who left for this reason had failed to grasp the essential element that made the company a unique place to work.

The people who left here, who were not a selection mistake, missed the point. They never should have tried to satisfy us. . . . Bob tells them going in that we will never be satisfied . . . that constant struggling to better satisfy the customer is on-going. . . . I guarantee if you do 1,000 boxes today I am going to praise you and tell everyone about it. But, I am going to want you to do 1,100 tomorrow, and *why aren't you doing it*? Not that we want to embarrass or place undue pressure, but we want to probe how you can do your job better to make the next record. The goals have meaning only within satisfying the customer. . . . 1,100 means that someone got their package quicker.

The organization took turnover seriously, and those who had the "Spirit of Replacements" had a feeling of personal rejection when people resigned.

When people leave saying, "I do not want to work Saturdays," it hurts our feelings. When you feel the way we do, and you invest the time to communicate why this is such a unique place to work, it hurts our feelings when you want to leave. It's not personal, but [when you leave] we just do not want to talk to you, really.

It is such a personal thing. Sometimes when we hire the wrong leaders, they feel like we need some guidance, that we ought to chill out. You can debate what is a fair expectation

---

[1]Turnover rates were 37 percent (148 employees) in 1996 and 36 percent (186 employees) in 1997.

of a person's commitment, but we only want 400–500 people . . . *this is not a national movement!* We've had only 2 dismissals in 2 years—most get the idea independently.

The company had recently initiated two innovative programs in response to turnover caused by burnout and by a relatively tight local labor market. The first program, known as the "30 for 40" program, targeted employees who would be willing to work 30 relatively unpopular hours (nights, weekends, and holidays) in exchange for 40 hours of pay. These employees typically were trained in and performed one job in an area that had consistent demand for employees during these hours (e.g., customer service). Employees in this program did not work a set shift; instead, the company provided them some flexibility in scheduling their 30 undesirable hours. The program appealed to moonlighters and mothers with small children whose spouses were available for child care during these times.

The second program, known as the "super part-timer" program, paid a 33 percent wage premium ($12 versus $9, for example) in exchange for the employee being willing to rotate among four designated jobs. This allowed the company some flexibility in giving employees in those areas a break when volume was high and the volunteerism system failed to provide sufficient support or taxed the stamina of those who would normally volunteer. Management believed that both of these programs were very successful.

Nondiscrimination toward Gay/Lesbian Employees

Replacements was the first company in North Carolina to offer same-sex partner benefits and to apply nepotism rules to same-sex partners. The early move toward offering gay/lesbian benefits may be attributed in part to Bob Page's sexual orientation. Having experienced considerable discrimination as a gay man in the Southeastern United States, he developed a strong distaste for discrimination in any form. Replacements personnel policies had been labeled "progressive," "liberal," and "gay friendly" and were consistent with Bob's philosophy that discrimination in any form was unacceptable. Replacements stated that its ethical standards did not promote homosexuality. Instead, they promoted the right to protection from discrimination for all employees.

> Bob is not pro-gay. He is antidiscrimination. We never promote homosexuality. The only thing we are promoting is the right to discrimination protection. What Bob wants is some sort of basic acceptance. An "in-your-face," gay-pride sort of environment is inappropriate. We are not into quotas. . . . We are just saying do not discriminate.

Though the company did not develop "gay-friendly" policies in an effort to attract gay or lesbian employees and customers, these policies had created business opportunities and problems both internally and externally. A customer participating in the Replacements' tour or browsing in the showroom might happen upon a framed cover page highlighting Bob Page, gay businessman, or an award plaque designating Bob Page as "Gay Entrepreneur of the Year." Although it was quite common for companies to display the achievements of their CEOs, the "discovery" that the owner was gay elicited varied reactions. Some customers reacted with indignation and left. Others felt a closer bond with the company. Some simply admired the founder's courage to be open and take a stand, while others were curious or indifferent. Although the thought of displeasing a customer was anathema to Replacements, the company was willing to risk losing customers if it was a consequence of doing what it thought was the right thing.

Doug pointed out one advantage Replacements had.

> Our position creates a number of marketing opportunities. The gay/lesbian population is somewhat hidden, but large and very loyal. When gay/lesbian individuals learn we are supportive, they are more likely to send their business this way, because so many [other] companies disassociate themselves.

When a controversial "coming out" episode of the network show *Ellen* was scheduled to air on network television, a number of large corporations bowed to pressure to remove their commercial sponsorship. In this void, Replacements decided to "do the right thing." It developed a short commercial describing the company that included a trailer stating: "The employees of Replacements, Ltd., both gay and straight, are proud to stand against discrimination, on any front."

Despite the relatively innocuous nature of the statement, only two local affiliates (Raleigh, North Carolina, and Washington, D.C.) of several solicited along the eastern seaboard were willing to run the ad. Despite the relatively low exposure, the company got a number of letters supporting the commercial.

Internally, having a reputation for being gay/lesbian friendly both attracted and repelled some potential job applicants. On the positive side, many highly qualified employees were attracted to the company.

> Our recruiting efforts are aided by coverage of the company in the gay/lesbian publications such as *The Advocate,* and the knowledge among gay/lesbian professional groups, that this is a "safe place." Many times, that alone can get us some very talented people. Here they can be free to serve the customer and not worry about factors unrelated to the company influencing their career. . . . You simply cannot underestimate how attractive that feature is to some. To affiliate with Bob and his leadership in this area. . . . But do not confuse gay friendly with gay preference. One employee once boasted that his job was safe because he was gay. . . . That gentleperson was eventually displaced.

On the negative side, Replacements' selection pool was unquestionably reduced through a process of self-selection. Though this impact had not been quantified, the organization was aware that a certain percentage of the population was not comfortable with and even fearful of alternative lifestyles. Just as some people would self-select themselves out of organizations based on racial composition, some potential employees would self-select themselves out of a gay/lesbian-friendly organization.

Replacements instructed all managers to tell the potential employee that the owner was gay and that the organization did not tolerate discrimination on any basis, including sexual orientation, before they made an offer to anyone. The company implemented this policy after an employee overheard a manager trainee state that if he had known when he came in that the owner was gay and that a number of employees were gay or lesbian, he would never have taken the job. Doug noted that due to this disclosure in the offer process, the issue of sexual orientation rarely came up in the day-to-day workplace.

CORPORATE STRATEGY

Finding Respect

Bob Page looked out his window toward Interstates 85/40. It was snowing heavily—very unusual for the first week of December in North Carolina. It was Friday, and everyone was exhausted but energized by the last two weeks' hectic activities. Sales on

Monday reached a record high of $417,000, smashing the previous one-day record of $286,000 set just a year ago on December 5, 1996. Tuesday's sales had topped $375,000.

A reporter from *The Wall Street Journal* had visited Replacements earlier in the week and made several follow-up telephone calls about an article that the paper would publish in late December. An issue of *Southern Living* that included an article on Replacements had just hit the newsstands. The president of Wedgwood USA and a representative from the office in England had come to see him. Five years ago, Bob had gone to England to see someone at Wedgwood only to be stood up. Now, it was Wedgwood that approached Replacements.

Trudy, one of his two dachshunds, interrupted his thoughts, begging for a dog treat. Her puppies would arrive in three weeks. Several employees had already adopted them and, like their parents, they would come to work every day.

He had never envisioned it being like this. He had thought that he would be lucky to have six employees. Now there were 500 people in the Replacements family, 50 hired in the last two months. He'd known there was demand, but he'd never dreamed how much demand there was.

It's not something that business school professors would want to hear, but we really don't talk about the bottom line. That would almost never come up in a conversation here. Our philosophy is that we do the things that we believe in and the bottom line will take care of itself. We take care of our customers.

I think that just by doing the things that we're doing today, sales are going to continue to grow. The articles in *Southern Living* and in *The Wall Street Journal*—that's exposure. More and more people find out about us, yet half of our business still comes from word of mouth.

There are dozens and dozens of companies that've started up since I started Replacements, but they're still on a level like when I operated out of my attic. We recently bought out a competitor in Washington state, and its entire inventory and office furniture fit in two tractor trailers. We ship out two tractor-trailer loads of merchandise daily.

We've established an impeccable reputation with our suppliers. They know that they can trust us to send them their money. I've heard some horror stories that when they've sent someone else something it would take them six months to get their money. In other cases, I've heard that the company said that it was going to pay one price and after they have shipped it the company said, "Well we're not going to pay that." I think that our real focus on computers and our index have made us different. We have one competitor who was sending out letters to our suppliers asking them to get our index but not let us know what they were doing. On certain items they would pay $2.00 or $5.00 per piece more—but then told the suppliers not to ship anything without telling them.

We recently purchased the mailing list of one of our former competitors. It also wanted to sell its inventory, but it had such depth in the pieces that it had. It had a fifty-year supply of cups and saucers in one pattern! What we look at is buying a lot of different pieces, but not in huge amounts. They just kept accumulating pieces, but it was their buying system that didn't work for them. They might pay $15 for a cup and saucer and then they would automatically pay $15 for the dinner plate because the system was so rigid. We may be paying $1 for the cup and saucer and $25 for the dinner plate based on demand or how much inventory we already have.

Our customers can't find the product anywhere else. Some of our patterns are more than 100 years old. We couple that with the level of customer service that we provide. What would it take for a substantial competitor to emerge? Money, experience, a customer list, inventory, and a period of time. At this time, I'm not really concerned about competitors, because if someone had all the money in the world, they wouldn't have the inventory. We have the largest stockpile in the world of discontinued products. It would take a competitor a period of time to accumulate the inventory.

When we put out our indexes, the first ones to buy them are our competitors. Of course, a lot of our competitors sell a good portion of their inventory to us. They don't have the client base that we do. It has taken us all these years to accumulate 2½ million customers. You couldn't do that overnight. If you had all the customers, what would you sell them? Now we have made lots of mistakes over the years. For example, we were buying a pattern called "Sylvia" from a German manufacturer. It turned out that Sylvia was a shape, not a pattern, and now we have 25 patterns with a Sylvia shape. This is something that was listed in our book, and if someone brought a piece in we would buy it—but it wasn't what we thought we were buying. These are the kinds of things that other people are going to have to learn, too. We have knowledge here that nobody else would have. And we keep documenting things. We have over 2,200 old Noritake patterns, forty years old or older. When we publish our book, it's just going to be a killer book. This is doing a service to the world.

We are constantly adding patterns. We computer-image hundreds of patterns a week. We'd love for our customers and suppliers to have access to this knowledge. We have suppliers who fax things in here or bring a piece in or try to describe it over the phone. If they had access to some of this knowledge, it would make it easier. Here is an example of a pattern to which we have assigned a number. For our purposes, it is an identifiable pattern. This would save on our own research time. We may also want to have customers place their own orders.

We entered the silver business because we kept getting more and more requests from people asking why we didn't handle silver, too. And, of course, we already had our mailing list. It's fairly cost effective to add silver. With our supplier base, we just had to let them know we were in the silver business. It was a natural expansion of our business . . . all tableware.

Refurbishment is a business that we want to do at some point when we get caught up ourselves. We have a large new kiln that we're operating; and in the last couple of weeks, we have gotten fire polishing for beveling stemware. We lost some pieces before we perfected that. There's a lot of experimentation involved. With the china patterns, we keep records of the temperature to fire various patterns, which patterns we can fire, and which we can't. We get better at what we do as time goes on. We have the ability to launch the business now, but we are processing so many things that we already bought but can't sell until we refurbish. If someone came in right now, we could do it—but we don't have the manpower. It's very time consuming, and it's a real art.

I went to England four or five years ago to meet with people from Wedgwood, and the man who I had an appointment with was out of town. Now, they want us to be their worldwide distributor for closeouts. The president of Wedgwood USA and another man from England were here. They approached us about this arrangement—we did not approach them. They have their own matching center for recently discontinued patterns (patterns discontinued within the last 5 years). They shared information with us on the total sales of various patterns in all markets. They gave us a breakdown of sales by those patterns in the U.S., U.K., Japan, and Australia. They want to sell us all the company's discontinued inventory, and they would refer to us all the customers who are looking for discontinued merchandise. We would supply that from the United States.

Over the years, we've bought thousands of pieces of stemware from Lenox crystal in recent patterns that have been out of production for three or four years. We had such demand that they'd produce those just for us. They also have produced some of their china patterns for us if they still had some of the decals to decorate the pieces. Once they've discontinued patterns, they'll sell them out to us because they want to dispose of them. They also have outlet stores, but we sell more Lenox pieces than all their outlet stores combined.

Back four or five years ago, we had a dip in employee morale. I'd say that now our employee morale is way up there. Everyone's working really hard. And we have people who're really thrilled to be here. It's really great. It's demanding, very demanding; but it's positive adrenaline for the most part. I really enjoy it.

I still try very hard to know everyone by name. I'd know 95 percent of them. We've got so many new ones. I get a picture of everybody, and they fill out a questionnaire giving a little bit of information about themselves, what attracted them to Replacements, and what's the most interesting thing about them. I took these home last night. In my spare time, I look at their pictures and read their comments. When we had 25 employees, I knew everybody and their brothers and sisters. I miss some of that, but I am still very close to a lot of people here. I like to think that this is my extended family.

It's our real intent to take care of our people. We've higher expectations of our employees than most places. Right now, they're overworked because it's our busy season. I think that people either love it here, or they hate it. Typically, people who just want a job won't be here long. We have others who just couldn't think of working anywhere else. They just love being here. And it's a very diverse group. For example, there's a guy who we hired down in imaging who's a vegetarian and is really new-wave looking. But he wrote the nicest little thing. He started working here through a temporary agency. And he wrote that this is the neatest job that he'd ever worked at or heard about, and he had been looking for over a year. He's very enthusiastic about being here. We want people who are really glad to be here. We feel like attitude is the most important thing.

There's a learning curve. The new employees train for two or three weeks out in the warehouse before they ever have anyone on the phone, and then they are not proficient at what they do. It takes six months to a year to really get familiar with the products, and still they wouldn't have the depth of knowledge needed to put that customer on file and send them a list. There are so many times that I get a customer on the phone and think that if somebody else in phone sales had gotten that customer that they'd not be able to talk them through and get the information to put that customer on file and send them a list. I'm able to talk them through because of my product knowledge. Right now our employee is just looking at a computer screen; it will be very educational when we get pictures on the screen and he or she can see what the product looks like.

The thing I love to do is to go to flea markets and antique shops and buy things. What would I do if I didn't own Replacements? I love what I do. I really enjoy it. I'm overworked right now. I enjoy going out in the warehouse and working. I go out there every day. And, of course, I do a lot of the identification. There were 750 pieces of mail today. Some days there are 1,100 or 1,200, so it was fairly light today. I go through and I can identify up to one-half of the pieces that come in. I love to take sales calls. I get ideas from everything I do, whether it's the mail or sales calls. If I'm out of town for a few days, I can hardly wait to get back. I'm always ready to get back.

The Kimpton Hotel and Restaurant Group

Armand Gilinsky Jr.
Sonoma State University

Richard L. McCline
San Francisco State University

When your strategy is deep and far reaching, then what you gain by your calculations is much, so you can win before you even fight. When your strategic thinking is shallow and nearsighted, then what you gain by your calculations is little, so you lose before you do battle. Therefore it is said that victorious warriors win first and then go to war, while defeated warriors go to war first and then seek to win.

—Sun Tzu, "The Art of War"

At 8:30 AM on June 3, 1999, Steve Marx, vice president of hotels for the Kimpton Hotel and Restaurant Group, Inc., left the office of Thomas La Tour, president of Kimpton. The hour-long breakfast meeting in the company's San Francisco headquarters had been bittersweet. On the previous day, Marx had accepted an "irresistible" offer from Jonathan Tisch, president of Loews Hotels, to manage its hotel operations based in New York City. Marx had wrestled with the decision but recognized that, professionally, he almost *had* to accept the offer from Loews. La Tour understood the dilemma and, with regret, accepted Marx's resignation and two-week notice. The two men anticipated a continuation of the friendship that had characterized their relationship from the beginning. The personal aspect of the decision was as difficult for Marx as the professional component had been. He, his wife, and their 10-year-old son loved living in the San Francisco Bay area and were not thrilled about the prospect of relocating to the New York metropolitan area.

Over the past six years, Marx and La Tour had built the ninth largest hotel management company in the United States, with groupwide revenues per available room (RevPAR) approaching $125 per night and occupancy rates an estimated 85 percent, placing it in the top tier of all U.S. hotel management companies. (RevPAR is a key industry benchmark that really indicates how one makes money in the hotel industry.) Since is formation in 1981, Kimpton Group (KG) had, by 1999, grown into a $250 million hotel company with 5,308 rooms and 5,325 employees, among which 40 staff

This case was presented at the 1999 meeting of the North American Case Research Association in Santa Rosa, CA.

managed its hotel division alone. In early 1998, La Tour had said publicly that he expected the growth pattern of opening three new hotel properties a year to continue "indefinitely." Whereas seed investment capital had originally come from some 200 loyal investors contributing $100,000 apiece, more recently a partnership with the Crow family in Texas provided a $300 million development fund to acquire new hotel properties. The company was privately held.

At 51 and now in his 26th year in the industry, Marx had previously worked his way up at Hilton to become a manager of several hotels. He then left Hilton in the late 1980s for London to manage Trusthouse Forte's hotel properties in the United Kingdom. Just before their son was born, Marx and his wife relocated to Monterey, California, where he managed a Doubletree hotel for three years before being headhunted by KG in 1992.

Prior to his 3:00 PM, June 3, 1999 meeting with his two senior direct reports, David Martin, director of operations, and Jeff Senior, vice president of hotel sales and marketing, Marx reflected on the several key strategic issues that he thought the senior management team would need to address in the near future. Among the strategic choices that he thought would require attention were (1) determining the feasibility of acquiring new properties in new markets on the East Coast and in the South; (2) evaluating the near-term potential to gain additional revenue by developing and adding new services such as Internet connectivity and related products; and (3) the pros and cons of developing product branding to increase market identification, using perhaps the Hotel Monaco as the flagship brand. Additionally, Marx would encourage the senior managers to consider how much longer Kimpton could continue to capitalize on the benefits of the rapidly closing "window" in the real estate market. Historically, Kimpton has prospered by purchasing and renovating buildings at a discount in strategic nationwide locations that matched Kimpton's niche segment. Aggressive national growth could potentially create a strong base of resources and core competencies to support an eventual long-term growth strategy of diversification and globalization. In the short term, maybe some forms of valued-added services could be added to the marketing mix to win the battle for more discriminating customers in a highly competitive marketplace. The hotel industry in general had been slow to enter the boutique niche, and Kimpton currently enjoyed a substantial edge in experience in developing value-added services for guests. Another potential strategic choice could have the Kimpton team focus on the individual brand equity of each hotel and embrace the entry of new boutique competitors into the competitive set, since they would help create and grow the category, in essence giving the "boutique category" the credibility necessary to generate long-term profitability and growth.

Marx would caution Senior and Martin that any future strategy would have to be guided by founder Bill Kimpton's original formula for acquiring undervalued assets:

> We are proud of our value engineering, construction, and design. We make very few mistakes. Kimpton doesn't build hotels from the ground up. We buy buildings and renovate them, primarily undervalued assets in downtown, urban locations. We try to outperform other hotels in our particular segment and create value for our owners.

Equally important, Marx would remind his executive team, is that the important strategic decisions that must be made must also uphold the company's mission of "getting and keeping guests, keeping and developing employees." He felt personally responsible for having developed an organization and management style to attract professional managers from other hotel chains to Kimpton. Martin and Senior were part of his recruited talent and would be expected to take increasingly more highly visible roles in determining the company's destiny after Marx's departure.

As the meeting began, Marx reflected on the Kimpton Group's rapid growth and strategic positioning within the hotel industry:

> Five or six years ago we made a conscious decision to grow. Life is growth; you can't ever stay where you are. Our investors see us as the future of the industry, as we have created a category and become a dominant player in that category. We offer personal, intimate service to our guests, people who live in an increasingly impersonal world. We provide five-star service at a four-star price. We need to become the most unique "four-diamond" hotel in each market we serve. That's our niche, and we welcome imitators because they validate what we're doing.

Since Marx joined the company, KG had grown from 14 hotels and restaurants in San Francisco to 23 boutique hotels and 24 upscale and popular restaurants in major cities such as San Francisco, Portland, Seattle/Tacoma, Chicago, Denver, and Salt Lake City. Two new properties, Serrano Hotel and Hotel Palomar, were scheduled to be opened in San Francisco in summer 1999. A list of KG's leading hotel and restaurant properties is provided in Exhibit 1.

THE U.S. HOTEL INDUSTRY

Global issues, changing industry fundamentals, increasing volatility in the capital markets, and a general unease with the direction of the economy created opportunities for Kimpton to aggressively expand nationally while its competitors were scrambling to refocus. For hotels, managing supply and demand was a top priority for decision makers. Since the hotel industry's recovery from the recession of the early 1990s, it had changed from the fragmented, high-growth state that dominated the 1980s to the fierce competitive environment of the late 1990s. As the industry approached the millennium, demand for hotel rooms increased by 3.1 percent in 1997–98 over 2.5 percent in 1996–97, while RevPARs also grew by 5.3 percent and 3.5 percent, respectively, according to Smith Travel Research. Exhibit 2 provides a summary of the generally upward trends of occupancy rates and RevPARs for the 1994–98 period. Exhibit 3 provides time series data on occupancy and average daily revenue trends in the U.S. lodging industry.

The American Hotel and Motel Association had forecast that both business and tourist travel would increase during the early 21st century, and that more than 1 billion people would be traveling worldwide by 2006, when international tourism dollars were projected to total more than $7.1 trillion. The United States would continue to be the first choice for tourists, attracting almost 50 million for 1999 alone. Employment was also expected to rise, with estimates of 1.89 million people working in the tourism industry by 2005, according to the U.S. Department of Commerce's *1998 Census of Service Industries.*

KG's competition in the full-service hotel segment included many well-known brand names such as Hilton, Hyatt, Marriott, Promus (Doubletree), and Starwood (Sheraton and Westin brands). For the year ending December 1998, revenues rose at Hilton by 35 percent, Promus by 25 percent, and Marriott by 20 percent. In 1998 RevPARs at these hotels demonstrated the continued strong recovery of the industry from the recession of the early 1990s, rising by 8 percent at Hilton, 6 percent at Promus, and 6 percent at Marriott. This upsurge in business made its way to the bottom line. Hilton's earnings before taxes and other nonoperating income rose by 75 percent; Promus's corresponding earnings rose 25 percent and Marriott's by 18 percent, according to *Moody's Industry Review* on January 22, 1999. Operating profit margins for some of the more profitable companies reached a high of 35 percent in 1997, according to *Moody's.* Selected 1998 operating results for the top 10 publicly traded U.S. hotel

exhibit 1 Kimpton Group Hotels and Restaurants as of June 1999

	Date Opened	Number of Rooms	Number of Seats
San Francisco			
Clarion Bedford Hotel at Union Square	April 1981	144	—
Hotel Vintage Court/Masa's	April 1983	107	100
Galleria Park Hotel/Perry's Downtown	June 1984	177	133
Juliana Hotel	September 1985	106	—
Villa Florence Hotel/Kuleto's Italian Restaurant	May 1986	180	176
Monticello Inn	October 1987	91	—
Puccini & Pinetti	June 1995	—	160
Prescott Hotel/Postrio	April 1989	158	150
Carlton Hotel	June 1989	165	—
Splendido	November 1989	—	150
Cartwright Hotel	January 1990	114	—
Tuscan Inn/Café Pescatore	July 1990	221	—
Harbor Court Hotel/Harry Denton's	April 1991	131	176
Hotel Triton	October 1991	140	—
Kuleto's Trattoria	September 1993	—	200
Sir Francis Drake Hotel	April 1994	417	—
Scala's Bistro	January 1995	—	200
Hotel Monaco/Grand Café	June 1995	201	260
Serrano Hotel	June 1999	236	—
Hotel Palomar/Fifth Floor	August 1999	198	75
Portland			
Hotel Vintage Plaza/Pazzo Ristorante	May 1992	107	200
Fifth Avenue Suites Hotel/ Red Star Tavern & Roast House	May 1996	221	200
Seattle/Tacoma			
Alexis Hotel	September 1982	109	—
The Painted Table	May 1992	—	100
Hotel Vintage Park/Tulio	August 1992	127	156
Hotel Monaco Seattle/Sazerac	August 1997	189	185
Sheraton Tacoma Hotel/Broadway Grill	May 1984	319	170
Chicago			
Hotel Allegro/312 Chicago	March 1998	489	244
Hotel Monaco Chicago/Mossant	November 1998	193	174
Denver			
Hotel Monaco Denver/Panzano	October 1998	189	244
Salt Lake City			
Hotel Monaco Salt Lake	July 1999	—	—

Source: The Kimpton Group.

corporations are presented in Exhibits 4 and 5. A brief overview of the strategies and competitive tactics of the three largest competitors is shown in Exhibit 6.

Some industry observers commented that the hotel industry's outlook remained uncertain. Joseph Tardiff, an analyst writing in *U.S. Industry Profiles, 1998,* reported that across the nation, room supply grew by about 4 percent in 1998 after 3.5 percent growth in 1997. In the July 1998 edition of *Lodging,* a leading industry trade publication, Smith

exhibit 2   U.S. Lodging Industry Supply and Demand, 1994–98

	% Change in Supply					% Change in Demand				
	1994	1995	1996	1997	1998	1994	1995	1996	1997	1998
	1.0	1.5	2.8	3.4	4.0	3.0	1.7	2.3	2.5	3.1

Sources: Bear Stearns & Co., Smith Travel Associates Research, Coopers & Lybrand LLP.

exhibit 3   U.S. Lodging Industry Occupancy and Average Daily Rates, 1991–99

	1991	1992	1993	1994	1995	1996	1997	1998	1999 (1st quarter)
Occupancy %	61.8	62.6	63.5	64.7	65.0	65.1	64.5	64.0	59.4
% change	(1.7)	0.8	0.9	1.2	0.3	0.1	(0.6)	(0.5)	(4.6)
Average daily rate	$58.10	$58.90	$60.50	$62.80	$65.80	$69.90	$75.20	$78.60	$81.90
% change	0.2	1.4	2.8	3.8	4.7	6.2	5.3	3.5	3.3

Sources: Bear Stearns & Co., Smith Travel Associates Research, Coopers & Lybrand LLP.

exhibit 4   U. S. Lodging Industry Rankings by Revenues, Fiscal Year 1998 ($ Millions)

Company Name	Latest Revenues
Sodexno Marriott Services, Inc.	$12,034
Hilton Hotels Corporation	5,316
Starwood Hotels & Resorts	4,700
Trump Hotels and Casino Resorts	1,399
Host Marriott Corporation	1,147
Promus Hotel Corporation	1,038
MGM Grand, Inc.	828
Red Roof Inns, Inc.	351
Prime Hospitality Corporation	341
Sunterra Corporation	338

Source: "Hotels and Motels," *Moody's Industry Review,* January 22, 1999.

Travel Research forecast that demand growth would average 2.4 percent through the year 2000. Analysts also cautioned that room supply growth would average 3.2 percent, raising fears of oversupply, declines in occupancy rates, and probable diminution of growth rates in RevPAR as well as industrywide profitability. Industrywide profits had risen by 20.5 percent from 1997 to a record $17.6 billion in 1998, and were forecast by Smith Travel Research to increase to $19.2 billion in 1999 and $21 billion in 2000, respectively. To partially offset the prospect of oversupply in the industry, some hotel companies (e.g., Marriott) were said to be pursuing diversification into retirement facilities and time-share programs, according to Bill Scatchard, publisher of *Hoteliers' Infosource.*

exhibit 5 Financial Ratio Data for Top 10 Hotel Chains (Ranked by Fiscal Year 1998 Revenues)

Company Name	Return on Capital	Return on Assets	Current Ratio	Operating Profit Margin	$ Revenues per Employee
Sodexno Marriott, Inc.	10.13%	5.30%	.88	6.03%	$61,713
Hilton Hotels Corporation	3.73	3.19	1.07	11.21	87.147
Starwood Hotels & Resorts	12.40	7.70	.50	7.62	36,154
Trump Hotels	nmf	nmf	1.55	10.23	12,580
Host Marriott Corporation	0.80	0.72	10.43	35.05	n/a
Promus Hotel Corporation	4.52	4.01	.55	17.72	25,317
MGM Grand, Inc.	9.47	8.24	.94	23.08	126,219
Red Roof Inns, Inc.	2.91	13.15	.71	25.05	60,517
Prime Hospitality Corporation	2.36	2.16	.76	26.64	50,147
Sunterra Corporation	3.23	2.83	4.67	15.89	81,445
Marcus Corporation	5.32	4.68	.43	17.16	48,000
Industry averages	4.00%	5.90%	1.00	2.99%	$62,343

nmf = not meaningful figure
n/a = not available
Source: "Hotels and Motels," *Moody's Industry Review,* January 22, 1999.

exhibit 6 Major Lodging Companies' Strategies

Marriott	Hilton	Promus
• Price segmentation • Customer segmentation • Global presence • Time-share segments • Senior care—bought senior living Forum Group, now largest operators of senior housing • Brand management • Selling non-industry-related businesses • Selling hotels that do not match strategy • Acquisitions in midpriced segment • Acquisition of small hotel companies	• Price segmentation • Customer segmentation • Global presence • All-suites segment • Gaming—now industry leader in facilities • Brand management • Acquisition of full-service hotels • Global expansion in midpriced segment • Electronic marketplace • Employee training in quality improvement	• Price segmentation • Customer segmentation • Global presence • Time-share segments • All-suites segments • Merger with other large hotel leader • Brand management • Partnership with food producer (Dole) • Sponsorship of sporting events • Restructuring of management in early 1999

Sources: www.mariott.com, www.hilton.com, www.prnewswire.com, May 12, 1999.

Ted Mandigo, an industry observer quoted in *Hotel & Motel Management,* felt that location was the key to success: "Finding a good location in a commercial district is an excellent way to enter a market. Many such opportunities have already been exploited. The operator looking for undervalued assets that can be turned into boutique hotels will

exhibit 7   Hotel Industry Growth, 1990–98

Year	Number of Hotels	% Growth	Number of Rooms	% Growth
1990	30,114		3,206,454	
1991	30,384	0.9%	3,234,673	0.8%
1992	30,516	0.4	3,249,699	0.5
1993	30,727	0.7	3,270,864	0.6
1994	31,152	1.4	3,306,304	1.1
1995	31,808	2.1	3,354,970	1.5
1996	32,851	3.3	3,455,087	2.9
1997	34,225	4.2	3,588,072	3.8
1998	35,013	2.3	3,662,524	2.1

Source: Smith Travel Associates Research.

need a sharp pencil to avoid buying bargain properties that do not create a situation of oversupply." Other critical success factors appeared to determine a firm's ability to remain competitive in the hotel industry. At the basic level, hotel owners strove to create a level of service that attracted and retained customers. The "experience" of staying at a particular hotel facility was intended to have a lasting and memorable effect if a hotel was to be distinguished from the competition.

The trend, noted in the *1994 Atlas of the American Economy,* toward hotel property and management consolidation, posed several threats for owners of small and midsized hotel chains. As the larger firms continued to grow and expand their operations, it became easy to expand beyond economies of scale factors and create an oversupply, driving down room rates. This threat was heightened during economic downturns and could significantly affect both the overall occupancy rate in the industry and profitability. In the early 1990s there was a notable and steady increase in the number of establishments, according to Smith Travel Associates (see Exhibit 7). The result was a surplus of rooms and low occupancy rates. High operating expenses diminished profit margins considerably in years with low occupancy rates, especially given that hotels had to keep room rates down in such years as well. The predictable outcome was that record losses were experienced by the industry during a period of oversupply (e.g., full-service hotels with significant departmental expenses particularly experienced this loss history). The occupancy rates for limited-service hotels were not significantly different from those of full-service hotels, according to Smith Travel Associates. This suggests why some large corporate hotel operators in the late 1990s were emphasizing a more limited-service facility that had lower operating costs yet retained good customer traffic and operating gross margins. Exhibit 8 presents 1995 data on hotel real estate selling prices and estimated costs of replacement per room.

Perhaps the most profound change in hotel industry strategy arose from the dramatic shift of hotel properties from private to public ownership. The volume of investment dollars for the hotel industry was significantly greater in the late 1990s than it had been historically. Banks, insurance companies, finance companies, equity investors and real estate investment trusts (REITs) entered the hotel industry with aggressive parameters as they perceived that the market oversupply had begun to dissipate. The latter instrument, REITs, which emerged in 1991, had become a major source of low-cost capital that fueled growth and construction in the hotel industry. Starwood Lodging had used REITs as a vehicle to acquire Westin Hotels and Sheraton Hotels from IT&T. The availability of low-cost capital became an especially important factor for the larger players in the industry, who moved increasingly toward consolidation via acquisition

exhibit 8   Hotel Real Estate Selling Prices and Estimated Costs of Replacement, 1995

Lodging Segment	Average Selling Price per Room	Estimated Cost of Replacement per Room
Budget	$11,804	$25,000–30,000
Economy—limited service	20,538	30,000–35,000
Economy—full service	19,239	35,000–50,000
Midmarket—limited service	42,244	35,000–50,000
Midmarket —full service	42,117	45,000–70,000
Luxury—limited service	65,174	80,000–150,000

Source: National Hotel Realty Advisor.

of other chains, according the Smith Travel Associates. However, the lowering of barriers to entry allowed disproportionate levels of new supply in the industry.

Aging of the baby boomers also emerged as a significant demographic factor. Seventy million Americans were moving into their midlives (over 50) and were expected to seek greater comfort and choose service over price in their choice of hotels. In the late 1990s, other emerging trends in the hotel industry included (1) the introduction of limited-service suites; (2) additional emphasis on higher-value-added business-related amenities such as data ports for laptops and interactive Web TV sets in rooms; (3) automation of labor-intensive functions via information technology; (4) development of extended-stay or "residence-style" hotels and time-share projects; (5) reduction in marketing expenses and long-term operating costs via standardization and branding of properties.

In spite of the many changes in the hotel industry, comments made by Kimpton executives suggest that, in addition to location, the factors still considered critical to success in the hotel industry include:

- Low-cost purchases of land or buildings.
- Greater latitude in product/service offerings at comparable profit margins.
- Customer service.
- Effective utilization of technology.
- Brand loyalty.
- Employee training and development.
- Complementary services.
- Revenue management systems.
- Clean and comfortable lodging.
- Strategic alliances.
- Convenience in making reservations.
- Access to growth capital.
- Value-added services.

The Boutique Hotel Niche

As the millennium approached, the emerging boutique or small luxury hotel niche began attracting new entrants, both large and small. For example, Starwood Hotels & Resorts announced in late 1998 that it was launching a new "W" line of boutique hotels with fewer than 400 rooms in an attempt to replicate the Kimpton formula for success.

Based in White Plains, New York, Starwood Hotels & Resorts managed, owned, and operated such branded properties as St. Regis and the Luxury Collection (luxury hotels), Westin (upscale full-service), Sheraton (full-service), and W (boutique full-service hotels for business travelers). It had sold its Caesars World properties in early 1999. Starwood's meteoric yet troubled rise had been guided by chairman Barry Sternlicht (German for "starlight"), an aggressive dealmaker who snatched ITT from Hilton Hotels. Sternlicht owned about 5 percent of the firm. In 1999 the company abandoned its paired-share real estate investment trust structure for a standard corporate structure with a property-owning REIT subsidiary; Starwood Hotels & Resorts Worldwide managed the operation of the properties. A 21-story W Hotel opened across from the Moscone Convention Center in San Francisco in April 1999. Despite heavy debt and the high costs of integrating operations acquired during the whirlwind buying spree that preceded the change in its structure, in mid-1999 Starwood announced that it planned to expand into Latin America.

The other national player in the boutique hotel category, according to a July 1999 story in the *San Francisco Examiner,* was New York hotelier Ian Schrager (formerly co-owner of the Studio 54 disco). Schrager ran the Royalton in New York, the Mondrian in Los Angeles, and had purchased the Clift Hotel in San Francisco for $80 million in June 1999. The Clift was undergoing a $25 million facelift prior to its reopening in October 1999.

Boutique hotels accounted for about 15 percent of San Francisco's estimated 31,000 rooms. In San Francisco, KG was the recognized market leader, with 67 percent of the city's boutique hotels, according to analyst Anwar Elgonomy of PKF Consulting. Chip Conley's Joie de Vivre Hotels enjoyed 20 percent of the San Francisco market, and Yvonne Lembi-Detert's Personality Hotels on Union Square, with four properties, had 12 percent of the market. Other operators split the remaining 1 percent. "It's a very specific group of people [boutique hoteliers] are going after: well-educated professionals," Elgonomy said recently in an interview in the *San Francisco Examiner,* "people who don't like generic activities. People who don't like Starbucks."

Chip Conley, president of Joie de Vivre, a $40 million chain of 14 boutique hotels and motels in the San Francisco Bay area, commented on the boutique lodging niche in an April 1999 interview with Neal Templin in the *Contra Costa Times*:

> The question is whether the big boys will have the agility to handle the boutique market. We look for aging hotels with "good bones"—good elevators, plumbing and electrical systems—and bad images. We spend our money on things that get a lot of bang for the buck. Our strategy is to make our Hotel del Sol a national brand by buying a portfolio of motels around the country and converting them to the same concept. There's a huge collection of 1950s and 1960s hotels waiting to be fixed up. Our next project to open will be a boutique camping resort south of San Francisco where guests will rough it in tents but still be able to order up caffé lattés after their hikes in the woods. It is aimed at the sort of people who buy sport-utility vehicles even though they rarely drive off-road. They can feel like they're connected with nature while not getting their hands dirty.

One reason San Francisco spawned so many boutique hotels is that it had had a big inventory of older hotels that could be cheaply acquired and converted. Analyst C. Jay Scott, of Scott Hospitality Services in San Francisco, noted, "Boutique hotels don't work everywhere. They work only in downtowns that are still vibrant relative to business and leisure travel markets. It's a concept that has been well received by the marketplace. Why try to continually reinvent yourself when you have a concept that works?"

As property values in San Francisco soared, KG's competitors were increasingly building all-new developments, which, in the opinion of Kimpton executives, were both more risky and less profitable than conversions. By contrast, most of the KG's hotels were converted buildings that had been built for other purposes. In the words of Jeff Senior, KG's director of marketing:

> Our lowered asset investment requires a lesser average rate to be successful. In other words, it costs us less, so we can charge less and still be as much or more profitable than our competitors. In reality, any full service hotel in markets we compete within is a competitor, including Sheraton, Westin, Hyatt, Starwood, etc. Other competitors include other boutique providers.

According to Bill Scatchard, publisher of *Hoteliers' Infosource*, the baby boomer generation was attracted to the boutique style hotel that Kimpton Group pioneered. The brightly trimmed decor with a hint of European luxury appeared to capture the taste of this lucrative segment. In general, the market appeared to favor properties that offered a fun atmosphere in an intimate surrounding. One hotel manager at the Kimpton Group suggested that his organization was one of two or three companies that had responded to this boutique hotel niche very well. This general manager, keenly aware of Kimpton's prominence in the San Francisco market, took a more global perspective. He emphasized the relative smallness of the company's presence overall and described the Kimpton Group niche in the hotel industry colorfully: "We're like a pimple on the ass of an elephant."

The Kimpton Organization

The Kimpton Hotel and Restaurant Group consisted of a family of 23 boutique-style hotels and 24 unique and often independently successful restaurants. Its hotels ranged in size from 91 to 483 rooms, and a typical hotel had between 100 and 200 rooms. KG's destination restaurants, each with its own local following, were located in the same buildings as the hotels.

Founder William Kimpton, now 63, bought his first hotel in 1981. Kimpton was born in Kansas City, Missouri, and in his schooldays was hampered by what he now believes was dyslexia. He noted that he did not learn to read until he reached high school. He struggled academically but was encouraged by his family to continue schooling. Kimpton earned a bachelor of science in economics from Northwestern University and was a graduate of the renowned University of Chicago Lab School. Prior to starting the Kimpton Group in 1981, Kimpton served for three and a half years as director and vice president of Lepercq de Neuflize, an international investment banking firm. During his stint at Lepercq, Kimpton participated in negotiating, structuring, and overseeing the projects of Lepercq de Neuflize. Preceding Lepercq, Kimpton was a partner in Shuman, Agnew & Co., Inc., in Belvedere, California, where he was responsible for project finance. Other experiences that helped shape his acumen for project financing included almost four years as a manager with Lehman Brothers (now Shearson–Lehman Brothers American Express, Inc.) in its San Francisco office. This assignment in San Francisco followed his three years as an associate for Lehman Brothers in its Chicago office.

Bill Kimpton's approach to the hotel industry was based on his prior career as an investment banker. Kimpton began his foray into the hotel industry by structuring a highly creative investment strategy for the Helmsley Hotel organization. He worked with Harry Helmsley (now probably best known for the exploits of his controversial wife, Leona Helmsley, the "Queen of Mean") to raise seed money for the $23 million renovation of the New York Palace Hotel. Through that project Kimpton became known for his imaginative approach to raising investment capital. Kimpton also handled the financing for the exclusive Kapalua Bay resort in Maui and brought in the Rockefeller family's RockResorts to manage the property.

Bill Kimpton recalled that he wanted to get into a business "that sells sleep, because sleep has high [profit] margins." He combined his bottom-line focus with a unique feel for offering value and comfort with a "personality" in all the Kimpton Group properties. He imprinted on his hotel and restaurant management team a flair for being different yet profitable. "My theory is, no matter how much money people have to spend on big, fancy hotels, they are intimidated," Kimpton said recently. "The psychology of how you build restaurants and hotels is very important. You put a fireplace in the lobby and create a warm, friendly restaurant and the guest will feel safe."

Bill Kimpton, by 1999, had served as chairman and chief executive of KG since its inception. Although he was by then no longer intimately involved in day-to-day management, Kimpton's entrepreneurial style was still very visible in the organization. His style was very personal, and he practiced a decentralized approach to decision making since the early days of the corporation. Following his entrepreneurial flair, each property emphasized guest room comfort rather than high overhead amenities such as fancy water fountains, ornate lobbies, or excessive brass and glass.

Guest rooms were tastefully decorated in cheerful colors with elegant bedspreads and thick carpeting, perhaps reflecting Bill Kimpton's trademark multicolor sweaters. Each room was meant to feel like a comfortable guest room in a friend's luxury home and was complete with good lighting; a stocked honor bar/refrigerator; and direct-dial phones with extralong cords to reach the bed, the desk, and other parts of the room. Hotel lobbies were furnished with the emphasis on comfort, not on waiting, and each had a cozy fireplace.

KG's strategy was to create each hotel as a stand-alone "personality" that appealed to its own unique customer group. The hotels shared a common upscale theme and appearance but priced the rooms below the full-service hotels such as Marriott or Hilton. A European style was visible in almost every KG property. Kimpton's aggressive expansion in San Francisco made it very difficult for other chains to find low-cost property in commercial locations that could compete on both price and amenities found at the KG properties.

A high degree of personalized service and numerous complementary amenities were also the hallmark of KG's hotels. Some KG hotels were testing a system to provide arriving guests with "desk-less" check-in via use of cellular and digital communications technology. Doormen were equipped with headsets and could escort new guests directly to their rooms without the usual paperwork and waiting around, considered to be some of the most unwelcoming experiences of tired travelers who just want to get into their rooms. Most hotels featured some or all of the following complementary services: limousines to the financial district, wine served in the lobby each evening, continental breakfast, and coffee and tea available throughout the day. Most hotels also offered same-day valet and laundry service, room service and express check-out with on-site parking. According to Kimpton executives, all of these services were provided at room rates that averaged 25 to 30 percent lower than comparable hotels in the same markets. Indicative of the success of KG's strategy was its annual occupancy rates, which averaged 85 percent over the group, compared to the industry average, which hovered between 68 and 75 percent, depending on the geographical market segment served.

Human Resources

Hotel general managers were strongly encouraged to innovate and provide their specific property with a personality that separated it from the other properties in KG's portfolio.

Senior management practiced reciprocal communication and was very reluctant to impose anything other than customer-related service standards on each property.

Nanci Sherman, general manager of the Hotel Monaco in San Francisco, confirmed this approach:

> Most of our general managers have a hotel background, but like me are refugees from patriarchal companies like Hilton, Disney, and Ritz-Carlton. People come to Kimpton because they see there's another way. Why is it that in 200,000 hotels around the world that the staff meet every Tuesday and Friday for two hours but no changes ever take place? We built our business around the 2 percent that rarely occurs, not on the 98 percent that happens regularly. We really want to look good. Very rarely do we (as industry people) want to take risks. Building a group culture starts with who we are as people: giving, teamwork, friendship, and confidence. People who get rewarded and promoted here are team players. But you can't run a highly bureaucratic, top-down management style anymore, even in a conservative industry like the hotel industry. That's a major reason why our staff turnover rate has been 18–21 percent over the past two years, far below the average rate of 50 percent in the industry. Low turnover rates are absolutely essential to us, because the hotels with the lowest turnover rates have the highest financial performance, particularly in the tight labor markets that we are experiencing now.

Each hotel manager and line staff member attended "Kimpton University," a program of in-house classes on front-desk service, housekeeping, finance and record-keeping, and corporate wellness. In keeping with KG's philosophy of the "gracious host," general managers poured wine for guests at the cocktail hour each night. It was on these occasions that feedback on amenities and service was most readily obtained on a firsthand basis. Feedback from guests was systematically gathered via comment cards in guest rooms. Some of its hotels were experimenting with using interactive TV in guest rooms to obtain comments at check-out. The company also had hired Pannell Kerr Foster (PKF), a San Francisco-based consulting firm, to obtain quality control information using "phantom guests." Executives were also considering the use of focus groups to obtain feedback about the efficacy of current and planned future service offerings. KG observed a "sundown rule," in that each general manager must respond to a guest's comments on their stay by the end of the business day.

KG hired people whose "light had been hidden under a bushel," according to Jim McPartlin, general manager of the Prescott Hotel in San Francisco and the citywide manager for KG's San Francisco Hotels. "We encouraged the operating managers to 'be different' and think 'outside of the box,'" said McPartlin. "The incentives are there, as we can earn up to 25 percent bonus on our salaries, paid out quarterly. Our typical wage percentage of sales is about 22 percent, of which 70 percent is 'raw' wages and 30 percent are benefits. We also have a 'Circle of Stars,' an employee luncheon once a month, where employees who are recognized by guests for outstanding service can win prizes in a 'Wheel of Fortune'–type game," he added.

KG did not have a formal organization chart. According to David Martin, the director of hotel operations:

> Perhaps this is because we try to create an entrepreneurial atmosphere. We hire managers who have the guts to make decisions. Internal competition—creativity—that we label as entrepreneurial is healthy, as long as it's in the customer's best interests. We must meet minimum customer standards. There's sort of a Maslow's hierarchy almost. We gotta be clean, personable, and offer quick service.
>
> We offer a "fireside chat" once a quarter, where we put Steve [Marx] on the firing line with the hotel general managers. He gets people to express their needs. We've challenged Steve on many occasions. We talk about real issues that are important to managers.

"Mongoose" Strategy

Since its inception in 1981, KG had followed a so-called mongoose strategy—named after the ferretlike animal that successfully kills poisonous animals by circling them until they tire, at which point it dives in quickly and finishes them off. Before the company successfully bought its Bellevue property, Kimpton bid $10 million and was outbid by investors who paid $15 million, according to the *New York Times* on January 16, 1994. The company watched the property for seven years until it was able to pick up that property from those owners for $5 million. Similarly, the firm bought the Sir Francis Drake property for $19.5 million, although the property had been on the market eight years earlier for $60 million. If a property possessed the three attributes of uniqueness in character, location, and design potential, it became a target for the patient capital of the KG and its co-investors. Each new property was typically financed by 60 percent equity and 40 percent debt, considered low leverage in the hotel industry.

In the San Francisco market, which by 1999 included 15 semiluxury hotels and 16 destination restaurants, KG began with the Bedford Hotel in 1981, which was followed by the Vintage Court, the Galleria Park, the Juliana, and so on until the firm controlled some 2,000 rooms in its home market. As a point of reference, the Hilton, which towered in the skyline of San Francisco, had almost as many rooms as the entire collection of KG properties in that city. Other properties were located in Seattle, Tacoma, Portland, Denver, Chicago, and the soon-to-be-opened Hotel Monaco in Salt Lake City.

By mid-1999, KG was considering expansion to the East Coast and had begun looking at properties in New York, Boston, and Washington, D.C. "It's time to start looking outside the West Coast," Bill Kimpton recently told the *San Francisco Examiner.* "It's difficult to find a building that hasn't already been worked over. We'd love to be in New York. We'd like to be in San Diego. We're going into Vancouver [in spring 2000]."

Customer Targets

The KG avoided targeting the 10 percent of customers who wanted absolute luxury. Nor was it after the backpacking student. Rather, KG had sought to serve the 50 to 60 percent of the market that was looking for "comfort and value." In 1994, Bill Kimpton summarized his approach quite succinctly in the *New York Times*: "We sell sleep, while corporation lodging [full-service hotels] is in the entertainment business because of all the extras it has to offer." Guests at those other hotel facilities paid for the meeting rooms, the ornate lobbies, the fabulous water fountains, the unused restaurants, and other services that most would never use. A hotel, according to KG's philosophy, should relieve a traveler of his or her loneliness. It should make guests feel "warm and cozy," Bill Kimpton told the *Chicago Tribune* in 1998. This vision shaped the organization's approach to the hotel industry in general and to its markets in particular.

In discussing KG's success, Steve Marx spoke of a "customer intimacy" that gave "personality" to each one of its properties. This focus on service details resembled the attention to cost details that characterized the property acquisition process for which KG had become noted.

According to Jeff Senior:

> How do we build brand equity? Classic brand management. We need to rely on the power of the individual hotel brands, a core premise in our niche/boutique hotel segment. We need to focus on the product positioning, ensuring uniqueness and legitimate competitive advantage; product and service delivery consistency with the positioning; distribution focus against the highest-yielding channels for our target; and performance management to ensure desired results are achieved, appropriate corrective action taken, and strategic revisions evaluated in

an ongoing manner. We compete within the deluxe category in urban markets . . . both reflecting much higher barrier to entry.

The target market for KG included both business and tourist travelers who were looking for a unique, intimate, and personal hotel experience. International guests represented about 11 percent of KG's total. The amenities offered by KG properties bordered on luxury but provided each guest with a clearly recognized bargain compared with the upscale chains such as Hilton or Marriott.

Restaurant Operations

Each of the restaurants that KG operated had a separate entrance and a separate identity from its hotel location. The company took pains to avoid having its restaurants perceived as "hotel restaurants." Niki Leondakis, vice president of restaurant operations for KG and six-year veteran of the organization, said that hotel restaurants were the antithesis of what her company did best. "The minute that we become a hotel-restaurant," Leondakis added, "that's death. A hotel-restaurant has a stigma: overpriced [and offering] poor service." KG strove to offer dining patrons a "handcrafted" experience—something that gave character and personality. "[We] want our guests to feel they're getting something they can't get anywhere else," commented Leondakis.

Jeff Senior commented:

> When I came to Kimpton less than a year ago, we were already structured with a separate restaurant division. While the downside is a duplication of resources to support the respective businesses, the upside is a focus on the core competencies of each business and the key drivers of profitability. The result: we have profitable restaurants and profitable hotels.

Following this strategy, each KG restaurant was custom-made for each property and market location. Each restaurant was allowed to run independently and to exist with renowned chefs including Julian Serrano (at Masa's), Wolfgang Puck (at the Postrio), and Gionvanni Perticone (at the Splendido). According to KG's San Francisco city manager Jim McPartlin, "We create freestanding restaurants that actually make an operating profit, around 5 to 15 percent versus the break-even margins at typical hotel restaurants."

Each of the KG-managed restaurants was individually themed and offered a variety of food styles, price ranges, and ambiences. Many of the restaurants featured exhibition kitchens and counter seating that made them user-friendly for single guests who wished to dine alone. "Our restaurants are run by restaurateurs," said Leondakis. "We provide service to the hotel, but our restaurants are more than a food and beverage outlet. We are a profitable, independent, and separate business."

In December 1998, a Smith Travel Associates report on the U.S. lodging industry noted that, on average, 73 percent of a hotel's revenue came from rooms, 20.6 percent from food and beverage, and 6.4 percent from minor operations such as telecommunications, space rentals, and other miscellaneous sources. KG depended on its restaurants to deliver extra perceived value to customers, much as the full-service hotel with much higher room rates would. The most obvious cross-marketing between the restaurant and hotel operations occurred when restaurant customers visited the restroom and inevitably had to walk through the lobby of the hotel. Diners would, hopefully, spread the word about the little boutique hotel that they had "discovered" while having a terrific dinner.

Thus, KG helped pioneer the strategy of a stand-alone restaurant as a lure to get word-of-mouth advertising for its hotels. However, other chains, such as Fairfield Inns by Marriott, Hilton Garden Inn, and Microtel were known to be operating some of their properties under a strategy very similar to the Kimpton Group's approach of attracting travelers by being closely associated with a world-class restaurant. A potential concern for all using this strategy is that there is a limited pool of quality chefs willing to work within the structure of a corporation, especially when the strong suit of the corporation is the hotel division.

The Future

As with most business situations, past success could turn out to be a double-edged sword for KG. A recent collaboration with the Trammel-Crow investment group made funds more or less readily available for property acquisition and rapid growth. Yet, it was not clear that KG's strategy could be easily transferred to other markets. KG needed to decide on its desired growth rate and how it could manage growth without losing the uniqueness and decentralized culture that its senior management held in high regard.

According to PKF, the San Francisco-based hotel and real estate research firm, the projected profitability of the industry could, by the year 2000, reach the highest in at least a half-century. Gross margins could exceed 30 percent, fattening returns on investment and permitting aggressive expansion by KG into untapped markets.

Still, KG has insisted that the organization does not do deals just to do deals. By 1999, the group was managing almost 4,000 rooms in increasingly far-flung locations. Although privately held, KG executives revealed that revenues had grown by an estimated 10 to 20 percent per year in the past six years. The organization had been generating a consistent 15 to 20 percent return for its investment partners, all high-net-worth individuals including movie stars Paul Newman and Harrison Ford, as well as members of the Getty family. The level of return also exceeds the 13 percent return on investment target set by the Crow family.

In order to continue to differentiate itself from the competition, in 1999 KG added new amenities in its guest rooms such as telephones that easily accommodated laptop computers, easy chairs, desks with large work surfaces, and improved lighting. Technological trends that may affect the competitive landscape of the hotel industry included the emerging use of "smart cards" to replace cash and capture unique preferences of the hotel guest. Technology similarly made hotel-specific Web sites and bargain-hunting at sites like www.priceline.com almost ubiquitous within the industry.

According to Jeff Senior, KG was experiencing difficulty entering the Internet age:

> Fear of technology and systems is serious around here. The infrastructure does not exist. We have only one management information system person in this entire organization. We're not using e-mail. Our high technology is voice mail.

Also in 1999, KG began to emphasize on-site revenue management systems. This information would help general managers decide what each part of their operation contributed to profitability, which, in turn, would help senior executives at the group level to understand the potential for increasing internal efficiencies. Additionally, information access improvements were expected to give each property general manager a sense of decentralized decision making in spite of living under a corporate umbrella.

Strategic Meeting at KG: Afterthoughts

Before the 3:00 PM meeting with David Martin and Jeff Senior ended, Marx had an opportunity to explore with them the range of strategic choices that he thought were critical to the continued success of KG. Looking back after that meeting, Marx noted:

There are people in integral positions in this organization who remain "small thinkers" and who are afraid to step up to the plate. Our greatest fault is that we're sometimes not ready to put our money where our mouth is. That's a real danger. From the top, you've got to send a signal that it's okay to take risks, that it's (sort of) okay to fail. Mind you, we have made very few mistakes. Still, we have to be more careful about seducing ourselves that every market is the right place for our hotels. The problem is the fragility of the tourism economies in other cities, making it difficult to expand into new markets.

We're sort of disorganized; I know we like to kid ourselves about how "seat-of-the-pants" we are, and we say we're strategic but we're really very tactical. This is typical of the hotel industry. We are trying to be strategic in what really is a tactical industry. We need to decide where we're going in the future. You can't have two sides of an organization in conflict. We have tension that is unnecessary, sort of a push-pull between those managers that advocate returning to what we used to be and those that advocate changing into what we're going to become. Even Bill [Kimpton, the founder and chairman of the Kimpton Group] is torn.

We need to preserve our philosophy to enable a general manager to imprint their personality on an individual hotel. We need to continue to go to great lengths to attract and nurture people who believe that their success is also the success of the company. Always stay in touch with line employees. I actually want to hear bad news. Be unreasonable. Set unreasonable expectations. And always be really hands-on with our owners. These are hallmarks of what we do.

After the afternoon meeting with Martin and Senior, Marx wondered to what extent his successors could cope with the changing dynamics in the hotel industry and at the same time continue the open management philosophy and participatory decision-making style that had served KG so well during his tenure. The strategic choices to be made now fell—at least, temporarily—on Martin and Senior's watch. He wondered in what direction they would take KG and which issues they would make their priorities.

bibliography

Allen, J. L. "San Franciscan Making More Room at Inns." *Chicago Tribune,* March 18, 1998.

Anderson, R. *Atlas of the American Economy.* Washington, D. C.: Congressional Quarterly, 1994.

Armstrong, D. "Keeping Hotels Hot." *San Francisco Examiner,* July 18, 1999, p. B1.

"Front Desk." *Lodging,* July 1998, p. 16.

Garfinkel, P. "Bed & Breakfast? No, Bed and Dinner." *New York Times,* January 16, 1994.

Higley, J. "Kimpton Group Broadens Its Horizon." *Hotel & Motel Management* 213, no. 13 (July 20, 1998).

"Motels and Hotels." *Moody's Industry Review,* January 22, 1999.

"Ratings of Hotels & Motels." *Consumer Reports,* July 1998, p. 17.

Scatchard, B. "Occupancy Was Down Last Year." *Hoteliers' Infosource* 7, no. 1 (January 1999).

Smith, R. A. "Lodging Outlook Survey for the Year Ending December, 1998." Smith Travel Associates Research, www.hotel-online.com, May 16, 1999.

Tardiff, J. C. *U.S. Industry Profiles.* New York: Gale Research, 1998.

Templin, N. "Eccentric Sells: S. F. Firm Finds a Profitable Niche with Boutique Hotels." *Contra Costa Times,* April 17, 1999, pp. C1–C2.

U. S. Department of Commerce. *Census of Service Industries.* 1998.

Brithinee Electric in 1999: Raising the Standards

Harold Dyck
California State University–San Bernardino

Sue Greenfeld
California State University–San Bernardino

As teenagers, identical twins Wallace Jr. and Don Brithinee helped when their father, Wallace Sr., started Brithinee Electric in 1963. Back then, the entire business consisted of repairing electric motors. Providing first-rate service to customers with critical motor repair needs became the primary mission and business of Brithinee Electric. On occasion, meeting the turnaround times desired by customers meant working around the clock. Hard work eventually earned the twin brothers PhDs in mathematics from the University of California–Riverside by the time they were 23 years old, and helped lay the foundation for the cultural values and success of the firm in the succeeding decades. Brithinee Electric had won an assortment of industry and manufacturers' awards, which were proudly displayed in the lobby of the company's offices. At the entrance to the company's conference room were pictures of Wally and Don Brithinee with a number of distinguished political figures, including former head of the Joint Chiefs of Staff, General Colin Powell, and former British prime minister Margaret Thatcher.

Brithinee Electric repaired industrial motors, distributed motor/control devices, and designed and built control panels, primarily for municipalities and other businesses. In 1988 this Colton, California, firm commemorated 25 years in business, had 23 employees, and brought in $4.6 million in revenue; that same year, a case study about the firm appeared in three strategic management textbooks.[1] At that time, the company had an implied mission based on quality and service, but did not have a formal mission statement. The most pressing issues facing the company then included employee development, job rotation, overdependency on the "Brithinee boys," and whether to undertake a major expansion. The company was located in the "Inland

---

[1]S. Greenfeld, "Brithinee Electric," in Smith, Arnold, and Bizzell, eds., *Business Strategy and Policy* (Boston: Houghton-Mifflin, 1991), pp. 180–200. Also in Stahl and Grisby, eds., *Strategic Management for Decision Making* (Boston: PWS-Kent, 1992), pp. 368–87, and Dess and Miller, eds., *Strategic Management,* (New York: McGraw-Hill, 1993), pp. 393–410.

exhibit 1   Brithinee Electric's Mission Statement

> **Brithinee Electric**
>
> Our mission:
>
> *to delight our customers by delivering products and services of superior quality, thereby raising their expectations.*

Empire," about 50 miles directly east of Los Angeles; the expansion then under consideration would have meant building a new facility to service customers in the San Diego area.

Eleven years later, in 1999, Brithinee Electric had grown to 50 employees and $6.7 million in revenues. The company had decided against expanding into the San Diego area. It had weathered a recession, struggled through the loss of a $1-million-per-year customer, coped with mounting competition in its industry, improved employee training through more formalized methods, worked through the job rotation issues encountered earlier, and solved most of the dependency issues. The Brithinee brothers had developed a formal mission statement centered on "enabling the customer." This had led to an effort to encourage and empower the company's multiethnic employees to "provide literature, materials, specifications, and some learning opportunities for our customers." The company had recently added the words "Brithinee Electric . . . Raising the Standards" to its "Customer Bill of Rights" (see Exhibits 1 and 2).

In 1999, Brithinee Electric had a different set of challenges. Competition in selling electric motors was now considerably stronger than it had been in the late 1980s. Moreover, customers wanted more sophisticated control devices than used to be the case. Wally and Don believed that for Brithinee Electric to grow and prosper in the years ahead they would need to resolve several strategic and organizational issues: How could an independent motor rewinding shop like Brithinee Electric best position itself against its rivals, many of whom were substantially larger? What could Brithinee Electric do to distinguish itself from its competitors? Could Brithinee successfully position itself as a high-quality service provider when a number of its customers didn't seem to appreciate the need for or the value of high standards for motor repair? What organizational changes, if any, did the company need to consider making? Exhibit 3 presents the company's current organizational chart.

COMPANY HISTORY

Wallace Brithinee Sr. started Brithinee Electric in 1963 after two previous ventures did not work out. The earlier ventures proved to be a springboard for getting into the business of repairing industrial motors. Wallace's young sons, Wally and Don Brithinee, worked alongside their father in starting and developing the fledgling company, gradually learning the rewinding business.

In 1970, when Lincoln Electric, a large manufacturer of electric motors, came out with an appealing low-priced motor, the Brithinees made a strategic decision to become distributors for Lincoln's new product line. Taking on the Lincoln line allowed

exhibit 2   Brithinee Electric's Customer Bill of Rights

CUSTOMER BILL OF RIGHTS

At Brithinee Electric, we believe both the customer and the supplier of electrical hardware and service will benefit if the purchase decision is an informed one. Assert your rights as customer by getting to know your vendor's business practices. Get maximum value by comparing the vendor's commitment as well as the price.

As a customer of Brithinee Electric, you have the right to expect:

RELIABILITY
- Stable workforce
- Work references
- Sound financial condition
- Environmental responsibility

QUALITY
- Qualified personnel
- Documentation
- Pride in workmanship
- Best available technology

COMMUNICATION
- Before and after tests reports
- Prompt and accurate quotations
- Product and service alternatives
- Accurate itemized invoices

COMMITMENT
- Service
- Investment in technology and our facility
- Investment in inventory
- Problem solving

BRITHINEE ELECTRIC

. . . Raising the Standards

Brithinee Electric to offer its customers the choice of repairing or replacing a malfunctioning motor. By 1972 Brithinee Electric had seven employees and enough business to feel optimistic about the future, so it built a 10,000-square-foot facility to house the business. The company's facilities were expanded to 16,750 square feet seven years later. By 1980 Brithinee Electric had 23 employees. In 1982 Wally and Don Brithinee took over management of the business when Wallace Sr. decided to retire.

In 1987, Brithinee had about $4.5 million in revenue, about 75 percent of which came from selling its Toshiba and Baldor lines of electric motors and about 25 percent of which came from motor repair work. Building customized electric control panels was a new venture with one full-time employee, but control panel sales were not yet large enough to be listed as a separate revenue category in the company's financial statements. Brithinee's main emphasis was in motors for water pumping and treatment areas, rock crushing, cement facilities, and the food industry, including wineries and breweries.

MOTOR REPAIR AND ENERGY EFFICIENCY

Various government agencies and utilities in the United States and Canada estimated that the use of electric motors in various types of equipment and appliances accounted for close to 70 percent of total electrical energy consumption, roughly equivalent to the energy consumption of all passenger automobiles. Just as proper maintenance and repair practices had a positive effect on reducing an automobile's gasoline consumption, proper maintenance and repair practices had a positive effect on the electric motor efficiency. A poorly repaired electric motor could end up using significantly more electricity than was

exhibit 3   Brithinee Electric's Organization Chart

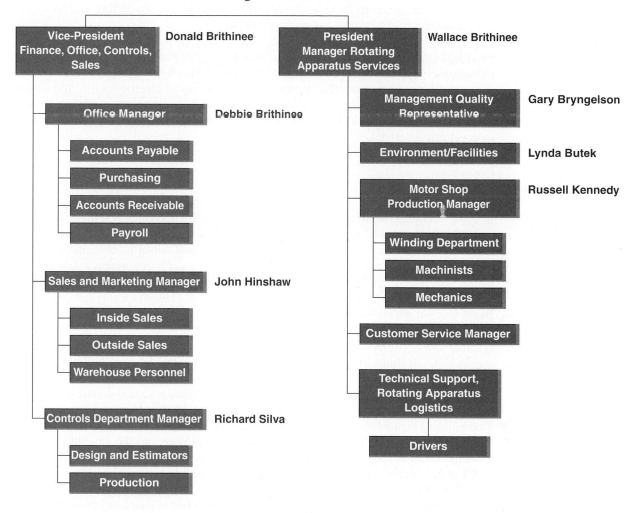

necessary. Most industrial users of electric motors were aware that using properly repaired electric motors not only improved the reliability of electric-powered equipment but also helped reduce their costs for electric power.

When Iraq invaded Kuwait in August 1990, threatening Western oil supplies, legislators in the United States and Canada passed more stringent requirements mandating greater electric motor efficiency. Noting that the horsepower of electric motors repaired far exceeded the horsepower of newly sold electric motors, regulators studied the repair process for electric motors as well as the purchasing practices of industrial firms. While considering draconian measures such as licensing schemes or even the banning of motor repair in favor of replacement with new, energy-efficient models, the sentiment for less government intervention led to voluntary-compliance programs to improve electric motor repair practices in ways that would boost efficiency and reduce electricity consumption. Wally Brithinee, as the chairman of the Engineering Committee of the Electrical Apparatus Service Association (EASA), had led the development of a set of standards and guidelines for repair of electric motors that met most of the regulators' concerns. These standards and guidelines subsequently became the building blocks for the motor repair industry, ushering in a new set of best practices in electric motor repair. Brithinee's adherence to these new standards was used as a marketing tool to attract new customers and win business away from rivals.

In addition to seeking to reduce U.S. dependency on foreign oil, the U.S. government had signed two climate-change treaties and agreed to pursue actions to reduce greenhouse gas emissions. Since fossil-fuel power plants were large contributors to such emissions, any actions that increased the efficiency of electric motors and dampened electricity consumption helped meet greenhouse gas emission standards. Hence, heightened environmental concerns were adding to the pressure to improve electric motor repair practices.

BRITHINEE ELECTRIC IN THE 1990S

In 1991, Brithinee Electric experienced its first significant decline in revenues. The company "hit a brick wall," says Don Brithinee. The U.S. economy went into a recession, which Brithinee weathered with some pain. Through no fault of its own, the company lost a $1-million-per-year customer because the customer's equipment could not accommodate the change in the size of the variable frequency drive that Brithinee was supplying. Brithinee's total revenue declined further in 1992 before turning upward again. But it was not until 1996 that revenues exceeded the level achieved in 1990. Brithinee was proud that no one was laid off during the downturn, though some employees were asked to take accumulated vacation time.

In 1992, Brithinee made three changes to enable it to handle the rebuilding of large quantities of locomotive motors from General Motors' Electro-Motive Division (EMD) and to expand inventory space. First, the company acquired a 13,000-square-foot building (called the 680 Building due to its address) about 100 yards south of the old site. This building cost $495,000, and another $141,000 was spent for remodeling. Second, $500,000 of inventory was moved out of the main building into the new building, the winding machine shop areas were enlarged, and special floor space was dedicated to EMD motor repair activities. Third, the company established more stringent quality procedures than had previously existed.

Acquiring the 680 Building pushed Brithinee Electric in a new strategic direction: designing and building control panels. Previously, Brithinee had dabbled in making control panels, but making customized control panels became a significant part of the business in order to broaden the company's revenue and customer base and avoid being too dependent on one customer or product category. The decline in aerospace and defense in the early 1990s taught many Southern California businesses not to have all their eggs in one basket. Expanding into control panels was a "Y in the road," according to Don Brithinee. "It is a different beast . . . It's a cleaner operation . . . It's not a repair operation at all. It is an assembly of new electronic components." As part of this new focus, Brithinee hired Richard Silva in 1992; Silva was instrumental in attaining Underwriter Laboratories (UL) certification for the company. UL certification paved the way for Square D and Telemecanique, both subsidiaries of French multinational Groupe Schneider, to become major new customers.

Lynda Butek, the environmental/facilities coordinator, who worked directly for Wally Brithinee, was responsible for the 1992 installation of a closed-loop aqueous parts washer for loads weighing up to 20,000 pounds. The installation improved efficiency by eliminating the need to dispose of large quantities of water from a washdown area. Exhibits 4 and 5 show Brithinee's current facilities.

exhibit 4   Layout of Brithinee Electric "620 Building" (Facility for Manufacturing Electric Motors and Headquarters Office)

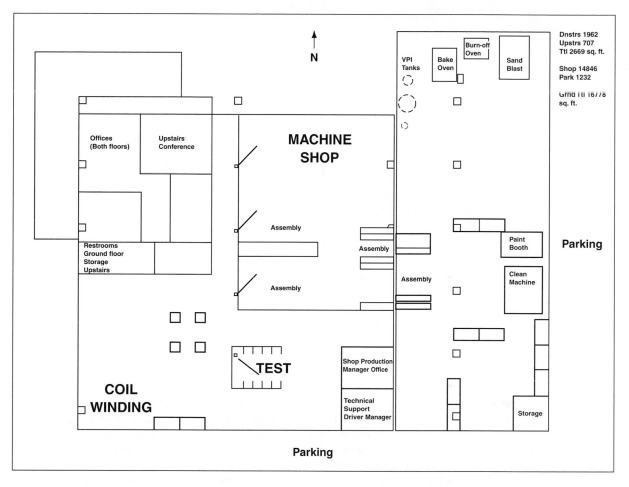

Wally described the circumstances surrounding the $315,000 renovation of the original 620 Building in 1997, stating that the reason for the remodel was

> to control the environment in the manufacturing area, and to make it reflect the quality of the products produced there. In that regard, we had specific goals and tasks. One was to reduce noise and increase the desirability of the eastern third of the building as a work area. That area has certain processes with air handlers and pumps that generate audible noise. These include the paint booth exhaust; the sand-blast cabinet and dust collector; and the parts washer, with its array of pumps. We evaluated all the lighting in the building and greatly increased it . . .
>
> At the same time, controls were centralized so that it would be easy to reduce lighting and electrical consumption when personnel were not in the work area. During the remodel, we added insulation with value of R-30 and covered the ceiling with a white plastic sheath. That moderated temperatures, further reduced noise, and increased the effectiveness of the light. The effects were dramatic.
>
> Shop offices were enlarged, allowing better supervisory control at the plant floor. A laser printer was added, with fax-modem, and the shop offices became much more efficient. There was far less cause for drivers, delivery persons, and shop personnel to come

exhibit 5   "680 Building" Layout

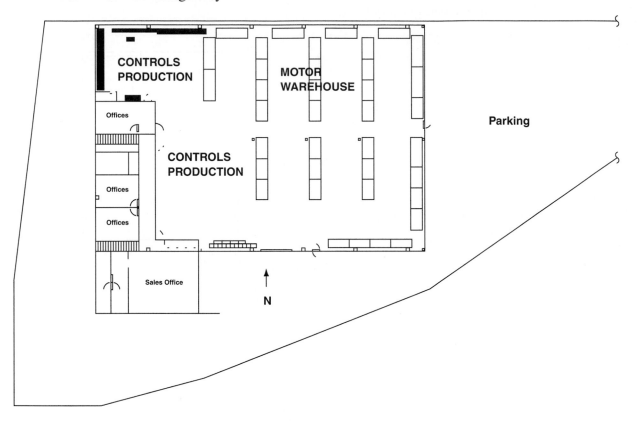

into the business office. The offices of this building were redone to eliminate the large, open office area. As we had grown, the open area seemed to create many distractions to the tasks at hand and to offer sound interference for telephone conversations.

    The conference room that existed was reshaped and enlarged, and today is fitted with a table for executive meetings. The decor has been completely redone from its early 1970s look to a more modern look.

Brithinee was installing a vacuum pressure impregnation (VPI) tank as an integral part of the company's repair capabilities. The closing of other motor repair shops in Southern California had resulted in an increase in larger motors coming into Brithinee for repair, creating the need for equipment to handle the larger stator and rotors on such motors. Putting in the new VPI tank required digging a 10- to 12-foot pit and getting various environmental protection permits.

    Brithinee primarily relied on personal selling to establish and cement relationships with customers. It also was the beneficiary of word-of-mouth advertising from satisfied customers. In late 1997, the company hired Cyd Sandefur as an assistant to Don Brithinee to work on advertising and other special projects.

    Brithinee's revenues in 1998 were $6.99 million; 43 percent came from motor repair work, 26 percent came from motor sales, and 31 percent were from custom-made control panel sales. While 11 years ago the company's accounting system provided separate itemized statements for repairs and sales, in 1999 there was a single consolidated statement. This system made it easy to move people from one area to another without making significant accounting changes but it provided less detailed information concerning specific labor charges to each different activity—motor repair, motor sales, and custom-made control panel sales.

THE INDUSTRY ENVIRONMENT FOR MOTOR SALES AND MOTOR REPAIR

Throughout the 1980s, sales of new electric motors grew at a 20 percent average compound rate. As the industry moved into the 1990s, growth slowed and the market matured, motor prices came down, and electric motor reliability went up. Features became user-friendly. Many types of electric motors became more standardized and more widely available from a variety of sources. By the late 1990s, competition had heated up to the point that 12 out of 13 of Toshiba's top distributors of variable-frequency drives (inverters) were selling fewer new motors. According to Don Brithinee, "What changed was better competition from some premium brand names." As Brithinee Electric lost market share to competing brands, the company's revenues from new motor sales dropped, contrary to management's expectations.

The introduction of electric motors with variable-frequency drives greatly changed the market by increasing motor system efficiency, reducing energy consumption, and changing repair requirements. Variable-frequency drives introduced high-voltage pulses, thousands each second, into the motor windings, resulting in partial discharge and corona. This produced highly corrosive ozone and charged particles that eroded the organic insulation from the windings. These problems increased the costs to rework a motor. Previously, insulation life could be 10 to 12 years without a failure, but with the new electronic frequency drives, wire failures could occur within a few hundred hours of operation.

The Engineering Committee for EASA had met with researchers from various electrical testing laboratories and with the suppliers making the various components of motor windings to make sure they understood the nature and costs of the repairs, to try to identify all the causes of the increase in winding failures, and to explore why the new motor inspection procedures and analysis used in the past were not working. Motor repair firms wanted to stay on top of what progress, if any, was being made in developing more resistant insulation materials.

The development of a microprocessor-controlled variable-frequency drive created opportunities for improved process control as well as improved energy efficiency of the driven system. With the more stringent energy-efficiency requirements mandated in the Energy Policy Act of 1992, motor manufacturers were redesigning electric motors. The design changes generally included increasing the active materials in the stator and rotor. In the stator (the part that is usually rewound) the active materials being used were laminated steel sheets ("core iron") and copper wire. In the case of copper wire, designers had increased the cross-section of the conductor, while reducing the length of the wire and cutting winding resistance. But in so doing, these design changes usually resulted in increased difficulty for coil insertion (trying to stuff more copper into a very crowded frame and core). Thus, motor repair firms needed thinner, tougher, slicker insulation in order to maintain the energy efficiency of the motor and withstand the harsh electrical environment that variable-frequency drives entailed.

The EASA Engineering Committee, chaired by Wally Brithinee, had brought all of these issues to the attention of Du Pont's Nomex and Kevlar researchers and marketers in Richmond, Virginia, as well as key industry suppliers of wire (Essex Group, Phelps Dodge) and resins (P. D. George Company). Additionally, the committee had met several times with the Technical Subsection of the NEMA Motors and Generators Committee in an effort to strengthen the information ties between manufacturers and the repair industry. All this had produced guidelines for motor rewinding that provided both an energy-efficient rewind as well as a winding that could give long life in the variable-frequency applications, using materials that were readily available.

Wally Brithinee's experiences in chairing the EASA committee helped him understand how the company could improve its motor repair practices to better address the maintenance problems that users were having, especially as concerned winding an "inverter-duty" motor. The repair process changes the company had implemented had been well received, enhancing the company's stature with several motor manufacturers. In a growing number of instances, the company's windings on repaired motors were proving superior and longer lasting than the windings on brand-new motors.

The Exit of Several Rivals from the Southern California Market

In 1999 Brithinee Electric confronted weaker competition in motor repair than it had in the late 1980s. Several large manufacturers with repair shops had withdrawn from the Southern California market. Don Brithinee observed, "The playing field is a lot more level when we are competing with another independent company than with the captive business of a major manufacturer. That has brought some positive changes for us because we don't have the pressure of competing with some of the majors." Some of the area closures included the 30,000-square-foot facility of Swiss-based ASEA Brown Boveri, located 30 miles to the west of Brithinee Electric. General Motors' Electro-Motive Division had closed its motor repair facility in Los Angeles, while Reliance Electric had shut its shop in Anaheim. Westinghouse had been gone for a number of years, and General Electric's facility no longer did rewind work and did very little repair work on high-voltage motors. The last big captive shop in the area was a McGraw-Edison facility that had recently been purchased by MagneTek and then resold to Eastern Electric, which was operating with a much smaller staff. The closing of the shops of the major manufacturers had boosted opportunities for small independents like Brithinee. Don and Wally were unsure exactly why the "big boys" had left the market but were eager to capitalize on what they saw as an opportunity to fill the gap left by the closings and pick up new customers.

Trade Association Participation and Regulatory Affairs

As part of Brithinee Electric's commitment to educating and raising the expectations of their customers, Wally Brithinee and Lynda Butek had cultivated leadership roles within EASA. Wally chaired the EASA Engineering Committee and Lynda had become chair of EASA's Environmental Affairs Committee, recently renamed the Governmental Affairs Committee. Lynda was also on the Insurance and Safety Committee of EASA. Lynda believed that being closely involved with EASA activities "really helped the business from a technical standpoint." Wally and Lynda's committee work had helped Brithinee gain access to the latest and best information about new materials and technology. Plus, it had afforded them the opportunity to initiate and maintain contacts with wire, insulation materials, and equipment manufacturers.

In addition, Brithinee Electric worked closely with several regulatory agencies, including the South Coast Air Quality Management District and the Air Resources Board of California, to help streamline regulations. There were several agencies in California with overlapping jurisdictions, but the agencies did not appear to coordinate and collaborate with each other. Every year Lynda filled out three sets of forms with basically the same information for three different state agencies. In one instance, Lynda was forced to spend half a day preparing a report documenting that Brithinee owed $6.95 for particulate matter emissions (e.g., sulfur oxide, methane, hydrogen oxide, 1.1.1 trichloroethane, and carbon monoxide). Lynda questioned the reasonableness of all the regulations and procedural requirements of the three agencies and was working to figure out how to best streamline the processes to minimize repetition and how to gather the information with the least work disruptions. She believed that "California is still the toughest state to get permits in." Regulatory developments in California were closely watched by regulatory agencies in other states, with several environmentally conscious states sometimes following California's lead in establishing regulatory requirements for emissions and waste disposal. In reflecting on the company's involvement with EASA and various agencies, Wally was uncertain how to best influence government regulatory policies and whether there was anything he or EASA could do to minimize agency overlap and duplication of effort for the industry. He thought there ought to be a role for EASA in lobbying state and federal agencies to become more business-friendly while also protecting the environment.

OPERATIONS AT BRITHINEE ELECTRIC

Motor Repair

Brithinee repaired motors up to 1,000 horsepower, 4,000 volts, and 5 tons in weight. According to Wally Brithinee, "95 percent of all motors 200 horsepower and above can be expected to be repaired once in their lifetime." The motor repair process began when incoming electrical motors were received. Using contract drivers and its own fleet of trucks, Brithinee picked up and delivered customers' motors; some customers brought motors in to the shop for repair. Incoming motors underwent initial inspection and testing before being dismantled. The core was tested and the old windings were burned off in a temperature-controlled oven. Then a second core test was performed. The motors were rewound with new quadruple-build or inverter-duty magnet wire. Connections were made and a preassembly inspection performed before additional assembly and final testing. Approximately 70 percent of the motor was used in the remanufacture; most of the rest was recycled. The motors Brithinee repaired were able to maintain energy efficiency within 0.5 percent of what the motor was originally designed to achieve when new. The final step in the repair process was to prepare the motor for shipping and delivery to the customer. Brithinee did not repair motors on a customer's site due to liability, the difficulty associated with burning off the old windings, the use of chemicals, and the equipment needed to rewind, assemble, and bond the new wire inside the industrial motor (see Exhibit 6).

Motor Repair Workflow Russ Kennedy, production manager since 1988, oversaw the workflow from start to finish. He made the work assignments and scheduled the repair process so that customers' motors could be returned and put back into service in a timely fashion. Kennedy documented the conditions of incoming motors using one of three digital cameras and stored the images electronically on a Macintosh.

exhibit 6   Activity Sequence for Motor Repair

1. Receipt	7. Rewind & Connect
2. Initial Inspection & Test	8. Pre-Assembly Inspection
3. Dismantle	9. Assembly
4. Core Test	10. Final Test
5. Burn Out Old Windings	11. Prepare for Shipping
6. Core Test	12. Ship

The use of digital cameras had improved the process tremendously over previously used Polaroid pictures. Benefits included lower costs, more flexibility, more views of each motor, and electronic file handling capability. Having digital pictures associated with work orders had decreased the number of misunderstandings with workers and customers. For example, one customer, after delivery of a repaired motor, thought a part was missing; the digital pictures of the motor in the company's file were used to clear up the problem of the missing part.

Brithinee had designed process flow charts for the jobs it did for GM's Electro-Motive Division because the procedures were more standardized for these types of motors than most of the other motors that it serviced. These procedures instituted for the GM jobs included calibration of all measuring instruments. Some aspects of the flow charts developed for GM's work had proved useful for other motor repair work and were incorporated into the company's motor repair process.

Workers went to Kennedy's office to pick up their repair assignments—with the photos attached to the work order. Motors at various stages of repair were stored in bins that were labeled both alphabetically and numerically. Supposedly, every job had a storage location home, but with three shifts and uneven pallet sizes, there were times when workers would put a motor or some of its parts "wherever," and finding them could become an Easter egg hunt. The motor repair area contained several motors that had been left for repair as far back as 1995. Customers who did not have sufficient funds to get their motors repaired immediately sometimes just left them with Brithinee indefinitely. Although Brithinee had cleared out a significant number of these older jobs, management was still pondering the issue of how long it should provide service to customers by storing their motors gratis versus when it should start charging them for storage service.

A typical repair could range from $600 to $7,000. When a motor came in for repair, an estimate of the repair costs was prepared and provided to the customer by fax or phone; customer authorization to proceed was required before Brithinee initiated the repair process. Work was scheduled at a daily production meeting where the day- and night-shift production and customer service team discussed work in progress and promised delivery times. At that time, the team determined the priority for open jobs and discussed what work would be performed during the night shifts. Each workstation was equipped with EASA-created laminated charts showing the acceptable tolerance values to allow the workers to compare the fit of each part. Various agencies recommended that motor owners patronize repair facilities using EASA guidelines and standards.

Work orders were color-coded: green for go, red for stop, and orange for a "hot" rush job. Orange jobs went to the head of the queue. An orange-coded priority job could preempt another job, "by the minute," according to Russ Kennedy. He cited a rush-order case where the city of Riverside didn't have water for 10 city blocks and

Brithinee Electric worked through the night to complete the rush job. Customers paid a premium for overtime on orange-coded jobs. Jobs might be assigned by workers' ability. Repairs on a hot rush job from a very big customer sometimes began before a repair quote had been accepted, causing consternation in the accounts receivable department. Kennedy did not want procedures to hold up emergency work. One of Wally Brithinee's goals was to reduce the company's overtime costs (though not necessarily on orange-coded rush jobs, where customers expected to pay for emergency work). Three-fourths of the costs of repairing a motor were labor costs; one-fourth went for parts and materials.

Plant Layout Issues and Outsourcing Potential With 75 to 110 work orders open at any one time and 18 workers on the day shift, 5 on the swing shift, and 3 on graveyard shift, there was seldom a time when a worker was idle. Occasionally a machine might be idle if workers were pulled off to work on a rush job. At one point the company encountered frequent bottlenecks in the shop floor area; thinking that more space would remedy the problem, Brithinee hired a consultant to redesign the plant layout. After conducting interviews and studying ways to reorganize the layout to get a better workflow, the consultant concluded that the company did not need more space and recommended a different plant layout. The basic problem of work frequently crossing paths as the repair process moved from department to department was corrected by relocating and widening aisles, adding electrical outlets and lighting, and redesigning each workstation. Hazardous repair operations were relocated to a different area.

Other operating problems included work stoppages that occurred when work crews ran out of propane gas because no one was assigned the task of monitoring the gas level on a regular basis. This problem was addressed by having a propane gas vendor make regular deliveries. Russ Kennedy was looking at whether there were any other tasks that could be outsourced, thereby freeing worker time for motor repair work.

Customer Reports Beginning in 1993, Brithinee Electric began providing customers a previously internal computer report on why a motor fails and the state of the motor when it arrived and when it left the shop. This report explained what Brithinee found, how the motor tested when it came in, and how it tested when it went out. Included were such items as vibration, resistance of the winding, and types of bearings installed that provided a baseline for the motor's performance. Brithinee decided to share this information with its customers as a value-added service and as a way of raising customer expectations about the caliber of Brithinee's expertise and capabilities. Wally explained, "We don't expect [the customer] to even ask for what they really need . . . With our training and outreach programs through the Department of Energy, [we ask ourselves,] 'How do you get the user of electrical motor systems to develop or purchase a good system—for both efficiency and reliability?'"

Lynda Butek added, "Brithinee Electric has always had a reputation for quality . . . and that reputation has tripled in the last 9 to 10 years. Wally has instituted a very rigorous testing and reporting system for our customers that they didn't even know they wanted." She indicated that at first customers appeared to pay little attention to the report, but "now you try not to send it and you get a phone call. 'Where is my report? I need my report!'" Some customers had even begun expecting such reports from Brithinee's competitors when they sent them motor repair work.

Customized Motor Control Panels Customized control panels involved building industrial integrated systems and dealing with programmable logic controllers, motor controls, and variable frequency drives. Brithinee did not consider itself to be either a mass producer or a low-price leader in providing custom control panels; rather, it saw this market niche as a value-added service it could provide. From one employee in 1987, this department had grown to eight employees in 1999. Sometimes the workload for control panels was heavy, necessitating "borrowing" up to nine people from the repair side to complete a project. Brithinee specialized in drives and soft-start applications that reduced stresses associated with each motor start, and increased the longevity of the motor. Depending on the complexity, motor control panels could cost $1,000 to $10,000 in labor time to design. Brithinee sometimes charged separately for designing the control panel and related software and for manufacture.

When Brithinee hired Richard Silva as controls department manager in 1992, one of his first assignments was to establish the procedures necessary to manufacture control panels meeting standards prescribed by Underwriters Laboratories (UL), specifically UL Standard 508 and, later, UL Standard 845. Panels carrying UL certification signaled that the product met accepted safety standards in its construction, thereby reducing the risk of liability. According to Richard Silva, "It legitimizes you . . . It has been real good for our business. It has opened doors, and been a plus for us."

It was Brithinee's practice to "overdesign" a product in order to guarantee product performance. Brithinee used a larger size wire and would dip it in tin to lessen problems associated with heat. Brithinee also investigated where the panel would be installed and serviced, including exposure to heat, moisture, wind, and other environmental conditions. One panel shipped to the United Arab Emirates was designed with parts that would be available locally should the need arise. The company's goal was to make sure its panels worked the first time and every time thereafter. If a panel failed, the company's reputation suffered and it had to incur the cost of sending someone to fix the problem.

Silva worked closely with several large companies to meet UL Standard 845 in building control panels. Square D found Brithinee's control panel operations very flexible and responsive to its requests. Brithinee could build control panels faster than Square D's own plant. Richard Silva explained the distribution pattern: "Brithinee is a subcontractor to Square D, who sells the product to a distributor, who sells it to an electrical contractor, who will sell it to the general contractor, who actually is providing the control panel to the municipality or utility company." Square D supplied Brithinee with some control panel parts.

Candace Winn, Square D's Oceanside, California, plant manager, described their relationship with Brithinee as "unique." She said, "We talk to them all the time on the phone three to six times a day . . . They have a real knack for educating the customer." She was confident that repairs by Brithinee were done correctly and almost considered them to be a sister company. David Whitney, a senior sales engineer at Square D who called on industrial-type end users in Orange County and part of Los Angeles County, characterized the Square D–Brithinee relationship as more like a partnership than a customer-supplier relationship. David remarked, "There is a lot of trust and shared information . . . Brithinee has a lot of product expertise. They will see what our customers want and design it for them."

Brithinee used AutoCAD software to design control panels on the computer and shorten the time it took to bid on projects. Once a project bid was accepted, it typically took four to six weeks to build a control panel. The longest lead time was needed for acquiring the metal structure that housed the electrical components. Building the control panel might take only a week or two.

In scheduling a control panel job, Richard planned for unexpected delays, but the control panel department took special pride in knowing that they had so far met all the deadlines for shipping their products. Richard stated, "We have never, ever, ever missed a ship date. Never. We will never miss a ship date . . . I have been here Saturday and Sunday to make a ship date . . . It is important to us. You are only as good as your reputation." He went on to say that the UL 508 directory looked "like a telephone directory," adding that Brithinee was among only 20 companies in the United States with UL 845 certification. Most were very large corporations like Siemens, Allen-Bradley, and Square D. The limited number of companies with UL 845 certification had elevated the company's visibility in the industry and helped it attract more business.

Several Brithinee employees told the case researchers that motor repair costs were fairly well known and manageable but that a good system for determining the labor costs and profit on control panels had so far eluded them. Richard stated, "Labor has been a real problem. Until recently, we did not have a good way to keep track of accounting hours." Sometimes Brithinee would not know for six months whether they had made money on a job. For bidding on a job, Brithinee based its cost estimates on historical data, but the unique and variable nature of each job made it difficult to estimate costs accurately. Richard was pondering how to develop a way to track the costs of building control panels so as to make better bids and increase the profitability of this part of the company's operations.

ISO and EASA Q Certifications

The International Organization for Standardization (ISO) had created worldwide guidelines to promote higher-quality engineering designs and product manufacturing practices in a variety of industries. The ISO 9000 concept took off in the early 1990s and helped manufacturers to implement a number of quality improvements. Manufacturers that met ISO standards had formal systems in place to produce their products in a consistent manner. Most large manufacturers of motors like Toshiba, General Motors, and Square D were ISO 9000 compliant. There were three levels of ISO 9000 certification, referred to as 9001, 9002, and 9003. (However, a forthcoming revision in ISO certification was expected to have only one level.) The most rigorous of the three ISO standards, ISO 9001, meant a company had certification in design, engineering, and manufacturing; ISO 9002 signified qualification in just manufacturing. The popularity of ISO 9000 certification among manufacturers and the recognition that it provided made Don and Wally Brithinee wonder if ISO certification could make their company more visible and more competitive in the electrical apparatus industry. David Whitney at Square D believed that Brithinee would be smart to attain ISO certification since many big customers, like Boeing or General Motors, inquired about a vendor's quality control programs and sometimes used ISO certification as a way to screen possible vendors. Whitney said, "It certainly helps to be able to say, 'We are working with customers with ISO.'"

The Electrical Apparatus Service Association (EASA) had initiated a related standard, the EASA Q. Lynda Butek asserted that this standard "is *more* than the ISO 9002 . . . [It is 9002] plus specific procedures only having to do with motor rewind. It also includes a customer satisfaction audit of certain selected customers, which the ISO 9002 does not have." The EASA Q was put together by the Technical Services Committee of EASA, chaired by Wally Brithinee. Russ Kennedy said he supported industry movement toward EASA Q and ISO 9002 because it "makes my job easier with the documentation. Procedures are being implemented that everyone's following. It helps change the mind-set of a 20-year mechanic to conform to today's standards and regulations . . . It's a great adventure we're in right now. It makes work very interesting, and these guys [the Brithinee brothers] are behind it."

On the other hand, it was not clear that meeting ISO 9002 standards at Brithinee was strategically important given the company's UL certification. Candace Winn, at Square D, said it was the UL certifications that distinguished Brithinee from other control panel makers. Of the three certifications—UL 845, ISO 9002 and EASA Q, the UL 845 was "drastically important," she claimed. The pressure for achieving ISO 9002 certification was internally driven by the two brothers, although Wally readily admitted, "It is not a big market issue here in Southern California." Don Brithinee agreed: "Most of our customers are not terribly concerned about [our being ISO 9002 certified] . . . For our size business, it doesn't seem to be an expectation. We have virtually no external pressure from our customers to become ISO certified. The principal benefit will be the internal side, the savings associated with going through the process of developing these systems." Wally and Don did acknowledge that GM's Electro-Motive Division used ISO 9000 certification as a qualifying screen when selecting new vendors (but continuing to get business from GM was not contingent on Brithinee's meeting new ISO standards). While ISO certification often helped a company compete in foreign markets, none of Brithinee's motor repair work came from customers in foreign countries due to the high cost of transporting heavy industrial motors. It was, however, economically feasible to make and ship custom control panels to foreign customers; Brithinee had not pursued this possibility because it lacked knowledge about the opportunities that might exist and because it made more sense to concentrate its resources on serving local area customers.

The company's goal was to achieve ISO 9002 certification in 2000, but Wally and Don acknowledged that while the company was working on a number of fronts to meet the necessary requirements, it was "still a ways off." Getting there in 2000 might not be realistic. Their hope was that the company's attaining ISO 9002 certification would awaken customers' interest in having their work done by a quality-conscious vendor and that the added reputation that accrued to Brithinee from ISO 9002 certification would translate into a competitive edge over rivals.

Efforts to Improve Internal Administrative Procedures and Practices

Don Brithinee was interested in developing better ways to detect and prevent errors in any and all aspects of the company's operations. He said, "Every point seems to be a spot in which we can make savings." He recited an instance where Brithinee had sold a vehicle and verbally canceled the cellular telephone service associated with that vehicle. The provider stated that it did not need anything in writing to cancel the telephone number. Debbie Brithinee wrote a memo to staff members to watch out for further charges that might come through on that telephone number. Sixteen months later, the company discovered it had been charged $70 a month for a telephone number that had zero calls on it. The vendor refused to refund the money. Don was contemplating whether it was worth the time and energy to change cellular telephone vendors or whether the company's procedures were basically at fault and should have been tight enough to reveal the error much sooner.

Another costly error occurred when the employee preparing the bid on a large customized control panel inadvertently made a mistake in handling the spreadsheet and deleted a line containing 18 percent of the materials in the final cost estimate. The mistake, which was not discovered until too late, wiped out the profits on the project. The error unfortunately occurred on the largest control panel job Brithinee had ever done.

Wally and Don believed that one of the greatest benefits of achieving ISO 9002 certification might ultimately prove to be the internal savings associated with improving the company's administrative procedures and eliminating clerical errors such as those just described.

Brithinee's Value Chain, Relationship Marketing, and Advertising

In 1999, Brithinee Electric was very alert to ways to add customer value to the activities it performed and was working with its suppliers in this respect as well. In earlier periods, Brithinee did not place much strategic emphasis on value-added assembly, but this had changed. The contract with EMD Locomotive provided one value-added dimension in the repair shop. Most of Brithinee's motor sales in the late 1980s were off-the-shelf packages made by Toshiba and Baldor and for which it was an authorized distributor. But over time Brithinee Electric found that having only one location and a relatively small volume of sales made it tough to compete against multioutlet discount houses that entered the market in the early 1990s and had greater sales volumes and buying leverage with manufacturers. Brithinee discovered that it was in better position to compete for the business of customers wanting customized electrical apparatus products and services such as sophisticated motor control panels. Brithinee had the expertise and capabilities to tailor-make certain types of electrical products to customer specifications, giving it the ability to add value through its own internal activities and deliver something to buyers other than a standard package stocked by a variety of electrical suppliers.

Brithinee applied the principles of relationship marketing whenever the opportunity presented itself. For instance, Brithinee worked closely with David Whitney at Square D to better satisfy Square D's customers. According to Whitney, "My customer may be a water district and I may ask where they get their motors repaired and suggest to the customer that they contact Brithinee." And when a Brithinee customer could profit from using Square D products, Brithinee suggested the customer get in touch with Dave Whitney at Square D.

Two outside salespeople generated business by calling on customers and identifying new prospects, whether in the repair area, sales, or control panels. Brithinee's competitors sometimes referred a customer to Brithinee when they could not fulfill a customer's request, and Brithinee reciprocated. Bill Gaborko, at C&M Electric, a small local competitor, did not repair large motors and referred those customers to Brithinee. Brithinee sent customers wanting repairs on single-phase motors to C&M.

Brithinee was exploring new ways to generate sales in order to run all three shifts at full strength and to increase revenues and profit margins. John Hinshaw, the sales and marketing manager, said, "Getting a new customer is the most expensive part of the business." His goal was to grow and maintain the business primarily with existing customers but to also search out new customers. One source of leads was business starts in the Inland Empire. Using a Dun and Bradstreet "Marketplace" CD-ROM set, the company had identified hundreds of prospects with profiles similar to its current customer base. Brithinee had learned that a number of its repair customers did not know the company could provide customized motor control panels and that some control panel buyers were unaware of the company's motor repair capabilities.

Hinshaw expressed a belief that the computer-generated repair report accompanying each particular job had been instrumental in raising the expectations of current customers. Those customers now required the same information from Brithinee's competitors. He also felt that the UL certification was the most important one in generating sales locally, especially for the control panel side of the business. He observed, "For electrical safety, UL is it."

exhibit 7   Selected Balance Sheet and Income Statement Data for Brithinee Electric, 1988–98

	1988	1989	1990	1991
Balance sheet				
Assets				
Current assets	$1,278,365	$1,644,500	$1,551,245	$1,229,799
Fixed assets less accumulated depreciation	121,739	82,625	139,922	193,562
Other assets	14,716	14,716	14,716	7,876
Total assets	$1,414,820	$1,741,841	$1,705,884	$1,431,238
Liabilities and Shareholders' Equity				
Current liabilities	$356,096	$563,656	$332,276	$328,377
Long-term liabilities				
Shareholders' equity	1,058,724	1,178,184	1,373,607	1,102,860
Total liabilities and shareholders' equity	$1,414,820	$1,741,841	$1,705,884	$1,431,238
Income statement				
Gross income	$4,836,401	$5,372,555	$5,643,979	$4,530,838
Cost of goods sold	3,349,853	3,766,378	3,751,243	3,013,072

*Projected.

As part of the company's effort to reach out to a new customer base, Don Brithinee and Cyd Sandefur had been attending a marketing class at a local community college to help them create presentation material for seminars and to learn other ways Brithinee could gain recognition with potential customers. Don and Cyd had given a number of presentations to groups of customers and EASA meeting attendees concerning such topics as how to hook up and safely use industrial motors, how to make the equipment run better, and how to do maintenance planning. Wally said, "Customers are better customers when they know what we do." Don and Cyd had also toyed with the idea of pursuing customer accounts in Arizona and Northern California because there were carrier services that guaranteed overnight delivery. Cyd said the company was still in the infancy stage of its marketing outreach efforts and was looking for further steps to take to grow its business.

Accounting and Information Technology

In 1999 Deborah Brithinee was responsible for Brithinee's general ledger and other types of accounting. Prior to marrying Don Brithinee and coming to work at Brithinee Electric, Deborah had worked for 17 years in accounting, purchasing, and trust operations in a county government, overseeing a $70 million budget. Periodically, she helped on special projects before becoming Brithinee's office manager in 1990. Exhibit 7 presents an 11-year overview of Brithinee's financial statements.

In 1998, Brithinee introduced a new 401(K) profit-sharing plan after company-wide meetings and a vote by employees. Previously, the company had paid annual year-end bonuses tied to company profitability into a guaranteed retirement fund managed by the company. With the 401(K) plan, Brithinee paid into each employee's fund monthly. Contributions were based on a percentage of each employee's salary rather than being linked to year-end profits, as had been the case with the prior plan. Deborah indicated that "our financial statements look very different month-to-month than they did in prior years . . . It was a big step for us to go into the 401(K)." Employees

1992	1993	1994	1995	1996	1997	1998*
$1,105,523	$997,596	$1,125,322	$1,195,479	$1,269,494	$1,501,129	$1,446,709
271,273	223,745	293,329	240,558	363,180	406,165	441,091
2,087	6,896	6,896	6,896	1,093	2,004	1,951
$1,378,883	$1,228,238	$1,425,546	$1,442,933	$1,633,767	$1,909,299	$1,889,752
$540,978	$376,593	$378,799	$292,863	$305,465	$550,758	$351,239
	28,079	19,036	26,708	36,106	27,662
837,905	851,644	1,018,668	1,131,034	1,301,593	1,322,434	1,510,850
$1,378,883	$1,228,237	$1,425,546	$1,442,933	$1,633,767	$1,909,299	$1,889,752
$4,405,211	$4,968,783	$5,127,066	$5,995,404	$5,696,261	$6,490,431	$7,037,731
3,045,850	3,260,598	3,344,487	3,854,561	3,525,998	4,370,105	4,483,012

*Projected.

were fully vested in the 401(K) the first day they began work. The two advantages, as Wally saw it, were (1) the employee awareness of the plan throughout the year and (2) employees' control of their own retirement funds. But the disadvantage to Wally was the lack of an obvious tie to the company's performance; he explained, "How do you get the employee to understand a tie-in between his or her performance and the company's performance? If they [the employees] are to succeed, the company needs to succeed."

A major accounting issue was how to track and measure the labor costs associated with control panel projects. "We don't do cost accounting," stated Deborah Brithinee. "In the repair shop, we have done considerable analysis on what goes into a repair . . . We have a handle on that. But in the control panel area, it's very, very difficult to get a handle on that. That's what we're working on now." Deborah was trying to determine what different systems would capture information to solve this problem. She was certain the company needed better methods for addressing the sometimes-dramatic differences between initial cost estimates and actual costs incurred in building the control panels. The big problems were in the labor cost estimates and changes in the prices of parts between the time the estimate was made and the work was done. Customer design changes could also complicate the process. Deborah suspected that the company needed to overcome its reluctance to adjust original estimates as a result of materials price changes and customer design changes. Tracking purchase orders was another problem area, according to Cyd Sandefur, who did the tracking manually. She said that "things change in the middle of the project. Something will be quoted in the bid that doesn't work." Making substitutions typically entailed renegotiating with suppliers for parts and prices.

Don said, "We don't have an integrated system for our order entry and accounting." While Brithinee had purchased some custom software to reduce paperwork and streamline processes, it had not yet been installed on the system and implemented. The goal was to reduce the amount of hours devoted to accounting, but no plan to do this was in place.

In the information technology area, Don stated, "We enjoy our computers . . . We probably have 30 computers scattered around . . . versus only one or two 10 years ago . . . This is a big plus." The company had both Macintosh and Windows NT-based machines operating on the same network. The company allowed both types of machines to be used for entering orders, sending mail, accessing data files, and exchanging data on the company's local area network (LAN). The LAN was connected to the Internet, but Brithinee did not yet have its own Web site. Don explained, "I don't find that most of the customers we deal with would find their way to us through [a Web site] . . . not yet." Brithinee hoped to find lower-cost ways of reaching out to new and existing customers, but didn't believe a Web page would serve this purpose very well. Wally had created spreadsheets that tracked progress of work orders through the shop; he said, "Computers for us are a shop tool. It is not universally acknowledged that you would put computers in the shop area."

Personnel Issues

Brithinee Electric's commitment to helping customers out with emergency repairs had attracted a lot of emergency repair work and fostered a high-pressure work environment driven by trying to meet tight time deadlines. To respond to the problem of being worn down by "always being in a panic mode" and to create a less stressful organizational climate, Brithinee had contracted with a psychological consultant and added second and third shifts. In 1996, the industrial psychologist began testing applicants and looking at ways to improve the work climate. Don Brithinee explained, "We have been trying to put together a company of more like-minded people. We have managed to remove some personnel who were a problem for us . . . This has made the organizational environment more pleasant and conveyed a better image to our customers and even our vendors." Brithinee had done personality profiles of job applicants and, with their permission, existing employees. Profiling had helped management better understand why certain personalities worked well together and why some were better suited to the company's work environment. The consultant's work had led to the development of a preferred profile that was used to screen job applicants. According to Russ Kennedy, "We want people to fit . . . the Brithinee profile." The profiles of existing employees had been used as a basis for reassigning some personnel; so far, the results had been quite satisfactory.

Brithinee had also instituted drug testing as part of its job applicant screening process and a no-tolerance drug use policy. Personnel found to be using illegal drugs were dismissed. The dismissal of one employee for drug use had boosted morale in the shop (the individual had crashed a truck and was a disruptive force on the shop floor). One employee described the management style at Brithinee as "very forgiving" when errors or mistakes were made.

The hiring of additional personnel with the right characteristics to staff the second and third shifts had alleviated attrition problems associated with employee burnout. Moreover, the new employees fit the Brithinee profile and seemed to work well together. To help add workforce flexibility, the company had hired three or four "all-purpose, no-purpose" entry-level people who were moved from task to task as needed. According to operation manager Russ Kennedy, "We have grown on all fronts . . . [and now] we take emergencies more in stride."

Brithinee Electric suffered from some common people-management problems associated with the growth of small, family-owned businesses. Longtime employees who had once worked side by side with Don and Wally sometimes had difficulty following the chain of command and going through the new managers who had been brought in. The industrial psychologist had improved matters by redefining job descriptions, creating better-documented employee manuals, and helping Wally and Don communicate better with each other. Wally remarked that he was sold on the value of using a psychologist to help managers better understand their staff and adopt a team approach. Pay increases were determined by Don and Wally, who factored in profitability, labor market conditions, and the value of the individual to the company. Employees were not automatically granted annual pay raises.

Growth and the Future

As the Brithinee brothers looked to the future, they knew the company faced a challenge trying to grow revenues by 10 to 15 percent annually in an industry predicted to shrink by 2 percent per year. They were uncertain whether to keep the company focused on expanding its existing electric motors sales, motor repair, and control panels departments or whether to branch out and diversify into other areas. Predicting what areas would offer the best growth opportunity was difficult. For example, since 1988 the rewinding portion of the company's business had grown 180 percent. Wally said, "I would have never expected that . . . We've never been good at predictions here." Brithinee Electric forecast its earnings only one year at a time, but the consultant had suggested setting longer-term goals and making longer-term financial forecasts.

In speculating on future business opportunities, Wally noted that the water industry nationwide was expected to spend $40 billion in upgrades of water and waste-water treatment facilities in the near future, a significant part of which was expected to involve converting the associated electric motors to variable frequency drives. He said, "Upgrading fits our controls arena. This is our greatest potential area for growth." Brithinee could readily accommodate growth by expanding its second- and third-shift skeleton crews into fully staffed crews. However, expanding repair capabilities for handling larger size motors would require extensive capital investment. Wally said, "Everything would have to be upsized to another level greater than what we have." It was unclear where the capital for such upgrades would come from.

There was room to expand the shop facilities if necessary by acquiring a vacant lot of about five acres between the two current buildings. According to Lynda Butek, it was a strange piece of property because it also wrapped around the back of both buildings and a cul-de-sac, and extended to the next street. At the moment, though, it was not clear whether the property would be best used for expansion of the warehouse, a parking lot, a bigger control panel area, or another building equipped to handle more repair work. Aside from how to grow, there was the issue of what to do about ISO 9002 certification and whether company emphasis on quality would pay off in the eyes of the company's existing and prospective customers.

Finally, as the Brithinee brothers approached celebration of their 50th birthdays, the issues of retirement and succession were not too far down the road. Don and Deborah Brithinee had one child, Nicole, age 10, while Wally remained single. The brothers carried substantial life and disability insurance policies on each other.

bibliography

Electrical Apparatus Service Association, Inc. (EASA). "Understanding A-C Motor Efficiency." Pamphlet, 1994.

———. "How to Get the Most from Your Electric Motors." Pamphlet, 1997.

————. "EASA AR 100 1998 Recommended Practice." Pamphlet, 1998.

Greenfeld, S. "Brithinee Electric." In *Business Strategy and Policy,* ed. Smith, Arnold, and Bizzel. Boston: Houghton-Mifflin, 1991, pp. 180–200. Also in *Strategic Management for Decision Making,* ed. Stahl and Grisby. Boston: PWS-Kent, 1992, pp. 368–87. Also in *Strategic Management,* ed. Dess and Miller. New York: McGraw-Hill, 1993, pp. 393–410.

Nailen, Richard L. "Building a Service Company's Numbers with Higher Mathematics." *Electrical Apparatus,* December 1997.

"You Got It Off the Ground and Flying, Now How Do You Safely Land It?" *Los Angeles Times,* December 16, 1998, p. C8.

case 24 The Roccoco New York Hotel

Anna S. Mattila

The Pennsylvania State University

The following customer complaint letter was submitted by a first-time customer at the Roccoco New York Hotel. Tony Richards, the general manager, had called a meeting with his executive committee to ponder the situation facing the hotel. The director of operations, Sylvia Jenkins, the human resource director, Paul Gordon, and the director of marketing, Nancy Wheeler, were glancing through the letter as Mr. Richards explained that, unfortunately, this customer encounter typified what many clients experienced during their stay at the hotel. Two members of the executive committee, the food and beverage director and the head of the engineering department, were absent due to a mandatory fire drill taking place in the main kitchen on snowy January 2, 1998.

To Whom It May Concern,

I stayed at your hotel last week and was disappointed in my overall experience. I travel to the city often and will probably not return to your hotel. I would, however, like to express my discontentment with the service I received.

As I sat in the bar waiting for my cocktail to be delivered, I became more and more frustrated with the service I had received since my arrival the day before. Upon booking my reservation, I was kind of wary about what I was in for. After all, I had not heard too much about this brand. It was not like going to a Hilton or Marriott where I know what type of service and atmosphere to expect. Needless to say, I was pleasantly surprised with the grand atmosphere at this hotel. It can be described as an oasis in the heart of Times Square. The lobby area is small, yet elegant and quaint. It is the type of hotel where I can feel comfortable entertaining my clients and holding negotiations. It is big enough to provide privacy, yet cozy enough to deliver a personalized type of service. Automatically, my expectations of service soared as I admired the care and beauty of the rooms and public areas. No detail has been left unfinished. Unfortunately, my expectations were quickly shot down as reality set in.

After an extremely long journey from halfway across the world, I was more than looking forward to a hot shower and warm bed. I checked in at about 6:00 PM on a Wednesday evening. Upon arrival, the doorman welcomed me graciously and collected my bags. I took the elevator to the lobby area to check in. I approached the desk and stood there for what seemed like an eternity before either of the two girls standing there acknowledged my existence. Finally, one of the girls looked up from her paperwork and, as if I were interrupting her, asked me if she could be of assistance. I gave her my last name and told her I had a reservation. She confirmed my room number, handed me my key, and in no time I was on my way—I could not wait. Upon entering the room, I noticed that there were two beds and a horrible smoky smell. I had asked for a king bed, nonsmoking. I immediately called down to the front desk. The girl who answered seemed a bit annoyed and said that I could return to the lobby, as she would try to accommodate my needs. With that, I went back to the elevator, down 20 floors and finally back to the front desk. She half-heartedly apologized for the inconvenience, gave me another key, and once again, I was on my way.

I waited nearly a half an hour before the boy at the entrance came up with my luggage. He placed my very expensive carryon piece in front of the door (to hold it open) and proceeded to take in the rest of my bags. He informed me about the amenities available at the hotel. You know, the usual—minibar, complimentary shoeshine, 24-hour room service, exercise room, and so on. With that, he smiled and wished me a pleasant stay. I wondered if he even knew my name or realized that I was upset with the time it took my luggage to arrive (not to mention the fact that my carryon piece had doubled as a doorstop).

After unpacking and settling in, I picked up the room service menu. It was pretty limited, but I was very tired and was not about to go out for a bite to eat. The girl who answered the phone knew who I was. Quite impressive, as I had only been there for about two hours: "Good evening, room service, this is Cary, how may I help you, Ms. Bressner?" The meal was delicious, although it arrived nearly an hour after I ordered it—the girl who took my order said it would be up in 25 minutes. After finishing my meal, I called back down to room service to tell the girl that I would leave my tray outside the door. Finally, with all that I had been through that day, it was almost midnight before I was finally able to get some rest.

The following morning, I stepped out of my room and almost onto the very same room service tray; it was right where I had left it the night before. That evening, upon checking out, the girl asked me if she could assist me in making reservations for a future trip to the hotel. I politely declined and told her that my stay was not a pleasant one. She apologized and wished me a good evening. As I walked away from the desk, thinking of what my stay had been like, I knew that I would never return.

I liked the hotel; in fact, it is definitely nicer than most of the Marriotts or Hiltons I had been to and the price was very reasonable for NYC. However, I do not think I will return. It is something about the service—it is definitely not what I had expected. Your staff should work on their attitudes and attention to detail. Very few were really friendly, and even fewer seemed interested in my happiness. I hope this situation is rectified, as you have already lost at least one guest.

Sincerely,

Laura Bressner

As the executive committee reviewed the hotel's performance, Tony Richards addressed the critical questions. "What can we do to avoid problems on this type in the future? How can we improve the level of service quality in our establishment? We need to do something to ensure that occupancy levels will remain high despite the rate increases imposed by our financial situation. Why don't we brainstorm to get some ideas? Nancy, what do you suggest from the marketing perspective?"

Nancy Wheeler responded, "Well, given the resistance to rate increases from our current guests, I feel that we should focus on attracting new customers. Weekends are clearly a problem for us; the occupancies drop to a mere 50 percent on most weekends. By offering attractive packages, we could get more leisure travelers to stay with us. Because we have such a high proportion of Asians in our client mix, I suggest that we get into Web marketing. We could place ads on Asian air carriers' sites or on Netscape or Yahoo! so that, when people are seeking travel information regarding New York City, they get an immediate exposure to our hotel. I have done some data searching, and the current monthly cost on travel sites is about $12,000."

"I hate to disagree with you, Nancy, but our main goal should be to satisfy our existing customers," Paul Gordon asserted. "Look, the data from our customer satisfaction surveys and the ever-increasing pile of complaint letters that I have in my office clearly indicate that our current guests are not happy. Or, have a look at the shopper report summary (see Appendix 1). I think that we should put our efforts into developing a service recovery policy. My informal talks with our front-line employees indicate that they feel lost with our operating manuals. They have to deal with upset customers without having the power to do anything about their complaints. At the moment, a supervisor's signature is required for any service recovery effort. I can just imagine how our guests feel about paying over $200 a night and having to wait for someone's approval to get a complimentary welcome drink because the room is not ready. In many cases, further referral to the department head is needed, causing unseemly delay and further guest irritation. These things should be handled on the spot by our customer-contact employees."

Sylvia Jenkins, the director of operations, joined the discussion. "Empowering the front line to deal with service failures is a good idea in theory, but how do you control the money involved? Free meals and free stays represent lost revenues, and I do not believe that our cash position is such that we could afford a dip in revenues. Moreover, as you know, we are in the process of hiring new food and beverage employees, and this additional expenditure will have an impact on our bottom line."

MANAGEMENT BACKGROUND

Tony Richards's first exposure to the hospitality business had come 25 years ago working as a busboy in his father's family restaurant. During college, he had worked summers at various resorts on Cape Cod. After graduating with an undergraduate business degree, he spent three years working for an insurance company in Hartford, Connecticut. His heart kept longing for the hustle and bustle of hospitality, and he then decided to return to school to earn a master's in hospitality management. After college, he worked for Bristol Hotels, mainly opening new properties for the fast-growing hotel chain. Since he had joined the Roccoco hotel two years ago, Tony had been working vigorously to bring the revenue stream to its optimal level while controlling costs and increasing demand. As a result of these efforts, the Roccoco New York Hotel realized its first positive cash flows in 1997.

The general manager hired a new food and beverage manager, Mr. Jean-Pierre Pottier, at the end of 1996. His dynamic character, combined with a prestigious culinary degree from Cordon Bleu in Paris, had made him successful in revamping the hotel's restaurant business. Jean-Pierre's reputation for superb banquets and creative menu concepts had resulted in a 22 percent increase in food sales during the past 12 months. Room service sales, in particular, had gone up by 50 percent since 1996.

Paul Gordon, the current director of human resources, had worked for Holiday Inns in the corporate training position for 15 years prior to joining the Roccoco Hotel six months ago. His wife had been relocated to New York City, and Paul was looking forward to a more stable family life. The hotel's former HR manager had implemented sizable budget cuts for employee training and hiring practices, and these efforts had indeed showed a positive impact on last year's bottom line. In the past, newly hired employees had completed a two-week formal training program, but this procedure had been replaced by a more cost-efficient, on-the-job "buddy" training system. In addition to on-the-job training, each new employee received the hotel's 500-page operations manual, which explained company policies for each department. The hotel had lost many of its middle managers to competitors over the past three years, but these positions had been left vacant to improve the bottom line.

The director of marketing, Nancy Wheeler, had joined the Roccoco Hotel nearly a year and a half ago. Her previous job as a middle manager of a mega-convention center had familiarized her with group business travel. Summarizing the situation facing Roccoco, she reported: "There is perceived guest resistance to higher rates, requiring our hotel to have a competitive edge when compared to similar hotel properties and hotel brands."

Sylvia Jenkins, the director of operations, was an old-timer at the Roccoco Hotel. In fact, she had been with the hotel over ten years and had personally seen the transformation from a typical mid-priced Restwell Inn to a quaint boutique hotel. Sylvia started her career as a housekeeper and worked her way up to a rooms division manager within the Restwell Corporation. When she was offered her current position five years ago, she gladly accepted. Sylvia strongly believed in "management by walking around" and was constantly fixing problems throughout the hotel.

PROPERTY OVERVIEW

The Roccoco was a full-service, 30-story boutique hotel with 305 rooms. Boutique hotels were relatively small, well-staffed properties that offered upscale, high-end and ample amenities. Corporate buildings, restaurants, shopping, and the theater district surrounded the Roccoco Hotel. The Times Square location was, however, less desirable than Central Park or the Upper East or West Side. Amenities offered included a full-service restaurant overlooking Times Square, a wine bar, a cocktail lounge, and 24-hour room service. The lobby was small and quaint, perfect for the business traveler who preferred a private, relaxing atmosphere. In addition, amenities such as complimentary shoeshines, coffee delivery with wake-up calls, and entertainment services were available to all guests.

In terms of meeting business travelers' needs, the property lagged behind the competition. Meeting facilities were limited to less than 2,000 square feet, and there was no business center. The guests could, however, request a personal fax machine in the room. The guest rooms themselves offered great convenience for computer and modem hook-up and had plenty of workspace.

Formerly a Restwell Inn, the Roccoco group purchased and reflagged the property in the early part of 1993. More than 25 million dollars was allocated to renovate the hotel. Because no structural upgrades were needed, all of the capital was used to enhance the property's appearance. The general manager contracted a famous New York City artist to design an art-deco lobby area, restaurant, and guest rooms. Marble and fine cherry woods replaced the original décor. Massive statues and fine, imported furnishings created a lavish environment, and a restaurant and a lounge area were created on the main lobby level.

COMPETITION

The New York City hotel market was fiercely competitive. (The 1996–97 statistics on the overall New York market are shown in Exhibit 1. For information on Manhattan rate structures, refer to Appendix 2.) There were two main competitive sets (see Exhibit 2). The Sheraton, Crown Plaza, Guest Suites, and Millennium were all relatively large

exhibit 1   New York Area Hotel Market—Selected Properties

Year	Occupancy		Room Rate		Annual Room Supply		Annual Room Demand	
	Current Year	Prior Year	Current Year	Prior Year	Current Year	Prior Year	Current Year	Prior Year
1996	81.9%	76.2%	$158.45	$144.60	2,533,794	2,328,794	2,075,177	1,744,469
1997	84.1%	81.9%	$176.90	$158.50	2,637,125	2,533,700	2,217,822	2,075,177

exhibit 2   Competitive Set Report

1996	Occupancy	ADR	REVPAR	Competitive Set I
Roccoco	79.8%	$167.13	$133.38	Sheraton
Competitive Set I	83.3%	$166.53	$138.72	H. I. Crown Plaza
Competitive Set II	84.1%	$176.95	$148.90	Marriott
				Guest Suites

1997	Occupancy	ADR	REVPAR	Competitive Set II
Roccoco	83.1%	$174.86	$145.30	H. I. Crown Plaza
Competitive Set I	86.5%	$169.65	$146.75	Millennium
Competitive Set II	85.1%	$184.23	$156.82	Guest Suites
				Leonardo Davinci

Source: Smith Travel Research. This information is taken from a sample of eight area hotels and general demand patterns. RevPar stands for revenue per available room. ADR refers to average daily rate.

properties that catered to a different clientele, as the properties offered a less personalized atmosphere and larger public areas; however, their geographic location and price similarity had enabled them to control a large portion of the market. A nearby property owned by the Roccoco group, previously considered a major competitor, had evolved into a support system for the Roccoco. Since becoming part of the same global distribution system, all overflow from the second property, which ran at full occupancy most of the year, was diverted to the Roccoco. The Sheraton had completed its renovation at the end of 1997; every guest room was now equipped with ergonomic chairs, in-room data ports, voice mail, and a Hewlett-Packard Office Jet Printer/fax/copier machine. The Sheraton was expected to increase its room rates to $240 per night within the next three months.

Perhaps the Roccoco's primary competitor was the Leonardo. Located only blocks away, this 178-room property offered its guests a more personalized and superior stay. Amenities such as fresh flowers in the rooms, standardized bath amenities (i.e., bubble bath), slippers, and fruit baskets were among the items all guests could expect. In evaluating the quality of the property and service at the Leonardo, even Roccoco's management admitted to the property's inherent superiority. One guest who had previously stayed at the Leonardo described it as, "The perfect place to stay—anywhere in the world. The staff there knows what you need even before you do. It is amazing. Every luxury you could expect, right in the heart of New York's finest. They even know your name before you introduce yourself. I do not know how they do, they just do."

CUSTOMER PROFILE

Because of its boutique orientation, the hotel attracted guests looking for a quiet, convenient place to stay. The property's mix was 70/30 between business and leisure guests. Accordingly, weekday occupancy levels were much greater than weekend, with little seasonal variation. Many of the hotel's business clients were mature, that is, between the ages of 45 and 65. They preferred to stay in the same hotel and quite often the same room. This had contributed to the property's repeat customer base of nearly 60 percent. Unfortunately, the customer retention rates had been consistently dropping over the past few years, as the repeat base had declined by about 10 percent in reaction to the hotel's increase in room rates (see Appendix 3A). To induce high response rates, Mrs. Wheeler had revamped the hotel's customer satisfaction instrument (see Appendix 3B). Many of the clients, up to 40%, were international travelers. With the hotel's luxury reputation in Asia, about 80% of the international guests came from this market. Customer satisfaction data indicated that Asian business travelers were particularly unhappy with the level of service provided by the Roccoco staff.

EMPLOYEE OVERVIEW

The Roccoco had approximately 250 employees. Because of the hotel's relatively small size and the complex labor market in the New York area, staffing issues posed a major problem. This hotel was a nonunion property in a market where approximately 96 percent of hotels were unionized. Thus, in order to keep the union out of the hotel, pay and benefit packages were slightly higher than union standards. The property realized an annual turnover rate of approximately 10 percent, although the industry standard for first-class hotels was 45 percent. Average seniority was 3.7 years, with 10–15 percent of the employees remaining from when the hotel was a Restwell.

Despite this seemingly low level of turnover, employee satisfaction was quite low. Morale and culture had been compromised through the shifts in management and the ambiguous nature of policies, procedures, and management support (see Appendix 4). In terms of management, turnover was extremely high. In fact, the current general manager was one of five who had been at the property since it opened. With the exception of Ms. Jenkins, the rest of the members in the executive office were also relatively new to the property (hired within the past two years). Ms. Jenkins was often heard to repeat the following phrases to her employees: "You should have seen this place before renovation took place . . . all the furniture and fixtures were getting worn out . . . really shabby. But look at it now; what a beauty this hotel has turned out to be. We should all be proud of it."

FINANCIALS

Although occupancy levels remained high and the New York market was booming, the Roccoco was struggling. In the first three years of operation, the property realized a net loss of nearly $12 million annually. This loss had since been reduced to approximately $1 million per year. The property showed its first positive cash flow in 1997. With this in mind, the management team had calculated that the rates must be increased by an additional 30 percent over the following two years.

In light of the relatively low ADR (average daily rate), the property had not realized its revenue goals. Guests had been paying a room rate that was, on average, $30.00 less than the projected $205.00 ADR budgeted for 1998. Additionally, many guests paid current rack rates (published, nondiscount rates) of $205 to $305 (the differentiation in rates can be accounted for by differences in weekend–weekday demand patterns). These mostly non–New York City residents would need to believe they were receiving value with personalized service and attention to detail that was worth the additional $30 over current rack rates (see Appendix 5).

A comparison of Roccoco's profitability against industry standards (ratios and publications published by consulting firms) showed that the level of gross operating income (income before fixed charges) was about 2 to 4 percentage points below the average for comparable properties. While Tony Richards acknowledged that opportunities for marginal cost-cutting might exist, these efforts might well conflict with the need to provide higher levels of service quality. For example, in a previous board of directors' meeting two months ago, one of the owners of the hotel had suggested that management should get rid of the hotel's full-service restaurant or its labor-intensive 24-hour room service. The executive committee strongly objected to this cost-cutting plan because reputable food service operations form an integral part of any upscale property's image and prestige value.

WHAT TO DO!

The slowly drifting snow had turned into a heavy mix of snow and rain by 5:30 PM. The traffic would be chaotic in a couple of hours, so Mr. Richards decided to call it a day. He would draft a letter of apology to Ms. Bressner the first thing in the morning. Driving home that night, he started to think about the board of directors' meeting scheduled for next Friday. "What can we do to add value to the guest experience? How can we enhance guest satisfaction? Should we aim at new target markets to increase occupancy levels? I need to have my recommendations ready by Friday."

appendix | 1 Roccoco Hotel Sample Executive Summary— Shopper Survey, September 1998

- The High Stars Consulting Company is a leading international firm specializing in quality management programs in the hospitality industry.
- The executive summary is based on the experience of four shoppers who stayed at your property for three nights during the week of September 15.
- Shoppers are trained by the corporate office to pay attention to the following areas: speed of service, cleanliness of the property, handling of special requests, and overall employee attitudes.

Reservations

- All reservationists with whom we spoke were polite and professional; however, one reservationist addressed us by first name, although a full, simple name had been provided.
- Inconsistent offers of smoking versus nonsmoking rooms and mention of the 6 PM check-in time.

- Only one on-site reservationist extended thanks or other words of appreciation, simply waiting for the caller to thank them, to which they would respond, "You are welcome."

Arrival

- Immediate, friendly assistance curbside with "Welcome to the Roccoco."
- During an evening arrival, prompt processing, but when arriving at the hotel at 2 PM, the room was not ready until 3:22 PM.
- The complimentary drink while waiting for the room to be ready never arrived.
- Baggage delivery was slow, requiring 18 to 51 minutes.
- Upon delivering of the luggage, the bellman made no introduction to the room's features, nor any other information.
- An on-arrival message was handled effectively.

Departure

- During one check-out, we were not asked if we enjoyed our visit, nor asked about late charges, nor specifically thanked.
- The folios were correct except for some minibar charges.
- When questioned a charge on our folio, the cashier explained that he needed to talk to his supervisor. We waited for 10 minutes for any action; at the end the charge was removed.

Concierge

- The concierge staff seems to be a genuine strength of the hotel. They seemed well trained, considerate, and thorough.
- Excellent assistance about local dining options was readily available. Restaurant A was one of the six options provided, not recommended either more or less enthusiastically than any other restaurant.
- A FedEx package arrived at the hotel at 9:52 AM, but we were first notified of this by a written message under the door at 1:15 PM. No message light was used, and there was no offer to deliver the package to us.

Telephone

- Unusually long delays in answering of inside and outside telephone lines.
- In one instance, a wake-up call was requested but never received.
- During the survey, we received a voice mail from a front-office manager that was actually addressed to another guest.

Housekeeping

- During the survey, rooms #243, 480, 115, and 755 were occupied.
- Rooms 243, 115, and 755 were generally very clean, although a rumpled hand towel was left on the bed in #115.

- During remakes in #480, there was incomplete attention given to restocking of guest supplies.
- Housekeeping staff consistently honored posted DND signs and was polite and smiled frequently when interacting with or passing guests.
- Responses to special requests were 23 minutes for an iron and 10 minutes for a DND sign.

Room Service

- Breakfasts were served in 45 and 37 minutes, far exceeding the estimated time of 20 minutes.
- During dinner, the order taker failed to mention any dinner specials.
- The ordering process was affected by numerous call-holds and by considerable background noise.

Restaurant A

- During all meals, the host staff seemed absolutely intent on getting guests' names recorded in the logbook, although they made no use of the name once learned.
- The breakfast buffet had a particularly imaginative impression, and all products were fresh and appetizing.
- One dinner was a poor experience from start to finish, and the dining-room manager did not seem able to control the situation.
- Impolite hostessing, greeting, and inaccurate seating, possibly resulting in our getting someone else's table. The hostess was overheard to interrupt some guests trying to speak to her, saying abruptly, "I will be with you in a minute," and command other guests to "wait over there."

Lounge Bar

- Four out of our five visits resulted in poor performance from staff.
- On Tuesday night, service at the bar counter was hectic and available to only those who were assertive.
- The server pick-up area was incredibly untidy, yet guests often walked through this area.
- When we were escorted to a table, it was unclean. The server appeared not to notice that some guests at the same table had coasters while others had none.

appendix|2 Manhattan Lodging Report, Average Daily Rates

	YTD November 1997	YTD November 1996
Manhattan	$171.39	$154.43
Hotel Type		
Deluxe	309.22	288.31
Luxury	236.32	208.38
First class	176.30	157.28
Convention	182.11	167.91
Affiliation		
Chain	176.96	165.78
Independent	205.39	189.50
Size		
Less than 200 units	167.04	154.59
201–500 units	184.12	173.53
501–1,000 units	204.67	186.53
More than 1,000 units	170.63	161.79

Source: Coopers & Lybrand, LLP.

appendix|3A Roccoco Hotel

An Analysis of Customer Satisfaction Survey Results, 1997			
Process Area	**Delighted**	**Satisfied**	**Dissatisfied**
Overall stay	32%	55%	13%
Room	54	40	6
Front-office service	20	68	12
Room service	19	50	31
Physical property	68	22	10
n = 547			

Source: Company records.

An Analysis of Customer Retention Rates, 1997	
Chance of Return	**Percentage of Guests**
100%	18
80	12
60	29
40	24
20	14
0	4

Source: Company records.

appendix|3B Sample Guest Survey

Hotel Roccoco New York

1. Please rate your experience with us by circling the number that best describes your feelings about the various aspects of your stay.

How did you feel about . . . ?	1 = delighted	2 = satisfied	3 = dissatisfied
Overall stay	1	2	3
Condition of your guest room	1	2	3
Service at the front desk	1	2	3
Room service	1	2	3
Condition of lobby and other public areas	1	2	3

2. On a scale from 0 to 100%, how certain is it that you will return to this hotel?

0%	20%	40%	60%	80%	100%
Chance that I'd come back					Chance

3. Your primary purpose of visit: 1 = business   2 = pleasure

4. How many times have you been a guest at this hotel?   1   2   3   4+

COMMENTS

Please give us any other comments you feel would help us:

_____

_____

_____

_____

_____

Please place this survey in the envelope provided. Seal the envelope and bring it to the front desk upon departure. Thank you.

appendix|4

Results of Roccoco Employee Survey (non-managerial employees)	
1 = strongly disagree, 7 = strongly agree	**Mean**
1. I have to do things that I think should be done differently.	4.8 (1.2)
2. There is a lack of policies and guidelines to help me.	4.0 (1.4)
3. I work under guidelines that are inconsistent with other guidelines for doing my job.	2.5 (.9)
4. I often get work to do without being given the right materials, training, or direction.	4.3 (1.3)
5. I do not know if my work will be acceptable to my supervisor.	4.3 (1.2)
6. I have to work under vague directives from management.	4.4 (1.1)
7. I know what is expected of me.	4.8 (1.8)
8. I receive clear guidance on how to resolve customer complaints.	2.5 (.6)
9. I work on unnecessary things.	2.3 (1.5)
10. I am allowed to perform work in a way that suits my own style and approach.	2.4 (1.5)
11. I have to ignore guidelines in order to do my job.	2.4 (1.3)
12. I receive clear guidance on how best to serve the guests.	2.1 (.8)
13. I receive clear guidance on how much time to spend on the various aspects of my job.	4.5 (1.5)
14. I receive clear guidance on how to plan and organize my daily work activities.	4.6 (1.4)
15. I receive clear guidance on where to get assistance in doing my job.	4.3 (1.2)
16. I receive clear guidance on the extent to which I can bend the rules to satisfy customers.	1.8 (1.0)
17. I receive clear guidance on how to operate hotel information systems.	4.7 (1.6)
18. I often receive incompatible requests from two or more people at work.	3.8 (.9)
19. The guests and management often expect different things from me.	5.1 (.5)
20. I often have to bend the rules to satisfy the guests.	5.3 (.6)
21. I receive clear, planned guidelines for doing my job.	2.3 (1.5)
22. I know what my responsibilities are.	4.8 (.9)
23. I know how to fulfill my work responsibilities.	5.1 (1.1)

Source: Company records. All the employees of the Hotel (excluding middle and top management) were surveyed in January 1997. $n = 239$. The standard deviations are in parentheses.

Results of Employee Satisfaction Survey (all employees)	
1 = very dissatisfied, 7 = very satisfied	**Mean**
1. your overall job	4.3 (1.2)
2. your fellow workers	5.1 (.8)
3. your supervisor(s)	4.2 (1.5)
4. hotel policies	3.1 (.7)
5. the amount of pay you receive	4.5 (1.3)
6. your opportunities for advancement	3.9 (1.3)
7. your hotel's customers	5.4 (.9)
8. the resources you have to do the job	5.1 (1.4)
9. the training you receive	3.5 (.6)

Source: Company records. $n = 247$. The standard deviations are in parentheses.

appendix|5 Roccoco New York Hotel, Statement of Income and Cash Flow after Debt Service

	1996	1997
Occupancy	79.8%	83.1%
Average Daily Rate	$ 167.13	$ 174.86
Revenues		
Rooms	14,847,386	16,176,487
Food & Beverage	2,534,920	3,235,297
Other	724,263	808,824
Total Revenues	**$18,106,569**	**$20,220,608**
Departmental Expenses		
Rooms	$ 5,493,533	$ 5,500,005
Food & Beverage	2,332,126	2,911,768
Other	579,410	582,354
Total Departmental Expenses	**8,405,069**	**8,994,127**
Total Departmental Profit	**$ 9,701,500**	**$11,226,481**
Undistributed Operating Expenses		
Administrative & General	$ 2,715,985	$ 2,729,782
Marketing	1,357,993	1,415,443
Energy	905,328	950,369
Property Operation & Maintenance	1,176,927	1,213,236
Total Undistributed Expenses	**6,156,233**	**6,308,830**
Income before Fixed Charges	**$ 3,545,267**	**$ 4,917,651**
Fixed Charges (*Insurance, Prop. Taxes . . .*)	**$ 1,267,460**	**$ 1,314,340**
Income before Debt Service Depreciation & Taxes	**2,277,807**	**3,603,311**
Debt Service	**3,183,777**	**3,183,777**
Cash Flow after Debt Service	**($ 905,970)**	**$ 419,534**

case 25

Developing a Global Mind-Set at Johnson & Johnson, 1998

Vladimir Pucik

International Institute for Management Development

In 1998, Johnson & Johnson (J&J) was the world's most comprehensive manufacturer of health care products. It was composed of more than 180 operating companies worldwide with three major business segments for consumer, pharmaceutical, and professional markets. In the late 1980s, its total revenue was close to $10 billion, but it more than doubled to $22.6 billion in 1997, generated from sales activities in more than 175 countries (refer to Exhibit 1).

The company's sales were evenly distributed between the United States and the rest of the world, but only one-third of profits were earned abroad, compared to one-half of corporate profits almost a decade before—a consequence of several recent U.S. acquisitions. By 1997, Europe accounted for 26 percent of J&J's total sales and 28 percent of operating profit. The Western Hemisphere (not including the United States contributed 9 percent to the total sales, and J&J's sales in Africa, Asia, and the Pacific region accounted for 13 percent of sales (refer to Exhibit 2). Over the same decade, the company's number of employees grew from 83,500 to 90,500 and the percentage of J&J's total workforce outside the United States had grown from half to two-thirds.

Before 1998, Johnson and Johnson had been organized around its operating companies established mostly on a country level (in some countries, J&J was represented by more than one operating company, and some companies operated in more than one country). The legacy of commitment to decentralized management was still evident in the company's customer-related functions. Marketing, sales, and country management functions remained largely decentralized. However, support functions such as finance, human resources, and information technology were increasingly shared among operating companies, and in an effort to streamline activities and reduce costs, J&J was moving toward a regional and global approach.

exhibit 1   Regional Sales as a Percentage of Total J&J Sales

	1989	1997
Africa	1.1	1.2
Asia	8.9	11.6
United States	50.0	51.9
Europe	27.6	26.3
Western Hemisphere (not including United States)	12.4	9.0

Source: Johnson & Johnson.

exhibit 2   Number of J&J Employees per Region

	1989	1997
Africa	1,985	1,568
Asia	9,449	11,962
United States	37,465	42,946
Europe	19,939	23,581
Western Hemisphere (not including United States)	14,258	10,447
Total number of employees	83,096	90,504

Source: Johnson & Johnson.

GLOBAL PLATFORMS

Due to the high cost of formulating new drugs, the company's pharmaceutical business segment had always used centralized research shared among operating companies worldwide. Johnson & Johnson consumer and professional businesses were pursuing a similar approach in a large portion of their value chains. J&J was seeking to utilize fewer company resources by implementing coordinated strategies, for example, a single, common marketing strategy for a given region rather than several different marketing tactics.

Johnson & Johnson's three business segments were subdivided into franchises, which could best be described as loose federations of individual products integrated across the company's three major operating groups. This integration was achieved through the company's new global platforms, defined as groupings of product franchises unified by use. J&J's new global platforms included such product franchise groups as wound care, skin care, women's health, and urology. The wound care global platform, for example, included a full range of Band-Aid products in the consumer business segment, and all types of surgical dressings in the professional business segment.

By 1998, the company's strategy had shifted from individual product-based operating companies to the new global platforms and integrated franchise management.

This shift to global platforms included shared marketing functions within geographic regions, consolidated production, and streamlining of product offerings to eliminate cost duplication. As recently as five years ago, J&J had marketed as many as 75 formulas for baby shampoo worldwide, but the product line had been streamlined to just a few formulas for differing hair types in world markets. Standardization of products within franchises allowed the company to make changes quickly to keep pace with global competition.

Consolidated production figured prominently in J&J's shift to global platforms. For example, rather than maintaining separate production facilities for different European markets, the company had started producing all its shampoo products for the European region at a single efficient plant in Italy. Globally, the company's Ethicon franchise (part of worldwide sutures platform) provided goods to Latin American markets from J&J's main facilities in Scotland, and Ethicon Brazil provided catgut and certain raw materials to Asia and Africa.

Before the shift to global platforms, individual manufacturing plants had been like silos of production activity—acting separately and producing different formulas. But the reduction of trade barriers and shipping costs in the era of globalization had increased opportunities to export, which allowed J&J to maximize plant capacities and increase efficiency.

J&J top management recognized that to compete in today's marketplace the company had to be nimble and agile and guided by a global mind-set, defined by Allen C. Anderson, J&J's vice president of education and development, as "the ability to think globally and act locally, and to understand the impact of worldwide strategies." The company's global approach, fueled by the reduction of trade barriers and unification of regional markets, required more communication among employees, an increased emphasis on matrix management, and more shared responsibility between managers worldwide.

GLOBAL HUMAN RESOURCES STRATEGY

With the ongoing globalization of J&J businesses, the firm's human resources management had also become increasingly global. The external forces of globalization created new business opportunities for increased efficiency through global integration in R&D, production, and marketing, but were also reshaping the opportunities and challenges in human resource management.

The unification of the EU labor market and the decline in barriers to labor mobility facilitated the movement of J&J employees within EU countries, both influencing staffing decisions and broadening career opportunities. At the same time, the shift to global platforms created new human resource challenges and expectations of the skills and competencies required from J&J managers in a globally integrated business environment. J&J managers also had to be able to share responsibility with J&J managers in other parts of the world, and the compensation system was intended to mirror this shared responsibility.

Johnson & Johnson's human resources organization reflected the company's recent changes in business strategy. J&J's regional human resource vice presidents spanned the globe, with one human resource vice president for each of the company's three business segments in Europe, three human resource vice presidents in the Asia Pacific region, and two in Latin America. The 28 human resource vice presidents in the United States represented each of J&J's companies operating in the United States and were equivalent in scope of responsibilities to human resource directors in Johnson & Johnson's international operations. In 1997, all of the company's human resource vice presidents and directors had met to develop J&J's worldwide human resource strategic plan, which centered all management education and development initiatives around the company's Standards of Leadership developed in 1996.

Standards of Leadership

The company's Standards of Leadership had helped make leadership relevant to J&J employees by identifying 60 specific behaviors that contributed to business results (refer to

Exhibit 3). These behaviors were grouped into categories: Customer/Marketplace Focus, Innovation, Interdependent Partnering, Masters Complexity, and Organizational and People Development. They were inextricably linked to the philosophy expressed in the well-known J&J Credo.

The J&J Credo (refer to Exhibit 4), which was periodically reviewed and updated, defined the company's view of its responsibility to customers, company employees, communities in which J&J operated, and finally, company stockholders. The values that underpinned Johnson & Johnson's Credo influenced how the company conducted its business. Upon this foundation, J&J's Standards of Leadership guided all aspects of the company's human resource function, from providing a basis for candidate assessment to evaluating managers' performance and potential.

International Recruitment

J&J's Standards of Leadership provided a basis for assessing an individual's potential fit with the company and helped the interviewer ask the right questions during the recruitment process. In the cast of upper-level management positions, candidates' previous international experiences were assessed, and their savvy regarding the global mind-set was evaluated through questions on cultural diversity. For lower-level managers, a global mind-set was not considered immediately necessary; to rise to a leadership position, the candidate was expected to acquire his mind-set on the job.

However, recruiters did examine entry-level candidates' résumés for evidence of a global orientation. Candidates who had taken advantage of educational exchanges outside their home countries were of interest to J&J, and those who had undertaken internationally focused degree programs in another country were actively pursued by J&J's international recruiters. For example, an Italian student studying for an MBA at the International Institute for Management Development (IMD) in Switzerland might well have been considered a prime prospect for an international management career with J&J.

J&J's international recruiters, based at J&J headquarters in New Jersey, sought candidates form the top U.S. and European MBA schools for J&J's overseas companies. Each year, the operating companies sent requests to international recruiting with the number of MBAs they were seeking and descriptions of the positions they needed to fill. J&J international recruiters then made campus visits seeking suitable candidates from among the world's most competitive MBA programs.

J&J's international MBA recruitment programs included the Leadership Development Program Europe and the Asia Global Managers Program. The Leadership Development Program Europe focused on top MBA students in Europe. Usually, these graduates were not placed in their home countries, but rather in other European countries in which they were authorized to work. This program required that candidates be multilingual and mobile, since after their initial assignments of 12 to 18 months in one country, they were likely to be moved to other European countries. During their initial assignments, new hires in this program were assigned development mentors who worked with them to improve their management skills.

The Asia Global Managers Program recruited Asian candidates from top U.S. and European MBA programs. J&J international recruiting manager Dina Da Silva explained: "After interviewing with the international recruiters, candidates were referred to top management for further interviews. Once selected the new hires were trained for approximately 18 months in the U.S. and Asia, always outside their home countries." Training consisted of broad, multidisciplinary overview assignments that helped define the type of position for which the new hire was best suited. After the training period, new hires were placed in Asia, usually in their home countries or in other countries in which they were authorized to work and had language fluency. The company's experience had

exhibit 3   Standards of Leadership

STANDARDS OF LEADERSHIP
Johnson & Johnson

CREDO VALUES/BUSINESS RESULTS	
Credo Values	**Business Results**
Behaves with honesty and integrity	Cash flow
Treats others with dignity and respect	Cost effectiveness
Applies Credo values	Customer satisfaction
Uses Credo Survey results to improve the business	Environmental/safety responsibility
Balances the interests of all constituents	Income growth
Manages for the long term	Market share
	New product flow
	People development
	Product quality
	Productivity
	Regulatory compliance
	Volume growth

"Credo values represent the foundation stone upon which leadership is built. Certainly within Johnson & Johnson you cannot be a good leader if you don't believe in and try to live up to the Credo."

Ralph S. Larsen, Chairman and Chief Executive Officer

"Business results are in the center of the model because all five leadership competency areas influence business results."

Clark H. Johnson, Vice President, Finance

shown that placing new hires in their home countries for initial assignments often offered the best environment for career growth and development.

The company was satisfied with the success of these international recruitment programs, and the numbers of new hires through the programs had increased substantially

exhibit 3   (*continued*)

CUSTOMER/MARKETPLACE FOCUS

Creates Value for Customers

Projects a sense of passion about customers

Recognizes the range of customers and their needs

Serves as the voice of the customer

Uses customer-perceived value as the key criterion for the design of current and future products and services

Focuses Externally

Analyzes market forces and positions Johnson & Johnson to capitalize on opportunities

Seizes the advantage of being first

Benchmarks competitive practices and performance

"Our raison d'être, as the French say, is the customer. We tend to forget that we do not have any role to play if the customer is not there. Its place in this model is a way of reminding everyone that this is what we're here for."

Christian Koffmann, Worldwide Chairman, Consumer & Personal Care

INNOVATION

Forges a Vision of the Future

Visualizes and communicates the future

Develops strategies for growth

Inspires others to commit to the vision

Executes vision and strategy

Fuels Business Growth

Acts and encourages others to be entrepreneurial

Finds and exploits new opportunities

Takes risks and manages them intelligently

Demands the pursuit of stretch goals for self and others

Promotes Innovation and Continuous Learning

Generates and encourages creative ideas

Finds new ways to do things better and faster

Challenges and encourages others to challenge the status quo

Transfers ideas and successes across boundaries

Promotes quality improvement as a value and as process

Finds new ways to use technology more effectively

Learns from personal and organizational experiences

"Our whole business is built on innovation and the ability to move rapidly ahead with new therapies, to be the first in a new treatment category. It is a key element of the Johnson & Johnson history and future, and a key competency of leaders within our company."

Robert N. Wilson, Vice Chairman, Board of Directors

INTERDEPENDENT PARTNERING

Builds Interdependent Partnerships

Cooperates across functions, business units and geographic boundaries

Leverages technology, products, and services across boundaries

Establishes mutually beneficial objectives; clarifies roles and accountabilities with partners

Fosters open communication with partners

Communicates commitment to the success of the partnership in both words and actions

"We can no longer afford to be independent silos, not worrying about what's happening on your left or right or with other sister companies or other departments. It just isn't going to work that way as the environment is changing. We need to do things differently and interdependent partnering is a very important part."

Ronald G. Gelbman, Worldwide Chairman, Pharmaceuticals & Diagnostics Group

(*continued*)

exhibit 3 (*continued*)

MASTERS COMPLEXITY	
Manages Complexity	**Implements Positive Change**
Thinks analytically and acts decisively	Recognizes and communicates the need for change
Thrives in uncertain circumstances	Embraces non-traditional ideas and practices
Knows when to act and when to wait	
Makes the complex clear and compelling	Engages in constructive conflict
Builds consensus and impacts outcomes with limited authority	Drives the change process
	Teaches and encourages others to deal with change

"As our business lives get more complex and we enter new businesses, we'll have to have a compass in the forest of all the information that comes at us every day and this model includes the leadership skills to handle it."

James T. Lenehan, Worldwide Chairman,
Consumer Pharmaceuticals & Professional Group

ORGANIZATIONAL AND PEOPLE DEVELOPMENT	
Creates an Achievement Environment	**Develops People for Optimal Performance**
Challenges and motivates people to reach their highest potential	Fosters the continuous professional development and career growth of a diverse workforce
Creates an environment that encourages risk taking	Provides challenging work assignments and development opportunities
Promotes the business value of diverse perspectives, ideas, backgrounds, styles and cultures	Identifies and champions high potential talent as a Johnson & Johnson resource
Fosters organizational flexibility	Coaches and mentors future leaders
Sets clear performance standards and holds people accountable for results	Requires people to expand their capabilities, knowledge and skills
Values, recognizes, and rewards the achievement of others	Functions as both team player and leader
Promotes teamwork	

"Our company is all about a large group of people engaged in a common endeavor. There's nothing more important than making our people better and better at what they do and at who they are."

Roger S. Fine, Vice President, General Counsel

"The organizational part is just as important. We need an environment in each of our business operations that encourages, fosters, and develops the kind of business activities and leadership we need to grow the business."

Russell C. Deyo, Vice President, Administration

Source: Johnson & Johnson.

over the last decade. By 1998, the programs were bringing in an average of 90 new hires a year, with about 45 in training at any given time.

Management Development

J&J's emerging regional and global strategies required managers to develop new skills to support the integration of company's business segments. These skills included partnering

exhibit 4   Johnson & Johnson's Credo

We believe our first responsibility is to the doctors, nurses and patients, to mothers and fathers and all others who use our products and services. In meeting their needs everything we do must be of high quality. We must constantly strive to reduce our costs in order to maintain reasonable prices. Customers' orders must be serviced promptly and accurately. Our suppliers and distributors must have an opportunity to make a fair profit.

We are responsible to our employees, the men and women who work with us throughout the world. Everyone must be considered as an individual. We must respect their dignity and recognise their merit. They must have a sense of security in their jobs. Compensation must be fair and adequate, and working conditions clean, orderly and safe. We must be mindful of ways to help our employees fulfill their family responsibilities. Employees must feel free to make suggestions and complaints. There must be equal opportunity for employment, development and advancement for those qualified. We must provide competent management, and their actions must be just and ethical.

We are responsible to the communities in which we live and work and to the world community as well. We must be good citizens— support good works and charities and bear our fair share of taxes. We must encourage civic improvements and better health and education. We must maintain in good order the property we are privileged to use, protecting the environment and natural resources.

Our final responsibility is to our stockholders. Business must make a sound profit. We must experiment with new ideas. Research must be carried on, innovative programmes developed and mistakes paid for. New equipment must be purchased, new facilities provided and new products launched. Reserves must be created to provide for adverse times. When we operate according to these principles, the stockholders should realise a fair return.

Source: Johnson & Johnson.

with colleagues, sharing responsibility with managers in other units, cross-border communication, and matrix management, along with a broad global perspective and international experience. J&J's Anderson said, "To develop these skills in J&J managers, the company depended largely on on-the-job training."

J&J's new corporate structure based on global franchises promoted on-the-job training for employees, which the company viewed as 80 to 85 percent of an employee's overall development. Since J&J believed formal education and training could be difficult to apply directly to employees' jobs, development programs utilized on-the-job learning to develop managers, both individually and in the context of their organizational roles. Cross-functional teams in global franchises were one potential source of hands-on training, which strengthened global franchises and enhanced employees' matrix management skills.

Formal Training Programs   J&J also provided formal training programs to support leadership development. In the late 1980s, J&J sponsored in-company management development programs at Northwestern University in Chicago (for North American employees), the University of California at Berkeley (for the Asia-Pacific region), and IMD in Switzerland (for Europe). J&J had also developed relationships with several other universities in the United States and the United Kingdom; however, since more and more training programs were being developed in-house, most of these relationships had disappeared.

After gaining experience through the earlier outside programs and opting not to invest in physical institutes of its own, J&J had developed in-house formal training programs which it viewed not only as more cost-effective but also more flexible in teaching employees as needed and where needed. As Anderson reported, "Essentially, J&J had decided to build its own management program to take on the road as needed, which could be tailored for different regions and thereby minimized travel costs by bringing training to the most cost-effective location." In recent years, the company had offered an Advanced Manager Program in Antwerp for European employees and a smaller program in Sao Paulo and Miami for the South American region.

Ethics Training   As J&J grew from a $1 billion company with fewer than 10,000 employees in 1970 to a $23 billion company with over 90,000 employees in 1998, much of this through acquisitions, it had been challenged to maintain a high level of ethics in accordance with the long-standing Johnson & Johnson credo. Dedicated to upholding J&J's ethics standards, top management considered the Credo to be the "heart and soul" of their leadership, and took ownership of ethics development throughout the company. J&J's human resource personnel recruited individuals who shared Johnson & Johnson's values and then developed these new employees around J&J's Standards of Leadership.

Adhering strictly to the company's ethical values throughout the global organization was difficult, considering the varying cultures of acquired companies and the varied countries in which J&J did business. To help employees deal with the variety of complex ethical issues that they might encounter in the company's extensive international operations, J&J's training organization had developed a case-based education program called "Ethics Toolkit" to help managers worldwide learn how to uphold the company's values regardless of prevailing cultural norms. Ethics Toolkit training examined front-line ethics situations (such as third party payments), taught managers ethical decision-making processes, and advised them whom to turn to for help and advice when ethical gray areas arose (refer to Exhibit 5).

Stretch Assignments   In order to accelerate development of high-potential managers, J&J used "stretch assignments" designed to extend a manager's range of skills by providing new challenges and career opportunities. Stretch assignments were the basis of J&J's succession planning, which focused on building dynamic leadership.

For example, the company might assign a manager who had performed particularly well in one turnaround situation to another turnaround assignment. However, J&J was aware of the limitation this could place on the employee's career development, and preferred to find an assignment in which the manager could gain additional experiences and skills. Still, international assignments were, by definition, well suited for a stretch.

Global Coordination and Development Programs   The key J&J global coordination and development programs were the executive development programs and executive conference sessions.

The objective of the executive development program was to help managers develop global mind-set through action learning. These high-impact programs, which were designed for high-potential managers, were driven by business needs (business issues addressed during the program were selected by each company's operating committee). Cross-border work groups, members of which were nominated by each company group chairman, were assigned to spend three weeks in the field abroad working on solutions for business issues and then present specific recommendations for action.

J&J's executive conference sessions were convened by global franchise leaders, who selected key franchise managers from around the world (usually numbering around 40 to 50 but as many as 130) and determined which specific business to address. Over a custom-developed session that lasted several days, the group worked to resolve specific business issues within the franchise with participants from across the globe. Executive conferences provided opportunities for managers to broaden their global perspectives by working with colleagues from other regions, deepen the communication channels and relationships among franchise members, and advance partnering between employees and shared responsibility between managers. To demonstrate senior management

exhibit 5   Ethics Toolkit (Sample Case)

Applying Credo Values in the Real World—A Diagnostic Survey Case: The Fine Line between Custom and Corruption

You are the new general manager of Utopia, a recently acquired subsidiary that does business in a country with a tradition of corruption. It is customary for businesses to make payments and gifts to government officials. You have been briefed by the company's legal counsel about the Credo's statements about good citizenship and about the Foreign Corrupt Practices Act (a U.S. law that makes the company criminally liable for improper payments to foreign officials). When you meet with the management to tell them that some of the practices they are used to may not be acceptable to the company, the reaction is disdain. One manager says flatly, "You don't understand what it takes to do business in this part of the world. If you can't make the traditional payments to politicians and bureaucrats we will be out of business within a year." You know that other U.S. companies try to avoid the problem by hiring independent expediting firms who take care of all the details and shield management from direct knowledge or involvement. You ask an executive to make a list of the kinds of payments they are talking about. Each of the following was on the list and you are to determine whether you will permit continuation of the payments.

1 = Yes—there is nothing legally or ethically wrong with this action.

2 = Yes—this may not be proper elsewhere but it is acceptable under local standards.

3 = Yes—if the amounts are relatively small. Tell your people to proceed with caution.

4 = No—it is not consistent with Credo values or the Company's worldwide reputation.

5 = No—don't even think about it; this is foolish and probably illegal.

1 2 3 4 5 When acquiring permits to ship good internationally, it is customary to pay an unofficial service fee to the official in charge equal to 10 percent of the permit fees that go to the government.

1 2 3 4 5 When goods arrive from outside the country they must go through customs. It can take months to get release of the goods and the custom official exercises broad discretion in assessing duty. Officials are given monthly "gifts" during visits to the plant.

1 2 3 4 5 When the electricity goes down, state-employed electrical workers expect to be "tipped" for performing their services. The more you tip, the faster the service.

1 2 3 4 5 One of Utopia's largest customers is a state-run medical facility. It is customary to provide the buyers with free products, trips, and cash.

1 2 3 4 5 The Minister of Health serves on the Company's "advisory council." A substantial fee is paid. The Company benefits from preferential treatment from the Ministry.

1 2 3 4 5 During busy times one has to "tip" the train ticket agent to get a ticket.

1 2 3 4 5 Occasionally, the local police stop Company vehicles for real or fictitious traffic violations. Employees are reimbursed for payments to avoid having the truck impounded.

Source: Johnson & Johnson.

commitment to managerial development, executive committee members actively participated in executive conferences.

International Mobility

Johnson & Johnson consistently worked to balance its use of in-country talent and expatriates. Since the 1980s, the number of expatriates had decreased, primarily to reduce costs. In addition, expatriate compensation packages had been reduced in recent years, making expatriate assignment less glamorous to many managers. However expatriate assignments were still used when in-country talent was unavailable, or for the cross-cultural development of managers. Expatriate assignments were usually to a single country for a limited time period, although some expatriate managers moved from one foreign country to another.

J&J's reduction in the use of expatriate managers had achieved significant cost reductions without diminishing the effectiveness of the organization. Still, maintaining the balance between using in-country talent and providing opportunities for cross-cultural experience through expatriate assignment remained a constant challenge. Expatriate assignments were often learning-driven, rather than solely driven by the demand for a manager in a foreign location, and were intended to develop managers' global mind-sets and international experience. Limiting the use of expatriate assignments to these development goals reflected the company's traditional preference for using in-country talent.

International experience was considered extremely important for young J&J managers, and international assignments were encouraged early in managers' professional careers. Ideally, the company tried to assign managers internationally when they were in their late 20s and early 30s, since young families usually relocated more easily than those already established in communities and schools.

Johnson & Johnson also found that a global mind-set was more readily adopted when managers were fairly young. To increase the likelihood of success of managers on international assignment, the company also worked to find challenging employment in the company for spouses in dual-career couples.

The International Recruitment and Development Program (IDP), J&J's broader umbrella development activity, also included career development programs for employees worldwide. Each year, the IDP moved 70 to 80 current J&J employees from different parts of the globe into one or two year assignments in the United States. Since each operating company had to pay for the program, and accordingly had to justify the expense, the recurrent choice of the IDP program to develop managers reflected the value it provided. The company was pleased with this success: roughly the same number of participants took part in 1998 as 10 years before, and the program had an excellent retention rate.

J&J had also launched a special program to globalize high-potential employees from the United States. A formalized structure which can best be described as a "reverse IDP" program was used to give young U.S. employees international exposure to prepare them for full time international experience. Each year, 5 to 10 U.S. employees sere sent abroad for up to 18 months for development purposes. These employees set out with clear individualized objectives specifically based on their own development requirements and the company's business needs. During the overseas assignment, the employee was expected to gain international experience through exposure to different cultures, markets, and products.

For example, a high-potential employee responsible for corporate compensation in the United States might have been assigned for 18 months to work in corporate compensation in Belgium. After the assignment was completed, the employee re-turned to the United States. J&J arranged work authorizations for employees in this program, since temporary assignments for current employees were easier to arrange than permanent assignments for new hires. Cost issues were always a factor in this program as well, since moving families, arranging spousal employment, and overall expatriate support were costly. This program was relatively new, and the company was watching the results closely to see if demonstrated success warranted expansion of the program.

Preparing for a Global Future

J&J top management believed that, from the point of view of doing business on a worldwide scale, leaders are leaders, no matter where. Having found commonalties among excellent managers around the globe, the company was fine-tuning its global franchise corporate strategy.

J&J was also constantly searching for new methods to develop crucial cross-cultural business skills and to provide international management experiences that were driven by business needs. Anderson explained, "Rather than just providing classroom cross-cultural training, or arranging an international experience—which often amounted to picking up managers and moving them to foreign countries for a short time, only to have them then come back to sit at the same desk, unable to fully utilize their cross-cultural experience—J&J was focusing on increasing the opportunities for bringing managers together to work on specific business issues."

Through this international work integration, managers both developed cross-cultural management skills and accomplished business tasks. By partnering with international colleagues to solve specific operational problems, managers also developed the ability to share responsibility with others, improve cross-border communication, and operate in an international matrix organization. The company believed this hands-on approach was well suited to prepare managers for future global management activities because it supported global coordination while developing managers' international management skills.

Motorola: Ethical Challenges in a Multicultural Environment

E. Brian Peach
The University of West Florida

Kenneth L. Murrell
The University of West Florida

In June 1999 Christopher Galvin, Motorola's CEO, wrote a memo to all Motorola employees concerning the company's continuing commitment to its code of business conduct and the ongoing efforts to get "Motorolans" worldwide to live up to the highest possible ethical standards:

> As we continue to focus on the future, we are changing many things in the corporation. However, we will never change or compromise our high principles—our superb business ethics and the dignity and respect we hold for the individual. This week, I met with the team responsible for revising and reissuing Motorola's code of business conduct. The updated code has been well researched and embodies insights of small group discussions with Motorolans around the world. You will hear more about it soon.
>
> The code is an important milestone in the Motorola Ethics Renewal Process, which has engaged us over the last few years. During that time, we established ethics committees and ethics compliance officers worldwide in our vigorous commitment to live up to the highest possible standards. We have always considered trust to be our competitive advantage and we continue to demand ethical behavior throughout the Corporation. Adherence to our code of business conduct ensures that we will disappoint neither ourselves nor the world.
>
> We are committed to behave honorably at all times when conducting business. Global implementation of our code is challenging because cultures, morals, value systems and business ethics standards vary widely from country to country. To address this, we have established an active, open, participative process where Motorolans worldwide can discuss how to determine right and wrong in various situations. Our process, which has been in place for years, is powerful, exciting and right. It will be expanded and re-emphasized over the next few months through training and employee communications, including Motorola's Intranet.

Financial support for this project was provided by a grant from the Shell Corporation, and a University of West Florida Research Grant. Copyright © 2000 by the case authors.

exhibit 1 Motorola's Revenues and Workforce Size, 1930–99

Year	Sales	Employees	Sales/Employee
1930	$ 287,256	—	—
1940	9,936,558	985	$ 10,088
1950	177,104,669	9,325	19,000
1960	299,065,922	14,740	20,300
1970	796,418,521	36,000	22,100
1980	3,098,763,000	71,500	43,340
1990	10,885,000,000	105,000	103,670
1998	29,398,000,000	133,000	221,000
1999	30,931,000,000	121,000	255,600

Source: Company annual reports.

Motorola had a long legacy of honorably and ethically conducting its business worldwide, and Christopher Galvin wanted to continue the company's tradition. But as Galvin and others at Motorola had come to recognize, this was easier said than done given that the company had over 121,000 employees scattered across company operations in nearly 100 countries.

COMPANY BACKGROUND

Founded in 1928 as the Galvin Manufacturing Company, Motorola manufactured radios for cars, developed home and police radios, and during World War II developed the walkie-talkie. The company's name was changed to Motorola in the 1940s. During the 1950s and 1960s, Motorola emerged as pioneer in developing semiconductor-related products and became a leading commercial provider of semiconductors for sale to other manufacturers. Motorola introduced computer microprocessors and high-capacity telephone systems in the 1970s and 1980s. It became a world leader in the cellular telephone and wireless communications industry during the 1980s and 1990s. Motorola initiated a companywide six sigma quality program in 1979 and won the Malcolm Baldrige Quality Award in 1988, the first year the award was given.

In 2000, Motorola was one of the world's leading providers of wireless communications; semiconductors; and advanced electronic systems, components, and services. Its major equipment businesses included cellular telephones, two-way radios, paging and data communications products, personal communications products, automotive products, defense and space electronics, and computers. Motorola semiconductors powered communication devices, computers, and thousands of other products. Exhibit 1 shows long-term trends in Motorola's revenues and workforce size.

Motorola competed in industries noted for extraordinarily intense competition, the exit of formerly significant competitors, and rapidly changing technology. Remaining on the cutting edge of technology was often insufficient—firms had to anticipate and lead the changes in technology. In addition, Motorola competed against some of the strongest and most competitive global firms in the world, including Intel in microprocessors, the leading Japanese firms in semiconductors, and Nokia and Ericsson in cellular telephones. Two of the seven arenas the Japanese government had targeted for development support as critical industries of the future were semiconductors and communications—the very industries in which Motorola derived most of its revenues and earnings.

Motorola's revenues tripled from approximately $10 billion in 1990 to almost $31 billion in 1999, but its 1996–99 bottom-line performance did not match its rapid growth and profitability during the 1990–96 period (see Exhibit 2). Rapid technology gains and product innovations by Motorola's rivals in wireless communications, combined with a downturn in demand for semiconductors and pagers and an economic meltdown in parts of Asia, contributed to a stunning reversal of fortune for Motorola in 1998. In two years, Motorola had gone from being a firm respected around the world for cutting-edge technology and six sigma quality to being a company bombarded by criticism for its management style, its lagging digital cellular phone technology, its focus on a wireless-equipment technology that only covered half the U.S. market potential, and its poor quality and performance in some of its product areas (which resulted in loss of customers). But, to Motorola's credit, things began to turn around in late 1999, with the company reporting full-year earnings of $817 million in 1999 versus a loss of $962 million in 1998 (after restructuring charges of $1.93 billion).

AN OVERVIEW OF MOTOROLA'S BUSINESSES IN 1999

Cellular Phones

Motorola invented the cellular phone and had excelled at improving analog technology, making its phones ever smaller and more feature-rich. Although dominant in the area of analog technology, Motorola made some missteps and errors in judgment during the 1995–98 period. In one instance, trying to maintain its high margins, Motorola attempted to leverage its dominant market share and limit wholesale sales to a few companies—a move that antagonized many of its major customers.[1] But its biggest error was continuing to put its emphasis on analog technology at a time when rivals were racing forward with advances in digital cellular technology. This mistake was compounded by the company's banking on a single digital technology. Globally, three competing digital technologies were being developed and in use: time division multiple access (TDMA), which was six times as fast as analog technology; code division multiple access (CDMA), which was three times as fast as analog; and global standard for mobile communications (GSM), which was two to three times as fast and was the primary system used in Europe and Japan.

Motorola had elected to abandon its early efforts on TDMA, where it had a technological lead, to concentrate on CDMA, which it viewed as having greater market potential. This decision prevented Motorola from competing for customers that used TDMA and also resulted in Motorola's losing the business of carriers that used CDMA (such as AT&T) and that therefore wanted equipment capable of interfacing with both analog and digital systems. Dual compatibility was necessary for carriers to provide national coverage, since most carriers had CDMA systems in some geographic locations and TDMA systems in other geographic locations. National coverage equipment was provided by Nokia, which had introduced a cellular phone that worked on analog networks and both CMDA and TDMA digital networks.[2]

---

[1]Daniel Roth, "Burying Motorola," Fortune, July 6, 1998, p. 28.

[2]"Sales Surge for Wireless Makers," The Wall Street Journal, February 8, 1999.

exhibit 2 Motorola's Financial Highlights, 1994–99

	Years Ended December 31					
	1999	**1998**	**1997**	**1996**	**1995**	**1994**
Operating results						
Net sales	$30,931	$29,398	$29,794	$27,973	$27,037	$22,245
Manufacturing and other costs of sales	22,652	20,886	20,003	18,990	17,545	13,760
Selling, general and administrative expenses	5,045	5,493	5,188	4,715	4,642	4,381
Restructuring and other charges	(266)	1,980	327	—	—	—
Depreciation expense	2,182	2,197	2,329	2,308	1,919	1,525
Interest expense, net	155	216	131	185	149	142
Total costs and expenses	29,763	30,722	27,978	26,198	24,255	19,808
Net gain on Nextel asset exchange	—	—	—	—	443	—
Earnings (loss) before income taxes	1,168	(1,374)	1,816	1,775	3,225	2,437
Income tax provision (benefit)	351	(412)	636	621	1,777	877
Net earnings (loss)	$817	($962)	$1,180	$1,154	$2,048	$1,560
Net earnings (loss) as a percent of sales	2.6%	(3.3)%	4.0%	4.1%	7.6%	7.0%
Per share data (in dollars)						
Diluted earnings (loss) per common share	$1.31	$(1.61)	$1.94	$1.90	$3.37	$2.66
Diluted weighted average common shares outstanding	624.7	598.6	612.2	609.0	609.7	591.7
Dividends declared	$0.480	$0.480	$0.480	$0.460	$0.400	$0.310
Balance sheet statistics						
Total assets	$37,327	$28,728	$27,278	$24,076	$22,738	$17,495
Working capital	4,087	2,091	4,181	3,324	2,717	3,008
Long-term debt	3,089	2,633	2,144	1,931	1,949	1,127
Total debt	5,593	5,542	3,426	3,313	3,554	2,043
Total stockholders' equity	$16,344	$12,222	$13,272	$11,795	$10,985	$9,055
Other data						
Current ratio	1.33	1.18	1.46	1.42	1.35	1.51
Return on average invested capital	3.9%	(6.2)%	8.4%	8.4%	16.7%	17.5%
Return on average stockholders' equity	5.0%	(7.6)%	9.4%	10.0%	20.2%	21.1%
Capital expenditures	$2,684	$3,221	$2,874	$2,973	$4,225	$3,322
% to sales	8.7%	11.0%	9.6%	10.6%	15.6%	14.9%
Research and development expenditures	$3,438	$2,893	$2,748	$2,394	$2,197	$1,860
% to sales	11.1%	9.8%	9.2%	8.6%	8.1%	8.4%
Year-end employment (in thousands)	121	133	150	139	142	132

Source: Motorola annual reports.

Lack of a competitive digital product also hurt Motorola in Asian markets. Motorola had spent 20 years developing and cultivating Asian markets and dominated the markets for two-way radios and pagers across most of the Asian-Pacific region; the region accounted for 20 percent of Motorola's revenue in 1997. In Japan, after spending considerable energy penetrating the market and attaining a 25 percent market share in

1995, Motorola's lack of digital phones working on GSM had reduced its market share to 3 percent in 1998. In Thailand, one of Motorola's top three Asian markets, Motorola lost its lead and fell behind Nokia and Ericsson. At year-end 1998, Nokia had 40 percent of the Thai market.[3] In China, Motorola lost its dominant position in the cellular phone market when China adopted GSM instead of CDMA, allowing Ericsson and Nokia to move in and control approximately two-thirds of the market by mid-1998.[4]

By 1998, the lack of a competitive digital cellular phone was really beginning to hurt Motorola. The company continued to dominate sales of analog phones, but these were now only 15 percent of worldwide sales. In 1998, Motorola had only a 20 share of the $28 billion global market for wireless telephones.

Wireless Technology Equipment

Motorola was a major supplier of wireless system infrastructure products—the support equipment that made pagers, two-way radio systems, and cellular phones work. Motorola had excellent base station equipment that sent and received signals from mobile phones. However, it had problems developing a reliable switching system. Digital systems offered a great many new capabilities and features, and digital switches were required to make many of the new digital services possible. Because many customers preferred to purchase a complete system infrastructure solution from a single supplier, between 1990 and 1999 Motorola lost a number of customers and contracts because of the poor switching capabilities of its digital equipment. By 1998, Motorola's market share had dropped to 13 percent versus Lucent's 38 percent share.

Satellite Systems

The Iridium Network   Motorola was a major backer and developer of Iridium, a satellite-based worldwide phone network that allowed users to make and receive calls anywhere in the world. Iridium was intended to be an anywhere, anytime communication device for people needing global mobile communications services. Iridium management had predicted that the network would garner a 40 percent share of an anticipated 12 million users by 2002, and projected that it would generate revenues of over $2.5 billion by the year 2000.[5] However, technical and construction problems delayed introduction of Iridium to consumers, and major problems were encountered. Iridium users found the handsets to be bulky and hard to work. In addition, the handsets required a clear line of sight to the satellites, which precluded their use in buildings and other obstructed sites. User costs were high—the Iridium handset itself cost $3,000, and airtime charges ran $2 to $7 per minute.

By mid-1999, although more than $5 billion had been invested in Iridium, there were only 10,000 subscribers (barely a fifth of the expected number) and revenues were a meager $1.45 million, well short of covering operating expenses and a $400 million annual debt service.[6] Iridium filed for Chapter 11 bankruptcy in August 1999.

---

[3]"Thailand: Motorola Undertakes a Marketing Drive," *Nation*, October 27, 1998.

[4]"Motorola Expands Operations in China," *The Wall Street Journal*, June 12, 1998.

[5]Roger Crockett, "How Motorola Lost Its Way," *Business Week*, May 4, 1998, pp. 140–48.

[6]"High Wireless Act," *Forbes*, June 4, 1999.

Motorola had set aside a reserve of $740 million to cover its exposure in case Iridium was unable to restructure its debt and avoid bankruptcy. Meanwhile, three more hand-held mobile phone services serving the rural areas of Latin America, Africa, and Southeast Asia were expected to be launched in 2000–2001, intensifying competitive pressures on Iridium.

Teledesic Motorola was a 26 percent owner of Teledesic, a low-earth-orbit (LEO) satellite network originally intended to begin operations in 2002. Other owners included billionaires Bill Gates of Microsoft and Craig McCaw of McCaw Cellular Communications (now part of AT&T), who each had a 21 percent stake in Teledesic; Saudi investor Prince Alaweed Bin Talal, with 11 percent; and Boeing, with 4 percent. Teledesic planned to have 288 LEO satellites and was designed to support millions of simultaneous users. Teledesic's business plan was to provide business users with Internet access at speeds up to 2,000 times faster than a dial-up modem.

In May 1999, Motorola shifted several hundred engineers from the Teledesic project, and rumors flew that Motorola was rethinking its support for Teledesic given its problems with Iridium. The satellite rocket launch industry had experienced a rash of satellite launch failures, and this raised concerns about possible increased costs for projects such as Teledesic in establishing its LEO network.[7] In July 1999, contracts were finalized for Motorola to build most of the satellites to be used in the Teledesic network. Cost estimates were revised to $9 billion, and the expected service date was moved to late 2003.[8]

Semiconductors

In mid-1999, Motorola was the third largest semiconductor manufacturer in the world, trailing Intel and NEC. Motorola's semiconductor business was organized around 23 decentralized product groups with responsibility for 82,000 commodity products. The groups were said to be reluctant to share designers or designs with each other. Each group had its own fabrication and systems design libraries and submicron laboratories. Believing that the future of embedded chips was evolving rapidly toward whole systems on a chip, Motorola's semiconductor group had recently changed its product emphasis, dropping generic products and moving to differentiated lines. As part of a plan to get out of low-end chip manufacturing, Motorola laid off over 17,000 employees and sold the commodity component of its semiconductor division for $1.6 billion in cash.

Recent Management Actions to Turn Motorola Around

CEO Christopher Galvin took a number of actions in 1998 to reverse Motorola's market share losses and return the firm to profitability. He reorganized Motorola into three major enterprises and replaced the heads of a number of divisions. The objective was

---

[7]Joanna Glasner, "Motorola Wavering on Teledesic"
(www.wirednews.com/news/news/business/story/19758.html), May 19, 1999.

[8]Joanna Glasner, "Motorola on Board for Teledesic"
www.wired.com/news/news/business/story/20655.html).

to reduce interdivision competition, encourage sharing of ideas, reduce development costs, and coordinate actions between Motorola's business units. He also instituted a bonus system for top executives based on companywide performance, rather than division performance, to encourage cross-unit cooperation and collaboration.

MOTOROLA'S CORPORATE CULTURE AND MANAGEMENT STYLE

Motorola's culture was grounded in its two "key beliefs" of "constant respect for people" and "uncompromising integrity," a long tradition of participative management, decentralized business divisions and groups that operated with considerable independence, a strong and pioneering commitment to six sigma quality, a technology-engineering orientation, and a deep commitment to operating honestly and ethically.

The Roots of Motorola's Culture

Motorola's ethical culture began with founder Paul Galvin's personal code, which had its roots in the ethical milieu of the small-town U.S. Midwest in the early 1900s. Whether accurately or not, this era is regarded by many as one of integrity and honesty in business dealings. Galvin's code was institutionalized as the "Key Beliefs of Uncompromising Integrity and Constant Respect for People." Motorolans believe that the value they place on these key beliefs is demonstrated by their everyday work habits and is measured by the sacrifices they have made to uphold them over the years.

The consistency of ethical behavior in the performance of business tasks is a critical aspect to understanding Motorola's approach to ethical behavior. Paul Galvin's son, Bob Galvin, who in turn became the company's chief executive and dominant figure from 1956 to 1990, declares that "there is no such thing as situational ethics"[9] and he also believes that you cannot predict or specify every situation and ethical challenge. Thus, the approach is to provide an ethical posture that enables Motorolans to act ethically when confronted with an unexpected or unfamiliar challenge. Just as culture provides members of a society a set of standards for their behavior in all aspects of their life, Motorola's two key beliefs provide Motorolans standards for their behavior across cultures in their accomplishment of business-related tasks.

Since 1973, Motorola has published and periodically updated a document entitled "For Which We Stand: A Statement of Purpose, Objectives & Ethics." Initially it was a response by Bob Galvin to what he perceived to be unfair criticism of American industry, where many were labeled with the sins of a few.[10] It is both notable and typical of Motorola that "ethics" would be a prominent part of a statement of purpose. The document was revised several times over the succeeding years, but the last revision, published in 1996, contained the same emphasis on integrity and ethics and could be

---

[9]Interview with author.

[10]Corporate Public Relations, Motorola, Inc., "For Which We Stand: A Statement of Purpose, Objectives & Ethics," October 1973.

exhibit 3   Motorola's Fundamental Objective, Key Beliefs, Key Goals, and Key Initiatives (Referred to by Motorolans as the Total Customer Satisfaction Card)

Our Fundamental Objective (Everyone's Overriding Responsibility): Total Customer Satisfaction

Key Beliefs—How we will always act
- Constant Respect for People
- Uncompromising Integrity

Key Goals—What we must accomplish
- Best in Class
    People
    Marketing
    Technology
    Product: Software, Hardware, and Systems
    Manufacturing
    Service
- Increased Global Market Share
- Superior Financial Results

Key Initiatives—How we will do it
- Six Sigma Quality
- Total Cycle Time Reduction
- Product, Manufacturing and Environmental
- Profit Improvement
- Empowerment for All, in a Participative, Cooperative, and Creative Workplace

Source: Company documents.

readily found in all parts of Motorola throughout the world. This document was incorporated in 1999 into the revised "Motorola Code of Business Conduct."

Motorola's Key Beliefs

Motorola has an informal, first-name-only culture that stresses the role and importance of individual employees. As noted earlier, Motorola has two key beliefs: constant respect for people and uncompromising integrity (see Exhibit 3). Both beliefs originated with Motorola's founder, Paul Galvin. Galvin consistently demonstrated a concern for people and integrity in business; his concerns ran so deep and were so strongly evident in his actions and behavior that they became ingrained in company practices during its early years. Motorola was recognized as a family-friendly place to work and for emphasizing a balance between work and family. The family orientation and the faithfulness with which the company lived up to its core values were prime reasons that Motorola was named to the *Fortune* list of the 100 best companies to work for in 1997.[11]

---

[11]"The 100 Best Companies to Work For," *Fortune,* January 12, 1998, p. 94.

Numerous Motorola employees had worked for the company many years. Employee longevity was reflected by the fact that in 1997 most of the employees hired in 1952 celebrated their 25th anniversary at Motorola.

Folklore and Stories   Part of Motorola's culture was rooted in stories about Paul and Bob Galvin, and in some of the company's policies and practices. Aspects of the culture included the following:

● In Motorola's early days, the company experienced serious financial struggles. Despite the almost overwhelming challenges, Paul Galvin kept all the regular employees on the payroll.

● In the 1950s Motorola withdrew from a potentially profitable contract in a foreign country because there were payments that had the appearance of a kickback.

● Paul Galvin initiated a policy of treating female employees fairly and with respect decades before sexual harassment issues became a matter of general concern and legislation was passed. The policy was continued by Bob Galvin. One oft-told story concerned Bob Galvin's visit to a Motorola manufacturing facility where he observed women working on the assembly lines. He expressed concern about what Motorola should do to protect the women from offensive behavior and harassment, making it clear that such behavior would not be tolerated. One senior official was dismissed for failure to enforce the behavior standards that Bob Galvin set forth.

● Several stories illustrated how, when the choice was money or ethics, Bob Galvin always went with ethics. Others were more about him as a role model. One person told about a meeting where Bob Galvin gave a 10-minute speech shortly after he had a heart bypass operation. He was very tired, but later in the meeting, when he saw women standing in the crowded room, he went around gathering chairs for them and gave up his chair so a woman could be seated.

● Motorola has an official policy of refusing to supply customers with any materials that would be used in making land mines.

● Motorola has a long-standing policy that no employee with over 10 years service can be fired without prior approval of the CEO.

Decentralization and Management Style

Paul Galvin had a highly participative management style that had become embedded in the company's culture. In the late 1980s and early 1990s, Motorola had a strong three-man office of the chief executive and a highly decentralized organization structure that placed operating and strategic authority at the business-unit level. While such functions as strategic planning, finance, human resources, legal, ethics, and quality were centralized at the corporate level, full authority to develop business strategies was delegated to the heads of Motorola's business units. Motorola's decentralized approach to running its different businesses and divisions was both a strength and a weakness. Divisions headed by strong managers operated as virtual fiefdoms, pursuing their own agendas and priorities. Divisions were often not cooperative or responsive to the requests and needs of sister divisions, prompting one outsider to label them "warring tribes."[12] The

---

[12]Crockett, "How Motorola Lost Its Way."

lack of cross-division collaboration was said to allow "stovepipe thinking." There were cases where divisions became so preoccupied with their own business issues and problems that they took little note of the rapidly changing nature of the global marketplace (unless it bore directly on the division's own business). Division autonomy and independence tended to result in strategies and behavior that appeared best for the division and that sometimes were contrary to the competitive interests of Motorola as a whole.

But case researcher interviews with Motorola insiders indicated that this characterization might be overblown, Motorola's organizational structure was basically relational, not hierarchical. While Motorola did have general managers with considerable authority over a particular business or group, most of life within Motorola consisted of collaborative relationships. Motorola made a practice of giving managers cross-functional tasks and assignments outside of their formal job descriptions. As a consequence, it was customary for Motorolans to have and use a network of contacts across the company that made the company's informal structure almost as influential as its formal structure. Moreover, the company's strong emphasis on ethical standards created trust between co-workers and promoted a good basis for information sharing and cooperation across departmental boundaries.

Technology-Engineering Climate

Another characteristic of Motorola's leadership culture was its engineering base. Motorola competed in industries with rapidly advancing technologies and high-velocity product innovation. Most of Motorola's key executives were well versed in technology, and over time the company had developed a high level of technological and engineering expertise. For many decades, Motorola had demonstrated an ability to stay on the cutting edge of technological advances. Going into the 1990s, however, some observers viewed Motorola's technology- and engineering-based culture as a liability in a world they saw as increasingly driven by marketing.

Other Motorola critics saw the company's top executives as insular and tradition bound. In 1998, 67 percent of Motorola's top executives had been with the company for more than 20 years.[13] Internally, this was viewed by many Motorola leaders as a source of strength and cohesion; externally, it was viewed by critics as evidence that Motorola was inbred and out of touch at the top.

The Ethics Component of Motorola's Culture

Motorola's ethical standards were set forth in its code of business conduct. Over more than five decades, company officials had issued interpretations and clarifications of the code to further communicate to all Motorolans what behaviors were expected and what behaviors were prohibited. The company's ethical standards were deeply ingrained in the Motorola culture. Respect for and appreciation of the company's high ethical standards were widely shared among employees and managers.

Top executives at Motorola had an unwavering conviction that maintaining high ethical standards was not only the right thing to do but also good business. This conviction extended to both countries where business was conducted in a manner that matched Motorola's ethical standards and countries where it was not. Motorola executives believed that the company's stance against bribery, extortion, and "lubricating

---

[13]Rick Tetzeli, "And Now for Motorola's Next Trick," *Fortune,* April 27, 1997, p. 122.

fees" (fees paid to local officials to speed needed actions) reduced costs in the long run and that Motorola's reputation for ethical behavior made it a desirable business partner. Other benefits they saw included higher morale, a higher level of mutual trust among Motorolans, and greater trust between Motorola and its customers and vendors. Case researcher interviews revealed a general opinion among Motorolans that the company's long-standing commitment to ethical behavior set a good example for other firms to follow in those foreign-country markets where corruption and questionable ethical behavior were still common. Motorolans took pride in the fact that the company's strong focus on providing quality products at competitive prices while conducting its business honorably showed to the world that a company could succeed in global markets without resorting to unethical or questionable acts.

ETHICS IN THE GLOBAL MARKET ARENA

Ethical standards, of course, vary widely in countries across the world. Each region of the world has its own interpretations of what is ethical and what is not, and many countries have implicit and explicit standards for appropriate business practices both at home and around the world. In the United States, the passage of the Foreign Corrupt Practices Act (FCPA) of 1977, prohibiting a variety of unethical actions and imposing severe sanctions for violations, had heightened the need of U.S. companies to exercise due diligence in how they did business anywhere in the world. Some of the actions considered illegal under the FCPA were considered acceptable business practices in parts of Europe, Asia, Africa, and Latin America.

But economic globalization was beginning to drive greater homogeneity of what was ethical and what was not. Whereas in the 1970s and 1980s it was hard to get government or business leaders to acknowledge that corruption existed, by the mid-1990s there was open talk about corruption and discussion of ways to curb it. The United Nations had begun to issue statements supporting the criminalization of bribery and extortion and to express concerns about various types of "facilitating payments." Bribery and extortion could range from passing a few dollars to a poorly paid border guard to gain exit from a country, to agreeing to the monetary demands of local government officials in return for their issuing the necessary permits to conduct business or open factories. Extortion payments were a permissible legal business expense for many European firms but were illegal for U.S. firms. Facilitating payments to expedite services of one kind or another were fairly widespread in many countries; but because they did not entail requests for actions that weren't ordinarily expected, they were acceptable under the FCPA. The United Nations Center on Transnational Corporations had put together a sample code of conduct to provide guidance on ethical conduct.

In Europe, the Organization for Economic Cooperation and Development, which had 29 European nations as members, adopted an accord in 1997 that called for firms in member countries to conduct business according to rules that were similar to those governing U.S. firms.[14] In Latin America, where bribery and other forms of corruption had long been common in business, there had been some movement by national leaders to curb such practices—the Interamerican Convention Against Corruption was adopted by the Organization of American States in 1996. The Caux Round Table, an international group of business leaders from the United States, Europe, and Japan that

---

[14]Paul Blustein, "Major Nations Agree to Ban Trade Bribery," *Los Angeles Times,* May 24, 1997, p. D1.

was formed in 1986 to foster international business relations, published a set of "Principles for Business" that advocated corporate responsibility for ethical concerns and business practices.[15]

In 1993, an organization called Transparency International began an effort to reduce corruption by encouraging nations to pass laws and anticorruption programs. Transparency International conducted an annual survey of businesspeople, risk analysts, investigative journalists, political analysts, and the general public to determine perceived corruption levels for various countries. In 1999, the five countries perceived as least corrupt were Denmark, Finland, Sweden, New Zealand, and Iceland. The five countries perceived as having the most corruption were Nigeria, Tanzania, Honduras, Paraguay, and Cameroon.[16]

MOTOROLA AND ETHICS IN A GLOBAL ENVIRONMENT

For much of its history, Motorola was unyielding in its definitions of what constituted ethical behavior and what did not. Virtually no official exceptions were made for any reason. As Motorola began to expand into foreign countries, company executives were adamant that its key beliefs and code of business conduct should be applied evenhandedly across the board everywhere it operated and that the well-defined ethical behaviors the company had always expected of Motorolans had to remain intact. But such strict black–white interpretations placed a mounting burden on Motorolans in foreign countries. In complying with the company's ethical expectations, Motorola managers and employees sometimes found themselves doing things they considered "business suicide" of one form or another. For example, many Motorolans in Japan knew that their Japanese counterparts expected them to participate in the gift-giving rituals so much a part of the Japanese culture. Yet, if Motorolans did participate in such rituals in direct violation of the company's code of business conduct, they were subject to dismissal and to feelings of guilt. Similar problems surfaced elsewhere. Growing numbers of Motorolans began to point to conflicts between Motorola's traditional ethical expectations and what were acceptable business practices and ethical standards in the countries where they operated.

Adjusting Ethical Standards and Interpretations to Make Room for Cultural Diversity

Over a period of time, Motorola executives came to the conclusion that there were legitimate circumstances in which the company's strict ethical requirements ought to permit some room for responsiveness to local customs, business practices, and ethical standards. Motorola began taking one of four stances when conflicts arose. One stance was to make no adjustment in expectations. The remaining three stances involved situations in which some responsiveness and modification in expectations appeared reasonable and appropriate without compromising basic principles; in these cases, company policy was to (1) make minor adjustments in its ethical expectations to respond to local

---

[15]See the Caux Round Table Web site (www.cauxroundtable.org).

[16]See the Transparency International Web site (www.transparency.de). The current Corruption Perceptions Index is at www.transparency.de/documents/cpi/index.html.

standards, (2) make major adjustments to be responsive to local standards, or (3) make global adjustments.

Enforcing Ethical Behavior Expectations without Adjustment to Local Conditions   One area where Motorola stood fast and refused to adjust its ethical behavior expectations to meet local standards was payment of bribes. Paying money to government officials or customers to gain a contract was clearly out of bounds at Motorola no matter what the local circumstances might be. Motorola executives believed this strict policy had served the company well. To make their point, they told the story of a time when Motorola had constructed a large and expensive factory and was ready to begin production, but a local official was in control of operating permits and the official would not issue the permit without a bribe. The choice was to either pay the official or experience a very expensive delay in opening the plant. Motorola elected to wait, and as word spread in the local community over a period of several months that Motorola wouldn't pay bribes, the necessary permits were issued.

Motorola also enforced a strict policy worldwide for not allowing Motorolans to enter into procurement arrangements with family members or be a party to any such negotiations, despite the fact that doing business with companies owned by family members is common practice in countries such as Russia and China.

In instances where senior management concluded that no adjustment in its ethical behavior expectations could be allowed, company officials met with the affected Motorolans to justify its expectations and/or explain why responsiveness to local standards should not be accommodated. Such meetings helped clarify the company's code of business conduct, reinforce the appropriateness of the company's behavioral expectations, and gain stronger employee acceptance of both the code and the company's ethical expectations of Motorolans.

Making Minor Adjustments to Respond to Local Standards   Historically, Motorola's prohibition against paying bribes had been extended to include accepting or giving gifts in any form to government officials, suppliers, customers, or other business associates. In some cultures, however, gift giving was a fundamental part of the business relationship. In Japan, it was considered an offense not to accept and give gifts in business. In a move to establish a behavior expectation that remained true to its overall ethical philosophy yet responsive to local standards and sensitivities, Motorola adopted an ethical expectation for Japan that permitted limited gift giving and acceptance under well-defined conditions. For example, there were cost and time-of-year limitations on gifts, and any gift to a Motorolan had to remain on display in the recipient's office rather than becoming his or her personal property.

Another area where adjustment was deemed appropriate was Motorola's long-standing policy against paying agent's fees (perceived as similar to bribes). In numerous countries where Motorola operated, it was common to engage the services of an agent when a firm was unfamiliar with a country's conventions, rules and regulations; agents introduced company officials to local government officials and businesspeople and helped a firm avoid violating local rules or customs. It was difficult if not impossible to do significant business with the government in Saudi Arabia without being properly introduced. After a time, Motorola determined it would agree to the payment of agent's fees, provided they were a relatively small amount of the total contract value. In the Middle East, where agents played a critical factor and demanded substantively larger payments, Motorola approved such payments on a case-by-case basis after taking steps to ensure that the payments were comparable to local practice and none of the money was used as a bribe or other illegal payment by the agent. Under the FCPA, it is illegal for U.S. firms to pay an agent if the firm knows that part of the payment will be used as a bribe.

Making Substantive Adjustments to Respond to Local Standards

On occasion, Motorola encountered situations where responding to local standards and customs required "substantive" adjustments in its ethical expectations or a different interpretation of what constituted a fundamental conflict with its key beliefs. For example, Motorola had historically rewarded outstanding individual performance as part of its "constant respect for people" belief, but in Malaysia the culture valued group rewards. To accommodate the Malaysian preference for group-based rewards, Motorola allowed one of its plants in Malaysia to shift to a group-based performance evaluation and compensation. Given Motorola's cultural tradition of rewarding employees for outstanding individual performance and the strong tie this practice had to Motorola's belief in constant respect for people, agreeing to group-based rewards in Malaysia was indeed a substantive adjustment. To combat any perception that this adjustment comprised or posed fundamental conflict with its key belief, in 1992 Motorola added a fifth key initiative ("Empowerment for all, in a participative, cooperative and creative workplace") to its Total Customer Satisfaction Card.

Substantive adjustments were also made in cases where local officials asked for monetary payments from Motorola. While bribes were never paid, Motorola did work to achieve a creative solution within the boundaries of its key beliefs and ethical principles. In a country where Motorola had a large production facility, local officials indicated that some critical services such as police or fire protection might not be available unless funds were transferred. Further investigation revealed that the officials intended for the funds to be used to improve the equipment and boost the caliber of local government services. Motorola decided to donate communications equipment in support of the government effort to better serve the local community.

Making Global Adjustments
Global adjustments occurred when Motorola extended what was a local adjustment to a number of different locales. The most significant instance of global adjustment was taking place in the company's reward structure, where there was a growing shift from individual incentives to group-based incentives. A number of Motorola plants in varying locales had been granted permission to shift to group-based incentives. The preference for group-based rewards in these locations had begun to affect management thinking more globally as the company shifted to the use of more team-based production and design units where group-based incentives worked well.

THE CHALLENGES POSED BY MOTOROLA'S RAPIDLY GROWING MULTICULTURAL WORKFORCE

When Motorola's activities were confined primarily to the United States, its growth involved new employees of relatively similar backgrounds. Maintaining a homogeneous culture and ethical posture was relatively straightforward. However, as Motorola sought to preserve and apply its ethical tradition in the face of global expansion, it faced a complex array of new cultural challenges.

During the 1990s, Motorola added 50,000 employees drawn from cultures around the world. Half of the company's 121,000 employees were in locations outside the United States. In 1999, its employees spoke more than 50 different home languages and belonged to as many or more cultures. Motorola's employee base resided in hundreds of subcultures based on region, dialect, gender, class, wealth, education, occupation, religion, age group, and other variables. In addition to the diversity among its employees, Motorola's supplier and customer base was already multicultural and becoming more so.

The addition of 50,000 new employees in less than 10 years posed a big challenge to Motorola in terms of assimilating such large numbers of new employees into its culture and instilling Motorola's core beliefs and ethical posture. Rapid workforce expansion meant that there were proportionally fewer experienced employees to help indoctrinate new employees in Motorola's culture and to help with the process of continuously reinforcing the company's key beliefs and ethical expectations. The employee influx problem was complicated further by the fact that the new employee pool consisted of people coming from not only a variety of countries and cultural backgrounds but also from other companies—Motorola recruited many of its new employees from jobs at other corporations. These new employees often had developed ethical practices based on societal or company cultures that were quite different from Motorola's. Historically, Motorola had assigned experienced managers to its new subsidiaries and business divisions who acted as mentors and role models and transmitted the Motorola philosophy of doing business. In both the 1980s and 1990s, the company's rapid growth, coupled with the retirement of many senior Motorolans of various nationalities who knew Motorola's ethics well, had depleted the pool of experienced, culturally aware managers available for new assignments. Still another factor compounding the problem was Motorola's efforts to flatten the organization structure, empower employees, and further involve them in decision making in their areas of responsibility. These changes in roles and relationships put enhanced responsibilities on each Motorolan to understand and support the values of the corporate culture.

Responding to the challenges of a rapidly expanding multicultural workforce, Motorola's senior leadership initiated and supported a number of programs to help all Motorolans operate with high ethical standards. One step was to reinstitute use of the Total Customer Satisfaction Card (Exhibit 3) which had been used in the 1940s and 1950s. The card was translated into all the needed languages and provided to all Motorola employees worldwide; the hope was that they would keep the card in their possession at all times and refer to it frequently. A second step was the development and execution of the Motorola Ethics Renewal Process (MERP).

The Motorola Ethics Renewal Process

In 1995 Motorola's board of directors asked a group of very senior retired Motorola officers to look into the status of ethics understanding and compliance around the world. The team spent about a year interviewing people both inside and outside Motorola and produced a recommendation to the board that an "ethics renewal process" be created and rolled out across the corporation. The board concurred with the proposal, and the Motorola Ethics Renewal Process (MERP) became the focal point for disseminating, maintaining, and modifying Motorola's ethical posture. Board members agreed to put their full weight behind the MERP initiative, and several personally participated in the process.

Responsibility for implementing and executing MERP was assigned to the human resources department rather than to legal personnel. A unit was formed to ensure ethics compliance; its charge was to be proactive rather than reactive. According to Motorola executive Glenn Gienko, "From the start, the objectives were to establish an honest dialogue on concerns about ethical compliance, ethical values and the code of conduct." A book providing information about ethics, along with a set of real-life cases, was prepared for use in training discussions and ethics workshops.[17] The cases presented real-world ethical dilemmas faced by Motorolans, along with commentaries by ethics experts on the issues that were raised. The cases were designed to bring to the surface what was keeping people awake at night, things they couldn't easily discuss with co-workers. The majority of ethical questions were local, making local workshops an essential part of MERP.

The rollout process was structured to build higher levels of participation from all regions of the world and eventually from all levels of the organization. The first MERP workshop was successfully piloted in 1996, and workshops were held in additional regions throughout 1997–99. Establishing MERP meant answering everyday questions and developing an escalation process for major problems; it also meant making ethical issues a part of local management's everyday decision-making process. Workshop sites were selected without regard to whether a country might be experiencing unusual levels of ethical problems. Management emphasized that the workshops were not a search for possible violations or violators. By mid-1999 the process had involved Motorola employees in Africa, Canada, the Caribbean, Central and Eastern Europe, China, France, Japan, Korea, Latin America, the Middle East, Mexico, the United Kingdom, and Southeast Asia.

However, the chief purpose of MERP was not to be a platform for teaching ethics or business conduct. Rather, it was to help Motorolans at all levels in all countries make ethically appropriate business decisions every day and to get them to take ownership and accountability for Motorola's key beliefs and ethical values. MERP was intended as a vehicle to (1) allow open and honest exchanges of ethical questions across businesses and regions; (2) make dialogues about ethics and values as common as discussions about quality, cycle time, or customer satisfaction; and (3) encourage employees to discuss and debate the most sensitive aspects of remaining ethically steadfast in daily behavior.

Ethics Committees   Part of the comprehensive MERP involved creating local, country, and regional ethics committees to be responsible for promoting a culture that embodied Motorola's key beliefs and for providing a forum to openly discuss issues surrounding these beliefs and the code of business conduct. Regional/country committees included senior managers from the region/country as well as other appointed members. Ethics committees were expected to address (and hopefully resolve) procedural issues, questions of interpretation, and the appropriateness of particular local exceptions. They had no responsibility for conducting investigations.

---

[17]R. S. Moorthy et al., *Uncompromising Integrity: Motorola's Global Challenge* (Schaumberg, IL: Motorola University Press, 1998).

When tough issues emerged that could not be resolved at the local level, the ethics committee structure provided a way for major problems and issues to work their way up the ladder to final resolution. In 1999, final authority for setting "big-issue" ethical standards still remained a corporate function, but handling specific case-by-case interpretations of the code and local exceptions had been largely decentralized to the regional, country, and local ethics committees. The establishment of ethics committees continued Motorola's move away from corporate absolutism and put in place a decentralized structure for determining when and under what circumstances corporate ethical expectations should be adjusted to fit local customs and business practices. Greater reliance on ethics committees for such determinations meant that senior corporate executives and the CEO could concentrate their full attention on handling major ethical issues and leading the ethics compliance process.

Ethics Compliance at Motorola

In Motorola's early years, the procedures for ethical enforcement were straightforward. The code of business conduct was clear and provided a list of "thou shalt nots." Possible breaches of the code were investigated by the human resources, legal, or finance departments. Any requests for exceptions or exemptions from the code were referred to the chief legal officer. But as Motorola began to expand its operation to countries around the world, it became increasingly impractical to set worldwide ethical standards for every situation from corporate headquarters and to enforce them in the same strict fashion in light of all the cultural diversity.

In 2000, compliance was considered the responsibility of all Motorolans at all levels. Supervisors at all levels were charged with enforcing ethical standards and ensuring compliance to company's code of business conduct. However, three of Motorola's functional departments—human resources, legal, and finance—had important roles in monitoring compliance, investigating complaints, and reporting problem areas. All three departments had representatives on the ethics committees that had been created as a part of MERP. Complaints and allegations of ethical misconduct from parties outside Motorola were received by the company's legal department; the department's investigative team was headed by a former U.S. attorney. Human resources also had investigators to look into internal allegations of ethics violations. Finance, through the auditing function, monitored financial activity for possible ethical violations. Over time, as potential violations were investigated and sanctions were meted out where violations had occurred, the compliance effort contributed to the storytelling that reinforced the fabric of Motorola's ethical culture.

Some authority to approve country-specific variances from the code of business conduct was delegated to regional managers. For example, say that in China either a local ethics committee or the national ethics committee determined that a variance to currently stated Motorola policies was appropriate. A recommendation would be made to the Asian regional manager for approval of a variance. If the Asian regional manager concluded that the variance did not compromise Motorola's Key Beliefs and did not violate either U.S. or local laws, then a variance for China could be authorized.

If a local or national issue had ramifications for conduct in other countries or parts of the world, then the issue was passed up to the regional and corporate level ethics committees. Recommendations for global variances had to be approved at the corporate level and were reviewed by the CEO.

THE ONGOING ETHICS COMPLIANCE CHALLENGE AT MOTOROLA

In interviews conducted with senior managers, the case researchers pressed on the issue of what types of ethical violations the company's investigative forces were currently encountering. Company officials stressed that Motorolans were complying with the company's code of ethical conduct in good faith and that violations were usually unintentional and occurred in "gray areas." They provided the following examples to give a sense of the type of problems being encountered:

- An Asian government official wanted a "scholarship" for his son. Motorola had programs where it provided scholarships, but the awards were never in response to such types of requests for aid. In this case Motorola determined that the government official's request involved paying tuition fees and was unacceptable.

- It came to Motorola's attention that a particular distributor who had obtained Motorola products was avoiding tariffs in a country by trucking them through a remote border post. This distributor was not officially connected to Motorola, and the Motorola products the distributor had obtained had changed hands several times after leaving the authorized Motorola distributor. The matter was referred to an ethical committee. The committee determined that the distributor's actions were a fairly common occurrence, and now that Motorola had knowledge, this violated the key belief of uncompromising integrity. Motorola directed its authorized distributor to no longer sell to this chain of buyers.

- A salesperson was working with a lobbyist to sell equipment to a municipal government. The lobbyist suggested an action that raised the salesperson's concerns about ethical propriety. In accordance with company policy, the salesperson went to his supervisor for approval. The supervisor also had concerns and went up a level to seek approval from a manager. The manager was heavily preoccupied with other business and gave the OK. During an annual audit, the auditor challenged the expenditure. The subsequent investigation determined that all three should have known that the action was unacceptable, and all three were disciplined.

- Entertainment expenses were an area rich for possible violations. Motorola sponsored a number of events, such as the Phoenix Open, to which current and potential customers were invited. But to guard against ethical violations the circumstances for an invitation were restricted. The restrictions for governmental customers were more strict than for business customers. Guest lists for all Motorola-sponsored events had to be cleared through Motorola's legal department.

- Agent's fees were cited as a constant compliance and enforcement problem. In the Middle East, many of Motorola's potential customers were extraordinarily wealthy. Thus, for an agent to maintain contacts, it required a very high lifestyle, and exceptions might be made for higher than "normal" agent's fees. Such exceptions were made very carefully. In China, it was critical to have an effective agent to make introductions. Despite their importance, Motorola worked hard to find effective agents who charged reasonable fees; the company did not authorize above-normal payments.

- When the Chinese government brutally suppressed student demonstrations in Tiananmen Square, Motorola had to decide whether to pull out or continue doing business in the country. Given the substantial financial investment Motorola had in China, and the size of the potential consumer market, some observers questioned the ethical standards Motorola used to decide to remain in China. Motorola's leaders issued statements saying that they carefully considered the options and decided that Motorola could have a more positive impact on China by remaining, and that many innocent people in China would be severely hurt if Motorola departed. In interviews conducted for this case, it was reiterated that there were many reasons for remaining in China, but a primary reason was the belief of Motorola's leaders that increasing the free flow of information would facilitate reforms. By manufacturing and supplying telecommunications equipment and improving the telecommunications infrastructure, Motorola could act as a change agent and in the long run help shape the society and its values.

- While it was a common practice for salespeople to buy tickets to events, a violation occurred when a salesperson unwittingly purchased tickets from what turned out to be a government agency, which was prohibited.

- Motorola officials cited a case where taking aggressive action to uphold ethical standards resulted in unexpected and undesirable consequences. Another Western multinational firm operating in a country where Motorola had operations reported one of its employees to local authorities for stealing. The police came, arrested the individual, and shot him on the spot. The incident had the effect of making Western firms doing business in this country reluctant to report employee theft. They were caught between letting a crime go unreported or taking action that might result in punishment out of proportion to the crime being committed.

MOTOROLA AND ETHICS: THE VIEWS OF COMPANY INSIDERS

The case researchers' interviews revealed a clearly discernible ethical attitude and demeanor among the top managers at Motorola. Ethical behavior was considered a given. The typical attitude was that Motorola's two key beliefs had "stood the test of time in all different cultures." Bob Galvin, the current chairman of Motorola's executive committee, said that a lot of people across the world believed that their traditions were different from those in other countries but in fact "all people value honesty, values, and fair compensation." Jack Bradshaw, Motorola's chief ethics compliance officer, made the comment that "ethics is good business" because "people like to work for an ethical company." The opinion was expressed that a company with high ethical standards attracted employees who had high ethical standards and wanted to work in an ethical environment. One vice president with Latin American heritage and work experience said that working in an ethical company "allows me to sleep at night." A manager noted that Motorolans were rarely asked to pay bribes or kickbacks because of the company's well-known reputation for not engaging in such practices—a condition that made ethics enforcement at Motorola easier.

While most managers interviewed agreed that Motorola' strong enforcement of ethical standards had cost it some business and some time in penetrating certain markets (there were stories of a lost contract here or a lost opportunity there), there was a strong consensus that in the long run Motorola got more business, even in countries with varying levels of corruption. Several reasons were given. First, buyers knew Motorola had high standards and that customers would get what they paid for because the price did not include allowances for bribes or kickbacks. One senior manager cited a case where a customer was offered $2 million to go with another supplier; the customer declined because it wanted to deal with an honest company. Second, a government official that contracted with Motorola did not have to be concerned about being charged with graft because it was well known that Motorola could not be bought and did not pay bribes.

Ethics at Motorola as Seen by Outsiders

The case researchers interviewed a sampling of people who conducted business with Motorola, either as suppliers or customers. Those interviewed were of the opinion that Motorola's employees as a rule tried to abide by the code of business conduct and to serve as ethical role models. But they expressed concerns about whether Motorola's conduct in certain situations reflected high ethical standards, and they related instances where they believed Motorolans had violated the company's code of business conduct.

One challenged Motorola's willingness to forgo profit to maintain its ethical posture. The individual commented that Myanmar had had riots that were suppressed similar to those in China in Tiananmen Square. Motorola had pulled out of Myanmar but remained in China, where it had substantially greater investments.

One consultant who had an association with Motorola extending over 20 years told the case researchers that Motorola had an ideal image of itself and the expected behaviors for its employees but that the actions of its 121,000 employees covered the spectrum of ethical behavior. This person expressed a belief that Motorolans in different countries held different interpretations as to what constituted ethical behavior and was allowable under the code. He also spoke of occasions where he had observed Motorolans engaging in actions he perceived as contrary to the code of business conduct. While he thought that the Motorolans in question may have believed they were acting within the code's parameter, he believed they were violating the code based on his familiarity with the company and its ethical expectations.

Several interviewees cited instances where lower-level Motorolans experienced conflict between the restrictions of the code and requirements of their job. When asked about the oft-stated beliefs of senior leaders that code violations were certainly rare exceptions rather than the rule, the responses varied. One source felt top managers could become somewhat disconnected from reality; the source said the practice of executives traveling to Asian countries in first-class or business-class cabins and being whisked through customs to waiting limousines did not mirror the travails of lower-echelon Motorolans. The source said that when lower-level Motorolans were in a dusty airport late at night in an insecure city with a departing airplane their only possible transportation, a few dollars as a "tip" were treated as an acceptable violation of the code.

Other interviewees also told of having observed occasional minor violations but contended that, at the corporate level, Motorola did not make concessions and that as a group Motorolans were likely to act ethically. One told the story of a Motorolan in India who refused to pay a bribe to keep the power at his residence from being turned off—stating to officials that Motorolans did not pay bribes. In another story, in Bangladesh, which was cited in the interview as a country noted for corruption, a Motorolan would not pay bribes to import critical items necessary for the operation of his office. He also told local officials, "Motorolans do not pay bribes." Eventually he got what he wanted and felt gratified that even in a country with high corruption one could work ethically.

Motorola's Response to the Comments of Outside Observers   When Motorola's managers were apprised of the foregoing comments, they responded, in essence, as follows:

1. Yes, we know that some Motorolans will occasionally feel their health or safety is threatened and pay sums of money or surrender items to value to extricate themselves from the situation. What outside observers may not know is that such cases are reported to supervisors and documented by Motorola. A number of examples in Eastern Europe and Asia were cited. Such actions were not considered a violation of the code because the company's key belief of constant respect for people took precedence over uncompromising integrity. They cited a statement by Bob Galvin: "Do not be embarrassed by embarrassment."

2. In response to the contention that interpretations of ethical conduct varied across cultures, Motorola managers indicated that varying interpretations were the motivating force behind MERP. MERP was designed to clarify ethical behavior in local terms and involve and empower local Motorolans in the ethical process.

3. Even senior managers flew business class, and the use of corporate drivers and vehicles was for security reasons.

case 27 Levi Strauss & Company

John E. Gamble
University of South Alabama

In 1999 Levi Strauss & Company was the world's largest branded apparel manufacturer and second largest manufacturer and marketer of blue jeans. Levi's 501 button-fly jeans, introduced in the 1800s, were available in 108 sizes and 20 different finishes and fabrics, and were the best-selling brand of blue jeans in the United States during 1999. The company also manufactured and marketed the L2, Silver Tab, and Red Line brands of blue jeans; Dockers khakis; and Slates men's dress pants. Dockers was the leading brand of khakis in the United States, and Slates was the best-selling brand of dress pants in department stores.

Levi Strauss & Company (LS&C) was widely regarded as a leader in promoting corporate social responsibility. It was active in advocating ethical labor practices in the apparel and textile industries and helping communities in North America, Europe, and Asia respond to critical societal issues. Each year during the 1990s, LS&C had awarded more than $20 million to programs that addressed AIDS prevention and care, economic empowerment of low-income people, youth empowerment, and social justice programs that attempted to eliminate racial prejudice and discrimination. The company had received numerous awards for its social responsibility efforts from such organizations as the U.S. Centers for Disease Control, Volunteers of America, Harvard University, the United Nations, and the U.S. Department of Commerce. The company's employee benefit plan was ranked number one by *Money* magazine in 1992, and *Fortune* magazine listed Levi Strauss 15th on its 1996 list of the 100 best companies to work for. LS&C management stressed building an organizational culture that empowered and fairly rewarded employees.

However, in 1999 the company's declining competitive position in its core jeans business was of considerable concern to CEO Robert Haas and other company managers and shareholders. Even though Levi's was still the best-selling brand of blue jeans, the company's share of the U.S. men's jeans market had declined from 48.2 percent in 1990 to 25.0 percent in 1998. Its overall share of the jeans market had fallen from 30.9 percent in 1990 to 14.8 percent in early 1999. Company revenues had declined from $6.9 billion in 1997 to $6.0 billion in 1998. Analysts estimated that Levi's plummeting sales and market share had driven the value of privately held Levi Strauss shares down by nearly 45 percent since 1996.

In an effort to reverse its deteriorating competitive position, the company announced it would close 11 of its 22 plants and cut nearly one-third of its workforce in

North America. In Europe, Levi Strauss said it would close three plants and trim its workforce by 20 percent. The announcements triggered alarm among the company's suppliers and in the communities where the affected plants were located. Several long-time fabric suppliers indicated that the Levi Strauss plant closings would force them to lay off many of their employees. Merchants in the small towns where LS&C plants were targeted for closure expressed concern that the lost jobs would hurt local economies.

COMPANY HISTORY

Levi Strauss was born in Buttenheim, Bavaria, in 1829 and came to New York in 1847 to join his brothers Jonas and Louis, who had preceded him in immigrating to America. Jonas and Louis had established a successful dry-goods business and eventually brought all three of their siblings to New York to work in the store. Levi became a skilled salesman and merchant under the tutelage of his brothers during his first five years in America. In February 1853 Levi left New York to go sell supplies to the multitude of miners lured to California during the gold rush. He packed such goods as thread, scissors, yarns, and bolts of canvas with him for his two-month voyage to California, which would take him down the Atlantic coast, through the Panama Canal, and then north up the Pacific coast to San Francisco.

Levi Strauss's independent venture into the dry-goods business met with a rocky start; the young man found it difficult to sell many of the items brought from New York to stock his new store. Strauss had hoped to sell canvas to miners to use to make tents but was largely unable to find a market for the heavy, durable fabric. Legend has it that at some point during his first year in San Francisco, a lamenting Strauss was approached in a saloon by a stranger who suggested that Strauss use the unsellable canvas to produce rugged pants for miners. Strauss believed that the idea had promise and began producing and selling canvas "waist overalls" to area miners. Strauss's garments quickly gained in popularity, providing the basis for a thriving wholesale dry-goods business and work-clothes manufacturer. The evolution from waist overalls to the blue jeans of today began when Strauss soon ran out of canvas and switched to denim fabric. Rivets were added in 1873 to reinforce the pants' pockets, and in 1886 the now-familiar Levi's Two Horse Brand leather patch was sewn to the back of the waistband. The 501 designation was given to the pants in 1890, belt loops were added in 1922, the red tab was added to the back pocket in 1936, and in 1960 waist overalls were renamed jeans.

Levi Strauss was the company's chief manager until his death in 1902; his four nephews inherited Levi Strauss & Company. A large number of Levi Strauss's heirs have since held management positions with the company throughout its history, including chairman and CEO Robert D. Haas, a great-great-grandnephew of the company's founder. Between the early 1900s and World War II, the company's jeans became the uniform of hardworking miners, factory workers, farmers, and ranchers. Levi's jeans became fashionable as well as functional in the 1950s when Marlon Brando and James Dean helped make Levi's a must-have brand for teenagers. The popularity of Levi's jeans continued to rise through the 1960s and 1970s before ebbing somewhat in the early 1980s. Blue jeans regained their popularity in the mid- to late 1980s and at the onset of the 21st century continued to be among the most frequently worn pants by teens and young adults in the United States and many other parts of the world.

OWNERSHIP STRUCTURE AND GOVERNANCE

Levi Strauss & Company was a private company controlled by heirs of the founder until 1971, when it offered shares to the public to finance its growth and diversification moves into such new apparel businesses as rainwear and wet suits. Levi Strauss's heirs retained control of the company through the collective voting rights of their shares. In 1985, confronted with the potential threat of hostile takeover, the family chose to initiate a $1.6 billion leveraged buyout (LBO) to again take the company private. The LBO resulted in 94 percent of the company's shares coming under the control of Levi Strauss's 203 descendents. Four percent of the shares were held by a company employee stock ownership plan and 2 percent of the remaining were held by outside investors led by F. Warren Hellman, a distant relative of the controlling Haas family.

Further ownership changes occurred in 1996 when members of the Haas family began to quarrel about the company's dividend policy and other potential uses of its $1 billion cash balance. Robert Haas, Warren Hellman, previous Levi Strauss & Company CEO Peter Haas Sr., and Peter Haas Jr. initiated a deal that would buy back all employee shares and the shares of discontented Haas family members. Employees and family members were initially offered $189 per share—a price established by a valuation analysis conducted by Morgan Stanley—but then offered $265 per share when advisers to disgruntled family members valued the stock at $315 to $387 per share. Thirty percent of the company's shares were repurchased through the buyout at a price of $4.3 billion. All shares were placed in a trust that was controlled by the four men who organized the buyback. The four trustees possessed all voting rights concerning company business issues and were required to approve any subsequent sale of Haas-family-member shares and were the only shareholders allowed to name successors as trustees. The trust was structured to remain in force for 15 years or until Robert Haas ceased to be a trustee, or unless two-thirds of the company's shareholders voted to alter the trust. Haas called the trust an insurance policy that "would allow the company to remain private and family-owned for years to come."[1] Exhibit 1 presents a list of LS&C's top 10 shareholders prior to the 1996 buyback.

In a Securities and Exchange Commission filing describing the company's ownership restructuring, it was noted that Robert Haas, Warren Hellman, and an investment banker and a company attorney who both played key roles in the buyback were allowed to purchase shares valued at nearly $90 million for $250,000 in return for organizing the buyback. At the $265 per share buyback price, Robert Haas received shares worth about $70 million, while Hellman and the other two men received shares worth a total of about $17.5 million. Employees who were required to sell their shares to the trust were promised a bonus roughly equal to each employee's 1996 annual compensation if the company's cumulative cash flow reached $7.6 billion by 2001. CEO Haas stated that if the company's cumulative cash flow between 1996 and 2001 was less than $7.6 billion, employees would receive a proportionately smaller bonus.

---

[1]"Levis Strauss Offers $265 a Share in Stock Buyback Plan," *Los Angeles Times,* February 10, 1996, p. D1.

exhibit 1   Levi Strauss & Company's 10 Largest Shareholders as of January 1995

Shareholder	Relationship	Total Shares (in millions)	Percent Ownership	Value of Shares (in billions)
Robert D. Haas	Great-great-grandnephew of Levi Strauss	4.2	8.0%	$1.1
Peter E. Haas Sr.	Robert Haas's uncle	11.5	22.3	3.1
Josephine B. Haas	First wife of Peter Haas Sr.	5.7	10.8	1.5
Peter E. Haas Jr.	Son of Peter Haas Sr.	4.5	8.6	1.2
Estate of Walter A. Haas Jr.	Robert Haas's father	4.3	8.2	1.1
Rhoda H. Goldman	Sister of Peter Haas Sr. and Walter Haas Jr.	3.7	7.1	0.9
Miriam L. Haas	Second wife of Peter Haas Sr.	3.0	5.7	0.8
Margaret E. Jones	Daughter of Peter Haas Sr.	2.9	5.5	0.8
Daniel E. Koshland Jr.	A Haas cousin	2.9	5.5	0.8
Frances K. Geballe	Sister of Daniel Koshland Jr.	2.7	5.2	0.7

Source: "Levi's Bold Plan for Reorganization," *San Francisco Chronicle,* February 13, 1996, p. C1.

In addition, if cumulative cash flows exceeded $7.6 billion, the employee bonuses would be increased.

Robert D. Haas—Levi Strauss & Company's CEO

Robert D. Haas was among a long line of Haas family members to hold high-ranking management positions with Levi Strauss & Company. Robert Haas's grandfather Walter Haas Sr. was the company's president between 1928 and 1955; his father, Walter Haas Jr., was president between 1958 and 1970; and his uncle Peter Haas Sr. was president between 1970 and 1981. Robert Haas began his career with Levi Strauss & Company in 1973 and held positions as marketing director and group vice president of Levi Strauss International, director of corporate marketing development, senior vice president of corporate planning and policy, president of the operating groups, and LS&C executive vice president and chief operating officer before being promoted to CEO in 1984 and named chairman of the board in 1989. Robert Haas was also the president of the Levi Strauss Foundation, a member of the Conference Board, and former director of the American Apparel Association.

Prior to joining LS&C, Haas was elected to Phi Beta Kappa and was valedictorian of the 1964 University of California–Berkeley graduating class. After then spending two years with the Peace Corps in Africa, Haas received an M.B.A. degree from the Harvard School of Business in 1968. Robert Haas was a White House Fellow under the Johnson administration for two years before joining consulting firm McKinsey & Company as an associate between 1969 and 1972.

When Haas became CEO in 1984, Levi Strauss & Company was troubled, with declining sales and market share. The company's profits had fallen by over $160 million in recent months as Levi Strauss lost market ground to designer jeans brands like Calvin Klein and Guess. Haas began a major overhaul of the business by divesting noncore businesses, creating a flatter organizational structure, cutting the workforce by one-third, and investing heavily in new product development, marketing, and process

exhibit 2   Levi Strauss & Company Sales and Operating Income, 1962–98

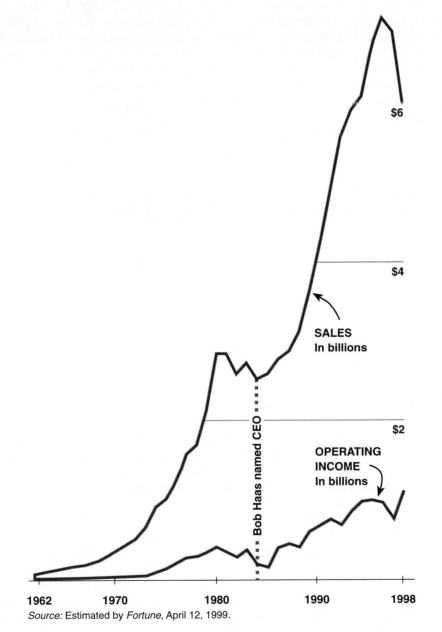

Source: Estimated by *Fortune,* April 12, 1999.

improvements. In 1985, Haas engineered the LBO to protect the company from an un-friendly takeover during its recovery period. By 1989 the company's sales had in-creased to $3.6 billion (a 31 percent increase over 1985 sales), and its profits grew by 500 percent between 1985 and 1989, to a record $272 million. The company regained its market-leading position with a 48 percent share of the U.S. jeans market in 1990. Exhibit 2 present s graph of Levi Strauss & Company's estimated sales and operating earnings between 1962 and 1998.

Robert Haas was instrumental in shaping the company's policies regarding its treatment of employees, its expectations for ethical business practices by suppliers, community involvement, and other issues concerning corporate social responsibility. Haas thought that after the turnaround the company could focus on its corporate values and social mission: "I said, let's fix the business issues first, but as soon as we have our business back on track we have to attend to our culture, because that's the glue that unites us, the beacon that guides our actions."[2] Robert Haas believed that the company's culture should promote ethical decision-making and that when making business decisions company executives should take into account the well-being of all stakeholders, not just shareholders. Haas said, "The key thing is that we try to look at our decisions from as many different points of view as we can. We look at the impact on the community, on the people involved."[3]

"ASPIRATIONAL MANAGEMENT" AT LEVI STRAUSS & COMPANY

Even though the company was forced to reduce its workforce by nearly 12,000 employees and close over 40 manufacturing and distribution facilities worldwide during its 1984–89 turnaround, Haas ensured that terminated employees were offered generous severance packages; these included 90 days of notice pay, one week of severance pay for each year of service, three months of health benefits beyond the 90-day notice period, job counseling, and relocation assistance. When labor leaders criticized the company's relocation of its production to such offshore locations as the Dominican Republic and Costa Rica, where hourly wages ranged between 30 cents and $1.00, Haas conceded that there were "no simple answers" but emphasized that "we are in business to make a fair profit" and that "we are not a government entity."[4]

The severance package LS&C offered to displaced workers was an illustration of how the Levi Strauss Mission, Vision, Aspirations, and Values Statement affected management decisions at the company (see Exhibit 3). Robert Haas orchestrated the development of the first such statement in 1987 when he saw a need to define the shared values that should guide the company's management and workforce. The values embodied in the document called for mutual trust and respect among management and employees and a commitment to strong ethical standards, teamwork, diversity, and empowerment. The Mission, Vision, Aspirations, and Values Statement guided strategic decisions, company operating policies, and company practices and, in management's view, promoted a corporate culture that recognized the demands of balancing a job and family.

The statement, for example, set the tone for how the company dealt with job responsibilities, performance appraisal, and training and resulted in personnel policies that provided employees with paid time off and leaves of absence for vacations, illness, medical appointments, or other personal emergencies. All LS&C employees were eligible for some type of incentive pay and were offered what *Money* magazine called the

---

[2]"How Levi's Trashed a Great American Brand," *Fortune,* April 12, 1999, p. 86.
[3]"Keeping a Shiny Corporate Image," *San Francisco Chronicle,* January 29, 1990, p. B1.
[4]Ibid.

exhibit 3   Levi Strauss & Company's Mission, Vision, Aspirations, and
Values (as revised in May 1999)

Mission

The mission of Levi Strauss & Co. is to achieve and sustain commercial success as a
global marketer of branded apparel.

Vision

Through a relentless focus on consumers, innovation, and people, Levi Strauss & Co. will
be the world's foremost authority in casual apparel.

Aspirations

All LS&C employees aspire to be part of a winning organization built on the strong
foundation of accomplishments, traditions, and values that we have inherited and that
continue to lead us to commercial success.

Values

Our values guide our success, unite us, and make LS&C unique.

- **Integrity and Ethical Behavior**
  Honesty, promise-keeping, fairness, respect for others, compassion, and integrity
  guide our conduct and actions, even when we are confronted by personal,
  professional, and social risks or economic pressures.

- **Commitment to People**
  We want LS&C to be known as a great place to work—a place where satisfaction
  grows out of the contributions we make and that offers opportunities for professional
  growth.

- **Diversity**
  We value and utilize the varying backgrounds, experiences, knowledge, and talents of
  all of our employees. Our global workplace will reflect the ethnic, cultural, and lifestyle
  diversity within the communities where we do business.

Behaviors

Our behaviors will support the achievement of the company's Mission, Vision, and
Aspirations.

- **Be Innovative**
  We will be innovative and embrace new and exciting ways of thinking. Innovative
  products, marketing programs, and business practices are the keys to our success.

- **Take Informed Risks**
  We will take informed risks that enable each of us to create new opportunities and to
  challenge established business practices.

- **Be Decisive and Results-Oriented**
  We will act decisively to assess and act swiftly on opportunities that will contribute to
  our commercial success. Our decision making will be results-oriented and guided by
  our strategic business vision and our values.

- **Seek Leverage**
  We will work together, actively exchanging ideas and information throughout the
  company, in order to achieve our business goals. Successful teamwork involves using
  the knowledge and opportunities created by our global presence.

- **Be Accountable**
  We will set clear and measurable responsibilities for individuals and teams, and will
  hold each other and ourselves accountable for the success of the company.

- **Recognize Results**
  We will recognize and reward superior contributions to our business success. We will
  also acknowledge our failures and shortcomings, and respond quickly with any
  necessary corrective actions.

Source: Levi Strauss & Company, www.levistrauss.com/about/vision.html.

exhibit 4   Highlights of the Levi Strauss & Company Employee
               Benefit Plan

- Health and dental insurance for employees, unmarried partners, and dependents.
  (Levi Strauss & Company was the first *Fortune* 500 company to offer medical and
  dental benefits to employees' unmarried partners and their dependents.)
- Vision plans.
- Life insurance.
- Accidental death and dismemberment insurance.
- Short- and long-term disability.
- 50 percent company-matched retirement plans.
- Time off with pay.
- Paid holidays.
- Three to seven weeks of annual vacation time.
- Child care subsidies.
- Friday afternoons off.
- Incentive pay for employees at all levels of the organization.

Sources: Levi Strauss & Company Web site and press releases.

United States' best employee benefits program in 1992. Exhibit 4 lists some of the traditional and less commonly offered benefits provided by LS&C to its employees.

Levi Strauss & Company's compensation was among the highest in the apparel industry, with hourly rates of pay that ranged from $8 to $10 per hour and incentives for
hourly employees like sewing machine operators as well as incentives for management.
The company's Global Success Sharing Plan, announced after the 1996 LBO, promised
all employees a onetime bonus roughly equal to their 1996 salaries if the company accumulated excess cash flow of $7.6 billion between 1996 and 2001. The bonus would
cost the company as much as $750 million, but Robert Haas believed the expense was
worth it. Haas commented that the company's managers, shareholders, and workforce
were "all in this together" and that a large lump-sum bonus could make a difference
in the lives of LS&C employees since it was so difficult for hourly employees to
accumulate wealth.[5] Some industry analysts questioned why the company would
promise such a large bonus while others in the industry were trying to reduce expenses
to better compete against rivals relying on contract manufacturers located in low-wage
countries. Robert Haas rebutted his critics by suggesting that Levi Strauss & Company
was "a company that zigs when other companies zag."[6]

Haas believed that the company's efforts to compensate employees fairly and
provide them with flexibility and participation in decision making would lead to a
stronger resource base and set of competitive capabilities. In a *Harvard Business Review* interview, Haas explained how the aspirations statement was a melding of the
"hard stuff" with the "soft stuff" and why the company's values were crucial to its
competitive success:

> If companies are going to react quickly to changes in the marketplace, they have to put
> more and more accountability, authority, and information into the hands of the people who
> are closest to the products and the customers. That requires new business strategies and

[5]"Levi's Pot o' Gold," *Business Week,* June 24, 1996, p. 44.
[6]"Levi Strauss Offers to Pay a Dividend to Workers," *New York Times,* June 13, 1996, p. D4.

different organizational structures. But structure and strategy aren't enough. This is where values come in. In a more volatile and dynamic business environment, the controls have to be conceptual. They can't be human anymore: Bob Haas telling people what to do. It's the ideas of a business that are controlling, not some manager with authority. Values provide a common language for aligning a company's leadership and its people.

The passivity and dependence of traditional paternalism—doing what you're told—doesn't work anymore. People have to take responsibility, exercise initiative, be accountable for their own success and for that of the company as a whole. They have to communicate more frequently and more effectively with their colleagues and customers.

The Aspirations encourage and support the new behaviors we need. For example, in an empowered organization there are bound to be a lot more disagreements. Because we value open and direct communication, we give people permission to disagree. They can tell a manager, "It doesn't seem aspirational to be working with that contractor because from what we've seen, that company really mistreats its workers." Or they can say, "It may help us conserve cash to be slow in paying our bills, but that company has been a supplier for a long time, and it's struggling right now. Wouldn't it be better in terms of the partnership we're trying to create with our suppliers to pay our bills on time?"[7]

Levi Strauss & Company attempted to make its Mission, Vision, Aspirations, and Values Statement an important part of the company's culture by covering leadership, employee empowerment, diversity, and ethical decision making in a three-part, 10-day course called Leadership Week. Haas had formed 80 task forces to study and make recommendations concerning the company's policies related to overseas labor practices, work-and-family issues, and diversity in the workforce. Managers were encouraged to practice and nurture the behaviors outlined in the statement and were trained in how to do so during the Leadership Week course. The company's compensation plan for management made one-third of managers' bonuses, raises, and other financial rewards contingent on their ability to manage in a style and manner that promoted deeper commitment to the company's mission, vision, aspirations, and values. Haas stated that the company could also ingrain the aspirations and values into its culture by encouraging managers to be explicit about their vulnerabilities and failings, talk about the bad decisions they've made, and talk about the limitations of their own knowledge. Haas also suggested that promotions were not in the future of managers who did not improve their ability to manage aspirationally.

LEVI STRAUSS & COMPANY'S PARTNERSHIPS WITH SUPPLIERS AND RETAILERS

As with the company's relationships with its employees, Haas also believed that the company needed to structure its supplier network to reflect LS&C's values and to emphasize long-term relationships. In the past, Haas said, the company maintained a large number of suppliers in order to promote strong price competition among suppliers: "The old way of thinking was, if you had enough different suppliers, the competition for your business would force them to drive their prices to the lowest possible point and to maintain the highest possible quality."[8] Haas believed that partnerships between the company and its suppliers would improve the overall quality of Levi's products and

---

[7]"Values Make the Company: An Interview with Robert Haas," *Harvard Business Review,* September–October 1990, p. 329.

[8]"Robert Haas' Vision Scores 20/20," *Industry Week,* April 2, 1990, p. 19.

allow the company to provide better service to its customers through more timely deliveries. Haas also believed that it was important to treat the company's retailing customers as partners by providing assistance in point-of-sale program support and a strong national advertising program plus the availability of information systems that aided retailers in improving inventory management and purchase ordering. In summarizing the importance of the company's supplier and customers partnerships, Haas suggested that Levi Strauss was forced to "change the way you look at things—your retailers and your suppliers as partners. If they're not successful and profitable, then we go down the tubes over time."[9]

Robert Haas also oversaw the development of the company's Global Sourcing and Operating Guidelines, drafted in 1991 and approved by the company's board of directors in 1992 to ensure ethical business practices on the part of LS&C suppliers. The guidelines called for LS&C's overall evaluation of the country-specific external issues beyond the control of individual business partners (e.g., health and safety issues and political, economic, and social conditions) to help the company assess the risk of doing business in a particular country. Levi Strauss managers could avoid suppliers and other potential business partners that were located in what were deemed to be high-risk countries where unethical or inhumane business practices were likely to occur. The Global Sourcing and Operating Guidelines also created terms of engagement that approved business partners were expected to adopt and follow. If LS&C determined that a business partner was in violation of the terms of engagement, it could withdraw production from that factory or require that the contractor implement a corrective action plan within a specified time period. Contractors were aware that if they failed to meet the corrective action plan commitment, Levi Strauss would terminate the business relationship. The Global Sourcing and Operating Guidelines' terms of engagement are presented in Exhibit 5.

LS&C's terms of engagement and its close relationships with suppliers helped improve the working conditions of those around the world who worked in factories where Levi's products were made. The company's supplier-monitoring program revealed that in Bangladesh several underage girls were working in two suppliers' factories. After a discussion of the situation, the suppliers agreed to discontinue hiring underage workers and to release existing underage workers from their job responsibilities but continue to pay a salary to the girls as long as they attended school. Levi Strauss & Company agreed to pay for the girls' tuition, books, and school uniforms until the completion of their education when their jobs would again be available at the factory if they desired to return. LS&C also negotiated safer work environments for workers employed by offshore suppliers and encouraged suppliers to offer medical treatment to employees and their families and find ways for employees to further their education.

LEVI STRAUSS & COMPANY'S COMMITMENT TO ADDRESSING BROAD SOCIAL ISSUES

The company's social mission and commitment to bettering the lives of others could be traced to its founder, who used his influence and wealth to benefit such charities as orphan homes, homes for the elderly, the Eureka Benevolent Society, and the Hebrew Board of Relief. Levi Strauss also provided funding to the California School for the Deaf and endowed perpetual scholarships at the University of California–Berkeley. At the time of Strauss's death, the San Francisco Board of Trade passed a special resolution noting his contributions to the community:

---

[9]Ibid.

exhibit 5 Levi Strauss & Company's Global Sourcing and Operating Guidelines' Terms of Engagement

1. **Ethical Standards**

   We will seek to identify and utilize business partners who aspire as individuals and in the conduct of all their businesses to a set of ethical standards not incompatible with our own.

2. **Legal Requirements**

   We expect our business partners to be law abiding as individuals and to comply with legal requirements relevant to the conduct of all their businesses.

3. **Environmental Requirements**

   We will only do business with partners who share our commitment to the environment and who conduct their business in a way that is consistent with Levi Strauss & Co.'s Environmental Philosophy and Guiding Principles.

4. **Community Involvement**

   We will favor business partners who share our commitment to contribute to improving community conditions.

5. **Employment Standards**

   We will only do business with partners whose workers are in all cases present voluntarily, not put at risk of physical harm, fairly compensated, allowed the right of free association and not exploited in any way. In addition, the following specific guidelines will be followed:

   Wages and Benefits: We will only do business with partners who provide wages and benefits that comply with any applicable law and match the prevailing local manufacturing or finishing industry practices.

   Working Hours: While permitting flexibility in scheduling, we will identify prevailing local work hours and seek business partners who do not exceed them except for appropriately compensated overtime. While we favor partners who utilize less than sixty-hour work weeks, we will not use contractors who, on a regular basis, require in excess of a sixty-hour week. Employees should be allowed at least one day off in seven.

   Child Labor: Use of child labor is not permissible. Workers can be no less than 14 years of age and not younger than the compulsory age to be in school. We will not utilize partners who use child labor in any of their facilities. We support the development of legitimate workplace apprenticeship programs for the educational benefit of younger people.

   Prison Labor/Forced Labor: We will not utilize prison or forced labor in contracting relationships in the manufacture and finishing of our products. We will not utilize or purchase materials from a business partner utilizing prison or forced labor.

   Health & Safety: We will only utilize business partners who provide workers with a safe and healthy work environment. Business partners who provide residential facilities for their workers must provide safe and healthy facilities.

   Discrimination: While we recognize and respect cultural differences, we believe that workers should be employed on the basis of their ability to do the job, rather than on the basis of personal characteristics or beliefs. We will favor business partners who share this value.

   Disciplinary Practices: We will not utilize business partners who use corporal punishment or other forms of mental or physical coercion.

Evaluation & Compliance

All new and existing factories involved in the cutting, sewing, or finishing of products for Levi Strauss & Co. must comply with our Terms of Engagement. These facilities are continuously evaluated to ensure compliance. We work on-site with our contractors to develop strong alliances dedicated to responsible business practices and continuous improvement.

Source: Levi Strauss & Company, www.levistrauss.com/about/code.html.

The great causes of education and charity have likewise suffered a signal loss in the death of Mr. Strauss, whose splendid endowments to the University of California will be an enduring testimonial to his worth as a liberal, public-minded citizen and whose numberless unostentatious acts of charity in which neither race nor creed were recognized, exemplified his broad and generous love for and sympathy with humanity.[10]

Many LS&C CEOs, including Robert Haas's father, grandfather, and uncle, continued the founder's commitment to social causes. Walter Haas Sr. established the Levi Strauss Foundation as an independent charitable organization in 1952 to support nonprofit organizations that addressed important social or community issues. Throughout the 1990s the company donated more than $20 million annually to fund nonprofit organizations in more than 40 countries. Walter Haas Jr. initiated Community Involvement Teams (CITs) in 1968 to provide employees with time off from work to take an active part in their communities through volunteerism. The CITs were promoted further by Peter Haas during his tenure as CEO, and in 1984 the White House presented Levi Strauss & Company with the President's Volunteer Action Award for Corporate Volunteerism for its support of employee community volunteer efforts. In 1999 LS&C employees had established over 100 CITs worldwide to donate time to projects as diverse as refurbishing homeless shelters to teaching computer skills to women in prison.

Levi Strauss & Company offered and promoted a variety of employee-giving programs in addition to Community Involvement Teams. The company awarded volunteer service grants to organizations where LS&C employees volunteered or served as board members. The company also matched employees' contributions to all types of nonprofit organizations and held campaigns to encourage employees to donate money to their favorite charities or disaster relief drives.

Robert Haas held a deep personal interest in many social issues and maintained and extended company's policy of providing funding to organizations that addressed what he saw as critical societal issues. Robert Haas was awarded Volunteers of America's Ballington and Maud Booth Award for Distinguished Service to Humanity in 1993 for his leadership in shaping Levi Strauss & Company's commitment to philanthropy and community service. He received an award from the United Nations for his commitment to improving the lives of LS&C employees and was recognized for his commitment to developing awareness of such social issues as racism and AIDS prevention and care.

Haas was frequently called on to make speeches on business ethics and once distributed AIDS leaflets to employees outside the company cafeteria. The U.S. Centers for Disease Control's National Business and Labor Award for Leadership on HIV/AIDS was presented to LS&C in 1997 in large part because of Haas' commitment to AIDS education. Robert Haas also encouraged employees to volunteer time and raise funds for community projects related to their interests and directed ample funding to the Levi Strauss Foundation which provided grants worldwide to organizations dedicated to such causes as social justice, AIDS awareness, youth empowerment, and economic empowerment.

Examples of programs funded by the Levi Strauss Foundation included Project Change which was launched in 1991 as an ongoing program to combat cultural beliefs and social norms that perpetuated discrimination in Albuquerque, New Mexico, El Paso, Texas, Valdosta, Georgia, and Knoxville, Tennessee. In 1998 President Clinton made Levi Strauss & Company the first recipient of the Ron Brown Award for Corporate Leadership in recognition of Project Change's efforts to promote social justice and end institutional racism. OCCUR was another social justice program funded by Levi

---

[10]Levi Strauss & Company—Biographies, www.levistrauss.com/about/bio_founder_downey.html.

Strauss that allowed the Japan Association for the Lesbian and Gay Movement to expand its peer-based telephone counseling services and begin a media campaign to promote positive images of lesbian and gay people. Levi Strauss also funded a youth empowerment program that allowed 100 youth from low-income and racial minority backgrounds to write short cultural diversity articles that were to be printed in various Canadian newspapers. In Mexico, LS&C funded an organization made up of university students and prostitutes that included AIDS workshops for prostitutes, their partners, and their clients. The president of the organization commented that Levi Strauss had made it "possible for these women to determine how to best stop the spread of HIV in the community—and to actually implement the program themselves."[11]

LEVI STRAUSS & COMPANY'S DECLINING SALES AND MARKET SHARE IN ITS CORE JEANS BUSINESS

Even though Levi Strauss & Company had reemerged during the 1990s as the leader of the jeans segment of the apparel industry, as 2000 approached it was again confronted with falling corporate sales and earnings resulting from the rapid decline its blue jeans business. The company's 1998 sales total of $6.0 billion was 13 percent lower than 1997's $6.9 billion total, and its market share in the jeans category had fallen from its 1990 high of 30.9 percent to 14.8 percent in 1999. The blue jeans segment of the apparel industry had grown by 6 to 8 percent in 1995 through 1997 and by 3 percent in 1998, but beginning in late 1997 LS&C began to lose sales to more stylish designer brands like Tommy Hilfiger and Polo and better-priced private-label brands offered by The Gap, Old Navy, J.C. Penney, and Sears. A retail analysis suggested that "Levi Strauss was zagging when the world was zigging"[12] as it failed to introduce new styles that appealed to consumers aged 15 to 24, who accounted for the largest percentage of blue jeans purchasers. Some analysts and competitors doubted that Levi's declining market share would be short lived, since appealing to the 15-to-24 age group was so important to the apparel industry. An executive at VF Corporation, the jeans segment leader and maker of Lee and Wrangler jeans, stated, "It's very important that you attract this age group. By the time they're 24, they've adopted brands that they will use for the rest of their lives."[13]

Robert Haas conceded that the company had missed trends like wide-legged pants, baggy jeans, and cargo pockets, but suggested that at the time the company was overly concerned with growing its newer Dockers and Slates brands: "When you try to take on too many things, you are not as attentive to the warning signs."[14] Levi's inability to introduce styles that appealed to teens was reflected in a Teenage Research Unlimited survey that found only 7 percent of teens in 1998 viewed Levi's as a "cool brand" and focus group results that pointed out that teens viewed Levi's as a brand more suitable for their parents or older siblings than teens. Levi's inability to keep its styles fresh was suggested to be in part related to the company's consensus management style and a

---

[11]Levi Strauss & Company Giving Program description, www.levistrauss.com/community/HIVAIDSstudy.html.

[12]"Levi's Is Hiking Up Its Pants," *Business Week,* December 1, 1997, p. 70.

[13]Ibid.

[14]Ibid.

management team that was characterized as "insular, paternalistic, and quite frankly, a little smug" by the president of a retail sector marketing research firm.[15]

A J. P. Morgan Securities analyst stated that LS&C managers were "still resting on their laurels at bit" and were ultimately responsible for "a brand that is really stale right now" and "doesn't have any momentum." The analyst also commented that Levi's had "not been able to aggressively move into the new trends" and that "they are definitely not being as hip as some of the new brands we've been seeing that focus on what the kids want."[16] Levi Strauss & Company's former president suggested that strategic decisions at the company were difficult to make: "[Some managers say,] 'Our objective is to be the most enlightened work environment in the world.' And then you have others who say, 'Our objective is to make a lot of money.' The value-based people look at the commercial folks as heathens; the commercial people look at the values people as wusses getting in the way."[17] LS&C's previous chief financial officer claimed that "it was very difficult to be responsive" at the company because of the "principled reasoning approach" promoted in the company's leadership courses that called for consensus decisions: "Unless you could convince everyone to agree with your idea, you didn't have the authority to make a decision."[18]

A previous head of marketing who left the company in 1998 after a 20-year tenure suggested that Levi's problems had been building for years but were ignored by some executive level managers: "A big brand like Levi's is an aircraft carrier. You can turn the engines off and the actual speed of the carrier will not slow perceptibly for a long time. With the Levi's brand we gradually dialed down our propeller speed and the carrier kept moving. People up on the deck said, 'We're still moving fast!' But those down in the engine room said, 'Whoa! We're going to be dead in the water!'"[19]

The president of a major Levi's retailer suggested that Robert Haas was partly to blame for the company's falling sales during a time when rival apparel manufacturer Gap had increased its market value from $7 billion to over $40 billion: "Typically in apparel you have merchants, men like [Gap CEO] Mickey Drexler. I'm not sure Bob Haas has ever been trained to be a merchant. I'm not sure he's even been in a store, waiting on customers, talking to them so that he could hear them say, 'Why are the legs on those jeans so tight?'"[20] Expressing similar concerns, a former Levi's executive stated, "Bob is very smart. But then the question is 'What's he smart at? Is he smart at running an apparel company?' I think that's an open question."[21]

Many longtime Levi's retailers complained that the company's inability to introduce new styles that appealed to teens and young adults caused sales decreases for retailers as well as the manufacturer. In noting that Levi's declining popularity had contributed to Sears' 4 percent decline in men's apparel sales during 1998, the company's chairman and CEO stated that "we've suffered because of our excessive dependence on Levi's."[22] In addition, Levi's declining sales also affected suppliers adversely.

---

[15]Ibid.

[16]"Bad Day at Levi's: 11 Plants to Close, Costing 5,900 Jobs," *WWD,* February 23, 1999, p. 1.

[17]"How Levi's Trashed a Great American Brand," p. 86.

[18]Ibid.

[19]Ibid., p. 85.

[20]Ibid., p. 84

[21]Ibid.

[22]"Bad Day at Levi's: 11 Plants to Close, Costing 5,900 Jobs," p. 1.

INDEXES

NAME

Abell, Derek F., 16n, 17n, 29, 34n

Adams, Barney, C–343

Ahlstrand, Bruce, 11n, 13n, 29, 70

Alexander, John, 412, 433

Alexander, Marcus, 280, 317, 334n, 343

Aleyne, Adrian, 135t

Allaire, Paul, 378

Amara, Roy, 100n

Amsden, Davida M., 387n

Amsden, Robert T., 387n

Anderson, P., 397n

Andrews, Kenneth R., 63n, 72

Anslinger, Patricia L., 297n

Argyris, Chris, 376

Armstrong, C. Michael, 344

Armstrong, Douglas, 247

Arnold, David J., 217n, 218n, 223

Athos, Anthony, 411

Austin, Nancy, 403n

Ayling, Robert J., 26

Badaracco, Joseph, Jr., 68n, 70, 440

Bales, Carter F., 297n

Baliga, B. R., 273n

Band, David C., 394n

Barney, Jay B., 119n, 184n, 197, 317

Barringer, Bruce, 13n

Bartlett, Christopher A., 207n, 371, 430n, 440

Beckard, Richard, 367

Beinhocker, Eric D., 263n, 264n, 265, 279

Bethune, Gordon, 274

Bhide, Amar, 148, 408

Bickford, Deborah J., 254n

Biesada, Alexandra, 134n

Birchall, David W., 122n, 147

Birinyi, Laszlo, 72

Bleeke, Joel A., 279

Bluedorn, Allen C., 13n

Bodenstab, Jeffrey, 194

Bodett, Tom, 170

Bogner, William C., 118n

Bolt, James F., 223

Bontis, Nick, 147

Bossidy, Lawrence A., 344, 378

Bourgeois, L. J., 23n

Brandenburger, Adam M., 148

Brenneman, Greg, 274, 279

Brodwin, David R., 23n

Bromiley, Philip, 17n, 29, 71

Brown, Robert, 17n, 29, 71

Brown, Shona L., 49n, 70, 253n, 254, 255n, 343

Burgelman, Robert A., 29, 39n

Burgers, Willem P., 315n

Byrne, John A., 331, 344, 352n, 353

Calantrone, Roger J., 279

Caligiuri, Paula M., 398n

Calloway, Wayne, 148

Camp, Robert C., 134n

Campbell, Andrew, 70, 280, 317, 334n, 343

Carlzon, Jan, 433

Carroll, Archie B., 436n, 440

Carroll, Lewis, 2

Carter, John C., 24n, 344, 430n

Cashman, Kristen M., C–479

Cassini, Barbara, 26

Castrogiovanni, Gary J., 273n

Chakravarthy, Bala, 253n

Chambers, John, 354

Champy, James, 136, 364n, 365n, 376, 378

Chandler, Alfred, 362n, 363n

Chaples, Sherry S., 113

Charan, Ram, 430n

Chatterjee, Sayan, 294n, 297n

Chen, Ming-Jer, 189n

Christensen, H. Kurt, 147

Chu, Jessica, 224

Clement, Ronald W., 440

Coffman, Vance, 437

Collins, James C., 29, 39n, 45n, 70

Collins, Jim, 383

Collins, John, 248

Collis, David J., 114, 123n, 125n, 147, 305n, 317, 318, 335n, 336n, 337n, 343

Colvin, Geoffrey, 351n

Colvin, Jeffrey G., 13n, 39n, 193n

Cooper, Robin, 129n, 133n

Copeland, Thomas E., 297n

Cowen, Tyler, 288

Crosby, Philip, 386

Cucuzza, Thomas G., 133n

Cusumano, Michael A., 188n, 197, 248

Darr, Eric D., 390n, 392n

Darwin, Charles, 72

Das, T. K., 223

D'Aveni, Richard A., 113, 197, 253n, 279

Dawar, Niraj, 198, 219n, 219n, 220n, 221n, 223

Day, George S., 279

Deal, Terrence E., 414n

Denton, Keith D., 405

Dess, Gregory G., 197

di Benedetto, C. Anthony, 279

Donaldson, Gordon, 27n

Downs, Harry, 64n, 65n, 66n

Doz, Yves L., 148, 172n, 177n, 210n, 214n, 215n, 216, 223, 301n, 302n, 308n, 313n, 314, 317

Dragonetti, Nicola C., 118n, 147

Dretler, Thomas D., 223

Driscoll, Dawn-Marie, 440

Note on page numbers: those in *italics* indicate figures; those followed by *t* indicate tables; those followed by *n* indicate material in footnotes.

Drucker, Peter F., 2, 70, 298n, 305n, 361n

Duncan, W. Jack, 127n, 147

Eccles, Robert G., 440

Eisenhardt, Kathleen M., 49n, 70, 253n, *254*, 255n, 292n, 317, 343

Ellig, Jerry, 288

Evans, Philip, 147, 165n, 246, 377

Fahey, Liam, 147, 188n

Falbe, Cecilia M., 39n

Farkas, Charles M., 29, 440

Feder, Barnaby J., 389

Feldman, Lawrence P., 279

Ferratt, Thomas S., 387n

Ferrier, Walter J., 266n

Fiegenbaum, Avi, 103n

Finkelstein, S., 397n

Finkin, Eugene F., 279

Fisher, Marshall L., 147

Floyd, Steven W., 23n, 345, 440

Fresius, Bernard, C–411

Friedman, Lawrence, 223, 279, 377

Frost, Tony, 198, *219*, 219n, 220n, 221n, 223

Gadiesh, Orit, 147

Gall, Gene, 367

Galli, Joseph, C–474

Galunic, D. Charles, 292n, 317

Galvin, Bob, C–586, C–598, C–600

Gates, J. Russell, 247

George, S., 386

Ger, Guliz, 219n, 223

Gerstner, Louis V., Jr., 30

Ghemawat, Pankaj, 79n, 108n, 113

Ghosh, Shikhar, 246

Ghoshal, Sumantra, 207n, 371, 430n, 440

Gilbert, James L., 147

Ginsburg, Lee, 440

Ginter, Peter M., 127n, 147

Goffee, Robert, 440

Goldsmith, Marshall, 367

Goleman, Daniel, 440

Gomez, Alain, 198

Goodman, Paul S., 390n, 392n

Goold, Michael, 280, 317, 334n, 343

Gordon, Geoffrey L., 279

Gordon, Mary Ellen, 100n

Gorman, Philip, 113, 223

Goss, Tracy, 411

Govindarajan, Vijay, 129n, 133n, 137n, 147

Grant, Robert M., 405

Griffith, David A., 247

Grimm, Curtis M., 266n

Grove, Andrew S., 39, 39n, 40, 198

Gunnarson, Sarah K., 428n, 440

Guth, William D., 63n

Haeckel, Stephan H., 391n

Hall, Gene, 376, 388n

Hall, William K., 273n

Hambrick, Donald C., 189n, 351n, 376

Hamel, Gary, 11n, 18n, 27n, 29, 45n, 49n, 70, 122n, 147, 148, 170n, 172n, 177n, 197, 214n, 215n, 216, 223, 229n, 232n, 247, 264n, 301n, 302n, 317, 377

Hamermesh, R. G., 259n, 260n, 267n

Hammer, Michael, 70, 136, 364n, 365n, 376, 378

Hardee, Camilla, 45n, 173n

Harrigan, Kathryn R., 180n, 189n

Haspeslagh, Phillippe C., 343

Hax, Arnoldo C., 100n, 317

Hayes, Robert H., 114, 183n, 197, 358n

Hedley, Barry, 338n

Heeley, Michael B., 193n

Hegert, M., 129n, 132n, 133n

Heifetz, Ronald A., 440

Henderson, Bruce D., 280

Herzberg, Frederick, 378, 405

Heskett, James L., 64n, 399n, 410n, 413n, 416, 416n, 417n, 418n, 432n, 440

Hesselbein, Frances, 367

Hewlett, Bill, 42

Hilmer, Frederick G., 361n

Hitt, Michael A., 45n, 70, 173n

Hodgetts, Richard M., 388n

Hofer, Charles W., 251n, 252n, 338n

Hoffman, W. Michael, 440

House, Charles H., 42n

Hout, Thomas M., 24n, 344, 430n

Huey, John, 64n

Humble, John, 422n

Hwang, Peter, 315n

Inkpen, Andrew C., 223

Ireland, R. Duane, 70

Iverson, Michael, C–349

Jackson, David, 422n

Jackson, Dist. Judge Thomas Penfield, 268

Jacobsen, Kristine, 118n, 147

Jamison, David B., 343

Jarvenpaa, Sirkka L., 366n

Jones, Gareth, 440

Jones, Ian W., 428

Juran, J., 386

Kahaner, Larry, 104n, 113

Kami, Michael, 2

Kanter, Rosabeth Moss, 214n, 223, 371n, 376

Kaplan, Robert S., 42n, 70, 116n, 129n, 133n, 147

Katzenbach, Jon R., 376, 405

Kennedy, Allen A., 414n

Kerr, Steven, 397n, 401, 401n, 403, 403n, 405

Khurana, Rakesh, 28n

Kidwell, Roland E., 273n

Kim, W. Chan, 315n

Kirkpatrick, Shelley A., 440

Klein, Harold E., 100n, 113

Kohn, Alfie, 400n, 403n, 405

Kotler, Philip, 186n, 187n, 190n, 251n, 265n, 275n

Kotter, John P., 64n, 399n, 410n, 413n, 416, 416n, 417n, 418n, 430n, 432n, 440

Kress, Donald, 114

Kriger, Mark, 39n

Krishnan, R., 405

Kulkarni, Shashank, 138n

Lampel, Joseph, 11*n*, 13*n*, 29, 70

Langley, Ann, 113

Larwood, Laurie, 39*n*

Laurie, Donald L., 440

Lei, David, 223

Leibovitz, Mitchell, 9

Lemak, David J., 388*n*

Leuchter, Miriam, 353

Levering, Robert, 383

Lieberthal, Kenneth, 201*n*, 217*n*, 218*n*

Liedtka, Jeanne M., 288*n*, 317, 369*n*

Lincoln, Abraham, 318

Linneman, Robert, 100*n*, 113

Lipinski, Andrew J., 100*n*

Lipton, Mark, 29, 70

Littlejohn, Michael, 366*n*

Locke, Edwin, 440

Lombardi, Vince, 344

Lorsch, Jay W., 28*n*

Lowy, Alex, 247

Lubatkin, Michael, 294*n*, 297*n*

Lublin, Joann S., 373

Luchs, Kathleen, 317

Luthans, Fred, 405

McCombs, Billy Joe, 179

McGill, A. R., 71

MacMillan, Ian C., 185*n*, 186*n*, 189*n*, 190*n*, 265*n*

McTavish, Ron, 39*n*, 70

Main, Jeremy, 135*n*, 136, 215*n*

Majchrzak, Ann, 367, 376

Majluf, Nicolas S., 100*n*, 317

Malone, John, 126

Markides, Constantinos C., 29, 114, 286*n*, 292*n*, 305*n*, 307*n*, 376

Mayer, Robert J., 279

Mays, Lowry, 179

Meeker, Mary G., 224

Middelhoff, Thomas, 224

Miesing, Paul, 39*n*

Miles, Morgan P., 13*n*, 39*n*

Miles, Robert H., 440

Miller, Neil, 440

Milne, A. A., 344

Milne, George R., 100*n*

Mintzberg, Henry, 11*n*, 29, 49*n*, 70, 71

Mokwa, Michael P., 103*n*

Moncrieff, James, 29

Montgomery, Cynthia A., 114, 123*n*, 125*n*, 147, 305*n*, 317, 318, 335*n*, 336*n*, 337*n*, 343

Moore, Gordon, 40

Moore, James F., 362*n*

Morris, D., 129*n*, 132*n*, 133*n*

Moscowitz, Milton, 383

Mroz, John Edward, 367, 368*n*

Murphy, Patrick E., 422*n*, 440

Nakache, Patricia, 355

Nalebuff, Barry J., 148

Nash, Laura, 70

Nash, Sarah, 254*n*

Ness, Joseph A., 133*n*

Newman, George, 30

Nielsen, Anders P., 118*n*

Niles-Jolly, Kathryn, 428*n*, 440

Noble, Charles H., 103*n*

Nocera, Joseph, 224

Nolan, Richard L., 391*n*

Norton, David P., 42*n*, 70, 116*n*, 147

Ohinata, Yoshinobu, 383*n*, 405

Ohmae, Kenichi, 72, 223, 286*n*, 339*n*

Olian, Judy D., 386*n*, 387*n*, 390*n*, 406, 420*n*, 433*n*

Olusoga, S. Ade, 103*n*

O'Neill, Hugh M., 223

Oster, Sharon M., 30

Page, Albert L., 279

Paine, Lynn Sharp, 440

Palmer, Jonathan W., 247

Paré, Terence P., 134*t*

Park, Daewoo, 45*n*, 173*n*

Parkhe, Arvinde, 223

Pascale, Richard T., 64*n*, 411

Pelosky, Robert, 198

Perot, H. Ross, 408

Peteraf, Margaret A., 119*n*

Pfeffer, Jeffrey, 376, 377, 394*n*, 396*n*, 397*n*, 398*n*, 406, 411, 430*n*

Picken, Joseph C., 197

Pisano, Gary P., 114, 183*n*, 197, 358*n*

Pollitt, Michael G., 428

Pollock, Timothy, 113, 223

Porras, Jerry I., 29, 39*n*, 45*n*, 70

Porter, Michael E., 29, 45*n*, 71, 77, 77*n*, 79–80, 80*n*, *81*, 82*n*, 84*n*, 87*n*, 88*n*, 90*n*, 93*n*, 94*n*, 100*n*, 113, 129*n*, *130*, 130*n*, *132*, 132*n*, 133*n*, 138*n*, 148, 149*n*, 150*n*, 151*n*, 153*n*, 159*n*, 164*n*, 165, 166*n*, 167*n*, 174*n*, 191*n*, 192*n*, 193*n*, 197, 203*n*, 204*n*, 209*n*, 211*n*, 214*n*, 248, 250*n*, 257*n*, 261*n*, 265*n*, 269*n*, 285*n*, 286*n*, 300*n*, 301*n*, 318, 337*n*, 340*n*, 343

Powell, Thomas C., 386, 387, 388*n*

Prahalad, C. K., 11*n*, 45*n*, 70, 122*n*, 147, 148, 201*n*, 210*n*, 217*n*, 218*n*, 308*n*, 313*n*, *314*, 377

Price, Raymond L., 42*n*

Quelch, John A., 217*n*, 218*n*, 223

Quinn, James Brian, 114, 139*n*, 140*n*, 184*n*, 356*n*, 361*n*, 367, 391*n*, 397*n*, 438*n*

Rackham, Neil, 223, 279, 377

Radosevich, Lynda, C–308*n*

Rakowski, Paul, C–369

Reed, Richard, 388*n*

Rigby, Darrell K., 386*n*

Roos, Goran, 118*n*, 147

Rosenoer, Jonathan, 247

Rosenthal, Jim, 367, 376, 388*n*

Ross, Joel, 2

Rothschild, William E., 188*n*

Ruff, Richard, 223, 279, 377

Rynes, Sara L., 386*n*, 387*n*, 390*n*, 406, 420*n*, 433*n*

St. Clair, L., 71

Santamaria, Jason A., 405

Sathe, Vijay, 415*n*

Scanlan, Gerald, 394*n*

Schendel, Dan, 251*n*, 252*n*, 338*n*

Schnarrs, Steven P., 197

Schneider, Benjamin, 428*n*, 440

Scholz, Christian, 440

Schulman, Lawrence E., 165*n*

Schulmeyer, Gerhard, 434

Selby, Richard W., 248

Shani, Rami, 405

Shank, John K., 129*n*, 133*n*, 137*n*, 147

Shaw, Gordon, 17*n*, 29, 71

Shulman, Lawrence E., 147, 377

Silas, C. J., 408

Silk, S. B., 259*n*, 260*n*

Simons, Robert, 369*n*, 393*n*, 406

Singh, Ravi, 186*n*

Slevin, Dennis P., 193*n*

Smith, Adam, 365*n*

Smith, Clayton G., 279

Smith, Douglas K., 376

Smith, Ken G., 266*n*

Smucker, J. M., 426

Somerville, Iain, 367, 368*n*

Son, Masayoshi, 227

Stajkovic, Alexander D., 405

Stalk, George, 147, 165*n*, 377

Stanley, Morgan, 198

Stepanek, Marcia, 381*n*, 418

Stoddard, Donna B., 366*n*

Stroh, Linda K., 398*n*

Stuart, T., 367

Stuckey, John, 180*n*, 197

Sugiura, Hideo, 223

Sun Zi, 408

Swayne, Linda E., 127*n*, 147

Tagiuri, Renato, 63*n*

Tapscott, Don, 247

Teece, David J., 122*n*, 147

Teets, John W., 30

Teng, Bing-Sheng, 223

Terry, Robert J., 280

Thomas, Howard, 103*n*, 113, 223

Thomson, Alan, 422*n*

Tichy, Noel M., 71, 408, 430*n*

Ticoll, David, 247

Timmers, Paul, 247

Torvalds, Linus, 5

Tovstiga, George, 122*n*, 147

Tully, Shawn, 215*n*

Twer, Doran, 401*n*

Tyler, Beverly B., 45*n*, 173*n*

Upton, David M., 114, 183*n*, 197, 358*n*

Vancil, Richard F., 63*n*

Veiga, John F., 377, 394*n*, 396*n*, 398*n*, 406

Venkatesan, Ravi, 197

Very, Philippe, 318

Wade, Judy, 367, 376, 388*n*

Waitt, Ted, 350–351

Walton, M., 386

Walton, Sam, 64, 64*n*, 410, 431

Wang, Qianwei, 367, 376

Waters, J. A., 11*n*, 13*n*, 49*n*

Watson, Gregory H., 134*n*, 147

Webb, Allen P., 440

Welch, Jack, 47, 180, 318, 329, 330, 331, 353, 431

Wernerfelt, Birger, 119*n*

Wetlaufer, Suzy, 29, 377, 434*n*, 440

White, David, 180*n*, 197

Williamson, Peter J., 114, 286*n*, 292*n*, 376

Wilson, Ian, 71

Wilson, Meena S., 412, 433

Woods, Tiger, 190, 357

Wooldridge, Bill, 23*n*, 345, 440

Wurster, Thomas S., 246

Yoffie, David B., 188*n*, 197

Zack, Michael H., 118*n*, 147

Zahra, Shaker A., 113, 118*n*, 223, 254*n*

Zimmerman, Frederick M., 273*n*, 279

ORGANIZATION

Aaeon Technology (Taiwan), 224

ABB, 370

ABC, 178, 190, 295

ABC Outdoor, 178

Accompany, 418

Acer Computer Group, 226, 255, 302

Acura, 169

Adidas, 46

Advanced Manufacturing Online, 161

Advanced Micro Devices (AMD), 89, 186–187, 397

A&E, *See* Arts & Entertainment Network

Aerospatiale, 216, 362

AES Corporation, 433–434

Airborne Express, 87, 159, 241, 391

Airbus Industrie, 176, 216

Alcan Aluminum, 11

Alcon, 310

Aligent Technologies, 304

Allied-Signal, 344, 378

AltaVista, 242

Altra Energy Technologies, 239–240

Amalgamated Sugar Company, 384–385

Amazon.com, 33, 46, 53, 83, 124, 139, 156, 163, 193, 232, 238, 243, 265, 352, 435

AMD (Advanced Micro Devices), 89, 186–187, 397

American Airlines, 124, 163, 390

American Express, 216, 241

American Greetings, 171, 243

American Red Cross, 8

American Standard, 296

American Tobacco, 270

America Online (AOL), 16, 23, 32, 46, 49, 173, 176, 177, 192, 193, 227, 242, 268, 352

AMFM, Inc., 178

Amgen, 396

Anaheim Angels, 295

Anaheim Mighty Ducks, 295

Andersen Consulting, 136, 176

Anheuser-Busch, 44, 67, 91, 265, 283, 363

AOL, *See* America Online

Apple Computer, 37, 270, 283

Arepa.com, 237

Ariba, 227, 232, 392

Armour, 159

Arrowhead, 310

Arthur Andersen, 384, 385, 391

Arthur D. Little, 387

Arts & Entertainment Network, 295, 329

A.T. Kearney, 136

AtHome/Excite, 177

Atlantic Southeast, 169

Atlas Corporation, 11

AT&T, 28, 36, 43, 100, 126, 137, 173, 176, 177, 215, 226, 235, 288, 306–307, 344, 362, 397

Atyouroffice.com, 240

Avis Rent-A-Car, 8, 190

Avon Products, 104, 416

Baan, 227

Baccarat, 270

Bailey's, 295

Bain & Co., 274

Bajaj Auto, 220

Bally Shoes, 270

Banc One Corporation, 11

Bandag, 169

BankAmerica, 416

Banker's Trust, 177

Bank of America, 50

Bank One Corp., 49, 50–51, 224, 400

Barnesandnoble.com, 83

Barnes & Noble, 124, 232

Beaird-Poulan, 161, 289

Beaulieu Vineyards, 295

Bechtel Group, 239

Bell, 173, 295

Bell Atlantic Corporation, 216, 226, 235, 365

BellSouth, 235

Ben & Jerry's Homemade, Inc., 63, 260

Benson & Hedges, 310

Bertelsmann AG, 224

Best Practices Benchmarking & Consulting, 136

Bethlehem Steel, 400

Bic, 161

Black & Decker Corporation, 161, 289, 290

Blaxxun, 227

Blockbuster, 133, 177, 304

Bloomberg, 242

Bloomingdale's, 241

Blue Diamond, 270

Bluefly.com, 18, 380–381

Blue Mountain Arts, 171

Bluemountain.com, 243

B&M, 295

BMW, 124, 163, 169, 177, 189, 302, 362

Boeing, 216, 362, 381

Bombardier, 289

Bombay, 270

Borders Bookstores, 124, 304

BP Amoco, 34, 204

Bridgestone, 131

Briefing.com, 227, 242

Briggs & Stratton, 43, 161

Bristol-Myers Squibb, 8, 11

British Aerospace, 216

British Airways, 26

British Telecom, 215, 226

Note: Page numbers followed by *n* indicate material in footnotes.

Broadcast.com, 193
Broadcom, 226
Buick, 169
Burger King, 175, 295
Business Week, 241–242
Buy.com, 227, 237

Cadillac, 124, 169
California Pizza Kitchens, 304
Calistoga, 310
Campbell's Soup Company, 163, 270, 283
Camstar Systems, 230
Canada Dry, 270
Canel, 170
Cannondale Corporation, 168–169, 270
Canon, 46, 290
Capital Cities/ABC, 177
Cardinal Health, 34–35
Carnation, 310
carOrder.com, 161, C–103, C–114, C–127
CarParts.com, 227
Carrier, 295
Castrol, 204
Caterpillar, 45, 46, 163, 382
CBS, 178, 190, 303, 304
CBS Cable, 304
CBS Marketwatch.com, 304
CBS Television Network, 304
CDW Computer Centers, 430
Cessna Aircraft, 295
CFM International, 216
Chanel, 163
Charles Schwab & Co., 49, 163, 227, 239, 242, 245, 396
Chase Manhattan, 161, 229
Chemdex, 161
Chevron, 258–259, 362
Chicago Cutlery, 270
Chick-fil-A, 436
Chrysler Corporation, 177, 362
Cinzano, 295
Circuit City, 90
Cisco Systems, 177, 180, 183–184, 185, 226, 227, 235, 351, 352, 353, 354–355, 396

Citicorp, 35, 416
Citigroup, 35, 44
Classic Sports Network, 295
Clear Channel Communications, 177, 178
Cloud 9 Shuttle, 384
CMGI, 227, 303
CNBC, 329
CNET, 329
CNN, 166
Coca-Cola, 32, 43, 100, 109, 124, 133, 217–218, 258, 283, 304, 326, 363
Columbia, 310
Comair, 169
Comedy Central, 304
Commerce One, 227, 232
Community Pride Food Stores, 436
Compaq Computer, 28, 91, 160, 220, 231, 255, 268
CompuServe, 177, 192
Computer Associates, 392
Contadina, 310
Continental Airlines, 273, 274
Cooper Industries, 295
Cooper Tire, 155
Coors, 91, 416
Corel, 177
Corning Glass Corporation, 173
Country Music Television, 304
Covad, 236
Cray, 357
Critical Path, 227
Cross, 163
CyberCenters, 176

Daimler-Benz Aerospace, 216
Daimler-Benz AG, 177, 362
DaimlerChrysler AG, 92, 216
Darden Restaurants, 291
Deere & Company, 33
Degussa-Huls, 296
Dell Computer Corporation, 23, 90, 92, 139, 160, 176, 183, 194, 207, 227, 231, 232, 241, 255, 268, 288, 352, 353, 362, 435
Delta Airlines, 124, 163, 390

Deutsche Bank, 177
Deutsche Telecom, 173, 226
Diageo PLC, 67, 175, 295
Diamond, 295
DiaSorin, 296
Direct TV, 176
Disney Channel, 295
Disney Radio, 295
The Disney Store, 295
Dr. Pepper, 163
Domino's Pizza, 11, 133, 283, 391
Dom Perignon, 295
DoubleClick, 46, 193, 227, 352–353
Dow-Jones, 241
Dr Pepper, 270
Du Pont, 100

E!, 295
Eastman Kodak, 8, 124, 265, 362, 416
eBay, 156, 168, 176, 193, 227, 228, 243, 265
EDS (Electronic Data Systems), 24, 351
Edward Jones, 430
Electronic Arts, 227
Electronic Data Systems (EDS), 24, 351
Eli Lilly, 43
Eller Media Company, 178
E-Loan, 46, 227, 229
Emerson Electric, 289
Emery Worldwide, 159
EMusic.com, 227, 229
Engage Technologies, 227
Enron, 65
Enterprise Rent-A-Car, 169
Epic, 310
Ericcson, 84, 173
Ernest and Julio Gallo Winery, 362
ESPN, 295
e-Steel.com, 95
eToys, 124, 139, 239, 241
E*Trade Group, 46, 227, 239
Excite, 176, 242
Excite@Home, 243
Exodus Communications, 44, 241

Exxon Company International, 34, 362

Exxon/Mobil, 204

E-Z-Go, 295

Fairmarket, Inc., 176

Famous Players, 304

FDX Corporation, 36

FDX Global Logistics, 36

Federal Express, 36, 87, 95, 159, 163, 166, 232, 241, 250, 283, 391, 396, 397, 411

Federated Department Stores, 241

Fingerhut, 241

Ford Motor Company, 11, 86, 92, 100, 136, 157, 163, 177, 216, 218, 283, 362, 416

Formby's, 270

Fox Network, 178, 190

Frescarina, 295

Frito-Lay, 304

Fujitsu, 226

Fuji-Xerox, 135

Furniture.com, 227, 229

Galderma, 310

Gardner-Denver, 295

Gateway, 139, 176, 194, 207, 226, 255, 268, 350

GE, *See* General Electric Company

GE Medical Systems, 397

General Electric Company (GE), 44, 47, 100, 161, 173, 176, 216, 227, 289, 290, 318, 328, 328*n,* 329–331, 351, 352, 366, 381, 397, 410, 413, 430, 431

General Foods, 270, 290

General Mills, 396

General Motors, 34, 49, 100, 177, 216, 221, 416, 417

George Dickel, 295

Gerber, 283

Gilbey's, 295

The Gillette Company, 37–38, 265, 291

Glaxo, 139–140

Glen Ellen Wines, 295

Global Crossing, 226

Godiva Chocolatier, 170

Go Fly, Ltd., 26

Goodyear Tire & Rubber, 131

Gordon's, 295

Granite Rock Company, 382, 383, 430

Great Plains Software, 384, 385

Greenfield Online, 242

Green Giant, 295

Greyhound Corporation, 30

Gucci, 165

Guinness, 295

Häägen-Dazs, 170, 175, 260, 295

Hain, 270

Hallmark, 171, 243

Hamilton Substrand, 295

Hanson, PLC, 307

Harley-Davidson, 396

Harris Corporation, 380

HealthSouth, 270

Health Valley, 270

Heftel Broadcasting Co., 178

Heinz, 91, 270

Henessey, 295

Hewlett-Packard Co., 2, 42, 64, 91, 160, 176, 183, 220, 226, 231, 268, 304, 351, 382

Hi-C, 32

Hilton Hotels, 204, 206

History Channel, 329

Hollywood.com, 304

The Home Depot, 14, 34, 90, 155, 163, 262

Home Team Sports, 304

Honda, 46, 92, 123, 163, 212, 220, 290, 313, 314, 356, 357, 435

Hoover's, 329

Horizon, 169

Hughes Electronics, 176

Hughes Satellite, 173

IBM Corporation, 30, 176, 183, 220, 226, 227, 268, 415, 416, 418

Ideal Standard, 296

Imperial Chemical, 307

Infinity Broadcasting, 304

Ingram Micro, 18, 231, *231*

Inktomi, 193, 227, 237

Intel Corporation, 8, 39, 40, 89, 176, 180, 186, 187, 198, 202, 226, 227, 229, 264, 268, 356, 415

International Red Cross, 41

Internet Capital Group, 303

Iomega, 226, 275

Iowa Beef Packers, 159

iShip, 241

ITT, 307

i2 Technologies, 392

iVillage, 227, 329

J&B, 295

J.D. Edwards, 230

J.D. Power & Associates, 169

The J. M. Smucker Company, 24, 423, 425–426

Jacobsen, 295

Jaguar, 169, 177

JDS Uniphase, 35

Jeep, 169

Jiffy Lube International, 169

John Deere, *See* Deere & Company

John Hancock, 61

Johnny Walker, 295

Johnson & Johnson, 163, 176, 291, 422, 423

Jollibee Foods (Philippines), 220

Jose Cuervo, 295

Karastan, 163

Kellogg, 218

Kentucky Fried Chicken (KFC), 206, 262, 304

King World Productions, 304

Kinko's, 430

KLM Royal Dutch Airlines, 215

Kmart, 28, 289, 304, 416, 417

Koch Industries, 288

Komatsu, 45, 46

Kraft Foods, 177, 270, 290, 310

Kroger Company, 68, 416

L.L. Bean, 165

Lands' End, 34, 396

Lee Memorial Hospital, 367
Lenscrafters, 430
Levi Strauss & Company, 241, 265
Lexmark, 230
Lexus, 124, 177, 189
Libby's, 310
Lifetime Network, 295
The Limited, 34
Lincoln, 103, 124, 169
Lincoln Electric, 161, 397, 400
Listerine, 163
Lockheed Martin, 423, 424, 436, 437
Long John Silver's, 8
Lotus, 357
Lucent Technologies Inc., 226, 306
Lufkin, 295
Lycos, 176

McCormick & Company, 44
McDonald's, 14–15, 44, 163, 166,
    206, 209, 218, 220, 250, 265,
    283, 363, 382, 410, 430
McGraw-Hill Companies, 36, 241–242
McKinsey & Company, 264, 351,
    373, 397
Macromedia, 227
Macy's, 241
Malden Mills Industries, 436
Marks & Spencer, 326
Marlboro, 310
Marriott Corporation, 204
Marriott International, 430
Martha White, 295
Maruti-Suzuki (India), 218
Mary Kay Cosmetics (MKC), 104,
    270, 400, 420, 430
MasterCard, 241
Matsushita, 161
Matsushita/Panasonic, 226
Mazda, 136, 395, 396
MCI WorldCom, 173, 177
MediaOne, 36, 235, 288, 306
Medscape, 304
Medtronic, 397
MEMC Electronic Materials, 296
Mercedes-Benz, 103, 124, 163, 169,
    177

Merck, 35, 139–140, 176, 177, 396,
    397
Merrill Lynch, 49, 169, 239, 362
Metalsite.com, 95
Michelin, 131, 163
Micron Technology, 241
Microsoft Corporation, 4, 5, 8, 23, 92,
    163, 166, 173, 176, 177, 188,
    188n, 209, 220, 227, 229, 258,
    265, 267, 268, 329, 351, 380,
    396, 397, 410, 415
Microsoft Network (MSN), 242
Miller Brewing Company, 290, 310,
    363
Minute Maid, 32
Mr. Coffee, 289
Mrs. Fields Cookies, 382, 392
Mitsubishi, 301
MKC, See Mary Kay Cosmetics
Mobil, 34
Moët, 295
Monsanto, 397, 418
The More Group, 178
Morgan Stanley Dean Witter, 224
Mortgage.com, 46, 49, 139, 229
Motel 6, 170
MotherNature.com, 227
The Motley Fool, 227, 242
Motorola, 44, 84, 123, 161, 173, 176,
    218, 226, 389
The Movie Channel, 304
MP3.com, 237
MSN (Microsoft Network), 242
MSNBC, 329
MTV, 304
MTV2, 304
mtv.com, 304

Nabisco, 270
The Nashville Network, 304
NBC, 178, 188, 190
NBCi, 329
NBC Television Network, 329
NCR, 306
NEC, 226
Nestlé, 175, 177, 209, 310
Netscape, 188, 188n, 268

Newspaper Association of America,
    95
Nicholson, 295
nick.com, 304
Nickelodeon, 304
Nike, Inc., 46, 190, 351, 362
Nikki, 204
Nintendo, 227, 309, 313
Nissan, 164, 169, 216
Nokia Group, 24, 84, 173, 435
Nordstrom, 383, 396, 411
Northwest Airlines, 215
Northwest Water, 367
Novell, 177, 227
Nucor Steel Corporation, 153, 154,
    155, 161, 260, 400, 420

office.com, 304
Office Depot, 240
OfficeMax, 240, 304
Officesupplies.com, 240
Old El Paso, 295
Oldsmobile, 169
Oracle, 227, 232, 392
Otis Elevator, 8, 295, 301, 391

Pacific Corp., 28
Paine Webber, 239
Palm, 176
Palm Pilot, 306
Panasonic, 290
Paramount Home Video, 304
Paramount Pictures, 304
Paramount Television, 304
Patagonia, 270
Paxton Communication, 178
Pennzoil, 204
The Pep Boys—Manny, Moe, & Jack,
    9
PepsiCo, Inc., 109, 124, 148, 291,
    304, 326, 351, 363
Perrier, 310
Peugeot, 175
Pfizer, Inc., 37, 176, 423, 424–425
Philip Morris Companies, 109, 177,
    290, 310, 326
Philips Electronics, 226

Pier 1, 241

Pillsbury, 175, 270, 295

Pizza Hut, 206, 262, 304

PlayStation, 310

PMC Sierra, 226

Polaroid Corporation, 275, 362

Popov, 295

Porcher, 296

Porsche, 168

Portera Systems, 418

Pratt & Whitney, 176, 295

PreussenElektra, 296

Priceline.com, 193, 227, 240

Procter & Gamble, 91, 92, 177, 290, 351, 356, 396

Progresso, 295

Publix Supermarkets, 430

PurchasingCenter.com, 229

Quaker State, 204

Quote.com, 242

Qwest Communications, 173, 176, 226, 235

Ralph Lauren, 163

Ransomes, 295

Redhat Linux, 4, 5

Red Rocket, 304

Remington Products, 400

Renault, 175, 216

Rich's, 241

Ritz-Carlton Hotels, 8, 37, 64, 163, 170

Roberts Express®, 36

Rolex, 103, 163

Rolls-Royce, 165, 170, 176

Royal Dutch/Shell, 34, 264

RPS®, 36

Russell Corporation, 35

Rutherford Estates, 295

Rx.com, 304

St. Vincent's Hospital, 367

Samsung, 211, 310, 311

SAP, 227, 232, 392

SAS Airlines, 433

SBC Communications, 226, 235

Schindler, 301

Seagate Technology, 226

Sears, 369n, 416, 417

Sega, 309, 313

Seibel Systems, 227

Sempra Energy, 61

7-Eleven, 262

7UP, 326

SGI, 184

Sharp Corporation, 123

Shell Oil, 49, 100, 204

Sheraton, 204

Sherwin-Williams, 178

Showtime, 304

Siebel Systems, 392

Siemens, 310

Siemens-Nixdorf Information Systems, 434

Sikorsky, 295

Silicon Graphics, 183

Simon & Schuster, 304

Singapore Airlines, 124

Smart & Associates, 351

Smirnoff, 295

SmithKline Beecham, 426, 427

Snap.com, 329

SNECMA, 216

Softbank Corporation, 227, 303

Solectron Corp., 231, *231*

Solutia, 418

SonicNet.com, 304

Sony, 160, 227, 260, 309, 310, 312, 313, 435

Sony Classical, 310

Southwest Airlines, 26, 34, 124, 159–160, 283, 353, 390, 396, 400

Sports Authority, 304

Sportsline USA, 304

Springstreet, 240–241

Sprint, 177

Standard, 296

Standard & Poors, 242

Staples, 240

Starbucks Coffee, 23, 63, 265, 368, 430

Stinnes, 296

Stouffer's, 310

Stride Rite, 161

Subaru, 103

Sunbeam, 289

Sundaram Fasteners (India), 221

Sun Microsystems, 92, 226, 227, 418

Swift, 159

Taco Bell, 206, 262, 304, 363

Taiwan Semiconductor Manufacturing, 161

Talk City, 329

Tandata, 241

Tanqueray, 270, 295

Taster's Choice, 310

Tata Finance, 216

TCI (Tele-Communications Inc.), 36, 126, 235, 288, 306

TDI Outdoor Advertising, 304

Tele-Communications Inc., *See* TCI

Telescan, 329

Televisa (Mexico), 220

Tellabs, 396

Texaco, 416

Texas Instruments (TI), 226, 302, 362

Textron, Inc., 295

Textron Automotive, 295

Textron Fastening Systems, 295

Textron Financial Services, 295

TGE, 216

TheStreet.com, 227

Thomson, S.A., 198

3Com, 8, 124, 226

3M Corporation, 11, 163, 255–256, 370, 371, 381, 430, 435

TI, *See* Texas Instruments

Ticketmaster, 176

Tiffany & Co., 103, 165, 270

Time Warner, 16, 178, 235

Timex, 103, 283

Toon Disney, 295

Toshiba Corporation, 22, 124–125, 160, 226

Totino's, 295

Towers Perrin, 136

Toyota Motor Corporation, 33, 123, 169, 173, 177, 193, 194, 207, 216, 397

Toys "R" Us, 34, 124, 239, 436

Trader Joe's, 8, 170–171

Trane, 296

Tree of Life, 270

Tricon Global Restaurants, 206, 262

Trinitron, 310

Tupperware, 430

24/7 Media, 329

Unilever, 177, 218

United Airlines, 124, 390

United Cinemas, 304

United Parcel Service (UPS), 95, 176, 241, 391

United Technologies, Inc., 295

Universal Outdoor, 178

UPN TV, 178, 304

UPS, *See* United Parcel Service

U.S. Postal Service, 36, 87, 97, 391

U.S. Steel, 400

U.S. West, 235

USA Waste, 177

VEBA Electronics, 296

Veba Group, 296

VEBA Oel, 296

VEBA Telecom, 296

VH1, 304

vh1.com, 304

Viacom, 177, 303, 304

Viacom/CBS, 178

Viking Freight, 36

Virginia Slims, 310

Visa, 241

Vist, 220–221

Viterra, 296

Vodaphone AirTouch PLC, 216, 226

Volkswagen, 164

Volvo, 175

The Wall Street Journal, 241, 242

Wal-Mart Stores, 14, 34, 45–46, 50, 64, 90, 91, 92, 103, 124, 155, 160–161, 163, 212, 239, 241, 265, 283, 289, 391, 400, 410, 420, 430, 431

Walt Disney Company, 177, 178, 227, 295, 430

Warner-Lambert, 176

Waste Management, 177

Waterhouse, 239

Webvan Group, 239

Wells Fargo, 50, 161, 229

Westinghouse, 307

Weyerhaeuser Company, 95

Whirlpool, 161

Whole Foods Markets, 397

Wilson, 159

WingspanBank.com, 50–51

Wit Capital, 8

W.L. Gore & Associates, 24, 170, 397, 400, 430, 435

WordPerfect, 177

WorldCom, 177, 226

Xerox Corporation, 46, 135, 283, 378, 417

XOOM.com, Inc., 329

Yahoo!, 46, 156, 190, 193, 227, 242, 245

Yamaha, 46, 260, 261

SUBJECT

Accounting, traditional, 133, *134*

Acquisitions, *See* Mergers and acquisitions

Action plans, 56

Activities, in mission statement, 34

Activity-based costing, 133, *134*

Adaptive cultures, 417–419

Adaptive strategy, *See* Reactive strategy

Administrative support activities, 290–291

Advertising in e-commerce, 238

Aggressive posture, 83, 276–277

Asset-reduction strategies, 272

Attractiveness-strength matrix, 327–328, *328,* 328*n*

Authority:
    for decision making, 368
    for employees, 366–370

Backward integration:
    competitive advantage and, 180, 181–182
    as competitive pressure, 91

Bargaining power, 88–92

Barriers to entry, *See* Entry barriers

Benchmarking:
    cost position, 133
    of costs of key activities, 134–137
    ethical conduct and, 137
    example of, 136
    strategy implementation and, 383–385

Benefit period, for competitive advantage, 185, *186*

Best-cost provider strategies, 150, *151,* 152*t,* 167–168, 169, 195
    global, 205

Best practices, 135, 136, 404–405
    benefits of, 388–390
    examples of, 384–385

Better-off test, of diversification, 285

Beverage industry, *See* Food and beverage industry

BHAGs (big, hairy, audacious goals), 45, 45*n*

Big, hairy, audacious goals (BHAGs), 45, 45*n*

Board of directors, role in strategy crafting, 27–28

Boundaryless organization, 330

Brand names, multinational diversification and, 312

Brand preferences, as entry barrier, 85

"Brick-and-click" strategies, for Internet economy, 239, 240

Broad differentiation strategy, 150, 152*t*

Budgets, strategy implementation and, 380–381, 404

Buildup period, for competitive advantage, 185, *186*

Business base, 316
    broadening, 302–304
    narrowing, 304–306

Business definition, broad or narrow, 35–37

Business environment:
    causes of change in, 93–100
    changing strategy and, 13–14, 16–17, *17*

Businesses, *See* Companies

Business-level strategy, crafting, 49, *54,* 54–56

Business mix, restructuring, 306–307

Business model(s):
    comparison of, 5
    defined, 3–4, 5
    five-forces model, 79–80, *81,* 92
    strategy as, 48

Business models for Internet economy, 233–243
    "brick-and-click" strategies, 239, 240

Business models for Internet—*Cont.*
    communications equipment suppliers, 234–235
    communications services suppliers, 235–236
    e-commerce services suppliers, 239–242
    hardware suppliers, 236
    media companies and content providers, 242–243
    retailers, 237–239
    software developers, 236–237
    traditional businesses, 243–244

Business philosophies:
    corporate culture and, 410
    role in strategy crafting, 62–63, 63*n*

Business position, *See* Strategic performance

Business process reengineering, *See* Process reengineering

Business-to-business merchants, 237–239

Business-to-business relationships, 92

Business-to-consumer merchants, 237–239

Business units:
    of diversified firms
        competitive strength of, 324–328, 331–332
        cross-unit coordination, 370, 371
        managing, 329–331
        performance and prospects of, 336–337
        priorities and direction for, 337–338
        ranking, 336–337, 342
        resource fits and, 332–336

Buyers:
    changes in buyer demographics, 96
    changes in preferences, 97–98
    enhancing satisfaction of, 165

Note: Page numbers in *italics* indicate illustrations; those followed by *t* indicate tables; those followed by *n* indicate footnotes.

Buyers:—*Cont.*
　first-time buyers, 250, 252
　maturing industries and, 257
　online, bargaining power of, 229
　seller-buyer relationships, 90–92
　See also Customer(s)

Cable TV companies, 235–236
Capabilities, *See* Competitive
　　capabilities
Capacity utilization, cost control and,
　　156
Capital requirements:
　in e-commerce, 232–233
　as entry barrier, 85
Cash cows, 333–334
Cash hogs, 333
CEO, *See* Chief executive officer
Change:
　adaptation to, 49
　in business environment, causes of,
　　93–100
　in corporate culture, 432–434
　high-velocity markets, 252–256,
　　254, 372–373
　hostility to, 416
　rapid, 173, 418
　strategic posture and, 16–17, *17*
Chief architect approach, 23, 25
Chief executive officer (CEO):
　chief architect approach of, 23, 25
　ethical standards and, 435–436
　evaluation by directors, 28
　as strategy manager, 21, 22
Clustering, 77, 77*n*
Codes of ethics, 421–422, 423
Collaboration:
　approach to strategy crafting,
　　24–25, 26
　competitive pressure and, 88, 92
　partnerships; *See* Strategic alliances
Combination strategies, 273
Command-and-control paradigm,
　　366–367
Communication:
　formal (written), 18, 41
　of strategic vision, 40–41, 41*n*

Communications, electronic,
　　226–227
　equipment suppliers, 234–235
　hardware suppliers, 236
　services suppliers, 235–236
　software developers, 236–237
Community, ethical duty to, 67
Companies:
　as coordinated whole, 4
　culture of; *See* Corporate culture
　diversified; *See* Diversification;
　　Diversified firms
　framework for strategy crafting,
　　277–278, 278*t*
　industry leaders, strategies for,
　　265–267
　Internet strategies for, 243–244
　local, *219,* 219–221
　multinational; *See* Multinational
　　corporations (MNCs)
　ownership structure of, C–603
　rapid growth, sustaining, 263–265,
　　265
　runner-up firms, strategies for,
　　267–271
　smaller; *See* Single-business
　　enterprises
　strengths and capabilities of, 62
Companies in crisis, 271–275
　corporate culture and, 412
　end-game strategies for, 273–275
　liquidation, 273
　turnaround strategies, 271–273
Company situation analysis, *See*
　　Situation analysis
Company-specific strategy, 12
Company value chains, *See* Value
　　chains
Compensation:
　in incentive systems, 402–403
Competencies, *See* Core
　　competencies
Competition:
　competitive conditions, 61
　global, 201, 204, 221
　international, 200, 257, 373
　maturing industries and, 256, 257
　multicountry, 203–204

Competitive advantage, 148–197
　competencies and capabilities,
　　211–212
　competitive strategies and,
　　150–172, *151, 152t*
　cooperative strategies and, 172–177
　cross-border activities and, 212
　of cross-business strategic fits, 53
　in cross-company rivalry, 82
　defensive strategies to protect,
　　191–193
　differentiation strategies and,
　　163–167, 195
　in diversified companies, 280–317
　dominating depth and, 357
　example of, 314
　of first-movers, 193–194
　in global markets, 209–212, 222
　locational advantages, 210–211
　merger and acquisition strategies,
　　176–178, 179, 196
　multinational diversification and,
　　308–315
　offensive strategies for, 185–191,
　　186, 196–197
　potential for, analysis of, 330–332,
　　332
　for single-business firms, *54,* 55–56
　sustainable, 276
　unbundling and outsourcing
　　strategies, 182–185, 196
　vertical integration/deintegration,
　　178–182, 196
Competitive advantage test, 69
Competitive capabilities, 122
　boundary decisions and, 184–185
　cross-border transfer of, 211–212
　developing, 357–358, 435
　differentiation and, 165–166, 195
　evaluation of; *See* Situation analysis
　for maturing industries, 258–259
　in organization-building, 350,
　　355–359, 375
　role in strategy crafting, 62
　as strength, 118
　strengthening, 357–358
　updating and reshaping, 358–359
　value chain activities and, 139–140

Competitive forces, 79–92, *81,* 111
 rivalry, 81–84, 103
 seller-buyer relationships, 90–92
 strategic group mapping of, 101, *102, 103*
 strategic implications of, 92–93
 substitute products, 87–88
 supplier-seller relationships, 88–90
 threat of entry, 84–87
Competitive intelligence:
 evaluating positions, 104–105
 monitoring strategies, 103–104, 105*t*
 predicting moves, 105–106
Competitive position, 140, 141*t*
 enhancing, 276
 strength assessments, 140–143, 142*t,* 146
Competitive strategies, 150–172, *151,* 152*t*
 best-cost provider strategies, *151,* 167–168, 195
 differentiation strategies, 163–167
 focused strategies, 168–172, 195–196
 low-cost provider strategies, 150, 151, 153–163, 194–195
Competitive strength assessment:
 for diversified firms, 319, 324–328, 331–332, 341
 nine-cell matrix for, 327–328, *328,* 328*n*
 rating systems, 141–143, 142*t,* 326–327, 326*t,* 327*n*
Competitors:
 international v. global, 200
 number and size of, 82–83
 predicting actions of, 105–106
 strengths of, exceeding, 186–187
 weaknesses of, 187–188
Compromise, avoiding, 276
Constituencies, *See* Stakeholders
Content followers, 271
Content providers, business models for, 242–243
Content of strategies, 12–13, *13*

Continuous improvement programs:
 benefits of, 388–390
 example of, 389
 TQM and, 387, 387*t*
Cooperative strategies, 172–177
Core competencies, 122
 building, 55–56
 cross-border transfer of, 211–212
 developing and strengthening, 356–357
 in e-commerce, 244
 as entry barriers, 86
 global markets and, 200
 kinds of, 120, 122–123
 in organization-building, 350, 355–359, 375
 role in strategy crafting, 62
 in SWOT analysis, 120, 122–125
 updating and reshaping, 358–359
Core values, 417
Corporate citizenship:
 considerations in strategy crafting, 59–61
 ethical duty to community, 67
 leadership in, 435–436
 social responsibility and, 436
Corporate culture, 19, 410, 438, 439
 adaptive, 417–419
 changing, 419–421
 cultural fit and, 305
 effects on strategy crafting, 63–64
 ethics and, 421–428, 422*t,* 429
 example of, 411
 leadership and, 432–434
 in multinational companies, 433–434
 origins of, 410–413
 perpetuating, 411–412
 policies and procedures and, 382
 spirit of high performance in, 428, 430
 strategy, strong fit with, 419–421
 strategy execution and, 413–414
 strategy-supportive, 410–430
 strong v. weak, 414–416
 total quality culture, 390
 turnaround strategy and, 274
 unhealthy, 416–417

Corporate intrapreneur approach, 25, 26–27
Corporate restructuring, 306–308, 317
Corporate strategy:
 crafting, 49, 50–51, *53,* 53–54, 338–341
 diversification opportunities, 340
 of diversified firms, 319, 320, *321*
 managing crafting process, 340–341
 performance test and, 338–339
 uniting strategic plans, 57–58, *59*
 See also Strategy(ies)
Corrective actions, 437–438
Cost(s):
 analyzing; *See* Strategic cost analysis
 benchmarking, 134–137
 changes in, 97
 competitiveness in, achieving, *130,* 137–139, 146
 cost disadvantages as entry barrier, 85
 locational advantages in, 211
 reducing, 258, 361
 See also Value chains
Cost competitiveness:
 achieving, *130,* 137–139
 in global markets, *200*
Cost control and reduction:
 cost drivers, 153–157
 turnaround strategies, 272–273, 274
Cost disadvantages, as entry barrier, 85
Cost drivers, controlling, 153–157
Cost-of-entry test, 285, 298, 300
Cost position, comparisons of, 133–134
Countercyclical diversification, 297
Courses of action, in strategic vision, 33
Credit card services, 241–242
Crosby's 14 quality steps (TQM), 386*t*
Cross-border activities:
 coordinating, 212
 culture-change activities, 433–434
 Internet and, 229

Cross-border activities:—*Cont.*
  transfer of core competencies, 211–212
Cross-company rivalry, 81–84
Cross-country differences, 201–203
  exchange rate fluctuations, 202–203
  in governmental restrictions, 203
  locational advantages, 202
Cross-market subsidization, 213
Cross-subsidization, 313, 315
Cross-unit coordination, 370, 371
Cultural fit, 305
Culture (cultural diversity):
  corporate; *See* Corporate culture
  foreign alliances and, 216
Currency exchange rates, 202–203
Customer(s):
  in e-commerce, 243
  in emerging-country markets, 218
  ethical duty to, 66
  in global markets, 200
  loyalty of, as entry barrier, 85
  major, 89
  maturing industries and, 258
  needs of, in mission statement, 34
  substitute products and, 88
  in value chain, 131, *132*
  See also Buyers
Customer service:
  Internet and, 232
  organization structure and, 365
Customization, for foreign markets, 201–202

Data, developing, 133–134, 134*t*
Decision making:
  authority for, 368
  boundary decisions, 184–185
  cost control and, 156–157
  process of, foreign alliances and, 217
Declining industries, 259–260
Defensive strategies, 191–193
  blocking challengers, 192
  retaliation, signaling, 192–193
Defensive strategy, 55, 62

Delegate/delegation approach, 23–24, 25–26
Delphi method, 100
Demand for product, rivalry and, 83
Deming's 14 points (TQM), 386*t*
Differentiation strategies, 163–167, 195
  broad strategies, 150, 152*t*
  competitive advantage and, 165–166
  controlling costs of, 166
  in declining industries, 260
  distinctive image strategy, 270
  focused strategies, 152*t*, 160, 170–171
  global, 205
  perceived v. signaling value, 166, 166*n*
  performance-enhancing, 165
  pitfalls of, 167
  timing of use, 166–167
  types of, 163–164
Digital signal line (DSL) technology, 235
Direction, 33, 337–338
Direction-setting tasks, 20, 30–70
  ethics and social responsibility in, 64–68
  objective setting in, 41–48
  situational factors in, 58–64, *60*
  strategic vision, 32–41
  strategy crafting in, 48–58
  tests of winning strategy, 68–69
Distinctive competencies, 122–123
Distinctive image strategy, 270
Distribution activities:
  diversification and, 289
  in organization structure, 364
Distribution channels:
  access to, as entry barrier, 86
  forward channel value chains, 131–132, 138
  Internet technology in, 243, 244
  upstream (supplier) costs, 138
Diversification, 282–284
  achieving, 50–51
  examples of, 288, 291, C–223 to C–224

Diversification—*Cont.*
  multinational; *See* Multinational diversification
  opportunities in, 308–315, 340
  rushing, risks of, 283
  shareholder value and, 284–285
  signals for, 284
  tests for, 284–285
  See also Related diversification; Unrelated diversification
Diversified firms, 280–317
  broadening business base of, 302–304
  business definitions of, 36
  business units of; *See* Business units
  corporate restructuring in, 306–307, 317
  decentralizing, problems of, 369
  multinational, 308–315
  strategies of
    competitive strength tests, 319, 324–328, 331–332, 341
    corporate strategy, 50–51, *53*, 53–54
    divestiture strategies, 304–306
    evaluating, 318–342
    example of, 329–331
    identifying present strategy, 320, *321*
    industry attractiveness tests, 321–324
    ranking business units, 336–337
    resource allocation in, 337–338
    resource fit analysis, 332–336
    strategic fit analysis, 330–332, *332*
    strategy crafting, 281–282, 338–341
    strategy-making pyramid, *52*
    strategy options, 302–315, *303*
    turnaround strategies, 307–308
  strategy managers in, 23–24
  See also Diversification
Diversity, rivalry and, 83–84
Divestiture(s):
  accomplishing, 305–306

Divestiture(s):—*Cont.*
  reasons for, 304–305, 337
  as strategy, 339
Dominance, achieving, 357
Dot-com companies:
  as adaptive cultures, 417–418
  entrepreneurship of, 16
  See also E-commerce
Driving forces, 93–99, 111–112
  environmental scanning of,
    99–100
  examples of, 95
  kinds of, 94, 96–99
  link with strategy, 99
  strategic group mapping of, 101,
    102, 103

E-business technologies, 157, 161
E-commerce, 16, 227
  diversification into, 303–304
  as driving force, 94
  order-fulfillment services for, 241
  strategy-shaping characteristics of,
    227–229, 231–233
  support systems in, 392
  See also Dot-com companies;
    Internet
Economic features of industry:
  causes of change in, 93–100
  industry and competitive analysis
    of, 76, 77–79, 78*t, 79,* 80*t,* 111
Economic value added (EVA), 9–10,
  9*n,* 43*n*
Economies of scale, 291
  as entry barrier, 84–85
  locational advantages and, 210
  multinational diversification and,
    309
  strategic alliances and, 214
Economies of scope:
  multinational diversification and,
    309
  strategic fits and, 291–292
Efficiency, changes in, 97
Egalitarianism, 397
Electronic value chain, 245
E-markets, 239–242

Emerging-country markets, 222–223
  competing in, 217–218
  local company strategies in, *219,*
    219–221
Emerging industries, strategy for,
  250–252
Employees:
  authority and independence for,
    366–370
  ethical duty to, 66
  MBWA and, 431–432
  motivational practices and, 395–399
  nurturing, 434–435
  recruitment of; *See* Recruitment
  training; *See* Training
  treatment of, 428, 430
  See also Empowerment; Human
    resources
Employment security, 395–396
Empowerment, 368–369
  controlling, 394–395
  organizational responsiveness and,
    434–435
  strategy implementation and, 390,
    393, 393*n*
End-game strategies, 273–275
End-run offensive strategies, 188–189
Enterprise resource planning (ERP)
  software, 230
Entrepreneurship, of managers,
  strategy and, 13–16
Entry:
  by diversified firms, 281
  into foreign markets, 204–207, 208
  of major firms, 97
  threat of, 84–87
Entry barriers, 84–87
  in e-commerce, 228–229
  in emerging industries, 250
Environmental scanning, 99–100
Erosion period, for competitive
  advantage, 185–186, *186*
ERP (enterprise resource planning)
  software, 230
Ethics:
  benchmarking, 137
  codes of, 421–422, 423

Ethics:—*Cont.*
  in corporate culture, 421–428, 422*t,*
    429
  enforcement procedures, 427–428
  ethical beliefs of managers, 62–63,
    63*n*
  examples of, 424–426
  proactive behavior and, 67–68
  strategic leadership in, 435–436,
    437
  in strategy crafting, 61, 64–68
  test of, 429
EVA (economic value added), 9–10,
  9*n*
Evaluation/measurement:
  competitor, evaluating, 104–105,
    105*t*
  of executives, 28
  performance evaluation, 19–20
  of prices and costs, 128–140
  in strategic vision, 33
  of strategies of diversified firms,
    318–342
Exit, of major firms, 97
Exit barriers, rivalry and, 83
Expansion:
  by diversified business units, 337
  into global markets, 200
  by maturing industries, 258
Experience curve effects, 78–79, *79,*
  79*n,* 80*t*
  in emerging industries, 250
  as entry barrier, 85
  locational advantages and, 210
  multinational diversification and,
    309
Expertise:
  cross-unit collaboration and, 371
  of local companies, 220
  mergers and acquisitions for, 234
  as strength, 117–118
  See also Technical knowledge
Export market, *See* Global markets
Export strategies, global, 205–206
External factors:
  in direction setting, 59–64, *60*
  in strategy crafting, 62

External relationships:
  seller-buyer, 90–92
  supplier-seller, 88–90

Financial incentives, 395, 396
Financial objectives, 9–10, 11, 69
  examples of, 44
  setting, 42–45, 42n
  strategic objectives compared, 43, 45
Financial performance, See Profitability
Financial resources:
  achieving dominance and, 357
  unrelated diversification and, 296, 298–299
Financial VP, role of, 21
First-mover advantages, 193–194
  in e-commerce, 238, 242
  for emerging industries, 251
Five-forces model, 79–80, 81, 92
Five-task process, See Managerial tasks
Focused strategies, 105t, 168–172, 195–196
  attractiveness of, 171
  in declining industries, 259–260
  differentiation strategy, 150, 152t, 170–171
  in e-commerce, 239
  global, 205
  lower-cost strategy, 150, 152t, 169–170
  risks of, 171–172
  vacant-niche strategy, 270
Followers, 193, 271
Foreign markets, See Global markets
Formal (written) communication, 18, 41
"Formula" facilities, 262
Fortify-and-defend strategy, 266–267, 271, 337
Forward channel value chains, 131–132, 138
Forward integration, 180–181
Fragmented industries, strategies for, 261–263
Franchising, 14, 205, 206

Full vertical integration, 179
Fully integrated firms, 34
Functional area managers, 22, 56–57
Functional departments:
  mission statements for, 37–38
  role of, 364
  strategy crafting for, 49, 56–57
Functional strategy, crafting, 49, 56–57

Global business leaders, 172, 174, 178
Global competition, 201, 204
  multicountry competition and, 203–204
  situational factors in, 200, 221
Globalization, 94, 96, 199
Global markets, 198–223
  competitive advantage in, 209–212
  cross-country differences in, 201–203
  emerging-country markets, 217–218
  entering and competing in, 200, 204–207, 208t
  export strategies, 205–206
  Internet and, 227–228
  joint ventures in, 301–302
  multicountry v. global competition, 203–204
  organizational approaches for, 373
  profit sanctuaries in, 213
  race for leadership in, 172, 174, 178
  rivalry in, 84
  strategic alliances in, 213–217
Global strategy, in foreign markets, 205, 206–207, 208t
Goals, See Objectives
Goodness of fit test, 68–69
Government, 22, 98, 203
Growth of company:
  examples of strategy for, 14, 263–265, 265
  multinational diversification and, 308–315
  rapid, sustaining, 263–265, 265
  via acquisitions, 269–270

Guerilla offensives, 189

Harvesting, 273–275, 337
Hidden strategy, 12–13
High-velocity marketplace, 252–256, 254
High-velocity markets, 252–256, 254, 372–373
Hostile takeover, 300, 300n
Human assets, 118
Human resources:
  in e-commerce, 233
  personnel strategy, example of, 15
  See also Employees; Recruitment; Training

Identity, in strategic vision, 33
Improvement programs, 19
Incentive systems, 405
  financial incentives, 395, 396
  guidelines for compensation, 402–403
  low-cost provider strategies and, 400
  in multinational firms, 403–404
  nonmonetary incentives, 395, 396–397, 398
  See also Reward systems
Industry(ies):
  changes in growth rate, 96
  declining, 259–260
  defined, 77–79, 78t, 79, 80t
  economic features of, 76, 77–79, 78t, 79, 80t, 111
  emerging, strategy for, 250–252
  fragmented, 261–263
  framework for strategy crafting, 277–278, 278t
  market opportunities for, 126
  maturing, strategies for, 256–259
  value chains varied in, 130, 132, 132–133
Industry and competitive analysis, 72–74, 74, 75, 111–112
  of attractiveness and potential, 108–109
  competitive forces, role of, 79–93
  competitive intelligence, 103–106

Industry and competitive analysis—
Cont.
  driving forces, role of, 93–100
  economic features of industries, 76,
    77–79, 78*t, 79, 80t,* 111
  findings of, format for, 109–111,
    110*t*
  key success factors, 106, 107*t,* 108
  methods of, 76, 111
  strategic group mapping, 100–103
Industry attractiveness:
  analysis of, 108–109
  competitive forces and, 92
  strategy crafting and, 61
Industry attractiveness tests:
  for diversification, 285, 298
  for diversified firms, 319, 321–324,
    341
  of individual industries, 322
  mix of industries, 324
  nine-cell matrix for, 327–328, *328,*
    328*n*
  rating systems, 323–324, 323*t*
  relative attractiveness, 323–324
Industry conditions, rivalry and, 83
Industry leaders, strategies for,
  265–267
Industry value chains, *110,* 131–133
  reconfiguring, 230, 231, 292
  variation in, *130, 132,* 132–133
Inflection points, 39, 40
Infomediaries, 239–242
Information systems, as support
  system, 393–394
Information technology (IT),
  outsourcing, 237
Innovation:
  empowered employees and,
    434–435
  in marketing, 97
  in products, 96, 256
  in value chains, 257–258
Intangible assets, 118
Internal communication systems,
  391
Internal factors:
  in direction setting, 62–64, 70
  high costs and, 139

International competition, 200,
  203–204, 257, 373
Internet:
  cross-border activities and, 212
  as driving force, 94, 95
  effect on organization structure, 368
  importance of, 225, 246
  online banking, 50
  organization structure and, 365
  in support systems, 391–392,
    393–394
  use of, 16
  See also E-commerce
Internet economy, 224–246
  business models and strategies,
    233–243
  characteristics of, 227–229,
    231–233
  key success factors in, 244–245
  strategy modification and, 18
  supply side of, 226–227
  traditional businesses and, 243–244
"Internet speed," 418
Investments, by diversified firms,
  53–54, 282
IT, *See* Information technology

Joint ventures:
  in global markets, 213–217
  new businesses, 301–302
Juran trilogy (TQM), 386*t*

Key activities, costs of, 134–137
Key resource inputs, costs of, 155
Key success factors (KSFs), 106,
  107*t,* 108, 112
  competitive position and, 141
  in e-commerce, 244–245
Knowledge, specialized, 85
KSFs (key success factors), 106, 107*t,*
  108, 112

Last-mile providers, 235–236
Late movers, 193–194
Leadership, *See* Strategic leadership
Learning curve effects, 210
Learning process, 217

Leveraged buyout, 306
Licensing, foreign, 205, 206
Life-cycle hypothesis, 93, 93*n*
Local companies, *219,* 219–221
  evading global entrants, 220–221
  expertise of, 220
  in global competition, 221
  home-field advantage, 219–220
Location, geographic:
  changing, 155, 188–189
  cross-country differences and, 202
  e-commerce and, 228, 229
  fragmented industries and, 263
  locational advantages, 210–211
Location/construction strategy, 14
Location variables, 155
Long-range objectives, 10, 42*n,* 43,
  45, 46
Low-cost provider strategies, 150,
  151, 152*t,* 153–163, 194–195
  achieving success with, 160–161
  cost advantage, achieving, 153–157
  in declining industries, 260
  example of, 154
  focused strategies, 150, 152*t,*
    169–170
  for fragmented industries, 262–263
  global, 205
  incentive systems and, 400
  pitfalls of, 162–163
  timing of use, 161–162
  value chain revamping, 157, *158,*
    159–160

Macroenvironment, 73, *74*
Made-to-order products, 97–98
Major customers, 89
Major suppliers, 89
Malcolm Baldrige National Quality
  Award, 383, 387
Management:
  in adaptive cultures, 418–419
  arrogance of, 416–417
  daily responsibilities of, 20
  direction-setting tasks of; *See*
    Direction-setting tasks
  in emerging-country markets, 218

Management:—*Cont.*
  importance of strategy to, 4–6
  incentive compensation for, 402
Management by walking around
  (MBWA), 431–432
Management team:
  approach to strategy crafting,
    24–25, 26
  forming, 331
  implementing strategy, 346–347,
    374
  self-managed teams, 397
  strength of, 350–351
Managerial decisions, cost control
  and, 156–157
Managerial tasks, 6–20, *7*
  building total quality culture, 390
  direction-setting; *See* Direction-
    setting tasks
  diversification and, 290
  evaluation and adjustment, 19–20
  objective setting, 9–10, 11
  strategic leadership, 4
  strategic vision, development of,
    6–7, 8
  strategy crafting, 10–18, *12*
  in strategy implementation; *See*
    Strategy implementation
  top-down guidance, 381–382
Managers:
  effects on strategy crafting, 62–63
  ethical beliefs of, 62–63, 63*n*
  levels of, 22, 58
  role in strategy implementation; *See*
    Strategy implementation
  strategy making role, 21
  See also Functional area managers;
    Operating unit managers
Manufacturers, pursuit of alliances,
  175
Manufacturing:
  diversification and, 288–289
  effect of Internet on, 231, *231*
  locational advantages and, 210
Manufacturing capability, 107*t*
Manufacturing execution system
  (MES) software, 230
Manufacturing share, 210

Market advantage, 118
Market conditions:
  adaptation to, 15–16
Marketing:
  direct-to-end-user, 157, *158,* 160
  diversification and, 289–290
  innovation in, 97
  as key success factor, 107*t*
  techniques for e-commerce, 157,
    158, 160
Marketing VP, role of, 21
Market-niche strategies, *See* Focused
  strategies
Market opportunities:
  global markets, 201
  identifying, 121*t,* 125–127
  strategy crafting and, 62
Marketplace:
  as economic battlefield, 82
  high-velocity, strategies for,
    252–256, *254*
  strategic positioning in, 39, 39*n*
Market segmentation declining
  industries and, 260, 261M
Market share, relative, 324–325, *325,*
  325*n*
Market value added (MVA), 10, 10*n,*
  43*n*
Maturing industries, 256–259
MBWA (management by walking
  around), 431–432
Media companies, business models
  for, 242–243
Mergers and acquisitions:
  acquisition of existing business,
    299–300
  corporate culture and, 412–413
  example of, 179
  growth through, 269–270
  hostile takeover, 300, 300*n*
  maturing industries and,
    257, 258
  rivalry and, 84
  strategies for, 176–178, 176*n,* 179,
    196
  for technological expertise, 234
MES (manufacturing execution
  system) software, 230

Mission statement(s):
  business definition in, 35–37
  defined, 6, 7
  elements of, 34–35
  examples of, 8, 37–38
  for functional departments, 37–38
  profit and, 33
  roles of, 32–38
  strategic vision compared, 6–7, 8,
    38–39
Mix of industries, attractiveness of,
  324
MNCs, *See* Multinational
  corporations
Motivation, 19
  corporate culture and, 413–414
  strategic vision and, 40–41, 41*n*
Motivational practices, 395–399, 406
Multi-business enterprises, *See*
  Diversified firms
Multicountry strategy:
  examples of, 209
  in foreign markets, 205, 206–207,
    208*t,* 221–222
Multinational competition, 200,
  203–204, 257, 373
Multinational corporations (MNCs):
  corporate culture of, 412–413,
    433–434
  cross-subsidization in, 313, 315
  diversified, 308–315
  incentive systems in, 403–404
Multinational diversification, 308,
  317
  brand names and, 312
  combined advantages of, 313, 315
  competitive advantage and,
    308–309
  economies of scale and, 309
  economies of scope and, 309
  examples of, 310–311
  rivalry and, 313
  transfer of resources in, 311–312
  See also Diversification
Municipal government, 22
Muscle-flexing strategy, 267, 268
Mutual benefit, foreign alliances and,
  216

MVA (market value added), 10, 10*n*

New businesses, 316
  acquisition of existing business, 299–300
  adding, 339
  internal start-up, 300–301
  joint ventures, 301–302
Nine-cell matrix, 327–328, *328, 328n*
No-frills products/services, 157, 159–160
Nonmonetary incentives, 395, 396–397, 398
Not-for-profit organizations, 22

Objectives:
  goals compared, 42*n*
  setting, 9–10, 11, 20
  See also Financial objectives; Strategic objectives
Objective setting:
  examples of, 44
  kinds of objectives, 42–45, 42*n*
  long- and short-range, 46
  reasons for, 41–42
  strategic intent and, 45–46, 45*n*
  stretch in, 46–47
  top-down, 47–48
Offensive strategies, 55, 62, 196–197
  to build market share, 269
  for businesses in crisis, 271
  choosing targets of, 190–191
  competitor strengths, exceeding, 186–187
  competitor weaknesses, using, 187–188
  cross-market subsidization, 213
  end-runs, 188–189
  guerilla offensives, 189
  for high-velocity markets, 253
  for industry leaders, 266
  preemptive strikes, 189–190
  simultaneous initiatives, 188
  timeline for, 185–186, *186*
Offensive strategy, 55, 62
Online banking industry, 50

Online brokerage firms, *See* Brokerage firms, online
Operating strategy, 15, 50, 57
Operating unit managers, 22, 57, 349
Opportunity(ies):
  for diversification, 308–315, 340
  opportunity sharing, cost control and, 155–156
  in SWOT analysis, 121*t*, 125–127
  See also Market opportunities
Order-fulfillment services:
  for e-commerce, 241
  as key success factor, 107*t*
  in organization structure, 364
Organizational assets, 118
Organizational behavior, proactive, ethics and, 67–68
Organizational capability, 107*t*
Organizational culture, *See* Corporate culture
Organizational learning, 20, 78–79, *79,* 79*n,* 80*t*
Organizational levels, objectives for, 47–48
Organizational responsiveness, 434–435
Organizational stretch, 46–47
Organizational structure, 350, 359–372, *360,* 375–376
  centralized or decentralized, 366–368, 369
  collaboration with outsiders and, 371
  cross-unit coordination in, 370, 371
  employee independence in, 366–370
  future trends in, 372–374
  outsourcing and, 361–362, 362*n*
  perspectives on, 372
  strategic alliances and, 362–363
  strategy-critical activities, 359–361, 363–366, 363*n*
Organization building, 19, 349–372, *350,* 374–375
  core competencies in, 350, 355–359
  staffing, 349, 350–355
  structuring, 350, 359–372, *360*

Outsourcing, 182–184, 196
  advantages of, 184–185
  competitive capabilities and, 358, 361–362, 362*n,* 375
  cost control and, 156
  high-velocity markets and, 255
  of information technology (IT), 237
  non-critical value chain activities, 361–362, 362*n*
Overhaul-and-reposition strategy, 337
Owners, *See* Shareholders

Partially integrated firms, 34
Partial vertical integration, 179
Partnerships, collaborative; *See* Strategic alliances
  strategy managers in, 22
Payoffs:
  rivalry and, 83
  of vision statement, 41
Peer-based systems:
  controlling empowered employees, 394–395
  corporate culture and, 413
  motivational, 397
Perceived value, 166, 166*n*
Performance:
  boosting, 281
  of business units, 336–337
  lowering objectives, 339
  problems with, strategy and, 4–6
  spirit of high performance, 428, 430
  strategy for diversified firms, 51
  stretch and, 46
  See also Profitability; Strategic performance
Performance evaluation, 19–20
Performance measures, 69
  in reward systems, 400
  in strategy crafting, 338–339
Performance outcomes, 399–404
Personal ambition, 62–63, 63*n*
Personnel, *See* Employees; Human resources
Physical assets, 118
Piecework plan, 397
Planned strategy, 10–12, *12*

Policies and procedures, 19
   strategy-supportive, 381–382, 404
Political considerations in strategy
   crafting, 59–61
Preemptive strikes, 189–190
"Prestige" buyers, 90–91
Prices:
   analyzing, 128–140, 147
   cutting, cautions in, 276
Proactivity:
   ethics and, 67–68
   in high-velocity markets, 255–256
Process departments, 364, 365–366
Process reengineering, 365–366
   example of, 366–367
   TQM contrasted, 388
Product(s):
   demand for, 83
   of diversified multinational
      companies, 314
   in e-commerce, 238
   innovation in, 96, 256
   made-to-order, 97–98
   marginal, pruning, 257
   new; See Product development
   simplifying design of, 157, 159
   substitute products, 87–88
   superior product strategy, 270
Product development, introducing
   new products, 188, 238
Production, one-country base,
   205–206
Production VP, role of, 21
Product line strategy, example of,
   14–15
Profit(s):
   industry attractiveness and, 86, 86n,
      87
   mission statement and, 33
Profitability, 9, 42
   analysis of, 108–109
   differences in, 103
   of diversified business units,
      336–337, 336n
   profit potential, 109
   strategic fits in, 334
   unrelated diversification and, 296

Profit sanctuaries, 213, 222
Promotion from within, 398

Quality improvement:
   in organization structure, 365
   programs, 330–331

R&D, See Research and development
   (R&D)
Rapid followers, 193
Rating systems:
   in competitive strength assessment,
      141–143, 142t, 326–327,
      326t, 327n
   in industry attractiveness tests,
      323–324, 323t
Reactive strategy, 10–12, 12
   adaptive cultures and, 418
   adjustments in, 16–17, 17
   prompt, 276
Recruitment:
   corporate culture and, 411–412
   examples of, 352–353, 354–355
   selectivity in, 351–355
Regulatory policies:
   changes in, 98
   as consideration in strategy crafting,
      59–61
   as entry barrier, 86
   governmental restrictions, 203
Related diversification, 285–286, 286,
      315–316
   benefits of, 292–293
   combination strategies, 299
   economies of scope and, 291–292
   opportunities in, 340
   strategic fit and, 286–287, 287
   value chain, strategic fits in,
      287–291
Relative attractiveness test, 323–324
Relative market share, 324–325, 325,
      325n
Research and development (R&D):
   in communications, 234
   in computer hardware, 236
   diversification and, 288
   high-velocity markets and, 254–255

Resource allocation, 19, 320,
   337–338, 342
Resource fit analysis:
   cash hogs and cash cows,
      333–334, 333n
   competitive and managerial
      resources, 334–336
   for diversified firms, 320,
      332–336, 342
Resources:
   competitive value of, 123–125
   disadvantages as entry barrier, 85,
      86
   of diversified firms, 282, 339
   evaluation of; See Situation
      analysis; SWOT analysis
   investments by diversified firms,
      53–54
   locational advantages and, 210–211
   matching strategy to, 125
   role in strategy crafting, 62
   transfer of, 311–312
   use of TQM as, 388
   See also Resource fit analysis
Response times:
   in high-velocity markets, 255
   Internet and, 229, 244
Restructuring strategies, 306–307, 317
Results, reward linked to, 401–402
Retailers, in e-commerce, 237–239,
   246
Retaliation, 192–193, 276–277
Revenue-increasing strategies, 272
Reward structure, 19
Reward systems, 395–404
   examples of, 398, 401
   motivational practices, 395–399
   performance outcomes and,
      399–404
   See also Incentive systems
Risk(s):
   attitudes toward, 63
   of diversification, 283
   of focused strategies, 171–172
   of foreign strategic alliances,
      214–215
   of multiple strategy horizons,
      264–265

Risk(s):—*Cont.*
   reductions in, 98–99
   of single-business enterprise, 283–284
   spreading, 200
   in unrelated diversification, 294, 297, 297*n*
Rivalry, 81–84, 103
   in fragmented industries, 262
   multinational diversification and, 313
   role of competitive intelligence in, 104
   targeting rivals, 190–191
   underestimating rivals, 276
   use of Internet and, 228
   See also Competition
Rule-breaking strategy, 49
Rule-makers, 49
Runner-up firms, 267–271

Sales, diversification and, 289–290
   See also Buyers; Customer(s)
Sales approaches, *See* Marketing
Self-managed teams, 397
Seller-buyer relationships, 90–92
Shareholders, ethical duty to, 65–66
Shareholder value:
   diversification and, 284–285
   unrelated diversification and, 296, 298–299
"Short pay" policy, 383
Short-range objectives, 10, 42*n,* 43, 45, 46
Signaling value, 166, 166*n*
Simultaneous offensive strategies, 188
Single-business enterprises:
   crafting strategy for, 49, *54,* 54–56
   risks of, 283–284
   strategy-making pyramid for, *52*
   strategy managers in, 22, 56
Situational factors:
   in direction setting, 58–64, *60*
   in global competition, 201, 221
   in strategy crafting, 55
   in strategy execution, 439–440
Situation analysis, 114–147

Situation analysis—*Cont.*
   competitive position, strength of, 140–143, 141*t,* 142*t*
   current strategy, effectiveness of, 116–117
   format for, 144, 145*t*
   prices and costs, evaluation of, 128–140
   strategic issues in, 143–144
   SWOT analysis, 117–127
Skills, 107*t,* 356
Social responsibility, 436
   example of, 15, 68
   in strategy crafting, 61, 64–68
Societal considerations:
   changing social issues, 98
   in strategy crafting, 59–61
Software developers, 236–237
Sole proprietorships, 22, 56
Specialization, 263, 270
Specialized firms, 34
Staffing:
   in organization building, 349, 350–355
   recruitment and training; *See* Recruitment; Training
   strong management team, 350–351
Stakeholders:
   culture change and, 432
   duty to, 65–67, 68
   ethical business conduct and, 422
Star businesses, 333–334, 333*n*
Start-up companies, 300–301
Stay-on-the-offensive strategy, 266
Stock options, as reward, 396
Stories, role in corporate culture, 411
Strategic alliances, 196, 234, 339
   advantages of, 174–176
   competitive capabilities and, 358, 362–363
   effective, 215–217
   for emerging industries, 251
   examples of, 176, 216
   with foreign partners, 175, 213–217, 222
   global, 205
   high-velocity markets and, 255

Strategic alliances—*Cont.*
   instability of, 176–177
   new businesses, 301–302
   pervasive use of, 172–173
   responsibility for, 371
   risks of, 214–215
   as strength, 118
Strategic analysis, *See* Industry and competitive analysis
Strategic balance sheet, 120, 121*t*
Strategic challenges, 143–144, 145*t,* 146–147
Strategic cost analysis, 129–134
   developing data for, 133–134, 134*t*
   value chain concept and, 129, *130*
   See also Value chains
Strategic fit analysis, 319, 330–332, *332,* 341–342
Strategic fits, 281–282
   benefits of, 292–293
   competitive advantage and, 53
   corporate culture and, 419–421
   diversification and, 286–287, *287*
   economies of scope and, 291–292
   unrelated diversification and, 294*n,* 297
   along value chain, 287–291
Strategic group, 100
Strategic group mapping:
   analyzing map, 101, 103
   constructing map, 100–101
   example of, *102*
Strategic inflection points, 39, 40
Strategic initiatives, 188, 312–313
Strategic intent, objective setting and, 45–46, 45*n*
Strategic leadership, 4, 19, 430–439
   in changing culture, 421
   corporate culture and, 432–434
   corrective adjustments, 437–438
   ethics leadership, 435–436, 437
   by example, 433
   monitoring strategy execution, 431–432
   as motivation, 398
   responsive organization and, 434–435

Strategic leadership—*Cont.*

in strategy implementation,
348–349

Strategic management process, 2–29

benefits of strategic approach,
28–29

defined, 6, *7*

managerial tasks in, 6–20, *7*

review and adjustment in, *7,* 20–21

as sign of good management, 4–6

strategy managers, roles of, 21–28

Strategic objectives, 10, 11, 69

examples of, 44

financial objectives compared, 43,
45

setting, 42–45, 42*n*

Strategic performance, 9, 42,
104–105, 105*t*

Strategic plans, 17–18

as collection of strategies, 57–58,
59

formal (written), 18

Strategic vision, 32–41, 69

communicating, 40–41, 41*n*

defined, 6

entrepreneurship and, 39, 39*n*

examples of, 8, 33

importance of, 7

inflection points and, 39, 40

mission statement and, 6–7, 8,
32–38

narrowing, 126

time horizon of, 38–39

Strategy(ies):

for businesses in crisis, 271–275

competitive forces and, 79–92, *81,*
111

of competitor, monitoring, 103–104,
105*t*

content of, 12–13, *13*

corporate; *See* Corporate strategy

defensive, 55, 62

defined, 3–4

driving forces and, 93–99, 111–112

effectiveness of, 116–117

in emerging-country markets, 218

for emerging industries, 250–252

Strategy(ies):—*Cont.*

end-game strategies, 273–275

ethics and social responsibility in,
64–68

example of, 14–15

for firms in declining industries,
259–260

fortify-and-defend strategy,
266–267, 271, 337

for fragmented industries, 261–263

for high-velocity markets, 252–256,
254

importance of, 4–6

for industry leaders, 265–267

liquidation, 273

for maturing industries, 256–259

muscle-flexing strategy, 267, 268

offensive; *See* Offensive strategies

organization structure and,
359–372, *360*

revising, 272

for runner-up firms, 267–271

stay-on-the-offensive strategy, 266

strategy-culture conflict, 414,
419–420

for sustaining rapid company
growth, 263–265, *265*

ten commandments of, 275–277

tests of, 68–69

trailblazing, advantages of, 28–29

See also Corporate strategy

Strategy crafting, 10–18, *12,* 23–27,
48–58, 69–70

analysis and; *See* Industry and
competitive analysis

business-level strategy, 49, *54,*
54–56

chief architect approach, 23, 25

collaborative (team) approach,
24–25, 26

comparison of approaches, 24–27

corporate intrapreneur approach, 25,
26–27

corporate strategy, 49, 50–51, *53,*
53–54

delegate/delegation approach,
23–24, 25–26

distinctive competencies and, 123

Strategy crafting—*Cont.*

diversification opportunities, 340

in diversified firms, 338–341, 342

entrepreneurship and, 13–16

evolution of, 16–17, *17*

example of, 50–51

functional strategy, 49, 56–57

managing process of, 340–341

operating strategy, 50, 57

performance test, 338–339

rapid changes in, 17

role of board of directors in, 27–28

situational factors in, 58–64, *60*

strategic plans and, 17–18

strategy-making pyramid, 49–50, *52*

tailoring to situations, 248–278

unifying strategies, 57–58, *59*

Strategy-critical activities:

as building blocks, 363–366, 363*n*

fragmented, 370

organization structure and,
359–361, 363–366, 363*n*

policies and procedures and,
381–382

Strategy execution, 408–440

corporate culture and, 410–430

exerting strategic leadership,
430–438

principal aspects of, 18–19

Strategy implementation, 344–376,
378–405

best practices and, 383–385

budgets and, 380–381

continuous improvement and,
385–388, 386*t,* 387*t*

framework for, 346–347

leading process, 348–349

as manager's task, 21, 345–346

organization-building, 349–372,
350

policies and procedures for,
381–382, 383

principal tasks of, 347, *348*

reward systems and, 395–404

support systems for, 390–395

total quality culture, benefits of,
388–390